Theory and Practice of Cryptography Solutions for Secure Information Systems

Atilla Elçi
Aksaray University, Turkey

Josef Pieprzyk
Macquarie University, Australia

Alexander G. Chefranov
Eastern Mediterranean University, North Cyprus

Mehmet A. Orgun
Macquarie University, Australia

Huaxiong Wang
Nanyang Technological University, Singapore

Rajan Shankaran
Macquarie University, Australia

A volume in the Advances in Information Security, Privacy, and Ethics (AISPE) Book Series

Managing Director: Lindsay Johnston
Editorial Director: Joel Gamon
Production Manager: Jennifer Yoder
Publishing Systems Analyst: Adrienne Freeland
Development Editor: Austin DeMarco
Assistant Acquisitions Editor: Kayla Wolfe
Typesetter: Henry Ulrich
Cover Design: Jason Mull

Published in the United States of America by
Information Science Reference (an imprint of IGI Global)
701 E. Chocolate Avenue
Hershey PA 17033
Tel: 717-533-8845
Fax: 717-533-8661
E-mail: cust@igi-global.com
Web site: http://www.igi-global.com

Library of Congress Cataloging-in-Publication Data

Theory and practice of cryptography solutions for secure information systems / Atilla Elçi, Josef Pieprzyk, Alexander G. Chefranov, Mehmet A. Orgun, Huaxiong Wang and Rajan Shankaran, editors.
pages cm
Summary: "This book explores current trends in IS security technologies,techniques, and concerns, primarily through the use of cryptographic tools to safeguard valuable information resources"-- Provided by publisher.
Includes bibliographical references and index.
ISBN 978-1-4666-4030-6 (hardcover) -- ISBN 978-1-4666-4031-3 (ebook) -- ISBN 978-1-4666-4032-0 (print & perpetual access) 1. Computer security. 2. Data encryption (Computer science) 3. Computer networks--Security measures. I. Elçi, Atilla, editor of compilation.
QA76.9.A25T4725 2013
005.8--dc23

2013001015

This book is published in the IGI Global book series Advances in Information Security, Privacy, and Ethics (AISPE) Book Series (ISSN: 1948-9730; eISSN: 1948-9749)

British Cataloguing in Publication Data
A Cataloguing in Publication record for this book is available from the British Library.

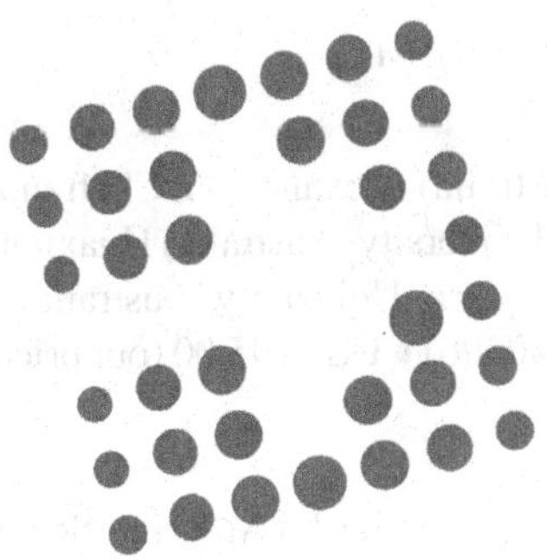

Advances in Information Security, Privacy, and Ethics (AISPE) Book Series

ISSN: 1948-9730
EISSN: 1948-9749

Mission

In the digital age, when everything from municipal power grids to individual mobile telephone locations is all available in electronic form, the implications and protection of this data has never been more important and controversial. As digital technologies become more pervasive in everyday life and the Internet is utilized in ever increasing ways by both private and public entities, the need for more research on securing, regulating, and understanding these areas is growing.

The **Advances in Information Security, Privacy, & Ethics (AISPE)** series is the source for this research, as the series provides only the most cutting-edge research on how information is utilized in the digital age.

Coverage

- Access Control
- Device Fingerprinting
- Global Privacy Concerns
- Information Security Standards
- Network Security Services
- Privacy-Enhancing Technologies
- Risk Management
- Security Information Management
- Technoethics
- Tracking Cookies

The Advances in Information Security, Privacy, and Ethics (AISPE) Book Series (ISSN 1948-9730) is published by IGI Global, 701 E. Chocolate Avenue, Hershey, PA 17033-1240, USA, www.igi-global.com. This series is composed of titles available for purchase individually; each title is edited to be contextually exclusive from any other title within the series. For pricing and ordering information please visit http://www.igi-global.com/book-series/advances-information-security-privacy-ethics/37157. Postmaster: Send all address changes to above address.

Editorial Advisory Board

List of Reviewers

Table of Contents

Foreword xviii

Preface xix

Acknowledgment xxvi

Section 1
Cryptographic Methods Analysis

Chapter 1
Ontology-Based Analysis of Cryptography Standards and Possibilities of Their Harmonization 1
Alexey Y. Atiskov, St. Petersburg Institute for Informatics and Automation of Russian Academy of Sciences, Russia
Fedor A. Novikov, St. Petersburg State Polytechnical University, Russia
Ludmila N. Fedorchenko, St. Petersburg Institute for Informatics and Automation of Russian Academy of Sciences, Russia
Vladimir I. Vorobiev, St. Petersburg Institute for Informatics and Automation of Russian Academy of Sciences, Russia
Nickolay A. Moldovyan, St. Petersburg Institute for Informatics and Automation of Russian Academy of Sciences, Russia

Chapter 2
GOST Encryption Algorithm and Approaches to its Analysis 34
Ludmila Babenko, Southern Federal University, Russia
Evgeniya Ishchukova, Southern Federal University, Russia
Ekaterina Maro, Southern Federal University, Russia

Chapter 3
Cryptography for the Forensics Investigator 62
Thomas Martin, Khalifa University, UAE

Chapter 4
Search in Encrypted Data: Theoretical Models and Practical Applications 84
Qiang Tang, University of Luxembourg, Luxembourg

Section 2
Cryptographic Systems

Chapter 5
Encryption Schemes with Hyper-Complex Number Systems and their Hardware-Oriented Implementation 110
Evgueni Doukhnitch, Istanbul Aydin University, Turkey
Alexander G. Chefranov, Eastern Mediterranean University, North Cyprus
Ahmed Mahmoud, Al-Azhar University-Gaza, Palestine

Chapter 6
Design Time Engineering of Side Channel Resistant Cipher Implementations 133
Alessandro Barenghi, Politecnico di Milano, Italy
Luca Breveglieri, Politecnico di Milano, Italy
Fabrizio De Santis, Technische Universität München, Germany
Filippo Melzani, STMicroelectronics, Italy
Andrea Palomba, Politecnico di Milano, Italy
Gerardo Pelosi, Politecnico di Milano, Italy

Section 3
Cryptographic Solutions for Distributed Systems

Chapter 7
An Efficient Attribute-Based Signature with Application to Secure Attribute-Based Messaging System 159
Piyi Yang, University of Shanghai for Science and Technology, China
Tanveer A Zia, Charles Sturt University, Australia

Chapter 8
SEcure Neighbor Discovery: A Cryptographic Solution for Securing IPv6 Local Link Operations 178
Ahmad AlSa'deh,Hasso-Plattner-Institute, Germany
Hosnieh Rafiee, Hasso-Plattner-Institute, Germany
Christoph Meinel, Hasso-Plattner-Institute, Germany

Chapter 9
Offline/Online Security in Mobile Ad Hoc Networks 199
Wen-Jung Hsin, Park University, USA
Lein Harn, University of Missouri – Kansas City, USA

Chapter 10
A Survey on Security in Wireless Sensor Networks: Attacks and Defense Mechanisms 223
Ilker Korkmaz, Izmir University of Economics, Turkey
Orhan Dagdeviren, Ege University, Turkey
Fatih Tekbacak, Izmir Institute of Technology, Turkey
Mehmet Emin Dalkilic, Ege University, Turkey

Section 4
Cryptographic Trust Solutions

Chapter 11
Secure Multiparty Computation via Oblivious Polynomial Evaluation 253
Mert Özarar, Middle East Technical University, Turkey
Attila Özgit, Middle East Technical University, Turkey

Chapter 12
PKI Trust Models 279
Audun Jøsang, University of Oslo, Norway

Chapter 13
Entity Authentication and Trust Validation in PKI Using Petname Systems 302
Md. Sadek Ferdous, University of Glasgow, UK
Audun Jøsang, University of Oslo, Norway

Chapter 14
Building a Trusted Environment for Security Applications 334
Giovanni Cabiddu, Politecnico di Torino, Italy
Antonio Lioy, Politecnico di Torino, Italy
Gianluca Ramunno, Politecnico di Torino, Italy

Chapter 15
Enhancing Security at Email End Point: A Feasible Task for Fingerprint Identification System....... 361
Babak Sokouti, Biotechnology Research Center, Tabriz University of Medical Sciences, Iran
Massoud Sokouti, Faculty of Electrical and Computer Engineering, Department of Computer Engineering, Shahid Beheshti University, Iran

Section 5
Engineering Secure Information Systems

Chapter 16
Cryptography in Electronic Mail 406
Hosnieh Rafiee, Hasso Plattner Institute, Germany
Martin von Löwis, Hasso Plattner Institute, Germany
Christoph Meinel, Hasso Plattner Institute, Germany

Chapter 17
Theory and Practice of Secure E-Voting Systems 428
Kun Peng, Institute for Infocomm Research, Singapore

Chapter 18
Sealed-Bid Auction Protocols 460

Kun Peng, Institute for Infocomm Research, Singapore

Chapter 19
Preserving the Privacy of Patient Records in Health Monitoring Systems 499
Mahmoud Elkhodr, University of Western Sydney, Australia
Seyed Shahrestani, University of Western Sydney, Australia
Hon Cheung, University of Western Sydney, Australia

Compilation of References 530

About the Contributors 559

Index 580

Detailed Table of Contents

Foreword xviii

Preface xix

Acknowledgment xxvi

Section 1
Cryptographic Methods Analysis

Cryptography is a field of great depth and breadth; its theory involves complex mathematics and its application rests on cutting-edge technology. Cryptographic methods are quite varied, thus their analysis helps to ascertain inherent worth of and security expectation from secure information systems. The chapters in this section set the basis to build an essential understanding and appreciation of cryptographic methods.

Chapter 1
Ontology-Based Analysis of Cryptography Standards and Possibilities of Their Harmonization 1
Alexey Y. Atiskov, St. Petersburg Institute for Informatics and Automation of Russian Academy of Sciences, Russia
Fedor A. Novikov, St. Petersburg State Polytechnical University, Russia
Ludmila N. Fedorchenko, St. Petersburg Institute for Informatics and Automation of Russian Academy of Sciences, Russia
Vladimir I. Vorobiev, St. Petersburg Institute for Informatics and Automation of Russian Academy of Sciences, Russia
Nickolay A. Moldovyan, St. Petersburg Institute for Informatics and Automation of Russian Academy of Sciences, Russia

Harmonization of standards involves problems due to lack of harmonized tools to support implementation. Ontology-based harmonized object models of standards would help but will not be sufficient. Ontological modeling should be used in order to provide an effective meta-description of standards in the form of formal computing models (for example, Semantic Web), automation of concept comparison by means of semantic analysis, and a software mechanism to access standards using Web-based technologies (XML, RDF, OWL, SPARQL). This chapter discusses Hybrid Ontology Technology using Unified Modeling Language, State Transitions Model, and a special tool based on Equivalent Transformations of Syntax Graph-Scheme.

Chapter 2
GOST Encryption Algorithm and Approaches to its Analysis 34
Ludmila Babenko, Southern Federal University, Russia
Evgeniya Ishchukova, Southern Federal University, Russia
Ekaterina Maro, Southern Federal University, Russia

The GOST symmetric block cipher is the basis for secure information systems in Russian Federation. Differential and algebraic analysis approaches are employed in demonstrating the most promising aspects for application of GOST. Use of several methods, such as correct text pairs, linearization, and eXtended Linearization, are discussed. Considering that the GOST algorithm structure includes simple cryptographic operations present in most modern cipher algorithms, the discussed approaches and findings of this chapter can be applied to the analysis of other ciphers found in various secure information systems.

Chapter 3
Cryptography for the Forensics Investigator 62
Thomas Martin, Khalifa University, UAE

There are many challenges for a forensic investigator when it comes to digital evidence. These include, among others, increasing use of cryptography, for example in communication protocols, file and whole-disk encryption, and individual applications. A forensics investigator does not need to be aware of all aspects of cryptography, yet there are certain practices that are vital. This chapter describes the steps necessary to protect the integrity of any information collected, and goes on to propose a set of best practices for use by an investigator encountering encrypted evidence.

Chapter 4
Search in Encrypted Data: Theoretical Models and Practical Applications 84
Qiang Tang, University of Luxembourg, Luxembourg

A systematic study is conducted on Search in Encrypted Data (SED) schemes. Three application scenarios are described identifying the desirable security requirements, providing two orthogonal categorizations and reviewing the related security models. Although SED schemes are provably secure in their respective security models, a brief analysis showed that there are a lot of potential security issues. Practical issues are analyzed, and future research directions are identified.

Section 2
Cryptographic Systems

Hardware related considerations of security have gained importance due to growing threats to the safety of dependable information systems. On the one hand, encryption algorithms are being implemented in hardware aiming for faster and securer operations and at the same time achieving better results. On the other hand, information leakage through techniques exploiting side-channels have driven concerns for securer design of hardware. Hardware design is the pivotal concern of this section.

Chapter 5
Encryption Schemes with Hyper-Complex Number Systems and their Hardware-Oriented Implementation 110
Evgueni Doukhnitch, Istanbul Aydin University, Turkey
Alexander Chefranov, Eastern Mediterranean University, North Cyprus
Ahmed Mahmoud, Al-Azhar University-Gaza, Palestine

Quaternion Encryption Scheme (QES), susceptible to the Known Plaintext-Ciphertext Attack (KPCA), is being modified towards resilience to KPCA and for obtaining a new effective hardware implementation called HW-OES. The frame size and the quaternion update procedure are adjusted; furthermore, mainly addition and shift operations are used. Experimental results show that the proposed HW-OES is more effective in the encryption quality of signals and images than the original QES. HW-OES provides higher encryption quality than AES at slightly slower speed than QES.

Chapter 6
Design Time Engineering of Side Channel Resistant Cipher Implementations 133
Alessandro Barenghi, Politecnico di Milano, Italy
Luca Breveglieri, Politecnico di Milano, Italy
Fabrizio De Santis, Technische Universität München, Germany
Filippo Melzani, STMicroelectronics, Italy
Andrea Palomba, Politecnico di Milano, Italy
Gerardo Pelosi, Politecnico di Milano, Italy

Security threats to embedded devices, like smart phones and PDAs, have grown of late mostly exploiting side-channel information leakage, aiming to recover secret keys. This chapter provides the background to understand the most common side-channel attacks based on power consumption, and reports the methodology to perform a side-channel security assessment of embedded devices. The advantage of performing power analysis at design time is that the leakage sources can be identified, isolated, and individually studied in a clean room environment. This enables the device designer to incorporate countermeasures during the regular design process.

Section 3
Cryptographic Solutions for Distributed Systems

Security issues of distributed systems such as IPv6, Mobile Ad Hoc Networks (MANETs), and Wireless Sensor Networks (WSNs) have become prominent interests to researchers and practitioners alike. This section provides a foundation towards better grasping the security issues involved and understanding measures in addressing them adequately. As a particular case, a secure attribute-based messaging system is studied.

Chapter 7
An Efficient Attribute-Based Signature with Application to Secure Attribute-Based Messaging System 159
Piyi Yang, University of Shanghai for Science and Technology, China
Tanveer A Zia, Charles Sturt University, Australia

Presented here is an efficient fully secure Attribute-Based Signature (ABS) scheme. The proposed scheme is highly expressive for it allows any signer to specify claim-predicates in terms of any predicate consisting of AND, OR, and threshold gates over the attributes in the system. ABS has found many important applications in secure communications, such as anonymous authentication system, and attribute-based messaging system. Also shown is how to apply this scheme to achieve user authentication, user privacy preserving, integrity protection of message, and freshness in a secure attribute-based messaging system. As the signature is based on attributes, the privacy of the user is protected. This work may be of good use in systems for instant messaging an attribute-based message routing.

Chapter 8
SEcure Neighbor Discovery: A Cryptographic Solution for Securing IPv6 Local Link Operations 178
Ahmad AlSa'deh, Hasso-Plattner-Institute, Germany
Hosnieh Rafiee, Hasso-Plattner-Institute, Germany
Christoph Meinel, Hasso-Plattner-Institute, Germany

Responding to the threats to Neighbor Discovery Protocol (NDP) of the IPv6 protocols suite, the SEcure Neighbor Discovery (SEND) was proposed. Relying on dynamically Cryptographically Generated Addresses (CGAs) and X.509 certificates, SEND's strong security extension renders the IPv6 local link safe. This chapter considers practical considerations of employing SEND, reviews other vulnerabilities, and provides recommendations.

Chapter 9
Offline/Online Security in Mobile Ad Hoc Networks 199
Wen-Jung Hsin, Park University, USA
Lein Harn, University of Missouri – Kansas City, USA

Characteristics of Mobile Ad Hoc Networks (MANETs) are discussed and security challenges are reviewed. The authentication and key management schemes are broadly classified into three categories in the literature, namely a MANET with a centralized server, a MANET with a distributed server, and a self-organized MANET by the mobile nodes themselves. Three offline/online Authentication and Key Agreement (AKA) schemes and one non-repudiation scheme are then presented. The timing analysis of the proposed schemes indicates minimalized online computation requirement for mobile nodes.

Chapter 10
A Survey on Security in Wireless Sensor Networks: Attacks and Defense Mechanisms.................. 223
Ilker Korkmaz, Izmir University of Economics, Turkey
Orhan Dagdeviren, Ege University, Turkey
Fatih Tekbacak, Izmir Institute of Technology, Turkey
Mehmet Emin Dalkilic, Ege University, Turkey

Attacks and respective defense mechanisms in Wireless Sensor Networks (WSNs) are surveyed in detail investigating security issues. Attacks are categorized according to the related protocol target layer. Open research issues and emerging technologies in security in WSNs are also investigated. This chapter is a state-of-the-art reference for the attacks and their defense mechanisms in WSN security.

Section 4
Cryptographic Trust Solutions

Privacy, trust, and cryptography are being linked in modern conversation. The most important property of an information system has become the protection of sensible information, be it personal or corporate, by providing privacy within trust limits among partners. Approaches differ, yet cryptography has been instrumental in helping to achieve that evasive goal in all cases. For example, the techniques for Secure Multiparty Computation (SMC) are quite relevant and practical to overcoming privacy gaps among partners alleviating anonymity-enabled computation through privacy preserving algorithms. Likewise, a Public-Key Infrastructure (PKI) can be used for propagating trust for authentication in online environments. Petname System combined with PKI assures user trust on identities. On the other hand, wider adoption of a trusted platform alleviating development of trusted applications can help increase security in information systems. An alternate would be dedicated, special purpose security measures, one of which is using biometric features, such as fingerprint.

Chapter 11
Secure Multiparty Computation via Oblivious Polynomial Evaluation 253
Mert Özarar, Middle East Technical University, Turkey
Attila Özgit, Middle East Technical University, Turkey

The techniques for Secure Multiparty Computation (SMC) are quite relevant and practical to overcome privacy gaps among partners alleviating anonymity-enabled computation through privacy preserving algorithms. This chapter presents the research on SMC demonstrating the concept using a cryptographic building block technique called Oblivious Polynomial Evaluation (OPE). Critical issues and challenges of adaptation future research directions are surveyed.

Chapter 12
PKI Trust Models 279
Audun Jøsang, University of Oslo, Norway

A Public-Key Infrastructure (PKI) can be used for propagating trust for authentication in online environments. Trust propagation takes place under an essentially syntactic trust model, whereas trust is primarily a semantic concept. Semantic trust models for PKIs consider semantic assumptions and human cognition of trust relationships between participants in a PKI, and by how identity information is displayed and represented. This chapter takes a closer look at the most prominent and widely used PKI trust models, and discusses related semantic issues.

Chapter 13
Entity Authentication and Trust Validation in PKI Using Petname Systems 302
Md. Sadek Ferdous, University of Glasgow, UK
Audun Jøsang, University of Oslo, Norway

Identity Management Systems facilitate management of identities but provide little support on the user side. PKI helps but involves difficulties for the general public in dealing with certificates giving way to vulnerabilities. Petname Systems are proposed in order to improve user friendliness and to further strengthen security. This chapter provides an analysis of the Petname Model by describing its essential properties, application domains, and usability issues. Petname System combined with PKI assures user trust on identities. The chapter also presents analysis of two applications integrating that combination.

Chapter 14
Building a Trusted Environment for Security Applications 334
Giovanni Cabiddu, Politecnico di Torino, Italy
Antonio Lioy, Politecnico di Torino, Italy
Gianluca Ramunno, Politecnico di Torino, Italy

An approach to building a trusted environment for running security-critical applications on a PC-class platform is being proposed. The Trusted Computing architecture exploits the low-cost TPM chip in monitoring the integrity of the computing platform detecting static unauthorized manipulation of binaries and configuration files, hence quickly detecting software attacks. The architecture provides enhanced security controls and remote attestation. Foundations of a trusted platform are presented, and the principles for developing trusted applications are explained. Wider adoption of such techniques can help increase security.

Chapter 15
Enhancing Security at Email End Point: A Feasible Task for Fingerprint Identification System....... 361
Babak Sokouti, Biotechnology Research Center, Tabriz University of Medical Sciences, Iran
Massoud Sokouti, Faculty of Electrical and Computer Engineering, Department of Computer Engineering, Shahid Beheshti University, Iran

A new secure email system based on fingerprint identification is proposed to provide recognition of the real identity of both the sender and the receiver of an email message. This method employs the user's username and password hashes, full name and personal image, and fingerprint hashes along with the email message hash in affecting endpoint security. The proposed method was successfully evaluated against security, maintenance, operational, and privacy issues. Employing a secure email system with fingerprint identification in real life email system infrastructures will allow users to draw the benefit of assured identities, thus averting many of the current pitfalls in email exchanges.

Section 5
Engineering Secure Information Systems

Engineering Secure Information Systems come in flavors always involving cryptography tools. Here a few case studies are presented. Securing email components through cryptography is taken up by the first chapter. Realizing secure e-voting systems more efficiently and achieving stronger privacy are the concerns of the second chapter. Securing electronic auctions through a new family of protocols called "Sealed-Bid Auction Protocols" is the subject of the next chapter. The final chapter considers preserving the privacy of patient records in health monitoring systems through a newly proposed authentication approach called "Ubiquitous Health Trust Protocol."

Chapter 16
Cryptography in Electronic Mail 406
Hosnieh Rafiee, Hasso Plattner Institute, Germany
Martin von Löwis, Hasso Plattner Institute, Germany
Christoph Meinel, Hasso Plattner Institute, Germany

The protocols to handle Electronic Mail (email) during transmission, downloads, and organizational processes are not secure; scammers and spammers misuse them. Cryptographic tools are applied in securing email components. This chapter introduces approaches and the most recent improvements in email security using cryptography, describing their advantages and disadvantages. Also examined is how such approaches would work in IPv6 as compared to IPv4.

Chapter 17
Theory and Practice of Secure E-Voting Systems 428
Kun Peng, Institute for Infocomm Research, Singapore

Electronic voting is a popular application of cryptographic and network techniques to e-government. In this chapter, the existing e-voting solutions are surveyed and analyzed. Key security properties are presented, and the existing e-voting schemes are checked against the corresponding security properties. Security and efficiency of the schemes are analyzed, and the strongest security and highest efficiency achievable is estimated. Problems and concerns about the existing solutions, including vulnerability to malicious voters and (or) talliers, possible failure of complete correctness, imperfect privacy, dependence on computational assumptions, and exaggerated efficiency are addressed. New approaches are proposed; the proposed e-voting scheme, compared against the existing ones, is more efficient and can achieve stronger privacy.

Chapter 18
Sealed-Bid Auction Protocols 460
Kun Peng, Institute for Infocomm Research, Singapore

Electronic auctions provide a key function in e-commerce, but face serious security threats as fraud can be committed by bidders or auctioneers. Open-cry bidding processes, although widely practiced, have serious difficulties in protecting bid confidentiality and bidder privacy. On the other hand, interactive auction techniques require many rounds of communication over insecure Internet, facing problems due to service availability and network security. Sealed-bid auctions can resolve these issues as the security requirements in e-auctions, including correctness, fairness, non-repudiation, robustness, public verifiability, bid privacy, and other desired properties, like price flexibility and rule flexibility, can be satisfied. Sealed-bid auction schemes are described and analyzed in this chapter.

Chapter 19
Preserving the Privacy of Patient Records in Health Monitoring Systems 499
Mahmoud Elkhodr, University of Western Sydney, Australia
Seyed Shahrestani, University of Western Sydney, Australia
Hon Cheung, University of Western Sydney, Australia

The challenges of generic security protocols and platforms for securing Electronic Health Records (EHR) in general and for their adoption in shared care environments in particular are taken up in this chapter. Various methods and security solutions based on existing protocols are introduced, discussing their potentials and describing experiences with their implementations. An authentication approach titled "Ubiquitous Health Trust Protocol" (UHTP) is proposed aiming at minimizing the security risk associated with remote access to EHRs using portable devices. The proposed approach is used to affect secure collaboration through a set of generic services such as read/write, authentication and trust management, as well as advanced functionality for mobile access. The experience in adopting the approach using Java on the Android platform is described.

Compilation of References 530

About the Contributors 569

Index 580

Foreword

Web services and service-oriented environments are key enablers for the migration of entertainment, business, sociability, science, and healthcare from the physical world to the virtual world. Cloud technologies today provide cost-effective platforms for such transition. Yet for this vision to become reality, security needs to be addressed. Security is a vital property of Internet-based interactions, service-oriented environments, and cloud. Whereas assuring security is already challenging in existing computing systems, it becomes much more complex because of the dynamic and adaptable nature of these environments, which are often large-scale and across domains. Comprehensive approaches to security need to combine different security techniques, ranging from cryptography to access control to identity management. Among all such techniques, a major role is played by cryptography, as this is a key technology for securing data and communication, for authentication, for privacy-preserving function computation, and many other security functions. Recent advances like homomorphic encryption have further expanded the application scope of encryption.

This book represents a comprehensive coverage of advances and applications of encryption. The book provides the key relevant foundations by looking at search protocols for encrypted data and novel encryption techniques that are more resistant to attacks. A central part of the book focuses on cryptographic protocols in a large variety of application domains, including attribute-based messaging systems, public key infrastructures, networks, e-auction systems, health-care records, voting systems, and e-mail systems. Techniques, systems, and applications are described in detail and illustrated with extensive examples.

This book is an invaluable reference for researchers in academia and industry who are interested in being acquainted with the applications of encryption and in exploring open research directions in encryption. Practitioners will find in the book many illustrative examples and tools for encryption that will help them in understanding the potential practical applications of this important security technology.

Elisa Bertino
Purdue University, USA

***Elisa Bertino** is Professor of Computer Science at Purdue University and serves as Director of Purdue Cyber Center (Discovery Park) and as Research Director of CERIAS. Previously, she was a faculty member in the Department of Computer Science and Communication of the University of Milan. Her main research interests include security, privacy, digital identity management systems, database systems, distributed systems, and multimedia systems. She is a fellow of the IEEE and a fellow of the ACM. She received the 2002 IEEE Computer Society Technical Achievement Award for outstanding contributions to database systems and database security and advanced data management systems and the 2005 IEEE Computer Society Tsutomu Kanai Award for pioneering and innovative research contributions to secure distributed systems.*

Preface

Information Systems (IS) play a central part in all aspects of our world, from science, medicine, and engineering, to industry, business, law, politics, government, arts, culture, society, health, operational support in daily life, surveillance of infrastructure and environment, and homeland protection and national security. Without proper security precautions, IS are prone to unexpected and intolerable side effects, such as leakage of operational and confidential data, identity theft and unauthorized access, and possibly modification of private data, services, and systems. Security services are required in order to guarantee information security and protection of privacy, such as data confidentiality, data authentication, anonymity, entity authentication, non-repudiation of origin and receipt, access control, protection against denial of service and phishing, and secure processing and deletion of data. In a nutshell, dependable and trustworthy security solutions based on strong cryptography are needed.

The collection of chapters in this book focuses on theory and the practice of cryptographic security solutions for deployment in Information Systems (IS). Given the rapid progress of tools, systems, and technologies, and the emergence of many new application areas of IS, it is essential for such solutions to be designed, implemented, tested, and verified using sound engineering approaches as they must support the core functionality of secure information systems. The theoreticians, designers, engineers, and practitioners of cryptography need to provide such cryptography solutions that balance the required level of security versus costs and risks involved in deploying those solutions in their targeted applications. Therefore, the successful deployment of cryptographic solutions requires a complete understanding of the requirements of IS at hand, their constraints and performance characteristics, the capabilities of the hardware and software platforms, and the nature of the network environments in which they operate. In some cases, especially in emerging areas, new cryptographic solutions based on new approaches and new theories may be required because off-the-shelf solutions may not work.

The editors of this collection have come together to compile and present the state-of-the-art in cryptographic security solutions from theory to implementations to applications in a comprehensive and definitive collection. They have a long-standing reputation in cryptography and several other allied and complementary areas of research, and have broad and recognized experience in leading international professional media, conferences, and the organization of special issues of international journals. The seeds of this collection were in fact laid in the ongoing cooperation of the editors in the organization of a conference series called International Conference on Security of Information and Networks (SIN).

The SIN series was inaugurated with SIN 2007, which was held in Gazimagusa, North Cyprus, hosted by Eastern Mediterranean University, and co-organized by İstanbul Technical University. SIN 2007 was chaired by Atilla Elçi, one of the editors of this collection, and served by an international program committee. Although the conference topics covered all areas of information and network security as intended from the outset, due to their critical importance and timeliness, several topical areas naturally emerged:

- **Cryptography:** This area featured papers on the development, design, and analysis of new cryptographic algorithms and methods, both software and hardware implementation of such algorithms and methods, and selected applications of cryptography.
- **Network Security:** This area featured papers on authentication, authorization, access control, privacy, intrusion detection, malware detection, and mobile and personal area networks.
- **IT Governance:** This area featured papers on information security management systems, risk and threat analysis, and information security guidelines and policies.

The conference main themes were supported by invited papers and talks, especially on the state-of-the-art in cryptography, given by some of the leading international researchers. Bart Preneel, Head of Computer Security and Industrial Cryptography (COSIC) at Katholieke Universiteit Leuven, Leuven, Belgium, talked about Research Challenges in Cryptology. He highlighted the recent developments in cryptography and how advanced cryptographic techniques could contribute to address future challenges related to privacy, trusted computing, distributed trust, and ambient intelligence. Marc Joye, Thomson R&D, France, talked about White-box cryptography techniques aimed at protecting software implementations of cryptographic algorithms against key recovery. Elisabeth Oswald, Cryptography and Information Security Group, University of Bristol, Bristol, UK, talked about Power Analysis Attacks that allow extracting keys from cryptographic devices with low effort. Çetin Kaya Koç, İstanbul Commerce University, Turkey, and Oregon State University, USA, gave an overview of side-channel attacks on commodity processors, particularly for computers running as servers. Mehmet Ufuk Çağlayan, Boğaziçi University, Turkey, delivered a survey on secure routing issues in MANETs, with a summary of the current state of the art in secure routing protocols and their resistance to known attacks. Karthik Bhargawan, Microsoft Research Cambridge, UK, overviewed the recent work in verifying security properties for protocols being standardized as part of the XML Web Services framework.

What was particularly notable at SIN 2007 was the participation of both the theoreticians and the practitioners who were interested in a holistic view of information and network security. In particular, the practitioners were interested in finding the latest research on information and network security and how best to benefit from that research in improving security solutions in information systems, and the theoreticians were interested in the challenges of actual security problems and how best to study and understand them so as to further foundational studies. The proceedings of the conference, co-edited by Atilla Elçi, S. Berna Örs, and Bart Preneel, was published by Trafford and sold internationally both as hardcopy and as an ebook. It was decided that the follow up conference SIN 2009 was also to be held in Gazimagusa, North Cyprus, but with an extended international cooperation that involved researchers from Eastern Mediterranean University, Macquarie University, and Southern Federal University. All of the editors joined the organization of SIN 2009 under various capacities: Atilla Elçi and Mehmet A. Orgun as conference co-chairs, Alexander Chefranov and Josef Pieprzyk as program co-chairs, and Rajan Shankaran as workshop co-chair. Huaxiong Wang joined the Program Committee of the conference and has been involved with the SIN series ever since.

As in SIN 2007, the conference program was supported by invited papers and talks, given by some of the leading international researchers. Elisa Bertino, Research Director of the Center for Education and Research in Information Assurance and Security at Purdue University, USA, who graciously agreed to write a foreword to this book, talked about "Assured Information Sharing: Concepts and Research Issues." Erdal Çayırcı, NATO JWC & University of Stavanger, Norway, talked about "Deployed Sensor Networks and Their Security Challenges in Practice." Sorin Alexander Huss, Director CASED Research

Center for IT Security, Technical University of Darmstadt, Germany, talked about "Embedded Systems for IT Security Applications: Properties and Design Considerations." In line with the international cooperation of the organizers, technical cooperation with the ACM Special Interest Group on Security, Audit, and Control (SIGSAC) was sought, and the conference proceedings was published by ACM for the first time and placed on the ACM Digital Library for perpetual access.

Encouraged by the successful cooperation of the organizers at SIN 2007 and 2009 and the resounding success of the conference, the SIN Conference was intended to be an annual event from 2009 onwards. SIN 2010 was held in Taganrog, Rostov-on-Don, Russia, organized by a team of researchers from Southern Federal University, Eastern Mediterranean University, Macquarie University, and Technical University of Darmstadt. Atilla Elçi and Mehmet A. Orgun served as conference co-chairs, Alexander Chefranov as program co-chair, and Rajan Shankaran as workshop co-chair. SIN 2010 was also held in technical cooperation with the ACM Special Interest Group on Security, Audit, and Control (SIGSAC), and the conference proceedings was published by the ACM once more. The very areas that emerged at previous SIN conferences were strong as ever, and several new frontier areas were also represented, including secure ontology-based systems, security-aware software engineering, trust management and privacy, and security standards, guidelines, and certification. Microsoft Russia and Russian Foundation for Basic Research also came to the party by providing sponsorship for the conference. As usual, the conference main themes were supported by invited papers and talks. Josef Pieprzyk, Macquarie University, Australia, talked about "Evolution of Cryptographic Hashing," and Alexander Tereshkin, Principal Researcher, Invisible Things Lab, Rostov-on-Don, Russia, talked about "Evil Maid goes after PGP Whole Disk Encryption."

As the research areas that underpin the SIN series continued to mature, it was felt that the time was ripe for a journal special issue which showcased the best and the most recent research efforts presented at SIN 2010. The authors of the papers presented at SIN 2010 were invited to submit the revised and substantially extended versions of their papers to a special issue of Security and Communication Networks (by Wiley) on the Design and Engineering of Cryptographic Solutions for Secure Information Systems. There was a strong interest in the special issue within the security and cryptography communities, and after several rounds of careful reviewing, nine high quality papers were finally accepted for publication. The special issue is scheduled to be published in early 2013. The papers which have been accepted for publication in the special issue cover several important topics in the design and engineering of cryptographic solutions for secure information systems, including hardware design, cryptographic fundamentals, auction design, protocol verification, detection of collusion attacks, and policy issues. The efforts to bring the special issue to fruition were but a prelude to a more substantial undertaking by the editors for the production of a comprehensive and up-to-date resource on cryptographic security solutions.

In order to further the goals of a truly international conference, SIN 2011 was held in Sydney, Australia, in November 2011, organized jointly by Macquarie University, Süleyman Demirel University, Southern Federal University, and Technical University of Darmstadt. All the editors took active roles in the organization of SIN 2011. Atilla Elçi and Mehmet A. Orgun served as conference co-chairs; Josef Pieprzyk, Alexander Chefranov, and Rajan Shankaran as program co-chairs; and Huaxiong Wang as the Asia-Pacific liaison. The Air Force Office of Scientific Research (AFOSR), Asian Office of Aerospace Research and Development (AOARD), Army International Technology Center-Pacific (ITC-PAC), and Office of Naval Research-Global (ONRG) provided sponsorship, which contributed substantially to the success of SIN 2011. There was yet again a strong presence of the discussion of latest cryptography solutions at the conference. The conference main themes were supported by invited papers and talks.

Professor Vijay Varadharajan, Microsoft Chair in Innovation in Computing, Macquarie University, Sydney, Australia, talked about "Rethinking Cyber Security"; and Dr. Kevin Kwiat, Principal Computer Engineer, the Cyber Science Branch of the U.S. Air Force Research Laboratory (AFRL), Rome, New York, USA, talked about "Fault Tolerance for Fight-Through: A Basis for Strategic Survival." The proceedings of the SIN 2011 conference was also published by the ACM and uploaded to ACM DL.

Now that the research areas represented at the SIN conferences have continued to grow and flourish, the organisers of SIN 2011 have arranged two special issues around two of those areas. A special issue of Concurrency and Computation: Practice and Experience (by Wiley) focussed on the theme of Trust and Security in Wireless Sensor Networks to address the design, development, and deployment of trust management schemes and security solutions that take into account the intrinsic features of wireless sensor networks. A special issue of Networking Science (Springer-Verlag) focussed on the theme of Next Generation Network Architectures, Protocols, Theory, Systems, and Applications to address security solutions for single packet switching networks that transports all kinds of information (voice, data, multimedia) as packets. Both the special issues are under progress and scheduled to appear in late 2013.

Continuing with the internationalization of the SIN series, and encouraged by the participation of a strong contingency of researchers from universities in India, SIN 2012 was held at Jaipur in India in October 2012, organized by Malaviya National Institute of Technology, Aksaray University, Southern Federal University, Macquarie University, and Indian Institute of Technology Bombay. Once again, all the editors have taken part in SIN 2012 under various but similar capacities, with a strong local participation from Indian researchers and practitioners in the organization of the conference. The strong technical program was supported by twelve invited speakers, seven of whom were from various institutions in India showcasing the fine cryptography research conducted in India as well as the latest advances in security in cloud computing. Continuing with the tradition of the past events, the proceedings of the SIN 2012 conference was also published by the ACM and uploaded to ACM DL.

After the successful conclusion of SIN 2012, it was decided that every few years the SIN series would be held in the region where it originated. Having taken a new post at Aksaray University, in the Cappadocia region, Turkey, Atilla Elçi has been spearheading the organization of SIN 2013, which will be held in Aksaray, Turkey, in November 2013. All the editors are looking forward to the next stage in their fruitful cooperation and welcome cryptography and security researchers as active participants both in the organization of the conference as well as on the conference program. They also welcome back Berna Örs Yalçın, İstanbul Technical University, Turkey, as program co-chair, who was conference co-chair of SIN 2007. If the resounding success and continuing growth of the past conferences is any indication, the future of the SIN series is bright indeed.

Every now and then, it is also essential to take stock of the progress in theory and practice of cryptographic security solutions, present the contributions scattered across many diverse forums such as conference proceedings and journal papers in a coherent way, and provide a broad picture of the recent achievements of the area, paving the way for future progress. Given the maturity of cryptography solutions and the recent advances in this area, these goals could not have been achieved within the time and page limitations of journal special issues, but they could be achieved in a book which would first introduce in an accessible style the nature of cryptography, then explore numerous established, advanced, and frontier topics in cryptography leading to illustrations of new frontiers in secure IS. As such, it would foster further research on the development, design, and engineering of cryptographic solutions in secure information systems ranging from theoretical to practical issues and of course to their ultimate applications. It would also serve the needs of advanced learners, faculty, and graduate students alike, and should be suitable for individual learners and classroom adoption.

To this end, the editors approached IGI Global in September 2011 with a view to the publication of such a book, which would primarily focus on cryptography and its use for security of IS in its broader context. It would also serve as a landmark resource for information and network security in IS, providing the reader with the state-of-the-art technologies and practices of putting cryptographic solutions to work for creating secure IS. To achieve these objectives, the book would naturally need to draw from a broader base of research efforts in cryptography solutions, not just those represented at the SIN conferences over the past few years. We were delighted when the book proposal was approved, and we had a worthwhile and timely challenge to bring it to its fruition.

Under the stewardship of the editors, an editorial board of international reviewers was formed, and the call for papers was widely circulated to the participants at the SIN conferences as well as to the broader scientific community. There was a strong response to the call for papers for the collection. Researchers and practitioners were first invited to submit a 2-3 page chapter proposal by November 2011, clearly explaining the contributions of the chapter and how it would address a cryptographic solution for IS. As a result, 35 chapter proposals from researchers from all over the world were received. The submitted chapter proposals were assessed by the editors for the significance and the originality of the proposed cryptographic solutions and how they would fit with the main theme of the collection. The authors of accepted proposals were duly notified and asked to submit full chapters of about 20 pages by February 2012. All the submitted full chapters were assessed by three reviewers of international standing on a double-blind basis, and the reviews were moderated by the editors for their significance, originality, quality, timeliness, and usefulness. The authors re-submitted full chapters after updating in response to reviewers comments. Finally, after a second round of reviewing, 19 high quality chapter submissions were accepted for publication in this collection.

The chapters in this collection are arranged in five sections, which can be read independently of one another. However, the natural progression of the material is from more foundational studies towards more applied ones at frontier areas such as e-voting, e-auctions, and health monitoring systems. In order to get the most out of the book and also to appreciate the holistic view of how cryptography solutions have been devised, implemented, and deployed, we strongly recommend a sampling of a few chapters from each of the sections 1-4 at the first reading, depending of course on the interests and expertise of the reader, followed by the chapters in section 5, which provide several case studies.

The chapters in Section 1 focus on Cryptographic Methods Analysis. Modern cryptographic methods are based on several branches of mathematics and computer science such as algebra, number theory, finite fields, complexity theory, algorithm design, and analysis. The implementation and application of cryptographic methods naturally draws from technological advances, in both hardware and software alike, which throw new challenges to theoreticians and practitioners of cryptography, literally on an ongoing basis. Cryptographic methods are quite diverse and have different underlying assumptions and constraints; thus, their analysis helps to ascertain inherent worth of and security expectations from secure information systems. The chapters in this section set the basis to build essential understanding and appreciation of cryptographic methods.

Chapter 1 proposes harmonization of tools to support the implementation of security standards in practice based on the use of ontologies. Chapter 2 discusses approaches to analysis of GOST 28147-89 encryption algorithm (also known as simply GOST), which is the basis of most secure information systems in the Russian Federation. Chapter 3 describes those aspects of cryptography that are vital to a forensics investigator who is not necessarily an expert in cryptography but must understand and analyse digital evidence. Chapter 4 presents a systematic study of Search in Encrypted Data (SED), which enables a client to have third-party server(s) to perform certain search functionalities on encrypted data.

The chapters in Section 2 focus on Cryptographic Systems. The rapid progress in hardware, such as the availability of multi-core processors, has had a major impact on security. It has now been possible to implement encryption algorithms in hardware aiming for faster and securer operations, while at the same time achieving better security. On the other hand, information leakage through techniques exploiting the physical properties of cryptosystems, such as measuring timing, power consumption, radiation emissions, has motivated further research towards the design of more secure hardware. On the opposite side of the coin, the wide availability of low-cost devices, such as tablets, mobile phones with weaker encryption / security mechanisms due to resource and processing constraints, has created further opportunities for attacks. Hardware related considerations of security are therefore the main concern of this section.

Chapter 5 proposes a modification of Quaternion Encryption Scheme (QES) called M-QES which is resistant to the Known Plaintext-Ciphertext Attack (KPCA) due to improper choice of the frame size and the procedure of secret quaternion updating. Chapter 6 summarizes the side-channel techniques based on power consumption and elaborates the issue of the design time engineering of a secure system, through the employment of the current hardware design tools.

The chapters in Section 3 focus on Cryptographic Solutions for Distributed Systems. With the advent of Mobile Ad-Hoc Networks (MANETs), Wireless Sensor Networks (WSNs), Body Area Networks (BANs) and vehicular networks, security of distributed systems operating in such networks has become a major interest to researchers and practitioners alike. Such systems usually have a dynamic, evolving topology, they are self-organizing, and often need to operate in hostile, uncertain environments. Most of the devices in such networks and systems often have severe communication, resource, and power limitations. Therefore, they present new security challenges and require new solutions, as most of the existing solutions are no longer feasible. This section provides a foundation towards understanding the security issues involved in such systems and designing and implementing cryptography solutions to address them adequately.

Chapter 7 presents an efficient fully secure Attribute-Based Signature (ABS) scheme in the standard model under certain assumptions which is more practical than the generic group model used in the previous schemes. Chapter 8 evaluates the practical considerations of a SEcure Neighbor Discovery (SEND) deployment, taking a cryptographic approach as a means of securing the IPv6 local link operations. It reviews the remaining vulnerabilities, and gives some recommendations with which to facilitate SEND deployment. Chapter 9 presents three offline/online authentication and key agreement schemes and one offline/online non-repudiation scheme, all aiming at fast online computation for mobile nodes in mobile ad hoc networks. Chapter 10 surveys attacks and their defence mechanisms in Wireless Sensor Networks (WSNs) and also investigates the open research issues and emerging technologies on security in WSNs.

The chapters in Section 4 focus on Cryptographic Trust Solutions. Trust plays an important role in secure IS. There is interplay between trust and cryptography towards achieving security and addressing privacy concerns. This section provides a discussion of cryptographic trust solutions in several representative areas such as Secure Multiparty Computation (SMC), Public-Key Infrastructure (PKI) trust models, and trusted computer architecture.

Chapter 11 surveys the significant research that has been carried out on Secure Multiparty Computation (SMC). It discusses the critical issues and challenges and the level of adaptation achieved as well as some future research directions. Chapter 12 takes a closer look at the most prominent and widely used

Public-Key Infrastructure (PKI) trust models, and discusses related semantic issues. Chapter 13 provides an analysis of the Petname Model and explains how a Petname System can be effectively combined with the PKI to recognise identities and impose certainty by validating the user trust on those identities. Chapter 14 introduces the features and foundations of Trusted Computing, an architecture that exploits the low-cost TPM chip to monitor the integrity of a computing platform. Chapter 15 proposes a new secure email system based on fingerprint identification to overcome the recognition of real identity of an email sender and the receiver.

The chapters in Section 5 focus on Engineering Secure Information Systems. Security considerations should not be add-ons, which can be incorporated into a functional system once it has been built and deployed. The development of secure IS requires the embedding of security considerations into the system analysis, design, implementation, and testing stages. In this way, the security requirements can be captured, analysed, and addressed in the design stage, implemented and tested together with the implementation and testing of the functional components, resulting in a more secure IS. This section presents a few representative case studies of engineering secure information systems.

Chapter 16 classifies the approaches used according to the protection mechanisms provided to the email components, and it also briefly describes these approaches. It concludes by examining how the use of these approaches will work in IPv6 as compared to IPv4. Chapter 17 presents an analysis of the existing e-voting solutions in both categories of homomorphic voting and shuffling-based voting. The key security properties in these two categories are discussed, and then the existing e-voting schemes are checked against their corresponding security properties. Chapter 18 addresses the main challenge of designing an e-auction while protecting bid privacy without compromising other critical requirements and properties. Chapter 19 discusses the challenges of generic security protocols and platforms for preserving the privacy of patient records in health monitoring systems.

Atilla Elçi
Aksaray University, Turkey

Mehmet A. Orgun
Macquarie University, Australia

Josef Pieprzyk
Macquarie University, Australia

Alexander G. Chefranov
Eastern Mediterranean University, North Cyprus

Huaxiong Wang
Nanyang Technological University, Singapore

Rajan Shankaran
Macquarie University, Australia

Acknowledgment

Many fine individuals contributed to this book. First, we would like to express our gratitude to Jan Travers, Director of Intellectual Property and Contracts of IGI Global, who was instrumental in the contracting stage of this project; we also would like to express our gratitude to Hannah Abelbeck and Austin M. DeMarco, Editorial Assistants from IGI Global, for their continuing support for the collection. We availed ourselves of their expert editorial advice at every junction of the whole process. Second, we would also like to thank our reviewers who unselfishly donated their time in reading the chapter proposals and providing very detailed, constructive, and insightful comments for the authors. Without their help and expert opinions, it would have been impossible to make decisions on each submitted chapter. Finally, we are truly grateful to the authors of all chapter proposals who responded to our invitation to submit their best works and made such a high quality collection possible in the first place. The authors and the reviewers of the chapters in this collection deserve all the credit, while the editors are only the ones to blame for any shortcomings and/or omissions.

To conclude, it has been a great pleasure and very rewarding experience for us to edit this collection, and we hope that the reader will have just as much pleasure while reading it.

Atilla Elçi
Aksaray University, Turkey

Mehmet A. Orgun
Macquarie University, Australia

Josef Pieprzyk
Macquarie University, Australia

Alexander G. Chefranov
Eastern Mediterranean University, North Cyprus

Huaxiong Wang
Nanyang Technological University, Singapore

Rajan Shankaran
Macquarie University, Australia

Section 1
Cryptographic Methods Analysis

Chapter 1
Ontology-Based Analysis of Cryptography Standards and Possibilities of Their Harmonization

Alexey Y. Atiskov
St. Petersburg Institute for Informatics and Automation of Russian Academy of Sciences, Russia

Fedor A. Novikov
St. Petersburg State Polytechnical University, Russia

Ludmila N. Fedorchenko
St. Petersburg Institute for Informatics and Automation of Russian Academy of Sciences, Russia

Vladimir I. Vorobiev
St. Petersburg Institute for Informatics and Automation of Russian Academy of Sciences, Russia

Nickolay A. Moldovyan
St. Petersburg Institute for Informatics and Automation of Russian Academy of Sciences, Russia

ABSTRACT

Security means for shared computer, networking, and information resources are not balanced, inefficient, and poorly integrative. This chapter gives a brief overview of certain discrepancies and incompletenesses of ISO standards ISO 15408, ISO 18045, ISO 27k, etc., which are not balanced. Formal methods for their harmonization and coordination are described. Then the chapter discusses Hybrid Ontology Technology using Unified Modeling Language, State Transitions Model (state machine diagrams), and a special tool based on Equivalent Transformations of syntax graph-scheme.

DOI: 10.4018/978-1-4666-4030-6.ch001

INTRODUCTION

Nowadays security means for shared computer, networking, and information resources are not balanced, inefficient, and poorly integrative. It is primarily caused by the fact that the security object is a highly complicated nonlinear system having many degrees of freedom, but also by lack of balanced standards, regulations, structures, and policies.

In particular, the use of Russian (national) cryptographic standards such as:

- GOST 28147-89 "Information processing systems. Cryptographic protection. Algorithm of a cryptographic transformation,"
- GOST R 34.10-2001 "Information technology. Cryptographic protection of information. Processes of construction and verification for digital signatures,"
- GOST R 34.11-94 "Information technology. Cryptography information protection. Hash function" makes it impossible to certify cryptography systems according to the Common Criteria (ISO / IEC 15408:2005 Information technology—Security techniques—Evaluation criteria for IT security).

It is important to note that the set of regulating documents recently approved by ISO / IEC 15408 still plays an important role in unification and structuring of IT-security activities from organizational and technological points of view.

As compared with existing solutions, in particular, expert methods for cryptography standards analysis, ontology approach has certain advantages:

- Ontology provides an integral systematic view for the user as regards the group of cryptography standards;
- All the data on the standards are presented uniformly;
- All the synonyms are reduced to one notion, multi-valued (poly-semantic) words are referred to different notions, so there is no room for duplications or contradictions;
- Ontological model is an open one.

Important applications of the above approach include the analysis of security assurance analysis in cloud computing, i.e., the problems of user non-participation in control and protection of their information resources, which causes distrust in security and regulation of user data access, especially for legally relevant data. Cryptography means are preferable for security assurance in cloud computations. Moreover, user activities are not always transparent; therefore, additional complications arise in the sphere of compliance with standards.

That is why the essential problem as regards risk decrease is to provide proofs of effectiveness of cloud computing since security services in cloud technologies have been proposed but cannot be verified by the user.

BASIC PROBLEMS

Preliminary content analysis of standards based on semiformal models to be mentioned below revealed certain discrepancies and incompletenesses, in particular, concerned with ill-conditioned interpretations of the basic domain concepts such as Threat, Vulnerability, Asset, Countermeasure, Threat agent, etc., uncertainty of some primary concepts, and consequently incompleteness or inconsistency of certain provisions and recommendations.

These facts are most noticeable in the secondary national standard version, but the English-language original can hardly claim to be the logical perfection. Therefore, Committee JTC 1/

SC 27/WG 2 has included the following activities in the Work program: improving the applicability of cryptographic standards, active review of the existing cryptographic standards, and elimination of weak schemes, including new and more effective schemes.

Due to high importance of IT-security and its international nature, all standards strongly lack harmonization, first of all in sematics, both on national and international scale.

It is clear that any agreed technical policy requires that conceptual apparatus be definite and unambiguous. However, the process of harmonization should not maintain at the level of linguistic discussions. Meaningful results can hardly be obtained without formalization and automation of this process. An example of unsuccessful harmonization attempt is GOST R ISO / IEC 10116-93 “Information technology. Modes of operation for an n-bit block cipher algorithm”; ISO / IEC 10116: 2006 “Modes of operation for an n-bit block cipher algorithm (3rd edition).”

From the practical standpoint, the standards harmonization should be implemented in the following directions.

The first one is the harmonization within the CC line, including the CC itself, the Common Evaluation Methodology (ISO 15408), national and international cryptographic standards, common methodology for IT security evaluation (ISO 18045) and the Guide to develop protection profiles and security targets. The focus here is made on harmonization and compliance of national standards with Common Criteria. Another much more pressing and universal problem is harmonization of Common Criteria and ISMS (ISO 27000).

The second direction is the harmonization between the CC line and ISMS standards. Contents and interpretations of line’s basic concepts may be surely brought together and the solution for these and similar problems is the primary goal of harmonization at the ontological level. At the methodical level, core (ontological) harmonization provides required tools for handling the normative risks. The only way to avoid double work and expenses is to create the information security system that would be acceptable for both framework requirements.

At the software development level there is the problem of tools’ adjustment to support standards. Solving this problem should help obtain significant results because of its strong attention to formalization and automation.

At the level of normative-methodical documents, ontological harmonization can successfully solve the problem of reducing normative risks for organizations. For example, it is a common situation (most often, in the financial sphere), when an organization needs both ISMS certification (required by the partners) and Common Criteria certification (required by the state institutions).

To avoid double work (and not to bear the double cost), the organization needs to build an information security system complying with both families of standards. This can hardly be done without harmonization of standards at the top conceptual level. Harmonization in the broadest sense can be interpreted as standardization of data.

It is proposed to achieve harmonization using ontological engineering, which includes construction of taxonomies of terms, predictive relationships between the terms, logical conclusions based on descriptive logic, and means of ontology integration such as mapping, alignment, and merging. The aim is to build a consistent formal description or formal unification of the subject area and to develop the application software to support the unified schema. To reach this aim, terminological taxonomies, predicative relations, and ontological restrictions should be developed to derive new data types and extend the set of inference rules. Clarification of terminology and relationships can (and probably will) occur directly in the course of development of ontologies (ontology series), due to the flexibility of ontological descriptions (atomicity, where an atom is a logical triple) unlike the descriptions of data structures based on relational tables.

At the next level, the following problem arises: harmonization of tools to support implementation of standards in practice. Currently, these tools are developed and exist independently. The tools are mostly developed using UML–tools or similar ones. The developers, however, have to develop their own object model of standards. Ontology-based harmonized object models would make it possible to coordinate the software and the process of IT security evaluation.

However, for long-term problems it is not sufficient. Ontological modeling should be used in further work. It will provide an effective meta-description of standards in the form of formal computer models (for example, semantic networks [Berners-Lee, Hendler, & Lassila, 2001]), automation of their notional comparison by means of semantic analysis, and a software mechanism to access standards using web-based technologies.

Another approach is to describe natural text of articles of standards as syntax of the algorithmic high-level languages using two-level WW-grammar, or attribute CF grammars, Wirth diagrams, syntax graph schema, etc. Ontology can be described using these powerful syntax-oriented mechanisms; the only question is how effectively they are used. We would like to believe that using meta-description of security standards ensures the conditions for their harmonization at different levels and in different directions.

The authors have experience in semantic analysis of the conceptual apparatus of Common Criteria and ISMS standards using semiformal means of modeling. This experience suggests the usefulness of such analysis. In particular, we have constructed the following models (Czarnecki & Helsen, 2003; Fedorchenko, 2011):

- Object-oriented model of the overall security context complying with Common Criteria;
- Object-oriented model of the threat complying with Common Criteria;
- Object-oriented model of the threat context complying with Common Criteria;
- Fully functional IT evaluation model complying with Common Criteria and Common Evaluation Methodology – ISO 18045;
- Fully functional model of ISMS requirements complying with ISO 27001;
- Object-oriented model of ISMS requirements complying with ISO 27001, etc.

The transition from standard texts to formalized ontological descriptions implies the definition of the ontological triples:

- Set of concepts (notions, terms);
- Set of relations between concepts;
- Rules of inference in the network of concepts and relationships (e.g., the rule of transitivity, symmetry, antisymmetry, reflexivity).

The process of logic inference can be divided into two stages. The first stage of derivation schemes yields regular expressions, which makes it possible to effectively use a special tool designed at St. Petersburg Institute for Informatics and Automation of Russian Academy of Sciences (SPIIRAS) to reduce the rule schemes and derivation schemes (e.g., to remove blind alleys [deadlocks], and cyclic conclusions, and modus ponens). The second stage requires the use of grammars containing context-sensitive rules, which can also be analyzed.

For ontological descriptions, we develop an automated interface with the export-import tool for describing in UML.

The main properties of our hybrid harmonization system are as follows:

- System modularity;
- Independence of input and output notation syntax (using JAXB- Java Architecture for

XML Binding), which facilitates access to XML documents from Java applications);
- Abstract definition of notation semantics using OWL-description (McGuinness & Deborah, 2009), which is determined by abstract transformation rules (in the form of logical triples);
- Possibility of using SPARQL for realization (SPARQL, 2008).

It can be noted that rule implementation of rules is controlled by the user, and the system should be self-adapting for input (for example, for descriptions of UML or IDEF standards). Therefore, a Semantic Web pyramid was applied to solve the transformation problem (Berners-Lee, Hendler, & Lassila, 2001). It is experimentally verified that semantic analysis and metadata transformation methods are suitable not only to for text but also for any other data formats (if they can be formalized in RDF standard [Manola & Miller, 2004]). Put shortly, the backbone of such technique is the extraction of data and their context or extraction of metadata from the original document, formalization of extracted information in the form of semantic Semantic web, and subsequent formal comparison of different standards.

HYBRID TECHNOLOGY

We introduce a new technology (Atiskov, 2012) to transform IDEF0 [IDEF0 Draft] diagrams into UML diagrams. There was mentioned in Meyer(1988), existing model-to-model transformation approaches can be classified into direct manipulation approaches, relational approaches, graph-transformation-based approaches, structure-driven approaches, and hybrid approaches. These approaches are described below:

- Direct manipulation is obviously the most low-level approach. It offers the user little or no support or guidance in implementing transformations. Basically all work has to be done by the user. In the long run, this approach will become impractical.
- The structure-driven category groups pragmatic approaches that were developed in the context of certain kinds of applications such as generating EJB implementations and database schemas from UML models. These applications require a strong support for transforming models with a 1-to-1 and 1-to-n (and sometimes n-to-1) correspondence between source and target elements.
- Graph-transformation-based approaches are inspired by heavily theoretical work in graph transformations. These approaches are powerful and declarative, but also the most complex ones. The complexity stems from the non-determinism in scheduling and application strategy, which requires careful consideration of termination of the transformation process and the rule application ordering (including the property of confluence). There is a large amount of theoretical work and some experience with research prototypes. However, experience with practical applications of these approaches is still limited.
- Relational approaches seem to strike a good balance between flexibility and declarative expression. They provide flexible scheduling and good control of non-determinism.
- Hybrid approaches allow the user to mix and match different concepts and paradigms depending on the application. Practical approaches are very likely to have the hybrid character.

That is why we have decided to create a hybrid technology for semiautomatic transformation of IDEF0 diagrams into UML class diagrams. We developed special extensions for OWL to use this language for describing IDEF0 and UML notations. A new algorithm of creating and implementation of transformation rules (SPARQL queries) has been implemented. Software using hybrid technology to semiautomatically transform IDEF0 diagrams into UML class diagrams has been developed.

Primitives for Ontology

The following primitives were used to describe the notations of modeling:

1. **owl:Class:** Class defining a group of objects with common properties. Classes are organized in special hierarchy by relation rdfs:subClassOf;
2. **owl:Thing:** Class combining all objects and being a super-class for all classes in this ontology;
3. **rdfs:subClassOf:** Hierarchy of classes formed by defining one or more relationships between classes showing that one class as a subclass of the other;
4. **rdf:Property:** Property defining special relations between objects or between object and data value. In the first case owl:ObjectProperty is used, in the second case, owl:DatatypeProperty is used; owl:Restriction – specifies the restriction of the use of property rdf: Property (relationships with owl: onProperty) for an object of a particular class;
5. **owl:onProperty:** The relation defining the property rdf: Property, for which a restriction owl:Restriction is stated;
6. **rdfs:domain:** The relation associated with the rdf: Property, defining the subject (in a logical triple subject-predicate-object), namely class, an object of which can only be determined by the property;
7. **rdfs:range:** Defines a logical triple unlike the rdfs:domain object;
8. **owl:cardinality:** Type of restriction. Shows how the ratio is related to the number that describes the exact number of elements of a particular property owl:Property to be defined for specific instances of the class owl:Class. In the ontology described the use of owl:cardinality is always associated with the number "1", meaning that the associated property should be defined only once;
9. **owl:minCardinality:** Type of restriction. Unlike the owl:cardinality defines the minimum number of elements of a particular property for a specific class.

Figure 1. Example of IDEF0 diagram

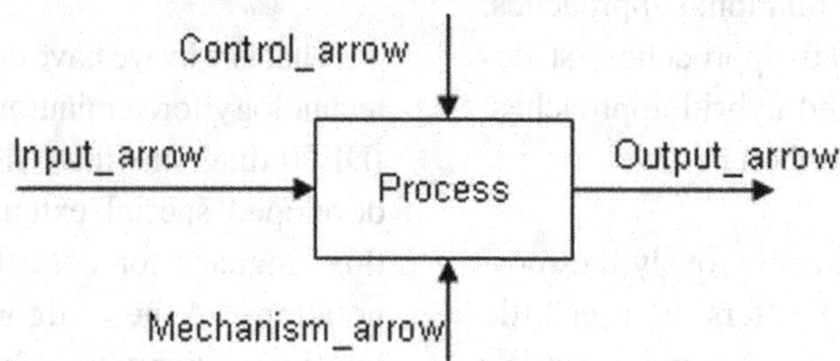

OWL-description of IDEF0 diagram structure is built using two types of elements (blocks and arrows) and the relations between them. Arrows may be of four types (input, output, control, and mechanism), and may begin and end on blocks or on sides of the diagram (Figure 1).

Blocks can also be decomposed (i.e., a unit may contain a number of others). Arrows can merge and split. Description of IDEF0 standard makes it possible to build its OWL-interpretation in Protégé software.

In course of development of OWL-description, combining the functional approach (diagrams IDEF0) and object-oriented approach (UML class diagrams), the following concepts were introduced: classes owl:Class, properties owl:Property, including owl:ObjectProperty and owl:DatatypeProperty, and relationships

- **tf:Functional:** owl:Class, which is a parent of all the classes describing the metadata of IDEF0 diagrams.
- **tf:ObjectOriented:** Unlike the tf:Functional its successors are the classes describing the metadata of UML class diagrams.

OWL-Description of IDEF0 Notation

Figure 2 shows the elements of IDEF0 diagram connected with parent class tf:Functional by using the relation owl:subClassOf: predefined in OWL (Algorithm in Algorithm 1):

- **tf:Arrow:** Class denoted by "arrow" in IDEF0 diagrams;
- **tf:Block:** Class denoted by "block" in IDEF0 diagrams;
- **tf:ArrowEnd:** Relationship between specific "arrow" and "block". It has the following varieties: tf:Control, tf:Input, tf:Output, tf:Mechanism.

OWL-Description of UML Class Diagram Notation

OWL-description of UML class diagrams uses the basic entities used in creating UML class diagrams: class, attribute, method, and method parameter, relation type (inheritance, association, composition, and dependency). This description should be based on primitives used for universal OWL-description of transformed diagrams. That's why we couldn't use approaches like in Mehrolhassani and Elзi (2008).

The elements of UML class diagrams (Figure 3) (relating to the superclass tf:ObjectOriented) include:

- **tf:Type:** Class representing the conventional concept of "type" with subclasses tf:Class and tf:PrimitiveType;
- **tf:Attribute:** Denotes the attribute of class tf:Class;
- **tf:Method:** Denotes the method of class tf:Class;

Figure 2. Graphical representation of OWL-description of IDEF0 notation

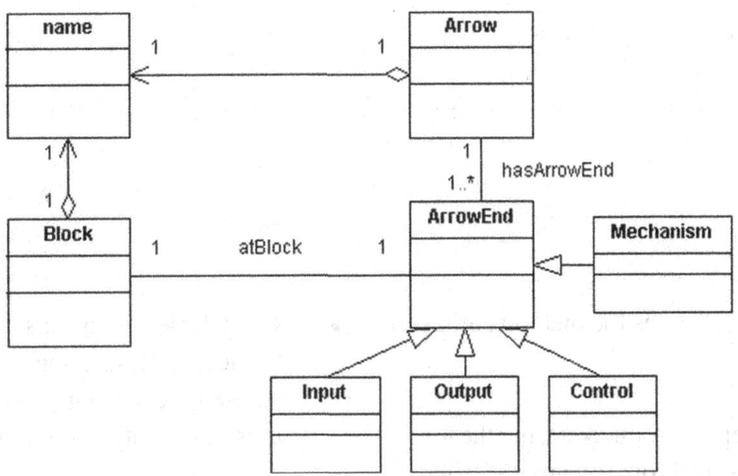

Algortihm 1. XML file for an example of IDEF0 diagram

```
<tf:Control rdf:ID="Control_3">
  <tf:atBlock>
    <tf:Block rdf:ID="Block_2">
      <tf:name rdf:datatype="http://www.w3.org/2001/XMLSchema#string">b2</
tf:name>
    </tf:Block>
  </tf:atBlock>
</tf:Control>
<tf:Control rdf:ID="Control_2"><tf:atBlock rdf:resource="#Block_2"/>
</tf:Control>
<tf:Arrow rdf:ID="Arrow_2">
  <tf:name rdf:datatype="http://www.w3.org/2001/XMLSchema#string">a2</tf:name>
  <tf:hasArrowEnd rdf:resource="#Control_3"/>
</tf:Arrow>
<tf:Arrow rdf:ID="Arrow_1">
  <tf:name rdf:datatype="http://www.w3.org/2001/XMLSchema#string">a1</tf:name>
  <tf:hasArrowEnd>
    <tf:Control rdf:ID="Control_1">
      <tf:atBlock>
          <tf:Block rdf:ID="Block_1">
              <tf:name rdf:datatype="http://www.w3.org/2001/
XMLSchema#string">b1</tf:name>
          </tf:Block>
      </tf:atBlock>
    </tf:Control>
  </tf:hasArrowEnd>
  <tf:hasArrowEnd rdf:resource="#Control_2"/>
  <tf:hasArrowEnd>
  <tf:Input rdf:ID="Input_1"><tf:atBlock rdf:resource="#Block_1"/>
  </tf:Input>
  </tf:hasArrowEnd>
  <tf:hasArrowEnd>
    <tf:Output rdf:ID="Output_1"><tf:atBlock rdf:resource="#Block_1"/>
    </tf:Output>
  </tf:hasArrowEnd>
</tf:Arrow>
```

- **tf:Parameter:** Denotes the method parameter tf:Method;

To link the concepts introduced earlier the following relationships rdf:Property: are identified

- **tf:atBlock:** Connects tf:ArrowEnd and tf:Block. Restriction owl:Restriction is defined, according to which tf:ArrowEnd must have only one relation tf:atBlock;

Figure 3. Graphical representation of OWL-description of UML class diagram notation

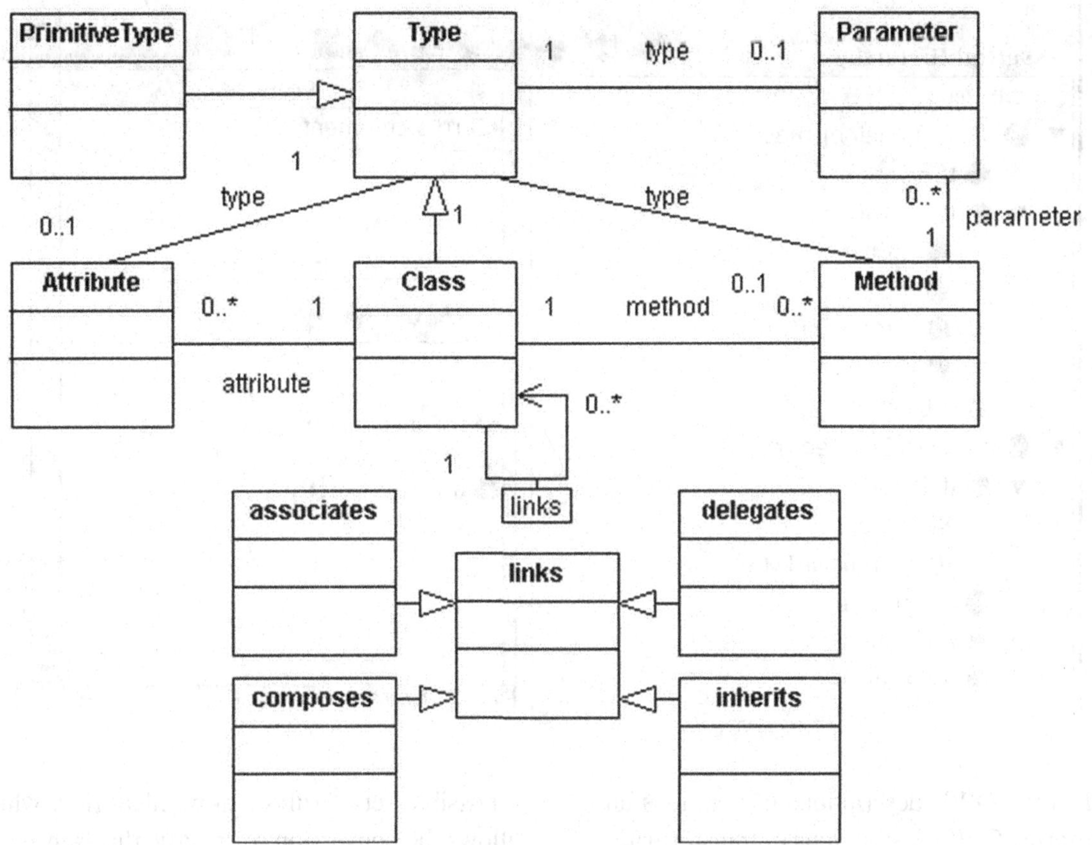

- **tf:hasArrowEnd:** Connects tf:Arrow and tf:ArrowEnd. Restriction is defined, according to which tf:Arrow must have at least one relationship (property) tf:hasArrowEnd;
- **tf:type:** Connects tf:Attribute, tf:Method, and tf:Parameter with tf:Type. Restriction is defined, according to which the logical triple must have only one such relation;
- **tf:parameter:** Connects tf:Method and tf:Parameter;
- **tf:attribute:** Connects tf:Class and tf:Attribute;
- **tf:method:** Connects tf:Class and tf:Method;
- **tf:links:** Connects various instances of tf:Class. This relationship has the following varieties: tf:composes, tf:inherits, tf:delegates, tf:associates.

The 'SUBCLASS EXPLORER' window (Figure 4) defines a hierarchy of owl:Class (with the root class owl:Thing), described in Protégé (Musen, 2012) for ontology linking of functional approach to tf:FunctionalApproach (Figure 2) in IDEF0 diagrams and object-based tf:ObjectOrientedApproach – in UML class diagrams (Figure 3). The lower right window shows the restriction owl:Restriction defined for the class of tf:Arrow.

OWL-Description of Transformation Rules

For a formal description of the rules (as a set of logical triples), we introduced additional concepts and relations and also used a number of predefined concepts and relations from RDF language (Table 1).

Figure 4. Screenshot of the Protégé software with OWL-description of notations

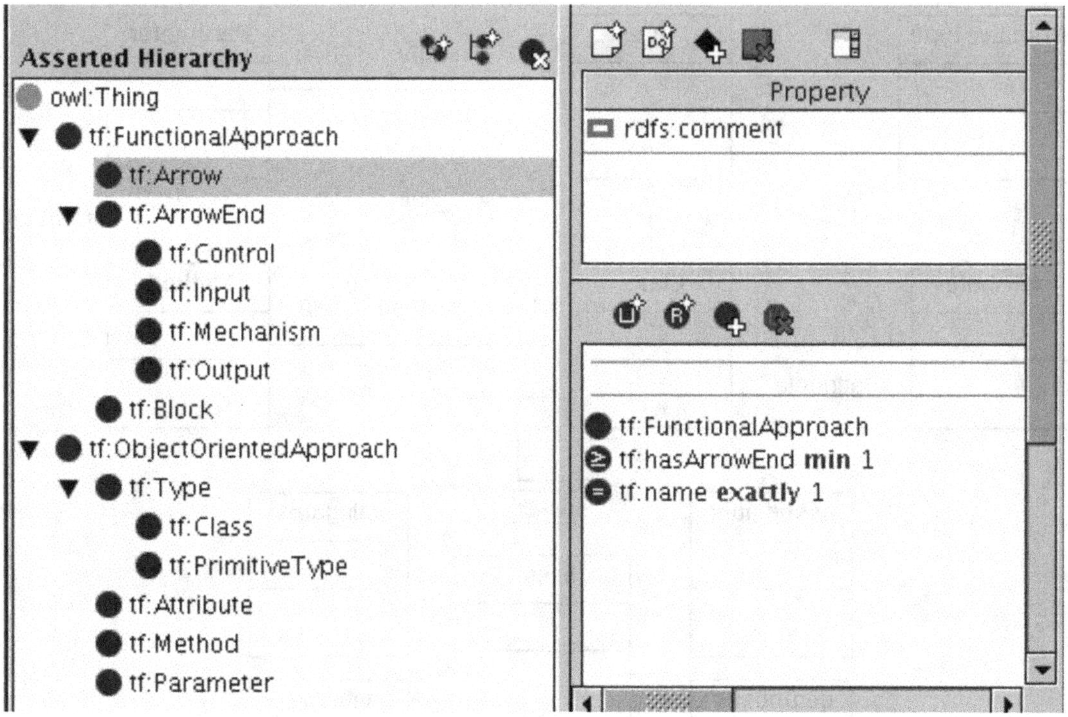

To bind OWL-descriptions of notations and to describe OWL-descriptions of transformation rules, the following concepts were introduced:

- **tf:Transform:** Concept denoting the rule;
- **tf:Object:** Bariable applied in the rule;

and relationships (properties):

- **tf:functionalTemplate:** Property of rule tf:Transform, which connects rule with the union of the set conditions of rdf:Statement, which describes the part of the rules relating to the IDEF0diagram;
- **tf:objectOrientedTemplate:** Unlike the tf:functionalTemplate it connects rule with the part that refers to the UML class diagram.

It should be noted that the rules cannot be regarded as stable and unchanging. In other words, a possible set of rules can be identified, which allows the conversion of specific diagram.

The rules are presented in the form of relationship of two sets – a set of elements of the transformed IDEF0 diagram and a set of elements from UML class diagrams. But for a consistent definition we used the list of logical

Table 1. RDF concepts and relations

RDF Definition	
rdf:Statement	denotes the rule condition (in the form of logical triple)
rdf:parseType=«Collection»	denotes the union of a finite set of concepts
rdf:subject	binds condition rdf:Statement to the subject, which is a part of a logical triple describing this condition
rdf:predicate	binds rdf:Statement to the predicate
rdf:object	binds rdf:Statement to the object

triples (subject-predicate-object), which should be complete enough for an unambiguous definition of the desired item in a particular transformation.

Consider the example of the transformation rule "Names of all IDEF0 mechanism arrows are transformed into class names of UML class diagram." Due to Protégé limited capacity as regards the description of relationships between the classes owl:Class, we used an abstract form of description, namely the description of this rule as a logical set of triples. This representation can be interpreted as a set of objects; relations between them are shown in Figure 5.

The root element is divided into three parts (original data functionalTemplate, target data objectOrientedTemplate, and the type of conversion is transformation).

Figure 6 shows the first triple in the form of logical expression, the result of this query is an Arrow (tf:Arrow), whose type (tf:hasArrowEnd) is a mechanism (tf:Mechanism).

Figure 7 shows the second triple in the form of a logical expression, the result of this query is an arrow (tf:Arrow), which has a name (tf:name) that can be converted into the target object (tf:Object).

Figure 8 shows the third triple in the form of a logical expression, the result of this query is a UML class (tf:Class), which has a name (tf:name) into which the target object (tf:Object) is transformed.

Figure 5. Set of logical triples for an example of transformation rule (statement_1 is shown in Figure 6, statement_2 — in Figure 7, statement_3 — in Figure 8)

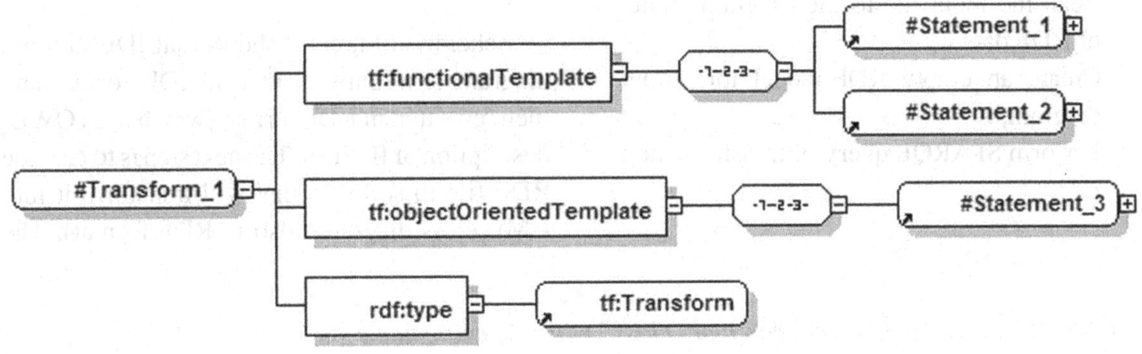

Figure 6. The expression for the search of "mechanism arrow"

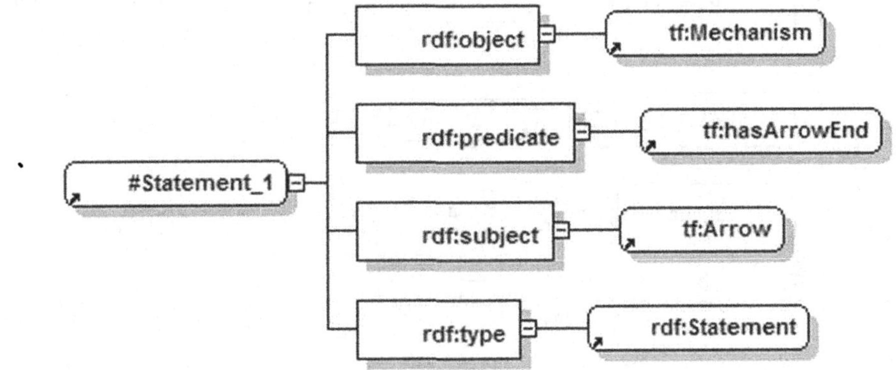

Figure 7. The expression for the search of "arrow" with a specific name

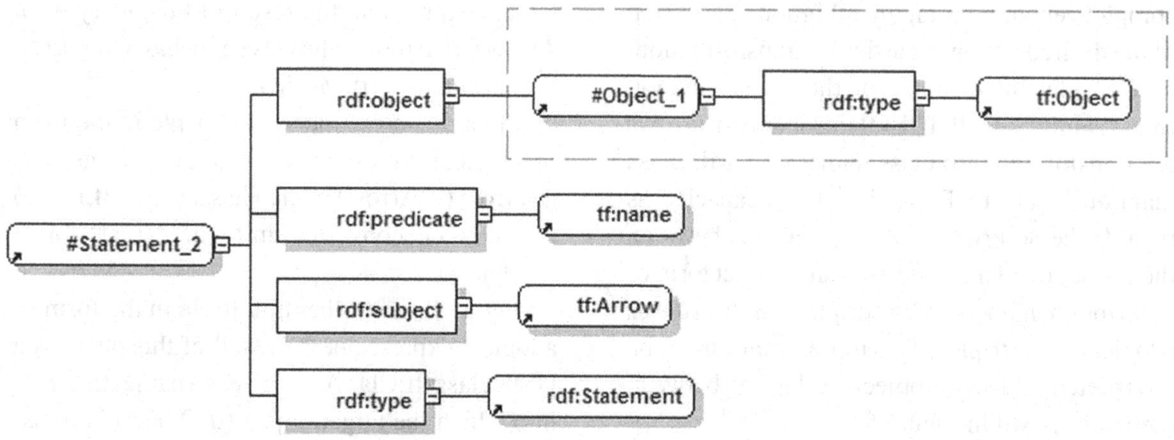

Algorithm of Transformation from IDEF0 to UML Class Diagram

The developed software uses the following algorithm:

- Read the input file to the program model of RDF data,
- Create an empty RDF-model for output diagram,
- Perform SPARQL query of transformation rule,
- Get result of query, combine it with RDF-model for output diagram and proceed to next rule,
- Repeat the steps 3-5 for all transformation rules,
- Write RDF-model into output file.

Scheme in Figure 9 shows that IDEF0 input diagram is initially written in IDL format and then rewritten in RDF format (which uses OWL-description of IDEF0). The next step is to provide RDF file to software that will transform it into UML class diagram (also in RDF format). The

Figure 8. The expression for the search of "class" with a specific name

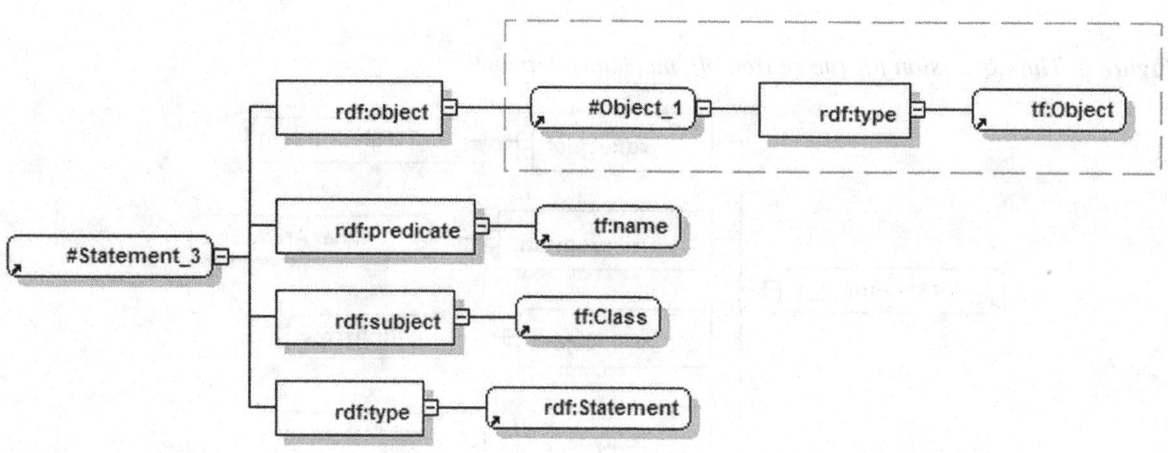

Figure 9. Hybrid semi-automatic transformation of IDEF0 diagrams into UML class diagrams

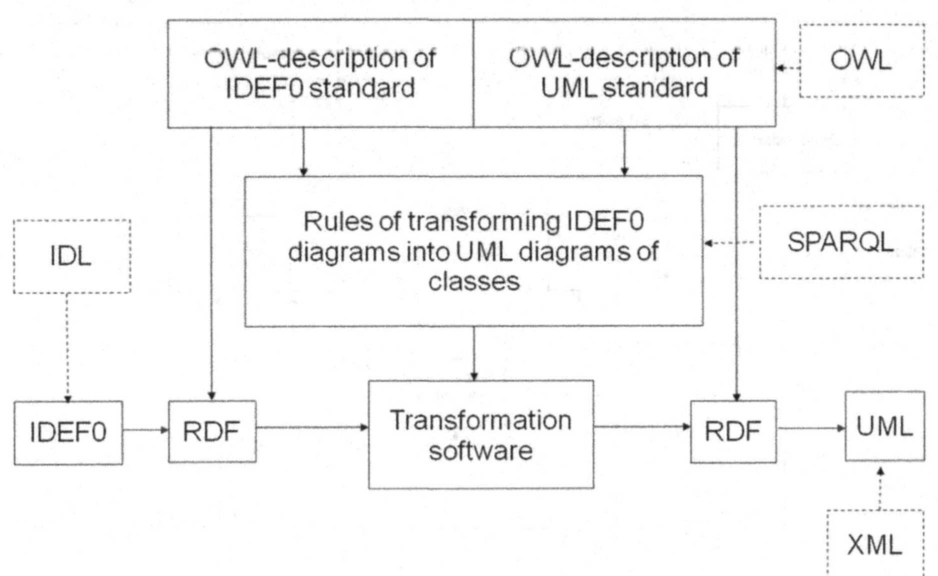

last step is to rewrite output file of UML diagram into format that can be used in external tools (such as Borland Together). Standards are given in dotted blocks.

We will show its capabilities by example of ontological formalization of transformation (translation) of IDEF0 diagrams into UML class diagrams UML (see Figure 10, Figure 11, Figure 12, and Figure13). Consider a rule which describes that the mechanism nodes in IDEF0 should be transformed into the objects of the UML class, which will own functional block, to which mechanism node is connected.

The proposed rule consists of several statements. Firstly, we formalize the transformation for the proposition: "Mechanism arrows in IDEF0 are objects of UML class." Since the conversion problem is reduced to the transformation of RDF-format data (describing the IDEF0-diagram) to another format (describing the UML-diagram), standardized query language SPARQL (Atiskov & Perminov, 2007) is used to extract data from the IDEF0-diagram.

RDF-identifiers will be kept while transforming.

Algorithm 2 is a part of SPARQL-query describing the class object is saved as a separate variable, because its text would be used in other queries.

To bring the request to the final (standardized) form it is quite sufficient to make some preprocessing, replace variable %class by its value and add the prefix data. The other side of transformation is generation of output data for the RDF-data for UML diagram. Since the standard SPARQL supports read-only format RDF-data

Algorithm 2. Part of SPARQL-query describing the class object

```
%class =
?class  a tf:Mechanism.
_:class a tf:Arrow.
_:class tf:hasArrowEnd ?class
Query:
SELECT  ?class  ?name
WHERE {
%class.
_:class tf:name ?name
}
```

Figure10. Source data to transform (IDEF0 diagram) (1 from 3)

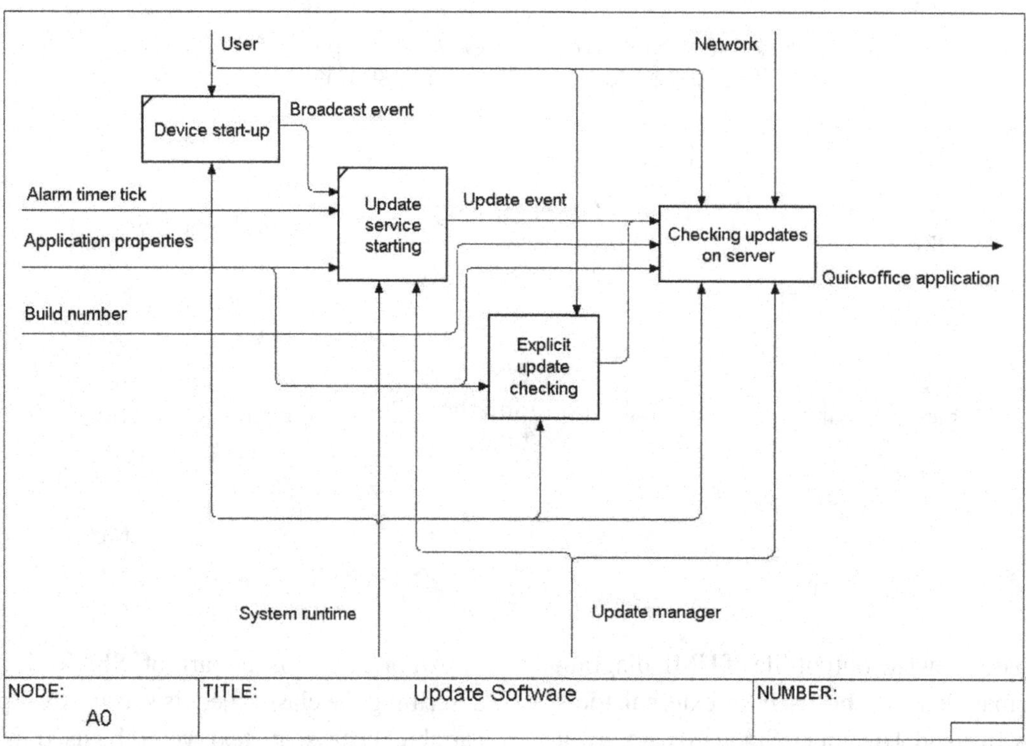

Figure 11. Source data to transform (IDEF0 diagram) (2 from 3)

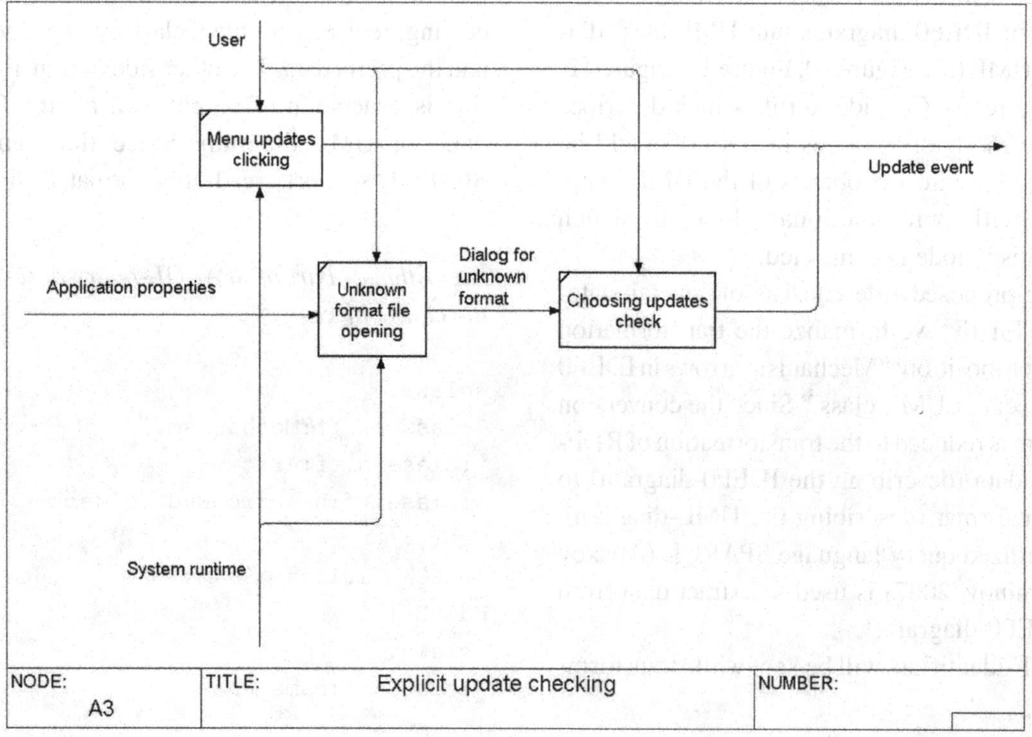

Figure 12. Source data to transform IDEF0

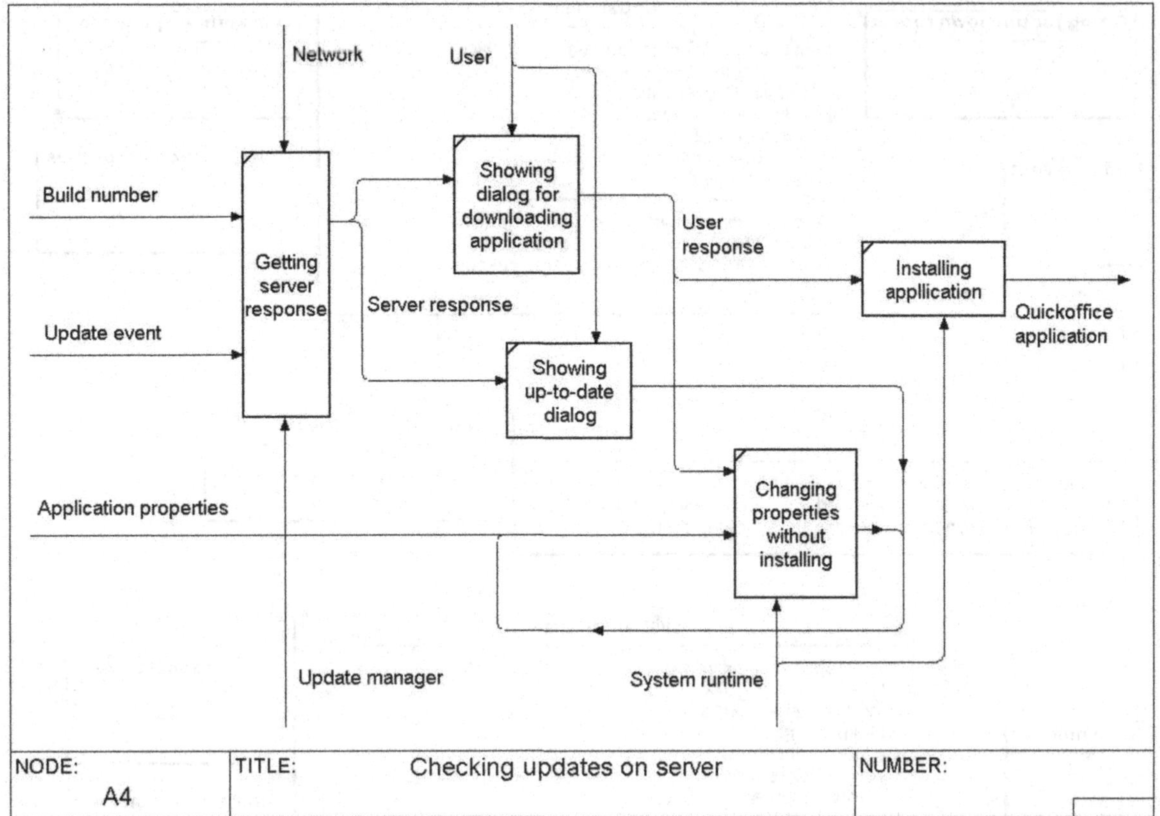

we use standard notation based on SPARQL primitives. The notation uses a logic triple created from the array for each result of the SPARQL processor.

It should be noted that in this case we applied several layers proposed in Semantic Web (Atiskov & Perminov, 2007), which is the experimental proof of the assumption that semantic search method using metadata is suitable for analysis and transformation of not only Internet data, but also for any other data, if it can be formalized for RDF presentation. The essence of this technique is to extract data and their context or metadata from the original document, formalize the presentation of the extracted information in the form of semantic web and the performed formal search.

The model library is permanently expanded; however, it is not an adequate solution for perspective problems. Ontological modeling is needed in future work because it provides effective meta-descriptions of standards using a formal computer model (Semantic Web), automation of their ontological merging and mapping using semantic analysis methods, and common software access using web-technologies for their description. This approach provides conditions for harmonization at different levels and in different directions. The developed interface will allow automated export-import to UML tools for using with ontological descriptions.

HARMONIZATION OF BEHAVIOR

Information security standards strongly lack the means for description of behavior of interacting

Figure 13. The result of transformation: UML diagram

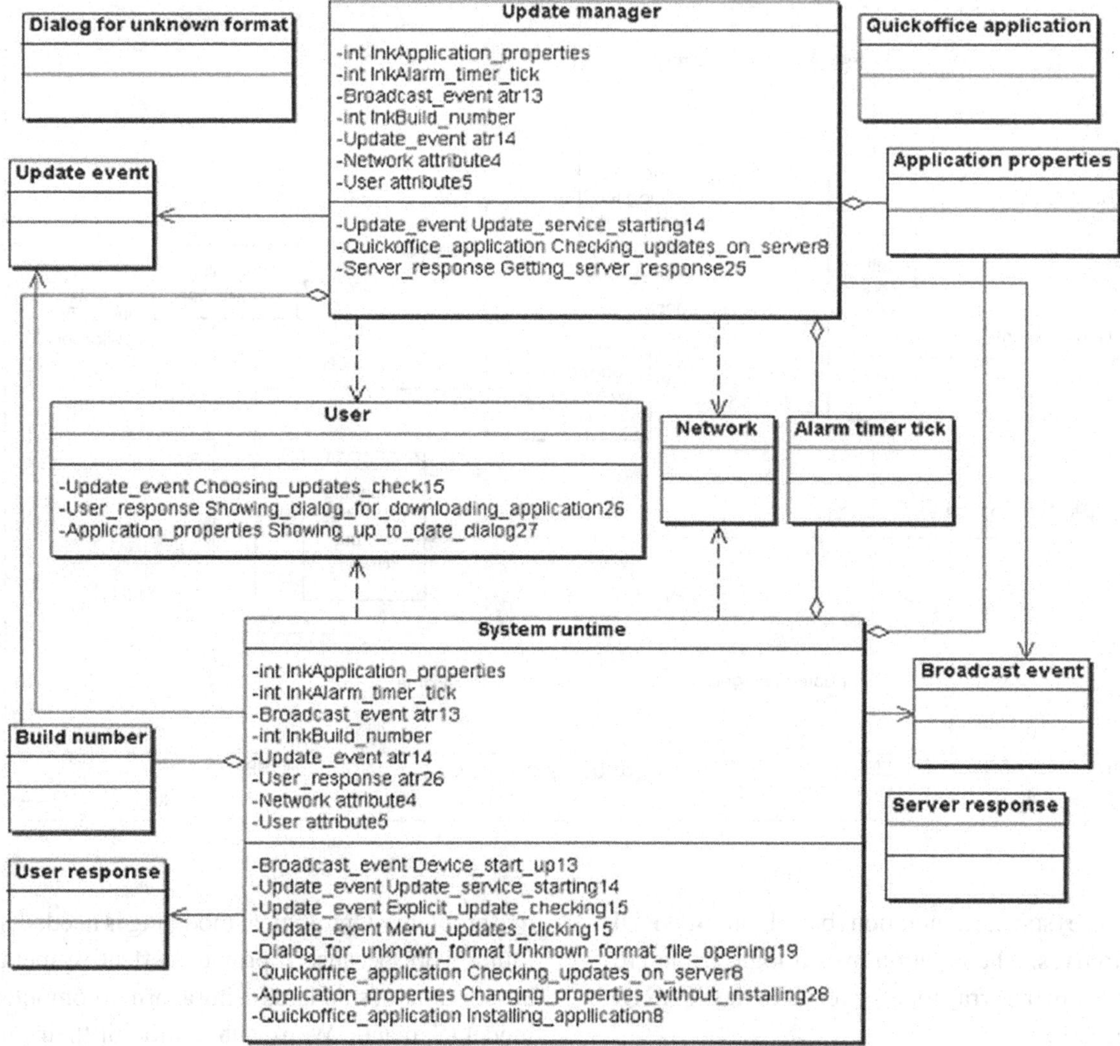

parties. For example, the public key infrastructure standards assume that public key owner should get valid certificate and the end user of the public key should check the validity of the certificate, otherwise they would fail to establish secure information connection. Therefore exact and exhaustive descriptions of action and event sequences form significant parts of many standards. Description of action and event sequence is generally referred to as behavior description or behavior model or, for short, behavior.

Most standards describe behavior in plain English. In ordinary cases it is quite sufficient, but not in a sophisticated cryptography algorithm. With account for the problems of national standards connected with the language peculiarities such as modality, imperative and subjunctive mood, etc., it becomes quite clear that formal description of behavior is preferable. There are a lot of behavior formal models (Bock, 1999), and the most popular of them are unified within UML frame. These are state transition model (state machine diagrams), control and object flow model (activity diagrams) and messaging model (sequence and other interaction diagrams). Description of behavior with these formal diagrams reveals discrepancies in standards, enables formal verification and gains other benefits. The problem is that these models work well in their particular fields, namely object-oriented software system design, and reveal lack of generalization at the ontological level. Thus we introduce state machine diagram extension, easy to use and at the same time general enough to meet the requirement of standard harmonization.

The next section contains a brief description of behavior model proposed, and then we demonstrate the model to be general enough due to its Turing completeness, and finally analyze a well-known example of behavior description.

Automata Objects Cooperation as a Behavior Model

First of all, we describe the behavior of several communication objects or actors, rather than behavior of one standalone object. One of the most important features we want to achieve in the introduced behavior model is modularity. Activity diagrams have no means of interaction with each other; therefore, they cannot be used. Sequence diagrams, especially in the form of communication diagram, do have such means, but these diagrams are obviously extremely low level, far below the level of ontology we need, so they are rejected too. A state machine diagram is the only suitable choice, but it needs some extensions. Therefore, we extend the notion of finite automaton specified by the UML state machine with features serving for interaction with other objects and/or with external environment. We assume the communicating object to be a first class real world object able to do whatever it has to. That is why there are no restrictions on the acceptable actions in the behavior model described. It draws us away from limited model of finite automata and leads us to a powerful model of automata objects cooperation.

Figure 14 shows the basic concepts of behavior model. Part (a) shows four principal interfaces for automata objects interaction. Part (b) shows the model of an automata object interacting with other objects.

Consider the model in detail. An automata object models a behavior. This behavior maps a sequence of events coming from an Event source object to a sequence of effects which may yield event performed by a Controlled object. The mapping is modeled through two interactions, as shown in Figure 14, one between Automata object and Controlled object and other one

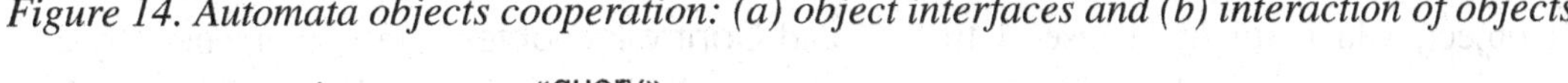

Figure 14. Automata objects cooperation: (a) object interfaces and (b) interaction of objects

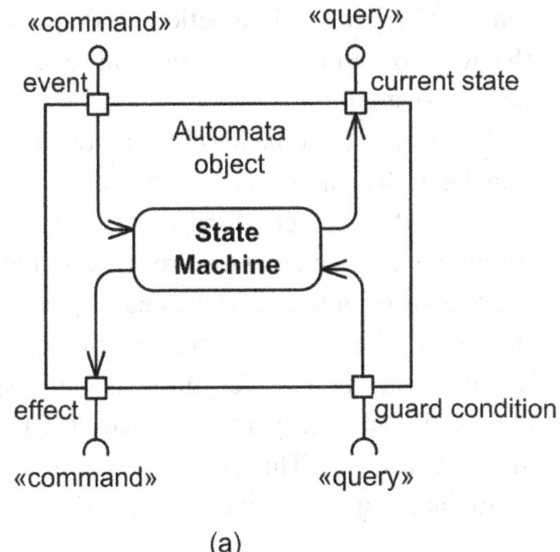

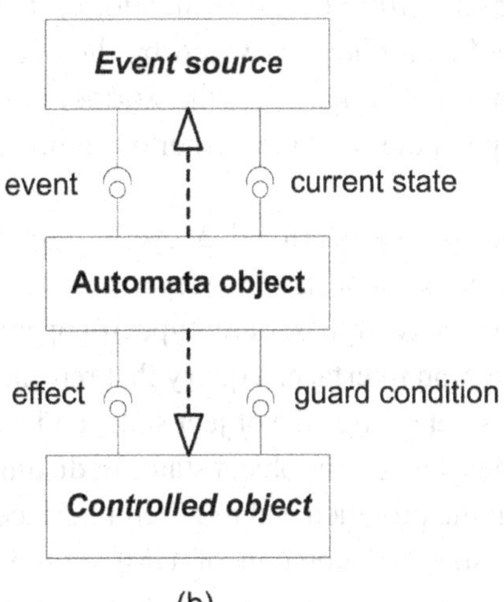

between Automata object and Event source object.

When the automata object receives an event, it handles it just as an ordinary state machine: it checks the guard condition, changes the current state and performs actions (effects) addressed to the controlled object. We model these four concepts as interfaces event, current state, effect and guard condition, shown in Figure 14(a).

- An event is a way to command the automata object and to transmit input to it. Therefore we model it as a command provided by the automata object: the ball with the «command» stereotype in the top left corner of Figure 14(a).
- An effect is the automata object's output, performed on the controlled object. It is modeled as the command required by the automata object: the socket with the «command» stereotype in the bottom left corner of Figure 14(a).
- A guard condition provides a possibility to consider the state of the controlled object. So we model it as a query required by the automata object: the socket with the «query» stereotype in the bottom right corner of Figure 14(a).
- A current state is internal data of the automata object, which might be useful to observe from outside. Therefore it is modeled as a query provided by the automata object – the ball with the «query» stereotype in the right top corner of Figure 14(a).

Here we use Bertrand Meyer's command-query separation principle (Meyer, 1988), which distinguishes two types (stereotypes) of operations of interaction interface: a query that returns data and does not change the object state, and a command that changes the object state. To distinguish between the provided and required interfaces we use the standard notation of UML component diagrams, namely, balls and sockets attached to the borders of objects. Note that all four possible combinations: provided commands, required commands, provided queries and required queries are used. It makes the model the most complete.

There is certain duality of the provided and required commands: an effect on required side turns out to be an event on provided side; similarly, current state on provided side constructs guard condition on required side. It means that Event source and Controlled object are not singular entities, but rather play specific roles as shown in Figure 14(b). In fact, every automata object acts as a source of events or as a controlled object for any other objects or even for itself. This possibility is modeled through realization of relationships between the Automata object and the Event source and the Controlled object, as shown in Figure 14(b). Note that names Event source and Controlled object are given in italics to show that these are roles, or abstract objects in terms of UML. This unification of all interacting components, when any automata object can play any role, provides the modularity declared above.

The interaction model described here can be used in two general ways. If Event source and Controlled object are implemented as external components, the interaction model captures the interaction of an Automata object with an external environment. On the other hand, if Event source and Controlled object are implemented by automata objects, the interaction model describes the way to assemble behaviors in an arbitrary desired system.

The last but not the least, the automata object may be at the same time a source of events and/or a controlled object. Moreover, automata object might be connected with arbitrary number of sources of events and controlled objects simultaneously. The model is extremely flexible, there are no restrictions: everything is permissible, provided conformity of interfaces (respect of signed contracts). That is why we call the model Automata Objects Cooperation (AOC).

Turing Completeness of the Behavior Model

In connection with the problem of standards harmonization, the question arises whether the formal model of behavior is rich enough to capture all practical needs? In the case of AOC the answer is positive: the model is Turing complete and thus sufficient to express any definite behavior. The proof is given in Figure 15 in a form of Turing machine emulator, whose behavior is captured by three cooperative automata objects: control unit, program memory (table of state transitions) and data memory (tape). Figure 15 gives an overview of notation used as well.

Control unit provides only one main command: it can only be started from outside. After the start the Turing machine sets program memory into initial state, gets ready and immediately (spontaneously, as called in UML), reads the symbol from the tape, moves along the tape if needed, writes the symbol to the tape and so on. The control unit uses local variables, denoted a, b, and m of enumerated types Symbol and Move. It does not matter what is inside the "black boxes" Environment, State transition table, and Tape. There might be AOCs of any kind, electronic devices, or human beings, etc. Everything works fine while declared interfaces are provided and the signed contracts are respected.

We see that behavior of Turing machine as it used to be described in manuals has been captured pretty well. But is this diagram of any practical interest? Is it useful in analysis, comparison, and harmonization of behavior descriptions? We believe it is. Even superficial analysis of the diagram in Figure 15 shows that common description of Turing machine behavior is essentially incomplete. For instance, we need the ability to populate the tape with arguments before starting the machine, and to review the results after Turing machine reached a final state. Similarly, we need the ability

Figure 15. Ordinary turing machine as automata objects cooperation

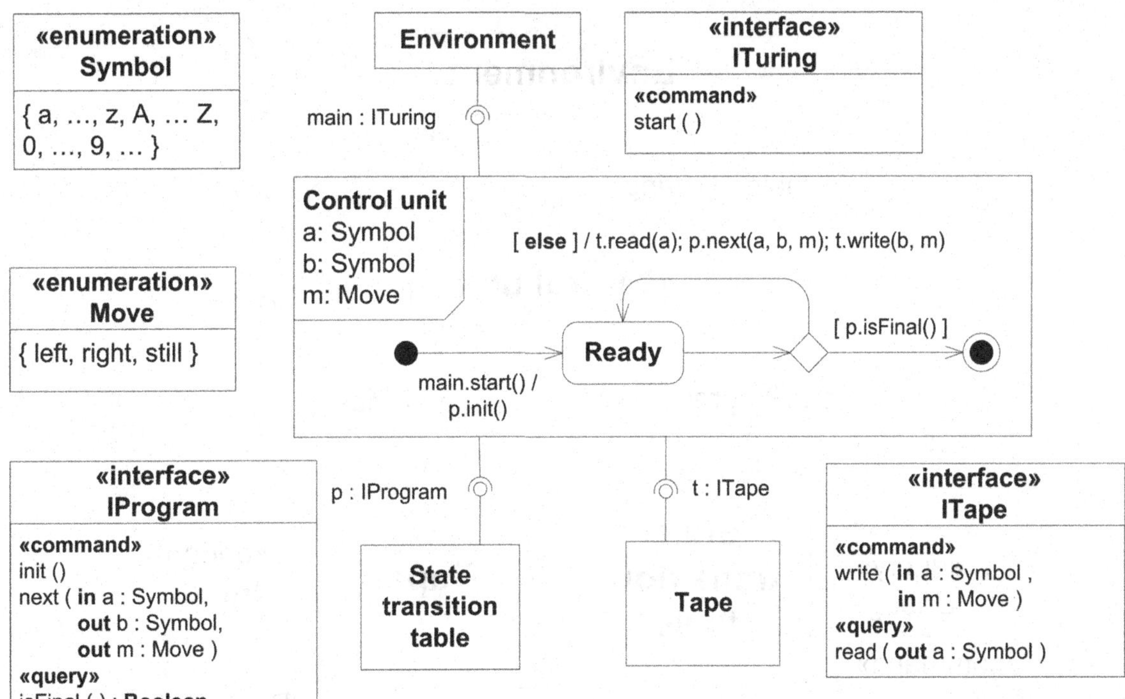

to fill the state transition table cells before starting the machine, and we might badly need the ability to watch its current state if we are going to debug Turing machine. Thus, we arrive at the necessity to construct more complicated AOC somewhat like depicted in Figure 16.

That is not all. An ideal Turing machine never crashes, but real world programs do fail sometimes. Their behavior under exceptional circumstances is crucial for the standards. The AOC technique allows modeling concurrent behavior with exceptions uniformly, as would be seen in the next section.

Producer and Consumer

Most processes in secure communications are concurrent; therefore, description of concurrent behavior is in the focus of standards harmonization. Let us consider a common example of communicating Producer and Consumer processes. Producer sequentially produces some products from time to time and consumer consumes them in the same sequence if any. Both are independent and have free will, but they are bounded with the contract. The Consumer must consume a product if it has placed an order. Of course, the Consumer cannot consume a product if it has not been produced, and the Producer should not produce a new product if the previous one hasn't been consumed. How should they communicate safely? Since 1965, when Dijkstra first introduced the problem, hundreds of solutions were proposed, more or less effective. The AOC solution does not claim to be scientifically new, it is simple (not to say trivial) and obvious (Figure 17). The only assumption is that handling any event is an atomic operation.

Of course, the solution in Figure 17 is not complete. For instance, it does not process indefinite waiting if one partner dies. The AOC technique allows refining the model in straightforward manner, reusing most of design (Figure 18).

Figure 16. Enhanced automata objects cooperation for turing machine

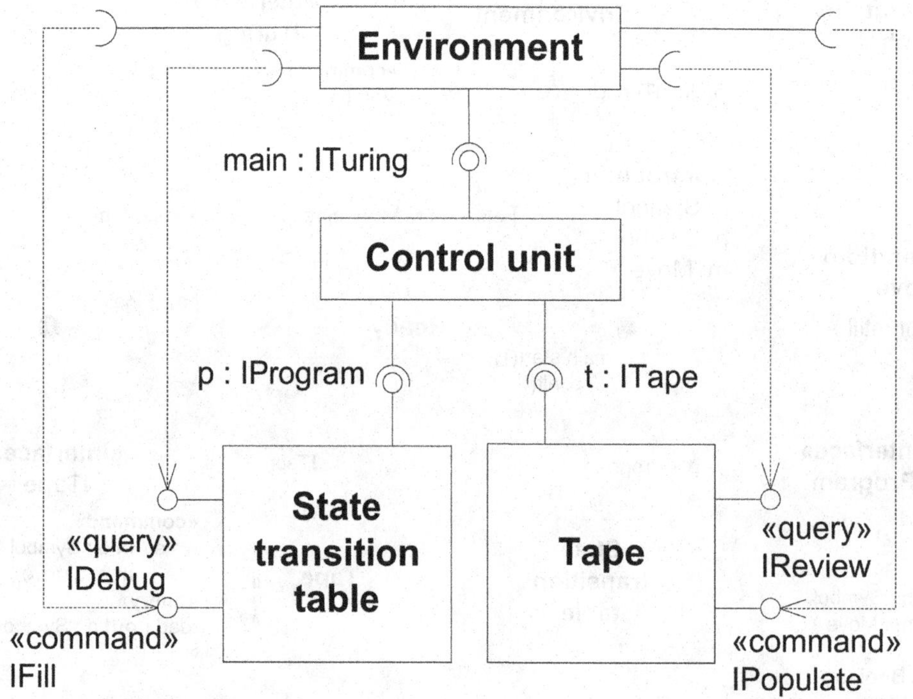

Figure 17. The producer and the consumer cooperation

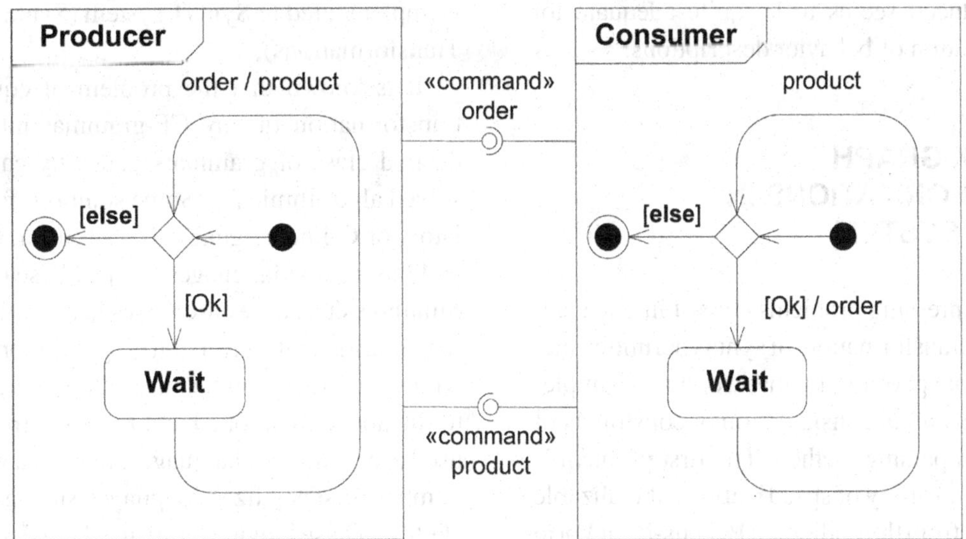

Figure 18. The producer and the consumer cooperation avoiding infinite waiting

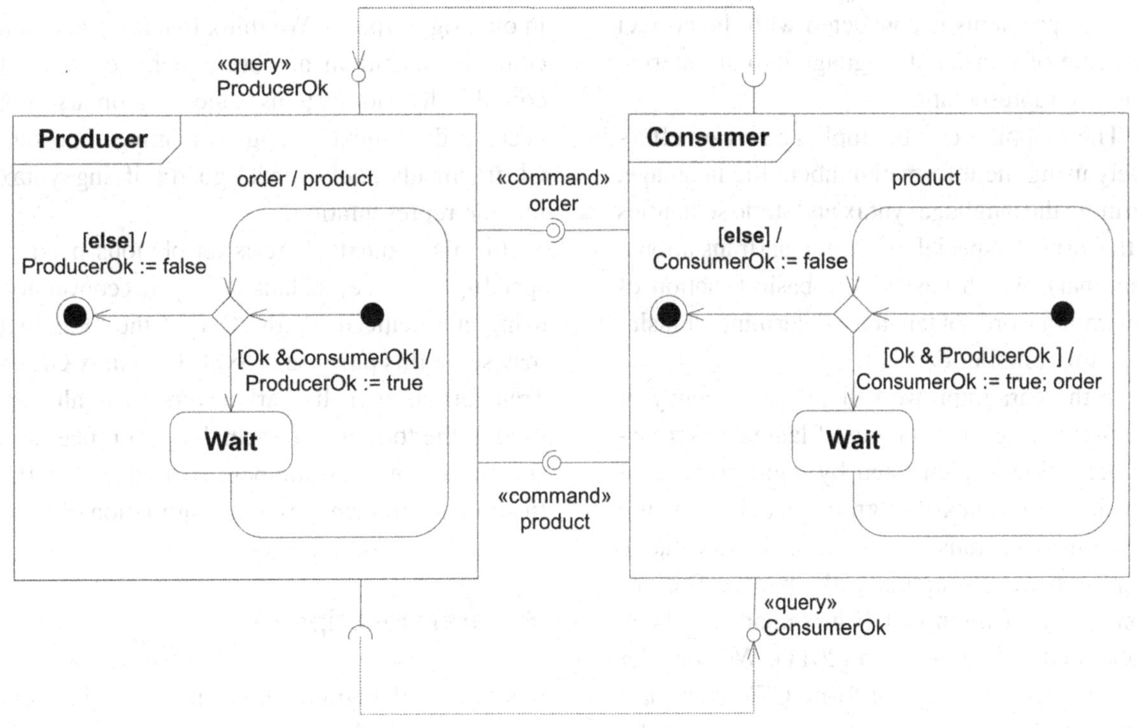

To sum it up, automata objects cooperation we introduced seems to be quite adequate for harmonization of behavior descriptions.

SYNTAX GRAPH TRANSFORMATIONS IN SYNGT SYSTEM

The most pressing problems consist in quick adjustment (transformation) of syntax definition into the form that permits automatic or manual implementation, and in consideration of constraints of the chosen parsing method. The first problem is caused by a variety of specifications of realizable languages from the traditional Backus-Naur Form (BNF) and markup language HTML to two-level, affix, and other types of grammar. The second one is leading either to linguistic ambiguity or nondeterministic recognizing automaton. Solution of these problems is connected with the correct mapping of translated language into an internal machine representation.

The mapping can be implemented by effectively using the information about the language, defining the language syntax and static semantics in the form of a special CF-grammar (translational grammar), which besides the basic function of generating words of language determines translations for compiler developers.

In the paragraph we validate the urgency of the problem of rapid tuning of language syntactic definition implemented by regularization of translational context-free grammar (TCFG) using the equivalent transformations of their syntactic graph-schemes to optimize the parser. The notion "regularization of CF grammar" has been elaborated in Fedorchenko (2011). We consider a CF grammar in a regular form (CFR-grammar) supplied with extended set of operations in regular expressions in the right hand side of rules. The known algorithms of equivalent grammar transformations have been presented in a new form for CFR-grammar (including the algorithm of extracting left (right) recursion nonterminals). It is implemented in SynGT system (Syntax Graph Transformations).

It is known that the problem of equivalent transformation of any CF-grammar into some desired class of grammars generally cannot be solved algorithmically. Some solutions for translators of C-line languages (C ++, Java, C#, etc) and Pascal-line languages (Object Pascal, ADA, Simula-3, etc.) were based on rather laborious and tiresome manual conversion of syntax (sometimes with the help of customary text editors). In addition to the above mentioned and the most frequently used programming languages, there is a growing number of specialized languages such as XML, HTML. These languages are used in AI-systems, in computer algebra, in 3D-graphics, and other performance-sensitive applications.

Recently some new applications of grammars attracted attention, such as the use of grammars in ontology aspects. We think that this approach could be useful in a more general context of complex hybrid systems, since grammars (not necessarily context-free but containing important CF-fragments) could provide good unifying syntax for rule representation.

In this context, there is an obvious need to speed up the process of language syntax conversion using automatic methods. One of the tools that may serve this purpose is SynGT (Syntax Graph Transformations). Its earlier version is already used in the toolkits for special signal processors and translators development carried out in the Institute for Informatics and Automation of Russian Academy of Sciences.

General Description

It is evident that grammar pre-processing should be performed, that is, bringing syntax definitions to the desired form. It is to be done using special tools improving the language syntax and optimizing the parser through regularization of initial translational grammar by equivalent transformations.

These tools should provide user-friendly interface and include a sufficient set of functions to implement the transformations. These transformations and their application in compiler development are presented in detail in classic papers, along with solutions to the problem of linguistic ambiguity and indeterminacy in automatic parser construction.

In 1980s, the mathematical model for definition and recognition of context-free language based on so called syntax graph schema (analog of syntactic flow-chart) was constructed and described. The model is used to check important grammar properties and to define its constraints for automatic synthesis of language recognizer. Later the model algorithm for grammar regularization based on equivalent transformations of syntax graph schema was developed, which optimizes the developed parser.

Presently there exist various methods of specifying translations in modern compiler technologies. Various and diverse syntax definitions dictate the need to adjust the source translational grammar to respective translational machine (MP-converter), and hence, the need for equivalent transformations of these grammars, since the original grammar can be regarded only as the initial form of the specification of language syntax. Instead, we use a different specification equivalent to the original one and represented in different formalism.

Review of publications on parsing methods since 1960-ies, detailed study of popular compiler tools such as Lex/Yacc, Flex/Bison, Eli, Antlr, Fort technology, TK SYNTAX, etc, and estimation of relationship between the parsing type and grammar equivalent transformations for the most demanding specifications (two-level grammar by Van Wijngaarden and affix grammar by Cornelis H.A. Koster [Nijmegen, The Netherlands]) suggests restricted use of automatic tools. To bridge the gap, equivalent grammar transformations should be performed to specify the translations and to construct optimal parsers while minimizing the parser control tables.

It is desirable to minimize the time of writing a new (input) grammar adapted for the chosen parsing method. This is achieved by developing a special tool for the developers.

A characteristic feature of these systems (tools) is redundant information on the conflict so that the programmer can hardly distinguish the main diagnostic messages among the others. For instance, the system Bison produces several hundreds of text pages with all the suspected errors in grammar rules, most of which are caused by automatic correction of one primary error.

Critical analysis of existing compiler (parser) development systems (according to the comp. compilers news group) reveals the absence of comprehensive methodologies providing correct analysis of grammar rules after detecting a conflict situation (error). The grammar rules must be transformed equivalently. Transformations are usually carried out either manually or partially, and transformation to the form where generated parser has minimal number of states is hardly possible. Therefore, special tools for automatic equivalent transformations should be developed. The method of equivalent transformations of so called syntax graph-scheme is the most promising one. Syntax graph-scheme is a graphical analog of the original (source) grammar, which is subjected to further regularization.

Mathematical formalization of constructing syntactic recognizers (parsers) is presented in Fedorchenko (2011), where the context-free grammars in the regular form (CFR-grammar) are defined. The right parts of grammar rules are treated as regular expressions over the terminal, nonterminal and semantic symbols.

The method description starts with a simple model: regular expressions as a means to describe an infinite language, and also a Finite State Automaton (FSA) as a language recognizer. This model is based on Kleene theorem: a class of regular sets is the minimal class containing all finite sets, closed as regards union, concatenation and closure operations, and the consequences of this theorem on the possibility of representing regular sets (recognizable by finite automata) by regular expressions. Step by step this simple model transforms into complex MP-transducer.

CF-Grammars in Regular Form

The language syntax is usually defined using Backus-Naur form. In SynGT, regular expressions with binary operations are used. They are much easier to transform into reversed Polish notation for subsequent analysis and processing. From the point of view of generated language these forms are equivalent.

Then we define CF-grammar in the regular form (CFR-grammar) and give examples of graphical representation of grammar rules (the examples are taken from the C-language grammar).

Suppose V is finite alphabet,

$$V = \{\xi_1, \xi_2, \ldots, \xi_n\}.$$

Let V^* be the set of all words in the alphabet V, and ε be the empty word (empty set of symbols). For any languages (subsets A and B of V^*). $A\,;B$ will denote their union, $A\,,B$ their product (concatenation) and $A\#B$ generalized iteration defined as follows.

Definition 1: Generalized iteration $(\#)$. (occasionally, iteration with separator, or Tseytin iteration) of the sets of words A and B is the set $C = A\#B$ that consists of all possible words of the form $x_1y_1x_2y_2\ldots y_{n-1}x_n$ with $x_i \in A$, $1 \le i \le n$, $y_j \in B$, $1 \le j \le n-1$, and n is a positive integer.

Definition 2: The regular sets of words (regular languages) in V are defined inductively.

The sets $\{\xi_1\}, \{\xi_2\}, \ldots \{\xi_n\}$ are regular;

- Sets e and $\varnothing$ are regular, where ($e = \{\varepsilon\}$, and $\varnothing$ is the empty set of words);
- If the sets B and C are regular, and $\otimes$ is one of the operations ($\#$; , } then the set $A = B \otimes C$ is regular.

Set of all regular languages in the alphabet V will be denoted by $\Re(V)$. It is the minimal subset of the set 2^{V^*} that contains $\{\xi_1\}, \{\xi_2\}, \ldots \{\xi_n\}$, e, $\varnothing$ and it is closed under operations in $\otimes$.

According to this definition, a set of words of V^* is regular if and only if it is either $\varnothing$, or $e = \{\varepsilon\}$, (ε is a blank character string), or $\{\xi\}$ for some $\xi \in V$, or it can be obtained from these sets by applying union, concatenation, unary and binary generalized iteration operations for a finite number of times.

If a first or a second operand of the generalized iteration represents the set $e = \{\varepsilon\}$ and if no confusion will occur, it can be omitted.

The ordinary Kleene iteration A^* may thus be identified with $\#A$, and the nonempty iteration A^+ with $A\#$.

As mentioned before, S.C. Kleene introduced the notion of regular expression in the alphabet V to represent a regular set of V. We shall introduce the notion of generalized regular expression for the set A in the alphabet V using operation $\#$.

Definition 3: Generalized regular expression for the set A is called a word $r(A)$ over the extended alphabet

$$W,\ W = V \cup \{\#, *, +, ;, (,), \varepsilon, \varnothing\}$$

defined inductively as follows:

1. if $A = \varnothing$ then the word $\varnothing$ is a regular expression;

2. if $A = e$ then the word ε is a regular expression;
3. if $A = \{\xi\}$ and $\xi \in V$ then the words ξ are regular expressions;
4. if A and B are regular expressions and $\otimes \in \{\#\, ,\, ;\}$ then the word $(A \otimes B)$ is a regular expression.

Denote the set of all regular expressions in V by $R(V)$. For each regular expression A let $L(A)$ be corresponding regular language.

Two regular expressions A and B from $R(V)$ are equivalent if they represent the same regular language in

$V,\ L(A) = L(B) : A \equiv B.$

It is known that the regular expressions representing the same regular language can be converted to each other using certain identities. Some of these identities are shown in Box 1 and $A, B, C \in R(V)$.

For every regular expression there is a regular language, and for each regular language there is a regular expression representing this language (it is shown by obvious induction by the process of construction). There exist the following well known problem: since a regular language can be generated using operations in many different ways, then generally there exist many regular expressions representing the same regular language. So, we can find minimal length regular expression corresponding source regular language. Note that operation $(\#)$ can be defined using the traditional (unary) Kleene operation $(^*)$ as follows:

$$A \# B = A, (B, A)^* \qquad (1)$$

That partially solves the problem of regular expression minimization by reducing the number of occurrences of nonterminal symbols and hence, of possible Shift/Reduce conflicts in the process of parser construction.

Thus, all operations may be binary in a generalized regular expression. It is convenient to operate a program stack during processing reverse Polish form of regular expressions.

Regular expressions can be used within a larger grammatical framework where the grammar productions are represented by the couples of the form $(A : R)$ with A being a nonterminal symbol of the grammar (nonterminal), and R being a regular expression that represents the set of words (strings) directly derived from the nonterminal A. Each couple can be interpreted as the set of rules

$$\{A \to x \mid x \in L(R) : L(R) \in \Re(V)\},$$

where V is the union of the alphabet T of terminal and the alphabet N of nonterminal symbols, $V = N \cup T$.

Following to Aho, Sethi, Ullman (1986), we shall call CF-grammars in regular form the grammars where all rules are represented by couples $(A : R)$ interpreted as above. The couple $(A : R.)$ will be called CFR-rule.

For practical purposes it is convenient to modify the definition of grammar adding to the alphabet some semantic symbols. The aim is to make possible the inclusion of some code into compiled text. Therefore, a context-free grammar in regular form (CFR-grammar) is the quintuple of finite sets $G_R = (N, T, \Sigma, P, S)$, where N is a set of nonterminals, T is a set of terminals, Σ

Box 1.

A;B≡B;A	(A;B);C≡A;(B;C)	(A,B),C≡A,(B,C)	(A;B),C≡A,C;B,C	C,(A;B)≡C,A;C,B
A,ε ≡ε ,A	A,A*≡ A*,A≡A+	(A,B)*,A≡A#B	(A#B)#C≡A#(B;C)	(A+)#B≡A#(ε;B)

is a set of semantics, P is a set of the CFR-rules, $P = \{A : R_A. \mid A \in N, R_A$ is a regular expression in the set $N \cup T \cup \Sigma\}$ NUTUΣ}, S is the initial nonterminal of the grammar.

CFR-Rules in Graphical Form in SynGT

Each CFR-rule is written in the form <nonterminal>:<regular expression>. The <nonterminal> denotes the left side of the rule and <regular expression> denotes its right side. Without loss of generality we may suppose that for each nonterminal there is a unique CFR-rule in P defining it. Two CFR-rules of the form (A, R_1) and (A, R_2) can be replaced by one CFR-rule $(A : R_1; R_2)$. In the examples below the basic symbols are given in quotes (“,”), and sign ($) is put before the semantic symbols. To check the regularity of input grammar in SynGT different coloring of metasymbols (operations, parentheses and separators), terminals, nonterminals, semantics and comments is used. Here is an example of a CFR-rule:

procedure_call: name,(”(“,((formal_parameter, “⇒”;ε), actual_parameter)#”,”,”)”; ε),”;”.

Here the basic symbols are in quotation marks. For typographic reasons, bold (and larger) font is used to display operations, parentheses, and separators. In fact on the screen they are colored red. There are no semantic symbols in the rules. In this way the CFR-rules are presented after their processing by the text editor in SynGT. The editor checks the correctness of regular expressions and performs some simple equivalent conversions of grammar (deletes empty results and infinite loops).

The regular expressions in the right side of CFR-rules generally define infinite regular sets of words. From practical point of view it is more convenient to represent those using finite oriented graphs with labels on nodes. This graph can be considered as a deterministic finite automaton scheme, where each node corresponds to some state, and its label specifies the generated character. The collection of these graphs representing the right sides of the CFR-rules is called the syntax graph-scheme of a CFR-grammar G.

Though the syntax graph-schemes (as a generation mechanism) are equivalent to regular expressions, they more clearly express the structure of CFR-rules. Conversion of the generating scheme into recognizing scheme, and then into the parsing scheme is easier; with the arcs of a graph-scheme it is easy to associate the calls of the semantic procedures and, last but not least, a syntactic graph-scheme allows the use of simpler structure instead of derivations in CF-grammars. This structure is the set of the paths in the graph-scheme, which is better suited to define (and describe) generation of words of the language $L(G)$ and to check its the grammar properties.

More formally each CFR-grammar G is associated with its counterpart (graph representation), a syntactic graph-scheme $\Gamma_G = (N, T, \Sigma, K, S)$ such that the language $L_\Gamma = L(G)$). Here N is the set of nonterminals, T is the set of terminals, Σ is the set of semantics, $K = \{K_A \mid A \in N, K_A$ is the component of the graph defining the nonterminal $A\}$, $S \in N$ is the initial nonterminal. Each component of the syntactical graph-scheme represents a syntactical definition of language construction (possibly with information on its semantics). The semantics is understood as a set of executable operations (evaluated before using semantic rules). The syntax graph-scheme is recursively created from the elementary graphs (base graphs) corresponding to the elementary regular expressions (Figure 19) and operations defined previously. Figure 20 represent elementary operations performed with regular expressions implemented in SynGT.

Graphical representationsof basic regular operations are shown in Figure 20, Figure 21, and Figure 22. The complex cases are recursively

Figure 19. Graphical representation of elementary regular expressions

Figure 20. Graphical representation of basical operations

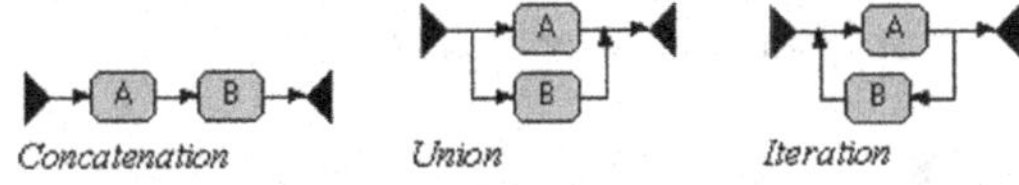

reduced by basic ones. The recursion is done by the structure of regular expressions using the standard convention concerning priority of main operations and their left associativity.

The representations of some composite (complex) functions are shown in the Figures 21–23.

The last examples also illustrate backward semantics which are placed in reverse order. The CFR-rule in visual graphical representation is the graphical representation of the corresponding regular expression with labels for entry and exit nodes. (see Figure 24).

SynGT and Its Main Functions

The system SynGT uses graphic user interface and graphical representation of CFR-rules as a basis for grammar processing. The purpose of grammar equivalent transformations in SynGT is maximal regularization and (in case of programming languages) construction of a deterministic parser.

The grammar is treated by SynGT several modules. First, correctness of the input grammar is checked. The grammar is transformed into a reduced one. The ordinary grammar code is transformed into inverse polish notation. The inaccessible symbols and useless rules are eliminated. Finally, CF-grammar is transformed into CFR-grammar.

Afterwards the well-formed regular expressions in textual form are transformed into their graph representation. SynGT contains an algorithm that will output this graph directly to the screen. A SynGT document is formed (SynGT document is an object containing the information about the syntax graph-scheme, state of desktop, source CFR-grammar and comments).

Graph-scheme editor is implemented. It allows for example reduction (of a subgraph), substitution (of a graph for nonterminal node), check of well formedness, use of clipboard, graphic operations on the screen etc. Inverse transformation of the graph-scheme into textual form is possible too.

Main Components and Operations inside the System SynGT

Informational components in SynGT:

- SynGT-document;
- working desktop and fields for dictionaries (terminals, nonterminals, semantics and others);
    1. SynGT-document may be:created, loaded from file, deleted, renamed, printed, saved.

Figure 21. Graphical representations of the complex expressions

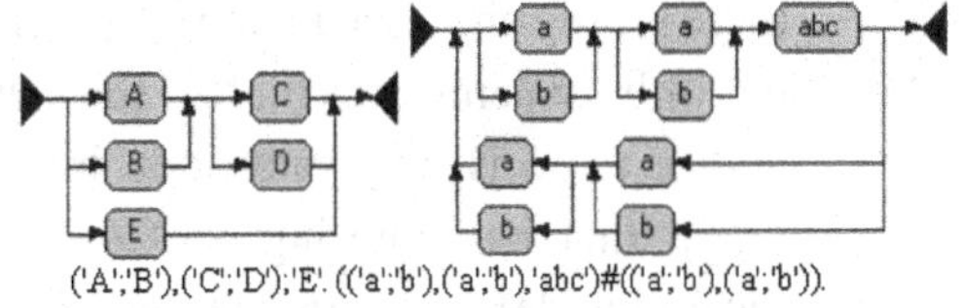

Figure 22. Graphical representations of the expressions

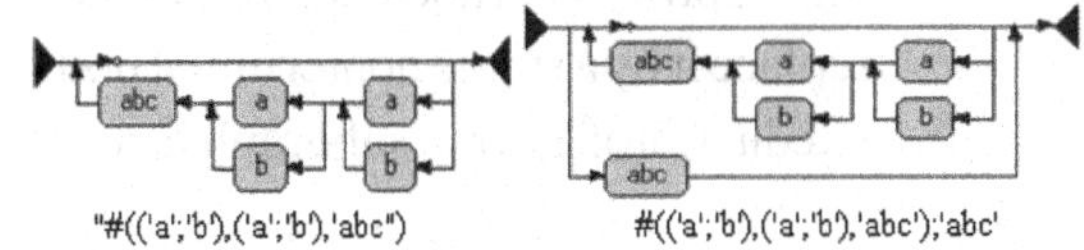

Figure 23. Examples of the expressions with semantics (S1, S2, S3, S4 – semantic symbols)

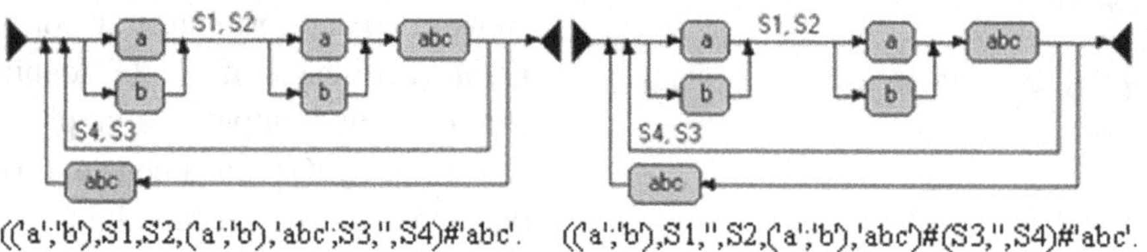

(('a';'b'),S1,S2,('a';'b'),'abc';S3,'',S4)#'abc'. (('a';'b'),S1,'',S2,('a';'b'),'abc')#(S3,'',S4)#'abc'.

Figure 24. Examples of the CFR-rules represented in SynGT

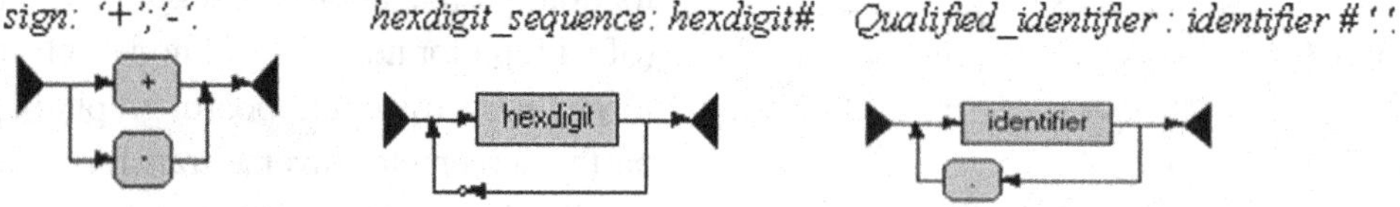

2. Desktop can occupy some part or the whole screen. It is used for manipulations with syntax graph-scheme. It contains the fields to carry out the following actions: edit graph for CFR-rule (nonterminal nodes of graph), list of nonterminals (dictionary), list of terminals, list of semantics, list of auxiliary symbols, represent CFR-rule in text format, scrolling, comments, etc.
3. As already discussed, the syntax graph-scheme in SynGT is a set of oriented pairwise disjoint graphs. They possess some special properties: every node may be marked by a label, every arc may be marked by a expression (semantic), there is only one node inside graph that has only issueing arcs (called the start node), there is only one node inside graph that has entering arcs (called the end node), every two nodes inside graph may be connected by only one directed arc.
4. The following operations for graph editing are provided: choose a subgraph and replace it by a single nonterminal node (Reduction); insert a subgraph instead of a nonterminal node (Substitution); check well-formedness of a graph; copy a graph into the Clipboard; insert a graph from the Clipboard; change the node position on the desktop; print a graph; zoom a graph image.
5. In a graph, some subgraph can be marked. If this marked subgraph is regular then following operations can be applied to it: transform into nonterminal node and simultaneous forming a new CFR-rule, delete, cancel deleting, move in the window, copy into the Clipboard, paste from the Clipboard, cancel paste.
6. In SynGT an arc may be updated by semantic and style. The semantic is a string of symbols. It can be edited in a usual way (copying, marking, deleting, etc). The style of an arc is a set of parameters describing the line width, its color, ets. In SynGT there are some default styles.
7. Nonterminal node is a node corresponding to some CFR-rule. The nodes can be created. Editing (like subgraphs in cl. 6) is possible.

8. Terminal node is a node corresponding to a symbol of the terminal alphabet of CFR-grammar. Here it is represented by a string of symbols. So, all text editor operations are allowed.
9. CFR-rule is represented in the form $A : R.$ where A is a nonterminal and R is a regular expression including nonterminals and terminals and semantics. In the field of nonterminals the cursor points to the nonterminal A. The regular expression R is printed in the bottom of the field of desktop. It can be copied into Clipboard.

Various equivalent transformations of the graph-scheme are implemented, for example simplification of regular expressions using identities, elimination of left or right recursion locally (for a given non-terminal) or globally, grammar reduction to one regular expression in case when all nonterminals are not self-embedded, etc.

It should be noted that in the process of parser development it is frequently required to transform a CFR-grammar into the grammar that has no left or right recursive nonterminals. This requirement reflects the necessity of parsing determinacy. For example, the algorithm for construction of recognizer states often requires finiteness of state decomposition for any nonterminal node in the syntax graph-scheme. Thus the lists of all paths from nonterminal nodes to terminal or exit nodes should have finite length. In case of infinite decomposition of a state for some nonterminal node the transformation of the source syntax graph-scheme Γ_{G_1} into an equivalent graph – scheme Γ_{G_2} i.e. $L(\Gamma_{G_1}) = L(\Gamma_{G_2})$ that has the required property should be done.

Regularization of CF grammars is the process of applying step by step equivalent transformations of the source CF grammars into new CF-grammar in regular form (CFR-grammar). Then all non self-embedded nonterminals are excluded.

Summing up the progress in the field of translator development, the following conclusions can be drawn.

Algorithms for equivalent grammar transformation for building compact and efficient language processors have been developed and implemented. Their performance is improved by 10% to 20% compared with the known GNU Compiler systems due to the effectiveness and the amount of memory. In these algorithms, the regularization scheme is constructed by translational CFR-grammar. Equivalent transformations and the method of regularization based on them are the only way to extend the applicability of the method of syntactic analysis, which is fixed in the choosen tool for automatic compiler construction.

FUTURE RESEARCH DIRECTIONS

- It is proposed to use ontological engineering to harmonize standards, including construction of taxonomies of domain terms, predictive relationships between the terms, the logical inference based on descriptive logic, and ontology integration tools: mapping, alignment, and merging. The aim is to build a consistent formal description or formal unification of the subject area and to develop application software to support the unified schema. The process of achieving the goal will be to construct terminological taxonomies, predicative relations, descriptive constraints (ontological restrictions) to display the new data types and the extension of the set of inference rules. Clarification of the terminology and relationships can (and probably will) occur in the course of development of ontologies (an ontology series) due to the flexibility of ontological descriptions (atomicity, where the atom is a logical triple) unlike the descriptions of data structures based on the relational tables.

- It is recommended to apply this techniques to validate the use of standards in cloud computing.

CONCLUSION

At a certain stage of standards harmonization, the following problem arises: harmonization of tools to support implementation of standards in practice. Currently, these tools are developed and exist independently. The tools are mostly developed using UML-tools or similar ones. The developers, however, have to develop their own object models of standards. Ontology-based harmonized object models would make it possible to coordinate the software, with future development of universal software or at least interfaces.

However, for long-term problems it is not sufficient. Ontological modeling should be used in further work. It will provide an effective meta-description of standards in the form of formal computer models (for example, Semantic Web [Berners-Lee, Hendler, & Lassila, 2001]), automation of their notional comparison by means of semantic analysis, and a software mechanism to access standards using web-based technologies (XML, RDF, OWL, SPARQL). Software for describing the algorithmic high-level languages such as Algol 68, Simula-6 etc (WW-two-level grammar, attribute CF grammars, Wirth diagrams, syntactic graph-schemes, etc.) can be used for meta-description of standards. Ontologies can be described by those powerful syntax-oriented tools; the only question is how effectively they are used.

These approaches using meta-description of safety standards will provide their harmonization at different levels and in different directions.

REFERENCES

Aho, Sethi, & Ullman. (1986). Compilers: Principles, techniques, and tools. Reading, MA: Addison-Wesley.

Atiskov, A. J. (2008). Integration of business-process modeling with object-oriented designing using hybrid technology of transformation. Informational. *Measuring and Controlling Systems*, *6*(4), 18–20.

Atiskov, A. J. (2012). *Transformation functional diagrams into UML diagrams*. Saarbrucken, Germany: LAP LAMBERT Academic Publishing GmbH & Co..

Atiskov, A. J., & Perminov, V. I. (2007). Adaptive hybrid technology of business-process modeling. SPIIRAS Proceedings, 4(1).

Berners-Lee, T., Hendler, J., & Lassila, O. (2001). The semantic web: A new form of web content that is meaningful to computers will unleash a revolution of new possibilities. *Scientific American*, *5*, 34–43. doi:10.1038/scientificamerican0501-34.

Blaha, M., & Rumbaugh, J. (2005). *Object-oriented modeling and design with UML* (2nd ed.). Upper Saddle River, NJ: Pearson Prentice Hall.

Bock, C. (1999a). Three kinds of behavior model. *Journal of Object-Oriented Programming*, *12*(4).

Bock, C. (1999b). Unified behavior models. *Journal of Object-Oriented Programming*, *12*(5).

Czarnecki, K., & Helsen, S. (2003). Classification of model transformation approaches. In Proceedings of the OOPSLA 2003 Workshop on the Generative Techniques in the Context of Model-Driven Architecture. Anaheim, CA: OOPSLA. Retrieved from http://www.swen.uwaterloo.ca/~kczarnec/ECE750T7/czarnecki_helsen.pdf

Fedorchenko, L. N. (2011). *Regularization of context-free grammar*. Saarbrucken, Germany: LAP LAMBERT Academic Publishing GmbII & Co..

IDEF0 Draft. (2012). Federal information processing standards publication. Retrieved from http://www.itl.nist.gov/fipspubs/idef0.doc

IDEF5. (2012). Ontology description capture method. Retrieved from http://www.idef.com/idef5.html

Lubimov, A. V. (2008). The functional structure of common criteria. In Proceedings of XI St. Petersburg International Conference "Regional Informatics–2008" (RI–2008), (pp. 103-104). St. Petersburg, Russia: RI.

Lunin, A. (2008). Government and business collaboration in the standardization of cryptographic methods. World and Security, 1.

Manola, F., & Miller, E. (2004). RDF primer. W3C Recommendation 10 February 2004. Retrieved from http://www.w3.org/TR/rdf-primer

McGuinness, D., & Deborah, L. (2009). OWL 2 web ontology language. W3C Recommendation 27 October 2009. Retrieved from http://www.w3.org/TR/owl2-overview

Mehrolhassani, M., & El3i, A. (2008). OLS: An ontology based information system. In Proceedings of International Workshop on Ontology Alignment and Visualization (OnAV-2008), held in conjunction with the Second International Conference on Complex, Intelligent and Software Intensive Systems (CISIS 2008), (pp. 892-896). Barcelona, Spain: IEEE.

Meyer, B. (1988). *Object-oriented software construction*. Hemel Hempstead, NJ: Prentice Hall.

Moldovyan, N. A., & Moldovyan, A. A. (2007). *Data-driven block ciphers for fast telecommunication systems*. New York, NY: Talor & Francis Group. doi:10.1201/9781420054125.

Musen, M. (2012). Protégé. Stanford, CA: Stanford University. Retrieved from http://protege.stanford.edu

SPARQL Query Language for RDF. (2008). W3C recommendation 15 January 2008. Retrieved from http://www.w3.org/TR/rdf-sparql-query

UML. (2012). Website. Retrieved from http://www.uml.org

ADDITIONAL READING

Delfs, H., & Kneble, H. (2002). *Introduction to cryptography*. Berlin, Germany: Springer-Verlag. doi:10.1007/978-3-642-87126-9.

Koblitz, N. A. (1994). *Course in number theory and cryptography*. Berlin, Germany: Springer. doi:10.1007/978-1-4419-8592-7.

Menezes, A. J., & Vanstone, S. A. (1996). *Handbook of applied cryptography*. Boca Raton, FL: CRC Press. doi:10.1201/9781439821916.

Pieprzyk, J., Hardjono, T., & Seberry, J. (2003). *Fundumentals of computer security*. Berlin, Germany: Springer-Verlag. doi:10.1007/978-3-662-07324-7.

Schneier, B. (1996). *Applied cryptography: Protocols, algorithms, and source code* (2nd ed.). New York, NY: John Wiley & Sons.

KEY TERMS AND DEFINITIONS

Common Criteria (CC): Common Criteria for Information Technology Security Evaluation, an international standard (ISO/IEC 15408) for computer security certification. It is currently in version 3.1.

IDEF0: Integration Definition for Function Modeling (IDEF0) is a functional modeling methodology for describing manufacturing functions, which offers a functional modeling language for the analysis, development, reengineering, and integration of information systems; business processes; or software engineering analysis. The IDEF0 Functional Modeling method is designed to model the decisions, actions, and activities of an organization or a system. It was derived from the established graphic modeling language Structured Analysis and Design Technique (SADT) developed by Douglas T. Ross and SofTech, Inc. In its original form, IDEF0 includes both a definition of graphical modeling language (syntax and semantics) and a description of comprehensive methodology for developing models. The US Air Force commissioned the SADT developers "to develop a function model method for analyzing and communicating the functional perspective of a system. IDEF0 should assist in organizing system analysis and promote effective communication between the analyst and the customer through simplified graphical devices." IDEF0 may be used to model a wide variety of automated and non-automated systems. For new systems, it may be used first to define the requirements and specify the functions, and then to design an implementation that meets the requirements and performs the functions. For existing systems, IDEF0 can be used to analyze the functions the system performs and to record the mechanisms (means) carried out by the functions. The result of applying IDEF0 to a system is a model that consists of a hierarchical series of diagrams, text, and glossary cross-referenced to each other. The two primary modeling components are functions (represented by boxes in the diagram) and the data and objects that interrelates those functions (represented by arrows).

ISMS: Information Security Management System. ISMS standards are as follows.

ISO/IEC 27001:2005 Information Technology: Security Techniques – Information Security Management Systems – Requirements.

ISO/IEC 27002:2005 Information Technology: Security Techniques – Code of Practice for Information Security Management.

ISO/IEC 27005:2011 Information Technology: Security Techniques – Information Security Risk Management.

SPARQL (a Recursive Acronym for SPARQL Protocol and RDF Query Language): is an RDF query language, that is, a query language for databases, able to retrieve and manipulate data stored in Resource Description Framework format. It was made a standard by the RDF Data Access Working Group (DAWG) of the World Wide Web Consortium, and considered as one of the key technologies of semantic web. On 15 January 2008, SPARQL 1.0 became an official Recommendation of World Wide Web Consortium (W3C). SPARQL allows for a query to consist of triple patterns, conjunctions, disjunctions, and optional patterns.

Unified Modeling Language (UML): is a standardized general-purpose modeling language in the field of object-oriented software engineering. The standard was created and is currently managed by the Object Management Group. It was first added to the list of OMG adopted technologies in 1997, and since then has become an industry standard for modeling software-intensive systems. In software engineering, a class diagram in the Unified Modeling Language (UML) is a type of static structure diagram that describes the structure of a system by showing the system's classes, their attributes, operations (or methods), and relationships between the classes. The class diagram is the main building block of object oriented modeling (Blaha & Rumbaugh, 2005). It is systematically used both for general conceptual modeling of the application, and for for detailed designing models transformations which is translated into programming code. Class diagrams can also be used for data modeling (Atiskov, 2008). The classes in a class diagram represent both the main objects and interactions in the application and the objects to be programmed. In the class diagram these classes are represented with boxes which contain three parts: 1) the upper part holds the name of the class; 2) the middle part contains the attributes of the class;

3) the bottom part gives the methods or operations the class can take or undertake. UML provides mechanisms to represent class members, such as attributes and methods, and additional information about them. The UML specifies two types of scopes for members: instances and classifiers. Classifier members are commonly recognized as "static" in many programming languages. In case of instance members, the scope is a specific instance. For attributes, it means that the value can vary between instances. For methods, it means that invocation affects the instance state, in other words, affects the instance attributes. Otherwise, in the classifier member, the scope is the class. For attributes, it means that the value is equal for all instances. For methods, it means that its invocation does not affect the instance state. To indicate that a member has the classifier scope, its name must be underlined. Otherwise the instance scope is considered by default.

Web Ontology Language (OWL): (McGuinness & Deborah, 2009) is a family of knowledge representation languages for authoring ontologies. The languages are characterized by formal semantics and RDF/XML-based serializations for the Semantic Web. OWL is endorsed by the W3C and has attracted academic, medical, and commercial interest. In October 2007, a new W3C working group has started to extend OWL with several new features as proposed in the OWL 1.1 member submission. W3C announced the new version of OWL on 27 October 2009. This new version, called OWL 2, found its way into semantic editors such as Protégé and semantic reasoners. The data described by ontology in the OWL family are interpreted as a set of "individuals" and a set of "property assertions", which relate these individuals to each other. Ontology consists of a set of axioms, which place constraints on sets of individuals (called "classes") and the types of relationships permitted between them. These axioms provide semantics by allowing systems to infer additional information based on the data explicitly provided. Languages in the OWL family are capable of creating classes and properties, defining instances and operations with them.

Chapter 2
GOST Encryption Algorithm and Approaches to its Analysis

Ludmila Babenko
Southern Federal University, Russia

Evgeniya Ishchukova
Southern Federal University, Russia

Ekaterina Maro
Southern Federal University, Russia

ABSTRACT

This chapter considers approaches to analysis of the GOST 28147-89 encryption algorithm (also known as simply GOST), which is the basis of most secure information systems in the Russian Federation. As soon as the GOST algorithm is characterized by a simple structure and uses widely known mathematical operations, approaches to its analysis can be easily propagated to other cryptographic systems. In the conclusion, the authors consider some interesting observations that are related to the structure of GOST encryption and can be useful for further development of cryptanalysis.

INTRODUCTION

The GOST encryption algorithm is a state encryption standard in Russian Federation. The GOST 28147-89 algorithm is recommended by the Federal Security Service of Russia for building cryptographic protection systems for data of limited distribution (commercial secrets, personal data, etc.) Any cryptographic system of data protection certified by the Federal Security Service has to be built using only the following algorithms: GOST R 34.10-2001, GOST R 34.11-94, GOST 28147-89. That is why the majority of information systems for confidential data protection are based on GOST 28147-89. Besides that, this algorithm is used in the hash function described in GOST R34.11-94 and is included into RFC4357 as "id-GostR3411-94-CryptoProParamSet." For example, correspondence of commercial enterprises with pension funds, tax inspection, online auctions cannot be implemented with foreign cryptographic algorithms. GOST 28147-89 is also

DOI: 10.4018/978-1-4666-4030-6.ch002

used in biometric passports of Russian citizens for calculating hash values. Nowadays activities are carried out in Russia on implementing universal e-cards that will also use national cryptographic standards. Many Russian hardware and software data protection tools are based on GOST, such as CryptoPro CSP, VipNet CSP, Lissi CSP, Secret Disk, SafeDisk, Accord trusted boot module, Strazh, etc. Therefore one can conclude that GOST is widely used in many modern information systems.

Originally, the algorithm became known to the international community in 1994 when it was declassified and translated into English. Despite the fact that GOST was designed more than 20 years ago, in 2010 it was among the candidates for codification as an international encryption standard as ISO 18033.

At the session of the 27th ISO committee in 2010, a decision was made to initiate inclusion of GOST into the international standard ISO/IEC 18033.3..The first version was prepared in January, 2011. However, in February 2011 a presentation (Isobe, 2011) was made at Fast Software Encryption (FSE) symposium that contained results of successful application of Reflection – Meet in the Middle Attack (R MITM) against GOST. The attack against full-round GOST encryption demands 232 encryptions, i.e. the complexity of this attack is 2225. Besides that, after when voting on inclusion of GOST into ISO/IEC 18033.3 started, another research (Courtois, 2011) was published that makes strong assumptions about the possibility to break GOST with improved differential cryptanalysis. We should note that this work considers fixed s-boxes, which are different from those offered in ISO/IEC 18033-3.

As of January 27th 2012, the addendum on GOST 28147-89 was deleted from ISO/IEC 18033-3. The Russian party proposes to continue negotiations on considering GOST algorithm as an international standard and to proceed to the second version of proposals. Based on the publications mentioned above, one can make a conclusion that in order to make the decision about inclusion of GOST into ISO/IEC 18033.3, further research on its cryptographic strength should be carries out.

GOST encryption algorithm has four operation modes: simple substitution mode, stream mode, stream mode with feedback and authentication mode. Simple substitution mode is the basic one and all other modes contain it in their structure. We will consider only this mode in the chapter.

GOST algorithm is a symmetric block cipher, which conforms to Feistel scheme. 64-bit blocks of data are submitted to the input and converted into 64-bit blocks of encrypted data by 256-bit key. In each round the right side of plain text messages is processed by function F, which converts data with three cryptographic operations: adding data and subkey modulo 232, substitution of data using S-boxes, and left cyclic shift by 11 positions. Output of F-function is added modulo 2 to the left part of the plaintext, then right and left sides are swapped for next round. The algorithm has 32 rounds. In the last round of encryption right and left parts are not swapped. The overall dataflow diagram of GOST is shown in Figure 1.

GOST uses 8 S-boxes, which convert 4-bit input to 4-bit output. Unlike most encryption algorithms, GOST has no predefined S-boxes and any values can be used for them.

Secret key contains 256 bits and is represented as a sequence of eight 32-bit words: K1, K2, K3, K4, K5, K6, K7 and K8. In each round of encryption one of these 32-bit words is used as a round subkey. When round subkey is calculated, the following principle is used: from round 1 to round 24 the order is straight, (K1, K2, K3, K4, K5, K6, K7, K8, K1, K2, etc.); from round 25 to round 32 reversed order is used (K8, K7, K6, K5, K4, K3, K2, K1).

The more detailed description of GOST and its modes can be found in (Popov, Kurepkin, & Leontiev, 2006). Thus, it appears that the same subkey K1 is used at both the first and the last rounds. As we can see from the description of the algorithm, the round transformation has a rela-

Figure 1. GOST dataflow

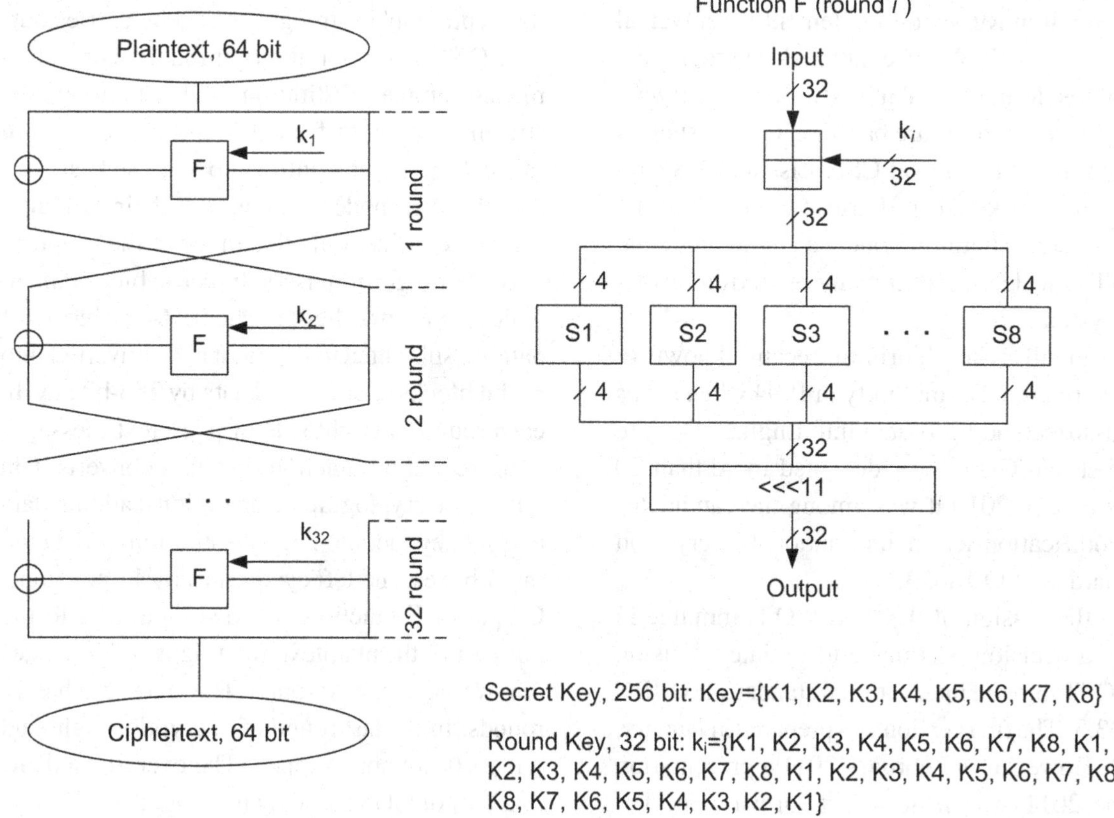

tively simple structure. The developers of GOST have probably accepted the paradigm that can be formulated as "simple structure – many rounds" and also they relied on long keys.

The characteristic feature of GOST algorithm is the use of customized S-boxes. It is assumed that any filling of S-boxes of thirty-two rounds of encryption is sufficient to resist effective analysis methods such as linear and differential cryptanalysis.

It was widely accepted that as long as S-boxes are kept secret, they can be considered as an extra key material. However, a method was proposed in (Saarinen, 1998) that allows to reconstruct S-boxes values relatively simply. In order to do this, one has to find a "zero vector" with a null encryption key that takes around 232 encryptions. Calculation of S-boxes values can then take approximately 211 operations. It is still an unresolved issue, how particular values of S-boxes influence the strength of GOST, however it is considered that many rounds and excessive key length is enough to guarantee sufficient strength. B. Schneier (1996) published the set of S-boxes that were used by the Central Bank of Russian Federation.

This chapter is devoted to the existing approaches to the analysis of symmetric block encryption algorithms in general and GOST in particular. More attention will be paid to some more promising methods of analysis in our opinion. These include differential and algebraic cryptanalysis. We will give their detailed description and sketch directions of their further development. In the conclusion, we will share some interesting observations in data encryption that can be used for further work on the analysis of GOST and other similar encryption algorithms.

BACKGROUND

In spite of the fact that GOST was designed more than 20 years ago, nowadays one can find relatively few papers devoted to its analysis. This is partly due to the fact that the algorithm was classified in the beginning and became publicly available only after 1994. Besides that, before the publication of (Saarinen, 1998) it was considered that S-boxes can contribute to the complexity of encryption that made analysis too complicated.

The fact that S-boxes are variable makes analysis more complicated anyway. This brings limitations to the methods that are based on the examination of their properties. These methods include linear, differential and algebraic cryptanalysis. Whenever S-boxes are changed, the analysis should be started from the beginning in contrast to the analysis of DES, for instance, which relies on predefined and fixed S-box values.

Vulnerability assessment of a cipher is often started from its simplified models (Oreku, Li, Pazynyuk, & Mtenzi, 2007). With regard to GOST, there are two factors in addition to variable S-boxes that make this approach hard to implement. These are addition modulo 232 and the use of reversed round subkeys for the last eight rounds of encryption. Results of cryptanalysis of a simplified GOST (GOST-H) are presented in (Biham & Shamir, 1991). Unlike GOST, GOST-H uses straight order of subkeys from K1 to K8 in the last eight rounds. It is shown that the modified algorithm is much weaker than the original and there is a subset of possible keys that make it even weaker. Another simplified version of GOST, in which integer addition is replaced with addition modulo 2 and the number of rounds is reduced to 20, was researched in (Birukov & Wagner, 2000).

In this section, we are reviewing existing approaches to the analysis of existing symmetric block systems in general and GOST in particular.

Brute Force Search

If encryption algorithm is known and there is at least one pair of plaintext and ciphertext, it is possible to implement an exhaustive search of the key. The search is performed up to the moment when encryption of the plaintext produces known ciphertext. The obvious advantage of this method is the fact that it guarantees to find the correct key with minimal initial data. The time needed to find the key depends on the length of the secret key, analyst's computational capacity, and a bit of luck. In case of GOST analysis, there are two problems. Firstly, the length of the secret key of 256 bits is too big to find a key in observable time with even the most productive supercomputer. Secondly, there is a problem of equivalent keys. As soon as the maximal volume of the plaintext is 264 and the number of possible keys is 2256, in average 2192 different keys will transform the same plaintext value X to the same result of encryption. This fact will be discussed in "Future research directions" section.

Linear Cryptanalysis

Linear cryptanalysis was proposed by M. Matsui in early 1990s. M. Matsui has shown how an attack against DES with the reduced complexity of 247 can be implemented (Matsui, 1998). The drawback of this method is necessity to obtain a large amount of data, which is encrypted with the same secret key. This fact makes linear cryptanalysis unsuitable for real applications.

Under the assumption that the analyst has a cipher text with important data and a black box (either hardware or software) that is capable of enciphering any number of text without disclosing the key, application of linear cryptanalysis becomes realistic. Many encryption algorithms, that were known before the publication of (Matsui, 1998), were tested for resistance against this method and some of them proved not strong enough. In order to fix this, they demanded improvements.

Any encryption algorithms can be presented as a function E, which receives an input message X and a secret key K and returns the cipher text Y = E(X, K). If the transformation E and the plaintext X are known, one still cannot predict any properties of Y. In this case, non-linearity of the function depends on internal logic of transformations of E and K. K.M Matsui has shown that there is a possibility to represent the encryption function as a system of equations, which hold with a certain probability of p. The further this probability from the value of 0.5, the more chance of success analysis has.

In order to implement linear cryptanalysis successfully, the following problems should be solved. First of all, the most effective statistical linear analogs or their estimations should be found. When finding the analogs, one has to ensure that as many private key bits as possible are involved in them. Then, the required statistical data should be obtained, namely a big enough set of plain text - cipher text pairs received using the same secret key. Finally, the key (or at least some of its bits) are found using statistical data and linear analogs.

The first stage of the analysis consists of finding effective statistical analogs. For the encryption algorithms with predefined S-boxes this stage can be passed once with regard to the analysis of linear properties of all the cryptographic elements of the cipher. This approach is not suitable for the analysis of GOST due to the variability of S-boxes. That is, whenever S-boxes are changed, it should be started from the beginning. As the result a system of equations is obtained, in which each equation holds with a certain probability. Left parts of the equations should contain sums of the bits of input and output messages, and right parts should contain secret key bits. While the first step of the analysis is purely theoretical and fully depends on the structure of the algorithm, the second step is practical and consists of the analysis of known plain text-cipher text pairs using the obtained systems of statistical analogs. The following algorithm is used for this:

Algorithm

Suppose N is the number of all plaintexts and T is the number of plaintext whose left part of linear statistical analog is 0. Two possible options can be considered here.

- If T>N/2, the number of plaintexts, whose analog's left part equals 0, is more than a half
- If the probability of this linear statistical analog p>1/2, this means that in most cases analog's left and right parts are equivalent, i.e. analog's left part, that contains key bits, equals 0.
- If the probability of this linear statistical analog p<1/2, this means that in most cases analog's left and right parts are not equivalent, i.e. analog's left part, that contains key bits, equals 1.
- If T<N/2, the number of plaintexts, whose analog's left part equals 0, is less than a half
- If the probability of this linear statistical analog p>1/2, this means that in most cases analog's left and right parts are equivalent, i.e. analog's left part, that contains key bits, equals 1.
- If the probability of this linear statistical analog p<1/2, this means that in most cases analog's left and right parts are equivalent, i.e. analog's left part, that contains key bits, equals 0.

Nowadays, there is not enough research data about the resistance of GOST against linear cryptanalysis. However, B. Schneier (1996) argues that linear cryptanalysis is inapplicable to full-round GOST because of the large number of rounds.

The Method of Differential Cryptanalysis

The method of differential cryptanalysis was proposed in early 1990s by A. Biham and A. Shamir for analysis of DES. Even though B. Schneier (1996) mentions that the designers of DES were aware about the possibility of differential cryptanalysis as early as in 1970s, this method became commonly after being mentioned in (Biham & Shamir, 1992; Biham & Shamir, 1991).

A. Biham and A. Shamir (1991, 1992) have decreased complexity of DES analysis to 237 using differential cryptanalysis. Even though analysis demanded 237 specially selected texts encrypted with the same key, it was a major breakthrough in the history of cryptanalysis. Further improvement of this method has demonstrated the possibility to apply it to a wide range of various ciphers revealing vulnerabilities of existing encryption algorithms. Nowadays, this method and its derivatives such as linear-differential cryptanalysis, the method of impossible differentials and boomerang attack, are widely used for testing of newly designed ciphers.

Cryptanalysis assumes consideration of text pairs, not individual texts. Obviously, two texts will have difference in some positions. In order to determine a difference, it is sufficient to add the texts modulo two with each other. By tracing text transformation when passing encryption rounds, one can make assumption about possible secret key values. Accumulated statistics sooner or later allows to find the secret key.

Just as in the case of linear cryptanalysis, the difficulty of differential cryptanalysis application is caused by the fact that S-boxes are not fixed constant. However, some achievements in application of differential analysis to GOST are published. An attack against full-round GOST using related keys is described in (Kelsey, Schneier, & Wagner, 1996). We revealed the possibility to analyze GOST, when S-boxes are intentionally made weak (Babenko & Ishchukova, 2010). Various approaches to the application of differential cryptanalysis to GOST algorithm will be discussed in the main section of this chapter.

Slide Attacks

Slide attacks were proposed in (Birukov & Wagner, 1999). This method of analysis is applicable to all block ciphers and does not depend on the number of encryption rounds.

While the two methods described before rely on widely used properties of encryption, slide attack uses self-similarity, which is its characteristic feature. Self-similarity means the use of the same cryptographic F-function, which is dependent on the same subkey in each encryption round. Depending on the structure of the encryption algorithm, the slide attack can use weaknesses of subkey formation or more common structural properties of the cipher. The simplest implementation of this attack can be resisted by eliminating self-similarity in encryption algorithm. The more complex variants of this attack use more sophisticated analysis, which is harder to resist.

The simplest variant of slide attack is designed for the encryption algorithms that consist of r rounds, each of which contains F-function that is dependent on the same key value of K. This type of encryption algorithms is called homogeneous. The algorithms which use periodically variable keys are also classified as homogeneous. This condition is mathematically defined as Fi = Fj for all i j (mod p). The idea is to match one encryption process and another in such a way that one encryption process follows another. The main problem here is to find this slide pair.

The GOST algorithm is characterized by a certain degree of self-similarity. This is typical for the first 24 rounds of encryption, in which round subkeys are repeated periodically. The difficulty here is caused by the fact that the last 8 rounds use reverse order of subkeys. In (Birukov & Wagner, 2000) authors consider the analysis of the simplified GOST using slide attack, which they called GOST.

Algebraic Analysis

The general idea of algebraic cryptanalysis is finding equations that describe nonlinear transformations of S-boxes followed by finding solution of these equations and obtaining the secret key. This method of cryptanalysis belongs to the class of attacks with known plaintext. It is enough to have a single plain text/cipher text pair for the success. Algebraic methods of cryptanalysis contain the following stages:

- Creation of the system of equations that describe transformations in non-linear cryptographic primitives of the analyzed cipher (i.e., S-boxes for most symmetric ciphers);
- Finding solution of this system.

The idea to describe an encryption algorithm as system of linear equations originated quite long time ago. However, until recent years it was a purely theoretical idea because it demanded huge memory capacities for storing variables and supplementary data. Nowadays, just a few research results are available that demonstrated the possibility to attack a full-round encryption algorithm. Analysis of full-round GOST is declared in (Courtois, 2011). However, this chapter does not contain any detailed description of the approach, only a brief outline. We will discuss in detail the basic mechanisms of algebraic analysis with regard to GOST.

Overview of Cryptographic Attacks against GOST

For the first time, description of GOST was translated into English and published in 1994 (Pieprzyk & Tombak, 1994). After that moment, results of its analysis made by international experts started to appear in publication. In this section, we summarize the most important results.

Attacks with linear and differential cryptanalysis are based on investigations of s-boxes features, i.e. whenever s-boxes are changed, results of earlier cryptanalysis become useless. Several publications, e.g. (Charnes, O'Connor, Pieprzyk, Safavi-Naini, & Zheng, 1994), contain false assumption that secret S-boxes values can be treated as a part of a key and increase its effective length. However, in (Saarinen, 1998) it is proven that secret S-boxes can be evaluated with the following attack, which can be implemented in practice.

In (Oreku, Li, Pazynyuk, & Mtenzi, 2007), results of cryptanalysis of modified versions of GOST are published, namely GOST-H (in which the order of subkeys is straight in all rounds, even from the 25th to the 32nd) and the 20-round GOST+ (in which XOR substitutes standard addition modulo 232). Conclusions are made that both GOST-H and GOST+ are weaker then the genuine GOST algorithm because both have classes of weak keys.

An interesting modification is proposed in (Yeh, Lin, & Wang, 1998): the tables of S1…S8 has to be different and they have to be mixed according to a predefined law in each round of encryption. This mixing can either explicitly depend on the encryption key or be secret. Both of these options significantly improve cryptographic strength of GOST according to the opinion of the authors.

Another modification connected with s-boxes is published in (Grosek, Nemoga, & Zanechal, 1997). Here the authors analyze possible methods of generating S-boxes from encryption keys. The authors conclude that this dependency weakens the algorithm because it leads to possible weaker keys and other potential vulnerabilities.

Attacks against the original and full-round GOST are also known. One of the first publications is (Kelsey, Schneier, & Wagner, 1996), which is devoted to the attacks that use weaknesses of key expansion by different encryption algorithms. In particular, the full GOST algorithm can be attacked with differential analysis on related keys although only if S-boxes are weak; the 24-round GOST (without the first 8 rounds) is successfully attacked in a similar fashion, however strong s-boxes (e.g. those described in (Schneier, 1996) make this attack unpractical.

In 2004, a group of experts from Korea proposed an attack, which makes possible to obtain 12 bits of the secret key on related keys with the probability of 91.7% (Ko, Hong, Lee, Lee, & Kang, 2004). The attack demands 235 chosen plain texts and 236 encryption operations. The complete analysis in this case demands 2224 operations. As can be seen, this attack is useless for use in practice. In 2011 the work (Isobe, 2011) was published which is directed to the investigation of Reflection - Meet in the Middle Attack applicability to GOST. Also, in (Courtois, 2011) there is an assumption on the possibility of attacking GOST with algebraic cryptanalysis when s-boxes are fixed.

Summarizing the considered results, we collect them in Table 1.

DIFFERENTIAL CRYPTANALYSIS

Differential Cryptanalysis in General

The method of differential cryptanalysis is based on tracking changes in dissimilarity between two texts. To determine the dissimilarity using the addition operation modulo 2 as a result of addition gives non-zero bits in those positions in which the two original texts have different values of bits.

Before proceeding to the solution, we introduce some basic definitions that are used for presentation. By difference we mean a result of the bitwise addition modulo 2 (XOR operation) of two separately encrypted texts with the same symmetric key, which are in the same position of the same encryption algorithm. Input difference means the difference of input values before cryptographic transformation; output difference is the difference obtained at the output of the transformation. By characteristic we mean a combination of input and output values for n rounds of the encryption algorithm. Correct pair of texts means a pair of plain text - cipher text combinations, for which the difference of plain text is equal to the input difference of the characteristic and the difference of cipher text is equal to the output difference of the characteristics.

Differential cryptanalysis is generally defined as a sequence of the following stages:

- Finding characteristics of the encryption algorithm that are characterized with maximal probabilities. Characteristics are searched according to differential properties of nonlinear cryptographic primitives of the encryption algorithm.
- Search of correct text pairs with the characteristics found before.
- Analysis of correct text pairs and accumulating statistics about possible secret key values.

The first stage is the most complicated; it characterizes the applicability of differential cryptanalysis to the considered algorithm. This

Table 1. Summarizing the considered results of cryptanalysis GOST

Number of rounds	Type of analysis	Number of plain texts	Number of operations for analysis
32	Exhaustive search	1	2256
32	Differential cryptanalysis on related keys	235	2224
24	Slide attack	264	263
30	Slide attack	264	2254
32	Slide attack with weak keys	264	264
32	Reflection - Meet in the Middle Attack	232	2225

stage is performed once for most algorithms. The values of characteristics fully depend on the structure of the encryption algorithm and used cryptographic primitives. The situation is different when it comes to the algorithms with variable elements. GOST algorithm, which is characterized by variable S-boxes, is one of them. Differential analysis should be started from the beginning for every new layout of S-boxes.

The basic approaches to the analysis of modern symmetric block ciphers are well described by the developers of this method in (Biham & Shamir, 1991; Biham & Shamir, 1992). That is why, we are not giving this information in detail, but describing the features that are typical for GOST only.

Differential Properties of GOST

Addition Modulo 232

Unlike DES, GOST data and key material are intermixing with the help of addition modulo 232. That complicates the analysis and produces nonlinearity. When observing text differences for DES encryption algorithm Biham and Shamir demonstrated that after addition with secret subkey the difference always remained unchanged but it is not true for GOST algorithm.

Therefore, it is necessary to investigate the influence of such additions to transformation of differences.

We carried out an analysis of 2, 3, 4 and 5-bit numbers, which were added with each other respectively, modulo 22, 23, 24 and 25. For each value of the input difference, not only possible variants of its formation were considered, but also different versions of secret key values. Using an inductive analysis method we formulated rules for determining the probability that the difference will remain unchanged when arguments are added modulo 2n:

- Any value of the input difference may remain unchanged. The probability of this mapping is defined as follows:

$$p = \frac{1}{2^k}, \text{if } \Delta_{in} < 2^{n-1} \quad (1)$$

$$p = \frac{1}{2^{k-1}}, \text{if } \Delta_{in} \geq 2^{n-1} \quad (2)$$

where k is the number of nonzero digits in the input difference Δ_{in}.

- For the input difference $\Delta_{in} = 0$, the output difference Δ_{out} reaches 0 with the probability of p = 1.
- For the input difference Δ_{in} = 2n-1 the output difference Δ_{out} reaches 2n-1 with the probability of p = 1.

Substitution with S-Boxes

The first step of the analysis is to identify regularities of difference transformation caused by non-linear cryptographic primitives. For symmetric block encryption algorithms (including GOST) substitution of data using S-boxes is a non-linear transformation.

Dissimilarity of different pairs of texts enciphered by cryptographic operations leads to dissimilarity of obtained cipher text with a certain probability. These probabilities can be found for S-boxes by building analysis tables. Tables are built according to the following principle: the columns contain all possible combinations of input difference of Δ A for a given S-box; rows correspond to all possible combinations of output difference of Δ C for the same S-box, and cells contain numbers of matching Δ C values with a predefined value of Δ A (or the ratio between the obtained number of matches and the total possible number of matches, which in turn can be defined as 2n, where n is the input capacity of S-boxes.) Pairs of differences Δ A and Δ C characterized by the highest probability (or the probability close to maximum) can be used for analysis in order to find the secret key.

General analysis algorithm for arbitrary S-box can be formulated as follows:

- We can take next S-box with n bits on its input.
- In the analysis table for this S-box all original values are considered to be 0.
- The first possible value of A=1 input difference is defined.
- Value of X=0 first input of analyzed S-box is defined.
- The second value of X' = X A input is calculated.
- For X и X' inputs Y and Y' outputs are defined respectively according to S-box operation principle.
- Value of C = YY' output difference is calculated.
- Value in the analysis table at the intersection of A line and C column increases by 1.
- X value increases by 1.
- If X<2n, move to Stage 5.
- A value increases by 1.
- If A<2n, move to Stage 4.
- If all S-blocks are not analyzed, move to Stage 1, or algorithm finishes its work.

We tried to analyze various table entries for S-boxes of GOST. The boxes, described in (Schneier, 1996), seemed to be a judgment sample for using by the Central Bank of the Russian Federation as they possess almost a uniform probability distribution for the built analysis tables thus they make cipher more stable to the method of differential cryptanalysis. Later we shall consider the use of analysis tables, those are weak with reference to differential cryptanalysis.

Cyclic Shift

Shift operation in GOST is one of three basic operations that comprise the round transformation function. Differential cryptanalysis usually implies the difference between two texts. Suppose we have two texts: A and B. Their difference is defined as $A \oplus B$. If we shift each of the values of A and B cyclically to the left by s bits, then we obtain the difference $(A <<s) \oplus (B <<s)$, characterized by the following property:

$$(A <<s) \oplus (B <<s) = (A \oplus B) <<s \quad (3)$$

If we consider this operation in relation to GOST, we get:

$$(A <<11) \oplus (B <<11) = (A \oplus B) <<11,$$

i.e., in order to obtain the correct difference at the output of a cyclic shift operation, one has to shift the input difference cyclically left by 11 digits.

Weak S-Boxes for GOST: Search and Analysis

GOST relies on eight S-boxes, which are not fixed. That is, it is implied that randomly generated S-boxes can be used. Cryptographic strength should be provided by a sufficient number of encryption rounds (i.e., 32).

We showed that there is a range of S-boxes with eased features with reference to differential cryptanalysis (Babenko & Ishchukova, 2010). In practice it will cause an attack on a cipher with similar boxes. To give a concept of weak, with reference to differential cryptanalysis, S-boxes, we remember that the difference remains unchanged after addition modulo 223 depends on the quantity of non-zero digits of the difference.

Therefore, we have assumed that the weak ones are the boxes for which the input difference ΔA contains only one high bit (i.e., only 4 variants of such difference exist, namely Δ A = 1, Δ A

= 2, $\Delta A = 4$, and $\Delta A = 8$) will be replaced by the output difference ΔC, which also contain only one high bit (i.e., $\Delta C = 1$, $\Delta C = 2$, $\Delta C = 4$, or $\Delta C = 8$).

The paper (Babenko & Ishchukova, 2010) illustrates the construction of interdependency graph to receive S-box with required probabilities for the analysis. It showed only 384 various S-boxes with weak features can be deducted.

It may seem at a glance that the constructed S-box cannot be used for attack because the probabilities in analysis table are either 0 or 1, but this is not so. In fact S-boxes are not the only component of GOST that affect variation of characteristic's probability. Integer addition modulo 232 affects difference transformation as well. Under these conditions, the probability that the difference remains unchanged depends on the quantity of non-zero digits of the difference, which is directed to transformation input. It is possible to find characteristics for algorithm analysis using S-boxes. In this case, the probability that the difference remains unchanged will be 1 while the common characteristic probability will depend on addition modulo 232.

Searching for Characteristics with Maximal Probabilities

For GOST 28147-89 S-boxes are unknown in advance, thus algorithm analysis cannot be carried out only once. Every time when box values change, it is necessary to start the analysis from the very beginning to detect the best possible differential value. Let us consider the facing problem in further detail. The GOST encryption algorithm operates on 64-bit blocks of data and conforms to Feistel scheme. Therefore, there are 264 cases of input differences which can be directed to the algorithm input. Each of input differences can produce an abundance of output differences with various probabilities. And yet, the solution of the problem is a pair of input-output difference values where difference possesses maximum probability value. Input difference value, which is 0, should be naturally excluded, as the output difference value will be 0 with p=1 probability, and which means to obtain maximum probability value.

A tree-branching structure of possible transformations for original similar difference from round to round is similar to building B-trees. B-trees are discussed in (Cormen, Leiserson, & Rivest, 2009) in detail. The definition of a B-tree, as well as its relationship to the discussed problem, is depicted below.

B-tree is a rooted tree with the following structure:

1. Every node of a tree includes fields packaging
    a. A number of n[x] keys kept there (i.e. in the problem discussed, n[x] is possible number of output differences of one round with concrete input difference);
    b. The keys themselves (i.e. difference values);
    c. Leaf[x] Boolean value, true, when x node is a leaf (in this case leaves are outputs of the last encryption round).
2. If x is an internal node, it also contains n[x]+1 pointers to its children. Leaves has no fields, thus these fields are not pinpointed for them.
3. All the leaves are on the same depth (which is equal to h of a tree, i.e. equal to the number of encryption rounds discussed).

Basing on the definition of B-tree given above, we can schematically depict (Figure 2) the tree for every input difference.

We stated that for any entry of GOST substitution tables nonzero value of input difference, which gives output zero difference value, will never occur. Therefore, the only way to miss one encryption rounds with p=1 possibility is that the left part of input difference agress to the difference value on F encryption function output of the first encryption round. In this case, value on F function input of the second encryption round is 0, and one

Figure 2. B-tree of input difference transformation

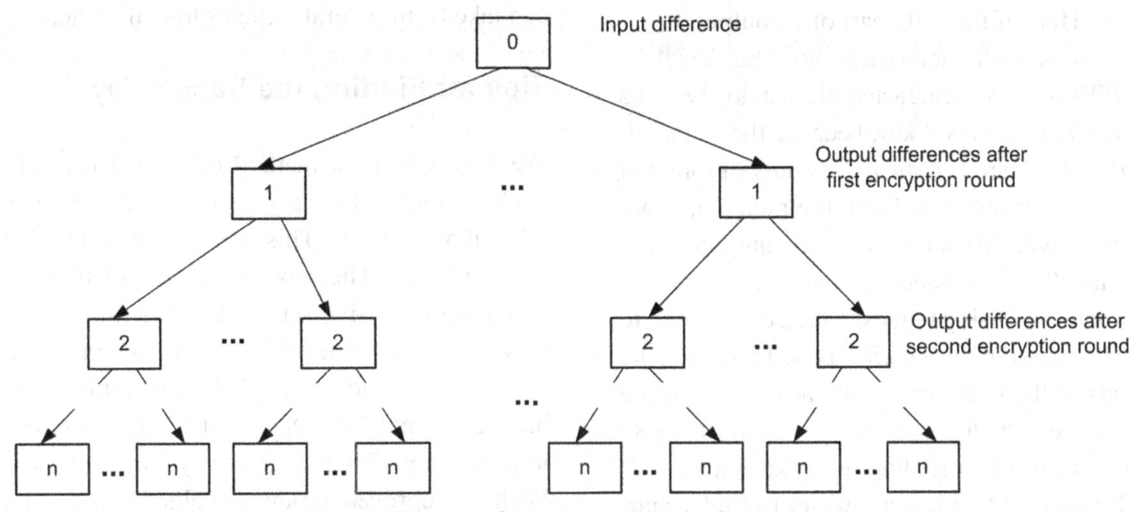

encryption round can be missed without changing general probability value.

It is no use to sort out all 264 combinations of input differences in order to find the most probable difference pairs. It is quite sufficient to sort out the right part values of input difference, and the left part values of input difference set equal to the probable output of F function of the first round. In this case the second difference transformation round will obtain p=1 probability value, and thus it will not have implications for general probability value.

Searching for difference pairs can be performed according to threshold probability value. There are two methods of setting threshold probability value. The first method is the direct setting. In this case we will find all difference pairs, their probability of occurrence is not lower than the set threshold value. The second method is a dynamic change of threshold probability value. In this case, the initial threshold value is taken to be equal to zero. When searching the next pair of input-output difference is defined. And if p probability of this pair is more than threshold value, then threshold probability is redefined and goes to p value. This method finds all difference pairs with maximum probability values from the search range.

Generally searching in B-tree is like to searching in a binary tree. The difference is that in every node only one variant is chosen of n[x], and not of two. On the input recursive searching in B-tree receives pointer to a subtree root and the key, which we are looking for in this tree (Cormen, Leiserson, & Rivest, 2009).

In the problem discussed, the key is probability value. If probability value is not more than threshold value when recursive procedure is called, the recursive procedure will return the pointer to the next tree level, otherwise backtracking & searching should be performed on another branch. If searching for x node is failed on any branch, transition to the previous level should be performed. Searching should last until all the rooted tree branches are tested.

The developed algorithm is a recursive algorithm for searching the most probable difference pairs for GOST, its speed depends upon differential properties of analysis tables. Thus, for the tables with maximum values, searching is very fast with the use of parallel computing in particular.

Before finding good characteristics, we have to find out which characteristics cannot be used for analysis. According to the rules of difference transformation caused by addition modulo 2n, if

Δ_{in} = 2n - 1, then Δ_{out} = 2n - 1 with probability p = 1. Thus, if the right part of an output difference of the characteristics will be equal to 80000000x, such characteristic cannot be used for finding the secret key, because the probability that the characteristic passes the last round of encryption is also p = 1. All the more so, in accordance with a round subkey searching algorithm, which will be discussed in Section 6, we estimate the secret key using tetrads, which correspond to the data passing through S-boxes. Therefore, the tetrads of the right part of characteristics output difference, which contain the values of 0x or 8x cannot be used for finding secret key either.

It turns out that it is necessary to find a characteristic, which contains values other than 0x or 8x in the right part of the output difference in each tetrad. According to a property integer addition modulo 232, finding unique characteristic with non-zero values in each tetrad leads to a little probability, because a difference containing at least 8 high bits passes through integer addition each round. It is much easier to receive some characteristics with sufficiently high probabilities, each of which involves one or more tetrads.

We tried the recursive searching algorithm for the most probable difference pairs, described above, to find all possible input differences with the tetrads containing one of five possible values: 0x, 1x, 2x, 4x и 8x.

As soon as the input of GOST contains only 64 bits (16 tetrads), we tried 516 ≈ 237.15 variants. Analysis of 32 rounds of GOST has shown that there is a large amount of input/output difference pairs for which the characteristic has quite high probability (from 2-25 to 2-33) and can be used for analysis. As we had expected, the input differences, for which several tetrads (at least three) contained non-zero tetrad, were not characterized by good probabilities. So there is a sound reason to conclude that there is no need to do exhaustive search of input differences. It suffices to consider several options, where different tetrads containing different values and use them later for analysis.

The similar reduction using recursive algorithm can take from several minutes to half an hour.

Tips for Finding the Secret Key

We have offered a method of correct text pair analysis for finding a secret key (Babenko & Ishchukova, 2010). This method has a number of drawbacks. The most important of those is searching excessive sets of key fragments (i.e., they contained values, which could be filtered as wrong ones in advance). This fact significantly hampered analysis, because it led to extremely large number of round secret keys combinations. We have improved the analysis algorithm in order to make as few excessive key fragments as possible.

As we have already mentioned, it is quite easy to find round characteristics whose probability belong to the interval from 2-25 to 2-33. If possible, the total number of characteristics should be such that no tetrads of output difference exist whose values are either 0x or 8x. These probabilities let us expect that correct pairs of texts, which are suitable for analysis, are found easily. According to the birthday paradox, in order to find a correct pair of texts corresponding to a characteristic with probability $\frac{1}{2^{25}}$, one has to analyze 233.5 text pairs.

For searching correct text pairs, we are using the approach proposed by Biham and Shamir (1992) for DES analysis. Correct text pairs are selected according to right part values of output characteristics, while left parts are not taken into account. The fact that right parts of correct text pairs matches right parts of the characteristics makes it possible to assume that text differences is transformed by the encryption rounds in the manner, which was determined by the design of the characteristic. Besides that, we can ignore the probability that the difference remains unchanged in the last encryption round, when the aggregate characteristic probability is calculated.

When this correct text pair selection procedure is applied, the analysis implies to get the difference from the output of integer addition modulo 232 by function F of the last round of encryption. To do so, the difference formed by the left halves of the encrypted messages of correct text pairs, i.e. the value Δ YL = YL $\oplus$ YL1, has to be added modulo two to the left part of the estimated value of the difference on the input of the last round, i.e. the value Δ YL-1. Thus, we obtain the value of the difference that occurred at the output of function F at the last round. Then the final value of the difference has to be shifted right by 11 digits and in accordance with the table of analysis for S-boxes and the value of the difference, which was received at the input of S-boxes, has to be found (we can do this as long as the weakest S-blocks are chosen for the analysis, i.e. those whose difference is mapped from the round's input to the round's output with the probability of 1). In order to conclude these ideas, we have to make the following transformations:

Δ Z= Δ S-1((Δ YL $\oplus$ Δ YL-1)<<<11),

where the operation Δ S-1(m) stands for replacing the output difference value m to the only possible input value of Δ Z difference according to the analysis table.

The Δ Z value is the estimated output difference value of the output of integer addition modulo 232.

For each correct text pair we will consider only the first and the last encryption round. According to the original GOST description, the same round subkey K1 is used by both of them. Therefore, the analysis of the first and the last round will make it possible to soundly assume the value of the first round subkey. We will consider the eight tetrads, namely k1, k2, k3, k4, k5, k6, k7, and k8, for the round subkey K1 in accordance with the number of S-blocks. Possible values of ki tetrad value are determined for the characteristic of Si-block.

The fact that the correct pair of texts corresponding to a given characteristic is found allows to assume that the difference was transformed at encryption rounds exactly as it was defined by the constructed characteristic. Thus, when the right pair of texts is known, right parts of the original message XR and XR1 that came to F of the first round, are known either. We also know that after integer addition modulo 232 the difference in these texts remains unchanged.

As we mentioned earlier, we will calculate the tetrad key value for each characteristic in accordance with a corresponding S-block. For instance, for the tetrad, which corresponds to S8-block, the lowest bits of the key are considered. That is why we are not considering the carry, which may occur in addition of previous tetrads. Analysis of the first characteristics, which involve the S8-block, makes it possible to extract some most probable values for the secret key lower tetrad. These values will be used later when analyzing correct text pairs for the found characteristics of the S7-block. The value of k8 tetrad allows us to find out if there was a carry from the lower tetrad to the higher tetrad when the analyzed data were summed with the key. Earlier, we carried out analysis considering the possibility of a carry from lower bits to higher bits by default, which led to many excessively searched secret key values.

For each analyzed tetrad, we will test 16 possible kij key fragment options (from 0000 to 1111), where i is an index of the S-block of the analyzed tetrad, j is a possible key tetrad value. That is, say the values kij such as holds ((XRi + kij + pi-1) mod 24) $\oplus$ ((XR1i + kij + p1i-1) mod 24) = Δ Zi will be considered possible options for round subkey fragments. The values of pi-1 and p1i-1 are the possible carries from addition of lower data tetrads and lower key tetrads.

Analyzing correct text pairs we can see that some values of each round subkey tetrads occur more often than others and this fact lets us to make assumptions about possible values of the round subkey.

As the result of this analysis, a certain number of possible K1 round subkey values will be formed.

After that, it is necessary to analyze the same right pairs of texts, though not with subkey fragments, but with selected values of the all possible 32-bit round subkey values. After the testing, only a few keys (less than ten) will remain and one of them will be the real round subkey.

The following algorithm summarizes the stages of finding a secret subkey.

1. Generate at least 8 round characteristics ($\Delta X = (\Delta XL, \Delta XR)$; $\Delta Y = (\Delta YL, \Delta YR)$) so that all S-blocks for both the first and the last encryption rounds are involved.
2. Arrange the characteristics according to the following principle: S8-block should be involved in the first characteristic, then S7 corresponding to the second one, etc. until S1-block is reached.
3. The following transformation should be carried out for each characteristic:
   a. Set the values p0 = 0, p10 = 0, p20 = 0 and p30 = 0 (the former two are to define carries for the texts XR and XR1 in the first round analysis; the latter two are to define carries for texts YR and YR1 in the last round analysis).
   b. Select several correct text pairs (X = (XL, XR); Y = (YL, YR)) и (X1 = (XL1, XR1); Y1 = (YL1, YR1)) so that holds $\Delta XL = XL \oplus XL1$; $\Delta XR = XR \oplus XR1$; $\Delta YR = YR \oplus YR1$. The value ΔYL is not taken into account for the selection.
   c. Find out the difference value for the first round, which is formed at the output of integer addition of the data and the possible keys: $\Delta Z1 = \Delta XR = XR \oplus XR1$.
   d. Find out the difference value for the last round, which is formed at the output of the integer addition of the data and the possible keys: $\Delta Z2 = \Delta S\text{-}1((\Delta YL \oplus \Delta YL\text{-}1) \lll 11)$ (Box 1).
4. Build a set of possible round subkeys.

Test the selected possible values of round subkeys and filter all the excessive ones.

Experimental Observations Made by GOST Differential Analysis

In order to verify the effectiveness of the method, we simulated an attack on GOST with the number of rounds reduced to 12. In this case we used 8 round subkeys so that in the first and last round

Box 1.

```
for j=0 to 15 do
kij = j
Calculate a= ((XRi + kij  + pi-1) mod 24) ⊕ ((XR1i + kij + p1i-1) mod 24)
Calculate b= ((YRi + kij  + p2i-1) mod 24) ⊕ ((YR1i + kij + p3i-1) mod 24)
If (a = b) then
Fix the value of kij as a possible key fragment value for i-th tetrad.
If kij ≥ XRi, then pi = 1
If kij ≥ XR1i, then p1i = 1
If kij ≥ YRi, then p2i = 1
If kij ≥ YR1i, then p3i = 1
```

the same round subkey is used. We used a weak S-box defined in (Babenko & Ishchukova, 2010). Attack on full GOST will look the same way except that it will demand much more text pairs for finding a correct pair.

At first we have found 10 characteristics for 12 rounds of GOST presented in Table 2. The table shows that right sides of output differences ΔY have from one to three non-zero tetrad while at least one tetrad is either 1x, 2x, or 4x.

For each characteristic in Table 2 we tested 100 000 pairs of texts in order to find a correct text pair. Received correct pairs were analyzed to find a secret key.

As the result of primary selection of tetrads of the secret key, 16384 possible keys have been selected from 232 total values. Subsequent testing of the full round subkey was selecting 5 possible values in average (depending on the number of the found correct text pairs, this value fluctuated

Table 2. Characteristics for 12-round GOST

Nº	ΔX	ΔY	ΔYL-1	p
1	00001000 00000001	00010000 10000000	00010100	$\frac{1}{2^{18}}$
2	00000800 00000004	00000004 00200804	00200800	$\frac{1}{2^{18}}$
3	00020000 00000008	00000008 04002008	04002000	$\frac{1}{2^{18}}$
4	00010000 00000010	00100000 00000001	00101000	$\frac{1}{2^{18}}$
5	00040000 00000020	00000020 08040020	08040000	$\frac{1}{2^{18}}$
6	00008000 00000040	00000040 02008040	02008000	$\frac{1}{2^{18}}$
7	00020000 00000080	00000080 40020080	40020000	$\frac{1}{2^{18}}$
8	00100000 00000100	01000000 00000010	01010000	$\frac{1}{2^{18}}$
9	00400000 00000200	00000200 80400200	80400000	$\frac{1}{2^{13}}$
10	80000000 00400000	00400000 80400200	80000200	$\frac{1}{2^{11}}$

from 2 to 10). Full analysis of 12 rounds of GOST using ten round characteristics took from 1 to 2 minutes in average (experiments were carried out with Intel Celeron M CPU 530 1.73 GHz, RAM 1Gb). We have carried out around 1000 experiments using different values of round subkeys and the result was always positive.

ALGEBRAIC CRYPTANALYSIS

Survey of Algebraic Cryptanalysis Methods

Claude Shannon (1949) assumed that cracking strong encryption algorithm requires as much work as for solving simultaneous equations with a large number of the unknown variables. While analyzing encryption algorithms much attention used to be directed to statistical analysis methods and algebraic attacks describing holistic approaches to the problem of cipher strength analysis.

The use of cipher internal structure is a characteristic property of algebraic analysis unlike statistical methods. Cryptanalyst reports enciphering transformation in terms of simultaneous equations and tries to solve the present simultaneous equation to obtain the encryption key. Algebraic attacks can be set as two stages. The first stage is to present an encryption algorithm and some extra algorithm data in a form of polynomial equation set over GF(2) field or other finite field. The second stage is to solve the simultaneous equations and obtain the encryption key. Cryptanalyst should generally know μ pair, (P1, …, Pμ) plain text and (C1, …, Cμ) cipher text, when E(Pi)=Ci condition holds for any $i \in \{1, \mu\}$. One or several solutions can be obtained in the course of algebraic analysis. In the simultaneous equation, set for the analyzed encryption algorithm, single unknown value corresponds to every key bit. Furthermore, there could be other unknown values connecting input and output encryption round values in the simultaneous equations. Cryptanalyst's task is to construct a sufficient number of equations from algebraic analysis in order to reduce the number of solutions of simultaneous equations to only one correct solution, but yet simultaneous equations should be solved within acceptable period of time. Fulfillment of the above conditions means that algebraic analysis attack will be performed faster than brute force attack. Different cryptanalysis approaches were developed to solve nonlinear systems of Boolean equations. Practical aspects of cryptanalysis state that methods based on linear approximations of initial system are the most efficient.

One of the first algebraic methods used in cryptography is based on determining Gröbner basis. One can take a close look at Buchberger algorithm for determining Gröbner basis in (Becker & Weispfenning, 1993; Cox, Little, & O'Shea, 1996; Kalkbrener, 1999). Later Jean-Charles Faugère (1999, 2002) recommended to use more efficient F4 and F5 algorithms for determining Gröbner basis.

In cryptography, the solution of system of nonlinear equations is NP complex task and requires exponential time. At the same time efficient solution algorithms of simultaneous linear equations can be used within polynomial time. Thus, if the number of unique monomials in the system is more or equal to the number of linearly independent equations, initial nonlinear system can be put in linear form with linearization method (Courtois, Goubin, Meier, & Tacier, 2002). The linearization method is based upon the substitution of all nonlinear elements for new variables. The linearization method can be represented in the following form. Suppose simultaneous linear equations are over GF(2) field with the equations are given by:

$$\sum_{i,j} a_{i,j,k} x_i x_j \oplus \sum_i b_{i,k} x_i \oplus c_k = 0$$

where xi, xj– variables:

ai,j,k, bi,k, ck ∈ GF(2) – constants;

k – equation number.

Solution of the present simultaneous linear equations involves substitution of each nonlinear monominal term (xixj) for new unknown ug and solution of the resulting simultaneous linear equations with respect to new variables, with further determination of the solutions for the initial simultaneous linear equations by solving xixj =ug, special systems for each solution of simultaneous linear equations.

If nonlinearity degree for each equation is not more than d value, the number of variables in the resulting simultaneous linear equations is not more than $t = C_i^1 + C_i^2 + \dots C_i^d$. Complexity of determining solutions for simultaneous linear equations when using Gaussian algorithm and neglecting the complexity of special systems, is evaluated at O(t)3. Cryptanalyst should generate additional equations using mathematics, i.e. when variable products are substituted, the list of the system unknowns increases (all the products are taken as self-unknowns).

Kipnis and Shamir (1999) devised an advanced relinearization method. Aware that there are efficient solution algorithms of linear systems, Kipnis and Adi Shamir suggested reducing MQ-task to linear form by relinearization, and then obtaining additional system equations with the help of connection between new variables. Authors illustrated that for over defined system of equations relinearization algorithm will be executed within polynomial time. In relinearization method all nonlinear elements are substituted for new variables as is in the case of linearization, and then the relations between the unknowns produce additional equations. For example, one can use the commutative law of multiplication. Let initial nonlinear system possess {x1, x2, x3, x4} variables, then their products can be substituted in the following way:

x1• x2 = y12,

x1• x3 = y13,

x1• x4 = y14,

x2• x3 = y23,

x2• x4 = y24,

x3• x4 = y34,

then the additional equations come out right, as presented in Box 2.

New yiyj monomials will appear in the system, they can be substituted for new variables and linear system can be solved. The present method made possible to solve many systems which were not solvable by linearization method. The weak point of relinearization method is its complexity. The complexity is difficult to estimate correctly and depends on the properties of the initial system.

Extended Linearization method (XL) (Courtois, Klimov, Patarin, & Shamir, 2000) can be evolution of relinearization method. The basis of XL method is to solve system of equations by linearization with linearly independent equations produced preliminarily. Additional equations are formed with multiplication system initial equations by monomials of the specified degree. Let

Box 2.

(x1 • x2) • (x3 • x4) = (x1 • x3) • (x2 • x4) ⇒ y12 • y34 = y13 • y24,
(x1 • x3) • (x2 • x4) = (x1 • x4) • (x2 • x3) ⇒ y13 • y24= y14 • y23,
(x1 • x2) • (x3 • x4) = (x1 • x4) • (x2 • x3) ⇒ y12 • y34 = y14 • y23.

us assume that initial system results from m equations with n unknowns connecting encryption key and known data. Then eXtended Linearization algorithm is given by the following:

- Evaluating of D parameter of eXtended Linearization method by:

$$\begin{cases} D = \left\lceil \dfrac{n}{\sqrt{m}} \right\rceil, & if \quad \dfrac{n}{\sqrt{m}} > 2 \\ D = 3, \quad if & \dfrac{n}{\sqrt{m}} \leq 2 \end{cases},$$

- Multiplication of all initial m system equations for every monomials to ≤ D-2 degree.
- Including additional equations, obtained on stage 2, into the initial system.
- Substitution of all unknown products for new variables (system is reduced to a linear form) by linearization.
- Solution of the obtained linear system by Gaussian elimination method.

The attack complexity by eXtended Linearization corresponds to the complexity of finding the solution of linear system. When using Gaussian elimination method for solution of linear system, XL complexity is calculated by:

$$T^{\omega} \approx \binom{n}{D}^{\omega} \approx \binom{n}{n/\sqrt{m}}^{\omega},$$

where $\omega \leq 3$ – exponent of Gauss transformation.

eXtended Sparse Linearization algorithm (XSL) was developed in (Courtois & Pieprzyk, 2002). This method is used for the solution of sparse systems, i.e. systems of equations lacking many possible unknown products. XSL method includes 5 steps:

- Analysis of initial system of equations and selection of a fixed list of monomials and equations for further usage.
- Selection of P parameter value and multiplication of the equations selected on the previous step and (P-1) product results of the selected monomials. It is the principle step of XSL method where it necessary to obtain sufficient number of linearly independent equations.
- T' method is additionally executed, where some selected equations multiplied by single variables.
- The use of linearization method by representing each monomial in the form of a new variable.
- Execution of Gaussian elimination method to find one or several solutions of the equation system.

The vital difference between XL and XSL methods lies in that in XL method initial system equations are multiplied by all possible monomials to the degree not more than D-2 (where D – attack property depending on the number of equations and the unknowns of the initial system). In XSL method several equations should be multiplied by the monomials selected earlier.

The research of applying algebraic attacks to block ciphers can be found in the following papers. Ferguson, Schroeppel, and Whiting (2001) proposed to represent the block cipher algorithm, Advanced Encryption Standard (AES), in the form of one equation with a great number of unknown values over GF(2) field. For 128-bit AES cipher this equation included 250 unknowns and didn't practically bring the threat to cipher strength. The obtain results showed that representing the block cipher algorithm in the form of polynomial equation does not mean its algebraic attack vulnerabilities. In (Courtois & Debraize, 2008; Weinmann, 2009) there are further investigations of AES standard analysis. Thus in (Courtois & Debraize, 2008) the authors described the attacks on simplified Serpent, Present and AES cipher algorithms, and illustrated potential vulnerability to algebraic attacks. The dissertation (Weinmann, 2009) describes the analysis results of full version of AES-128 and Cryptomeria algorithms by finding Gröbner basis. The paper (Courtois & Bard, 2007) describes the attack on Data Encryption Standard (DES) cipher algorithm. In this research the authors executed the attack on 6 full rounds of DES encryption with the only known open text/ciphertext pair. Book (Bard, 2009) allows to take a closer look at algebraic attack on Keeloq block cipher. The paper (Bulygin, 2011) describes the analysis results by SAT-solving method, 8 rounds of PRINTCipher-48 block cipher algorithm with two text known and analysis of 9 rounds with processing some assumptions.

Today, despite the growing interest to the algebraic attacks, the use of such attacks in Russian symmetric encryption standard GOST is poorly reviewed. When reviewing GOST analysis, we should mention the work (Courtois, 2011); it executed the attack 239 times as fast than brute force attack with known 264 texts. However, in this work the author doesn't reveal GOST attack algorithm; that is why further research of GOST attack is important.

GOST Algebraic Cryptanalysis

Consider the use of algebraic attack on GOST with eXtended Linearization method. From the beginning the authors considered the attack on the simplified version of GOST. The algorithm was chosen in view of simplifying of addition modulo 232 with round key in the system of equations. Thereafter when passing to GOST analysis addition modulo 232 with round key should be presented as additional equations as described in Courtois and Debraize (2008).

Based on previous research of attack applicability to block ciphers, generation of equation system connecting cipher key and the known data is executed for nonlinear substitution transformation in GOST, presented by S-boxes. GOST substitution boxes are known as additional secret encryption element, and accordingly the authors considered the implementation of attack preparatory stage directed to calculation of secret substitution tables (Saarinen, 1998). The complexity of preparatory stage is not more than 232 encryption operations for guaranteed finding of substitution table. For recovery of substitution tables, as a part of study, 230 encryptions, and 26 minutes to calculate were required on IntelCore 2 Duo T8100 with 2 GB RAM. Algorithm of equation system generation for a fixed substitution table was illustrated in (Babenko, Ishchukova, & Maro, 2011). For the substitution boxes of 4x4 bit, described in (Popov, Kurepkin, & Leontiev, 2006), 237 possible equations were tested, and 221 equations appeared to be correct transformation of substitution block. 21 linearly independent equations were found for every block. Transformations in one encryption round were produced by the system which included 168 linearly independent equations with 64 unknowns and 288 various monomials. Linearly independent equations for the first substitution box under research are given by Box 3.

For two GOST rounds shown in Figure 3, the initial system depicting encryption transformation includes 336 equations, 128 unknowns and 576 various monomials. Using linearization method without additional reducing will not allow to find the solution as the number of equations is less than the number of monomials. Using GOST structure one can substitute output bits of substitution boxes for evaluated values by formulas:

$Y1=(PL \oplus CR)>>>11$, for the first round,

$Y2=(PR \oplus CL)>>>11$, for the second round.

After substitution the system will obtain 64 unknowns instead of 128 and the number of monomials in the equations will be reduced to 160.

Box 3.

```
x4⊕x4y2⊕x3y3⊕x3y1⊕x2y4⊕x2y1=0
x3⊕x3x2⊕x4y1⊕x3y3⊕x3y2⊕x2y4⊕x2y3⊕x2y2⊕x2y1⊕x1y4⊕x1y3⊕x1y2⊕x1y1=0
x2⊕x3x2⊕x2y3⊕x2y2⊕x2y1=0
x1⊕x4y1⊕x3y2⊕x2y4⊕x2y2⊕x2y1⊕x1y4⊕x1y3⊕x1y1=0
y4⊕x4y1⊕x3y1⊕x2y3⊕x2y1⊕x1y4⊕x1y3⊕x1y1=0
y3⊕x3x2⊕x2y2⊕x2y1⊕x1y4⊕x1y3⊕1=0
y2⊕x4y2⊕x1y2⊕x1y1=0
y1⊕x3y1⊕x2y3⊕x2y1⊕x1y3⊕x1y1=0
x4x3⊕x4y1⊕x3y4⊕x3y2⊕x3y1⊕x2y4⊕x2y2⊕x2y1⊕x1y4⊕x1y2⊕x1y1=0
x4x2⊕x4y1⊕x3y2⊕x1y3⊕x1y1=0
x4x1⊕x4y1⊕x3y4⊕x3y1⊕x2y4⊕x2y3⊕x2y2⊕x2y1⊕x1y4⊕x1y2=0
x3x1⊕x3y3⊕x3y1⊕x2y2⊕x1y4⊕x1y3⊕x1y2=0
x2x1⊕x4y1⊕x3y4⊕x3y1⊕x2y4⊕x2y3⊕x2y1⊕x1y4⊕x1y2⊕x1y1=0
y4y3⊕x4y1⊕x3y4⊕x3y2⊕x2y4⊕x2y2⊕x2y1⊕x1y4⊕x1y3⊕x1y2⊕x1y1=0
y4y2⊕x4y1⊕x3y2⊕x2y4⊕x2y2⊕x2y1⊕x1y3⊕x1y2⊕x1y1=0
y4y1⊕x3y3⊕x3y2⊕x2y4⊕x2y3⊕x1y1=0
y3y2⊕x4y4⊕x4y2⊕x4y1⊕x3y3⊕x3y2⊕x3y1⊕x2y4⊕x2y1⊕x1y1=0
y3y1⊕x4y4⊕x4y1⊕x3y4⊕x2y4⊕x2y3⊕x2y2⊕x2y1⊕x1y4⊕x1y2=0
y2y1⊕x4y4⊕x3y2⊕x1y3=0
x4y4⊕x3y4⊕x3y3⊕x3y2⊕x2y3⊕x2y2⊕x1y4⊕x1y3⊕x1y2⊕x1y1=0
x4y3⊕x4y2⊕x4y1⊕x3y4⊕x3y1⊕x2y4⊕x2y2⊕x2y1⊕x1y4⊕x1y3⊕x1y2=0
```

The requirement of linearization applicability will be fulfilled, thus, we will apply linearization method to find encryption key for two GOST rounds in the second attack stage. As it was mentioned above, the attack complexity determines the complexity of linear system solution, so the cryptanalysis complexity of two GOST rounds is 1603≈222, that is in 242 times less than the complexity of brute force attack (264).

The attack on two rounds of GOST+ algorithm was similar to the attack on two rounds of GOST encryption algorithm. The system of equations remains the same for GOST algorithm but round key calculation with the obtained input values of substitution boxes were affected. Considering that addition is performed modulo 232, carry between digits is verified when the sum is calculated. For example, suppose the original attack data as follows:

plain text 58b7e5e8a13a,
cipher text c3a09d847e1aa55e

X1=95771861,
X2=2DA91C85.

If we know S-box inputs, we can calculate round encryption keys by the formulas:

K=PR + X, if X>PR,
K=232 - PR+X, if X≤PR.

We have found the following keys for two rounds:

K1= AF8E7727
K2= AF8E7727

Figure 3. Two GOST rounds in ordinary substitution mode

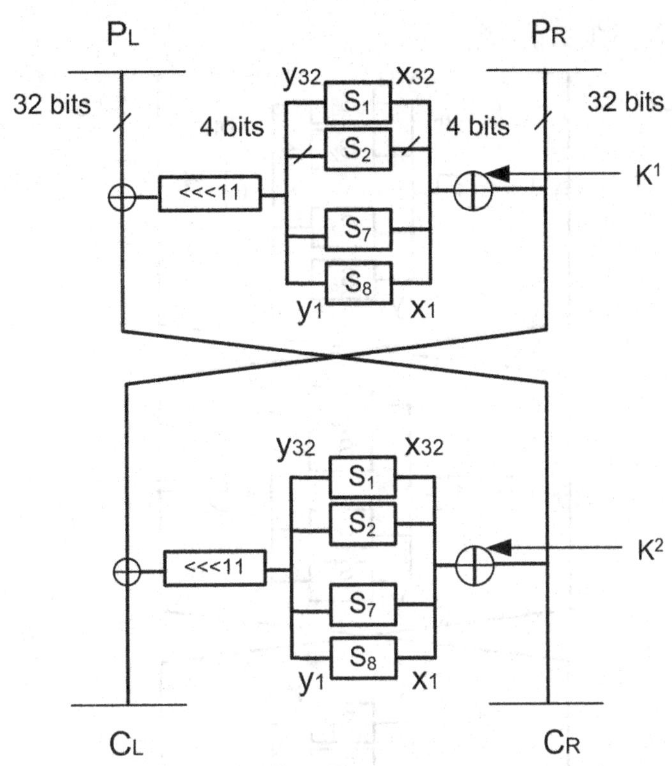

When passing to the analysis of three GOST encryption rounds illustrated in Figure 4, the system with 504 equations, 192 unknowns and 864 various monomials.

Reduction of the number of the system unknowns for three rounds was not successful and searching of the solution was executed with XL method. When applying eXtended Linearization method the authors consider every substitution box individually. In this case D parameter of XL method is 3, i.e. each of 21 equations for substitution box is multiplied by unknowns power 1. Then we obtain 189 equations for one substitution box, the majority of these equations are linearly independent. For three encryption rounds after resulting in additional equations, the system includes 4536 equations with 192 unknowns and 2208 various monomials.

The system can be solved by linearization. Attack complexity for GOST encryption rounds will be 22083≈234 that is 262 times as little as the complexity of finding round keys with brute force method.

For 32-round GOST encryption algorithm, the system contains 48384 equations with 2048 unknowns and 23552 various monomials. Attack complexity is 235523≈244.

Note that implementation of GOST attack algorithms mentioned above with GOST cipher attack is complicated by carry between digits when addition modulo 232 with round key. Implementation of unfixed substitution tables is the difference between attack on GOST algorithms and GOST in comparison with other box ciphers, that every time causes the necessity to restore substitution tables and generate system of equations. It is noteworthy that there is a possibility of efficient parallelization of equation system generation for substitution boxes and solution of simultaneous linear equations.

Figure 4. Three rounds of GOST encryption algorithm

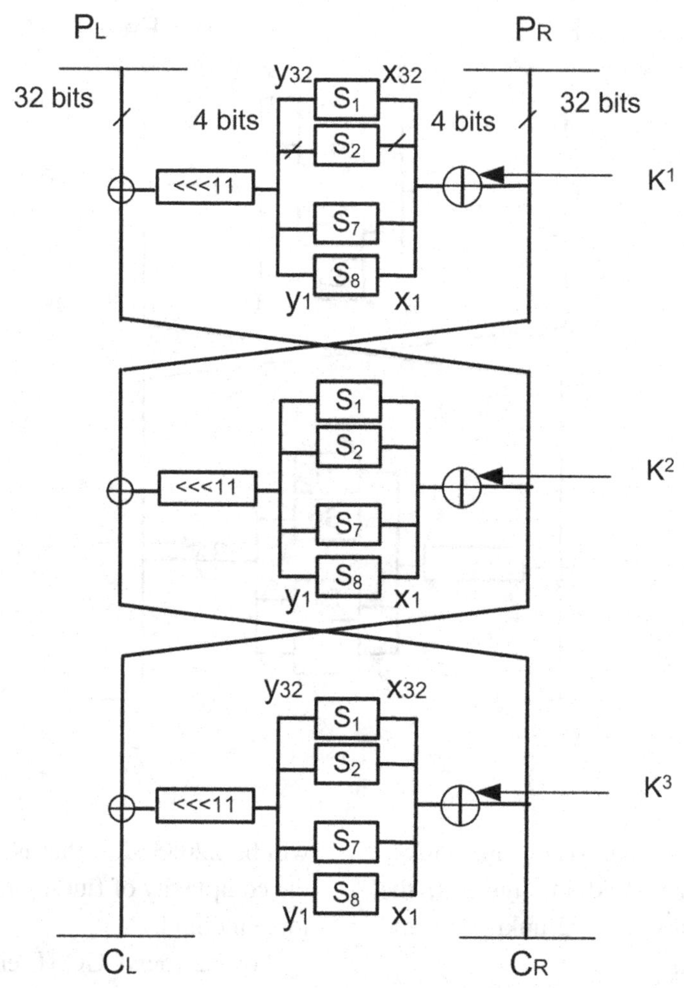

Nowadays the implementation of eXtended Linearization algorithms for GOST full-function 32-round algorithm is still under investigation.

FUTURE RESEARCH DIRECTIONS

We reviewed various approaches to the analysis of GOST algorithm. Particular attention was paid to differential and algebraic analysis methods. Today GOST algorithm is not considered as vulnerable within implementation of one of those methods. Implementation of differential cryptanalysis when breaking GOST becomes possible when algorithm uses weak substitution boxes which are hardly encountered in practice. Full GOST algorithm analysis poses severe difficulties as well, and today we have got only theoretical prediction for its complexity. However, cryptanalysis research is developing and new data on GOST algorithm analysis may appear in the nearest future. We hope that this research work contributes it.

One final comment to be shown is several curious regularities connected with encryption in GOST algorithm. The first interesting observation is the existence of equivalent keys. So as the length of scrambled information unit is 264, and the length of the key is 2256, there is a number of patterns (about 2192) of X input message with different variants of K key, which result in the same Y value after encryption. It makes the analysis with exhaustive method more complicated. So if the key suits one text pair after testing, it doesn't need to be the searched key but one of 2192 equivalent keys.

Our second observation is connected with the fact that within last 8 rounds encryption the subkeys are used in reverse order. In case the values of left and right text parts match after 24 rounds, further carries from the 25th to the 32nd round cancel (decipher) the carries performed from the 17th to the 24th round. That is, information is actually encrypted with 16 rounds. We concentrate on checking our hypothesis and revealed a great number of such coincidences. Unfortunately, today we cannot suggest an approach to select text pairs like those of the whole encrypted information. But if one finds the approach to it, the compexity of GOST algorithm analysis will be reduced to 16 encryption rounds that will make it vulnerable.

CONCLUSION

The chapter is aimed at the analysis of GOST symmetric block cipher which is the basis for secure information systems, in Russian Federation. We reviewed two common analysis techniques exhibiting the most promising for application GOST, namely the methods for differential and algebraic analysis.

We demonstrated that implementation of differential cryptanalysis with weak S-boxes for full 32-round GOST algorithm causes fast finding of characteristics with probabilities in the range from 2-25up to 2-33, that makes the attack possible. The method of correct text pairs was also described to define secret key encryption.

We have also given examples of linearization method applied to the modern block cipher algorithms. The attack algorithm of the standard of GOST symmetric block encryption and its GOST simplified version by eXtended Linearization method is reviewed.

As a part of the study for 32 round GOST algorithm we received the system of equations consisting of 48384 equations with 2048 unknowns and 23552 various monomials. The solution complexity of this system is 244.

Considering that GOST algorithm structure includes simple cryptographic operations, presented in most of modern cipher algorithms, the discussed approaches can be applied to the analysis of other ciphers found in various secure information systems.

ACKNOWLEDGMENT

The authors would like to thank Maxim Anikeev for valuable comments.

REFERENCES

Babenko, L. K., & Ishchukova, E. A. (2010). Differential analysis GOST encryption algorithm. In Proceedings of the 3rd International Conference of Security of Information and Networks, (pp. 149-157). New York, NY: Association for Computing Machinery, Inc.

Babenko, L. K., Ishchukova, E. A., & Maro, E. A. (2011). Algebraic analysis of GOST encryption algorithm. In Proceedings of the 4th International Conference of Security of Information and Networks, (pp. 57-62). New York, NY: Association for Computing Machinery, Inc.

Bard, G. V. (2009). *Algebraic cryptanalysis*. New York, NY: Springer. doi:10.1007/978-0-387-88757-9.

Becker, T., & Weispfenning, V. (1993). *Gröbner bases: A computational approach to commutative algebra (corrected edition)*. New York, NY: Springer–Verlag.

Biham, E., & Shamir, A. (1991). Differential cryptanalysis of DES-like cryptosystems. *Journal of Cryptology*, *4*(1), 3–72. doi:10.1007/BF00630563.

Biham, E., & Shamir, A. (1992). Differential cryptanalysis of the full 16-round DES. *Lecture Notes in Computer Science*, *740*, 487–496. doi:10.1007/3-540-48071-4_34.

Biryukov, A., & Wagner, D. (1999). Slide attacks. *Lecture Notes in Computer Science*, *1636*, 245–259. doi:10.1007/3-540-48519-8_18.

Biryukov, A., & Wagner, D. (2000). Advanced slide attacks. *Lecture Notes in Computer Science*, *1807*, 589–606. doi:10.1007/3-540-45539-6_41.

Bulygin, S. (2011). Algebraic cryptanalysis of the round-reduced and side channel analysis of the full PRINTCipher-48. Retrieved May 31, 2011 from http://eprint.iacr.org/2011/287.pdf

Charnes, C., O'Connor, L., Pieprzyk, J., Safavi-Naini, R., & Zheng, Y. (1994). *Further comments on GOST encryption algorithm*. Wollongong, Australia: The University of Wollongong.

Cormen, T. H., Leiserson, C. E., & Rivest, R. L. (2009). *Introduction to algorithms*. Cambridge, MA: The MIT Press.

Courtois, N. (2011). Algebraic complexity reduction and cryptanalysis of GOST. Retrieved November 19, 2011 from http://eprint.iacr.org/2011/626.pdf

Courtois, N., & Bard, G. V. (2007). Algebraic cryptanalysis of the data encryption standard. In Proceedings of the Cryptography and Coding, 11th IMA Conference, (pp. 152-169). New York, NY: Springer.

Courtois, N., & Debraize, B. (2008). Specific s-box criteria in algebraic attacks on block ciphers with several known plaintexts. *Lecture Notes in Computer Science*, *4945*, 100–113. doi:10.1007/978-3-540-88353-1_9.

Courtois, N., & Debraize, B. (2008). Algebraic description and simultaneous linear approximations of addition in snow 2.0. *Lecture Notes in Computer Science*, *5308*, 328–344. doi:10.1007/978-3-540-88625-9_22.

Courtois, N., Goubin, L., Meier, W., & Tacier, J.-D. (2002). Solving underdefined systems of multivariate quadratic equations. *Lecture Notes in Computer Science*, *2274*, 211–227. doi:10.1007/3-540-45664-3_15.

Courtois, N., Klimov, A., Patarin, J., & Shamir, A. (2000). Efficient algorithms for solving overdefined systems of multivariate polynomial equations. *Lecture Notes in Computer Science*, *1807*, 392–407. doi:10.1007/3-540-45539-6_27.

Courtois, N., & Pieprzyk, J. (2002). Cryptanalysis of block ciphers with overdefined systems of equations. *Lecture Notes in Computer Science*, *2501*, 267–287. doi:10.1007/3-540-36178-2_17.

Cox, D. A., Little, J. B., & O'Shea, D. (1996). *Ideals, varieties, and algorithms* (2nd ed.). New York, NY: Springer-Verlag.

Faugère, J.-C. (1999). A new efficient algorithm for computing Gröbner bases (F4). *Journal of Pure and Applied Algebra*, *139*(1-3), 61–88. doi:10.1016/S0022-4049(99)00005-5.

Faugère, J.-C. (2002). A new efficient algorithm for computing Gröbner bases without reduction to zero (F5). In Proceedings of the 2002 International Symposium on Symbolic and Algebraic Computation (ISSAC 2002), (pp. 75–83). New York, NY: Association for Computing Machinery, Inc.

Ferguson, N., Schroeppel, R., & Whiting, D. (2001). A simple algebraic representation of Rijndael. In *Proceedings of Selected Areas in Cryptography* (pp. 103–111). New York, NY: Springer–Verlag. doi:10.1007/3-540-45537-X_8.

Grosek, O., Nemoga, K., & Zanechal, M. (1997). Why use bijective S-boxes in GOST-algorithm. Retrieved July 30, 1997 from http://www.mat.savba.sk/preprints/1997/97-11.PS

Isobe, T. (2011). A single-key attack on the full GOST block cipher. *Lecture Notes in Computer Science, 6733*, 290–305. doi:10.1007/978-3-642-21702-9_17.

Kalkbrener, M. (1999). On the complexity of Gröbner bases conversion. *Journal of Symbolic Computation, 28*(1-2), 265–273. doi:10.1006/jsco.1998.0276.

Kelsey, J., Schneier, B., & Wagner, D. (1996). Key-shedule cryptanalysis of IDEA, G-DES, GOST, SAFER, and Triple-DES. *Lecture Notes in Computer Science, 1109*, 237–251. doi:10.1007/3-540-68697-5_19.

Kipnis, A., & Shamir, A. (1999). Cryptanalysis of the HFE public key cryptosystem by relinearization. *Lecture Notes in Computer Science, 1666*, 19–30. doi:10.1007/3-540-48405-1_2.

Ko, Y., Hong, S., Lee, W., Lee, S., & Kang, J.-S. (2004). Related key differential attacks on 27 round of XTEA and full round of GOST. *Lecture Notes in Computer Science, 3017*, 299–316. doi:10.1007/978-3-540-25937-4_19.

Matsui, M. (1998). Linear cryptanalysis method for DES cipher. *Lecture Notes in Computer Science, 765*, 386–397. doi:10.1007/3-540-48285-7_33.

Oreku, G. S., Li, J., Pazynyuk, T., & Mtenzi, F. J. (2007). Modified s-box to archive accelerated GOST. *International Journal of Computer Science and Network Security, 7*(6), 88–98.

Pieprzyk, J., & Tombak, L. (1994). *Soviet encryption algorithm*. Wollongong, Australia: The University of Wollongong.

Popov, V., Kurepkin, I., & Leontiev, S. (2006). Additional cryptographic algorithms for use with GOST 28147-89, GOST R 34.10-94, GOST R 34.10-2001, and GOST R 34.11-94 algorithms. Retrieved January 2006 from http://www.ietf.org/rfc/rfc4357

Saarinen, M.-J. (1998). A chosen key attack against the secret s-boxes of GOST. Retrieved August 12, 1998 from http://www.researchgate.net/publication/2598060_A_chosen_key_attack_against_the_secret_S-boxes_of_GOST

Schneier, B. (1996). *Applied cryptography, protocols, algorithms and source code in C* (2nd ed.). New York, NY: John Wiley & Sons, Inc..

Shannon, C. E. (1949). Communication theory of secrecy systems. *The Bell System Technical Journal, 28*, 656–715.

Weinmann, R.-P. (2009). Algebraic methods in block cipher cryptanalysis. (Doctoral Dissertation). Technische Universität. Darmstadt, Germany.

Yeh, Y.-S., Lin, C.-H., & Wang, C.-C. (1998). Dynamic GOST. *Journal of Information Science and Engineering, 16*(6), 857–861.

ADDITIONAL READING

Ajwa, I. A., Liu, Z., & Wang, P. S. (1995). Gröbner bases algorithm. Retrieved February 1995 from http://icm.mcs.kent.edu/reports/1995/gb.pdf

Albrecht, M., Cid, C., Faugère, J.-C., & Perret, L. (2011). On the relation between the MXL family of algorithms and Gröbner basis algorithms. Retrieved April 1, 2011 from http://eprint.iacr.org/2011/164.pdf

Armknecht, F., & Krause, M. (2003). Algebraic attacks on combiners with memory. *Lecture Notes in Computer Science, 2729*, 162–176. doi:10.1007/978-3-540-45146-4_10.

Bardet, M., Faugère, J.-C., & Salvy, B. (2003). Complexity of Gröbner basis computation for semi-regular overdetermined sequences over F2 with solutions in F2. Technical Report 5049. Paris, France: National Institute for Research in Computer Science and Control.

Ben-Aroya, I., & Biham, E. (1994). Differential cryptanalysis of lucifer. *Lecture Notes in Computer Science*, 187–199. doi:10.1007/3-540-48329-2_17.

Biham, E., Dunkelman, O., & Keller, N. (2007). Improved slide attacks. *Lecture Notes in Computer Science*, *4593*, 153–166. doi:10.1007/978-3-540-74619-5_10.

Biham, E., & Shamir, A. (1992). Differential cryptanalysis of Snefru, Khafre, REDOC-II, LOKI and lucifer. *Lecture Notes in Computer Science*, *576*, 156–171. doi:10.1007/3-540-46766-1_11.

Biryukov, A., & Kushilivitz, E. (1998). Improved cryptanalysis of RC5. *Lecture Notes in Computer Science*, *1403*, 85–99. doi:10.1007/BFb0054119.

Carlet, C., Faugère, J.-C., Goyet, C., & Renault, G. (2012). Analysis of the algebraic side channel attack. In *Proceedings of Journal Cryptographic Engineering* (pp. 45–62). IEEE. doi:10.1007/s13389-012-0028-0.

Charnes, C., O'Connor, L., Pieprzyk, J., Safavi-Naini, R., & Zheng, Y. (1995). Comments on Soviet encryption algorithm. *Lecture Notes in Computer Science*, *950*, 433–438. doi:10.1007/BFb0053459.

Courtois, N. (2002). Higher order correlation attacks, XL algorithm and cryptanalysis of toyocrypt. *Lecture Notes in Computer Science*, *2587*, 182–199. doi:10.1007/3-540-36552-4_13.

Courtois, N. (2005). General principles of algebraic attacks and new design criteria for components of symmetric ciphers. *Lecture Notes in Computer Science*, *3373*, 67–83. doi:10.1007/11506447_7.

Courtois, N., & Misztal, M. (2011). Differential cryptanalysis of GOST. Retrieved June 14, 2011 from http://eprint.iacr.org/2011/312.pdf

Dolmatov, V. (2010). GOST 28147-89 encryption, decryption and MAC algorithms. Retrieved March 2010 from http://tools.ietf.org/pdf/rfc5830.pdf

Fuhs, C., & Schneider-Kamp, P. (2010). Synthesizing shortest linear straight-line programs over GF(2) using SAT. *Lecture Notes in Computer Science*, *6175*, 71–84. doi:10.1007/978-3-642-14186-7_8.

Kim, K., Lee, S., Park, S., & Lee, D. (2003). Securing DES s-boxes against three robust cryptanalysis. *Lecture Notes in Computer Science*, *2595*, 145–157. doi:10.1007/978-3-540-45229-4_15.

Kleiman, E. (2005). The XL and XSL attacks on baby Rijndael. (Master Thesis). Iowa State University. Ames, IA.

Knudsen, L. R. (1994). Block ciphers analysis, design, applications. (Doctoral Dissertation). Aarhus University. Aarhus, Denmark.

Koblitz, N. (1998). *Algebraic aspects of cryptography*. New York, NY: Springer-Verlag. doi:10.1007/978-3-662-03642-6.

Langford, S. K., & Hellman, M. E. (1994). Differential-linear cryptanalysis. *Lecture Notes in Computer Science*, *8399*, 17–25. doi:10.1007/3-540-48658-5_3.

Mendel, F., Pramstaller, N., Rechberger, C., Kontak, M., & Szmidt, J. (2008). Cryptanalysis of the GOST hash function. *Lecture Notes in Computer Science*, *5157*, 162–178. doi:10.1007/978-3-540-85174-5_10.

Mohamed, M. S. E., Bulygin, S., Zohner, M., Heuser, A., Walter, M., & Buchmann, J. (2012). Improved algebraic side-channel attack on AES. Retrieved February 22, 2012 from http://eprint.iacr.org/2012/084.pdf

Patarin, J., Goubin, L., & Courtois, N. (1998). Improved algorithms for isomorphisms of polynomials. *Lecture Notes in Computer Science*, *1403*, 184–200. doi:10.1007/BFb0054126.

Poschmann, A., Ling, S., & Wang, H. (2010). 256 bit standardized crypto for 650 GE GOST revisited. *Lecture Notes in Computer Science*, *6225*, 219–233. doi:10.1007/978-3-642-15031-9_15.

Rudskoy, V. (2010). On zero practical significance of "key recovery attack on full GOST block cipher with zero time and memory". Retrieved February 24, 2010 from http://eprint.iacr.org/2010/111.pdf

Seki, H., & Kaneko, T. (2000). Differential cryptanalysis of reduced rounds of GOST. *Lecture Notes in Computer Science*, *2012*, 315–323. doi:10.1007/3-540-44983-3_23.

Shorin, V. V., Jelezniakov, V. V., & Gabidulin, E. M. (2001). Linear and differential cryptanalysis of Russian GOST. *Electronic Notes in Discrete Mathematics*, *6*, 538–547. doi:10.1016/S1571-0653(04)00206-9.

Stinson, D. R. (2002). *Cryptography theory and practice* (2nd ed.). London, UK: Chapman and Hall.

Talbot, J., & Welsh, D. (2006). *Complexity and cryptography: An introduction*. Cambridge, UK: Cambridge University Press. doi:10.1017/CBO9780511755286.

Yang, B.-Y., & Chen, J.-M. (2004). All in the XL family: Theory and practice. *Lecture Notes in Computer Science*, *3506*, 67–86. doi:10.1007/11496618_7.

KEY TERMS AND DEFINITIONS

Characteristic: Value pair input difference – output difference for n rounds of encryption algorithm.

Correct Pair of Texts: A pair of plain text-cipher text combinations, for which the difference of plaintext is equal to the input difference of the characteristic and the difference of cipher text is equal to the output difference of the characteristics.

Differential Cryptanalysis: Cryptanalytical method, devised by E. Biham and A. Shamir, based on reviewing the change of difference of two texts when passing encryption rounds.

Extended Linearization Method: Method of obtaining additional linearly independent equations and solution of nonlinear systems of Boolean equation.

GOST: Russian symmetric encryption standard consists of 32 round and applies 256-bit encryption key, as well as GOST algorithm is used to calculate hash-values according to GOST P 34.11-94.

Input Difference: Difference between two texts (calculated by addition modulo 2), coming to the input of the cryptographical transformation discussed.

Linearization Method: Solution method of nonlinear system of equations by reducing to a linear form.

Output Difference: Difference between two texts (calculated by addition modulo 2), at the output of the cryptographical transformation discussed.

S-Boxes: Substitution tables, used in block encryption algorithms, constructed on the principles of Feistel network or SPN.

Chapter 3
Cryptography for the Forensics Investigator

Thomas Martin
Khalifa University, UAE

ABSTRACT

There are many challenges for a forensic investigator when it comes to digital evidence. These include the constantly changing technology that may store evidence, the vast amounts of data that is stored, and the increasing use of cryptography. This last problem can prevent any useful information being retrieved and is encountered in the use of communication protocols, whole-disk encryption, and individual applications. Cryptography is a field of great depth and breadth, encompassing both complex mathematics and cutting-edge technology. A forensics investigator does not need to be aware of all aspects of this field, but there are certain areas that are vital. The knowledge described in this chapter can assist an investigator in obtaining information that may otherwise be obscured, and also prepare them to defend the integrity of any evidence obtained.

INTRODUCTION

Computer Forensics, the study of digital evidence relevant to legal matters, has long been considered solely the domain of law enforcement. And while this has been true in the past, there is an increase in the use of forensics in other areas. Outside of criminal cases, forensics can be relevant to Industrial Tribunals, E-Discovery and Incident Management. Information Systems need be designed to support the forensics investigator in satisfying these legal procedures. But beyond mere satisfying obligations, good forensics capabilities can strengthen the security of Information Systems. Gone is the notion that any system can be completely secure. When a breach does happen, a

DOI: 10.4018/978-1-4666-4030-6.ch003

well designed forensics capability (supported by staff trained to perform the analysis) can quickly determine the cause of the incident without major disruption. The sensitive nature of such investigations that require unrestricted access, as well as the potentially damning conclusions, has lead many organizations to develop such capabilities in-house.

Cryptography is seeing increased usage, in response to problems of data leakage, both commercial and personal. Criminals have also been known to use encryption to hide the details of their crimes. As encryption products become more easy to use and freely available, they are going to be encountered in more investigations. Encryption is a potential barrier to a forensics investigator. The physical media may be successfully captured, but encryption can prevent any information from being retrieved.

In this chapter, we will describe those aspects of cryptography that are vital to a forensics investigator. First, we describe the fundamental goals of cryptography and briefly describe the algorithms that achieve them. Second, we explain all the steps necessary to protect the integrity of any information collected. Finally, we propose a set of best practices that can be conducted when an investigator encounters encrypted evidence.

BACKGROUND

Ideally, a forensics investigator would have a back door to any cryptography encountered. Such mechanisms have long been proposed (Denning, 1996) but have not seen widespread adoption. Occasionally there are mistakes in the implementation of cryptography that have lead to weaknesses (e.g. a software bug caused predictable keys in the Debian Openssl package (Bello, 2008), or low entropy causing repetition of RSA primes (Lenstra et al., 2012)), but the number of cases is small, and one cannot rely on them being present.

In spite of the obstacles, a good deal of research has been undertaken on what can be done by a forensics investigator in the face of encrypted evidence. The majority of the work to date has focused on capturing keys from live memory. Shamir and Someren proposed a method for looking for the high entropy as a tell-tale aspect of RSA keys (Shamir & Van Someren, 1999). Klein instead looked for the common formats and syntax of keys and certificates (Klein, 2006). Halderman extended the timeframe that keys could be captured in memory by freezing the memory and using error-correction techniques (Halderman, Schoen, Heninger, Clarkson, Paul, Cal, Feldman, & Felten, 2006). The work of (McGrath, Gladyshev, & Carthy, 2010) identified many useful artefacts from the use of PGP/X509 public key encryption, including file headers, times, dates, identities, etc. Tromer demonstrated that inter-process information leakage can allow an unprivileged process to gain access to AES keys of processes running in parallel (Tromer, Osvik, Shamir, 2010).

FUNDAMENTALS

Forensics investigators require at least a superficial knowledge of cryptography. In this section we will describe the specific objectives of integrity and confidentiality aspired for in cryptography. We will briefly cover some of the algorithms currently used to achieve these objectives. We will also mention some of the upcoming advances in cryptography (fully homomorphic encryption, quantum computers) and the impacts they will have.

Confidentiality

Cryptography has been primarily been used to ensure the confidentiality of information. Encrypted information whether stored or in transit, must be prevented from being accessed by all but authorized parties. Encryption can be either symmetric or asymmetric. Symmetric encryption requires the sender and receiver to agree a common, secret key. Symmetric ciphers can either be stream ciphers (encrypt a bit at a time) or block ciphers (encrypt blocks of data at a time). Asymmetric encryption has two keys for every user, one public and one private. The public key is used to encrypt messages and the private to decrypt. All parties can use the same public key to encrypt messages for a given user, without being able to read each other's traffic.

Integrity

Cryptography can also be used in preserving the integrity of information, ensuring that only authorized parties are allowed to modify documents. Hash functions are frequently used for this purpose. A hash function produces a fixed length digest from any input. Typical lengths for common digests are 16 bytes (MD5), 20 bytes (SHA-1), 28, 32, 48, and 64 bytes (SHA-2 family). Functions that produce a similar output but that also include as input secret information are called Message Authentication Codes (MAC). MACs can be based on hash functions or block ciphers.

A similar goal is to prove the authorship of a document, or message authentication. While MACs can provide this to a certain extent, digital signatures are more frequently used. A digital signature requires the same keys as public key encryption, one public and one private. However, the private key is used by the sender and the public by the recipient. Anyone can use the public key to assure themselves that the owner of the corresponding private key is the only one who could have created the message.

Cryptographic Limitations

It is worth noting that modern cryptography does not aspire to complete protection. Nowhere is it stated that all attacks must be impossible. Instead, the probability of any attack should be so low as to be practically infeasible. For example, an attack that succeeds with probability of 1 in 280 is not considered a threat. Even if each attempt was extremely quick (say a microsecond), and a great deal of effort is applied to the attack (1 million devices executing the attack), current technology will not provide the result in a reasonable amount of time (around 20,000 years). While this is sufficient for the purposes of protection, care has to be taken with definitive statements about security derived from cryptography, especially in court testimony. Useful comparisons can be made with lotteries to put these figures in context. The odds of winning the jackpot in the Mega Millions lottery1 are roughly 1 in 227. The success of the above attack is approximately the same as winning the lottery three times out of three attempts.

Future Advances

Modern cryptography has been relatively free of major disasters. The most popular algorithms (DES and RSA) have stood the test of time. The most practical attack on DES is still a brute-force attack, the short key length is the reason it has been phased out. RSA key lengths are still a safe margin from published factoring efforts. However, this does not mean to say that discoveries that could have a disastrous impact on existing systems are not around the corner. Any such discovery would be a double-edged sword for the forensic investigator. On the one hand, new cryptanalysis techniques may provide the means to quickly recover data encrypted using older algorithms (either from evidence collected a long time ago or evidence from a suspect still using old versions of encryption software). On the other hand, such attacks call into question the validity of claims based on the security of the algorithms, i.e. who could have accessed certain data, who could have created such messages, etc.

One new area of cryptanalysis research that is bound to eventually cause a huge upheaval is Quantum Computing. First proposed in Shor

(1994), it has been practically demonstrated that a Quantum Computer can factor composites and solve the discrete log problem (Lu, Browne, Yang, & Pan, 2007), two problems that support the majority of asymmetric encryption currently in use. The reason this has not lead to a catastrophe for information security is that the technology currently only exists to create enough "qbits" to factor composites of a handful of bits (compared to composites with thousands of bits used in practice). It is possible we may see a revolution in the technology that will allow the creation of a device that can attack real RSA and DSA keys. Alternatively, we may see a growth similar to the one predicted by Moore for transistors, with a regular doubling of size over time. There are many different estimates for the expected maturity of Quantum Computers, but no one can really know for certain. The importance of any breakthrough does make the field important enough to require at least a passing knowledge.

Conversely, there are also advances in cryptography that can have important consequences for forensics. Fully Homomorphic Encryption (FHE) is currently receiving a great deal of attention and has had some successful breakthroughs (Gentry, 2009). The aim of FHE is to encrypt data such that a third party can perform any operations on the data without having to decrypt it. Currently, if anyone wants to store data in the "cloud", and be able to modify it in place it needs to be unencrypted and consequently available to the cloud service provider. While the cloud can be used for storage today, with data encrypted before upload and decrypted after download, offloading a database onto the cloud would require that it be completely unencrypted. Cloud computing does introduce problems regarding access to information stemming from different jurisdictions, but there are no technical hurdles to the provider handing the data over. With Fully Homomorphic Encryption, the user would have the benefit of being able to modify their data remotely without requiring the provider have access. While techniques exist to achieve this, they are not sufficiently mature to be used in practice. Gentry, Halevi and Smart (2012) implemented one of the recently discovered algorithms (Brakerski, Gentry, & Vaikuntanathan, 2012). They produced "packed" ciphertexts of data and a key schedule. This was then transformed into FHE-encrypted data. The former operation took 30 minutes, the latter over 36 hours. Due to the fact that the FHE allows for processing multiple AES blocks at the same time, this works out at roughly 40 minutes per block. The biggest technical hurdle was using a machine with enough RAM to handle all the data (the implementation ran on a machine with 256GB). These costs are prohibitive now, but advances in the field will no doubt bring these down (or technology will improve to catch up). Running AES homomorphically allows the following scenario:

1. The end user creates a ``packed'' AES key schedule and provides it to their provider
2. The end user uploads any AES ciphertext encrypted with this key
3. The provider can use homomorphic AES decryption to transform this ciphertext to FHE-encrypted data
4. Any computation can be performed on the transformed data without leaking any information to the provider
5. At any point the user can download and decrypt the processed data

Like Quantum Computers, Fully Homomorphic Encryption could considerably change the security landscape and developments should be closely monitored.

PRESERVING EVIDENCE USING HASH FUNCTIONS

The use of hash functions is common in forensics tools, and is reasonably well understood. But there is sometimes an over-reliance. Hash digests by themselves do not prove the integrity of files, they merely provide fingerprints. A lack of appreciation of the subtleties of hash functions has resulted in unnecessary dismissal of evidence. In this section, we will describe the necessary procedures to ensure the integrity of obtained evidence. We will make use of examples we have created specifically for this purpose. We will also place the relevance of known attacks on hash and signature algorithms into the correct context for the forensics investigator.

Proper Use of a Hash

As has already been stated, hash digests do not protect the integrity, nor prove the integrity of data by themselves. A hash digest is more akin to a digital fingerprint than a seal of authenticity. A fingerprint is never used in isolation. Any fingerprint found at the scene of a crime is of no value in and of itself. It is only when this fingerprint is matched with another, e.g. the fingerprint of a suspect, that a useful link can be proven, namely that the suspect touched an item that was at the crime scene. Similarly, hash digests by themselves are of no use.

Suppose a file is entered as evidence in a court case. The prosecution argues that the file has not been modified since it was collected from the crime scene because a hash digest of the file was stored in the same location. Unfortunately, the defense can argue that anybody could have made any modification to the file they wished, and simply changed the hash digest to the one calculated from the modified file. The prosecution may argue that extra protections were also used to protect the file; the storage device was kept in a locked room, time stamps from the file system, etc. Whether or not this holds, in this case the hash digest serves no function. If instead, the investigator who collected the file from the crime scene took a digest of the file at the scene and recorded the digest in his notebook, the evidence could not have been modified in this way. When later questioned on the veracity of any file submitted as evidence, the hash can be recalculated and compared with the digest in his notebook. The defense may still be able to argue that the file presented is not the same as the file that was originally at the crime scene, by arguing the notebook was not adequately protected, or the hash not calculated on the correct file initially. The hash digest still does not guarantee the integrity of the file, but used correctly it makes it hard to disprove. The problem of ensuring the integrity of the whole file has been reduced to ensuring the integrity of a much smaller digest.

It is rare that a single file be collected as evidence, capturing a whole drive is much more common. We will explore in-depth the steps involved in the creation and verification of the hash digests of such evidence. First, the data on the drive needs to be copied (typically via a write-blocker). Drives can be cloned or stored in one of several image file formats. The most commonly used are E01 (Encase) or Raw (dd), but there is also SMART (ASR Expert Witness) and dmg (Apple). The next step is to calculate the hash digest of the entire disk. Performing this manually in Windows is problematic, so a Linux boot disk has been used instead. The necessary command-line tools (md-5sum and sha1sum) are not natively available in Windows and would need to be installed. Also, Windows does not provide the facility of using file handles to access devices such as hard disks. Calculating the md5 digest of a drive in Linux is as simple as presented in Box 1.

Box 1.

```
# md5sum /dev/sde
7a7b8515e691d83269ceb02320e080ca  /dev/sde
```

The image of this drive has been captured in three different ways: using the Encase E01 format, Raw format split into 2GB files and Raw without splitting (see Table 1). The next step is to verify that the image is the same as the original disk. It is enough to show that the digests are the same. When trying to verify the E01 image, we have the immediate problem that the image is now two files. One might try to calculate the hashes of the individual files that make up the image, and combine them somehow. This will not work, as hash functions are specifically designed to prevent any such simple relationship between the hash of the whole and the hash of the parts. The files could simply be copied together and then hashed, but Linux has a more elegant solution. Both files are piped directly to the md5sum command, avoiding the need for creating a separate, temporary file, as presented in Box 2.

Despite the fact that this is an image of the original drive, the digest is not the same. Logically, the image contains all the information from the drive. Importing the image into a forensics tool such as FTK or EnCase would give the exact same results as importing the actual drive. All the same data would be available. However, md5sum operates on the files it is passed, not on information that can be derived from them. The original disk was 6GB, but the E01 image is only 1.5GB. For two digests to be the same, both inputs must be exactly the same size as well as having exactly the same content. The E01 format compresses the data before storing it. This saves storage spaces as many disks are mostly blank data. The image of an 80GB disk can be as little as 150MB if it is mostly 00's.

For the purposes of verifying the hash, the E01 image is of no use. If we look at the md5 digests of the Raw image, either the image of the combined parts using a pipe or the image of the single file, we get the same digest as the original drive. The Raw image is an exact byte for byte copy of the original drive (as suggested by the fact that it is the same size). It is only through hashing this image that we can verify that it is the same as the original drive.

This exercise would be unnecessary in most cases. Raw images are usually larger in size than other formats. Most imaging software automatically calculates hashes of the disk and the image as part of the imaging processes, and when requested can perform the verification of the data as well. However, with a Raw image, verification of the hash is relatively straightforward. And what a

Box 2.

```
# cat Test.E01 Test.E02 | md5sum
16265ecbeda49c42c30bed59f97adca1  -
```

Table 1. File size and hash digests from a single disk and its images

Format	Filename	Size(M)	MD5 Digests
Original Drive	NA	5730	7a7b8515e691d83269ceb02320e080ca
E01	Test.E01 Test.E02 <combined>	1500 50 1550	de0ef2f88bba60b8dfa8da6c4bb66c1c e35ebe75b78c5e9c34f12e857ba9a92f 16265ecbeda49c42c30bed59f97adca1
Raw/dd (fragments)	Test_frag.001 Test_frag.002 Test_frag.003 <combined>	2000 2000 1730 5730	5a4e9dbb3676324b2c7c474141dffa62 2c49fdb4fd94bc70d69d0b3f2a5e5c26 aa1180c8fa1e9a23eafe133ef815bbe0 7a7b8515e691d83269ceb02320e080ca
Raw/dd (single file)	Test.001	5730	7a7b8515e691d83269ceb02320e080ca
Raw/dd (single file, modified)	Modified.001	5730	07d6b3de44afbbff3415f532f9b223d5

miss-match looks like is also simple to create. Changing the first byte of the raw image from \x33 to \xFF gives the different hash in the last row of Table 1. A deeper appreciation of hash functions is necessary to be able to confidently defend the authenticity of digital evidence. And as the following sections will show, they can provide other positive features, but do have limitations.

While manual verification of hash digests is seldom necessary, it is always important to adequately protect the hashes of important evidence. Writing down the hashes can accomplish this, although it may be tedious and error-prone if there are many devices. Copying the hashes to a write-once-read-many medium (such as a CD) may be more appropriate where there are many devices being collected. At roughly 70 bytes for a digest plus identifier, a single 600MB CD has the capacity for millions of digests. Also, for reasons that will be covered later, one of the SHA-2 family of hashes should be used instead of MD5. Physical protection of the hashes can be achieved by locking the hashes in a safe or other secure container. A Cryptographic mechanism can be used to protect the hashes, in the form of either a MAC or a digital signature. A MAC can be calculated more quickly, but a digital signature allows for greater flexibility in verification. Only the private key holder can generate the signature but anyone can verify, whereas with the MAC the secret key is used for both. As usual, neither option provides absolute security, but it does reduce the set of people who could possibly modify the evidence from those who have access to the hashes to those who have access to the hashes and have the key.

Effective Searching

Hash functions can be useful in analyzing evidence as well as protecting its integrity. Consider a case where the investigator wishes to prove communication between two individuals. If hard drives are obtained from each, there are various ways to look for files common to both. The most obvious would be by file name, but this may have a high risk of false negatives as file names are easily changed (sometimes done automatically by the Operating System, e.g. older versions of Windows truncating longer file names to 8.3 format). The next method might be by file size, but this would be likely to have too many false positives as many files have the same size. Directly comparing all files is theoretically possible, but would take too long in practice. If each device had 10,000 files, then that would mean 100 million comparisons. Instead a simpler approach can be taken using hashes and a few commands.

The md5deep command2 provides the facility to create a list of hashes of all files recursively through an entire directory tree. For this particular problem, the command is executed on both drives; with the output saved as text files (each line having the digest first followed by the full filename). The "sort" command is used to order the outputs by the digests. We wrote a simple perl script that can then be used to go through both lists to find matches. Since the lists are ordered, it will only take a single pass through each (much less than the millions of comparisons needed for direct checking). The common files themselves do not prove communication between the parties; they may simply be due to common OS or applications. A manual inspection would still be required to determine if this is the case or not (and also to verify that the files are actually the same in the unlikely case of a collision).

Another application of this technique is in evaluating certain tools. In Martin and Jones (2011) we looked to test the performance of tools designed to overwrite existing data. As most tools overwrote with random data, it was often the case that the analysis would carve files with correct headers and footers for a given file type, but were just random data and not from the original dataset. The hashes of the dataset and derived files were calculated and compared to tell the difference. This instantly indicated if any recovered files were part of the original dataset.

Hash Function Security

As previously mentioned, cryptographic security is never absolute. There are always attacks that can work, but are usually too expensive one way or another. As time goes on, algorithms are weakened by both faster processors reducing attack times and more effective methods of attacks being discovered. Cryptographic algorithms need to be continually re-evaluated for security. Hash functions are no exception to this. Consider the case of the contested speeding ticket in New South Wales, Austraila (AAP 2005). The main evidence was an image of the vehicle speeding, along with an MD5 digest. The defense sited the recently discovered attacks on MD5 (Wang, Feng, Lui & Hu, 2004) as evidence that called the effectiveness of the camera system into question. They claimed it there was no way to prove that the images had not been altered after they were taken. The prosecution was unable to find an expert to testify on the matter and the case was dismissed.

The cited attack has been accepted, reproduced and enhanced by the cryptographic community (Wang, Yu, and Yin, 2005; Wang and Yu, 2005); there is no doubt to its correctness. There have since been calls for the phasing out of MD5 and related algorithms in favor of a more secure hash function (Kayser, 2007). However, it should have been argued that these matters were not relevant to this specific instance. Up to this point, we have been ignoring the inner workings of MD5 and other hash algorithms. It is not actually necessary for a forensics investigator to understand the internals of cryptographic algorithms. However, he must understand the implications of any discovered attacks on these algorithms.

There are two basic types of attacks on hash functions: pre-images and collisions. To perform a pre-image attack, one must construct a file that will hash to a given digest. To find a collision, one must construct any two files that hash to the same digest. In the former case, the target digest is determined and fixed; in the later it can take any value. The attack of Wang, Feng, Lui and Hu (2004) showed how to construct collisions in MD5. Collisions are considered a weaker attack than pre-images: if one can calculate a pre-image one can use it to also calculate collisions, but the opposite does not hold. There is a major difference in the expected effort for these attacks. A brute force attack to find a pre-image would take on the order of O(2L) operations, where L is the number of bits in the digest. A brute force attack to find a collision would take on the order of O(2L/2) operations. Both brute force attacks are impractical for modern hash functions, but the latter is orders of magnitude faster than the former.

In the New South Wales case, the defense argued that the presented image could not be shown to be the original. They were saying it would have been possible for someone to replace this image with another that gave the same digest, thanks to the discovered weakness of MD5. However, this would require a pre-image attack. The weakness of MD5 was just the discovery of collisions, not pre-images. Creation of collisions would not have helped someone trying to replace the image with a modified version. The reliability of the system was not actually affected. The discovery of collisions does highlight a flaw in the algorithm, and suggests the possibility that calculation of pre-images may be discovered in the near future. One advance in attacks on MD5 that have practical implications was the discovery of chosen-prefix collisions (Stevens, Lenstra, & Weger, 2007). While not a full pre-image attack, it is almost as powerful. The attacker can choose any two documents, then work out two values that need to be appended respectively for them to hash to the same value. The example they gave was an attacker obtaining a X.509 certificate for one domain and using this to forge a CA certificate that would be trusted by browsers. Table 2 has some common terminology used in the literature describing attacks on cryptographic algorithms.

The process of selection of a new hash standard has obvious importance to forensics investigator,

Table 2. List of common terms in cryptanalysis

Name	Definition	Applicability
	Hash functions	
Pre-image	Find input that hashes to a given digest	High: Undermines claimed integrity hashed objects, also effects algorithms/protocols that rely on hashes, e.g. signatures.
Collisions	Find two inputs that hash to the same value	Limited: Only valid when the attacker controls the creation of documents that are hashed
Semi-free collision	Collision, but with different IV	None: Attack on variant of algorithm
Pseudo collision	Collision, but with two different IVs	None: Attack on variant of algorithm
Reduced round attack	Any attack, but on simpler version of algorithm	None: Attack on variant of algorithm
Chosen-prefix collision	Collision, but attacker can choose start of both messages.	High: Forged certificates created for real-world systems.
	Ciphers	
Known plaintext	Gain information on key using knowledge of some plaintext	High: Attacker likely to have partial knowledge of plaintext
Chosen plaintext	Manipulate user into encrypting text chosen by attacker	Likely: Many protocols require challenge and responses
Chosen ciphertext	Manipulate user into decrypting text chosen by attacker	Less likely: Returning decrypted text is unusual, but still may occur
Related key attack	Knowledge of plaintext encrypted with several related keys	Little: Highly unlikely attacker has control of generation of keys
Reduced round attack	Any attack, but on simpler version of algorithm	None: Attack on variant of algorithm
	Side Channel Attacks	
Timing attack	Using length of time of operations to infer information on the key	High: Timing information usually readily available
Padding oracle attack	Using information in error messages to infer information on the key	Variable: Can be successful depending on implementation
Power Analysis	Measures power consumption during encryption to find the key	Low: Requires physical access and complex equipment

once selected the new hash should be used wherever possible. However, it is also important that a forensics investigator be aware of changes in how security is evaluated for hash functions. Rogaway and Shrimpton (2004) expanded the three basic attacks (Collision, Second Pre-image, and Pre-image) into seven notions. These apply to keyed-hash functions, and consider the different attacks when they key/challenge is fixed from when they are chosen at random.

There is another limitation on hash functions related to forensics analysis. This is due to the disconnect that the hash digest is always calculated on the data, not the information. Consider a simple search function that returns the offset of the first match along with the digest of the entire file. From any result, it is simple to verify:

1. That the string at the provided offset does contain the search parameter (by jumping to the offset value of the input file)
2. That the file that was searched by the function is the same as the file currently in the possession of the verifier (by comparing the hashes)

Combined, these two provide strong assurance of the validity of the results. Suppose instead we consider a more complex data analysis function, an analysis of the Windows 7 Registry (Alghafli, Jones, & Martin, 2011). This program uses the API of the Windows OS itself to analyze the data, and consequently the input files need to be loaded into the live registry. The program provides a report on different details gathered from the registry files (including user accounts, applications used, IM chats, networks accessed, devices attached, various history lists, etc.) with a hash digest of the input files. The input files can be hashed to show that they are the same after the program has run as before. Despite also using a hash before and after the analysis, we do not get the same assurances of the results. For a start, there is no offset to directly verify the results from the output directly (too much interpretation of the data is required for this to be practical). Also, the analysis was not done on the data that was hashed, but on the data after it had been processed by the OS.

Programs that obtain pertinent information from large quantities of data are necessary in forensics. Verification of the integrity of the data is not sufficient to verify the results of any derived data. In cases where the analysis is done on processed data, but the results can be viewed in the data directly, this can validate the output. Where this is not possible, other methods must be used, such as using two separate tools to check if they give the same results (while one tool may potentially produce an error, the odds of two independent tools coincidentally giving the same error are slim to none). As a tool is used and studied over time, eventually it becomes sufficiently well tested and trusted to be acceptable.

To finish this section, we will briefly discuss the merits of multiple hash digests. Most forensic imaging tools will typically calculate two distinct hashes of any evidence using two different algorithms (e.g. MD5 and SHA-1). Security is often viewed as possessing the same quality as a chain: only as strong as its weakest link. For example, a hybrid encryption scheme might encrypt a message using AES and a random key, but encrypt the AES key using RSA. Any attack on either AES or RSA will break the hybrid encryption. However, integrity protected by multiple hashes is as secure as the combined strength of the individual hashes. It is equivalent to double encryption, using two different encryption algorithms on the plaintext, one after the other. It could be argued that the integrity protection is slightly greater than the combined strength of each algorithm. Collisions have been found for both MD4 and MD5, but no-one has yet published a collision for both hash algorithms (two different files whose MD4 and MD5 digests are equal). Should someone discover a way to compute pre-images for MD4 and again for MD5, there may not necessarily be a way to combine the attacks to compute a single pre-image for a pair of MD4 and MD5 digests. This is not to suggest that combining multiple hashes allows one to ignore individual vulnerabilities. Any attack shows a weakness in the underlying algorithm, and should be taken seriously. However, given digests short size, it makes sense to have multiple for redundancy. Suppose there is some older evidence being preserved using an obsolete hash. Naturally, a hash of the data with a newer algorithm should be calculated and added to the record, but there is no need to get rid of the old hash as well. Best practices should be to use a combination of the two most secure, widely accepted algorithms, currently SHA-1 and (any of) SHA-2, with a move to SHA-2 and SHA-3 once the later has been selected.

ENCOUNTERING ENCRYPTION

In order to prepare the forensics investigator to deal with encrypted evidence, we will describe the facilities that they have available. To start with, we will explain how to identify the different artifacts of cryptographic applications, ciphertexts and keys, using OpenPGP software as an example. Then, we will discuss the relationships between passwords and cryptography. Finally, we will explain how live-memory captures can be inspected to provide cryptographic keys directly.

Encryption Artefacts

One of the first concerns of an investigator is to detect the presence of the use of cryptography on any suspect device, followed by location of the relevant files (ciphertexts and keys). Through the use of examples from GnuPG 2.0.17, we will explore some of the benefits and pitfalls in a straightforward approach. GnuPG is a free and opensource package for performing public key encryption. Creating keys and encrypting/signing files is straightforward, and can be done through the command-line or with a GUI using one of the many frontends. Verifying someone else's public key is done through a web-of-trust. When you look up a public key through one of the dedicated servers, it will have a number of signatures. If it is signed by someone you trust, it is likely a reliable public key. If the connection is less direct (the public key is signed by someone who has a key signed by someone who has a key signed by someone you trust), it may be less reliable. The web-of-trust provides the user information to make such judgments.

The typical way of finding files of a particular type is to determine if they have a unique starting byte pattern, and then look for files that also have the same pattern (the same idea can be applied to obtain files from disks that do not have an intact filesystem, i.e. file carving). Through some basic experimentation in creating keys and encrypted files (using mainly default values), the important files in GnuPG seem to have the pattern shown in Table 3.

GnuPG complies with the OpenPGP message format3, which would suggest the first 3 or 4 bytes are predictable (as the standard explains, subsequent bytes are used for date or recipient ID so will vary). However, there are some complications. The key sizes shown are those commonly used, but not comprehensive. GnuPG can create RSA public keys of any size from 1024 to 4096, and the size clearly has an impact on the file pattern. Indeed, GnuPG supports other public key algorithms, for example DSA and El Gamal with support for Elliptic Curve Cryptography in development. Within the standard there is also a great deal of variation, with older versions having different encodings of byte lengths, flags, etc. The file patterns in Table 3 will not necessarily work for older versions of GnuPG and are unlikely to work for future versions. File carving requires a known pattern to the start of a given file type, but this cannot be reliably done for cryptographic keys/ciphertexts. GnuPG also stores several public keys in a single file, meaning that if the first key in the file does not use the pattern searched for, no keys will be found. It is better to search for a common artifact. For example, almost every RSA implementation uses the public exponent 65,537. In the standard format, this will be encoded as \x0011010001. This is also an area where commercial products can assist4. Alternatively, a forensics investigator could first look for the cryptographic software.

Table 3. File signatures for GnuPG

RSA Key Length	1024	2048	3072	4096
Public Key	988D04	99010D04	99018D04	99020D04
Private Key	9501D804	95039804	95055804	95071804
Private Key (password protected)	9501FE04	9503BE04	95057E04	95073D04
Ciphertext	848C03	85010C03	85018C03	85020C03

It is possible that a suspect device has encrypted material and no encryption software. Possible explanations are:

1. Suspect received encrypted material, but had not yet made necessary arrangements to decrypt
2. Suspect stores all encryption software on removable media (i.e. portable app on USB drive)
3. Suspect routinely erases all cryptographic software to frustrate any investigation

In the first case, the investigator is unlikely to be able to decrypt the data if the suspect had never done so. In the second case, the software may still be found as part of a thorough search when any digital evidence is collected. The third case is unlikely due to the high level of effort required. Where the software is located and identified, the forensics investigator can recreate the environment and determine the appropriate file patterns by creating test keys and ciphertexts.

Encountering MACs or digital signatures will not necessarily provide an investigator with more information, but they can provide useful ties between information and individuals (i.e. evidence not just of what was written but of who wrote what). It should be noted that while it may be mathematically impossible for someone to repudiate their signature on a document, there is the equivalent of the "malware defense". With the malware defense, the suspect claims that an illegal act was done by a piece of malware run on the machine. It is possible to disprove this by examination of the device and of what malware remains/was removed. With a digital signature, all someone has to do is claim that a backup of the private key was made, copied to removable media, and then lost. The signature can then be claimed to have been made by someone who recovered the backup. While unlikely, there is no way to disprove this claim (GnuPG does not make a record of exporting private keys).

Passwords and Cryptography

One could be forgiven for thinking that encryption is not important and not prevalent. This has less to do with the majority of people not coming across encrypted data, but rather that they do not recognize it when they do. It might be more comprehensible or intuitive if users were to see a scrambled version when attempting to open an encrypted file, but typically, they are prompted for a password. Passwords are important for cryptography in practice, but not in theory. It is quite clear that the security of any system takes a dramatic reduction when having to rely in part on a person's ability to remember random strings. However, the vast majority of cryptographic keys are either protected by passwords, or key encrypting keys (which may themselves be password protected). More effective protections for keys exist, but are often expensive. Just about every device that contains data to be protected will have a keyboard, but not nearly as many have smartcard readers or biometric scanners.

Passwords straddle the border of two important access control mechanisms: logical and cryptographic. There are often similarities between the two. For example, a user who must enter a username and password before gaining access to their computer may be undergoing a logical or cryptographic control. Superficially, they may be the same, but for the forensics investigator there are significant differences. Cryptographic protections are almost always more secure. If the previous example were a logical control, say the Windows login process, then it can be circumvented by removing the hard drive and viewing the data directly. If it were a cryptographic control instead, such a method would not work. Naturally, where passwords are used in cryptographic controls, they are important to the subject of this chapter. However, passwords in logical systems can be important to a forensics investigator too. As most users have many passwords to remember, password reuse is common. Determining a suspect's Windows login password may not give the investigator any more information than could be obtained from inspecting the drive directly, but may give him a password used to protect individual files within the drive. Even if the exact same password is not used, knowing one password can suggest the methods that the individual uses to generate passwords (e.g. name, date, lyrics to a song, etc.).

The problem with securing password authentication is that the information used to verify a password can never be made completely secret. It needs to be available to the system for authentication. Certain protections are possible while the system is running, but once it is shutdown, the information can be found from the system at rest. While it may be encrypted, the key used also needs to be stored; moving the problem of protecting the password information to protecting the key. The information is obscured, not secret. However, the information used to verify a password does not need to be the password itself. A function can be applied to the password before it is stored. If the same function is applied to any submitted password, then a match in the output and the stored value implies a match in the passwords (provided collisions are sufficiently rare). Not only does it not matter if the function is one-way (cannot easily be undone), it is actually preferable. We do not want the original password to possibly be derived from the stored information, only that it be verified. Consequently, hash functions are used for this purpose, but with some variation. The end result is that unless the security is particularly poor, passwords cannot be recovered directly, but the necessary information to check that a guessed password is correct is almost always present. If this check can be performed once with this information, it can be performed any number of times.

Attempting to retrieve passwords from stored digests essentially comes down to time. The amount of time an investigator is willing to devote to the effort and the length of time each attempt takes will determine how many passwords can be checked. A simple example is how Windows stores passwords. Up until Windows XP, DES was used (password is the key and a fixed string is the plaintext) while since Vista the passwords were hashed with MD4. More complex systems use a salt with the password, a unique random value that is combined with the password before hashing. This has the effect that any efforts placed into breaking one password hash cannot be used against another. More sophisticated systems still use key stretching, iterating the hash function many times. The extra operations will have a similar multiplication on the time it takes to perform an attack.

To demonstrate the impact of these different protections, we have performed a number of cracking attempts on password hashes. Table 4 shows the results of these experiments. The weakest hash is Windows LM. The lack of a salt means it can take advantage of a time/memory trade-off in the form of a rainbow table (Oechslin, 2003). Windows LM hashes suffer a further weakness not represented in Table 4: only seven characters are hashed at a time. This means that attacking passwords of length up to 14 effectively only requires attacking passwords of length up to 7. The difference in time taken to attack 1 and to attack 38 hashes is much less than might be expected. This is because both require loading the rainbow tables into memory, which takes the same time in both cases. There is a significant decrease in the cracking rate for the salted passwords. Unique salts per user mean pre-computed tables are of no use, and all effort needs to be repeated for each hash. The final hash further decreases the rate due to key stretching.

We have described the issues involved in retrieving passwords from digests, and demonstrated some simple techniques. We previously mentioned that passwords are often used to derive cryptographic keys. Used literally, passwords make incredibly poor keys. A cryptographic key needs to be a specific length, while passwords vary in length. This means either some characters of the password will not be used, or part of the key will be fixed zero values. Characters are most

Table 4. Various computation times for verifying/guessing password hashes

Password hash type	Number of hashes	Time taken (sec)	No. passwords checked*	Average rate (Million passwords per second)
Windows LM (XP)	1	515	80,603,140,212	156.5
Windows LM (XP)	38	623	80,603,140,212	4916.3
Salted (MD5)	2775	115,099	3,160,120	0.076
Salted (SHA1)	2090	161,028	3,160,120	0.041
OpenSSL passwd –apr1 (Salt and key stretching)	1	922.15	3,160,120	0.0034

likely to be represented in ASCII, which only uses 7 of the 8 bits. Certain characters are more likely to be used (letters and numbers), and some cannot be entered with a keyboard (control characters), reducing the randomness of the key. At the very least, a hash of the password will be used instead.

There are two problems involved in applying the previous password recovery methods to any use of cryptography. The first is that all the techniques used to enhance the protection of hashed passwords can equally be applied to key derivation. Keys derived from passwords are likely to have salts added and key stretching used. The second problem is that of verification. If one has digests stored for authentication, then you are guaranteed to be able to verify if a guessed password is correct. If a file has been encrypted with a password-derived key, there is nothing intrinsic in the operation that will acknowledge a correctly guessed password or give an error on an incorrect attempt.

The Openssl package5 provides commands for encrypting with a wide array of algorithms. A single command such as presented in Box 3

would create an encrypted file very difficult to attack. A command to decrypt can be given with any guessed password and will always produce an output file. Some knowledge of the plaintext is required to be able to tell if the correct password was chosen. The mode of operation chosen here was deliberate. Ciphertext FeedBack mode (CFB) and Output FeedBack mode (OFB) operate similar to a stream cipher, XOR'ing a keystream with the plaintext. The length of the plaintext does not matter. Other modes (CBC being the most common) can only encrypt an exact multiple of the block length. Where padding is added, it is done in a deterministic way, meaning that ciphertexts decrypted with the wrong key are unlikely to be correctly padded.

Fortunately, direct encryption with command line tools is unlikely to be encountered in any investigation. Users prefer, and the majority use, complete packages that automate most of the mundane details of encryption, e.g. PGP/GnuPG for email, TrueCrypt/BestCrypt for whole disk encryption. Most encryption tools will include redundancy for the explicit purpose of validating correct decryption. For example, a PGP private key encrypted with a passphrase will include an (encrypted) hash (as well as various other known flags and packet lengths). Only the correct passphrase will yield a private key that hashes to the same value as the decrypted hash. Unfortunately, encryption software can (and often does) utilize

Box 3.

```
openssl enc aes-128-cfb -in text.txt -out file.dat -k pass
```

the same methods as protecting password digests; salting and key stretching.

The simplest way to retrieve data from encrypted evidence is to attack the password. A number of possible passwords can be obtained from different sources (observing the scene the device was used, information about the suspect, generic lists from public sources), collected in a dictionary. There are essentially three approaches to using this dictionary in an automated attack on password-based encryption, listed in increasing ease of use:

1. Direct calculation
2. Scripted commands
3. Commercial password recovery tool

Direct calculation involves independently developing the code to mimic the translation of the password into cryptographic key and attempting to decrypt the ciphertext. Naturally, this will require a great deal of effort and understanding of the implementation. Cryptographic algorithms enjoy considerable standardization. AES is by far the most common block cipher (some legacy systems will still use DES/Triple DES). Asymmetric systems are usually based on RSA, but some use discrete log/elliptic curve systems. Unfortunately, there can still be a great deal of variation between implementations. Block ciphers can be used in a number of different modes of operation, a wide range of different password-to-key methods exist and data can be stored in different ways (the methods of storage of encrypted data in hard disks, SQL databases, SQLlite databases, email, etc., differ greatly). This approach is time-consuming, even when there are standards and open source implementations available. Where the software is closed and proprietary, it can be impractical. On the positive side, it can be applied in any instance, and may avoid logical lockouts of the original software (e.g. three failed attempts lead to delays).

Where there are command line tools to perform encryption/decryption, the effort to mount an automated attack is greatly reduced. For example, GnuPG provides commands for all operations on keys and plain/ciphertexts. As GnuPG is based on public/private keys, the ciphertexts are unlikely to be password protected, but the private keys are. A script can be written to repeatedly try to decrypt the private key using each password in a dictionary, demonstrated in Box 4.

The return value of the command will communicate if the private key was successfully decrypted. We wrote a short perl script to do so, and when executed was found to take 171 seconds to check 10,000 passwords. This rate of 58.5 passwords per second is much less than OpenSSL password hash that similarly had a salt and key stretching (which could perform 3,400 checks a second). The difference is that gpg has to also perform the decryption of several blocks to get the private key before checking if the password was correct.

This approach can easily be tailored by the investigator (use of customized dictionary, execute on many machines, etc.). While the same script can be used on different encryption products, it does require some familiarity with the commands and minor adjustments. The biggest downside is that command line tools are not always available. Linux software (including cross-platform software) is more likely to provide this feature than software designed solely for Windows.

The third approach is to use a dedicated commercial password recovery tool. Many individual

Box 4.

```
gpg --decrypt -passphrase <currentpassword> <privatekeyfile>
```

point solutions exist for particular cryptographic protections of common file types (MS Word, Excel, zip, etc.), and there are suites of tools that can support a number of different encrypted files, e.g. FTK Password Recovery Toolkit. The advantage of using a commercial tool is the ease of use. No familiarity with the implementation is needed, nor is any knowledge of the plaintext. All that is needed is for the investigator to be able to identify the filetype. The tool will either exploit weaknesses in the protections mechanisms (can occur with older formats) or automate the dictionary/brute-force attack. One downside of this approach is the cost. Most tools will provide free demos with limited support. Another issue is the range of supported products. While the common formats and encryption suites will have corresponding password recovery tools available, not every possible product will be supported. More recent products and niche tools are unlikely to be supported, for example browser password-managers or any smartphone encryption app.

Live Memory Capture of Cryptographic Keys

Cryptography can cause problems in the first two stages of any forensics investigation: identification and collection of evidence. Typical identification of files of interest is done by filename, type, path and header/footers. File encryption can remove most of these (encryption does not necessarily modify the file name, but the software implementation may also do this, or alternatively the user themselves), but can also replace them with alternative identifying artefacts.

In one sense, detecting whole disk encryption is straightforward. Once a disk has been removed and is forensically imaged, it will be immediately apparent if the data is random or a recognizable file system. Unfortunately, when whole disk encryption is present, steps need to be taken before the device is shutdown and the disk is removed, e.g. all files should be copied from the device. Therefore, efforts have been made to determine ways to quickly detect the presence of whole disk encryption on live systems. Individual procedures exist to detect specific products6, and some tools that can detect a number of different encrypted volumes7. These solutions are tied to some extent to the implementations of the disk encryption, and may need updating as the technology changes/new technologies appear. What we will describe in the rest of this section is what we believe to be a good general approach. Not only is it independent of the implementation, but can apply to multiple encryption algorithms, operating systems, and is possible to implement on a locked device.

We propose that when running machines are encountered in an investigation, capturing a memory dump should become part of the standard evidence collection process. Memory capture has traditionally been shunned by forensics investigators as it does involve accessing and potentially modifying the evidence before collection. It is going to become a necessary countermeasure as criminals become more proficient with using encryption tools to cover up their crimes. Every encryption tool must have the key in memory to function. So while encryption can frustrate any analysis of encrypted media, if a machine is encountered while running it will be possible to extract the keys from memory. Even if the machine is locked, a hard reset and a boot disk can circumvent this to capture the memory (although a certain degree of loss of data in RAM is guaranteed).

Up to this point, we have treated cryptographic algorithms as black boxes. We have argued that a forensics investigator needs to be aware of the objectives that cryptography attempts to achieve, the requirements to correctly implement these algorithms, and the implications of any published attacks on the algorithms. However, for the purposes of the following section, it is necessary to delve into the details of parts of modern encryption algorithms.

We have noted that passwords make poor cryptographic keys due to their having some predictable bits. Block ciphers require completely random keys, which makes locating keys in memory problematic. Fortunately, block ciphers do not use the key as is. Most block ciphers operate over several rounds, and generate a different sub-key for each round, collectively known as the key schedule. Since the key schedule is derived from the key in a deterministic fashion (needs to be repeatable both during encryption and decryption), this represents a redundancy that can be used for locating key schedules within memory. AES has a particularly distinctive pattern in its key schedule (NIST, 2001). The key is divided into four 32-bit words. The fourth word is rotated, bytes are substituted using a fixed lookup table, and XOR'd with a round constant. The word is then XOR'd with the first word of the key to produce the first word of the first subkey. The next three words are generated in a similar manner to this last step; each word is produced by XOR'ing the last word generated with the third previous word8. Each subsequent subkey is generated in a similar fashion, with a different round constant. The end result is that the first word of a subkey has a complex relation with the previous key words, but the other three words obey a straightforward XOR relation with previous key words. In a large data object where there is known to be a key schedule (such as a memory dump), the latter pattern can be efficiently searched for.

To demonstrate this technique, we created an encrypted volume with TrueCrypt. Figure 1 gives a screen shot of the creation (and also shows a portion of the Master key). The memory of the device was captured four times, twice before and twice after the encrypted volume was mounted (with a reboot in between). Searching each images for AES keys took approximately 45 minutes. Note that no other applications were running, nor had been run. Table 5 contains (portions of) the keys recovered. In both cases, three keys were present in memory after the TrueCrypt volume was mounted that were not present before, and one of these is the Master key displayed in the setup.

This process is not without its downsides. Very few tools provide the facility to decrypt with the key directly. This would need to be implemented separately for each encryption software. Nor would

Figure 1. Creation of a TrueCrypt encrypted volume

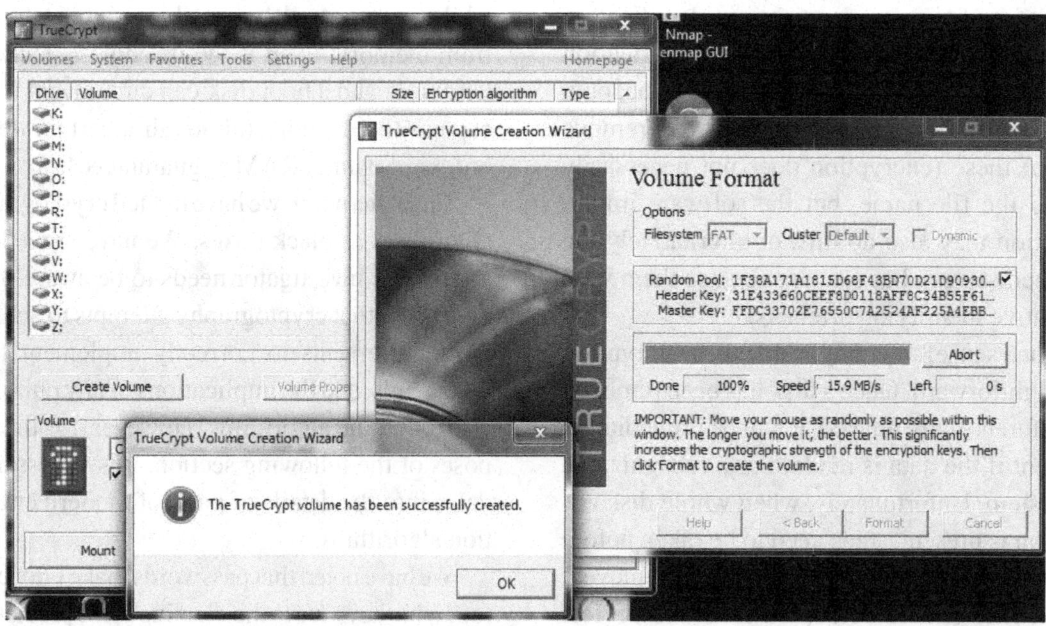

Table 5. Examples of AES keys retrieved from memory images

	Image 1		Image 2		Image 3		Image 4	
	Size	Key	Size	Key	Size	Key	Size	Key
1	128	d0e4c0...	128	d0e4c0...	128	e8b565...	128	e8b565...
2	128	48a644...	128	48a644...	128	63268a...	128	63268a...
3	128	aae8b6...	128	aae8b6...	128	fdb840...	128	fdb840...
4	256	72cde8...	256	72cde8...	128	aae8b6...	128	aae8b6...
5	128	99d7e7...	128	99d7e7...	256	72cde8...	256	72cde8...
6	256	b24a39...	256	b24a39...	256	3182b9...	256	3182b9...
7	256	88dbc0...	256	88dbc0...	128	48a644...	128	48a644...
8	128	3e1994...	128	3e1994...	256	30bff7...	256	30bff7...
9	256	af2b01...	256	af2b01...	128	3e1994...	128	3e1994...
10	256	30bff7...	256	30bff7...	128	249a8e...	128	249a8e...
11	128	326c38...	128	326c38...	256	88dbc0...	256	88dbc0...
12			256	ffdc33...	128	72f24c...	128	72f24c...
13			256	c15504...	128	b96184...	128	b96184...
14			256	b7325d...	128	63268a...	256	af2b01...
15					128	fdb840...	256	ffdc33...
16					128	fdb840...	256	c15504...
17					128	63268a...	256	b7325d...
18					256	af2b01...		

an investigator have a "before and after" image to compare. However, even if there were hundreds of AES keys found in memory, checking them would be many times more efficient than performing a dictionary attack on passwords, and certainly better than trying to brute force the key. The benefit of this approach is that a simple step during collection can provide the ability to perform this analysis at a later date, if it is deemed necessary (whole disk encryption turned out to be used) and worth the effort (the importance of the investigation justifies the effort).

One of the new areas of cryptographic research has been leakage-resistant cryptography. This is attempting to address the problem of attackers using side-channels (e.g. power analysis) to gain information about keys in use. While it has not yet reached maturity, such systems may limit the usefulness of memory analysis. Much work has been done on systems that modify the key used over time (Dziembowski, Kazana, & Wich, 2011). Such a system would limit what could be learned from a key in memory (at the very least it would prevent decryption of anything encrypted previously). But the applicability of key evolution schemes to systems that require random access (i.e. full-disk encryption) is likely to be problematic.

FUTURE RESEARCH DIRECTIONS

Live memory analysis has the potential to solve problems arising from criminals using encryption to better hide their tracks. However, there is still much work needed to be done to be able to provide useful and reliable results. Obtaining the key can often be the simple task, the real effort being required to use the key to decrypt data in an unknown and proprietary format. Even an open tool such as TrueCrypt has nine different possible encryption options, including double and triple encryption. Research is also needed in determining how often different keys for different products remain in memory, to better prepare an investigator as to what may or may not be recoverable. Another avenue of possible research is applying these techniques to swap space.

CONCLUSION

Recent research has brought a number of interesting cryptanalytic attacks to light. The collisions found for MD5 have lead to the drive to select a replacement. As has been discussed, this does not immediately invalidate all methods for preserving the integrity of evidence. However, the upcoming standard should be accepted and integrated as a matter of course, and further enhancements to attacks monitored. Attacks have also surfaced on the AES algorithm (Bogdanov, Khovratovich, & Rechberger, 2011). While these attacks are not considered cause for concern, future breakthroughs may change this position.

Live memory capture provides both risks and rewards. The risk of modification of evidence is outweighed by the reward of capturing encrypted data. This chapter has attempted to convey the concepts to an investigator not proficient in cryptography, but much of the necessary software tools are still lacking. A wide range of tools do exist for memory capture. Work is needed on developing the analysis that will capture keys of a number of different algorithms and provide the facility to use them to decrypt data.

REFERENCES

AAP. (2005). NSW speed cameras in doubt. The Age. Retrieved March 27, 2012, from http://www.theage.com.au/articles/2005/08/10/1123353368652.html

Alghafli, K., Jones, A., & Martin, T. (2011). Forensic analysis of the Windows 7 registry. Journal of Digital Forensics, Security and Law, 5(4).

APCO. (2007). Good practice guide for computer-based electronic evidence. Retrieved April 25, 2012, from http://7safe.com/electronic_evidence/ACPO_guidelines_computer_evidence_v4_web.pdf

Bello, L. (2008). DSA-1571-1 Openssl – Predictable random number generator. Debian Project. Retrieved April 22, 2012, from http://www.debian.org/security/2008/dsa-1571

Bogdanov, A., Khovratovich, D., & Rechberger, C. (2011). Biclique cryptanalysis of the full AES. In D. Lee & X. Wang (Eds.), 17th International Conference on the Theory and Application of Cryptology and Information Security – AsiaCrypt, (pp. 344-371). Berlin, Germany: Springer.

Brakerski, Z., Gentry, C., & Vaikuntanathan, V. (2012). Fully homomorphic encryption without bootstrapping. In Proceedings of Innovations in Theoretical Computer Science (ITCS 2012). ITCS.

Denning, D., & Branstad, D. (1996). A taxonomy for key escrow encryption systems. *Communications of the ACM*, *39*(3). doi:10.1145/227234.227239.

Donnerhacke, L., Finney, H., Shaw, D., & Thayer, R. (2007). OpenPGP message format. IETF. Retrieved April 25, 2012, from https://tools.ietf.org/html/rfc4880

Dziembowski, S., Kazana, T., & Wichs, D. (2011). Key-evolution schemes resilient to space-bounded leakage. In P. Rogaway (Ed.), Advances in Cryptology - CRYPTO 2003, 23rd Annual International Cryptology Conference, (pp. 617-630). Berlin, Germany: Springer.

Gentry, C. (2009). Fully homomorphic encryption using ideal lattices. Paper presented at the 41st ACM Symposium on the Theory of Computation. Bethesda, MD.

Gentry, C., & Halevi, S. (2011). Implementing Gentry's fully-homomorphic encryption scheme. In Paterson, K. (Ed.), *Advances in Cryptology -- Eurocrypt 2011* (pp. 129–148). Berlin, Germany: Springer. doi:10.1007/978-3-642-20465-4_9.

Gentry, C., Halevi, S., & Smart, N. (2012). Homomorphic evaluation of the AES circuit. *Lecture Notes in Computer Science*, *7417*, 850–867. doi:10.1007/978-3-642-32009-5_49.

Halderman, J., Schoen, S., Heninger, N., Clarkson, W., Paul, W., & Cal, J. et al. (2006). Lest we remember: Cold-boot attacks on encryption keys. *Communications of the ACM*, *52*(5).

Kayser, R. (2007). Federal register. Government Printing Office. Retrieved March 27, 2012, from http://csrc.nist.gov/groups/ST/hash/documents/FR_Notice_Nov07.pdf

Klein, T. (2006). All your private keys are belong to us - Extracting RSA private keys and certificates from process memory. Trapkit. Retrieved April 22, 2012, from http://www.trapkit.de/research/sslkeyfinder/keyfinder_v1.0_20060205.pdf

Lenstra, A., Hughes, J., Augier, M., Bos, J., Kleinjung, T., & Wachter, C. (2012). Ron was wrong, Whit is right. Report 2012/064. Cryptology ePrint Archive.

Lu, C. Y., Browne, D., Yang, T., & Pan, J. W. (2007). Demonstration of a compiled version of Shor's quantum factoring algorithm using photonic qubits. *Physical Review Letters*, *99*(25). doi:10.1103/PhysRevLett.99.250504 PMID:18233508.

Martin, T., & Jones, A. (2011). An evaluation of data erasing tools. Paper presented at the 9th Australian Digital Forensics Conference. Perth, Australia.

McGrath, N., Gladyshev, P., & Carthy, J. (2010). Cryptopometry as a methodology for investigating encrypted material. *International Journal of Digital Crime and Forensics*, *2*(1), 29–35. doi:10.4018/jdcf.2010010101.

National Institutes of Standards and Technology. (2001). Announcing the advanced encryption standard (AES). Retrieved April 25, 2012, from http://csrc.nist.gov/publications/fips/fips197/fips-197.pdf

Oechslin, P. (2003). Making a faster cryptanalytic time-memory trade-off. In D. Boneh (Ed.), Advances in Cryptology - CRYPTO 2003, 23rd Annual International Cryptology Conference, (pp. 617-630). Berlin, Germany: Springer.

Rogaway, P., & Shrimpton, T. (2004). Cryptographic hash-function basics: Definitions, implications, and separations for preimage resistance, second-preimage resistance, and collision resistance. In Proceedings of the Fast Software Encryption, 11th International Workshop, (pp. 371-388). Springer.

Shamir, A., & Van Someren, N. (1999). Playing hide and seek with stored keys. In M. Franklin (Ed.), Financial Cryptography, Third International Conference Proceedings, (pp. 118-124). Springer.

Shor, P. (1994). Algorithms for quantum computation: Discrete logarithms and factoring. In Proceedings of the 35th Annual Symposium on Foundations of Computer Science, (pp. 124-134). IEEE.

Stevens, M., Lenstra, A., & Weger, B. (2007). Chosen-prefix collisions for MD5 and colliding X.509 certificates for different identities. In Naor, M. (Ed.), *Advances in Cryptology -- Eurocrypt 2007* (pp. 19–35). Springer. doi:10.1007/978-3-540-72540-4_1.

Tromer, E., Osvik, D., & Shamir, A. (2010). Efficient cache attacks on AES, and countermeasures. *Journal of Cryptology, 23*(2), 37–71. doi:10.1007/s00145-009-9049-y.

Wang, X., Feng, D., Lai, X., & Yu, H. (2004). Collisions for hash functions MD4, MD5, HAVAL-128 and RIPEMD. Cryptology ePrint Archive. Retrieved March 27, 2012, from http://eprint.iacr.org/2004/199

Wang, X., & Yu, H. (2005). How to break MD5 and other Hash functions. In Cramer, R. (Ed.), *Advances in Cryptology -- Eurocrypt 2005* (pp. 19–35). Springer. doi:10.1007/11426639_2.

Wang, X., Yu, H., & Yin, Y. (2005). Efficient collision search attacks on SHA-0. In V. Shoup (Ed.), Advances in Cryptology - CRYPTO 2005, 25th Annual International Cryptology Conference, (pp. 1-16). Springer.

ADDITIONAL READING

Casey, E. (2008). The impact of full disk encryption on digital forensics. *ACM SIGOPS Operating Systems Review, 42*(3), 93–98. doi:10.1145/1368506.1368519.

Casey, E. (2009). *Handbook of digital forensics and investigation*. Waltham, MA: Academic Press.

Casey, E. (2010). *Digital evidence and computer crime: Forensic science, computers, and the internet*. Waltham, MA: Academic Press.

Maartmann-Moe, C., Thorkildsen, S., & Arnes, A. (2009). The persistence of memory: Forensic identification and extraction of cryptographic keys. In Casey, E. (Ed.), *Digital Investigation* (pp. 132–140). Amsterdam, The Netherlands: Elsevier. doi:10.1016/j.diin.2009.06.002.

Menenzes, A., Oorschoot, P., & Vanstone, S. (Eds.). (1996). *Handbook of applied cryptography*. Boca Raton, FL: CRC Press. doi:10.1201/9781439821916.

Siegfried, J., Siedsma, C., Countryman, B., & Hosmer, C. (2004). Examining the encryption threat. *International Journal of Digital Evidence, 2*(3), 1–11.

Stinson, D. (Ed.). (1995). *Cryptography: Theory and practice*. Boca Raton, FL: CRC Press.

Walters, A., & Petroni, N. (2007). Volatools: Integrating volatile memory forensics into the digital investigation process. Paper presented Black Hat. Washington, DC.

KEY TERMS AND DEFINITIONS

Confidentiality: Ensuring that data may only be accessed by authorized parties.

Cryptography: Processes of modifying data and/or deriving values from data in order to preserve its confidentiality or integrity. Typically involves the use of a secret key known to certain parties.

Dictionary: A collection of commonly used passwords/words and phrases that may be passwords.

File Carving: Analysis of media, which may have been deleted/formatted, to attempt to recover files. Typically searches for known patterns at the start and end of files, e.g. <html to </html>.

Forensics: The identification, collection, preservation, and presentation of evidence.

Hash: A method of creating a digital fingerprint of a file or piece of data.

Integrity: Ensuring that data may only be modified by authorized parties.

ENDNOTES

1. http://www.mcgamillions.com/
2. http://md5deep.sourceforge.net/
3. http://tools.ietf.org/html/rfc4880
4. http://www.forensicinnovations.com/fitools.html
5. http://www.openssl.org/
6. http://www.forensicfocus.com/potential-impact-windows-vista
7. http://www.jadsoftware.com/encrypted-disk-detector/
8. The key schedule described is for 128-bit key AES. The process involved in generating the 192 and 256-bit keys are slightly more complex but follow the same basic rules.

Chapter 4
Search in Encrypted Data: Theoretical Models and Practical Applications

Qiang Tang
University of Luxembourg, Luxembourg

ABSTRACT

Recently, the concept of Search in Encrypted Data (SED) has become a highlight in cryptography. A SED scheme enables a client to have third-party server(s) perform certain search functionalities on the encrypted data. In this chapter, the authors conduct a systematic study on SED schemes. First, they describe three application scenarios and identify the desirable security requirements. Second, they provide two orthogonal categorizations and review the related security models for each category of SED schemes. Third, the authors analyze the practical issues related to SED schemes and identify some future research directions.

INTRODUCTION

A Search in Encrypted Data (SED) scheme allows third-party server(s) to search on behalf of a client without the need to recover the plaintext data while preventing the server(s) from learning any plaintext information. SED has become a very active research area in cryptography in recent years. Two seminal SED schemes are the one by Song, Wagner, and Perrig (2000) and the one by Boneh, Crescenzo, Ostrovsky, and Persiano (2004). The first scheme allows a client to encrypt its database and store the encrypted database at a remote server. Later on, the client can instruct the server to search in the encrypted database and return the relevant data. The second scheme is often referred to as PEKS, namely public key encryption with keyword search. With a PEKS

DOI: 10.4018/978-1-4666-4030-6.ch004

scheme, a client publishes his public key so that any entity can encrypt messages for him. Later on, the client can allow a third-party server to search in the encrypted messages by assigning a token to it. Following these two schemes, a lot of variants have been proposed to extend the concepts in many aspects. For instance, Yang, Tan, Huang, and Wong (2010) proposed the concept of public key encryption supporting equality test. In contrast to the scheme by Boneh et al. (2004), the scheme by Yang et al. (2010) allows a third-party server to search on the ciphertexts which are encrypted with public keys from multiple different clients. With the wide adoption of cloud computing applications, SED schemes have been regarded by many to be an important technology in securing outsourcing databases while preserving data utility and confidentiality.

In this book chapter, we aim at a systematic study on existing SED schemes and their security implications. In particular, we reflect on the related theoretical security models and try to understand their practical security guarantees.

In the first step, we study three representative application scenarios, which have motivated a variety of theoretical SED schemes. Despite the frequent citations, the security requirements of these scenarios have not been investigated in depth in the literature. This fact means that there may be a gap between the theoretical security guarantees of existing SED schemes and the practical needs of the application scenarios. In the second step, we present two categorizations for SED schemes. One is based on whether a scheme supports full-domain or index-based search. The other is based on the answers to two questions, namely "Who can contribute searchable data in the outsourced database?" and "Who can issue search queries to the third-party server(s)?" Due to the desired storage and search functionalities, outsourcing data storage and search operations to third-party server(s) inevitably results in some privacy loss for the client. The answers to the above two questions define the characteristics of the search functionalities provided by a SED scheme, and consequently determine the inevitable information leakage of the scheme. In the third step, based on the results in the first two steps, we provide some practicality analysis against the existing provably secure SED schemes. The analysis shows that many practical security concerns have not been covered by theoretical security models. As a result, we are able to identify some future research directions for SED schemes.

Organization. The rest of this chapter is organized as follows. In the second section, we describe three application scenarios and identify their security requirements. In the third section, we categorize the existing SED schemes. In the fourth section, we review the security models for SED schemes. In the fifth section, we analyze the practical issues facing SED schemes. In the sixth section, we conclude the chapter.

SED APPLICATION SCENARIOS

In this section, we describe three representative application scenarios for SED schemes and the related security requirements. In addition, we also mention some possible variants.

Search in Outsourced Personal Database

Suppose Alice is a frequent traveler and needs to access her database during her travel anytime and anywhere in the world. For this, Alice can outsource her personal database to a third-party service provider, such as Google or Dropbox. With this approach, Alice needs to reveal everything (the data and search criteria) to the third-party service provider, which makes the solution undesirable from the privacy perspective. To achieve a privacy-preserving solution, Alice can employ a SED scheme to encrypt her database and outsource the ciphertext. Later on, Alice can issue a search query (containing encrypted search criteria) to the service provider, which can then search in the database and return the encrypted documents which match the search criteria. As to this scenario, we distill the following security requirements.

- Only Alice can generate contents for the outsourced database and decrypt the encrypted contents in the database, and only Alice can issue meaningful search queries.
- No entity, including the server, should learn what Alice has searched for.

This application scenario was firstly mentioned by Song et al. (2000), and has motivated the investigation of SED schemes in the symmetric-setting described in the third section.

Email Routing Service

Among all outsourcing services, email may be one of the most well known examples, where users' email data is stored and related services are managed by the email service providers. In email services, the service providers normally have access to all emails of their customers in plaintext so that a lot of privacy concerns exist (e.g. sensitive email messages and targeted advertisements). Now, suppose that there is an email service provider, which wants to provide secure email service and allow users to receive encrypted emails. In this situation, a user Alice can employ a SED scheme and have all her emails encrypted under her (public) key. Later on, Alice can ask the service provider to search in her encrypted emails and then selectively retrieve the interesting ones. For instance, during her vacation, Alice can simply retrieve the emails labeled as "urgent" through her smart phone, without being bothered by other emails. As to this scenario, we distill the following security requirements.

- Every entity should be able to generate encrypted emails for Alice, but only Alice can read her emails.
- Only Alice can issue meaningful email retrieval queries. In addition, Alice may also want the service provider to scan her encrypted emails, in particular the attachments, to detect viruses or malwares without learning unnecessary plaintext information. This functionality has been described by Ibraimi, Nikova, Hartel, and Jonker (2011).
- No entity, including the server, should learn what Alice has searched for.

This application scenario was firstly mentioned by Boneh et al. (2004), and has motivated the investigation of SED schemes in the asymmetric-setting described in the third section.

Matching in Internet-Based PHR Systems

An Internet-based PHR (personal healthcare record) system, such as Microsoft Health Vault, helps users store their PHRs and allow the information to be accessed and edited via a web browser or some APIs, and they may also help users find kindred spirits (i.e. build social networks) and share their information. Considering a user, say Alice, her PHR data can come from a lot of sources. For example, she can get prescription results from her doctor, treatments from a hospital, test results from a laboratory, and monitoring results from home-based sensors. Quite often, a lot of Alice's PHR data may be directly sent to Alice's account, while the rest will be input by Alice herself. Figure 1 shows a general picture of an Internet-based PHR system.

In most existing Internet-based PHR systems, users will be provided privacy controls. However, there are a number of concerns that stop users from sharing their data. One concern is that the system providers, say Microsoft, are always able to fully access the data. Although there will be some privacy agreement, but users may still worry about that these providers may abuse their

Figure 1. An illustration of outsourced PHRs

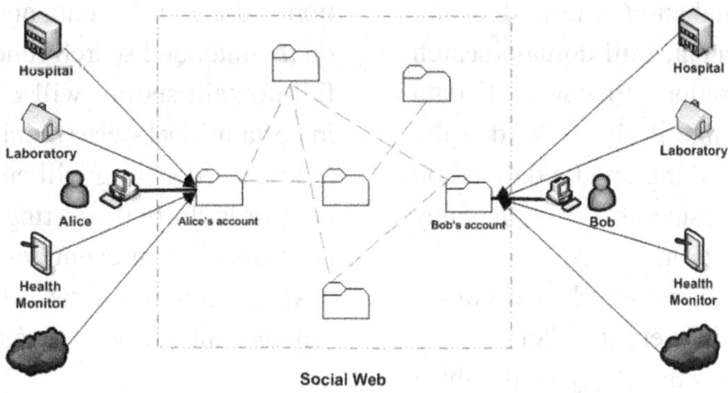

data. The other concern is that, even if the service providers behave honestly, their databases may be compromised, in which case all data may be leaked. Since PHRs are sensitive information to individuals, and information leakage may cause undesirable consequences, such as being discriminated by the potential employer because of a disease.

To solve the privacy problem, users can employ a SED scheme and have all their PHR data encrypted under their own (public) keys. Moreover, the users can authorize third-party server(s) to match their encrypted data without recovering the plaintext information. As to this scenario, we distill the following security requirements.

- A user, say Alice, should be able to allow multiple entities to generate contents for her, and only Alice should be able to decrypt the encrypted contents intended for her.
- Together with another user, Alice can authorize third-party server(s) to match their ciphertexts. The authorization should support different levels of granularity, and third-party server(s) should not be able to learn any information more than the match result, such as "equal" or "not-equal" in exact matching.

This application scenario has motivated the SED schemes for joint databases in the asymmetric-setting, as described by Tang (2011).

CATEGORIZATION OF SED SCHEMES

In this section, we review and categorize the existing SED schemes which follow the work of Boneh et al. (2004) and Song et al. (2000). Boneh, Sahai, and Waters (2011) have regarded functional encryption as a general form of searchable encryption, where a client out-sources its encrypted data to third-party server(s) and assigns tokens to them so that they recover certain plaintexts if the tokens satisfy some conditions. Nevertheless, we omit discussions of these generalized primitives.

Full-Domain vs. Index-Based

Given a data item, which can be of various forms (e.g. an email, a document, a video clip, etc.), search can be done in two ways.

- One is to perform full-domain search, in which a search will sequentially go through every data item in order to test some criteria. For instance, a search can be to test whether some term appears more than a threshold times and another term does not appear in the content. Full-domain search takes linear operations to cover all data items, and is flexible in the sense that the criteria can be anything and be defined on the fly. The downside is its inefficiency when the data items are of big size.

- The other is index-based search or keyword-based search, where every data item is firstly characterized by a list of keywords which are then used to build a search index for the data item. Later, when a search takes place, the criteria will be tested based on the indexes instead of the contents of data items. In the literature, there are two basic ways to construct indexes, namely forward index shown in Figure 2 and inverted index shown in Figure 3. With this approach, search can be done much more efficiently since it does not need to go through the contents of all data items. The downside is that search criteria may not be as flexible as in the case of full-domain search. The performance will depend on the selection of keywords and how the index is constructed.

The above description assumes that no encryption is done on the data and indexes. Depending on the intended search functionality, SED in the full-domain setting will encrypt the data items in certain block-wise manner, while SED in the index-based setting will encrypt the indexes and keywords. In both set-tings, search queries will be blinded to prevent information leakage. In next subsection, we categorize the existing SED schemes into these settings.

Symmetric-Setting vs. Asymmetric-Setting

Based on the answer to the questions "Who can contribute searchable data in the outsourced database?" and "Who can issue search queries to the third-party server(s)?" SED schemes can be divided into two categories, which are referred to as symmetric-setting and asymmetric-setting. This categorization is orthogonal to that in previous subsection.

In the symmetric-setting, as described in the seminal paper by Song et al. (2000), only the client is able to generate the searchable contents, generate valid search queries, and decrypt the

Figure 2. Forward index

Item Identifiers	Keywords
Item ID1	keyword1, keyword3, keyword5
Item ID2	keyword5
Item ID3	keyword2, keyword4
Item ID4	keyword2, keyword3
Item ID5	keyword1, keyword2, keyword4
Item ID6	keyword4, keyword5, keyword6
Item ID7	keyword2, keyword3, keyword4, keyword5

Figure 3. Inverted index

Keywords	Item Identifiers
keyword1	Item ID1, Item ID5
Keyword2	Item ID3, Item ID4, Item ID5, Item ID7
Keyword3	Item ID1, Item ID4, Item ID7
Keyword4	Item ID3, Item ID5, Item ID6, Item ID7
Keyword5	Item ID1, Item ID2, Item ID6, Item ID7
Keyword6	Item ID6

encrypted contents. This setting matches the application in the second section. The SED scheme in the paper assumes full-domain search and the encryption is word by word. Along the line, a number of variants exist.

- Despite of its more general purpose, the seminal work of Goldreich and Ostrovsky (1996) on Oblivious RAMs gives us techniques for performing full-domain search on encrypted data stored on a server. Compared with other schemes, the advantage of Oblivious RAMs is allowing the client to hide data access patterns (i.e. achieving query result privacy as defined below). The downside of this approach is that it requires polylog rounds of communication and significantly more inefficient than other schemes.
- Following the work by Song et al. (2000), the concept of index-based SED schemes in the symmetric-setting was investigated. Goh (2003) formalized the IND-CKA property (i.e. indistinguishability against chosen keyword attack), namely semantic security against an adaptive chosen keyword attack, and an improved IND2-CKA property which is slightly stronger than IND-CKA. Goh also proposed two schemes based on bloom filters, which can result in some false positive incidents in the query results. Chang and Mitzenmacher (2005) formalized a property similar to IND2-CKA, and proposed two SED schemes without bloom filters. Curtmola, Garay, Kamara, and Ostrovsky (2006) improved these security definitions by taking into account trapdoor privacy which has not been adequately covered by Goh (2003) and Chang and Mitzenmacher (2005). Note that the construction by Curtmola et al. (2006) uses inverted index while the constructions in the other two papers use forward index.
- Shen, Shi, and Waters (2009) formulated the full security property for symmetric-key predicate-only encryption (Setup, Encrypt, GenToken, Query), which is a building block for predicate encryption. Though the primitive is not initially designed for the purpose of SED, but it can be regarded as a general formulation of SED with forward index: the client runs Setup to generate his secret key; given a document, the index is computed as an encryption of the keywords by the function Encrypt; by representing the search criteria with a

predicate, a trapdoor can be generated by the function GenToken; a search is done by running the function Query to test whether the keywords in an index satisfy the predicate or not. In this regard, it is more general than formulations by Goh (2003) and Chang and Mitzenmacher (2005).

- The seminal work by Song et al. (2000) considers a single-user setting, where the client is the intended receiver of encrypted data items. How to extend index-based SED to multi-user setting has been investigated afterwards. In the formulation by Curtmola et al. (2006), multiple intended receivers can submit search queries. The client (who contributes the searchable data) dynamically manages the receivers' search capability and the scheme construction is based on the concept of broadcast encryption. In the formulation of Bao, Deng, Ding, and Yang (2008), a new party, namely user manager, is introduced into the system, to manage multiple clients' search capability. Unlike the formulation by Curtmola et al. (2006), all clients can contribute searchable contents and can search. The downside of this formulation is that the user manager is also capable of submitting search queries and decrypting encrypted data items. In practice, all clients are required to fully-trust the user manager, who may be a single point of failure for the whole system. In addition, the clients need to interact with the user manager to generate an index. This may be an efficiency drawback. In the formulations by Agrawal, Kiernan, Srikant, and Xu (2004) and Boldyreva, Chenette, Lee, and O'Neill (2009), any entity can search in all encrypted data. These SED schemes are termed order preserving encryption, where the ciphertexts preserve the order the plaintexts, so that every entity can perform an equality comparison. One drawback of these schemes is that they do not define standard security notions. In contrast, the scheme by Tang (2010) allows similar functionality but with standard security notions.
- Golle, Staddon, and Waters (2004) proposed two SED schemes which allow the client to attach multiple keywords to a data item and then perform conjunctive keyword search. In both schemes, an index tells the number of encrypted keywords.
- Most SED schemes assume that a search is either a sequential scan in the encrypted data or a direct matching in the index. Chase and Kamara (2010) specifically studied SED for structured data (e.g. matrices, labeled data, graphs, and labeled graphs) and investigated its application in controlled disclosure.
- Islam, Kuzu, and Kantarcioglu (2012) investigated an attack with respect to data access pattern leakage and presented experimental results. Moreover, they proposed a generic mitigation technique, which introduces a certain degree of false positive rate in the searching. Bosch, Tang, Hartel, and Jonker (2012) proposed an interactive SED scheme based on the recent advances in fully homomorphic encryption schemes. The proposed scheme is secure in a security model which is at least as strong as that by Shen et al. (2009). The original scheme supports equality test, but can be easily adapted to support many useful search features, including aggregating search results, supporting conjunctive keyword search queries, advanced keyword search, search with keyword occurrence frequency, and search based on inner product. With all the schemes, the client can protect his access pattern by retrieving the matched documents through some Private Information Retrieval (PIR) protocols. Compared with the solution by Islam et al. (2012), PIR will not introduce any false positive results,

although it may suffer from complexity penalties.

- Hore, Mehrotra, Canim, and Kantarcioglu (2012) investigated the problem of supporting multidimensional range queries on encrypted data, and proposed a solution based on the idea of computing a secure indexing tag of the data by applying bucketization. Kerschbaum and Sorniotti (2011) proposed a SED scheme in the symmetric-setting, which supports range queries, relying only on Diffie-Hellman assumptions in the random oracle model. Kuzu, Islam, Mohammad, and Kantarcioglu (2012) and Raykova, Cui, Vo, Liu, Malkin, Bellovin, and Stolfo (2012) investigated SED schemes that allow searching based on keyword similarities.

In the asymmetric-setting, as described in the seminal paper by Boneh et al. (2004), every entity is able to generate searchable contents without any explicit authorization from the client. By default, only the client can generate valid search queries and decrypt the encrypted contents. This setting matches the application in the second section. The SED formulation in the paper is often referred to as PEKS (public key encryption with keyword search). The concept formulation and scheme construction of PEKS are limited in many aspects, and a lot of variants have proposed thereafter.

- The PEKS formulation only considers the encryption of single keyword and only supports exact matching in the search. It has been extended to support search queries with conjunctive keywords by Boneh and Waters (2007), Hwang and Lee (2007), and Iovino and Persiano (2008). These extensions are straightforward in the sense that the keywords are somehow still encrypted one by one, and an index tells the number of encrypted keywords. Moreover, the solution by Boneh and Waters (2007) also supports subset and range queries. Katz, Sahai and Waters (2008) proposed schemes supporting disjunctions, polynomial equations, and inner products. Note that the above schemes except for that by Hwang and Lee (2007) have been under the name of predicate encryption, which can provide the functionality of SED.
- The PEKS formulation only covers the encryption and matching of keywords, but it does not touch on the encryption of affiliated messages. A natural question is whether we can use the same public key for encrypting both the keywords and the messages. The concept of integrating PKE and PEKS has been investigated by Baek, Safavi-Naini, and Susilo (2006) and Zhang and Imai (2007). It is worth noting that these formulations do not address the linkability concern discussed in the fifth section.
- When applying a PEKS scheme, it is assumed that the trapdoor should always be transmitted from the client to the server through a secure channel. Baek, Safavi-Naini, and Susilo (2008) and Rhee, Park, Susilo, and Lee (2010) argued that this additional requirement is not realistic in some application scenarios, so they proposed the concept of PEKS with designated tester (referred to as dPEKS), by letting the encryption of keywords done under both public keys from the client and a specific server. On one hand, dPEKS successfully gets rid of the security channel requirement of PEKS. On the other hand, it has very limited applications due to the following facts: the message sender must obtain both public keys and, for one ciphertext, only one server can search. For both PEKS and dPEKS, the schemes may still be vulnerable to offline keyword recovery attacks against a curious server, as noted by Byun, Rhee, Park, and Lee (2006). In

addition, Baek et al. (2008) emphasized that keyword ciphertext is secure against a malicious client, but it is unclear why this makes any difference because the client can always recover the message and somehow determine the encrypted keywords any way.

- With respect to index-based SED schemes in the asymmetric-setting, the keyword set is certainly required to be public so that every entity can generate searchable contents. Byun et al. (2006) showed that the server can mount an offline message recovery attack to recover the keywords in the received trapdoors. The attack is straightforward. The server first generates fake tags based on the keywords it chooses, and then analyses the results of the client's search queries. If a trapdoor matches a fake tag (say, from keyword w), then the server can conclude that other matched tags also contain w and those unmatched tags do not contain w. To address this type of attack, Tang and Chen (2009) proposed the concept of PEKS with registered keywords. In this new formulation, the message senders need to be authorized by the client before being able to generate meaningful indexes. With the extra authorization process, the client can prevent entities such as the server from mounting an attack. The downside of this approach is that the setup phase becomes more complex. Another countermeasure is to use the computational puzzle technique, as shown in Tang (2011, 2012b). With this approach, a brute-force attack can be made computationally expensive, but the downside is that the message sender needs to compute a puzzle in order to construct an index. Baek et al. (2008) suggested refreshing the keyword set to mitigate attacks from the server. The problem with this approach is that new trapdoors cannot be used to search old contents, and this may cause usability problem in many applications. Moreover, it is still possible for the server to recover the keywords in trapdoors.
- By definition, a PEKS scheme only allows the server to search the client's ciphertexts, and there are scenarios two clients may want a server to perform certain forms of search in their joint database. Yang et al. (2010) proposed the concept PKEET (public key encryption supporting equality test). The drawback with their formulation is that any entity can perform the search without any explicit authorization. Tang (2011, 2012a, 2012b) introduced the concept of fine grained PKEET and presented corresponding constructions. Under the new formulations, two clients can authorize a third-party server to perform equality test based on their ciphertexts and some simple form of fuzzy equality testing. The authorization can come with different levels of granularity. This extension matches the internet-based PHR application described in the second section.
- In PEKS and most of its variants (and SED in the symmetric-setting as well), the server always knows the search results, namely the documents matched by every search request. This pattern itself leaks some information about the encrypted documents (and keywords), although no entity except the client can decrypt anything. Boneh, Kushilevitz, Ostrovsky, and Skeith III (2007) investigated the concept of public key storage with keyword search, which is an extension of PEKS that allows PIR queries. Compared with PEKS, the extension is substantial because a message sender and the server may need to engage in an interactive protocol for storing the encrypted contents. Moreover, a search operation may also need to be done through an interactive protocol. With all these changes, a stron-

ger security model has been designed for this primitive and the search results can be hidden from the server. The construction is constrained in the sense that the number of data items associated to every keyword is required to be bounded by a constant.

- Hwang and Lee (2007) extended the PEKS concept to multiple-user setting, where multiple clients can submit search queries for encrypted data which is intended for them all. The intuition behind their formulation is very straightforward, i.e. the index for every data item is generated based on the public keys of all clients.
- For most SED schemes in the asymmetric-setting (and SED in the symmetric-setting as well), a search request will typically require the server to sequentially scan all the encrypted data items or indexes therefore result in linear complexity. Bellare, Boldyreva and O'Neill (2007) introduced the concept of efficiently full-domain searchable deterministic encryption, which allows any entity to generate searchable contents and generate trapdoors to search in encrypted contents (generated by all entities) with logarithmic complexity. The downside with this approach is that the ciphertext is deterministic, so that an adversary can test any guessed plaintext by an encryption operation, and this is strictly weaker than the security guarantees provided by any other security model.
- For almost all SED schemes in the asymmetric-setting, including some constructions of the deterministic encryption by Bellare et al. (2007), search is done in the encrypted "index" instead of the ciphertexts of messages. For some application scenarios, the linkability problem described in the fifth section may be a serious issue. Ibraimi et al. (2011) proposed the concept of public key encryption with delegated search (referred to as PKEDS) which allows a server to search directly in the ciphertext. The drawback with their formulation is that the security model only considers the one-wayness property against a server and it is even weaker than the notion by Bellare et al. (2007). Fuhr and Paillier (2007) investigated the concept of full-domain searchable encryption and presented a solution in the random oracle model. Hofheinz and Weinreb (2008) revisited the concept and proposed a solution in the standard model. In both works, the authors only consider information leakage from ciphertexts and allow the server to access the information encoded in the trapdoors.

To give an intuitive view of the categorization results, we summarize the mentioned SED schemes in Figure 4. We emphasize that the summary only contain representative SED schemes mentioned above, and it is not intended to be a full list of all existing SED schemes.

In Figure 5, we classify the existing SED schemes based on the types of queries they support.

SED SECURITY MODELS

In this section, we review SED security models and analyze their security guarantees. It is worth noting that these models only focus on the confidentiality of data, namely preventing the server(s) from learning any plaintext information. In practice, integrity may also be an important concern for SED, but it has not attracted much attention so far so that we ignore the issue in our analysis.

In the following discussion, we assume the data items come from the set M while the keywords come from the dictionary D. For the generality, we use a predicate set F to represent all possible (non-encrypted) queries. One of the simplest types of predicates is the equality test, denoted as $F = \{f_w \mid w \in D\}$. In this case, $w' \in W$ satisfies f_w

Figure 4. Summary of categorizations

	Symmetric-Setting	Asymmetric-Setting
Full-domain	Agrawal et al. (2004), Boldyreva et al.(2009), Goldreich and Ostrovsky (1996), Song et al. (2000), Tang (2010)	Bellare et al. (2007), Fuhr and Paillier (2007), Hofheinz and Weinreb (2008), Ibraimi et al. (2011), Tang (2011, 2012a, 2012b), Yang et al. (2010)
Index-based	Bao et al. (2008), Bosch et al. (2012), Chang and Mitzenmacher (2005), Chase and Kamara (2010), Curtmola et al. (2006), Goh (2003), Golle et al. (2004), Hore et al. (2012), Islam et al. (2012), Kerschbaum and Sorniotti (2011), Kuzu et al. (2012), Raykova et al. (2012), Shen et al. (2009)	Baek et al. (2006, 2008), Boneh et al. (2004), Boneh et al. (2007), Boneh and Waters (2007), Hwang and Lee (2007), Iovino and Persiano (2008), Katz et al. (2008), Rhee et al. (2010), Tang and Chen (2009), Zhang and Imai (2007)

Figure 5. Classification based on supported queries

	SED Schemes
Equality test	All schemes in Figure 4.
Conjunctive and Disjunctive keyword queries	Boneh and Waters (2007), Bosch et al. (2012), Golle et al. (2004), Hwang and Lee (2007), Iovino and Persiano (2008), Katz et al. (2008)
Range queries	Agrawal et al. (2004), Bellare et al. (2007), Boldyreva et al. (2009), Boneh and Waters (2007), Hore et al. (2012), Kuzu et al. (2012)
Inner product queries	Bosch et al. (2012), Katz et al. (2008), Shen et al. (2009)

if and only if $w' = w$. For a set X, the notation $x \in_R X$ means that x is chosen from the set X uniformly at random. Probabilistic polynomial-time is abbreviated as P.P.T.

Index-Based SED in Symmetric-Setting

Generally, an index-based SED scheme in the symmetric-setting consists of the following polynomial-time algorithms.

- KeyGen(k): Run by the client, this algorithm takes a security parameter k as input, and outputs a secret key K. Let the data space be M and the predicate set be F.
- BuildIndex(m, K): Run by the client, this algorithm takes a data item $m \in M$ and the secret key K as input, and outputs an index Im which encodes a set of keywords u(m) for m. Let |u(m)| be the cardinality of the set u(m).
- Trapdoor(f, K): Run by the client, this algorithm takes a predicate $f \in F$ and the secret key K as input, and outputs a trapdoor Tf.
- Test(Tf, Im): Run by the server, this algorithm takes a trapdoor Tf and an index Im as input, and outputs 1 if u(m) satisfies f and 0 otherwise.

This definition is a generalization of those by Bao et al. (2008), Chang and Mitzenmacher (2005), Goh (2003), Golle et al. (2004), and Shen et al. (2009) with a forward index structure. The SED definition by Curtmola et al. (2006) adopts an inverted index structure, in which the BuildIndex algorithm takes a collection of data items and outputs a single index for all the items. Despite this structural difference, security definitions for both cases stay similar so that we only describe security models according to the above definition. Note that some of the schemes, such as that by Bao et al. (2008), support special properties, and we do not discuss them in detail here.

For an index-based SED scheme, regardless the setting (either symmetric or asymmetric), information leakage may come from three sources, namely index, trapdoor, and query results. Correspondingly, there are three types of privacy concerns, including index privacy, trapdoor privacy, and query result privacy.

- Index privacy, which means that indexes should not leak unnecessary information about the encoded keywords. Ideally, an index should be constructed in such a way that the server only learns whether the predicate in the trapdoor is satisfied or not in an execution of the Test algorithm. Intuitively, an index should not allow the server to recover the encoded keywords. However, how much information an index leaks in an execution of the Test algorithm also depends on how the trapdoor is constructed (or trapdoor privacy). Informally speaking, a trapdoor containing predicate in plaintext possibly may cause more information leakage than a trapdoor only containing encrypted keywords.
- Trapdoor privacy, which means that trapdoors should not leak unnecessary information about the encoded predicates. Ideally, in an execution of the Test algorithm, a trapdoor should only allow the server to tell whether the encoded predicate is satisfied by the index or not. For example, a trapdoor should not allow the server to recover the encoded predicate. Analogy to the statement in index privacy, the amount of information a trapdoor leaks in an execution of the Test algorithm also depends on whether the index privacy is achieved or not. Due to this dependency, index privacy and trapdoor privacy should be considered simultaneously.

- Query result privacy, which means that a search query should not leak unnecessary information about the searched results to the server. It is not difficult to imagine that, in a specific application scenario, the pattern of how a data item matches the client's search request can already leak some information about the data item. We elaborate on this in the fifth section.

With respect to all these privacy concerns, the adversary is an honest-but-curious (or, semi-honest) server, which will faithfully executing the protocol algorithms while they will also try to perform any operations possible to obtain private information. Essentially, the server will not deviate from the protocol specification in executing the Test algorithm to forge invalid results. Any outsider attacker is always less privileged than an honest-but-curious server, so that we will mention it only when it is necessary.

Among the security models available for SED in this setting, the security model by Shen et al. (2009) is the strongest one in the sense that it covers index privacy and trapdoor privacy simultaneously. However, none of them considers query result privacy. Formally, the definition is rephrased below.

Definition 1: An index-based SED scheme in the symmetric-setting is fully secure if no P.P.T. attacker has non-negligible advantage in the attack game defined in Figure 6. The attacker's advantage is defined to be $|\Pr[b = b'] - 1/2|$.

This definition simultaneously models index privacy and trapdoor privacy because the challenge contains both indexes and trapdoors. With respect to index privacy, the definition implies that an attacker cannot distinguish two index vectors of the same cardinality, namely

(BuildIndex(m1,0, K), BuildIndex(m2,0, K), ···),

(BuildIndex(m1,1, K), BuildIndex(m2,1, K), ···),

given that the available trapdoors perform identically between pairwise indexes from the two vectors. With respect to trapdoor privacy, the definition implies an attacker cannot distinguish two trapdoor vectors of the same cardinality, namely

(Trapdoor(f1,0, K), Trapdoor(f2,0, K), ···),

(Trapdoor(f1,1, K), Trapdoor(f2,1, K), ···),

Figure 6. Attack game

1. Setup. The challenger runs the *KeyGen* algorithm and obtains the secret key K, data space be **M**, and the predicate set **F**. The challenger publishes **M**, **F** and picks a random bit b.

2. Challenge. The attacker adaptively makes the following types of queries.

   - On the j-th index query, the attacker outputs two data items $m_{j,0}$, $m_{j,1} \in \mathbf{M}$, where $|u(m_{j,0})| = |u(m_{j,1})|$. The challenger responds with *BuildIndex*($m_{j,b}$, K).
   - On the i-th trapdoor query, the attacker outputs two predicates $f_{i,0}$, $f_{i,1} \in \mathbf{F}$. The challenger responds with *Trapdoor*($f_{i,b}$, K).

   The attacker's queries are subject to the restriction that, for all index queries $(m_{j,0}, m_{j,1})$ and all trapdoor queries $(f_{i,0}, f_{i,1})$, the following is true: $u(m_{j,0})$ satisfies $f_{i,0}$ if and only if $u(m_{j,1})$ satisfies $f_{i,1}$.

3. Guess. The attacker outputs a guess b′.

given that the pairwise trapdoors from the two vectors perform identically on the available indexes. The restriction stated in the attack game eliminates the attacker's trivial winning situations. To satisfy the above security definition for the inner product predicate, Shen et al. (2009) proposed a scheme by relying on bilinear pairings with composite-order groups, where the order is a product of four big prime numbers. So far, there is no implementation for such bilinear pairings, and the complexity is theoretically very high.

In the above definition, the value of Test(Tf, Im) directly tells whether u(m) satisfies the predicate f or not. As a result, it does not model query result privacy. The security model by Curtmola et al. (2006) provides similar security guarantee, although it is intended only for SED schemes that support an equality test predicate. The construction by Curtmola et al. (2006) employs an inverted index structure and uses padding to hide the number of data items associated with every keyword, and employs pseudorandom functions to provide the security. The security model by Bosch et al. (2012) covers all three privacy properties, but it is specifically designed for interactive SED schemes.

Full-Domain SED in Symmetric-Setting

Generally, a full-domain SED scheme in the symmetric-setting consists of the following polynomial-time algorithms.

- KeyGen(k): Run by the client, this algorithm takes a security parameter k as input, and outputs a secret key K. Let the data space be M and the predicate set be F.
- Encrypt(m, K): Run by the client, this algorithm takes a data item m ∈ M and the secret key K as input, and outputs a ciphertext Cm.
- Decrypt(Cm, K): Run by the client, this algorithm takes a ciphertext Cm and the secret key K as input, and outputs a plaintext m or an error message.
- Trapdoor(f, K): Run by the client, this algorithm takes a predicate f ∈ F and the secret key K as input, and outputs a trapdoor Tf.
- Test(Cm, Tf): Run by the server, this algorithm takes a ciphertext Cm and a trapdoor Tf as input, and outputs 1 if m satisfies f and 0 otherwise.

This definition is a generalization of those by Agrawal et al. (2004), Boldyreva et al. (2009), Goldreich and Ostrovsky (1996), Song et al. (2000), and Tang (2010). The definitions by Agrawal et al. (2004), Boldyreva et al. (2009), and Tang (2010) do not have Trapdoor and Test algorithms, because the order of ciphertexts is identical to the order of encrypted data items in the formulations by Agrawal et al. (2004) and Boldyreva et al. (2009) and there is a public function any entity can run to compute the order of the plaintexts in any ciphertexts in the formulation by Tang (2010).

For a full-domain SED scheme in either symmetric-setting or asymmetric-setting, information leakage may come from three sources, including ciphertext, trapdoor, and query results. Correspondingly, there are three types of privacy concerns, including ciphertext privacy, trapdoor privacy, and query result privacy. Ciphertext privacy means that indexes should not leak unnecessary information about the encoded data items, the other two types of privacy properties are similar to those for an index-based SED scheme described in the fourth section.

- The aim of Song et al. (2000) is to design a SED scheme with some level of ciphertext privacy and trapdoor privacy, although the security analysis is not done through a well-defined security model. It is clearly stated that query result privacy is not an intended property. The proposed scheme relies on pseudorandom functions and symmetric-key encryption schemes.

- For the security models by Agrawal et al. (2004), Boldyreva et al. (2009), and Tang (2010), trapdoor privacy is not a concern since there is no trapdoor, and query result privacy is not the aim. As to ciphertext privacy, the security models guarantees that only the ordering of the data items is leaked from the ciphertexts. The proposed scheme by Agrawal et al. (2004) uses some bucketization technique, the proposed scheme by Boldyreva et al. (2009) uses block ciphers, and the proposed schemes by Tang (2010) use bilinear pairings.
- The security model by Goldreich and Ostrovsky (1996) can cover all privacy concerns, although it is not explicitly designed for SED.

Index-Based SED in Asymmetric-Setting

Generally, an index-based SED scheme in the asymmetric-setting consists of the following polynomial-time algorithms.

- KeyGen(k): Run by the client, this algorithm takes a security parameter k as input and generates a public/private key pair (PKr, SKr). Let the data space be M and the predicate set be F.
- Tag(m, PKr): Run by a sender, this algorithm takes a data item $m \in M$ and the public key PKr as input and outputs an index Im which encodes a set of keywords u(m) for m. Let |u(m)| be the cardinality of the set u(m).
- Trapdoor(f, SKr): Run by the client, this algorithm takes a predicate $f \in F$ and the private key SKr as input, and outputs a trapdoor Tf.
- Test(Im, Tf, PKr): Run by the server, this algorithm takes an index Im, a trapdoor Tf, and the client's public key PKr as input, and outputs 1 if u(m) satisfies f and 0 otherwise.

This definition is a generalization of those from Baek et al. (2006, 2008), Boneh et al. (2004), Boneh et al. (2007), Boneh and Waters (2007), Hwang and Lee (2007), Iovino and Persiano (2008), Katz et al. (2008), Rhee et al. (2010), Tang and Chen (2009), and Zhang and Imai (2007). Nevertheless, some of the schemes, such as those by Baek et al. (2008), Rhee et al. (2010), Tang and Chen (2009), and Zhang and Imai (2007), support special properties, and we do not discuss them in detail here.

As stated in the fourth section, a SED scheme in this setting has the same privacy concerns, namely index privacy, trapdoor privacy, and query result privacy. Similarly, an honest-but-curious server is regarded as the attacker in the security models. Below, we rephrase the definitions by Boneh and Waters (2007), Iovino and Persiano (2008), and Katz et al. (2008) to this generalized SED definition.

Definition 2: An index-based SED scheme in the asymmetric-setting is secure if no P.P.T. attacker has non-negligible advantage in the attack game defined in Figure 7. The attacker's advantage is defined to be $|\Pr[b = b'] - 1/2|$.

In the above attack game, if we let u(m) contain only one keyword and the predicate be equality test one described at the beginning of this section, then it is identical to the security definition for PEKS. As to the construction of SED schemes in this category, most existing schemes make use of bilinear pairings, and use the bilinear property to perform search operations.

This definition only models index privacy, while without explicitly touching upon trapdoor privacy. Given a trapdoor, it is unclear how much information the attacker can learn about

Figure 7. Attack game

1. Setup. The challenger runs the *KeyGen* algorithm and obtains a key pair (PK_r, SK_r), the data space be **M**, and the predicate set **F**. The challenger publishes **M**, **F** and PK_r .
2. Phase 1. The attacker adaptively makes *Trapdoor* queries. For a *Trapdoor* query with the predicate f, the challenger responds with *Trapdoor*(f, SK_r). At some point, the attacker outputs two data items m_0 and m_1, where $|u(m_0)| = |u(m_1)|$. In this phase, the attacker's queries are subject to the following restriction: for any trapdoor query with the input f, $u(m_0)$ satisfies f if and only if $u(m_1)$ satisfies f.
3. Challenge. The challenger chooses $b \in_R \{0,1\}$ and responds with the challenge $I_{mb} = \text{Tag}(m_b, PK_r)$.
4. Phase 2. The attacker can issue the same type of queries as in Phase 1, subject to the same restriction.
5. Guess. The attacker outputs a guess b'.

the encoded keywords in a secure SED scheme under this definition. For example, in the PEKS construction by Boneh et al. (2004), the trapdoor is a deterministic function of the keyword, while, in the constructions by Fuhr and Paillier (2007) and Hofheinz and Weinreb (2008), the server can recover the keyword in any trapdoor. Among all security models, the model by Rhee et al. (2010) considers trapdoor privacy against an outsider attacker but not an honest-but-curious server. Boneh et al. (2007) assume a very special setting for SED where all algorithms except for KeyGen can be interactive protocols, and the security model covers all three privacy properties. Due to its special setting, the security model does not fit other SED schemes.

Full-Domain SED in Asymmetric-Setting

Generally, a full-domain SED scheme in the asymmetric-setting consists of the following polynomial-time algorithms.

- KeyGen(k): Run by the client, this algorithm takes a security parameter k as input, and and generates a public/private key pair (PKr, SKr). Let the message space be M and the predicate set be F.
- Encrypt(m, PKr): Run by the client, this algorithm takes a data item m ∈ M and the public key PKr as input, and outputs a ciphertext Cm.
- Decrypt(Cm, SKr): Run by the client, this algorithm takes a ciphertext Cm and the private key SKr as input, and outputs a plaintext m or an error message.
- Trapdoor(f, SKr): Run by the client, this algorithm takes a predicate f ∈ F and the private key SKr as input, and outputs a trapdoor Tf.
- Test(Cm, Tf, PKr): Run by the server, this algorithm takes a ciphertext Cm, a trapdoor Tf, and the client's public key PKr as input, and outputs 1 if m satisfies f and 0 otherwise.

This definition is a generalization of those by Bellare et al. (2007), Ibraimi et al. (2011), Tang (2011, 2012a, 2012b), and Yang et al. (2010), but the specific definitions differ in certain aspects and provide different security guarantees.

- In the definition by Bellare et al. (2007), the Trapdoor algorithm takes only the predicate and the public key as input; therefore any entity can generate a trapdoor. Under this definition, a SED scheme can only achieve an enhanced version of one-wayness. The enhancement means, in addition to prevent an attacker from recovering the plaintexts, ciphertexts also hide other characteristic information of the plaintexts. The proposed schemes can be realized based on a public-key encryption scheme and a hash function in the encrypt-then-hash manner.
- In the definition by Ibraimi et al. (2011), the predicate set is the equality test one. There are two trapdoor functions: one is similar to the one in the above definition for generating item-dependent trapdoors, and the other is for generating master trapdoors. Correspondingly, there are two Test functions: one is based on an item-dependent trapdoor to test whether the item in the trapdoor is identical to that in a ciphertext, and the other is based on a master trapdoor to test whether a ciphertext contain any chosen plaintext data item. Note that both Test functions need to take a master trapdoor as input. As to security, one-wayness property is defined in the presence of an honest-but curious server, while ciphertext privacy and trapdoor privacy are defined against an outside attacker. The proposed scheme makes use of bilinear pairings in the asymmetric setting.
- In the definition by Yang et al. (2010), there is no Trapdoor function required and the Test function takes two ciphertexts as input. In the definitions by Tang (2011, 2012a, 2012b), the Trapdoor function is replaced with an authorization function Aut which allows two clients to generate an authorization token. Correspondingly, the Test function takes two ciphertexts and a token as input. The security models by Tang (2011, 2012a, 2012b) give better security control to the clients, in contrast to that by Yang et al. (2010) where clients have no security control at all. All these schemes make use of bilinear pairings.

PRACTICALITY ANALYSIS

In the plaintext case, both full-domain search and index-based search can be easily implemented and they are usually supported at the same time. However, according to the discussions in the third section, existing SED schemes are much more constrained in this perspective so that they may not satisfy the needs of the practical application scenarios, such as those described in the second section. As to security, the analysis in the fourth section has shown that most SED schemes do not achieve the strongest security we may hope for from a theoretical perspective. Moreover, we will show below that, even in the existing strongest security models, a SED scheme may still put a client's privacy at risk in reality.

Analysis of Full-Domain SED Schemes

For full-domain SED schemes, the first practical concern is the encryption block size, due to the fact that encryption techniques, either symmetric or asymmetric, only take a binary string of certain length as input. This means that a data item is potentially needed to be split into blocks before encryption is done in a block-wise manner. For instance, in the SED scheme by Song et al. (2000), every word is treated as a block and only exactly matching is supported. In order to support search in a fuzzy manner, the data item may need to be encrypted letter-wise instead of word-wise. Referring to the analysis by Song et al. (2000), the downgrade of encryption granularity may result in additional security issues, such as more severe statistical analysis. In practice, the encryption block size will not only be limited by the encryption algorithms, it also depends on the search criteria to be supported. Moreover, considering the personal database outsourcing scenario in the second section and the Internet-based PHR scenario, there can be many different types of data items such as photos, videos, and audios. How to support a variety of search criteria on different types of data items without further deteriorating security and efficiency is an interesting research question.

Another concern is the computational and storage efficiency, in particular for SED schemes in the asymmetric-setting. For the schemes by Ibraimi et al. (2011), Tang (2011, 2012a, 2012b), and Yang et al. (2010), suppose that encryption is required word-wise for a data item with x words, then the encryption will take O(x) public key operations (e.g. exponentiation and pairing) and the storage may become significantly larger than the plaintext case. The more severe efficiency bottleneck lies in the fact that every search request in a single encrypted data item will also take O(x) operations, which may be overwhelming for a data item of moderate size. In contrast, if the SED scheme by Bellare et al. (2007) is used, a search only requires logarithmic number of integer comparisons. But the downside is that the scheme achieves only a somewhat one-wayness property.

Yet another concern is that, for the schemes by Tang (2011, 2012a, 2012b), and Yang et al. (2010) and one scheme by Bellare et al. (2007) in the asymmetric setting, the encryption of every data block contains two parts: one part is a standard encryption used for data recovery, the other part is an encryption of a checksum of the data block used for searching. This structural construction may result in a linkability problem, in which a malicious sender may put a bogus checksum for a data block. We will discuss this problem in more detail for index-based search in the asymmetric-setting in next subsection.

Analysis of Index-Based SED Schemes

In contrast to full-domain SED schemes, index-based SED schemes face other challenges although they suffer less from the above concerns. The index for a data item is constructed based on the related keywords. For many applications, such as the personal database outsourcing scenario and the email routing scenario, it is likely that the keyword space is of limited size and the distribution of keywords is non-uniform. Moreover, the keyword set might be public knowledge. These factors may result in some security issues.

- By observing the client's search results, the server may infer the embedded keywords in search queries and the keyword information in the indexes. For instance, if a lot of search queries match the same index, then the server can infer that the index contains some keywords which have high distribution probabilities in the keyword set. To prevent the information leakage, the property of query result privacy is required.
- SED schemes in the asymmetric-setting are generally vulnerable to the offline message recovery attack and existing solutions such as those by Baek et al. (2008), Tang and Chen (2009), and Tang (2011, 2012b) suffer from efficiency and usability problems, as we have mentioned in the third section. Regardless the aforementioned solutions, how to practically solve this issue is still an open problem.

Another concern is information leakage from indexes. Take the forward index shown in Figure 2 in the third section as an example, suppose a SED scheme straightforwardly encrypts both the data items and their associated keywords. The server and any other entity can notice how many keywords are associated with each data item, and they may infer that the more keywords a data item has the more important it is to the client. The schemes by Boneh and Waters (2007) and Hwang and Lee (2007) suffer from this problem. The scheme by Chang and Mitzenmacher (2005) mitigates this problem by using a pre-defined and fixed dictionary of size x, and every index contains x bit showing whether each keyword is in the related data item or not. In the scheme by Goh (2003), it is required to estimate the upper bound of the possible keywords from all data items, and then random values will be added in every index to hide keyword occurrence differences. For the inverted index shown in Figure 3 in the third section, if a SED scheme encrypts straightforwardly the keywords and their associated data items. Then, the server and any other entity know how many data items are associated to each keyword, and they may infer that the popularity of encrypted keywords. The issue becomes more obvious when the keywords are from a set of limited size and are not uniformly distributed. To mitigate the problem, a SED scheme such as that by Curtmola et al. (2006) may try to add dummy values to the pad the indexes in the case of forward index or to pad item identifiers in the case of inverted index. Unfortunately, this mitigation measure may cause issues when the indexes need to be updated (e.g. new data items or new keywords to be added).

Yet another concern is the linkability issue between the data items and their indexes. In more detail, the potential problem is that a malicious party can try to generate contents and indexes in a malicious manner in order to gain some benefits. Here, the malicious party refers to any entity except for the receiver and the server, which will often be regarded as semi-trusted in practice. We illustrate an attack by taking the email routing scenario described in the second section and a PEKS scheme by Boneh et al. (2004) as example. In this scenario, any sender can send encrypted messages to the client and attached encrypted keywords to every message, and later on search can be done based on the encrypted keywords and message retrieval follows. In this situation, some message senders can always encrypt the keyword "urgent" and attach it to the spams so that the client always retrieve the spams with a higher priority. All existing index-based SED schemes in the asymmetric-setting may suffer from this problem. Note that this problem falls beyond all existing security models. A straightforward countermeasure is to combine an index-based scheme with a full-domain scheme so that the server can filter the encrypted data items to identify malicious contents. However, it is an open problem to design a more elegant solution. In contrast, in the symmetric-setting, this may not be a problem because the client will generate the searchable contents by himself so that no third-party entities will be allowed to contribute anything.

In addition, for index-based SED schemes, how to update indexes has not been discussed much even though they are very practical issues in deploying SED schemes. For these schemes using a forward index structure, updating may be quite straightforward. But it may be more complicated for those using inverted index structures, since straightforwardly adding new index information to old indexes will leak information to the server. Chang and Mitzenmacher (2005) and Curtmola et al. (2006) proposed methods to add new indexes, which will be generated based on new secret keys. As a result, old trapdoors cannot be used to search new indexes and it will result in different groups of indexes which can be only searched by certain trapdoors (generated based on different secret keys). This approach may cause problems in key management and search flexibility in reality.

More General Issues

Referring to the application scenarios described in the second section, we have mentioned that the client may want a SED scheme which supports queries with flexible search criteria. For instance, exact matching, fuzzy matching, and conjunctive keywords should be supported at the same time. To our knowledge, no existing index-based SED scheme can provide this functionality. Generally speaking, almost all SED schemes only support certain types of search criteria. In order to support a variety of search criteria, the only way is to encrypt the data items with several SED schemes simultaneously, each of them is used for some search criteria. Besides the obvious increase in storage, this approach may result in additional information leakage because the server will learn some search pattern information (i.e. which search criteria has been invoked).

For most SED schemes other than those by Baek et al. (2008), Ibraimi et al. (2011), and Kerschbaum and Sorniotti (2011) if an outsider attacker can eavesdrop on the transmission of encrypted contents and trapdoors, then it is as privileged as the server so that it may infer a lot of private information about the client. In the schemes by Baek et al. (2008) and Kerschbaum and Sorniotti (2011), the searchable contents are protected between message senders and the server. Clearly, this approach is very inflexible and not practical, because the client should trust all message senders who may not have the motivation to treat the issue seriously. In the scheme by Ibraimi et al. (2011), the trapdoor transmission from the client to the server is encrypted so that an outsider attacker cannot obtain a useful trapdoor. However, the attacker may still eavesdrop on other communications such as the transmission of the search results, and it can still learn a lot about the index and trapdoor as shown by Tang and Chen (2009).

Except in the schemes by Boneh et al. (2009) and Goldreich and Ostrovsky (1996), query result privacy has not been touched upon in SED schemes, although it is a practical concern for many underlying application scenarios such as the personal database outsourcing scenario described in the second section. For a more concrete example, suppose that Alice stores both her work-related documents and personal documents on a remote server protected by a SED scheme. Moreover, she only queries her work-related documents in her office, and queries personal documents at home. One day, if the server notices at 10:00 pm that Alice is querying the same document as that she queried at 11:00 am, and then the server can guess that Alice is working over the time in her office (it is likely that nobody is in her house). Due to the fact that the server is allowed to know the search results in existing SED schemes, there is no straightforward enhancement to provide query result privacy.

Besides confidentiality, data integrity (or, more specifically operation correct-ness) is another serious concern in practice, such as in all the scenarios described in the second section. Due to a lot of reasons, a server may try to provide an incomplete or wrong result to the client. For example, the server may try to search 10 percent of the database in order to save computing resources. Another situation is that if some of the client's data has been lost, the server may try to provide some wrong result to the client to hide the truth. For data outsourcing in general, the concept of proof of retrievability or proof of storage has been investigated, such as the work by Ateniese, Kamara, and Katz (2009), Bowers, Juels, and Oprea (2009), and Shacham and Waters (2008). But, specifically for SED, there has not been rigorous treatment although it is informally investigated by Chai and Gong (2011). The investigation of data integrity in SED setting is an open research area.

CONCLUSION

In this chapter, we have categorized the existing SED schemes, reviewed their security models, and provided some practicality analysis. The brief analysis has showed that there are a lot of potential security issues facing SED schemes which are provably secure in their respective security models. How to resolve these identified issues may be interesting theoretical work in the future. Besides, there are other interesting future research directions. One is that a lot of experimental research work is needed to advance the research in the area of SED, despite very few efforts so far such as that by Pappas et al. (2011). Without real-world implementations, it is difficult to evaluate and compare the performances of existing SED schemes. The other is that, all algorithms are non-interactive in most of the definitions of SED, and it is interesting to investigate the case of allowing some algorithms to be interactive. On one hand, non-interactive algorithms are preferable than interactive ones because they do not require additional interactions between the client and the server. On the other hand, the requirement of non-interactive algorithms results in intensive usage of complicated structures (e.g. pairing operations) to have provable secure SED schemes. In addition, as shown by Boneh et al. (2009) and Bosch et al. (2012), allowing interactive algorithms can enable a SED scheme to achieve stronger privacy guarantees. Along this direction, it is also interesting to investigate the trade-off between the computational efficiency and communication efficiency.

REFERENCES

Agrawal, R., Kiernan, J., Srikant, R., & Xu, Y. (2004). Order preserving encryption for numeric data. In Proceedings of the 2004 ACM SIGMOD International Conference on Management of Data, (pp. 563–574). ACM.

Ateniese, G., Kamara, S., & Katz, J. (2009). Proofs of storage from homomorphic identification protocols. *Lecture Notes in Computer Science*, *5912*, 319–333. doi:10.1007/978-3-642-10366-7_19.

Baek, J., Safavi-Naini, R., & Susilo, W. (2006). On the integration of public key data encryption and public key encryption with keyword search. *Lecture Notes in Computer Science*, *4176*, 217–232. doi:10.1007/11836810_16.

Baek, J., Safavi-Naini, R., & Susilo, W. (2008). Public key encryption with keyword search revisited. *Lecture Notes in Computer Science*, *5072*, 1249–1259. doi:10.1007/978-3-540-69839-5_96.

Bao, F., Deng, R. H., Ding, X., & Yang, Y. (2008). Private query on encrypted data in multi-user settings. *Lecture Notes in Computer Science*, *4991*, 71–85. doi:10.1007/978-3-540-79104-1_6.

Bellare, M., Boldyreva, A., & O'Neill, A. (2007). Deterministic and efficiently searchable encryption. *Lecture Notes in Computer Science*, *4622*, 535–552. doi:10.1007/978-3-540-74143-5_30.

Boldyreva, A., Chenette, N., Lee, Y., & O'Neill, A. (2009). Order-preserving symmetric encryption. *Lecture Notes in Computer Science*, *5479*, 224–241. doi:10.1007/978-3-642-01001-9_13.

Boneh, D., Di Crescenzo, G., Ostrovsky, R., & Persiano, G. (2004). Public key encryption with keyword search. *Lecture Notes in Computer Science*, *3027*, 506–522. doi:10.1007/978-3-540-24676-3_30.

Boneh, D., Kushilevitz, E., Ostrovsky, R., & Skeith, W. E. III. (2007). Public key encryption that allows PIR queries. *Lecture Notes in Computer Science*, *4622*, 50–67. doi:10.1007/978-3-540-74143-5_4.

Boneh, D., Sahai, A., & Waters, B. (2011). Functional encryption: Definitions and challenges. *Lecture Notes in Computer Science*, *6597*, 253–273. doi:10.1007/978-3-642-19571-6_16.

Boneh, D., & Waters, B. (2007). Conjunctive, subset, and range queries on encrypted data. *Lecture Notes in Computer Science*, *4392*, 535–554. doi:10.1007/978-3-540-70936-7_29.

Bosch, C., Tang, Q., Hartel, P., & Jonker, W. (2012). Selective document retrieval from encrypted databse. *Lecture Notes in Computer Science*, *7483*, 224–241. doi:10.1007/978-3-642-33383-5_14.

Bowers, K. D., Juels, A., & Oprea, A. (2009). Proofs of retrievability: Theory and implementation. In Proceedings of the 2009 ACM Workshop on Cloud Computing Security, (pp. 43–54). ACM Press.

Byun, J. W., Rhee, H. S., Park, H., & Lee, D. H. (2006). Off-line keyword guessing attacks on recent keyword search schemes over encrypted data. *Lecture Notes in Computer Science*, *4165*, 75–83. doi:10.1007/11844662_6.

Chai, Q., & Gong, G. (2011). *Verifiable symmetric searchable encryption for semi-honest-but-curious cloud services. Technical Report CACR 2011-22*. Ontario, Canada: University of Waterloo.

Chang, Y., & Mitzenmacher, M. (2005). Privacy preserving keyword searches on remote encrypted data. *Lecture Notes in Computer Science*, *3531*, 442–455. doi:10.1007/11496137_30.

Chase, M., & Kamara, S. (2010). Structured encryption and controlled disclosure. *Lecture Notes in Computer Science*, *6477*, 577–594. doi:10.1007/978-3-642-17373-8_33.

Curtmola, R., Garay, J., Kamara, S., & Ostrovsky, R. (2006). Searchable symmetric encryption: Improved definitions and efficient constructions. In Proceedings of the 13th ACM Conference on Computer and Communications Security, (pp. 79–88). ACM.

Fuhr, T., & Paillier, P. (2007). Decryptable searchable encryption. *Lecture Notes in Computer Science*, *4784*, 228–236. doi:10.1007/978-3-540-75670-5_17.

Goh, E. J. (2003). Secure indexes. Technical Report 216. IACR.

Goldreich, O., & Ostrovsky, R. (1996). Software protection and simulation on oblivious RAMs. *Journal of the ACM*, *43*(3), 431–473. doi:10.1145/233551.233553.

Golle, P., Staddon, J., & Waters, B. (2004). Secure conjunctive keyword search over encrypted data. *Lecture Notes in Computer Science*, *3089*, 31–45. doi:10.1007/978-3-540-24852-1_3.

Hofheinz, D., & Weinreb, E. (2008). Searchable encryption with decryption in the standard model. Retrieved from http://eprint.iacr.org/2008/423

Hore, B., Mehrotra, S., Canim, M., & Kantarcioglu, M. (2012). Secure multidimensional range queries over outsourced data. *The VLDB Journal*, *21*(3), 333–358. doi:10.1007/s00778-011-0245-7.

Hwang, Y. H., & Lee, P. J. (2007). Public key encryption with conjunctive keyword search and its extension to a multi-user system. *Lecture Notes in Computer Science*, *4575*, 2–22. doi:10.1007/978-3-540-73489-5_2.

Ibraimi, L., Nikova, S., Hartel, P. H., & Jonker, W. (2011). Public-key encryption with delegated search. *Lecture Notes in Computer Science*, *6715*, 532–549. doi:10.1007/978-3-642-21554-4_31.

Iovino, V., & Persiano, G. (2008). Hidden-vector encryption with groups of prime order. *Lecture Notes in Computer Science*, *5209*, 75–88. doi:10.1007/978-3-540-85538-5_5.

Islam, M., Kuzu, M., & Kantarcioglu, M. (2012). Access pattern disclosure on searchable encryption: Ramification, attack and mitigation. In Proceedings of the Network and Distributed System Security Symposium, NDSS 2012. NDSS.

Katz, J., Sahai, A., & Waters, B. (2008). Predicate encryption supporting disjunctions, polynomial equations, and inner products. *Lecture Notes in Computer Science*, *4965*, 146–162. doi:10.1007/978-3-540-78967-3_9.

Kerschbaum, F., & Sorniotti, A. (2011). Searchable encryption for outsourced data analytics. *Lecture Notes in Computer Science*, *6711*, 61–76. doi:10.1007/978-3-642-22633-5_5.

Kuzu, M., Islam, M., Mohammad, S., & Kantarcioglu, M. (2012). Efficient similarity search over encrypted data. In Proceedings of the 2012 IEEE 28th International Conference on Data Engineering, (pp. 1156–1167). IEEE Computer Society.

Pappas, V., Raykova, M., Vo, B., Bellovin, S. M., & Malkin, T. (2011). Private search in the real world. In Proceedings of the 27th Annual Computer Security Applications Conference, (pp. 83–92). ACM.

Raykova, M., Cui, A., Vo, B., Liu, B., Malkin, T., Bellovin, S. M., & Stolfo, S. J. (2012). Usable, secure, private search. *IEEE Security & Privacy*, *10*, 53–60.

Rhee, H. S., Park, J. H., Susilo, W., & Lee, D. H. (2010). Trapdoor security in a searchable public-key encryption scheme with a designated tester. *Journal of Systems and Software*, *83*(5), 763–771. doi:10.1016/j.jss.2009.11.726.

Shacham, H., & Waters, B. (2008). Compact proofs of retrievability. *Lecture Notes in Computer Science*, *5350*, 90–107. doi:10.1007/978-3-540-89255-7_7.

Shen, E., Shi, E., & Waters, B. (2009). Predicate privacy in encryption systems. *Lecture Notes in Computer Science*, *5444*, 457–473. doi:10.1007/978-3-642-00457-5_27.

Song, D. X., Wagner, D., & Perrig, A. (2000). Practical techniques for searches on encrypted data. In Proceedings of the IEEE Symposium on Security and Privacy, (pp. 44–55). IEEE Computer Society.

Tang, Q. (2010). Privacy preserving mapping schemes supporting comparison. In Proceedings of the 2010 ACM workshop on Cloud Computing Security Workshop, (pp. 53–58). ACM Press.

Tang, Q. (2011). Towards public key encryption scheme supporting equality test with fine-grained authorization. *Lecture Notes in Computer Science*, *6812*, 389–406. doi:10.1007/978-3-642-22497-3_25.

Tang, Q. (2012a). Public key encryption schemes supporting equality test with authorization of different granularity. *International Journal of Applied Cryptography*, *2*(4), 304–321. doi:10.1504/IJACT.2012.048079.

Tang, Q. (2012b). Public key encryption supporting plaintext equality test and user-specified authorization. In *Security and Communication Networks*. New York, NY: Wiley. doi:10.1002/sec.418.

Tang, Q., & Chen, L. (2009). Public-key encryption with registered keyword search. *Lecture Notes in Computer Science*, *6391*, 163–178. doi:10.1007/978-3-642-16441-5_11.

Yang, G., Tan, C., Huang, Q., & Wong, D. S. (2010). Probabilistic public key encryption with equality test. *Lecture Notes in Computer Science*, *5985*, 119–131. doi:10.1007/978-3-642-11925-5_9.

Zhang, R., & Imai, H. (2007). Generic combination of public key encryption with keyword search and public key encryption. *Lecture Notes in Computer Science*, *4521*, 159–174. doi:10.1007/978-3-540-76969-9_11.

ADDITIONAL READING

Atallah, M. J., Pantazopoulos, K. N., Rice, J. R., & Spafford, E. H. (2001). Secure outsourcing of scientific computations. *Advances in Computers*, *54*, 216–272.

Ballard, L., Green, M., de Medeiros, M., & Monrose, F. (2005). Correlation-resistant storage via keyword-searchable encryption. Report 2005/417. Cryptology ePrint Archive.

Blum, M., Luby, M., & Rubinfeld, R. (1991). Program result checking against adaptive programs and in cryptographic settings. In *Discrete Mathematics and Theoretical Computer Science* (pp. 107–118). DIMACS.

Boneh, D., & Franklin, M. K. (2001). Identity-based encryption from the Weil pairing. *Lecture Notes in Computer Science, 2139*, 213–229. doi:10.1007/3-540-44647-8_13.

Byun, J. W., Lee, D. H., & Lim, J. (2006). Efficient conjunctive keyword search on encrypted data storage system. *Lecture Notes in Computer Science, 4043*, 184–196. doi:10.1007/11774716_15.

Fang, L., Wang, J., Ge, C., & Ren, Y. (2010). Decryptable public key encryption with keyword search schemes. Journal of Digital Content Technology and its Applications, 4(9), 141–150.

Gennaro, R., Gentry, C., & Parno, B. (2010). Non-interactive verifiable computing: Outsourcing computation to untrusted workers. *Lecture Notes in Computer Science, 6223*, 465–482. doi:10.1007/978-3-642-14623-7_25.

Girault, M., & Lefranc, D. (2005). Server-aided verification: Theory and practice. *Lecture Notes in Computer Science, 3788*, 605–623. doi:10.1007/11593447_33.

Goldwasser, S., Kalai, Y. T., & Rothblum, G. N. (2008). Delegating computation: Interactive proofs for muggles. In Proceedings of the ACM Symposium on the Theory of Computing (STOC), (pp. 113–122). ACM Press.

Hwang, Y. H., & Lee, P. J. (2007). Public key encryption with conjunctive keyword search and its extension to a multi-user system. *Lecture Notes in Computer Science, 4575*, 2–22. doi:10.1007/978-3-540-73489-5_2.

Jeong, I. R., Kwon, J., Hong, D., & Lee, D. H. (2009). Constructing peks schemes secure against keyword guessing attacks is possible? *Computer Communications, 32*(2), 394–396. doi:10.1016/j.comcom.2008.11.018.

Khader, D. (2006). Public key encryption with keyword search based on k-resilient IBE. *Lecture Notes in Computer Science, 3982*, 298–308. doi:10.1007/11751595_33.

Park, D. J., Kim, K., & Lee, P. J. (2004). Public key encryption with conjunctive field keyword search. *Lecture Notes in Computer Science, 3325*, 73–86. doi:10.1007/978-3-540-31815-6_7.

Parno, B., Raykova, M., & Vaikuntanathan, V. (2012). How to delegate and verify in public: Verifiable computation from attribute-based encryption. *Lecture Notes in Computer Science, 7194*, 422–439. doi:10.1007/978-3-642-28914-9_24.

Ristenpart, T., Tromer, E., Shacham, H., & Savage, S. (2009). Hey, you, get off of my cloud: Exploring information leakage in third-party compute clouds. In Proceedings of the 16th ACM Conference on Computer and Communications Security, (pp. 199–212). ACM.

Shi, E., Bethencourt, J., Chan, H. T.-H., Song, D. X., & Perrig, A. (2007). Multi-dimensional range query over encrypted data. In Proceedings of the 2007 IEEE Symposium on Security and Privacy, (pp. 350–364). IEEE Computer Society.

Yao, A. (1982). Protocols for secure computations (extended abstract). In Proceedings of the 23rd Annual Symposium on Foundations of Computer Science, (pp. 160–164). IEEE.

KEY TERMS AND DEFINITIONS

Data Security: It means protecting a database from destructive forces and the unwanted actions of unauthorized users.

Database Index: It is a data structure that improves the speed of data retrieval operations on a database table at the cost of slower writes and increased storage space.

Encryption: It is the process of encoding messages in such a way that eavesdroppers or hackers cannot read it, but that authorized parties can.

Information Leakage: It happens whenever a system that is designed to be closed to an eavesdropper reveals some information to unauthorized parties nonetheless.

Outsourcing: It is the contracting out of a business process, which an organization may have previously performed internally or has a new need for, to an independent organization from which the process is purchased back as a service.

Personal Health Record: It is a health record where health data and information related to the care of a patient is maintained by the patient.

Searchable Encryption: It is a special type of encryption, where an authorized party can search in the ciphertexts.

Section 2
Cryptographic Systems

Chapter 5
Encryption Schemes with Hyper-Complex Number Systems and Their Hardware-Oriented Implementation

Evgueni Doukhnitch
Istanbul Aydin University, Turkey

Alexander G. Chefranov
Eastern Mediterranean University, North Cyprus

Ahmed Mahmoud
Al-Azhar University-Gaza, Palestine

ABSTRACT

Quaternion Encryption Scheme (QES) is shown to be susceptible to the Known Plaintext-Ciphertext Attack (KPCA) due to improper choice of frame size and the procedure of secret quaternion updating. In this chapter, the authors propose a modification of the QES (M-QES) that is resistant to the KPCA. The M-QES is based on adjusting the frame size and the quaternion update procedure. An approach for effective hardware implementation of the proposed algorithm, HW-QES, is discussed. The HW-QES uses addition and shift operations. Extension of quaternion approach to another hyper-complex number systems, octonions, is used for designing a new hardware-oriented encryption algorithm, HW-OES. Experimental results show that the proposed M-QES and HW-QES are six-eight times more effective in the encryption quality of signals than the original QES. Additionally, M-QES and HW-OES are shown to be significantly more effective in the encryption quality of images than the original QES and well-known AES. The results show that the performance of the HW-QES is only 10% worse than that of QES.

DOI: 10.4018/978-1-4666-4030-6.ch005

INTRODUCTION

There are two hyper-complex number systems which are used in modern encryption systems: quaternions and octonions (Ward, 1997). The quaternion number system was discovered by a physicist Hamilton (1843) (Hamilton, 1847); it is an extension of the complex number system (so called hyper complex number). It has two parts, a scalar part and a vector part which is a vector in three-dimensional space $\Re^3$. Since the introduction of quaternion, it has been applied in several areas in computer science and engineering problems such as graphics and robotics (Kuipers 1999; Marins et al., 2001). It can be used to control rotations in three-dimensional space. The application of the quaternion number system is attractive in computation models due to its matrix representation. It has been applied as a mathematical model in encryption by several researchers. In (Nagase et al., 2004, 2005), a new Quaternion Encryption Scheme (QES) is proposed for signal encryption providing good hiding properties.

The octonion (Cayley numbers or octaves) number system was suggested by John T. Graves (1843) and discovered by Arthur Cayley (1845) (Ward, 1997). An octonion has two parts, a scalar part and a vector part which is a vector in seven-dimensional space $\Re^7$. It is used in physics for 8-D rotation description and for quaternion valued matrix decomposition (Doukhnitch & Ozen, 2011). Recently in (Malekian & Zakerolhosseini, 2010), new encryption schemes based on non-associative octonion algebra were proposed for signal encryption with better security against lattice attack and/or more capability for protocol design.

Hyper-complex number based ciphers are attractive not only because they may be represented using matrix-vector multiplication but also that the inverse matrix for such transformation is a transpose of the original matrix. Matrix operations are rather simple and can be efficiently implemented that is especially important for multimedia data transmission.

The QES works as follows. A sequence of signal samples is arranged as a sequence of frames containing three three-component vectors, represented as a 3x3 matrix B, i-th column B_i of which is the i-th mentioned above sample-vector ($i = \overline{1,3}$). Each vector B_i in a frame is encrypted by applying to it one and the same transformation represented by its multiplication from one side by some quaternion q and from the other side by its inverse q^{-1} producing the ciphertext vector B_i'

$$B_i' = q^{-1}B_i q, i = \overline{1,3}, \tag{1}$$

or, in the terms of plaintext-ciphertext matrices, (1) may be rewritten as

$$B' = q^{-1}Bq, \tag{2}$$

where $B' = (B_1', B_2', B_3')$. Transformation (2) may be also represented using matrix multiplication of the plaintext matrix B by a secret key matrix depending on q and producing the ciphertext matrix B'. It was expected that QES provides high security due to using dynamic key matrix obtained by changing the next quaternion components. But, this algorithm is a particular case of the well-known Hill cipher (HC) (Stallings, 2006). The HC is susceptible to the Known Plaintext-Ciphertext Attack (KPCA); therefore, QES can be broken with the KPCA, and the secret key matrix can be obtained.

One aim of the paper is to show that QES is susceptible to KPCA and to overcome (repair) this weakness of QES. To improve QES security, we propose a QES modification (M-QES) resistant to the KPCA by adjusting the frame size and the quaternion update procedure. In addition, hardware-oriented implementation of the QES modification (HW-QES) is proposed based on the ideas from (Doukhnitch & Ozen, 2011; Hsiao & Delosme, 1994). To give adequate performance comparison, we also examined the proposed QES modifications versus original QES and well-known AES (Stalling, 2006) for signal and image encryption.

Another aim of the paper is to extend the ideas of HW-QES algorithm to designing octonion encryption algorithms (OES and HW-OES) for signals and color image encryption.

The rest of the paper is organized as follows. We introduce main notions for quaternion and provide necessary details for QES. Then we show that actually QES is susceptible to the known plaintext-ciphertext attack. Next section is devoted to the proposed M-QES resistant to the KPCA. Next we give a description of the effective hardware-oriented proposed HW-QES using mainly operations of addition and shift. OES and HW-OES are suggested in the next section. Then we give experimental results of signal and image encryption quality and the performance of the proposed methods versus the original QES and AES. Statistical analysis and cryptanalysis resistance of the proposed methods is discussed next, followed by Directions of future work and Conclusions. Appendix contains a proof of zero determinant value for sine signal used in experiments with QES (Appendix A.1), and description of measures used to evaluate image encryption quality (Appendices A.2, A.3).

QES DETAILS

The quaternion q is a hyper complex number represented by

$$q = w + xi + yj + zk = (w, V), \tag{3}$$

where w, x, y, z are real numbers, (i, j, k) forms an orthonormal basis in R^3, $V = xi + yj + zk$,

$$i^2 = j^2 = k^2 = ijk = -1. \tag{4}$$

Inverse q^{-1} of the quaternion q is a quaternion such that

$$q^{-1}q = qq^{-1} = 1, \tag{5}$$

and

$$q^{-1} = \frac{w - xi - yj - zk}{| q |^2} = \frac{(w, -V)}{| q |^2}, \tag{6}$$

where

$$| q |= \sqrt{w^2 + x^2 + y^2 + z^2} \tag{7}$$

is the norm of q. Vector transform (1) is rotation if $| q |= 1$, and may be represented as a matrix-vector product

$$B_i' = \Gamma(q)B_i, i = \overline{1,3}, \tag{8}$$

where

$$\Gamma(q) = \frac{1}{| q |^2}\begin{bmatrix} | q |^2 - 2(y^2 + z^2) & 2(xy + wz) & 2(xz - wy) \\ 2(xy - wz) & | q |^2 - 2(x^2 + z^2) & 2(yz + wx) \\ 2(xz + wy) & 2(yz - wx) & | q |^2 - 2(x^2 + y^2) \end{bmatrix}. \tag{9}$$

Equation (8) may be written similar to (2) as

$$B' = \Gamma(q)B. \tag{10}$$

Plaintext matrix B can be restored from (10) using (9)

$$B = (\Gamma(q))^{-1}B', \tag{11}$$

where $(\Gamma(q))^{-1}$ is the inverse of $\Gamma(q)$, i.e.

$$(\Gamma(q))^{-1}\Gamma(q) = \Gamma(q)(\Gamma(q))^{-1} = E, \tag{12}$$

where E is 3×3 unity matrix such that

$$e_{ij} = \begin{cases} 1, i = j \\ 0, i \neq j \end{cases}; \text{ note that } (\Gamma(q))^{-1} = \Gamma(q)',$$

where X' is a transpose of the matrix X. The QES assumes that each next frame is enciphered using another quaternion, three vector V components (x, y, z) of which are obtained as three row elements of the matrix (9) used for encryption of the previous frame whereas its scalar component, w, is set to zero, that is

$$q_m = \begin{cases} w + xi + yj + zk, m = 0 \\ 0 + x_m i + y_m j + z_m k, m > 0 \end{cases}, \quad (13)$$

where

$$x_m = (\Gamma(q_{m-1}))_{11}, y_m = (\Gamma(q_{m-1}))_{12}, z_m = (\Gamma(q_{m-1}))_{13}, m > 0,$$

and the key matrix used for the m-th frame is $\Gamma(q_m)$. The next quaternion components may be taken not from the first row as shown above but from the other rows of the matrix (9) as well, or from its columns. Hence, encryption algorithm (Nagase et al, 2004a, 2004b, 2005) uses dynamically changing matrices of the form (9) in (10), (11) that are claimed to allow increasing its security contrary to the usage of static matrix (9).

ATTACKS ON QES

The QES is susceptible to KPCA as a particular case (for three component vectors) of the well-known HC algorithm (Stallings, 2006) which takes some vector as a plaintext, and produces the ciphertext by multiplication of the plaintext by a key matrix just similar to (8). The KPCA assumes that an opponent is able to get some number of plaintext-ciphertext pairs not knowing the key matrix. In the result of the attack, the opponent reveals the key matrix. Actually, if the opponent gets the number of such pairs equal to the number of the components of the vectors used (in the case of QES, three pairs) then s/he composes a plaintext matrix with the plaintext vector and a ciphertext matrix with the ciphertext vectors. Together with the key matrix they meet a matrix equation similar to (10) but with the key matrix K instead of $\Gamma(q)$. If the plaintext matrix is invertible then the key matrix can be easily obtained as

$$K = B' \cdot B^{-1}. \quad (14)$$

As far as QES actually enciphers frames (three three-component vectors), the secret key matrix $\Gamma(q)$ can be easily obtained from (9) as

$$\Gamma(q) = B' \cdot B^{-1}, \quad (15)$$

if B is invertible. Signal used in (Nagase et al, 2004a, Figure 3) is 400Hz sine (its period is 2.5 ms) sampled with 8 KHz frequency (its period is 0.125 ms), hence, the plaintext matrix has the following form

$$B = \begin{bmatrix} \sin\varphi & \sin(\varphi + 3x) & \sin(\varphi + 6x) \\ \sin(\varphi + x) & \sin(\varphi + 4x) & \sin(\varphi + 7x) \\ \sin(\varphi + 2x) & \sin(\varphi + 5x) & \sin(\varphi + 8x) \end{bmatrix} \quad (16)$$

and determinant of B is zero (see Appendix A.1.) that does not allow to apply (15) for the key matrix disclosing. However, usually signals are represented by a mixture of harmonic signals, and then the determinant of the plaintext is non-zero, and it can be inverted as shown below. The first nine values of the signal $y(t) = \sin t - \cos 3t$ for $t = 0, 0.2, .., 1.6$, are shown in (Figure 1) and arranged as a 3x3 matrix with the determinant equal to -0.3109 in Table 1. As far as this matrix has non-zero determinant, it is invertible (Table 1).

Figure 1. The first nine values of the signal $y(t) = \sin t - \cos 3t$ for t=0, 0.2, ..., 1.6

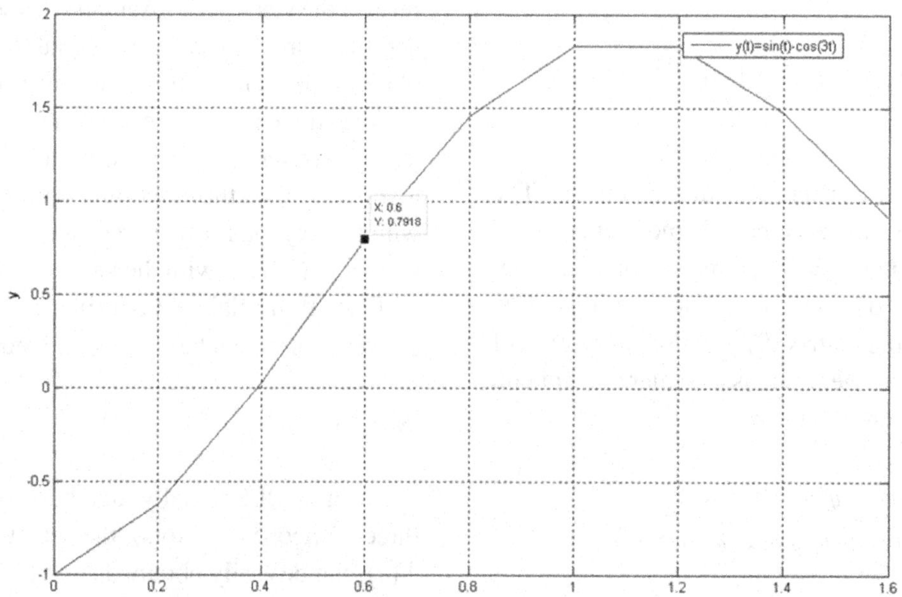

Let us consider some quaternion

$$q = w + xi + yj + zk = 1 + 2i + 3j + 4k$$

with

$$w = 1, x = 2, y = 3, z = 4. \quad (17)$$

From (7),

$$|q| = \sqrt{w^2 + x^2 + y^2 + z^2} = \sqrt{1+4+9+16} = \sqrt{30}. \quad (18)$$

From (9), (17), and (18),

$$\Gamma(q) = \frac{1}{|q|^2}\begin{bmatrix} |q|^2 - 2(y^2 + z^2) & 2(xy + wz) & 2(xz - wy) \\ 2(xy - wz) & |q|^2 - 2(x^2 + z^2) & 2(yz + wx) \\ 2(xz + wy) & 2(yz - wx) & |q|^2 - 2(x^2 + y^2) \end{bmatrix}$$
$$= \frac{1}{30}\begin{bmatrix} 30 - 2(9+16) & 2(6+4) & 2(8-3) \\ 2(6-4) & 30 - 2(4+16) & 2(12+2) \\ 2(8+3) & 2(12-2) & 30 - 2(4+9) \end{bmatrix}$$
$$= \frac{1}{30}\begin{bmatrix} -20 & 20 & 10 \\ 4 & -10 & 28 \\ 22 & 20 & 4 \end{bmatrix}. \quad (19)$$

From (10), (19), and Table 1,

Table 1. a) The first nine values of the signal $y(t) = \sin t - \cos 3t$. for $t = 0, 0.2, .., 1.6$, rounded to four decimal digits in the fractional part and arranged as a 3x3 matrix with the determinant equal to -0.3109, b) inverse of the matrix from (a)

-1	0,7918	1,8288
-0.6267	1,4547	1,4757
0.0271	1,8315	0,9121

(a)

4.4240	-8.447	4.7969
-1.9665	3.0920	-1.0597
3.8173	-5.9578	3.0818

(b)

$$B' = \Gamma(q)B = \frac{1}{30}\begin{bmatrix} -20 & 20 & 10 \\ 4 & -10 & 28 \\ 22 & 20 & 4 \end{bmatrix}\begin{bmatrix} -1 & 0.7918 & 1.8288 \\ -0.6267 & 1.4547 & 1.4757 \\ 0.0271 & 1.8315 & 0.9121 \end{bmatrix} = \begin{bmatrix} 0.2579 & 1.0524 & 0.0686 \\ 0.1009 & 1.3301 & 0.6032 \\ -1.1475 & 1.7947 & 2.4465 \end{bmatrix}. \quad (20)$$

From (15), (20), and Table 1b, the key matrix can be restored as follows

$$\Gamma(q) = B' \cdot B^{-1} = \begin{bmatrix} 0.2579 & 1.0524 & 0.0686 \\ 0.1009 & 1.3301 & 0.6032 \\ -1.1475 & 1.7947 & 2.4465 \end{bmatrix}\begin{bmatrix} 4.4240 & -8.4474 & 4.7969 \\ -1.9665 & 3.0920 & -1.0597 \\ 3.8173 & -5.9578 & 3.0818 \end{bmatrix} = \begin{bmatrix} -0.6667 & 0.6667 & 0.3333 \\ 0.1333 & -0.3333 & 0.9333 \\ 0.7333 & 0.6667 & 0.1333 \end{bmatrix},$$

which is the same as (19). Hence, QES is not secure.

Another weakness of QES originates from (13) dictating that all the key matrices except the first one use only three components of the quaternion (3). The key matrix in spite of its size is 3×3, has only four independent variables defining all its nine elements. With the use of (13), the number of independent elements in the key matrix becomes equal to three, and having three equations, it is possible to solve them with respect to three unknowns. Also QES fails to encrypt the vector with zero (black colour) components.

QES MODIFICATION M-QES

As we have shown, the weakness of QES follows from the use of the frame having nine samples comprising a 3×3 matrix with a non-zero determinant in the general case. If to reduce the frame size to less than nine samples (say six, or three), and change the key matrix for each new frame as proposed in QES, then there is no opportunity to apply the known plaintext-ciphertext attack due to the number of unknowns (nine) is greater than the number of equations (six or three) and the opponent does not have enough equations to solve such equations now. But due to (13), actually all the key matrices starting from the second one are built using only three-component quaternion (3), and even using a three-component vector as a plaintext, the opponent is able to find three unknowns from three equations if he has the plaintext-ciphertext pair. Hence, to counter this line of attack, additionally, modified QES shall not use (13) for getting the next key matrix from the previous one, but it uses a similar procedure with four quaternion components. Such an opportunity is mentioned in (Nagase et al. 2004a, 2004b, 2005) but it was not considered as an important. That is why, the way of producing the next key matrix may be as follows

$$q_m = \begin{cases} w + xi + yj + zk, m = 0 \\ w_m + x_m i + y_m j + z_m k, m > 0 \end{cases}, \quad (21)$$

where $w_m = (\Gamma(q_{m-1}))_{31}$, $x_m = (\Gamma(q_{m-1}))_{12}$, $y_m = (\Gamma(q_{m-1}))_{23}$, $z_m = (\Gamma(q_{m-1}))_{13}$, $m > 0$, and the key matrix used for the m -th plaintext vector is $\Gamma(q_m)$. In such a case, the key matrix is defined by four numbers specified in (21), and using three equations from the known plaintext-ciphertext pair, it is not possible to determine them uniquely: there is one free parameter on which all other values depend. The number of possible variants of such a matrix is defined by the number of possible values of the free parameter. In the case of the use of n-byte float point numbers, this number is equal to 2^{8n}, e.g., if $n=4$, then this number is 2^{32} that does not provide enough cryptographic strength. If one plaintext vector is subjected to l subsequent such kind transformations then an opponent sees results only after l iterations, and he is not able to have a matrix depending on a quaternion providing transformation from input to output. He can work in that direction trying to determine all quaternions used but each matrix depends of *4* numbers and there are l such matrices hence number of parameters is $4l$ and number of equations is *3*. Hence number of free unknowns is $4l-3$ that is equal to *1* only in the case of $l=1$. For $l=2$, it is *5* and with $n=4$ it yields already $2^{8nl}=2^{160}$ variants. If the opponent tries just to find a matrix providing total transformation, he faces a problem with *9* unknowns and *3* equations; hence he has 6 free unknowns that results in 2^{192} variants. Hence, with $l=2$, we have secure encryption with search space of 2^{160} variants at least.

Thus far, the proposed QES modification, M-QES, is as follows:

1. Each plaintext three-component vector P_i is subjected to l subsequent transformations (8), where quaternion q_m and its transformation matrix $\Gamma(q_m)$ are defined by (21) and (9) respectively, m=0,1,.. resulting in the ciphertext vector C_i :

$$D_{il} = P_i,$$
$$D_{il+m+1} = \Gamma(q_{il+m})D_{il+m}, m = \overline{0, l-1}$$
$$C_i = D_{(i+1)l}, i = 0,1,..$$

2. Decryption is performed as follows

$$D_{(i+1)l} = C_i,$$
$$D_{il+m-1} = \Gamma(q_{il+m})' D_{il+m}, m = l, l-1,..,1$$
$$P_i = D_{il}, i = 0,1,..$$

Note that, to overcome zero to zero mapping, we XOR (bit-by-bit exclusive OR operation) the plaintext components with the quaternion elements and then we perform encryption. Note also that instead of the use of (21), to get the next quaternion defining the next transformation matrix and defined by the previous transformation matrix, a pseudo-random number generator can be used with the seed value known to both the sender and receiver of the transferred text.

HARDWARE-ORIENTED QES (HW-QES)

To simplify implementation of the transform (8) used in QES and its modification, M-QES, we can use the quaternion $d = w + t(\dot{x}i + \dot{y}j + \dot{z}k)$ where $w^2 = \dot{x}^2 + \dot{y}^2 + \dot{z}^2$, $t = 2^{-i}$, to form matrix (9) with

$$w = 2^m + 1, m =$$
$$2k + 1, x = 2^{m-i}\alpha, y = 2^{\frac{m+1}{2} - i}\beta, z = 2^{-i}\gamma,$$
$$|d|^2 =$$
$$(2^m + 1)^2(1 + 2^{-2i}), \alpha, \beta, \gamma \in \{-1, 1\}, K > k \geq 0,$$
$$|i| < I \tag{22}$$

as shown in Box 1.

Entries of the matrix (23) are integers if $i<0$. Let us consider plaintext signal and transformation (23) having values from Z_N, where $N=2^n$. In such a case all operations are done modulo 2^n. Division by square of the norm in (23) is correct since according to (22) square of the norm is an odd number having multiplicative inverse modulo 2^n. As far as entries of (23) contain contributors being powers of two, when these powers exceed n, they vanish modulo 2^n, and matrix (23) degenerates to the unity matrix not providing hiding of the plaintext. To avoid the matrix degeneration, we require not vanishing of entries in (23) modulo 2^n:

$$\min(2m - 2i, m + 1 - 2i, -2i) < n$$
$$\min(3(m+1)/2 - 2i, m - i + 1, -i + 1) < n$$
$$\min(m - 2i + 1, 3(m+1)/2 - i, (m+3)/2 - i) < n$$
$$\min((m+3)/2 - 2i, 2m - i + 1, m - i + 1) < n, \tag{24}$$

Box 1.

$$\Gamma(d) = \frac{1}{|d|^2}\begin{bmatrix} (2^m+1)^2+2^{2m-2i}-2^{m+1-2i}-2^{-2i} & \alpha\beta 2^{3(m+1)/2-2i}+\gamma(2^{m-i+1}+2^{-i+1}) & \alpha\gamma 2^{m-2i+1}-\beta(2^m+1)2^{(m+3)/2-i} \\ \alpha\beta 2^{3(m+1)/2-2i}-\gamma(2^{m-i+1}+2^{-i+1}) & (2^m+1)^2+2^{m+1-2i}-2^{2m-2i}-2^{-2i} & \beta\gamma 2^{(m+3)/2-2i}+\alpha 2^{-i+m+1}(2^m+1) \\ \alpha\gamma 2^{m-2i+1}+\beta(2^m+1)2^{(m+3)/2-i} & \beta\gamma 2^{(m+3)/2-2i}-\alpha 2^{-i+m+1}(2^m+1) & (2^m+1)^2+2^{-2i}-2^{2m-2i}-2^{m+1-2i} \end{bmatrix}, \quad (23)$$

Since $m > 0, i < 0$,

$$2m \geq m+1, -2i \geq -i+1. \quad (25)$$

Hence, from (24), (25), one gets

$$\begin{aligned} &-2i < n, \\ &(m+3)/2 - i < n \\ &m - i + 1 < n. \end{aligned} \quad (26)$$

From (22) and (26), one gets

$$\begin{aligned} &-2i < n, \\ &2k + 2 - i < n. \end{aligned} \quad (27)$$

For example, if n=8, i may take values of -1, -2, -3, and k may take values 0, 1, 2 for i=-1; 0, 1for i=-2; and 0, 1 for i=-3. If n=8, i=-3, k=1, then the matrix (23) is as follows in Box 2.

The transform (8) may be implemented with matrix (23) very fast (without the division by the quadratic norm) using simple shift-add operations. Compensation of the scaling factor may be executed with hardware once after l such transformations using a product:

$$P = \frac{1}{\prod_{j=1}^{l}(2^{m_j}+1)^2(1+2^{-2i_j})},$$

where m_j, i_j are the values m, i for the j-th consecutive transformation.

The hardware-oriented QES, HW-QES, is based on the use of (23) and is similar to M-QES. HW-QES is defined as follows:

1. Each plaintext three-component vector P_t is subjected to l subsequent transformations (8) (quaternion $q = d$ and its transformation matrix $\Gamma(q)$. are defined by (22) and (23), respectively, m=0,1,..), resulting in the ciphertext vector C_t :

Box 2.

$$\Gamma(d) = \frac{1}{|d|^2}\begin{bmatrix} (2^3+1)^2+2^{12}-2^{10}-2^6 & \alpha\beta 2^{12}+\gamma(2^7+2^4) & \alpha\gamma 2^{10}-\beta(2^3+1)2^6 \\ \alpha\beta 2^{12}-\gamma(2^7+2^4) & (2^3+1)^2+2^{10}-2^{12}-2^6 & \beta\gamma 2^9+\alpha 2^7(2^3+1) \\ \alpha\gamma 2^{10}+\beta(2^3+1)2^6 & \beta\gamma 2^9-\alpha 2^7(2^3+1) & (2^3+1)^2+2^6-2^{12}-2^{10} \end{bmatrix}$$

$$= \frac{1}{(2^3+1)^2(1+2^6)}\begin{bmatrix} (2^3+1)^2-2^6 & \gamma(2^7+2^4) & -\beta 2^6 \\ -\gamma(2^7+2^4) & (2^3+1)^2-2^6 & \alpha 2^7 \\ \beta 2^6 & -\alpha 2^7 & (2^3+1)^2+2^6 \end{bmatrix} \bmod 2^8$$

$$D_{tl} = P_t,$$
$$D_{tl+m+1} = \Gamma(q_{tl+m})D_{tl+m}, m = \overline{0, l-1}$$
$$C_t = D_{(t+1)l}, t = 0,1,..,$$

where q_s is a value of the quaternion d obtained from (22) for some s-th combination of the values of five parameters ($i, k, \alpha, \beta, \gamma$) chosen according to some enumeration procedure (e.g., using pseudo-random number generator with agreed secret seed value).

2. Decryption is performed as follows

$$D_{(t+1)l} = C_t,$$
$$D_{tl+m-1} = \Gamma(q_{tl+m})D_{tl+m}, m = \overline{l, l-1,..,1}$$
$$P_t = D_{tl}, t = 0,1,..$$

Note that, to overcome zero to zero mapping, we XOR (bit-by-bit exclusive OR operation) the plaintext components with the quaternion elements and then we perform encryption. The HW-QES cipher uses dynamically generated transformation matrices number of different variants of which determines cryptographic strength of the cipher. This number is calculated as the number of possible different combinations of the parameters of the set of numbers (22). This set has five parameters: $\alpha, \beta, \gamma \in \{-1,1\}$, $i \in \{-1,-2,-3,...,-I\}$ (we consider only negative values for this parameter to have integer-valued entries of (23)), $k \in \{0,..,K-1\}$; and the numbers are in Z_N where $N = 2^n$. Let us estimate the number of possible combinations of these five parameters. Taking into account (27), number of possible variants of *i* is $\min(\frac{n}{2}-1, I)$, and the number of possible combinations of (*i, k*) is

$$\min(IK, \sum_{i=1}^{n/2-1}\frac{n-i-2}{2}) = \min(IK, (n/2-1)(3n/8-1))$$

if $\frac{n}{2}-1 \le I$. The number of combinations of all five parameters is

$$8\min(IK, (n/2-1)(3n/8-1))$$

since α, β, γ are binary. If *n*=24, *I*=30, *K*=15, then the number of combinations is 704. If a plaintext vector is subjected to *l*=14 consecutive transformations, as it is assumed in the M-QES, the number of all possible combinations of the parameters of transformations is $704^{14} \approx 10^{40}$ thus providing large cryptographic strength of such a cipher.

OES DETAILS

The use of quaternions to represent color images has been introduced by Sangwine (1996). A color image is represented as a pure quaternion image:

$$B(x,y) = 0 + r(x,y)i + g(x,y)j + b(x,y)k, \quad (28)$$

where *r(x,y)*, *g(x,y)*, *b(x,y)* are respectively the red, green and blue components of a pixel at position *(x,y)* in the image *B(x,y)*. This representation has allowed the definition of powerful tools for color image processing such as Fourier transforms, correlation or edge detection.

The typical matrix operation for an encoding process is an one-sided matrix multiplication of the plaintext matrix B by a secret key matrix $\boldsymbol{M}$ to produce the ciphertext matrix B':

$$B' = M \times B \quad (29)$$

The plaintext quaternion valued matrix *B* may be considered as a block-matrix where each block (or frame) consists of two pixels from (28) in form of quaternion valued vector $X=(q1, q2)^T$ as a column of *B*. Then we can describe with matrix M an 8-D rotation of equivalent 8-D real vector $X=(q11, q12, q13, q14, q21, q22, q23, q24)^T$, where quaternion l has components $q_l=(ql1, ql2, ql3, ql4)$ $(l=1,2)$.

There is a natural way to describe an 8-D rotation using octonions (Ward, 1997). The octonion o is a hyper-complex number represented as

$$o = w + xe_1 + ye_2 + ze_3 + ae_4 + be_5 + ce_6 + de_7 = (w, V) \tag{30}$$

where w,x,y,z,a,b,c,d are real numbers, $e_i (i=1...7)$ form an orthonormal basis in R^7,

$$V = (xe_1 + ye_2 + ze_3 + ae_4 + be_5 + ce_6 + de_7),$$

$$e_i^2 = -1, (i = 1..7), e_i e_j = -e_j e_i, e_i e_{i+1} = e_{i+3} \tag{31}$$

where addition is made modulo 7 (e.g., $e_6 e_7 = e_2$). Inverse $\boldsymbol{o}^{-1}$ of the octonion $\boldsymbol{o}$ is an octonion such that

$$o^{-1} o = oo^{-1} = I, \tag{32}$$

and

$$o^{-1} = \frac{(w - v)}{| o |^2} \tag{33}$$

where

$$| o | = \sqrt{w^2 + x^2 + y^2 + z^2 + a^2 + b^2 + c^2 + d^2} \tag{34}$$

is the norm of $\boldsymbol{o}$.

If an octonion has a unit norm ($|o|=1$), it can be represented in "polar" form

$$o = \cos\varphi + \sin\varphi(\alpha e_1 + \beta e_2 + \gamma e_3 + \delta e_4 + \lambda e_5 + \mu e_6 + \rho e_7) \tag{35}$$

Vector transform with octonion (35) is an 8-D rotation by angle φ, and may be represented as a matrix-vector product (Doukhnitch & Ozen, 2011)

$$B' = \cos\varphi R_8 B, \tag{36}$$

where

$$R_8 = \begin{pmatrix} 1 & \alpha t & \beta t & \gamma t & \delta t & \lambda t & \mu t & \rho t \\ -\alpha t & 1 & -\delta t & -\rho t & \beta t & -\mu t & \lambda t & \gamma t \\ -\beta t & \delta t & 1 & -\lambda t & -\alpha t & \gamma t & -\rho t & \mu t \\ -\gamma t & \rho t & \lambda t & 1 & -\mu t & -\beta t & \delta t & -\alpha t \\ -\delta t & -\beta t & \alpha t & \mu t & 1 & -\rho t & -\gamma t & \lambda t \\ -\lambda t & \mu t & -\lambda t & \beta t & \rho t & 1 & -\alpha t & -\delta t \\ -\mu t & -\lambda t & \rho t & -\delta t & \gamma t & \alpha t & 1 & -\beta t \\ -\rho t & -\gamma t & -\mu t & \alpha t & -\lambda t & \delta t & \beta t & 1 \end{pmatrix}, \tag{37}$$

and $t = \tan(\varphi)$.

8-D rotation with octonion (30) may be used for encoding (29) as

$$B' = \Gamma(o)B, \tag{38}$$

where

$$\Gamma(o) = | o |^{-1} \begin{pmatrix} w & x & y & z & a & b & c & d \\ -x & w & -a & -d & y & -c & b & z \\ -y & a & w & -b & -x & z & -d & c \\ -z & d & b & w & -c & -y & a & -x \\ -a & -y & x & c & w & -d & -z & b \\ -b & c & -z & y & d & w & -x & -a \\ -c & -b & d & -a & z & x & w & -y \\ -d & -z & -c & x & -b & a & y & w \end{pmatrix}, \tag{39}$$

Transform (38) represents multiplication of octonions o and B resulting in octonion B'.

Plaintext vector B can be restored from (38) using (39)

$$B = \Gamma(o)^{-1} B', \tag{40}$$

where $\Gamma(o)^{-1}$ is inverse of $\Gamma(o)$, i.e.

$$\Gamma(o)(\Gamma(o))^{-1} = (\Gamma(o))^{-1}\Gamma(o) = E, \quad (41)$$

where E is 8×8 unity matrix such that

$$e_{ij} = \begin{cases} 1, i = j \\ 0, i \neq j \end{cases}; \text{ note that } (\Gamma(o))^{-1} = (\Gamma(o))^{T},$$

where X^T is a transpose of the matrix X. The OES assumes that each next 8-component frame is enciphered using another octonion, components (30) of which are obtained from the elements of the matrix (39) used for encryption of the previous frame, for example, by addition of elements of some two rows, i and j, $i, j \in \{1,..,8\}, i \neq j$, that is

$$\begin{aligned} w_m &= (\Gamma(o_{m-1}))_{i1} + (\Gamma(o_{m-1}))_{j1}, \\ x_m &= (\Gamma(o_{m-1}))_{i2} + (\Gamma(o_{m-1}))_{j2}, \\ &.. \\ c_m &= (\Gamma(o_{m-1}))_{i7} + (\Gamma(o_{m-1}))_{j7}, \\ d_m &= (\Gamma(o_{m-1}))_{i8} + (\Gamma(o_{m-1}))_{j8}, m > 0 \end{aligned} \quad (42)$$

and the key matrix used for the m-th frame is $\Gamma(o_m)$. Values i,j shall be shared by the communicating parties. Contrary to QES (see (21)), we need applying some operations (as shown in (42) or other) to the elements of the previous matrix because otherwise new matrix (39) contains the same (by modulo) elements as the previous one. As far as the matrix is defined by *8* elements and the frame size is also *8*, such transformation as (38) is susceptible to KPCA, because if the plaintext and ciphertext are known then we may have *8* equations with *8* unknowns which can be uniquely solved. Hence, we need more secret parameters. If a ciphertext is obtained after $l=2$ consecutive applications of (39), then an opponent is to solve a system of nonlinear square equations (because of twice applied (39) coefficients are multiplied) to find *8* octonion components from *8* equations, or to find *64* elements of the matrix resulting after two transformations. In the first case the number of effective unknowns is 8^2, and in the second it is also *64*. With *8* equations and *64* unknowns, opponent faces with necessity of enumeration of *56* free unknowns. If each such unknown has *8* values then 2^{168} variants are to be considered that is not feasible.

Hence, OES method may be represented as shown in Algorithm 1.

Use of the secret numbers *SN[1..l]* with n binary digits extends key space of the algorithm 2^{ln} times, XOR operation with the first row of the current transformation matrix is used to avoid mapping of zero to zero. Decryption in OES method is straightforward and assumes l times applying of XOR operation, multiplication by inverses of *SN[1..l]*, and applied (40) for each ciphertext block *C[m]*.

So, encryption algorithm uses dynamically changing matrices of the form (39) in (38), (40) for increasing its security contrary to the usage of static matrix (39).

Hardware-Oriented OES

To simplify implementation of the transform (39) used in OES we can take the octonion

$$o = w + t(xe_1 + ye_2 + ze_3 + ae_4 + be_5 + ce_6 + de_7),$$

where $x^2+y^2+z^2+a^2+b^2+c^2+d^2=w^2$ and $t = 2^{-i}$, to form matrix (39), with

$$w=2^m+1,\ m=2k,\ x=2^{m-1}\alpha,$$

$$y=2^{m-1}\beta, z=2^{m-1}\gamma, a=2^{m-1}\delta, b=2^{m/2}\lambda, c=2^{m/2}\mu, d=\rho,$$
$$|o|^2=(2^m+1)^2(1+2^{-2i}),\ \alpha,\beta,\gamma,\delta,\lambda,\mu,\rho$$

$$\in \{-1,1\}, K \geq k > 0, I \geq i \geq -I, \quad (43)$$

Obtained from (39), (43) matrix looks as follows in Box 3.

Algorithm1. OES

```
Input: P[1],P[2],.., - plaintext, o1 - octonion with 8 components, l≥2 - num-
ber of consecutive iterations (l=2 is default for OES), SN[1..l] - secret
integers each having multiplicative inverse
Output: C[1], C[2],..
m=1;o[m]=o1; B=P[1];
While not end of input plaintext{
 For (i=1,l){
  Calculate Γ(o[m]) according to (39);
  Calculate B' according to (38);
  B'=SN[i]·B' + Γ(o[m])_{1,1:8};
  m++;
  Calculate o[m] according to (42), (39);
 }
 C[m/l]= B';
 B=P[m/l+1];
 Calculate o[m] according to (42), (39);
}/*end*/
```

Hence, method HW-OES is the same as OES but octonions are generated now not by (42) but by (44) (all appearances of (42) shall be replaced by (44) in Algorithm OES description) using a pseudo-random number generator with the specified seed value shared by the sender and receiver. Initial octonion *O1* used in OES is also obtained by (44) using the pseudo-random number generator. If a plaintext is represented as integers from Z_N, as for image processing where $N=256$, then all operations are to be done modulo N, including calculation of the square root according to (34), (39). If $N=2^n$, norm (34) must be invertible modulo N because of division used in (39). According to (43), the norm is an odd number, and, hence its inverse exists. From the other side, the norm needs square root operation. According to (43), the square root (34) exists and

Box 3.

$$\Gamma(o)=\begin{bmatrix} 2^m+1 & \alpha 2^{m-1-i} & \beta 2^{m-1-i} & \gamma 2^{m-1-i} & \delta 2^{m-1-i} & \lambda 2^{m/2-i} & \mu 2^{m-1-i} & \rho 2^{-i} \\ -\alpha 2^{m-1-i} & 2^m+1 & -\delta 2^{m-1-i} & -\rho 2^{-i} & \beta 2^{m-1-i} & -\mu 2^{m-1-i} & \lambda 2^{m/2-i} & \gamma 2^{m-1-i} \\ -\beta 2^{m-1-i} & \delta 2^{m-1-i} & 2^m+1 & -\lambda 2^{m/2-i} & -\alpha 2^{m-1-i} & \gamma 2^{m-1-i} & -\rho 2^{-i} & \mu 2^{m-1-i} \\ -\gamma 2^{m-1-i} & \rho 2^{-i} & \lambda 2^{m/2-i} & 2^m+1 & -\mu 2^{m-1-i} & -\beta 2^{m-1-i} & \delta 2^{m-1-i} & -\alpha 2^{m-1-i} \\ -\delta 2^{m/2-i} & -\beta 2^{m-1-i} & \alpha 2^{m-1-i} & \mu 2^{m-1-i} & 2^m+1 & -\rho 2^{-i} & -\gamma 2^{m-1-i} & \lambda 2^{m/2-i} \\ -\lambda 2^{m/2-i} & \mu 2^{m-1-i} & -\gamma 2^{m-1-i} & \beta 2^{m-1-i} & \rho 2^{-i} & 2^m+1 & -\alpha 2^{m-1-i} & -\delta 2^{m/2-i} \\ -\mu 2^{m-1-i} & -\lambda 2^{m/2-i} & \rho 2^{-i} & -\delta 2^{m-1-i} & \gamma 2^{m-1-i} & \alpha 2^{m-1-i} & 2^m+1 & -\beta 2^{m-1-i} \\ -\rho 2^{-i} & -\gamma 2^{m-1-i} & -\mu 2^{m-1-i} & \alpha 2^{m-1-i} & -\lambda 2^{m/2-i} & \delta 2^{m/2-i} & \beta 2^{m-1-i} & 2^m+1 \end{bmatrix} \quad (44)$$

$$|o| = (2^m + 1) \bmod 2^n \qquad (45)$$

for

$$i \le -n/2. \qquad (46)$$

The HW-OES cipher uses dynamically generated transformation matrices (44) (with the norm (45)) number of different variants of which determines cryptographic strength of the cipher. This number is calculated as the number of possible different combinations of the parameters of the set of numbers (43). This set has nine parameters:

$$\alpha, \beta, \gamma, \delta, \lambda, \mu, \rho \in \{-1, 1\}, i \in \{-n/2, .., -I\},$$

(we consider only negative values for this parameter to have integer-valued entries of (39), (44), and take into account (46)), $k \in \{1, .., K\}$; and the numbers are in Z_N where $N = 2^n$. The number of combinations of all the nine parameters is $2^7(I - n/2 + 1)K$. If I=32, K=32, then the number of combinations is $O(2^{16})$. If *n=32*, then number of values for each element from *SN[1..l]* is 2^{32}, and the number of variants is $O(2^{48})$. For OES, $l=2$, and hence the key space is $O(2^{48l}) = O(2^{96})$ that corresponds to a strong enough cipher. We can further increase its security using *l>2*.

EXPERIMENTAL RESULTS AND DISCUSSIONS

We developed programs for simulating the encryption schemes in C# on an Intel(R) Core(TM) 2 Duo 1.8 GHz processor with 2-GB RAM and Windows XP.

We study encryption quality and performance of QES, M-QES, and HW-QES, when encrypting integer-valued signals and images. HW-OES is applied for image encryption. First 90 values of the signal (47) encrypted by QES, M-QES, and HW-QES are shown in Figure 2:

Figure 2. The first 90 values of the signal (47) for (a) $t = 0, 0.2, .., 18$ and N=256 encrypted by (b) QES, (c) M-QES, (d) HW-QES, (e) HW-OES, and (f) AES

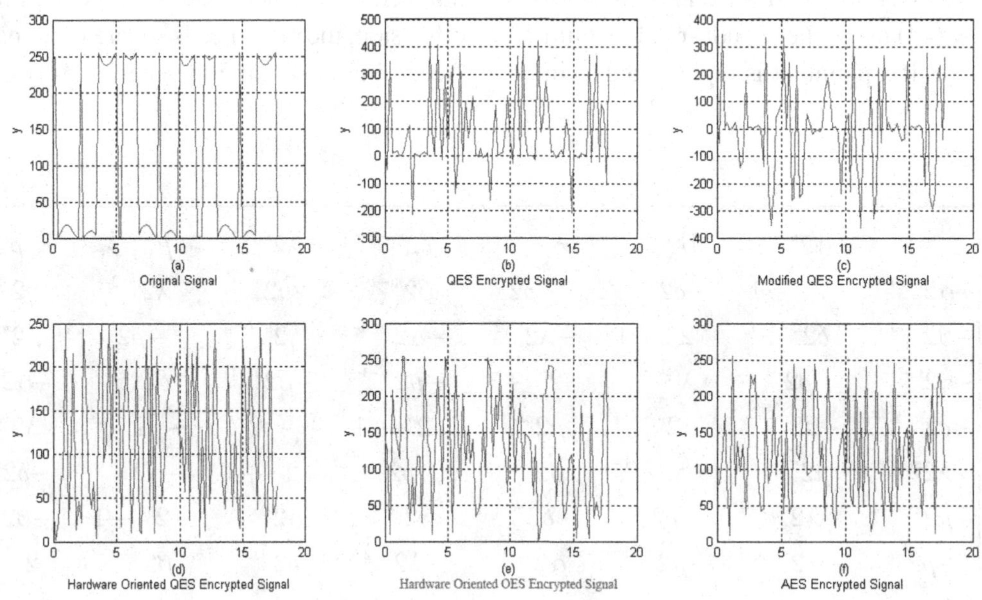

$$y(t) = (\text{int})(10 \cdot (\sin t - \cos 3t)) \bmod N, \quad (47)$$

where N=256 and $t = 0, 0.2, .., 18$. It was not possible to distinguish between the encryption times of the inspected algorithms for the first 90 elements of the signal (47), therefore, we encrypt the first 180000 values in (47) for N=256 and t=0, 0.2, …, 36000. Table 2 presents correlation coefficients C.C ((48), see Appendix) for the first 180000 values of the signal in (47) for N=256 and t=0, 0.2, …, 36000. It is clear from visual inspection of Figure 2 that HW-QES and HW-OES give better encryption quality than the original QES. Table 2 shows that the HW-QES has the best encryption quality among the inspected algorithms. Note that the closer C.C to zero the better.

The encryption time measured when applying QES, M-QES, HW-QES, and HW-OES is given in Table 3, which shows that the original QES has the best execution time. Table 3 shows that HW-QES is roughly two times faster than M-QES and only 10% slower than QES. HW-OES as working with greater sized than for HW-QES matrices shows three times worse time but its quality according to Table 2 is more than 10 times better than that of HW-QES.

For encrypting images, firstly, the image P of size $N \times M$ is converted into its RGB components. Afterwards, each colour matrix R, G, and B, is converted into a vector of integers within $\{0,1,...,255\}$. Each vector has the length $L = N \times M$. Then, the obtained three vectors are concatenated into one-dimensional array $\text{onedim}[3 \cdot L]$ thus representing the plaintext $P(3 \times L)$. which is encrypted.

We examine the encryption quality for five different images: Tick.bmp (Figure 3), Symbol.bmp (Figure 4), and Blackbox.bmp (Figure 5), containing very large single colour areas, Lena.bmp (Figure 6), that does not contain many high frequency components, and Girl.bmp (Figure 7), containing many high frequency components. From visual inspection of Figures 3-7, it follows that M-QES, HW-QES, and HW-OES are better than QES in hiding all the features of the image containing large single colour areas. The AES fails to hide the data patterns for the images containing large single colour areas. That is, the proposed HW-QES and HW-OES have advantage in encryption of identical plaintext blocks over the AES.

Table 4 and Table 5 present irregular deviation ID (see Appendix A.3) and correlation coefficient C.C (48) calculated for each encrypted image; they show that M-QES has the best encryption quality among the inspected algorithms, with AES competing with it for images (Figures 6 and 7) containing many high-frequency components.

Table 2. Correlation coefficients C.C of the first 180000 values for the signal (47) for N=256 and t=0, 0.2, …, 36000 encrypted by QES, M-QES, HW-QES, HW-OES, and AES

Algorithm	C.C
QES	0.1070
M-QES	0.0860
HW-QES	0.0604
HW-OES	0.0044
AES	-0.0093

Table 3. Encryption time (ms) of the first 180000 values of the signal (47) for N=256 and t=0, 0.2, …, 36000

Algorithm	Time (ms)
QES	98
M-QES	205
HW-QES	109
HW-OES	340
AES	389

Figure 3. Tick.bmp encrypted by: a) QES, b) M-QES, c) HW-QES, d) HW-OES, e) AES

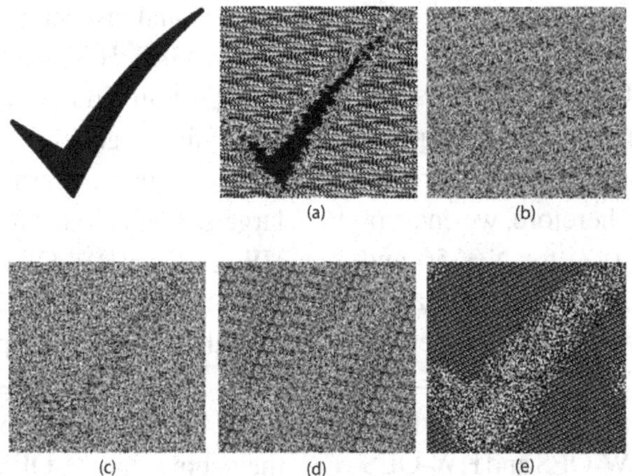

Figure 4. Symbol.bmp encrypted by: a) QES, b) M-QES, c) HW-QES, d) HW-OES, e) AES

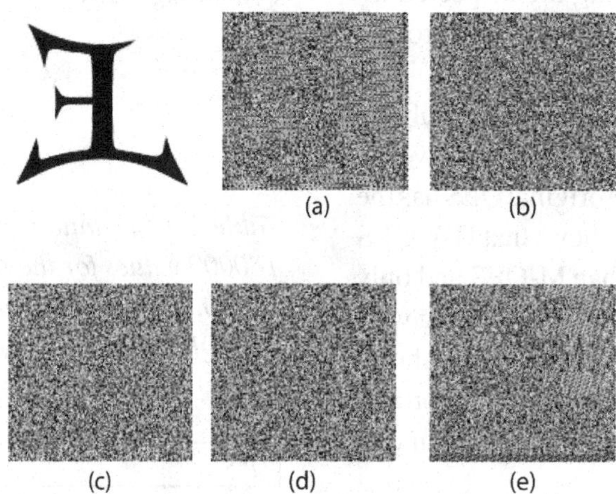

Figure 5. Blackbox.bmp encrypted by: a) QES, b) M-QES, c) HW-QES, d) HW-OES, e) AES

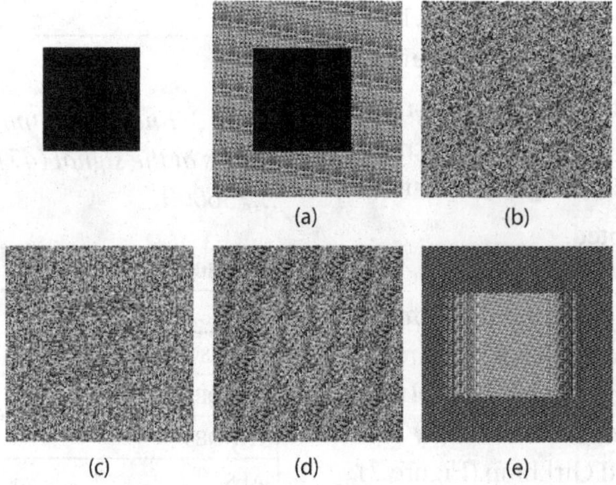

Figure 6. Lena.bmp encrypted by: a) QES, b) M-QES, c) HW-QES, d) HW-OES, e) AES

(a) (b)
(c) (d) (e)

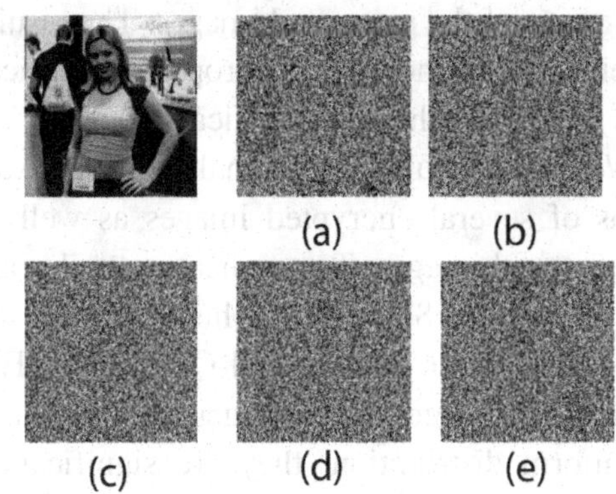

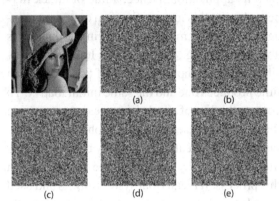

Figure 7. Girl.bmp encrypted by: a) QES, b) M-QES, c) HW-QES, d) HW-OES, e) AES

Table 4. Irregular deviation ID for encrypted images using QES, M-QES, HW-QES, HW-OES, and AES. The less ID, the better.

Image/Algorithm	QES	M-QES	HW-QES	HW-OES	AES
Tick.bmp	28874.66	13154.33	24579.91	18017.41	26562.30
Symbol.bmp	14558.21	6162.89	11828.54	15900.17	49911.39
Blackbox.bmp	28566	11348.83	22805.03	10521.33	29957.78
Lena.bmp	19789.33	10957.33	16464	15905.33	10149.33
Girl.bmp	22535.64	11136.62	18621.06	17820.63	9898.90

Table 5. Correlation coefficients C.C for encrypted images using QES, M-QES, HW-QES, HW-OES, and AES. The closer C.C to zero, the better.

Image/Algorithm	QES	M-QES	HW-QES	HW-OES	AES
Tick.bmp	0.30163	0.00540	0.03536	-0.0366	-0.13139
Symbol.bmp	0.01520	0.00049	0.01524	-0.0006	0.01998
Blackbox.bmp	0.68185	0.00788	0.02457	-0.0728	-0.2556
Lena.bmp	-0.00158	0.00496	0.00603	-0.0063	-0.0020
Girl.bmp	0.01726	-0.00265	0.00195	0.0012	-0.0012

STATISTICAL ANALYSIS AND CRYPTANALYSIS RESISTANCE

The ability to withstand all kinds of cryptanalysis and attacks (Alvarez & Li, 2006; Hossam et al, 2007; Yaobin & Guanrong, 2004a; Yaobin et al., 2004b) is a good measure of the security of a cryptosystem. Robustness against attacks is used to evaluate the security of our schemes. In (Hossam, 2007), it is mentioned that in (Shannon, 1948), Shannon said "it is possible to solve many kinds of ciphers by statistical analysis". A good cipher should be robust against any statistical attack. To prove the robustness of the proposed scheme, the statistical analysis has been performed. It is usually evaluated by the following measures (Cheng &

Xiaobo, 2000; Hossam, 2007; Lian et al., 2005; Marvel et al., 1999; Yaobin et al., 2004c): the histograms of the encrypted images. The results presented below show that our proposed modifications strongly withstand statistical attacks.

We have calculated and analyzed the histograms of several encrypted images as well as their original images. Two typical examples are given in Figures 8 and 9. The histograms of the encrypted by our proposed M-QES, HW-QES, and HW-OES algorithms images are very close to uniform distribution; they are significantly different from those of the original image, and bear no statistical resemblance to the original image. QES and AES show particular peaks in histograms for Tick.bmp (Figure 8), but both show good histograms for Lena.bmp (Figure 9).

The proposed methods use dynamically changing transformation matrices and XOR-ing with dynamically changing vector to counter all kinds of differential, linear, and integral cryptanalysis because continuously changing transformation matrix does not allow tracking of differences. Thus, security of the proposed ciphers is based on the feature of changing of the matrix just after each its application. Hence, a line of attack may be to disrupt this feature. So, if an opponent manages to use one matrix several times, then he is able to apply, e.g., KPCA attack. It might be possible, if for example, resetting of the cipher each time produces one and the same initial matrix. To counter this line of attack, it is necessary to provide that each new resetting of the ciphers yields new matrices not repeating previously used ones. This might be done by the use of the timestamps in this process. It means that system clocks and used pseudo-random generators must be carefully protected from compromising. Resistance to algebraic attacks was estimated when we described proposed algorithms as far as these attacks are most natural for such ciphers. Chosen plaintext attack (e.g., plaintext having all zeroes excepting one component equal to one) is countered by the use of addition (XOR-ing). Many attacks on conventional ciphers use their multi-round structure and substitution-permutation networks used in them but our ciphers do not have such features.

Figure 8. Histogram of RGB layers for original/encrypted Tick.bmp: a) histogram of the original image, b) histogram of QES-encrypted, c) histogram of M-QES-encrypted, d) histogram of HW-QES-encrypted, e) histogram of HW-OES-encrypted, f) histogram of AES-encrypted

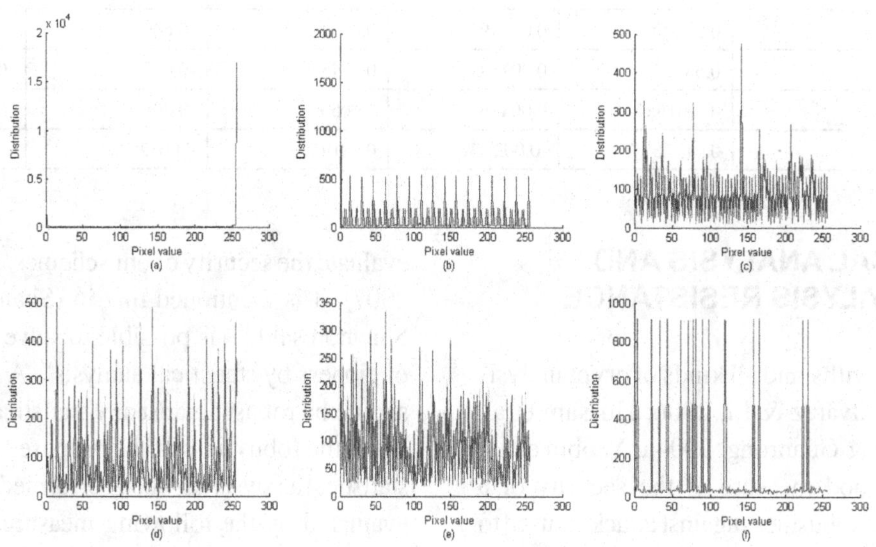

Figure 9. Histogram of RGB layers for original/encrypted Lena.bmp: a) histogram of the original image, b) histogram of QES-encrypted, c) histogram of M-QES-encrypted, d) histogram of HW-QES-encrypted, e) histogram of HW-OES-encrypted, f) histogram of AES-encrypted

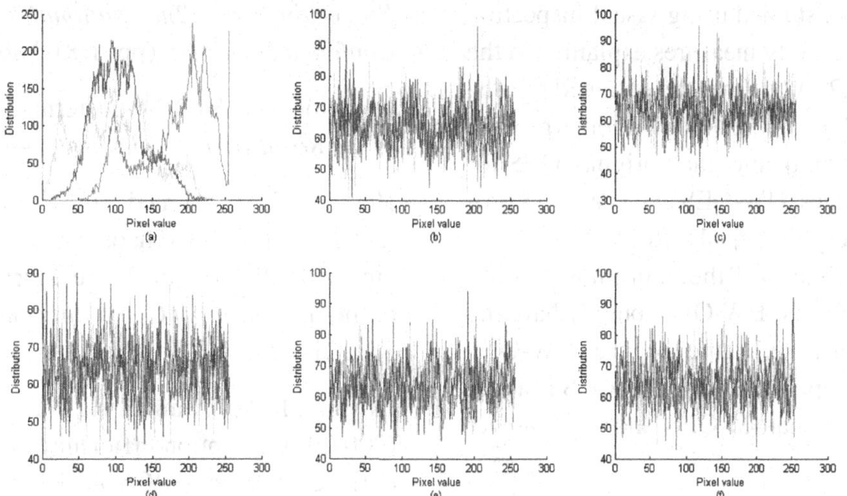

FUTURE RESEARCH DIRECTIONS

Future research may concern effective parallel implementation of the algorithms, e.g. using FPGA. Another direction of research may be extending of application of hyper-complex numbers in cryptographic realm (e.g., to hash functions, asymmetric cryptography).

CONCLUSION

Thus far, the QES cipher (Marins et al., 2001; Nagase et al., 2004a, 2004b) susceptibility to the KPCA is shown. There are two reasons for it:

- The frame size is equal to nine that allows getting nine equations for a key matrix having nine elements;
- The key matrix (9) depends on four independent variables (quaternion (3) components); only three of them (imaginary part) are assumed to be used for the key matrix generation beginning from the second frame according to (13).

We propose a modification of QES making it resistant to KPCA by

- Reducing the frame size to three,
- The use of all four quaternion components for each new plaintext vector, i.e. use of (21) instead of (13) or a pseudo-random number generator for the choice of the next quaternion value,
- One plaintext vector is subjected to l consecutive transformations to get a ciphertext that allows security increasing to the sufficient level.

Approach to effective hardware implementation of M-QES is proposed which is based on the restriction of the rotation parameters to the powers of two that allows escaping of the use of multiplication when additions and shifts are necessary only. The number of consecutive transformations of a plaintext increases to $l=14$ in that case. Octonions are used in the proposed OES and HW-OES algorithms, the latter, similar to HW-QES, can be implemented effectively in hardware as using also shifts and additions. Algorithm HW-OES showed good results for signal and image encryption.

Quality of signal and image encryption for all algorithms is studied using visual inspection and numerical quality measures explained in the Appendices A.2, A.3. From the obtained results, it follows that the proposed modifications provide higher encryption quality than original QES for signals and images. HW-QES and HW-OES provide higher encryption quality than AES.

Encryption time for all the algorithms has been considered, QES and HW-QES roughly have the same encryption time, but the proposed HW-QES is better in encryption quality. HW-QES is about two times faster than M-QES and 10% slower than QES.

ACKNOWLEDGMENT

The authors are grateful to anonymous reviewers for their valuable comments.

REFERENCES

Alvarez, G., & Li, S. (2006). Some basic cryptographic requirements for chaos-based cryptosystems. *International Journal of Bifurcation and Chaos in Applied Sciences and Engineering*, *16*, 2129–2151. doi:10.1142/S0218127406015970.

Cheng, H., & Xiaobo, L. (2000). Partial encryption of compressed images and videos. *IEEE Transactions on Signal Processing*, *48*, 2439–2451. doi:10.1109/78.852023.

Doukhnitch, E., & Ozen, E. (2011). Hardware-oriented algorithm for quaternion valued matrix decomposition. *IEEE Transactions on Circuits and Wystems. II, Express Briefs*, *58*(4), 225–229. doi:10.1109/TCSII.2011.2111590.

Elkamchouchi, H., & Makar, A. M. (2005). Measuring encryption quality of bitmaps images with Rijndael and KAMKAR block ciphers. In *Proceedings of 22nd National Radio Science Conference (NRSC)*, (pp. 1-8). NRSC.

Hamilton, W. (1847). On quaternions. *Proceedings of the Royal Irish Academy*, *3*, 1–16.

Hossam, E. H., Ahmed, H. M., & Osama, S. F. (2007a). An efficient chaos-based feedback stream cipher (ECBFSC) for image encryption and decryption. *Journal of Computing and Informatics*, *31*, 121–129.

Hossam, E. H., Ahmed, H. M., & Osama, S. F. (2007b). Encryption efficiency analysis and security evaluation of RC6 block ciphers for digital images. *International Journal of Computer and Information Technology*, *3*(1), 33–39.

Hsiao, S.-F., & Delosme, J.-M. (1994). Parallel processing of complex data using quaternion and pseudo-quaternion CORDIC algorithms. In *Proceedings of the ASAP 1994 Conference*, (pp. 125-130). University of California.

Ismail, A. I., Amin, M., & Diab, H. (2006). How to repair the hill cipher. *Journal of Zhejiang University of Science A*, *7*(12), 2022–2030. doi:10.1631/jzus.2006.A2022.

Kuipers, J. B. (1999). *Quaternions and rotation sequences*. Princeton, NJ: Princeton University Press.

Lian, S., Sun, J., & Wong, Z. (2005). Security analysis of chaos-based image encryption algorithm. *Physics Letters. [Part A]*, 645–661.

Malekian, E., & Zakerolhosseini, A. (2010). NTRU-like public key cryptosystems beyond dedekind domain up to alternative algebra. *Transactions on Computational Science*, *10*, 25–41.

Malekian, E., & Zakerolhosseini, A. (2010). OTRU: A non-associative and high speed public key cryptosystem. In *Proceedings of the 15th CSI International Symposium Computer Architecture and Digital Systems (CADS)*, (pp. 83-90). CADS.

Marins, J. L., Xiaoping, Y., et al. (2001). An extended kalman filter for quaternion-based orientation estimation using MARG sensors. In *Proceedings of the 2001 IEEE/RSJ, International Conference on Intelligent Robots and Systems*, (pp. 2003-2011). Maui, HI: IEEE.

Marvel, L. M., Boncelet, G. G., & Retter, C. T. (1999). Spread spectrum image steganography. *IEEE Transactions on Signal Processing*, *8*, 1075–1083. PMID:18267522.

Nagase, T., Koide, R., Araki, T., & Hasegawa, Y. (2004b). A new quadripartite public-key cryptosystem. In *Proceedings of the International Symposium on Communications and Information Technologies 2004 (ISCIT 2004)*, (pp. 74-79). Sapporo, Japan: ISCIT.

Nagase, T., Koide, R., Araki, T., & Hasegawa, Y. (2005). Dispersion of sequences for generating a robust enciphering system. *ECTI Transactions on Computer and Information Theory*, *1*(1), 9–14.

Nagase, T., Komata, M., & Araki, T. (2004a). Secure signals transmission based on quaternion encryption scheme. In *Proceedings 18th International Conference on Advanced Information Networking and Application (AINA 2004)*, (pp. 35-38). IEEE Computer Society.

Sangwine, S. J. (1996). Fourier transforms of color images using quaternions, or hypercomplex numbers. *Electronics Letters*, *32*(21), 1979–1980. doi:10.1049/el:19961331.

Shannon, C. E. (1948). Communication theory of secrecy systems. *The Bell System Technical Journal*, *28*, 656–715.

Stallings, W. (2006). *Cryptography and network security*. Upper Saddle River, NJ: Prentice Hall.

Ward, J. P. (1997). *Quaternions and cayley numbers*. Dordrecht, The Netherlands: Kluwer Academic Publishers. doi:10.1007/978-94-011-5768-1.

Yaobin, M. A., & Guanrong, C. H. (2004a). Chaos-based image encryption. In Bayro-Corrochano, E. (Ed.), *Handbook of Computational Geometry for Pattern Recognition, Computer Vision, Neural Computing and Robotics*. Berlin, Germany: Springer-Verlag.

Yaobin, M. A., Guanrong, C. H., & Shiguo, L. (2004b). A symmetric image encryption scheme based on 3D chaotic cat maps. *Chaos, Solitons, and Fractals*, *21*, 749–761. doi:10.1016/j.chaos.2003.12.022.

Ziedan, I., Fouad, M., & Salem, H. D. (2006). Application of data encryption standard to bitmap and JPEG images. In *Proceedings* of *20th National Radio Science Conference (NRSC)*, (pp. 1-16). NRSC.

ADDITIONAL READING

Encryption. (2012). *Wikipedia.* Retrieved November 26, 2012 from http://en.wikipedia.org/wiki/Encryption

Huy, H. N., Xianping, W., Phu, D., Campbell, W., & Balasubramaniam, S. (2010). Dynamic key cryptography and applications. *International Journal of Network Security, 10*(3), 161-174. Retrieved November 26, 2012 from http://ijns.femto.com.tw/contents/ijns-v10-n3/ijns-2010-v10-n3-p161-174.pdf

Hyper Complex Number. (2012). *Wikipedia.* Retrieved November 26, 2012 from http://en.wikipedia.org/wiki/Hypercomplex_number

Known Plaintext Attack. (2012). *Wikipedia.* Retrieved November 26, 2012 from http://en.wikipedia.org/wiki/Known-plaintext_attack

Matrix. (2012). *Wikipedia.* Retrieved November 26, 2012 from http://en.wikipedia.org/wiki/Matrix_(mathematics)

KEY TERMS AND DEFINITIONS

Dynamic Key: A variable key taking a new value for each next plaintext block.

Encryption/Decryption: Hiding/revealing plaintext/ciphertext by applying an encryption/decryption algorithm transformation to each plaintext/ciphertext block using some parameter (a key, usually secret).

Hyper-Complex Number: Similar to a complex number, it has a real part. Its imaginary part, contrary to a complex number, has more than one component.

Known Plaintext-Ciphertext Attack: Finding a secret key using a set of known plaintext and ciphertext pairs.

Matrix: A rectangular table of numbers having rows and columns.

APPENDIX

A.1. The Determinant of (16)

The determinant of (16) is as follows:

$$
\begin{aligned}
&\det(B) = \sin\varphi(\sin(\varphi+4x)\sin(\varphi+8x) - \sin(\varphi+5x)\sin(\varphi+7x)) - \\
&\sin(\varphi+3x)(\sin(\varphi+x)\sin(\varphi+8x) - \sin(\varphi+2x)\sin(\varphi+7x)) + \\
&\sin(\varphi+6x)(\sin(\varphi+x)\sin(\varphi+5x) - \sin(\varphi+2x)\sin(\varphi+4x)) = \\
&\sin\varphi(\sin(\varphi+4x)(\sin(\varphi+7x)\cos x + \cos(\varphi+7x)\sin x) - \\
&(\sin(\varphi+4x)\cos x + \cos(\varphi+4x)\sin x)\sin(\varphi+7x)) - \\
&\sin(\varphi+3x)(\sin(\varphi+x)(\sin(\varphi+7x)\cos x + \cos(\varphi+7x)\sin x) - \\
&(\sin(\varphi+x)\cos x + \cos(\varphi+x)\sin x)\sin(\varphi+7x)) + \\
&\sin(\varphi+6x)(\sin(\varphi+x)(\sin(\varphi+4x)\cos x + \cos(\varphi+4x)\sin x) - \\
&(\sin(\varphi+x)\cos x + \cos(\varphi+x)\sin x)\sin(\varphi+4x)) = \\
&\sin\varphi\sin x(\sin(\varphi+4x)(\cos(\varphi+7x) - \cos(\varphi+4x)\sin(\varphi+7x)) - \\
&\sin(\varphi+3x)\sin x(\sin(\varphi+x)\cos(\varphi+7x) - \cos(\varphi+x)\sin(\varphi+7x)) + \\
&\sin(\varphi+6x)\sin x(\sin(\varphi+x)\cos(\varphi+4x) - \cos(\varphi+x)\sin(\varphi+4x)) = \\
&-\sin\varphi\sin x\sin 3x + \sin(\varphi+3x)\sin x\sin 6x - \sin(\varphi+6x)\sin x\sin 3x = \\
&\sin x(-\sin\varphi\sin 3x + \sin(\varphi+3x)\sin 6x - \sin(\varphi+6x)\sin 3x) = \\
&\sin x(-\sin\varphi\sin 3x + 2(\sin\varphi\cos 3x + \cos\varphi\sin 3x)\sin 3x\cos 3x - \\
&(\sin\varphi\cos 6x + 2\cos\varphi\sin 3x\cos 3x)\sin 3x) = \\
&\sin x(-\sin\varphi\sin 3x + 2\sin\varphi\cos^2 3x\sin 3x - \sin\varphi(\cos^2 3x - \sin^2 3x)\sin 3x) = \\
&\sin x(-\sin\varphi\sin 3x + \sin\varphi(\cos^2 3x + \sin^2 3x)\sin 3x) = \\
&\sin x(-\sin\varphi\sin 3x + \sin\varphi\sin 3x) = 0.
\end{aligned}
$$

A.2. Correlation-Based Quality Measure

A good encryption algorithm must produce an encrypted image of totally random patterns hiding all the features of the original image/signal, and the encrypted image/signal must be independent of the original image/signal (Elkamchouchi & Makar, 2005; Ismail et al., 2006; Ziedan et al., 2006). This means that the two images/signals must have a correlation coefficient very close to zero. The correlation coefficient, CC, is given by the following expression:

$$
C.C = \frac{\sum_{i=1}^{N}(x_i - E(x))(y_i - E(y))}{\sqrt{\sum_{i=1}^{N}(x_i - E(x))^2}\sqrt{\sum_{i=1}^{N}(y_i - E(y))^2}}. \tag{48}
$$

The closer C.C to zero is the better.

A.3. Irregular Deviation-Based Quality Measure

This quality measuring factor is based on how much the deviation affected by encryption is irregular (Elkamchouchi & Makar, 2005; Ismail et al., 2006; Ziedan et al., 2006). This quality measure can be formulated as follows:

1. Calculate the matrix, D, which represents the absolute value of the difference between each pixel value of the original and the encrypted image respectively:

$$D = |O - E|,$$

where O is the original (input) image and E is the encrypted (output) image.

2. Construct a histogram distribution of the D we get from step 1:

h=histogram (D).

3. Get the average value of how many pixels are deviated at every deviation value by:

$$DC = \frac{1}{256}\sum_{i=0}^{255} h_i,$$

4. Subtract this average from the deviation histogram and take the absolute value by:

$$AC(i) = |h_i - DC|.$$

5. Count:

$$ID = \sum_{i=0}^{255} AC(i).$$

The smaller ID is the bet.

Chapter 6
Design Time Engineering of Side Channel Resistant Cipher Implementations

Alessandro Barenghi
Politecnico di Milano, Italy

Luca Breveglieri
Politecnico di Milano, Italy

Fabrizio De Santis
Technische Universität München, Germany

Filippo Melzani
STMicroelectronics, Italy

Andrea Palomba
Politecnico di Milano, Italy

Gerardo Pelosi
Politecnico di Milano, Italy

ABSTRACT

Dependable and trustworthy security solutions have emerged as a crucial requirement in the specification of the applications and protocols employed in modern Information Systems (IS). Threats to the security of embedded devices, such as smart phones and PDAs, have been growing since several techniques exploiting side-channel information leakage have proven successful in recovering secret keys even from complex mobile systems. This chapter summarizes the side-channel techniques based on power consumption and elaborates the issue of the design time engineering of a secure system, through the employment of the current hardware design tools. The results of the analysis show how these tools can be effectively used to understand possible vulnerabilities to power consumption side-channel attacks, thus providing a sound conservative margin on the security level. The possible extension of this methodology to the case of fault attacks is also sketched.

INTRODUCTION

Recent advances in the complexity of modern information systems lead to their employment for treating a variety of security sensitive data. This has a direct impact on the everyday's life of the layperson, since quite a few secure devices are commonly employed to perform payments (e.g., credit cards and e-ticketing) and to regulate the access to infrastructures and automotive systems (e.g., remote access control systems). Another key area where the security and privacy of personal

DOI: 10.4018/978-1-4666-4030-6.ch006

data should be guaranteed is the one of mobile and embedded devices: voice and data communications have their confidentiality guarded by a plethora of crypto-schemes. These infrastructures have created the need to design mathematically secure cryptographic primitives and to engineer effective implementations thereof. Indeed, even if the security margin warranted by the mathematical properties of the cipher is adequate, the security of the system can be undermined by the information leakage via environmental parameters (i.e., by side-channel leakage).

One of the first official notes related to this concept dates back to 1956, when P. Wright reported that MI5 (the British intelligence agency) were stuck in their efforts to break an encryption machine employed by the Egyptian Embassy in London (Wright & Greengrass, 1988). The hand-operated, mechanical encryption machine was a rotor-based device including a number of wheels, each of which was associated to an alphabet letter in order to set the secret key employed to encipher a "plaintext" message. The enciphered message was printed on a paper ribbon, while the wheel-pins were set each day according to a "key sheet" shared only with the intended receiver. In order to sidestep the statistical cryptanalysis of the system, Wright suggested to place a microphone for eavesdropping on the tones (clicks) produced by the encryption machine during its usage. Indeed, Wright discovered that the click frequency could enable to determine the position of some rotors and, consequently, to reduce the computational effort needed to break the cipher.

Nowadays, Side-Channel Attacks (SCA) are a widespread and well recognized threat to digital embedded systems, which rely on gathering information on the cipher key from the observation of environmental parameters (Kocher, 1996; Kocher et al., 1999; Messerges et al., 1999a, 1999b; Brier et al., 2004; Mangard et al., 2007) despite the fact that such a secret is stored in a protected memory. Commonly observed parameters are represented by the power consumption of the device (Kocher et al., 1999; Mangard et al., 2007; Eisenbarth et al., 2008) or the electromagnetic emissions during the computation (Gandolfi & Mourtel, 2001; Quisquater & Samyde, 2001; Agrawal et al., 2002; Peeters et al., 2007; Gebotys & White, 2008; Barenghi et al., 2011c; Enev et al., 2011). Since these observed parameters depend on the switching activity of the circuit, which in turn depends on the values employed in the computation, it is possible to correlate the actual measurements on a real-world device with hypothetical values of the parameter predicted using a model depending on a part of the secret key. If the secret key portion is small enough, it is possible to examine exhaustively the correlation for all the possible values taken by the secret key portion and to detect which one is actually correlated with the exhibited device behavior. In this way, an attacker can recover the whole key one part at a time, with a limited computing effort (Mangard et al., 2007).

Until recently, both Differential Power Attacks (DPA) and Differential Electromagnetic Attacks (DEMA) have proven very successful in retrieving the embedded secret key even in very large, commercial grade devices such as FPGA (Moradi et al., 2011), through dealing with measurements issued with proper digital signal processing techniques (Barenghi et al., 2010b). A different approach from the passive observation of an environmental parameter during the regular functioning of a device, is to induce a device misbehavior, in such a way to cause errors during the execution of cryptographic primitives (Boneh et al., 2001; Joye & Tunstall, 2012). In this case, an attacker is said to mount a fault attack, by means of some injection technique such as focusing a laser beam on the chip, micro-carving it with a Focused Ion Beam, or inducing temporary alterations of the power supply or clock signals. An analysis of the results of the faulted computations, together with a suitable model of the fault injection technique (Differential Fault Attack, DFA), helps the attacker recover the secret key with a computational effort drastically reduced compared to the one needed for a traditional cryptanalytical attack (Boneh et al., 2001; Barenghi et al., 2009; Joye & Tunstall, 2012).

Research Challenges

Since side-channel attacks may effectively compromise the security of a system (Renauld et al., 2011), it is of a paramount relevance to investigate the security margin against them offered by an implementation of a crypto-scheme. The most straightforward evaluation method of the side-channel resistance, is to test directly if the attack works on a real target device. This kind of analysis is usually performed during the prototyping phase of the device, but it requires a rather mature version of the prototype, because the computations should be performed as close as possible to the final version. However, this resistance evaluation approach implies that the feedback in terms of the entity of the actual security margin is provided in a very late stage to the Integrated Circuit (IC) design workflow, thus imposing a strong delay if an architectural redesign or fix is needed to ensure protection from some attacks.

This slow feedback, coupled with the high cost of building a large number of prototypes, has spurred research efforts in the direction of the evaluation at design time of the security against SCA. The main goal of the major research branch on this topic is to understand whether the available tools for the estimation of the power consumption of digital circuits can provide precise enough results to quantify the security margin of the device against power attacks, without resorting to an actual implementation of the chip. The current results show that the power estimation tools are accurate in predicting the actual power consumption up to capturing correctly the effect of the wiring among transistors (Tiri & Verbauwhede, 2005; Tiri, K., 2010). In particular, the simulations are so accurate that they can provide more information than what may be measured on the real chip, due to the technological limitations of the measurement setup (Barenghi et al., 2011b). This in turn suggests that it is possible to build a methodology to perform an evaluation at design time in order to estimate an upper bound for the resilience of a countermeasure to power attacks, which does not involve any kind of silicon prototyping of the device.

Contributions

An overview of the most important side-channel attacks is provided, with the main focus on power analysis techniques. The goal of the first part is to allow the reader to familiarize with the key concepts related to SCA and to provide a convenient entry point into the field of embedded system security. As mentioned before, the security evaluation of a digital device, designed to execute either a software or a hardware cryptographic function, requires the manufacturer to have a working prototype of the chip. This forces the security analyst to act as one of the last elements of the production chain, thus involving high re-engineering costs in the case a product is found to be vulnerable to power attacks. Currently, there is not any common practice to address such an issue since no specific tool is available to support the side channel security assessment at design time. The second part of this chapter describes the methodology to simulate the power consumption signals of a real target device, and discusses the accuracy and reliability of the common power estimation tools (used in the design workflow of digital circuits) when they are employed for SCA assessments. A comparative analysis of the security margin inferable from performing differential power attacks both in the simulated and in the practical scenarios, is reported. A case study with an industrial grade implementation of AES (Daemen & Rijmen 2002; NIST, 2001) on a common 32-bit microprocessor is also described to support the validation of the presented methodology. Furthermore, the extension of the simulation methodology to the case of fault attacks is also sketched. There are a few possible approaches, none of which at present appears to be preferable. A few references to the existing case studies are listed and briefly discussed.

BACKGROUND

A cryptographic algorithm is an abstract mathematical object that transforms some inputs into some outputs, but it is embodied by a concrete instance running on a physical device placed in a real environment. While a mathematical object can be attacked only by exploiting its theoretical weaknesses, its physical realization can be attacked exploiting weaknesses intrinsic to the implementation. The objective of side-channel attacks is to determine the secret key stored in a cryptographic device through exploiting the information leaked via a physical side-channel left open by an insecure implementation. In general a side-channel can be defined as an unintended channel of a system, over which security sensitive information (i.e., related to the secret key) is leaked. Typical side-channels are, for instance, the power consumption absorbed by the device or the electromagnetic radiation it emits during the computation. Figure 1 depicts the typical side-channels over which the information is leaked, together with their position in the cryptographic computation dataflow. The device boundary wherein the cipher key is contained, is assumed to be tamper-proof or at least to prevent a straightforward readout of the cipher key. Among the depicted side-channels, we will tackle in depth the issues regarding the power consumption one, which is the side-channel with the strongest exploitability evidence provided by a wide and sound corpus of open literature. In order to provide the background notions pertaining to this kind of analysis, we now proceed to recap the key points of the power consumption modeling for digital devices, and subsequently we will present the most significant attack techniques described in the open literature.

Modeling Power Consumption of Digital Devices

The building blocks of any integrated circuit are the logic cells (Mangard et al., 2007). Logic cells

Figure 1. Typical side-channels for a physical cipher implementation

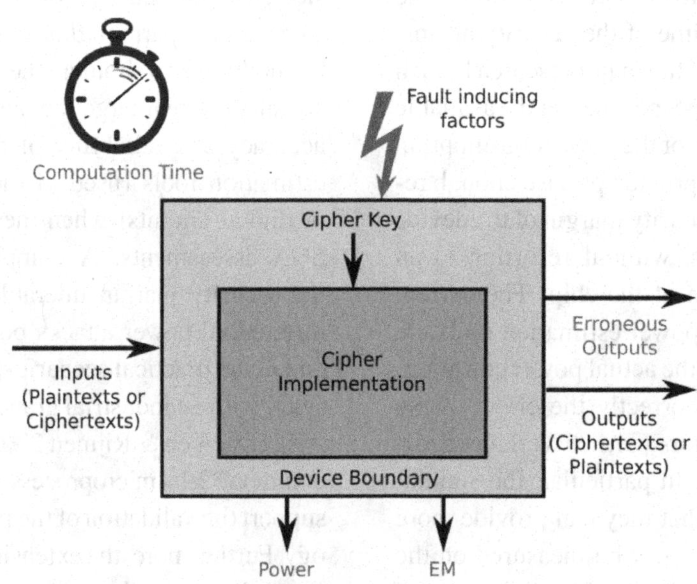

are typically supplied with a voltage referred to as V_{DD}, while the ground voltage is typically denoted by *GND*. The logic style defines how the logic input and output of the cells are represented by physical signals. In the Voltage Mode Logic (VML) style circuits, the V_{DD} and GND voltage levels are used to represent the logic values of the cells. Another common logic style is pre-charged (or pre-discharged) logic, where the output signals are pre-charged (or pre-discharged) to V_{DD} (or GND) and the logic output values are associated with the transitions from one level to the other one. The cells of digital circuits can be built employing different types of transistor: bipolar and the Metal-Oxide Semiconductor (MOS). The most common process technology is the Complementary Metal-Oxide-Semiconductor (CMOS) one.

The power absorbed by a CMOS cell W basically consists of two components: the power W_{leak} dissipated when the cell is powered on, and is in a steady state (i.e., not switching), which is called static or leakage power, and the power W_{dyn} absorbed when the cell switches its logic state, which is in turn denominated dynamic power: $W = W_{leak} + W_{dyn}$. The leakage power W_{leak} depends on the specific semiconductor technology employed to build the cell as well as on the working values of both temperature and voltage. The dynamic power consumption W_{dyn} is influenced by the switching activity of the circuit and is usually modeled as linearly dependent on both a cell-specific capacitance load and the transition rate of the physical signals driving the circuit (i.e., on the working signal frequency):

$$W_{dyn} = \frac{1}{2} C_{load} f \, V_{DD}^{\;2}$$

The split of the total power consumption of the cell in the two terms depends on the employed technology and on the fabrication process, but usually W_{leak} is much smaller than W_{dyn}. At a higher abstraction level, since the larger part of the power consumption depends on the switching activity of the physically flowing signals, the power dissipation of n logic cells between two consecutive time instants is (roughly) proportional to the exclusive-or between the output binary configurations $(x_1, x_2, \cdots, x_n) \in \{0,1\}^n$ of the cells at the mentioned time instants:

$$W \approx HW((x_1^{(t)}, x_2^{(t)}, \cdots, x_n^{(t)}) \oplus (x_1^{(t+1)}, x_2^{(t+1)}, \cdots, x_n^{(t+1)}))$$

also known as the Hamming distance between the two binary values. In case a pre-charged logic style is employed, the power consumption at a given time instant is proportional to the Hamming weight (HW) of the considered binary configuration:

$$W \approx HW(x_1^{(t)}, x_2^{(t)}, \cdots, x_n^{(t)})$$

As a practical example applied to a cryptosystem, in order to model the power consumption of a key dependent operation (f.i., addition via **xor** to the input value), we define the output v of the operation as $v = f(k, i)$. From the previous considerations we can define a power model $f_S(v)$, which provides us with an estimate of the actual power required to compute v, as $f_S\left(v\right) = HW(v)$. Another possible power model, in case the value to be modeled is stored in a register, is the Hamming distance between the former value contained in the register and the latter one which gets loaded into it. For instance, denoting as v and $f(i, k)$ the former and latter values contained in the register, the power consumption is proportional to $f_S\left(v, f(d, k)\right) = HW(v \oplus f(i, k))$.

Simple Power Analysis (SPA)

A SPA attack is a technique that aims at revealing the secret key of a cryptosystem by directly observing the power consumption of a device, as first described in (Kocher et al., 1999). SPA exploits the hypothesis that, if at a specific execution point the control flow of a cryptosystem depends on the key value, then the measurement of few executions may reveal the key. The simplest case is when an instruction is executed only depending on a specific value of the secret key, as in the key dependent branches that can be found in the implementation of the straightforward square-&-multiply (or double-&-add) exponentiation (addition) algorithm. If the multiplication operation has a power consumption different from the squaring one, it is possible for an attacker to distinguish them by simply looking at the recorded power trace of an exponentiation operation; consequentially, he can easily infer the bit values of the exponent (i.e., the secret key) (Mangard et al., 2007; Messerges et al., 1999b).

Differential Power Analysis (DPA)

Differential power analysis is a statistical power analysis technique, first introduced in (Kocher et al., 1999) and later formalized in (Messerges et at., 1999a), that relies on the Difference-Of-Means (DOM) statistical test (Moore, 2009) to find the secret key stored in a device. The fundamental difference between SPA and DPA is that the SPA attacks exploit the difference in the power consumption of the control flow branches, which are key-dependent, while the DPA attacks exploit the difference in the power consumption caused by the computation of different input data with the same key value. The main idea of DPA is to predict the power consumption caused by the combination of an intermediate value of the cipher with a small portion of the key, and to employ the actual measurements to distinguish which value of such key portion gives the correct prediction. To this end, a statistical test is employed to detect the dependences between the measurements and the predictions: once the correct prediction is found, the value of the corresponding key portion is retrieved. Depending on the particular statistical test used to verify the hypotheses, DPA attacks take a different denomination in the literature (Mangard et al., 2007, 2011).

In the practice, DPA attacks are mounted in five steps:

In the first step, an intermediate value v of the cryptographic algorithm must be chosen. This value must be computed as a function of a non-constant input data element d and a small portion of the secret key value $v = f(d,k)$. Note that the portion of the key should be small enough to keep small the set K of its possible values (i.e. the hypothesis space). Usually, 6-8 bits are considered a viable portion of the key to mount an attack.

In the second step, N power traces t_i using N different known data d_i and a fixed secret key are collected. The measurements are stored in the form of a matrix of power traces T of size $N \times M$, where each power trace represents a row vector, and the input data are recorded in the form of a vector d:

$$\boldsymbol{T} = \begin{bmatrix} \boldsymbol{t}_1 \\ \boldsymbol{t}_2 \\ \vdots \\ \boldsymbol{t}_i \\ \vdots \\ \boldsymbol{t}_N \end{bmatrix} = \begin{bmatrix} t_{1,1} & t_{1,2} & \cdots & t_{1,j} & \cdots & t_{1,M} \\ t_{2,1} & t_{2,2} & \cdots & t_{2,j} & \cdots & t_{2,M} \\ \vdots & \vdots & \ddots & \vdots & \ddots & \vdots \\ t_{i,1} & t_{i,2} & \cdots & t_{i,j} & \cdots & t_{i,M} \\ \vdots & \vdots & \ddots & \vdots & \ddots & \vdots \\ t_{N,1} & t_{N,2} & \cdots & t_{N,j} & \cdots & t_{N,M} \end{bmatrix} \qquad \boldsymbol{d} = \begin{bmatrix} d_1 \\ d_2 \\ \vdots \\ d_i \\ \vdots \\ d_N \end{bmatrix}$$

In the third step, the hypothetical intermediate values $v_{i,l}$ for each data d_i and every possible key portion guess $k_l \in K = \{k_1, k_2, \cdots, k_l, \cdots, k_{|K|}\}$ such that $v_{i,l} = f(d_i, k_l)$, are computed. This step produces a matrix V of size $N \times |K|$ that contains every intermediate value for each possible key guess k_l, as follows in Box 1.

Thus, each column $\boldsymbol{l}$ contains the intermediate values that have been computed through assuming a specific key guess $\boldsymbol{k}_l$, and the input data $\boldsymbol{d}_i$. The goal of DPA is to identify which column

Box 1.

$$
V = \begin{bmatrix}
v_{1,1} = f(d_1,k_1) & v_{1,2} = f(d_1,k_2) & \cdots & v_{1,l} = f(d_1,k_l) & \cdots & v_{1,|K|} = f(d_1,k_{|K|}) \\
v_{2,1} = f(d_2,k_1) & v_{2,2} = f(d_2,k_2) & \cdots & v_{2,l} = f(d_2,k_l) & \cdots & v_{2,|K|} = f(d_2,k_{|K|}) \\
\vdots & \vdots & \ddots & \vdots & \ddots & \vdots \\
v_{i,1} = f(d_i,k_1) & v_{i,2} = f(d_i,k_2) & \cdots & v_{i,l} = f(d_i,k_l) & \cdots & v_{i,|K|} = f(d_i,k_{|K|}) \\
\vdots & \vdots & \ddots & \vdots & \ddots & \vdots \\
v_{N,1} = f(d_N,k_1) & v_{N,2} = f(d_N,k_2) & \cdots & v_{N,l} = f(d_N,k_l) & \cdots & v_{N,|K|} = f(d_N,k_{|K|})
\end{bmatrix}
$$

actually contains the intermediate values computed by the device. Then, the key value $\boldsymbol{k}_l$ is recovered by the column index $\boldsymbol{l}$.

In the fourth step, a power model $f_S(\boldsymbol{v})$ that maps the matrix V of hypothetical intermediate values to a matrix $\boldsymbol{P}$ of hypothetical power consumption values, must be chosen according to the cipher implementation, as follows in Box 2.

Finally, in the fifth step each predicted power consumption, given a fixed key value $\boldsymbol{k}_l$ is compared by means of a statistical test, with the actual ones recorded in the power traces. This implies that the predicted consumption model represented by the $\boldsymbol{l}$-th column of $\boldsymbol{P}$ is compared against each of the columns of the trace matrix $\boldsymbol{T}$, as the attacker does not know in which time instant of the recorded trace the predicted operation happens. When a predicted power consumption matches, with a high statistical significance, the consumption of the device for a precise time instant, the key value hypothesized for the prediction is the correct one.

We will now describe the most common statistical tests employed to mount an attack, together with the name under which the attack is found in the open literature.

Difference-of-Means Test

The earliest proposed method to validate the consumption prediction relies on the test of the difference-of-means (Moore, 2009). To employ this statistical tool, the attacker needs to classify the traces into two sets $\boldsymbol{S}_0, \boldsymbol{S}_1$, in such a way that the sample-wise mean consumptions of the two sets differ significantly for some time instant. To this end, the attacker follows the procedure below:

The attacker chooses a so-called selection function, $\boldsymbol{g}(\cdot)$, that is a criterion to decide to which set $\boldsymbol{S}_0, \boldsymbol{S}_1$, a trace $\boldsymbol{t}_i$ belongs, relying on

Box 2.

$$
P = \begin{bmatrix}
p_{1,1} = f_s(v_{1,1}) & p_{1,2} = f_s(v_{1,2}) & \cdots & p_{1,l} = f_s(v_{1,l}) & \cdots & p_{1,|K|} = f_s(v_{1,|K|}) \\
p_{2,1} = f_s(v_{2,1}) & p_{2,2} = f_s(v_{2,2}) & \cdots & p_{2,l} = f_s(v_{2,l}) & \cdots & p_{2,|K|} = f_s(v_{2,|K|}) \\
\vdots & \vdots & \ddots & \vdots & \ddots & \vdots \\
p_{i,1} = f_s(v_{i,1}) & p_{i,2} = f_s(v_{i,2}) & \cdots & p_{i,l} = f_s(v_{i,l}) & \cdots & p_{i,|K|} = f_s(v_{i,|K|}) \\
\vdots & \vdots & \ddots & \vdots & \ddots & \vdots \\
p_{N,1} = f_s(v_{N,1}) & p_{N,2} = f_s(v_{N,2}) & \cdots & p_{N,l} = f_s(v_{N,l}) & \cdots & p_{N,|K|} = f_s(v_{N,|K|})
\end{bmatrix}
$$

the value of the predicted power consumption $p_{i,l} = f_S(v_i, l) = fs(f(d_i, k_l))$, where $1 < i < N, 1 < l <| K |$, previously computed with the data input d_i corresponding to the trace t_i and the key hypothesis k_l. For instance, if we need a selection function to classify the power consumption of loading an 8 bit value from a lookup table, a viable one is the following:

$$g(p_{i,l}) = 1 \text{ if } p_{i,l} > 4, g(p_{i,l}) = 0 \text{ if } p_{i,l} < 4$$

The attacker employs the selection function to split the traces into the two sets S0, S1 according to the value taken by it. This phase is repeated for every possible key hypothesis k_l, as each key will generate different partitions of the traces: $S_{0,l}$ and $S_{1,l}$.

For each of the possible partitions, the attacker computes the sample-wise mean $m_{0,l}$ of all the traces belonging to $S_{0,l}$, and the sample-wise mean $m_{1,l}$ of the ones belonging to $S_{1,l}$.

The attacker computes the sample-wise differences $\delta_l = m_{0,l} - m_{1,l}$ for all possible key hypotheses k_l. If the key hypothesis is correct, the value of δ_l is expected to be significantly large for some time instant ***j***, since the selection function has operated a correct partitioning of the traces into two sets, where the average power consumption of the operation fits the prediction. If the key hypothesis is wrong, the selection function simply operates a random partitioning of the traces into two sets, which are thus expected to have the same average consumption at every time instant.

Following this procedure, the attacker retrieves a portion of the correct key and repeats the attack (changing the guessed key portion and employing the same measurements), until either the whole cipher key is found or the security margin (i.e., the nvumber of remaining unknown bits) is low enough to be overcome through an approach based on exhaustive searching. A critical choice in the procedure, besides choosing the correct power model and collecting well synchronized and noise-free measurements, is a proper choice of the selection function, which is usually made through algorithm-dependent heuristics. For instance, a common choice to attack the DES cryptosystem is to employ as a selection function the value of the first output bit of the first S-Box of the first round, while attempting to guess the first 6 bits of the round key (Kocher et al., 1999). For the AES cryptosystem, the most common choice is to employ the previously mentioned selection function on the output of the s-box in either the first or the last round, i.e, to classify the traces depending on whether the hamming weight of the result of the operation is greater or less than half the length of the result.

Correlation Power Analysis (CPA)

Correlation power analysis uses the Pearson's (linear) correlation coefficient as a statistical test to distinguish the correct key hypothesis (Brier et al., 2004; Mangard et al., 2007). The correlation coefficient of two random variables, ***A*** has a value in the range $[-1,1]$ and is defined as the ratio between the covariance of the two variables and the product of their variances. High values of the correlation coefficient (regardless of the sign) express a high correlation between the two random variables, while a value close to zero indicates that they are not linearly correlated. A CPA considers as first random variable, the device power consumption in a precise time instant, ***j***. Therefore the j-th column of the aforementioned T matrix is intended as an array that includes the available instances of such a random variable:

$$T[:, j] = [t_{1,j}, t_{2,j}, \cdots, t_{i,j}, \cdots, t_{N,j}].$$

The second random variable is identified with the power consumption model corresponding to a generic key hypothesis k_l. As a consequence, the l-th column of the aforementioned power model matrix $\boldsymbol{P}$ is considered as an array that includes the available instances of such a random variable:

$$\boldsymbol{P}\left[:,l\right]=\left[p_{1,l},\ p_{2,l},\cdots,p_{i,l},\cdots,p_{N,l}\right].$$

Given the two array random variables instances, the CPA technique computes the sample estimator of ρ for every time instant and every key hypothesis in order to obtain $|\boldsymbol{K}|$ different time series: rl(j), with $\boldsymbol{j} \in \{1,\cdots,\boldsymbol{M}\}$, and $\boldsymbol{l} \in \{1,\cdots,|\boldsymbol{K}|\}$. The time sequence including the highest value (in a certain time instant j^*) is recognized as the one corresponding to the correct key hypothesis. The accuracy of the result depends on the number of measurements (for the statistical significance of the estimator), on the correct temporal alignment among measurements corresponding to different inputs, on the correctness of the power model, and on the environmental noise of both the target device and the employed measurement setup.

Fault-Based Attacks

A different methodology is based on using fault injection as a side-channel for the attack, and is known as active or fault attack. The attacker tries to force the device under attack to perform erroneous computations. In order to reach this goal, a couple of techniques have been developed, relying on a reproduction of the natural fault induction causes. The workflow for a typical fault attack methodology begins with the induction of an unexpected behavior of the device, subsequently collecting the erroneous output data and finally analyzing them under suitable hypotheses. Usually, it is necessary for the attacker to compare the correct and erroneous results corresponding to an execution of the cryptographic primitive with the same inputs, in order to recover the secret information contained in the device. However, in case of a public key cryptosystem, it is possible to devise attacks that are effective even without being in possess of the correct result of the cryptographic primitive (Boneh et al., 2001; Barenghi et al., 2011d).

Usually, the secret keys are held on the device in a form of storage that cannot be read in a straightforward way. Common solutions to achieve this are: write-only EEPROM buffers, SRAM buffers backed up by a battery or key derivation from hardware features of the etched die. These methodologies can also be complemented by sensor circuits detecting tamper attempts aimed at extracting the key.

A high-level taxonomy of the fault attack techniques may be stated as follows

- **Non-Invasive Attacks:** The attacker limits his actions to conventional access means to the device, without physically tampering with it in order to add extra interaction channels. An example of such an attack technique is represented by tampering with the supply voltage or external clock line.
- **Semi-Invasive Attacks:** This class of attacks usually requires the attacker to remove the chip packaging, usually through acid etching, before the attack commences. Typical attacks belonging to this class involve the irradiation of the chip with concentrated light or laser beams, or resort to chemical etching to highlight the contents of memory cells.
- **Invasive Attacks:** This class of attacks involve a direct action by the attacker on the silicon die. Typically, it is possible, through the use of a focused ion beam or microprobes, to either modify, rebuild or cut the on-die wiring among transistors, and to directly inject anomalous signals. The cost of the equipment employed in these techniques restricts their usage to extremely valuable targets, for the attacker to reach an economic break-even in breaching the security provided by the device.

A number of physical techniques exist to induce a faulty behavior during the computation of a cryptographic device. A quick summary of the available means is the following: high energy radiations (Govindavajhala & Appel, 2003; Bar-El et al., 2006), heat (Govindavajhala & Appel, 2003; Bar-El et al., 2006), die irradiation with either light or lasers (Leveugle et al., 2007; Monnet et al., 2006; Skorobogatov & Anderson, 2002), focused ion beams, power line tampering (Aumuller et al., 2002; Kim & Quisquater, 2007; Schmidt & Herbst, 2008; Barenghi et al., 2009), clock line tampering (Anderson & Kuhn, 1996), and strong electromagnetic pulses (Quisquater & Samyde, 2002).

The aforementioned techniques differ in terms of cost, technical effort, and achievable precision in the control of the position and time instant where the fault is injected. Consequently, in order to decouple the technologies with which the fault is injected from its effects, they are usually described through a fault model and an error model. The fault model characterizes the way the physical modifications of the device are obtained, while the error model characterizes the logical effect on the execution of a cryptographic algorithm.

It is possible to devise a taxonomy of the precision in both the space and time that a technology provides, as follows:

- Depending on the control the attacker has on the location of the fault: no control (it is impossible to control the location of the fault), approximate control (e.g., it is possible to choose a target register), complete control (e.g., a particular bit can be targeted by the fault).
- Depending on the control over the timing of the fault: no control (it is impossible to control the timing of the fault), approximate control (e.g., a block of few operations is targeted), precise control (e.g., the exact time is chosen and a certain operation is affected).

The error model describes the effect on either the data flow or the control flow of the program. Usually, alterations in the data flow are characterized as single or multiple bit flips, which can also be regarded as a random change in the value of the affected variable. The alterations to the control flow are usually caused by a modification of the instruction counter of a software implementation of the cipher, which translates in either a deviation of the control flow or in an instruction skipping. In case the underlying architecture supports conditional instructions (e.g. ARM, PowerPC), the possible effect of an alteration may also induce instruction skipping through changing the opcode of the executed instruction.

Example of a Fault Attack

A simple example of a fault attack, known as the Bellcore attack (Boneh et al., 2001), is now presented. Let RSA be the target cryptosystem (Rivest et al., 1978), and consider its signature generation algorithm. The generation of the RSA signature is the computation of the modular exponentiation $s = m^d \, mod \, N$, where $N = pq$ is the product of two large primes: m the message and d the private key. The publicly available variables are N and e, the public key, which satisfies the relationship $ed \, mod\left(N\right) = 1$. The signing device knows also the private variables p, q, and d, which are used to compute the signature in an efficient way by exploiting the Chinese Remainder Theorem. Instead of the full modular exponentiation, two smaller exponentiations $s_p = m^d \, mod \, p$ and $s_q = m^d \, mod \, q$ are calculated, and are then combined calculating the signature through one of the two following formulas:

$$s = s_q + q\left(\left(s_p - s_q\right)\left(q^{-1} \, mod \, p\right) mod \, p\right)$$

$$s = s_p + p\left(\left(s_q - s_p\right)\left(p^{-1} \, mod \, q\right) mod \, q\right)$$

Considering a technique able to induce any kind of error during the computation of either s_p or s_q (a rather easy to achieve error model, as almost any fault model for a fault induction technique fits), it is possible to successfully factor the modulus through the following computations. Indeed, suppose that the computation is disturbed in such a way that the calculated s_p is wrong. Computing the final value leads to a wrong signature $\tilde{s}$ such that $(s - \tilde{s}) mod\, q = 0$. An attacker can now break the security of the cryptosystem by easily factorizing N as $\gcd\left(N,\, s - \tilde{s}\right) = q$. Further details on this attack can be found in (Boneh et al., 2001).

OVERVIEW OF HARDWARE DESIGN WORKFLOW

The design of modern Integrated Circuits (ICs) follows a well established design workflow, which is largely or completely automated. This workflow is employed to describe, verify, synthesize, simulate, validate and fabricate the digital circuit. The outcome of the workflow is provided to semiconductor foundries to fabricate the IC samples made from silicon wafers, each of which may hold hundreds of dies (Mano, 1998). The design process is divided into a series of phases, which today are rather well established. Here is a brief list thereof:

- **Logic Design:** Given the functional and non-functional requirements of a target chip design, the hardware designer comes up with a formally specified functional and structural description of the whole system architecture. In order to simplify the design of a complex system, this description is normally broken down into a top level system and several sub-systems. These components are specified using a variety of methodologies and formalisms: behavioral (i.e. algorithmic) descriptions, finite state machines, combinatorial logic or sequential logic. This phase is called Logic Design or also Register Transfer Level (RTL) design. A behavioral or RTL specification is expressed in a Hardware Description Language (HDL), of which a few standardized and widely used examples exist, e.g., Verilog or VHDL. To clarify a little, the VHDL language allows to describe a digital (sub)system by giving its algorithmic function, or its state-transition graph, or by modeling it as a sequential circuit made of memories, registers, combinatorial functions, busses, etc.
- **Formal Verification:** In order to guarantee the adherence of the design to both the original specification and constraints, automatic functional/logical verification tools are employed, before passing to the next design phases. These tools check that the description is coherent with the functional specifications. In principle the formal verification may be skipped if the design is already granted to be functionally correct.
- **Logic Synthesis:** The (verified) circuit description has to be translated into a lower-level description that is suited for physical fabrication. A synthesis tool takes an RTL hardware description and a "standard cell library" as input, i.e. takes a description of each component in terms of logic gates with silicon area, timing and power model, and produces a gate-level netlist as output, through considering constraints such as timing, area and power consumption. The RTL description is converted into a gate-level netlist through a logic/RTL synthesis tool, such as: "Design Compiler" (Synopsys™), "RTL Compiler" (Cadence™) or "Blast Create" (Magma™). These synthesis tools try to meet the constraints, through calculating the cost of various possible implementations and through generating the best

gate level implementation for the given set of constraints.

- **Logic Simulation:** In order to check the consistency of the results provided by the logic synthesis, a phase of logic level simulation is performed through tools such as "ModelSim" (Mentor Graphics™) or "Incisive" (Cadence™). These tools provide a logic level simulation of the circuit, i.e. they consider the values "high" and "low" for each possible wire and take into account the delays proper of the target cell library chosen for the synthesis. In some cases, the simulation may consider more electric parameters, like parasitic capacitances, etc., as well as evaluate other interesting circuit features, like the average power consumption or the resilience to faults.
- **Pre-Layout Validation (or Testing):** The functional validation is performed through HDL described testbenches, which provide the correct response of the circuit to a large number of inputs. An alternative to testbench-based verification is represented by some specific formal verification tools such as "Formality" (Synopsys™) and "Verplex" (Cadence™), which check for the logic equivalence of the HDL and netlist level implementations.
- **Place and Route:** The gate-level netlist is subsequently synthesized into a physical layout using floor-planning and Place-&-Route (PNR) tools that provide a geometric representation of the netlist in a data format known as Graphic Database System II (GDSII), which can be transferred onto silicon. This is done according to the guidelines and limitations specified by the provided fabrication process library that specifies the circuit level characterization of the cells implementing the logic gates as well as the timing and power dissipation parameters of the cells. Common tools employed in this phase are: "IC Compiler" (Synopsys™), "Encounter" (Cadence™), and "Blast Fusion" (Magma™).
- **Post-Layout Validation (or Testing):** Finally, physical verification procedures are performed to check whether the chip layout still satisfies the requirements and constraints of the project, before providing the GDSII design description to the foundry to fabricate the a chip prototype. The physical verification procedures are performed with the so-called sign-off validation tools, such as "PrimeTime" (Synopsys™) or "Encounter Timing System" (Cadence™). For instance, these tools check whether the PNR description of the chip still matches the timing constraints imposed and does not exceed the thermal dissipation and power consumption specifications.

This outline of the design workflow of a digital circuit is sufficiently general to model the automated toolchains that are commonly employed to obtain the commercial as well as experimental chips today.

METHODOLOGY FOR POWER ANALYSIS AT DESIGN TIME

This section will describe the methodology employed in order to generate simulated power consumption traces for the considered platform.

Analysis Principle

Simulated power traces can be generated through a proper use of the hardware design tools previously mentioned. The simulation can be performed at different accuracy levels, depending on the designer needs. The most accurate way to predict the power consumption for a given design is to perform a simulation of the transistor network (e.g., by the HSpice tool), thus computing the value of the electric currents circulating for each time instant and obtaining the instantaneous power consumption value by multiplying them times the value of the supply voltage. However, the computational load imposed by this kind of simulation does not allow the designer to simulate large, real world circuits within reasonable time limits.

In order to reduce the simulation cost, a less accurate but more reasonable approach is to model the behavior of every logic gate, instead of the transistors. This is obtained by employing the power consumption figures included in the standard cell library (power library) and the capacitance loads associated with the wiring (as provided by the PNR tool). An overview of the workflow for obtaining simulated power traces at gate-level is provided in Figure 2. In particular, the first step to perform in order to obtain simulated power traces is the logic synthesis of the design under attack.

Our practical examples adopt this second more viable approach. This has been carried out by using the RTL Compiler from the Encounter suite by Cadence Design Systems. Subsequently, the gate-level simulation step has been performed through recording the switching activity of each gate in the circuit using the Incisive Enterprise Simulator by Cadence Design Systems. Then, the design has been further refined with a floorplanning tool (Encounter by Cadence Design Systems) in order to obtain information on the length of the physical wires on the chip, and therefore to deduce the parasitic capacitances which will affect both the timing and power consumption of the device. This information is output by the Encounter tool in the form of an annotated netlist, which provides the grounds for an accurate power simulation of the actual circuit, without the burden of taking into account the whole geometric representation of the circuit. The final power simulation of the target circuit, needed in order to obtain a design-time estimate of the leaked information through the power consumption, is performed via the Synopsys PrimeTime sign-off tool, giving it both the annotated netlist and the switching activity of the circuit.

Through combining the information available from the power library with the switching activity of the circuit obtained from a gate-level simulation, the power profile of the device is recorded. The simulated power consumption recordings can be computed with a maximum time precision that matches the smallest time delay among those of the cells in the power library, in the range of a few tenths of picoseconds.

Figure 2. Workflow employed to obtain simulated power traces at gate level

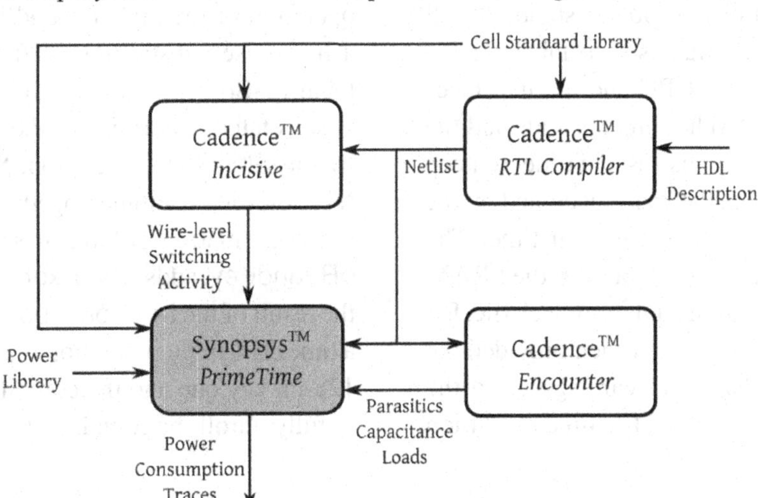

Case Study

In the following section we describe the target hardware architecture and the software implementation of the cryptographic primitive employed as a case study. Then we provide a comparison between the simulation estimates of the power consumption and the actual measures on a physical sample of the chip.

Target Device

The target device of our evaluation is a development board by STMicroelectronics, hosting an ultra low-power microprocessor geared towards healthcare applications, a typical scenario where security concerns are critical. The board features a MIPS-based 32-bit microprocessor fabricated with a 90 nm cell library tuned for ultra low-power applications. The platform is equipped with a 66 KiB on-die SRAM and an external 384 KiB Flash memory, and works in the 4-48 MHz system clock range. The regular operating frequency of the CPU clock is 4 MHz. Further details on the board model cannot be disclosed due to confidentiality issues.

Simulation Methodology of the Target Device

During the evaluation, the chip was synthesized using the same ultra low power standard cell library at 90 nm that was used to fabricate the physical chip. Only the CPU and the interfaces to and from the SRAM holding the code and the data were simulated in this case, in order to keep within feasibility both the space occupied by the simulated traces and the simulation time. The storage and retrieval of the data from the SRAM was simulated through an HDL testbench file, fed to the Cadence Incisive tool, which provided the correct values on the signal wires going to the SRAM interface of the chip. The time resolution used for the simulations was 10 ns, thus resulting in simulated power traces capturing an effective bandwidth of 50 MHz. The choice of this time resolution limits the amount of data produced by the simulations to an analyzable one, without losing significant information about the analyzed device. This is reasonable as the switching activity of the circuit is driven by a 4 MHz clock, which is far slower than the 10 ns simulation step. It is confirmed by the results, where we report that the information loss from the attack evaluation standpoint was negligible.

Target Algorithm

The algorithm chosen for the evaluation is the Advanced Encryption Standard (AES): the symmetric key cipher chosen as the standard for secret key encryption by NIST (Daemen & Rijmen, 2002). The AES algorithm processes 128 bits of plaintext at once and encrypts it using a key that is 128-, 192- or 256-bit wide depending on the security requirement of the application. The input plaintext is represented as a 16-byte square matrix and the cipher processes it through iterating a sequence of operations, known as the round, for a variable number of times depending on the selected key length. The cipher key is expanded by a KeySchedule procedure into a set of 128-bit sub-keys, one per round of the cipher. The first operation of the cipher round is the SubBytes, a byte-wise substitution of the state through a table (S-Box) lookup. The result is then byte-wise rotated according to the pattern specified by the ShiftRows operation. Subsequently, the MixColumns combines together the output values of the ShiftRows column-wise. Finally, the AddRoundKey, adds, via an xor addition, the key to the result of the MixColumns operation 32-bit at a time. The implementation is an industrial grade 128-bit key one and the compiler was instructed to fully unroll the rounds of the cipher.

Measurement Setup

Figure 3 provides an outlook of the acquisition setup employed to record the power traces on the real world device. The measured power traces were obtained with an Agilent Infiniium 80000B series oscilloscope and an active Agilent differential voltage probe. The oscilloscope features 4 independent analog channels, a 2 GHz analog bandwidth, coupled with an 8-bit ADC capable of recording 40 GSamples/s, with a noise floor of 3 mV RMS, and a minimum vertical resolution of 10 mV. The measured power traces were acquired using a sampling frequency of 50 MSamples/s over an acquisition window of 2.6 ms. The sampling frequency of the oscilloscope matches the one of the simulations, in order to provide a fair comparison among the results obtained with the two techniques. The measurements were taken by sampling the voltage drop variations over a 1 kΩ resistor Rsh inserted in series between the power pin of the chip and a low-drop voltage regulator (LDO) supplied by an external power supply. The choice of a relatively big shunt resistor (commonly the value of the shunt resistor is in the 1-2 Ω range) was driven by the amount of current (in the μA range) absorbed by the chip. The beginning and end of the acquisition of the power consumption measurement were driven by a digital General Purpose Input Output (GPIO) signal on the device under test.

Comparison Between Design-Time Simulated Traces and Real Measurements

The plot at the top of Figure 4 provides the estimated power consumption of one AES-128 encryption starting at time 0, while the plot at the bottom of Figure 4 provides the measured power consumption of one encryption: the beginning of the encryption operation can be spotted from the spike in the power consumption caused by the assertion of the trigger signal. In both cases, the activity of the ten AES rounds is clearly distinguishable in the traces and lasts roughly 1.74 ms. To reduce the measurement noise, the measured trace depicted in the bottom plot of Figure 4, is obtained as the average of 32 measurements of the same encryption. To achieve a deeper understanding of

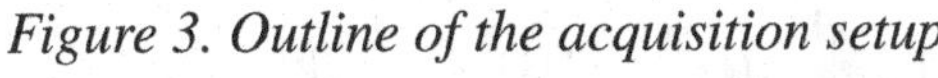
Figure 3. Outline of the acquisition setup

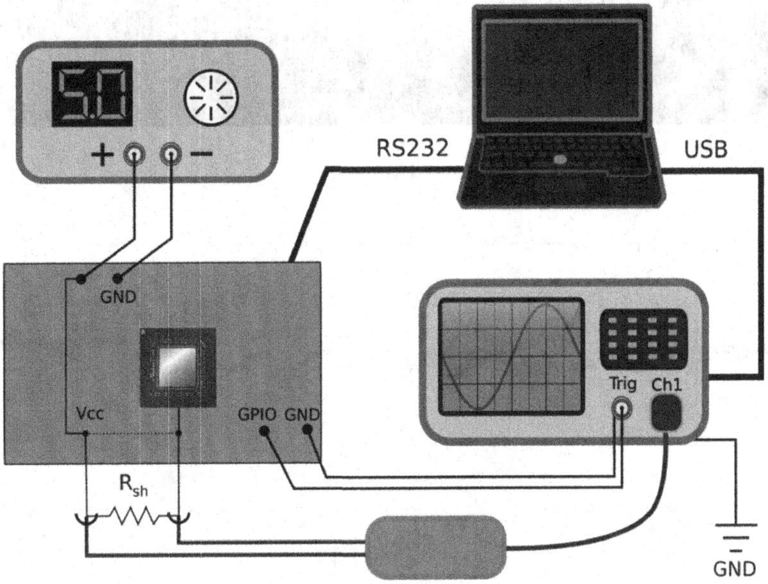

the differences between simulated and measured traces, the plots in Figure 5 show a comparison between the estimated and the measured power consumption of a single AES encryption in the frequency domain. The figures depict the single side amplitude spectrum of both the measured signal and the simulated one.

The first fact to be noticed is that the harmonic component of the simulated power traces with the greatest amplitude is the one located at 4 MHz, exactly the clock frequency of the device under exam. This comes from the fact that the switching activity, and thus the dynamic power consumption, of a clocked circuit mostly happens in correspondence with the clock edge. The simulated signal has a large effective bandwidth, since the last significant harmonic component showing a peak is located at 24 MHz. In particular, comparing the spectrum of the averaged signal with the one of the simulation, it is possible to notice that some of the harmonics are significantly damped. This is due to the RLC circuit that is established on the path from the measurement point to the ADC of the oscilloscope (Li, 2006). These parasitics are typically due to the capacitances that are intentionally placed by the analog designers between VDD and GND in order to stabilize the voltage supplied to the chip.

Moreover, another effect to be taken into account is the one due to the bonding wires connecting the pins of the package to the solder pads of the chip. In practice, this results in the measured power traces always being to some extent band-pass filtered when compared to the simulated power traces. Since the time-wise alignment of the measurements is a critical issue when performing side-channel attacks, we note that the simulated traces are always perfectly time-aligned, while the measured ones may suffer from an, albeit small, jitter in the timescale. In this case, simulated and

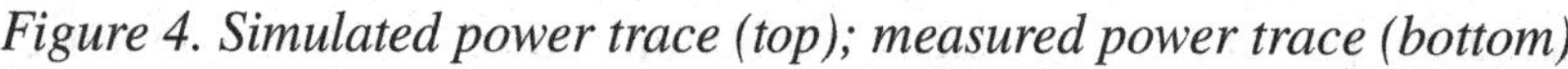

Figure 4. Simulated power trace (top); measured power trace (bottom)

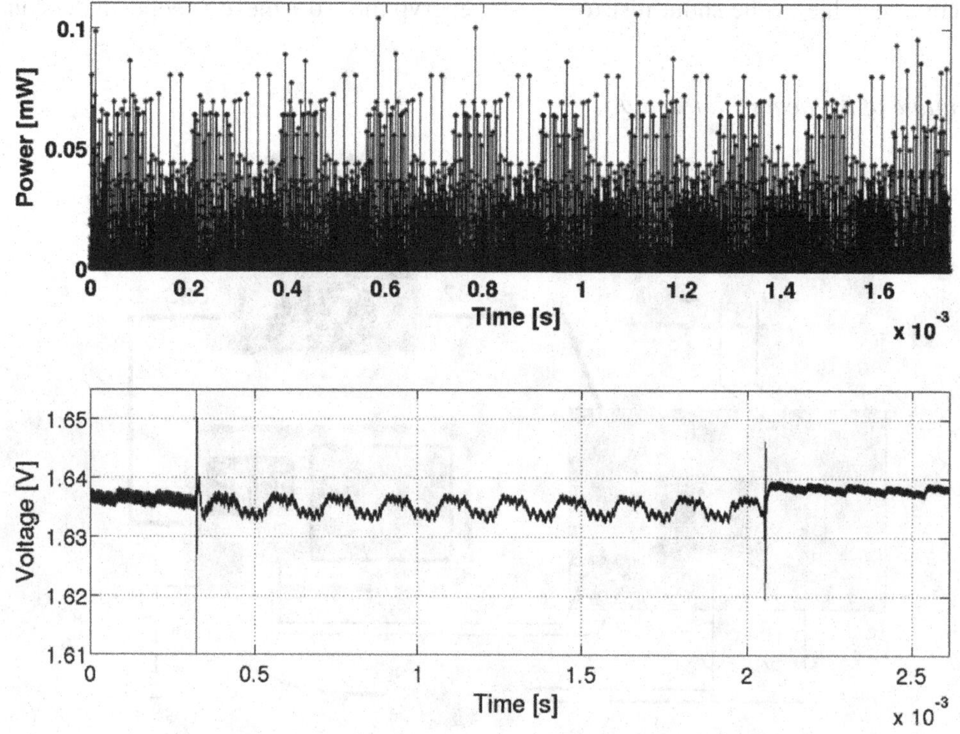

Figure 5. Power spectrum of the simulated trace (top); power spectrum of the measured trace (bottom)

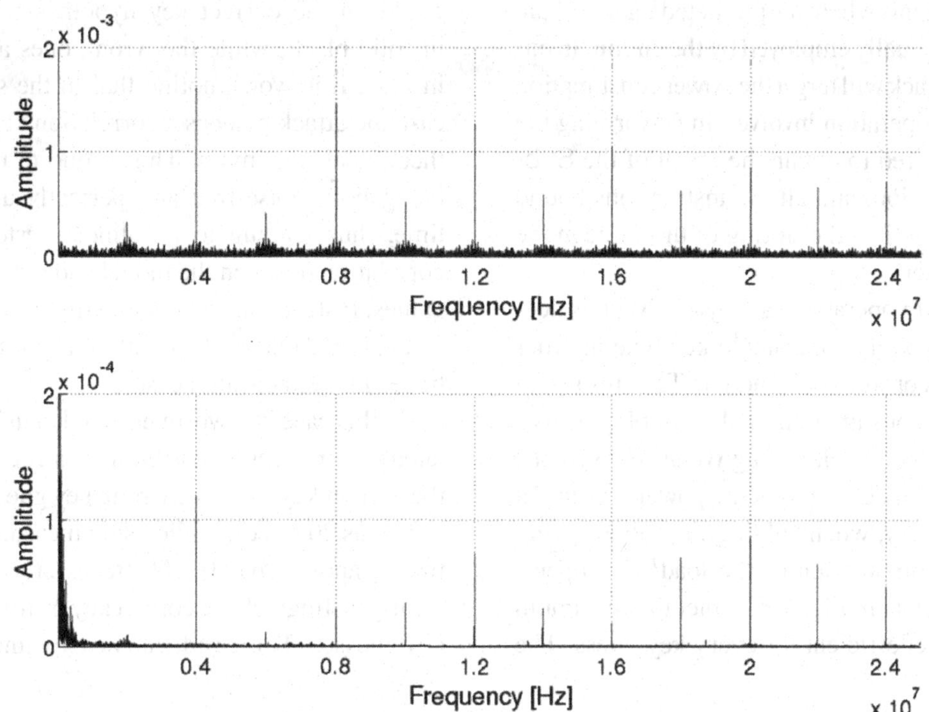

measured power traces have exactly the same execution time with an average of 1.731 ms and a standard deviation of 1.2 μs.

Since the execution times between the simulations and the experimental setup match, we can say that the timing of the practical measurements is correctly performed. Additionally, we can observe that the non-zero standard deviation highlights that the encryptions do not always take the same amount of time on the target platform.

The maximum distance between the shortest and the longest execution is roughly 16 clock cycles in our measurements. Since there are not either mechanisms such as caches or control flow divergences (implemented either via predicated instructions or common jumps), which may affect the execution time, the cause of the different duration has to be sought in the design of the instruction set. In fact, the decode stage of the CPU needs a different amount of time to fully decode some instructions, depending on the value of their actual operands. This phenomenon leads to a spread of the time instants where the correct model will have non-negligible correlation with the trace (Mangard, 2004), while lowering the absolute value of the correlation coefficient for those points. However the differences in the execution time depending on the data, represent another side-channel that can be exploited by an attacker for mounting timing attacks (Bernstein, 2004).

Comparison Between CPAs Mounted on Simulated and Measured Traces

As described in the previous sections, the typical way to carry out a correlation power attack is to calculate the Pearson's correlation coefficient between the hypothesized power consumption of an encryption operation for every possible key guess, and each sample of the power traces. In order to analyze the results, the values of the Pearson's correlation coefficient for the different key hypotheses at each time instant, are compared. The correlation for the correct key is expected to have a significant value in correspondence with the time instants where the predicted intermediate values are actually employed by the circuit. In our case, this attack will target the power consumption of the load operation involved in performing the lookup required to obtain the result of the SubBytes operation, and all the instructions bound to the lookup (i.e., the storing of the value in the target register).

Since both operations act byte-wise, it is necessary to hypothesize a single key byte in order to build a consumption model. This results in building 28 consumption models employing as a power estimator the Hamming Weight (HW) of the result. This model captures the power consumed by the circuitry, when holding the value, during either the computation or the load/store operations. The plots in Figure 6 depict the maximum correlation coefficient for every key guess. The trend of the correlation coefficient of the model based on the correct key hypothesis, is drawn in solid black, while the wrong ones are drawn in grey. It is worth noting that in the simulated case the attack reaches a correlation close to the theoretical maximum. This is due to the traces being both noise-free and perfectly aligned in time, thus leading to an almost perfect linear correlation between the model and the simulated values. Instead, only a low maximum correlation (roughly 0.2) is reached with ten times as many traces in the measured case.

In this case it is worth noting that using simulated power traces is possible to clearly distinguish the correct key from the wrong key guesses, with as low as 20 traces; while using measured power traces, approximately 700 traces are needed to clearly distinguish the correct key from the wrong key guesses. This result can be explained by ob-

Figure 6. Maximum value for Pearson's correlation coefficient on simulated traces (top); maximum value for Pearson's correlation coefficient on measured traces (bottom)

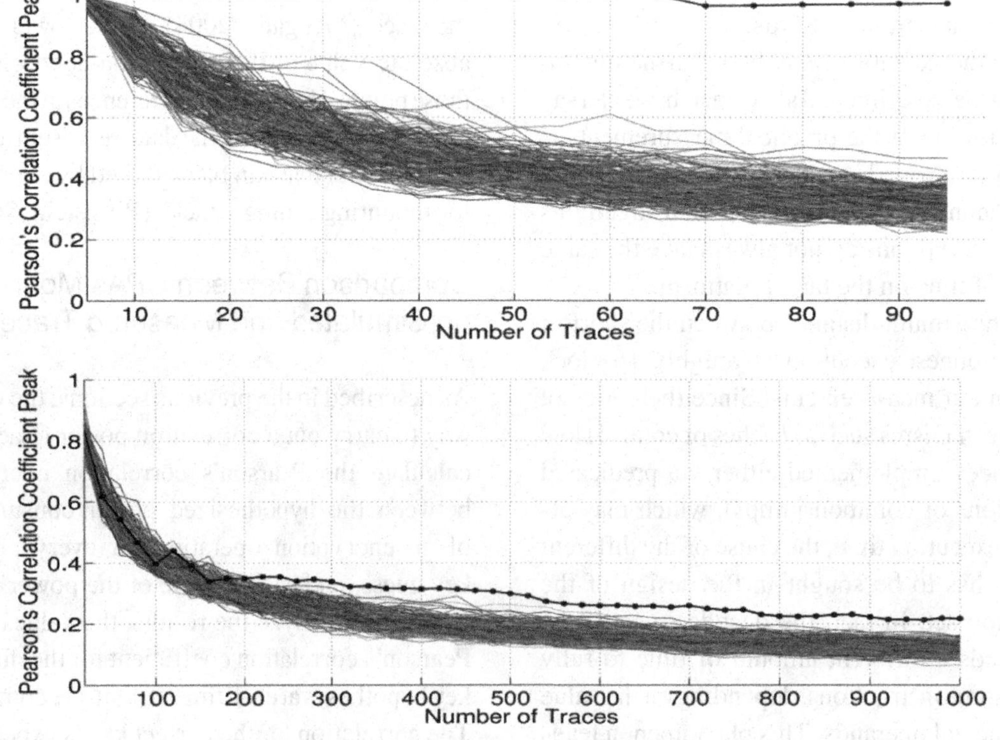

serving that the simulated power traces are noise-free, while the measured traces have a relative low Signal-to-Noise Ratio (SNR) due to the practical difficulties to precisely measure the power absorbed by an ultra low power device.

In order to better understand the relationship between the two results, plots in Figure 7 show a superposition of simulated and measured traces for the second attack considered in this section. For the sake of clarity, the traces were realigned in time to the beginning of the AES encryption and only the correlation coefficients for the correct key hypothesis are shown. As it can be noticed in the plot at the top of Figure 7, the lone peak in the correlation of the measurements matches perfectly in time one of the peaks predicted by the simulation. Willing to understand the multiple peaks on the simulated traces, we analyzed the code executed on the CPU. All the time intervals where the attacked value is in use, are highlighted by the dashed zones in the bottom plot in Figure 7. It is worth noting that the byte under attack is used by several different instructions in the code and every time it generates a correlation peak in the simulated power traces, while this does not happen in the measured power traces where the correlation peak is well visible only when load operations are executed. We can thus state that the load operation consumes a greater overall amount of energy, and thus the differences in the power consumption are easily measurable even with the technical difficulties imposed by the real world setup.

It is worth noting that the small correlation peaks that show up in the simulated traces do not emerge on the measured ones due to the naturally occurring low-pass filtering behavior of the real world measurement setup (Li, 2006). This

Figure 7. Correlation coefficients for the correct key hypothesis of simulated and measured traces (top); zoom over the vulnerable region of the cipher execution (bottom)

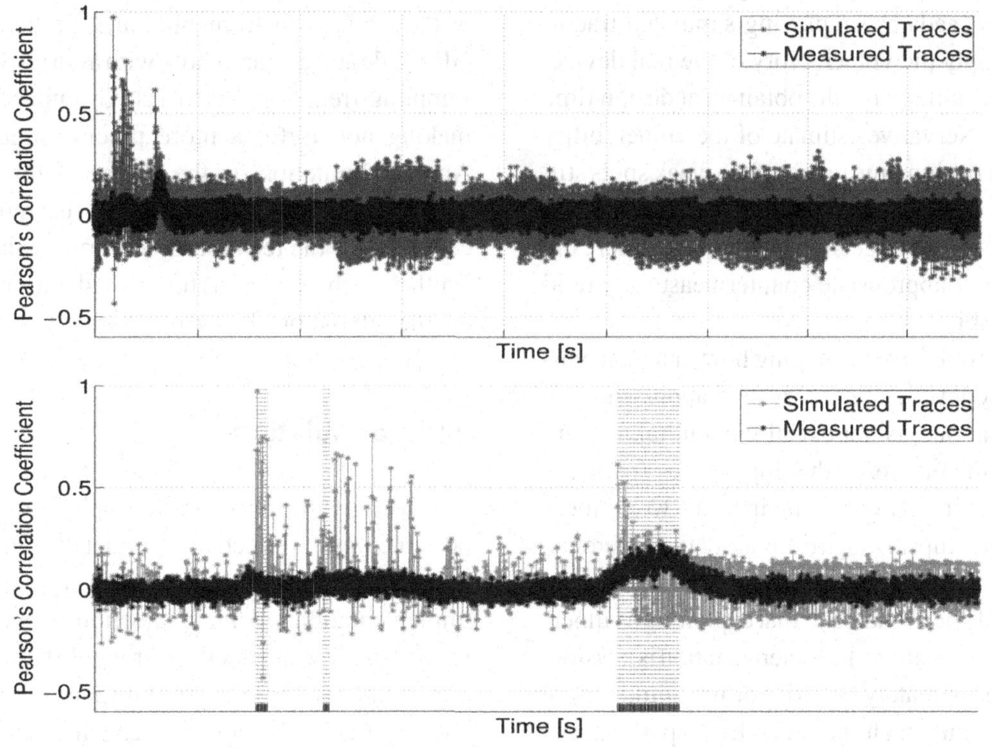

low-pass filtering effect is particularly evident in the large peak (the first from the right), appearing in the bottom plot of Figure 7, which contrasts with the sharp correlation peaks obtained in the simulated trace. In addition to the low-pass effect, the presence of non-systematic noise in the measurement workbench further reduces the value of the correlation coefficient. Moreover, observing the peaks in the simulated traces, we can deduce that the operations sensitive to side-channel attacks are executed at different time points, as there are instants where the correlation coefficient is not maximum, spread around in a short time interval. This is the consequence of a peculiarity of the ISA under exam, which has a data dependent decoding phase for a few instructions, thus causing misalignments even in the simulated traces.

Discussion

After analyzing a realistic case study, we discuss some of the key insights we have obtained and we point out the strong assets of this methodology for security evaluation at design time. If a DPA attack succeeds by employing simulated traces, it may imply the vulnerability of the real device. In fact, even if the results obtained at design time give a conservative estimate of the vulnerability level, the design time report of the weak spots still provides useful information on the most vulnerable parts of the target implementation, where the insertion of appropriate countermeasures would be advisable.

The problem of estimating how much the vulnerability level is a conservative approximation of the real one, is not trivial without taking into account the effects of the impedances (parasitic and not) naturally occurring in a real-world measurement setup. A rough estimate of the difference between the attack sensitivity of simulated and measured traces, indicates that exploiting a vulnerability in the real-world implementation is possible with approximately an order of magnitude more measurements than those needed to perform the attack on simulated traces. On the other hand, if a DPA attack does not succeed on simulated traces, which represent an idealized situation with respect to both the technical effort and the measurement accuracy necessary in a practical scenario, it is safe to assume that the device is not vulnerable to such an attack technique.

The timing accuracy employed in the simulations for the design time vulnerability assessment, strongly depends on the ideal security margin the designer whishes to obtain, because the accuracy of the results is proportional to both the computation time and the storage space needed to lead the attack. Indeed, the real-world attacker is constrained on the budget required to mount the attack by the actual foreseen gains derived by breaching the security of the device. In practice, it is thus safe to stop doing DPA attacks on simulated traces when the actual sampling frequency of the simulated traces exceeds the one of the measurement setups available to a real-world attacker within his budget.

However, in addition to the budget limit, the upper bound for the physical measurement, imposed by the available instrumentation, is limited to a 45 GHz wide analog bandwidth with a corresponding sampling frequency up to 120 Gsamples/s, thus making not useful a more precise simulation. Another limitation on the choice of the timing accuracy is the one imposed by the minimum cell delay of the technology library employed to synthesize the device, as this provides a hard limit on the simulator ability to provide meaningful power estimations in time.

Fault Simulation

A challenge in applied cryptography is to outline possible ways to effectively predict the sensitivity of both the hardware and software cryptographic implementations to fault injection attacks. The results about fault attacks (Barenghi et al., 2010a, 2011a) are by far less general than those based on power consumption side-channels, since the fault attacks are usually devised ad-hoc and thus are strongly coupled with the algorithms and implementations they target. Furthermore, there is no systematic approach either to analyze the fault resistance of a given implementation, or to design a device protected from the possible consequences of fault injection. Therefore, evaluating at design time the effectiveness of possible fault attacks is a topic of growing importance for both the research and industrial communities. At the time of writing, a few methodologies have been developed to assess the reliability of a device against fault injection.

Starting from the HDL description of the design, there are mainly two classes of techniques to simulate the injection of faults into the device under design. Both approaches are described in (Jenn et al., 1994). The first approach requires to modify the design, by replacing the basic blocks with ad-hoc entities that replicate the functionality but also allow to alter (i.e., to fault) their output signals. Such entities behave in a normal way most of the time, but have the option of triggering a faulty condition which causes a somehow different behavior, simulating the actual fault happening. Different methods to achieve this objective exist, as mentioned in (Jenn et al., 1994). The advantage of this approach lies in its ease of development and flexibility, and its main drawback consists in altering the actual structure of the synthesized circuit.

The second way to achieve a fault simulation is to use some additional features of the simulation software tools, i.e., the existence of commands that allow to alter the normal execution of the simulation while it is running. This is obtained by selectively forcing the target signals within the device design. The advantage is that the original design is left untouched, but the technique strongly relies on the control features offered by the simulation tool. The overall realization of the fault injection procedure may become quite complex compared to the driving of modified entities.

The performances reached by the simulation environment may become a limit in some cases, where the number of faults to apply is high and the gate count of the design under test is huge. The limit can be relaxed through replacing the simulation tool with the hardware implementation of the design on a FPGA, as described in (Janning et al., 2011). Following the first aforementioned approach for simulations, the technique is based on using an automatic tool able to modify the design components so that it becomes possible to emulate the effects of faults. In order to speed up the whole process, in addition to the modified design, the FPGA also includes a dedicated block for the control and management of fault injection. The system is then run several times and the subsequent statistical analysis of the outputs provides useful information to the designer.

Recent works (Sugawara et al., 2012) have shown that it is possible to efficiently simulate the class of faults induced by clock manipulation. The authors propose a way to analyze the VCD (Value Change Dump) data produced by the simulation tool, in order to study the influence of an alteration in the clock signal on the computation. The technique can be employed to simulate any attack relying on faults obtained via the manipulation of the clock signal. Therefore it can be applied to the recently proposed Fault Sensitivity Analysis class of attacks (Li et al., 2010).

CONCLUSION AND FUTURE RESEARCH DIRECTIONS

This chapter has provided the required background to understand the most common side-channel attacks based on power consumption, and has reported the methodology to perform a side-channel security assessment of embedded devices at design time. The advantage of performing power analysis with simulated traces is that the leakage sources can be easily identified, isolated, and individually studied in a clean room environment. This enables an early feedback to be sent to the device designer, who thus can integrate the countermeasure in the regular design workflow. As demonstrated by the case study for software implementations, this type of analysis can reveal how some instructions (e.g., "load" and "store") may leak more information than others, thus highlighting the possible weak spots in the secure chip under exam. The fact that an attacker is unable to perform a power attack over simulated traces represents a sound evaluation of the security margin, as the conditions in which a regular attacker is forced to work are by far worse in terms of measurement noise, precision, and synchronization of the data acquisition workbench. A similar approach can be used also for fault attacks, although this approach is still at its very beginning.

REFERENCES

Agosta, G., Barenghi, A., & Pelosi, G. (2012). A code morphing methodology to automate power analysis countermeasures. In Proceedings of the Design Automation Conference, (pp. 77–82). IEEE Press.

Agrawal, D., Archambeault, B., Rao, R., & Rohatgi, P. (2002). The EM side- channel(s). *Lecture Notes in Computer Science*, *2523*, 29–45. doi:10.1007/3-540-36400-5_4.

Aitken, R., Leveugle, R., Metra, C., & Nicoladis, M. (Eds.). (2006). 12th IEEE international on-line testing symposium (IOLTS 2006). Como, Italy: IEEE Computer Society.

Alioto, M., Giancane, L., Scotti, G., & Trifiletti, A. (2010a). Leakage power analysis attacks: A novel class of attacks to nanometer cryptographic circuits. *IEEE Transactions on Circuits and Systems. I, Regular Papers*, *57*(2), 355–367. doi:10.1109/TCSI.2009.2019411.

Alioto, M., Poli, M., & Rocchi, S. (2010b). A general power model of differential power analysis attacks to static logic circuits. IEEE Transactions on Very Large Scale Integration (VLSI). *Systems*, *18*(5), 711–724.

Anderson, R., & Kuhn, M. (1996). Tamper resistance: A cautionary note. Retrieved from http://www.cl.cam.ac.uk/~rja14/tamper.html

Aumuller, C., Bier, P., Fischer, W., Hofreiter, P., & Seifert, J.-P. (2002). Fault attacks on RSA with CRT: Concrete results and practical countermeasures. *Lecture Notes in Computer Science*, *2523*, 260–275. doi:10.1007/3-540-36400-5_20.

Bar-El, H., Choukri, H., Naccache, D., Tunstall, M., & Whelan, C. (2006). The sorcerer's apprentice guide to fault attacks. *Proceedings of the IEEE*, *94*(2), 370–382. doi:10.1109/JPROC.2005.862424.

Barenghi, A., Bertoni, G., Parrinello, E., & Pelosi, G. (2009). Low voltage fault attacks on the RSA cryptosystem. Retrieved from http://home.dei.polimi.it/barenghi/files/FDTC2009.pdf

Barenghi, A., Bertoni, G., Santis, F. D., & Melzani, F. (2011a). On the efficiency of design time evaluation of the resistance to power attacks. In Proceedings of DSD, (pp. 777-785). IEEE Press.

Barenghi, A., Bertoni, G. M., Breveglieri, L., Pelosi, G., & Palomba, A. (2011b). Fault attack to the elliptic curve digital signature algorithm with multiple bit faults. [ACM Press.]. *Proceedings of SIN*, *2011*, 63–72.

Barenghi, A., Pelosi, G., & Teglia, Y. (2010b). Improving first order differential power attacks through digital signal processing. In Proceedings of the 3rd International Conference on Security of Information and Networks, (pp. 124-133). ACM Press.

Barenghi, A., Pelosi, G., & Teglia, Y. (2011c). Information leakage discovery techniques to enhance secure chip design. *Lecture Notes in Computer Science*, *6633*, 128–143. doi:10.1007/978-3-642-21040-2_9.

Bernstein, D. (2005). Cache-timing attacks on AES. Technical Report. Retrieved from http://cr.yp.to/antiforgery/cachetiming-20050414.pdf

Boneh, D., DeMillo, R., & Lipton, R. (2001). On the importance of checking cryptographic protocols for faults. *Journal of Cryptology*, *14*(2), 101–119. doi:10.1007/s001450010016.

Brier, E., Clavier, C., & Olivier, F. (2004). Correlation power analysis with a leakage model. Retrieved from http://www.iacr.org/archive/ches2004/31560016/31560016.pdf

Daemen, J., & Rijmen, V. (2002). *The design of Rijndael: AES - The advanced encryption standard*. Berlin, Germany: Springer. doi:10.1007/978-3-662-04722-4.

Eisenbarth, T., Kasper, T., Moradi, A., Paar, C., Salmasizadeh, M., & Shalmani, M. T. M. (2008). On the power of power analysis in the real world: A complete break of the Keeloq code hopping scheme. Retrieved from http://emsec.ruhr-uni-bochum.de/media/crypto/veroeffentlichungen/2010/09/11/crypto2008_keeloq_slides.pdf

Enev, M., Gupta, S., Kohno, T., & Patel, S. N. (2011). Televisions, video privacy, and powerline electromagnetic interference. Retrieved from http://homes.cs.washington.edu/~sidhant/docs/TVEMI.pdf

Gandolfi, K., Mourtel, C., & Olivier, F. (2001). Electromagnetic analysis: Concrete results. [London, UK: Springer.]. *Proceedings of CHES*, *2001*, 251–261.

Gebotys, C. H., & White, B. A. (2008). EM analysis of a wireless java-based PDA. ACM Transactions on Embedded Computer Systems, 7(4).

Govindavajhala, S., & Appel, A. W. (2003). Using memory errors to attack virtual machine. Retrieved from http://www.cs.princeton.edu/~sudhakar/papers/memerr.pdf

Janning, A., Heyszl, J., Stumpf, F., & Sigl, G. (2011). A cost-effective FPGA-based fault simulation environment. In Proceedings of FDTC 2011. Tokyo, Japan: FDTC.

Jenn, E., Arlat, J., Rimen, M., Ohlsson, J., & Karlsson, J. (1994). Fault injection into VHDL models: The MEFISTO tool. In Proceedings of FTCS, (pp. 66-75). IEEE Press.

Joye, M., & Tunstall, M. (2012). *Fault analysis in cryptography*. Berlin, Germany: Springer. doi:10.1007/978-3-642-29656-7.

Kim, C. H., & Quisquater, J.-J. (2007). Fault attacks for CRT based RSA: New attacks, new results, and new countermeasures. *Lecture Notes in Computer Science*, *4462*, 215–228. doi:10.1007/978-3-540-72354-7_18.

Kocher, P. C. (1996). Timing attacks on implementations of Diffie-Hellman, RSA, DSS, and other systems. Retrieved from http://www.cryptography.com/public/pdf/TimingAttacks.pdf

Kocher, P. C., Jaffe, J., & Jun, B. (1999). Differential power analysis. Retrieved from http://www.cryptography.com/public/pdf/DPA.pdf

Leveugle, R., Ammari, A., Maingot, V., Teyssou, E., Moitrel, P., & Mourtel, C. … Tria, A. (2007). Experimental evaluation of protections against laser-induced faults and consequences on fault modeling. In Proceedings of DATE 2007, (pp. 1-6). IEEE Press.

Li, H. (2006). Security evaluation at design time for cryptographic hardware. Tech. Rep. UCAM-CL-TR-665, 1:1. Cambridge, UK: University of Cambridge.

Li, Y., Sakiyama, K., Gomisawa, S., Fukunaga, T., Takahashi, J., & Ohta, K. (2010). Fault sensitivity analysis. *Lecture Notes in Computer Science*, *6225*, 320–334. doi:10.1007/978-3-642-15031-9_22.

Mangard, S. (2004). Hardware countermeasures against DPA: A statistical analysis of their effectiveness. *Lecture Notes in Computer Science*, *2964*, 222–235. doi:10.1007/978-3-540-24660-2_18.

Mangard, S., Oswald, E., & Popp, T. (2007). *Power analysis attacks - revealing the secrets of smart cards*. Berlin, Germany: Springer.

Mangard, S., Oswald, E., & Standaert, F. (2011). One for all - All for one: Unifying standard differential power analysis attacks. *Information Security*, *5*(2), 100–110. doi:10.1049/iet-ifs.2010.0096.

Mano, M. (1988). *Computer engineering hardware design*. Upper Saddle River, NJ: Prentice-Hall, Inc..

Messerges, T. S., Dabbish, E. A., & Sloan, R. H. (1999a). Investigations of power analysis attacks on smartcards. Retrieved from http://static.usenix.org/events/smartcard99/full_papers/messerges/messerges.pdf

Messerges, T. S., Dabbish, E. A., & Sloan, R. H. (1999b). Power analysis attacks of modular exponentiation in smartcards. Retrieved from http://saluc.engr.uconn.edu/refs/sidechannel/messerges99power.pdf

Monnet, Y., Renaudin, M., Leveugle, R., Feyt, N., Moitrel, P., & Nzenguet, F. M. (2006). Practical evaluation of fault countermeasures on an asynchronous des crypto processor. In Proceedings of IOLTS, (pp. 125-130). IEEE Press.

Moore, D. (2009). *The basic practice of statistics*. New York, NY: WH Freeman & Co..

Moradi, A., Barenghi, A., Kasper, T., & Paar, C. (2011). On the vulnerability of FPGA bitstream encryption against power analysis attacks: Extracting keys from XILINX Virtex FPGAs. Retrieved from http://eprint.iacr.org/2011/390

NIST. (2001). FIPS-197: Advanced encryption standard (AES). [Washington, DC: NIST.]. *Federal Information Processing Standards Publication*, *197*, 441–0311.

Peeters, E., Standaert, F.-X., & Quisquater, J. (2007). Power and electromagnetic analysis: Improved model, consequences and comparisons. *Integration (Tokyo, Japan)*, *40*(1), 52–60.

Quisquater, J., & Samyde, D. (2001). Electromagnetic analysis (EMA): Measures and counter-measures for smart cards. [London, UK: Springer.]. *Proceedings of E-SMART*, *2001*, 200–210.

Quisquater, J.-J., & Samyde, D. (2002). Eddy current for magnetic analysis with active sensor. In Proceedings of E-Smart 2002. Nice, France: E-Smart.

Renauld, M., Standaert, F.-X., Veyrat-Charvillon, N., Kamel, D., & Flandre, D. (2011). A formal study of power variability issues and side-channel attacks for nanoscale devices. Retrieved from http://perso.uclouvain.be/fstandae/PUBLIS/94.pdf

Rivest, R. L., Shamir, A., & Adleman, L. M. (1978). A method for obtaining digital signatures and public-key cryptosystems. *Communications of the ACM*, *21*(2), 120–126. doi:10.1145/359340.359342.

Schmidt, J.-M., & Herbst, C. (2008). A practical fault attack on square and multiply. Retrieved from http://conferenze.dei.polimi.it/FDTC08/fdtc08-schmidt.pdf

Skorobogatov, S. P., & Anderson, R. J. (2002). Optical fault induction attacks. Retrieved from http://www.cl.cam.ac.uk/~sps32/ches02-optofault.pdf

Sugawara, T., Suzuki, D., & Katashita, T. (2012). Circuit simulation for fault sensitivity analysis and its application to cryptographic LSI. In Proceedings of FDTC, (pp. 16-23). IEEE Press.

Tiri, K. (2010). Side-channel resistant circuit styles and associated IC design flow. *Secure Integrated Circuits and Systems*, *1*, 145–157. doi:10.1007/978-0-387-71829-3_8.

Tiri, K., & Verbauwhede, I. (2005). Simulation models for side-channel information leaks. Retrieved from http://www.cosic.esat.kuleuven.be/publications/article-669.pdf

Wright, P., & Greengrass, P. (1988). *Spycatcher: The candid autobiography of a senior intelligence officer*. New York, NY: Dell.

KEY TERMS AND DEFINITIONS

Differential Power Analysis (DPA): Attack technique which deduces the values of the secret key in a cipher through exploiting the differences in power consumption through modeling the data dependent power consumption of the device, and validating the model through statistical tools.

Hardware Design Workflow: The procedure which, starting from a high-level description of a digital device in VHDL or Verilog, produces all the data needed for a foundry to fabricate the chip.

Hardware Synthesis Process: The procedure which takes a high level description (VHDL/Verilog) of a circuit and produces in output a register transfer level description of it in the form of a netlist.

Place and Route Process: The procedure which takes in input a register transfer level description of a circuit and produces in output the physical layout of the silicon which will be fabricated. The process takes into account the effects of the latencies introduced by the wiring.

Side-Channel: Unintentional channel over which a digital device transmits information on its inner state. Common side-channels include the power consumption of a device, its radiated Electro-Magnetic (EM) emissions and the computation time.

Simple Power Analysis: Attack technique which deduces the values of the secret key in a cipher through exploiting the differences in power consumption caused by the key dependent control flow of the algorithm.

(Simulated) Power Trace: Recording of the power consumption of a digital device during the computation of a cryptographic primitive. It may be obtained as either an actual recording via a digital oscilloscope or simulated with common Electronic Design Automation (EDA) tools.

Section 3
Cryptographic Solutions for Distributed Systems

Chapter 7
An Efficient Attribute-Based Signature with Application to Secure Attribute-Based Messaging System

Piyi Yang
University of Shanghai for Science and Technology, China

Tanveer A Zia
Charles Sturt University, Australia

ABSTRACT

A set of attributes instead of a single string to represent the signer's identity is a challenging problem under standard cryptographic assumption in the standard model. Therefore, designing a fully secure (adaptive-predicate unforgeable and perfectly private) Attribute-Based Signature (ABS) that allows a signer to choose a set of attributes is vital. Existing schemes are either too complicated or have only been proved in the generic group model. In this chapter, the authors present an efficient fully secure ABS scheme in the standard model based on q-parallel BDHE assumption, which is more practical than the generic group model used in the previous schemes. The proposed scheme is highly expressive since it allows any signer to specify claim-predicates in terms of any predicate consisting of AND, OR, and Threshold gates over the attributes in the system. ABS has found many important applications in secure communications, such as anonymous authentication systems and attribute-based messaging systems.

INTRODUCTION

Identity-based signature is a powerful mechanism for providing the authentication of the stored and transmitted information where the identity can be an arbitrary string such as an email address or a registration number, etc. While this is useful for applications, where the data receiver knows specifically the identity of the data signer, in many applications the signer will want to have fine-grained control over how much of their personal information is revealed by the signature.

DOI: 10.4018/978-1-4666-4030-6.ch007

Maji, Prabhakaran, and Rosulek (2008) presented a new vision of identity-based signature that they called Attribute-Based Signature (ABS), in which a signer is defined by a set of attributes instead of a single string representing the signer's identity. In ABS, a user obtains a set of attributes from one or multiple attribute authorities. An attribute-based signature assures the verifier that a signer, whose set of attributes satisfies a (possibly) complex predicate, has endorsed the message. The following example illustrates the concept. Suppose we have the following predicate:

Professor **OR** (((Biology Department **OR** Female) **OR** above 50 years old) **AND** University A).

Alice's attributes are (University A, Female). Bob's attributes are (above 50 years old, Professor). Although their attributes are quite different, it is clear that Alice and Bob can generate a signature on this predicate, and such a signature releases no information regarding the attribute or identity of the signer, i.e. Alice or Bob, except that the attribute of the signer satisfies the predicate.

This kind of authentication required in attribute-based signatures differs from that offered by identity-based signatures. An ABS solution requires a richer semantics, including privacy requirements, similar to more recent signature variants like group signatures (Chaum & Heyst, 1991), ring signatures (Rivest, Shamir, & Tauman, 2001), and mesh signatures (Boyen, 2007). All of these primitives share the following semantics:

- **Unforgeability:** By verifying the signature, one is assured that the message was indeed endorsed by a party who satisfies the condition described in the claim.
- **Privacy:** The signature reveals no information about the signer other than the fact that it satisfies the claim. In particular, different signatures cannot be identified as generated by the same party.

Besides these two semantics, ABS has another important property which is called collusion resistance. It assures different parties should not be able to pool together their attributes to sign a message with a claim which none of them satisfy alone. For instance, if Alice has an attribute Female, and her friend Bob has an attribute Professor, they should not be able to sign a message claiming to have both the attributes.

ABS has found many important applications. For instance, it helps to provide fine-grained access control in anonymous authentication systems (Li, Au, Susilo, Xie, & Ren, 2010). Another application of ABS, given by (Maji, Prabhakaran, & Rosulek, 2008, 2011), is to fulfill a critical security requirement in attribute-based messaging (ABM) systems using ABS.

BACKGROUND STUDY ABOUT ABS

Attribute-Based Signatures were first introduced by Maji, Prabhakaran, and Rosales (2008) as a way to let a signature attest not to the identity of the individual who endorsed a message, but instead to a (possibly complex) claim regarding the attributes they possess. They constructed an ABS scheme that supports a powerful set of predicates, namely, any predicate consists of AND, OR, and Threshold gates. However, the security of their scheme is weak as their construction is only proved in the generic group model. Since then, there have been lots of works on this subject (Escala, Herranz, & Morillo, 2011; Khader, 2007a, 2007b; Li, Au, Susilo, Xie, & Ren, 2010; Li & Kim, 2007, 2010; Maji, Prabhakaran, & Rosulek, 2011; Okamoto & Takashima, 2011; Shahandashti & Safavi-Naini, 2009).

Recently, Maji, Prabhakaran, and Rosulek (2011) presented an ABS scheme that is proven secure in the standard model. But it is much less efficient and more complicated than the scheme in (Maji, Prabhakaran, & Rosulek, 2008), since it employs the Groth-Sahai NIZK protocols (Groth &

Sahai, 2008) as building blocks. Okamoto and Takashima (Okamoto & Takashima, 2011) presented a fully secure Attribute-Based Signature (ABS) scheme in the standard model. The admissible predicates of the scheme support non-monotone predicates. Escala, Herranz, and Morillo (2011) proposed a fully secure Attribute-Based Signature (ABS) scheme in the standard model. This scheme supports an additional property of revocability, so that an external judge can break the anonymity of a signature when necessary.

Another related notion to ABS is fuzzy identity-based signature which was proposed and formalized in (Shanqing & Yingpei, 2008; Yang, Cao, & Dong, 2011). It allows a user with identity ω to issue a signature which could be verified with identity ω' if and only if ω and ω' are within a distance judged by some metric. However, this kind of signatures does not consider the anonymity for signer.

Maji, Prabhakaran, Rosulek (2008, 2011) and Okamoto, Takashima (2011) pointed that the future work of ABS, on the theoretical front, is to base the security of ABS on a standard hardness assumption, while still preserve the efficiency for the most part. In this chapter, we propose such an ABS scheme which is secure in the standard model based on decisional parallel bilinear Diffie-Hellman exponent assumption (Waters, 2011) which is more practical than the generic group model of (Maji, Prabhakaran, & Rosulek, 2008).

MATHEMATICAL AND SECURITY MODEL

We first give formal definitions for claim-predicate (access structure) and relevant background on monotone span program. Then, we give the formal definitions for the security of Attribute-Based Signature (ABS). Finally, we give the background information on bilinear map and our cryptographic assumption.

Notations

We denote the finite field of order q by $\mathbb{F}_q$. We also denote the group $\{0,1,\ldots,p\text{-}1\}$ under addition modulo p by Z_p, and $Z_p\backslash\{0\}$ by Z_p^*, where p is a large prime number satisfying $p = 2p' + 1$ with p' itself prime. A vector symbol denotes a vector representation over Z_p, e.g. $\vec{x}$ denotes $(x_1,\ldots,x_n) \in Z_p^{1\times n}$. $y := z$ denotes that y is defined by z. We use $\mathbf{span}\langle\vec{x_1},\ldots,\vec{x_2}\rangle$ denotes the subspace generated by $\vec{x_1},\ldots,\vec{x_n}$. For two vectors $\vec{x} = (x_1,\ldots,x_n)$ and $\vec{y} = (y_1,\ldots,y_n)$, $\vec{x}\cdot\vec{y}$ denotes the inner-product $\sum_{i=1}^{n} x_i y_i$. X^T denotes the transpose of matrix X. **det**(**M**) denotes the rank of matrix M. We denote a monotone span program (Beimel, 1996) over a field $\mathbb{F}_q$ as Z_p **M**:=(**M**,ρ) in which there exists a linear secret sharing scheme (Okamoto; Takashima, 2011).

Monotone Span Program

Let a claim-predicate (access structure) Y be a monotone boolean function and $\{x_1,\ldots,x_n\}$ be a set of input variables of Y. We define a monotone span program that computes the claim-predicate (access structure) Y as follows.

Definition 1: (Monotone Span Program (Beimel 1996)) A monotone span program over a field $\mathbb{F}_q$ is a labeled matrix, **M**:=(**M**,ρ), where **M** is a $l\times r$ matrix over $\mathbb{F}_q$ and ρ is labeling function that associates each row of **M** with an input variable of Y.

A monotone span program accepts or rejects an input by the following criterion. Every input sequence $\delta\in\{0,1\}^n$ of Y defines submatrix $\mathbf{M}_\delta$ of **M** consisting of those rows whose labels are set to 1 by the input δ. (Define $\gamma:\{1,\ldots,l\}\rightarrow\{0,1\}$ as

$\gamma(j)=1$ if $[\rho(j)=x_i]\wedge[\delta_i=1]$. Then we have $\mathbf{M}_\delta := (\mathbf{M}_j)_{\gamma(j)=1}$, where $\mathbf{M}_j$ is the *jth* row of $\mathbf{M}$). A monotone span program $\mathbf{M}$ accepts δ if and only if $\vec{1} \in \mathbf{span}\langle \mathbf{M}_\delta \rangle$, i.e., some linear combination of the rows of $\mathbf{M}_\delta$ gives the target vector $\vec{1}(\exists \vec{v} \in \mathbb{F}^{1\times l}$ s.t. $\vec{v}\mathbf{M}_\delta = [1,0,0,\ldots,0]0)$. A monotone span program computes boolean function Y if it accepts exactly those inputs δ where Y(δ)=1.

We call *l* the *length* and *r* the *width* of the span program. Every monotone boolean function can be represented by some monotone span program. Note that for any unauthorized set of rows *I*, the target vector is not in the span of the rows of the set *I*. Moreover, there will exist a vector w such that $\vec{w}\cdot(1,0,0,\ldots,0) = -1$ and $\vec{w}\cdot\mathbf{M}_i = 0$ for all $i\in I$.

We now describe the secret-sharing scheme for a monotone span program presented by Okamoto and Takashima (2011).

Definition 2: A secret-sharing scheme for monotone span program $\mathbf{M}:=(\mathbf{M},\rho)$ is:

- Let $\mathbf{M}$ be an $l\times r$ matrix, and randomly selects column vector $\vec{f} := (f_1,\ldots,f_r)^{\mathrm{T}}$ from $\mathbb{F}_q^r$. Then, $s_0 := \vec{1}\vec{f}^{\mathrm{T}} = f_1$ is the secret to be shared, and $\vec{s}^{\mathrm{T}} := (s_1,\ldots,s_l)^{\mathrm{T}} := \mathbf{M}\vec{f}^{\mathrm{T}}$ is the vector of l shares of secret s_0. Share s_i belongs to $\rho(i)$.
- If monotone span program $\mathbf{M}:=(\mathbf{M},\rho)$ accepts S, i.e., $\vec{1} \in \mathbf{span}\langle(\mathbf{M}_i)_{\gamma(i)=1}\rangle$, then there exist constants $\alpha_i \in I$ such that $I\subseteq\{i\in\{1,\ldots,\}|\gamma(i)=1\}$ and $\sum_{i\in I}\alpha_i s_i = s_0$. In addition, these constants $\{\alpha_i\}$ can be computed in time polynomial in the size of matrix $\mathbf{M}$.

Attribute-Based Signature

An attribute-based signature scheme consists of four algorithms, namely, setup algorithm Setup, private key generation algorithm KeyGen, signing algorithm Sign, and verification algorithm Verify. The algorithms are defined as follows.

- **Setup(λ,U):** On input the security parameter λ and attribute universe description U, the setup algorithm outputs the public parameters PK and a master key MSK.
- **KeyGen(PK, MSK, *S*):** On input the public parameters PK, the master key MSK and a set of attributes *S* that describes the key, the key generation algorithm outputs a private key SK.
- **Sign**$(\mathrm{PK},\mathcal{M},\mathrm{Y},\mathrm{SK}_S)$**:** Assume a user wants to sign a message $\mathcal{M}$ with a claim-predicate (access structure) Y, he runs the signing algorithm using his private key SK_S, which is a private key for a set *S* of attributes and the set *S* of attributes satisfies the claim-predicate (access structure) Y and outputs the signature σ. We will assume that the signature σ implicitly contain Y.
- **Verify**$(\mathrm{PK},\sigma,\mathcal{M})$**:** After receiving a signature on message $\mathcal{M}$, the verification algorithm outputs a boolean value accept or reject to denote if the signature is correct or not.

Correctness and Security Definitions of Attribute-Based Signatures

The minimal requirement of ABS schemes is to meet the correctness definition.

Definition 3: (Correctness) We say an ABS scheme is correct if for all (PK, MSK) ←**Setup** all message $\mathcal{M}$, all attribute sets *S*, all private keys SK←**KeyGen**(PK, MSK, *S*), and all claim-predicates (access structures) Y such that *S* satisfies Y,

$$\mathbf{Verify}(\mathrm{PK},\mathcal{M},\mathbf{Sign}(\mathrm{PK},\mathcal{M},\mathrm{Y},\mathrm{SK})) = \mathbf{accept},$$

with probability 1 over the randomness of all the algorithms.

We now describe two formal security definitions for ABS schemes.

Definition 4: (Perfect Privacy) An ABS scheme is perfectly private if, for all (PK, MSK)←**Setup**, all attribute sets S_1, S_2 all SK_1←**KeyGen**(PK, MSK, S_1), SK_2←**keyGen**(PK, MSK, S_2), all messages $\mathcal{M}$, and all claim-predicates (access structures) Y such that attribute sets S_1, S_2 satisfies Y, the distributions
$\textbf{Sign}(\mathrm{PK}, \mathcal{M}, \mathrm{Y}, \mathrm{SK}_1)$ and
$\textbf{Sign}(\mathrm{PK}, \mathcal{M}, \mathrm{Y}, \mathrm{SK}_2)$ are equal.

If the perfect privacy requirement holds, the signature reveals nothing about the attributes or other identifying information of the signer beyond what is explicitly revealed by the access structure. Thus, the signature is simply independent of everything except the message, the access structure and the public parameters.

For an ABS scheme with perfect privacy, we define algorithm **AltSign**(PK, MSK, $\mathcal{M}$, Y) with the claim-predicate Y and Master Secret Key MSK instead of S and SK_S. First, generate SK_S←**KeyGen**(PK, MSK, S) for arbitrary S that satisfies Y, then $\sigma \leftarrow \textbf{Sign}(\mathrm{PK}, \mathrm{SK}_S, \mathcal{M}, \mathrm{Y})$. Return σ.

Definition 5: (Unforgeability) An ABS scheme is (adaptive-predicate) unforgeable if the success probability of any polynomial-time adversary in the following experiment is negligible.

- **Setup Phase:** The challenger runs the **Setup** algorithm to generate (PK, MSK). It retains the master key MSK and gives the public parameters PK to the adversary.
- **Query Phase:** After receive the public parameters PK, the adversary can perform a polynomially bounded number of queries to oracles **KeyGen**(PK, MSK) and **AltSign**(PK, MSK).
- **Forgery:** Finally, the adversary outputs a signature σ* on message $\mathcal{M}^*$ with respect to Y*.

We say the adversary succeeds if $(\mathcal{M}^*, \mathrm{Y}^*)$ was never queried to the **AltSign** oracle, and S doesn't satisfy the access structure Y* for all S queried to the **KeyGen** oracle, and

$$\textbf{Verify}(\mathrm{PK}, \sigma^*, \mathcal{M}^*) = \textbf{accept}.$$

If the (adaptive-predicate) unforgeability requirement holds, then the only valid *new* signatures that a group of signers can produce are signatures that a single member of the group could legitimately generate by himself. This is because if a group of signers can construct a signature that none of them could individually produce, then they can build another adversary and output a forgery to win the above game. Thus, colluding behavior does not confer any advantage in generating signatures.

Bilinear Map and Assumptions

- **Bilinear Map:** Let $\mathbb{G}$ and $\mathbb{G}_T$ be two multiplicative cyclic groups of prime order p. Let g be a generator of $\mathbb{G}$, and e be a bilinear map, e:$\mathbb{G} \times \mathbb{G} \rightarrow \mathbb{G}_T$. The bilinear map e has the following properties:
  - **Bilinearity:** For all $u, v \in \mathbb{G}$ and $a,b \in Z_p$, we have $e(u^a, u^b) = e(u, v)^{ab}$.
  - **Non-Degeneracy:** $e(g, g) \neq 1$.

We say that $\mathbb{G}$ is a bilinear group if the group operation in $\mathbb{G}$ and bilinear map e:$\mathbb{G} \times \mathbb{G} \rightarrow \mathbb{G}_T$ are both efficiently computable.

SECURITY ASSUMPTIONS

Decisional Parallel Bilinear Diffie-Hellman Exponent Assumption

We describe the decisional q-parallel Bilinear Diffie-Hellman Exponent problem which is defined by Brent Waters (2011) as follows. Choose a group $\mathbb{G}$ of prime order p according to the security parameter. Let $a, s, b_1, \ldots, b_q \in Z_p$ be chosen at random and g be a generator of $\mathbb{G}$. The adversary is given $\vec{y} =$

$$g, g^{s}, g^{a}, \ldots, g^{a^q},, g^{a^{q+2}}, \ldots, g^{2q}$$

$$\forall_{1 \le j \le q}\, g^{s \cdot b_j}, g^{a/b_j}, \ldots, g^{a^q/b_j},, g^{a^{q+2}/b_j}, \ldots, g^{a^{2q/b_j}}$$

$$\forall_{1 \le j,k \le q, k \ne j}\, g^{a \cdot s \cdot b_k/b_j}, \ldots, g^{a^q \cdot s \cdot b_k/b_j}$$

It is called decisional q-parallel BDHE problem, if the adversary attempts to distinguish $e(g,g)^{a^{q+1}s} \in \mathbb{G}_T$ from a random element in $\mathbb{G}_T$.

The advantage of an algorithm $\mathcal{B}$ that outputs $z \in \{0,1\}$ for decisional q-parallel BDHE problem is defined as

$$Adv_{\mathcal{B}}^{q-BDHE} = \mid \Pr[\mathcal{B}(\vec{y}, T = e(g,g)^{a^{q+1}s}) = 0] - \Pr[\mathcal{B}(\vec{y}, T = R) = 0] \mid.$$

Definition 6: (Decisional Parallel Bilinear Diffie-Hellman Exponent Assumption) We say that the decisional q-parallel BDHE assumption holds if no polynomial time algorithm has a non-negligible advantage in solving the decisional q-parallel BDHE problem.

Collision Resistant (CR) Assumption

We define Collision Resistant (CR) assumption as follows.

Definition 7: (Collision Resistant (CR) Assumption) A hash function $H \leftarrow \mathcal{H}(k)$ is a collision resistant if for all PPT algorithms $\mathcal{A}$ the advantage

$$Adv_{\mathcal{A}}^{CR}(k) = Pr[H(x) = H(y) \wedge x \ne y \mid (x,y) \leftarrow \mathcal{A}(1^k, H) \wedge H \leftarrow \mathcal{H}(k)]$$

is negligible as a function of the security parameter.

DESCRIPTION OF THE ABS SCHEME

Our construction is inspired by the Attribute-Based Encryption (ABE) scheme of Waters (2011). Roughly speaking, a secret signing key SK_S with attribute set S corresponds to a secret decryption key SK_S with S in ABE (Waters, 2011). No counterpart of a signature σ in our construction exists in the ABE (Waters, 2011). In order to meet the privacy condition for σ, a novel technique is applied to randomly generate a signature from the private key SK_S and the claim-predicate Y. And there are many subtleties in the proof of unforgeability, e.g., we need to cancel all the unknown terms in order to answer the queries and solve the q-BDHE problem. We develop a novel technique to resolve the difficulty. See the proof for more details.

Let $\mathbb{U}$ be the universe of possible attributes. A *claim-predicate* over $\mathbb{U}$ is a monotone boolean function, whose inputs are associated with attributes of $\mathbb{U}$. We say an attribute set $S \subset \mathbb{U}$ satisfies a claim-predicate Y if Y(S)=1.

- **Setup (*U*):** The input parameter U is the number of attributes in the system. Choose suitable cyclic groups $\mathbb{G}$ and $\mathbb{G}_T$ of prime order p, equipped with a bilinear pairing $e: \mathbb{G} \times \mathbb{G} \rightarrow \mathbb{G}_T$. Choose a generator g and U random group elements $h_1, \ldots, h_U \in \mathbb{G}$ that are associated with the

U attributes in the system. Pick random number $\alpha, a \in Z_p$. Choose a collision resistant hash function $H:\{0,1\}^* \to Z_p$. The master key is $\mathrm{MSK} = g^{\alpha}$. The public key PK is a description of the groups $\mathbb{G}, \mathbb{G}_T$ and their pairing function, as well as, $g, e(g,g)^{\alpha}, g^{a}, h_1, \ldots, h_U$.

- **KeyGen (MSK, *S*):** On input the master secret key MSK and a set S of attributes, the algorithm fist picks a random $t \in Z_p$. Create the private key SK as

$$K = g^{\alpha} g^{at} \quad L = g^{t} \quad \forall x \in S\, K_x = h_x^{t}.$$

- **Sign (PK, SK_s, $\mathcal{M}$, Y):** On input the private key SK_s for an attribute set s, a message $\mathcal{M}$, and a claim-predicate Y such that Y(S)=1 First convert Y to its corresponding monotone span program $\mathbf{M} \in (Z_p)^{l \times n}$, with row labeling function ρ associates rows of **M** to attributes. Computes $\vec{\alpha} = (\alpha_1, \ldots, \alpha_l)$ such that $\sum_{i \in I} \alpha_i \mathbf{M}_i = \vec{1}$ and $\alpha_i = 0, i \notin I$, where $\mathbf{M}_i$ is the vector corresponding to the ith row of **M**, and $I := \{i | \rho(i) \in S\}$. If there is no such α_j' and J that $\sum_{j \in J} \alpha_j' \cdot M_j = \vec{0}$, let $\vec{\beta} = (\beta_1, \ldots, \beta_l) = (0, \ldots, 0)$ (in this case, any attribute set from $\{\rho(i) | 1 \le i \le l\}$ satisfies the claim-predicate Y); otherwise, chooses $\vec{\beta} = (\beta_1, \ldots, \beta_l)$ randomly from $Z_p^{*1 \times l}$. It solves the equation $\mathbf{M}^{\mathrm{T}} \vec{\gamma}^{\mathrm{T}} = \vec{\beta} \mathbf{M}$ to obtain $\vec{\gamma} = \gamma_1, \ldots, \gamma_l$. In addition, the algorithm chooses random $r, r_1, \ldots, r_l \in Z_p$.

The signature σ is computed as follows in Box 1., along with description of Y. Three points should be noted here.

1. The signer may not have $K_{\rho(i)}$ for every attribute $1 \le i \le l$. But when this is the case, $\alpha_i = 0$ and so the value is not needed.
2. $t\alpha_i H(\mathcal{M} \| \mathrm{Y}) + r\beta_i + r\alpha_i H(\mathcal{M} \| \mathrm{Y}) = 0$ will not leak any information about the signer's attribute. Because this only occurs when $\vec{\beta} = \vec{0}$, which means any attribute set from $\{\rho(i) | 1 \le i \le l\}$ satisfies the claim-predicate Y. Therefore, α_i could be zero whether $i \in I$ or not, so α_i being zero has no relationship with the signer holding the attribute $\rho(i)$. Because if α_i is chosen zero, the remaining $\alpha_j (j \in I \setminus \{i\})$ still guarantees $\sum_{j \in I \setminus \{i\}} \alpha_j \mathbf{M}_j = \vec{1}$. In this case, when

$$t\alpha_i H(\mathcal{M} \| \mathrm{Y}) + r\beta_i + r\alpha_i H(\mathcal{M} \| \mathrm{Y}) = 0,$$

the signer may either hold the attribute $\rho(i)$ or not hold the attribute $\rho(i)$. As a result, people gain no knowledge about whether the signer has the attribute $\rho(i)$ giving the knowledge of

$$t\alpha_i H(\mathcal{M} \| \mathrm{Y}) + r\beta_i + r\alpha_i H(\mathcal{M} \| \mathrm{Y}) = 0.$$

Box 1.

$$A = (K \cdot g^{ar})^{H(\mathcal{M} \| \mathrm{Y})}$$

$$(B_i = g^{r_i \gamma_i}, C_i = h_{\rho(i)}^{-r_i \gamma_i}, E_i = K_{\rho(i)}^{\alpha_i H(\mathcal{M} \| \mathrm{Y})} \cdot h_{\rho(i)}^{r_i \beta_i} \cdot h_{\rho(i)}^{r\alpha_i H(\mathcal{M} \| \mathrm{Y})}, F_i = L^{\alpha_i H(\mathcal{M} \| \mathrm{Y})} \cdot g^{r_i \beta_i} \cdot g^{r\alpha_i H(\mathcal{M} \| \mathrm{Y})})$$

for $1 \le i \le l$

3. $\vec{\gamma}$ is a random vector from $Z_p^{1\times n}$ and has no relationship with $\vec{\beta}(\vec{\beta} \neq \vec{0})$. Since $\vec{\beta} \neq \vec{0}$, we have **det(M)**$<l$. Given $\vec{\gamma}$, there are $p^{l-\mathbf{det}(\mathbf{M})}$ possible $\vec{\beta}$ for $\mathbf{M}^{\mathrm{T}}\vec{\gamma}^{\mathrm{T}} = \vec{\beta}\mathbf{M}$. Here, **det(M)** is the rank of matrix **M**. Therefore, the probability to deduce $g^{r_i\beta_i}$ successfully from $\{g^{r_i\gamma_i}\}_{i=1,\ldots,n}$ is negligible, since ρ is a large prime number.

- **Verify(**$\mathrm{PK}, \sigma, \mathcal{M}$**):** On input public parameters PK, the message $\mathcal{M}$, and the signature σ which is generated under the claim-predicate Y such that Y(S)=1. First convert Y to its corresponding monotone span program $\mathbf{M} \in (Z_p)^{l\times n}$ with row labeling function ρ. Choose a random vector $\vec{v} \in Z_p^{1\times n}$. Computes

$$\vec{s}^{\mathrm{T}} = (s_1,\ldots,s_l)^{\mathrm{T}} = \mathbf{M}\cdot\vec{v}^{\mathrm{T}}, s_0 = \vec{1}\cdot\vec{v}^{\mathrm{T}}.$$

Check the following constraints,

$$e(B_i, g) \stackrel{?}{=} e(C_i, 1/h_{\rho(i)}),$$

$$e(E_i, g) \stackrel{?}{=} e(F_i, h_{\rho(i)}), \quad \text{for } 1 \leq i \leq l$$

$$\frac{e(A, g^{s_0})\cdot\prod_{i=1}^{l} e(B_i, g^a)^{s_i}}{\prod_{i=1}^{l}(e(C_i, F_i)\cdot e(g^a, F_i)\cdot e(B_i, E_i))^{s_i}} \stackrel{?}{=} e(g,g)^{\alpha\cdot H(\mathcal{M}\|\mathrm{Y})\cdot s_0},$$

returns accept if the above check succeed, and reject otherwise (Box 2).

Box 2.

[Correctness]

$$\frac{e(A, g^{s_0})\cdot\prod_{i=1}^{l} e(B_i, g^a)^{s_i}}{\prod_{i=1}^{l}(e(C_i, F_i)\cdot e(g^a, F_i)\cdot e(B_i, E_i))^{s_i}}$$

$$= \frac{e(g^{\alpha H(\mathcal{M}\|\mathrm{Y})} g^{atH(\mathcal{M}\|\mathrm{Y})} g^{arH(\mathcal{M}\|\mathrm{Y})}, g^{s_0})\cdot\prod_{i=1}^{n} e(g^{r_i\gamma_i}, g^a)^{s_i}}{\prod_{i=1}^{l}(e(h_{\rho(i)}^{-r_i\gamma_i}, g^{t\alpha_i H(\mathcal{M}\|\mathrm{Y})} g^{r_i\beta_i} g^{r\alpha_i H(\mathcal{M}\|\mathrm{Y})})\cdot e(g^a, g^{t\alpha_i H(\mathcal{M}\|\mathrm{Y})} g^{r_i\beta_i} g^{r\alpha_i H(\mathcal{M}\|\mathrm{Y})})\cdot e(g^{r_i\gamma_i}, h_{\rho(i)}^{t\alpha_i H(\mathcal{M}\|\mathrm{Y})} h_{\rho(i)}^{r_i\beta_i} h_{\rho(i)}^{r\alpha_i H(\mathcal{M}\|\mathrm{Y})}))^{s_i}}$$

$$= \frac{e(g,g)^{\alpha\cdot s_0 H(\mathcal{M}\|\mathrm{Y})}\cdot e(g,g)^{as_0 tH(\mathcal{M}\|\mathrm{Y})}\cdot e(g,g)^{ars_0 H(\mathcal{M}\|\mathrm{Y})}\cdot\prod_{i=1}^{l}\prod_{j=1}^{n} e(g^{r_i\gamma_i\cdot\mathbf{M}_{*j}}, g^a)^{v_j}}{\prod_{i=1}^{l} e(g^a, g^{t\alpha_i H(\mathcal{M}\|\mathrm{Y})} g^{r_i\beta_i} g^{r\alpha_i H(\mathcal{M}\|\mathrm{Y})})^{s_i}}$$

$$= \frac{e(g,g)^{\alpha\cdot s_0 H(\mathcal{M}\|\mathrm{Y})}\cdot e(g,g)^{as_0 tH(\mathcal{M}\|\mathrm{Y})}\cdot e(g,g)^{ars_0 H(\mathcal{M}\|\mathrm{Y})}\cdot\prod_{i=1}^{l}\prod_{j=1}^{n} e(g^{r_i\gamma_i\cdot\mathbf{M}_{*j}}, g^a)^{v_i}}{e(g^a, g^t)^{H(\mathcal{M}\|\mathrm{Y})\sum_{i=1}^{l} s_i\alpha_i}\cdot\prod_{i=1}^{l}\prod_{j=1}^{n} e(g^{r_i\beta_i\cdot\mathbf{M}_{*j}}, g^a)^{v_i}\cdot e(g^a, g^{rH(\mathcal{M}\|\mathrm{Y})})^{\sum_{i=1}^{l}\alpha_i s_i}} = e(g,g)^{\alpha\cdot s_0 H(\mathcal{M}\|\mathrm{Y})}$$

SECURITY PROOF

Theorem 1: Our construction is correct (Definition 3) and perfectly private (Definition 4).

Proof: Correctness can be seen by straight-forward substitutions as in Correctness section illustrated above. To prove perfect privacy it suffices to show that for any claim-predicate Y and any attribute set S that satisfies Y, the output of $\mathbf{Sign}(\mathrm{PK}, \mathrm{SK}_S, \mathcal{M}, \mathrm{Y})$ is uniformly distributed among signatures σ under the constraint that $\mathbf{Verify}(\mathbf{PK}, \sigma, \mathcal{M}) = 1$.

For $\sigma = (A, (B_i, C_i, E_i, F_i)_{i=1,\dots,l})$ it is easy to see that for any setting of $A,(B_1,\dots,B_l), (E_1,\dots,E_l)$, there is a unique value of $(C_i, F_i)_{i=1,\dots,l}$ for which the signature successfully verifies. Thus, we conclude our construction is of perfect privacy by observing that $A,(B_1,\dots,B_l), (E_1,\dots,E_l)$ output by **Sign** are distributed uniformly and independently in their respective domains and that the signature output by **Sign** successfully verifies.

Note that it is obvious that $A,(B_1,\dots,B_l)$ is distributed uniformly and independently. And $E_1,\dots,E_l$ is distributed uniformly and independently, because $\vec{\beta}$ is independent from $\vec{\gamma}$. The reader could refer to note 2 and 3 in the note section of Sign algorithm for more details.

Theorem 2: Our construction is (adaptive-predicate) unforgeable under the decisional q-parallel BDHE assumption (Waters, 2011) and the existence of collision resistant hash functions.

Proof: In this proof, we embed a random k attribute $\mathbf{M}^*$ into the public parameters h_x using q-parallel BDHE assumption. For each row i of $\mathbf{M}^*$ the simulator programs n pieces of information $\left(M =\right)(\mathbf{M}^*_{i,l},\dots,\mathbf{M}^*_{i,n})$ into the h_x related to the attribute assigned to that row. With this method, the simulator is able to cancel the unknown terms during private key queries and signature queries, as well as combine the forged signature to solve the q-parallel BDHE problem.

Suppose an adversary $\mathcal{A}$ has a non-negligible advantage $\epsilon = \mathbf{Adv}_{\mathcal{A}}$ advantage in attacking our scheme. We show how to build a simulator $\mathcal{B}$ that solves the decisional q- parallel BDHE problem.

- **Initial Phase:** The simulator takes in a decisional q- parallel BDHE challenge $\vec{y}, T$. The simulator randomly chooses a $k = \lfloor U - \log_2 3t \rfloor$ attribute predicate Y^* and converts Y^* to its corresponding monotone span program $(\mathbf{M}^*, p^*)$, where $\mathbf{M}^*$ has l^* rows and n^* columns. Here, $\lfloor\ \rfloor$ is the round down operation, t is the maximum number of private key queries and signature generation queries, and $l^*, n^* < q$.
- **Setup Phase:** The simulator chooses random $\alpha' \in \mathrm{Z}_p$ and implicitly sets $\alpha = \alpha' + a^{q+1}$ by letting

$$e(g,g)^{\alpha} = e(g^{a}, g^{a^{q}})e(g,g)^{\alpha'}.$$

We describe how the simulator programs $h_1,\dots,h_U$.

For each x where $1 \leq x \leq U$, it begins by choosing a random value z_x Let X denotes the set of indices of i such that $p^*(i)=x$. The simulator programs h_x as:

$$h_x = g^{z_x} \prod_{i \in X} g^{aM^*_{i,1}/b_i} \cdot g^{a^2 M^*_{i,2}/b_i} \cdots g^{a^{n^*} M^*_{i,n^*}/b_i}$$

If $X=\varnothing$ then we have $h_x = g^{z_x}$. Note that h_x are distributed randomly due to the g^{z_x} value.

The simulator gives to $\mathcal{A}$ the public key: $g, e(g,g)^{\alpha}, g^{a}, h, \dots, h_U$.

The corresponding master key, $\mathrm{MSK} = g^{\alpha}$, is unknown to the simulator.

- **Query Phase:** In this phase the simulator answers private key queries and signature queries. Suppose the simulator is given a private key query for a set S.

If S satisfies Y^*, then the simulator aborts and randomly chooses its guess β of the q-parallel BDHE problem. Otherwise, the simulator first picks a random $r \in Z_p$. Next it finds a vector $\vec{w} = (w_1, \ldots, w_{n^*}) \in Z_p^{1 \times n^*}$ such that $w_1 = -1$ and for all i where $\rho^*(i) \in S$ we have that $\vec{w} \cdot \mathbf{M}_i^* = 0$. By the definition of monotone span program such a vector must exist.

The simulator begins by implicitly defining t as $r + w_1 a^q + w_2 a^{q-1} + \cdots + w_{n^*} a^{a^{a-n^*+1}}$. It performs this by setting $L = g^r \prod (g^{a^{q+1-i}})^{W_i} = g^t$.

We observe that by our definition of t, g^{at} contains a term $g^{-a^{q+1}}$ which will cancel out the unknown term in g^a when generating K. The simulator can compute K as:

$$K = g^{\alpha'} g^{ar} \prod_{i=2,\ldots,n^*} (g^{a^{q+2-i}})^{w_i}.$$

Now we calculate the key components K_x for $\forall x \in S$. First, we consider $x \in S$ for which there is no i such that $\rho^*(i)=x$. For those we can simply let $K_x = L^{Z_x}$.

The more difficult task is to create keys for attribute $x \in S$, where there exists an i such that $\rho^*(i)=x$ and $i \leq n^*$. To compute these keys we must make sure that there are no terms of the form g^{a^{q+1}/b_i} that we can't simulate. Notice that in calculating $K_x = h_x^t$ all terms of this form come from $g^{a^{q+1}/b_i M_{i,j} w_j}$, where $\rho^*(i)=x$. However we have that $\vec{w} \cdot \mathbf{M}^* = 0$, all of these terms cancel.

Again, let X be the set of all i such that $\rho^*(i)=x$. The simulator creates K_x in this case as follows.

$$K_x =$$

$$L^{z_x} \prod_{i \in X} \prod_{j=1,\ldots n^*} (g^{(a^j/b_i)r} \prod_{\substack{k=1,\ldots,n^* \\ k \neq j}} (g^{a^{a+1+j-k}/b_i})^{w_k})^{M^*_{i,j}}.$$

The simulator $\mathcal{B}$ returns $(K, L, (K_\chi)_{\chi \in S})$ to the adversary $\mathcal{A}$.

To answer a signature query on $(\mathcal{M}, Y)$. If $\forall S$ that satisfies Y also satisfies Y^*, the simulator aborts and outputs a random guess for β Otherwise, the simulator randomly chooses a set S that satisfies Y but does not satisfy Y^*, and asks the private key generation oracle to get the private key for S. Next, it uses the private key to generate the signature on $(\mathcal{M}, Y)$, and returns it to the adversary $\mathcal{A}$.

- **Forgery:** After a polynomially bounded number of private key queries and signature queries, the adversary outputs a forged signature $\sigma' = (A', (B_i')_{i=1,\ldots,n}, (C_i', D_i', E_i', F_i')_{i=1,\ldots,l})$ on message $\mathcal{M}'$ for the claim-predicate Y', such that $(\mathcal{M}', Y')$ was never queried to the signature generation oracle and Y' does not accept any S queried to the key generation oracle. If $\exists S$ that is accepted by Y' but not accepted by Y^*, the simulator aborts and outputs a random guess for β Otherwise, the simulator can solve the decisional q-parallel BDHE problem as follows.

First, convert Y' to its corresponding monotone span program $\mathbf{M'} \in Z_p^{l^* \times n^*}$ with row labeling function ρ'. The tricky part is to compute the g^{as_i} since it contains terms $(g^{a^i s})$ that we must cancel out. However, the simulator can use secret splitting to make these terms cancel out. Intuitively, the simulator chooses random $y_{2'}, \ldots, y_{n^{*\prime}}$. Then the simulator shares the secret using the vector

$\vec{v} = (s, sa + y_{2'}, sa^2 + y_{3'}, \ldots, sa^{n-1} + y_{n^*}) \in Z_p^{1 \times n}$.

Next, we define

$R_i = \{k \mid \rho^*(k) = \rho'(i) \wedge k \neq i, i = 1, \ldots, n\}$.

Suppose $r_1', \ldots, r_l'$ are random values, we have the following equations,

$$B_i' = g^{r_i \gamma_i} = g^{-r_i'} g^{sb_i},\ C_{i'} = h^{-r_i \gamma_i} = h_{\rho'(i)}^{r_i' - sb_i}$$

$$g^{as_i} C_i' = h_{\rho'(i)}^{r_i'} \Big(\prod_{j=2,\ldots,n^*} (g^a)^{M_{i,j}^* y_j'} \Big) (g^{b_i \cdot s})^{-z_{\rho'(i)}} \Big(\prod_{k \in R_i} \prod_{j=1,\ldots,n^*} (g^{a^j \cdot s \cdot (b_i / b_k)})^{M_{k,j}^*} \Big)$$

Thus, the simulator could compute g^{as_i} and $g^{r_i'}$ as follows,

$$g^{as_i} = h_{\rho'(i)}^{r_i'} \Big(\prod_{j=2,\ldots,n} (g^a)^{M_{i,j}^* y_j'} \Big) (g^{b_i \cdot s})^{-z_{\rho'(i)}} \Big(\prod_{k \in R_i} \prod_{j=1,\ldots,n} (g^{a^j \cdot s \cdot (b_i / b_k)})^{M_{k,j}^*} \Big) / C_i'$$

$$g^{r_i'} = g^{sb_i} / B_i'$$

Thus, the simulator compute $e(F_i', g^{as_i})$ and $e(B_i', g^{as_i})$ as follows in Box 3.

If

$$(e(A', g^s) \cdot \prod_{j=1}^{n} e(B_i', g^{as_i})) / \prod_{i=1}^{l} e(F_i', g^{as_i}) = T^{H(\mathcal{M}' \| \mathrm{Y}')} \cdot e(g^s, g^{\alpha'})^{H(\mathcal{M}' \| \mathrm{Y}')},$$

the simulator then outputs β=1 to guess that $T = e(g, g)^{a^{q+1} s}$; otherwise, it outputs β=0 to indicate that it believes T is a random group element in $\mathbb{G}_T$.

Next, we calculate the lower bound of the probability that the simulator completes without aborting. Without loss of generality we can assume the adversary always makes *t* queries which are the maximum number of the private key query and signature generation query. For any set of *t* private key queries on set $S_1, \ldots, S_t$ and *t* signature queries on set $(\mathrm{Y}_1, \mathrm{M}_1), \ldots, (\mathrm{Y}_t, \mathrm{M}_t)$ and the forged matrix $\mathbf{M}'$, we have

$$\Pr[\overline{\mathbf{abort}}] = \Pr[(\wedge_{i=1}^t \mathrm{Y}^*(S_i) = 0) \wedge (\wedge_{i=1}^t K(\mathrm{Y}_i) \not\subseteq K(\mathrm{Y}^*)) \wedge (K(\mathrm{Y}') \subseteq K(\mathrm{Y}^*))]$$

Box 3.

$$e(F_i', g^{as_i}) = e(F_{i'}, h_{\rho'(i)}^{r_i'}) \cdot e(F_i', (\prod_{j=2,\ldots,n} (g^a)^{M_{i,j}^* y_{j'}}) (g^{b_i \cdot s})^{-z_{\rho'(i)}} (\prod_{k \in R_i} \prod_{j=1,\ldots,n} (g^{a^j \cdot s \cdot (b_i / b_k)})^{M_{k,j}^*}) / C_i')$$
$$= e(E_i', g^{r_i'}) \cdot e(F_i', (\prod_{j=2,\ldots,n} (g^a)^{M_{i,j}^* y_j'}) (g^{b_i \cdot s})^{-z_{\rho'(i)}} \cdot (\prod_{k \in R_i} \prod_{j=1,\ldots,n} (g^{a^j \cdot s \cdot (b_i / b_k)})^{M_{k,j}^*}) / C_i')$$

$$e(B_i', g^{as_i}) = e(B_{i'}, h^{r_i'}) \cdot e(B_i', (\prod_{j=2,\ldots,n} (g^a)^{M_{i,j}^* y_j'}) (g^{b_i \cdot s})^{-z_{\rho'(i)}} \cdot (\prod_{k \in R_i} \prod_{j=1,\ldots,n} (g^{a^j \cdot s \cdot (b_i / b_k)})^{M_{k,j}^*}) / C_i')$$
$$= e(C_i', g^{r_i'}) \cdot e(B_i', (\prod_{j=2,\ldots,n} (g^a)^{M_{i,j}^* y_{j'}}) (g^{b_i \cdot s})^{-z_{\rho'(i)}} \cdot (\prod_{k \in R_i} \prod_{j=1,\ldots,n} (g^{a^j \cdot s \cdot (b_i / b_k)})^{M_{k,j}^*}) / C_i')$$

Here, $K(\mathrm{Y})$ is defined as the set of all attribute sets that satisfy Y. We can then lower bound the probability of not aborting as follows in Box 4.

Equations 1.4 comes from the fact that

$$\Pr[\mathrm{Y}^*(S_i) = 1] = \Pr[K(\mathrm{Y}_i) \subseteq K(\mathrm{Y}^*)]$$
$$= \Pr[K(\mathrm{Y}') \subseteq K(\mathrm{Y}^*)] = \frac{1}{2^{U-k}}$$

We can optimize the last equation by setting $k = \lfloor U - \log_2 3t \rfloor$ (as we did in the simulation), where t is the maximum number of private key queries and signature generation queries. Solving for this gives us a lower bound

$$\lambda = (1 - t / 2^{U-\lfloor U-\log_2 3t \rfloor})^2 \cdot (1/2)^{U-\lfloor U-\log_2 3t \rfloor}.$$

Suppose the adversary succeeds with probability ϵ after q private key queries and signature generation queries, and this probability is independent of the random choices made by the simulator, we conclude that the simulator succeeds with probability,

$$\tilde{\epsilon} =$$
$$\Pr[\beta = 1 \mid \overline{\mathbf{abort}}]\Pr[\overline{\mathbf{abort}}] = \epsilon\Pr[\overline{\mathbf{abort}}]$$
$$\geq (1 - t / 2^{U-\lfloor U-\log_2 3t \rfloor})^2 (1/2)^{U-\lfloor U-\log_2 3t \rfloor}\epsilon.$$

PERFORMANCE ANALYSIS

The proposed ABS scheme is efficient and practical. We give the comparison between our scheme and the existing ABS schemes in the standard model: Maji, Prabhakaran, and Rosulek's (2011) (two typical instantiations), Okamoto and Takashima's (2011), and Escala, Herranz, and Morillo's (2011), as well as the ABS scheme in the generic group model (Maji, Prabhakaran, & Rosulek, 2008) (as a benchmark). All of these schemes can be implemented over a pairing group and the size of a group element is about the size of Zp (e.g., 256 bits). We summarize the comparison as follows.

In Table 1, l and r represent the size of the underlying access structure matrix M for a predicate, i.e. $M \in Z^{l \times r}$. We also give comparison of two examples, the predicate with 4 AND and 5 OR gates as well as 10 variables which is expressed by a 10×5 matrix, and the predicate with 49 AND and 50 OR gates as well as 100 variables which is expressed by a 100 × 50 matrix (see the appendix of Lewko & Waters, 2011). λ is the security parameter (e.g. 128).

Box 4.

$$\begin{aligned}
&\Pr[(\wedge_{i=1}^{t} \mathrm{Y}^*(S_i) = 0) \wedge (\wedge_{i=1}^{t} K(\mathrm{Y}_i) \not\subseteq K(\mathrm{Y}^*)) \wedge (K(\mathrm{Y}') \subseteq K(\mathrm{Y}^*))] \\
&= (1 - \Pr[\vee_{i=1}^{t} \mathrm{Y}^*(S_i) = 1]) \cdot (1 - \Pr[\vee_{i=1}^{t} K(\mathrm{Y}_i) \subseteq \mathrm{Y}^*]) \cdot \Pr[K(\mathrm{Y}') \subseteq K(\mathrm{Y}^*)] \\
&\geq (1 - \sum_{i=1}^{t} \Pr[\mathrm{Y}^*(S_i) = 1]) \cdot (1 - \sum_{i=1}^{t} \Pr[K(\mathrm{Y}_i) \subseteq \mathrm{Y}^*]) \cdot \Pr[K(\mathrm{Y}') \subseteq K(\mathrm{Y}^*)] \qquad (1.4) \\
&= (1 - \frac{t}{2^{U-k}}) \cdot (1 - \frac{t}{2^{U-k}}) \cdot \frac{1}{2^{U-k}}
\end{aligned}$$

Table 1. Comparison of ABS systems in terms of signature size, model, assumptions, predicates, two examples of signature size

	MPR08 (Maji; Prabhakaran; Rosulek, 2008)	MPR11 (Maji; Prabhakaran; Rosulek, 2011) (Boneh-Boyen based)	MPR11 (Maji; Prabhakaran; Rosulek, 2011) (Waters based)	OT (Okamoto; Takashima, 2011)	EHM (Escala; Herranz; Morillo, 2011)	Proposed
Signature size (# of group elts)	1 + r + 2	51l + 2r+18λl	36l + 2r+9λ + 12	7l + 11	9l + 7	4l + 1
Model	Generic group model	Standard model	Standard model	Standard model	Standard model	Standard model
Security	full	full	full	full	full	full
Assmuptions	CR hash	q–SDH and DLIN	DLIN	DLIN and CR hash	CHD and Sub-group Decision	q–BDHE and CR hash
Predicates	monotone	monotone	monotone	non-monotone	monotone	monotone
Sig. size example 1 (l=10,r=5, λ = 128)	17	23560	1534	81	97	41
Sig. size example 2 (l=100,r=50, λ = 128)	152	282400	4864	711	907	401

APPLICATION TO SECURE ATTRIBUTE-BASED MESSAGING SYSTEM

An important application of ABS deals with Attribute-Based Messaging (ABM) system. As mentioned by Boba et al. (2006), Attribute-Based Messaging (ABM) enables message senders to dynamically create a list of recipients based on their attributes as inferred from an enterprise database. Since ABM can enhance the relevance of messages to the recipient and allow the sender to send confidential messages knowing that the messages would be delivered only to the intended recipients, many applications such as multiparty email messaging in an enterprise can benefit greatly from integration of ABM.

In ABM, to provide end-to-end message privacy, one can use ciphertext-policy attribute-based encryption, as proposed by Bethencourt, Sahai and Waters (2007). However, access control (i.e., for the receiver to verify that the sender also satisfied a particular policy) in an ABM system is still a challenge until now.

Our ABS scheme provides an attractive solution to access control in ABM system. We use our ABS scheme (**Setup**, **Keygen**, **Sign**, **Verify**) as the underlying algorithm. Our ABM architecture is based on the architecture presented by Boba et al. (2006). It distinguishes three phases: policy specialization phase, message transmission phase, address resolution phase. Figure 1 gives an illustration of our protocol.

Our protocol performs as follows.

Policy Specialization Phase

This phase is represented by green dashed lines in Figure 1.

PS1: The user starts the phase by sending his attribute expression *exp* to the web server.

PS2: The web server sends the user's attribute expression to the ABM Server.

Figure 1. The proposed ABM architecture

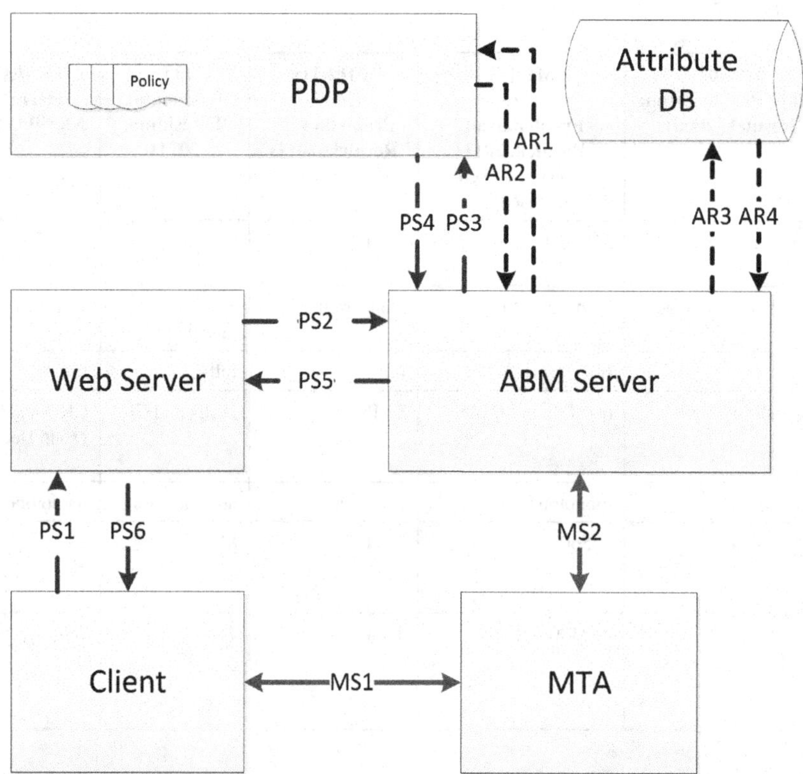

PS3: The ABM sends the user's attribute expression to the PDP (policy decision point) and requests a special policy.

PS4: The PDP evaluates all the policies in a policy file against the user's attribute expression and returns the specialized policy which is a list of <attribute, value> pairs that the user can route on.

PS5: The ABM server returns the specialized policy to the web server.

PS6: The web server generates a timestamp *t*. The user composes an ABM address and downloads it together with *t*. The user computes the hash of his sending message as *h*. The user then generates the ABS signature σ=**Sign**(*sk exp, h*||*t*). The ABM address created using the web interface includes a pre-specified enterprise email id, σ, timestamp *t* and attribute expression *exp*.

Message Transmission Phase

This phase is represented by purple solid lines in Figure 1.

MS1: Users send ABM messages using any standard Mail User Agent (MUA) to a pre-specified email address such as abm@localdomain.com, with the ABM address included in the message as an attachment.

MS2: When receiving a message for the pre-specified address, the Mail Transfer Agent (MTA) notifies the ABM server. The ABM server first verifies if the difference between *t* and current time is within a predefined value Δ, verifies that the from address in the message is same as the enterprise e-mail id included in the ABM address and verifies the ABS signature σ using *t,* hash value of the message and the sender's attributes expression *exp*. Next, it will process the message in the address resolution phase and invoke the MTA to deliver the message to the recipients as specified by the ABM address.

Address Resolution Phase

This phase is represented by black dotted lines in Figure 1.

AR1: The ABM server checks with the PDP if the sender is authorized to send the message to the attached ABM address.

AR2: The PDP evaluates the policies for accessing the attributes in ABM address against sender's attribute expression *exp* and responds in the affirmative only if the user is allowed access to all attributes in the ABM address.

AR3: The ABM server queries the attribute database to resolve the ABM address.

AR4: The attribute database returns a list of email addresses corresponding to the ABM address. The ABM server forwards the message to each member in the list via the MTA.

Security Analysis

In the following, we will analyze the security of our proposed ABM architecture.

- **User Authentication:** As described above, in order to pass the signature verification of the ABM server, each user has to register to the key generation center and obtain his private key. To send a valid ABM message, a user needs to sign the timestamp with his private key and the attribute expression. Therefore, the system owner enforces strict and fine-grained access control by user registration.
- **User Privacy-Preserving:** As before, the use of ABS can ensure user privacy-preserving. More specifically, ABS signature can lead to desirable user privacy-preserving property: We assume that an access structure satisfying *m* users attribute sets have been chosen to generate the signature. The ABS signature is signer-ambiguous in the sense that the verifier (e.g. the system owner, the ABM server, the PDP, the MTA) is unable to determine the identity of the actual signer with probability greater than *1/m*.
- **Integrity Protection of Message:** In our proposal, an authorized user uses an ABS signature technique to authenticate the sending message. The attribute expression of the user is attached, so the ABM server can verify the message. Therefore, an adversary cannot modify the message and then pass the verification of the ABM server.
- **Freshness:** The use of the timestamp included in the ABS signature can ensure the freshness of the message. In addition, nonces can be used to prevent replay attacks instead of timestamp. A user sends the request for nonce to the web server. The web server directs the request to the ABM server. The ABM server returns random or pseudo-random numbers *n* to the web server which sends *n* back to the user. Subsequently, the user includes hash of *n* in its ABS signature. When the ABM server verifies the signature, it checks whether hash of *n* is included in the signature.

FUTURE RESEARCH DIRECTIONS

The kind of authentication required in attribute-based signatures differs from that offered by identity-based signatures. An ABS solution requires richer semantics including privacy requirements, unforgeability, and collusion resistance. The identity-based signature provides a powerful mechanism for authentication of the stored and transmitted information where the identity can be an arbitrary string such as an email address or a unique identification number. While this is useful for applications, where the data receiver knows specifically the identity of the data signer, in many applications the signer will want to have fine-grained control over how much of their personal information is revealed by the signature.

As part of our future work, we intend to enhance the ABS scheme which will be secure in the standard model based on decisional parallel bilinear Diffie-Hellman exponent assumption (Waters, 2011) which is more practical than the generic group model (Maji, Prabhakaran, & Rosulek, 2008) by ensuring the privacy requirements, unforgeability, and collusion resistance. We also plan to work on key management for ABS and extend our model to multiple enterprises.

CONCLUSION

We have presented an efficient and fully secure attribute-based signature system that is expressive and provably secure under decisional q-parallel BDHE assumption (Waters, 2011) in the standard model. We have proved that our scheme is (adaptive-predicate) unforgeable against adaptively chosen message attack and perfectly private in the standard model. Our method of embedding a monotone span program into the public parameters allowed us to create clean, modular proof of security. The new construction is most efficient ABS scheme in the standard model comparing with the state-of-the-art (Escala, Herranz, & Morillo, 2011; Maji, Prabhakaran, & Rosulek, 2011; Okamoto & Takashima, 2011) construction.

Furthermore, we have shown how to apply our scheme to achieve ''User authentication'', ''User privacy-preserving'', ''Integrity Protection of Message'' and "Freshness" in ABM system. Since in our proposal the signature is based on attributes, the privacy of the user is protected. We anticipate this work will be of good use in instant messaging system or systems that mainly use attributes to route message.

ACKNOWLEDGMENT

This work was supported by the Foundation for Young Teachers in Higher Education Institutions of Shanghai under Grant No. Slg11004 and Centre for Research in Complex Systems (CRiCS) at Charles Sturt University.

REFERENCES

Beimel, A. (1996). *Secure schemes for secret sharing and key distribution*. (PhD Thesis). Israel Institute of Technology. Haiifa, Israel.

Bethencourt, J., Sahai, A., & Waters, B. (2007). Ciphertext-policy attribute-based encryption. In *Proceedings of the IEEE Symposium on Security and Privacy*, (pp. 321-334). IEEE Press.

Bobba, R., Fatemieh, O., Khan, F., Gunter, C. A., & Khurana, H. (2006). Using attribute-based access control to enable attribute-based messaging. In *Proceedings of ACSAC*, (pp. 403-413). IEEE Computer Society.

Boneh, D., & Franklin, M. (2003). Identity-based encryption from the weil pairing. *SIAM Journal on Computing*, *32*, 586–615. doi:10.1137/S0097539701398521.

Boyen, X. (2007). Mesh signatures. *Lecture Notes in Computer Science*, *4515*, 210–227. doi:10.1007/978-3-540-72540-4_12.

Chaum, D., & Van Heyst, E. (1991). Group signatures. In *Proceedings of the 10th Annual International Conference on Theory and Application of Cryptographic Techniques, EUROCRYPT 1991*, (pp. 257–265). Berlin, Germany: Springer-Verlag.

Escala, A., Herranz, J., & Morillo, P. (2011). Revocable attribute-based signatures with adaptive security in the standard model. *Lecture Notes in Computer Science*, *6737*, 224–241. doi:10.1007/978-3-642-21969-6_14.

Groth, J., & Sahai, A. (2008). Efficient non-interactive proof systems for bilinear groups. *Lecture Notes in Computer Science*, *4965*, 415–432. doi:10.1007/978-3-540-78967-3_24.

Khader, D. (2007a). *Attribute based group signature with revocation*. Report 2007/241. Cryptology ePrint Archive.

Khader, D. (2007b). *Attribute based group signatures*. Report 2007/159. Cryptology ePrint Archive.

Lewko, A., & Waters, B. (2011). Decentralizing attribute-based encryption. *Lecture Notes in Computer Science*, *6632*, 568–588. doi:10.1007/978-3-642-20465-4_31.

Li, J., Au, M. H., Susilo, W., Xie, D., & Ren, K. (2010). Attribute-based signature and its applications. In *Proceedings of the 5th ACM Symposium on Information, Computer and Communications Security, ASIACCS 2010*, (pp. 60–69). New York, NY: ACM.

Li, J., & Kim, K. (2007). *Attribute-based ring signatures*. Report 2008/394. Cryptology ePrint Archive.

Li, J., & Kim, K. (2010). Hidden attribute-based signatures without anonymity revocation. *Information Sciences*, *180*(9), 1681–1689. doi:10.1016/j.ins.2010.01.008.

Maji, H., Prabhakaran, M., & Rosulek, M. (2008). *Attribute-based signatures: Achieving attribute-privacy and collusion-resistance*. Report 2008/328. Cryptology ePrint Archive.

Maji, H., Prabhakaran, M., & Rosulek, M. (2011). Attribute-based signatures. *Lecture Notes in Computer Science*, *6558*, 376–392. doi:10.1007/978-3-642-19074-2_24.

Okamoto, T., & Takashima, K. (2011). Efficient attribute-based signatures for non-monotone predicates in the standard model. *Lecture Notes in Computer Science*, *6571*, 35–52. doi:10.1007/978-3-642-19379-8_3.

Rivest, R., Shamir, A., & Tauman, Y. (2001). How to leak a secret. *Lecture Notes in Computer Science*, *2248*, 552–565. doi:10.1007/3-540-45682-1_32.

Shahandashti, S., & Safavi-Naini, R. (2009). Threshold attribute-based signatures and their application to anonymous credential systems. *Lecture Notes in Computer Science*, *5580*, 198–216. doi:10.1007/978-3-642-02384-2_13.

Shanqing, G., & Yingpei, Z. (2008). Attribute-based signature scheme. In *Proceedings of the 2008 International Conference on Information Security and Assurance (ISA 2008)*, (pp. 509–511). Washington, DC: IEEE Computer Society.

Waters, B. (2011). Ciphertext-policy attribute-based encryption: An expressive, efficient, and provably secure realization. *Lecture Notes in Computer Science*, *6571*, 53–70. doi:10.1007/978-3-642-19379-8_4.

Yang, P., Cao, Z., & Dong, X. (2011). Fuzzy identity based signature with applications to biometric authentication. *Computers & Electrical Engineering*, *37*(4), 532–540. doi:10.1016/j.compeleceng.2011.04.013.

ADDITIONAL READING

Bethencourt, J., Sahai, A., & Waters, B. (2007). Ciphertext-policy attribute-based encryption. In *Proceedings of IEEE Symposium on Security and Privacy*, (pp. 321-334). IEEE Press.

Bobba, R., Fatemieh, O., Khan, F., Gunter, C. A., & Khurana, H. (2006). Using attribute-based access control to enable attribute-based messaging. In *Proceedings of ACSAC*, (pp. 403-413). IEEE Computer Society.

Bobba, R., Fatemieh, O., Khan, F., Gunter, C. A., Khurana, H., & Prabhakaran, M. (2010). Attribute-based messaging: Access control and confidentiality. *ACM Transactions on Information and System Security*, *13*(4). doi:10.1145/1880022.1880025.

Cao, D., Zhao, B., Wang, X., Su, J., & Ji, G. (2011). Multi-authority attribute-based signature. In *Proceedings of the Third International Conference on Intelligent Networking and Collaborative Systems (INCoS)*, (pp. 668 – 672). INCoS.

Escala, E., Herranz, J., & Morillo, P. (2011). Revocable attribute-based signatures with adaptive security in the standard model. *Lecture Notes in Computer Science*, *6737*, 224–241. doi:10.1007/978-3-642-21969-6_14.

Fan, C.-I., Wu, C.-N., Chen, W.-K., & Sun, W.-Z. (2012). Attribute-based strong designated-verifier signature scheme. *Journal of Systems and Software*, *85*(4), 944–959. doi:10.1016/j.jss.2011.11.1008.

Khader, D. (2007a). *Attribute based group signature with revocation*. Report 2007/241. Cryptology ePrint Archive.

Khader, D. (2007b). *Attribute based group signatures*. Report 2007/159. Cryptology ePrint Archive.

Li, J., Au, M. H., Susilo, W., Xie, D., & Ren, K. (2010). Attribute-based signature and its applications. In *Proceedings of the 5th ACM Symposium on Information, Computer and Communications Security, ASIACCS 2010*, (pp. 60–69). New York, NY: ACM.

Li, J., & Kim, K. (2007). *Attribute-based ring signatures*. Report 2008/394. Cryptology ePrint Archive.

Li, J., & Kim, K. (2010). Hidden attribute-based signatures without anonymity revocation. *Information Sciences*, *180*(9), 1681–1689. doi:10.1016/j.ins.2010.01.008.

Maji, H., Prabhakaran, M., & Rosulek, M. (2008). *Attribute-based signatures: Achieving attribute-privacy and collusion-resistance*. Report 2008/328. Cryptology ePrint Archive.

Maji, H., Prabhakaran, M., & Rosulek, M. (2011). Attribute-based signatures. *Lecture Notes in Computer Science*, *6558*, 376–392. doi:10.1007/978-3-642-19074-2_24.

Okamoto, T., & Takashima, K. (2011). Efficient attribute-based signatures for non-monotone predicates in the standard model. *Lecture Notes in Computer Science*, *6571*, 35–52. doi:10.1007/978-3-642-19379-8_3.

Qian, Y., & Zhao, Y. (2010). Strongly unforgeable attribute-based group signature in the standard model. In *Proceedings of the 2010 IEEE International Conference on Intelligent Computing and Intelligent Systems (ICIS)*, (pp. 843 – 852). ICIS.

Shahandashti, S., & Safavi-Naini, R. (2009). Threshold attribute-based signatures and their application to anonymous credential systems. *Lecture Notes in Computer Science*, *5580*, 198–216. doi:10.1007/978-3-642-02384-2_13.

Shanqing, G., & Yingpei, Z. (2008). Attribute-based signature scheme. In *Proceedings of the 2008 International Conference on Information Security and Assurance (ISA 2008)*, (pp. 509–511). Washington, DC: IEEE Computer Society.

Wang, H.-X., Zhu, Y., Feng, R.-Q., & Yau, S. S. (2010). Article. *Journal of Computer Science and Technology*, *25*(6), 1293–1304. doi:10.1007/s11390-010-9406-1.

Waters, B. (2011). Ciphertext-policy attribute-based encryption: An expressive, efficient, and provably secure realization. *Lecture Notes in Computer Science*, *6571*, 53–70. doi:10.1007/978-3-642-19379-8_4.

Weber, S. G., Kalev, Y., Ries, S., & Mühlhäuser, M. (2011). MundoMessage: Enabling trustworthy ubiquitous emergency communication. In *Proceedings of the ACM International Conference on Ubiquitous Information Management and Communication (ICUIMC 2011)*. ACM Press.

Weber, S. G., Ries, S., & Mühlhäuser, M. (2010). *Concepts and scheme for multilaterally secure, user-friendly attribute-based messaging*. Technical Report No. TUD-CS-2010-2381. Darmstadt, Germany: Technische Universität Darmstadt.

Yang, P., Cao, Z., & Dong, X. (2011). Fuzzy identity based signature with applications to biometric authentication. *Computers & Electrical Engineering*, *37*(4), 532–540. doi:10.1016/j.compeleceng.2011.04.013.

KEY TERMS AND DEFINITIONS

Attribute-Based Signature: It is a kind of digital signature which assures the verifier that a signer, whose set of attributes satisfies a (possibly) complex predicate, has endorsed the message.

Attribute-Based Encryption: It is a kind of public key encryption in which the data provider can express how he wants to share data by providing a formula over a set of strings called "attributes" and a user will be ascribed a secret key associated with attributes.

Attribute-Based Messaging: It is a messaging system which enables message senders to dynamically create a list of recipients based on their attributes as inferred from an enterprise database.

Privacy: The signature reveals nothing about the attributes or other identifying information of the signer beyond what is explicitly revealed by the access structure.

Unforgeability: The only valid new signatures that a group of signers can produce are signatures that a single member of the group could legitimately generate by himself.

Chapter 8
SEcure Neighbor Discovery: A Cryptographic Solution for Securing IPv6 Local Link Operations

Ahmad AlSa'deh
Hasso-Plattner-Institute, Germany

Hosnieh Rafiee
Hasso-Plattner-Institute, Germany

Christoph Meinel
Hasso-Plattner-Institute, Germany

ABSTRACT

SEcure Neighbor Discovery (SEND) was proposed to counteract threats to the Neighbor Discovery Protocol (NDP). It is a strong security extension that can make the IPv6 local link very safe. SEND relies on dynamically Cryptographically Generated Addresses (CGAs) and X.509 certificates. However, SEND is not easily deployed and is still vulnerable to some types of attacks. This chapter evaluates the practical considerations of a SEND deployment taking a cryptographic approach as a means of securing the IPv6 local link operations. It reviews the remaining vulnerabilities and gives some recommendations with which to facilitate SEND deployment.

INTRODUCTION

The free pool of IPv4 address space will be depleted soon. On 3 February 2011, the Internet Assigned Numbers Authority (IANA) (2012, March 14) allocated the last remaining blocks of IPv4 address space to the Regional Internet Registries (RIRs). Therefore, the world is responding by transitioning from IPv4 to IPv6. On 8 June 2011, top websites and Internet Service Providers (ISPs) around the world joined together with more than 1000 other participating websites in a "World IPv6 Day". Because of the success of this global-scale event, the Internet Society organized the "World IPv6 Launch Day" on 6 June 2012 (Internet Society, 2012). On this day major ISPs and companies around the world permanently enabled IPv6 for their products and services.

DOI: 10.4018/978-1-4666-4030-6.ch008

However, businesses need to migrate to IPv6 in a secure manner in order to avoid the possible security risks inherent in an IPv6 deployment. One of the security concerns comes from the new IPv6 features and mechanisms, which can expose the network to new security threats. For instance, StateLess Address Auto-Configuration (SLAAC) (Thomson, Narten, & Jinmei, 2007) and Neighbor Discovery (ND) (Narten, Nordmark, Simpson, & Soliman, 2007) messages are essential portions of the IPv6 suite. Both ND and SLAAC, together, are known as Neighbor Discovery Protocol (NDP). IPv6 nodes use NDP for several critical functions: to discover other nodes (routers/hosts) on the link, to find the mapping between the MAC and link local addresses, to detect duplicate addresses, and to maintain reachability information about the paths to active neighbors. Also, NDP plays a crucial role in mobile IPv6 (MIPv6) networks (Perkins, Johnson, & Arkko, 2011). However, NDP is vulnerable to spoofing and Denial-of-Service (DoS) attacks (Nikander, Kempf, & Nordmark, 2004) and attackers have already developed a set of tools to use in attacking ND functionalities (Hauser, 2012).

NDP specifications do not include any security provisions. It was designed to work in trustworthy links where all nodes on the link trust each other. However, we cannot assume that being on the same network is trustworthy as this assumption does not hold in number of different scenarios, such as, over wireless networks, where anyone can join a local link either with minimal or with no link layer authentication. Today people use public networks such as Wireless LAN at airports, hotels, and cafes, where a malicious user can impersonate legitimate nodes by forging NDP messages to generate serious attacks. RFC 3756 (Nikander, et al., 2004) shows a list of potential threats to NDP. Therefore, if NDP is not secured, it will be vulnerable to these various attacks. Some such attacks are Neighbor Solicitation (NS)/ Advertisement (NA) spoofing, Neighbor Unreachability Detection (NUD) faller, Duplicate Address Detection (DAD), Denial of Service (DoS), Malicious Last Hop Router, Spoofed Redirect Message, Bogus On-Link Prefix, Parameter Spoofing, and Replay attacks.

Therefore, RFC 3971 "SEcure Neighbor Discovery (SEND)" (Arkko, Kempf, Zill, & Nikander, 2005) was proposed as a set of enhancements to make the IPv6 neighbor and router discovery secure. SEND was designed to ensure message integrity, prevent IPv6 address theft, prevent replay attacks, and provide a mechanism for verifying the authority of routers. It uses Cryptographically Generated Addresses (CGA) (Aura, 2005), digital signature, and X.509 certification (Lynn, Kent, & Seo, 2004) to offer significant protection for NDP. A SEND-enabled node must generate or obtain a public-private key pair before it can claim an address. Then it generates the CGA address based on the public key and other auxiliary parameters. The associated private key is used to sign the outgoing ND messages from that address. For router authorization, every router must have a certificate from a trust anchor and the hosts provisioned with a trust anchor(s) list and picks routers that can show a valid certificate from a trust anchor. The SEND verifier node checks that the received address is a hash of the corresponding public key and that the signature, from the associated private key, is valid. If both verifications are successful, then the verifiers know that the address is not a stolen address and that it is from the address corresponding to public private key pairs.

Although SEND is considered to be a promising technique with which to protect NDP and to make IPv6 a very safe protocol, its deployment is not easy and thus is very challenging. SEND lacks mature implementations by developers of operating systems. It is compute-intensive and bandwidth-consuming. Moreover, SEND itself can be vulnerable to some types of attacks.

This chapter will introduce SEND functionalities and messages, discuss the practical considerations of SEND deployment as a cryptography solution in securing IPv6 local networks, survey the SEND implementation status, analyze the CGA security and computation complexity, and review the proposals made to optimize SEND in order to make it work in real networks.

The chapter is organized as follows. An overview of NDP and possible attacks against it is presented in section 2. Section 3 explores the theory of SEND and shows how SEND can be used to protect NDP. In Section 4 we highlight the deployment challenges of SEND and survey the existing SEND implementations. Section 5 discusses some possible approaches to optimize SEND and to provide some recommendations for SEND deployment. The last section concludes this work.

BACKGROUND

In an IPv4 network, a host does not get an IP address by it itself. The IP address is assigned manually by a human or retrieved from a Dynamic Host Configuration Protocol (DHCP) daemon. However, DHCP (Droms, 1997) is not a native part of the TCP/IP suite. The DHCP exchange utilizes a broadcast/response method. Initially, a DHCP client does not have an IP address and does not know the IP address of any DHCP servers. The client sends a broadcast discovery message with a source IP address of 0.0.0.0 and with a destination address of FF.FF.FF.FF. The DHCP server responds to the Media Access Control (MAC) address from the sender with a message including parameters like the IP address and subnet of the proposed lease, the length of the lease, and the real IP address of the DHCP server. No matter which way IPv4 is configured (manual or from DHCP), a host must test if the address is already in use by sending an Address Resolution Protocol (ARP) probe (Cheshire, 2008).

IPv6 replaces ARP and DHCP with a mechanism built into the IPv6 specifications thereby eliminating the need for daemons or extra configuration. This mode is called Stateless Address Auto-configuration. It is an integral part of IPv6. A new host attached to a new network automatically obtains all information needed for full connectivity with Zero-configuration. The following subsection briefly shows how the Stateless Auto-configuration works in IPv6. However DHCPv6, (Droms, et al., 2003) called Stateful Auto-configuration, is out of the scope of this chapter.

IPv6 Stateless Address Auto-Configuration (SLAAC)

Stateless auto-configuration is one of the most novel features of the IPv6 design. Each active network interface gets a default IPv6 address called the Local-Link address. A new host attached to a new network automatically obtains all the information needed for full connectivity. In IPv6 Stateless Address Auto-Configuration (SLAAC), the node creates the rightmost 64-bit (interface identifier), which identifies an individual node within a local network. The Interface Identifier (IID) is often configured from the Extended Unique Identifier (EUI-64) that is generated based on the interface hardware identifier, i.e., the Media Access Control (MAC). Then the node combines the subnet prefix with the IID to form a complete 128-bit IPv6 address as depicted in Figure 1. The IID includes two bits which are reserved by the IPv6 addressing architecture for special purposes. The 7th bit from the left in the 64-bit IID is called the Universal/Local bit (u bit) which, when set to "1", identifies the local IID as being globally unique. The 8th bit from the left is the Individual/Group (g bit) which is set to "1" to identify multicast addresses.

The subnet prefix part is used for routing packets across the network. The subnet prefix can be the reserved local link prefix (FE80::) used to generate local link addresses. The formation of local link addresses is done without any communications with the other hosts or by any human interaction beyond the enablement of the IPv6 network. These addresses are fully functional

Figure 1. IPv6 address format

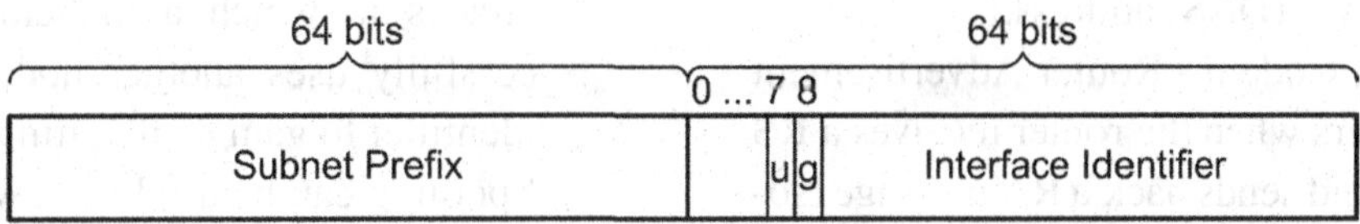

within the local segment, i.e., hosts can use these addresses to communicate with other hosts on the same network segment. However, routers are prohibited from forwarding any packets with local-link addresses. The router uses the link-local address as an identifier. One valid link-local works as an identifier. Once a host configures a link-local address, the next step is to obtain information about its neighbors (hosts and routers) residing on the same link, i.e., the nodes of a multicast group. Hosts also use link-local address generation for their global IPv6 addresses.

When a host receives a Router Advertisement (RA), it proceeds to create a global IPv6 address. A router will send out a RA message periodically to the link or when a Router Solicitation (RS) is received from a host. A RA message contains the routing prefix, Hop limit, Maximum Transfer Unit (MTU), lifetime, etc. The global IPv6 address is created by concatenation of the prefix to the interface identifier. This address is a tentative address until it can be shown to be unique and that there are no other detectable matching addresses on the subnet (address collision). Duplicate Address Detection (DAD) is a procedure used to ensure that there are no address conflicts on the same link. The host achieves DAD by sending a Neighbor Solicitation (NS) message to the solicited-node multicast group of the target address. If there is a collision, a Neighbor Advertisement (NA) message will be sent from the node that has the same address. If no conflict is detected, the tentative address is approved for use as a valid address. It is common to have multiple valid addresses on each Network Interface Card (NIC). More than one global address can be bound to an interface and one link-local address is permitted per interface.

IPv6 Neighbor Discovery Protocol (NDP)

Neighbor Discovery (NDP) is one of the most important functions of the Internet Control Message Protocol for IPv6 (ICMPv6), RFC 4443 (Conta, Deering, & Gupta, 2006). Its messages are implemented as a set of ICMPv6 Types and Options and follow the ICMPv6 message formats. NDP was designed to be at this position in the IP protocol stack to keep it simple and to let NDP benefit from the services provided by IP, such as security and multicast. NDP messages consist of an ICMPv6 header, ND message specific data, and zero or more options. ND message options provide additional information such as link-layer addresses, on-link network prefix, on-link Maximum Transmission Unit (MTU) information, redirection data, mobility information, and router specifications. In this section, we give further details about NDP messages and operations and list some possible ways to attack it.

NDP Functionalities and Messages

NDP is used for several functions including router and prefix discovery, parameter discovery, address auto-configuration, address resolution, Duplicate Address Detection (DAD), Neighbor Unreachablility Detection (NUD), next-hop determination, and redirect. To achieve these functions and services between the neighbor nodes, NDP uses the following five ICMPv6 messages:

- Type 133, Code 0 - Router Solicitation (RS), RS is sent by IPv6 host to discover the default router and to glean network information such as prefixes and the Domain Name Server (DNS) address.

- Type 134, Code 0 - Router Advertisement (RA) occurs when the router receives a RS message and sends back a RA message (solicited router advertisement). Also, RA is sent by IPv6 routers periodically (unsolicited multicast router advertisements).
- Type 135, Code 0 - Neighbor Solicitation (NS) is used to resolve the neighbor nodes IPv6 address with its MAC address or to verify if the node is still reachable.
- Type 136, Code 0 - Neighbor Advertisement (NA) occurs when the node that receives a NS message sends back a NA message with its own MAC address.
- Type 137, Code 0 - Redirect is used by the router to inform other nodes of a better first-hop toward a destination.

NDP Inherent Threats

NDP is not secure and there is a potential for breaking the local network protection. NDP has some basic protection mechanisms based on the scope of NDP. It is a link-local protocol, so the source address must be either unspecified (::/128) or a link-local address, and the hop limit must be set to 255. Also, the routers do not forward link-local addresses. Thus NDP messages cannot be injected into the network infrastructure from beyond the directly connected layer 2 access networks. This protection shield is not enough to completely protect IPv6 local networks. Therefore, without securing NDP, it is vulnerable to various attacks which can be categorized as spoofing, Denial-of-Service (DoS), Replay, Redirect, and Rogue routing information attacks. RFC 3756 (Nikander, et al., 2004) describes and categorizes some of the possible attacks against NDP. In addition, the Hacker's Choice IPv6 (THC-IPv6) (Hauser, 2012) provides an implemented tool set that can be used to attack IPv6. The following list presents brief reviews of these possible attacks:

- **Spoofing Attack:** Spoofing is a class of attacks in which a malicious node successfully uses another node's address or identifier to gain an illegitimate advantage. Spoofing can be used for a wide variety of purposes. It can be used to leverage Man-In-The-Middle (MITM) attacks, create a DoS attack, hide the attacker's identity, abuse the trust relation between the legitimated nodes, etc. ARP spoofing is a well known attack in the IPv4 network. Instead of ARP, IPv6 relies on the NDP to carry out the address resolution operation. Without the IPv6 authentication mechanism, the attacker can generate crafted IPv6 packets with spoofed source addresses and send them across the network.
- **Denial-of-Service (DoS) Attack:** DoS is a class of attack that eats up system resources when a malicious node prevents the communication between the legitimate node and other nodes. An attacker can generate DoS on Duplicate Address Detection (DAD) in order to prevent a network node from obtaining a network address. DAD is used to ensure that there is no address collision on the same link. A malicious node may hinder the legitimate host from getting a new IPv6 address by always responding to every duplicate address detection attempt with a spoofed message saying "I have this address". The victim would thus find out that every IPv6 address it tries to use is being used by other nodes on the link and so the victim would not be able to configure an IP address for accessing the network.
- **Replay Attack:** In this form of attack the attacker captures the messages exchanged between two nodes and later changes them. NDP messages are prone to replay attacks. One example occurs when HostA wants to communicate with HostB. It sends a NS message to get the MAC address of HostB.

An attacker on the same link can capture the NS message and change it to take command of the traffic flow between HostA and HostB. Another example is the replay of a RA message. The attacker can receive the RA and change some RA parameters, and later, resend this message, which now contains false router information, back to the link.

- **Redirect Attack:** Redirect attack is a class of attacks in which a malicious node redirects packets away from the legitimate receiver to another node. In IPv6, Redirect messages are used by routers to inform nodes of a better first hop router. An attacker can fabricate such a message and then take over routing from the legitimate router and act as a MITM by intercepting all messages between the two nodes.
- **Rogue Router Attack:** In this type of attack, a malicious node injects rogue information to poison the routing tables, reroute the traffic, or prevent the victim from accessing the desired network. It is very easy for an attacker to configure a rogue router on an unsecured link. On the other hand, it is difficult for a node to distinguish between fake and authorized router advertisements, especially for a newly connected node, because it cannot validate the routers without having an IP address to communicate. Thus a malicious node can advertise itself as a router and send a bogus address prefix, or advertise itself as the last hop router to act as a MITM and effectively receive, drop, or replay the packets. Such kinds of attacks can cause serious problems since they affect all other nodes that are connected to the same segment.

In practice, an attacker can use several of the above types of attacks simultaneously. For example, spoofing and DoS can be used together. The attacker can fabricate packets with a fake source IP address to hide his identity which makes it more difficult to detect the attack.

NDP Privacy Implications

SLAAC may lead to serious privacy implications. Generating the Interface Identifier (IID) part of IPv6 based on the MAC address results in a static IID, which remains constant over time. This one-to-one mapping between the MAC address and IID remains the same regardless of the network location. Therefore, every network card will be set to the same local-link address. Consequently, the attacker can correlate the captured traffic from a specific IID to a certain device. This makes it possible for the attacker to track a node from anywhere. Once the location and the identity of the user are determined, the attacker can target the user for identity theft or other related crimes.

RFC 4941 (Narten, Draves, & Krishnan, 2007) addresses this problem and introduces a solution whereby a global scope address is generated from interface identifiers that change over time. Changing the IID part over time makes it more difficult for eavesdroppers and other information collectors to collect the information they desire. The RFC 4941 approach, however, while protecting the privacy, does not provide protection against IP address spoofing attacks.

IPsec and Auto-Configuration

To secure the IPv6 network, security must be established in the initial state, when the node gets its address. Secured hosts must only be allowed to communicate with other secured hosts. The challenge to the NDP occurs when a host first joins a new network because it does not know who the other nodes are or how to discern legitimate hosts from malicious hosts. Although the original specification of NDP called for the use of IPsec (Kent & Seo, 2005) to protect NDP messages, it does not specify how to use it. IPsec is not suitable for securing the NDP auto-configuration process due to a bootstrapping problem. When using the Internet Key Exchange (IKE), the nodes need to be addressable, first, before the IPsec can use them. The automatic key exchange can occur after the hosts have already established the IPv6 addresses. Therefore, the IETF developed the SEcure Neighbor Discovery Protocol (SEND) to counteract the vulnerabilities in NDP. The focus of CGA and SEND is on securing the initial stage, when a host does not have a valid address and is trying to establish its own address on a new network.

SECURE NEIGHBOR DISCOVERY (SEND)

SEND is an extension of the NDP which offers three additional features; address ownership proof, message protection, and a router authorization mechanism. To achieve these enhancements, SEND encodes its messages in ICMPv6 by creating new Option Types. Four new options can be appended to the regular NDP message in order to create a SEND packet; CGA, RSA Signature, Nonce, and Timestamp. In addition, SEND came up with two new ICMPv6 messages for use in the router authorization process; Certificate Path Solicitation (CPS) and Certificate Path Advertisement (CPA).

CGA Address Ownership Proof (CGA Option and RSA Signature Option)

Cryptographically Generated Addresses (CGAs) form the basic foundation of SEND, which was proposed to prevent address theft. The main idea behind CGA is to use asymmetric cryptography to authenticate IPv6 Auto-configuration addressing without changing the zero configuration paradigm of SLAAC. CGA can work alone as a "zero configurations" security approach without the need to rely on any security infrastructure or any third party. CGAs are IPv6 addresses where the Interface Identifiers (IIDs) are generated by one-way hashing of the node's public key and other auxiliary parameters. Thus the IPv6 address for a node is bound to its public key. This binding can be verified by re-computing the hash value which is then compared to the interface identifier of the sender's address.

The idea of using CGA first appeared in the Childproof Authentication for MIPv6 (CAM), which was proposed by O'Shea and Roe (2001). In the CAM approach, the hash of the owner's public key is written into the interface identifier part of IPv6 address. Later Nikander (2002) suggested an improvement, and an extension, to the CAM approach to make it more resistant to birthday collision by adding some "random" data to the hash input. The final form of CGA was proposed by Aura (2003) and standardized in RFC 3972 (Aura, 2005). In this chapter the term CGA is used to refer to the standardized CGA which appears in RFC 3972.

The introduction of the Hash Extension is the main difference between Aura's proposal (Aura, 2003) and earlier proposals. The Hash Extension increases the security of the hash functions where the hash value can only have a limited number of bits. The use of a 64-bit value is not adequate for the protection of the address from a security standpoint. The Hash Extension technique increases the hash length beyond the 64-bit limit without actually increasing its length. Instead of a single hash value, the standard CGA (Aura, 2005) computes two independent one-way hash values (Hash1 and Hash2). The Hash2 (112-bit) calculations determine an input parameter for the Hash1 (64-bit) calculation. The purpose of the second hash (Hash2), Hash Extension, is to increase the cost (computing time) to the hacker for doing a brute-force attack, without increasing the length of the hash output value, which is written to the interface identifier portion of the IPv6 address.

This technique increases both the cost of generating a new CGA address and the cost of initiating a brute-force attack against the address. A scaling factor, called the Security Parameter (Sec), is used to determine the level of security for each generated address. The Sec is an unsigned 3-bit integer having a value between 0 and 7 (0 being the least secure while 7 the most).

CGA Generation

The procedure for the CGA generation process is depicted in Figure 2(a). The algorithm uses as input values; Public Key, Modifier, Subnet Prefix, and Sec value. The output from the CGA algorithm is a CGA address and a CGA Parameters Data Structure which is comprised of the following fields:

- **Modifier (128 bits):** Initialized to a random value.
- **Subnet Prefix (64 bits):** Set to the routing prefix value advertised by the router at the local subnet.
- **Collision Count (8 bits):** A collision counter used for Duplicate Address Detection (DAD) to ensure the uniqueness of the generated address.
- **Public Key (Variable Length):** Set to the Distinguished Encoding Rules (DER)-encoded public key of the address owner.
- **Extension Field:** Variable length field for future use.

CGA generation begins with the determination of the address owner's Public Key and by selecting the proper Sec value to use. The process continues with the Hash2 computation loop which finds the Final Modifier that will satisfy the condition where the 16*Sec-leftmost bits of the Hash2 are equal to zero. The Hash2 value is a hash created by the combination of the Modifier, concatenation of (64 + 8) zero bits and the Public Key. The address generator tries different values for the Modifier until the 16*Sec-leftmost bits of Hash2 computes to zero. Once a match is found, the Hash2 loop computation terminates. At this point the Final Modifier value is saved and used as an input to the Hash1 computation. The Hash1 value is a hash created from the combination of the whole CGA Parameters Data Structure. The interface identifier (IID) is then derived from the Hash1 value. The hash value is truncated to the appropriate length (64-bit). The Sec value is encoded into the three leftmost bits of the IID. The 7th and 8th (u and g) bits, from the left of IID, are reserved for a special purpose; they are set to "1" to identify the field as a CGA address. Now, part of the hash output of the CGA Parameters Data Structure is distributed across the remaining 59 bits of the IID. The concatenation of the subnet prefix (64-bit leftmost bits) with the IID portion forms the completed IPv6 address. The subnet prefix can be a routable address prefix which is obtained by listening for the local Router Advertisement (RA) or local link prefix. Finally, a Duplicated Address Detection (DAD) process is done against this tentative address to ensure that there is no address collision within the same subnet. If an address conflict does occur, then the Collision Count will be incremented and the Hash1 process will be repeated until a link-unique address is obtained or the Collision Count reaches 2, i.e., after three collisions. The CGA Option includes the associated CGA Parameters Data Structure which allows the receiver to validate the proper binding between the public key and the CGA.

To assert the ownership of the address, the address owner uses a corresponding private key to sign messages sent from that address. Signing a message using CGA requires the combined use of the CGA address, the associated CGA Parameters Data Structure, the message, and the private key that corresponds to the public key that has been used in the CGA's generation algorithm. Finally, the node will send the message, the CGA Parameters Data Structure, and the signature to the receiver node. SEND uses the RSA Signature Option to authenticate the identity of the sender and to prevent an attacker from spoofing CGA addresses. The RSA digital signature contains the following fields:

Figure 2. CGA algorithm: (a) generation; (b) verification

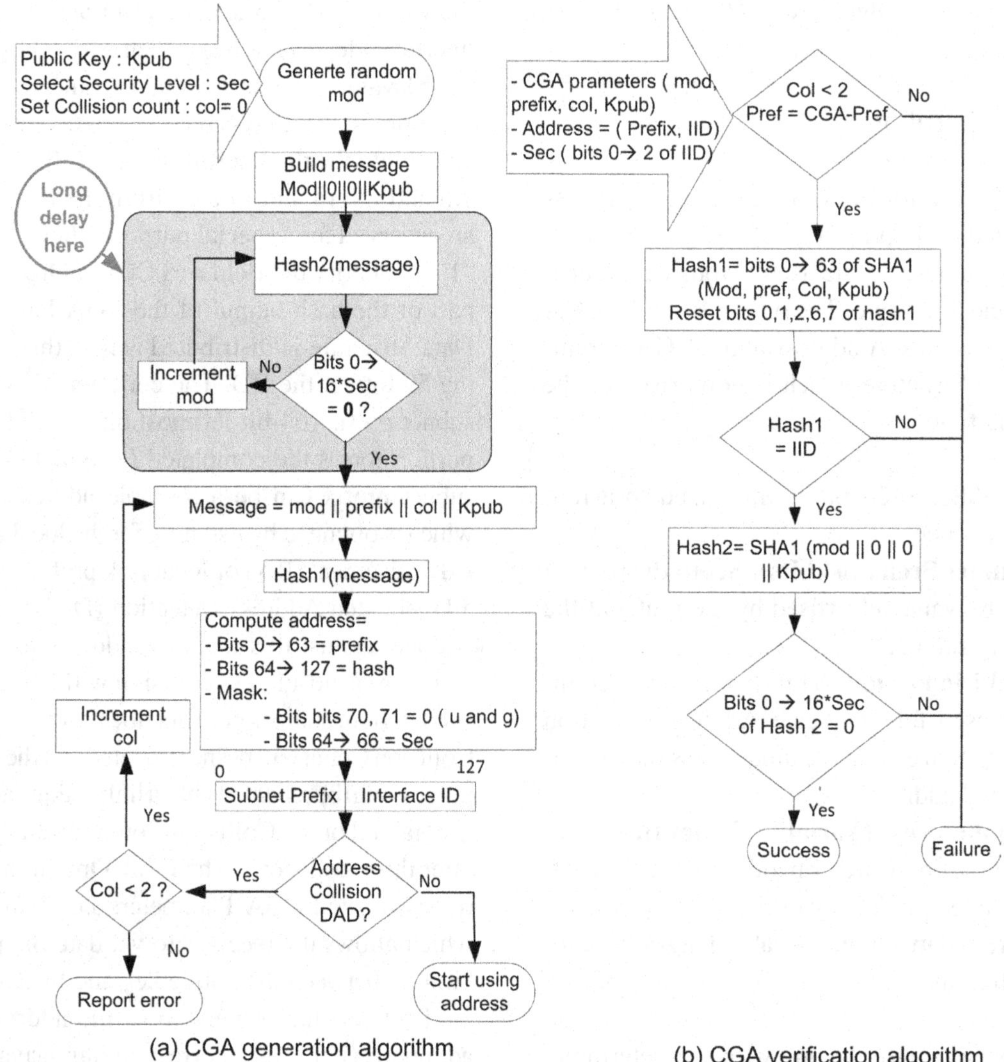

- 128 bit CGA Message Tag value for SEND.
- 128 bit Source Address from the IPv6 header
- 128 bit Destination Address from the IPv6 header
- 8 bit Type, 8 bit Code and 16 bit Checksum fields from the ICMPv6 header
- ND protocol message header, starting after the ICMPv6 checksum, and up to, but not including, the ND protocol options
- ND protocol options preceding the RSA signature option

CGA Verification

CGA verification takes as an input the IPv6 address and CGA Parameters Data Structure. If the verification succeeds, the verifier knows that the public key belongs to that address. The verifier can then use the public key to authenticate the signed messages received from the address owner. The verification process is shown in Figure 2(b). According to RFC3972, the verification of address ownership is achieved by executing the following steps:

- Check that the Collision Count value is 0, 1 or 2, and that the "Subnet Prefix" value is equal to the subnet prefix of the address. The CGA verification fails if either check fails.
- Concatenate the CGA Parameters Data Structure and execute the hash algorithm (SHA-1) on the concatenation. The 64 leftmost bits of the result are Hash1.
- Compare Hash1 with the interface identifier of the address. Differences in the "u" and "g" bits and in the three leftmost bits are ignored. If the 64-bit values differ (other than in the five ignored bits), the CGA verification fails.
- Read the security parameter (*Sec*) from the three leftmost bits of the interface identifier of the address.
- Concatenate the Modifier, 64+8 zero bits and the Public Key. Execute the hash algorithm on the concatenation. The leftmost 112 bits of the result are Hash2.
- Compare the 16*Sec leftmost bits of Hash2 with zero. If any one of these is non-zero, CGA verification fails. Otherwise, the verification succeeds. If Sec=0, verification never fails at this step.

In addition to the CGA verification process outlined above, the verifier uses the public key to verify the signature of the message. If the signature is valid, the verifier knows that the message was sent by the owner of a specific IPv6 address. It is important to note that once the address has been created, the cost of using and verifying a CGA address does not depend on the Sec value.

Replay Protection: Nonce Option and Timestamp Option

SEND includes a Nonce Option (a random number) in the solicitation message and requires the advertisement to include a matching option to ensure that an advertisement is a fresh response to a solicitation sent earlier by the node. This option is used to prevent a replay attack in solicited messages, such as NS/NA and RS/RA, when there is two-way communication. The Nonce Option cannot be used for one-way communication messages. SEND uses the Timestamp Option to provide replay protection against unsolicited advertisements such as periodic RA and Redirect messages. Here the assumption is that all nodes have synchronized clocks and that the node can prevent a replay attack by executing a Timestamp checking algorithm.

The conceptual layout of a router solicitation message with SEND Options is shown in Figure 3.

Router Authorization: Certificate Path Solicitation (CPS)/ Advertisement (CPA)

CGA Option and RSA Option together are used for IPv6 address authentication. This authentication proves only that the owner of the claimed IPv6 address is the owner of the corresponding public-private key pair. However, the CGA authentication does not provide anything about the privilege of using this address. An attacker can generate his own private-public key and start the communication in which he easily advertises himself as a router.

SEND uses third parties for router authorization. This process is known as the Authentication Delegation Discovery (ADD). SEND uses the ADD process to validate and authorize IPv6 routers which act as default gateways, and to specify IPv6 prefixes that a router is authorized to announce on the link. ADD relies on an electronic certificate issued by a trusted party. Before any node can accept a router as its default router, the node must be configured with a trust anchor(s) that can certify the router via certificate paths. The node requests the "router" to provide its X.509 certificate path to a Trust Anchor (TA), which is preconfigured on the node. The "router" should not be trusted if it fails to provide the path to the TA.

Figure 3. Router solicitation message with SEND options

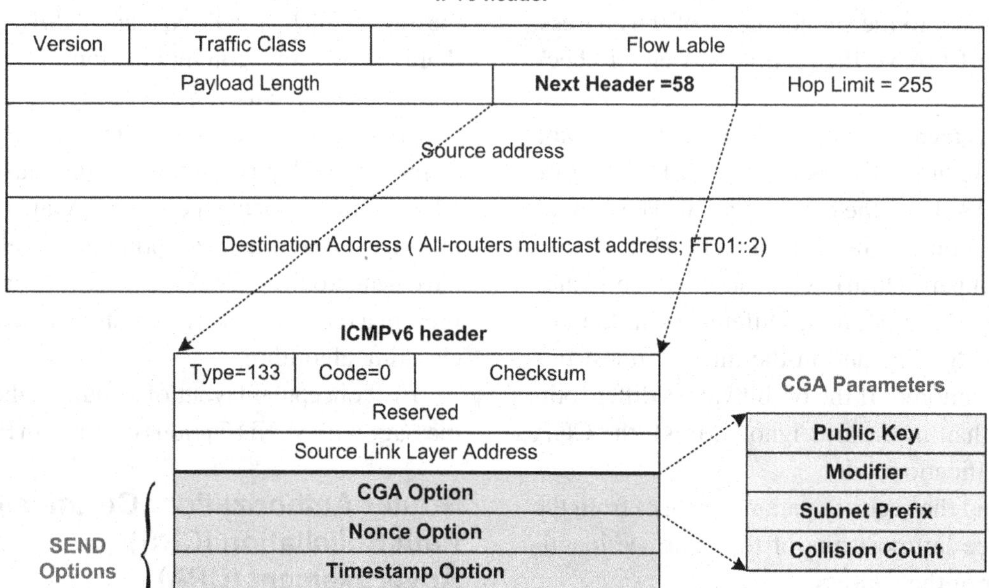

This feature is achieved by the use of two new ICMPv6 message types; the Certificate Path Solicitation (CPS) and the Certificate Path Advertisement (CPA). A CPS message, ICMPv6 type 148, is sent by hosts during the ADD process to request a certification path between a router and one of the host's trust anchors. The CPA message, ICMPv6 type 149, is sent in reply to the CPS message and contains the router certificate. In addition, new rules describe the preferred behavior when a SEND node receives a message, whether supported by SEND or not. Figure 4 shows a simplified view of the router authorization mechanism.

THE MAIN CHALLENGES AND LIMITATIONS OF SEND

Although SEND seems to be a promising technique for protecting NDP messages, it is lacking in several respects with regard to computation, implementation, deployment, and security. These limitations may prevent the use of SEND and leave NDP messages vulnerable to potential attacks. In this section we give further details about these limitations and challenges.

SEND Security and Privacy Considerations

SEND Security Limitations and Remaining Attacks

SEND can prevent the theft of another node's address but it cannot provide assurance about the identity of the real node and it is not capable of guaranteeing that the CGA address is being used by the appropriate node. Since CGAs are not certified, an attacker can come up with a new and valid address from its own public key, and start the communication. However, the address owner uses the corresponding private key to assert its ownership and to sign NDP messages sent from the address. Therefore, an attacker can impersonate another node address from a valid public key, but cannot take over an address of an

Figure 4. Simplified view of router authorization delegation discovery in SEND

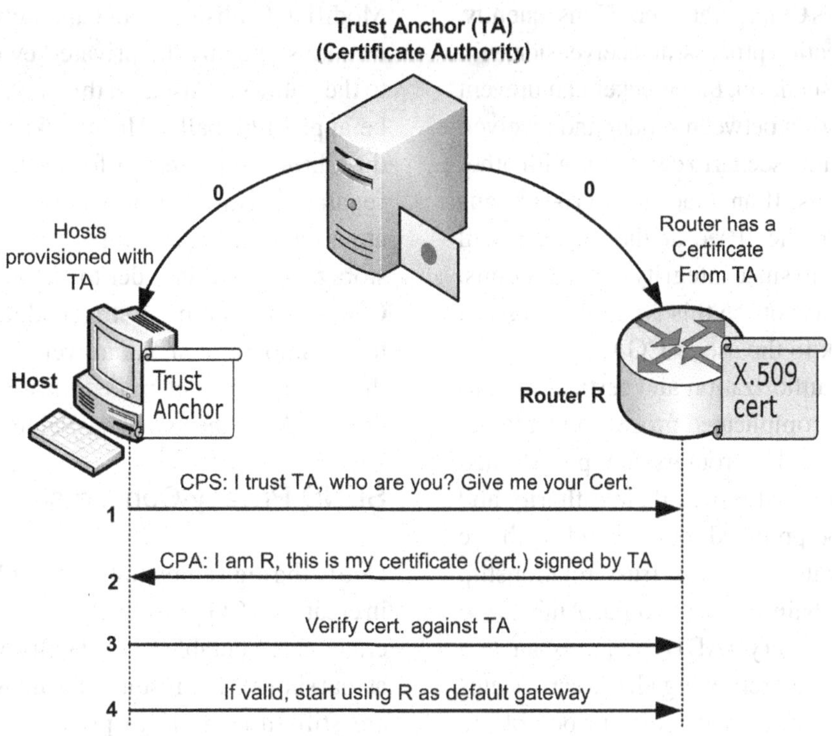

existing host because the attacker does not have the private key and he would have to find a collision of the cryptographic hash values, which would cost $2^{(59+16*Sec)}$ compute operations, on average. To insure greater security, a certificate authority is needed in order to validate the keys.

Moreover SEND can be susceptible to Denial-of-Service (DoS) attacks. An attacker can conduct DoS attacks on some particular steps within the CGA verification process (AlSa'deh, Rafiee, & Meinel, 2012b). He can perform a DoS attack against the DAD check and the CGA parameter verification in order to prevent a new CGA node from joining a link. When an attacker receives a DAD message sent by a CGA node, he can immediately copy the IP address, CGA parameters, and Signature. Then he replies with an NA message that has the same valid Signature and CGA parameters. The victim's node receives the reply via a secure NA message and checks its validity as defined by the CGA verification algorithm. If it is valid, because the signature is valid and the reply was received in the allotted time frame, the victim will increment its Collision Count value, and try another address. If the attacker replies again and the Collision Count reaches 2, the victim stops and reports an error. In this way the attacker does not need to do any brute-force searches against the CGA in order to carry out this attack. Even though this attack is limited to DoS attacks because the attacker does not have the private key needed to sign messages, the attacker can prevent the CGA address configuration for all new nodes that want to attach to the local link. Therefore, the CGA algorithm may need to be extended to verify the response to the DAD messages before incrementing the Collision Count. The CGA node should discard the DAD response message in two cases; if it comes from a non-CGA and gives the priority to the new CGA address, or if it has the same tentative address, CGA parameters, and signature that was sent before.

An attacker can also capture ND messages and change a sender's CGA parameters. Consequently, the CGA verification process, at receiver side, will fail. So, in this scenario, the attacker can prevent the communication between sender and receiver. However, the same scenario can occur with other security protocols. If an attacker inserts a bogus IPsec datagram, the IPsec at the receiver will drop the datagram since integrity check is bogus. Therefore, we do not see this type of attack as a major drawback to the use of CGA.

The router authorization and certificate validation can be a complicated process and a target for DoS attacks. The routers are provisioned with a certificate that proves their authority and hosts need to be prepared, beforehand, with the anchor certificate. But this trust relationship can be a long chain of trust, so the Authorized Delegation Discovery (ADD) requires an end node for storing and retrieving all the certificates in the certification path in order to be able to verify the authorized router. Thus the router is required to perform a large number of operations for generating, verifying, and signing NDP messages, especially when a high frequency of router advertisements is required, which can affect the routers' performance. Also, attackers may target hosts by sending a large number of unnecessary certification paths thus forcing hosts to spend useless memory and verification resources on them. The numerous computations required by a host to generate and verify CGAs and the certificates chain make it vulnerable to DoS attacks.

The CGAs can also be vulnerable to another type of attack known as the global Time-Memory Trade-Off (TMTO) attack. The attacker needs to do an exhaustive search for hash collision or must create a large, pre-computed database from the interface identifiers of the attacker's own public key(s) used to find matches for many addresses. A more secure version, called CGA++ (Bos, Özen, & Hubaux, 2009) has been proposed to resist this type of attack. In CGA++, the subnet prefix is included in the calculation of Hash2 and all the Modifier, Collision Count and Subnet Prefix values are signed by the private-key corresponding to the public key used. In this way, TMTO cannot be applied globally. The attacker would have to do a brute-force search for each address prefix separately. However, it is not easy to impersonate a random node in a network because of the storage required in order to carry out this attack. CGA++ also comes with an additional cost due to the amount of signature verifications needed, thus requiring much more time for the generation of a CGA for the same Sec value.

SEND Privacy Concerns

Due to the high computation complexity involved in creating a CGA it is likely that once a node generates an acceptable CGA it will continue to use it at that subnet. The result is that nodes using CGAs are still susceptible to privacy related attacks. However, we think the CGA privacy implication (when the node uses the same subset for a long time) can be solved by setting a valid time limit for the use of a CGA address. If the time has elapsed, a new CGA, with a new CGA parameter, should be generated. But to avoid the long CGA generation time, it is not recommended to choose a Sec value greater than "1" for the current applications. There should be a balance between the valid time and the security level. For a mobile node, CGA can provide the necessary privacy protection. When a node moves to new subnet, Hash1 should be recalculated by including the new subnet prefix. Consequently, a new IPv6 address with new IID will be generated without the need to recalculate Hash2. The process of generating a new address only costs one Hash calculation. In this case, the only concern is the possibility of tracking the node based on its public key if it remains fixed. But it is not easy to track the node based on its public key. Normally tracking over the Internet is done based on the IP address.

SEND Computation Cost and Bandwidth Consumption

In reality, the average CGA address generation time depends on the Sec bit setting. Even there is a probabilistic guarantee that the CGA address generation will stop after a certain number of iterations, but it is impossible to tell exactly how long it will take for the CGA generation when Sec is not zero. It might vary significantly because the Modifier field of the CGA parameter is randomly generated. Theoretically, the computation time needed to generate a Hash2 value is increased by 2^{16} for each Sec value.

Performing 1000 tests on an Intel Duo2 2.67 GHz CPU we found the average CGA generation time to be 402 Milliseconds for Sec = 1. A test on an unrepresentative set of 5 samples carried out with 2.67 GHz CPU gave an average CGA generation time of 5923857 Milliseconds (1 hour and 39 minutes). Accordingly, Sec values higher than "1" are not recommended, as they require a lot of processing power and too much time when using the current technologies. Bos, & et al., (2009) expected that CGA generation time for Sec=3 would take around 24 years on a modern workstation (AMD64).

Furthermore, SEND requires that each node include the public key and other parameters with the message and then to affix its Signature to every signaling packet that it generates. This means that more than 1K bytes is added to each packet. This increases the communication overhead and consumes network bandwidth and computational resources. Moreover, the transportation of all the certificates and keys between routers and hosts increases the local network traffic. Also, the certification path information exchange requires a lot of Certificate Path Solicitation/Advertisement CPS/CPA messages, especially if there is an error on the network and retransmission is required.

Lack of Sophisticated Implementation at End-Nodes

SEND-aware implantation is still scarce. NDP is supported by most modern operating systems, but it lacks support for SEND, and it is a security standard without sophisticated implementations. Even though some major vendors, such as Cisco and Juniper, have various levels of support for SEND in their routers, there is no major operating system providing a good level of support for SEND. Current SEND implementations for specific OS distribution are, basically, a proof of concept rather than production-ready software.

DoCoMo's SEND

NTT DoCoMo USA Labs (2008) implemented the first open source of SEND. Their implementation works exclusively with Linusx 2.6 or FreeBSD 5.4 and later. It uses a Berkley Packet Filter (BPF) interface embedded in a netgraph node to get traffic from the kernel to the user-space daemon, and vice versa. The user-space daemon handles the SEND options. The communication between the NDP stack in the kernel and the SEND daemon flows through the chain of netgraph nodes, rather than passing through the normal layer processing. The DoCoMo implementation has some limitations. First, all network traffic has to traverse through packet filtering hooks which introduces significant processing overhead. Second, it depends on the subsystem, which is only available for the FreeBSD operating system family and thus makes it non-portable for other operating systems. Additionally, users need to have a good knowledge of firewall rules (ip6tables) since this knowledge is essential for the configuration of the application. Finally, DoCoMo USA Labs no longer supports the SEND project and the source code is no longer available for downloading at their web site since their support has been stopped. Figure 5 shows the DoCoMo SEND general architecture.

Figure 5. DoCoMo SEND architecture

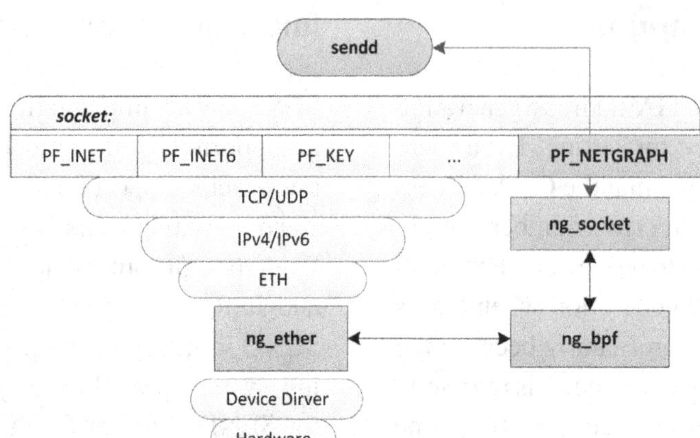

Native SeND kernel API for *BSD

This implementation (Kukec & Zeeb, 2010) is an attempt to overcome the major drawbacks of DoCoMo's implantation by implementing a new kernel-user space API for SEND and eliminating the use of the netgraph and Berkley Packet Filter (BPF). Avoiding the use of netgraph reduces the overhead and speeds up packet processing and makes the implementation more portable to other operating systems. Native SeND uses routing control sockets for exchanging messages between the kernel and the user-space. It handles the packets that may be affected by SEND, rather than processing all packets, thus allowing the existing kernel to process the other packets. This implementation uses a kernel module (send.ko) which acts as a gateway between the network stack and the user-space interface.

Huawei and BUPT (ipv6-send-cga)

Beijing University of Post and Tele-communications (2009) introduced an implementation for SEND within the Linux kernel IPv6 module. The "C" code is partially built into the real NDP code at the kernel, where direct access to neighbor caches and routing tables are available. However, the cryptographic processing remains in the user-space. This work is a research prototype under development which still lacks interoperability testing. Bugs that can cause the kernel to crash can be expected. Figure 6 shows the architecture of Huawei and BUPT SEND implementation.

Easy-SEND

Easy-SEND (Chiu & Gamess, 2009) is another Linux user-space implementation of SEND developed in Java. Easy-SEND is an open source project which has been developed for educational purposes. Easy-SEND does not implement the router authorization portion of SEND.

NDprotector

NDprotector (Cheneau, 2011) is another implementation of CGA and SEND for Linux based on Scapy6. NDprotector follows the same principle of the DoCoMo implementation with its dependency on iproute2, ip6table, and the netfilter queue. The implementation can be divided into initialization and runtime phases. During the initialization, CGA addresses are set up and ip6tables rules are defined. These rules route all NDP messages to specific netfilter queues. NDprotectror's runtime

Figure 6. Huawei and BUPT SEND (ipv6-send-cga) architecture

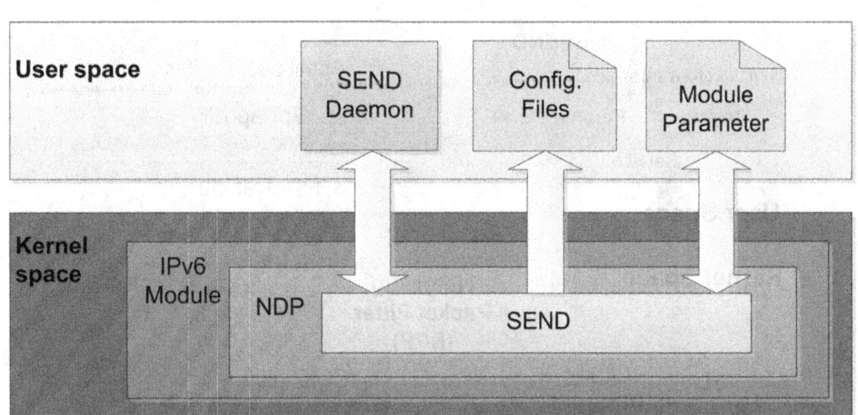

component takes the NDP messages out of these queues and secures the outgoing NDP messages or verifies the incoming messages. NDprotector supports Elliptic Curve Cryptographically (ECC) keys in addition to the standard RSA keys. It is implemented in Python and therefore uses a python wrapper to access the netfilter. For packet manipulation, NDprotector uses a modified version of Scapy6 (scapy6send).

WinSEND

Windows SEcure Neighbor Discovery (WinSEND) (Rafiee, AlSa'deh, & Meinel, 2011) is the first SEND implementation for Windows families. It is a user-space implementation which is developed in Microsoft.NET. WinSEND works as a service for Windows families with a user interface which allows the setting of security parameters for the proper Network Interface Card (NIC). This implementation came in response to a lack of SEND support for Windows operating system. Since the Windows family is the most popular operating system in use today, and accounts for almost 80% of the operating systems in use (W3Schools, 2012), it was felt that support for SEND was necessary. Figure 7 shows the architecture of the WinSEND implementation.

FUTURE RESEARCH DIRECTIONS TO FACILITATE SEND DEPLOYMENTS AND PROTECT LOCAL IPV6 NETWORK

There are some proposals to optimize and facilitate SEND deployment and protect IPv6 local networks. Some of these proposals come solely within the SEND domain without needing to rely on other deployments. Others are proposed as alternative approaches to avoid the difficulty of SEND deployments.

Proposals to Facilitate SEND Deployments

Cheneau, Boudguiga, and Laurent (2010) propose an improved method for generating CGA by using an Elliptic Curve Cryptograph (ECC) key instead of a standardized RSA key. ECC has a shorter key for the same security level as RSA, which leads to creation of smaller packets. Thus, the use of ECC is more suitable for resource-limited environments.

Another idea that has potential is to delegate the expense of the computation to a powerful machine where a key sever does the computation on behalf of the nodes in advance or offline. Jiang and Xia (2012) propose to use the DHCPv6

Figure 7. WinSEND architecture

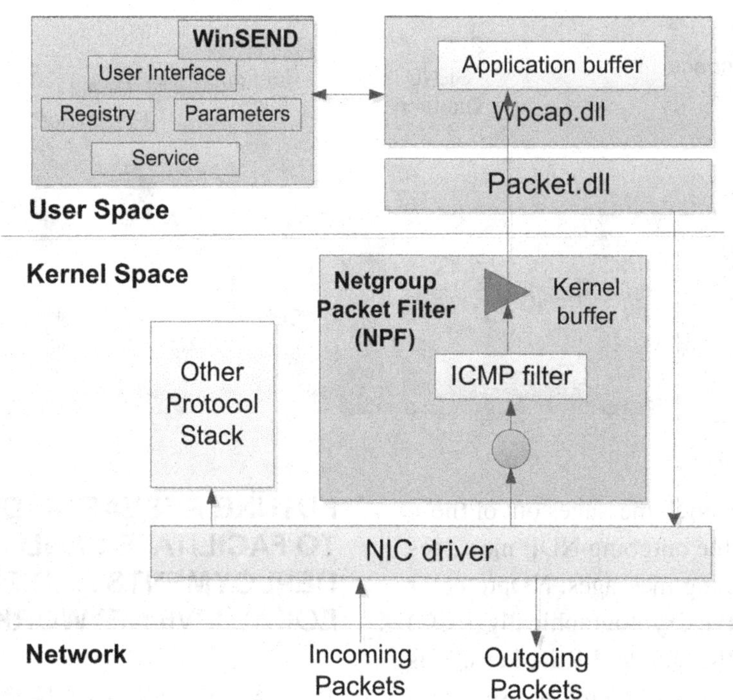

server to manage the CGA. DHCPv6 is extended to propagate the parameters that a host needs to generate a CGA. A host may send a request to a DHCPv6 server to have the CGA computed for it.

Another solution, to achieve faster CGA computations, would be to use cryptographic accelerator cards to compute the CGA or to use parallelized algorithms in the computation of the CGA modifier. Rafiee, AlSa'deh, and Meinel (2012) implemented a parallelizing CGA generation algorithm in order to speed up the CGA computation. With the parallel approach, the computation time has been reduced dramatically by increasing the number of cores in the computing device, which allows for parallel processing.

In order to avoid an unreasonable and unacceptable delay in CGA generation, the use of a time termination condition may be a practical approach to make using CGA feasible. For example, based on the CPU speed, the algorithm recommends a proper value for Sec, or the setting of a time termination condition. The termination condition will definitely depend on the application requirement, e.g., MIPv6 needs to finish the address generation within hundreds of a millisecond. AlSa'deh, Rafiee, and Meinel (2012a) proposed a modified CGA generation algorithm, called Time-Based CGA (TB-CGA), to put a limit on the maximum time that the user/application is willing to invest for CGA generation. TB-CGA takes the upper bound of the CGA running time as an input, and the Sec value is determined as an output of the brute-force computations. Also, this paper proposes to reduce the granularity of the security level from "16" to "8", in order to increase the chances of having a better Sec value within the time limit.

An additional possible way to speed up the CGA generation is to use the Optimistic DAD (Moore, 2006) with CGA. The Optimistic DAD approach is a method to minimize address configuration delays by making an address available for use before completing the DAD. The DAD in the CGA generation algorithm can be one reason for the delay.

Other Approaches to Protect IPv6 Local Network

Other approaches try to avoid the complexity of the SEND deployment and to propose alternative protection models. IPv6 Router Advertisement Guard (IPv6 RA-Guard) (Levy-Abegnoli, et al., 2011) proposes an alternative and complementary approach to SEND based on filtering at layer-2 in order to avoid router authorization and certificate validation complexity. IPv6 RA-Guard is proposed to counter the rogue-RA problem by applying a layer-2 switching device in order to identify invalid RAs and then blocking them. However, IPv6 RA-Guard still cannot prevent IP address theft if it is deployed alone. Maybe a combination of CGA and RA-Guard would be a solution to a secure IPv6 network.

Other approaches, such as the NDPMon (Beck, Cholez, Festor, & Chrisment, 2007) tool, have been proposed to protect the local network by monitoring the NDP messages in order to detect malicious activity. However, monitoring techniques cannot prevent attacks: attacks may be capable of damaging the network before a response is received from the administrator. Also, it is not easy to determine which node did the attack because the attacker may be using a spoofed address.

CONCLUSION

Neighbor Discovery Protocol (NDP) is one of the main protocols in the IPv6 suite, but it is not secure, and it is vulnerable to malicious attacks. These security issues are what led to the birth of SEcure Neighbor Discovery (SEND). The SEND approach eliminates most attack vectors levied against IPv6 link operations. SEND uses Cryptographically Generated Addresses (CGAs) in order to prove the ownership of a claimed address. It is also based on the use of X.509 certificates and a router authorization delegation mechanism to prevent fake router advertisement attacks. In addition, SEND uses the Nonce Option and Timestamp Option in order to prevent replay attacks.

However, a SEND deployment is a challenge. There are several reasons for this: first, SEND is compute-intensive, especially when high security values are used, second, the SEND Authorization Delegation Discovery (ADD) mechanism is, so far, mostly theoretical rather than practical, and third, the operating systems lack sophisticated SEND implementations. After several years of standardizing the SEND, it is, sorry to say, still in trial stages. Therefore, enhancing CGAs and SEND, in order to make them lightweight and practical, while maintaining some level of security and privacy, is very important for the deployment of IPv6 in a secure manner. If this is not accomplished, then the IPv6 network will be left vulnerable to IP spoofing related attacks.

REFERENCES

W3Schools. (2012). OS platform statistics. Retrieved from http://www.w3schools.com/browsers/browsers_os.asp

AlSa'deh, A., Rafiee, H., & Meinel, C. (2012a). Stopping time condition for practical IPv6 cryptographically generated addresses. In Proceedings of 2012 International Conference on Information Networking, ICOIN 2012, (pp. 257-262). Bali, Indonesia: IEEE.

AlSa'deh, A., Rafiee, H., & Meinel, C. (2012b). Cryptographically generated addresses (CGAs): Possible attacks and proposed mitigation approaches. In Proceedings of 12th IEEE International Conference on Computer and Information Technology (IEEE CIT'12). Chengdu, China: IEEE.

Arkko, J., Kempf, J., Zill, B., & Nikander, P. (2005). Secure neighbor discovery (SEND). RFC 3971. Retrieved from http://tools.ietf.org/html/rfc3971

Aura, T. (2003). Cryptographically generated addresses (CGA). *Lecture Notes in Computer Science*, *2851*, 29–43. doi:10.1007/10958513_3.

Aura, T. (2005). Cryptographically generated addresses (CGA). RFC 3972. Retrieved from http://tools.ietf.org/html/rfc3972

Beck, F., Cholez, T., Festor, O., & Chrisment, I. (2007). Monitoring the neighbor discovery protocol. In Proceedings of the International Multi-Conference on Computing in the Global Information Technology, (pp. 57-62). IEEE.

Bos, J. W., Özen, O., & Hubaux, J. P. (2009). Analysis and optimization of cryptographically generated addresses. In Proceedings of the 12th International Conference on Information Security, (pp. 17-32). Pisa, Italy: Springer-Verlag.

Cheneau, T. (2011). NDprotector an implementation of CGA & SEND that works on Linux. Retrieved from http://amnesiak.org/NDprotector/

Cheneau, T., Boudguiga, A., & Laurent, M. (2010). Significantly improved performances of the cryptographically generated addresses thanks to ECC and GPGPU. *Computers & Security*, *29*(4), 419–431. doi:10.1016/j.cose.2009.12.008.

Cheshire, S. (2008). IPv4 address conflict detection. RFC 5227. Retrieved from http://tools.ietf.org/html/rfc5227

Chiu, S., & Gamess, E. (2009). Easy-SEND: A didactic implementation of the secure neighbor discovery protocol for IPv6. In Proceedings of the World Congress on Engineering and Computer Science, WCECS 2009, (pp. 260-265). San Francisco, CA: WCECS.

Conta, A., Deering, S., & Gupta, M. (2006). Internet control message protocol (ICMPv6) for the internet protocol version 6 (IPv6) specification. RFC 4443. Retrieved from http://tools.ietf.org/html/rfc4443

DOCOMO Communications Laboratories USA. (2008). SEND project. Retrieved April 23, 2012, from http://www.docomolabs-usa.com/lab_opensource.html

Droms, R. (1997). Dynamic host configuration protocol. RFC 2131. Retrieved from http://tools.ietf.org/html/rfc2131

Droms, R., Bound, J., Volz, B., Lemon, T., Perkins, C., & Carney, M. (2003). Dynamic host configuration protocol for IPv6 (DHCPv6). Retrieved from http://tools.ietf.org/html/rfc3315

Groat, S., Dunlop, M., Marchany, R., & Tront, J. (2010). The privacy implications of stateless IPv6 addressing. In Proceedings of the Sixth Annual Workshop on Cyber Security and Information Intelligence Research, CSIIRW '10, (pp. 52:1-52:4). New York, NY: ACM.

Hauser, V. (2012). THC-IPv6: The hackers choice. Retrieved April 23, 2012, from http://www.thc.org/thc-ipv6

Huawei Technologies Corp. & BUPT. (2009). IPv6-send-CGA an implementation of SEND protocol in LINUX kernel. Retrieved from http://code.google.com/p/ipv6-send-cga/

Internet Assigned Numbers Authority. (2012). IANA IPv4 address space registry. Retrieved from http://www.iana.org/assignments/ipv4-address-space/

Internet Society. World IPv6 Launch. (2012). Internet society. Retrieved April 23, 2012, from http://www.worldipv6day.org/

Jiang, S., & Xia, S. (2012). Configuring cryptographically generated addresses (CGA) using DHCPv6. Retrieved from http://tools.ietf.org/html/draft-ietf-dhc-cga-config-dhcpv6-02

Kent, S., & Seo, K. (2005). Security architecture for the internet protocol. RFC4301. Retrieved from http://tools.ietf.org/html/rfc4301

Kukec, A., & Zeeb, B. A. (2010). Native SeND kernel API for* BSD. [Tokyo, Japan: Tokyo University of Science.]. *Proceedings ofAsiaBSDCon, 2010*, 1–9.

Levy-Abegnoli, E., Van de Velde, G., Popoviciu, C., & Mohacs, J. (2011). IPv6 router advertisement guard. RFC 6105. Retrieved from http://tools.ietf.org/html/rfc6105

Lynn, C., Kent, S., & Seo, K. (2004). X.509 extensions for IP addresses and AS identifiers. RFC 3779. Retrieved from http://tools.ietf.org/html/rfc3779

Moore, N. (2006). Optimistic duplicate address detection (DAD) for IPv6. Retrieved from http://tools.ietf.org/html/rfc4429

Narten, T., Draves, R., & Krishnan, S. (2007). Privacy extensions for stateless address autoconfiguration in IPv6. RFC 4941. Retrieved from http://tools.ietf.org/html/rfc4941

Narten, T., Nordmark, E., Simpson, W., & Soliman, H. (2007). Neighbor discovery for IP version 6 (IPv6). RFC 4861. Retrieved from http://tools.ietf.org/html/rfc4861

Nikander, E. P., Kempf, J., & Nordmark, E. (2004). IPv6 neighbor discovery (ND) trust models and threats. RFC 3756. Retrieved from http://tools.ietf.org/html/rfc3756

Nikander, P. (2002). Denial-of-service, address ownership, and early authentication in the IPv6 world. In Proceedings of the 9th International Workshop on Security Protocols, (pp. 12–21). London, UK: Springer-Verlag. Retrieved from http://dl.acm.org/citation.cfm?id=647219.720869

O'shea, G., & Roe, M. (2001). Child-proof authentication for MIPv6 (CAM). *ACM SIGCOMM Computer Communication Review*, *31*(2), 4–8. doi:10.1145/505666.505668.

Perkins, C., Johnson, D., & Arkko, J. (2011). Mobility support in IPv6. RFC 6275. Retrieved from http://tools.ietf.org/html/rfc6275

Rafiee, H., AlSa'deh, A., & Meinel, C. (2011). WinSEND: Windows secure neighbor discovery. In Proceedings of the 4th International Conference on Security, SIN 2011, (pp. 243-246). Sydney, Australia: ACM.

Rafiee, H., AlSa'deh, A., & Meinel, C. (2012). Multicore-based auto-scaling secure neighbor discovery for windows operating systems. In Proceedings of the 2012 International Conference on Information Networking, ICOIN 2012, (pp. 269-274). Bali, Indonesia: IEEE.

Thomson, S., Narten, T., & Jinmei, T. (2007). IPv6 stateless address autoconfiguration. RFC 4862. Retrieved from http://tools.ietf.org/html/rfc4862

ADDITIONAL READING

Arkko, J., Aura, T., Kempf, J., Mäntylä, V.-M., Nikander, P., & Roe, M. (2002). Securing IPv6 neighbor and router discovery. In Proceedings of the 1st ACM Workshop on Wireless Security, WiSE '02, (pp. 77–86). New York, NY: ACM.

Arkko, J., & Nikander, P. (2004). Weak authentication: How to authenticate unknown principals without trusted parties. In Christianson, B., Crispo, B., Malcolm, J. A., & Roe, M. (Eds.), *Security Protocols* (pp. 5–19). Berlin, Germany: Springer. doi:10.1007/978-3-540-39871-4_3.

Arkko, J., & Nikander, P. (2005). Limitations of IPsec policy mechanisms. In Christianson, B., Crispo, B., Malcolm, J. A., & Roe, M. (Eds.), *Security Protocols* (pp. 241–251). Berlin, Germany: Springer. doi:10.1007/11542322_29.

Sarikaya, B., Xia, F., & Zaverucha, G. (2011). Lightweight secure neighbor discovery for low-power and lossy networks. Retrieved from http://tools.ietf.org/html/draft-sarikaya-6lowpan-cgand-02

Zhang, J., Liu, J., Xu, Z., Li, J., & Ye, X. (2007). TRDP: A trusted router discovery protocol. In Proceedings of the International Symposium on Communications and Information Technologies, 2007, (pp. 660 –665). ISCIT.

KEY TERMS AND DEFINITIONS

ADD: Authorization Delegation Discovery is a process by which a SEcure Neighbor Discovery (SEND) node can acquire a certificate path, from a router to a trust anchor, in order to certify the authority of a router. A trust anchor is a third party that the host trusts, and to which the router has a certification path. SEND uses two messages for ADD process: Certificate Path Solicitation (CPS) and Certificate Path advertisement (CPA).

ARP: Address Resolution Protocol is used by the Internet Protocol version 4 (IPv4) to associate IP network addresses with hardware addresses. It is used when IPv4 is used over Ethernet.

CGAs: Cryptographically Generated Addresses are IPv6 addresses where the interface identifier portion of the address is generated by hashing the address owner's public key and other parameters. The address owner uses the corresponding private key to assert address ownership and to sign messages sent from that address.

DAD: Duplicate Address Detection is a procedure for verifying the uniqueness of the addresses on a link before they are assigned to an interface. The DAD algorithm is performed on all IPv6 tentative addresses, independently, whether they are obtained via stateless autoconfiguration or DHCPv6.

DoS Attack: A Denial-of-Service attack is an attempt made to make a machine or other network resources unavailable to legitimate users.

IID: Interface Identifier is comprised of the last 64 bits of an IPv6 address. It can be determined using different methods: Extended Unique Identifier (EUI-64), randomly-generated interface identifier that changes over time, or manually configured.

NDP: Neighbor Discovery Protocol is a protocol contained within Internet Protocol Version 6 (IPv6). It is a part of ICMPv6. It is used by IPv6 nodes on the same link to discover each other's presence, to determine each other's link-layer addresses, to find routers, and to maintain reachability information about the paths to active neighbors.

SEND: SEcure Neighbor Discovery is designed as a countermeasure to NDP threats. It enhances NDP with three additional capabilities: Address ownership proof based upon Cryptographically Generated Addresses (CGAs), Message replay protection by including Nonce and Timestamps, and Router authorization to enable routers to act as default gateways based on X.509 certificates.

SLAAC: StateLess Address Auto-Configuration is a process by which an IPv6 node (host or router) can configure IPv6 addresses for interfaces automatically, when connected to a routed IPv6 network using the Neighbor Discovery Protocol. The node builds various IPv6 addresses by combining an address prefix with either the Media Access Control (MAC) address of the node or a user-specified interface identifier. The prefixes include the link-local prefix (fe80::/10) and prefixes of length 64 that are advertised by local IPv6 routers via a Router Advertisement (RA) message.

Chapter 9
Offline/Online Security in Mobile Ad Hoc Networks

Wen-Jung Hsin
Park University, USA

Lein Harn
University of Missouri – Kansas City, USA

ABSTRACT

Mobile ad hoc network is a network comprised of mobile nodes quickly forming an autonomous network for a particular purpose such as emergency search and rescue. One of the most prominent security challenges for such a network is the limited capacity in the mobile nodes, thereby preventing costly computation operations. However, this limitation on a mobile node manifests itself only when the mobile node is dispatched on an active duty (i.e., online). One can prepare the mobile nodes as much as possible offline in anticipation of an upcoming deployment. In this chapter, the authors present three offline/online authentication and key agreement schemes and one offline/online non-repudiation scheme, all aiming at fast online computation for mobile nodes in mobile ad hoc networks.

INTRODUCTION

A Mobile Ad hoc NETwork (MANET) is a set of mobile nodes rapidly and dynamically forming an autonomous network. A mobile node is a generic term for a mobile communication device such as a router, a laptop, a Personal Digital Assistant (PDA) and a smartphone in which the device can freely move around. The main attraction of a MANET is its self-organizing, roaming, and swiftly deployable features among the mobile nodes. Initially, a MANET was for use in military (Taneja & Patel, 2007). Over the years, it has also been applied to the communication among entities in many other settings, e.g., emergency rescuers, conference and meeting attendees, sensors for collecting environmental and ecological data, devices for monitoring human physiological data (Saha, Bhattacharyya,

DOI: 10.4018/978-1-4666-4030-6.ch009

& Banerjee, 2012), learners in an instantaneous classroom (Luo, Zerfos, Kong, Lu, & Zhang, 2002), taxicabs dispatching and booking services (Boukerche, Camara, Loureiro, & Figueiredo, 2009; Huang, Hu, Crowcroft, & Wassell, 2005), and vehicle-to-vehicle and vehicle-to-roadside in vehicular MANETs (Raya & Hubaux, 2007).

A MANET has been studied extensively due to its distinct challenges. These challenges include energy and memory limitation in the mobile nodes, low bandwidth, limited transmission ranges, unreliable transmission links, changing topology due to the roaming feature of the mobile nodes, and network forming without requiring fixed network infrastructure (Taneja & Patel, 2007). As routing is essential to the feasibility of a MANET, the study in routing was one of the focal points in the early stage of a MANET. Many routing protocols (such as ARAN – Authenticated Routing for Ad Hoc Networks, SAODV – Secure Ad Hoc On-Demand Distance Vector Routing, and SEAD – Secure Efficient Ad Hoc Distance Vector Routing) have been proposed for a MANET since then (Karlsson, Dooley, & Pulkkis, 2012; Kaur & Rai, 2012; Lee, 2011; Singh, Yadav, & Ranvijay, 2007).

Outside of feasibility study, security is very important for a MANET especially when one of the first applications of a MANET is to be used in battlefields where a secure MANET is important in the midst of attacks by the enemies. Considering the distinct challenges mentioned above, it is difficult to directly use the traditional cryptography techniques in a MANET. For example, when using public-key cryptography within an autonomous MANET, public-key infrastructure such as a Certificate Authority (CA) may not exist (Chlamtac, Conti, & Liu, 2003). Additionally, public-key cryptography usually incurs high computational overhead (Kumar, Munjal, & Sharma, 2011; Liang & Wang, 2005). Thus, it is not feasible for energy and memory limited mobile nodes. Consequently, it may not be practical to directly apply some of the current public-key cryptosystems in a MANET. In spite of the challenging considerations mentioned above, as MANETs become increasingly popular for the applications that they can support, it is imperative to strengthen the security of MANETs.

For the literature up to date, one can broadly categorize the schemes that deal with the secure association in MANETs into three categories:

1. A MANET with a centralized server (also referred to as an organized MANET by Lin and Slay [2005]; as an authority-based MANET by Van der Merwe, Dawoud, and McDonald [2007]).
2. A MANET with a distributed server (Di Crescenzo, Ge & Arce, 2007; Murugan & Shanmugam, 2012).
3. A MANET self-organized by the mobile nodes themselves (also referred to as an open MANET by Capkun, Buttyan, and Hubaux [2003]; as a pure MANET by Lin and Slay [2005]; as a public MANET by Van der Merwe, Dawoud, and McDonald [2007]).

A MANET with a centralized server is frequently used for applications such as military or emergency relief where the mobile nodes are to follow certain authority so that they can access the network services robustly (Van der Merwe, Dawoud, & McDonald, 2007). For a MANET with a distributed server, a collective service is distributed among a set of mobile nodes. In a MANET self-organized by the mobile nodes themselves, there is no centralized or distributed server as such this kind of MANET tends to be open (i.e., the mobile nodes can come in and out of a MANET at ease [Van der Merwe, Dawoud, & McDonald, 2007]).

Depending on the duration of the MANET applications, Saxena, Tsudik, and Yi (2009) distinguished MANETs into long-lived MANETs and short-lived MANETs. Saxena, Tsudik, and Yi gave an example of a long-lived MANET in which military ships travel overseas in a group. Examples of a short-lived MANET are for sensors gathering environmental data for an afternoon, and for firefighters putting out a fire in a civilian property. A long-lived MANET exists for a long period of time, therefore, the security scheme built for it should be robust and can withstand for a long time. In contrast, a short-lived MANET is temporary; therefore, it may be sufficient to have a security scheme that can sustain "weaker static adversaries" as referred in (Saxena, Tsudik, & Yi, 2009, p. 159). A security mechanism built for a long-lived MANET is also suitable for a short-lived MANET. Saxena, Tsudik, and Yi pointed out that many applications of a MANET are short-lived. Therefore, without jeopardizing the security of the MANET, an efficient way of establishing authentication and key association is essential for the short-lived MANET.

As stated above, one of the biggest challenges in MANETs is the resource limitation in mobile nodes. For ease of mobility, a mobile node is typically running on battery. Therefore, it is particularly important to limit the tasks running on the mobile node so as to conserve the energy. However, this restriction is placed on a mobile node only when the mobile node is dispatched on an active duty. For example, an emergency worker carrying a PDA is assigned to respond to a situation, or a sensor is actively gathering data in a field. To clarify the terminologies, for a mobile node, the period of time during deployment is referred to as the online phase, and the period of time before deployment is referred to as the offline phase. Based on these terminologies, the PDA or the sensor is actively performing an assignment in the online phase. When the PDA or the sensor is not actively carrying out a task, it is in an offline phase in which the quantity of the resource is generally not an issue.

The objective of this chapter is to provide specific algorithms such that mobile nodes can quickly authenticate each other and agree on the shared keys (also known as Authentication and Key Agreement – AKA) to be used in the online phase, and quickly generate non-repudiation evidences in the online phase. The foundation of our joint offline and online effort is the Online/Offline Digital Signature Scheme. The first online/offline digital signature scheme was introduced by Even, Goldreich, and Micali (1990). Note that Even, Goldreich, and Micali named their scheme as online/offline (rather than offline/online) digital signature scheme. Since the work in the offline phase needs to be performed before the work in the online phase, in this chapter, we call this kind of two-phase scheme as an offline/online scheme to accurately reflect the timing sequence. To fulfill our objective, in this chapter, three practical offline/online AKA schemes (proposed in our prior work in Hsin & Harn, 2007), and one offline/online non-repudiation scheme suitable for the MANET environment are presented. Specifically, these schemes are:

1. Offline/Online AKA Scheme: Peer-To-Peer
   a. This scheme is used for a MANET in which the mobile nodes self-organized in the online phase.
2. Offline/Online AKA Scheme: Using a Registration Agent
   a. This scheme is used for a MANET with a centralized server.
3. Offline/Online AKA Scheme: Hybrid
   a. This is a hybrid scheme between the peer-to-peer offline/online AKA scheme and the offline/online AKA scheme via a registration agent.
4. Offline/Online Non-Repudiation Scheme:
   a. This scheme is for a MANET with a centralized server.

In the rest of the chapter, we first give the background information about the security of a MANET. We then present the offline/online AKA schemes, and the offline/online non-repudiation scheme. Finally, we describe the future research directions, and give a summary and conclusion.

BACKGROUND

This section discusses the distinct features and security considerations of a MANET, and provides the literature review on the authentication and key management, and non-repudiation in MANETs.

Distinct Features of MANET

As stated in the Introduction section, a MANET has several distinct features. These features can significantly impact the design of the security of a MANET. Here, we discuss some of these distinct features. Interested readers are directed to (Van der Merwe, Dawoud, & McDonald, 2007) for an excellent review on this subject.

1. **Limited Power Supply:** For mobility, a mobile node usually runs on a battery, hence limited power supply. This in turn affects the choices of the operations that can run on the node.
2. **Dynamically Changing Topology:** Due to the roaming feature of the mobile nodes, the topology (hence the routing information) of a MANET is dynamically changing.
3. **Susceptible to Security Attacks:** Due to the MANET's features such as self-organization without a trusted server, a MANET is susceptible to security attacks. For example, the Sybil attack is an attack in which an entity possesses multiple identities in the same network (Grover, Gaur, Laxmi, & Prajapati, 2011; Schreiber, 1973). Douceur (2002) pointed out when a network that is fully self-organized without a trusted server, it is relatively easy for an imposter to process multiple identities. Van der Merwe, Dawoud, and McDonald indicated that the accountability of a mobile node's action will be hard to enforce when the node has different identities. Xu and Capkun (2008) pointed out that when a network that is built upon distributed authority via threshold cryptography or secret sharing, an imposter can obtain a large share based on its multiple identities, so that it has a considerable leverage in the threshold scheme.
4. **Susceptible to Physical Attack:** A small, portable mobile node is relatively easy to be captured by an intruder. When it is captured, an intruder can launch an attack within the network. Van der Merwe, Dawoud, and McDonald pointed out that this kind of attack is especially risky in a centralized authority based MANET such as the one used for the military.

Security Considerations of MANET

As described previously, a MANET has its own kind of security attacks along with the attacks in the traditional networks. While it may be unlikely to have a completely attack-free MANET, one can try to provide the following security services so as to minimize the possible attacks.

1. **Service Availability:** Service availability means that the service is available to the legitimate users when they want it. The most pronounced attack on the service availability is the Denial of Service (DOS) attack in which an attacker injects many bogus requests to bombard a server such that legitimate users cannot be served. Service availability can be a problem for a self-organized MANET in that mobile nodes in the MANET typically share the same goal (Hubaux, Buttyan, & Capkun, 2001; Shirude, Muley, Nikam, & Marathe, 2012). For example, mobile nodes, sometimes needing to function as routers, transmit packets for other nodes to keep the network going. If a mobile node acts selfishly, not transmitting the packets for other nodes, the network service is disabled for other nodes and the network may not function as it should. Thus, individual mobile nodes are restrained from disabling or saturating the

network, as they are expected to cooperate to achieve the same goal.

2. **User Authentication:** User authentication is used to validate the intended communicating parties. It is important to have an authentication service in a MANET to prevent unauthorized use of network resources by an outsider (Boonkrong & Bradford, 2004).
3. **Data Confidentiality:** With data confidentiality, an attacker cannot understand the message even if he can eavesdrop on a communication. This is usually achieved by using cryptography as in the traditional networks.
4. **Data Integrity:** Data Integrity ensures that what is sent by a sender does not get altered on the way to the destination. A misbehaving mobile node can compromise the network with falsified data. The problem of data integrity happens more often in a heterogeneous MANET than a homogeneous MANET since the mobile nodes typically do not share the same goal in a heterogeneous MANET (Gavidia & Van Steen, 2007).
5. **Non-Repudiation:** When non-repudiation is applied to a message originator, it means that the originator of a message cannot deny the origination of the message at a later time. The traditional symmetric key system cannot provide this service because a common shared key is known by the communicating entities and any entity can use the shared key and later deny using it. Public-key cryptosystems can provide this kind of service since each entity has its own private key.

In providing some of the above security services, usually user authentication is performed first. Once a user is authenticated by the network, a shared key can be produced for use to achieve data confidentiality and data integrity. As a mobile device is governed by the light weight requirement, resulting in limited capacity which can be put in a mobile device, the capacity confined mobile device is the major challenge. In the following sections, we will show how to bring some of these security services into the capacity limited mobile devices.

Literature Review

This section reviews the literature related to authentication and key management, and non-repudiation in MANETs.

For the literature dealing with authentication and key management, one can broadly categorize them into the following three categories. Note that in the following, the term "server" under both centralized and distributed server categories is a generic term for providing services such as membership identification, keying material, or public-key certificate endorsement.

A MANET with a Centralized Server

In a MANET with a centralized server, the centralized server can provide many functions such as an authority for giving out keys, or as a trusted third party for the purpose of endorsing public-key certificates. It is frequently achieved by having the mobile nodes loaded with pre-determined keys or public-key certificates through a centralized server before deployment.

Capkun, Hubaux, and Buttyan (2003, 2006) considered a MANET with an offline centralized server which manages the mobile nodes' membership for the network. Each node first goes to the centralized server to obtain its identification, public key, and public-key certificate that is signed by an authority. Once a mobile node is equipped with these information, it can then establish a peer-to-peer association with other mobile nodes that are close within certain range. For establishing a peer-to-peer association between two mobile nodes, many tasks involved include obtaining the certificate of the other mobile node, verifying the authority's signature, and generating shared keys, and others tasks for secure communication.

Lu and Pooch (2005) proposed an authentication protocol for use in a MANET by using one-way hash chains. Through a one-way hash chain, each mobile node pre-calculates offline a sequence of one-way hash values, and then signs the last hash chain value using its private key. A certificate authority is used to endorse the mobile nodes' public-key certificates. Upon deployed in the field, all mobile nodes exchange their hash chain values and the public-key certificates, and verify the authenticity of the hashed chain values by using others' public-key certificates. This method incurs high traffic volume for authentication. Specifically, due to the mobility of the mobile nodes, coming in and out of the network, it is necessary for the nodes to periodically broadcast their current use of the hash chain values so that all other nodes in the network are informed and synchronized. This is costly for a typical MANET with limited bandwidth.

Our work in (Hsin & Harn, 2007) proposed an offline/online authentication and key agreement scheme with a registration agent, which is also described in section "Offline/Online AKA Scheme: Using a Registration Agent" of this chapter. Unlike Lu and Pooch's approach, our approach does not require any periodic updates. Our approach is different from Capkun, Hubaux, and Buttyan's approach in two ways. Since the computation in public-key cryptography is costly as compared to symmetric-key cryptography, if Capkun, Hubaux, and Buttyan's approach uses public-key cryptography to setup peer-to-peer associations in the online phase, the setup will be costly. If symmetric-key cryptography is used, it is impossible to create secure one-way association in Capkun, Hubaux, and Buttyan's approach. In our approach, we adopted a challenge-response mechanism via a hash function for most of the computation in the online phase. Additionally, in our approach, one can establish secure one- or two-way associations at ease.

A MANET with a Distributed Server

In a MANET with a distributed server, the authority or the duty of a collective server is distributed among a set of mobile nodes. Threshold Cryptography has been popularly adopted for this category (Murugan & Shanmugam, 2012). Threshold cryptography, typically utilizing public-key cryptography for underlying operations, is widely used for multi-party communications. In particular, in order to accomplish a group service, a number of cooperating authorized entities must exceed a certain threshold. For example, to obtain an intended message, a number of entities in the group exceeding a certain threshold are required to decrypt the message. A message obtained by the number of entities below the threshold is not the intended message. For a MANET with threshold cryptographic key distribution, the trust of a server function (such as Certificate Authority (CA)) is distributed among a set of n mobile nodes. Out of n mobile nodes, a certain number of nodes, each trustworthily performing a partial server function, are required to exceed a certain threshold to properly perform a jointly trusted server function.

Based on the threshold secret sharing technique, Castelluccia, Saxena, and Yi (2005) proposed two shared key establishment schemes, Matrix Threshold Key Pre-Distribution and Polynomial Threshold Key Pre-Distribution, for MANETs. Rizvi, Sultana, Sun, and Islam (2010) used threshold cryptography in a MANET with mobile agents.

The main feature of the threshold cryptography is that it avoids a single point of failure. That is, it is difficult to jeopardize the function of the distributed server by a deceitful mobile node. However, this cryptosystem has a high cost with regard to both computation and memory. It is therefore infeasible for resource-constraint mobile nodes. In an attempt to solve the resource limitation for using threshold cryptography, several approaches have been proposed. For example, based on the secret sharing idea, Saxena, Tsudik, and Yi (2009) used bi-variate polynomials for non-interactive node admission control in short-lived MANETs. For long-lived MANETs, Saxena and Yi (2009) used bi-variate polynomials and threshold signature for non-interactive self-certification.

A MANET that is Self-Organized by the Mobile Nodes Themselves

In a MANET that is self-organized by the mobile node themselves, there is no centralized or distributed server.

Capkun, Hubaux, and Buttyan (2003, 2006) considered a fully self-organized scheme in which the peer-to-peer association can be established when the distance between two mobile nodes is close within certain range such that the mobile nodes can identify each other visually via, for example, an infrared mechanism. The mobile peers, then, exchange cryptography values and authenticate each other. In their approach, a trust of the acquaintance is utilized. Rafsanjani and Shojaiemehr (2012) presented a hierarchical self-organized public key management scheme in which the authentication between the mobile nodes is done based on their local information.

Our work in (Hsin & Harn, 2007) proposed a peer-to-peer offline/online authentication and key agreement scheme, which is also described in section "Offline/Online AKA Scheme: Peer-To-Peer" of this chapter. Our approach differs from Capkun, Hubaux, and Buttyan's approach in that we do not assume any trusted relationship among the mobile nodes. Comparing our work with Rafsanjani and Shojaiemehr's approach, they used a public-key certificate based authentication method which can be computationally costly. In our approach, the mobile nodes pre-arrange shared keys among themselves before deployment, and immediately upon deployment, the mobile nodes execute the online authentication and key agreement algorithm which is a challenge-response method with a hash function to authenticate each other and produce shared keys for use in the online phase.

For non-repudiation in a MANET, Lin and Slay (2005) proposed a non-repudiation protocol and addressed the fairness of exchanging non-repudiation evidences between two entities in a MANET. Lin and Slay (2006) pointed out several QoS issues associated with their non-repudiation protocol in a MANET. Tandel, Valiveti, Agrawal, and Kotecha (2010) gave a review of non-repudiation in both conventional networks and ad hoc networks. In section "Offline/Online Non-repudiation Scheme" of this chapter, we present an offline/online non-repudiation scheme in which the computation work is performed in two phases, i.e., offline and online.

OFFLINE/ONLINE AKA SCHEMES

Authentication and Key Agreement (AKA) scheme first authenticates a mobile node in a MANET. After a mobile node is authenticated by its peer, a shared key can be established under a mutual agreement between the mobile peers so that the mobile node can perform an active duty in a MANET in a cryptographically secure manner. In the following, we propose three offline/online AKA schemes.

Offline/Online AKA Scheme: Peer-to-Peer

This scheme was first proposed in our work in (Hsin & Harn, 2007). In particular, in this scheme, we assume that the set of to-be-deployed mobile nodes is known beforehand. This is akin to a team of fire fighters who have been trained together to respond to fire incidents. In the offline phase when the resource is bountiful, not confined to the capacity of mobile nodes, the mobile nodes can establish pairwise authenticated shared keys so that they can communicate with each other securely in the online phase. In the case where a mobile node itself is not equipped or not capable to execute pairwise authenticated shared keys with other nodes in the offline phase, other device (such as a desktop computer) can perform the computation for the mobile node and store the resulting keys in the mobile node. For pairwise authenticated public key establishment, readers are directed to (Harn, Mehta, & Hsin, 2004) and (Liu & Li, 2010) for Diffie-Hellman key exchange with Digital Signature Algorithm (DSA), or (Law, Menezes, Qu, Solinas, & Vanstone, 2003) for authenticated key agreement. Each pairwise authenticated shared key between a pair of mobile nodes is computed only once during the offline phase. In the following, for ease of reference, denote the pairwise authenticated shared key established in the offline phase between a pair of mobile nodes A and B as KAB.

Based on the offline pairwise authenticated share keys, in the online phase upon deployment, a pair of mobile nodes can quickly execute our work in (Hsin & Harn, 2007)'s Peer-to-Peer On-line Light-Weight AKA Algorithm, also shown in Figure 1 of this chapter, to establish session keys for use in an online communication session.

Specifically, our peer-to-peer online light-weight AKA algorithm uses a 3-way challenge and response authentication via a hash function. The following explains how two mobile nodes A and B establish two session keys, one for each direction of the communication in the online phase. Each of mobile nodes A and B selects a nonce. Denote nA and nB as the nonce selected by mobile nodes A and B respectively. Mobile node A uses nA to challenge mobile node B, and mobile node B uses nB to challenge mobile node A. In step p1 of the peer-to-peer online light-weight

Figure 1. Peer-to-peer online light-weight AKA algorithm (©2007, International Conference on Security of Information and Networks. Used with permission). The following describes the suitable scenario and assumption for using the peer-to-peer online light-weight AKA algorithm. The set of to-be-deployed mobile nodes is known beforehand, therefore, during the offline phase, the pairwise authenticated shared key such as KAB between mobile nodes A and B are established before invoking this online AKA algorithm.

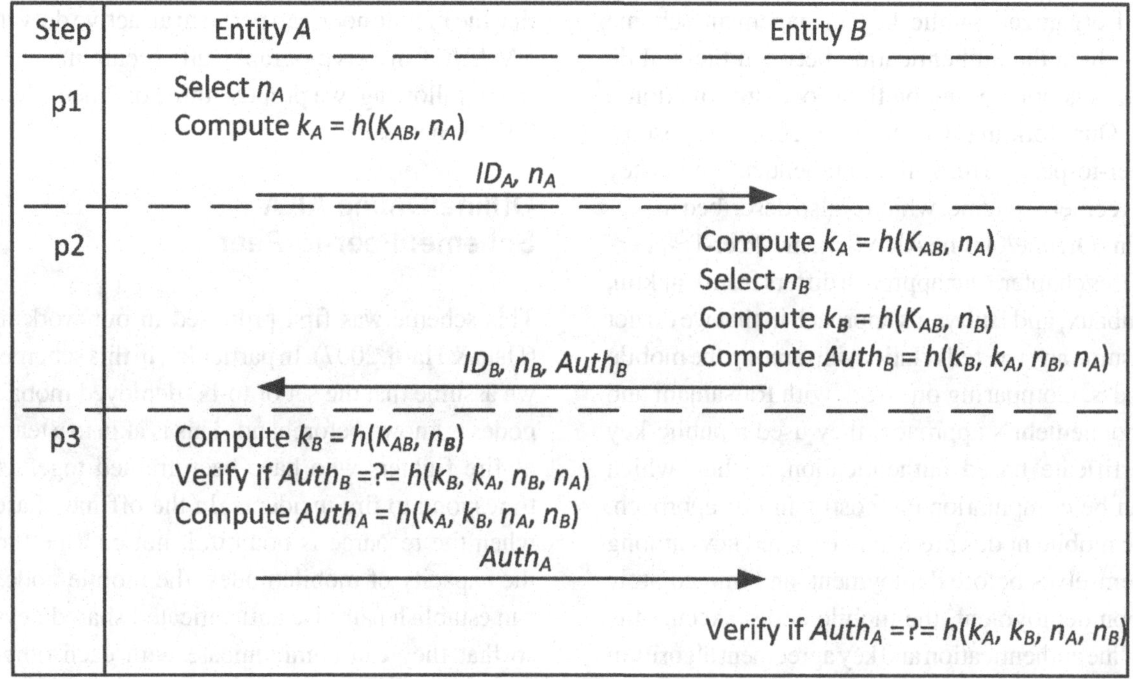

AKA algorithm (shown in Figure 1), mobile node A computes kA using an agreed upon hash function h and KAB, the pre-shared key established offline, and sends its identification and nonce nA over to mobile node B. In particular, kA = h(KAB, nA), where h() is a one-way hash function, and KAB and nA are concentrated as an input to the one-way hash function. Mobile node B, using KAB and nonce nA, computes its value of kA. Mobile node B computes kB. Using kB, kA, nB, and nA, mobile node B computes AuthB, and then sends IDB, nB, and AuthB over to mobile node A. Mobile node A computes its value of kB, and then computes the hash value of kB, kA, nB, and nA to see if the result is equal to AuthB sent by mobile node B. If so, mobile node B has been authenticated by mobile node A. Mobile node A also computes AuthA by hashing the values of kA, kB, nA, and nB, and sends it over to mobile node B. Mobile node B computes the hash value of kA, kB, nA, and nB and checks to see its value equal to AuthA sent by A. If so, mobile node A has been authenticated by mobile node B. Once mobile nodes A and B have been mutually authenticated, the shared session keys kA (for the communication direction from A to B), and kB (for the communication direction from B to A) are established.

As can be seen from the above 3-way algorithm, the computation is via a hash function. It does not invoke extensive computation as that in public-key cryptosystems, hence the term "light-weight" in the name of the peer-to-peer online light-weight AKA algorithm. Additionally, no trusted relationship among the mobile nodes is assumed in this scheme.

Offline/Online AKA Scheme: Using a Registration Agent

This scheme was first proposed in our work in (Hsin & Harn, 2007). In particular, in this scheme, we assume that the mobile nodes to be deployed are not known beforehand. This is akin to a large disaster requiring relief workers from out of states to assist in recovering from the disaster. In this scheme, we adopt a key registration agent to assist in establishing the shared keys. In the offline phase, before joining in the relief effort, each mobile node first establishes a pairwise authenticated shared key with the registration agent R so that the mobile nodes can communicate with the registration agent R securely in the online phase. If a mobile node is not able to compute the offline shared key, other device can perform the computation and load the resulting key in the mobile node. Some examples of pairwise authenticated public key algorithms can be found in (Harn, Mehta, & Hsin, 2004; Law, Menezes, Qu, Solinas, & Vanstone, 2003; Liu & Li, 2010). Each pairwise authenticated shared key between a mobile node and the registration agent R is computed only once during the offline phase. For ease of reference, denote the pairwise authenticated shared key established in the offline phase between mobile node A and the registration agent R as KAR, and the key between mobile node B and the registration agent R as KBR.

In the online phase, the online light-weight AKA algorithm via a registration agent, shown in Figure 2, will be used. In particular, in step d1 of Figure 2, the peer-to-peer online light-weight AKA algorithm (Figure 1) between mobile nodes and registration agent R is invoked. At the end of step d1, session keys kA, kR, kB, and kR' are established, where kA is the shared key between mobile node A and registration agent R for the messages from A to R, kR is the shared key between mobile node A and registration agent R for the messages from R to A, kB is the shared key between mobile node B and registration agent R for the messages from B to R, and kR' is the shared key between mobile node B and registration agent R for the messages from R to B.

Step d2 of Figure 2 shows how kA is securely passed to mobile node B, and kB is securely passed to mobile node A. In particular, registration agent R uses kR to encrypt kB, resulting in c1. Registration agent R then uses kA and c1 to obtain hashed

Figure 2. Online light-weight AKA algorithm via a registration agent (©2007, International Conference on Security of Information and Networks. Used with permission.), where E() is an encryption function, and D() is a decryption function. The following describes the suitable scenario and assumption for using the online lightweight AKA algorithm via a registration agent. The mobile nodes to be deployed are not known beforehand. Therefore, in the offline phase, a mobile node such as A or B, must establish a pairwise authenticated shared key (KAR and KBR, respectively) with the registration agent R before invoking this online AKA algorithm.

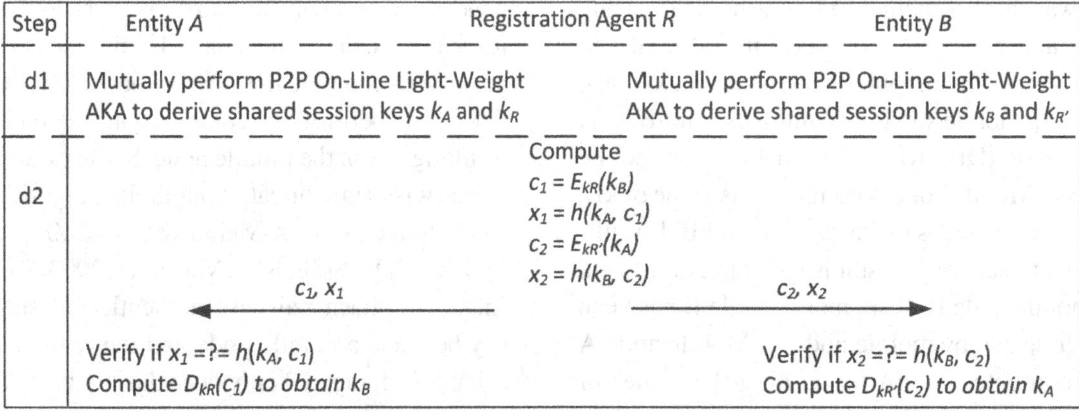

result x1. Both c1 and x1 are then sent over to mobile node A. Similarly, registration agent R uses kR' to encrypt kA, resulting in c2. Registration agent R then uses kB and c2 to obtain hashed result x2. Both c2 and x2 are then sent over to mobile node B. Mobile node A computes a hash of kA and c1, and checks to see if it is equal to the received value x1. If so, mobile node A uses kR to decrypt c1 to obtain key kB. Now, mobile node A shares a key (i.e., kB) with mobile node B. This key will be used for the messages sent from B to A. Similarly, mobile node B computes a hash of kB and c2, and checks to see if it is equal to the received value x2. If so, mobile node B uses kR' to decrypt c2 to obtain key kA. Now, mobile node B shares a key (i.e., kA) with mobile node A. This key will be used for the messages sent from A to B.

As can be seen from the above scheme, the computation in the mobile nodes is via a hash function, along with encryption and decryption in which traditional symmetric-key computation can be used. It does not invoke extensive computation as that in public-key cryptosystems, hence the term "light-weight" in the name of the online light-weight AKA algorithm via a registration agent. Additionally, no trusted relationship among the mobile nodes and the registration agent is assumed in this scheme.

Offline/Online AKA Scheme: Hybrid

This scheme was first proposed in our work in (Hsin & Harn, 2007). In particular, our hybrid offline/online AKA scheme, shown in Figure 3, is a joint scheme between the peer-to-peer offline/online AKA scheme and the offline/online AKA scheme via a registration agent. It is used for the cases in which, in the offline phase, some mobile nodes have established authenticated shared keys, and other mobile nodes have not. This is akin to a disaster relief crew which involves both local and out-of-state relief members. An out-of-state relief crew member may be on-call on a needed basis, therefore having not established key agreement with other mobile nodes in the offline phase beforehand.

Figure 3. Hybrid offline/online light-weight AKA algorithm between mobile nodes A and B. The following describes the suitable scenario and assumption for using the hybrid offline/online AKA algorithm. The mobile nodes to be deployed may be known or not known beforehand, therefore, some nodes have established pairwise authenticated keys with each other, while other nodes have not. Regardless of the situation, all mobile nodes must each establish an offline pairwise authenticated shared key with the registration agent R.

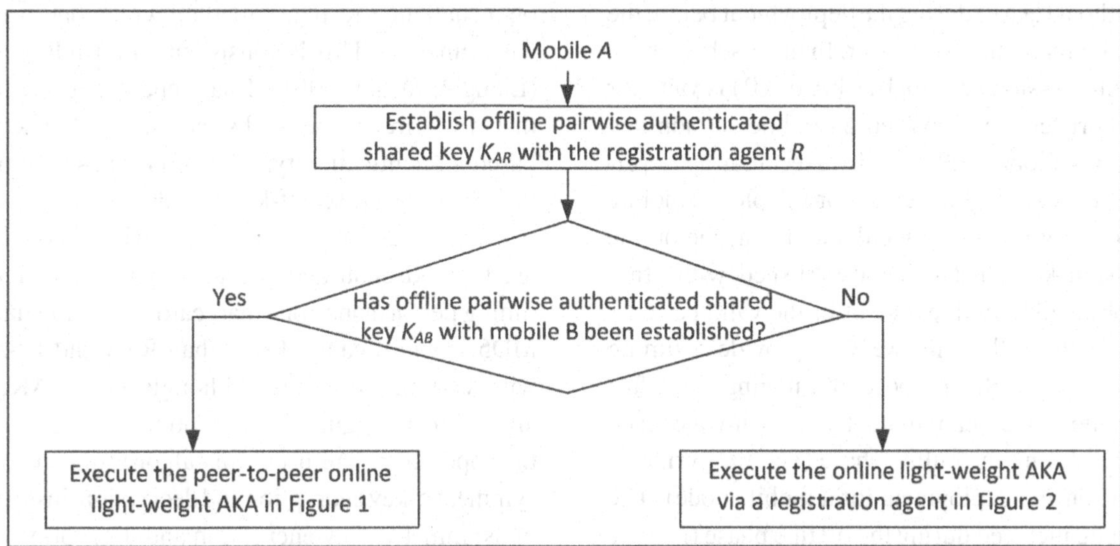

A local relief crew member, having established offline pairwise authenticated shared keys with other mobile nodes, can adopt the peer-to-peer online light-weight AKA algorithm (Figure 1) to establish shared keys in the online phase. An out-of-state relief crew member who has not established an offline pairwise authenticated shared key must first establish a pairwise authenticated shared key with the registration agent R in the offline phase, and then adopts the online light-weight AKA algorithm via a registration agent in Figure 2 to establish shared keys with other mobile nodes in the online phase.

Note that regardless whether the mobile nodes are local or from out-of-state, all mobile nodes must each establish an offline authenticated shared key with the registration agent R. This is required so that a mobile node joining the network later can communicate, in the online phase, with any other nodes in the network.

Discussion

This section discusses various aspects of the AKA schemes in the previous sections. These aspects include whether the schemes allow a new mobile node to join an existing MANET, how the schemes take care of a deployed mobile node needing to leave early before the deployment mission is over, and how the algorithms fare in terms of computation time.

The peer-to-peer online lightweight AKA algorithm described in Figure 1 assumes that the set of to-be-deployed mobile nodes is known beforehand, therefore, the mobile nodes can establish pairwise authenticated shared keys with each other in the offline phase. Once the set of mobile nodes is deployed onto the field forming a MANET, a new mobile node outside of the known set of mobile nodes will not be able to join the established MANET. For a new mobile node to join an established MANET, the AKA scheme via a registration agent or the hybrid AKA scheme can be used.

All three AKA schemes can handle the case in which a deployed mobile node is on leave, or re-assigned to other mission, or AWOL (Absent Without Leave) during the deployment before the deployment mission is over. In these schemes, an online session key (such as kA or kB) is valid for a short term only. When an online session key expires, mobile nodes need to execute an appropriate AKA algorithm again. For a deployed mobile node leaving during the deployment, the online session keys that it has established with other mobile nodes will expire after the valid period.

In the following, we will provide a timing analysis for the purpose of judging how fast mobile nodes can mutually authenticate each other during the online phase (i.e., the period of time during deployment for a mobile node). The timing incurred during the offline phase (i.e., the period of time before the deployment of a mobile node) is not critical since if it ever becomes critical, other devices (such as desktop computers) can perform the computation for a mobile node and store the result in the mobile node. For the peer-to-peer online lightweight AKA algorithm in Figure 1, each mobile node requires 4 one-way hash function computations. For the online lightweight AKA algorithm via a registration agent in Figure 2, each mobile node requires 5 one-way hash function computations and 1 decryption, and the registration agent R requires 10 one-way hash function computations and 2 encryptions. The computation requirement in the online phase for the hybrid AKA algorithm in Figure 3 is the same as that in Figure 1 or Figure 2 depending on whether the offline pairwise authenticated shared key has been established.

In terms of computation time, it is well known that symmetric (secret) key operations are, in general, more efficient than the asymmetric (pubic) key operations (Kumar, Munjal, & Sharma, 2011) Specifically, Kumar, Munjal, and Sharma pointed out that because of high computational processing power requirement, asymmetric techniques for encryption are nearly 1000 times slower than the symmetric counterparts. In our online lightweight AKA schemes in Figures 1 to 3, the online authentication mechanism is based on a challenge-response method with a one-way hash function. This is consistent with finding in (Liang & Wang, 2005). Liang and Wang stated that, for wireless networks, because public-key based authentication typically consumes a lot of time and power, secret-key based authentication with challenge-response mechanism is commonly used. Handschuh and Paillier (2000) compared timing performance on smart cards, showing that MD5 is significantly faster than RSA and DSA with varying key sizes. Although, in the AKA algorithm in Figure 2, encryption and decryption operations are used, this algorithm can use symmetric-key encryption and decryption, instead of asymmetric-key encryption and decryption.

In terms of our algorithm framework, in the offline/online AKA schemes, the online authentication mechanism establishing online session keys between a pair of mobile nodes is based on a pairwise authenticated key established offline between the peer nodes. This key-derive-key approach is widely adopted in network communication. For examples, the popular applications such as SSL (Secure Sockets Layer) for HTTPS (Secure HTTP) and IEEE 802.11i standard for secure WLAN (Wireless LAN) adopt this approach.

OFFLINE/ONLINE NON-REPUDIATION

In this section, we propose an offline/online non-repudiation scheme for a MANET with an online centralized server in which the server has more computing resource as compared to that in a typical mobile node in the online phase. In this model, during the online phase, mobile nodes are the non-repudiation originators, generating messages along with their non-repudiation evidences; whereas the centralized server is the receiver of the messages and non-repudiation evidences, and the verifier of the non-repudiation evidences. Some of the applications for this type of MANETs include (1) a sensor network in which sensors collect environmental data and report the collected data to an online base station, and (2) a combative situation in which mobile nodes are dispatched in a field to collect and report data to an online central authority.

Using our proposed scheme, a non-repudiation originator (i.e., a mobile node which generates a message and its non-repudiation evidence) cannot deny originating the message later. This is achieved by having a mobile node provide a message along with essential crypto values to a verifier. Based on the data received from the mobile node along with the mobile node's public information, the verifier can check to see if the data is indeed genuinely from the non-repudiation originator.

The structure of this proposed non-repudiation scheme is different from the AKA schemes in the previous section in that this scheme is built on top of our work in (Harn, Hsin, & Lin, 2009)'s offline/online digital signature scheme based on multiple-collision trapdoor hash family, whereas the above offline/online AKA schemes do not use the crypto characteristics described in (Harn, Hsin, & Lin, 2009).

In the following, we first reviewed the multiple-collision trapdoor hash family under the Factoring assumption. We then propose our offline/online non-repudiation scheme based on the multiple-collision trapdoor hash family under the Factoring assumption for a MANET.

Multiple-Collision Trapdoor Hash Family under the Factoring Assumption

Shamir and Tauman (2001) proposed a trapdoor hash family under the Factoring assumption. They then built an offline/online digital signature scheme based on the trapdoor hash family. Shamir and Tauman's offline/online digital signature scheme produces a one-time signature in that the crypto data generated under the trapdoor hash family can be used for signing exactly one message.

To alleviate Shamir and Tauman's one-time signature constraint, our work in (Harn, Hsin, & Lin, 2009) proposed multiple-collision trapdoor hash families under both Factoring and Discrete Logarithm assumptions, and built an offline/online digital signature scheme that can be used to sign multiple messages. This is achieved by adding an additional secret value k, as compared to Shamir and Tauman's trapdoor hash family.

Specifically, in Harn, Hsin, and Lin's Factoring based approach, one first randomly selects two prime values p and q. The primes p and q are safe primes in that p and q must satisfy the constraints such that p' = (p-1)/2 and q' = (q-1)/2, and that p' and q' are primes as well. Compute n such that n is equal to p multiplied by q. Then, select an element g of order λ(n) in which λ(n) is equal to lcm(p-1, q-1) = 2p'q'. Randomly choose k, and then compute r as gk (mod n). The private trapdoor key TK is equal to (p, q, k), and the public hash key HK is equal to (n, g). Given f as a cryptographic hash function, the trapdoor hash function hHK(m, r, s) is defined to be rg f(m, r) s (mod n).

By utilizing the offline/online digital signature scheme in (Harn, Hsin, & Lin, 2009), we will present an offline/online non-repudiation scheme based on multiple-collision trapdoor hash family under the Factoring assumption for use in a MANET environment.

The Placement of Public Hash Key and Trapdoor Hash Value

In Shamir and Tauman's offline/online signature scheme, after a message is signed in the online phase, a sender also signs the trapdoor hash value hHK(m, s) and then sends it to a verifier along with the message. A verifier first uses the public key of a certificate authority to verify the sender's public-key certificate, obtains the public key of the sender, and then uses the public key to verify the signature of the trapdoor hash value hHK(m, s) to make sure that it is genuine. The verifier can then verify the message's signature.

In our approach, the public hash key HK and the trapdoor hash value hHK(m, r, s) are used for many messages. In order for an online centralized server to verify the authenticity of HK and hHK(m, r, s) of a mobile node, we recommend a couple of approaches here.

Approach 1: In the offline phase before sending a mobile node out on active duty, one can load the mobile node's public hash key HK and trapdoor hash value hHK(m, r, s) in the centralized server's local storage.

Approach 2: This approach utilizes an offline certificate authority, and assumes to be used for a short-lived MANET for dealing with public-key certificate revocation. Specifically, in the offline phase, a mobile node stores its HK and hHK(m, r, s) in its public-key certificate, and has the certificate authority endorse its public-key certificate. Additionally, the centralized server is loaded with the public key of the offline certificate authority. Readers are referred to the Introduction section for the discussion of short-lived vs. long-lived MANETs.

Offline/Online Non-Repudiation Scheme

The following describes our offline/online non-repudiation scheme under the Factoring-based multiple-collision trapdoor hash family. Similar to Shamir and Tauman's offline/online digital signature scheme, our proposed scheme has three algorithms, i.e., Key Generation, Non-Repudiation Evidence Generation, and Verification. In the following, for ease of notation, A stands for a mobile node (i.e., a non-repudiation originator) providing a message and its non-repudiation evidence to a verifier V, which is an online centralized server in a MANET. The online centralized server V checks to see if the data sent by mobile node A is indeed non-repudiably A's data.

Key Generation Algorithm: Offline

In this algorithm, an arbitrary mobile node, denoted as A, performs the actions and computations in Figure 4 in the offline phase. If mobile node A is not able to perform the computations in the algorithm, other devices can perform the computation and load the resulting keys and values in mobile node A.

Non-Repudiation Evidence Generation Algorithm: Online

This algorithm, depicted in Figure 5, is executed in the online phase. Specifically, for a message, mi, that mobile node A wishes to generate a non-repudiation evidence, mobile node A follows the algorithm in Figure 5 to send the message and its non-repudiation evidence to a verifier V. If Approach I in section "Placement of Public Hash key and Trapdoor Hash Value" is used, the non-repudiable evidence for message mi is the combination of ri, si, and the pre-loaded A's HK and hHK(m, r, s) in V's local storage. If Approach II is used, the non-repudiable evidence for message mi is the combination of ri, si, and A's public-key certificate.

Verification Algorithm: Online

The Verification algorithm is depicted in Figure 6. This algorithm is executed online by a verifier V. Specifically, the verifier V first retrieves mobile node A's HK and hHK(m, r, s) from V's local storage or from mobile node A's public-key certificate, depending on the placement of these

Figure 4. Key generation algorithm for offline/online non-repudiation scheme. This algorithm is executed offline. Mobile node A is an arbitrary mobile node wishing to provide non-repudiation evidences to a verifier. The Approach II mentioned in the figure can be found in section "Placement of Public Hash key and Trapdoor Hash Value."

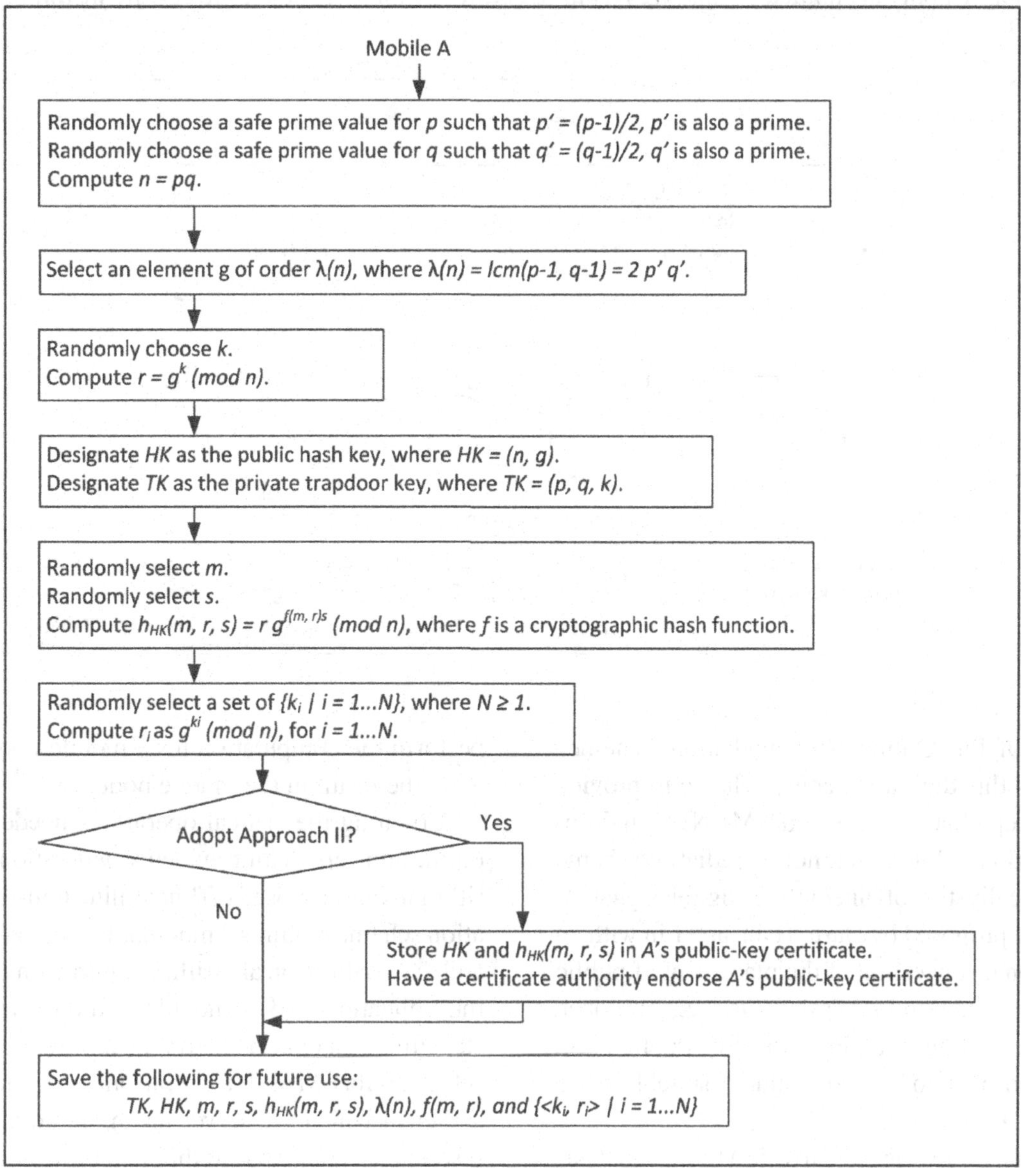

values (see section "The Placement of Public Hash key and Trapdoor Hash Value"). Verifier V then computes hHK(mi, ri, si). Finally, verifier V checks to see if hHK(m, r, s) is equal to hHK(mi, ri, si). If they are equal, verifier V has obtained a non-repudiable evidence from mobile node A.

Discussion

In our prior work (Harn, Hsin, & Lin, 2009), we proposed an offline/online digital signature scheme based on multiple-collision trapdoor hash family with Factoring assumption. Sec-

Figure 5. Non-repudiation evidence generation algorithm for offline/online non-repudiation scheme. This algorithm is executed by an arbitrary mobile node, denoted as A, who wishes to produce a non-repudiation evidence for a message. The Approaches 1 and 2 mentioned in the figure can be found in section "Placement of Public Hash key and Trapdoor Hash Value." Assumptions for using this algorithm: (1) A mobile node has limited computing resource online; (2) there is no online certificate authority in a MANET.

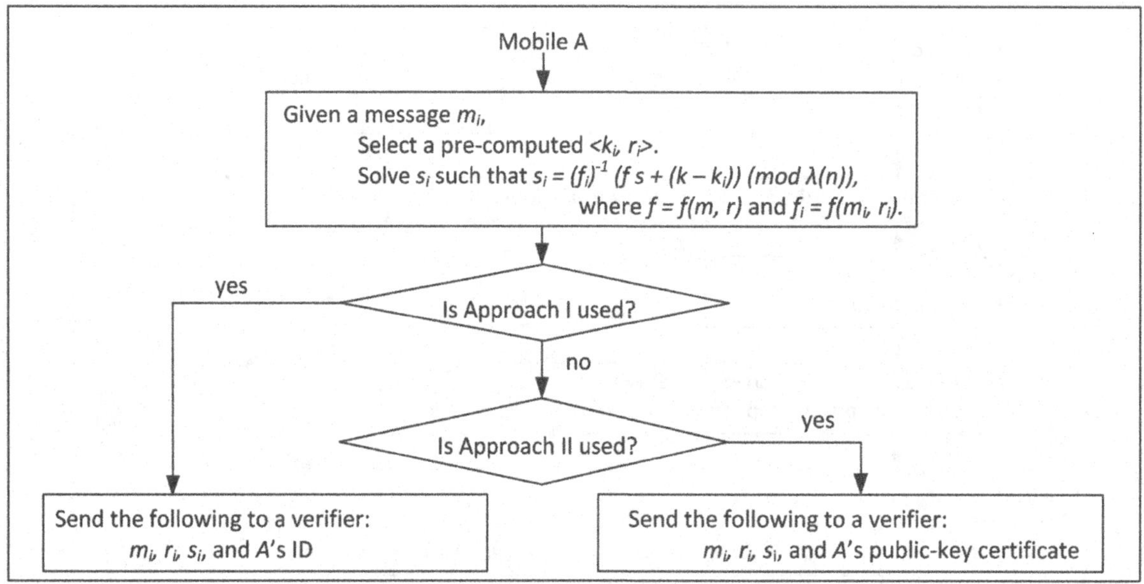

tion "Offline/Online Nonrepudiation Scheme" utilizes this digital signature scheme to provide a non-repudiation service in a MANET environment. This offline/online non-repudiation scheme is basically the offline/online digital signature scheme proposed by Harn, Hsin, and Lin with an additional suggestion of the placement of public hash key and trapdoor hash value (i.e., Approach I of the section "The Placement of Public Hash key and Trapdoor Hash Value") suitable for a MANET environment.

In the following, we provide a timing analysis for the purpose of judging how fast a mobile node can produce a non-repudiation evidence during the online phase (i.e., the period of time during deployment for a mobile node). We assume that the timing incurred during the offline phase (i.e., the period of time before the deployment of a mobile node) is not critical. If it ever becomes critical, other devices (such as desktop computers) can perform the computation for a mobile node and store the result in the mobile node.

Counting the critical operations needed, the online non-repudiation evidence generation algorithm in our proposed offline/online non-repudiation scheme requires 2 modular multiplications, and the verification algorithm requires 1 modular multiplication and 3 modular exponentiations. Recalling that our offline/online non-repudiation scheme is for a MANET with an online centralized server in which the server has more computing resource as compared to that in a typical mobile node in the online phase. Mobile nodes are the ones generating non-repudiation evidences, and the centralized server is the verifier of the non-repudiation evidences.

Public key cryptosystems commonly use modular exponentiation with large modulus and exponent where a modular exponentiation is usually carried out via modular multiplications repeatedly (Sutter,

Figure 6. Verification algorithm for offline/online non-repudiation scheme. This algorithm is executed by a verifier V (which is an online centralized server in a MANET) during the online phase. The Approaches I and II mentioned in the figure can be found in section "Placement of Public Hash key and Trapdoor Hash Value." Assumptions for using this algorithm: (1) Verifier V is an online centralized server in a MANET. It has more computing resource online as compared to that in a typical mobile node; (2) there is no online certificate authority in a MANET.

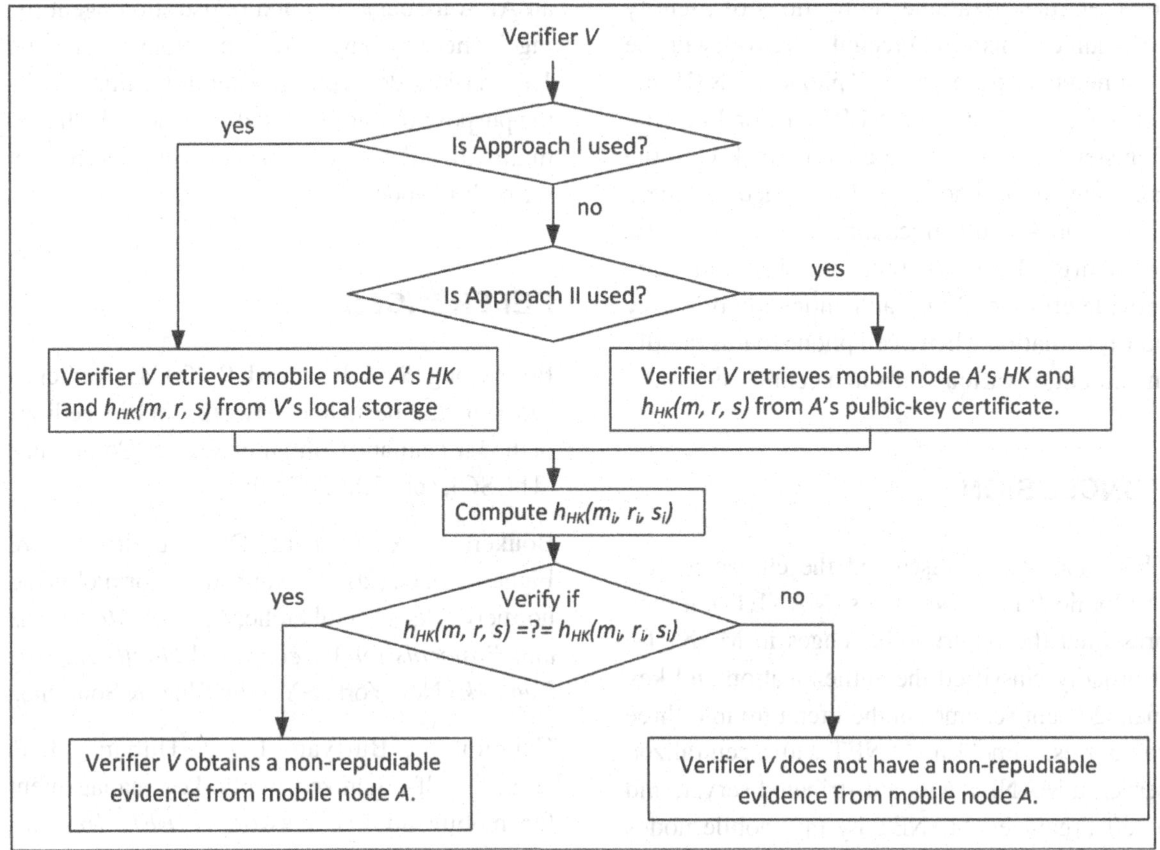

2011). Depending on the values of the modulus, the exponent, and the base of the exponent, sometimes one modular exponentiation can incur several hundreds or thousands of modular multiplications. For specific empirical timing performance on various platforms, Handschuh and Paillier (2000) reported the timing of public key computations on smart cards under various crypto coprocessors by various manufacturers (such as Hitachi, Toshiba, and Siemens) using various public-key algorithms with various key sizes (such as RSA512, RSA1024, RSA2048, DSA512, DSA1024, Elliptic Curve DSA 135, and Elliptic Curve DSA255).

FUTURE RESEARCH DIRECTIONS

Currently, the mobile devices are limited in energy and memory. However, as the technology advances, this limitation may be eased gradually in the future (Moore's Law) such that a full-blown public-key cryptosystem can be utilized in a MANET. However, until then, research can consider a hybrid approach with a mix of symmetric-key and public-key cryptosystems. For example, in a typical client-server model, a server is usually an entity with more capacity, whereas a client has less capacity. Thus, one can utilize public-key cryptography in a mobile server, and utilize symmetric-key cryptography in a mobile client.

In this chapter, the offline/online AKA and non-repudiation schemes are proposed for use between two entities. The future research can extend these schemes to the communication among three entities. Example applications of 3-entity communications are (1) a cellular network with the communication among a cell phone, HLR (Home Location Register), and VLR (Visitor Location Register), and (2) a local area network with the communication among a mobile device, an access point, and an authentication server. A specific problem to address is how one can algorithmically provide efficient 3-way authentication or 3-way non-repudiation when a cell phone roams rapidly in and out of various cells in a cellular network.

CONCLUSION

This chapter first discussed the characteristics of Mobile Ad Hoc Networks (MANETs). It then presented the security challenges in MANETs. It broadly classified the authentication and key management schemes in the literature into three categories, namely, a MANET with a centralized server, a MANET with a distributed server, and a self-organized MANET by the mobile nodes themselves.

We then presented three offline/online Authentication and Key Agreement (AKA) schemes, and one offline/online non-repudiation scheme. Specifically, three AKA schemes are a peer-to-peer offline/online AKA for use in a self-organized MANET, an offline/online AKA scheme via a registration agent for use in a MANET with a centralized server, and a hybrid offline/online AKA scheme to dynamically use the above two AKA schemes. Our proposed offline/online non-repudiation scheme is for use in a MANET with a centralized server.

From the timing analysis of our proposed schemes, during the online phase, a mobile node can (1) generate a non-repudiation evidence using only 2 modular multiplications, (2) establish a peer-to-peer AKA association using 4 one-way hash function computations, and (3) establish an AKA association via a registration agent using 5 one-way hash function computations and 1 secret-key decryption. Therefore, this fulfills the purpose of our proposed schemes which is to minimalize the online computation requirement for mobile nodes.

REFERENCES

Boonkrong, S., & Bradford, R. (2004). Authentication in mobile ad hoc networks. In Proceedings of the 1st Thailand Computer Science Conference (ThCSC), (pp. 202-207). ThCSC.

Boukerche, A., Camara, D., Loureiro, A., & Figueiredo, C. (2009). Algorithms for mobile ad hoc networks. In Boukerche, A. (Ed.), *Algorithms and Protocols for Wireless and Mobile Ad Hoc Networks*. New York, NY: John Wiley & Sons, Inc..

Capkun, S., Buttyan, L., & Hubaux, J.-P. (2003). Self-organized public-key management for mobile ad hoc networks. *IEEE Transactions on Mobile Computing*, *2*(1). doi:10.1109/TMC.2003.1195151.

Capkun, S., Hubaux, J.-P., & Buttyan, L. (2003). Mobility helps security in ad hoc networks. In Proceedings of the 4th ACM International Symposium on Mobile ad Hoc Networking & Computing (MobiHoc). ACM Press.

Capkun, S., Hubaux, J.-P., & Buttyan, L. (2006). Mobility helps peer-to-peer security. *IEEE Transactions on Mobile Computing*, *5*(1), 43–51. doi:10.1109/TMC.2006.12.

Castelluccia, C., Saxena, N., & Yi, J.-H. (2005). Self-configurable key pre-distribution in mobile ad hoc networks. In Proceedings of the 4th IFIP-TC6 International Conference on Networking Technologies, Services, and Protocols. IFIP.

Chlamtac, I., Conti, M., & Liu, J. (2003). Mobile ad hoc networking: Imperatives and challenges. *Ad Hoc Networks*, *1*, 13–64. doi:10.1016/S1570-8705(03)00013-1.

Di Crescenzo, G., Ge, R., & Arce, G. (2007). Threshold cryptography in mobile ad hoc networks under minimal topology and setup assumptions. *Security Issues in Sensor and Ad Hoc Networks*, *5*(1), 63–75. doi:10.1016/j.adhoc.2006.05.006.

Douceur, J. (2002). The sybil attack. In Proceedings of the 1st International Workshop on Peer-to-Peer Systems (IPTPS). IPTPS.

Even, S., Goldreich, O., & Micali, S. (1990). Online/offline digital signatures. *Crypto*, *435*, 263–277.

Gavidia, D., & Van Steen, M. (2007). Enforcing data integrity in very large ad hoc networks. In Proceedings of the 2007 International Conference on Mobile Data Management, (pp. 77-85). IEEE.

Grover, J., Gaur, M., Laxmi, V., & Prajapati, N. (2011). A sybil attack detection approach using neighboring vehicles in VANET. In Proceedings of the 4th International Conference on Security of Information and Networks, (pp. 151-158). IEEE.

Handschuh, H., & Paillier, P. (2000). Smart card crypto-coprocessors for public-key cryptography: Smart card research and application. *Lecture Notes in Computer Science*, *1820*, 372–379. doi:10.1007/10721064_35.

Harn, L., Hsin, W.-J., & Lin, C.-L. (2009). Efficient online/offline signature schemes based on multiple-collision trapdoor hash families. *The Computer Journal*. doi: doi:10.1093/comjnl/bxp044.

Harn, L., Mehta, M., & Hsin, W.-J. (2004). Integrating Diffie-Hellman key exchange into the digital signature algorithm (DSA). *IEEE Communications Letters*, *8*(3). doi:10.1109/LCOMM.2004.825705.

Hsin, W.-J., & Harn, L. (2007). Practical public key solution in mobile ad hoc networks. In Proceedings of the International Conference on Security of Information and Networks. Gazimagusa, Cyprus: IEEE.

Huang, E., Hu, W., Crowcroft, J., & Wassell, I. (2005). Towards commercial mobile ad hoc network applications: A radio dispatch system. In Proceedings of the 6th ACM International Symposium on Mobile Ad Hoc Networking and Computing. Urbana-Champaign, IL: ACM Press.

Hubaux, J.-P., Buttyan, L., & Capkun, S. (2001). The quest for security in mobile ad hoc networks. In Proceedings of the ACM Symposium on Mobile Ad Hoc Networking and Computing (MobiHOC). ACM Press.

Karlsson, J., Dooley, L., & Pulkkis, G. (2012). Routing security in mobile ad-hoc networks. Issues in Informing Science and Information Technology, 9.

Kaur, R., & Rai, M. (2012). A novel review on routing protocols in MANETs. Undergraduate Academic Research Journal, 1(1).

Kumar, Y., Munjal, R., & Sharma, H. (2011). Comparison of symmetric and asymmetric cryptography with existing vulnerabilities and countermeasures. *International Journal of Computer Science and Management Studies*, *11*(3).

Law, L., Menezes, A., Qu, M., Solinas, J., & Vanstone, S. (2003). An efficient protocol for authenticated key agreement. *Designs, Codes and Cryptography*, *28*(2), 119–134. doi:10.1023/A:1022595222606.

Lee, E. (2011). Security in wireless ad hoc networks. Science Academy Transactions on Computer and Communication Networks, 1(1).

Liang, W., & Wang, W. (2005). On performance analysis of challenge/response based authentication in wireless networks. *International Journal of Computer and Telecommunications Networking*, *48*(2), 267–288.

Lin, Y.-C., & Slay, J. (2005). Non-repudiation in pure mobile ad hoc network. In Proceedings of the Australian Information Security Management Conference, (pp. 59-66). IEEE.

Lin, Y.-C., & Slay, J. (2006). QoS issues of using probabilistic non-repudiation protocol in mobile ad hoc network environment. In Proceedings of the 4th Australian Information Security Management Conference. Perth, Australia: IEEE.

Liu, J., & Li, J. (2010). A better improvement on the integrated Diffie-Hellman-DSA key agreement protocol. *International Journal of Network Security*, *11*(2), 114–117.

Lu, B., & Pooch, U. (2005). A lightweight authentication protocol for mobile ad hoc networks. *International Journal of Information and Technology*, *11*(2).

Luo, H., Zerfos, P., Kong, J., Lu, S., & Zhang, L. (2002). Self-securing ad hoc wireless networks. In Proceedings of the 2002 IEEE Symposium on Computers and Communications. IEEE.

Murugan, R., & Shanmugam, A. (2012). Cluster based node misbehaviour detection, isolation and authentication using threshold cryptography in mobile ad hoc networks. *International Journal of Computer Science and Security*, *6*(3).

Rafsanjani, M., & Shojaiemehr, B. (2012). Improvement of self-organized public key management for MANET. *Journal of American Science*, *8*(1).

Raya, M., & Hubaux, J.-P. (2007). Securing vehicular ad hoc networks. *Journal of Computer Security*, *15*, 39–68.

Rizvi, S., Sultana, Z., Sun, B., & Islam, W. (2010). Security of mobile agent in ad hoc network using threshold cryptography. World Academy of Science, Engineering and Technology, 70.

Saha, H., Bhattacharyya, D., & Banerjee, P. (2012). A novel approach for attacks mitigation in mobile ad hoc networks using cellular automata. International Journal of Ad Hoc, Sensor & Ubiquitous Computing, 3(2).

Saxena, N., Tsudik, G., & Yi, J.-H. (2009). Efficient node admission and certificateless secure communication in short-lived MANETs. *IEEE Transactions on Parallel and Distributed Systems*, *20*(2), 158–170. doi:10.1109/TPDS.2008.77.

Saxena, N., & Yi, J.-H. (2009). Noninteractive self-certification for long-lived mobile ad hoc networks. *IEEE Transactions on Information Forensics and Security*, *4*(4), 946–955. doi:10.1109/TIFS.2009.2031946.

Schreiber, F. (1973). *Sybil*. New York, NY: Warner Books.

Shamir, A., & Tauman, Y. (2001). Improved online/offline signature scheme. *Advances in Cryptology*, *2139*, 355–367.

Shirude, A., Muley, G., Nikam, A., & Marathe, S. (2012). Detection node misconduct in MANET. *International Journal of Engineering and Social Science*, *2*(5), 2249–9482.

Singh, K., & Yadav, R., & Ranvijay. (2007). A review paper on ad hoc network security. *International Journal of Computer Science and Security*, *1*(1).

Sutter, G. (2011). Modular multiplication and exponentiation architectures for fast RSA cryptosystem based on digital serial computation. *IEEE Transactions on Industrial Electronics*, *58*(7), 3101–3109. doi:10.1109/TIE.2010.2080653.

Tandel, P., Valiveti, S., Agrawal, K., & Kotecha, K. (2010). Non-repudiation in ad hoc networks. Communication and Networking. *Communications in Computer and Information Science*, *120*, 405–415. doi:10.1007/978-3-642-17604-3_48.

Taneja, K., & Patel, R. (2007). Mobile ad hoc networks: Challenges and future. In Proceedings of the National Conference on Challenges & Opportunities in Information Technology (COIT-2007). RIMT-IET.

Van der Merwe, J., Dawoud, D., & McDonald, S. (2007). A survey on peer-to-peer key management for mobile ad hoc networks. *ACM Computing Surveys*, *39*(1).

Xu, S., & Capkun, S. (2008). Distributed and secure bootstrapping of mobile ad hoc networks: Framework and constructions. *ACM Transactions on Information and System Security*, *12*(1). doi:10.1145/1410234.1410236.

ADDITIONAL READING

Aboud, S., & Al Ajeeli, A. (2012). Efficient multiple-collision trapdoor hash family. *Security and Communication Networks*, *5*(6), 681–688. doi:10.1002/sec.363.

Aboudagga, N., Refaei, M., Eltoweissy, M., DaSilva, A., & Quisquater, J.-J. (2005). Authentication protocols for ad hoc networks: Taxonomy and research issues. In Proceedings of the 1st ACM International Workshop on Quality of Service & Security in Wireless and Mobile Networks, (pp. 96-104). ACM Press.

Al-Bayatti, A., Zedan, H., & Cau, A. (2009). Security solution for mobile ad hoc network of networks. In Proceedings of the IEEE 5th International Conference on Networking and Services, (pp. 255-262). IEEE Press.

Al-Bayatti, A., Zendan, H., & Cau, A. (2012). Security management for mobile ad hoc network of networks (MANoN). In Proceedings of Advancing the Next-Generation of Mobile Computing – Emerging Technologies, (pp. 1-18). IEEE.

Aldabbas, H., Alwada'n, T., Janicke, H., & Al-Bayatti, A. (2012). Data confidentiality in mobile ad hoc networks. *International Journal of Wireless & Mobile Networks*, *4*(1). doi:10.5121/ijwmn.2012.4117.

Ammayappan, K., Negi, A., Sastry, V., & Das, A. (2011). An ECC-based two-party authenticated key agreement protocol for mobile ad hoc network. *Journal of Computers*, *6*(11), 2408–2416. doi:10.4304/jcp.6.11.2408-2416.

Armknecht, F., Festag, A., Westhoff, D., & Zeng, K. (2007). Cross-layer privacy enhancement and non-repudiation in vehicular communication. In Proceedings of the 4th Workshop on Mobile Ad-Hoc Networks. Bern, Switzerland: IEEE.

Carvalho, M. (2008). Security in mobile ad hoc networks. *IEEE Security Privacy*, *6*(2), 72–75. doi:10.1109/MSP.2008.44.

Chandrasekhar, S. (2011). *Construction of efficient authentication schemes using trapdoor hash functions. (Ph.D. Dissertations)*. Lexington, KY: University of Kentucky.

Chauhan, K., & Sanger, A. (2012). Securing mobile ad hoc networks: Key management and routing. *International Journal on Ad Hoc Networking Systems*, *2*(2), 65–75. doi:10.5121/ijans.2012.2207.

Chen, S., Zhang, Y., Liu, Q., & Feng, J. (2012). Dealing with dishonest recommendation: The trials in reputation management court. *Ad Hoc Networks*, *10*(8), 1603–1618. doi:10.1016/j.adhoc.2011.07.014.

Conrad, M. (2006). Non-repudiation mechanisms for peer-to-peer networks. In Proceedings of the 2006 ACM CoNEXT Conference. ACM Press.

Dahshan, H., & Irvin, J. (2010). A robust self-organized public key management for mobile ad hoc networks. *Security and Communication Networks*, *3*, 16–30.

Fan, X.-X. (2010). *Efficient cryptographic algorithms and protocols for mobile ad hoc networks. (Ph.D. Dissertations)*. Ontario, Canada: University of Waterloo.

Freudiger, J., Raya, M., & Hubaux, J.-P. (2009). Self-organized anonymous authentication in mobile ad hoc networks. In Proceedings of the Conference on Security and Privacy in Communication Networks (Securecomm), (pp. 350-372). Securecomm.

Gangwar, R. (2011). Secure and efficient group key agreement protocol for mobile ad hoc network. *International Journal of Research and Reviews in Computer Science*, *2*(4).

Gangwar, S. (2012). Mobile ad hoc network: A comprehensive study and survey on intrusion detection. *International Journal of Engineering Research and Application*, *2*(1).

Ge, M., & Lam, K.-Y. (2009). Self-healing key management service for mobile ad hoc networks. In Proceedings of the First International Conference on Ubiquitous and Future Networks. IEEE.

Haboub, R., & Ouzzif, M. (2012). Secure and reliable routing in mobile ad-hoc networks. *International Journal of Computer Science & Engineering Survey*, *3*(1). doi:10.5121/ijcses.2012.3105.

Hegland, A. M., Winjum, E., Mjolsnes, S. F., Rong, C., Kure, O., & Spilling, P. (2006). A survey of key management in ad hoc networks. *IEEE Communications Surveys & Tutorials*, *8*(3), 48–66. doi:10.1109/COMST.2006.253271.

Hoeper, K. (2007). References for authentication, key exchange and key revocation in mobile ad hoc networks. Retrieved April 30, 2012, from comsec.uwaterloo.ca/refadhoc.html

Hoeper, K., & Gong, G. (2007). Pre-authentication and authentication models in ad hoc networks. In Xiao, Y., Shen, X., & Du, D.-Z. (Eds.), *Wireless Network Security*. Berlin, Germany: Springer Verlag. doi:10.1007/978-0-387-33112-6_3.

Hu, R., Chi, Y., Xu, F., Wei, Z., & Li, R. (2009). A password-authenticated key agreement scheme for ad hoc networks. In Proceedings of the 5th International Conference on Wireless Communications, Networking, and Mobile Computing. IEEE.

Jarecki, S., & Saxena, N. (2010). On the insecurity of proactive RSA in the URSA mobile ad hoc network access control protocol. *IEEE Transactions on Information Forensics and Security*, *5*(4), 739–749. doi:10.1109/TIFS.2010.2058104.

Kaur, S., Singh, T., & Das, V. (2012). Security threats in mobile adhoc network: A review. *International Journal of Computer Networks and Wireless Communications*, *2*(1).

Kettaf, N., Abouaissa, H., & Lorenz, P. (2008). An efficient heterogeneous key management approach for secure multicast communication in ad hoc networks. *Telecommunication Systems*, *37*, 29–36. doi:10.1007/s11235-008-9074-4.

Liaw, S.-H., Su, P.-C., Chang, H., Lu, E.-H., & Pon, S.-F. (2005). Secured key exchange protocol in wireless mobile ad hoc networks. In Proceedings of the 39th Annual International Carnahan Conference, (pp. 171-173). IEEE.

Mafra, P. (2012). A distributed IDS for ad hoc networks. In Proceedings of the Advanced Information Networking and Applications Workshops (WAINA). WAINA.

Mangai, S., & Tamilarasi, A. (2001). An improved location aided cluster based routing protocol with intrusion detection system in mobile ad hoc networks. *Journal of Computer Science*, *7*, 505–511. doi:10.3844/jcssp.2011.505.511.

Manikan, S., & Manimegalai, R. (2012). Survey of mobile ad hoc network attacks and mitigation using routing protocols. *American Journal of Applied Sciences*, *9*(11), 1796–1801.

Manulis, M. (2005). Key agreement for heterogeneous mobile ad-hoc groups. In Proceedings of the 11th International Conference on Parallel and Distributed Systems, (pp. 290-294). IEEE.

Mehul, E., & Limaye, V. (2009). Security in mobile ad hoc networks. In Unhelkar, B. (Ed.), *Handbook of Research in Mobile Business* (2nd ed., pp. 541–558). Hershey, PA: IGI Global.

Mishra, A., & Nadkarni, K. (2003). Security in wireless ad hoc networks. In *The Handbook of Ad Hoc Wireless Networks*. Boca Raton, FL: CRC Press LLC.

Moses, G., Varma, P., Supriya, N., & Satish, G. (2012). Security aspects and challenges in mobile adhoc networks. In *Proceedings of Computer Network and Information Security* (pp. 26–32). IEEE. doi:10.5815/ijcnis.2012.06.04.

Qabajeh, L., Kiah, L., & Qabajeh, M. (2012). A more secure and scalable routing protocol for mobile ad hoc networks. In *Security and Communication Networks*. New York, NY: John Wiley & Sons, Ltd. doi:10.1002/sec.563.

Safdar, G. A., McGrath, C., & McLoone, M. (2006). Limitations of existing wireless networks authentication and key management techniques for MANETs. In Proceedings of the 7th IEEE International Symposium on Computer Networks, (pp. 101-107). IEEE Press.

Samara, G. (2010). Security issues and challenges of vehicular ad hoc networks (VANET). In Proceedings of the 4th International Conference on New Trends in Information Science and Service Science (NISS), (pp. 393-398). NISS.

Sanzgiri, K., LaFlamme, D., Dahill, B., Levine, B. N., Shields, C., & Belding-Royer, E. M. (2005). Authenticated routing for ad hoc networks. *IEEE Journal on Selected Areas in Communications*, *23*(3), 6598–6610. doi:10.1109/JSAC.2004.842547.

Shafigh, A., Soleimany, A., Mohammadzadeh, H., & Mohseni, S. (2011). A persuading approach for cooperating nodes in mobile ad hoc networks. *World Applied Sciences Journal*, *15*(5), 921–931.

Sima, (2011). Security issues in ad hoc networks. International Journal of Information and Communication Technology Research, 1(4).

Su, X., & Boppana, R. V. (2007). On mitigating in-band wormhole attacks in mobile ad hoc networks. In Proceedings of the IEEE International Conference on Communications, (pp. 24-28). IEEE.

Viswanatham, V. M., & Chari, A. A. (2008). An approach for detecting attacks in mobile ad hoc networks. *Journal of Computer Science*, *4*, 245–251. doi:10.3844/jcssp.2008.245.251.

Xiao, Y., Shen, X., & Du, D. (2007). *Wireless network security*. New York, NY: Springer. doi:10.1007/978-0-387-33112-6.

Yan, G., Olariu, S., & Weigle, M. (2009). Providing location security in vehicular ad hoc networks. *IEEE Wireless Communications*, *16*(6), 48–55. doi:10.1109/MWC.2009.5361178.

Zhang, Y., Liu, W., Lou, W., & Fang, Y. (2006). Location-based compromise-tolerant security mechanisms for wireless sensor networks. *IEEE Journal on Selected Areas in Communications*, *24*(2), 247–260. doi:10.1109/JSAC.2005.861382.

Zhu, L., Zhang, Y., & Feng, L. (2008). Distributed key management in ad hoc network based on mobile agent. In *Proceedings of Intelligent Information Technology Application* (pp. 600–604). IEEE. doi:10.1109/IITA.2008.444.

KEY TERMS AND DEFINITIONS

A MANET with a Centralized Server: A centralized server provides essential services for the mobile nodes in a MANET.

A MANET with a Distributed Server: The authority or the duty of a collective server is distributed among a set of mobile nodes.

A Self-Organized MANET: A MANET is self-organized by the mobile nodes themselves without a centralized or distributed server.

Authentication and Key Agreement: Communicating parties first authenticate each other and then agree on a shared key for the subsequent communication.

Light Weight: When the term is applied to an authentication and key agreement algorithm, it means the algorithm takes an insignificant amount of computation to execute the algorithm.

Mobile Ad Hoc NETwork (MANET): Is a set of mobile nodes rapidly and dynamically forming an autonomous network.

Non-Repudiation: When the term is applied to a message originator, it means that the originator of a message cannot deny the originating of the message at a later time.

Offline/Online Digital Signature Scheme: Is a signature scheme in which the computation to produce a signature is broken down into two phases, i.e., offline and online.

Offline: Is the period of time before the deployment of a mobile node.

Online: Is the period of time during deployment for a mobile node.

Chapter 10
A Survey on Security in Wireless Sensor Networks: Attacks and Defense Mechanisms

Ilker Korkmaz
Izmir University of Economics, Turkey

Orhan Dagdeviren
Ege University, Turkey

Fatih Tekbacak
Izmir Institute of Technology, Turkey

Mehmet Emin Dalkilic
Ege University, Turkey

ABSTRACT

Wireless Sensor Network (WSN) is a promising technology that has attracted the interest of research in the last decade. Security is one of the fundamental issues in sensor networks since sensor nodes are very resource constrained. An attacker may modify, insert, and delete new hardware and software components to the system where a single node, a specific part of the sensing area, and the whole network may become inoperable. Thus, the design of early attack detection and defense mechanisms must be carefully considered. In this chapter, the authors survey attacks and their defense mechanisms in WSNs. Attacks are categorized according to the related protocol layer. They also investigate the open research issues and emerging technologies on security in WSNs.

INTRODUCTION

In the last few years, with the advancements in technology, new device designs that are different than the personal computers, laptops and servers have been introduced and used extensively all over the world. These devices are smaller and cheaper, and use less energy than the ordinary designs. Besides, they are designed on the integrated circuits having a low power communication unit. Their design techniques provide the use of Wireless Sensor Networks (WSNs). A microprocessor of

DOI: 10.4018/978-1-4666-4030-6.ch010

a sensor node not only includes volatile memory and processor but also includes non-volatile memory, digital to analog converter, analog to digital converter, universal asynchronous receiver transmitter and interrupt controller interfaces. In addition, low range radio frequency, infra-red and optical communication techniques are used in these nodes. Moreover nodes can sense heat, light, acceleration and chemical contaminants from the environment and can send these information through a wireless communication channel.

WSNs are ad hoc networks that are composed of hundreds to thousands self-organizing sensor nodes. An example WSN is given in Figure 1. Each sensor node may collect information from the sensing area and relay its data to the sink node on a multi-hop path. Sink is a gateway node that collects data from the other nodes located on sensing area and aggregates the delivered data. Sink node may communicate with a repository in order to deliver its collected data. The data repository may store data in various forms in order to give query service to the users through Internet.

WSNs have many application areas in today's world (Garcia-Hernandez, 2007). One of the most important applications is habitat monitoring. In the Great Duck Island (GDI) application, the life cycle of storm petrel birds are monitored by researchers from UCB and Intel (Mainwaring, 2002). In the PODS application (Biagioni, 2002) developed in Hawaii University, some endangered plant species are investigated. ALERT system is developed for the early detection of flood threat by measuring water level, heat and wind power. Another application area of WSN is patient's health monitoring. Schwiebert (2001) developed a system for blind people to sense the objects in their environment. Remote patient monitoring and management of drug usage are the other type of health-based applications (Akyildiz, 2002).

Figure 1. WSN integrated information system example

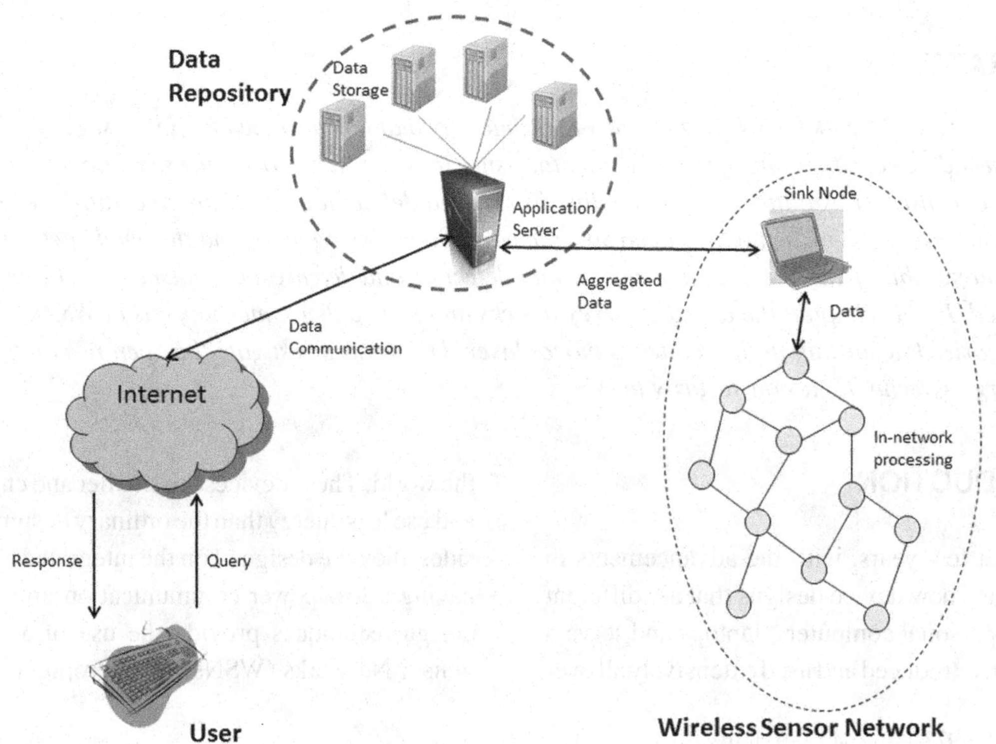

Another WSN application is home and office deployment. Srivastava (2001) developed a kinder garden project for educating children.

An attack on a WSN can be defined as a bad behavior by a single node, malicious invasion on a specific part of the sensing area, or an action to defect the operation of the whole system (Sokullu, 2008). The adversary is used synonymously with the attacker which is the originator of an attack (Wood, 2004). The adversary attacks to the network with the aim of damaging a single or group of nodes in order to gain more selfish benefits on the related services than the other nodes of the WSN (Sokullu, 2009). The attacker may exploit protocol weakness to gain network resources, may create fake packets, may overwhelm the nodes, may behave strangely like switching between on and off status or even may simply reach and reprogram the sensor nodes. The basic feature of these attacks is that they are entirely unpredictable (Radosavac, 2007). Identification and investigation of these attacks are very important to design defense mechanisms or counterattacks.

Today, WSNs in various topologies are used with many different applications that are integrated into kinds of Information Systems. To us, the security of those Information Systems is strongly associated with the security of the WSN used within. For that reason, we believe that a chapter covering the WSN attacks and their defense mechanisms as a detailed survey on the security in WSNs would be properly related to the content of Secure Information Systems.

In this chapter, we classify the WSN attacks by considering the related protocol layers as physical layer, data link layer, routing layer, transport layer and application layer. For each attack, we give its definition, effects and defense techniques. We also provide the open research issues for WSN attacks as use of privacy homomorphism, overhearing, integrating IPv6 to WSN, emerging wireless sensor and actor network problems. The chapter is organized as follows: The attacks and defense mechanisms are covered in Section Attacks and Defense Mechanisms, open issues are discussed in Section Open Issues and Future Research Directions, and the conclusions are drawn in Section Conclusion.

ATTACKS AND DEFENSE MECHANISMS

Any possible attack to WSN is a threat for the Information System integrated to the corresponding WSN. As an attack to any part of the hardware or software of the WSN may give a significant damage to the Information System in use, the defense mechanisms to that attack should be taken into consideration at every stage of the system. From this perspective, the possible attacks and defense mechanisms against these attacks need to be discussed and a trade-off analysis of pros and cons for handling the defense mechanisms is also needed to be considered for a compact risk assessment of the used WSN infrastructure.

A view on top of all types of attacks in WSNs, an attack to a WSN may target mainly the followings: 1) the hardware/software of any part of the WSN; 2) the communication protocol at any part of the WSN. The attackers may directly access to at least one node of the WSN or may give harm to the data communication by interfering with the communication channel or may get into the network without being recognized. From both the point of view of the attacker and the attacked network, the incurred damage is the essential criteria to evaluate the result of the attack. Rather than evaluating the attack results and then comparing the attacks one another, the researchers consider any different attack independently and generally based on a scenario. From this point, the view of the researchers on attacks in WSN literature has been categorized in various ways. In many classifications, the common criterion of the attacks is generally the targeted protocol layer of the sensor network; however there are also some other criteria such as regarding the objectives of the attacks, the security services targeted by the attacks or some hybrid classifications. On this point, Karlof (2002) discusses the attacks to routing layer of WSN and their countermeasures. Sharma (2011) also gives a brief survey of the attacks distressing the routing layer. Chan (2003) makes a categorization for the attacks based on the physical, MAC, and routing layers. As a more general view, Raymond (2008) categorizes the denial of service attacks and defenses by protocol layer taking into consideration all OSI layers, physical, link, network, transport, and application layers. Sokullu (2008), Sokullu (2009) and Lupu (2009) survey the attacks with a classification based on all protocol layers. Sokullu (2008) and Sokullu (2009) also introduce a new attack on MAC protocol layer (defined as GTS attack targeting to the frame structure of IEEE 802.15.4, which is used as a standard MAC protocol for WSN) and explain the different behaviors of the attacker based on different scenarios. Deng (2005) proposes to deal with the attacks aiming the traffic analysis and gives countermeasures to make the base station not to be located easily by such an attack. Padmavathi (2009) gives a classification of WSN security attacks based on their objectives of being passive or active in the sensor network. According to the availability, authentication, integrity, and confidentiality services, the security issues for ad hoc wireless networks are taken into consideration by Stajano (1999). Sen (2009) gives a categorization of the WSN attacks based on the security services and requirements, in addition to this, attacks are also categorized according to their target layers. Yu (2012) describes the trust mechanisms in WSNs and categorizes the trust related attacks in WSNs.

This section mainly gives the state-of-the-art of the attacks and their defense mechanisms in WSNs. The important attacks to WSNs are categorized by their target protocol layers. A general summary of the WSN attack classification according to protocol layers are depicted in Figure 2. As the section surveys probably every known attack in WSN literature, we propose that it is an essential up-to-date reference to the study area of the WSN security literature.

Physical Layer

Radio Jamming: In this attack, adversary emits just signals to interfere in the communication (Raymond, 2008). Because of this behavior, the attack is simple to implement on any type of sensor network environment. It is very effective since it corrupts the communication channel due to frequency interferences. For example assume that two nodes are communicating to transmit a critical data. At this moment, the adversary can emit signals in order to interfere with the data packet. This leads to corruption of the data packet and retransmission of it causing energy consumption. If the jammer is located at a critical position, the effect of the attack can be more harmful. An example case is depicted in Figure 3 where 7 nodes are forming a sensor network. The transmission range of each node is shown with dashed circles where node is in the center of it. The jammer node is node 7 where it is depicted with black filled style. As seen on the figure, jammer node can affect all the other nodes since they are within transmission range of it.

One of the defense techniques against this attack is implementing spread spectrum communication in radio units of sensor nodes (Raymond, 2008). Although this defense mechanism is effective, it is not feasible in many aspects to implement spread spectrum in sensor network radio units. Because of this fact, this defense strategy can be theoretical solution of low cost sensor nodes. The other technique is adjusting the sleep durations by switching from radio on mode to radio off mode. This adjustment can also be implemented by encrypting protocol packets which announce sleep/wake intervals. For example beacon packets in IEEE 802.15.4 includes sleep/wake intervals to synchronize sensor nodes. So

Figure 2. WSN attack classification

- WSN Attacks
  - Physical Layer
    - Radio Jamming
    - Node Tampering
  - Data Link Layer
    - Link Layer Jamming
    - Back-off Manipulation
    - Same Nonce Attack
    - Replay Protection Attack
    - ACK Attack
    - PANId Conflict Attack
    - GTS Attack
    - Unintelligent Replay Attack
    - Unauthenticated Broadcast Attack
    - Full Domination Attack
    - Exhaustion (Interrogation) Attack
  - Routing Layer
    - Bad Mouthing Attack
    - Ballot Attack
    - On-Off Attack
    - Newcomer Attack
    - Conflicting Behavior Attack
    - Intelligent Behavior Attack
    - Identity Spoofing Attack
    - Hello Flood Attack
    - Sybil Attack
    - Sinkhole Attack
    - Wormhole Attack
    - Fake Route Information Attack
    - Blackhole Attack
    - Greyhole (Selective Forwarding) Attack
  - Transport Layer
    - SYN Flood Attack
    - Session Hijacking
    - Desynchronization Attack
  - Application Layer
    - Overwhelming Nodes
    - Path-based DoS Attack
    - Reprogramming Attack

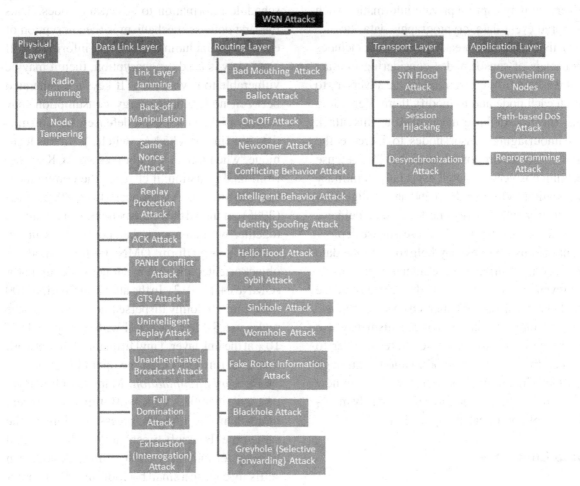

Figure 3. An example jammer located at a critical position

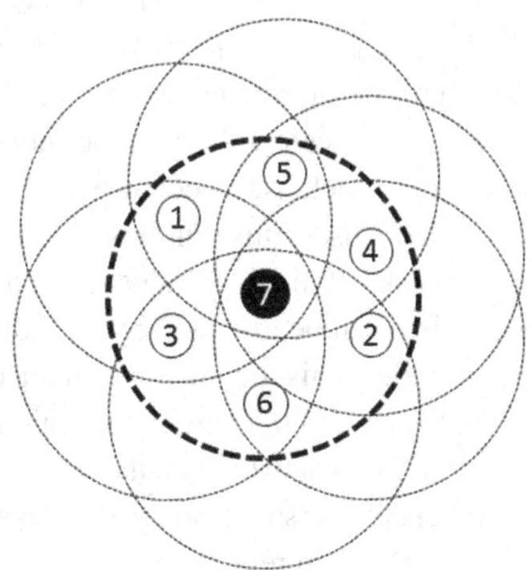

these beacon messages can be encrypted not to inform possible jammers about sleep/wake intervals. This action causes not to receive jamming signals and to protect corruption of data message. Moreover, the adversary redundantly consumes its energy by emitting signals while ordinary nodes are sleeping.

Node Tampering: This attack is done by an adversary who can freely enter to the sensing area and can physically handle sensor nodes (Raymond, 2008). In this case, attacker can simply modify the software in sensor nodes in order to disrupt the operation or can install harmful software to make the sensor node as a new adversary. The attacker may also modify or insert new hardware components for the same purposes. Moreover, the adversary may capture private information such as stored event data, cryptographic data, etc.

This attack can be weak when network includes thousands of sensor nodes considering the fact that it is very time consuming for the adversary to reach each node and to modify them. Regarding this, the first defense mechanism to this attack is camouflaging sensor nodes to increase the physical search time of sensor nodes. This defense technique is very common especially in military applications. On the other hand an intelligent attacker may select critical nodes on data delivery paths to tamper them. In this case a dense deployment of sensor nodes may help to continue data delivery. In addition to these defense mechanisms to prevent data capture, a self-destruction defense mechanism can be implemented on sensor nodes. Furthermore, an encryption mechanism may also be implemented to sensor software in order to protect from software modification. Although this mechanism may not protect node from new software installation, it may prevent easily modification of complicated applications.

Data Link Layer

Link Layer Jamming: In this attack, adversary knows the logics of the link layer protocol and creates collision at the link layer (Law, 2005). The adversary sends link layer packets at data transmission time of the target nodes. By this action, the adversary misinterprets the channel use rules to prevent the legitimate users from accessing to the medium. In contrast to blind attacks in radio jamming, link layer jamming is an intelligent and energy efficient attack that aims to attack at planned times to preserve the energy of the adversary.

In most of the link layer protocols, message schedule is shared by sensor nodes before beginning synchronous data transmission. This provides a common schedule for the nodes involved in data transmission. Although this technique can be useful for communication, it can also cause to leak schedule information to adversary nodes. Thus the first defense mechanism is the encryption of each packet including scheduling information. If single key is used for encryption, then it may be vulnerable to key stealing. If keys are generated between nodes, then energy consumption may be very high. The second defense mechanism is data blurting or schedule switching. In this technique, when a node cannot receive ACK packet from its destination, it changes the communication schedule and announces (Law, 2005). Law (2005) simulated the implementation of this attack together with an appropriate countermeasure in OMNeT++ platform. OMNeT++ is a modular object oriented discrete event network simulator (OMNeT++, 2012). In the attack simulation, 100 nodes are randomly dispersed in test area. These nodes use S-MAC protocol with a duty cycle of 10% at the link layer, TinyDiffusion at the network layer and run TinyOS as the operating system.

Back-off Manipulation: Many data link layer protocol includes a back-off timer to prevent more than one node to access medium at the same time. Back-off timers are usually designed to sleep for randomly chosen times. A node can selfishly choose a small back-off interval in order to sleep less and gain unfair access to the medium (Radosavac, 2007). Famous CSMA-CA based protocols such as IEEE 802.11 and IEEE 802.15.4 are prone to this attack.

This attack is hard to detect in nature because attacker's behavior is hard to be characterized. Attacker can choose any integer for back-off timer, thus it can communicate with the other nodes at any time it wants. A defense mechanism is to check attacker whether it uses truly random numbers for exponential back-off timer (Radosavac, 2007). This mechanism can be executed by an ordinary monitoring node. This defense mechanism is implemented with OPNET simulator which is a high level event based network simulator (OPNET, 2012). Another defense strategy can be encryption of back-off mechanism related protocol packets;

the encryption might not permit selfish attacker to choose small back-off intervals.

Same Nonce Attack: Sensor nodes may store an Access Control List (ACL) which has the list of nodes for communication. Each ACL entry has a destination address, the key, the nonce, and option fields. These fields are used in an encrypted message communication. If the same key and nonce pairs are used within two transmissions, an adversary who obtains those ciphertexts may retrieve useful information (Xiao, 2005).

Same nonce can be occurred in many situations such as sleep mode, power failure, hardware malfunction, etc. Besides, same keys can be occurred when situations such as using broadcasting keys and grouping keys. The defense mechanism to same nonce attack is firstly to add new fields to the message such that separating nonce field from the frame counter (Xiao, 2005), so two fields are both used at the same time. The security of the message is enhanced in this case, but an additional field transmission overhead will be added to the system. The other defense mechanisms are to use timestamp instead of frame counter and dynamically dividing nonce spaces such that different entries with the same key will use different space of nonce values. Xiao (2005) proposed separating nonce field from the field counter and using timestamp instead of frame counter techniques for IEEE 802.15.4 based sensor networks. Nevertheless, these proposed methodologies are explained without their real implementations.

Replay Protection Attack: Replay protection mechanism in IEEE 802.15.4 is used to accept a frame by checking if the counter of the recent message is larger than the previous message. An adversary in a sensor network may target this replay protection mechanism (Xiao, 2005). For example an adversary sends many frames with large counters to an ordinary sensor node. After this attack, the ordinary sensor node will reject the legitimate frames with small counters from other legitimate nodes.

In IEEE 802.15.4, to prevent replay protection attack the frame counter is used. As mentioned in same-nonce attack, the frame counter may cause problems in some situations. To provide sequential freshness, the defense mechanism is to use timestamp instead of frame counter as also mentioned in same-nonce attack. With this mechanism, there will not be a replay counter to be incremented. The drawback of this approach is the increasing message size. Besides a time-synchronization mechanism should be provided. Although there are not given any specific implementation details of these mechanisms, the methodologies of the approaches are noted in (Xiao, 2005).

ACK Attack: Assume a channel is used by two parties where first node sends a data packet, the other node replies with an ACK packet after successful reception of the data packet. In ACK attack, an adversary should firstly eavesdrop the channel of communicating two parties (Xiao, 2005). Then the adversary should block the data packet of the first node to prevent successful packet transmission. Lastly, the adversary generates a fake ACK packet as generated from the first node, and sends this packet to the second node.

ACK frames do not have any integrity protection mechanism. In order to provide this mechanism, Message Integrity Code (MIC) can be appended at the end of the ACK frame (Xiao, 2005). MIC can be obtained by AES-CBC-MAC authentication algorithm provided in IEEE 802.15.4 security suites where whole ACK frame can be used as the authentication field. As replay protection and same nonce attacks, no specific implementation of the countermeasure for ACK attack is given in any specific format.

PANId Conflict Attack: A PANId conflict occurs in a Personal Area Network (PAN) if there exists more than one PAN coordinator operation in same Personal Operating System (POS). PANId conflict attack is created by creating fake conflict messages within a PAN (Sokullu, 2007). In this attack, an adversary may send fake PANId conflict notification messages to overwhelm the PANId coordinator. After PANId coordinator receives PANId conflict notification messages, PAN coordinator executes conflict resolution procedure that prevents the data transmission between PAN coordinator and legitimate nodes at the same time.

In order to defend against PANId conflict attack, the coordinator may simply check two parameters: the conflict count for any node and the maximum conflict count in a deterministic time interval (Sokullu, 2007). If PAN coordinator detects the attacker, it can ignore any packets originating from the adversary node. These rules can be integrated to IEEE 802.15.4 MAC layer protocol. The implementation details of this attack and its defense mechanisms are set up in version 2.34 of ns2 platform, which is a discrete event simulator and developed at ISI, California (Ns2, 2012). Single attacker, double attacker and triple attacker scenarios are implemented within a fixed size star topology with the fixed coordinator parameters.

GTS Attack: PAN coordinator can assign dedicated slots to network devices in IEEE 802.15.4 standards. Guaranteed Time Slot (GTS) is a slot assigned by the coordinator to a device to warrant collision free transmission. The applications with predefined bandwidth requirements can be supported by GTS based communication. In GTS attack, the adversary may disrupt the communication between a device and its PAN coordinator (Sokullu, 2009). The attacker first synchronizes with the PAN coordinator by receiving beacon messages. At the same time attacker may learn the GTS times of the legitimate nodes. To accomplish the GTS attack, the adversary sends data packets at GTS moments in order to create interference and collision. Sequence diagram of this attack is given in Figure 4.

GTS attack is hard to detect and defend. Since the adversary synchronizes its time with the PAN coordinator, the attacker creates collision at exact GTS moments where it is hard to detect by PAN coordinator. In this case, the PAN coordinator cannot perceive the ID of the attacker. On the other hand, if attacker and PAN coordinator do not synchronize in a fine-grained way, the coordinator may detect the attack and extract the ID of the adversary (Sokullu, 2009). But this case is also unrealistic since an intelligent attacker may hide its ID from packets. To derive a defense solution to this attack, we can firstly characterize the basic nature of the GTS attack. In GTS attack, the communication between two legitimate nodes is corrupted by an intelligent and synchronized attacker. From this fact, we may state that attacker behaves like an

Figure 4. GTS attack sequence diagram

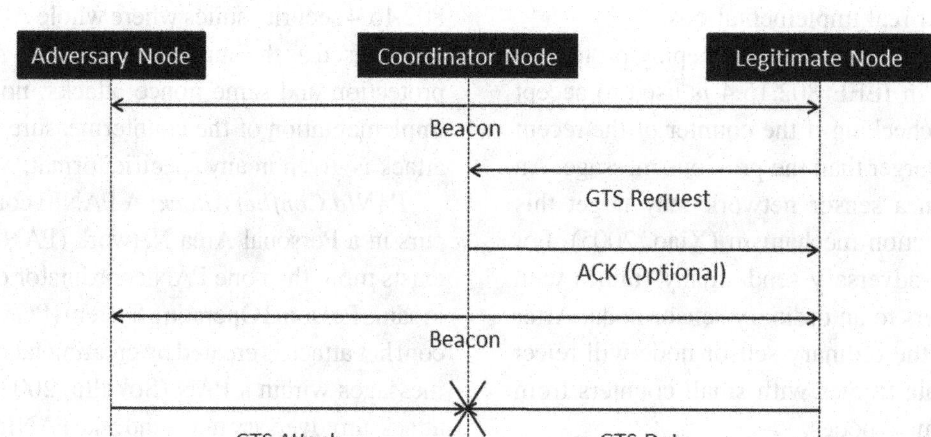

intelligent jammer. So that some defense mechanisms which are covered for jamming can be applied to GTS attack. For example, although it is an expensive solution, different frequencies can be assigned to each node by PAN coordinator for GTS transmission. In this case, adversary should learn frequencies of each transmission. Besides that, the GTS fields in beacon message can be removed not to leak information to adversary. To support this operation, protocol rules should be reorganized. Finally, GTS request messages can be encrypted in order to prevent information leak to the attacker. This encryption technique can be chosen as asymmetric key cryptography if total node count in a PAN is small. In this small sized star topology case, memory allocation for public keys will not be a problem. Conversely, symmetric key cryptography will probably be more suitable for large scale sensor networks. As a popular implementation tool for the use of symmetric key cryptography in sensor networks, SPINS (Perrig, 2004) can be chosen since it provides broadcast authentication, two-party authentication, data confidentiality and integrity. We think that using SPINS in the countermeasure implementation of GTS attack is appropriate because the focus point of the defense involves the communication with base station (PAN coordinator).

Unintelligent Replay Attack: In this attack type, the attacker sends recorded events into the network in order to prevent nodes from entering to the sleeping state, thus the adversary causes significant energy consumption (Pawar, 2012). If sensor nodes do not have anti-replay mechanism, the previously sent data messages are redelivered into the network. Because of this operation, network-wide energy consumption increases. This attack causes both local and global waste of energy.

The defense mechanism is the anti-replay protection technique. In this technique, sequence numbers are tracked as packets arrive. As mentioned previously in replay protection attack, timestamps may be used instead of sequence numbers to provide sequential freshness.

Unauthenticated Broadcast Attack: The adversary knows MAC rules in this attack, but cannot penetrate the network (Pawar, 2012). The attacker follows the MAC rules and broadcasts unauthenticated traffic into the network. These packets consume the energy of nodes in two ways: Energy consumption from radio transmission and energy consumption from decreasing sleeping period. This energy consumption reduces the network lifetime. To defend against this attack, schedule switching and spread spectrum communication may be used. Another idea as a general defense solution is using encryption. Protocol packets can be encrypted in order to prevent leaking of schedule information from legitimate nodes. However, encrypting all packets adds so much extra cost to the whole system. An indirect solution, which mainly changes the context of this attack and the view of the communication to the attacker, may be to use authentication in only broadcast messages. Authenticated broadcast problem have been attractive for the sensor network researchers and its more energy constrained implementation may still be seen as an open issue. A very popular implementation tool for the authentication for data broadcast in sensor networks is μTesla, which is one of the main secure components of SPINS (Perrig, 2004).

Full Domination Attack: The adversary knows MAC rules in this attack and can penetrate the network in contrast to unauthenticated broadcast attack (Pawar, 2012). The attacker follows the MAC rules and produces trusted traffic to gain maximum benefit. This attack is very dangerous since attacker intelligently uses all protocol rules in a selfish manner. One or more attacker nodes can participate in full domination attack. The defense mechanism for full domination attack is not unique and depends on the attack type. For example, similar to defense mechanism of unauthenticated broadcast attack, protocol packets can be encrypted not to leak information to attacker.

Exhaustion (Interrogation) Attack: The exhaustion attacks are applicable on WSN when nodes use

MAC protocols based on Request To Send (RTS) and Clear To Send (CTS) packet exchanges. In this type of MAC protocol, a sender node initiates the data transmission by sending a RTS packet. The receiver node receives RTS packet and replies with a CTS packet. Any other node receiving RTS and CTS messages cannot send data and waits for a period of time. This approach solves the hidden node problem in wireless ad hoc networks. In this attack, the adversary node sends RTS packets repeatedly (Raymond, 2008). The RTS receiver node replies with CTS packets repeatedly causing energy consumption and exhaustion of its battery.

The defense mechanism for this attack can be similar with PANId conflict attack's defense mechanism. The receiver node may check the RTS count and maximum RTS count in order to detect exhaustion attack. If receiver node finds that RTS count exceeds maximum RTS count, it decides sender node is an attacker and it can ignore any packets originating from that adversary. Since RTS and CTS packets are small in size, using an encryption will not be a convenient countermeasure suggestion for this attack.

Routing Layer

Trust Related Attacks and Defense Mechanisms

Reputation is simply the idea about trustworthiness of an entity about another entity. Historical knowledge affects the entity to have positive, negative or neutral thought for the intended element. In daily life, people make good connections with whom they have good reputations about. The amount of reputation implies having a trust level about the related person (or entity). Thus, reputation may be concerned as input to calculate trust values. The main notion is to obtain trust values according to trustworthiness of individual nodes by using the collaborative behavioral messages from related node's neighbors (Sun, 2008). So the trust value about a node helps giving a decision to interact with it. In accordance with defense mechanism, nodes with low trust values may be suspected to misbehave.

In WSNs, nodes can produce reputation about other nodes. The increasing positive reputation about a trusted node helps determining a goal as forwarding packets through other nodes in WSN. In a reputation and trust-based system, reputation is recorded and utilized to create trust information where trust affects nodes how to act in the network (Srinivasan, 2008).

In trust-based systems, sensor nodes should be initialized to get starting reputation values. There are three initialization choices for sensor nodes. Firstly, every sensor node can be considered as a trusted node and they trust each other (initially positively reputed nodes). When nodes act in WSN, the reputation of nodes decrease and they can be untrusted by time. Secondly, every sensor node can be considered as an untrusted node and they do not trust each other (initially negatively reputed nodes). When they behave positively their reputation will increase. As the last approach, all nodes are supposed to have neutral reputation (initially neutrally reputed nodes). The interaction of nodes helps them to increase or decrease their reputation values (Srinivasan, 2008).

Sensor nodes can update their reputation with first-hand or second-hand observation. In first-hand observation, nodes directly sense the state changes and update reputation without external effect (direct trust). However, direct trust is calculated by the value of successful interactions between subject node and interacted node. There is a special kind of direct trust named as recommendation trust. Recommendation trust considers direct observations and the recommended nodes from its neighbors. Subject node compares the reputations (good or bad recommendations) supplied by its neighbors with first-hand observations and calculates a trust value. In second-hand observation, subject node tries to discover the trustworthy collaborative nodes to achieve its goal. Therefore, subject node requires the information of neighbor nodes to update its local data (indirect trust). If neighbor nodes send recommendations (positive reputation) about a third node to subject node, indirect trust is provided by trust propagation (Sun, 2008).

In distributed multicast networks, secure authentication and authorization are crucial issues if the members of a multicast group change frequently. To be used in such multicast ad hoc networks, Chang (2008) proposed a two-step secure authentication approach. In the first level, the trust value of each one-hop neighbor is calculated by a Markov chain trust model. In the second level, a node with the highest trust value of a group is chosen and it is labeled as central authentication (CA) server. For reliability issues, node with second highest trust value is selected as backup CA server and secure authentication for group management is formed via trust.

Trust mechanisms look promising in terms of strategic defense approaches. However, there are also trust related attacks at routing layer and the explained followings are some popular ones.

Bad Mouthing Attack: Adversaries supply negative reputation of compromised sensor nodes to the neighboring nodes. The negative reputation from adversaries makes trustworthy sensors calculate the trust value of compromised node negatively (Pathan, 2010). In a WSN including positively or neutrally initialized nodes with second-hand information, sensors can share negative feedback to neighboring nodes and bad mouthing attack may be appeared.

By the viewpoint of subject node, historical recommendations acquired by that node are used for defense mechanism. However, trust is taken into account by good or bad recommendations. In defense mechanism of bad mouthing attack, malicious nodes may be detected using malicious node detection performance metric (Sun, 2008). Each node detects the malicious interacted node locally using Average Detection rate (AVD) and false alarm rate parameters. AVD is calculated dividing total number of nodes in good behavior, which detect malicious nodes, by the set of malicious nodes. False alarm rate is calculated similarly to AVD except changing denominator with the set of good nodes. Sun (2008) shows that recommendation trust approach increases the detection rate of attacks with malicious node detection performance metric. There is a threshold value for trust recommendation which affects trust propagation. If threshold passes a predefined value between two neighbor nodes (A-B) for a trusted path (A-B-C), trust propagation is permitted for the third node from its neighbor (B-C).

Ballot Attack: Ballot attack is the opposite of bad mouthing attack according to adversary's behavior (Pathan, 2010). Adversary supplies positive reputation of compromised nodes to their neighboring nodes. Adversary forwards reputation of malicious or badly reputed nodes to trustworthy nodes positively. In a WSN including negatively or neutrally initialized nodes with second-hand information, nodes can share positive feedback to neighboring nodes and ballot attack may be appeared.

The defense mechanism explained for bad mouthing attack may also be used similarly for ballot attack.

On-Off Attack: In this attack type, adversary behaves in nondeterministic manners not to be detected by the other nodes in WSN (Sun, 2008). Adversary sends alternatively positive and negative reputation values to neighbors. So its misbehavior cannot be detected easily and negative reputation values can be distributed to WSN for a long time before detection. The trust value for the adversary node may dynamically change.

As a countermeasure, the trust value should be weighted during a timeline using a parameter named as forgetting factor. Forgetting factor is based on observing the good actions for different time intervals. On-Off attack's defense mechanism uses the social life rules. Being a trustable entity takes a long time while decreasing that reliability happens in a short period. Therefore, forgetting factor should be defined adaptively for the periods of good and bad behaviors (adaptive forgetting scheme) (Sun, 2008).

Newcomer Attack: In initially positive or neutral reputed node manner, reputation of adversaries decreases by time with their hazardous behavior to other nodes. Thus they may not attend routing links and act as a passive entity in the network. To erase its bad reputation and perform actively, adversary may rejoin the network as a newcomer and starts functioning with an initial reputation. Attack of reentering the network with a new ID is also called as whitewasher attack (Lopez, 2010). Attacker may also impersonate or compromise nodes to erase its bad history to be known as a trusted node. If adversary is able to reenter the system repeatedly, detection of untrusted nodes becomes meaningless and defense mechanism in the system should be redesigned.

Authentication and access control are the main concerns to defend against newcomer attack. Therefore new nodes may not reenter continuously to the network by getting new IDs. As another approach, if newcomers have initially negative reputation values and have to behave positively for a long time, this may help decreasing their attacking behavior. Lastly, "pay their dues" approach for a node is based on supplying more service than it receives (Hoffman, 2009). So adversary node should continually behave positively to stay its trust value high for obtaining the service that it needs to acquire.

As a tool to be used for protecting the nodes against bad mouthing and newcomer attacks, a trust evaluation scheme is simulated for Mobile Ad Hoc Networks (MANETs) on a self-organized virtual trust network (Misaghi, 2012). To disseminate the trust information through nodes, each node periodically exchanges its trust network with its neighbors. Each node creates a virtual layer to keep trust information of other networks. That information should be obtained by direct or indirect trust approaches. Trustworthiness for the network of the node is computed locally. Performance and effectiveness of the scheme is evaluated with ns2 (Ns2, 2012). The simulation environment covers 100 trustworthy and malicious nodes using IEEE 802.11 with Distributed Coordination Function (DCF) as MAC protocol. For bad mouthing attack and newcomer attack, the scheme may resist up to 10% attackers of whole nodes.

Conflicting Behavior Attack: Adversary behaves differently to different group of nodes. So different nodes have different reputations for the attacker and inconsistent trust values between different groups of nodes occur. While on-off attack is concerned on the unnoticed misbehaviors in time domain, conflicting behavior attack determines the inconsistent behavior in node domain (Yu, 2012). Figure 5 shows a conflicting behavior attack scenario. Node A behaves good to Node C and forwards the packets coming from C. However, Node A misbehaves to Node B and does not forward its packets. When Node B and Node C share their reputations about Node A, there will be conflict on their values and they will not trust each other anymore.

In this attack mechanism, the adversary node drops the packets of a group of nodes (GNd) and routes packets of another group of nodes (GNr) successfully. Attack percentage is defined by the division of GNd to total number of nodes (Sun, 2008). If attack percentage is low, honest recommendations of attacker make it a trustable node. If it keeps its honesty for a period of time, attacker detection will be difficult. If attack percentage is high and malicious node continues sending bad recommendations to its neighbors, attacker can be easily detected. If attacker does not want to be detected easily in the network, it does not interact in the network intensely.

Intelligent Behavior Attack: Attacker tries to detect the important information like reputation values or trust ranking in the messages and it adapts its behavior according to that information (Yu, 2012).

To defend against this attack, messages may be encrypted and just the destination node may be permitted to read the content of the message.

Figure 5. A sample scenario for conflicting behavior attack

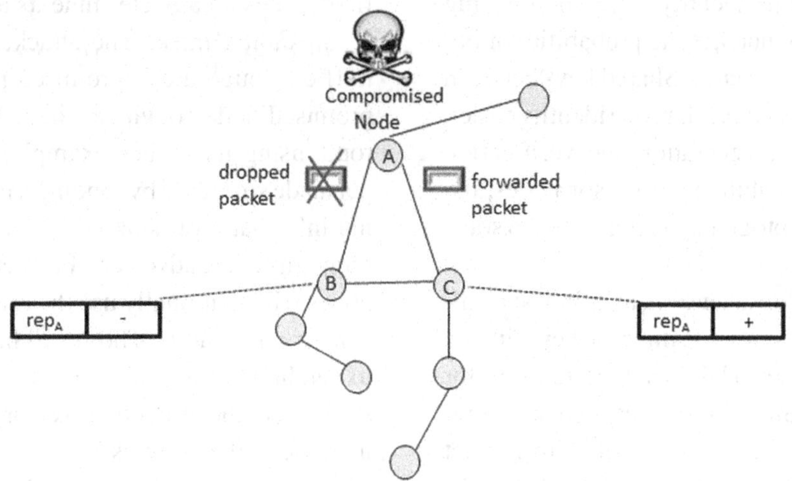

Thus, the nodes whose goal is forwarding messages may not be aware of the data inside the message and the attacker may not impair the network as long as it does not compromise destination node.

Other Routing Attacks and Defense Mechanisms

Identity Spoofing Attack: In identity spoofing attack, an adversary may capture sensor nodes, replicate them and put them to planned locations in network (Parno, 2005). This may cause disconnection of the network topology and routing cycles. As countermeasures to identity spoofing attack, two distributed techniques can be used (Parno, 2005). In randomized multicast technique, node location information is distributed to randomly-selected witnesses, to exploit the birthday paradox. The other technique is line-selected multicast where topology of the network is used to select witnesses for a node's location and to detect identity spoofed nodes.

HELLO Flood Attack: In some routing protocols of WSNs, announcing the node to its neighbors is realized by broadcasting HELLO packets. Therefore, the sensors which receive radio message from the broadcaster node will assume that node as a neighbor. In reality, adversary node may have a large transmission power to convince the nodes to use itself as a routing node. If the base station is compromised by the adversary, convinced nodes of WSN will send their packets to a geographically further located adversary and the whole network may be in a complicated state (Singh, 2010).

A defense mechanism against HELLO flood attacks is defined as multi-path routing to multi-base stations (Hamid, 2006). In this approach, node authentication is used between regular nodes and multiple base stations. All of the base stations are assigned with the specific keys shared by the ordinary nodes. According to Karlof (2002), a bidirectional link between nodes should be constructed to verify the message traffic. Therefore messages may just be forwarded through this link. A trustworthy sink node defines limitations for verified neighbors of each node to control a large network configuration. Singh (2010) also proposed a detection and prevention method for HELLO flood attack. Nodes that have known radio range strength classify neighbor nodes as "friend" or "stranger" according to the signal quality. If a node is labeled as stranger, it is tried to be verified by client puzzles. However, the puzzles get more complicated with increasing number of non-replied HELLO messages to verify the suspected node's trustworthiness.

Sybil Attack: Adversary node enters the system with more than one identity by compromising different nodes to increase the probability of being chosen on many routes. Shared keys between nodes enable having more than one identity easier. Although signature generation and verification are beyond the capabilities of sensor nodes, using public key cryptography is suggested to solve this problem.

An approach for defense is as follows: Ordinary nodes share a unique symmetric key with the sink node and those nodes create session keys for confidential communication between neighbor nodes (Karlof, 2002). Sink's goal is to restrict the number of neighbors for a node and an error message is sent when the limit is exceeded. If a node is compromised by an attacker, it just may interact with verified number of neighbors, not the whole network. So the negative effect of the attacker to whole network can be reduced until adversary does not create a wormhole which precipitates a verified neighbor having a virtual neighbor.

Newsome (2004) proposed radio resource testing which assumes that every physical device has a radio that may not use different channels simultaneously for message transfer. The node assigns different channels for each of its neighbors (if there are enough channels) to prove the identity of neighbors. Probabilistically, it broadcasts messages to different channels and listens to the related channel to verify the neighbor. If the node does not have enough channels, it may not cover all the neighbor nodes and Sybil node may affect the network indifferently. At this condition, a random subset of nodes and channels are chosen to listen to the traffic for increasing the probability of adversary node detection.

Lazos (2004) proposed a cryptographic and localization based approach for finding the correct position of the node as long as the locator node is not compromised. Sensor encrypts a nonce with pairwise key and concatenates its ID for each locator and then broadcasts those messages to the network. Since the closest located node replies firstly, sensor can determine its actual location.

Sinkhole Attack: The attacker tries to direct traffic through a compromised node. The compromised node convinces the neighbor nodes to route using itself. For example, adversary may persuade sink node by sending a fake quality routing information if sink node does not verify the reliability of the adversary. Furthermore, neighbor nodes will continually use the route that includes compromised node. Those neighbors will inform its neighbors with positive reputation about adversary where the effect of adversary will gradually increase in the network.

Krontiris (2007) proposed an intrusion detection mechanism in which each node has its Intrusion Detection System (IDS) client. These clients monitor the traffic with the owner node's neighbors. The monitoring process is based on the detection of anomaly behaviors by the rules defined for each node. If anomaly detection is observed by a sensor node, a cooperative mechanism should be enacted for decision of attack with neighboring nodes.

Wormhole Attack: Attackers store the transmitted packets by the legitimate nodes in the network and replays them into the network through the "low-latency out-of-bound" channel (Yu, 2012). Out-of-bound channel, which may not be perceptible by the network, makes detection hard. Wormhole attack is especially harmful at neighborhood discovery phase of a node. Attacker node Y replays the routing request packet of node X to a non-neighbor node Z that causes an unreal neighborhood link.

Karlof (2002) proposed a routing protocol based on the exchange of coordinate information for routing of geographically indicated packets. The packets which are assumed to be forwarded from neighbor nodes may be detected as suspicious if the geographical position information is far from expected. This approach requires the position of node's own location, one-hop neighbors and the location of destination.

Fake Route Information Attack and Blackhole Attack: In fake route information attack, adversary node advertises routing information that the shortest path is routed through itself. Additionally, blackhole attacker drops those received messages.

REWARD is a routing method to obtain a distributed database for the black hole attack in the network (Karakehayov, 2005). This algorithm uses MISS and SAMBA broadcast messages for algorithm utilization. For route discovery, when destination receives a query, it sends its location and waits for new packets. If destination node does not receive a packet in a defined time slot, it sends a MISS broadcast message, which includes the list of the querying nodes' names until that time. The names listed in this message are suspicious nodes which may act as blackhole attackers. Nodes in the network collect those MISS messages and compare the information with their lists to be aware of adversary nodes. On the other hand, SAMBA messages provide suspicious locations of the candidate adversary nodes.

Greyhole (Selective Forwarding) Attack: In this attack, adversary nodes do not forward certain type of messages and drop those packets to prevent dissemination of them anymore. To decrease the suspicion on itself, the attacker selects and modifies the contents of desired packets while others are forwarded unchanged.

If the compromised node is located near the sink node, it may attend data flow directly. According to Karlof (2002), multipath routing is a defense mechanism for this attack. A probabilistic defense mechanism is designed for protection using n different routes that include disjoint nodes even if more than n compromised nodes exist in the network.

Transport Layer

SYN Flood Attack: SYN flood is a kind of Denial of Service (DoS) attack that attacker creates huge number of half-opened (uncompleted handshaking) TCP connections with a node. A sample sequence diagram for this attack is drawn in Figure 6. Three way handshaking is used to prove that two nodes are ready to make a TCP communication. For this attack, handshaking process never ends between the adversary and the chosen node which means ACK message does not reach to victim node. Adversary learns the return addresses obtained from SYN-ACK packets replied to large number of SYN packets. Victim node starts waiting for beginning the connection by getting the adversary node's message although it will never come. The nodes store the connection requests in a limited size buffer and the buffer will overflow after some number of unsuccessful connection attempts. Therefore, victim node may not accept any more valid connections.

The defense mechanism for this attack is SYN cookies technique. With this technique, connection requests are not kept in target side and the buffer overflow of victim node may be prevented. Responder encodes the SYN message's information and sends it back to requestor to give the responsibility of holding the state (Raymond, 2008).

Session Hijacking: Adversary node captures the session information between victim and target. Adversary spoofs the victim's IP address and the message sequence numbers. Then it may continue session with sending correct sequence numbered messages to target with acting as regularly communicated node. Therefore victim node may not be aware of the interruption of session.

Although the usual sensor networks are not based on the use of sessions, in the context of studying the use of IP-based sensor networks, this attack may be a threat. A kind of lightweight protocol providing the Secure Socket Layer (SSL) services may be used as a defense approach. Jung (2009) performed such a protocol for IP-WSN regarding key exchange, authentication and data encryption on their developed sensor node hardware.

Desynchronization Attack: Attacker interrupts an active connection and sends fake sequence numbered messages to connected nodes. Then the synchronization of message is disrupted and the

Figure 6. SYN flood attack sequence diagram

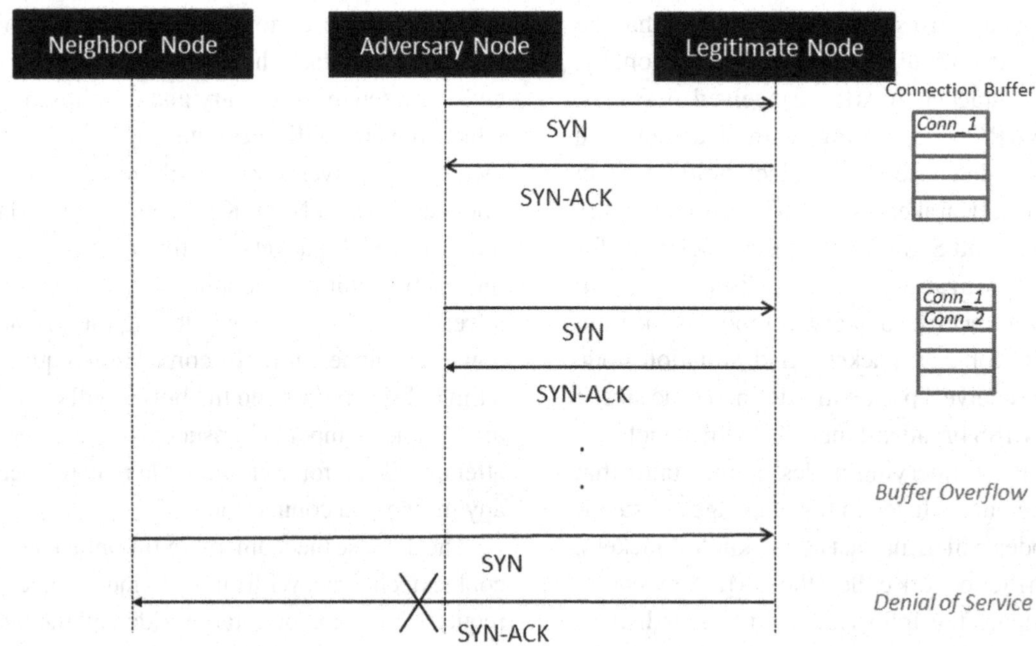

nodes start retransmitting packets. Authentication of headers or full packets may prevent desynchronization attack (Raymond, 2008).

Application Layer

Overwhelming Sensor Nodes: An adversary node may generate application messages to overwhelm sensor nodes (Raymond, 2008). By applying this attack, network bandwidth is decreased, energy consumption is increased and lifetime of the network is reduced. The adversary can realize this attack if the application is dynamic in nature. For example target tracking application is a dynamic application that uses motion detection mechanism. In contrast to target tracking, a periodical heat measurement application is static and it is not suitable for overwhelming the sensor nodes attack. To defend against this attack, efficient data aggregation algorithms can be used (Raymond, 2008). The aim of this defense technique is to reduce the message count disseminated into the network. Encryption of application layer packets can also be a solution for especially newcomer attackers.

Path-Based DoS Attack: In this attack type, an adversary leaf node injects replayed application messages into the network (Raymond, 2008). This causes forwarding of these messages along the path to the sink node. Hence, the total energy of the network is consumed and network lifetime is reduced. Besides bandwidth for legitimate traffic can be reduced because the attack causes resource consumption on the path to the sink node. The defense mechanisms of path-based DoS attack are packet authentication and anti-replay protection. An alternative method can be packet encryption.

Reprogramming Attack: Sensor nodes can be remotely reprogrammed by protocols such as TinyOS's Deluge (Raymond, 2008). Considering the fact that many sensor network applications are operating on harsh conditions, remotely reprogramming is reasonable. But most of the systems are assumed to be running on trustworthy environments. This brings vulnerability that systems can be reprogrammed by hijackers where large portions of the networks can be controlled by the attackers. In this case, attacker can reprogram the sensor node to take maximum benefit from the application. The defense mechanism against this attack is using authentication streams for reprogramming. Similar to defense mechanism against node tampering, an encryption mechanism may be implemented to sensor software in order to protect it from reprogramming.

OPEN ISSUES AND FUTURE RESEARCH DIRECTIONS

This section discusses the open research issues in the WSN security. Actually, there may be various suggestions on many subjects for directing the researchers to WSN security area. For example, any effort to propose a different countermeasure technique on any attack described in Section ATTACKS AND DEFENSE MECHANISMS would be valuable and appreciated by the academia and industry as well. The motivation on searching for a new countermeasure proposal may be as the following: To propose a defense mechanism which brings up at least the same level of security but consumes at most the same amount of energy than that of an existing one. The pros and cons of the defense mechanism, the cost and benefit on securing the system against the corresponding attack should be taken into account at the beginning. In addition, it needs to prepare a well designed timing schedule whether studying and searching for a new defense mechanism is worth or not. If the study time consumed is too long, different communication protocols or mechanisms may be developed meanwhile and the subject of concerned attack may not be a matter then. On the other hand, we explicitly want to mention that studying on the new attacks, defense mechanisms, or counter attacks in WSN is always an open research area since the security of Information Systems is strongly related to the security of the WSN used within. In addition, to study on the alternative trust mechanisms to prevent WSN from any trust related attacks would also be valuable.

Yet another advising section, we prefer to take a general top level view on the security issues in the WSNs. Rather than searching for a specific countermeasure against a specific attack in a WSN, we suggest the WSN security researchers to work for a general approach to secure the whole sensor network infrastructure that will provide a secure communication service in the network. It is worth spending effort to the theoretical and practical studies that may come up with solutions to any security issues in WSN. On this motivation, we focus on the general view approaches and defense mechanisms for the communication in the network that seem promising for the future of sensor networks to be used practical and secure within the Information Systems.

Privacy Homomorphism

The fundamental security services that should be provided in any type of Networked Information Systems which are based on the data distribution over wired and/or wireless communication channels are mainly the followings: confidentiality, integrity, authentication, and freshness. Perrig (2002) emphasizes those services as to be the first requirements of sensor network security. Perrig (2004) notes that secure data aggregation is also a network security service for WSN. Data aggregation is mainly the technique for aggregating the logically same data in physically different data packets to reduce the number of total packets delivered within the network to the sink node. Data aggregation term is also used where in-network processing of data is concerned and when the result of gathered data from the sensor nodes is computed at sink as well. On this point, if end-to-end data confidentiality and data aggregation are to be offered in a sensor network, Privacy Homomorphism (PH) is a promising solution.

PH technique supports a set of restricted mathematical modular arithmetic and so computations can be done on encrypted data. With the help of PH use, any node in the sensor network encrypts the sensed data (confidentiality service) and forwards it to a neighbor node on the path where the sink is targeted to, the forwarding nodes can process and aggregate the received encrypted messages without decrypting (data aggregation via PH method) and sends the new aggregated message in encrypted format. In-network processing through data aggregation is sustained till the sink is reached. Only the sink node decrypts (end-to-end confidentiality service) and recovers the result data in the packet using PH rules. By without decrypting the messages at the intermediary nodes, the total energy of those nodes will be conserved and so the network life time can be prolonged. By reducing the packet number in the network delivered along the sink path, not only the communication bandwidth will be conserved but the total energy consumption to send and receive packets will be decreased as well.

PH is a mathematical base for homomorphic encryption approaches. In a homomorphic encryption scheme that supports data aggregation via PH and so allows modular arithmetic operations on encrypted data, the encryption and the decryption techniques are based on the privacy homomorphic transformations to preserve the privacy. An encryption algorithm E() is homomorphic if given ciphertexts E(x) and E(y), E(x OPERATOR y) could be obtained without decrypting them for some operation OPERATOR. In this manner, a privacy homomorphic transformation is operatively homomorphic on the ciphertext. If the OPERATOR is the addition operator on rings, the transformation scheme is called as additively homomorphic; whereas the transformation is called as multiplicatively homomorphic if the OPERATOR is multiplication. More clearly as in Westhoff (2006), a privacy homomorphic encryption scheme can be denoted as in the following formula:

$$x \text{ OPERATOR } y = Dk[Ek(x) \text{ OPERATOR } Ek(y)]$$

After the PH had first been investigated by Rivest (1978) and had been mathematically proven that it is prone to ciphertext-only attacks, there have been many researches on its use in different areas. In Domingo-Ferrer (1996) and Domingo-Ferrer (2002) the homomorphic encryption mechanisms based on PH were proposed for the first time. Then, Girao (2004) introduced the concealed data aggregation concept which facilitates data aggregation by homomorphic encryption in WSN. Some alternative methods for the aggregation of encrypted data in WSN through PH were also proposed by Castelluccia (2005) and Castelluccia (2007). Yet another asymmetric homomorphic encryption technique with a performance analysis for an application-specific scenario for tree based WSN is presented by Viejo (2011). All those publications have focused on the use of PH in WSNs from a particular point of view. When they concentrated on a general application, they could not probably extend the solution to all different topologies; likewise, when they concentrated on general topologies including the tree-based WSN infrastructures they could only propose solution to specific application scenarios.

Nevertheless, the researchers have been trying to offer solutions to the drawbacks in the use of homomorphic encryption in WSN. There are still many open issues to carry on research on this subject; with this motivation the followings may be the research directions: Number theoretical restrictions on the functional operators, such as addition, multiplication, mixed operation; the investigations on the resilient (Wagner, 2004) and precise calculations on data aggregation; homomorphic encryption techniques operating on the real number data instead of only integer data; facilitating the tree based WSN hierarchies instead of only star networks or cluster-based WSN topologies; last but not least, any new proposal of or any extension modification to concealed data aggregation mechanisms based on PH.

As considering the first challenge issue of the energy constrained networks to be the network lifetime and another challenge issue of the wireless networks to be the secure data communication, the academia have been studying the PH use for data aggregation in WSNs over a decade now and it still seems to be an open research issue for academia and the industry as well in the coming years.

Overhearing

Conceptually, overhearing a packet in a wireless network may help a node to monitor the communication around it. Terminology of overhearing may refer to the behavior of either an adversary or a legitimate node. From the perspective of the adversaries, overhearing is a general behavior of passive or active attackers of hearing the wireless communication between the legitimate sensor nodes without their awareness. From the view of the legitimate sensor nodes, overhearing may be used for securing the transmission between the neighbor nodes; in this manner, the nodes themselves can monitor their own packets when routed by their corresponding forwarding nodes. In this section the overhearing issue is discussed for its help on detection of any modification on the forwarding packet where all sensor nodes know that some part of the neighboring nodes knowingly overhear their packets at their forwarding time.

There have been many researches in wireless networks literature that use overhearing concept for the benefit of the total energy consumption of the network. One of them, (Lim, 2005) studied on the appropriate balance in overhearing amounts. Overhearing may be used in favor of underlying routing protocol of the MANETs, however overhearing by any node at any time in an uncontrolled way will probably give a poor communication design regarding to the energy cost. Lim (2005) proposed a randomized communication mechanism by which the set of nodes and the amount of overheard transmissions are to be balanced in MANETs. Lim (2005) compared their scheme against the power saving mechanism and on-demand power management protocol of IEEE 802.11 and showed that their proposal is more energy efficient in terms of both total energy consumption and the energy consumption variance among the nodes.

Brownfield (2006) and Le (2007) also suggested controlling the message overhearing to facilitate the MAC protocol of WSNs for energy savings. Brownfield (2006) proposed in their Gateway MAC (GMAC) protocol to reduce the number of sensor nodes overhearing by controlling the transmission requests and also transition times to sleep state among nodes. GMAC also suggests extra energy prevention by preventing nodes to overhear unrelated control messages and so allowing them to be able to sleep for longer times regarding to their duty cycle. OBMAC (Le, 2007) is another MAC proposal based on overhearing use. Le (2007) suggested overhearing use to reduce the number of redundant transmissions in the sensor network and to prolong the network lifetime, and also showed with simulations that OBMAC outperforms the standard IEEE 802.15.4 MAC protocol regarding to energy consumption. Iima (2009) and Kanzaki (2010) proposed overhearing based data aggregation method for WSNs using data interpolation. ODAS (Iima, 2009) uses the spatial data interpolation, and the nodes only send their actual data after comparing it to the previous overheard values and unless they decide that there is trivial information in terms of spatial redundancy. ODAST (Kanzaki, 2010) proposes to reduce the total number of transmitted packets using not only the spatial but also the temporal correlation of sensed data based on the previous overheard communication around. However, processing the sensed payload data in the overheard messages might give a delay to the whole system. The investigation of overhearing use in delay-tolerant systems might also be another research subject.

As a common property of the above mentioned studies, overhearing may be used in sensor networks to lead higher energy efficiencies. Any contribution to this subject would be appreciated by the academia and industry since energy efficiency is the first concern of such resource constrained networks. As stated before, the security services have also been the requirements for WSN. Not only for their military based applications but also for the integration of WSNs into any Information System using critical private data, any contribution proposals to the security of the WSN are worth to work on. In this motivation, it is needed to state that overhearing may facilitate the security of the transmitted data to make sure that the forwarded packets are monitored and any modification of the forwarded packets are detected. On the other side, primitive security services such as confidentiality through encryption, authentication and integrity through hash chains may be used in WSNs. Overhearing is not mentioned here as to take place of those services. Nevertheless, overhearing may be seen as another concept to help for reliable communication between the nodes. The scenario is mainly as follows: A node first sends a packet to its parent on the path to the sink node, secondly overhears that packet within the time interval when the parent forwards it to the grandparent. In this scheme, there may also be used encryption or any other service. However, if overheard packet is required to be processed to read the data, it would take much energy consumption on the nodes. There may be used any service that does not require to process the overheard data for their actual meaning. Even, the privacy homomorphic encryption techniques for data aggregation may be used. The forwarding packet may be checked with the previous sent and stored packet in physical bit level without considering the logical meaning of data. The only restriction for theoretical use of overhearing and deciding if the packet is modified is to consciously not change the packet in the protocol. If it's decided that the overheard packet is modified compared to the previous sent packet, a fault will be detected. Detection and recovery mechanisms of such faults are also some other research directions. After a monitoring time period passes, reputation-based trust can be established between the node and its overheard parent according to the observed behavior of the parent. This reputation mechanism may also lead to a framework for the reliable transmission based on overhearing. These are all significant overhearing based issues to research over.

Sensor nodes using the standard IEEE802.15.4 MAC layer protocol consume already a significant amount of their energy for listening. When used, the overhearing presents extra energy consumption for the nodes. To prevent uncontrolled energy consumption due to overhearing at any time and in anywhere, at some times of the communication and/or in some parts of the network the overhearing can be used. Working for optimizing the overhearing use in WSNs may lead to some other valuable solutions. There may also be used probabilistic overhearing mechanisms in which a node occasionally overhears its transmitted packets in terms of a ratio and the parent always behaves as it is monitored in all transmissions since the parent cannot understand overhearing and the ratio is not clearly known by the parent.

Another problematic issue on using overhearing mechanisms in wireless and resource constrained networks is synchronization. Time synchronization problem in WSN has always been a main challenge to solve. Here the issue is not about the general time synchronization in the network, it's partially about the time synchronization between two nodes, child and parent. When the parent forwards the data to grandparent located on the path to the sink, child overhears the same packet. In order to succeed to receive the correct packet at correct time the child requires the forwarding time of its parent. Such a system may be established via a scheduling plan. The scheduling plan may statically be given to each node before network deployment. Instead, as generally sensors are deployed without full control mechanisms on their locations, it's better to use a self organizing communication scheduling mechanism based on the topology of the network. The scheduling plan may be designed in a type of time division approach and the communication may be kept on a TDMA based structure. By this way, at the establishment phase for a self organized WSN, every node can learn its scheduling plan to send, receive, forward and also learn the parent's corresponding forwarding interval to overhear. In contrast, CSMA based infrastructures may also be used dynamically later at any time in any part of the network; whereas the cost of overhearing together with contention would be higher energy consumption. To the authors, these are seen as future research directions about the optimal use of overhearing in WSN.

Integrating IPv6 to WSN

A usual WSN is consisted of massive sensor nodes working for the common objectives in a self organized manner and a sink node as the base station. Such a WSN has a kind of autonomous structure internally. The WSN can be integrated to the external networks (any private or public network of an Information System or the global Internet) through its sink node as being a gateway connection. In some application-specific cases multiple sinks may also be used. The global world uses Internet Protocol as a general routing layer standard, whereas the WSN uses one of various WSN routing protocols based on the application. The general standards for the WSN only define the physical and MAC interfaces for the nodes, but no standard definition is offered for the upper layers. Considering the exchange of the information between the WSN and its integrated IP based network the packet frame formats need to be tuned and a negotiation is required unless the payload of one frame format is fully captured and then recapsulated in the other format. On this motivation, any research on the integration of any different kind of network to WSN and providing their coexistence in ubiquitous environments would be a valuable asset for the pervasive computing.

Indeed, the node devices use IEEE 802.15.4 MAC layer as the standard link layer protocol, which has a specific protocol frame regarding a wireless link throughput of 250 kbps at most (IEEE Std 802.15.4TM-2003). WSN applications consider this and prefer using any convenient routing protocol taking care of not only bandwidth limitation but energy constraint as well. IP packets are not able to be forwarded directly in WSN. It requires a kind of compression on the IP packets to be encapsulated in IEEE 802.15.4 MAC frame. Today the IP packets are considered as both IPv4 and IPv6 structures, the latter is the recent version that expands the IP address notation to 128 bits from 32 bits. The initial deliverables of the standardization process of the Internet Engineering Task Force (IETF) about supporting IPv6 packets over IEEE 802.15.4 networks have been published as RFC 4944 (Montenegro, 2007). The recommendation proposal has been updated in 2011 as RFC 6282 (Hui, 2011) to specify IPv6 header compression format for IPv6 datagrams to be transmitted in IEEE 802.15.4-based networks.

Although the efforts on transmission of IPv6 packets on sensor networks are valuable as the emerging technology is to use IPv6 in the global Internet, there are still open issues for WSN in terms of security considerations. In RFC 4944, it is suggested that the security services provided inherently by IEEE 802.15.4 standard MAC protocol are to be used on the frame data if possible. However, that might not be practical for some applications in terms of the total energy consumption and the network lifetime. It would be an important research to categorize the criteria that require using link layer security service capabilities in 802.15.4-based applications. Another issue stated in RFC 4944 is that the full function devices (FFD) in 802.15.4-based personal area networks may communicate with off-link IPv6 peers and such IPv6 devices may use Transmission Layer Security (TLS) protocol services to secure their communication. TLS mainly aims to provide the security services for an end-to-end secure communication to prevent eavesdropping, tampering, or message forgery. It would not be a big problem for the IPv6 devices to handle a type of TLS mechanism since those devices have no energy limitations. However to handle the similar issues in the sensor devices would lead too much power consumption. In addition to the defense mechanisms to eavesdropping, tampering, or any other attacks defined in Section ATTACKS AND DEFENSE MECHANISMS, those corresponding TLS capabilities may be investigated to be arranged for sensor networks which do not cover a specific transport layer. Taking care of the energy use, similar capabilities could be studied to be handled generally at MAC layer rather than upper layers. As another approach a way of cross layer design involving MAC and network layers could be studied. Reducing this problem to the issue of securing data frame at MAC layer may also lead the researchers to investigate on the optimal use of security services at link layer in WSN.

Emerging Wireless Sensor and Actor Network Problems

WSNs can be used in many applications where distributed sensing and wireless communicants meet the requirements of the application. Although WSN is a very important technology for today's applications, physical actuation to the environment can be needed by emerging applications where static sensor nodes can be inadequate to handle such operations (Nayak, 2010). Wireless sensor and actor networks (WSAN) are emerging technologies for these types of applications in which actuators are introduced into the sensing area in order to physically effect to the system. The actuators interact with the environment to collect information or to make actions. These actuators can be humans, robots, mobile sensors, etc.

Actuator-based approaches can be new solution perspectives for common problems in sensor networks. For example, one of the fundamental issues is covering all the sensing area by the sensing ranges of the nodes, also known as the sensor coverage problem. Another problem is the connectivity in WSNs in which topology should be a single connected component. Any faults in individual nodes may cause to disrupt connectivity and coverage. In this case, intelligent actuators may move to planned locations or may carry sensor nodes to repair connectivity and coverage. Another fundamental problem, data collection can be solved by mobile actuators. Similar to these approaches, mobile robots may execute other complicated algorithms centrally. For example, security services such as security primitives based on asymmetric cryptography which are not suitable for distributed implementation in resource constraint sensor networks can be implemented on mobile robots centrally.

Although actuator usage brings new solution perspectives to common problems in sensor networks, it causes the formation of new vulnerable points. It could be harder to camouflage mobile actors than doing so the ordinary static sensor nodes. This makes WSAN vulnerable to the actor node tampering. A jamming attack performed by a compromised mobile actor node can be much more harmful than the same attack applied by an ordinary node. The harm will also be much larger for the back-off manipulation, same nonce attack, GTS attack, unintelligent replay attack, replay protection attack, ACK attack, PANId conflict attack, identity spoofing attack and reprogramming attack. Considering this fact, all of these attacks should be reevaluated for WSANs.

CONCLUSION

This chapter mainly investigates the security issues in sensor networks via the following two subjects: an updated attack literature survey and the future research directions on open issues in WSN security.

A detailed survey of the known attacks in WSN is given, the categorization of the attacks according to their target layers are drawn, and the probable defense mechanisms in WSN security literature are also outlined. In addition, some possible suggestions as alternative security approaches are given, such as an available defense mechanism is also proposed to be used as a challenge to protect the sensor network from a GTS attack. The content can be seen as a state-of-the-art reference for the attacks and their defense mechanisms in WSN security.

Although many studies have been made on many issues in WSNs, it is emphasized that there are still many challenges to be faced. Especially considering the pervasive technologies, WSN is a potential environment for any Information System in the future of the ubiquitous platforms. There are many open issues to research on. Our chapter focuses on the future directions for security issues in WSN. To be clear, the significant priorities among the research topics in WSN security are stated with their study motivations. The significance of using trust mechanisms in WSN is underlined. Moreover, any alternative defense mechanism to any attack would be worth to focus on if the energy constraint is taken care of. Among many efforts on WSN security issues some current research directions are indicated. Working on the use of privacy homomorphism and homomorphic encryptions for secure data aggregation in WSN is pointed out, studying the use of synchronized overhearing to secure the communication between nodes is suggested, the transmission of IPv6 packets on sensor networks is emphasized, and the emerging wireless sensor and actor network problems are listed.

We believe the chapter is a current and timely reference to the attacks and their countermeasures in WSN, and also calls attention to the future research directions in WSN security.

REFERENCES

Akyildiz, I. F., Su, W., Sankarasubramaniam, Y., & Cayirci, E. (2002). A survey on sensor networks. *IEEE Communications Magazine*, *40*(8), 102–114. doi:10.1109/MCOM.2002.1024422.

Biagioni, E., & Bridges, K. (2002). The application of remote sensor technology to assist the recovery of rare and endangered species. *International Journal of High Performance Computing Applications*, *16*(3). doi:10.1177/10943420020160031001.

Brownfield, M. I. (2006). Energy-efficient wireless sensor network MAC protocol. (Doctoral Dissertation). Virginia Polytechnic Institute and State University. Blacksburg, VA.

Castelluccia, C. (2005). Efficient aggregation of encrypted data in wireless sensor networks. In *Proceedings of MobiQuitous* (pp. 109–117). IEEE Computer Society. doi:10.1109/MOBIQUITOUS.2005.25.

Castelluccia, C. (2007). Securing very dynamic groups and data aggregation in wireless sensor networks. In Proceedings of the IEEE Internatonal Conference on Mobile Adhoc and Sensor Systems, (pp. 1-9). IEEE.

Chan, H., & Perrig, A. (2003). Security and privacy in sensor networks. *IEEE Computer*, *36*(10), 103–105. doi:10.1109/MC.2003.1236475.

Chang, B. J., Kuo, S. L., Liang, Y. H., & Wang, D. Y. (2008). Markov chain-based trust model for analyzing trust value in distributed multicasting mobile ad hoc networks. In Proceedings of the IEEE Asia-Pacific Services Computing Conference, (pp. 156-161). IEEE.

Deng, J., Han, R., & Mishra, S. (2005). Countermeasures against traffic analysis attacks in wireless sensor networks. In Proceedings of the 1st IEEE Conference on Security and Privacy for Emerging Areas in Communication Networks, (pp.113-124). IEEE.

Domingo-Ferrer, J. (1996). A new privacy homomorphism and applications. *Information Processing Letters*, *60*(5), 277–282. doi:10.1016/S0020-0190(96)00170-6.

Domingo-Ferrer, J. (2002). A provably secure additive and multiplicative privacy homomorphism. *Lecture Notes in Computer Science*, *2433*, 471–483. doi:10.1007/3-540-45811-5_37.

Garcia-Hernandez, C. F., Ibarguangoytia-Gonzalez, P. H., Garcia-Hernandez, J., & Perez-Diaz, J. A. (2007). Wireless sensor networks and applications: A survey. *International Journal of Computer Science and Network Security*, *7*(3), 264–273.

Girao, J., Schneider, M., & Westhoff, D. (2004). CDA: Concealed data aggregation in wireless sensor networks. In Proceedings of the ACM Workshop on Wireless Security. ACM Press.

Hamid, A., Rashid, M. O., & Hong, C. S. (2006). Defense against lap-top class attacker in wireless sensor network. In Proceedings of the 8th International Conference on Advanced Communication Technology. IEEE.

Hoffman, K., Zage, D., & Nita-Rotaru, C. (2009). A survey of attack and defense techniques for reputation systems. *ACM Computing Surveys*, *42*(1). doi:10.1145/1592451.1592452.

Hui, J., & Thubert, P. (2011). Compression format for IPv6 datagrams over IEEE 802.15.4-based networks. IETF Request for Comments (RFC): 6282. Retrieved April 20, 2012, from http://tools.ietf.org/html/rfc6282

IEEE Std 802.15.4TM-2003. (2003). IEEE standard for information technology-telecommunications and information exchange between systems-local and metropolitan area networks-specific requirements-part 15.4: Wireless medium access control (MAC) and physical layer (PHY) specifications for low-rate wireless personal area networks (WPANs). IEEE.

Iima, Y., Kanzaki, A., Hara, T., & Nishio, S. (2009). Overhearing-based data transmission reduction for periodical data gathering in wireless sensor networks. In Proceedings of the International Workshop on Data Management for Information Explosion in Wireless Networks, (pp. 1048-1053). IEEE.

Jung, W., Hong, S., Ha, M., Kim, Y.-J., & Kim, D. (2009). SSL-based lightweight security of IP-based wireless sensor networks. In Proceedings of the International Conference on Advanced Information Networking and Applications Workshops, (pp. 1112-1117). IEEE.

Kanzaki, A., Iima, Y., Hara, T., & Nishio, S. (2010). Overhearing-based data transmission reduction using data interpolation in wireless sensor networks. In Proceedings of the Fifth International Conference on Mobile Computing and Ubiquitous Networking. IEEE.

Karakehayov, Z. (2005). Using REWARD to detect team black-hole attacks in wireless sensor networks. In Proceedings of the Workshop on Real World Wireless Sensor Networks. IEEE.

Karlof, C., & Wagner, D. (2002). Secure routing in wireless sensor networks: Attacks and countermeasures. In Proceedings of the First IEEE International Workshop on Sensor Network Protocols and Applications, (pp. 113-127). IEEE.

Krontiris, I., Dimitriou, T., & Giannetsos, T. (2007). Intrusion detection of sinkhole attacks in wireless sensor networks. In Proceedings of the 3rd International Conference on Algorithmic Aspects of Wireless Sensor Networks, (pp. 150-161). IEEE.

Law, Y. W., Hartel, P., den Hartog, J., & Havinga, P. (2005). Link-layer jamming attacks on S-MAC. In Proceedings of the Second IEEE European Workshop on Wireless Sensor Networks, (pp. 217-225). IEEE.

Lazos, L., & Poovendran, R. (2004). SeRLoc: Secure range-independent localization for wireless sensor networks. In Proceedings of the 3rd ACM Workshop on Wireless Security, (pp. 21-30). ACM Press.

Le, H.-C., Guyennet, H., & Felea, V. (2007). OB-MAC: An overhearing based MAC protocol for wireless sensor networks. In Proceedings of the International Conference on Sensor Technologies and Applications, (pp. 547-553). IEEE.

Lim, S., Yu, C., & Das, C. R. (2005). Rcast: A randomized communication scheme for improving energy efficiency in MANETs. In Proceedings of the 25th International Conference on Distributed Computing Systems, (pp. 123-132). IEEE.

Lopez, J., Roman, R., Agudo, I., & Fernandez-Gago, C. (2010). Trust management systems for wireless sensor networks: Best practices. *Journal of Computer Communications*, *33*(9), 1086–1093. doi:10.1016/j.comcom.2010.02.006.

Lupu, T. G. (2009). Main types of attacks in wireless sensor networks. In Proceedings of the 9th WSEAS International Conference on Signal, Speech and Image Processing, (pp. 180-185). WSEAS.

Mainwaring, A., Culler, D., Polastre, J., Szewczyk, R., & Anderson, J. (2002). Wireless sensor networks for habitat monitoring. In Proceedings of the 1st ACM International Workshop on Wireless Sensor Networks and Applications. ACM Press.

Misaghi, M., da Silva, E., & Albini, L. C. P. (2012). Distributed self-organized trust management for mobile ad hoc networks. *Communications in Computer and Information Science*, *293*, 506–518. doi:10.1007/978-3-642-30507-8_43.

Montenegro, G., Kushalnagar, N., Hui, J., & Culler, D. (2007). Transmission of IPv6 packets over IEEE 802.15.4 networks. IETF Request for Comments (RFC): 4944. Retrieved April 20, 2012, from http://tools.ietf.org/html/rfc4944

Nayak, A., & Stojmenovic, I. (2010). *Wireless sensor and actuator networks: Algorithms and protocols for scalable coordination and data communication*. New York, NY: Wiley-Interscience. doi:10.1002/9780470570517.

Newsome, J., Shi, E., Song, D., & Perrig, A. (2004). The sybil attack in sensor networks: Analysis and defenses. In Proceedings of the Third International Symposium on Information Processing in Sensor Networks, (pp. 259-268). IEEE.

Ns2. (2012). Website. Retrieved September 5, 2012, from http://www.isi.edu/nsnam/ns/

OMNeT++. (2012). Website. Retrieved September 5, 2012, from http://omnetpp.org/

OPNET. (2012). Website. Retrieved September 5, 2012, from http://www.opnet.com/

Padmavathi, G., & Shanmugapriya, D. (2009). A survey of attacks, security mechanisms and challenges in wireless sensor networks. *International Journal of Computer Science and Information Security*, *4*(1&2).

Parno, B. J. (2005). Distributed detection of node replication attacks in sensor networks. (MSc. Thesis). Carnegie Mellon University. Pittsburgh, PA.

Pathan, A. S. K. (Ed.). (2010). *Security of self-organizing networks: MANET, WSN, WMN, VANET*. Boca Raton, FL: CRC Press. doi:10.1201/EBK1439819197.

Pawar, P. M., Nielsen, R. H., Prasad, N. R., Ohmori, S., & Prasad, R. (2012). Behavioral modeling of WSN MAC layer security attacks: A sequential UML approach. *Journal of Cyber Security and Mobility*, *1*(1), 65–82.

Perrig, A., Stankovic, J., & Wagner, D. (2004). Security in wireless sensor networks. *Communications of the ACM*, *47*(6), 53–57. doi:10.1145/990680.990707.

Perrig, A., Szewczyk, R., Tygar, J. D., Wen, V., & Culler, D. E. (2002). SPINS: Security protocols for sensor networks. *Wireless Networks*, *8*(5), 521–534. doi:10.1023/A:1016598314198.

Radosavac, S., Crdenas, A. A., Baras, J. S., & Moustakides, G. V. (2007). Detecting IEEE 802.11 MAC layer misbehavior in ad hoc networks: Robust strategies against individual and colluding attackers. *Journal of Computer Security*, *15*(1), 103–128.

Raymond, D. R., & Midkiff, S. F. (2008). Denial-of-service in wireless sensor networks: Attacks and defenses. *IEEE Pervasive Computing / IEEE Computer Society [and] IEEE Communications Society*, *7*(1), 74–81. doi:10.1109/MPRV.2008.6.

Rivest, R. L., Adleman, L., & Dertouzos, M. L. (1978). On data banks and privacy homomorphisms. In *Foundations on Secure Computation* (pp. 169–179). New York, NY: Academia Press.

Schwiebert, L., Gupta, S. K. S., & Weinmann, J. (2001). Research challenges in wireless networks of biomedical sensors. In Proceedings of the 7th Annual International Conference on Mobile Computing and Networking, (pp. 151-165). New York, NY: ACM.

Sen, J. (2009). A survey on wireless sensor network security. *International Journal of Communication Networks and Information Security*, *1*(2), 55–78.

Sharma, S., & Jena, S. K. (2011). A survey on secure hierarchical routing protocols in wireless sensor networks. In Proceedings of the International Conference on Communication, Computing & Security, (pp. 146-151). IEEE.

Singh, V. P., Jain, S., & Singhai, J. (2010). Hello flood attack and its countermeasures in wireless sensor networks. *International Journal of Computer Science*, *7*(3), 23–27.

Sokullu, R., Dagdeviren, O., & Korkmaz, I. (2008). On the IEEE 802.15.4 MAC layer attacks: GTS attack. In Proceedings of the Second International Conference on Sensor Technologies and Applications, (pp. 673-678). IEEE.

Sokullu, R., Korkmaz, I., & Dagdeviren, O. (2009). GTS attack: An IEEE 802.15.4 MAC layer attack in wireless sensor networks. *IARIA International Journal on Advances in Networks and Services*, *2*(1), 104–114.

Sokullu, R., Korkmaz, I., Dagdeviren, O., Mitseva, A., & Prasad, N. R. (2007). An investigation on IEEE 802.15.4 MAC layer attacks. In Proceedings of the International Symposium on Wireless Personal Media Communications. IEEE.

Srinivasan, A., Teitelbaum, J., Liang, H., Wu, J., & Cardei, M. (2008). Reputation and trust-based systems for ad hoc and sensor networks. In Boukerche, A. (Ed.), *Algorithms and Protocols for Wireless, Mobile Ad Hoc Networks*. New York, NY: Wiley. doi:10.1002/9780470396384.ch13.

Srivastava, M. B., Muntz, R. R., & Potkonjak, M. (2001). Smart kindergarten: Sensorbased wireless networks for smart developmental problem-solving enviroments. In Proceedings of the 7th Annual International Conference on Mobile Computing and Networking, (pp. 132-138). New York, NY: ACM.

Stajano, F., & Anderson, R. (1999). The resurrecting duckling: Security issues for ad-hoc wireless networks. In Proceedings of the 7th International Workshop on Security Protocols. IEEE.

Sun, Y., Han, Z., & Liu, K. J. R. (2008). Defense of trust management vulnerabilities in distributed networks. *IEEE Communications Magazine*, *46*(2), 112–119. doi:10.1109/MCOM.2008.4473092.

Viejo, A., Wu, Q., & Domingo-Ferrer, J. (2011). Asymmetric homomorphisms for secure aggregation in heterogeneous scenarios. Information Fusion. Retrieved April 20, 2012, from http://dx.doi.org/10.1016/j.inffus.2011.03.002

Wagner, D. (2004). Resilient aggregation in sensor networks. In Proceedings of the 2nd ACM Workshop on Security of Ad Hoc and Sensor Networks. New York, NY: ACM.

Westhoff, D., Girao, J., & Acharya, M. (2006). Concealed data aggregation for reverse multicast traffic in sensor networks: Encryption, key distribution, and routing adaptation. *IEEE Transactions on Mobile Computing*, *5*(10), 1417–1431. doi:10.1109/TMC.2006.144.

Wood, A. D., & Stankovic, J. A. (2004). A taxonomy for denial-of-service attacks in wireless sensor networks. In *Handbook of Sensor Networks: Compact Wireless and Wired Sensing Systems*. Boca Raton, FL: CRC Press.

Xiao, Y., Sethi, S., Chen, H. H., & Sun, B. (2005). Security services and enhancements in the IEEE 802.15.4 wireless sensor networks. In Proceedings of IEEE Global Telecommunications Conference. IEEE.

Yu, Y., Li, K., Zhou, W., & Li, P. (2012). Trust mechanisms in wireless sensor networks: Attack analysis and countermeasures. *Journal of Network and Computer Applications*, *35*(3), 867–880. doi:10.1016/j.jnca.2011.03.005.

ADDITIONAL READING

Alzaid, H., Foo, E., Nieto, J. G., & Ahmed, E. (2012). Mitigating on-off attacks in reputation-based secure data aggregation for wireless sensor networks. *Security and Communication Networks*, *5*(2), 125–144. doi:10.1002/sec.286.

Alzaid, H., Foo, E., Nieto, J. G., & Park, D. (2012). A taxonomy of secure data aggregation in wireless sensor networks. *International Journal of Communication Networks and Distributed Systems*, *8*(1), 101–148. doi:10.1504/IJCNDS.2012.044325.

Bonnet, P., Gehrke, J., & Seshadri, P. (2001). Towards sensor database systems. In Proceedings of the Second International Conference on Mobile Data Management, (pp. 3-14). IEEE.

Bulusu, N., & Jha, S. (Eds.). (2005). *Wireless sensor networks: A systems perspective*. Norwood, MA: Artech House Inc..

Cerpa, A., Elson, J., Hamilton, M., Zhao, J., Estrin, D., & Girod, L. (2001). Habitat monitoring: Application driver for wireless communications technology. In Proceedings of Workshop on Data communication in Latin America and the Caribbean, (pp. 20-41). IEEE.

Gao, T., Greenspan, D., & Welsh, M. (2005). Improving patient monitoring and tracking in emergency response. In Proceedings of the International Conference on Information Communication Technologies in Health. IEEE.

Karl, H., & Willig, A. (2005). *Protocols and architectures for wireless sensor networks*. Chichester, UK: John Wiley & Sons Ltd. doi:10.1002/0470095121.

Kim, T. H., & Choi, S. (2006). Priority-based delay mitigation for event-monitoring IEEE 802.15.4 LR-WPANs. *IEEE Communications Letters*, *10*(3), 213–215. doi:10.1109/LCOMM.2006.1603388.

Krishnamachari, B. (2005). *Networking wireless sensors*. Cambridge, UK: Cambridge University Press. doi:10.1017/CBO9780511541025.

Kung, H. T., & Vlah, D. (2003). Efficient location tracking using sensor networks. In Proceedings of IEEE Wireless Communications and Networking Conference, (pp. 1954-1962). IEEE.

Malan, D., Fulford-Jones, T., Welsh, M., & Moulton, S. (2004). CodeBlue: An ad hoc sensor network infrastructure for emergency medical care. In Proceedings of the International Workshop on Wearable and Implantable Body Sensor Networks. IEEE.

Misic, J., & Misic, V. B. (2007). Security issues in wireless sensor networks used in clinical information systems. In Xiao, Y., Shen, X. S., & Du, D.-Z. (Eds.), *Wireless Network Security* (pp. 325–340). Springer. doi:10.1007/978-0-387-33112-6_13.

Ozdemir, S. (2008). Functional reputation based reliable data aggregation and transmission for wireless sensor networks. *Computer Communications*, *31*(17), 3941–3953. doi:10.1016/j.comcom.2008.07.017.

Raghavendra, C. S., Sivalingam, K. M., & Znati, T. (Eds.). (2004). *Wireless sensor networks*. Dordrecht, Netherlands: Kluwer Academic Publishers Group. doi:10.1007/b117506.

Sabbah, E., & Kang, K. D. (2009). Security in wireless sensor networks. In S. C. Misra, I. Woungang, & S. Misra (Eds.), Guide to Wireless Sensor Networks: Computer Communications and Networks, (pp. 491-512). London, UK: Spring-Verlag.

Steere, D. C., Baptista, A., McNamee, D., Pu, C., & Walpole, J. (2000). Research challenges in environmental observation and forecasting systems. In Proceedings of the Sixth Annual International Conference on Mobile Computing and Networking, (pp. 92-299). New York, NY: ACM.

Taban, G., & Gligor, V. D. (2008). Efficient handling of adversary attacks in aggregation applications. In Proceedings of the 13th European Symposium on Research in Computer Security, (pp. 66-81). IEEE.

Wang, H., Elson, J., Girod, L., Estrin, D., & Yao, K. (2003). Target classification and localization in habitat monitoring. In Proceedings of the IEEE International Conference on Acoustics, Speech, and Signal Processing, (pp. 844-847). IEEE.

Xiao, Y. (Ed.). (2007). *Security in sensor networks*. New York, NY: Taylor & Francis Group.

Zahariadis, T., Leligou, H. C., Karkazis, P., Trakadas, P., Papaefstathiou, I., Vangelatos, C., & Besson, L. (2010). Design and implementation of a trust-aware routing protocol for large WSNs. *International Journal of Network Security & Its Applications*, *2*(3), 52–68. doi:10.5121/ijnsa.2010.2304.

Zahariadis, T., Leligou, H. C., Trakadas, P., & Voliotis, S. (2010). Trust management in wireless sensor networks. *European Transactions on Telecommunications*, *21*, 386–395.

Zhang, W., & Cao, G. (2004). Optimizing tree reconfiguration for mobile target tracking in sensor networks. In Proceedings of the 23rd IEEE International Conference on Computer Communications, (pp. 2434-2445). IEEE.

Zhao, F., & Guibas, L. (2004). *Wireless sensor networks: An information processing approach*. San Francisco, CA: Morgan Kaufmann Publishers Inc..

KEY TERMS AND DEFINITIONS

Actuator: A mechanism/entity that interacts with the environment and acts in response to the environment.

Adversary: A malicious node/entity that either attacks to a part of the network or disrupts the operation of legitimate nodes/users in the network.

Guaranteed Time Slot: A scheduled time slot in IEEE 802.15.4 standard frame format assigned by the coordinator to a device to warrant collision free transmission.

Homomorphic Encryption: An encryption technique that performs a mathematical operation on ciphertexts where the result is equal to the output after encrypting the result of the same mathematical operation on the corresponding plaintexts.

Overhearing: Listening the message communication between the other nodes/parties in the neighborhood.

Sensor: A small electro-mechanical device that senses/measures the amount of a relevant physical/environmental data.

Wireless Sensor and Actor Network: A distributed network that involves a large number of sensors and actuators.

Wireless Sensor Network: A wireless and ad hoc network that is composed of a large number of self-organizing sensor nodes.

Section 4
Cryptographic Trust Solutions

Chapter 11
Secure Multiparty Computation via Oblivious Polynomial Evaluation

Mert Özarar
Middle East Technical University, Turkey

Attila Özgit
Middle East Technical University, Turkey

ABSTRACT

The number of opportunities for cooperative computation has exponentially been increasing with growing interaction via Internet technologies. These computations could occur between almost trusted partners, between partially trusted partners, or even between competitors. Most of the time, the communicating parties may not want to disclose their private data to the other principal while taking the advantage of collaboration, hence concentrating on the results rather than private data values. For performing such computations, one party must know inputs from all the participants; however, if none of the parties can be trusted enough to know all the inputs, privacy will become a primary concern. Hence, the techniques for Secure Multiparty Computation (SMC) are quite relevant and practical to overcome such kind of privacy gaps. The subject of SMC has evolved from earlier solutions of combinational logic circuits to the recent proposals of anonymity-enabled computation. In this chapter, the authors put together the significant research that has been carried out on SMC. They demonstrate the concept by concentrating on a specific technique called Oblivious Polynomial Evaluation (OPE) together with concrete examples. The authors put critical issues and challenges and the level of adaptation achieved before the researchers. They also provide some future research proposals based on the literature survey.

DOI: 10.4018/978-1-4666-4030-6.ch011

INTRODUCTION

The number of opportunities for cooperative computation has exponentially been increasing with growing interaction via Internet technologies. These computations could occur between trusted partners, between partially trusted partners, or even between competitors. Most of the time, the communicating parties may not want to disclose their private data to the other principal while taking the advantage of collaboration, hence concentrating on the results rather than private and perhaps useless data values. For example, two or more competing large organizations might jointly invest in a project that must satisfy all organizations' goals while preserving their private and valuable data (Du, 2001). For performing such computations, one party must know inputs from all the participants; however if none of the parties can be trusted enough to know all the inputs, privacy will become a primary concern. Hence the techniques for secure multiparty computation are quite relevant and practical to overcome the privacy gaps.

Secure Multiparty Computation

If multiple parties want to perform a computation based on their private inputs, but neither party is willing to disclose its own input to anybody else, then the basic problem is how to conduct such a computation while preserving the privacy of the inputs. This is referred to as Secure Multiparty Computation problem (SMC) in the literature.

For example, consider the following real life scenarios where SMC can directly be applicable;

1. Some hospitals situated in various different countries having their medical databases and patient's history stored on some remote database sites. They want to wish to jointly mine their patient's data for the purpose of medical research and prevention of data is to be maintained due to confidentiality of patients' records.
2. In a given exam, the results are privately shared with the students. No student wants to disclose its exam grade yet all the students want to calculate the average of the exam.
3. Let us assume that an airline company that has a reservation database for each country exists. If a person wishes to make a reservation from city A located in country X to a city B located in country Y, then we need to consult each intermediate countries databases. These databases provide only the queried details without disclosing their whole reservation database.

In general, a secure multiparty computation problem deals with computing any function on any input, in a distributed network where each participant holds one of the inputs, ensuring independence of the inputs, correctness of the computation, and that no more information is revealed to a participant in the computation other than that can be inferred from the participant's input and output (Du, 2002).

Currently, to solve the above problems, a common strategy is to assume the trustworthiness of the service providers, or to assume the existence of a trusted third party, which is risky in nowadays' dynamic and malicious environment. Consider a trusted party who collects all participants' data and then performs the computation and sends the results to the participants. Without having a trusted party, some communication among the participants is certainly required for any related computation; yet we do not know how to ensure that this communication does not disclose anything. Therefore, protocols that can support joint computations while protecting the participants' privacy are of growing importance.

In theory, the general secure multiparty computation problem is solvable (Yao, 1986; Goldreich, 1987; Goldreich, 2004) but using the solutions derived by these general results for special cases of multiparty computation can be impractical; special solutions should be developed for efficiency reasons. One solution is to allow non-determinism in the exact values sent for the intermediate communication and demonstrate that a party with just its own input and the result can generate a predicted intermediate computation that is as likely as the actual values.

Model Paradigms

Many models have been proposed in the literature for the study and analysis of SMC problems. Among them, two model paradigms are popular:

1. Ideal Model Paradigm
2. Real Model Paradigm

In ideal model, a third party whom we assume that it is trusted performs computations. The parties send their data in secure mode to such Trusted Third Party (TTP). There are a number of protocols proposed by researchers for this model. In this model, if some party behaves maliciously, the result of the computation may be incorrect because the party may supply invalid input to the TTP but the privacy can be preserved.

The ideal model of SMC is not preferred due to the cost of working with the TTP. One more drawback of this model is that the trustworthiness of the TTP is significant. When TTP turns into a corrupted one, the whole notion of the SMC becomes worthless. However, today this model is frequently used due to easy implementation and use of tools that prevent the TTP from becoming malicious.

On the other hand, in real model there is no TTP for computation. Cooperating parties in this model agree on some protocol, which is to be run among themselves for privacy preservation and computation of correct result. Parties do not share actual inputs with each other. The values sent by parties are some function of their private data. What exists between parties is a theoretical computation machine. The real model of SMC is said to be secure if an adversary can carry out some attack, which is also possible in the ideal model of SMC.

We concentrate on the real model paradigm. In this model, the type and activity of adversaries should be carefully investigated.

Adversarial Behavior

Privacy preserving algorithms are designed in order to preserve privacy even in the presence of adversarial participants that attempt to gather information about the inputs of their peers. There are, however, different levels of adversarial behavior. Cryptographic research typically considers two types of adversaries: A semi-honest adversary (also known as a passive, or honest but curious adversary) is a party that correctly follows the protocol specification, yet attempts to learn additional information by analyzing the messages received during the protocol execution. On the other hand, a malicious adversary (active) may arbitrarily deviate from the protocol specification. For example, consider a step in the protocol where one of the parties is required to choose a random number and broadcast it. If the party is semi-honest then we can assume that this number is indeed random. On the other hand, if the party is malicious, then he might choose the number in a sophisticated way that enables him to gain additional information.

It is of course easier to design a solution that is secured against semi-honest adversaries, than for malicious adversaries. A common approach is therefore, first to design a secure protocol for the semi-honest case, and then transform it into a protocol that is secure against malicious adversaries. This transformation can be done by requiring each party to use zero-knowledge proofs to justify that each step that it is taking follows the specification of the protocol. More efficient transformations are often required, since this generic approach might be rather inefficient and add considerable overhead to each step of the protocol. It is remarkable that the semi-honest adversarial model is often a realistic one. This is because deviating from a specified protocol which may be buried in a complex application is a non-trivial task, and because a semi-honest adversarial behavior can model a scenario in which the parties that participate in the protocol are honest, but following the protocol execution an adversary may obtain a transcript of the protocol execution by breaking into a machine used by one of the participants.

We consider the semi-honest case throughout this chapter.

BACKGROUND

Background on SMC

There has been a solid work in cooperative computation between entities that mutually distrust one another. This computation may be of any sort: scientific, data processing, or even secret sharing. The first paper on SMC belongs to Yao who has stated the famous problem called "Millionaire's Problem" (Yao, 1986). How can two millionaires know who is richer without disclosing their individual wealth to each other? Yao has used cryptographic techniques to solve the problem. Goldreich et al. extended the idea from two party case to multiparty case (Goldreich, 1987). These works are directly related with the field called "Secret Sharing," which is close to SMC (Shamir, 1979).

The early solutions to SMC problems used combinatorial circuit where each party cooperatively runs a short protocol for every gate in the circuit. Every participant gets (randomly chosen) shares of the values of the input and output for each gate; the exclusive or of the shares is the actual value. One share alone carries no information about the input or function value, as which party gets which share is determined randomly. At the end, the parties exchange their shares, enabling each to compute the final result. This protocol has been proven to give the desired result without disclosing anything other than the result. This approach, though appealing in its simplicity and generality, implies that the size of the protocol depends on the size of the circuit, which depends on the size of the input. Other general techniques have been proposed by Chaum et al. (Chaum, 1988) and Naor et al. (Naor, 2001). While this approach is appealing in its generality and simplicity, the generated protocols depend on the size of the circuit. This size depends on the size of the input domain, and on the complexity of expressing such a computation.

Du and Atallah complete an excellent survey of secure multiparty computation problems and their applications (Du, 2001). They defined various SMC problems for their specific computations such as Privacy-Preserving Data mining, Privacy-Preserving Intrusion Detection and Privacy-Preserving Geometric Computation. On the other hand, Du and Zhan suggest a practical approach to applying secure multiparty computation by accepting a compromise on security (Du, 2002). Verykios et al. present an overview of the new and rapidly emerging research area of privacy preserving data mining, also classify the techniques, review and evaluation of privacy preserving algorithms (Verykios, 2004). Clifton et. al. present some tools and show how they can be used to solve several privacy preserving data mining problems (Clifton, 2004). Agrawal and Srikant propose a novel reconstruction procedure to accurately estimate the distribution of original data value by these reconstructed distributions (Agrawal, 2000). Pinkas focuses to demonstrate basic ideas from a large body of cryptographic research on secure distributed computation and their applications to data mining (Pinkas, 2003). Vaidya et al. survey approaches about secure multiparty computation and propose a method by presenting an efficient two-party (Vaidya, 2003).

Specific Notable SMC Problems

Many specific SMC problems and theirs solutions are devised by the researchers. The notable SMC problems can be presented together with their solutions:

Privacy-Preserving Decision Trees

Lindell et al. focused on the problem of Decision Tree learning with the ID3 algorithm and protocol is quite efficient (Lindell, 2000). Vaidya et. al. also tackle the same problem of classification and they introduce a generalized privacy preserving variant of the ID3 algorithm for vertically partitioned data distributed over two or more parties (Vaidya, 2003). Fang et al. present a novel privacy preserving Decision Tree learning method (Fang, 2008). Emekci et al. also focuses on the same problem and develop a privacy-preserving ID3 algorithm as well (Emekci, 2007). Agrawal and Srikant define the problem as how one party can be allowed to perform data mining operation on the private database of another party without the first party knowing any details of the database of the second party (Agrawal, 2000). Different from previous ones, they use data perturbation method to solve the problem. Dowd et al. present a data perturbation technique based on random substitutions and showed that the resulting privacy-preserving decision tree mining method is immune to attacks that are seemingly relevant (Dowd, 2006). Systematic experiments show that it is also effective.

Privacy-Preserving Naïve Bayes Classification

Vaidya and Clifton solve the same problem on vertically partitioned data (Vaidya, 2003). Kantarcioglu et al. present protocols to develop a Naive Bayes classifier on horizontally partitioned data (Kantarcioglu, 2004). Vaidya et al. compare the results of the both horizontal and vertical case and combined a solution for hybrid model as well (Vaidya, 2004).

Private Information Retrieval

Private Information Retrieval (PIR) is a protocol that allows a client to retrieve an element of a database without the owner of that database being able to determine which element was selected. While this problem admits a trivial solution—sending the entire database to the client allows the client to query with perfect privacy—there are techniques to reduce the communication complexity of this problem, which can be critical for large databases. Additionally, Strong Private Information Retrieval (SPIR) is private information retrieval with the additional requirement that the client only learn about the elements he is querying for, and nothing else. This requirement captures the typical privacy needs of a database owner. This problem was introduced by Chor et al. (Chor, 1995). The problem was extended by Gertner et al. (Gertner, 1998). Many solutions are proposed for the PIR problem focusing on reducing the communication cost (Chor, 1997; Kushilevitz, 1997; Di-Crescenzo, 1998; Cachin, 1999; Ishai, 1999).

Privacy-Preserving Clustering

Recently privacy-preserving data mining has been a very active area of research. Initial focus in this area was on construction of decision trees from distributed data sets (Agrawal, 2000; Lindell, 2000). There is also a solid body of research on privacy-preserving mining of association rules (Evfimievski 2002; Rizvi 2002). In general, there are two approaches for designing privacy-preserving machine learning algorithms. The first approach is to use transformations to perturb the data set before the algorithm is applied. This approach for designing privacy-preserving clustering algorithms is taken by several researchers (Klusch, 2003; Merugu, 2003; Oliviera, 2003). The second approach to designing privacy preserving algorithms is to use algorithms from the secure-multiparty computation literature. The advantage of this approach over the perturbation approach is that formal guarantees of privacy can be given for these algorithms. Vaidya and Clifton present a privacy-preserving k-means algorithm for vertically-partitioned data sets (Vaidya, 2003). There are distributed clustering algorithms where the goal is to reduce communication costs (Dhillon, 1999; Kargupta, 2001; Jha, 2005).

Privacy-Preserving Statistical Analysis

Franconi and Merola give a more recent survey on the subject, with a focus on aggregated data released via web access (Franconi, 2003). Evfimievski et al. give a very nice discussion of work in randomization of data, in which data contributors independently add noise to their own responses (Evfimievski, 2003). Many papers in the statistics literature deal with generating simulated data while maintaining certain quantities, such as marginals. Other widely-studied techniques include cell suppression, adding simulated data, releasing only a subset of observations, releasing only a subset of attributes, releasing synthetic or partially synthetic data, data-swapping, and post-randomization. Agrawal and Srikant begin to address privacy in data mining (Agrawal, 2000). That work attempts to formalize privacy in terms of confidence intervals and also shows how to reconstruct an original distribution from noisy samples.

Background on OPE

The usage of OPE in privacy preserving applications is presented by Naor by the introduction of "oblivious transfer" (Naor, 1999). Oblivious transfer is a basic protocol that is the main building block of secure computation. It might seem strange at first, but its role in secure computation should become clear later. It was shown by again Naor that oblivious transfer is sufficient for secure computation in the sense that given an implementation of oblivious transfer, and no other cryptographic primitive, one could construct any secure computation protocol (Naor, 2005).

OPE is applied to SMC problems especially under privacy preserving data mining concept which is introduced by designing privacy preserving ID3 decision tree algorithm (Lindell, 2000). Jha et al. solve weighted average problem by two techniques (Jha, 2005). Former is by OPE and latter is by encryption techniques based on homomorphism yet both of them is used as a tool for k-means clustering for two parties. Neural network applications are studied using OPE methods as well within the context of privacy-preserving data mining (Chang, 2001), Goethals et al. present a private scalar product protocol based on standard cryptographic techniques and proved that it is secure (Goethals, 2004).

Özarar and Özgit pay special attention to the subject and do extensive research on it. They solve the secure multiparty mean computation problem using OPE (Özarar, 2007). Moreover, they develop algorithms for matrix algebraic concepts like eigenvalue, eigenvector and determinant computations using OPE in horizontally partitioned data (Özarar, 2008). The presentation of a novel protocol for secure multiparty Hamming Distance algorithm exists which is designed to be used as a building block for Hierarchical Agglomerative Clustering (HAC) of documents in Özarar et al (Özarar, 2011).

METHODS TO SOLVE SMC PROBLEMS

In the literature, there are three types of solutions available to SMC problems:

1. Randomization methods.
2. Cryptographic techniques.
3. k-Anonymization methods.

Randomization Method

The randomization procedure furnishes a viable yet effortless way of staying away from the single from thinking about sensitive informative content, which could be effectively connected at informative data determination stage for solace securing qualified data investigation, being as how the unsettling influence incorporated to a given history is partitioned of the movements of different informative data records. In the randomization strategy, occasions utilize interesting figures for disguising their informative data and execute computations over undetectable informative content. Systems are made such that the conclusions of the counts over undetectable informative data are the same as the conclusions of estimations over honest qualified data.

Data randomization technique represents one common approach to solve some kind of SMC problems where the original (private) dataset is perturbed and the result is released for data analysis. Data perturbation includes a wide variety of techniques including: additive, multiplicative (Kim, 2003), matrix multiplicative, k-anonymization (Sweeney, 2002) and micro-aggregation (Li, 2006).

The additive perturbation is a technique for privacy-preserving data mining in which noise is added to the data in order to mask the attribute values of records (Agrawal, 2000). Agrawal and Srikant discuss how to use the approach for solving the privacy preserving classification problem (Agrawal, 2000). Besides, Evfimievski et al. propose a solution to the privacy preserving distributed association mining problem (Evfimievski, 2002). The problem of association rules is especially challenging because of the discrete nature of the attributes corresponding to presence or absence of items.

Cryptographic Techniques

The cryptographic techniques solutions to SMC problems include some basic building blocks which are used as components while handling secure computations. Some of the building blocks are as follows (Oleschchuk, 2007):

The Millionaires' Problem

It is a secure multiparty communication problem which was introduced by Yao (1986). The problem discusses two millionaires, Alice and Bob, who are interested in knowing which of them is richer without revealing their actual wealth. This problem is analogous to a more general problem where there are two numbers a and b and the goal is to solve the inequality b>a without revealing the actual values of a and b.

Many solutions have been introduced for the problem, among which the first solution developed by using symmetric cryptography, presented by Yao himself, was exponential in time and space (Yao, 1986).

This component for SMC is useful in applications such as online bidding and auctions. Many researchers propose solutions to this problem (Cachin, 1999; Ioannidis, 2003; Amirbekyan, 2009). The same problem can be extended to multiparty case and is useful for the SMC solution. Thus solution to this problem can work as the building block for many SMC problems

Homomorphic Encryption

The SMC problem becomes more complex when asking for the possibility to compute (publicly) with encrypted data or to modify functions in such a way that they are still executable while privacy is ensured. That is where homomorphic cryptosystems can be used.

A homomorphic encryption scheme is an encryption scheme which allows certain algebraic operations to be carried out on the encrypted plaintext, by applying an efficient operation to the corresponding cipher text. For a concrete instance, an additively homomorphic encryption scheme (Paillier, 1999) that is comparable with the encryption process of RSA in terms of the computation cost, while the decryption process of the additive homomorphism is faster than the decryption process of RSA can be presented.

An additively homomorphic cryptosystem has the nice property that for two plain text message m_1 and m_2:

$$E(m_1) + E(m_2) = E(m_1 + m_2)$$

This essentially means that we can have the sum of two numbers without knowing what those numbers are. Moreover, because of the property of associability,

$$E(m_1) + E(m_2) + \ldots + E(m_n) = E(m_1 + m_2 + \ldots + m_n)$$

and we can easily have the following corollary:

$$E(m_1)^{m}{}_2 = E(m_2)^{m}{}_1 = E(m_1 . m_2) \text{ where } E(m_i) \neq 0.$$

Many homomorphic systems with semantic security are proposed in the literature (Benaloh, 1994; Naccache, 1998; Paillier, 1999). There are a lot of important works related to usage of homomorphic encryption as a tool for SMC (Lindell, 2002; Du, 2002; Vaidya, 2002).

Gentry using lattice-based cryptography showed the first fully homomorphic encryption scheme where in his scheme, he supports evaluations of arbitrary depth circuits. His construction starts from a somewhat homomorphic encryption scheme using ideal lattices that is limited to evaluating low-degree polynomials over encrypted data. He then shows how to modify this scheme to make it bootstrappable in particular, he shows that by modifying the somewhat homomorphic scheme slightly, it can actually evaluate its own decryption circuit, a self-referential property. Finally, he shows that any bootstrappable somewhat homomorphic encryption scheme can be converted into a fully homomorphic encryption through a recursive self-embedding (Gentry, 2009).

Oblivious Transfer and Oblivious Polynomial Evaluation

The oblivious transfer protocol involves two parties, the sender and the receiver. The sender's input is a pair (x_0, x_1) and the receiver's input is a bit $\sigma \in \{0, 1\}$. At the end of protocol, the receiver learns x_σ (and nothing else) and the sender learns nothing. Oblivious transfer is often the most computationally intensive operation of secure protocols and is repeated many times. Each invocation of oblivious transfer typically requires a constant number of invocations of trapdoor permutations (i.e. public-key operations or exponentiations). It is possible to reduce the amortized overhead of oblivious transfer to one exponentiations per a logarithmic number of oblivious transfers, even for the case of malicious adversaries (Pinkas, 2003).

Oblivious polynomial evaluation is a technique based on oblivious transfer. To design a secure protocol for computing a function f(x,y) with two parties, a receiver who knows x and a sender who knows y, one needs to use oblivious transfer to jointly compute the value of f(x, y) in a privacy preserving way. The fact that for every computable function f(x,y) in polynomial time, there exists such a (polynomially-computable) protocol is already achieved in the cryptographic research (Naor, 2005). In the OPE, the input of the sender is a polynomial P of degree k over some field F. The receiver can get the value P(x) for any element $x \in F$ without learning anything else about the polynomial P and without revealing to the sender any information about x. The input and output for the functionality of OPE as a two party protocol run between a receiver and a sender over a field F as follows:

- Input
    - Receiver: an input $x \in F$.
    - Sender: A polynomial P defined over *F*.

- Output
    - Receiver: P(x).
    - Sender: nothing.

There are various protocols to solve the OPE yet the protocol given by Naor et. al. is preferred for the target algorithms (Naor, 2005).

The literature survey on OPE is given in the previous section.

Private Matching

Agrawal et al. present a paper that explores the following private matching problem: two parties each have a database and they wish to determine common entries without revealing any information about entries only found in one database (Agrawal, 2003). This paper has generated significant interest in the research community. While the Agrawal/Evfimievski/Srikant (AgES) protocol described in the paper is correct within in its assumptions, it is not robust in a variety of different scenarios. In fact, in many likely scenarios, the AgES protocol can easily be exploited to obtain a great deal of information about another database. The private matching problem has very different solutions depending on assumptions about the different parties, the way they interact, and cryptographic mechanisms available.

The protocols used for private matching use the properties of homomorphic encryption. Different protocols are available for semi honest parties and that for malicious parties (Freedman, 2004).

k-Anonymization

In order to preserve privacy, Sweeney et al. propose the k-anonymity model which achieves anonymity using generalization and suppression, so that, any individual is indistinguishable from at least k-1 other ones with respect to the quasi-identifier attributes in the anonymized dataset (Sweeney, 2002).

In recent years, numerous algorithms have been proposed for implementing k-anonymity via generalization and suppression. Bayardo and Agrawal present an optimal algorithm that starts from a fully generalized table and specializes the dataset in a minimal k-anonymous table (Bayardo, 2005). Lefevre et al. describe an algorithm that uses a bottom-up technique and a priori computation (Lefevre, 2005). Fung et al. present a top-down heuristic to make a table to be released k-anonymous (Fung, 2005). As to the theoretical results, Sweeney prove the optimal k-anonymity is NP-hard and provided approximation algorithms for optimal k-anonymity (Sweeney, 2002). However, Machanavajjhala et al. pointed out that the user may guess the sensitive values with high confidence when the sensitive data is lack of diversity, and introduced the l-diversity method (Machanavajjhala, 2007).

IMPLEMENTATION OF OPE PROTOCOL

Assume that there are two parties, Alice who has a function **f** and Bob who has an input **x**. They want to collaborate in a way for Alice to learn nothing and for Bob to learn **f(x)** and nothing more. A protocol achieving this task for any function **f** and any input **x** is called an "Oblivious Function Evaluation" protocol.

Note that any function from **m** bits to **m** bits can be represented as a polynomial over a finite field $\mathbf{GF(2^m)}$, but its degree could go as high as $\mathbf{2^m - 1}$. Thus one would like to focus on those functions that can be represented by low degree polynomials. This turns out to have several interesting applications (Gilboa, 1999; Naor, 1999). The scheme proposed in Naor et al. is much more efficient than the conventional way of going through oblivious circuit evaluation protocols, but its security is based on two assumptions (Naor, 1999). One assumption is the existence of a secure

OT protocol while the other, a new one, is the intractability of a Noisy Polynomial Interpolation problem. It was later shown in Bleichenbacher et al. that this new assumption may be much weaker than expected and suggested the use of a possibly stronger intractability assumption on a Polynomial Reconstruction Problem (Bleichenbacher, 2000). The protocol presented in Gilboa et al. is based on an assumption that the Decisional Diffie-Hellman (DDH) assumption also holds over the group Z_{nxn} (Gilboa, 1999), where **n** is the product of two large primes. Contrary to the well studied DDH over Z_n, the hardness of this problem in this new setting is yet to be studied. A novel OPE protocol is proposed in 2009 and we strongly recommend to use this novel one for the implementation of OPE (Vanishree, 2009).

Analyses show that the protocol provides unconditional security as against the computational security provided by the previously existing protocols. The main computational bottleneck of the existing constructions is the OT protocol, the computational cost of which is essentially exponentiations in finite fields. As another major asset of the protocol, this overhead is obviated and hence the protocol is proved to be more efficient.

One attractive feature of our protocols is that they can be modified very easily to handle floating-point numbers. This is not the case for existing OPE protocols which rely on some particular properties of finite fields. Many important applications in real life involve numerical computation over floating-point numbers, instead of over integers or arbitrary finite fields. There is no efficient mapping known that embeds floating-point numbers into finite fields where arithmetics can be carried out easily.

The target approach is to scale floating-point numbers up to integers with some book- keeping, apply some existing OPE protocol over integers, and then do a normalization to get back floating-point numbers. The extra work of scaling up, scaling down and book-keeping makes their algorithm less appealing. We show how our OPE protocols over finite fields can be easily modified to operate directly on floating-point numbers, and we believe that such protocols are more applicable in practice.

Preliminaries

We fix a security parameter τ, so that any number within a small factor of $2^{-\tau}$ is considered negligible.

For a distribution D over a set S, let D(i), for $i \in S$, denote the probability of i according to D, and define D(A), for $A \subseteq S$, to be $\Sigma_{i \in A}$ D(i).

Definition 1

Let D and D' be two distributions over a set S. Let $d_A(D,D') = |D(A)-D'(A)|$. The distance of D and D' is defined as $d(D,D') = \max_{A \subseteq S} d_A(D,D')$.

Note that $d(D,D') = \Sigma_{i \in S} |D(i)-D'(i)|$, which is a useful way for calculating d(D,D').

Definition 2

Let D and D' be two distributions. They are statistically indistinguishable, if d(D,D') is negligible. They are computationally indistinguishable, if $d_A(D,D')$ is negligible for any subset A decided by a polynomial-size circuit.

An important cryptographic primitive is the 1-out-of-2 oblivious transfer, denoted as 1-OT-2. There are several variants which are all equivalent, and the one most suited for us is the following string version of 1-OT-2.

Definition 3

A 1-OT-2 protocol has two parties, Sender who has input $(x_0, x_1) \in F^2$ and Chooser who has a choice $c \in \{0, 1\}$. The protocol is correct if the Sender learns x_c for any (x_0, x_1) and c. The protocol is secure if both conditions below are satisfied for any (x_0, x_1) and c:

Chooser cannot distinguish the distribution of Sender's messages from that induced by Sender having a different value of $x_{1-c.} \sum_{i=0}^{d}$

Sender cannot distinguish the distributions of Chooser's messages induced by c and 1 − c.

Definition 4

A protocol for oblivious polynomial evaluation has two parties, Alice who has a polynomial P over some finite field F and Bob who has an input $x_* \in$ F. An OPE protocol is correct if Bob learns P(x*) for any x_* and P. It is secure if both conditions below are satisfied for any x_* and P:

Alice cannot distinguish the distribution of Bob's messages from that induced by Bob having a different x_*'.

Bob cannot distinguish the distribution of Alice's messages from that induced by Alice having a different $P'(x_*) = P(x_*)$.

Protocol for OPE

We will present an OPE protocol in this section. Assume that both parties have agreed that polynomials are over a finite field F and have degrees at most d. The set of such polynomials can be identified with the set $T = F^{d+1}$ in a natural way. Suppose now Alice has a polynomial $P(x) = a_i x^i \in T$ and Bob has $x_* \in F$.

To make the picture clear, we only discuss the case GF(p) for some prime p. The generalization of GF(p^k) with k>1 is straightforward. Each coefficient a_i in the polynomial can be represented as $a_{ij} = \Sigma_{j\in[\log 2|F|]}\, a_{ij}2^{j-1}$ with $a_{ij} \in \{0, 1\}$. For i ∈ [d] and j ∈ [log2|F|], let $v_{ij} = 2^{j-1}\, x_*^{\,i}$. Note that for each i ∈ [d], $\Sigma_{j\in[\log 2|F|]}\, a_{ij}v_{ij} = a_i x_*^{\,i}$. The idea is to have Bob prepare $(v_{ij})_{\,j\in[\log 2|F|]}$ and have Alice get those v_{ij} with $a_{ij} = 1$, in some secret way. This is achieved by having Bob prepare the pair $(r_{ij}, v_{ij}+r_{ij})$ for a random noise r_{ij}, and having Alice get what she wants via 1-OT-2. Note that what Alice obtains is $a_{ij}v_{ij}+r_{ij}$.

Protocol 1

1. Bob prepares d[log2|F|] pairs $(r_{ij}, v_{ij}+r_{ij})$, i∈[d], j∈[log2|F|], with each r_{ij} chosen randomly from F.
2. For each pair $(r_{ij}, v_{ij}+r_{ij})$, Alice runs an independent 1-OT-2 with Bob to get r_{ij} if $a_{ij} = 0$ and $v_{ij}+r_{ij}$ otherwise.
3. Alice sends to Bob the sum of a_0 and those d[log2|F|] values she got. Bob subtracts $\Sigma_{i,j} r_{ij}$ from it to obtain $P(x_*)$.

Lemma 1

Protocol 1 is correct when parties are semi-honest.

Proof

The sum Bob obtains in Step 3 is $a_0 + \Sigma_i \Sigma_j (a_{ij}v_{ij}+r_{ij}) = P(x_*) + \Sigma_{i,j} r_{ij}$.

Lemma 2

Protocol 1 is secure when parties are semi-honest.

Proof

First, we prove Alice's security. Suppose P and P' are two distinct polynomials with $P(x_*) = P'(x_*) = y_*$. According to Lemma 1, it suffices to show that for any fixed r_{ij}, Alice's respective message distributions D and D' induced by P and P' are indistinguishable. Note that the last message from Alice is $y* + \Sigma_{i,j} r_{ij}$ for both P and P' can be ignored. So we focus on Alice's d[log2|F|] messages from the d[log2|F|] independent executions of OT's. For 0 ≤ k ≤ d[log2|F|], let D_k denote the distribution with the first k messages from D and the remaining messages from D'.

Assume that there exists a distinguisher C for D and D'. A standard argument show that C can also distinguish D_{s-1} and D_s for some s. Note that Alice must select different elements from that pair in the s'th OT, as otherwise the two distributions are identical.

Then one can break Chooser's security in 1-OT-2 when Sender has this input, because with Chooser's messages for different choices replacing the s'th message of D_{s-1}, we get exactly D_{s-1} and D_s, which can be distinguished by C. As 1-OT-2 is assumed to be secure, D and D' are indistinguishable, and Alice is secure.

Next, we prove Bob's security. Note that Bob sends dm messages to Alice for the d[log2|F|] independent executions of OT's. Let $x_* \neq x_*'$. let E and E' be Bob's respective message distributions, and let E_k denote the distribution with the first k messages from E and the remaining messages from E'.

Suppose a distinguisher for E and E' exists. Then it can also distinguish E_{s-1} and E_s for some s. The pairs in that s'th OT have the forms (r, v+r) and (r', v'+r'), for some fixed v and v' and for random r and r'.

Alice's polynomial is fixed, so which element to choose in that s'th OT is also fixed. Suppose Alice chooses the first one in that pair. Then according to Lemma 1, there is a fixed r_0 such that E_{s-1} conditioned on Bob having $(r_0, v+r_0)$ and E_s conditioned on Bob having $(r_0, v'+r_0)$ are distinguishable. Similarly as before, one can distinguish Sender's messages when Sender has $(r_0, v+r_0)$ and $(r_0, v'+r_0)$ respectively and Chooser selects the first element, which violates Sender's security in 1-OT-2.

The case when Alice chooses the second one in that pair can be argued similarly, by noticing that the distribution (r, v+r) and the distribution (−v+r, r) are identical. As 1-OT-2 is assumed to be secure, so is Bob.

Theorem 1

Protocol 1 is correct and secure when parties are semi-honest.

Proof

Note that only dm invocations of 1-OT-2 are required and they can be done concurrently. If 1-OT-2 can be carried out in one round, Protocol 1 runs in one round. Also observe that if 1-OT-2 can achieve perfect security for Chooser, then Protocol 1 is perfectly secure for Alice, in the information-theoretical sense.

SECURE MULTIPARTY COMPUTATION VIA OBLIVIOUS POLYNOMIAL EVALUATION

In this section, the application of OPE (as a building block) is discussed to handle SMC problems. Two concrete examples together with solution algorithms are presented to demonstrate the usage. Moreover, under given security assumptions like passive adversaries, the privacy validities of the algorithms are justified using statistical indistinguishability and semantic security.

Another important concept while developing a secure algorithm is the model of computation. We introduce a transformation framework that systematically transforms normal computations to secure multiparty computations.

Statistical Indistinguishability

Before all, the privacy proof concept in SMC and semantic security should be defined. The definition of privacy is based on the intuition that parties should learn nothing more from the messages used in privacy-preserving protocol, i.e., the messages received by a party during an execution of a privacy-preserving protocol can be "effectively computed" by only knowing its input and output. This idea is formalized below:

Definition 5

Let x and y be inputs of the two parties and $<f_1(x, y), f_2(x, y)>$ be the desired functionalities, i.e., the first party wants to compute $f_1(x, y)$, and the second wants to compute $f_2(x, y)$. Let P be a two-party protocol to compute f. The view of the first party after having participated in protocol P (denoted by $VIEW_1(x, y)$) is $(x, r, m_1 \ldots m_t)$, where r are the random bits generated by party 1 and $m_1 \ldots m_t$ is the sequence of messages received by party 1, while participating in protocol P. $VIEW_2(x, y)$, for the second party can be defined in a similar manner.

We say that P privately computes f if there are probabilistic polynomial-time algorithms (PPTA), denoted by S_1 and S_2 such that,

$$\{S_1(x, f_1(x, y))\}_{x,y} \equiv s \, \{VIEW_1(x, y)\}_{x,y}$$

$$\{S_2(x, f_2(x, y))\}_{x,y} \equiv s \, \{VIEW_2(x, y)\}_{x,y}$$

In the equation given above, ≡s denotes statistically indistinguishable.

Two probability ensembles $X = \{X_w\}_{w \in S}$ and $Y = \{Y_w\}_{w \in S}$ indexed by S are statistically indistinguishable if for some negligible function $\mu: \aleph \rightarrow [0, 1]$ and all $w \in S$,

$$\sum_{\alpha} \left| Prob\left(X_w = \alpha\right) - Prob\left(Y_w = \alpha\right) \right| < \mu\left(\left|w\right|\right)$$

A function $\mu: \aleph \rightarrow [0, 1]$ is called negligible if for every positive polynomial q, and all sufficiently large n's, $\mu(n) < q(n)^{-1}$. There is a weaker notion of indistinguishability called computationally indistinguishable.

We will use statistical indistinguishability throughout the chapter, but all the results hold even if the weaker notion of indistinguishability is used. Goldreich has provided a formal definition of privacy and has provided a solid theoretical background that solutions to a specific secure multiparty computation problem should base on (Goldreich, 2004).

Models of Computation

Assume that the input to be processed is a set D of data items. If we can divide D into two disjoint data sets D1 and D2, we will have a multiple-input computation model. There are many ways to divide D into two data sets, and each way could lead to a different SMC problem. We are focusing on two types of transformations: homogeneous transformation and heterogeneous transformation.

In the homogeneous transformation (horizontal partitioning), D's data items are divided to two sets, but each single data item is not cut into two parts. For example, if D is a database of patient records, the homogeneous transformation will put a subset of the records into one data set, and the rest of the records into another data set; however, each patient's record is not cut into two parts. In other words, the two generated datasets maintain the same set of features.

In the heterogeneous transformation (vertical partitioning), each single data item is cut into two parts, with each part going to a separate dataset. Taking the same example used above, if each patient record contains a patient's ID record and medical record, the heterogeneous transformation could put all patients' ID records into one data set, and all patients' medical records into another data set. In other words, the two generated data sets maintain different set of features.

In the next two subsections, we demonstrate the usage of OPE to concrete problems like secure overall mean and Hamming distance computations, respectively. The notion and role of OPE can be explained best by those examples.

Application of OPE to Secure Multiparty Overall Mean Computation

In this subsection, the problem definition for privacy preserving two party and multiparty overall mean computation problems are defined mathematically whose algorithms are presented.

Privacy Preserving Two-Party Overall Mean Computation Problem (OMP)

Suppose that Alice (party 1) has n samples and Bob (party 2) has m-n samples of real numbers. Each party wants to get the mean of their samples without revealing any private information. We are assuming that finding the mean of the union of samples from the two parties is more desirable than calculating the two samples individually.

Let μ_A represents the mean of Alice's samples and μ_B represents the mean of Bob's, respectively. The means are weighted with respect to their cardinalities and joined together with multiplication and then divided by the total size of samples. Hence the result to be computed is,

$$\mu = (\mu_A \bullet n + \mu_B \bullet (m-n)) / m \qquad (1)$$

Remark that the terms in the first product (μ_A, n) are only known by Alice and (μ_B, m-n) are only known by Bob.

Privacy Preserving Two-Party OMP Algorithm (via OPE)

To develop such an algorithm, a functional should be taken as a target to place the terms in the OPE. Let f be the functional for such a computation, its domain set must be two-dimensional vectors (i.e. mean and cardinality) for both parties and range set must be the same value (overall mean) as a two dimensional vector. Since the cardinalities are multiplied with individual means in the numerator and the total sum of samples exist in the denominator of (1), f is constructed as

$$f: \mathbb{R}^2 \times \mathbb{R}^2 \rightarrow \mathbb{R}^2$$

$$f((x,m),(y,n)) = ((x \bullet m+y \bullet n)/(m+n), (x \bullet m+y \bullet n)/(m+n)) \qquad (2)$$

The straight forward solution is approximating f by a circuit. However, it is well known that the cost for implementing such a circuit is so inefficient that a new solution should be developed for the specific case (via OPE). We describe the protocol in a top-down fashion. The steps are as follows:

1. Define the private Rational Polynomial Evaluation problem (RPE)
2. Develop a protocol for RPE using OPE.
3. Find a suitable case for RPE by placing polynomials and field elements for OMP. (Reduction from private-RPE)
   a. RPE Problem

For any finite field F, construct f as;

$$f: \mathbb{R}^2 \times \mathbb{R}^2 \rightarrow \mathbb{R}^2$$

$$f((P,Q), (\alpha, \beta)) = (P(\alpha)/Q(\beta), P(\alpha)/Q(\beta)) \qquad (3)$$

where P, Q ϵ F[x] (polynomials for party 1) and $\alpha, \beta \ \epsilon$ F (field elements of party 2).

b. RPE Protocol

The protocol can be developed via OPE in the following scheme:

- Party 1 blinds the polynomials P and Q by multiplying with a predetermined field element $\gamma \ \epsilon$ F.
- Party 2 computes $\gamma P(\alpha)$ and $\gamma Q(\beta)$ by applying OPE twice.
- Party 2 computes $P(\alpha)/Q(\beta)$, by computing $\gamma P(\alpha) / \gamma Q(\beta)$, and sends it to party 1.

The first two steps are adapted from Jha et. al. where the aim is to solve Weighted Average Problem which is relatively more trivial than OMP (Jha, 2005). In the below, the reduction from private-RPE to OMP is stated by placing suitable polynomials and field elements.

c. Reduction from private-RPE

Recall that party 1 has inputs (x,m) and party 2has inputs (y,n). Since the reduction is from RPE, in the format of (3), party 1 needs to construct polynomials and party 2 needs to choose field elements. The polynomials for party 1 are:

$P(w) = w+x$

$Q(w) = w+m$

$R(w) = w \bullet x$

$S(w) = w \bullet m$

Note that all polynomials are linear and coefficients are known by party 1. On the other hand, the field elements of party 2 are:

$\alpha = n$

$\beta = y$

$\gamma = -y$

$\delta = -n$

The field elements γ and δ are well-defined since every field is an algebraic group and inverse with respect to the addition exists for y and n.

Let us define the $T(w_1,w_2,w_3,w_4)$ as the linear combination of P, Q, R and S polynomials in the following way:

$$T(w_1, w_2,w_3,w_4) = P(w_1) \bullet Q(w_2) + R(w_3) + S(w_4)$$

T is nothing but a dummy polynomial to handle the bilinear terms. Since addition and multiplication are closed operations in a field, T is also well-defined. If $(w_1, w_2,w_3,w_4) = (\alpha, \beta, \gamma, \delta)$ variable replacement is done then it yields:

$$T(w_1, w_2,w_3,w_4) = x \bullet m+y \bullet n$$

The numerator of the desired functional is constructed and the denominator is nothing but $Q(\beta)$. Using OPE, the reduction is complete by choosing suitable field elements together with constructing the polynomial, T as a combination of party 1's polynomials.

Proof of Privacy of the Algorithm

Two lemmas are critical for the proof that f computes the overall mean privately. The former belongs to Canetti (Canetti, 2000) and the latter belongs to Jha et al. (Jha, 2005). Their proofs are not given here as they can be reached from original sources.

Lemma 3. Composition Theorem for Passive Adversary

If ***g*** is privately reducible to ***f*** and there exists a protocol for computing ***f*** privately then there exists a protocol for computing ***g*** privately.

Lemma 4. Private RPE

The protocol given as RPE protocol privately computes RPE problem.

Theorem 2. Two-Party Private OMP

The protocol formed by ***f*** yields a privacy preserving algorithm for two-party OMP.

Proof

It is clear that OMP is privately reducible to RPE by choosing the numerator as T and the denominator as Q and there exists a protocol for private-RPE (Lemma 2) then by Lemma 1, given protocol is privately computes two-party OMP. It is trivial that reduction is polynomially-computable.

The multiparty case is nothing but extension of two parties to multiple.

Multiparty OMP Protocol

Assume that there are N parties in the computation. The protocol for multiparty OMP can be designed from two-party OMP in the following way:

1. Parties are ordered from 1 to N in a manner that consecutive parties are involved to two-party OMP computation. This can be done with a common share or coin-tossing into well protocol (Özarar, 2007).
2. Between party j and j+1, 0<j<N, the two-party OMP protocol works and

$((\mu_j, c_j), (\mu_{j+1}, c_{j+1})) \rightarrow ((\mu_j \bullet c_j + \mu_{j+1} \bullet c_{j+1})/ (c_j + c_{j+1}), (\mu_j \bullet c_j + \mu_{j+1} \bullet c_{j+1})/ (c_j + c_{j+1}))$

   is computed.
3. Furthermore, party j and j+1 privately compute their cardinality sum via the functional given in lemma 3. In other words, consecutive parties compute the partial mean and partial size of their samples:

$((\mu_j, c_j), (\mu_{j+1}, c_{j+1})) \rightarrow (c_j + c_{j+1}, c_j + c_{j+1})$

4. The mean and cardinality values are updated for party j+1 with the new values calculated at the end of the protocol involved with the previously ordered party. (i.e. party j+1 gets the partial mean and partial sum of samples up to her)
5. Apply the previous two steps for all consecutive parties. Total computation is linear in size and k-1 times for k parties.
6. At the end of the computation, the last party gets the overall mean together with total sample size and share them with remaining parties.

The unimportant gap of the protocol is; party j learns the size of the total previous samples yet it is not give the size of the each individual party. The only exception is for the first party, party 2 gets the size of its sample. This can be overcome by choosing the order in a circular round-robin fashion so the order of consecutive parties are preserved but only the first party changes. The probability to be the first party is 1/N which is Pareto-optimal for such a scheme.

After demonstrating the usage of OPE in overall mean case, let us analyze one more concrete application.

Application of OPE to Secure Multiparty Hamming Distance Computation

Privacy Preserving Two-Party Hamming Distance Computation Problem (HDP)

Suppose Alice has a binary vector $X = (x_1,..., x_k)$ and Bob has also another binary vector $Y = (y_1,..., y_k)$. They want to determine the Hamming Distance of X and Y without revealing each other's vector. In information theory, the Hamming distance between two bit sequences of equal length is the number of positions at which the corresponding symbols are different. In another way, it measures the minimum number of substitutions required to change one string into the other, or the number of errors that transformed one string into the other.

For the remaining scope, we have the following assumption on the model of computation:

Assumption 1

N-Party Homogenous Cooperation: There exist N parties each having a matrix M_i. The dimension of each M_i is $m_i \times k$. Party A communicates with party B to compute the Hamming Distance of an arbitrary row of M_A with respect to an arbitrary row of M_B. The Hamming distance is well-defined since the cardinality of any row in the computation is constant.

Privacy Preserving Two-Party HDP Algorithm (via OPE)

In this subsection, an algorithm (in a more programmer-friendly way) for privacy preserving two-party Hamming Distance Problem (HDP) is designed. A function should be taken as a target to place the terms in the OPE for developing such an algorithm.

Let f be the function for such a computation, its domain set must be n-dimensional vectors for both parties and range set must be a singleton numeric value (Hamming Distance). f can be constructed as:

$$f: \mathbb{Z}_2^{\,k} \times \mathbb{Z}_2^{\,k} \rightarrow \mathbb{Z}$$

The straightforward solution is approximating f by a circuit. Yet it is well known that the cost for implementing such a circuit is so inefficient that a new solution should be developed for the specific case. We now develop a protocol using OPE by placing meaningful polynomials and field elements for HDP.

Party 1 and Party 2 have binary vectors X = $(x_1,..., x_k)$ and Y = $(y_1,..., y_k)$, respectively. Moreover, Party 1 generates a random vector R= $(r_1,... r_k)$ where each $r_i \in Z$ and Party 2 generates a singleton random value S from the set of integers as well. Party 1 is the sender who determines the polynomials and Party 2 is the receiver who chooses the field elements. The result should be known by Party 2. Let $P_i(x)$ denotes the ith polynomial of Party 1 during the protocol hence P = $(P_1(x),..., P_k(x))$. The return value **d** denotes the Hamming Distance of X and Y.

The construction of the algorithm via OPE is as follows in Box 1.

At the beginning, Party 2 initializes the output (Hamming distance) to 0. In the main loop, both parties apply OPE protocol. Party 1 determines two types of linear polynomials according to the value of the vector element. Party 2 chooses nothing but the corresponding value at each step.

At line 4, Party 1 blinds the polynomials P by adding with a pre-determined random integer. This is because at line 6, Party 2 cannot get any intermediate result about the distance. Between lines 3-7, OPE is applied between parties. The cardinality of the loop is equal to the cardinality of input vectors. Party 1 prepares the polynomials and sends them to Party 2. Party 2 evaluates the polynomials and keeps the summation.

At line 8, Party 2 has calculated the distance yet the result has been blinded. If he directly sends the

Box 1.

```
Inputs; k, X, Y, R, P, S
Output: d
Algorithm P_HDP(P,X,Y):
1       d:= 0;                                   /* Party 2 */
2       for i = 1 … k
3       begin                                    /* OPE starts*/
4           if (x_i = 0) then P_i(x) = r_i+x;    /* Party 1 */
5           else P_i(x) = r_i+1-x;               /* Party 1 */
6           d:= d + P_i(y_i);                    /* Party 2 */
7       end                                      /* OPE ends*/
8       d:= d + S;                               /* Party 2 */
9       d:= d - Σ_i r_i;                         /* Party 1 */
10      d:= d - S;                               /* Party 2 */
```

result to Party 1 then Party 1 will have a chance to get the exact distance. It is time for Party 2 to blind the result by adding a singleton value and sends it to party 1. Party 1 sums up the total value of random array, extracts the summation from the value sent by Party 1. Party 1 still cannot determine the distance because it was blinded with S. After that, it sends the value to party 2 again at line 9. At line 10, party 2 obtains the final distance value by subtracting S from d.

Privacy Proof of Private HDP

It is time to prove that Private HDP is privacy preserving. We need to use Composition Theorem stated in Lemma 1 for Passive Adversary as a lemma for main proof.

A protocol to solve OPE was given by Naor and Pinkas (Naor, 2005). Let $P_{OPE}(P,\alpha)$ denote the privacy-preserving protocol for OPE. We provide a protocol $P_{HDP}(P,X,Y)$ for HDP, which uses $P_{OPE}(P,\alpha)$ as an oracle.

Theorem 3. Two-party Private HDP

The algorithm $P_{HDP}(P,X,Y)$ yields a privacy preserving algorithm for two-party HDP.

Proof

The views of the two parties are;

$VIEW_1\,(P) = (P, d+(\Sigma_i\, r_i)+S)$

$VIEW_2\,(Y) = (Y_,\, d+P_1(x), d+P_2(x), \ldots\, d+P_k(x), d+ (\Sigma_i\, r_i), d)$

We have to show two PPTAs, $S_1(P,d)$ and $S_2(Y,d)$ are statistically indistinguishable with respective views, $VIEW_1(P)$ and $VIEW_2(Y)$.

Let z, z', $z_1, \ldots z_k$ are random elements from $\mathbb{Z}$. Define,

$S_1(P,d) = (P, d+z)$

$S_2(Y,d) = (Y, d+z_1, \ldots, d+z_k, d+z', d)$

It is easy to see that the following two ensembles are statistically indistinguishable:

$(P, d+z)$

$(P, d+(\Sigma_i\, r_i)+S)$

The reason is that is z is a random integer then d+z is a random element of $\mathbb{Z}$ as well. $P(d+z) = P(d+z|z)$ since the cardinality of $\mathbb{Z}$ is equal to the cardinality of the integers greater than or equal to z.

Similarly,

$(Y_,\, d+P_1(x), d+P_2(x), \ldots, d+P_k(x), d+ (\Sigma_i\, r_i), d)$

$(Y, d+z_1, \ldots, d+z_k, d+z', d)$

are also statistically indistinguishable in accordance with the previous approach.

Recall that P_{HDP} uses the protocol P_{OPE}. Using the Canetti's composition theorem as a lemma, we conclude that P_{HDP} is privacy preserving.

Applications of OPE

There are two major applications of an OPE protocol. One is whenever k-wise independence can replace full independence or pseudo-randomness. Such property is required, for example, for the application of constructing anonymous coupons that enable anonymous usage of limited resources (e.g., for constructing an anonymous complaint box). The other types of applications uses OPE for comparing information without leaking it, or preserving anonymity when Receiver must compute the value of a polynomial at a certain point. Applications of this nature include a protocol that allows reliable and privacy preserving metering.

Implementation and Complexity of OPE

Note that any function from m bits to m bits can be represented as a polynomial over a finite field GF(2^m), but its degree could go as high as $2^m - 1$. Thus one would like to focus on those functions that can be represented by low degree polynomials. This turns out to have several interesting applications (Gilboa, 1999; Naor, 1999). The scheme proposed in Naor et. al. is much more efficient than the conventional way of going through oblivious circuit evaluation protocols, but its security is based on two assumptions (Naor, 1999). One assumption is the existence of a secure OT protocol while the other, a new one, is the intractability of a Noisy Polynomial Interpolation problem. It was later shown in Bleichenbacher et. al. that this new assumption may be much weaker than expected and suggested the use of a possibly stronger intractability assumption on a Polynomial Reconstruction Problem (Bleichenbacher, 2000). The protocol presented in Gilboa et. al. is based on an assumption that the Decisional Diffie-Hellman (DDH) assumption also holds over the group $\mathbb{Z}_{nxn}$ (Gilboa, 1999), where n is the product of two large primes. Contrary to the well studied DDH over $\mathbb{Z}_n$, the hardness of this problem in this new setting is yet to be studied. A novel OPE protocol is proposed in 2009 and we strongly recommend to use this novel one for the implementation of OPE (Vanishree, 2009).

Analyses show that the protocol provides unconditional security as against the computational security provided by the previously existing protocols. The main computational bottleneck of the existing constructions is the OT protocol, the computational cost of which is essentially exponentiations in finite fields. As another major asset of the protocol, this overhead is obviated and hence the protocol is proved to be more efficient.

FUTURE RESEARCH DIRECTIONS

A new method for solving SMC problems will be tamper-resistant devices. This can be added as a fourth alternative to already existing methods or techniques.

SMC with Tamper-Resistant Devices

The solutions discussed so far meet some of the objectives of the ideal architecture, but require a group of mutually distrustful providers running peer-to-peer SMC protocols. Setting up and operating such a consortium is rather difficult in practice. Also, the cryptographic methods used in these protocols offer limited, rather poor support for real life applications, even for the passive adversary model.

We can extend the methods and tools used in SMC by including tamper-resistant cryptographic co-processors. These devices combine cryptographic methods and physical protection to provide integrity of executable code, data secrecy, and data integrity. Several solutions using tamper-resistant devices have recently been proposed, but this line of research has not received sufficient attention (Benenson, 2006; Katz, 2007). In a server-based solution, we propose the use of such devices to realize ideal functionalities for secure computation tasks, as trusted implementations of the tasks, running in a closed, secure execution environment.

A powerful cryptographic co-processor has sufficient resources to run internally a secure computation, for simple applications and a small number of parties. The device can interact with the parties using the ideal case, extended to enable the parties to verify that the device is genuine and runs trusted code. These devices are expensive and their resources are inherently limited. A more general solution uses hardware security modules only for a small set of tasks that cannot be (efficiently) done by cryptographic protocols, such as generation and distribution of threshold decryption keys and a comprehensive set of arithmetic operations and mathematical functions needed in business applications.

Using this approach, straight-line programs for mathematical computations could be done quite easily in a singleserver setting. Handling control flow and decryption of the results without compromising privacy seems more difficult. Threshold decryption could still help, and if the server may learn the result, direct interaction between parties is not necessary for decryption.

CONCLUSION

Privacy is one of the most important properties of an information system must satisfy, in which systems the need to share information among different, not trusted entities, the protection of sensible information has a relevant role. Thus secure distributed computation, which was done as part of a larger body of research in the theory of cryptography, has achieved remarkable results. These results were shown using generic constructions that can be applied to any function that has an efficient representation as a circuit. Privacy preserving algorithms have been recently introduced with the aim of preventing the discovery of sensible information.

Cryptographic protocols for secure computation achieved remarkable results: it was shown that generic constructions can be used to compute any function securely and it was also demonstrated that some functions can be computed even more efficiently using specialized constructions. Still, a secure protocol for computing a certain function will always be more costly than a naive protocol that does not provide any security. By making use of cryptographic techniques to store sensitive data and providing access to the stored data based on an individual's role, we ensure that the data is safe from privacy breaches.

In this chapter, the broad concept of Secure Multiparty Computation is analyzed especially concentrating on a cryptographic building block called Oblivious Polynomial Evaluation. The model paradigms in SMC are given and two types of adversarial behavior are explained. The literature survey and notable specific problems on SMC are briefly discussed. Methods to solve SMC problems are given and mainly focused on a cryptographic one, namely OPE. The usage of OPE to concrete problems like secure overall mean and Hamming Distance computations are demonstrated including privacy proofs. The applications and complexity of OPE protocols are presented.

The most common drawback of SMC protocols with OPE is their inefficiency. They require considerable computation and communication costs. We believe that further research in this area is crucial for the development of secure and efficient protocols in this field with the help of tamper-resistant hardware to provide low-cost practical solutions as well.

REFERENCES

Agrawal, R., Evfimievski, A., & Srikant, R. (2003). Paper. In *Proceedings of the 2003 ACM SIGMOD International Conference on Management of Data*, (pp. 86-97). ACM Press.

Agrawal, R., & Srikant, R. (2000). Privacy-preserving data mining. In *Proceedings of the 2000 ACM SIGMOD on Management of Data*, (pp. 439–450). ACM Press.

Amirbekyan, A., & Estivill-Castro, V. (2009). Practical protocol for Yao's millionaires problem enables secure multiparty computation of metrics and efficient privacy-preserving k-NN for large data sets. *Knowledge and Information Systems*, *21*, 327–363. doi:10.1007/s10115-009-0233-z

Atallah, M. J., & Du, W. (2001). Secure multiparty computational geometry. In *Proceedings of 7th International Workshop on Algorithms and Data Structures*, (pp. 165-179). IEEE.

Bayardo, R., & Agrawal, R. (2005). Data privacy through optimal k-anonymization. In *Proceedings the 21st International Conference on Data Engineering*, (pp. 217-228). IEEE.

Benaloh, J. (1994). Dense probabilistic encryption. In *Proceedings of the Workshop on Selected Areas of Cryptography*, (pp. 120-128). IEEE.

Benenson, Z. (2006). TrustedPals: Secure multiparty computation implemented with smart cards. In *Proceedings of the 11th European Symposium on Research in Computer Security (ESORICS 2006)*, (pp. 306-314). ESORICS.

Bleichenbacher, D., & Nguyen, P. (2000). Noisy polynomial interpolation and noisy Chinese remaindering. [EURO-CRYPT.]. *Proceedings of EURO-CRYPT, 2000*, 53–69.

Cachin, C., Micali, S., & Stadler, M. (1999). Computationally private information retrieval with polylogarithmic communication. *Lecture Notes in Computer Science*, *1592*, 402–414. doi:10.1007/3-540-48910-X_28

Canetti, R. (2000). Security and composition of multiparty cryptographic protocols. *Journal of Cryptology*, *13*(1), 143–202. doi:10.1007/s001459910006

Chang, Y., & Lu, C. (2001). Oblivious polynomial evaluation and oblivious neural learning. In *Proceedings of Theoretical Computer Science* (pp. 369–384). IEEE. doi:10.1007/3-540-45682-1_22

Chaum, D., Crepeau, C., & Damgard, I. (1988). Multiparty unconditionally secure protocols. In *Proceedings of the 20th ACM Symposium on the Theory of Computing*, (pp. 11-19). ACM Press.

Chor, B., & Gilboa, N. (1997). Computationally private information retrieval. In *Proceedings of 29th Annual ACM Symposium on Theory of Computing*, (pp. 304–313). ACM Press.

Chor, B., Kushilevitz, E., Goldreich, O., & Sudan, M. (1995). Private information retrieval. In *Proceedings of the 36th Annual IEEE Symposium on Foundations of Computer Science*, (pp. 41–50). IEEE.

Clifton, C., Kantarcioglu, M., & Vaidya, J. (2004). Tools for privacy preserving distributed data mining. *ACM SIGKDD Explorations Newsletter*, *4*(2), 28–34. doi:10.1145/772862.772867

Dhillon, I. S., & Modha, D. S. (1999). A data-clustering algorithm on distributed memory multiprocessors. In *Proceedings of Large-scale Parallel KDD Systems Workshop (ACM SIGKDD)*, (pp. 245-260). ACM Press.

Di-Crescenzo, G., Ishai, Y., & Ostrovsky, R. (1998). Universal service-providers for database private information retrieval. In *Proceedings of the 17th Annual ACM Symposium on Principles of Distributed Computing*, (pp. 91–100). ACM Press.

Dowd, J., Xu, S., & Zhang, W. (2006). Privacy-preserving decision tree mining based on random substitutions. [ETRICS.]. *Proceedings of ETRICS, 2006*, 145–159.

Du, W., & Atallah, M. J. (2001). Secure multiparty computation problems and their applications: Review and open problems. In *Proceedings of the New Security Paradigms Workshop*, (pp. 11-20). IEEE.

Du, W., & Atallah, M. J. (2002). a practical approach to solve secure multiparty computation problems. In *Proceedings of the New Security Paradigms Workshop*, (pp. 127-135). IEEE.

Du, W., & Zhan, Z. (2002). Building decision tree classifier on private data. In *Proceedings of Electrical Engineering and Computer Science* (pp. 11–20). IEEE.

Duda, R. O., Hart, P. E., & Stork, D. G. (2001). *Pattern classification*. New York, NY: John Wiley & Sons.

Emekci, F., Sahin, O. D., Agrawal, D., & El Abbadi, A. (2007). Privacy preserving decision tree learning over multiple parties. *Data & Knowledge Engineering*, *63*, 348–361. doi:10.1016/j.datak.2007.02.004

Evfimievski, A., Gehrke, J., & Srikant, R. (2003). Limiting privacy breaches in privacy preserving data mining. In *Proceedings of the Twenty-Second ACM SIGACT-SIGMOD-SIGART Symposium on Principles of Database Systems*, (pp. 211-222). ACM Press.

Evfimievski, A., Srikant, R., Agrawal, R., & Gehrke, J. (2002). Privacy preserving mining of association rules. In *Proceedings of the Eighth ACM SIGKDD International Conference on Knowledge Discovery and Data Mining*, (pp. 217–228). ACM Press.

Fang, W., & Yang, B. (2008). Privacy preserving decision tree learning over vertically partitioned data. In *Proceedings of the 2008 International Conference on Computer Science & Software Engineering*. IEEE.

Franconi, L., & Merola, G. (2003). *Implementing statistical disclosure control for aggregated data released via remote access*. Working Paper No. 30. Geneva, Switzerland: United Nations Statistical Commission and European Commission.

Freedman, M., Nissim, K., & Pinkas, B. (2004). Efficient private matching and set intersection. [Eurocrypt.]. *Proceedings of the Advances in Cryptology Eurocrypt*, *2004*, 1–19.

Fung, B., Wang, K., & Yu, P. (2005). Top-down specialization for information and privacy preservation. In *Proceedings of the 21st IEEE International Conference on Data Engineering*, (pp. 205-216). IEEE Press.

Gertner, Y., Ishai, Y., Kushilevitz, E., & Malkin, T. (1998). Protecting data privacy in information retrieval schemes. In *Proceedings of the Thirtieth Annual ACM Symposium on Theory of Computing, STOC '98*, (pp. 151–160). ACM Press.

Gilboa, N. (1999). Two party RSA key generation. [CRYPTO.]. *Proceedings of CRYPTO*, *1999*, 116–129.

Goethals, B., Laur, S., Lipmaa, H., & Mielikäinen, T. (2004). On private scalar product computation for privacy-preserving data mining. *Lecture Notes in Computer Science*, *3506*, 104–120. doi:10.1007/11496618_9

Goldreich, O. (2004). *Foundations of cryptography: Basic applications*. Cambridge, UK: Cambridge University Press. doi:10.1017/CBO9780511721656

Goldreich, O., Micali, S., & Wigderson, A. (1987). How to play any mental game - A completeness theorem for protocols with honest majority. In *Proceedings of the 19th Symposium on Theory of Computer Science*, (pp. 218–229). IEEE.

Ioannidis, I., & Grama, A. (2003). An efficient protocol for Yao's millionaires problem. In *Proceedings of the 36th Hawaii International Conference on System Sciences*, (pp. 6–9). IEEE.

Ishai, Y., & Kushilevitz, E. (1999). Improved upper bounds on information-theoretic private information retrieval (extended abstract). In *Proceedings of the Thirty-first Annual ACM Symposium on Theory of Computing*, (pp. 79–88). ACM.

Jha, S., Kruger, L., & McDaniel, P. (2005). Privacy preserving clustering. In *Proceedings of the 10th European Symposium on Research in Computer Security (ESORICS)*, (pp. 397-417).

Kantarcioglu, M., & Clifton, C. (2004). Privacy preserving data mining of association rules on horizontally partitioned data. *Transactions on Knowledge and Data Engineering*, *16*(9), 639–644. doi:10.1109/TKDE.2004.45

Kantarcioglu, M., & Vaidya, J. (2003). privacy preserving naive bayes classifier for horizontally partitioned data. In *Proceedings of the Workshop on Privacy Preserving Data Mining held in association with The Third IEEE International Conference on Data Mining*. IEEE.

Kargupta, H., Huang, W., Sivakumar, K., & Johnson, E. (2001). Distributed clustering using collective principal component analysis. *Knowledge and Information Systems, 3*(4), 405–421. doi:10.1007/PL00011677

Katz, J. (2007). Universally composable multiparty computation using tamper-proof hardware. *Lecture Notes in Computer Science, 4515*, 115–128. doi:10.1007/978-3-540-72540-4_7

Kim, J. (1986). A method for limiting disclosure in microdata based on random noise and transformation. In *Proceedings of the American Statistical Association on Survey Research Methods*, (pp. 370–374). IEEE.

Klusch, M., Lodi, S., & Moro, G. (2003). Distributed clustering based on sampling local density estimates. In *Proceedings of the Eighteenth International Joint Conference on Artificial Intelligence (IJCAI 2003)*, (pp. 485–490). IJCAI.

Kushilevitz, E., & Ostrovsky, R. (1997). Replication is not needed: Single database, computationally private information retrieval. In *Proceedings of the 38th Annual IEEE Computer Society Conference on Foundation of Computer Science*, (pp. 20–22). IEEE.

Lefevre, K., Dewittd, J., & Ramakrishnan, R. (2005). Incognito: Efficient full-domain k-anonymity. In *Proceedings of the 2005 ACM SIGMOD International Conference on Management of Data*, (pp. 49-60). ACM.

Li, B., & Sarkar, S. (2006). A tree-based data perturbation approach for privacy-preserving data mining. *IEEE Transactions on Knowledge and Data Engineering, 18*(9), 1278–1283. doi:10.1109/TKDE.2006.136

Lindell, Y., & Pinkas, B. (2000). Privacy preserving data mining. In *Proceedings of Advances in Cryptology (Crypto 2000)*, (pp. 36–54). Crypto.

Machanavajjhala, A., Gehrke, J., & Kifer, D. (2007). l-Diversity: Privacy beyond k-anonymity. In *Proceedings of ACM Transactions on Knowledge Discovery from Data*, (pp. 24-35). ACM Press.

Merugu, S., & Ghosh, J. (2003). Privacy-preserving distributed clustering using generative models. In *Proceedings of the 3rd IEEE International Conference on Data Mining (ICDM 2003)*, (pp. 211–218). IEEE.

Naccache, D., & Stern, J. (1998). A new public key cryptosystem based on higher residues. In *Proceedings of the 5th ACM Conference on Computer and Communications Security*, (pp. 59–66). ACM Press.

Naor, M., & Nissim, K. (2001). Communication preserving protocols for secure function evaluation. In *Proceedings of the 33rd Annual ACM Symposium on Theory of Computing*. Heraklion, Greece: ACM.

Naor, M., & Pinkas, B. (1999). Oblivious transfer and polynomial evaluation. In *Proceedings of the 31st Symposium on Theory of Computer Science*, (pp. 245–254). IEEE.

Naor, M., & Pinkas, B. (2005). Computationally secure oblivious transfer. *Journal of Cryptology, 18*(1), 245–254. doi:10.1007/s00145-004-0102-6

Oleshchuk, V., & Zadorozhny, V. (2007). Secure multiparty computations and privacy preservation: Results and open problems. *Telektronikk: Telenor's Journal of Technology, 103*(2).

Oliveira, S., & Zaiane, O. R. (2003). Privacy preserving clustering by data transformation. In *Proceedings of XVIII Simp'osio Brasileiro de Bancos de Dados*, (pp. 304–318). IEEE.

Özarar, M., & Özgit, A. (2007). Secure multi-party overall mean computation via oblivious polynomial evaluation. In *Proceedings of First International Conference on Security of Information and Networks (SIN 2007)*, (pp. 84-95). IEEE.

Özarar, M., & Özgit, A. (2008). Secure homogeneous matrix algebra with oblivious polynomial evaluation. In *Proceedings of Third Information Security and Cryptology Conference (ISCTURKEY)*, (pp. 157-163). ISCTURKEY.

Özarar, M., & Özgit, A. (2011). *Privacy preserving hierarchical agglomerative document clustering*. Technical Report. METU.

Paillier, P. (1999). Public-key cryptosystems based on composite degree residuosity classes. In *Proceedings of Advances in Cryptology (EUROCRYPT'99)*. EUROCRYPT.

Pinkas, B. (2003). In Explorations, S. I. G. K. D. D. (Ed.), *Cryptographic techniques for privacy-preserving data mining* (pp. 12–19). ACM.

Rizvi, S. J., & Harista, J. R. (2002). Maintaining data privacy in association rule mining. In *Proceedings of 28th International Conference on Very Large Data Bases (VLDB)*, (pp. 682-693). VLDB.

Shamir, A. (1979). How to share a secret. *Communications of the ACM*, *22*(11), 612–613. doi:10.1145/359168.359176

Sweeney, L. (2002). k-Anonymity: A model for protecting privacy. *International Journal on Uncertainty. Fuzziness and Knowledge-Based Systems*, *10*(5), 557–570. doi:10.1142/S0218488502001648

Vaidya, J., & Clifton, C. (2003). Leveraging the "multi" in secure multiparty computation. In *Proceedings of the Workshop on Privacy in the Electronic Society*, (pp. 53-59). IEEE.

Vaidya, J., & Clifton, C. (2003). Privacy-preserving k-means clustering over vertically partitioned data. In *Proceedings of the Ninth ACM SIGKDD International Conference on Knowledge Discovery and Data Mining*, (pp. 206–215). ACM.

Vaidya, J., & Clifton, C. (2004). Privacy preserving naive bayes classifier for vertically partitioned data. In *Proceedings of the 2004 SIAM International Conference on Data Mining*, (pp. 522-526). SIAM.

Vanishree, H., & George, K. (2009). A novel unconditionally secure oblivious polynomial evaluation protocol. In *Proceedings of 2009 International Workshop on Information Security and Application (IWISA 2009)*. IWISA.

Verykios, V. S., Bertino, E., Parasiliti, L., Favino, I. N., Saygin, Y., & Theodoridis, Y. (2004). State-of-the-art in privacy preserving data mining. *ACM SIGMOD, 33*(1).

Yao, A. C. (1986). How to generate and exchange secrets. In *Proceedings of the 27th IEEE Symposium on Foundations of Computer Science*. IEEE.

ADDITIONAL READING

Aggarwal, G., Mishra, N., & Pinkas, B. (2004). Secure computation of the k-th ranked element. *Lecture Notes in Computer Science*, *3027*, 40–55. doi:10.1007/978-3-540-24676-3_3

Aiello, W., Ishai, Y., & Reingold, O. (2001). Priced oblivious transfer: How to sell digital goods. *Lecture Notes in Computer Science*, *2045*, 119–135. doi:10.1007/3-540-44987-6_8

Aumann, Y., & Lindell, Y. (2007). Security against covert adversaries: Efficient protocols for realistic adversaries. *Lecture Notes in Computer Science*, *4392*, 137–156. doi:10.1007/978-3-540-70936-7_8

Beaver, D. (1991). Foundations of secure interactive computing. *Lecture Notes in Computer Science, 576*, 377–391. doi:10.1007/3-540-46766-1_31

Beaver, D., Micali, S., & Rogaway, P. (1990). The round complexity of secure protocols. In *Proceedings of STOC*, (pp. 503-513). STOC.

Bellare, M., & Micali, S. (1989). Non-interactive oblivious transfer and applications. *Lecture Notes in Computer Science, 435*, 547–557. doi:10.1007/0-387-34805-0_48

Ben-Or, M., Goldwasser, S., & Wigderson, A. (1988). Completeness theorems for non-cryptographic fault-tolerant distributed computation. In *Proceedings of the 20th STOC*, (pp. 1-10). STOC.

Canetti, R., & Herzberg, A. (1994). Maintaining security in the presences of transient faults. *Lecture Notes in Computer Science, 839*, 425–438. doi:10.1007/3-540-48658-5_38

Cleve, R. (1896). Limits on the security of coin flips when half the processors are faulty. In *Proceedings of the 18th STOC*, (pp. 364-369). STOC.

Cramer, R., Damgard, I., & Nielsen, J. B. (2001). Multiparty computation from threshold homomorphic encryption. *Lecture Notes in Computer Science, 2045*, 280–300. doi:10.1007/3-540-44987-6_18

Damgard, I., & Jurik, M. (2001). A generalisation, a simplification and some applications of Paillier's probabilistic public-key system. *Lecture Notes in Computer Science, 1992*, 119–136. doi:10.1007/3-540-44586-2_9

Even, S., Goldreich, O., & Lempel, A. (1985). A randomized protocol for signing contracts. *Communications of the ACM, 28*(6), 637–647. doi:10.1145/3812.3818

Fagin, R., Naor, M., & Winkler, P. (1996). Comparing information without leaking it. *Communications of the ACM, 39*(5), 77–85. doi:10.1145/229459.229469

Franklin, M., & Haber, S. (1996). Joint encryption and message-efficient secure computation. *Journal of Cryptology, 9*(4), 217–232. doi:10.1007/s001459900013

Gentry, C. (2009). Fully homomorphic encryption using ideal lattices. In *Proceedings of the Symposium on the Theory of Computing (STOC)*, (pp. 169-178). STOC.

Goldreich, O. (2001). *Foundations of cryptography: Basic tools*. Cambridge, UK: Cambridge University Press. doi:10.1017/CBO9780511546891

Goldreich, O. (2003). Cryptography and cryptographic protocols. *Distributed Computing, 16*(2), 177–199. doi:10.1007/s00446-002-0077-1

Goldwasser, S., & Levin, L. (1990). Fair computation of general functions in presence of immoral majority. *Lecture Notes in Computer Science, 537*, 77–93. doi:10.1007/3-540-38424-3_6

Goldwasser, S., & Micali, S. (1982). Probabilistic encryption and how to play mental poker keeping secret all partial information. In *Proceedings of the 14th STOC*, (pp. 365-377). STOC.

Halevi, S., & Kalai, Y. T. (2005). Smooth projective hashing and two-message oblivious transfer. *Lecture Notes in Computer Science, 3494*, 78–95. doi:10.1007/11426639_5

Ishai, Y., Kilian, J., Nissim, K., & Petrank, E. (2003). Extending oblivious transfers efficiently. *Lecture Notes in Computer Science, 2729*, 145–161. doi:10.1007/978-3-540-45146-4_9

Jarecki, S., & Shmatikov, V. (2007). Efficient two-party secure computation on committed inputs. *Lecture Notes in Computer Science, 4515*, 97–114. doi:10.1007/978-3-540-72540-4_6

Kilian, J. (1988). Founding cryptography on oblivious transfer. In *Proceedings of the 20th STOC*, (pp. 20-31). STOC.

Kissner, L., & Song, D. (2007). Privacy-preserving set operations. *Lecture Notes in Computer Science*, *3621*, 241–257. doi:10.1007/11535218_15

Lindell, Y., & Pinkas, B. (2007). An efficient protocol for secure two-party computation in the presence of malicious adversaries. *Lecture Notes in Computer Science*, *4515*, 52–78. doi:10.1007/978-3-540-72540-4_4

Malkhi, D., Nisan, N., Pinkas, B., & Sella, Y. (2004). Fairplay - A secure two-party computation system. In *Proceedings of the 13th USENIX Security Symposium*, (pp. 287-302). USENIX.

Micali, S., & Rogaway, P. (1991). Secure computation. *Lecture Notes in Computer Science*, *576*, 392–404. doi:10.1007/3-540-46766-1_32

Ostrovsky, R., & Yung, M. (1991). How to withstand mobile virus attacks. In *Proceedings of the 10th PODC*, (pp. 51-59). PODC.

Polat, H., & Du, W. (2005). Privacy-preserving collaborative filtering. *International Journal of Electronic Commerce*, *9*(4), 9–35.

Rabin, T., & Ben-Or, M. (1989). Verifiable secret sharing and multiparty protocols with honest majority. In *Proceedings of the 21st STOC*, (pp. 73-85). STOC.

KEY TERMS AND DEFINITIONS

Oblivious Polynomial Evaluation: It is a protocol involving two parties, a sender whose input is a polynomial P, and a receiver whose input is a value x. At the end of the protocol, the receiver learns P(x) and nothing more about P, while the sender remains oblivious of both x and P(x).

Oblivious Transfer: In cryptography, an oblivious transfer protocol (often abbreviated OT) is a type of protocol in which a sender transfers one of potentially many pieces of information to a receiver, but remains oblivious as to what piece (if any) has been transferred.

Privacy Preserving (Algorithm): The aim of these algorithms is the extraction of relevant knowledge from large amount of data, while protecting at the same time sensitive information.

Rivest-Shamir-Adleman (RSA) Algorithm: RSA is an algorithm for public-key cryptography that is based on the presumed difficulty of factoring large integers, the factoring problem.

Secure Hamming Distance Problem: A secure multiparty problem for calculating Hamming Distances between vectors.

Secure Multiparty Computation: The goal of methods for secure multi-party computation is to enable parties to jointly compute a function over their inputs, while at the same time keeping these inputs private.

Secure Overall Mean Problem: A secure multiparty problem to calculate overall mean of samples.

Trusted Third Party: In cryptography, a Trusted Third Party (TTP) is an entity which facilitates interactions between two parties who both trust the third party.

Chapter 12
PKI Trust Models

Audun Jøsang
University of Oslo, Norway

ABSTRACT

A PKI can be described as a set of technologies, procedures, and policies for propagating trust from where it initially exists to where it is needed for authentication in online environments. How the trust propagation takes place under a specific PKI depends on the PKI's syntactic trust structure, which is commonly known as a trust model. However, trust is primarily a semantic concept that cannot be expressed in syntactic terms alone. In order to define meaningful trust models for PKIs it is also necessary to consider the semantic assumptions and human cognition of trust relationships, as explicitly or implicitly expressed by certification policies, legal contractual agreements between participants in a PKI, and by how identity information is displayed and represented. Of the many different PKI trust models proposed in the literature, some have been implemented and are currently used in practical settings, from small personal networks to large-scale private and public networks such as the Internet. This chapter takes a closer look at the most prominent and widely used PKI trust models, and discusses related semantic issues.

INTRODUCTION

Trust is a directional relationship between two parties that can be called the relying party and the trusted party. One must assume the relying party to be a 'reasoning entity' in some form (Jøsang, 1996), meaning that it has the ability to make evaluations and decisions about trust based on received information and past experience. The trusted party can be anything from a person, organization or physical entity, to abstract notions such as information or a cryptographic key.

A trust relationship has a scope, meaning that it applies to a specific purpose or domain of action, such as "to be authentic" for a cryptographic key, or "to provide quality service and repair" for car

DOI: 10.4018/978-1-4666-4030-6.ch012

mechanics (Jøsang et al., 2005). The literature uses the term trust with a variety of meanings (McKnight and Chervany, 1996), so it is not always clear what authors mean by it. In order to avoid misunderstanding it is always useful to be specific and define the meaning of trust when using the term in a particular context.

A distinction should be made between interpreting trust as an evaluation or as a decision. When interpreting trust as a subjective evaluation of the reliability or correctness of something or somebody, it is called evaluation trust. When interpreting trust as a decision to enter into a situation of dependence on something or somebody, it is called decision trust. This distinction can appear subtle but is in fact quite fundamental. For example, having high evaluation trust in an entity is not necessarily sufficient to make a decision to enter into a situation of dependence on that entity if the risk is perceived as being too high. Evaluation trust reflects the reliability of the trusted party and is application and context independent, whereas decision trust depends on the particular application and on the context in which it is embedded. It can be shown that decision trust is a function of evaluations trust and risk (Jøsang and Lo Presti, 2004).

Both evaluation trust and decision trust reflect a positive belief about something on which the relying party potentially or actually depends for his welfare. Evaluation trust is most naturally measured as a discrete or continuous degree of reliability or belief, whereas decision trust is most naturally measured in terms of a binary decision. Several authors have proposed to let certificates express levels of trust on a discrete or continuous scale, e.g. (Kohlas et al., 2008). However, this would only be meaningful in case CAs are uncertain about the correctness of what they certify, and expressing levels of trust in the certificate seems to be incompatible with CA business models. It would be rather strange if a CA states in a certificate that the certified public key e.g. is authentic with probability 0.9, as no user would want to buy such certificates. Certificates are issued according to a certification policy. In practice this policy is often published as two separate documents called the Certificate Policy and the Certificate Practice Statement where the former specifies high level requirements and the latter how these requirements are fulfilled in detail. We will here refer to both with the term "certification policy." The relying party can judge the adequacy of the policy for the intended certificate usage. The relying party must also consider whether the certification policy is properly adhered to by the CA. Evaluation trust in a validated certificate can be defined as "the quality of the certification policy combined with the belief in the CAs adherence to that policy." However, relying parties often do not have the expertise to judge the certification policy, and it would be practically difficult for relying parties to audit the CA's adherence to the certification policy.

A validated certificate never provides 100% assurance that the public key actually is authentic. It could for example be possible for an attacker to trick the CA to issue a public-key certificate with the wrong name, thereby enabling the attacker to spoof the corresponding identity (Microsoft, 2001). It is up to the relying party how the assurance provided by a particular public-key certificate is to be used and depended upon in a real situation. For example, a relying party may take a validated public-key certificate as evidence of authenticity but still only be 90% convinced that the certified public key is authentic, which would be equivalent to 90% evaluation trust. The same relying party can nevertheless decide to accept and use the public-key certificate despite not being totally convinced about the correctness of the identity, and this would be a case of binary decision trust. Decision trust in a validated certificate can be defined as "the acceptance of the certificate based on evaluation trust and other contextual factors."

A certificate only partially provides the trust needed for a particular transaction. Relying parties should interpret a validated public-key certificate as evidence of its authenticity, but not as evidence of honesty and reliability. The relying party usually needs to consider both types of trust, but public-key certificates can only provide identity trust.

PKIs and public-key certificates enable authentication of the key owner and thereby support identity management. An identity is a representation of an entity in a specific application domain. Identities traditionally represent physical world entities, but online identities with anonymous entities are now common on the Internet. Typical physical world entities are people and organizations. In case of online identities, it must be assumed that an underlying physical world entity exists, even if it is unknown to relying parties.

An identity consists of a set of attributes, where an attribute is typically called a name or an identifier when used for identification purposes. These attributes may or may not be unique within the identity domain. They can have various properties, such as being transient or permanent, self-selected or issued by an authority, suitable for human interpretation or only by computers. The possible attributes of an identity may differ, depending on the type of entity being identified. For example, date of birth is an often used attribute for people, but not for organizations; companies often use logos to represent themselves, people usually do not.

It should be noted that the distinction between identity and name/identifier is blurred in common language. The term 'identity' is often used in the sense of 'name,' especially when an identity is recognized by a single unique name within a given context. For clarity, this chapter will use the terms 'identity' and 'name' with their separate specific meanings.

A name space of unique names in a domain allows a one-to-one relationship between identities and names. Not every identity characteristic can be used as unique name: for example, a date of birth does not uniquely identify an individual person, because two or more people can have the same date of birth. It can be quite challenging to define a suitable name space, and in general, the larger the domain (i.e. the more entities to identify), the more difficult it gets. For example, a name space of unique names for all humans seems to be politically and practically impossible to achieve. Name spaces must be carefully designed, because a poor name space design that must be changed at a later stage can result in significant extra costs. For example, when it became clear that the current 32-bit name space of fixed length IP (Internet Protocol) addresses in IPv4 would become too small, a new name space with 128 bits was designed for IPv6, with the result that IPv4 and IPv6 addresses are incompatible.

A pseudonym may be used as unique name in some systems for practical or privacy reasons in order to provide an anonymous identity (UK eEnvoy, 2002). The pseudonym is a name where only the party that assigned the pseudonym knows the real world identity behind it. The pseudonyms can be self-assigned, so that the real world identity (e.g. that of a legal persona) behind the pseudonym is only known by the owner, and otherwise is hidden to all other parties. Alternatively, the pseudonym can be defined and escrowed by a trusted third party who knows the real world identity, and who is able to reveal it under special circumstances such as law enforcement.

Identities can be established in various ways. It can happen formally through a registration process managed by a registration authority, or informally through repeated interactions with other entities where various characteristics of the identity are exposed. The etymological meaning of identity is "the same one as last time." A requirement for establishing an online identity is therefore that a process exists for first time definition or registration of identity attributes. The registration of a new identity does not necessarily take physical world characteristics or other pre-existing attributes of the entity. A new identity can be defined from scratch with totally new attributes, in which case it becomes a virtual or pseudonymous identity. The important property is that the entity can be recognized with the same attributes in future interactions. This principle also applies to PKIs, so that the unique name and the other identity attributes in a certificate are not necessarily tied to a known real world entity. It is even possible to use the public key itself as unique name, in which case the user's identity is formed by the public key as well as other characteristics emerging from the user's online presence. The SPKI/SDSI model described below applies this principle.

Traditional public-key certificates establish a cryptographic binding between a public key and a unique name in a specific identity domain. Other (possibly non-unique) names may also be specified. It is crucial that the names are meaningful to relying parties. The identity with which a user is commonly recognized by relying parties do not necessarily contain the unique name stored in the certificate. In such case it must be possible to link the unique name to a meaningful identity, otherwise the certificate might become meaningless to relying parties. This problem will be discussed in the section on the Semantics of Trust and Identity below.

PKI TRUST STRUCTURES

The difficulty of ensuring secure key distribution is a major obstacle to practical use of cryptography. With traditional symmetric-key cryptography each pair of parties that want to communicate securely must exchange cryptographic keys out-of-band and thereby establish a direct trust relationship. The term out-of-band denotes an external channel, i.e. outside the communication channel that the PKI is intended to protect. Secure out-of-band channels and direct trust relationships are typically expensive to set up and maintain, so finding ways to reduce their number can lead to significant cost savings. The main purpose of a PKI is to simplify key distribution by reducing the number of secure out-of-band channels needed. Trust in user public keys is then cryptographically derived from a limited set of direct trust relationships. In that sense, a PKI allows trust to be propagated from where it exists to where it is needed (Simmons and Meadows, 1995).

A public-key certificate represents a trust edge from the CA to the owner of the certified public key. The traditional trust scope is that: "The owner of the public key rightfully holds the unique name specified in the certificate." Such certificates are often called identity certificates. Any user who can prove that they control the private key corresponding to the public key, will have proved that they also own the unique name written on the certificate. The proof is typically given through a cryptographic security protocol. An identity certificate thus creates a binding between a public-key and an identity. A certificate can also express other semantic concepts than a unique name, in which case it is called an attribute certificate. In theory, any assertable concept that can be related to a public key can be certified in an attribute certificate. Expressing access authorization is the most common usage of attribute certificates, whereby the trust scope could be: "The owner of the public key is authorized to access resource X." An attribute certificate thus creates a binding between a public key and specific attributes of the owner.

A relying party who trusts the CA, who has validated the certificate, and who has successfully executed an authentication protocol proof with the user, will be able to derive trust in the authenticity of the user identity as represented by the unique name specified in the certificate. A linked chain of certificates represents a trust path, and a collection of interlinked certificates represents a trust network. In general, any such trust network based on certificates can be called a PKI, but only a few trust network classes represent practical PKIs with viable business models. Recipients of public-key certificates, also called relying parties, do not themselves need certificates in order to authenticate a user's public key, they only need an authentic copy of the root public key. Only users that want to be authenticated need to have public-key certificates. In this chapter, a leaf certificate owner is called a user. A user can be a legal entity such as an individual or an organization, or it can be a system or process entity, or even an abstract role.

Figure 1 illustrates the typical internal trust structure of a PKI and the graphical notation used in this chapter. The left hand side shows how the trust structure where the indexes indicate the order in which the trust relationships and digital signatures are formed. The right hand side shows the corresponding graphical PKI representation. It is assumed that a RA (Registration Authority) is part of both the root CA and the intermediate CA. The role of the RA is to pre-authenticate user identities based on physical world artifacts, and communicate the user identity (consisting of a set of attributes) to the CA. In reality, the RA can be separate from the CA in which case additional trust relationships between the CA and the RA are required.

The public and private keys are illustrated as a white and a shaded key respectively in Figure 1. The root CA, as well as intermediate CAs and users, are assumed to have complete trust in the authenticity of their own public-private key pair (index 1). The root CA generates a self-signed certificate (index 2) which is distributed through any suitable secure out-of-band channel to potential relying parties. When the root CA is assured about the identity of the intermediate CA and the authenticity of its public key it has established trust in the binding between the identity and the public key (index 3). The CA then issues a certificate to assert this fact according to a specific policy (index 4). Similarly, when the intermediate CA is assured about the binding between the user identity and the user's public key (index 5), it issues the user's public-key certificate that testifies this fact according to a specific policy (index 6). It should be noted that the root CA must also trust the intermediate CA regarding its reliability (competence and honesty) to correctly register and issue user certificates, so that the trust relationship between the root CA and the intermediate CA (index 3) normally has a double scope consisting of the explicit binding between the CA name and public key, as well as implicit reliability of the CA. The leaf trust relationship between the intermediate CA and the user (index 6) only has the explicit scope of binding between name and public key, i.e. it does not say anything about the reliability of the user. In practice this means that a CA will not check whether the user or organization buying a certificate is honest or competent in any regard because this is not within the trust scope of the user certificate.

Figure 1. Detailed trust structure for certificate generation

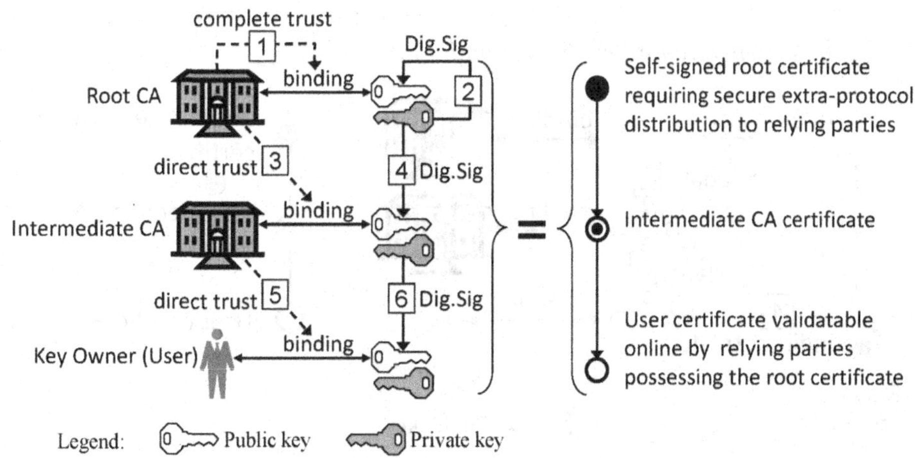

There are various business models for CAs. Commercial CAs generate revenue by selling certificates, whereas internal CAs in an organization issue certificates to units in the organization as part of their function or role. Individuals can also act as CAs, such as in PGP described below, in which case they issue certificates for the benefit of their friends and connections.

Software systems are designed to store and process public keys in the form of certificates, and are usually unable to handle naked public keys. For that reason, root public keys are normally distributed and stored in the form of a self-signed certificates. A root public key is thus part of a certificate that has been signed by the corresponding private key, as illustrated on the top of Figure 1 (index 2). Note that a self-signed certificate provides no assurance whatsoever regarding the authenticity of the root public key, it only makes the distribution, storage and processing of root public keys more practical. This is because validation of the self-signed public key would have to be done with the same public-key. This would clearly be meaningless as a public key cannot validate itself, and PKIs would be obsolete if public-keys were self-validating.

Certificate validation, normally done by the relying party, consists of verifying the correctness of the digital signature on the certificate. Data extracted from a validated certificate, such as name, public key, and other attributes are assumed to be authentic. A detailed illustration of the validation procedure and the derived trust in the user's public key is illustrated in Figure 2. A relying party who holds an authentic copy of the root CA public key contained in a root certificate received through a secure extra-protocol channel, will be able to derive trust in the binding between the user public key and the user name.

The identity of the root CA, normally represented by a unique name, must be known and recognized by users and relying parties in order to make trust in the root CA meaningful. Without recognition of root CA identity it is not possible to know who and what the self-signed root CA certificate represents. Relying parties must trust the root CA to be a genuine authority that is competent in issuing correct and authentic certificates. This makes it possible to depend on a certified key e.g. for authentication and digital signature verification. Owners of public keys must also trust the root CA to support authentication of their public keys e.g. by facilitating secure distribution of the root public key to potential relying parties. Users and relying parties can get this assurance for example when it is required that the root CA and intermediate CAs shall be accredited by government or other authoritative bodies to manage identity registration and public-key certification. This represents the trust anchor for users and relying parties.

Figure 2. Detailed trust structure for certificate validation

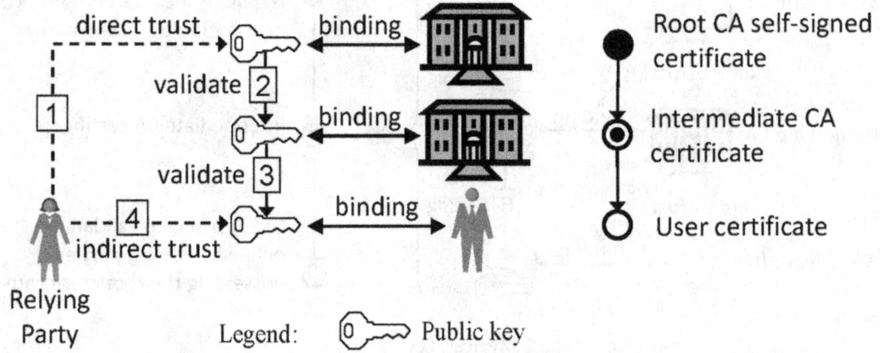

When the authority of a root CA is based on governmental or other authoritative accreditation bodies, the decision to trust a root CA ultimately becomes a political and philosophical question. For a PKI that is only used internally in an organization, the directors of the organization represent the ultimate authority for establishing the root CA as a trust anchor. In social networks between people, the decision to trust a public key or certificate can be discretionary typically based on personal relationships.

In some PKIs the CA generates the public/private key pair on behalf of the user. It is also possible that users generate their own public/private key pairs, in which case the CA must verify that the user controls the private key corresponding to the public key to be signed. Whether the signing party generates the public and private keys for the owner, or receives it from the owner is only a practical issue, and is not important for a particular PKI trust model. However, it should be noted that a CA that generates a public/private key pair for a user is technically able to masquerade as the user and to decrypt confidential messages sent to the user, and must therefore be trusted not to do so. Identity trust provided by a PKI is only as strong as the underlying trust relationships on the left hand side of Figure 1. It is normally assumed that the identity trust relationships from the root to the intermediate CAs, and onwards to the users are established out-of-band. This represents first hand direct trust relationships that form the basis for trust in PKIs. Such trust relationships are expensive, but the subsequent automated large-scale distribution and validation of user certificates is supposed to make it worthwhile.

The exact method of establishing the trust relationships on the left hand side of Figure 1 must be specified in the Certification Policy. For low assurance certificates, a requirement can be that the identity is provided to the CA online in the form of an email address, and that the verification of the claim to hold a particular email address is verified by sending a message to the specified address and requiring a specific reply message. For a high assurance level certificate a requirement can be that the user individual or a representative of the user organization physically present themselves to the CA/RA with evidence of identity and authority.

Attribute certificates can express anything that the certifying party wants to assert in the certificate or in the corresponding policy. Roles and access authorization privileges are typical examples of attribute certificates. The subsections below describe the most common PKI structures and their corresponding trust relationships.

Single Hierarchic PKI

The PKI class with the most optimal key distribution characteristics is when all users depend on a single hierarchical PKI. The advantage of this structure is that only one root public key needs to be distributed to relying parties through a secure out-of-band channel. More specifically, each relying party must have the assurance that the received root CA public key is authentic. Note that the root public key can only be trusted by parties who have this assurance, and that it should be distrusted by parties who cannot obtain this assurance.

The root CA must be trusted to represent a recognized authority that is competent and possibly accredited by a government or other authoritative body to manage identity registration and public-key certification. As already mentioned, the authenticity of the root public-key must be established with means external to the PKI itself. A trusted root CA with an out-of-band authenticated public key is called a trust anchor. Figure 3 illustrates a hierarchic PKI anchored on a self-signed root CA certificate.

Assuming that a relying party receives a user public-key certificate and that the root CA represents its trust anchor, then the relying party is able to authenticate the certified public key through resolution of the certification path from the root CA to the user certificate that contains the public

Figure 3. Hierarchic PKI

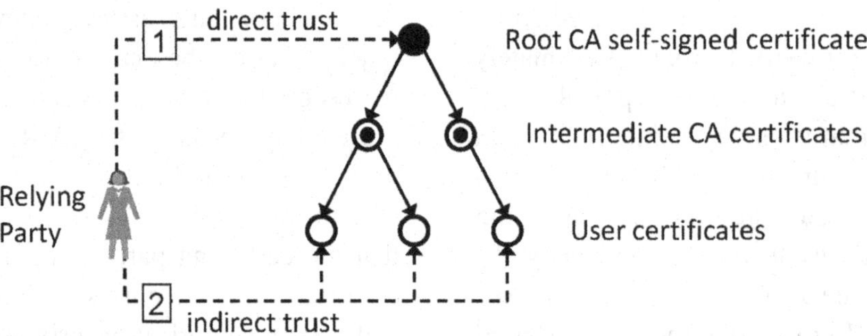

key. This also assumes that all intermediate certificates in the path between the root and certificate are also available to the recipient.

Single hierarchic PKIs can be operated by a single organization that operates the root and multiple intermediate CAs, or by a set of separate organizations under one common root CA. EuroPKI (http://www.europki.org/) is an example of the latter trust model which also could be described in terms of the bridge CA model described below.

Multiple Hierarchic PKIs

In case of multiple hierarchic PKIs it is possible that different user certificates belong to different PKIs. Assuming that each relying party shall be able to validate any user certificate from any PKI, then it is required that all root CAs represent trust anchors for the relying parties. In other words, all relying parties need to receive every root CA public key through a secure out-of-band secure channel. This situation is illustrated in Figure 4

The main problem with this model is the increased burden on relying parties to obtain root CA certificates out-of-band. As already mentioned, out-of-band channels are expensive, and this model therefore does not scale well. Having a dynamic set of root CA certificates will only exacerbate this problem. A specific form of this PKI model is the so-called browser PKI implemented in combination with Web browsers. The channel for distributing the root CA certificates is by hard coding them in the Web browser distributions. Whether the Web browser distribution represents a secure out-of-band channel is questionable. The hard coding of root CA certificates enables automated validation of server certificates for SSL/TLS and digital signatures on software. There are typically a few dozen root CA certificates in any major browser distribution. In Microsoft

Figure 4. Multiple hierarchic PKIs

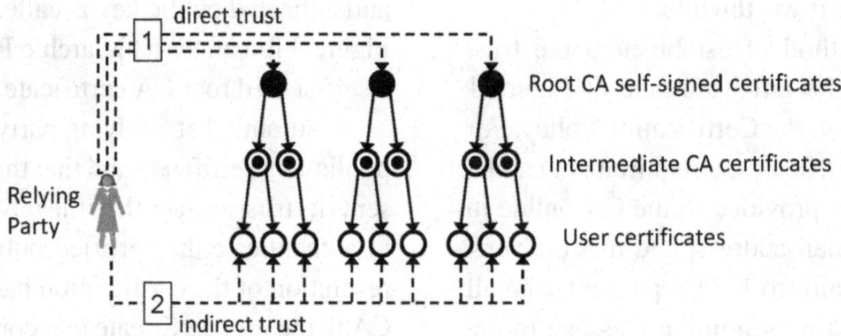

IE the list of root certificates can be viewed by clicking 'Tools' → 'Internet Options' → 'Content' → 'Certificates' → 'Trusted Root Certification Authorities'.

Typically in a browser, a substantial proportion of the pre-installed root certificates have expired several years back, even for newly downloaded browsers. Expired certificates are shipped with browsers e.g. in order to allow validation of legacy software, but shows that the model in fact is broken. Ignoring the validity period specified in a certificate for the sake of legacy functionality is a breach of the policy under which the certificates were issued.

The set of root CA certificates in the Web browser PKI model is dynamic, meaning that root certificates can be deleted and new root certificates can be added. This represents a real spoofing threat because it could be possible for attackers to replace a genuine root certificate with a false one. This attack could for example be executed by malware that gets installed on a victim computer. The authenticity of a root certificate depends on the security of the out-of-band channel through which it is obtained. Once a false certificate has been installed e.g. because the installation channel was insecure, it will not be possible for a relying party to detect that it actually is false. In practice, many people install browser PKI certificates and even root certificates based on discretionary ad hoc trust decisions, as described in the next section. This represents a real spoofing threat for identities on the Web.

Unfortunately, the Browser PKI is affected by serious vulnerabilities. One aspect is the fact that the Browser PKI is only as secure as the weakest of each separate PKI it contains, and each separate PKI is only as strong as the weakest of each CA member it contains. Thus, the more root certificates and the more subordinate CAs there are, the less secure the browser PKI becomes. There are several realistic scenarios for exploiting vulnerabilities in the Browser PKI, as explained below (Hayes, 2004; Soghoian and Stamm, 1995).

1. **Attack Against a CA:** VeriSign, the world's largest CA, issued false certificates in the name of Microsoft in 2001 when VeriSign staff failed to recognized that the persons buying the certificates were not Microsoft representatives (Microsoft, 2001). The false certificates were never used and VeriSign survived the breach with only a scratch to its reputation. In 2001 the Dutch CA DigiNotar was attacked by hackers who managed to gain access to DigiNotar's systems and generate false certificates. These certificates were used by criminals to conduct a man-in-the-middle attack against Google services (Mills, 2011). A few months later DigiNotar was declared bankrupt.
2. **Pressure or Blackmailing Against a CA:** As part of the Stuxnet affair (Shakarian, 201) two separate Taiwanese software companies—Realtek Semiconductor Systems and JMicron Technology Corp—used their genuine software signing certificates to produced digital signatures for the malicious Stuxnet software, which enabled the attackers to install malicious software on computer systems inside Iran's nuclear production facility. The companies in question have not been sanctioned, and it is likely that the companies were pressured to use their private keys to sign the Stuxnet software.
3. **Malicious CA:** Technically seen any CA that is part of the Browser PKI is able to generate false certificates and false signatures that will be automatically validated by all standard computers worldwide. There would be many possibilities for a criminal CA, or for criminal staff members in an otherwise legal CA, to get financial profit or other advantages from issuing false certificates or generating false signatures.

The Browser PKI market is largely held by a small number of multinational companies. This market has significant barriers to entry since new providers must undergo annual security audits (such as Web-Trust3 for Certification Authorities: http://www.webtrust.org/) to be included in the list of web browser trusted authorities. Once approved as member of the Browser PKI, a CA will get its root certificate distributed with the major web browsers and other application software to billions of users worldwide. More than 50 root certificates are installed and thereby automatically trusted by the most popular web browsers. A 2009 market share report from Netcraft (Netcraft Ltd., 2003) showed that VeriSign and its acquisitions (which include Thawte and Geotrust) held a 47.5% share of the Browser PKI certificate market, followed by GoDaddy (23.4%), and Comodo (15.44%).

Discretionary Direct Trust

The Discretionary Direct Trust model is not officially a PKI model because it breaches basic PKI trust principles. It is included here because it is extensively used on the Web and in other contexts where PKIs are implemented. In the discretionary direct trust model, the relying party receives a user certificate—or even a root certificate—online, and makes a discretionary decision to trust the certificate, as illustrated in Figure 5. The discretionary direct trust model ignores the requirement of having secure out-of-band channels for receiving root certificates. Instead, in the discretionary direct trust model the relying party decides to trust a user certificate without a reliable root certificate as trust anchor, or decides to import a root certificate without verifying its authenticity. Convenience and cost saving are the main reasons for discretely trusting certificates in this way.

This model can be used with low risk in situations where certificates are being used for non-sensitive applications. It is quite common that a certificate cannot be validated because there is no available root, or because the policy for validation cannot be satisfied, e.g. when the root certificate has expired. A certificate that fails normal validation typically blocks service access, unless the certificate can be accepted in some other way. In such situations the relying party can simply make a discretionary decision to trust the certificate in order to access the service. However, this model is commonly used in situations where there is a real risk, such as when e.g. downloading and installing software. The problem with this model is that binary trust decisions are being made purely out of convenience, despite weak or non-existing direct evaluation trust. It can be argued that all PKI trust models are affected by this problem, because in many cases relying parties ignore the existence of root certificates, and even if relying parties know about root certificates there is often little or no basis for judging the authenticity of these certificates.

This is a fundamental problem for all PKIs: the existence of a syntactic chain from root to user certificates is in itself meaningless; it is only when

Figure 5. Discretionary direct trust decisions

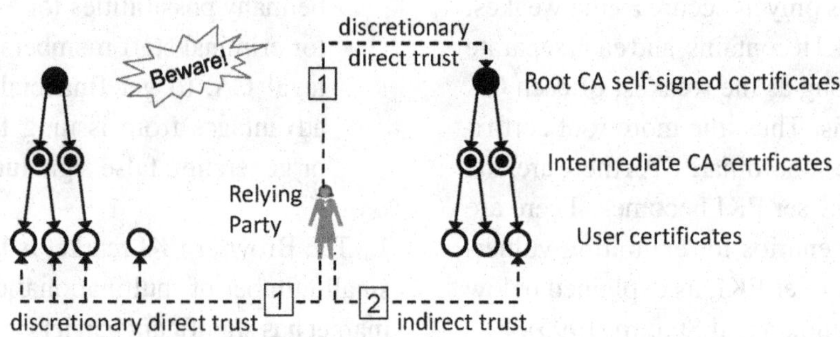

certificate chains have a reliable anchor that they provide a basis for reliable trust. So the morale is: Relying parties beware when making discretionary trust decisions in a PKI!

Cross Certification of Multiple Root CAs

A theoretically simple way to reduce the burden on relying parties is to let the root CAs cross certify their certificates. In that way, each relying party only needs to obtain one single root CA certificate, and still be able to validate any user certificate from other PKIs. This is illustrated in Figure 6.

The disadvantage of the cross-certified PKI model is that it significantly increases the burden on root CAs because each root CA must cross certify all other root CA certificates. The number of required cross certifications is $(n(n - 1)/2)$ where n is the number of separate PKIs. This is the same as the number of symmetric keys needed in a community of n parties. Policies must be established for each cross certification, and this can become a significant burden on the root CAs, and some CAs might not want to participate in the cross certification, e.g. for political reasons. The cross certified PKI model therefore does not scale well and is impractical to implement.

Bridge CA with Multiple PKIs

An improvement over the previous model is to use a bridge CA between multiple root CAs. This has the advantage that the relying parties only need to obtain one root CA certificate through a secure out-of-band channel, and that each root CA only needs to cross certify with the bridge CA. This is illustrated in Figure 7.

The disadvantage of the bridge PKI model is that it might be difficult to define an acceptable policy for cross certification that is acceptable by all parties. Certain root CAs might not be willing

Figure 6. Cross certified PKIs

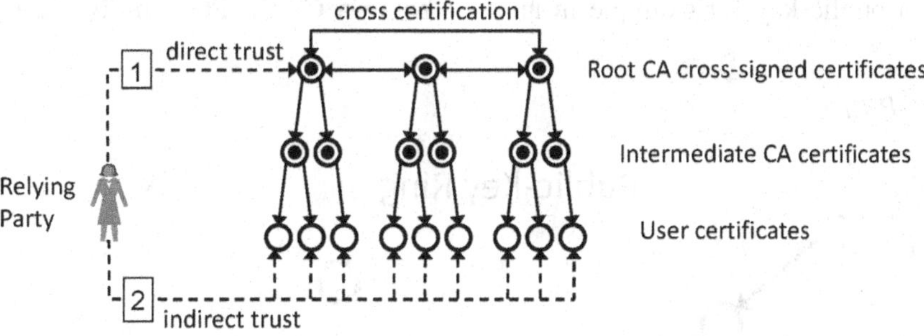

Figure 7. Multiple PKIs with bridge CA

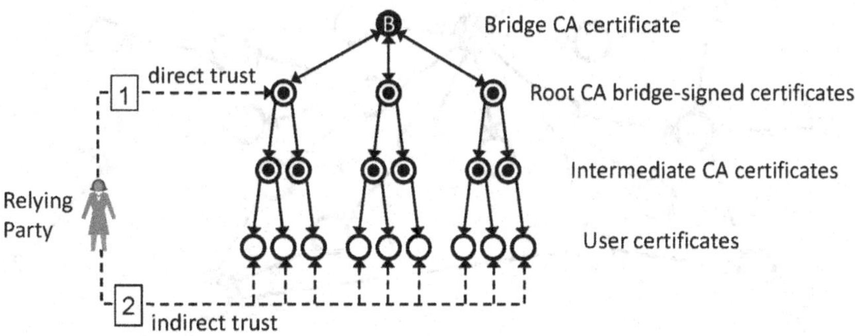

to cross certify with the bridge CA, e.g. for political reasons. The bridge CA might refuse to cross certify with a root CA for similar reasons.

The PGP Trust Model

The commercial encryption tool called PGP (Pretty Good Privacy) (Lucas, 2006), and its free version called GPG (Gnu Privacy Guard) (Callas et al., 2007), provide support for managing public keys and public-key certificates. PGP represents a practical model for public key distribution and usage, and is therefore a PKI, but which not is based on a hierarchical model. In PGP/GPG every user plays the role of relying party, user and CA at the same time, which means that users can send and recommend certificates to each other. There are several methods for a user and relying party to obtain public keys of other users. It can take place through a secure out-of-band channel such as a physical meeting, it can happen through online trust decisions based on introductions of new certificates from previously trusted users, or it can be based on a discretionary trust decision when receiving a public key for example in an email message or downloaded from a website. Imported public keys are stored in a file called Public-Key Ring as illustrated in Figure 8.

The relying party can sign imported keys and specify the trust level in key as it is stored on the Public-Key Ring. Discretionary trust should be based on contextual evidence such as agreeing over the phone to send a public key via email, and then checking that the email is timely received as expected. Otherwise such trust decisions would have a weak basis.

Computed trust in imported public keys is derived using PGP's particular trust model which is described in (Lucas, 2006). For example, the PGP tool can be configured to trust an imported public-key when it has been signed by a specific number of trusted users. The PGP tool will typically not trust a received key that has been signed by unknown or by untrusted users, but the relying party can always make a discretionary decision to trust and sign the imported public key.

It is worth mentioning that nobody makes a business out of selling certificates (i.e. signed keys) for PGP, so there is no business model for being a CA in PGP. Individuals and organiza-

Figure 8. The PGP PKI

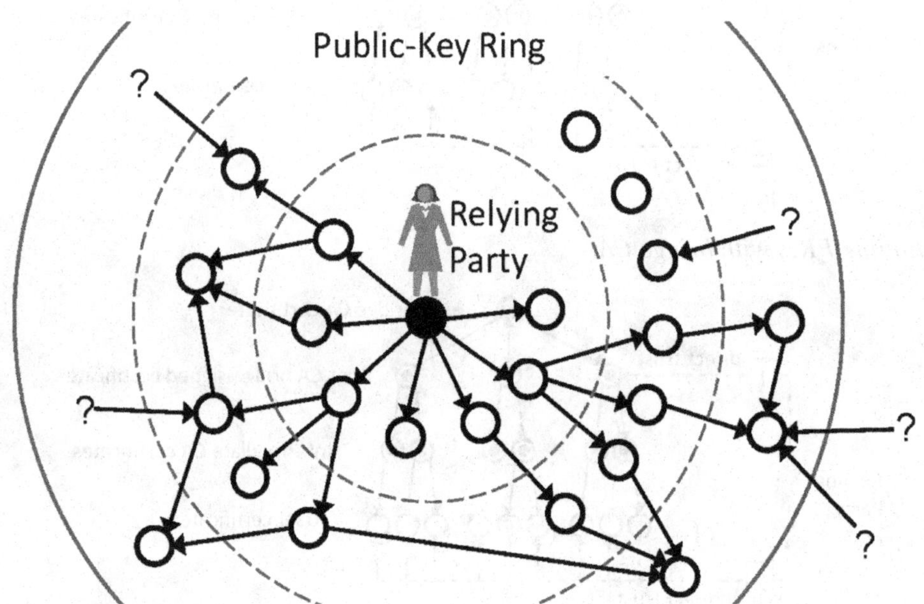

tions adopt PGP/GPG for its simplicity and low start-up cost. The popularity PGP/GPG is due to the simplicity of using it and the fact that it fills a real need among users.

Validation Authority with PKIs

The task of obtaining root CA public keys through secure out-of-band channels and validating user certificates represent the the main burden for relying parties. Introducing a separate role to take this burden and to validate user certificates on behalf of the relying party introduces a new trust anchor called a VA (Validation Authority). This is illustrated in Figure 9.

It is not necessary for a VA to be a CA. An organization can operate a CA only, a VA only, or both at the same time. To have a certificate validated the relying party needs an online secure channel to the VA. This must be based on an initial exchange of cryptographic keys through a secure out-of-band channel. Validation is different from certification, so the initial key exchange does not need to be based on publickey cryptography. An initial exchange of symmetric keys is for example possible. The two important security aspects to consider is that the relying party must be able to authenticate the VA in order to have trust in the validated certificates. It might also be necessary for the VA to authenticate the relying party for accounting purposes.

The validation authority model fills a real need for relying parties, and represents a recent trend in the PKI industry (Ølnes, 2006). VAs are independent of CAs, and their introduction makes it possible to connect multiple independent PKIs. While large and expensive PKI implementations often do not meet expectations in the market, the VA model might be the critical factor that can make PKI business models viable.

SPKI/SDSI and Delegation Certificates

A simple extension of the traditional hierarchical model is to let the certificate chain start from the relying party, so that the relying party in fact becomes a CA. The SPKI/SDSI model (Clarke et al., 2001; Ellison et al., 1999) is a PKI of this type, as illustrated in Figure 10.

Because every party, including the relying party, plays the role of a CA, the trust relationships in SPKI/SDSI will be similar to the internal trust relationships of traditional PKIs, as e.g. illustrated in Figure 1. There are several reasons why this model is not widely used. It would for example require that every relying party obtains a public/private key pair, and it makes certificate chain discovery more complicated than in hierarchical models.

An original element of SPKI/SDSI is that public keys are used as unique names. It is thus

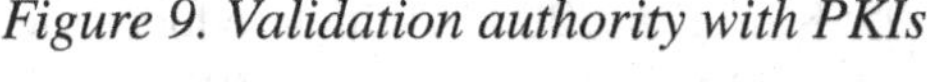
Figure 9. Validation authority with PKIs

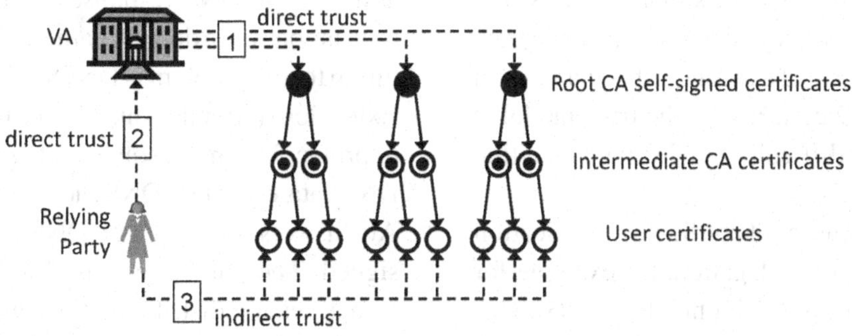

Figure 10. SPKI/SDSI model with known and anonymous users

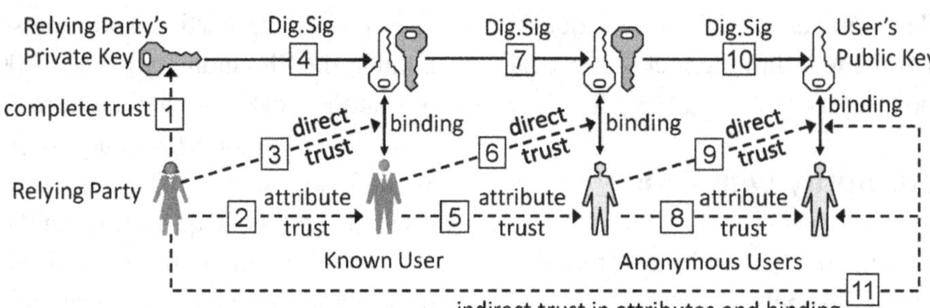

possible for users to stay anonymous and only expose their online identities, as illustrated by the online trust relationships (index 5 and 8) in Figure 10. Users also have the option to expose their physical world identities so that out-of-band trust in users (index 2) and public-keys (index 3) can be established. The distinction between trust in anonymous online users (index 5 and 8) and trust in their public keys (index 6 and 9) is quite subtle. Names represented by public keys are abstract notions that cannot by themselves perform actions or apply digital signatures, only users can. It must therefore be assumed that public keys in SPKI/SDSI correspond to real users that potentially can be trusted. A user can of course delegate the signing and certification to a software process, but it must be assumed that the user ultimately controls it.

Trust in the public key is the belief that it correctly and uniquely represents the assumed user. The scope of the trust in anonymous users (index 5 and 8) is that they correctly issue the next certificate in the chain (index 10). Although SPKI/SDSI certificates are simpler than X.509 certificates because they do not contain a separate attribute in the form of a distinguished name as in traditional X.509 certificates, the trust model is more subtle and difficult to understand than that of traditional PKIs.

An additional usage of public-key certification chains is to support delegation, for example for authorization purposes (Ninghui et al., 2003). This is the basis for the KeyNote authorization system (Blaze et al., 1999) where a certificate represents an authorization capability or privilege issued by the signing party. The relying party is the root of the delegation chain and will be able to validate and thereby trust the sink certificate in the chain and grant access as a function of the authorizations specified in the certificate. This represents an alternative to the traditional ACL (Access Control List) model of specifying access authorization policies. In a certificate based delegation model, the system does not even need to know the physical world identity of the certificate owner because the authorization is issued to an online identity represented by a public key. Whoever can prove that they control the private key corresponding to the certified public key will be granted access according to the authorization policy expressed in the certificate.

The DNSSEC PKI

Security threats against the DNS are many (Bellovin, 1995; Kaminsky, 2008), which reduces the assurance in DNS responses such as IP address translations from domain names. The technical solution to this problem is DNSSEC (DNS Security Extension) (Arends et al. 2005) which is designed to protect Internet resolvers (clients) from forged DNS data, e.g. due to DNS cache poisoning attacks. All answers received with DNSSEC are digitally signed. The public keys used for validating the signatures are distributed through the DNSSEC PKI which has a single root. Through validation of the digital signature a DNS resolver gets assurance that the information received is identical (correct and complete) to the information on the authoritative DNS server, i.e. that the information has not been corrupted.

Interestingly, the leaf nodes of the DNS (Domain Name System) are the same as those of the browser PKI, thereby making them adjacent hierarchic structures as illustrated in Figure 11 where the multi-hierarchic browser PKI at the bottom is turned upside-down.

By looking at the diagram of Figure 11, it becomes obvious that the hierarchic structure of the DNS itself can be used as a PKI structure for user certificates. In fact DNSSEC is already an overlay PKI on top of the DNS making it possible for DNS resolvers (clients) to authenticate replies to DNS requests.

A recent draft RFC (Hoffman et al., 2012) proposes to use the DNSSEC as a basis for distributing certificates for TLS. This would allow the elimination of trust required in third party CAs, and would therefore provide stronger security assurance than is currently possible with the Browser PKI. With ratification of (Hoffman et al., 2012) as an Internet standard and proper implementation of the required software, it would be possible to phase out the problematic Browser PKI described above. With this solution it is possible to let server certificates be signed by the DNS zone where the corresponding server is located, as illustrated in Figure 12.

Figure 11. Adjacent structure of DNS and the browser PKI

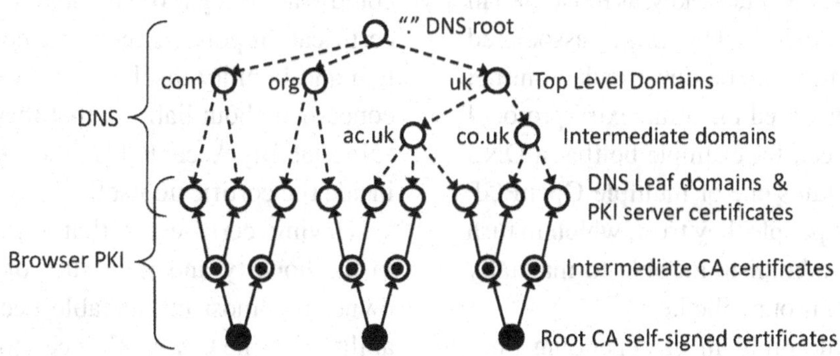

Figure 12. DNSSEC as a platform for server certificates

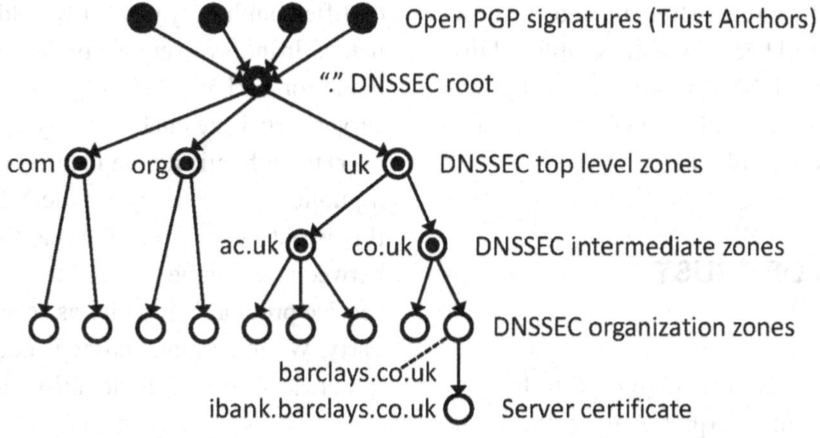

In the example, Barclays bank's online banking server is called ibank.barclays.co.uk where the certificate is used for TLS connections. The public-key certificate for this server is signed by the public key of the DNS zone barclays.co.uk. The certificate can be stored as a RR (Resource Record) on the DNS server for barclays.co.uk so that it is available to all clients accessing the server.

In case of DNSSEC the trust structure is taken very seriously and multiple trust anchors represented by trusted individuals in the Internet community. Online validation of the DNS root public key is not possible, and is therefore called a DURZ (Deliberately Unvalidatable Root Zone). It does not mean that the DNS root public key cannot be validated at all, instead the root public key can be manually (or semi-automatically) validated through the multiple OpenPGP signatures (Callas et al., 2007) on the root public key, as illustrated in Figure 12. So while the root public key associated with the." DNS root can be downloaded online; its authenticity is based on some extra-protocol procedure. This can for example be that a DNS administrator obtains one or multiple OpenPGP public keys from people they trust, which in turn makes the DNS administrator able to manually validate the DNS root public key.

This solves the problem of depending on a separate trust structure in the form of the Browser PKI which in addition must be characterized as relatively unreliable. Not only will the reliability of server authentication be strengthened, the cost can also be reduced because of the simplified infrastructure. When DNSSEC is deployed anyway it might well be used as a platform for signing and distributing server certificates.

SEMANTICS OF TRUST AND IDENTITY

In a trust relationship the relying party has an implicit or explicit interpretation of the trust involved. The trust scope is the specific type(s) of trust assumed in a given trust relationship. In other words, the trusted party is relied upon to have certain qualities, and the scope is what the relying party assumes those qualities to be.

In the case of PKIs, the trust scope is specified in a certification policy. It is crucial for the relying party to correctly understand the trust scope expressed in the policy. Misunderstanding the trust scope of a certificate is the same as misplaced trust, which is a vulnerability that can be exploited by attackers. A typical misunderstanding is that identity certificates somehow provide assurance of the honesty and reliability of the identity owner. However, the fact that a user is authenticated does not say anything about whether that user is honest or malicious. This common misunderstanding is for example the basis for phishing attacks.

CAs must take care to avoid any liability that could lead to legal or financial risk, and typical certification policies therefore contain legal jargon and liability disclaimers. Some CAs are so concerned about liability that they even specify: "No Liability Accepted" in the issuer name field inside the certificate itself.

Having certificates that provide assurance in the honesty and reliability of the certificate owner is almost unthinkable because of the liability risk the CA would need to accept. While a typical certification policy can be several pages long, the essence of it can usually be expressed in one simple sentence, such as "The owner of the certified public key rightfully holds the specified name." In the browser PKI, the key owner's domain name (or URL) is the unique name. In theory, a server certificate enables a relying party (service user) to authenticate the identity of the owner of a public key (service provider), but in practice this is not always possible due to the mismatch between the unique name (domain name) and the service provider's identity as seen by the relying party. When a unique name is not recognized as a representative of the identity, then it becomes meaningless to authenticate the identity by the unique name, as the example below will illustrate. The semantic distance between what is certified and what people think is certified is a problem for digital signatures in general (Jøsang, Povey and Ho, 2002).

To authenticate is to verify the correctness of a claim to a specific identity. In case the verification succeeds, the identity has been confirmed and the relying party can decide to proceed with the transaction. In case the verification fails, the relying party should interrupt the transaction. Authentication therefore involves a decision by the relying party. With the browser PKI it is often impossible to make an informed and meaningful decision because the URL often does not represent a meaningful name in the eyes of a human relying party.

The most common usage of the web PKI is to support TLS, where a closed padlock in the corner of the web browser indicates that the session is secured with TLS. The relying party can inspect various types of information about the server certificate, but unfortunately, this information is not necessarily sufficient to make an informed and meaningful conclusion about the identity of the web server.

We will consider the real fraudulent phishing site with the URL http://www.hawaiiusafcuhb.com that targeted the online Hawaii Federal Credit Union bank in March 2007 (Jøsang et al., 2007).

Assuming that potential victims want to inspect the server certificate for its authenticity and validity, it is interesting to see that it actually provides very little useful information. Figure 13 shows

Figure 13. Fake certificate general info

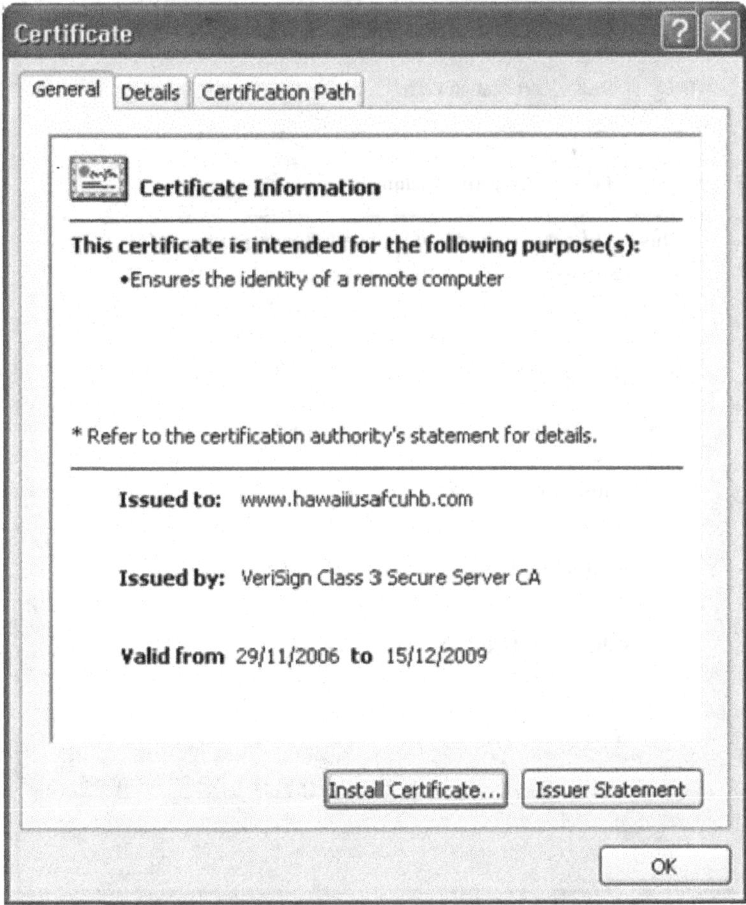

general information about the attacker's certificate as it can be viewed through the Microsoft Internet Explorer browser.

More detailed information can be viewed by selecting the "Details" and "Certification Path" placeholders on the certificate window. This gives the fraudulent certificate's validity period and the certification path from the root to the fraudulent certificate. However, this additional information gives no indication that the certificate is fraudulent.

The unique name in the fraudulent certificate is the domain name to which the fraudulent certificate is issued, specified as www.hawaii-usafcuhb.com, which is equal to the URL of the fake login page. The question now arises whether this represents sufficient evidence for the relying party to detect that the certificate is fraudulent. In order to find out, it is necessary to compare the fraudulent certificate to the genuine certificate of the genuine Hawaii Federal Credit Union illustrated in Figure 14.

The unique name of the genuine certificate's owner is the domain name to which the genuine certificate is issued, specified as hcd.usersonlnet.com. Interestingly this domain name does not correspond to the URL of the genuine Hawaii Federal Credit Union which is www.hawaiifcu.com.

Intuitively this fact seems to indicate that the login page is not related to the genuine Hawaii Federal Credit Union. Based on this evidence, relying parties who inspect the certificate could therefore falsely conclude that the genuine login page is fake.

Figure 14. Genuine certificate general info

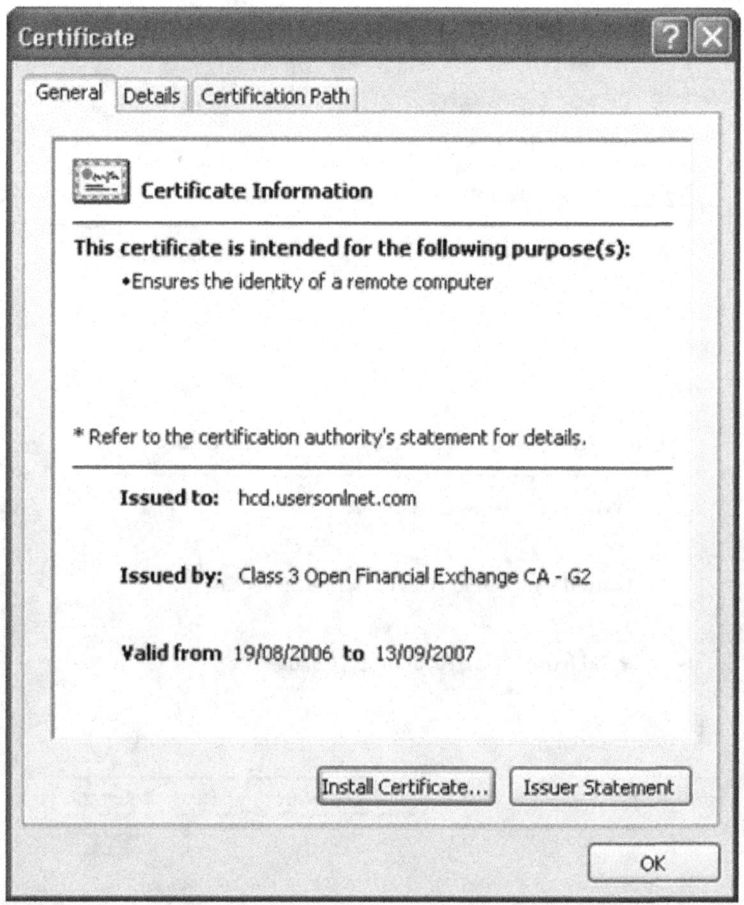

This analysis indicates that not even information found in certificates is sufficient to make the correct security conclusion and trust decision. The certificate window of Figure 14 provides a clickable button called "issuer statement" that opens a new window with the certificate issuance policy, which is a 2,666 word document (approximately four full standard pages in MS Word). While it might provide sufficient information to judge the legal status of the certificate, the size of this document alone makes the mental load of reading it intolerable for a human. In order to better understand why TLS can lead to a false positive authentication conclusion, it is useful to look at the very meaning of authentication.

According to the standard definition, peer-entity authentication is "the corroboration that a peer entity in an association is as claimed" (ISO, 1988). However, even if the claimed name can be verified, it is insufficient to make an informed trust decision in case the name itself is not recognized by the relying party. The identity of the genuine bank as recognized by the customer is not the same as the URL name of the same genuine bank recognized by the TLS client. Thus, the bank is an entity with multiple identities.

From the customer's perspective, the ordinary name and logo of the bank constitute a large part of the identity. From the client browser's perspective, this identity cannot be used because normal names are ambiguous and visual/graphical logos cannot be interpreted.

Certificates, which must be unambiguous, require globally unique names in order to allow efficient automated processing. Domain names mostly satisfy this requirement (although they can change over time: http://www.taguri.org/) and have therefore been chosen to represent the identity of online banks in server certificates. Having different identities for the same user can obviously cause problems. A theoretical solution to this problem could be to require that relying parties learn to identify online service providers by their domain names. Unfortunately this solution is jeopardized by banks often using multiple and different domain names depending on the specific service being offered.

As illustrated by the certificate of the genuine Hawaii Federal Credit Union bank of Figure 14, it is common that a company's secure web site has an URL with a non-obvious domain name that does not correspond to the domain names of its main web site. An additional vulnerability is the fact that distinct domain names can be very similar, for example differing only by a single letter so that a false domain name may pass undetected. How easy is it for example to distinguish between the following URLs?

http://www.bellabs.com,
http://www.belllabs.com,
http://www.bell-labs.com.

The crux of the problem is that domain names provide relatively poor usability for identification of organizations by people. This is because domain names are globally unique and therefore are not memorable. Ordinary names are suitable for dealing with organizations in the real world, but not for automated online authentication. The consequence of this is that relying parties do not know which service provider identity to expect when accessing online services. This is thus a case of cryptographically strong authentication which is semantically meaningless. In other words, the relying parties do not know which security conclusion to draw and trust decision to make. This vulnerability is for example the basis for phishing attacks. An early description of this problem and how it can be exploited by attackers is provided in (Jøsang et al., 2001).

Current approaches to solving the phishing problem include anti-phishing toolbars. Most anti-phishing toolbars are based on one or a combination of the following elements: blacklists, whitelists, ratings, heuristics (Cranor et al., 2006). However, none of these elements attempt to solve the fundamental problem of mapping the unique domain name contained in the certificate to a user-friendly identity that a human relying party can recognize. Thus they do not improve the relying party's ability to authenticate the server, but is a tool for flagging and avoiding potential malicious servers.

A more fundamental approach to solving the phishing problem is the Mozilla TrustBar (Herzberg and Gbara, 2004) which aims at making authentication meaningful for the relying party. The Mozilla TrustBar solution consists of personalizing every server certificate that the relying party needs to recognize. The personalization can e.g. consist of linking the certificate to an image or an audible tune of the relying party's choice. This method, called a Petname System, allows users to define their own personal "petnames" for services that they frequently use (Ferdous et al., 2009). This makes authentication meaningful, and represents a user-centric approach to identity management (Jøsang and Pope, 2005). Petname Systems are described in more detail in the chapter entitled Entity Authentication & Trust Validation in PKI using Petname Systems in this book.

FUTURE RESEARCH DIRECTIONS

In the evolutions of PKIs the main focus has traditionally been the PKI architecture and syntactic structure of certification, as well as policies and legal context in which PKIs are embedded. There are many unsolved problems under these categories, such as the overhead of certificate revocation, complexity of automated validation, as well as weak liability of erroneous certificates.

Areas that have received relatively less attention are the semantic and cognitive aspects of PKIs, which is unfortunate because the most frequent cause of authentication failure is precisely that relying parties misinterpret or ignore the syntactic identity that technically is being authenticated through the PKI. Research challenge for solving the latter problem should focus on usability and identity cognition.

Another crucial aspect that is commonly ignored is the method and assurance of obtaining root certificates. Policies are often silent on this issue, and CAs have an interest in ensuring simple and low cost distribution of their respective root certificates, which obviously runs into conflict with requirements for having secure out-of-band distribution channels for root certificates.

Given the many issues of PKIs that potentially can lead to authentication failure there is a need to consider the factors underlying the authentication assurance level that a particular PKI can provide. There are e.g. proposals for establishing service provider authentication frameworks, similarly to national user authentication frameworks (Jøsang et al., 2012). The method for distributing root certificates would naturally be included as one such assurance factor.

Although apparently simple, a PKI is much more complex to design and more expensive to operate than was first anticipated. In a nutshell, the challenge is to find satisfactory solutions to the remaining design issues, and to establish sound practices that have viable business models.

CONCLUSION

Assurance provided by a PKI is based on a set of direct trust relationships established out-of-band between the CAs within a PKI as well as between the external relying parties and root CAs of the PKI. While the establishment of direct trust relationships is slow and expensive, a PKI can be leveraged to support automated and efficient large-scale distribution of user public-keys which in turn can support cryptographic security services.

Having a sound basis for trust in a PKI is crucial for the security of the applications and services it supports. Misplaced trust could lead to large-scale vulnerabilities and attacks, so correct interpretation of the assurance provided by PKIs is crucial. The wave of recent phishing attacks is in fact a result of misunderstood trust in the security provided by the browser PKI and server certificates. It is often incorrectly believed that certificates provide assurance of reliability of a user or a service provider, whereas in reality they only provide assurance about identities or specific attributes.

The assurance that certificates provide must be described in the certification policies, but most relying parties never read the policies, and even if they did the policies would be difficult to interpret. In case of human relying parties, the difficulty of understanding and interpreting certification policies is a security usability problem. There is a great potential for improving the security of applications that depend on PKIs by improving the usability of interpreting certificates and their corresponding certification policies.

REFERENCES

Arends, R., Austein, R., Larson, M., Massey, D., & Rose, S. (2005). RFC 4033 - DNS security introduction and requirements. Retrieved from http://www.rfc-editor.org/

Bellovin, S. M. (1995). Using the domain name system for system break-ins. In Proceedings of the Fifth Usenix Unix Security Symposium. IEEE.

Blaze, M., Feigenbaum, J., Ioannidis, J., & Keromytis, A. D. (1999). RFC 2704 – The keynote trust management system version 2. Retrieved from http://www.ietf.org/rfc/rfc2704.txt

Callas, J., Donnerhacke, L., Finney, H., Shaw, D., & Thayer, R. (2007). RFC 4880 - OpenPGP message format. Retrieved from http://www.rfc-editor.org/

Clarke, D., Elien, J. E., Ellison, C., Fredette, M., Morcos, A., & Rivest, R. L. (2001). Certificate chain discovery in SPKI/SDSI. *Journal of Computer Security*, *9*(4), 285–322.

Cranor, L., Egelman, S., Hong, J., & Zhang, Y. (2006). Phinding phish: An evaluation of anti-phishing toolbars. Technical Report CMU-CyLab-06-018. Pittsburgh, PA: Carnegie Mellon University CyLab.

Ellison, C., et al. (1999). RFC 2693 - SPKI certification theory. Retrieved from http://www.ietf.org/rfc/rfc2693.txt

Ferdous, M. S., Jøsang, A., Singh, K., & Borgaonkar, R. (2009). Security usability of petname systems. In Proceedings of the 14th Nordic Workshop on Secure IT systems (NordSec 2009). Oslo, Norway: IEEE.

Hayes, J. M. (1998). The problem with multiple roots in web browsers - Certificate masquerading. In Proceedings of the 7th Workshop on Enabling Technologies, Infrastructure for Collaborative Enterprises (WETICE '98), (pp. 306–313). IEEE.

Herzberg, A., & Gbara, A. (2004). Protecting (even na¨ive) web users from spoofing and phishing attacks. Technical Report 2004/155. Cryptology ePrint Archive.

Hoffman, P., & Schlyter, J. (2012). The DNS-based authentication of named entities (DANE) protocol for transport layer security (TLS) draft-ietf-dane-protocol-18. Retrieved from http://tools.ietf.org/html/draft-ietf-dane-protocol-18

ISO. (1988). *IS 7498-2: Basic reference model for open systems interconnection - Part 2: Security architecture*. Geneva, Switzerland: International Organisation for Standardization.

Jøsang, A. (1996). The right type of trust for distributed systems. In C. Meadows (Ed.), Proceedings of the 1996 New Security Paradigms Workshop. ACM.

Jøsang, A., AlFayyadh, B., Grandison, T., Al-Zomai, M., & McNamara, J. (2007). Security usability principles for vulnerability analysis and risk assessment. In Proceedings of the Annual Computer Security Applications Conference (ACSAC'07). ACSAC.

Jøsang, A., & Lo Presti, S. (2004). Analysing the relationship between risk and trust. In T. Dimitrakos (Ed.), Proceedings of the Second International Conference on Trust Management (iTrust). Oxford, UK: iTrust.

Jøsang, A., Møllerud, P. M., & Cheung, E. (2001). Web security: The emperors new armour. In Proceedings of the European Conference on Information Systems (ECIS2001). Bled, Slovenia: ECIS.

Jøsang, A., & Pope, S. (2005). User-centric identity management. In A. Clark (Ed.), Proceedings of AusCERT 2005. Brisbane, Australia: AusCERT.

Jøsang, A., Povey, D., & Ho, A. (2002). What you see is not always what you sign. In Proceedings of the Australian UNIX and Open Systems Users Group Conference (AUUG2002). Melbourne, Australia: AUUG.

Jøsang, A., Varmedal, K. A., Rosenberger, C., & Kumar, R. (2012). Service provider authentication assurance. In Proceedings of the 10th Annual Conference on Privacy, Security and Trust (PST 2012). Paris, France: PST.

Kaminsky, D. (2008). Details. [Blog]. Retrieved from http://dankaminsky.com/2008/07/24/details/

Kohlas, R., Jonczy, J., & Haenni, R. (2008). A trust evaluation method based on logic and probability theory. In Proceedings of the Joint iTrust and PST Conferences on Privacy, Trust Management and Security (IFIPTM 2008). IFIPTM.

Li, N., Grosof, B., & Feigenbaum, J. (2003). Delegation logic: A logic based approach to distributed authorization. *ACM Transactions on Information and System Security*, *6*(1), 128–171. doi:10.1145/605434.605438.

Lucas, M. W. (2006). *PGP & GPG: Email for the practical paranoid*. New York, NY: No Starch Press Inc..

McKnight, D. H., & Chervany, N. L. (1996). The meanings of trust. Technical Report MISRC Working Paper Series 96-04. Minneapolis, MN: University of Minnesota, Management Information Systems Reseach Center.

Microsoft. (2001). Microsoft security bulletin MS01-017 (March 22, 2001): Erroneous VeriSign-issued digital certificates pose spoofing hazard. Retrieved from http://www.microsoft.com/technet/security/bulletin/MS01-017.asp

Mills, E. (2011). Fraudulent Google certificate points to internet attack. Retrieved form http://news.cnet.com/

Netcraft Ltd. (2010). Certification services: Netcraft report. Retrieved from https://ssl.netcraft.com/ssl-samplereport/CMatch/certs

Ølnes, J. (2006). PKI interoperability by an independent, trusted validation authority. In Proceedings of the 5th Annual PKI R&D Workshop. Gaithersburg, MD: NIST.

Shakarian, P. (2011, April). Stuxnet: Cyberwar revolution in military affairs. Small Wars Journal.

Simmons, G. J., & Meadows, C. (1995). The role of trust in information integrity protocols. *Journal of Computer Security*, *3*(1), 71–84.

Soghoian, C., & Stamm, S. (2011). Certified lies: Detecting and defeating government interception attacks against ssl (short paper). Financial Cryptography, 250–259.

UK e Envoy. (2002). Registration and authentication. Retrieved from http://e-government.cabinetoffice.gov.uk/assetRoot/04/00/09/60/04000960.pdf

ADDITIONAL READING

Adams, C., & Lloyd, S. (2003). *Understanding PKI: Concepts, standards, and deployment considerations*. Reading, MA: Addison-Wesley Professional.

Gasson, M., Meints, M., & Warwick, K. (2005). D3.2: A study on PKI and biometrics. FIDIS Deliverable, 3(2).

Karamanian, A., Tenneti, S., & Dessart, F. (2011). *PKI uncovered*. Indianapolis, IN: Cisco Press.

Trček, D. (2006). *Managing information systems security and privacy*. New York, NY: Birkhauser.

Vacca, J. R. (2004). *Public key infrastructure: Building trusted applications and web services*. Boca Raton, FL: CRC Press. doi:10.1201/9780203498156.

Viega, J. et al. (2002). *Network security with OpenSSL*. New York, NY: O'Reilly Media.

Wilson, S. (2005). The importance of PKI today. China Communications. Retrieved from http://www.china-cic.org.cn/english/digital%20 library/200512/3.pdf

KEY TERMS AND DEFINITIONS

Decision Trust: The extent to which one party is willing to depend on something or somebody in a given situation with a feeling of relative security, even though negative consequences are possible.

Evaluation Trust: The subjective probability by which an individual, A, expects that another individual, B, performs a given action on which its welfare depends.

Identity: Set of attributes of an entity. One of the attributes is typically a unique name within a domain.

Out-of-Band Channel: A communication channel that is separate and independent from the communication channel that is cryptographically protect by the PKI. Can also be called an Extra-Protocol Channel.

Public-Key Certificate: A data record containing a public key, a set of attributes as well as a digital signature on the attributes. The digital signature is interpreted as a binding of the public key to the attributes. When one of the attributes is a unique name the certificate is an identity certificate.

Public Key: One of a pair of cryptographic keys that are mathematically related, the other key being the private key. As the name says, the public key is publicly known within a domain. The private key is only known to the user who owns the public-private key pair.

Relying Party: In the context of PKI, the relying party needs to authenticate the user, or some data originating from the user. The relying party relies on the correct validation of the public-key certificate for this purpose.

User: In the context of PKI, the user owns a public-key certificate.

Validation: To verify the correctness of a public-key certificate.

Chapter 13
Entity Authentication and Trust Validation in PKI Using Petname Systems

Md. Sadek Ferdous
University of Glasgow, UK

Audun Jøsang
University of Oslo, Norway

ABSTRACT

Recognition of identities and certainty about identity ownership are crucial factors for secure communication in digital environments. Identity Management Systems have been designed to aid users as well as organisations to manage different user identities. However, traditional Identity Management Systems are primarily designed to facilitate the management of identities from the perspective of the service provider, but provide little support on the user side to manage organisational identities. Public Key Infrastructures (PKI) is the primary tool in aiding users to manage such identities on their sides as well as to establish trust during online transactions. Nevertheless, the complexities and difficulties involved in managing and understanding such certificates from the general public's point of view are overlooked. This causes vulnerabilities that open up for serious attacks such as identity theft and Phishing. Petname Systems have been proposed for managing organisational identities on the user side in order to improve the user friendliness and to strengthen security. This chapter provides an analysis of the Petname Model by describing its history and background, properties, application domains, and usability issues, and explains how a Petname System can be effectively combined with the PKI to recognise identities and impose certainty by validating the user trust on those identities. The chapter also presents an analysis on two applications that integrate the Public Key Infrastructure with the Petname Model.

DOI: 10.4018/978-1-4666-4030-6.ch013

INTRODUCTION

Entity identification and trust are two important factors that help people decide whether or not to engage in transaction with other people in the real world. We humans inherit these qualities as part of our human endeavours in the society, and as our boundary of social interactions expand over time so does our ability to utilise those qualities to our benefit. But trust can misleads us while engaging in transactions with other human beings due to the complex and unpredictable nature of human behaviour, and when expectation does not meet in transaction, it results in erosion of trust. With the ever growing expansion of the Internet, technologies have enabled us to engage in transactions much like the way we transact in real world. However, with the absence of the face-to-face interaction, trust assessment through the Internet is typically much more challenging. At the initial growing stage of the Internet, the web and web-based services were not foreseen in its current form and the necessity of formal verification of entity identities was not felt. This led to the omission of the much needed Identity Layer. This causes the identification of entities to be very difficult in online world which in turn makes it difficult to establish and validate trust with other entities.

Authentication was subsequently added for verifying the correctness of claimed and assumed identities. Authentication requires prior registration of identities, and is based on a set of security mechanisms combined with a credential or security token. As authentication became necessary for accessing many online services, more and more identities and credentials were issued, and their management became problematic, both for service providers and for users. Identity Management (IdM, in short) Systems were introduced by the industry to facilitate the server-side management of user identities. Initially, the client-side management of user identities was not considered to be an issue. However, many people currently feel overloaded with identities and passwords that security policies require them to memorise. The growing number of identities that users need to handle and the inability of users to comply with credential management policies now makes client (user) side IdM a critical issue. It is important to consider that users need to manage their own identities as well as SP (Service Provider) identities. The latter aspect of IdM has received relatively little attention. Users have been provided with only PKI and digital certificates for identifying and authenticating SPs. In practice PKI on the Internet is used for automatic authentication of SP entities through their domain names. Although technically sound, PKI suffers from serious usability issues which make it difficult for general people to use it effectively and efficiently. This creates precisely the vulnerability that makes phishing attacks potent and successful. Petname Systems can be an effective solution against such threats. In this chapter we highlight the shortcomings of PKI and show how a Petname System can effectively be used to improve security and usability.

An essential part of an IdM is the namespace which provides a set of unique names (identifiers) for all entities it deals with. Different types of namespaces will have different properties. It is desirable that the namespace enables names to be 1) Global, 2) Memorable and 3) Unique (Called "Secure" in Wilcox, 2001). Unfortunately, no single namespace have all the three properties simultaneously (Wilcox, 2001). However, by combining a global namespace with a local namespace, all three properties can be combined (Miller, 2000). A so-called Petname System is a solution for achieving this. The combination of IdM and Petname Systems therefore seems to be an ideal choice for client-side Identity Management.

In this chapter, we present an extensive elaboration of our previous work on Petname Systems that can be found in (Ferdous et al., 2009). In addition, we focus on PKI and show how a Petname System and PKI can be combined for entity authentication as well as for establishing and validating trust on the web. The contributions of this chapter in comparison with the previous work are:

- An introductory section that provides definitions of basic terminology of Identity and Identity Management, aimed at audiences that are not familiar with Identity Management.
- A brief introduction on the PKI that describes its mechanisms and highlights its shortcomings.
- The background of the Petname System.
- Real world examples to familiarize readers with the abstract concept of the Petname Systems.
- Fundamental properties of Petname Systems.
- An analysis of how the Petname System and PKI can be combined to remove many shortcomings of the current implementation of PKIs.
- Security usability analysis of Petname Systems combined with PKIs.

The structure of the paper is as follows. Sec.2 explains frequently used basic terms that are necessary for understanding Petname Systems. We use the term Petname Model to denote the abstract properties of Petname Systems. An implementation of the Petname Model is then a Petname System.

Sec.3 provides a very short primer on PKI. It explains the mechanisms behind the digital certificate and techniques highlighting the inner working of the PKI for entity authentication. The section also underlines the shortcomings of the PKI System.

To understand the Petname Model it is essential to understand why Petname Systems were proposed in the first place. The Petname Model was formally described by Marc Stiegler in his 2005 paper (Stiegler, 2005). The potential of the Petname Model, however, was discovered by different people in several successive steps. Elements of the fundamental Petname System concept are scattered among several papers and web articles, and the combined efforts of these authors have shaped the formulation of the Petname Model. Sec.4 aims to summarise the existing literature.

Sec.5 defines the Petname Model by outlining its different components and establishing the connections among them. A Petname System has several properties and its potential applications can span over several disciplines of computing and networking. A long list of properties as well as several application scenarios was listed in (Stiegler, 2005). Sec.6 formalises the properties in a more systematic way by dividing them into two broad categories: 1) Functional properties and 2) Security usability properties, as well as usability requirements. We analyse mechanism for integrating the Petname Model in PKIs in Sec.7. In Sec.8, different applications of the Petname Model are explained. Section 9 analyses the usability issues of two PKI based applications that utilize the Petname Model. Sec.10 provides some hints on potential future works on Petname Systems and concluding remarks are provided in Sec.11.

DEFINITION

Entity

An entity is a physical or logical object which has a separate distinctive existence either in physical or in the logical world (Wikipedia Entity, 2012). In the scope of this chapter, a person, an organisation or a machine (computer) operated by any person or organisation will be denoted as an entity. It is to note here that examples of entity could be used for both server-side and client-side. In traditional server-side identity management, an entity can be a person, another organisation or a computer, where the identity of the respective entity typically is managed automatically by the server. In client-side identity management, users manage their own identities as well as identities of SP organisations.

Identity

Different disciplines (Philosophy, Social Science, etc.) interpret identity in different ways. There are also different definitions of identity which can be quite complex to understand and sometimes even contradictory. By putting aside the philosophical debates and contradictory arguments, a simple but intuitive definition can be provided (Thanh & Jørstad, 2007): Identity is the fundamental property of any entity that declares the uniqueness or sameness of itself and makes it distinctive from other entities in a certain context. Readers who would want to explore the philosophical debates and other advanced concepts over Identity such as Identity over time, Absolute and Relative Identity, etc. please refer to the work of (Geach, 1967; Sider, 2000; Deutsch, 2008; Gallois, 2011, 2012).

In general, an entity can have multiple unique identities, but a unique identity cannot be associated with more than one entity. Each identity can consist of multiple attributes (Jøsang & Pope, 2005). Here, the same attribute can be associated with multiple identities. Attributes can have different properties, such as being transient or permanent, self-selected or issued by an authority, suitable for human interpretation or only by computers. The possible attributes of an identity may differ, depending on the type of real world entity being identified. For example, gender applies to people, but not to organisations; stock exchange listing applies to a company, but not to a person. Some attributes are shared and some are unique within a given identity domain (a logical boundary governed by a single organisation), but each identity has to be unique within a specific identity domain. It is usually the case that one of the attributes is a unique name within a specific namespace, in which case that attribute cannot be shared with other identities. The unique name is then used to identify the identity within the specific identity domain. The diagram below illustrates the conceptual relationship between identities, entities and attributes. It should be noted that the distinction between identity and name is blurred in common language usage. The term "identity" often used in the sense of "name", especially when an identity is recognised by a single unique name within a given context. For clarity, the terms "identity" and "name" will be used with their separate specific meanings throughout this chapter.

Human beings are equipped with the ability to intuitively identify an entity based on an ad hoc set of characteristics and also in varying contexts but a machine is not. To enable a machine to identify other entities, Digital Identity is required (see Figure 1).

Digital Identity and Name

The digital encoding of the attributes of an identity can be defined as a digital identity. It is the representation of an identity in a form that is suitable for representation and processing in computer systems. The digital encoding of a name is then a digital name. In all types of digital communication (Internet, telecommunication) digital names are being used in the form of the URL, user-id, phone number, etc. In many digital communications, digital name uniquely identify an entity and are confused to be an identity. Like the identity and the name, digital identity and digital name should be treated separately. For a good introduction to the concepts of identity and digital identity, (see Jøsang & Pope, 2005; Thanh & Jørstad, 2007).

Identity Management

ID management consists of technologies, policies and practices for recognising and authenticating entities in online environments. All parties that engage in the online activities have identities that need to be managed. In particular, not only user identities, but also the identities of servers and

Figure 1. Relationship between entities, identities, and identifiers

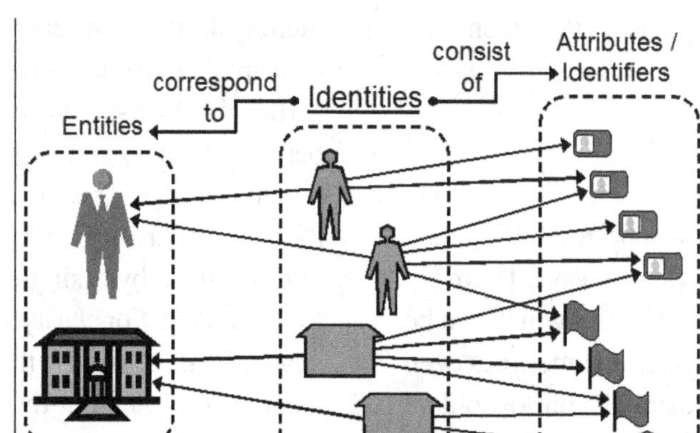

SPs must be managed. Given that Id management must cover both the identities of the user and service provider, and given that there are always two parties involved (the relying party or the service provider and the target) it is necessary that the Id management have a component both on the client and the server side. This leads to four main types of Id management, as illustrated in Table 1. Type 1A ID Management was the first form of Id management, where SPs typically implemented the Silo Model. In the Silo Model, each service is exclusively managed by a separate SP that provides a separate identity service, so that each user must maintain separate user-id and password for each service (Jøsang, Al Zomai, and Suriadi, 2007). THs silo model is still the most widely used IdM model on the Web. Type 1B ID management focuses on how users manage their own identities, and typically consists of memorising user names and passwords, although various types of password wallet applications have been around for many years. Id management of Type 2 focuses on the management of SP identities, where Type 2A is about how SPs manage their own identities, and Type 2B is about how users manage SP identities. Unfortunately Type 2 Id management is hardly ever discussed, although there are serious issues with current Type 2 Id management, as e.g. shown by the relatively high success rate of phishing attacks. The industry's attempt to solve this problem is to compile blacklists of "bad" server names (some commonly used blacklist sites are: Spamhaus [www.spamhaus.org], Spews [www.spews.org], DSBL [www.dsbl.org], MAPS [www.mail-abuse.org/rbl/], etc.) that can be used for triggering warnings in browsers, which in fact represents a form of trust management, not Id management. Because server names are often meaningless to users, server authentication based on server certificates and SSL also becomes meaningless which we will show later. Only when server certificates are combined with petnames server names and server certificates become meaningful.

The term "User-Centric Id Management" is often used with different meanings. In the most general sense it means Id management that improves the user experience. The so-called federated Id management models fall under this category. In a more specific sense, user-centric Id management means that there is local technology

Table 1. Identity management types

IdM Type 1A: SP-side management of user Ids and credentials	IdM Type 1B: User-side management of user Ids and credentials
IdM Type 2A: SP-side management of SP Ids and credentials	IdM Type 2B: User-side management of SP Ids and credentials

on the client side that assists users in managing identities, as e.g. proposed in (Jøsang & Pope, 2005), and the term local user-centric Id management captures this interpretation. Petname Systems resides on the client side, and therefore represent technology for local user-centric Id management.

Petname Systems are applicable in different domains (to be elaborated in subsequent sections), however, we mainly focus on how the combination of Petname Systems and PKI can provide support for Type 2B IdM, i.e. the management of SP identities on the client side. This specifically solves problems related to the authentication of Web site identities, so that it e.g. can be used to prevent phishing attacks.

PUBLIC KEY INFRASTRUCTURE

A PKI is a framework based on public key cryptosystems (also known as the asymmetric cryptography) and consists of a set of policies that governs how cryptosystems should operate and defines the procedure for generating and publishing digital certificates (Menezes, Oorschot, and Vanstone, 1997). In a public-key cryptosystems an entity generates a key pair known as the public key and the private key. The public key, denoted as pub hereafter, is intended to be publicly available while the private key, denoted as priv hereafter, is intended for the entity only and to be a kept as a secret strictly. RSA is the most widely used public key cryptosystem however other popular public key cryptosystems exist such as Diffie–Hellman key exchange, ElGamal Encryption, etc. (Menezes, Oorschot, and Vanstone, 1997).

Public key cryptosystems are used to exchange data securely (e.g. using encryption) over any insecure channel such as the Internet. It is suitable for a situation when it is not possible to exchange the shared secret (to be used as a key for encrypting data) between two parties a priori. In such cases, the data is encrypted before transmission in the insecure channel using pub of the recipient. Upon receiving the data, the recipient uses the corresponding priv to decrypt the data. Such mechanism would allow achieving data confidentiality over the transmission medium, however, does not guarantee any data integrity. To achieve data integrity, digital signature is used. To digitally sign a message, a hash function is used to generate a hash of the message which is then encrypted using the priv of the sender. This encrypted hash message usually accompanies the message. Upon receiving this pair (message and the encrypted hash message), the recipient uses the pub of the sender to decrypt the hash message, uses the same hash function to generate a hashed message of the message and then compares the hash message with the decrypted hash message. If they are equal, the integrity of message is thought to be intact, otherwise not. Typically the operations of encryption and signing are combined to achieve confidentiality and data integrity altogether. To visualise the scenarios, let's assume that we have two parties Alice and Bob and Alice wants to send an encrypted message to Bob accompanied by the digital signature over an insecure channel. They first generate the corresponding key pair (pub_{alice}, $priv_{alice}$) and (pub_{bob}, $priv_{bob}$) respectively. They also share their public keys with other so that Alice gets hold of pub_{bob} and Bob gets hold of pub_{alice}. We also need three operations encryption, decryption and hash and will be denoted by enc(message, key) and dec(message, key) where message is the message to be encrypted and the key is the encryption key and hash(message) respectively. Now the following operations take place:

1. Alice hashes the message m using the hash operation to generate $hash_m = hash(m)$.
2. Alice encrypts the $hash_m$ using the $priv_{alice}$: $enchash_m = enc(hash_m, priv_{alice})$.
3. Alice combines a pair of the message and hash: pair = (m, $enchash_m$).
4. Alice encrypts the pair with the pub_{bob} to generate e: e = enc (pair, pub_{bob}).

5. Alice transmits e to Bob over an insecure channel.
6. Bob uses $priv_{bob}$ to decrypt e and get the pair: pair = dec (e, $priv_{bob}$).
7. Bob retrieves the message m and $enchash_m$ from the pair.
8. Bob uses the same hash function to generate hash´: $hash_m´$ = hash(m).
9. Bob decrypts the $enhash_m$ using the pub_{alice} to get back the $hash_m$: $hash_m$ = dec($enchash_m$, pub_{alice}).
10. Bob compares $hash_m´$ with $hash_m$.
11. $hash_m´$ = $hash_m$ signifies that the message remained intact during transmission which completes the process.

One of the key challenges in the public key cryptosystem is to share the corresponding public key securely between different entities. PKI has been developed to enable a secure distribution of public with the help of a trusted third party called the Certificate Authority (CA in short) using a key component called Digital Certificate. A digital certificate is used to bind the name of a subject with a piece of information. The name of a subject can be of different types such as email address, DNS name, IP address, URI, etc. (Kesterson II, 2007). There are different types of digital certificates as well. Two major examples of different certificates are public key certificate and attribute certificate. When the name of a subject is bound with its public key, the certificate is known as the public key certificate whereas when the name is bound with an attribute of the subject, the certificate is called the attribute certificate. For the scope of this chapter, we are mainly interested about public key certificates. X.509 version 3 is the most commonly used industry standard for public key and attribute certificate (Housley, Ford, Polk, and Solo, 1999).

Each CA is responsible for generating and issuing digital certificates as well as revoking and archiving certificates that have been generated and signed by the CA. To preserve the authenticity of the binding, each digital certificate is signed by the CA. Additionally, the CA also generates and issues a self-signed certificate called the root certificate. Any entity that wants to use a digital certificate must trust the CA and possess the root certificate to validate the signature on the certificate. A transport layer protocol, known as the Secure Socket Layer/Transport Layer Security (SSL 3.0/ TLS 1.2), has been developed and widely used to exchange and validate digital certificates between communicating entities over the Internet which ultimately is used for entity authentication (Thomas, 2000). We briefly explain this process in the next section.

Entity Authentication Using PKI

A public key certificate usually consists of the name of the entity presenting the certificate, name of the CA which has signed it, the public key associated with the entity, a validity period for the certificate and other information regarding the cryptographic algorithms used to sign this certificate. All these information are added to the certificate and signed by the CA. The first step after receiving a certificate is to validate it. A certificate is deemed valid if:

1. The certificate is signed by a trusted a CA.
2. The certificate has not expired as indicated by the validity period in the certificate.
3. The certificate has not been revoked by the CA.
4. The content of certificate is unaltered which can be checked by the signature of the certificate. This requires possessing the public key of the CA itself.

Once the verification is complete, authentication phase begins. During the authentication phase, the sender has to prove its possession of the corresponding private key. This process can be quite complex in nature. However, a very general form is like the following:

The recipient sends a nonce (a one-time random data) to the sender. The sender is asked to encrypt it with the private key and return back to the recipient. Upon receiving the encrypted nonce, the recipient decrypts it with the sender's public key and compares it with the previously sent nonce. If both match, the sender is verified to be the holder of the presented certificate and the entity seems to be properly authenticated.

PKI Shortcomings

Despite being a sound technical system, PKI suffers from several critical flaws. A long list of such flaws can be found in (Ellison & Schneier, 2000; Linn & Branchaud, 2004). Some of the major technical concerns are:

1. Retrieval of Keys and Certificates are difficult.
2. Complexities in certificate processing.
3. Management of trust in cross domain scenarios.
4. Ensuring security at different ends.
5. Naming semantics

All these flaws lead into further significant usability vulnerabilities that allow attackers to launch different types of phishing attacks. The core problem here is the user's lack of knowledge regarding the domain name system and the user's inability to identify a fake domain name from the real one. Attackers may exploit the technique of typo squatting, a technique in which similar domain names that only vary in one or two letters are utilized, e.g. as represented by PayPa1 (the last character here is number 1) instead of PayPal. When the fake website looks identical to the genuine PayPal website, most users will be tricked into believing that the fake website is genuine. An attacker even may use a legitimate digital certificate for the fake domain and the browser will validate it without any problem whatsoever indicating that the server is fully authenticated by showing a closed padlock sign that it would usually show for other legitimate PKI-validated sites. Such a visual cue entices the user to establish trust with an invalid entity and thereby making the whole point of using PKI useless. In this sense, PKI with TLS is a technically sound solution, but lacks to provide any semantic meaning. In addition, users are suggested to follow a series of careful steps: 1) check if the target URL in the address uses the encrypted https protocol instead of the unencrypted http protocol, 2) check if the received server certificate is issued by some trusted authority, and 3) check if the domain of the accessed site matches the domain specified in the certificate. Not only do these steps pose a significant mental load on the user, but also become very tedious when the users need to do it over and over again even for the same entity tempts the user to overlook any warning related to the problem of entity authentication (Jøsang, Al Fayyadh, Grandison, AlZomai, and McNamara, 2007). It is also observed that security is a secondary consideration from the user's point of view (Dhamija & Tygar, 2006). The primary issue is to conclude the transaction and buy the desired item. This leads the user to ignore the required steps and creates precisely the vulnerability that makes phishing attacks potent and successful. Things would improve considerably if the process of trust validation could be incorporated into the system which would allow users to establish trust like before and validate their trust when they would visit the website again. Currently, the Web and browser PKI do not have any such facility and we believe that the Petname System fits perfectly in this scenario.

BACKGROUND OF PETNAME SYSTEMS

The identity management process can roughly be divided into three phases (Wikipedia Identity, 2012):

1. **Registration Phase:** An identity with a unique name is created. A corresponding credential may also be supplied along with the name. The name and the credential are kept as long as there is a relationship between the entity and any relevant relying party.
2. **Operations Phase:** The entity produces the name and the corresponding credential to the IdM system of the relying party for authentication and access control.
3. **Deregistration Phase:** When the relationship between the user and the relying party(ies) ceases, the identity is normally deregistered so that it can no longer be used for authentication or for accessing services.

In the first phase the Identity Management System (IdMS) has to generate and issue a unique name for each entity. The IdMS uses a namespace from which a name is selected or chosen. Simply, a namespace is a logical and abstract lot of names that can be used to uniquely select an entity. The main requirement for a name is uniqueness such that each name maps to a unique entity. It is obvious that the same name can be used to represent different entities in different namespaces. The larger the namespace, the more unique names it contains. However, a global namespace will normally suffer from the shortcoming that interpretation and memorization by humans becomes problematic. IP address is an example of such a global namespace. While it is possible to remember a few IP addresses, the mental load of remembering and accessing a large number of web sites by their IP addresses would be intolerable for normal users.

Three desirable properties of a name were defined by Zooko Wilcox-O'Hearn in his influential web article published in 2001 (Wilcox, 2001). According to him, a name should ideally be Global, Unique and Memorable (Called "Decentralized" "Secure" and "Human-Meaningful" respectively in Wilcox, 2001; Internet, 2012; Wilcox, 2001). To be memorable, a name has to pass the so-called "moving bus test" (Miller, 2000). That is, if one can correctly remember a name written on a moving bus for a definite amount of time, that name can be considered memorable. A name will be unique if it is collision-free within the domain (Stiegler, 2005) and has the property that it cannot be "forged or duplicated" or "mimicked." Wilcox-O'Hearn also claimed with supporting evidence that no name could have all the three desirable properties simultaneously, and suggested to choose any two of them according to different scenarios. Clay Shirky in his web article also came up with the same conclusion (Shirky, 2002). Any attempt to achieve all the three properties by any name could lead into the following problems:

1. Dependency on a third party which could monopolise the system and create a single point of failure (Wilcox, 2001).
2. Political and legal conflict may arise when a name becomes a trademark for different companies locally in several region and those companies compete for the same name when it reaches the global scale (Shirky, 2002).
3. Unintentional confusion between almost similar names, for example any confusion between two email addresses, e.g. rahim@bd.com and rahim@bd.net, can be very dangerous in a life critical situation. Intentional confusion caused by e.g. phishing attacks can also be disastrous (Stiegler, 2005).

A triangle where the three properties are placed in the three corners is commonly known as the Zooko's triangle, and represents the basic foundation for the Petname Model. Zooko's triangle is illustrated in Figure 2.

The idea of placing the three properties at the three corners of a triangle can be explained as follows. In a triangle the three corners are never connected by a single line, only pairs of corners are connected. Placing those three properties in the three corners of the triangle provides a visual analogy to the fact that a name can only achieve two of the desirable properties at any one time.

Figure 2. Zooko's triangle

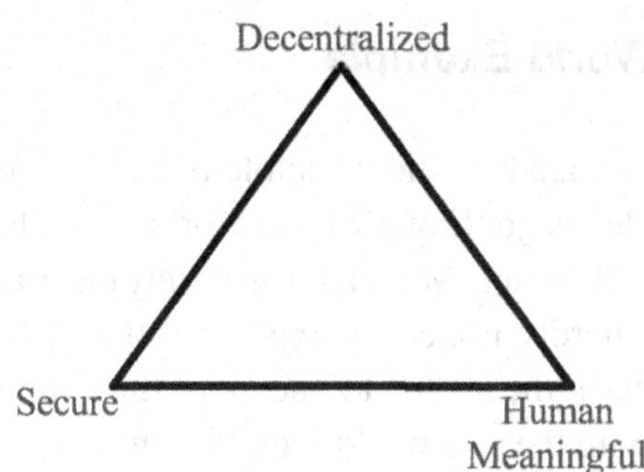

In 2000, Jonathan S. Shapiro, being inspired by the idea of Marc Miller et al. while at Electric Communities, described in a web article his scheme of adopting a system which utilised three types of naming conventions: Petname, True Name and Nickname (Shapiro, 2000). He adopted this idea for a configuration management system. A True Name is synonymous to a global unique name, the Nickname is a global memorable assigned name of an entity by its creator, and the Petname is a memorable and locally unique user-assigned name for that entity.

A few months later, Mark Miller published another article (Miller, 2000) in which he, for the first time, documented the structure of the Petname Model with three components: Petname, Key and Nickname. These three components are essentially equivalent to Shapiro's Petname, True Name and Nickname respectively. Miller suggested to use the term Key instead of True Name, and pointed out that the Petname Model satisfies all the three desirable properties of Zooko's triangle. This idea was actually elaborated by Marc Stiegler when he formalised the Petname Model. Tyler Close suggested adopting the term Pointer instead of Key (Close, 2003) and the term Pointer will be adopted instead of Key in this chapter. This topic will be described in greater details in the subsequent sections.

In 2003, Tyler Close of Waterken Inc. pointed out the possibility of using Petname Systems for better trust management (Close, 2003a). Waterken Inc. developed the Petname Toolbar for the Firefox web browser. The main motif was to show the potential implementation of the Petname Model to counter phishing attacks. According to Tyler Close, humans are not capable of managing the transition of trust from one entity to another in digital communications and this leads to identity-theft as a result of phishing attacks. The next paragraph explains his view on the rationale behind Petname Systems.

Whenever we move from one website to another by clicking a hyper-link at the first site, there are two types of transitions that take place. One is the website transition that takes us to the next website and the second one is the transition of trust which enables us to retain or discard the trust relationship with the next website. We have different types of trust relationships with different entities. We may trust one entity more than another and with different scopes. As an analogy, when a user wants to buy something from an e-commerce website, she may not trust to give her credit card credentials to that site but she may trust PayPal. In this case, after choosing the item, the website may take her to the PayPal web page and she completes the transaction there. But the problem here is to make sure that the e-commerce site takes her to the right PayPal site, not to a fraudulent one. As mentioned earlier, users find it difficult to evaluate and validate their trust during transitions of website. That is, transition of trust may not take place as desired. So Tyler Close concluded that it was unwise to perform both transitions on the recommendation from a non-trustworthy entity, and therefore suggested to use Petname Systems to enable manual trust evaluation by the user while the transition takes place.

It is interesting to note at this point the relationship between identity management and trust management, where applying them improperly may lead to identity theft attacks. A realistic scenario can be used as an example. In the brick-and-mortar world, we come across different people where the different biological differences help us identify each person uniquely. Interactions with them enable us to decide who to trust. Sometimes recommendations play a crucial role. When our near and dear tell us not to trust somebody, we usually do not trust him or her, though this perspective may change over time. So we usually identify a person at first and place trust afterwards. Now in the digital world this scenario is somewhat different. To trust a digital entity, recommendation is the best and sometime the only option. We read website reviews, blogs, etc. and receive advice from relatives and friends on which digital entity to trust for online transactions. We may learn from them that there is a website www.paypal.com (there are also other trusted websites for online transactions) which we can trust for online transactions, even before we have accessed and identified it. Once the trust is placed, the only thing remaining is to identify the website which is truly the recommended one. It can also be the other way around, as for example we may browse and identify several unknown websites that are potentially suitable for a specific transaction, and then choose to transact with a specific one that subsequently will be trusted based on positive experiences. The first way obviously is the most hassle-free, and the second one requires the user to accept a certain risk of transacting with an unknown entity. Whichever is the best option, trust management and identity management are closely tied to each other when we try to derive a solution for the identity theft. As we will see, the Petname Model provides a solution for both scenarios.

In 2005, Marc Stiegler extended the Petname Model based on Mark Miller's suggestion and also explained the detailed interaction among the components of the Petname Model (Stiegler, 2005). He also formalised the properties and requirements for the Petname Model and gave examples of some applications of Petname Systems. The evolutionary time-line in this section illustrates how the different topics of namespace, identity management, and trust management are interrelated, and how they were combined to formulate the Petname Model.

THE PETNAME MODEL

Real World Example

Before we analyse the principle of the Petname Model, let us go through a real world example in which the Petname Model is so naturally integrated that we hardly notice its existence. It will help to link back the abstract concept of the Petname model with the real world scenarios and to grasp some of the key concepts of the Petname Model. Let us first analyse how people actually recognise each other. This process is very simple and natural to us: through several physical attributes like face, voice, physique or maybe combinations of them. These combinations can be thought of as the Pointer in the Petname terminology (see below) to uniquely identify a single person. That single person introduces herself to us by stating her name XYZ which is actually a Nickname in the Petname Model terminology (See below). From then on we may perceive that the person's identity as Mrs XYZ, which actually represents a Petname in the Petname terminology (see below). Now if another person also introduces herself as XYZ, then our mind does not simply assign that name as her Petname because it was already assigned to another person. Here things may evolve in different directions. One possible direction can be that our mind distinguishes between those two persons and changes the Petname for the first person as Mrs XYZ of London and Mrs XYZ of Paris for the second person or whatever seems practical.

Rationale

As mentioned in the previous section, the Zooko's triangle visualises the hypothesis that no name can at the same time be Global, Memorable and Unique, but can only have two of the properties. Three unique pairs can be created using these three properties: 1) Global-Memorable, 2) Memorable-Unique, and 3) Global-Unique. Even if no name can have all the three properties, a naming system can be designed to achieve all the three properties. The Petname Model represents one such naming system.

Components

The Petname Model uses three different types of names that in our terminology are called: Pointer, Nickname and Petname. These three name types actually represent the three sides of the Zooko's triangle and hence are synonymous to the three pairs discussed above. Detailed explanation of each of them is given below.

- **Pointer:** The Pointer was defined as "True Name" in Shapiro's interpretation and as "Key" in Miller's interpretation. A Pointer implies a globally unique and securely collision free name which can uniquely identify an entity. In this sense, it is actually a Name (Identifier). It inter-connects the Global and Unique corners of the Zooko's triangle. The security of the Petname Model mainly depends on these factors: 1) Difficulty to forge a Pointer (meaning it should be difficult to duplicate one pointer from another), 2) Difficulty to mimic a Petname (meaning it should be difficult to create two petnames so similar that users will have difficulty to differentiate them) later and 3) It should reasonably difficult in spoofing the trusted path and context (e.g. the browser chrome within the scope of this paper) in which the petname is displayed. A public/private key pair and a fully qualified pathname of a file in an Internet file server are good examples of Pointers. They are globally unique and difficult to forge. However, a Pointer (e.g. a public key, IP address, etc.) may not be memorable to the human.
- **Nickname:** The Nickname inter-connects the Global and Memorable corners of the Zooko's triangle. It is an optional non-unique name created by the owner of the Pointer. The purpose of the Nickname is to aid in identifying the entity easily. The title of a web page that is displayed in the title bar of the browser is an example of a Nickname. Users may remember that web page by the title, but another website may have the same title and can create a collision on the user's mind. Thus a Nickname is not necessarily unique.
- **Petname:** The Petname is a name created by the user to refer to a specific Pointer of an entity. Within the domain of a single user a bi-directional one-to-many mapping exists between Petnames and Pointers. A Petname connects the Memorable and Unique corners of the triangle. Petnames only have a local scope and may only be relevant for local jurisdiction. The trusted path and context mentioned in the Pointer section above highlights the importance of confining the Petname only in a local context. The same Petname can be used by different users to refer to either the same Pointer or to different Pointers. The security of a Petname System also depends on the privacy of Petnames and the difficulty to mimic a Petname. Here it is interesting to note that a Petname does not necessarily mean a text-based name. In addition to text, it can also be an image or a sound or any combination of all of the items in different ways.

The concept of Referral is also related to the Petname Model (Stiegler, 2005). A Referral from a third party can consist of a Pointer and a so-called Alleged Name which is the introductory/referred name for an entity, like the Nickname. The distinction between a Nickname and an Alleged Name is that the Nickname is created by the owner of the entity and the Pointer, whereas the Alleged Name is provided by a third party. In a trivial case, the Nickname and the Alleged

Name can be identical. If your friend sends you a message with the text "Best e-auction site" with the link www.ebay.com, then it can be thought as Referral where the text "Best e-auction site" can be interpreted as the Alleged name.

A couple of naming conventions, global names and local names, found in the Simple Public Key Infrastructure (SPKI, in short) (Ellison, Frantz, Lampson, Rivest, Thomas, and Ylonen, 1999) has strong similarities with the Petname model. Therefore it is useful to analyse the similarities and dissimilarities between these names of the two models. The suggested globally unique name (or global name) in the SPKI model is essentially a Pointer in the Petname model. Both share the same properties of a name; they are global and unique, however may not be memorable. The local name of the SPKI, also known as the Simple Distributed Security Infrastructure (SDSI, in short) name, is similar to the concept of the Petname as both are locally created name residing only the domain of a user with one major dissimilarity: a SDSI name can be used globally by prefixing the local namespace with the local name, however a Petname will never reach global scale and will always be kept under local jurisdiction. The SPKI has no concepts of the Nickname or Alleged name whatsoever.

Relationship Among the Components

There is a bidirectional one-to-many mapping between Petnames and Pointers within the domain of each user. A Nickname has a one-to-many relationship to the set of Pointers. A Pointer is assumed to map to a single Nickname, but can map to several Alleged Names in the global domain. The relationship between Petnames and Nicknames can be confusing sometimes when first described without a good example. In some situations, a Nickname can be used as a Petname or in other situations a Petname can be derived from the Nickname. A single Nickname can always be uniquely resolved from the Petname, but the Nickname is not necessarily unique for the Petname. For that reason, a Petname cannot be uniquely resolved from a Nickname. Figure 3 illustrates this relationship. As seen from the figure, the Petname Model is actually a naming convention built on top of the Zooko's triangle.

It is fascinating to note here that other than providing a trivial bi-directional mapping, the relationship between the Pointer and the Petname offers a subtle indication of the trust transition that was mentioned previously. Thus a Petname can also be thought of as a trust indicator for the

Figure 3. Petname model

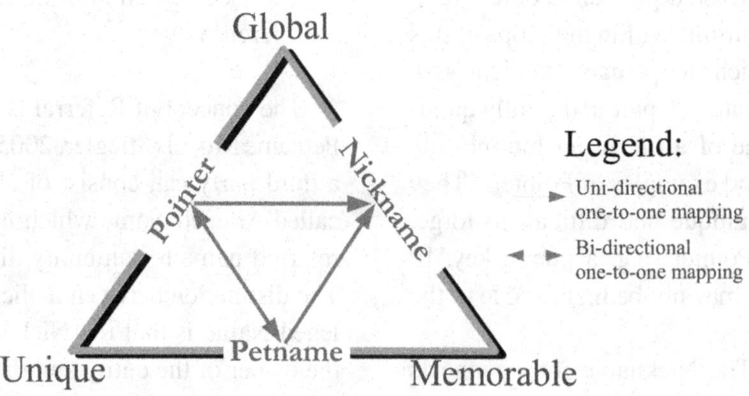

Pointer. In the following sections, it will be explained how Petnames can act as a trust indicator for Pointers.

PROPERTIES OF PETNAME SYSTEMS

The properties of a Petname System can be divided into two broad categories: Functional properties and Security Usability properties.

Functional Properties

F1: A Petname System must consist of at least a Pointer and a Petname.

F2: Nickname is optional.

F3: Pointers must be strongly resistant against forgery so that the Pointer cannot be used to identify a false entity, meaning that there should not be any second pointer that has been created from another pointer and at the same time both pointers refer to different entities, or simply, two same pointers must refer to the same entity. However, it is always possible to have two different pointers referring to the same entity.

F4: For every user there must be a bi-directional one-to-many mapping between the Petname and the Pointer of each entity only if these pointers refer to the same entity, otherwise a bidirectional one-to-one mapping between the Petname and Pointer of each entity has to be enforced. That is, the same Petname can be used for different pointers only if all these pointers refer to the same entity. It is suitable for situations when an entity has different pointers and the user wants to use the same Petname for all these pointers. It also enforces that the same Petname cannot be used for different pointers if each of those pointers refers to different entities.

Security Usability Properties

Security usability will ensure the reliability of using the system and enables the user to draw conclusion on the actual security of the system. These properties will ensure that the Petname System is not affected by usability vulnerabilities. Usability properties can again be categorized in two types (Jøsang, Zomai, and Suriadi, 2007):

Security Action. A security action is when users are required to produce information and security tokens, or to trigger some security relevant mechanisms. Security actions enable a user to interact securely with an entity. For example, typing and submitting a password is a security action. Properties related to the security action in the Petname System are (Stiegler, 2005):

SA1: It is the user who must assign the Petname for each Pointer.

SA2: Users must assign the Petname for the Pointer with explicit actions.

SA3: As the relationship between the user and other entities evolve, the user should be able to edit the previously applied Petname for a Pointer to a new Petname.

SA4: Suggestion on the Petname based on the Nickname can be provided as an aid for the user to select a Petname for a Pointer. If the Nickname is missing, other criteria could be chosen for the suggestion.

SA5: If a suggestion is provided and the user wants to accept it as the Petname, then she must do so with explicit actions. This is to ensure that the suggestion is not automatically assigned as the Petname and users are well informed that a suggested name is being assigned as the Petname.

SA6: Petname Systems must make sure that the user-selected, created or suggested Petname is sufficiently distinct from the Nickname so that the user does not confuse them with each other. This is needed to ensure that two same nicknames do not result in the same Petname and thus violating the F4. It might be acceptable that a Petname is equal to the Nickname in case a specific Nickname is unique within the user's local domain, but it would cause confusion and security usability vulnerabilities in case two or more Pointers correspond to the same Nickname in the user's domain. An alternative formulation of the SA6 property can therefore be that the Petname System must enforce that a Petname is different from the Nickname in case the Nickname is non-unique.

SA7: Petname Systems must make sure that the user-selected, created or suggested Petname must be sufficiently different from existing Petnames unless they refer to the same entity. In that case, the Petname even be the same as any existing one. This is needed to reduce the risk of mimicry of the Petname upon which the security of the Petname System largely depends.

SA8: If the user chooses a Petname that may resemble a Nickname or other Petnames, she should be warned explicitly. This property actually supplements SA6 and SA7.

SA9: The User should be alerted to apply a Petname for the entity that involves in highly sensitive data transmission.

Security Conclusion. A security conclusion is when users observe and assess security relevant evidence in order to derive the security state of systems. Security conclusions enable the user to conclude on the security state of the system by observing security relevant evidence and assessing this together with assumptions. For example, observing a closed padlock on a browser, and concluding that the communication is protected by TLS is a security conclusion. Properties related to the security conclusion are (Stiegler, 2005):

SC1: The Pointer and the corresponding Petname must be displayed at all times through the user interface of the Petname System. This will make the user confident about her interaction and help to draw the security conclusion easily.

SC2: The Petname for a Pointer should be displayed with enough clarity at the user interface so that it can attract the user's attention easily.

SC3: The absence of a Petname for a Pointer should be clearly and visually indicated at the user interface so that the user is surely informed about its absence.

SC4: The visual indications distinguishing actual petnames from suggestions (like Nicknames) should be unambiguous enough so that the user does not confuse them with each other.

SC5: The warning message that will be provided when there is a direct violation of any of the above properties should be clear enough so that the user can understand the problem and take the necessary security action.

PKI AND PETNAME SYSTEMS

Now, let us analyse the ways a Petname System can be used for entity authentication as well as for trust validation. In line with context of this chapter, the ideal place to utilise any Petname System is inside the chrome of a browser as a browser add-on or extension much like the Petname Tool (Close, 2005), developed by Tyler Close, TrustBar (Herzberg & Gbara, 2004), developed by the TrustBar team at the Dept. of Computer Science in the Bar Ilan University, Israel and Passpet (Yee & Sitaker, 2006), developed at the University of California, Berkeley. All of them are Firefox extensions and work only with the Firefox. They allow the user to define a Petname for a website and display the Petname when she visits it later.

The first step of using the Petname System is, as we call it and happens to be the most important one, Trust Bootstrapping in which the user visits the intended (secure) website with an intention to involve in an online transaction. It follows the Entity Authentication phase as described in the PKI Section in which the certificate is validated and the website is authenticated. During the bootstrapping phase, the user needs to investigate the domain name and the certificate carefully. When she is confident that this is the correct entity, she will define a Petname against a Pointer for this website satisfying the functional and security usability requirements mentioned above. Different Petname Systems utilise different mechanisms to define a Pointer. For example, the Petname Tool uses the pair CA public key fingerprint, end entity Organisation name or Common Name if absent to define the Pointer for that site. It does not work with non-https sites because it depends on certificate to retrieve the public key. Passpet extends the idea of the Petname tool also for non-https sites. It utilises the combination of root key, field name and field value to generate the Pointer. For https sites, root key is the hashed public key of the site, field name is "O" and field value is the organisation name if organisation name is available in the certificate, otherwise field name is "CN" and field value is the certificate's common name. For the non-https sites, root key is empty, field name is "D" and field value is the last n+1 level for the n-level TLD (Top level domain). Users can assign a Petname for each site by clicking an icon in the browser. The domain name represents the Pointer in case of TrustBar.

The second step is called the Trust Validation in which the user visits the aforementioned secure site once again. If the user visits the same site (identified and authenticated by the certificate) and the calculated Pointer matches with a pointer for which a Petname was assigned beforehand, her defined Petname will be displayed in the Petname System. The absence of the Petname would indicate that her trust has not been validated properly and would provide the required visual cue that this site may be a fraudulent site and hence she needs to be more vigilant in engaging any sort of transaction with this site. Different systems may utilise different visual cues which will be explained in the next section. As mentioned previously, a Petname needs not to be a Text only; it can be an image, sound or any combination of them.

To summarise, PKI and the Petname Model should be considered as supplementary technologies for entity authentication and trust validation on the web; not as complimentary technologies. The PKI lacks significantly in providing a semantically consistent trust bootstrapping and validation mechanism which can be provided consistently by the Petname Model as long as the bootstrapping process is carefully carried out. On other hand, the Petname model may not function properly without the automatic entity authentication mechanism service provided by the PKI.

At this point it is worth exploring recently popular trust ensuring mechanisms based on recommendation systems where the reputation data is provided by the community of users of the respective system. There are different such systems namely McAfee's SiteAdvisor and SiteAdvisor Plus (McAfee, 2012), Trend Micro's TrendProtect (Trend, 2012) and WOT Services Ltd.'s Web of Trust (WoT) (WOT, 2012). To keep our analysis concise, here we analyse the WoT only.

WoT provides a browser add-on for different browsers. Using this browser add-on, WoT allows users to rate the trustworthiness, vendor reliability, privacy and/or child safety of a website as they perceive while using the websites or the services they offer. The rating scale ranges from poor to excellent. That rating input is transferred to the WoT Server where the reputation of any websites are computed algorithmically through a combination of user ratings and data from trusted sources such as hpHosts Legit Script Panda Security, PhishTank, and TRUSTe. That reputation data for a specific website is displayed on the WoT add-on using the traffic-light style color rating system

(Green for provable safe sites, Red for provable dangerous sites, etc.) when a user visits that site.

Theoretically, any such recommendation system coupled with the PKI can provide the trust bootstrapping and validation similar to the Petname Model. However, any such recommendation system suffers from some significant disadvantages such as:

1. Like any other recommendation systems, the accuracy of the rating of a website largely depends on the active participation of users and on the aggregated trust users have in that website. Therefore, they system may rate a website as a potentially unsafe one even though the website may be technically safe if a significant enough portion of the community has indicated lack of trust for the site (WOT Wiki, 2012). Conversely, the system may rate a website as a potentially safe one even though the website may be technically unsafe if a significant enough portion of the community has (maliciously) given a positive feedback for the site. That is, the displayed result may be significantly biased.
2. A new website which is not properly recognised in the system may do significant damage before it is negatively rated creating a window of opportunity for malicious websites.
3. Such systems may alternate the ratings of different websites to gain financial incentives (e.g. via sponsored result, etc.). For example, it has been reported that McAfee's figures show a higher percentage of potentially dangerous sites among sponsored results in their systems (Rubenking, 2009).
4. Relying on a specific recommendation system run by a third party for ensuring trust may be potentially problematic for users in case the respective company goes bankrupt and all the reputation data is gone.

Having no central dependency on a specific third party, the Petname Model is free from almost all these disadvantages. It does not depend on any third party that can influence the outcome of any trust bootstrapping and trust validation result. There is no window of opportunity for malicious websites as long as the user can bootstrap the trust. There is no need for a significant amount of participation from the users of a community to establish and validate trust in the Petname Model. In such we believe that the Petname Model coupled with the PKI can be a more suitable choice for entity authentication and trust validation on the web.

OTHER APPLICATION DOMAINS

The presence of the Petname Model is so ubiquitous that people may sometimes be unaware of its existence. Here we will highlight the possible domains in which the Petname Model is used, intentionally or unintentionally, or could be used. For each of the applications we will try to determine the suitability of applying the Petname Model (Stiegler, 2005).

Phone/E-mail Contact List

A phone/email contact list is another classic example of a Petname System. The phone number with international format (preceding the number with + or 00 and country code) may represent the Pointer and it is unforgeable and globally unique. We save the number in our contact book by placing a name for it which is nothing but a Petname for that number. Nicknames are absent here. The same analogy applies for email contact lists. Email addresses represent Pointers. A From-field in an email header may contain only the email address: xyz@yahoo.com or a given name by the sender with her email address: Mr. XYZ <xyz@yahoo.com>. Here the given name (Mr. XYZ) represents the Nickname. After receiving a mail from a new sender one can save the sender's email address in the email contact list. At that time a Petname is created by inserting a name suitable to identify that person, or by simply keeping the Nickname. It should be noted that many email systems violate the petname model by not adequately distinguishing between a nickname that was automatically accepted by the system without any user action, and a petname that the user explicitly accepted. In such systems, it was not uncommon to start a series of email with one person and end the day with a completely different person who happens to have the same nickname and thus causing lots of confusion just because the system has tried to be helpful. This particular example stresses out the need for SA1 and SA2 properties.

IM Buddy List

In the domain of a particular Instant Messaging Service each entity has a unique Id (email Id for yahoo, Hotmail or Passport service) which represents the Pointer for that entity. But sometimes those Ids can have quite close resemblance (logicman and 1ogicman, the second one actually is a 1 not a small L) to each other and thus can be quite confusing for the user to differentiate. A better option is used in the interface of the Instant Messenger where one can put a name for each of the IDs. Such a name is actually a Petname. In the user interface all the interactions with the Id is usually done with the Petname and thus making the IM Buddy list a good example of a Petname System. Nicknames are absent here.

IP Address

Not all IP addresses have domain names. If one would like to communicate only utilizing IP address, a Petname Model can be applied locally as a substitute for domain names. IP addresses are hard to remember, and Petnames will make it easy to refer to them. IP addresses will represent the Pointer, and the corresponding Petname will be used at the user interface. All communication from the user's side will be based on Petnames.

CapDesk and Polaris

CapDesk is a desktop environment that applies the principle of least authority and utilises the Petname Model to provide security to the user for applications (Corporation, 2012). Whenever a new application is installed, CapDesk will feature a Pet Text and Pet Graphic for that application. The user may accept it or modify it. Once provided, Pet Text and Graphics will be used in the window of the application while it runs. Like CapDesk, Polaris is also based on the principle of least authority and also uses Pet Text similar to CapDesk and attaches it to the window of the application while it runs (Stiegler, Karp, Yee, and Miller, 2004).

OpenPGP

The OpenPGP key is the Pointer and it carries the Nickname given by the owner of the Pointer. Some implementations of OpenPGP allow the user to change the Nickname and implement a Petname System (Stiegler, 2005).

Process Handling

Every modern OS runs a number of processes simultaneously. ps-e command in Linux or the process tab in the task manager for Windows shows a long list of processes. Some of the process names are so obscure that it is impossible for the user to understand their functionalities. A Petname Model could be applied to improve the situation significantly. When a process would run for the first time it would present a short description of what it would do. Then the user could create an informative Petname for that process. This Petname would be displayed in the memory map, for example in the process tab in task manager or with ps-e command. In this case the Pointer does not have to be global. It is simply the unique process name or unique command used to run the process.

EVALUATION OF SECURITY USABILITY FOR PKI-BASED PETNAME SYSTEM

The usability of security is crucial for the overall security of the system, but is still a relatively poorly understood element of IT security. Therefore it is important to evaluate the Security Usability of Petname Systems as it is directly related to the security of client-side Identity Management. A set of general Security Usability principles related to Identity Management were proposed in (Jøsang, Al Zomai, and Suriadi, 2007). We will use these principles as a basis to evaluate the Security Usability of the Petname System by analysing if the Security Usability properties of the Petname System satisfy these principles. The Security Usability principles are described below:

Security Action Usability Principles

A1: Users must understand which security actions are required of them.

A2: Users must have sufficient knowledge and the ability to take the correct security action.

A3: The mental and physical load of a security action must be tolerable.

A4: The mental and physical load of making repeated security actions for any practical number of instances must be tolerable.

Security Conclusion Usability Principles

C1: Users must understand the security conclusion that is required for making an informed decision.

C2: The system must provide the user with sufficient information for deriving the security conclusion.

C3: The mental load of deriving the security conclusion must be tolerable.

C4: The mental load of deriving security conclusions for any practical number of instances must be tolerable.

The Security Usability properties of Petname Systems can now be analysed according to these security principles. When a Petname System satisfies SA1-SA3 and SA6-SA9 of the Security Action properties, it implicitly implies that principles A1 and A2 are also satisfied, because the former properties enable a user to select a unique and unambiguous Petname for a Pointer. This selection of a unique and unambiguous Petname for a Pointer can be thought of as the correct security action as it enables the user to securely identify an entity. Security Action properties SA4-SA8 will act as the aid for the user to select a Petname for a Pointer. We believe that selecting an unambiguous Petname will pose the most significant mental load for the user in the Petname System when repeated for several entities. Such mental load will be reduced significantly if these five properties are satisfied in a Petname System because users do not have to think about the ambiguity of the new Petname with other existing Petnames. Automated suggestion could also be a great aid in such selection. Therefore satisfying these five properties will implicitly lead to the principles A3 and A4 also being satisfied.

To analyse the Security Conclusion properties of the Petname System, we have to first define Security Conclusion in the Identity Management perspective. Security Conclusion in the Identity Management perspective is to correctly identify a specific entity. Displaying the Petname for a Pointer that points to the desired entity at the user interface will enable the user to draw conclusion that this Pointer and in turn the entity the user is interacting with is the intended one. The presence and absence of the Petname will provide the user with enough information to draw the security conclusion easily. So whenever a Petname System satisfies SC1-SC3, it will explicitly satisfy C1 and C2. Different visual techniques should be applied to help the user reduce their mental load in deriving security conclusions. Using different eye-catching colours to indicate the presence or absence of a Petname for a specific Pointer can be an example of one such visual technique. The security conclusion properties SC2-SC5 should be applied to enable a user to draw conclusion with ease and thus if followed will satisfy principles C3 and C4.

From the above analysis we can conclude that a complete implementation of all the properties of a Petname System will satisfy all the security usability principles.

Having formalized the properties of Petname Systems, and having analysed security usability issues on a general level, the security usability for two existing Petname System applications are analysed with the Cognitive Walkthrough method. The applications to be analysed are: 1) Petname Tool and 2) TrustBar. Both toolbars are designed only to work with the Firefox browser, and are aimed at simplifying client-side management of SP identities and at providing a better defence mechanism against Phishing attacks. Though the application domains for the Petname System is much broader, as described in Sect. 8, we have decided to confine our evaluation only to these two in order to focus on managing SP identities at the client side. These two particular applications exactly meet this criterion. The Passpet mentioned earlier could not be evaluated as it was not compatible with the Firefox that was used for evaluation or with the current version of the Firefox.

The Cognitive Walkthrough method is a usability evaluation method in which an evaluator or a group of evaluators participate to identify the usability issues of an application by visually inspecting the user interface. It focuses on evaluating the understandability and the ease of use for a user at the user interface to accomplish a task using that application. Among several usability evaluation methods the Cognitive Walkthrough was chosen as our preferred method because of its main focus on the understandability of the user at the user interface (Whitten & Tygar, 1999). Because Petname Systems affect the user interface, Cognitive Walkthrough is a suitable method for evaluating their usability. While performing the Cognitive Walkthrough for each application, it will be noted if the application satisfies the usability properties discussed in Sect. 5. The degree of compliance with the specified security usability properties will give an indication of the level of security usability of each application. For the evaluation, Firefox with the Nightly Tester Tool, a Firefox add-on, was used. It is important to note here that the evaluations were performed by the authors of this chapter.

The Petname Tool

Setup

The Petname Tool is available as a Firefox add-on in (Close, 2012). The current version of the Petname Tool is compatible with the latest Firefox version, and can be easily installed by just clicking the "Add to Firefox" button in the respective Firefox Add-on website. Once installed the toolbar will look like Figure 4.

Functionality

The first thing to note about the Petname Tool is its simplicity. It consists of only a text field in

Figure 4. The petname tool in Firefox

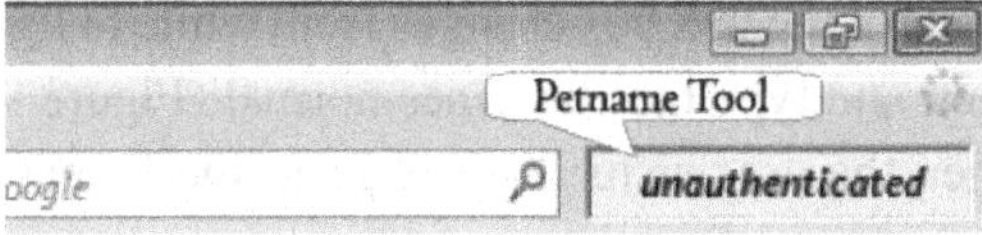

the navigation toolbar of the browser. Its main purpose is to allow a user to assign a Petname for a website that she wants to correctly recognize and to display that Petname in the text field when she visits the site later. The Petname will be absent if the visited site is not the intended one. A user can judge if a webpage comes from a previously identified website by observing the presence or absence of the Petname. The Petname Tool utilizes different font properties and graphical user interface elements to achieve its goal: 1) The text in the text field, 2) The typeface of the text, 3) Color of the text field, 4) Tooltip, and 5) Dialog box. Different texts with different typefaces are displayed in the text field in different situations, color of the text field change, different tooltips are provided accordingly when mouse pointer is placed over the text field, and warnings are displayed using dialog boxes.

Some examples can illustrate how the Petname Tool operates. It is worth noticing here that the Petname Tool does not work for non-https sites, as it uses the pair CA public key fingerprint, end entity Organisation name or Common Name if absent as the Pointe for that site. While visiting a non-https site, e.g. www.wikipedia.org, the text in the text field will be unauthenticated with italic typeface and it will be disabled with grey colour so that nobody can assign a Petname for the site (Figure 5). The corresponding tooltip is: Don't give this page sensitive information; it was not received securely (Figure 6). During the visit to a https site for the first time, e.g. www.paypal.com, the text in the text field becomes unknown site with italic typeface and the text field colour changes to white (Figure 7) with the corresponding tooltip-Assign a Petname to this site before exchanging sensitive information (Figure 8). At this point, user can assign a Petname by just writing it in the text field and hitting the Enter key. The colour of the text box changes from white to light green and type face becomes normal (Figure 9). When the user visits that site later, the Petname with normal typeface is displayed in the green text field. Different dialog boxes are prompted to warn users whenever something goes wrong.

Evaluation

As mentioned earlier, the Petname Tool is very simple; however, one may almost feel that it is too simple. It does not come with any text label; only a text field to enter Petnames. Absence of a text label can confuse unfamiliar users because they might not understand its purpose. The Petname Tool does not work for non-https sites; therefore it will not be possible for a user to assign Petnames to non-https sites. Many sites with server certificates do not use https in the initial log-in stages, though the log-in name and the related password may be encrypted before transmission. An example is the famous social networking website www.facebook.com. A potential vulnerability is caused by Facebook because email addresses represent user names. People often use the same passwords for different accounts, so a password used on Facebook will often allow access to the user's web email account. The lack of support, therefore, for non-https sites in the Petname Tool is a major drawback. Another thing is worth to note that the Petname Tool uses the pair CA public key fingerprint, end entity Organisation name or Common Name if absent as a Pointer.

Figure 5. Disabled text field for a non-https site

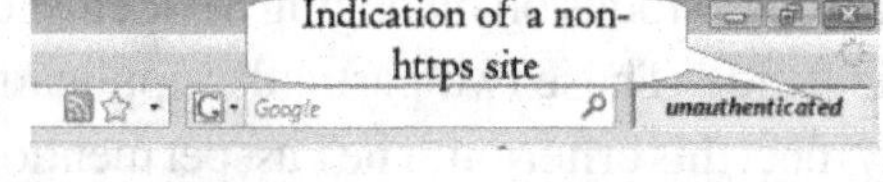

Figure 6. Tooltip for a non-https site

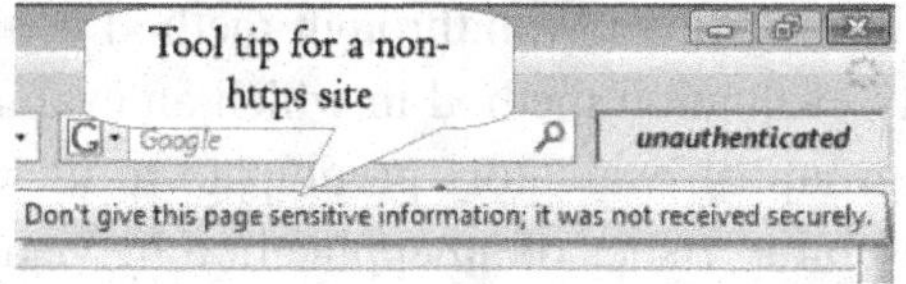

Figure 7. Indication of an https site

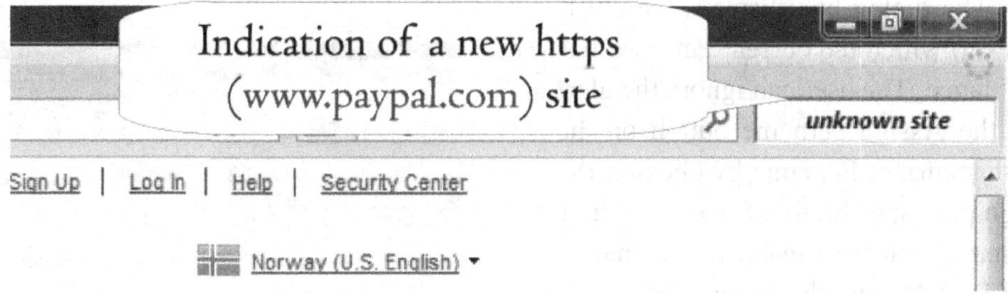

Figure 8. Tooltip for an https site

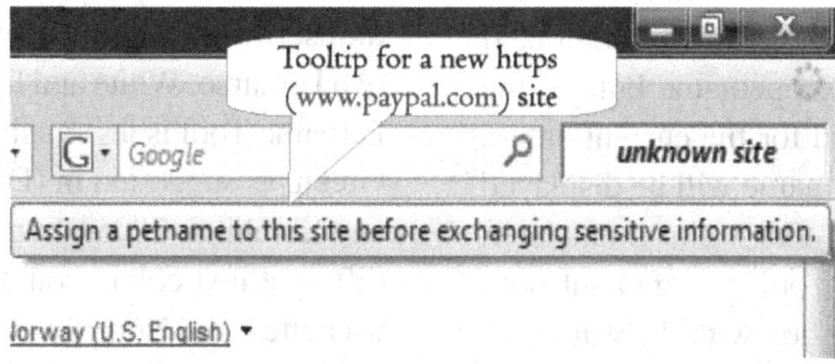

Figure 9. Assigned petname for a new https site

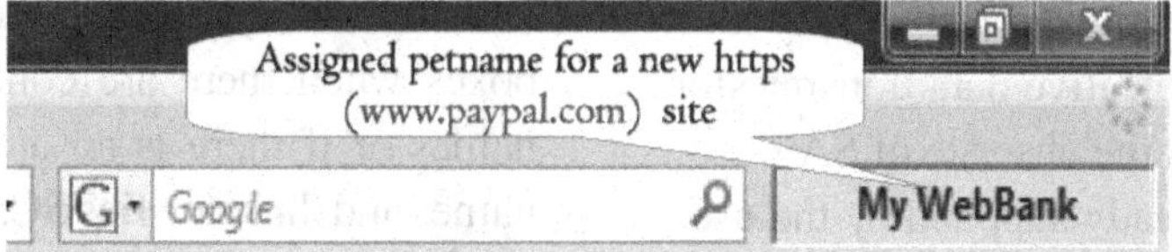

Therefore if the site receives a new certificate and thus a new public key, the Petname Tool will fail to map between the already assigned Petname and the Pointer. A possible solution could be to let URL or domain name be the Pointer that will also remove the restriction of applying Petnames for https sites only.

In the following, the Petname Tool will be analysed for compliance with the Petname System properties. The Petname Tool, obviously, deploys Petnames. The pair, CA public key fingerprint, end entity Organisation name or Common Name if absent, is used to define the Pointer and is strongly resistant against forgery. Therefore we conclude that the Petname Tool satisfies F1 and F3. But a serious restriction of the Petname Tool is that it allows users to assign exactly the same Petname for different entities as demonstrated in the next paragraph, thus violates F4. It does not deploy Nicknames and therefore does not satisfy the optional property F2.

The Petname Tool enables users to explicitly assign a Petname for each entity, e.g. to select the text field, write down a Petname and hit the Enter key. This satisfies SA1 and SA2. Users can change any Petname any time, thereby satisfying SA3. No suggestion is provided for aiding the user to select a Petname, thereby, is not compliant with SA4 and SA5. Also Nicknames are not used in the Petname Tool, resulting in non-compliance with SA6. Whenever a user selects a Petname that closely resembles existing Petnames, the user is alerted with an informative dialog box (Figure 10). The dialog box displays the existing Petnames to which the current Petname has close resemblance. The user can ignore the alert by clicking the Assign petname button or she can cancel this current Petname by clicking the "Don't assign petname" button. If a user assigns a Petname that is similar to an existing Petname, the Petname Tool displays the dialog box (Figure 11). The dialog box contains the name of the existing similar Petname with its creation date. The user has the option to discard the current Petname by clicking the Don't assign petname button. If the user clicks the Assign petname button, the Petname will be assigned for the current entity. In this case, the same Petname will be displayed for both websites when she visits them later. Therefore, the Petname Tool is compliant with SA8 (showing the dialog box with the warning), but directly violates SA7 as the same Petname is possible for two different entities. The Petname Tool allows a user to assign a Petname at her will whenever she feels and does not show any alert when there is highly sensitive data transmission and therefore indicates the absence of SA9.

Figure 11. Dialog box warn about the similarity between two petnames

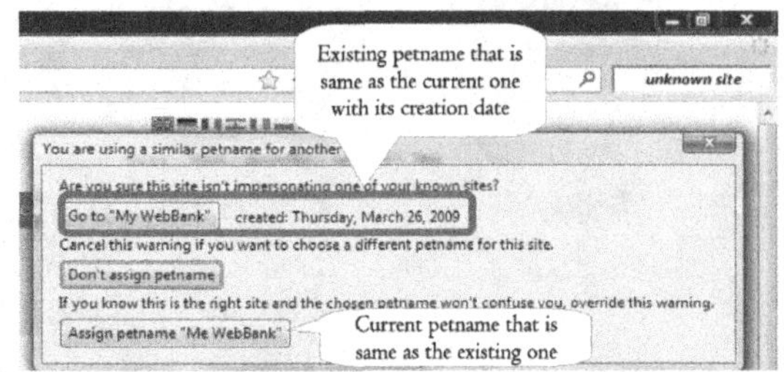

The Petname, if already supplied by the user, is displayed on the Petname Tool toolbar, thereby satisfying SC1. Different typefaces, tooltips, and colors have been used in the Petname Tool to catch the user attention to indicate the presence or absence of a Petname. White and light green as used by the Petname Tool is less visible than Red, Yellow, or Green, as suggested in (Drelie Gelasca, Tomasic, and Ebrahimi, 2005). In addition, blinking text or different text colors could be used to draw more user attention. Nevertheless, we can conclude that the Petname Tool is compliant with SC2 and SC3. As there is no suggested Petname or Nickname in the Petname Tool, it does not satisfy SC4. The Petname Tool provides warning through dialog boxes when there are conflicts with other Petnames or if there is an ambiguity between Petnames and thus satisfies SC5. However, it does not provide a warning message when there is a violation for other properties.

Figure 10. Dialog box warning about the close ambiguity among different petnames

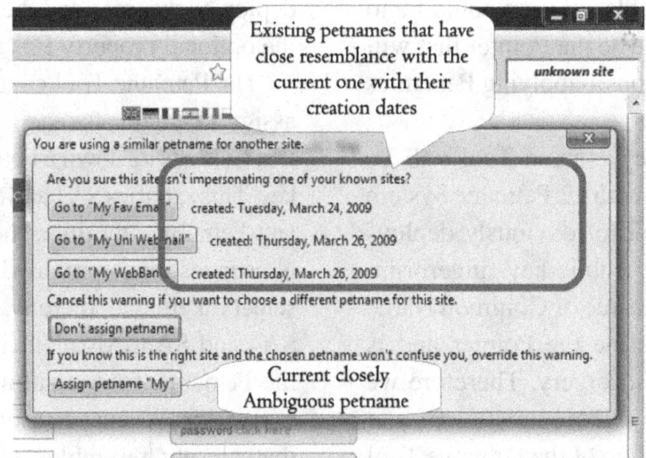

Apart from security usability issues, there are some other weaknesses in the Petname Tool. For example, there is no help button that could explain what the user has to do to utilise it properly. It does not provide the standard About menu item that could explain the purpose of the Petname Tool.

TrustBar

Setup

The TrustBar Tool is available as a Firefox add-on in (Herzberg, 2006). The current version of TrustBar is not compatible with the latest Firefox version. Therefore the Nightly Tester Tool, another Firefox add-on, was used to resolve the compatibility issues. Once installed the toolbar looks like Figure 12.

Functionality

TrustBar consists of a text field, a menu and a Security Status field. The text field allows users to enter a Petname for an entity, the menu provides the user with options, and the Security Status field provides visual indication of various security statuses based on the certificate. Unlike the Petname Tool, it also allows user to assign a logo as a Petname for an entity. When a logo is used, an image replaces the text field and such logos can be called Petlogos. A user can assign a Petname text or Petlogo for a website that she wants to correctly recognise and to display that Petname or Petlogo when she visits the site later. The Petname or Petlogo will be absent if the visited site is not the intended one. A user can

Figure 12. TrustBar installed in Firefox

judge if a webpage comes from a previously identified website by observing the presence or absence of the Petname or Petlogo. TrustBar utilizes different graphical user interface elements to achieve its goal: 1) The Petname field for text or logo, 2) Colour of the Petname field, 3) Drop down menu, 4) Tooltip, and 5) Security Status field. The Petname field changes as a user visits different sites. At the same time the colour of the Petname field changes and different tooltips over the Security Status field are provided. The Security Status field provides a visual indication of the status of the server certificate, and changes according to different circumstances. Options in the menu allows users to set the Petname or Petlogo, to edit the Petname or Petlogo, remove the defined Petname(s), report fraudulent websites and display help regarding TrustBar (Figure 13). The menu also contains an About menu item that, if clicked, displays some relevant information regarding TrustBar, e.g. what is TrustBar, why is it used for, etc.

Some examples can illustrate the TrustBar functionality. Unlike the Petname Tool, TrustBar works both with https and non-https sites. When users visit a non-https site, e.g. www.wikipedia.org, the Petname field contains the domain name for that site (Figure 14). A user can assign a Petname by writing directly in the text box and hitting the enter key. The colour of the text field will turn from white to light green. The Security Status filed displays a No lock icon indicating that the site does not have a server certificate and that TLS is not used, and also provides the tooltip "This site is not protected. Click here for more information" (Figure 15). Clicking the icon will redirect the user to the TrustBar website that explains the necessary concept on TrustBar. A user can edit the Petname later just by writing the new one and hitting the enter key. The drop-down menu also provides methods to assign, edit or delete Petnames. Assigning and editing a Petlogo happens in a similar way, except that the user has to select an image from her computer. When the user vis-

Figure 13. Components of TrustBar

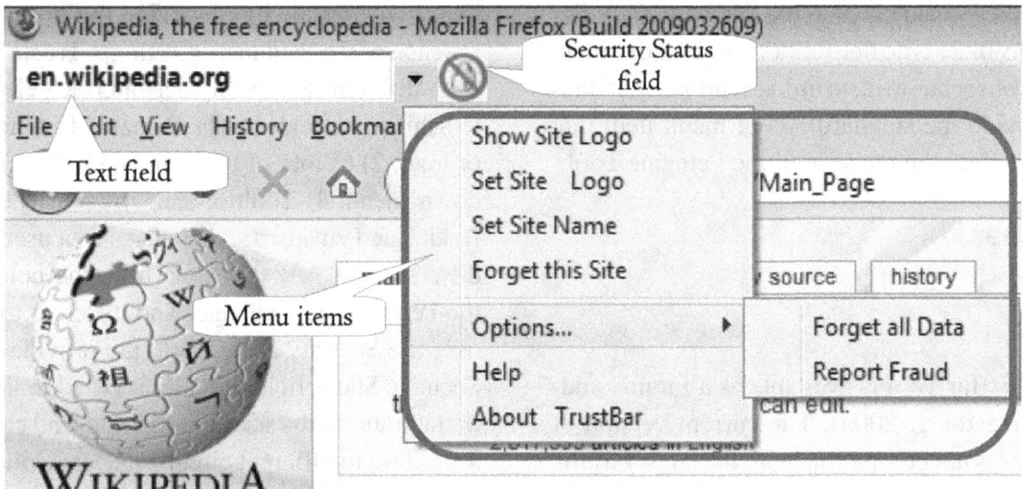

its an https site, e.g. mail.yahoo.com, the text field contains the organisation name from the certificate. The colour of the text field turns to pale yellow. The Security Status field is modified with a lock icon and the text "Identified By:". The name of the CA and another drop-down menu are displayed adjacent to the Security Status field. This second menu allows the user to set, edit or delete a logo for CA, to ignore the CA, and some other options (Figure 16). The user can assign a Petname or Petlogo to override the organisation name like before. Once a Petname is assigned, the Petname field turns to light green (Figure 17).

Evaluation

TrustBar overcomes some of the shortcomings of the Petname Tool. For example, it works for non-https sites, provides an excellent "Help" feature

Figure 14. Indication of a non-https site in TrustBar

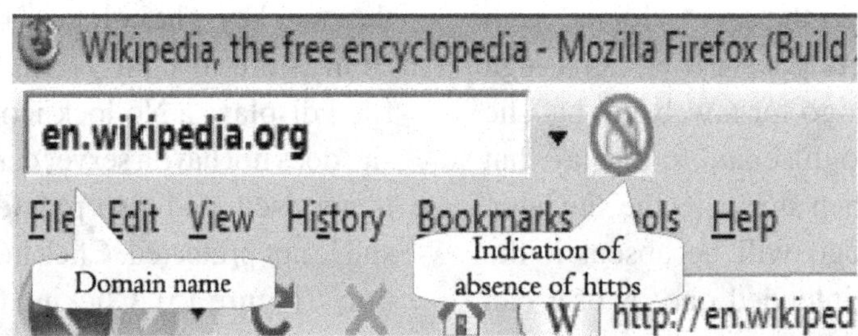

Figure 15. Assigning a Petname for a non-https site in TrustBar

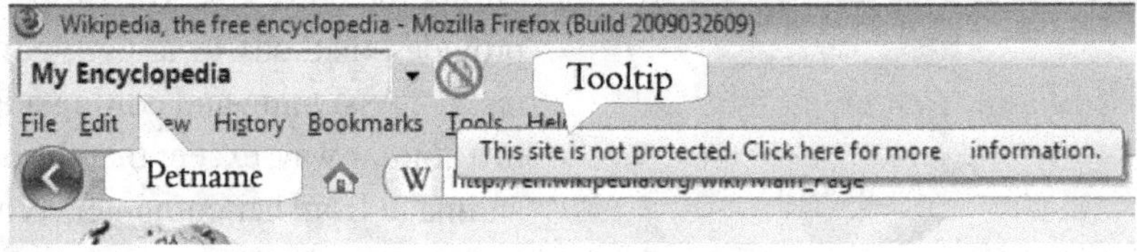

Figure 16. TrustBar interaction with an https site in TrustBar

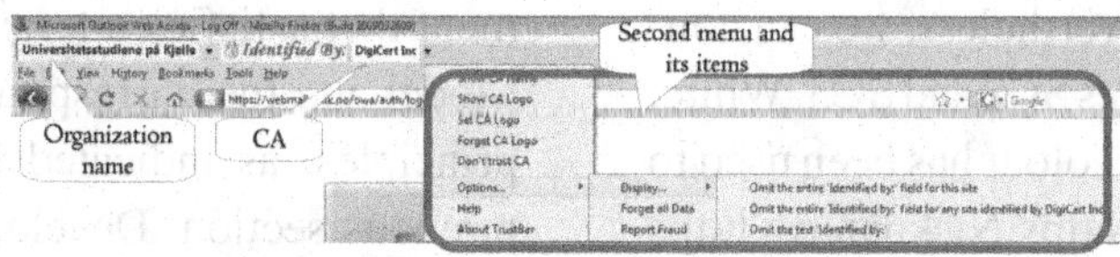

Figure 17. Assigning a Petname for an https site in TrustBar

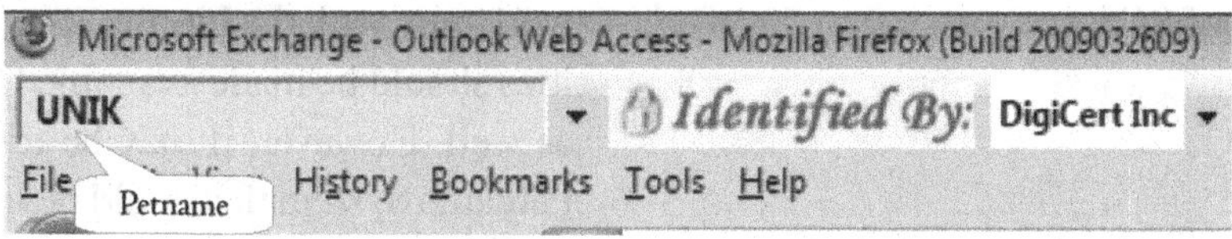

and also comes with the standard About menu item that provides a short description of what it does.

The following simple analysis of TrustBar gives an indication of how it satisfies the properties of the Petname Model. TrustBar utilizes Petnames, and thereby complies with F1. The domain name or URL represents the Pointer. Therefore we conclude that TrustBar satisfies F1 and F3. TrustBar also displays a Nickname in the form of the organisation name, if a certificate is available or in the form of the domain name for non-https sites and thus satisfies F2. However, a serious restriction of TrustBar is that it allows users to assign exactly the same Petname for different entities as demonstrated in the next paragraph, thus violates F4.

TrustBar enables a user to assign a Petname for each entity so she has to act explicitly, e.g. select the text field, write down a Petname and hit the Enter key, to enable the Petname and this satisfies SA1 and SA2. Users can change any Petname any time and thus TrustBar meets the requirement of SA3. A suggestion is provided in the form of a Nickname for aiding the user to select a Petname if a server certificate is available and this satisfies SA4 partially, and the user has to act explicitly, e.g. by hitting the Enter key so the text field turns to light green (an indication for accepting the Petname) to accept the Nickname as the Petname. This satisfies SA5 too. However, it is important to note here that if the Nickname is accepted as the Petname without any modification then it represents a temporary Petname, because when the user visits it again, the Petname turns into the Nickname, also indicated by the pale yellow colour of the text field. This means that TrustBar tries to ensure S6. But this approach is rather contradictory and that a better approach could be taken that would not allow users to accept the Nickname as the Petname without any modification. As mentioned earlier, a serious restriction of TrustBar is that it allows users to assign ambiguous Petnames or even equal Petnames for different entities. It does not provide any sort of warning to users about the ambiguity or similarity of the Petnames and thus directly violates SA7 and SA8. TrustBar allows a user to assign a Petname at her will whenever she feels and does not show any alert when there is highly sensitive data transmission and therefore violates SA9.

The Pointer and the related Petname in the TrustBar, if already supplied by the user, are displayed all the time in the browser toolbar, thereby satisfying SC1. Different icons, tooltips and colours have been used in the TrustBar to catch the user attention to indicate the presence or absence of Petnames. It would have been better to use more flashy colours like Red, Yellow or Green instead of pale yellow and light green. Blinking text or different text colours could be used to draw more user attention to potential security problems in websites. Nevertheless, we can conclude that TrustBar satisfies SC2 and SC3. White, pale yellow or light green colour has been used to differentiate among non-https Nicknames, https Nicknames and Petnames respectively, thereby satisfying SC4. TrustBar does not provide any sort of warning to the user and this indicates the complete absence of SC5.

Summary

Table 2 summarises the distinction between the Petname Tool and TrustBar in terms of the properties of Petname Systems.

It can be noted that TrustBar satisfies more properties of the Petname model than the Petname Tool, though TrustBar has one major shortcoming: absence of any type of warning message. Both tools suffer from the absence of the crucial property F4. As neither of them satisfies all the main properties of Petname Systems, we can conclude that none of them fully satisfies the security usability principles.

FUTURE WORK

The next natural step is to conduct a large-scale usability study of the mentioned Petname Systems performed by several users. It would be very interesting to compare both results and also to determine the understandability and ease of use for Petname Systems by general users.

No tool (assuming the inapplicability of the Passpet tool with any current browser) is currently available for Petname based identity management that satisfies all the properties of Petname Model and the corresponding security usability principles, as indicated by our analysis in the previous section. Developing a Petname Model based tool that satisfies the security usability principles should be a priority in future research and development. The extensions described earlier work only with the Firefox. The same functionalities should be made available for other browsers as well. However, it may be tricky to develop a Petname System that could be integrated into every browser since different browsers use different mechanisms and frameworks for their extensions. A better approach could be to develop a central Petname System and provide services to each browser when required. Unfortunately, it will require a considerable amount of research and development effort to build such a central system.

As the Petname Model is based on the Zooko's triangle, any shortcut in the triangle may collapse the relationships among the components of the Petname Model or may create a new dimension of relationship. Bob Wyman in his web blog proposed to update the Zooko's triangle into a pyramid by inserting a new attribute called "Persistent" and connecting it to the other corners. The new attribute was proposed to signify the longevity of each name (Wyman, 2006). This proposal to change the shape of the Zooko's triangle can be another potential topic for research which could give Petname Systems additional security properties.

Smart phones are becoming increasingly popular and the number of people that access the Internet from their smart phones is growing every day. Investigations into how the Petname

Table 2. Comparison between the petname tool and TrustBar

Tool Name	F				SA									SC				
	1	2	3	4	1	2	3	4	5	6	7	8	9	1	2	3	4	5
Petname Tool	Y	N	Y	N	Y	Y	Y	N	N	N	N	Y	N	Y	Y	Y	N	Y
TrustBar	Y	Y	Y	N	Y	Y	Y	Y	Y	Y	N	N	N	Y	Y	Y	Y	N

Model can be implemented and adapted for the tiny screen of a mobile phone can be a challenging task and another scope for future research. Typing in mobile phones is still very challenging. Sound or image based Petname Systems could be an ideal choice in this regard.

CONCLUSION

The Petname Model is naturally embedded in human perception to identify different entities. Implementing it in computer networks and system is a natural extension of human cognitive capabilities and represents a great aid for humans in digital environments. This fact has been demonstrated through several applications, experiments, and proposals. It could actually be a necessary component of digital certificates and has been recommended in the W3C Security Context: User Interface Guidelines (Roessler & Saldhana, 2010). A large-scale adaptation of the Petname Model is therefore timely.

In this chapter, we have focused on providing the link between PKI and Petname Systems. We have provided a brief overview of Petname Systems starting from the history and evolution of the Petname Model. We have formally defined the properties of Petname Systems and explained how this set of properties can satisfy essential security usability principles. It is our belief that the integration of the Petname Model into applications will improve the user experience and improve overall security by removing security vulnerabilities related to poor usability. We have also explained the necessity, suitability and applicability of the Petname Model in combination with traditional PKIs. The chapter has also analysed two available Petname-based applications for SP identity management on the client side, and have shown that they represent a significant improvement in usability, but unfortunately do not fully satisfy every desirable security usability principle.

REFERENCES

Close, T. (2003a). Naming vs. pointing. Retrieved April 17, 2012, from http://www.waterken.com/dev/YURL/Analogy/

Close, T. (2003b). Waterken YURL: Trust management for humans. Retrieved April 17 2012, from http://www.waterken.com/dev/YURL/Name/

Close, T. (2005). Petname tool: Enabling web site recognition using the existing ssl infrastructure. Retrieved April 17, 2012, from http://www.w3.org/2005/Security/usability-ws/papers/02-hp-petname/

Close, T. (2012). Petname tool 1.7. Retrieved April 17 2012, from https://addons.mozilla.org/en-US/firefox/addon/957

Corporation, C. (2012). Capdesk. Retrieved April 17 2012, from http://www.skyhunter.com/marcs/CapDeskSpec.html

Deutsch, H. (2008). Relative identity. In E. N. Zalta (Ed.), The Stanford Encyclopedia of Philosophy. Retrieved from http://plato.stanford.edu/archives/win2008/entries/identity-relative/

Dhamija, R., & Tygar, J. D. (2006). Why phishing works. In Proceedings of the SIGCHI Conference on Human Factors in Computing Systems, (pp. 581–590). ACM Press.

Drelie Gelasca, E., Tomasic, D., & Ebrahimi, T. (2005). Which colors best catch your eyes: A subjective study of color saliency. Retrieved April 17, 2012, from http://infoscience.epfl.ch/getfile.py?mode=best&recid=87215

Ellison, C., Frantz, B., Lampson, B., Rivest, R., Thomas, B., & Ylonen, T. (1999). SPKI certificate theory. RFC 2693. Retrieved from http://www.ietf.org

Ellison, C., & Schneier, B. (2000). Ten risks of PKI: What you're not being told about public key infrastructure. Computer Security Journal, 16(1).

Entity. (2012). Wikipedia. Retrieved April 17 2012, from http://en.wikipedia.org/wiki/Entity

Ferdous, M. S., Jøsang, A., Singh, K., & Borgaonkar, R. (2009). Security usability of petname systems. In Proceedings of the 14th Nordic Workshop on Secure IT systems (NordSec 2009). Oslo, Norway: NordSec.

Gallois, A. (2011). Occasional identity: Thereby hangs the tale. *Analytic Philosophy*, *52*(3), 188–202. doi:10.1111/j.2153-960X.2011.00527.x.

Gallois, A. (2012). Identity over time. In E. N. Zalta (Ed.), The Stanford Encyclopedia of Philosophy. Retrieved from http://plato.stanford.edu/archives/sum2012/entries/identity-time/

Geach, P. T. (1967). Identity. *The Review of Metaphysics*, *21*, 3–12.

Herzberg, A. (2006). Trustbar firefox addon. Retrieved April 17, 2012, from http://u.cs.biu.ac.il/~herzbea/TrustBar/

Herzberg, A., & Gbara, A. (2004). Protecting (even naïve) web users from spoofing and phishing attacks. Technical Report 2004/155. Cryptology ePrint Archive.

Housley, R., Ford, W., Polk, T., & Solo, D. (1999). Internet X.509 public key infrastructure – Certificate and CRL profile. RFC 2459 (RFC 3280–2002). Retrieved from http://www.ietf.org

Identity. (2012). Wikipedia. Retrieved April 17 2012, from http://en.wikipedia.org/wiki/Identity_management.

Internet Archive Wayback Machine. (2012). Snapshot on zooko's writing. Retrieved on April 17 2012, from http://web.archive.org/web/*/http://zooko.com/distnames.html

Jøsang, A., Al Fayyadh, B., Grandison, T., Al-Zomai, M., & McNamara, J. (2007). Security usability principles for vulnerability analysis and risk assessment. In Proceedings of the Computer Security Applications Conference, Annual, (pp. 269-278). ACSAC.

Jøsang, A., Al Zomai, M., & Suriadi, S. (2007). Usability and privacy in identity management architectures. In L. Brankovic & C. Steketee (Eds.), Fifth Australasian Information Security Workshop (Privacy Enhancing Technologies) (AISW 2007), (vol. 68, pp. 143–152). Ballarat, Australia: ACS.

Jøsang, A., & Pope, S. (2005). User centric identity management. In Proceedings of the Asia Pacific Information Technology Security Conference, AusCERT2005, (pp. 77-89). AusCERT.

Kesterson, H. L., II. (2007). PKI & identity: Technical and legal aspects. Retrieved April 17, 2012, from http://www.itu.int/dms_pub/itu-t/oth/15/04/T15040000110001PDFE.pdf

Linn, J., & Branchaud, M. (2004). An examination of asserted PKI issues and proposed alternatives. In Proceedings of the 3rd Annual PKI R&D Workshop. Gaithersburg, MD: NIST.

McAfee. (2012). SiteAdvisor and SiteAdvisor plus. Retrieved September 09, 2012, from http://home.mcafee.com/store/siteadvisor-live?ctst=1

Menezes, A., van Oorschot, P., & Vanstone, S. (1997). *Handbook of applied cryptography*. Boca Raton, FL: CRC Press.

Micro, T. (2012). TrendProtect. Retrieved September 09, 2012, from http://www.trendsecure.com/portal/en-US/tools/security_tools/trendprotect

Miller, M. (2000). Lambda for humans: The PetName markup language. Retrieved April 17, 2012, from http://www.erights.org/elib/capability/pnml.html

Roessler, T., & Saldhana, A. (2010). W3C security context: User interface guidelines. Retrieved April 17 2012, from http://www.w3.org/TR/wsc-ui/

Rubenking, N. J. (2009). Web of trust review and rating, August 13, 2009. Retrieved September 09, 2012, from http://www.pcmag.com/article2/0,2817,2351536,00.asp

Shapiro, J. S. (2000). Pet names, true names, and nicknames. Retrieved April 17 2000, from http://www.eros-os.org/~majordomo/dcms-dev/0036.html

Shirky, C. (2002). Domain names: Memorable, global, non-political? Retrieved April 17, 2012, from http://shirky.com/writings/domain_names.html

Sider, T. (2000). Recent work on identity over time. *Philosophical Books*, *41*(2), 81–89. doi:10.1111/1468-0149.00183.

Stiegler, M. (2005). Petname systems. Retrieved April 17 2012, from http://www.financialcryptography.com/mt/archives/000499.html

Stiegler, M., Karp, A. H., Yee, K. P., & Miller, M. (2004). Polaris: Virus safe computing for windows xp. Retrieved April 17 2012, from http://www.hpl.hp.com/techreports/2004/HPL-2004-221.pdf

Thanh, D. V., & Jørstad, I. J. (2007). The ambiguity of identity. *Telektronikk*, *103*(3/4), 3–10.

Thomas, S. (2000). *SSL and TLS essentials, securing the web*. New York, NY: Wiley.

Whitten, A., & Tygar, J. D. (1999). Why johnny can't encrypt: A usability evaluation of PGP 5.0. In Proceedings of the 8th USENIX Security Symposium. USENIX.

Wilcox-O'Hearn, Z. (2001). Names: Decentralized, secure, human-meaningful: Choose two. Retrieved April 17 2012, from http://www.zooko.com/distnames.html

WOT. (2012). Wiki. Retrieved September 09, 2012, from http://www.mywot.com/wiki/WOT

WOT Services Ltd. (2012). Web of trust. Retrieved September 09, 2012, from http://www.mywot.com/

Wyman, B. (2006). The persistence of identity. Retrieved April 17, 2012, from http://www.wyman.us/main/2006/12/the_persistence.html.

Yee, K. P., & Sitaker, K. (2006). Passpet: Convenient password management and phishing protection. In Proceedings of SOUPS, (pp. 32–43). SOUPS.

ADDITIONAL READING

Alpár, G., Hoepman, J., & Siljee, J. (2011). The identity crisis. In Proceedings of Security, Privacy and Usability Issues in Identity Management. CoRR.

Camp, J. L. (2004). Digital identity. *IEEE Technology and Society Magazine*, *23*(3), 34–41. doi:10.1109/MTAS.2004.1337889.

Chadwick, D. W. (2009). Federated identity management. *Lecture Notes in Computer Science*, *5705*, 96–120. doi:10.1007/978-3-642-03829-7_3.

COSIC. (2011). Modinis – Common terminological framework for interoperable electronic identity management. Retrieved from https://www.cosic.esat.kuleuven.be/modinis-idm/twiki/bin/view.cgi/Main/GlossaryDoc

Ferdous, M., & Poet, R. (2012). A comparative analysis of identity management systems. In Proceedings of the International Conference on High Performance Computing and Simulation (HPCS), (pp. 454-461). HPCS.

FIDIS. (2005). Future of identity in the information society WP3: Study on mobile identity management, May 2005. Retrieved from http://www.fidis.net/fileadmin/fidis/deliverables/fidis-wp3-del3.3.study_on_mobile_identity_management.pdf

ITU-T. (2009). Baseline capabilities for enhanced global identity management and inter-operability. Retrieved from http://www.itu.int/ITU-T/recommendations/rec.aspx?rec=X.1250

Jøsang, A., Fabre, J., Hay, B., Dalziel, J., & Pope, S. (2005). Trust requirements in identity management. In Proceedings of the Australasian Information Security Workshop (AISW'05). Newcastle, Australia: AISW.

Jøsang, A., Keser, C., & Dimitrakos, T. (2005). Can we manage trust? In Proceedings of the Third International Conference on Trust Management (iTrust'05). iTrust.

Kölsch, T., Zibuschka, J., & Rannenberg, K. (2011). Digital privacy. In *Privacy and Identity Management Requirements: An Application Prototype Perspective* (pp. 735–749). Berlin, Germany: Springer-Verlag.

NIST. (2006). Electronic authentication guideline: Information security. Retrieved from http://csrc.nist.gov/publications/nistpubs/800-63/SP800-63V1_0_2.pdf

OAuth 2.0. (2012). Website. Retrieved from http://oauth.net/2

OpenID Authentication 2.0. (2007). Final. Retrieved 5 December, 2007, from http://openid.net/specs/openid-authentication-2\0.html

Pötzsch, S., Borcea-Pfitzmann, K., Hansen, M., Liesebach, K., Pfitzmann, A., & Steinbrecher, S. (2011). Requirements for identity management from the perspective of multilateral interactions. *Lecture Notes in Computer Science*, *6545*, 609–626. doi:10.1007/978-3-642-19050-6_22.

Pötzsch, S., Meints, M., Priem, B., Leenes, R., & Husseiki, R. (2009). D3.12: Federated identity management – What's in it for the citizen/customer? Retrieved from http://www.fidis.net/fileadmin/fidis/deliverables/new_deliverables/fidis-wp3-del3.12.Federated_Identity _Management.pdf

Priem, B., Leenes, R., Kosta, E., & Kuczerawy, A. (2011). The identity landscape. *Lecture Notes in Computer Science*, *6545*, 33–51. doi:10.1007/978-3-642-19050-6_3.

Shibboleth. (2012). Website. Retrieved from http://shibboleth.internet2.edu/

Standard, O. A. S. I. S. (2005). Assertions and protocols for the OASIS security assertion markup language (SAML) V2.0. Retrieved 15 March, 2005, from http://docs.oasis-open.org/security/saml/v2.0/saml-core-2.0-os.pdf

Suriadi, S., Ashley, P., & Jøsang, A. (2007). Future standardization areas in identity management systems. In Proceedings 2nd PRIME Standardization Workshop. Zurich, Switzerland: PRIME.

Tatli, E. I., & Lucks, S. (2009). Mobile identity management revisited. *Electronic Notes in Theoretical Computer Science*, *244*, 125–137. doi:10.1016/j.entcs.2009.07.044.

KEY TERMS AND DEFINITIONS

Authentication: Authentication is the process of proving an association between a name (identifier or an attribute) and an entity supplying the name (identifier). To prove the association, the entity usually has to supply a credential that accompanies the name (identifier). Authentication is the process of verifying the association using the credential.

Cognitive Walkthrough: The Cognitive Walkthrough method is a usability evaluation method in which an evaluator or a group of evaluators participate to identify the usability issues of an application by visually inspecting the user interface. It focuses on evaluating the understandability and the ease of use for a user at the user interface to accomplish a task using that application.

Identity Management: Identity management consists of technologies, policies and practices for recognising and authenticating entities in online environments.

Petname System: The Petname System is an implementation of the Petname Model which is a naming system that is designed to achieve all the three properties (Global, Memorable and Unique) of the Zooko's triangle.

PKI: Public Key Infrastructure is a framework based on the public key cryptosystem (also known as the asymmetric cryptography) and consists of a set of policies that governs how the cryptosystem should operate and defines the procedure for generating and publishing digital certificates.

Security Usability: The usability of security is crucial for the overall security of the system since it ensures the reliability of using the system and enables the user to draw conclusion on the actual security of the system.

Security: Security is the inherent property of each information system that safeguards the system from unauthorised access, use, disclosure, modification, etc. Security of a system is governed by three essential properties: Confidentiality, Integrity, and Availability, combinedly known as the CIA property. It is extremely essential to maintain the security of a system which is involved in online transactions especially during financial transactions.

Trust Validation: Trust validation is the mechanism for evaluating the trust that is placed on an entity during a particular transaction or operation.

Chapter 14
Building a Trusted Environment for Security Applications

Giovanni Cabiddu
Politecnico di Torino, Italy

Antonio Lioy
Politecnico di Torino, Italy

Gianluca Ramunno
Politecnico di Torino, Italy

ABSTRACT

Security controls (such as encryption endpoints, payment gateways, and firewalls) rely on correct program execution and secure storage of critical data (such as cryptographic keys and configuration files). Even when hardware security elements are used (e.g. cryptographic accelerators) software is still—in the form of drivers and libraries—critical for secure operations. This chapter introduces the features and foundations of Trusted Computing, an architecture that exploits the low-cost TPM chip to measure the integrity of a computing platform. This allows the detection of static unauthorized manipulation of binaries (be them OS components or applications) and configuration files, hence quickly detecting software attacks. For this purpose, Trusted Computing provides enhanced security controls, such as sealed keys (that can be accessed only by good applications when the system is in a safe state) and remote attestation (securely demonstrating the software state of a platform to a remote network verifier). Besides the theoretical foundation, the chapter also guides the reader towards creation of applications that enhance their security by using the features provided by the underlying PC-class trusted platform.

INTRODUCTION

Cryptography is routinely used to protect data and communication from tampering and disclosure. However cryptographic operations and keys must themselves be protected against direct attacks: if an attacker gets hold of a key or can replace a library, then he can easily bypass the cryptographic protection. In most cases, purely software protection techniques are used, but these kind of protection often fail against skilled attackers.

DOI: 10.4018/978-1-4666-4030-6.ch014

As an example, let us consider a Web server which uses the Transport Layer Security (TLS) protocol to protect its transactions. This requires access to a private asymmetric key for the server authentication and key-exchange phases. A simple solution is to store the private key in clear in the file system, relying on the access control mechanisms of the operating system to prevent unauthorized access, but this can be bypassed if an attacker can run a process impersonating the identity of the server process or has direct access to the underlining storage (e.g. being a backup operator or having physical access to the server). Even when hardware elements are used (such as a HSM, Hardware Security Module) there is still room for effective attacks based on manipulation of software building blocks (e.g. drivers, libraries) or direct memory access by privileged processes (e.g. for reading in-memory keys or sensitive data). Last but not least, if the attacker can modify the TLS configuration file then it can disable or reduce protection for certain pages by shortening the length of the negotiated symmetric encryption key.

It should be clear that a trusted environment for program execution and data storage is needed and this is actually the mission of the Trusted Computing Group (TCG) (http://www.trustedcomputinggroup.com). It introduced a set of technologies to create a "Trusted Platform," based on a hardware trust anchor capable of protecting sensitive information and identifying the components running in a computer system.

A Trusted Platform is built around a cost-effective and tamper-resistant chip called Trusted Platform Module (TPM). Most of the commercial desktop and notebook computers sold nowadays include this component, although it is usually disabled by default and rarely used by system administrators and applications developers, mostly due to ignorance of its features and difficulties in management and programming.

Key features of the TPM are its cryptographic primitives (hashing and asymmetric encryption), key and random number generation capabilities, and shielded locations to store keys and sensitive data. These features can be used for measuring the platform's integrity (and reliably reporting such data) and protecting application data and execution.

Although TPM is widely available, building a Trusted Platform is not an easy task. For a PC-class platform we aim to fill this gap with this chapter, that first briefly describes the key features of the TPM, and then explain how its cryptographic capabilities can be used to build a Trusted Platform (e.g. able to detect tampering of cryptographic libraries). Finally, we show how the TPM's capabilities are exposed to applications and how they can be used to protect the cryptographic operations and keys of a generic application.

The rest of the chapter is organized as follows: Section 2 introduces the foundation of Trusted Computing in terms of building blocks for a Trusted Platform; Section 3 defines how to build a trusted environment by leveraging the building blocks; Section 4 describes how to write an application for a trusted environment, in particular using a software library called Trusted Platform Agent; Section 5 presents related works and finally Section 6 concludes the chapter.

TRUSTED COMPUTING

Computer security is normally associated to the concepts of data confidentiality and integrity and system availability. We rarely think of security as related to trust, but for special cases (e.g. when we talk of a trusted third-party in specific protocols, such as Kerberos). However all solutions to provide security rely on some software not being altered, being executed in the proper way, and behaving as expected: these three elements can be collectively associated to the word "trust."

In social science, trust is a personal and fuzzy concept, but in the computer world, we are interested in a clear definition and exact quantitative evaluation. The Internet Security Glossary (Shirey, 2007) provides the following definitions:

- **Trust:** Generally, an entity is said to "trust" a second entity when the first entity makes the assumption that the second entity will behave exactly as the first entity expects. This trust may apply only for some specific function.
- **Trustworthy:** A system that not only is trusted, but also warrants that trust because the system's behavior can be validated in some convincing way, such as through formal analysis or code review.

These definitions are at the heart of the work of the TCG, "a not-for-profit industry standards organization formed to develop, define and promote open, vendor-neutral, industry standards for trusted computing building blocks and software interfaces across multiple platforms."

Trusted Platform

According to the TCG's vision, a Trusted Platform must provide three main features: protected capabilities, integrity measurement, and integrity reporting.

The protected capabilities are commands which have exclusive access to the shielded locations. The latter are places where sensitive data can be securely stored and manipulated. Integrity information and cryptographic keys are examples of data to be stored into the shielded locations. Examples of protected capabilities are functions which report the integrity information or that use the cryptographic keys, e.g. for digital signature or data encryption.

The integrity measurement is the procedure of gathering all platform aspects which influence its trustworthiness (the integrity information, from the BIOS to the Operating System, including the applications) and storing their digests into the protected capabilities.

Integrity logging is an optional procedure of storing all integrity metrics for a later use, e.g. recognizing single components running on a platform.

The integrity reporting is the procedure of accounting the integrity information stored in the protected locations to a (remote) verifier.

As the purpose of the TCG's work is to protect computer systems from software attacks, the features of a trusted platform cannot be implemented by relying purely on software solutions: a hardware module is required and this has been specified in the form of TPM, the Trusted Platform Module. This element provides a hardware implementation of the basic cryptographic and protection features needed to build a trusted platform. Note that this is not a cryptographic hardware accelerator: its purpose is to provide a trust anchor and hence its cryptographic functions are minimal and merely adequate to the specific functions assigned to this element. This has been a deliberate design choice both to minimize the complexity (and so simplify the verification) and the cost (to encourage wide adoption).

The Trusted Platform Module (TPM)

The TPM (Trusted Computing Group, 2007) is a hardware device with cryptographic capabilities, usually implemented as a low-cost chip. The TPM provides both shielded locations and protected capabilities and implements the Roots of Trust for Storage and Reporting, through an internal architecture consisting of several inter-connected components (see Figure 1): Input and Output, Cryptographic co-processor, Power detection, Opt-in, Execution engine, Platform Configuration Registers (PCR) Non-volatile and Volatile storage.

The Input/Output component manages the data exchanged over internal and external communication buses: it performs encoding/decoding of protocol messages, routes the messages to the destination components and enforces access con-

Figure 1. TPM internal components (adapted from TCG)

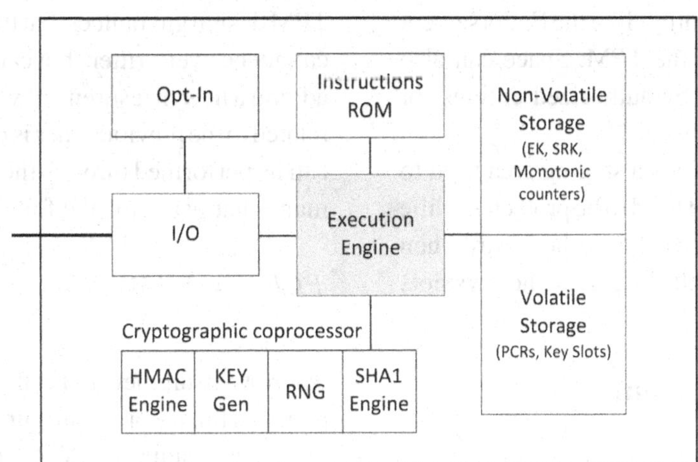

trol policies. It also checks that the length of the parameters is correct for the requested command.

The Cryptographic co-processor provides the cryptographic primitives needed by the TPM to build its capabilities upon. The component must support RSA for key generation and encryption/decryption, SHA-1 for digest calculation and a Random Number Generator (RNG). Other asymmetric encryption algorithms may be supported while symmetric encryption algorithms could be used internally but should not be exposed for direct use. The implementation and formats for RSA digital signature and encryption must be compliant with PKCS#1 (Jonsson & Kaliski, 2003) specification; the supported schemes are PKCS#1-v1_5 for both digital signature and encryption and OAEP for encryption only. The SHA-1 algorithm is implemented as a trusted primitive: it constitutes the foundation for many TPM operations, like accumulating measurements and authentication.

Power detection is required to notify the TPM of all power state changes. This component also reports assertions about physical presence (i.e. operator input via keyboard): they are used by TPM to restrict some operations (like TPM_TakeOwnership), also according to the current power state.

The Opt-In component manages the operational states related to TPM activation and provides protection mechanisms to enable state transition only in a controlled manner, e.g. via authentication or physical presence. The operational states are pairs of mutually exclusive states: TPM can be (1) turned on or off, (2) enabled or disabled, (3) activated or deactivated. State management is implemented via volatile (PhysicalPresenceV) and persistent flags (PhysicalPresenceLifetimeLock, PhysicalPresenceHWEnable, PhysicalPresenceCMDEnable).

The Execution Engine is the processing unit that runs the program code stored in the Read-Only instructions memory. Since the TPM is a passive component, it is not allowed to initiate any transaction toward the external bus. As a result, the execution flow depends uniquely on the received command. The set of commands supported by each TPM is documented in (Trusted Computing Group, 2011).

The program executed by the Execution Engine can be thought as a big loop that reads the command type, delegates the execution of a function to an engine and return the results.

The Platform Configuration Registers (PCR) are registers used to store the taken measurements; details will be given in the next subsection.

The Non-volatile storage provides persistent storage to keep the identity (like the Endorsement Key) and the state of the TPM. Space can also be allocated inside it by authorized entities for other purposes.

The Volatile storage is a staging area used to store sensitive data that need to be protected while the TPM is on but that can be flushed away when switched off; in particular PCRs and the keys slots reside in this storage.

Integrity Measurement

Normally in the security field the concept of integrity is associated to the ability to prevent or detect unauthorized data manipulation, and this is offered by security components such as access control or cryptographic protection (e.g. MAC, Message Authentication Code, or digital signature). On the contrary, in the specific area of trusted computing, integrity is referred to the state of a computing platform and can be static or dynamic: if the software components of a platform have not been manipulated, then we have static integrity, while dynamic integrity refers to the components being actually executed at a certain point in time and to their behavior (it is out of the scope of this chapter).

Static platform integrity can be easily measured by means of a SIV (System Integrity Verifier) such as Tripwire (http://www.tripwire.org/). However such tools do not detect firmware modifications (e.g. to the BIOS) or modifications that a malicious software like a rootkit would hide. The TCG schema explicitly addresses these issues through the provision of hardware elements in the TPM—the PCRs (Platform Configuration Registers)—and specific procedures to update their values.

The PCRs are shielded locations within the TPM. They are 160 bits wide volatile registers used to accumulate the measurements of the system components and permit only four types of operations: modification, reset, read and use. The TPM design guarantees that the value of each PCR cannot be overwritten, but can be only updated by adding a new measurement while the information related to the previous ones is retained. This update can be performed through the TPM_Extend command that performs the following computation:

$$PCR_{new} = SHA1\left(PCR_{old} \mid\mid Measurement\right)$$

where Measurement is usually the digest of a component's binary or a configuration file, PCRold is the current value of a PCR, || is the concatenation operator, and PCRnew is the new value calculated internally by the TPM and stored into the PCR. At any time, the value of a PCR comprises the whole history of the measurements accumulated up to that moment, i.e. it must be considered as the cumulative digest of all added integrity values.

The TPM_Extend command is designed to achieve two main objectives:

- Storing an unlimited number of measurements into a single PCR, and
- Preventing the deletion or replacement of a measurement, e.g. by a rogue component wanting to replace its integrity measurement with the one of a good component.

This guarantees the integrity of the stored chain of measurements, irrespective of the access control actually enforced onto the TPM_Extend command.

The properties of the hash function (and the way it is used by the TPM_Extend command) have the consequence that each PCR contains a time-ordered sequence of measurements; changing the ordering of measurements results in different PCR values:

PCR { TPM_Extend(A) then TPM_Extend(B)} ≠
PCR { TPM_Extend(B) then TPM_Extend(A)}

Moreover the one-way property of the hash function guarantees that given a PCR value an attacker cannot guess the value used to extend it, and the value of a PCR after an update can be derived only upon knowledge of the previous PCR value or the complete sequence of accumulated measurements since the last reset.

TPM_Extend is the only operation that can affect the value of a PCR, which is initialized to a default value (all bits set to zero or one). All PCRs are reset during the execution of a TPM_Init command sent by the platform to the TPM at bootstrap time. A single PCR can also be reset via the TPM_PCR_Reset command. Its execution can be restricted on a per-PCR basis through the hard-coded attribute pcrReset and by Locality (a way to recognize which trusted process is accessing the TPM), through up to four hard-coded locality modifiers, one for each type of operation that can be performed on a PCR.

The value of a PCR can be read from outside the TPM via the TPM_PCR_Read command or can be used directly within the TPM for attestation and sealed storage, i.e. respectively during the operations TPM_Quote or TPM_Seal/TPM_Unseal.

The whole chain of trust may be stored into a single PCR. However using many PCRs for holding a single chain is convenient: indeed each chosen PCR could be used to store only measurements bound to the same "entity", such as the host platform. Therefore a specific instance of the entity (e.g. a specific platform model from a specific vendor) can be easily identified through a single PCR value (e.g. holding the measurements of the BIOS and Embedded ROM) and this piece of information is completely decoupled from the one carried by other measurements. However, the values of all PCRs are not sufficient information if the identification of all measured components is required. In this case a Stored Measurement Log (SML) is necessary, keeping the records of all measurements.

According to the architecture-independent specification, every TPM must be manufactured with at least 16 PCRs.

Key Management in the TPM

The TPM provides several key types. Three are special keys: Endorsement Key, Attestation Identity Key and Storage Root Key. Additionally there are six standard key types according to the permitted application (storage, signing, binding, migration, legacy and authentication key types) and some properties common to all key types. The main properties are related to the possibility for a key to be migrated from a TPM to another one or not (non-migratable key) or to be used only when the platform is in a specific state (sealed key), represented by the values of a set of PCRs.

The Endorsement Key (EK) is a 2048 bits RSA key pair embedded in each TPM. The EK represents the cryptographic "identity" of the TPM and, as a consequence, of the platform which the TPM is installed on. The key is generated before the end user receives the platform, usually by the TPM manufacturer, and can be created within the TPM or externally and then securely injected. This key constitutes the Root of Trust for Reporting (RTR): ideally it could be used to sign the integrity reports generated when executing the command TPM_Quote. A valid signature verified through the public part of the EK would let a remote verifier consider a TPM as genuine and trust the integrity report it produced, i.e. the values of a (sub)set of PCRs. However this approach would let the platform be identified at every remote attestation, thus making possible tracking the platform user and linking together its operations. Due to the nature of the EK, the private part incurs a security problem (confidentiality and usage control) while the public part is privacy-sensitive. The private part must be properly protected: it is stored in a shielded location and never leaves the TPM. The public part, certified by the TPM manufacturer in the EK credential, should not be unnecessarily exposed. To counter this privacy problem, the design of the TPM requires an alias for the EK to be used upon execution of TPM_Quote to sign the PCRs values: the Attestation Identity Key (AIK).

Thus the EK cannot be used for signing but only for encryption/decryption in a specific procedure during the process of certifying an AIK.

The Attestation Identity Key (AIK) is a 2048 bits RSA key pair used as an alias of the EK for privacy protection. It can be generated only by the TPM Owner, it is non-migratable and usually resides protected outside the TPM (i.e. encrypted by a Storage Key). It can be used only for signing the PCR information (during the execution of TPM_Quote, the core operation of a remote attestation) and the public part of non-migratable keys generated by the TPM upon execution of TPM_CertifyKey, which creates a signed evidence that the key is actually protected by a TPM (Trusted Computing Group, 2005). The AIK cannot be used to sign data external to the TPM, to avoid fake PCR data being signed by the TPM as genuine. To prevent the tracking of the platform during these operations, the TPM supports an unlimited number of AIKs: a different AIK should be used for each remote verifier. Each AIK requires an authorization secret (set at the creation time) to be used, to prevent a user from using AIKs assigned to other users.

The use of AIKs instead of an EK prevents the correlation among different remote attestations. However, to trust the signatures made by AIKs, they must be linked to a genuine TPM, that is to the EK credential which represents the TPM identity and states its genuineness. This link is created through the creation of the AIK credential, in the form of a public-key certificate created by a Trusted Third Party called Privacy CA (PCA) (e.g. http://www.privacyca.com).

The Storage Root Key (SRK) is a 2048 bits RSA key pair used for encryption/decryption. It is the root of the Protected Storage, ideally a tamper-resistant storage which guarantees data confidentiality and integrity. Conceptually the Protected Storage is needed to hold application data (such as encryption or authentication keys used by various applications running on the trusted platform). For generality and to avoid space problems inside the TPM, the actual storage data is held protected outside the TPM in form of a binary "blob", usually on a mass storage device, and can be accessed/used only when loaded into a shielded location of the TPM. The size of the Protected Storage is limited only by the capacity of the external storage but its protection is rooted in the TPM as it is implemented through a key hierarchy whose root is the SRK.

The SRK is non-migratable and is the foundation of the TPM key hierarchy: SRK (together with EK) is the only keys which never leaves the TPM and it is used to recursively encrypt the keys needed by specific applications (Figure 2). The SRK is freshly generated during the Take Ownership operation, when an authorization secret is optionally set. The key is deleted when the Owner is deleted, thus making the key hierarchy not accessible anymore, i.e. virtually destroyed. Cryptographic keys of interest for applications (such as the private key used by a web server for SSL authentication), can be guarded through the Protected Storage. These keys are leafs of the key hierarchy: when stored outside the TPM they are encrypted through a storage key, which is eventually encrypted using another storage key up to the SRK. If these application keys (together with the storage ones) are stolen or copied/moved to another platform, they cannot be used as they are encrypted. This is true even if the destination is another Trusted Platform, because its SRK will be different from the source platform's one. However there are cases when it is useful copying or moving some keys from a Trusted Platform to another one: application migration, redundant server for fault tolerance (namely backup of keys to another platform), or server hardware upgrade. To satisfy these legitimate needs, the TPM provides mechanisms to "migrate" the keys from a Trusted Platform to another one (i.e. between their protected storages). The keys on the source platform can be kept or deleted according to the motivation for the migration.

Figure 2. The TPM key hierarchy (adapted from TCG)

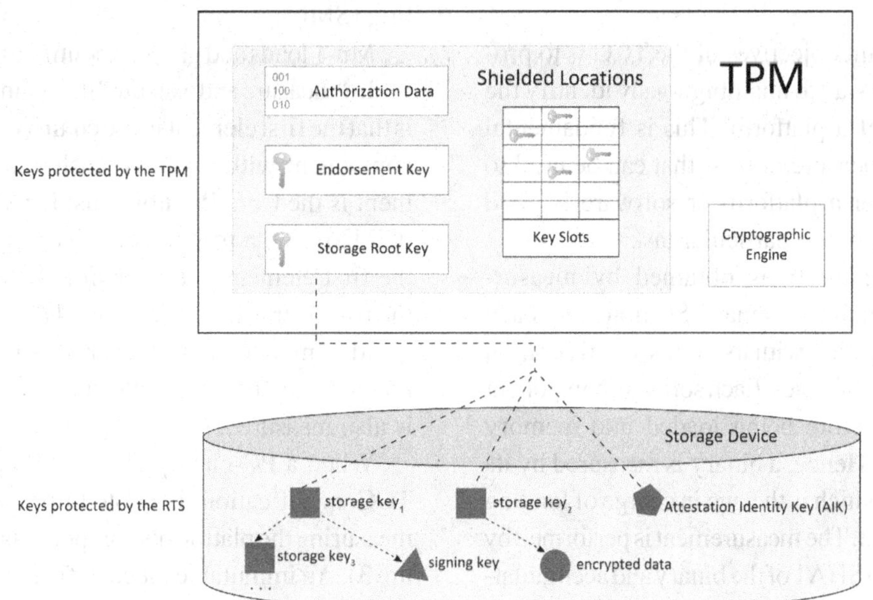

The TPM's Authentication Protocols

Using protected capabilities or directly accessing the TPM may require proving proper authorization as platform Owner or User. To accomplish this task two protocols have been designed, OIAP and OSAP.

The Object Independent Authorization Protocol (OIAP) can be used to authorize access to multiple protected capabilities using multiple commands: only one setup is necessary. This protocol guarantees the authentication and the integrity of the authorized command byte stream and of the TPM reply.

The Object Specific Authorization Protocol (OSAP) can be used to authorize the access to a single protected capability using multiple commands. In addition to authentication and integrity, it allows the agreement of a shared secret to be used for encrypting a TPM command session. It is normally used for setting or changing the authorization data for protected entities respectively through the Authorization Data Insertion Protocol (ADIP) and the Authorization Data Change Protocol (ADCP).

BUILDING A TRUSTED ENVIRONMENT

Having described the basic features and capabilities of the TPM, we are now in the position to use them for building a trusted environment. We refer here to a PC-class platform.

We will proceed with a bottom up approach that describes how the TPM is used to identify the running components of a platform, from the power-on stage, through the bootstrap of the operating system, and up to the application services. This permits to identify tampered software components or untrusted components that are executed against the will of the platform owner. In turn this will deny access to special keys (called sealed keys) protected by the TPM if the system is not in a trusted state.

The section also presents the remote attestation, i.e. the process of vouching the configuration of a Trusted Platform to a remote verifier, and different examples of remote attestation protocols developed in research. This is particularly useful to permit identification of the software state of a network peer and deny connection to peers in an unsafe state.

Trusted Boot

One of the main objectives of the TCG is to provide a reliable way to unambiguously identify the components of a platform. This is fundamental to provide a measure of trust that can be used to decide whether a platform or software is good enough to perform a particular task.

Software identity is obtained by measuring—following the schema in Section 2.3—each executable together with its inputs, configuration files and linked libraries. Each software component is measured before being loaded into memory and executed. Hence, a binary is measured by its predecessor, which is the one in charge of loading and executing it. The measurement is performed by calculating the SHA1 of the binary and accumulating this value in a PCR through the TPM_Extend command. This process is called "measure and execute" and continues recursively establishing a so called Chain of transitive Trust (CoT) and can be summarized as follows:

A module Mn-1 computes the hash of its successor Mn;

Mn-1 records the measurement of Mn in the TPM by extending PCRi and optionally appends the measurement to the Storage Measurement Log (SML);

Mn-1 loads and gives up control to module Mn.

In "measure and execute" the main prerequisite is that the first element in the chain is a trustworthy component with a known hash value. This element is the Core Root of Trust for Measurement (CRTM), i.e. a trustworthy piece of code. Since the first element in the chain is a Root of Trust, the trust is transitively extended through all measured components. However, this is only true if the PCRs are not resettable and all executed code is also measured.

When a PC-class platform, compliant to the TCG specification, is booted up, the process of measuring the platform's components begins (Figure 3). An immutable piece of firmware code (the CRTM) initiates the chain of trust by measuring the BIOS. The BIOS then measures and executes the boot loader which in turn will measure and transfer the control to the OS kernel and so forth, up to applications. At the end of the boot sequence, if every component has been measured, the PCRs values will reflect the actual state of the platform. The TCG has defined this procedure as Static Core Root of Trust for Measurement (S-CRTM) since the CRTM is executed once at fixed time.

Figure 3. Chain of trust (adapted from TCG)

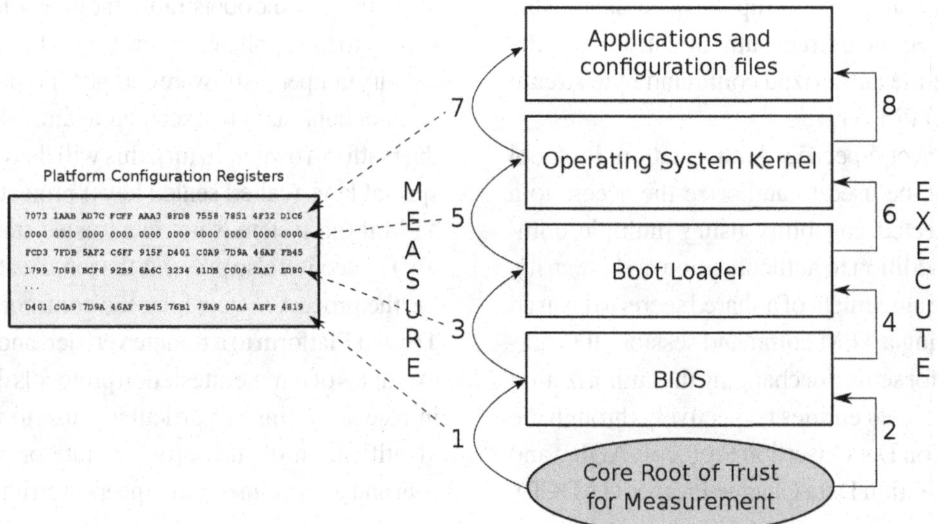

In particular, this process, known as Trusted Boot or authenticated boot, for a PC-class platform is definite in (Trusted Computing Group, 2012) and follows exactly this sequence: (1) after a platform reset all PCRs between 0 and 15 are cleared, (2) the CRTM measures itself and the BIOS, extends PCR[0] and PCR[1] with these measurements and executes the BIOS, (3) the BIOS measures the option ROMs and the configuration data and extends PCR[2] and PCR[3], (4) the BIOS measures the Master Boot Record (MBR) and the partition table, extends PCR[4] and PCR[5] and gives control to the MBR. Afterwards (5) PCRs from 0 to 7 are populated with the Pre-Operating System State.

After a Trusted Platform is booted, it could happen that evil software could compromise one of the previously measured components. At the next reboot, the compromised software will be measured and executed. Therefore, if the CRTM is immutable, at the end of the boot phase the value of the PCRs has to reflect a known configuration otherwise it is a clear evidence of tampering. This allows identifying compromised software or untrusted components that have been installed and executed against the will of the platform owner. In turn, this will deny access to sealed keys protected by the TPM or sealed data if the system is not in a known state.

Trusted Boot does not prevent the execution of any software in a platform; instead, it only records the measurements of each component before its execution and leaves to a verifier the trust decision. This is in contrast with the Secure Boot model, which enforces the execution of authorized software in a machine and interrupts the boot sequence if a component in the chain has been altered.

With Trusted Boot and a Static Core Root of Trust for Measurement, the main problem is that from the CRTM to the applications every single component has to be trusted. In order to overcome this limitation, TCG defined the Dynamic Core Root of Trust for Measurement (D-CRTM). The D-CRTM allows jumping to an isolated environment and executing a measured piece of code. This reduces the number of components to trust in the chain. In the isolated environment, the only element to trust is an initialization code, written by the CPU vendor, with a known identity. Indeed, the trusted environment is implemented through a CPU instruction that performs a soft reset and executes the trusted code. The implementation of D-CRTM is different for each CPU vendor (Intel, 2011; AMD, 2005). D-CRTM can be executed at any time after the platform boot, but very often it is used at boot time to run a Virtual Machine Monitor (Kauer, 2007; Trusted Boot Project, 2012) and hence create an isolated trusted environment.

Secure Integrity Measurement System

PCs which embed a TPM are usually shipped with a CRTM and BIOS which are compliant to the TCG Specification but identifying CRTM and BIOS is not enough to prove that an application has not been modified and it is running on a trustworthy system. Indeed a TCG-compliant Trusted Platform implements the Trusted Boot up to the Boot Loader: the Master Boot Record of the boot medium is the last object being measured. We therefore need to extend the Chain of Trust from the RTM up to a Trusted Application, by measuring all the running software and this process must be done correctly. This is what a secure integrity measurement system is supposed to do.

A secure integrity measurement system is an OS component which dynamically identifies any change in the state of a platform and records it in the TPM. This module operates after the system has booted up and traces every binary executed in the system as well as its configuration. The design of this system must guarantee efficiency (i.e. low performance overhead), flexibility, and transparency to the user.

An example of a secure integrity measurement system is the Integrity Measurement Architecture

(IMA) designed and developed by IBM (Sailer, Zhang, Jaeger, & van Doorn, 2004). IMA extends the Linux kernel with a runtime mechanism that measures each user binary, shared library or kernel module in the system. The measurement is computed as soon as a component is mapped in memory, but before its execution, and is stored in an ordered list that implements the SML. This list is kept inside the kernel and represents the history of the system since its boot.

The IMA model differs slightly from the TCG one. In the latter, integrity reports are dependent from the order of execution, thus, all executable content is measured and reported to the TPM (even multiple times) as soon as is loaded in memory. Differently, IMA reports to the TPM only if the component's hash is not present in the list or the component might have been modified since last measurement (i.e. its hash doesn't match the previous one). Consequently, the TPM is used to protect the integrity of the list. A corruption of the list is detected by re-computing the aggregate and comparing this value with that stored in the PCRs. The design of IMA has been thought to reduce performance overhead. Therefore, caching the list of measurements prevents an intensive usage of the TPM that otherwise would dramatically slow down the system. Furthermore, it allows having a manageable representation of the system state.

In order to extend the Chain of Trust in IMA's architecture, the Linux kernel must be loaded using a TCG compliant boot loader. IMA uses a modified version of the standard bootloader GRUB similar to Trusted GRUB (Sirrix AG, 2010) that measures and executes the kernel. In addition, IMA provides a mechanism to set measurement policies that allow to define which operation (read, execute) performed by which user context (root, standard users, services) must trigger the measurement of the object of the operation. This mechanism can be used, for example, to measure configuration files.

Integrity Reporting

Trusted Computing provides a tool which allows capturing the metrics that represent the state of a platform. Evidence of the state of a platform is provided by the TPM by signing a subset of PCRs. The signature is computed by using a non-migratable TPM key, the AIK.

Every AIK is generated by the TPM and it is certified by a PCA. The PCA assesses the trustworthiness of the TPM by verifying the EK and the Platform certificates and requiring a proof of possession for the EK.

The steps to generate an AIK and a corresponding certificate are:

1. The TPM internally generates a 2048 bit RSA key pair, AIK;
2. The TPM generates a request for a AIK (through a Collate Identity request) that contains the EK certificate, the public part of AIK, and a signature of the public part of AIK with the corresponding private part;
3. A request for the PCA is built in software, encrypted with the public key of the PCA and then sent to the PCA;
4. The PCA decrypts and validates the request, extract the EK certificate and the Platform certificate and it they are good it issues and AIK certificate. It encrypts this certificate with the public part of EK;
5. The TPM, as it owns the EK private part, is able to decrypt the AIK certificate and use the corresponding AIK.

A signature over a set of PCRs is made through the TPM_Quote function. The TPM generates an RSA signature σ_{Quote} with an AIK over a set of PCRs and a *nonce* (used for freshness) by computing

$$\sigma_{Quote} \leftarrow \mathrm{TPM}_{\mathrm{Quote}}(SAIK, PCR_{set}, nonce)$$

where SAIK is the private part of the AIK key, PCR_{set} are the values of the selected PCRs that represent the current state of the platform and $nonce$ is a random chosen by the remote verifier.

PCRs values can be reliably reported to an external entity through a challenge-response protocol, the Remote Attestation. This protocol allows a remote Verifier to perform an on-line verification of an Attestor's platform metrics and detect if the platform has been modified (either compromised or updated). With this information the Verifier can make a trust decision and choose if the platform is good enough to perform a certain task.

A basic attestation protocol runs as follows:

The Verifier generates a non-predictable $nonce$ (used for freshness in the protocol), builds a remote attestation request specifying a list of PCRs and sends the request to the Attestor;

1. The Attestor receives the request, selects a AIK, and requires the TPM the execution of TPM_Quote specifying the list of PCRs provided by the Verifier; The TPM performs a cryptographic signature σ_{Quote} over the list of PCRs using SAIK and returns the result of the Quote to the Attestor;
2. The Attestor builds a response containing the Quote from the TPM, the AIK certificate and optionally a log of the measurements (SML) collected in the platform. The response is then sent to the Verifier;

The Verifier verifies the σ_{Quote} and eventually the takes a trust decision.

The process of verification of σ_{Quote} is split in three steps:

1. Verification of the AIK, that implies checking the certificate validity, the chain and if the issuer of the certificate is trustworthy; Cryptographic verification of σ_{Quote}, which aims to guarantee that the signature over the set of PCRs and the nonce has not been forged and therefore the measurements have been reported by a genuine TPM;
2. Semantic verification of the PCRs' values, which aims to decide whether measurements are acceptable or not against reference values (also including the verification of SML, if provided).

Platform measurements are not only employed in the remote attestation protocol but they are also used to give a high level of protection to sensitive data. More exactly, the TPM allows encrypting data which can be released only inside a certain platform and only if its PCRs match specific values decided at the encryption time. This operation is called sealing and can be used locally to check the integrity of a platform.

Remote Attestation Protocols

Protocols like TLS (Dierks & Rescorla, 2008) or IPSec (Kent & Seo, 2005) are extensively used across the Internet to build secure channels between two nodes. These protocols guarantee integrity, freshness, and confidentiality of the information transferred in the channel in addition to authentication of endpoints.

Although secure channels allow to reliably identify both parties involved in the communication, they do not provide any additional information about the integrity of the software stack running in the endpoints. This means that even if a connection is established with a node whose identity is known, it is not possible to recognize if that node has been compromised or not. This is a problem since the majority of attacks on the Internet aims to compromise endpoints rather than the communication channels.

A simple way to guarantee the integrity of the endpoint would be to run a simple attestation protocol (such as that described above) within a secure channel. Nevertheless, this solution is not secure because it is subject to Man-In-The-Middle (MITM) and relay attacks. Indeed, if the attestation server has been compromised and it pretends to be a "good" one, as soon as the secure channel is established with the victim, the rogue server forwards the request to a third good server providing the nonce sent by the victim. Then, the rogue server gets the result of the Quote from the good server and forwards it to the victim.

This problem can be circumventing with a Trusted Channel which provides reliable evidence of the integrity of the counterpart through a strong linkage between the attestation data and the secure channel.

A first attempt to build a Trusted Channel is presented in (Goldman, Perez, & Sailer, 2006). In this work three simple solutions based on the SSL protocol are proposed. In the first one, the binding is achieved extending one of the PCRs with the public key of the certificate used for the SSL channel. In the other two, the PCA-issued certificate is linked to the SSL one through an external certificate. This paper provides only a preliminary solution to the problem.

A different solution to this problem is in (Gasmi, Sadeghi, Stewin, Unger, & Asokan, 2007) where the authors modified the TLS handshake to transfer attestation data. An enhancement of this solution is proposed in (Armknecht, et al., 2008) and it is fully compliant to the TLS standard. Both these two solutions do not use the Quote but a sealed key that is bound to a set of PCRs and can be retrieved only if the PCRs match the expected ones. A similar solution for IPsec is proposed in (Sadeghi & Schulz, 2010).

WRITING APPLICATIONS THAT USE THE TPM

As seen in the previous sections, the TPM and TCG specification provide primitives to write applications that exploit the TPM to increase their own protection in two areas: secure storage of cryptographic material (or other sensitive data) and secure connection to a trusted network peer.

In order to implement these ideas avoiding low-level programming tasks (e.g. directly sending binary commands to the TPM), the TCG Software Stack (TSS, Trusted Computing Group, 2007) has been defined: this is a standard complete interface to develop interoperable applications that access the TPM. However, although the TSS exposes APIs for C and Java programming, it is still quite complex to be used. A simpler interface is offered by the Trusted Platform Agent (TPA), a library that hides from the programmer many of the technical details of the TSS. In this section we explain the structure and main features of the TSS and TPA, along with programming examples that are targeted to PC-class platforms.

The TCG Software Stack (TSS)

The TCG Software Stack (TSS) is the software stack used by applications to interact with the TPM. TSS multiplexes accesses from different applications, hides details about how a TPM command is built and, finally, manages the TPM limited resources.

The TSS specification defines a set of classes (e.g. for keys, data, PCR registers, non-volatile memory storage) and methods to deal with TPM or to perform correlated tasks. It also introduces a TPM class to perform administrative operations, a policy class to specify secrets to protect particular objects and a context class necessary to multiplex connections from different applications and to group resources used in the same session.

The TSS architecture consists of three layers, each one exposing an interface for the upper layer (Figure 4):

- **TCG Service Provider (TSP):** This module is linked to the application and provides a rich object oriented interface to developers. It does the work necessary to create

Figure 4. TCG software stack (adapted from TCG)

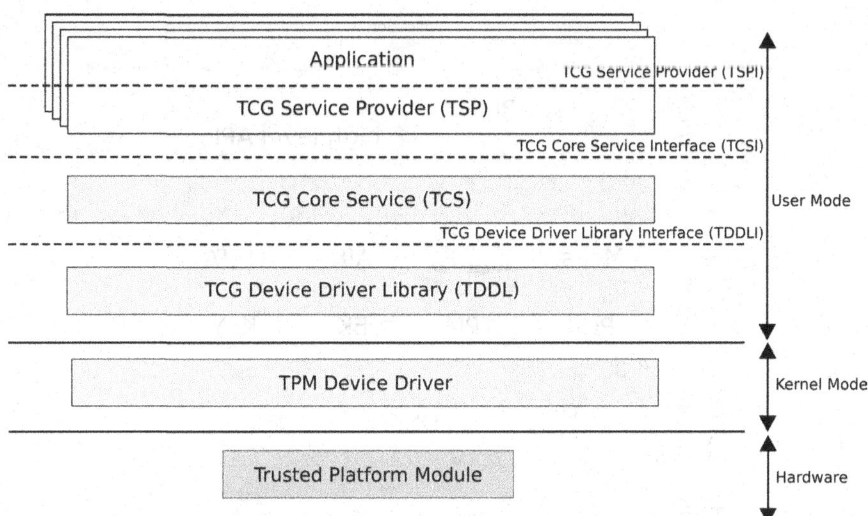

and manage TPM objects and to supply secrets when authorization is required. It also provides abstraction for calling the underlying TCS interface through an RPC channel. It provides the programming interface, called TSP Interface (TSPI) to applications.

- **TCG Core Services (TCS):** This component runs as system service and multiplexes requests made by the TSP. It consists of functional blocks that manage applications contexts keys and credentials, retrieve the logs of the measurements taken in the platform, and build commands to be sent to TPM through the TDDL layer.
- **TCG Device Driver Library (TDDL):** This layer provides a user space interface to TPM and is designed to be the only component accessing the driver.

The Trusted Platform Agent (TPA)

The TPA (Cabiddu, Cesena, Sassu, Vernizzi, Ramunno, & Lioy, 2011) (http://security.polito.it/trusted-computing/trusted-platform-agent/) is a C library built on top of the TSS and designed to minimize the effort required to write applications that use TC technology. It is worth noting that TPA is explicitly designed to address high-level operational tasks. It is not intended as a replacement of the TSS, on the contrary it requires a working TSS and also depends upon other widespread open source libraries (e.g. OpenSSL).

TPA exposes a high level API that allows developers to access all its features. However, most applications do not fully take advantage of such a rich interface, thus the TPA also provides a μAPI, a light interface built on top of the full one which implements the most common patterns used by applications.

The TPA was developed following principles of simplicity, modularity and security, and features the following architecture (Figure 5):

- The lower layer wraps all the libraries needed by the TPA (e.g. TSS, cryptographic and network) to provide a unified interface to the upper layers.
- The core is organized in several modules, one for each functionality exposed by the TPA. Each module defines abstract objects that map onto TSS-specific objects and composes lower layer functions into aggregated operations.

Figure 5. TPA architecture

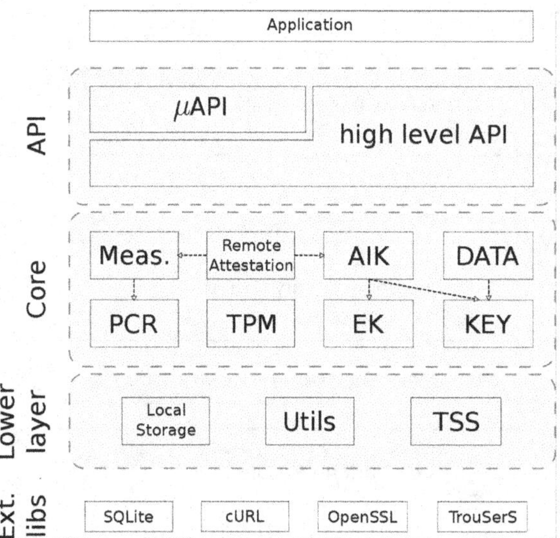

- The high level API allows developers to access all of the TPA features. While the TPA simplifies the TSS interface, it still permits the same level of flexibility.
- The μAPI is a light interface built on top of the high level API, which implements the most common patterns used by applications; at the expense of some limitations (e.g. it is single-threaded). In order to make the most of both APIs, the TPA allows switching between the two at any time. Note that the TPA functions have been defined by factorizing and generalizing the TC-related code fragments most frequently found in Trusted applications. As such, TPA supports code reuse by avoiding tedious and error-prone repetitions of the same code fragments.

TPA is available for Linux and Windows and works with TrouSerS (http://trousers.sourceforge.net) as TSS, with the Infineon TPM and TPM emulator (http://tpm-emulator.berlios.de/). TPA also requires OpenSSL for cryptographic operations, SQLite (http://www.sqlite.org/) as database library to implement its local storage and cURL (http://curl.haxx.se/) for networking interaction.

The main features of the TPA are listed below.

- **TPM Basic Commands:** TPA provides basic commands related to TPM management, for instance to verify if the ownership has already been taken or to take ownership, i.e. set the owner secret and create a new SRK.
- **PCR, SML and System State:** TPA inherits from TSS the concept of PCR set and implements an application-specific SML. These describe the system state needed for sealing and remote attestation. TC is based on the concept that a component must be measured before it is used. It is crucial that these two operations are executed as an atomic one, to prevent an attacker to substitute the component between the measurement and the usage. TPA implements this concept on common functions (e.g. file open, library load, SSL connect/accept) providing wrappers where relevant data for the function is measured before usage. In future works we plan to employ database protection mechanisms to protect privacy-sensitive measurements.

- **Key Management and SMK:** TPA exposes a set of functions for managing the life cycle of TPM keys. Applications can use TPA to create, load and delete keys. Built upon TSS, keys are hierarchically organized and identified by labels. Moreover, TPA permits to limit key visibility to application keys only, introducing an application specific database while TSS only supports system/user-level storage. TPA also guarantees isolation from other applications by transparently wrapping any stored object with a unique TPM key, called Storage Master Key (SMK), which is protected by a secret only known to the application.
- **Binding and Sealing:** TPA abstracts binding and sealing of data, by removing the TSS constraint on the data size. Therefore, TPA (1) generates a symmetric key, (2) encrypts the data with this key, (3) binds (or seals) the symmetric key, and (4) eventually encodes the resulting blob.
- **Backup and Restore:** Availability of bound data, as well as of any wrapped key, is a concern in case of TPM failure. Currently, TPA provides a simple way to backup and restore bound (or sealed) data, by returning to the application the symmetric key used to actually encrypt the data, together with the encrypted blob itself. By default, TPA protects the symmetric key with a passphrase; however, the application may recover the symmetric key in clear and protect it with any alternative method.
- **EK and AIK:** TPA manages the complete lifecycle of an AIK before it can be used for remote attestation, i.e. generation and certification according to TCG specifications. After successful certification, the AIK can be used for remote attestation because its certificate proves that the TPM is genuine, without exposing any part of the EK.
- **Remote Attestation:** TPA offers support for remote attestation by providing functions for: (1) computing a quote, i.e. a signature over a set of PCR values with an AIK; (2) serializing/deserializing the quote, together with the corresponding measurement logs and AIK certificate chain; (3) verifying the remote attestation data. TPA implements cryptographic verification and returns a list of validated measurements to the application which is in charge of the semantic verification. In some specific contexts, TPA also provides functions useful for semantic verification.

The next subsections show programming examples for two use cases, Secure Storage and Remote Attestation, which represent a mean for securing an encryption endpoint using Trusted Computing, like a service provided through a web server over a SSL channel. The SSL keys can be protected using the TPM and can be sealed, so that they can be only used if the platform running the web server is in a good state. The client of the service can verify the integrity of the web server through the Remote Attestation procedure.

Use Case: Secure Storage

Figure 6 presents a simple example that uses the TPA for generating a cryptographic key protected by the TPM (i.e. a key that never leaves the TPM unencrypted).

First, in order to use the TPA μAPI, the application must initialize the library with TPA_init, providing TPM owner, SRK and SMK secrets. The TPM key is created using the TPA_KEY_create function that internally implements all the logic that is needed to request the TPM the generation of a new non-migratable key. This function requires a pointer to the parent key (if it is NULL the key will have as a parent the SMK), a label that identifies the key and a secret. The key is

Figure 6. Create key

```
#include "TPA.h"

// ...

if (TPA_init(TPM_OWNERPWD, TPM_SRKPWD) != TPA_SUCCESS)
    goto error;

// ...

/* create key */
if (TPA_KEY_create(NULL, KEY_LABEL, KEY_SECRET, &key)
        != TPA_SUCCESS)
    goto error;
// ...

/* retrieve key */
if (TPA_KEY_retrieve(KEY_LABEL, KEY_SECRET, &key) != TPA_SUCCESS)
    goto error;

// application logic using key
// ...

error: /* free */
TPA_finish();
// ...
```

retrieved using TPA_KEY_retrieve. At the end, the code terminates cleaning up the allocated resources with TPA_finish.

Figure 7 presents a sample application which uses the Trusted Computing technology to seal confidential data plain_data against a known system state. The application is organized in two phases: an initialization run at setup time that protects plain data and creates a backup, and the application core that retrieves both before performing its task.

In order to use the TPA µAPI the application must initialize the library with TPA_init, providing TPM owner, SRK and SMK secrets, and terminate cleaning up the allocated resources with TPA_finish.

In the initialization phase (lines 10–34), the application: (1) seals plain data, (2) creates a backup with TPA_BLOB_backup to be stored in a secure location (e.g. a USB disk) and (3) securely cleans the instance of plain data in memory with TPA_BLOB_destroy. It is noteworthy that there is no need for the developer to guarantee isolation from other applications since TPA stores all data under an application-specific Storage Master Key (SMK).

Of all the above operations, sealing deserves closer attention. First, the application selects a set of PCRs describing the system state (TPA_PCR_select, in our example only PCR 10). Then, sealing is performed with TPA_BLOB_seal, which returns a blob composed of a randomly generated symmetric key which is actually sealed by the TPM, and the encryption of plain data with such key. Using a symmetric key is necessary because the TPM can only seal input with limited size.

Before performing its tasks, the application unseals the sealed blob with TPA_BLOB_unseal.

Figure 7. Sealing

```
#include "TPA.h"

// ...

if (TPA_init(TPM_OWNERPWD, TPM_SRKPWD) != TPA_SUCCESS)
        goto error;

// ...

if (initialization) {

        /* select PCR registers */
        if (TPA_PCR_select(10) != TPA_SUCCESS)
                goto error;

        /* seal plain_blob */
        if (TPA_BLOB_seal(NULL, plain_data, plain_data_len,
            &sealed_blob, &sealed_blob_len) != TPA_SUCCESS)
                goto error;

        // store sealed_blob on the disk
        // ...

        if (TPA_BLOB_backup(sealed_blob, sealed_blob_len,
            &backup_blob, &backup_blob_len) != TPA_SUCCESS)
                goto error;

        // store backup_blob in a secure location (e.g. USB pendrive)
        // ...

        if (TPA_BLOB_destroy(&plain_data, &plain_data_len)
                    != TPA_SUCCESS)
                goto error;
}

// ...
/* unseal blob */
if (TPA_BLOB_unseal(sealed_blob, sealed_blob_len, NULL,
    &unsealed_data, &unsealed_data_len) != TPA_SUCCESS) {

        /* if unseal fails, provided that we are in a safe mode
         * of operation, we can restore from backup */
        if (safemode) {
                // retrieve backup_blob from secure location
                // ...

                if (TPA_BLOB_restore(backup_blob, backup_blob_len,
                    &unsealed_data, &unsealed_data_len) != TPA_SUCCESS)
                        goto error;
        } else
                goto error;
}

// application logic using the unsealed_blob
// ...
```

If unseal fails, the application can still retrieve plain data from backup through TPA_BLOB_restore. It is the responsibility of the developer to provide a secure way to verify if the user has the privileges to access the backup: we encoded this requirement assuming the application can restore only in a safe mode of operation.

Use Case: Remote Attestation

In Figure 8, we present another example, where the TPA is used to perform a remote attestation over an SSL channel. A server accepts incoming connections and reports its configuration to vouch for its integrity. In this scenario, it is fundamental to bind the SSL channel to the remote attestation data, avoiding relay attacks where a malicious

Figure 8. Remote attestation (server side)

```
#include "TPA.h"

// ...
TPA_init(OWNERPW, SRKPW, SMKPW);
TPA_PCR_select(11);
TPA_MEASURE_init(11);

// ...
/* measure and open config_file */
TPA_MEASURE_fopen(config_file, "r", &config);

// code to read config (e.g. PORT, KEYFILE, PASSWORD)
// ...

fclose(config);

/* build SSL context */
ssl_ctx = initialize_ctx(KEYFILE, PASSWORD);

/* create TCP socket */
listen = tcp_listen(PORT);

while (1) {
      /* accept on TCP socket */
      if ((conn = accept(listen, 0, 0)) < 0)
            err_exit("TCP accept error");

      /* fork */
      if (!(pid = fork())) {
            /* child */
            // code to create SSL socket (cf. client)
            // ...

            /* measure and accept on SSL socket
               (bind SSL channel and remote attestation) */
            TPA_MEASURE_SSL_accept(ssl, &r);
            if (r <= 0) err_exit("SSL accept error");

            /* remote attestation */
            nonce_len = SSL_read(ssl, nonce, sizeof(nonce));

            TPA_RA_quote("aik_label", nonce, nonce_len,
                        &ra_blob, &ra_blob_len);

            SSL_write(ssl, ra_blob, ra_blob_len);

            // application logic
            // ...
      } else {
            /* parent */
            close(conn);
            // ...
}
// ...
```

(or compromised) server forwards the attestation request to a different, trusted server.

The skeleton for the SSL client-server is created using OpenSSL. In the following we concentrate only on the TC-related details. The server initializes the TPA, selects a set of PCRs describing its state (TPA_PCR_select, e.g. PCR 11) and initializes the local measurements database by specifying the PCR where measurements will be accumulated (TPA_MEASURE_init, e.g. PCR 11). Then, it measures (TPA_MEASURE_fopen) and reads its configuration file, setting up the relevant configuration properties, for instance its SSL certificate.

As usual, the server accepts incoming TCP connections, then forks a child to serve each connection. The child creates an SSL socket and measures-and-accepts (TPA_MEASURE_SSL_accept) on this. Internally this function measures the SSL certificate (i.e. it extends the PCR and appends an entry to the SML), then calls the OpenSSL SSL accept, performing the SSL handshake. This serves to bind the remote attestation data to the SSL channel, avoiding relay attacks (Goldman, Perez, & Sailer, 2006).

When the SSL socket is connected, the remote attestation protocol can start. First, the client sends a nonce used for freshness. Subsequently, the server calls TPA_RA_quote, which asks the TPM to generate a quote (i.e. a signature done with an AIK over a set of PCRs and the nonce) and serializes the quote, the AIK certificate chain and the stored measurement logs into a blob. Finally, the server sends this blob to the client (Goldman, Perez, & Sailer, 2006).

Upon receiving this data, the client performs a three-step process verification. Step one, (TPA_RA_verify) is a cryptographic verification that (1) all the measurements are well-formed, (2) the quote is correct and (3) the AIK is certified. The second step (TPA_RA_verifySSL) is a SSL-specific verification, to check that the SSL server certificate is valid and is exactly the measured one. Step three is a semantic verification carried out by the application logic, for instance to check that the measurement corresponding to the server configuration file is in a database of reference measurements.

The remote attestation protocol is run over SSL, after the handshake completion and before application data are sent over the secure channel.

RELATED WORKS

This chapter focused on the building blocks required to build a Trusted Environment for applications which increase their security by leveraging the Trusted Platform Module chip. We illustrated that, under some constraints, it is possible to build a complete chain of trust using TC-enabled boot loader and operating system. The limitation of this approach is that identifying the running components, and the relative configuration, through their digest is a difficult task due to the multitude of acceptable configurations. Work has been done in this area to address the scalability problem and several alternative solutions have been proposed: property-based (Sadeghi & Stüble, 2004) and model-based (Alam, Zhang, Nauman, Ali, & Seifert, 2008) attestation.

Another limitation of our approach is that we don't limit the size of the Trusted Computing Base (TCB), the combination of hardware and software that must be immutable and trustworthy. Indeed, the TCB should be as small as possible since misbehavior of this cannot be detected. Recent work has been done in this direction to reduce the size of the TCB and provide a minimized trusted environment for software execution (McCune, et al., 2010; Vasudevan, Parno, Qu, Gligor, & Perrig, 2012; Vasudevan, McCune, Newsome, Perrig, & van Doorn, 2012).

The target system's environment of this work is a commodity PC. Nevertheless, research has been done in this area to define a trusted environment for mobile devices and embedded systems (Trusted Computing Group, 2010). In (3G

Americas, 2008) security and trust requirement and technology building blocks are analyzed for mobile applications, ranging from financial and content protection to access, authentication and identity selection.

Emin, Bruijn, Reynolds, Shieh, Walsh, Williams, and Schneider (2011) reports about a new operating system, Nexus, that implements the Logical Attestation, an approach based on property descriptions represented as logical formulas, focused to reasoning about the run-time behavior of applications (i.e. dynamic integrity), in contrast with the TCG approach, devoted to static integrity.

Harris and Hill (2010) presents PlugNPlay Trust, a framework for embedded systems to be trusted based on TPM and live-CD technology (file system on read-only images).

This work also presented the Trusted Platform Agent, an open source library designed to minimize the effort of writing applications that use TC technology. Through some examples, we showed how it simplifies the development of secure applications which include complex operations like sealing and remote attestation. The TPA is explicitly designed to address high-level operational tasks and simplify the TSS interface. Furthermore, the TPA is not intended as a replacement of the TSS, on the contrary it requires a working TSS. In particular, it leverages TrouSerS (TrouSerS project, 2008), an open source implementation of the TSS developed by IBM available for Linux and Windows. TrouSerS is written in ANSI C and it is considered the TSS reference implementation.

Other projects related to TSS are jTSS (jTSS project, 2009), µTSS (Stüble & Zaerin, 2010) and JSR 321 (Toegl, Winkler, Nauman, & Hong, 2009). jTSS is an open source library written in the Java language. It is a platform independent TSS alternative to TrouSerS. µTSS is an object oriented TSS written in C++. It exposes a lightweight and intuitive API based on the TPM main specification. It allows the use of only a subset of the functionality as it is required—such as for embedded systems or in the contexts of security kernels. JSR321 (Java specification request) is a Java API for TC that is an alternative to the TSS. It reduces the complexity of TC-aware applications and makes TC accessible to a large group of developers. These libraries are intended to be alternatives to TrouSerS, whilst the TPA focuses on higher-level application programming providing a complete solution that integrates TC functionality with cryptographic and network-related functions.

FUTURE RESEARCH DIRECTIONS

Building a trusted environment is a theme being investigated and developed in multiple directions. Some relevant research paths are: reducing the trust assumptions on the hardware platform, minimizing the Trusted Computing Base (TCB), facing the scalability of remote attestation, and attesting the dynamic behavior of Operating Systems and applications.

TCG Trusted Computing technologies are essentially designed to counter software attacks using hardware Root of Trusts mounted on commodity x86 or mobile platforms. One direction for enhancement is lowering the trust assumptions to be assumed on the hardware platforms. For instance, Intel Trusted Execution Technology (TXT) goes in the direction of mitigating the risks of simple hardware attacks (so called "open case") by introducing the integrity verification of the platform firmware and secure boot capability, among the others. Hardware resistance can be further pushed forward to resist against more sophisticated attacks in order to increase the platform trustworthiness.

Another relevant research direction to follow is on minimizing the size of the TCB. This can be done both at software level and at hardware level. For the former, some approaches have already been proposed: the usage of (hardware-assisted) virtualization to isolate security critical components and applications from the untrusted ones. Disaggregation of hypervisors like Xen goes in this direction: the core services of the hypervisor are split and executed in tiny virtual machines, typically rootless, and isolated from each other. Another way to reduce the TCB size is implemented in Trustvisor, a minimal hypervisor that uses the Intel TXT and AMD-V capabilities (Dynamic Root of Trust for Measurement, or D-CRTM) to provide code and data integrity as well as data secrecy for selected portions of an application (e.g. to protect a private key) running on a commodity OS. For TCB minimization at hardware level, instead, an example is currently given by CARMA, where the only platform component to be trusted is the CPU.

Another research direction is related to remote attestation techniques. First the use of different approaches to overcome the limitations—e.g. the scalability—of the so called binary attestation that the TCG technology puts in place. Along this path, for instance, the property-based or the model-based attestation that have been proposed. Another approach to face the scalability problem is the usage of databases for high volumes queries (like Apache Cassandra) to store the white lists of reference measurements, e.g. taken from official OS distribution metadata. Finally, the TCG attestation, based on the load-and-measure model, cannot report on the dynamic behavior of processes, because it only identifies the executables with their libraries and configurations. Therefore another relevant research path is the run-time checking of Operating System processes and applications. As an example on this path, one technique currently being investigated is the Virtual Machine (VM) introspection, i.e. the possibility that critical data structures of an Operating System running in a user VM are checked by a rootless, privileged and trusted VM that accesses the user VM with the mediation of the hypervisor.

CONCLUSION

This chapter has presented a specific approach (the one by the Trusted Computing Group) to build a trusted environment for running security-critical applications on a PC-class platform. Although the prerequisites to create such an environment are widely available, misconceptions and complexity have insofar stopped developers and system managers to adopt this approach. We have presented here the basics behind a trusted platform and explained as also the principles for developing trusted applications.

Limitations of this approach are the scalability of remote attestation due to a multitude of acceptable configurations and components, only addressing the static integrity of the components and the lack of minimization of the TCB.

We hope that this will contribute to a wider adoption of these techniques and increase our security.

REFERENCES

Alam, M., Zhang, X., Nauman, M., Ali, T., & Seifert, J. (2008). Model-based behavioral attestation. In Proceedings of the 13th ACM Symposium on Access Control Models and Technologies, (pp. 175-184). ACM.

AMD. (2005). AMD64 virtualization codenamed ''pacifica'' technology. Publication No. 33047. Secure Virtual Machine Architecture Reference Manual, Revision 3.01.

3G. Americas. (2008). Security and trust in mobile applications. Technical Report. Retrieved September 16, 2012, from http://www.gemalto.com/telecom/download/security_trust_in_mobile_applications.pdf

Armknecht, F., Gasmi, Y., Sadeghi, A.-R., Stewin, P., Unger, M., Ramunno, G., et al. (2008). An efficient implementation of trusted channels based on OpenSSL. In: Proceedings of the 3rd ACM Workshop on Scalable Trusted Computing, (pp. 41-50). ACM.

Cabiddu, G., Cesena, E., Sassu, R., Vernizzi, D., Ramunno, G., & Lioy, A. (2011). The trusted platform agent. *IEEE Software*, *28*(2), 35–41. doi:10.1109/MS.2010.160.

Dierks, T., & Rescorla, E. (2008). RFC-5246: The transport layer security (TLS) protocol version 1.2. Retrieved from http://www.ietf.org

Emin, E. G., Bruijn, W., Reynolds, P., Shieh, A., Walsh, K., Williams, D., & Schneider, F. B. (2011). Logical attestation: An authorization architecture for trustworthy computing. In Proceedings of the 23rd ACM Symposium on Operating Systems Principles, (pp. 249-264). ACM.

Gasmi, Y., Sadeghi, A.-R., Stewin, P., Unger, M., & Asokan, N. (2007). Beyond secure channels. In Proceedings of the 2nd ACM Workshop on Scalable Trusted Computing, (pp. 30-40). ACM.

Goldman, K., Perez, R., & Sailer, R. (2006). Linking remote attestation to secure tunnel endpoints. In Proceedings of the 1st ACM Symposium on Applied Computing, (pp. 21-24). ACM.

Harris, J., & Hill, R. (2010). Building a trusted image for embedded systems. In Proceedings of the 6th Annual Cyber Security and Information Intelligence Research Workshop, (pp. 65:1-65:4). IEEE.

IAIK TU Graz. (2009). jTSS project (jTSS). Retrieved May 2, 2012, from http://trustedjava.sourceforge.net

IBM. (2008). TrouSerS project – The open-source TCG software stack (TrouSerS). Retrieved May 2, 2012, from http://trousers.sourceforge.net/

Intel. (2011). Intel trusted execution technology (TXT), measured launched environment developer's guide. Document Number: 315168-008. Retrieved May 2, 2012, from http://download.intel.com/technology/security/downloads/315168.pdf

Jonsson, J., & Kaliski, B. (2003). RFC-3447 - PKCS#1: RSA cryptography specifications version 2.1. Retrieved from http://www.ietf.org

Kauer, B. (2007). OSLO: Improving the security of trusted computing. In Proceedings of the 16th USENIX Security Symposium, (pp. 1-9). USENIX.

Kent, S., & Seo, K. (2005). RFC-4301: Security architecture for the internet protocol. Retrieved from http://www.ietf.org

McCune, J. M., Li, Y., Qu, N., Zhou, Z., Datta, A., Gligor, V., & Perrig, A. (2010). TrustVisor: Efficient TCB reduction and attestation. In Proceedings of the 2010 IEEE Symposium on Security and Privacy, (pp. 143-158). Washington, DC: IEEE Computer Society.

Sadeghi, A.-R., & Schulz, S. (2010). Extending IPsec for efficient remote attestation. In Proceedings of the 14th International Conference on Financial Cryptograpy and Data Security, (pp. 150-165). IEEE.

Sadeghi, A.-R., & Stüble, C. (2004). Property-based attestation for computing platforms: Caring about properties, not mechanisms. In Proceedings of the 2004 Workshop on New Security Paradigm, (pp. 67-77). New York, NY: ACM.

Sailer, R., Zhang, X., Jaeger, T., & van Doorn, L. (2004). Design and Implementation of a TCG-based integrity measurement architecture. In Proceedings of the 13th USENIX Security Symposium, (pp. 223-238). USENIX.

Shirey, R. (2007). RFC-4949: Internet security glossary, version 2. Retrieved from http://www.ietf.org

Sirrix, A. G. (2010). Trusted GRUB project (tGRUB). Retrieved May 2, 2012, from http://projects.sirrix.com/trac/trustedgrub

Stüble, C., & Zaerin, A. (2010). µTSS - A simplified trusted software stack. In Proceedings of the 3rd International Conference on Trust and Trustworthy Computing, (pp. 124-140). IEEE.

tBook. (2012). Trusted boot project (tboot). Retrieved May 2, 2012, from http://tboot.sourceforge.net/

Toegl, R., Winkler, T., Nauman, M., & Hong, T. (2009). Towards platform-independent trusted computing. In Proceedings of the 2009 ACM Workshop on Scalable Trusted Computing, (pp. 61-66). ACM.

Trusted Computing Group. (2005). TCG infrastructure working group (IWG) subject key attestation evidence extension: Version 1.0 revision 7, 2005. Retrieved September 16, 2012, from https://www.trustedcomputinggroup.org/files/resource_files/876A7F79-1D09-3519-AD321B21144AE93C/IWG_SKAE_Extension_1-00.pdf

Trusted Computing Group. (2007). TCG software stack: Version 1.2 level 1 errata A, 2007. Retrieved September 16, 2012, from http://www.trustedcomputinggroup.org/files/resource_files/6479CD77-1D09-3519-AD89EAD1BC8C97F0/TSS_1_2_Errata_A-final.pdf

Trusted Computing Group. (2010). TCG mobile trusted module, specification, v. 1.0, revision 7.02. Retrieved May 2, 2012, from http://www.trustedcomputinggroup.org/files/static_page_files/3D843B67-1A4B-B294-D0B-5B407C36F4B1D/Revision_7.02-_29April2010-tcg-mobile-trusted-module-1.0.pdf

Trusted Computing Group. (2011a). TCG TPM main part 1 design principles: Version 1.2 level 2 revision 116, 2011. Retrieved September 16, 2012, from https://www.trustedcomputinggroup.org/files/static_page_files/72C26AB5-1A4B-B294-D002BC0B8C062FF6/TPM%20Main-Part%201%20Design%20Principles_v1.2_rev116_01032011.pdf

Trusted Computing Group. (2011b). TCG TPM main part 2 TPM structures: Version 1.2 level 2 revision 116, 2011. Retrieved September 16, 2012, from https://www.trustedcomputinggroup.org/files/static_page_files/72C2B624-1A4B-B294-D0E07C5F7F49140D/TPM%20Main-Part%202%20TPM%20Structures_v1.2_rev116_01032011.pdf

Trusted Computing Group. (2011c). TCG TPM main part 3 commands: Version 1.2 level 2 revision 116, 2011. Retrieved September 16, 2012, from https://www.trustedcomputinggroup.org/files/static_page_files/72C33D71-1A4B-B294-D02C7DF86630BE7C/TPM%20Main-Part%203%20Commands_v1.2_rev116_01032011.pdf

Trusted Computing Group. (2012). TCG PC client specific implementation specification for conventional BIOS, version 1.21 errata, revision 1.00. Retrieved May 2, 2012, from http://www.trustedcomputinggroup.org/files/resource_files/CB0B2BFA-1A4B-B294-D0C3B9075B5AFF17/TCG_PCClientImplementation_1-21_1_00.pdf

Vasudevan, A., McCune, J., Newsome, J., Perrig, A., & van Doorn, L. (2012). CARMA: A hardware tamper-resistant isolated execution environment on commodity x86 platforms. In Proceedings of the 7th ACM Symposium on Information, Computer and Communications Security. IEEE.

Vasudevan, A., Parno, B., Qu, N., Gligor, V. D., & Perrig, A. (2012). Lockdown: Towards a safe and practical architecture for security applications on commodity platforms. In Proceedings of the 5th International Conference on Trust and Trustworthy Computing, (pp. 34-54). Vienna, Austria: IEEE.

ADDITIONAL READING

Balfe, S., Gallery, E., Mitchell, C. J., & Paterson, K. G. (2008). Challenges for trusted computing. In Proceedings of IEEE Security and Privacy, (pp. 60-66). IEEE.

Brickell, E., Camenisch, J., & Chen, L. (2004). Direct anonymous attestation. In Proceedings of the 11th ACM Conference on Computer and Communications Security, (pp. 132-145). Washington DC: ACM.

Castelluccia, C., Francillon, A., Perito, D., & Soriente, C. (2009). On the difficulty of software-based attestation of embedded devices. In Proceedings of the 16th ACM Conference on Computer and Communications Security, (pp. 400-409). Chicago, IL: ACM.

Catuogno, L., Dmitrienko, A., Eriksson, K., Kuhlmann, D., Ramunno, G., Sadeghi, A.-R., et al. (2010). Trusted virtual domains - Design, implementation and lessons learned. In Proceedings of the 1st International Conference on Trusted Systems, (pp. 156-179). Beijing, China: Springer-Verlag.

Cesena, E., Ramunno, G., Sassu, R., Vernizzi, D., & Lioy, A. (2011). On scalability of remote attestation. In Proceedings of the 6th ACM Workshop on Scalable Trusted Computing, (pp. 25-30). Chicago, IL: ACM.

Challener, D., Yoder, K., Catherman, R., Safford, D., & Van Doorn, L. (2007). *A practical guide to trusted computing*. New York, NY: IBM Press.

Davi, L., Sadeghi, A.-R., & Winandy, M. (2009). Dynamic integrity measurement and attestation: Towards defense against return-oriented programming attacks. In Proceedings of the 2009 ACM Workshop on Scalable Trusted Computing, (pp. 49-54). Chicago, IL: ACM.

England, P. (2008). Practical techniques for operating system attestation. In Proceedings of the 1st International Conference on Trusted Computing and Trust in Information Technologies: Trusted Computing - Challenges and Applications, (pp. 1-13). Villach, Austria: Springer-Verlag.

England, P., Lampson, B., Manferdelli, J., Peinado, M., & Willman, B. (2003). A trusted open platform. *Computer*, *36*(7), 55–62. doi:10.1109/MC.2003.1212691.

Garfinkel, T., Pfaff, B., Chow, J., Rosenblum, M., & Boneh, D. (2003). Terra: A virtual machine-based platform for trusted computing. In Proceedings of the 19th ACM Symposium on Operating Systems Principles, (pp. 193-206). Bolton Landing, NY: ACM.

Grawrock, D. (2009). *Dynamics of a trusted platform: A building block approach*. New York, NY: Intel Press.

Jaeger, T., Sailer, R., & Shankar, U. (2006). PRIMA: Policy-reduced integrity measurement architecture. In Proceedings of the 11th ACM Symposium on Access Control Models and Technologies, (pp. 19-28). Lake Tahoe, CA: ACM.

Kuhlmann, D., Landfermann, R., Ramasamy, H. V., Schunter, M., Ramunno, G., & Vernizzi, D. (2006). *An open trusted computing architecture: Secure virtual machines enabling user-defined policy enforcement*. OpenTC Consortium.

Loscocco, P. A., Wilson, P. W., Pendergrass, J. A., & McDonell, C. D. (2007). Linux kernel integrity measurement using contextual inspection. In Proceedings of the 2007 ACM Workshop on Scalable Trusted Computing, (pp. 21-29). Alexandria, VA: ACM.

Lyle, J., & Martin, A. (2009). On the feasibility of remote attestation for web services. In Proceedings of the 2009 International Conference on Computational Science and Engineering, (pp. 283-288). IEEE Computer Society.

McCune, J. M., Li, Y., Qu, N., Zhou, Z., Datta, A., Gligor, V., & Perrig, A. (2010). TrustVisor: Efficient TCB reduction and attestation. In Proceedings of the 2010 IEEE Symposium on Security and Privacy, (pp. 143-158). IEEE Computer Society.

McCune, J. M., Parno, B., Perrig, A., Reiter, M. K., & Seshadri, A. (2008). How low can you go? Recommendations for hardware-supported minimal TCB code execution. In Proceedings of the 13th International Conference on Architectural Support for Programming Languages and Operating Systems, (pp. 14-25). Seattle, WA: ACM.

McCune, J. M., Parno, B. J., Perrig, A., Reiter, M. K., & Isozaki, H. (2008). Flicker: An execution infrastructure for TCB minimization. In Proceedings of the 3rd ACM SIGOPS/EuroSys European Conference on Computer Systems 2008, (pp. 315-328). Glasgow, UK: ACM.

McCune, J. M., Perrig, A., Seshadri, A., & van Doorn, L. (2007). Turtles all the way down: Research challenges in user-based attestation. In Proceedings of the 2nd USENIX Workshop on Hot Topics in Security, (pp. 6:1-6:5). Boston, MA: USENIX Association.

Mitchell, C. (Ed.). (2005). *Trusted computing*. London, UK: IEE. doi:10.1049/PBPC006E.

Murray, D. G., Milos, G., & Hand, S. (2008). Improving Xen security through disaggregation. In Proceedings of the 4th ACM SIGPLAN/SIGOPS International Conference on Virtual Execution Environments, (pp. 151-160). Seattle, WA: ACM.

Parno, B., McCune, J. M., & Perrig, A. (2011). *Bootstrapping trust in modern computers*. Berlin, Germany: Springer. doi:10.1007/978-1-4614-1460-5.

Pirker, M., Toegl, R., Hein, D., & Danner, P. (2009). A PrivacyCA for anonymity and trust. In Proceedings of the 2nd International Conference on Trusted Computing, (pp. 101-119). Oxford, UK: Springer-Verlag.

Sailer, R., Jaeger, T., Zhang, X., & van Doorn, L. (2004). Attestation-based policy enforcement for remote access. In Proceedings of the 11th ACM Conference on Computer and Communications Security, (pp. 308-317). Washington, DC: ACM.

Seshadri, A., Luk, M., Shi, E., Perrig, A., van Doorn, L., & Khosla, P. (2005). Pioneer: Verifying code integrity and enforcing untampered code execution on legacy systems. In Proceedings of the 20th ACM Symposium on Operating Systems Principles, (pp. 1-16). Brighton, UK: ACM.

Seshadri, A., Perrig, A., van Doorn, L., & Khosla, P. (2004). SWATT: SoftWare-based ATTestation for embedded devices. In Proceedings of the 2004 IEEE Symposium on Security and Privacy. IEEE Computer Society.

Strasser, M., & Stamer, H. (2008). A software-based trusted platform module emulator. In Proceedings of the 1st International Conference on Trusted Computing and Trust in Information Technologies: Trusted Computing - Challenges and Applications, (pp. 33-47). Villach, Austria: Springer-Verlag.

KEY TERMS AND DEFINITIONS

Attestation: Process of reporting to third party the measurements of a platform.

Measurement: Cryptographic hash of a component's binary or a configuration file which represent the identity of a component.

Protected Capabilities: Set of functions with exclusive control of the shielded locations.

Sealing: Feature of the TPM. It allows the encryption of data which can be conditionally released in a certain platform only if its state matches the one defined at encryption time.

Shielded Locations: Storage area accessible exclusively through the protected capabilities where sensitive data can be safely stored and modified.

TCG Software Stack (TSS): Software stack specified by the TCG which provides an API to Trusted applications to communicate with the TPM. It multiplexes accesses from different applications and abstract hardware details.

Trusted Computing: Technology developed by the Trusted Computing Group (TCG) which aims to increase the security of a computing node providing hardware and software mechanism to measure and to report the state of a platform.

Trusted Platform Module (TPM): Low-cost cryptographic device designed to protect cryptographic keys and assist the measurement of a computing platform. It provides protected capabilities and shielded locations.

Chapter 15
Enhancing Security at Email End Point:
A Feasible Task for Fingerprint Identification System

Babak Sokouti
Biotechnology Research Center, Tabriz University of Medical Sciences, Iran

Massoud Sokouti
Faculty of Electrical and Computer Engineering, Department of Computer Engineering, Shahid Beheshti University, Iran

ABSTRACT

Although email security needs more attention, a small amount of research has been conducted. Most of the security properties that can be applied to the email messages are based on encryption and digital signatures. The cryptography techniques that can be both symmetric and asymmetric algorithms cannot prove the identity of the sender and receiver in the real world, which is related to the end point security. Additionally, these techniques are not capable of preventing the spams, scams, and spoofing attacks. A new secure email system based on fingerprint identification is proposed to overcome the recognition of the real identity of the email sender and receiver. This method uses the user's username and password hashes, their full name and personal image, and fingerprint hashes along with the email message hash. The proposed method is successfully evaluated against security, maintenance, operational, and privacy issues.

INTRODUCTION

Electronic mail or email is a popular form of communication between computer users. This has led it to forcefully get used to hosting the malware, for example, viruses, spam email, Trojans and other phishing scams. The use of email will allow attackers (Garfinkel, Margrave, Schiller, Nordlander, & Miller, 2005)—an entry wedge as a means of getting personal information—if the person trusts the received email. Sometimes sensitive data is transmitted clearly in Internet.

DOI: 10.4018/978-1-4666-4030-6.ch015

This allows the messages to be intercepted or to be read by an unauthorized person; also messages can be re-created, altered and sent to the recipient from an unauthorized sender (Garfinkel, et al., 2005). By using cryptographic techniques a secure channel can be created for protecting the email contents; this is the only way used to protect the messages from previous years. Nowadays, although encryption and signing messages based on cryptography are integrated into email client software, small numbers of messages are transmitted securely (Gutmann, 2004).

Some of the standards of securing emails are PEM (Privacy Enhanced Mail), MIME (Multipurpose Internet Mail Extensions), S/MIME (Secure/ Multipurpose Internet Mail Extensions)), PGP (Pretty Good Privacy) and PKCS#7 (Public Key Cryptography Standard #7). These are being used to provide security services such as confidentiality, data origin authentication, message integrity and non-repudiation of origin. By using these standards within the email process, a digital signature can be added to email to provide the authenticity of the sender to make a message tamper resistant and encrypting makes it undecipherable by anyone else (Garfinkel, 2003; Housley, 1989).

These techniques are all based on the asymmetric or public key cryptography in which we do not need to share a secret key between sender and receiver. The public and private key pair production is done by special mathematical formulas in which the private key can be used for both decrypting and signing processes and the public key for both encrypting and verifying processes. The security of this system is totally relying on the key management issue, i.e. by compromising the private key or by altering the public key the whole sensitive data will be revealed to an unintended person.

Up to now, protecting the email content by providing the related security service is being presented which has its own pros and cons in special situations. Now at this stage it is critical to see how previous methods can solve it. In this chapter, a new email security model is presented to answer this question that none of the previous methods can solve this problem. Though the security of the communication channel is being discussed, the real authenticity of the endpoints (sender and receiver) is not provided. This can be resulted in the threats such as Spam emails and Phishing threats or even a non-repudiation security service issue.

Suppose a simple scenario in which Alice (Sender), Bob (Intended Receiver), and Sarah (Secretary Receiver) are included. Alice signs or/ and encrypts the message by her private key and sends it to Bob's email address. Sarah, as Bob's secretary receiver, knows the Bob's Public key as she is his trusty secretary, receives the message, verifies or/and decrypts the message. The message is very urgent and Bob should also have a reply to Alice's email. For some reasons, Sarah forgot to tell Bob about the received message. After some days, Alice asks Bob about the reply of her message and Bob does not know about the email she is talking about as Sarah has not informed him. Now, the problem is how Bob will know whether the email sent to him has been deleted or read while he did not get informed.

In this situation, a means is needed to reveal the real authenticity of the message receiver/sender as cryptographic techniques are just a combination of ASCII characters and are not based on an individual's characteristics. Biometrics technology is the most common way of determining the identity; for solving this problem a biometric solution is used to authenticate individuals for which fingerprint identification is more reliable and user-friendly than other biometric features (Jain, Ross, & Prabhakar, 2004).

A fingerprint recognition system consists of a fingerprint sensor input, feature extractor, a database of stored fingerprint features, and decision making section. Finally, the system will make the comparison between the input data and the stored data in database. If the input extracted features are close to the templates extracted features, the person will be identified; otherwise he or she will be rejected.

In this chapter, a new email security based on fingerprint identification system for communication endpoints is presented. This will reveal the real sender and receiver of the message by providing his or her fingerprint while sending and receiving messages. The identity will be known by comparing its features with a templates database. Using a cryptographic technique for signing and verifying the messages can be also advisable.

The following sections will review existing email security standards and issues. Also, fingerprint systems, fake finger problems and how to detect a live finger will be discussed there. Finally, a new security email model based on fingerprint identification and its related issues will be proposed.

This chapter aims at providing a secure traceable access to mailbox by means of a fingerprint identification system. This will employ a database in which the hash of sent messages and fingerprints are being stored for message verification and person identification purpose.

This makes a feeling that this sets out a chapter that will look at fingerprints to achieve some form of secure access. This motivates us to propose a secure email system based on fingerprints for real human identity authentication.

BACKGROUND

Electronic Mail (Email): What is It?

In this section, a brief look will be given to the history and development of the email system and components along with the important security threats that could be encountered when using emails. The aim is to provide the current state of email security system.

History

Email is a 46 year-old term that exists since the computers were around or at least after the first programs of the computers came into existence. The early form of the email was to leave messages for others on the same computer in which was used by the other person. As a matter of fact, the number of computers was not that much in the 1960s and the "networking" term was not fully introduced then. By development of computer networking the email really got its meaning.

The earliest network, Advanced Research Projects Agency Network (ARPANET), was developed and later became a key part of the internet. Engineers and scientists working on ARPANET were encouraged to make use of email to communicate with each other and even schedule their meetings.

Experientially, the need for providing security services for the email system was felt to be essential. There were some previously achieved works, standards, technologies, and algorithms on securing emails which will be reviewed in this section. Six known solutions have been presented ever since to secure the email contents. In the mid 1980s, Privacy Enhanced Email (PEM) (Crocker, 1982) was first proposed by Privacy and Security Research Group (PSRG). Later, it was updated by IETF three times as (Crocker, 1982; Namestnikova, 2012; Rojkovic, 2010) a four part standard consisting of RFC1421 (Linn, 1993), RFC1422 (Kent, 1993), RFC1423 (Balenson, 1993), RFC1424 (Kaliski, 1993). At this stage, email security was not developed because of its single hierarchical CA root (PEM's PKI) and non-support MIME attachment property. End-to-end encryption was the fundamental for securing email message contents (Garfinkel, et al., 2005). Pretty Good Privacy (PGP) proposed by Phil Zimmermann, was standardized in 1996. The aim was for distributing the trust between trusted participants to digitally sign and encrypt the messages. By using PGP, one is able to produce his public key certificate and store them (Atkins, Stallings, & Zimmermann, 1996). PGP and GnuPG (GPG) are both based on public/private key pair encryption technologies in which GPG is an equivalent to the PGP (Callas, Donnerhacke, Finney, & Thayer, 1998). The Multipurpose Internet Mail Extensions (MIME) added some more specifications to PEM. MIME supports special character coding for representing non-English texts and object attachments such as images, documents, and videos (Borenstein & Freed, 1993).

Secure Multipurpose Internet Mail Extensions (S/MIME) was developed by RSA based on PEM. Unlike PEM, S/MIME offered as many trusted CA as needed. Nowadays, S/MIME is mostly used in many mail clients such as Microsoft office outlook and Lotus Notes, but it is not commonly used in web-based mail clients such as Gmail, yahoo, hotmail, and etc (Dusse, Hoffman, Ramsdell, Lundblade, & Repka, 1998).

At the same time with PEM, Message Security Protocol (MSP) was also used by US military standards for securing messages. The main purpose was to secure X.400 email messages; X.400 standard is an alternative to SMTP standard mostly used in EU and Canada (NISTIR 90-4250, 1990).

Public-Key Cryptography Standard#7 (PKCS#7), a data protection standard, was proposed by RSA Data Security Inc. PKCS#7 was mostly used for export control by using strong signature and weak encryption keys (Kaliski, 1998).

In 2003, an Email Mining Toolkit (EMT) was introduced that was based on the behaviour-oriented methods different from the content-oriented methods to add security to email systems. Real-time email profiling is used on accounts usage to detect email violations (Stolfo, et al., 2003), for example Malicious Email Tracking system (Bhattacharyya, Hershkop, Eskin, & Stolfo, 2002). In this project two special behavioural properties user cliques (the mostly used groups that email are sent to) and Hellinger distance (the frequency of user communication with his recipients) (Stolfo, et al., 2003) model were being used.

In 2004, a PractiSES secure system was simulated based on several domain networks. The public/private key pair distribution management was done by means of an inter-domain communication to provide user's public keys, when a user in other domains needs the key to exchange encrypted messages. In this system, PractiSES server is known as trusted to all users (Levi & Özcan, 2005).

In 2007, a Facemail secure webmail system was proposed that was aimed at lessening wrong directed emails by showing the email sender's face while one is composing or sending email messages (Lieberman & Miller, 2007). A Crypto-Biometric Secure email system for wireless environment based on three factor scheme was also presented in 2008 (Sukarno & Bhattacharjee, 2008), which added a biopass phrase to sender's private key by using iris biometric and cryptography algorithms. Also, Obied (2006) reported a secure email based on fingerprint authentication in 2006. However, the method needs to be examined against spam, fraudulent, phishing attacks and real-human identity authentication.

Operation Overview

In this section, email system processes will be reviewed to find out how an email system works. The sender using an email client is supposed to send an email message to the recipient in the same or different place from that of the sender's. The steps A to E are followed for a message to be sent by a sender and received by an intended recipient.

In step A, the sender creates an email message by the means of sender's Mail User Agent (MUA) such as Eudora, Outlook and sends email message by clicking on "Send" button.

In step B, MUA passes email message to sender's Mail Delivery Agent (MDA) or Mail Transport Agent (MTA) which is similar to mail transfer Protocol (SMTP). In this stage, MDA/MTA will route email messages to a local network. If there is no local network, message will be forwarded to sender's MTA to be ready to be sent through the Internet.

In step C, there is a network cloud into which email message enters. Sometimes the network cloud can be private that will route all email messages to the nearest available MTA through a unique gateway.

In step D, as entered email message is intended for another person other than a local network's user, email messages will be queued until the MTA is free to process. Finally, email message is forwarded to recipient's MTA because of large email message loads. Sometimes there may be multiple MTAs between sender's and recipient's MTA while it is forwarded through the Internet.

In step E, sender's MTA will hold all responsibilities of mail delivery while communicating with recipient's MTA. A set of servers are distributed along the Internet from which recipient's IP address will be found and directed through several Domain Name Systems (DNS).

After passing through many spam and antivirus software, email message will be accepted by receiver's MTA. After that, receiver's MTA will look for a local MDA to find a correct mailbox to be waited until the receiver reads it by receiver's MUA.

In real email system, there is an email server which is responsible for outgoing and incoming email messages. For this purpose email server is consisting of two servers, SMTP (Simple Mail Transfer Protocol) and POP3 (Post Office Protocol) or IMAP (Internet Mail Access Protocol) servers. These servers are listening to particular port numbers for being able to find out about the current status of email messages within mail server. SMTP, POP3, and IMAP will listen to port numbers 25, 110, and 143, respectively.

Technically speaking, SMTP on both sides plays the MTA role, communicating with each other by interconnecting with DNS paths to deliver email messages. While an email message is received by receiver's MUA, client connects to POP3 server which acts as an interface between client and message. The copies of email messages will be taken to receiver's local personal computer and then email messages will be deleted from the server. This makes it difficult to read email messages when a receiver is both working on a laptop and personal computer. For resolving this issue IMAP can be helpful. By using IMAP, email message will remain in mail server and all the commands such as folders searching and inbox reading are done on mail server rather than on a local machine. This technique makes it easy to access email messages from everywhere without getting into POP3 problems (Edulog, 2005).

Message Format

This part describes a simple email message format. The email which is fully specified in RFC 822 can be divided as two separate parts, message envelope and message contents. The message envelope, regarded as header, includes transmission and delivery information. The message content is the actual email message which only contains lines of ASCII texts. Other binary object attachments and special character sets are not supported. This structure is regarded as a problem in RFC 822 message format (Crocker, 1982).

Multipurpose Internet Mail Extensions (MIME), proposed by IETF in RFCs 2045-2049, unlike RFC 822 message format supports all long binary object attachments and special non-English ASCII character sets in message contents. While sending a MIME message, it will be translated in to ASCII format as an RFC 822 message format. MIME header field includes information about message body, so it is backward compatible to RFC 822 Message format. The header fields are illustrated as below where the first three are mandatory and the last two are optional.

- **MIME-Version:** This is the MIME message format version whose value must be equal to 1.0. This number is set to default. So if a number other than one is used, it will not be compliant with RFC 2045 document.

- **Content-Type:** MIME content uses seven types for being used in recipient's client software:
  - **Application:** Postscript (Executable files) / binary code objects is being transmitted.
  - **Audio:** Audio data format.
  - **Video:** MPEG movie format.
  - **Image:** GIF, JPG, and JPEG graphic images.
  - **Message:** Supports RFC 822 messages, partial messages, and external-body messages.
  - **Multipart:** Documents' multiple parts can be used by Mixed, Parallel, alternative, and digest subtypes.
  - **Text:** Specifies enriched and plain text content.
- **Content-Transfer-Encoding:** Available choices for transforming encoded document into 7-bit format are being indicated as below:
  - **7-Bit:** US-ASC data is sent.
  - **8-Bit:** Short lines will contain 8-bit character.
  - **BASE64:** This is used for Binary file formats.
  - **Binary:** Long lines which are not transportable using SMTP are using 8- bit character.
  - **Quoted-Printable:** This is used by ASC text with 76 character line length limitation.
  - **X-Token:** This uses private encoding values with prefix "X-".
- **Content-ID:** The possibility of a body of information reference is allowed.
- **Content-Description:** This provides a body of information description (Freed & Borenstein, 1996)

Table 1 shows the header lines in an MIME message.

Email Security Threats

At this stage of information security era, the way that email systems are working, is mostly based on SMTP servers, so attention should be given to its security issues. Recalling that preserving the CIA (Confidentiality, Integrity and Availability) triad is the main specific information security principle. This can be directly considered as email security issues as well.

Providing confidentiality of email messages means to make sure of a message being protected from an unauthorized access. This property is essential for two reasons. Firstly, the message content is sent clearly through a distrusted network and secondly, email messages are stored in clear in client and servers which are not secure enough to trust. To guarantee that message content is not altered or changed in an unauthorized manner is regarded as providing integrity property for an email message.

To provide availability of mail servers is to make assurance of servers being on-line and ser-

Table 1. Header lines in an MIME message

Return-Path:	< SenderEmailID@DomainName >
Received:	from DomainName ([IP Address]) by dredd.mcom.com (Netscape Messaging Server 3.0) with ESMTP id AAA24896; Sat, 04 Dec 2010 20:08:19 -0800
Sender:	SenderEmailID
Message-ID:	<34D93795.C1F48C83@netscape.com>
Date:	Sat, 04 Dec 2010 19:52:53 -0800
From:	Name Family <SenderEmailID@DomainName>
X-Mailer:	Mozilla 4.03C-NSCP [en] (X11; U; SunOS 5.5.1 sun4u)
MIME-Version:	1.0
To:	ReceiverEmailID@DomainName
Subject:	A Reliable Subject
Content-Type:	multipart/mixed; boundary = "------------BFA9E722569728E3111F0326"

vice the users at any time that they need to use email client to communicate with mail servers.

By defining CIA triad, the next step is to find out threats that are threatening email security and are enabled by using email system itself in a company environment. The threats to email security can be summarized as below:

1. **Loss of Confidentiality:** As given in the above sentences, there are two issues that will be counted towards the email security threats if message confidentiality is not provided. One is the clear messages being transferred by a distrusted public network and the other one is their clearly storage in insecure clients and mail servers.
2. **Loss of Content Integrity:** As default there is no content integrity applied to email messages, they are vulnerable and can be changed or altered on the server or in transit by an active or passive attacker.
3. **Lack of Data Origin Authentication (Known as Masquerading or Forging of Email):** According to the use of SMTP, by telnet command, it is possible to forge all email fields including the "FROM" field. Even if the "FROM" field is not altered, how can one be sure who has logged in as the intended legitimate sender to compose the email? Because, sharing passwords is common between friends or in companies between the boss and secretary!
4. **Lack of Non-Repudiation of Origin:** There is no evidence that who has sent the email message. So the email content may not be reliable or in other time sender can deny of his email sending. In other words non-repudiation security property is the assurance that the sender cannot deny his authenticity of sending message. Stock trading by email is an example of this threat.
5. **Lack of Email Receipt Notification:** When this threat is enabled, there is no evidence that intended recipient has read the email message. Having an email message marked locally as "Sent" does not assure its reception and being read, because they can be deleted by the sender after they are being sent.

The threats that can be enabled by using emails are summarized as below:

1. **Disclosure of Sensitive Information:** This is directly connected with the first email security threat namely "Loss of Confidentiality." Delivering information by email is the easiest way in comparison with writing the information realms by hand and delivering it. In this situation, sensitive information can be disclosed either accidental or deliberately. Disclosure can be also an internal (about a sacked person in an organization) or external (a message being sent to outside environment) event. Losing reputation or staff's job losing is the result of companies' internal and external information disclosure.
2. **Exposure of Systems to Malicious Code:** Viruses are the most dangerous and high risk of all security issues. Whenever they are delivered and opened by the receiver, an executable file or a visual basic script or java script code is found on its attachment part. If the virus script runs, it will cause harmful results and destructive payloads which can make a mail server system to crash and lose its availability status. As SMTP servers are always connected to the Internet and are communicating with each other, they are vulnerable to this threat. The vulnerability of making SMTP connections will use system's memory that is a result of a Denial of Service attack (DoS attack). It is worth mentioning that in some occasions, exploiting a system by the operating system, memory, CPU computing cycles and network bandwidth needs some user interaction.
3. **Exposure of Systems to Denial of Service (DoS) Attacks:** Nowadays, the use of email

has dramatically increased; this makes email a primary communication tool (Rojkovic, 2010). By this, it can be known that a general mail server which can be used by anyone is a target for attackers to exposure the mail server by DoS attacks. By a successful DoS attack, other network services of infected server will be compromised. This will threaten the availability of mail server.

4. **Exposure of Individuals to Denial of Service Attacks:** One of the most important threats that stop someone from reading their incoming emails is by sending many useless emails to a person which is an overused manner of using the email system. Though a person may go over the email subject, he will either delete or leave them as they are. So he may prefer face-to-face communication or contacting person by phone. Mail bombing is a known worldwide threat which makes mailbox full of over 1000 unread messages in which the real intended email will be lost.
5. **Unauthorized Access to Mail Server Systems:** Mail servers which include Operating System, network, and email applications are important to be protected against the security threats and vulnerabilities. If the latest security patches are not applied to mail servers, all known vulnerabilities can be employed to compromise it easily by loading a Trojan horse code on the system. After a Trojan horse is loaded on victim's system, attacker will be able to watch and control everything that goes on the mail server which can be spread to the user's machine as well. After all, this makes the users unsatisfied with provided mail services and may lead to loss of company reputation as mail server is not protected securely.
6. **Spamming:** Spam known as a junk mail, is an email security threat. Spams can affect email security by either huge volumes to threaten the system availability or the malicious code accompanied as an attachment to steal the personal information. Kaspersky Lab reported that an average of 75% of email sent traffic are detected as spam in which the USA and India are the leaders (17.2% and 9%, respectively). The most promising rate (over 10%) in July 2010 was occupied by UK, Germany, and Italy which had a 50% increase in comparison with previous months (Namestnikova, 2012). What most security professionals worry the most about is the collaboration between virus writers and spammers to compromise large networks (Plante, 2004).
7. **Relaying and Blacklisting:** Mail servers can be easily compromised by misconfiguration of relaying router and exchange servers which makes the guilty server blacklisted by the Spam and Open-Relay Blacklist (SORBS, 2002). As a result all incoming email messages from a particular mail sever will be blocked and blacklisted as mail servers are using the blacklists for accepting incoming email messages.
8. **Phishing and Pharming:** One of the newest threats known as phishing and pharming, developed in recent years (Pharming, 2009), is a criminally fraudulent process. This threat known as identity theft gets the sensitive information such as username/ password and credit card details by masquerading as a legitimate website by an electronic communication. Phishing is the action after pharming which sends spoof emails to find the above information. A research carried out by Gartner Research estimates that over 3/4 of the entire known phishing attacks had occurred in five-month period. The Anti-Phishing Working Group (APWG, 2011) also reported over 1000 unique phishing attacks and this number is reported nearly seven times repeatedly. It is expected that the number of phishing attacks will grow drastically while an effective solution to this security issue will take some time to find.

EXISTING EMAIL SECURITY MODELS

Privacy Enhanced Mail (PEM)

Privacy Enhanced Mail (PEM) is an email encryption protocol. This is an internet standard to provide a secure email by providing security properties including confidentiality, message integrity, authentication, and key management. This is done by employing various symmetric and public key encryption algorithms (Linn, 1993). In this standard protocol, confidentiality is provided by DES/AES encryption algorithms and origin authentication is provided by RSA signing/verifying algorithms (Kent, 1993). Additionally, non-repudiation security service is supported by using asymmetric key management and some privacy related issues such as access control, reuse of PCs by multiple users, and assurance of message reception are not well addressed. A CA-managed hierarchy of digital signatures for key management can also be used in PEM which is compatible with the authentication architecture in CCITT 1988 X.509. But PGP is just using the "Web of Trust" instead of CA hierarchy (Kent, 1993).]. The X.509 certification (CCITT, 1988) profile was firstly defined by PEM.

The PEM is consisting of four standard parts as given below:

- **Message Encryption and Authentication Procedures:** In this part, message structures are defined as MIC-CLEAR, MIC-ONLY, and ENCRYPTED; where MIC stands for Message Integrity Check. MIC-CLEAR provides authentication and message integrity without providing the message confidentiality. It is being told to be clear-signed as the message can be read in clear by anybody. Though MIC-ONLY is the same as MIC-CLEAR security services, as its message content cannot be read by anybody; it uses an MIME similar encoding which provides all three security services including authentication, message integrity, and message confidentiality (Kent, 1993).
- **Certificate-Based Key Management:** RFC1422 (Kent, 1993) defines a method for key management architecture which supports both public key and symmetric key management.
- **Algorithms, Modes, and Identifiers:** This defines the cryptographic algorithm types and modes with special parameters being used in PEM. RSA algorithm is used for signing/verifying messages and DES/AES in ECB (Electronic Code book) or CBC (Cipher Block Chaining) mode are used to provide confidentiality security service. MD2 and MD5 are the one-way functions used in this part.
- **Key Certification and Related Services:** In this RFC, PEM supports some services such as key certification, CRL (Certificate Revocation List) storage, and retrieval.

PEM had two main drawbacks. The first issue was PEM's PKI single hierarchical root CA; the implementation cost was awesome and when a root CA with more power than others did not like company A, the root CA will revoke the certificate of company A. So the related company will not be able to send secure email any more. The second issue is about the PEM's ability to send text messages but not attachments as MIME can.

Pretty Good Privacy (PGP)

Pretty Good Privacy (PGP) was firstly written by Phil Zimmerman in 1991 (Zimmermann, 1993) and standardized in 1996 in RFC 1991 (Atkins, et al., 1996). PGP was created for message encryption and signature using its own public and private key pairs which is known as an asymmetric cryptography algorithm. It also defines its own public key certificates and the way of its storage;

X.509 certificate (CCITT, 1988) support was added later in OpenPGP (Callas, Donnerhacke, Finney, Shaw, & Thayer, 2007). The following concepts are supported by using PGP (Turner & Housley, 2008):

In Web of Trust, trust point is not centralized in which the trust degree depends on how much may the person know. For example if Bob knows Alice and trusts her, and Alice knows Betty and introduces her to Bob, then Bob will trust Betty, too.

Key generation in PGP is fully customized by users and PGP allows its users to create their own keys freely that may be based on user's thought and characteristics. PGP does not have the X.500 and X.509 Internet Name limitations. It supports various Internet Name forms in certificates on the issuer's side.

PGP has the ability to add a key fingerprint in the certificate to assure the key has not been changed or altered. So PGP certificate will include a key fingerprint in the authority key identifier and subject key identifier certificate extensions.

In PGP, optional message compression can decrease the message size. By default the compression processing is applied to message, before it is being signed and after the encryption is applied, but the other order will not work. The PGP usage was not so broad, as its standardization was taken place so late. Five years later after it was introduced, user involvement in PGP Web of Trust chain is not that much impressive.

GnuPG (GPG)

Gnu Privacy Guard (GPG) has its technical, legal and social issues, which is designed for situations with different security needs. Since 1999, according to the digital signature and encryption laws which are differing from country to country, the use of GPG as legal is still a debating issue among international governments (Ashley, Copeland, Grahn, & Wheeler, 1999).

GPG can be used to protect user's privacy from eavesdroppers (not exactly an adversary) in sender's and receiver's communication path. Four issues effecting customizing GPG are given below (Ashley, et al., 1999):

1. The Public – Private key pairs key size
2. Private key protection
3. Expiration date setting and using subkeys
4. Web of Trust management

The master signing key in GPG is a DSA key that a 1024 bit key must be used and the encryption sub-keys are ELGamal keys which can be of any size. The GPG public key in a hybrid public-key cryptography system is used to encrypt the 128-bit session key and the private key will decrypt it. Considering the speed and storage space for large public private key pairs, the key size should be so large that can resist brute force attacks (Ashley, et al., 1999).

The private key protection is so important because if it is compromised by an attacker, the encrypted message will be decrypted easily. Also, if the private key is lost, user will not be able to decrypt documents in the future. Therefore, regardless of how one may use the GPG, a backup of private/public key revocation certificate must be backed up on a media such as CD-ROM or DVD ROM in a safe place. In this matter GPG supports a safeguard using a symmetric encryption algorithm to access the private key by a passphrase rather than storing raw private key on the hard disk. So using a good passphrase which is easy to remember and hard to guess is essential (Ashley, et al., 1999).

When a new key pair is generated, a DSA master signing key and ELGamal encryption sub-key are created by default. For this different key lifetimes may be applied to the generated keys. As the master signing key is used for making digital signatures and gathers the signature keys of anyone who has trusted you, it would be better to set a lifetime expiration date for the master key. On the other hand for improving the security, it is essential to change the encryption sub-key periodically. After the key is changed, there is no guarantee for protecting the past encrypted documents, but the future documents will be protected. So having a valid encryption sub-key on key ring is a good decision and one key must be made active from the key ring at any given time (Ashley, et al., 1999).

Building the Web of Trust plays an important role in protecting privacy. Regardless of security needs, assigning trust to other's signatures must be done accurately. If a wrong trust decision is assigned to someone, the whole Web of Trust users who are communicating with each other in the trust shelter will be in danger. So it is better to sign close friends' signature that are known and slightly trust all others on the key ring until their confirmed key become trusted by more people in the Web of Trust system (Ashley, et al., 1999).

Multipurpose Internet Mail Extensions (MIME Object Security Services MOSS)

The email message contents format which provides both textual and non-textual message bodies is based on MIME. The header is based on RFC 822 message and the body is defined according to MIME. The MIME itself does not provide security services. MIME Object Security Services (MOSS) based on PEM, holding the most PEM features, was designed to support MIME features (Crocker, Freed, Galvin, & Murphy, 1995). At least one user or a process must have a public private key pair in order to use the MOSS Services. The public keys are known to user of secure communication and the private key must not be revealed to anybody.

The sender's private key will be used to sign MIME objects and sender's public key at recipient's side is used for verifying MIME objects' digital signature. In the encryption process, recipient's public key is used for encrypting the message and its corresponding private key is used to decrypt MIME object message. MOSS can also support Internet Names and encrypted-unsigned MIME objects, but it was not widely used after the S/MIME came to existence.

Message Security Protocol (MSP)

Message Security Protocol (MSP), the U.S military's email security standard, was used in Defense Messaging System (DMS). Supporting the X.400 email messages were the first aim of this design which was carried out about the same time as development of PEM (NISTIR 90-4250, 1990). At the later time, it was also used for securing emails. X.400 message consists of two parts: envelope and content. After the MSP is applied to X.400 email message, X.400 content is encapsulated by MSP. As a result an MSP header will add a secure header for future MSP trusted endpoint communications.

Five security services were provided by MSP. These services are confidentiality, integrity, authentication, non-repudiation of origin (by message signature), and non-repudiation of delivery (by signed receipts). There are some X.509 certificate types provided in MSP that supports signing, encrypting, and both processes by using two keys. After that S/MIME and PGP were the most popular methods being employed for email security while MSP couldn't follow the market.

Public Key Cryptography Standard #7 (PKC#7)

Public Key Cryptography Standard #7, a Cryptographic Message Syntax Standard from RSA Data Security Inc., includes plaintext or ciphertext or a digital signature or one or more certificates and certificate revocation lists (Ramsdell, 1999; RSA, 2009). At first, it was not particularly designed to be used in email security application. PKCS #7 was published by RSA Data Security as a group of Public Key Cryptography Standards (PKCS).

RSA Data Security starts to overcome PEM security shortcomings by adding an encapsulating layer. The keys for signing and encrypting processes are not the same. So PKCS #7 becomes fully compatible with PEM in a manner that any signed data in PEM mode is convertible to PEM messages without cryptographic operations. Similarly, the same thing in reverse manner can happen to PEM messages.

PKCS #7 was widely used in literature even in providing architectures for certificate-based key management.

Secure/ Multipurpose Internet Mail Extensions (S/MIME)

Secure Multipurpose Internet Mail Extensions (S/MIME) is working based on PKCS #7 (Ramsdell, 1999) (an asymmetric cryptography system) and MIME to encrypt and digitally sign email messages. The latest version is described in RFC 2633. This effort was developed by RSA Data Security Inc. (RSA, 2009).

As for performance enhancement, S/MIME does encrypting and signing email message a bit differently by providing confidentiality and authentication. "Smime-type" field as an extra MIME content type is used to specify if an email message is encrypted or digitally signed. An MIME entity can be bounded to an encrypted or signed Cryptographic Message Syntax (CMS) object, a base64 encoded (Hoffman & Ramsdell, 2005), this structure is specified in Abstract Syntax Notation (ANS.1) (Kaliski, 1998).

The content-type application/pkcs7-mime is usually included in CMS object.

If a clear-text message is sent, clear-text part and CMS object will be joined in a multipart/signed content and CMS object will be part of the content-type application/pkcs7-signature (Moser, 2002).

Assume a plaintext email as presented in Box 1 which is not encrypted, not signed and can be read clearly.

It is obvious from the S/MIME Clear-Signed Message presented in Box 2 that Content-Type: application/x-pkcs7-signature may contain original message in clear. This enables all email client software to be able to read it. The message modification/alteration is detectable as the digest will be different from the original one.

As this message, presented in Box 3, is encrypted, the intended recipient will be able to read it. But there is one drawback in here; the encrypted message can be replaced by another en-

Box 1. Original Message

```
From: "Name1 Family1" <Family1@DomainName1>
To: "Name2 Family2" < Family2@DomainName2>
Subject: test
Date: Sat, 11 Dec 2010 01:38:36 +03 00
MIME-Version: 1.0
Content-Type: text/plain
This is a test message.
```

Box 2. S/MIME Clear-Signed Message

```
From: "Name1 Family1" <Family1@DomainName1>
To: "Name2 Family2" < Family2@DomainName2>
Subject: S/MIME test
Date: Sat, 11 Dec 2010 01:38:36 +03 00
MIME-Version: 1.0
Content-Type: multipart/signed;
protocol="application/x-pkcs7-signature";
micalg=SHA1; boundary="ABCDE"
--ABCDE
Content-Type: text/plain
This is a test message.
--ABCDE
Content-Type: application/x-pkcs7-signature
Content-Transfer-Encoding: base64
This part includes S/MIME clear-signed message
--ABCDE--
```

Box 3. S/MIME Encrypted Message

```
From: "Name1 Family1" <Family1@DomainName1>
To: "Name2 Family2" < Family2@DomainName2>
Subject: S/MIME test
Date: Sat, 11 Dec 2010 01:38:36 +03 00
MIME-Version: 1.0
Content-Type: application/x-pkcs7-mime;
smime-type=enveloped-data
Content-Transfer-Encoding: base64
This part includes S/MIME encrypted message
```

crypted message. An encrypted session key and the sender's public key are included in the message (Moser, 2002).

At the present, S/MIME is supported by most popular email clients such as Microsoft Outlook Express and can be used by world users as a default encrypting/signing client to secure their email messages.

Issues with Email Encryption

It is known that by encrypting a simple message, more security can be added to the whole message; so the following issues should be considered while using the encryption processes for email messages (Tracy, Jansen, Scarfone, & Butterfield, 2007):

- By encrypting a message, virus/malware scanning and email content filtering will be dramatically complex at firewall and mail server side. If a decrypting method is not supported by firewall or mail server, as a result the encrypted message cannot be decrypted and acted on malicious message content. In some situations the encrypted message for scanner can be decrypted on the other end if the scanner is an intended recipient. If the malware scanner is infected or exploited, these techniques will cause serious results.
- The organizations hardwares upgrade should be considered if a load of encryption and decryption calculations are needed.
- Significant use of encrypting message by organizations will be need. This causes an overload task for system administrators for managing, recovering, and revocating keys.
- Email message reading will not be supported by some law enforcement parties.
- The result of using weak encryption algorithm or small key makes the recipient contact the sender to tell him to use a strong encryption algorithm or send the message securely through other tools.

FINGERPRINT SYSTEMS

Overview of Biometrics

The knowledge of finding out the identity of a distinct entity based on the physical, behavioural or chemical characteristics of a person is called Biometrics. It originates from two words bios (means life) and metron (means measure). The biometrics is mostly used for employing the identity management in wide-ranging situations in which precise individual identification is fundamental.

Some of the biometric applications are employed in situations where the networks are being shared between the users, in electronically business deals (such as e-shopping and ATM stations) and in any other commercial transactions.

The identity identification may be essential for a variety of factors though the major goal, in most programs, will be to avert invaders from penetrating to the covered property. Three ways of creating a person's identity comprise the following mechanism:

- What you know (for example. Knowledge-based Passwords)
- What you have (for example. Token-based ID cards)
- What you are (for example. Biometrics such as fingerprint)

The security of an infrastructure can be easily threatened by the first two above mentioned mechanisms. By "What you are" it is meant a pure and unfailing key to particular characteristics of identity identification and management by using computerized schemes to be recognized by biological features (Jain, et al., 2004). Also, there are several attacks that can be applied to the traditional authentication forms which offend the effectiveness of these systems to be recognized as compromised (O'Gorman, 2003). Although some of these attacks can be prevented by using security defense software, it is impossible to overcome all problems by using tokens and passwords.

By employing biometric properties in a system, non-repudiation security property can be guaranteed (a kind of original person identification) (Poh & Bengio, 2005). Non-repudiation makes the assurance of not refusing after a person has accessed the resource in a computer. Various properties such as fingerprint, iris, hand geometry, retina scan, hand vein, ear geometry, DNA data, signature/signature motion, gait, voice waves, retina, and palm print can be offered by using the biometrics systems (Jain, Bolle, & Pankanti, 2005; Wayman, Jain, Maltoni, & Maio, 2005). With some limits that are accompanied by biometrics systems (O'Gorman, 2002), there are more advantages over the non-biometric-based authentication systems. The biometric properties are included in person and are credible for who always are unable to remember their multiple passwords.

The properties listed in Table 2 are considered to be chosen as a biometric property for individual authentication and verification (Jain, et al., 2005; Molle, Connell, Pankanti, Ratha, & Senior, 2003). Choosing one or more of listed properties are essential in identity verification:

- **Universality:** The property should be included in everybody.
- **Uniqueness:** The property has to be specific to anybody.
- **Permanence:** The property must remain unchanged through individual's lifetime.
- **Collectable:** The property should be easy to measure and be gathered by a sensor.
- **Performance:** The property should match required FAR and FRR during design and test process.
- **Acceptability:** All parties should accept to present their biometric property in all conditions including the religious issues.
- **Circumvention:** The easiness ratio in fooling the designed system

Depending on absence of one or more properties mentioned in the Table 2 biometrics identifier can not be employed to be used in a verification/authentication biometric system. An individual is identified by a biometric system through a process that includes two stages: The first stage is to enroll the individual in the biometric system by collecting data from user's biometric properties. After, data will be processed by image processing algorithms to extract features from this data. The extracted features are called Templates which will be securely stored in a database to finish the enrolling process.

In second stage, biometric system will get user's biometric for authentication or identification. This is called the verification stage. The gained data is processed to extract user's biometric features. Then, extracted features are compared to all stored

Table 2. A comparison of properties of biometric identifiers (high=H, medium=M, low=L)

Biometrics	Face	Fingerprint	Iris & Retina Scan	Signature	Voice	Vein	DNA
Universality	H	M	H	L	M	M	H
Uniqueness	L	H	H	L	L	M	H
Permanence	M	H	H	L	L	M	H
Collectable	H	M	M	H	M	M	L
Performance	L	H	H	L	L	M	H
Acceptability	L	M	L	H	H	M	L
Circumvention	H	H	H	L	L	H	L

Templates in the database to make a decision on accepting or rejecting the user based on a defined threshold.

So it is obvious that a biometric system response is performing such a non-linear system whose response is not a 1/0 output for identification/verification process; because the presented user property is a color/black and white image. The produced Temples cab affected according to various environments once it is being taken from the sensor; the biometric systems performance can be assessed according to FRR (False Rejection Ratio) and FAR (False Acceptance Ratio).

From the FRR and FAR matching score and frequency portions with the threshold portion, it can be determined that a less shaded conceptual map will be resulted in to a better performance system on accepting and rejecting right and wrong persons which is a must in the fingerprint email system.

History of Fingerprints

Ridges and valleys are main components of a fingerprint pattern (Jain, Maltoni, Maio, & Prabhakar, 2003). Fingerprint is a unique property of every individual even for twins (Jain, Prabhakar, & Pankanti, 2001). The DNA genetic acts like a computer program to shape skin and fingerprint in an unborn baby. After the baby is born, his fingerprints will be fully grown and will not be changed unless an accident takes place (Babler, 1991). If a fingerprint is destroyed, there are ways to reconstruct it by using nano silvers to stimulate the remained active stem cells. This is reported in six case reports for developing the foot, fingers and face skins (Pramod, 2010).

The development on fingerprint identification systems was vastly increased that makes it to be used in global parties to identify a person by using a criminal database (Lee & Gaensslen, 2001). For the first time, the FBI constructed his fingerprint database from some fingerprint samples in which several fingerprint identification algorithms were employed to get, classify and match fingerprints (FBI, 1991).

Fingerprints have been used for years in criminal investigation work. What is new is the ability to read and compare fingerprints using electronic equipment. This makes them ideal for biometrics.

Soon, the FBI started to improve the AFIS (Automatic Fingerprint Identification Systems). Because of rapid improvements in AFIS system, it is now suitable in forensics applications (FBI, 1991). Nowadays, using fingerprint technology in many applications is increasing as recognition performance of these systems is good and cost effective.

Fingerprint Feature Extraction

Once a fingerprint image (with terminations or bifurcations) is digitally acquired, fingerprint pattern can be studied according to image analysis techniques. The existing noises will be removed from fingerprint ROI (region of interests) to classify them based on pixel, minutia and singularities. Singularities can be divided into three parts as loop, delta and whorl. The minutia (called Galton's characteristics) (Galton, 1892; Mohsen, Zamshed, & Hashem, 2004) is formed by various ways of ridges. Termination is shaped when ridges are focused to an end and Bifurcation is formed if ridges are extracted from one point. Achieving a high accuracy is a final aim in computerized classifying various mentioned types of minutiae.

In a desired fingerprint feature extraction after the fingerprint image is obtained from the fingerprint sensor, there are noises and some in-complete ridges which needs to get improved (Bansal, Sehgal, & Bedi, 2010). For improving obtained image, mean of gradient estimations is calculated in recent studies (Bazen & Gerez, 2002; Donahue & Rokhlin, 1993; Ratha, Chen, & Jain, 1995).

The local orientation, local frequency (Alonso-Fernandez, Fierrez-Aguilar, & Ortega-Garcia, 2005) and segmentation are applied to the obtained input image to improve and enhance the image. The segmentation process will separate the background and fingerprint. In this stage, thresholding is not useful as the fingerprint pattern is complicated and cannot be separated in to two regions. Some of the good segmentation algorithms for this problem are mentioned in (Mosorov, 2001; Shen, Kot, & Koo, 2001; Teddy & Lockheed, 2002). The next step is detecting fingerprint singularities to extract the loop, delta, whorl, and core region of the images.

Although one of the perfect algorithms used in this era is based on continuous fingerprint index (Msiza, Leke-Betechuoh, Nelwamondo, & Msimang, 2009), there are still some other options for detecting the image singularity (Babler, 1991; Bansal, et al., 2010).

The fingerprint image quality is an important factor in extracting minutia which affects fingerprint recognition performance. So it is essential to apply an enhancement algorithm such as Hong's algorithm and contextual filters (Alonso-Fernandez, et al., 2005; Hong, Wan, & Jain, 1998) to improve the fingerprint image quality which will improve the clarity of ridges.

The last stage is related to minutia extraction. In this stage, the grey scale image needs to be converted in to (0,1) binary image (black and white). The width of one pixel is resulted after thinning process is applied. After all, the minutia can be extracted according to the termination and bifurcation ridge types easily.

Fingerprint Identification

Fingerprint identification is a method of person identification based on the features extracted from the person's fingerprint image. There are several methods proposed for identifying a person's fingerprint. These methods can be classified as minutiae matching (Rokbani & Alimi, 2005), spectrum matching (Teddy & Lockheed, 2002; Xu, et al., 2009), and template matching (Ismail & Schnabel, 2004).

While a fingerprint sample is matched to its corresponding features stored as template in a dataset, the fingerprint will be identified. There is no difficulty on identifying the high quality fingerprint images with the existing methods; the only problem is on the low quality fingerprints which are hard to identify. Various errors can arise from feature extracting, image noises, finger movement, pressure ratio are the point of identification failure to the fingerprint identification systems such as FVC2002 (Maio, Maltoni, Cappelli, Wayman, & Jain, 2002). Some rotated fingers may have the same imprints of the other person's fingerprints and consequently the wrong user will be accepted as a legitimate person or vice versa. A legitimate user can also easily be rejected.

A minutia matching method, a widely used technique, was proposed to overcome the problems related to the non-linear fingerprint deformities by using thin plate splines which also performs better than other algorithms (Bazen & Gerez, 2002a, 2002b). In this method, $m = \{x, y, \theta\}$ is a representation for extracted fingerprint minutiae (where (x,y) shows pixel position and θ I direction of minutia) which is stored as a two-dimensional template in the biometric database (Jain, et al., 2003). Some researchers have proposed successful and different minutia matching algorithms based on local minutia arrangements (Chen, Tian, Yang, & Zhang, 2006; Jiang & Yau, 2000; Ratha, Pandit, Bolle, & Vaish, 2000). Though transform based methods are used for global minutia arrangements in which rotation of the minutia is not an important problem (Chang, Cheng, Hsu, & Wu, 1997; Ratha, Karu, Chen, & Jain, 1996).

Extracting minutia from the low quality image is troublesome and time consuming. Also for reaching high performance and accuracy, extra features should be added along with the minutiae features.

A ridge-based method (Jain, Prabhakar, Hong, & Pankanti, 2000) was proposed to find the centre point as a reference point, and then divides the image in sectors like a mosaic. In the next step, sectors are normalized and Gabor filtering is applied to them in eight distinctive directions. Then, Average Absolute Deviation of grey values (A.A.D) feature of mean images is computed. Finally, FingerCode is calculated by Euclidian distance among two FignerCodes (template and input FingerCodes) compared against a matching threshold (Jain, et al., 2000) in order to identify the fingerprints.

Fake Finger Problems

The fingerprint identification systems are known to have a good performance and accuracy. From the security perspective, it has been reported that these systems are vulnerable to artificial fingers at the input fingerprint acquisition device. Some kind of artificial fingerprints such as gummy fingers and liquid silicone rubber fingers and other materials are reported which are recognized as live fingers (Matsumoto, Matsumoto, Yamada, & Hoshino, 2002). The artificial fingers can be made from either a plastic mold or residual fingerprints. From the images of a live finger and the cloned fingers of the same live finger, it is shown that they all are almost the same.

The average acceptance ratio of these gummy fingers is reported 68%-100%. In some fingerprint devices silicone fingers are not accepted. This value will be more than 67% of acceptance ratio while cloning from the residual fingerprint (Matsumoto, et al., 2002).

Live Finger Detection

To protect against spoofing, the vitality detection of fingerprints is essential. Some novel approaches can differentiate between live and artificial fingers from each other (Cappelli, 2003; Endo & Matsumoto, 2002; Matsumoto, 2001; Schuckers, Hornak, Norman, Derakhshani, & Parthasaradhi, 2002). For a device to determine the liveness characteristics, it is enough to work on fingertip features. The outstanding features for liveness detection are based on finger's skin distortion and pores properties, temporal features (Endo & Matsumoto, 2002; Matsumoto, 2001), and some static feature analysis (Cappelli, 2003).

Using the finger presenting to a fingerprint sensor system in special orders is also a new cost-effective method (Prabhakar, Pankanti, & Jain, 2003). In this case, system security will be enhanced as it is infeasible to guess which fingerprints has been presented and the order is also unknown!

Another method for liveness detection is to analyze the image noises which are integrated with valleys. The accuracy detection of 90.9% - 100% is resulted by some fingerprint sensors including optical, electro optical, and capacitated DC fingerprint acquiring devices (Tan & Schuckers, 2008).

The fingertip papillary lines can be processed for both fine movements and calculating the distance of the fingertip surface from the sensor (Drahansky & Lodrova, 2008). In this optical implementation, there is no need for finger contact and it is cost-effective to add it to a fingerprint sensor for liveness detecting.

There are two optical –based methods for measuring the fingertip movements (Drahansky, Funk, & Nötzel, 2006). The first one is using a CCD camera system and the next one is using a laser beam system.

The original idea in the CCD camera system (Drahansky & Lodrova, 2008) is to make a 6mm hole on the glass, so at the fingerprint acquiring image phase, the whole image of the fingerprint will be stored. In this phase, the system is acting as a normal fingerprint acquiring device. Then, the liveness of the finger will be analyzed by using a second CCD camera by rotating the semi-permeable mirror to reflect the image to the macro lens of the CCD camera. The sequences of video will be created from these two images to detect liveness of the finger. The main aspect of this method is to find out the volume changes in finger papillary lines generated by heartbeats and make a 4.5 micro meter fine movement differentiation.

In the laser based system (Drahansky & Lodrova, 2008), the fingerprint acquiring image is the same as the camera based system. The only difference is on using the laser module for measuring fine movements according to heartbeat movements. The laser module is able to discover the movements at the micrometer scale. Once the finger is situated fixed on the glass, there is no movements, so fingerprint aliveness cannot be detected. If enough attention is given to this drawback, laser system can be used efficiently for aliveness detection of fingers.

FINGERPRINT-BASED EMAIL SECURITY MODEL

Most email messages are sent without any additional message encryption. The sender will send a message through internet via Sender's SMTP server which will be later passed to the recipient via recipient's POP/IMAP server. Although encryption is not added, the opportunity of identity spoofing, unauthorized message modification or interception is still possible.

Once a sender wants to send an encrypted message to an intended recipient, the sender should recognize whether the recipient has the reliable decryption tools or not; after that, he will get his public key K_R^{Public} corresponding to his private key $K_R^{Private}$. Then, sender should load recipient's public key K_R^{Public} in the mail client and produce his own private/public key pairs $K_S^{Public}, K_S^{Private}$ for signing purpose. Finally, signed text $C_1 = S_{K_S^{Private}}(M_1)$ will be encrypted by recipient's public key K_R^{Public} to form ciphertext $C_2 = E_{K_R^{Public}}(C_1)$ to be sent to the recipient. The recipient will decrypt the received message by his private key and verify sender's signature by his verification tool and sender's public key to reveal the message.

To make users comfortable in sending and receiving emails securely, a confidential secure system was proposed in 2003 named Stream which does all actions transparently (Matsumoto, et al., 2002). This system extracts sender's email address and creates public and private key pair if there is none. It adds a copy of public key to message header, checks for the existence of recipient's public key. Then, it encapsulates original mail's header within the message. For encapsulating header, a key fingerprint will be produced for any recipient's public key. After all, the whole message is encrypted by recipient's public key and is sent through SMTP server. Although this is an appealing scenario for users, Stream is vulnerable to man-in-the-middle attack, as it does not use any digital signature scheme. The recipient will never differentiate the real data sender whether he is an adversary or intended sender.

Another system, Enigma, was proposed in 1999 which was based on a proxy approach to add security to email. In this system, the client agent is interacting with enigma proxy that consists of "Encryptor / Signer" (interacts with SMTP Server) and "Decryptor / Verifier" (interacts with POP3 Server). The first part uses a local public key database to find recipient's public key for encryption and signs the message by sender's private key (which is kept in Enigma) (Endo & Matsumoto, 2002). Once the decryption and verification is done on the recipient part, message can be viewed. This secure model also lacks the property of identifying original sender and receiver.

Model Design

Though various securing email models were proposed by encrypting and signing messages, all of them are lacking the assurance of real message sender and receiver to defend spoofing and spamming attacks. According to proposed models, employing cryptography algorithms were prosperous in their applications which make it easy to be used by users, as all of the cryptographic processes are computed without user awareness. A new approach model is proposed to enhance email security property by acquiring user's fingerprint image for identifying them along with signing and verifying messages. In this model, user's fingerprint image is acquired for enrolling process. This image will be stored in a database in which the unique properties of users are kept. Finally, fingerprint image with corresponding unique user properties (such as first name, last name, personal picture, mail account and password, identification number) are used to identify which user has sent or received email messages. This approach can be implemented as an application to be responsible and interacted with all of relating parts shown in Figure 1.

The application details and components can be described as following sections.

SSL Connection for Servers (Mail/Database)

In this model, several types of mail servers which support POP3 and SMTP services can be used. A simple mail server based on Microsoft windows 2003 server can be installed for this purpose, if any SSL connections are needed; a web based mail system such as gmail.com can also be used. The Microsoft windows 2003 server includes POP3 and SMTP services as its built-in services. Gmail server is used because its POP3 and SMTP ports are freely open which provide SSL connection and 2-way authentication for resisting attacks mentioned in next sections.

Figure 1. Secure email endpoints model

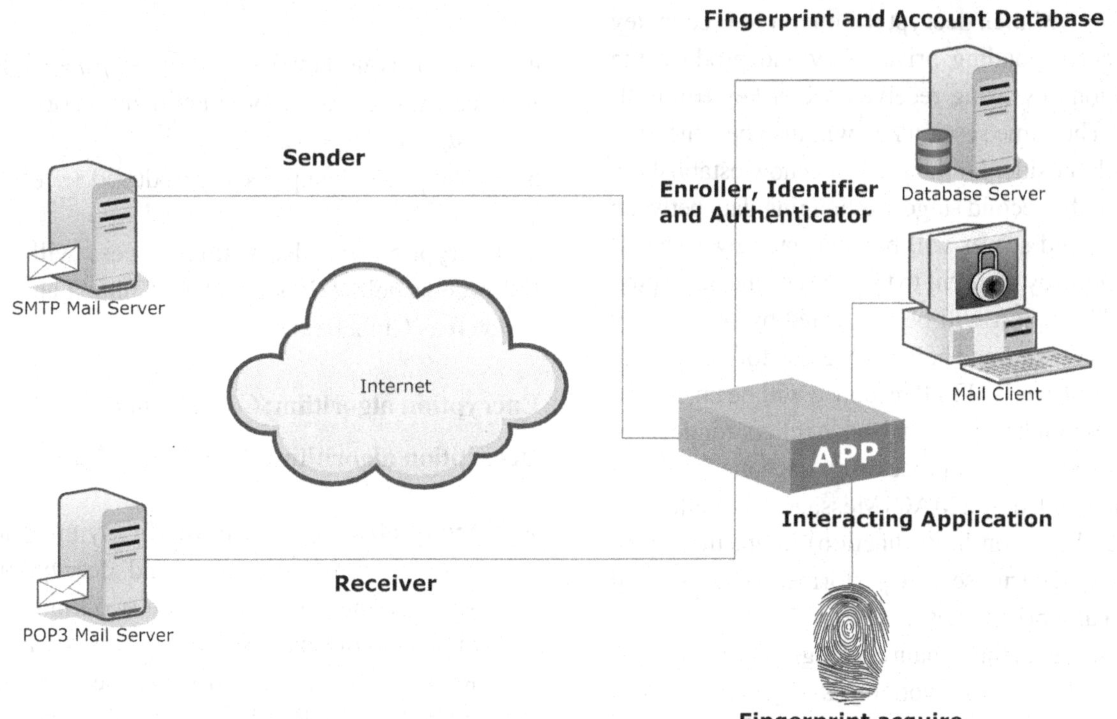

For setting up a secure communication channel between clients and servers, privacy, integrity and authentication security services should be provided. By providing privacy, it is ensured that no third parties can access and view the data exchange between two systems. By providing integrity, it is ensured that exchanged data has not been modified or altered by attackers through transmission channel. And by providing authentication, one can be sure about the end systems (not end users) are the ones who they claim they are. In Figure 2, SSL handshake protocol sequence diagram is illustrated which exchanges message in two stages: (1) session negotiation stage (handshake) and (2) bulk data transfer stage. In the first stage, client sends a connection session request message which will be responded a SSL certificate including server's public key and other cipher suit (i.e. session id, secret keys for bulk data transfer) by mail/ database server. The server's certificate will be validated by third party CA validator, which makes the client produce secret key and send encrypted secret key using server's public key to the server. The server will then decrypt the encrypted secret key by corresponding private key and produce the session key using received secret key from client. The same session key will also be generated on client side. So the session is now established.

In the second stage, exchanging data between client and server will be encrypted by a shared session key and sent to the server. The encrypted HTTP request will be decrypted by session key on server side and being processed for a response. Then, server's HTTP response will be encrypted by session key and sent back to client for decryption and response processing. Each message will be appended by a MAC (Message Authentication Code based on hash function) to ensure the integrity security service performed on transferred data and private keys.

SSL uses three main cryptographic operations as public key encryption (RSA [Menezes, Van Oorschot, & Vanstone, 1996; Ruby, Zhijie, & Xiao, 2001], Diffie Hellman [Diffie & Hellman, 1976]), symmetric encryption based on session key (AES [NIST, 2001], 3DES, DES, RC4 [Menezes, et al., 1996; Ruby, et al., 2001]), and one-way hash functions (MD5 [Menezes, et al., 1996; Ruby, et al., 2001], SHA-1 [NIST, 2002]).

For the proposed fingerprint secure email model, following widely used cryptography algorithms are used that their basic ideas will be introduced and discussed.

- **Asymmetric Encryption:** The RSA cryptosystem, the most widely used cryptographic algorithm, is used to provide digital signature. Its security is based on factoring a number to two prime numbers. Key generation steps are as follows:

1. Two large random distinct prime numbers p, q are generated
2. $n = p.q$ and $\varphi = (p-1)(q-1)$ are computed.
3. A random integer number $1 < e < (p-1)(q-1)$ is chosen such that e and φ don't have prime numbers in common.
4. The Private key $1 < d < (p-1)(q-1)$ is calculated based on Euclidian algorithm $ed \equiv 1 \pmod{\varphi}$
5. The public key pairs are produced (n, e)

Encryption and decryption process will be followed as below (P denoted as Plaintext and C denoted as Ciphertext):

Encryption algorithm: $C = P^e \bmod n$

Decryption algorithm: $P = C^d \bmod n$

- **Symmetric Encryption:** In symmetric cryptosystem, encryption and decryption keys are the same. There are two kinds of ciphers in this part. Stream ciphers (such as RC4) in which encryption is based on one bit or byte XORed by a randomly generated Initialization Value (IV). Block ciphers

Figure 2. A sequence diagram for SSL handshake protocol

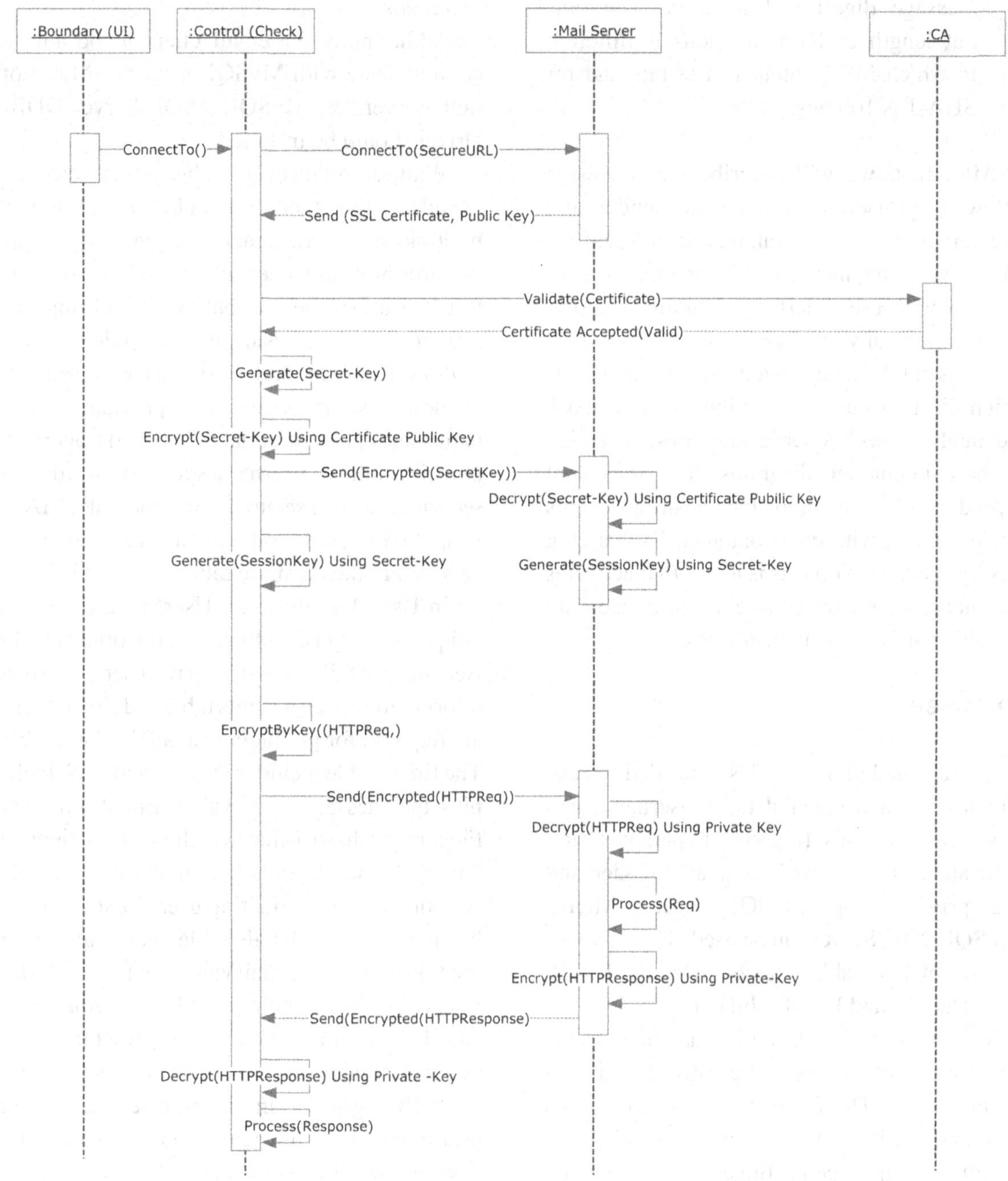

(AES, 3DES/DES) in which encryption is based on blocks of data using methods such as diffusion, substitution and transposition. RC4 algorithm is a default cipher used in SSL connection for encryption or decryption purposes for both servers.

- **Hash Functions:** In SSL connection channel MD5 (calculation of finish messages in first stage (handshake)) and SHA-1 (MAC calculations) hash functions are used for message digest and integrity. The output length of hash functions is different in which MD5 output is 128 bits and for SHA-1 is 160 bits.

After that, we will describe the processes followed by user to authenticate sender and receiver to each other, sending/signing and receiving/verifying messages, that is, how the user interacts with user interface of future windows system. Generally, we have to model each task by means of UML specialized sequence diagrams which illustrates user interactions with database and mail servers sequence diagrams, so called database interaction diagrams. It is important to produce these diagrams for transitions/events which interact with data container. Exchanging messages between objects is a task that activates a sequence of messages to consult/update data containers using transitions/events.

Database

A database including 4 tables is needed to save person's email account details (username and password), person's fingerprint, person's first name and last name, hash of email message and fingerprint. A simple MySQL server or Microsoft SQL 2000 Server can be used. The database consists of four tables: AccountDetails, Email, User_Details, and EmailValidator.

The AccountDetails table has three fields including username, hash of password, and hash of fingerprint. The Email table has five fields including email from, email to, EmailCode, and hash of email message and fingerprint. EmailCode is a unique code assigned for emails used for making relationship between tables. The User_Details table has four fields including first name, last name, personal image, and hash of fingerprint (as a primary key). The required database tables for this purpose are shown in Figure 3. The forth table is just for creating relationship transparently between User_Details and Email tables by using two fields.

Additionally for email client to be able to communicate with MySQL server or Microsoft SQL server, the MySQL / SQL Server ODBC Driver should be installed.

While enrolling users to the system, Account_Details table is there to enable users to provide multiple username email accounts with same fingerprint hash values while it will be possible to use a username and password with multiple fingerprints. As a result, it is possible to assign multiple username and password hashes to a user. So the user is being registered by providing his first name, last name, personal image, and fingerprint plus his multiple usernames and passwords. For security reasons, secure Hash function (SHA-2) is applied to password and fingerprint that will be saved in the database tables.

In User_Details table, UserName is set as a unique primary key which is in relationship with Account_Details table to derive user's personal information. User_Details table and Email tables are required for producing EmailValidator table. The Email table includes "From" and "To" Fields plus the message hash value, EmailCode, and Fingerprint hash value which is in relationship with both User_Details and EmailValidator table. Additionally, for extracting user's first name and last name, User_Details table should also be in relationship with EmailValidator table as well. Users can check their provided information in enrolling program whenever they want to be sure that their fingerprint and personal details are successfully registered in database server. While a user provides his username and password to the system according to Account_Details table, user will be authenticated to system by providing his fingerprint according to User_Details table. If the user is authenticated, he will be allowed to continue and according to his actions (sending or receiving the message), the application will ask for acquiring his fingerprint. The application will show error messages if:

Figure 3. The relationships of AccountDetails, EMail, EMailValidator, and User_Details tables

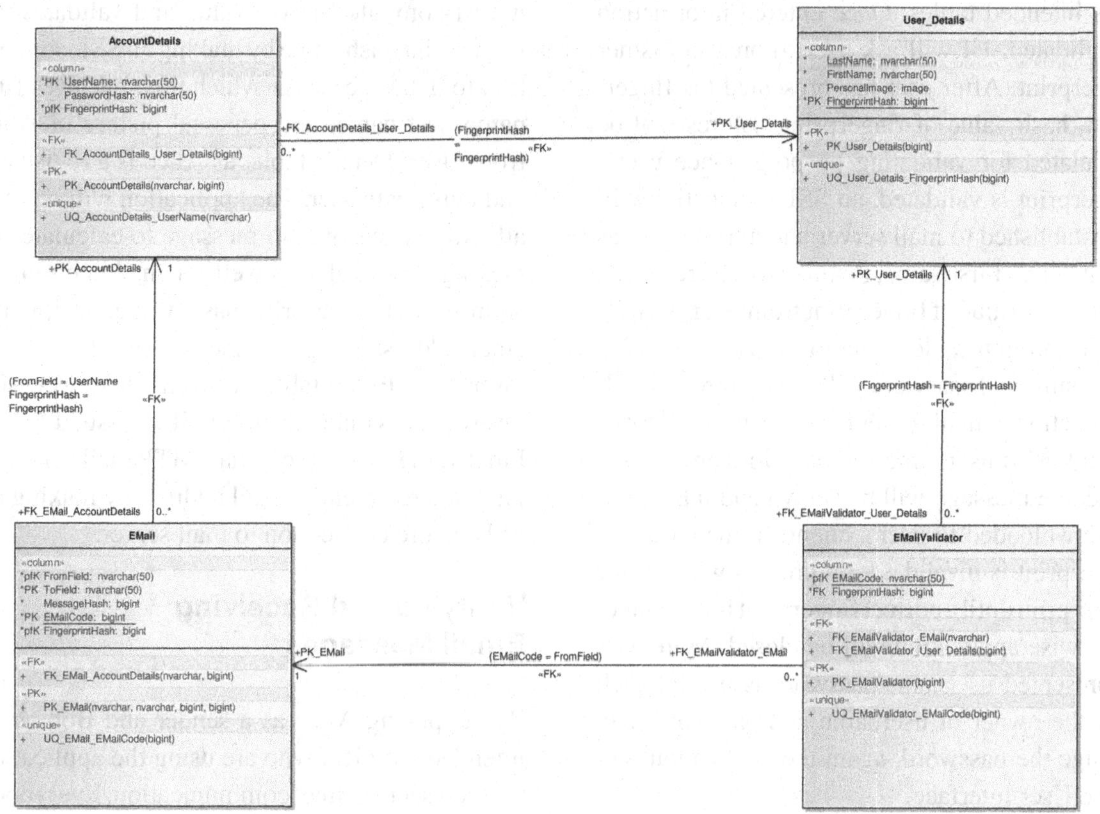

- The user tries to register a First Name and Last Name with another fingerprint
- The provided fingerprint by user is not recognized by application

In login process, a Two-Factor Authentication (TFA) is used including both a knowledge-based (password) and a biometric-based (user fingerprint). Security of this application is based on presenting both username/password and user's fingerprint. Once the user presents his username and password to application, the application will connect to POP3 and SMTP mail servers by using provided username and password. For this purpose, application should have special codes based on email RFC documents to be able to talk and communicate with POP3 and SMTP mail servers. If any errors occurred in POP3 and SMTP mail servers' communications, application will stop functioning by popping up an error dialog box message. As soon as user's singing process is done successfully, application will derive inbox contents to email client. In the next sections, sending/signing process and receiving/ verifying email messages is described in details.

Sending Email Messages

In sending email message process, according to illustrated sequence diagrams (Figure 4 and Finger 5) for authenticating and sending processes, when the user starts to sign in to his/her mailbox using the application, a login request will be issued to User Interface (UI), UI will show a login window box which asks the user to enter his/her username and password. UI will calculate hash value of password and validates entered information by making an SSL connection (using SSL sequence diagram i.e. Figure 4.) to database server to access intended tables. Once entered information is validated, UI will ask user to present his/her fingerprint. After user has presented his fingerprint, hash value of fingerprint features will be calculated for validating purpose. Once user's fingerprint is validated, an SSL connection will be established to mail server and a triple data as (LastName, FirstName, Picture) will be retrieved using hash value of fingerprint from User_Details Table through table's relationships (Figure 2.). Username and password will be sent through SSL connection to mail server for validation and loading inbox. If username and password are valid, a welcome message will be shown and inbox will be downloaded to user's client. In the case that fingerprint is invalid a loop process will ask for fingerprint until a correct fingerprint is presented; otherwise application will be closed. Moreover, if presented username/password is invalid such that the owner of username and password may change the password, again the application will close User Interface.

The next sequence diagram illustrated in Figure 5 is used for message sending process. After the user is signed in and is successfully authenticated by application, sender (namely Alice) is trying to send an email message via the application. Alice's message is ready to be sent by clicking on send button. So, message sending is issued by sender. Then, application will pop up a dialog box which asks for presenting Alice's fingerprint to application. Alice needs to present fingerprint every time for signing, sending, and receiving a message. This is for providing integrity and data origin authentication of real email sender. In some cases, the email address that the sender is using may not belong to sender. If everyone on Internet network who is using this application integrated to his mail client sends and receives email messages through this application, it makes an assurance that received message is from a person who is the real email sender or receiver to provide a robust non-repudiation security property.

After the application gets Alice's fingerprint, it will compute SHA-2 value and validates the fingerprint hash value by making an SSL connection to database server which then retrieves first name, last name, and personal picture of Alice from User_Details table, as Alice is a registered and legitimate user. The application will remove all extra spaces within message to calculate the message hash value as well. Then, Alice's email address and fingerprint hash value, recipient's email address along with message hash value, are inserted to Email table, respectively. Successful insert process notification will be issued to UI. Finally, message is sent via SMTP mail server to intended recipient's email address by making an SSL secure connection to mail server.

Verifying and Receiving Email Messages

By supposing Alice as a sender and Bob as an intended recipient who are using the application for their secure email communication. Everybody who is using this application for sending email messages is a legal user known to this application whose fingerprints are stored in database server. The signing process is done by calculating message hash value and identifying the user is done by fingerprint hash value stored in database server. Once Bob successfully signs in and authenticates himself to the application according to Figure 4, the inbox can be viewed by a successful or failure status message box. At this stage as illustrated in Figure 6, verification process, identification process and receipt acknowledgment will be invoked.

In verification process which is performed transparently to ease user's interactions, message will be verified when a request for reading message is invoked. The application downloads email message to email client by negotiating with POP3 mail server by syntaxes described in POP3 RFC documents through an SSL connection to mail server. Then, email addresses located in "From" and "To" are derived from the whole email mes-

Figure 4. A sequence diagram for sender / receiver authentication (identification) to each other

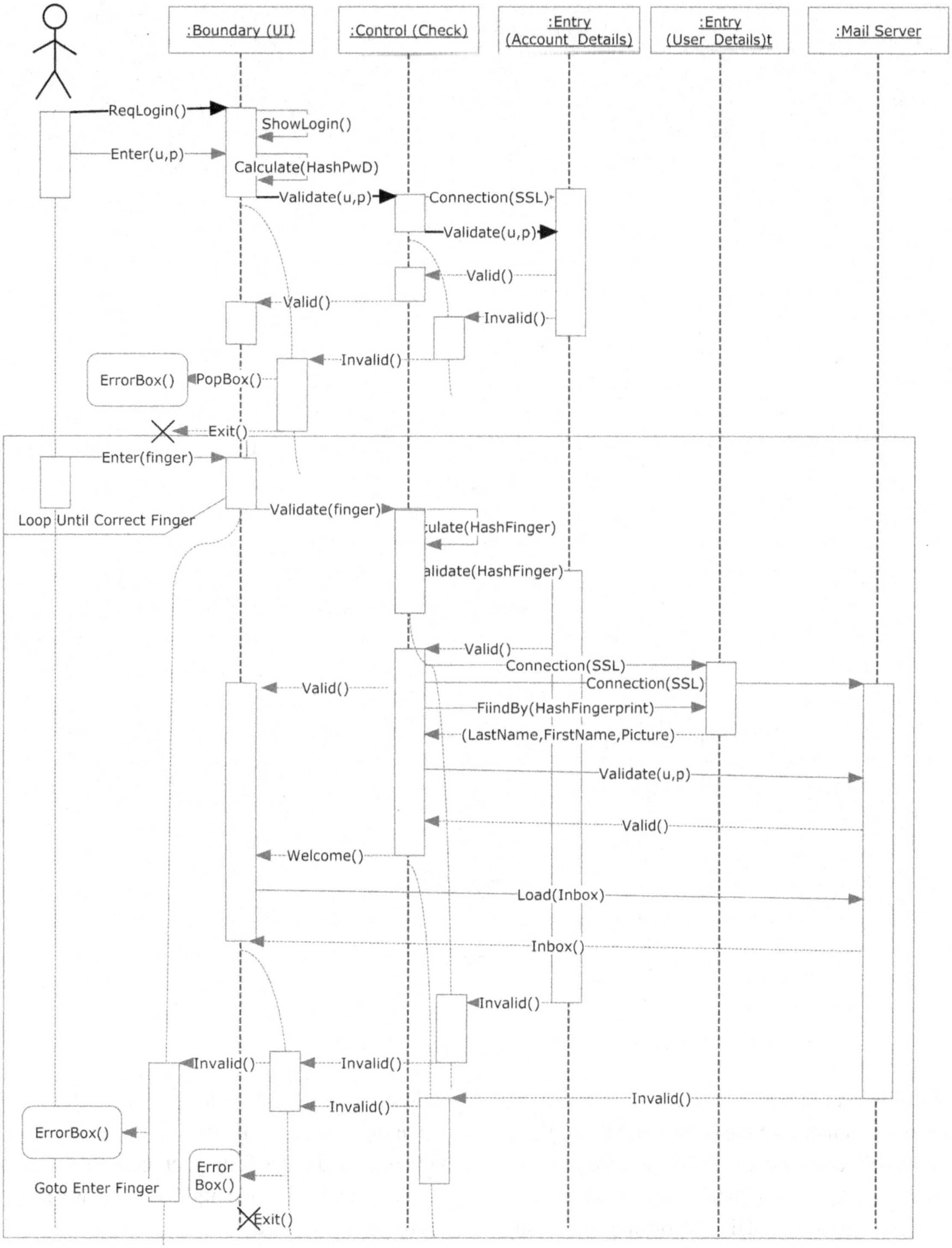

Figure 5. A sequence diagram for sending email message

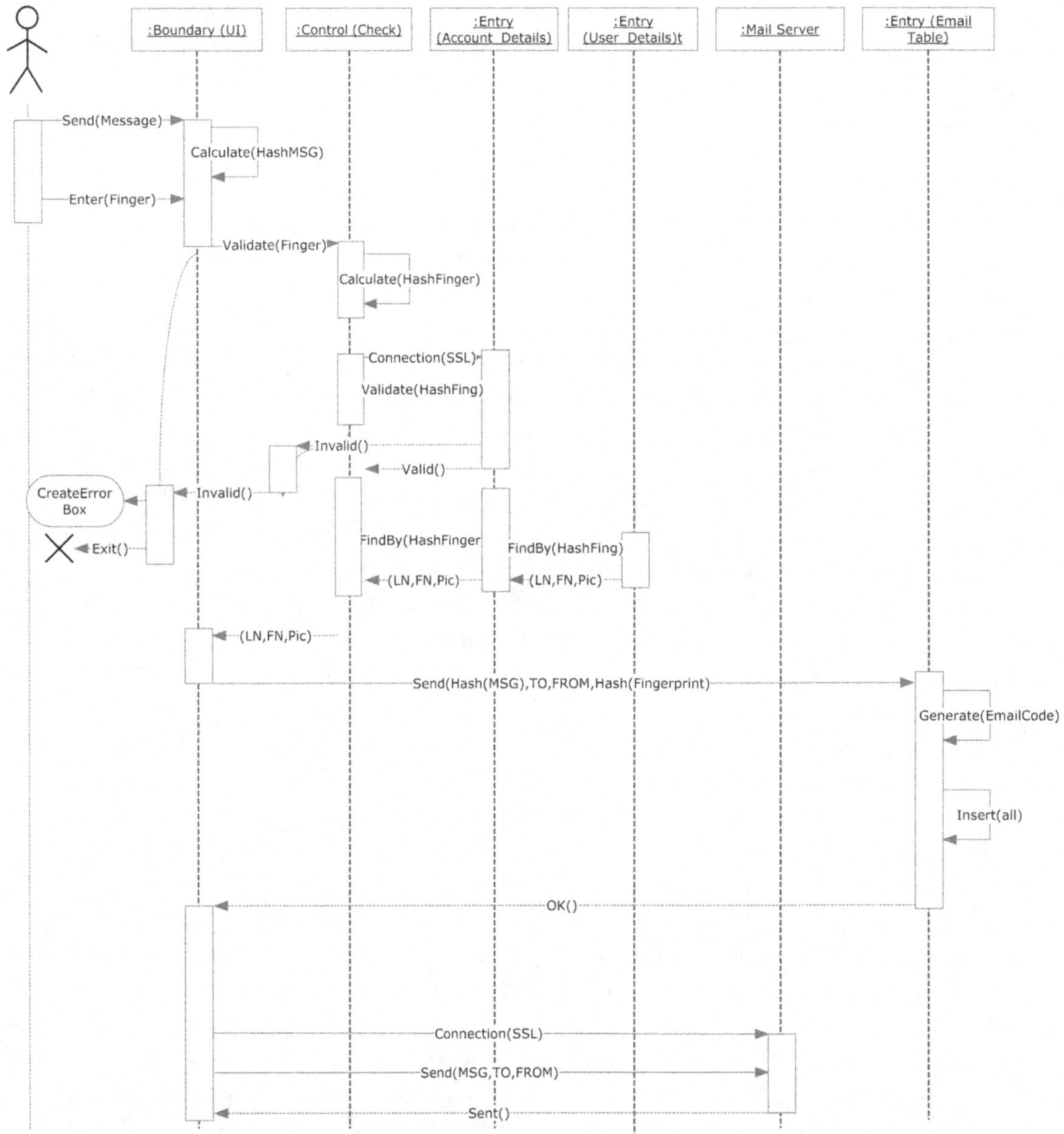

sage fields. By removing all spaces, message hash value is calculated by SHA-2 hash function. Then a secure SSL connection will be made to database server from Control (Check) object which has interconnection with UI. According to Email table, message hash value is checked which corresponds to intended "From" and "To" fields. If hash values are equal, then verification process is successful; otherwise it will turn to "verification failure" status. As there are no entries for hashed value of message in the Email table, application will regard it as a forged or non-authenticated message and will pop up with the warning as verification is failed.

In identification process that its purpose is based on real person identification according to his/her fingerprints and corresponding personal details, after the message is verified as successful;

Figure 6. A sequence diagram for receiving and verifying email message

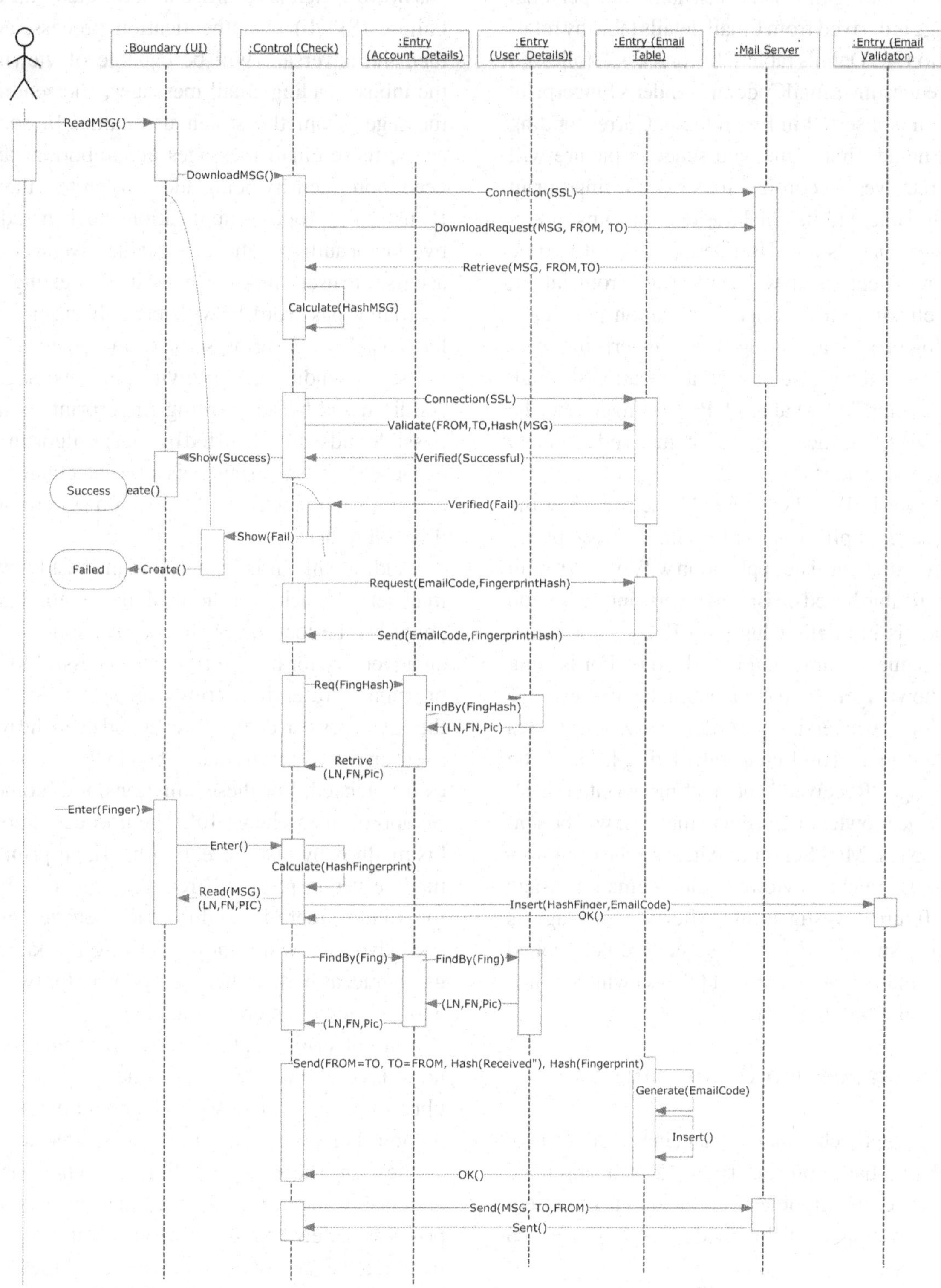

corresponding first name, last name, and personal image is derived from Email details table by relating to UserDetails table. This process is followed by requesting EmailCode and sender's Fingerprint which is inserted in Email table. Corresponding last name, first name, and sender's picture will be retrieved according to sender's fingerprint hash value and its database relationships in Accounts_Details and UserDetails. Now it is time for recipient to view his message from inbox. By clicking on message, application pops up a dialog box for acquiring Bob's fingerprint; after Bob is authenticated to the application through calculating hash value of Bob's fingerprint, he can view the message, real name, and personal image of sender.

Once Bob authenticates himself to view the message, application will produce a receipt acknowledgment. The application will insert a row in Email table based on Bob's fingerprint hash value which is in relationship with Bob's First name, last name, picture, and Email Code. For issuing acknowledgement receipt email, the process will be done by reversing the order of email addresses in "From", "To" fields, calculating hash of the message "Received" and his fingerprint. The receipt acknowledgment email message will be sent via SMTP Mail Server to Alice, so she can know who has read and viewed Alice's email message for future investigations. After the message is sent, a successful sent message will be invoked from mail server to control (check) which is also transparent to the user.

Advantages and Disadvantages

A new approach towards enhancing email security endpoint based on fingerprint identification and SHA-2 cryptographic hash function is proposed. The advantages of this model can be described as below.

Previously and recently, user authentication was performed by presenting a username and a password. So a bad guy can guess or steal the password which is regarded as a Single Point Of Failure (SPOF) in authentication process, and then the adversary will be capable of viewing the inbox, reading email messages, and sending messages from the stolen username. In some cases, these email messages are important and need more security being added to protect them. By using the proposed application which includes two-factor authentication, even if the adversary get accessed to user's inbox by guessing or stealing the username/ password, he will not be able to present legal user's fingerprint; so he cannot view email messages, sending, and receiving email messages. As discussed before, forging fingerprints is not possible and can be detected by special algorithms because liveness of fingers is also detectable. As a result, the biometric authentication systems are difficult to hack.

Additionally, it is known that in most known mail servers such as Yahoo! Mails, an email account can be locked for almost twelve hours by an adversary for his multiple unsuccessful login or trying to reset the victim's account password; the adversary can do this forever and even the real user can not access his mail inbox in this occasion as it is locked. For these situations, the biometric approach can be useful. The user can unlock his mailbox by just presenting his fingerprint to mail server in password recovery process. But for Yahoo!, there is no difference between user and adversary while they are using the known username, as both of them should wait for twelve hours to unlock intended email account.

One of critical attacks which are increased nowadays is email spoofing. The proposed application does not let users send email messages without being successfully authenticated to the application. The track of sending/ receiving emails and hash value of the sent messages and fingerprints are safely kept in database server. If in this matter, adversary tries to send an email message from a forged email address, the application will search for the forged email address with its corresponding hashed message in the Email table. If message hash value is not found, an error message will be popped up.

By taking advantage of cryptographic hash functions (SHA-2) for signing and verifying email messages and hashing fingerprints, expensive computations of signing and verifying using public key cryptographic techniques is not essential anymore.

The man-in-the-middle-attack can also be prevented by using the proposed fingerprint identification model. Recalling from previous sections, after Alice has sent a legitimate email message to Bob by providing his fingerprint to the application. Bob will try to view his inbox to view Alice's email message via POP3 mail server. If an adversary has changed the message contents by intercepting the proposed application, then application will download adversary's modified message from POP3 mail server, and calculates hash value of message by SHA-2 function. This hash value will be different in comparison with hash value inserted in Email table. As one of the important properties of hash functions (one-way function) is that it is impossible to find a and b in a way that Hash(a)=Hash(b).

So the adversary's modified message will have a different hash value. As a result, the hash value will not match with the one in Email table and verification process will be failed. So the recipient will know that the message has been altered in transmission path.

Spam emails are unwanted emails sent by unknown parties in order to make a fraudulent, scam, phishing by malicious codes, Trojan, and worms that may result in a denial of service attack. As a matter of fact, tracking spammers and defeating spam emails is a hard task for antivirus and anti spam software. From years ago, researchers are working to stop spammers from sending spam emails, up to now it is known there is no means that can be used to stop these spam emails and being sure about the origin of sender being a human. By using the proposed application, senders of email messages are surely humans and other emails which are not authenticated by the application can be stopped and deleted. This means that the spam emails can be identified, filtered, and deleted easily.

Liao's 10 requirements (Liao, Lee, & Hwang, 2006) provided a criterion for the robust remote authentication scheme. The details are as follows:

R1: The passwords or verification tables are not stored within the computer.

The hash value of passwords is stored in database server which is not within the user's client computer so R1 is provided.

R2: The password can be chosen and freely changed by the owner.

The password is related to his mail account which has been chosen freely by user. So R2 is provided.

R3: The password cannot be revealed by the administrator of the server.

As the password' hash value, a one-way function, is stored in database server, so the administrator of the server can not reveal user's password. R3 is provided.

R4: The passwords are not transmitted in plaintext on a network.

The user's details are transferred via SSL connection which is consisting of a secure channel of encryption (RC4), message digest (MD5, SHA-1) and key exchange (RSA). R4 is also provided.

R5: No one can impersonate a legal user to login to the server.

By using fingerprints as unique biometric property of a person, no one can present another person's fingerprint as a legal user to database server. R5 is provided.

R6: The scheme must resist the replay attack, guessing attack, modification attack and stolen verifier attack.

Our scheme is using a fingerprint and hash of email message for providing end to end email security (person identification) in addition to other security services. So it resists the replay attack, modification and stolen verifier attack. And by enabling the two factor authentication of gmail account, one can resist guessing attack as well which can work both in web page and application-specific model. For web page model, a random six character number additional to his real password is sent to user's mobile for 2 way authentication while in application-specific model, a random sixteen character number is generated for a specific application such as outlook to be provided as user's password. R6 is provided.

R7: The length of a password must be suitable for memorization.

The length of password is depending on the user's memorization capabilities. R7 is provided.

R8: The scheme must be efficient and practical.

According to its computational costs (3200 bits), our scheme is practical and efficient not only in application based software but also it is convenient for portable devices as well. R8 is provided.

R9: The scheme can achieve mutual authentication. Not only can the server verify legal users, but users can also verify the legal server.

Our scheme achieve a double mutual authentication which means not only server verify legal users and users also verify legal server, but also sender verify receiver and receiver verify sender as well. R9 is provided in a robust manner such that another requirement should be added to this list as below:

R10: The scheme can achieve mutual authentication. Not only can the sender verify legal receiver users, but receivers can also verify the legal sender.

R11: The password cannot be broken by a guessing attack even if the smart card is lost.

In the case of losing the mobile phone which receives random codes for 2 way authentication or using a application-specific password, user can revoke the one-time passwords and generate new ones. On the other hands, no one can send successful verified messages without presenting a legal user's fingerprint. R10 is provided.

According to R1-R11 requirements, our secure fingerprint based email model can provide those requirements to resist attacks such as Insider Attack (R2, R3, R7), Stolen Verifier Attack (R1, R6), Impersonation Attack (R4, R5, R9, R11), Replay Attack (R6), Denial of Service Attack (R8), Password Guessing Attack R10.

Any system that is proposed in the literature is surely not a complete one and has its own disadvantages. The proposed approach has a single of point of failure on the database server. This can be critical while the database server is attacked by DOS/DDOS attacks which make a disconnection between the application and database server. No one can be authenticated to the application and email messages cannot be verified. For overcoming this problem, distributed database servers can be implemented, so if one of the database servers are out of functioning, others will reply to the application as databases are replicated to other distributed database servers such as done in Microsoft windows servers for authenticating users in domain controllers.

Except DDBMS approach, another low price solution in single database server approach is to focus on three solutions. The first one is using parallelism techniques to enhance and increase data reliability and accessibility. The second one is to make a tight integration between database system and database operating system. The Last one is to upgrade hardware parts of a database server by using strong double / quad core microprocessors or PC clusters which will improve database server performance and database availability.

Distributed Database Server Design and Issues

As discussed above, a centralized database server can provide high degree of security, concurrency, backup and recovery control. One of the most important disadvantages of these databases is their availability problem, when all data is accessed through database communication lines. So when a database server goes down it will become a bottleneck in our network communications. One solution to this problem is to distribute data as a single logical database over multiple database servers known as distributed database servers in which their location will remain transparent to users who are creating a query from their desktop client. In designing a distributed database server, response time for queries is an important factor, furthermore, local autonomy including security, backup and recovery, concurrency control and distributed joins are the issues which will be resolved in its best manner.

So we need to allow database servers to duplicate database tables that make a replication process between 2 or more database servers. This will strengthen the availability of database server. For controlling concurrency in distributed database, lost updates should be prevented. A basic process known as 2 phase commit is used to lock the replicated copies of database table according to a special log file situated in each computer on the database network. After related table, which is not in use by other computers, is locked, the update process will be assigned to the locked table. If update process is done successfully, locked table will be unlocked and consequence processes will be resumed. In the case that tables are in use and an update is issued, the systems will decide to abort and make updates in routine schedule. Regarding distributed joins DDBMS should have a built in expert system to decide on which tables to choose for table joining process depending on their number and size transmitting distances and shipping distance based on query issued by user. The built in expert system should decide on following issues to make the best decision:

(Supposing 2 tables A [Computer A] and B [Computer B] should be joined according to a query issued by computer C)

- Table A is copied to computer B; the join result will be calculated and sent to computer C.
- Table B is copied to computer A; the join result will be calculated and sent to computer C.
- Tables A and B are copied to computer C, the join result will be calculated in computer C.

Each database server system should know where the database servers are situated; for this purpose, the DDBMS should keep a track of tables in a directory to automatically retrieve required database tables. These tracks should be stored in a directory that their copies are better to be saved on all database servers. As the directory data are mostly constant so it will only get updated when database tables are altered, added or moved.

For implementing the proposed secure finger print email system in distributed database servers, 4 sites can be supposed in which tables "Account-Details" and "User_Details" can be copied over 4 sites and EMail table is copied over 3 sites and EmailValidator table is just in one site. This design can ensure us about database server availability, security management, concurrency controlling and distributed joins (shown in Figure 7).

Figure 7. Sample distributed database implementation for secure fingerprint email system

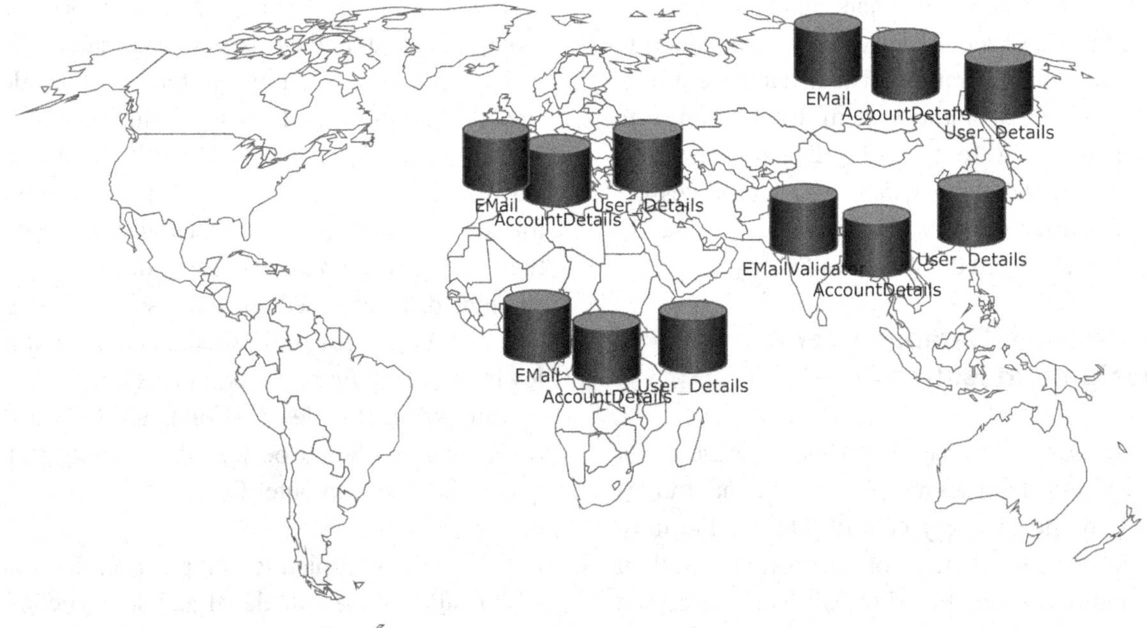

ANALYSIS OF FINGERPRINT BASED EMAIL SECURITY MODEL

Security Issues

The security issues and vulnerabilities which are directly or indirectly depending on fingerprint verification system architecture can be illustrated in Figure 8. These ten vulnerability points can be used in several parts to attack fingerprint systems directly or indirectly. At the first point, the vulnerability belongs to Fingerprint sensor in which it causes some security issues. The possibility of making fake fingerprints or a person's finger is being modified in several ways by cutting fingerprints, and fingerprint uniqueness even in twins are first vulnerability points which arose direct attacks. Accessing a system illegally is possible by producing copy versions of fingerprints (Ratha, Connell, & Bolle, 2001). The rest points in Figure 8 are vulnerable to indirect attacks. Points 2, 4, 5, 7, and 9 are regarded as communication channel weaknesses which can be exploited to implement an attack in processing images, adding and reading extracted features from database server and presenting a fake matching score for accepting or rejecting person's fingerprint.

In indirect attacks, inner algorithms and techniques used for fingerprint verification should be known.

According to wide use of fingerprint verification systems, they have a high acceptability rate in industry and could be easily integrated in devices (such as door locks, mice, flash memories, Mobile phones, etc.), this turns them to an important attack point for intruders.

Recent researches on direct attacks show that various optical and solid state sensors are vulnerable to a fake gummy finger (Putte & Keuning, 2000) or even to gelatin fingers; the acceptance rate was over 60% (Matsumoto, et al., 2002) where that of gummy fingers was over 68%. By using different verification algorithms based on minutiae and ridge patterns on over 1000 real and fake samples, the systems (optical and thermal) defense performance against direct attacks were dramatically increased (Galbally, et al., 2006). To prevent direct attacks, some researches based on

Figure 8. Fingerprint verification architecture

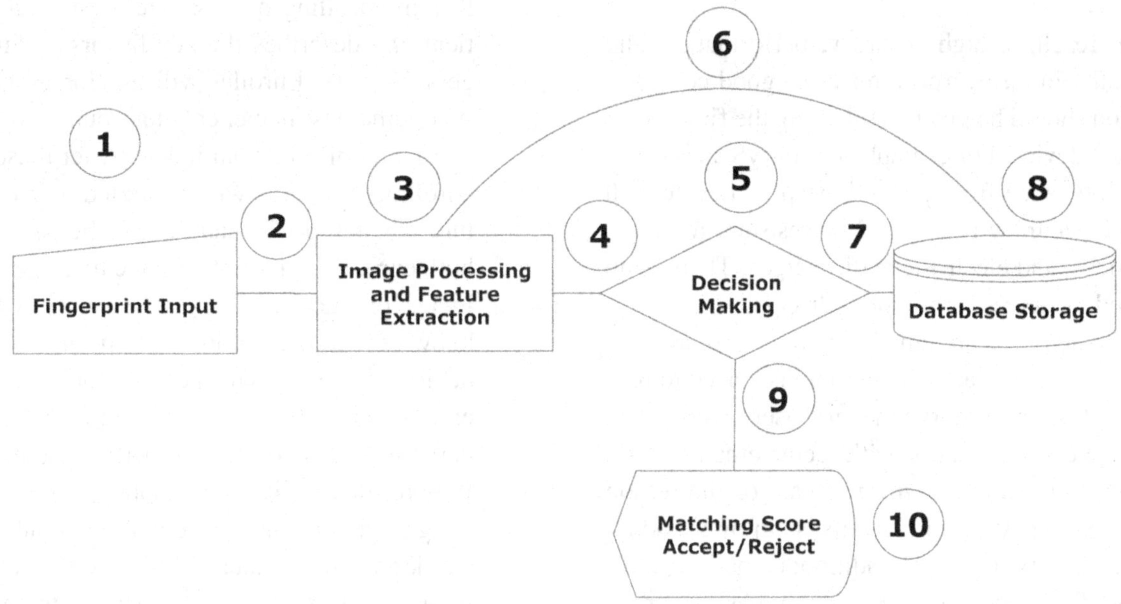

intensity (Schuckers & Abhyankar, 2004), wavelet (Cappelli, Maio, & Maltoni, 2001), odor sensor (Antonelli, Capelli, Maio, & Maltoni, 2006) (to differentiate odor from plastic and gelatin) and elasticity properties of skin (Baldiserra, Franco, Maio, & Maltoni, 2006) have been conducted to detect liveness (Tan & Schuckers, 2006) of real and fake fingers which shows a good performance on detecting fake fingers. Hill climbing techniques are known as indirect attacks which can be implemented against the database and matching device. This basic technique is used to grant an access by increasing the matching score by presenting a random template that will be changed until it is matched by the system (Hill, 2001; Soutar, 2002).

As discussed in previous sections, uniqueness of fingerprint in everybody whether he is a single person or multiple twins is a proven fact. So no different persons have same fingerprints. The existence of fingerprints from human's birth is also discussed and proved in previous sections. Additionally it has been told that even person's fingers are modified or cut, body biology system structure will produce it within one month. The percentage of crossover accuracy for different biometrics is illustrated in Table 3. As it is obvious, the accuracy mentioned for retinal scan and iris scan is higher than others. By considering about various device vendors, enrollment process, FAR (False Acceptance Rate), and FRR (False Rejection Rate) rates fingerprint biometric will act better than other biometric properties.

According to NIST's comments on attacking SHA-1 or any 160-bit hash functions which are based on finding a hash collision (i.e. two different messages will result in same hash values). This was firstly announced in 2005 by Professor Wang by performing 263 operations which seems to be infeasible by simple systems. This method affects digital signature applications of SHA-1. As a matter of fact, SHA-2 is also a family of SHA-1, there is no practical attacks reported on this hash function yet. It is also announced to stop using digital signatures based on SHA-1. For the next years, SHA-2 will be the target for attackers, so NIST has announced for new algorithms for hash functions before the latest one is turned to be an insecure one (NIST, 2012).

Maintenance Issues

For reaching high accuracy, performance, and quality in a fingerprint reader, a good consideration should be given in selecting the fingerprint input device. For example M2-EasyScanTM is a maintenance-free optical fingerprint device with high accuracy rates which is resistant to drops, shocks, and electrostatic discharges. There is no need for its re-calibration if dropped.

When a secure email system is needed to be used for an infrastructure, there is a need to provide training programmes for users who are in direct communication with secure email system. The users should be made aware of the reason for using new secure email system by introducing security threats of traditional email systems. The difference between a public message and a sensitive message should be announced to users, so they will know that sensitive messages should be transferred via secure email system. Making sure that users know that new system ID and accounts are not different from the ones they used before. An email security best practices document should also be written by the agency for user's awareness. So users' responsibility includes their using secure email system whether sending or receiving sensitive email messages, followed by email security documents written by agency experts.

In enrolling users, there are some issues that should be considered:

Table 3. Percentage of crossover accuracy

Biometric	Crossover Accuracy %
Retinal Scan	0.0000001%
Iris Scan	0.000763%
Fingerprints	0.2%
Hand Geometry	0.2%
Signature Dynamics	2%
Voice Dynamics	2%

- **Enroller:** The enroller plays an important role in enrolling process. He must be patient and describes the key factors of fingers to users. Enroller will ask for user's first name, last name, email account, password, and his personal image. After these, enrollment process will be started. For future's better performance, it is better for both enroller and user to see the fingerprint image on monitor's screen, so user will know how to present his fingerprint to the device efficiently. On the other hand, the enroller himself can be counted as a vulnerability to all of the biometric systems. In here, if the Civil Registration Office is integrated to email system for a double check on person's identity will prevent this weakness from happening. "Two watching eyes are better than one"
- **Fingerprint Reader Area:** The user must cover the whole fingerprint reader area by his finger regarding the pressure and moisture of his fingers applied to fingerprint device. Presenting his fingers to the device can be done more than one time to get a better result in matching score.

As the fingerprints can be reconstructed from their templates, they should be stored in database securely, providing the secure templates to be stored in fingerprint database is done by hashing extracted features using SHA-2 hash function. Previous researches show that securing fingerprints is done by hashing the minutiae of fingerprints which reaches the EER (Equal Error Rate) of 1.96-3% (Tulyakov, Farooq, Mansukhani, & Govindaraju 2007) which is a good rate.

Operational Issues

Evaluating a fingerprint system to be used in secure email systems from operational view is a hard task. Worldwide, there are several fingerprint vendors with different sensor characteristics (optical, solid-state, etc.) that result in different features according to their accuracy and performance rates. The temperature and percentage of humidity of enrolling / presenting infrastructure will affect the fingerprint enrolling and acquiring rates which may result in access failure to a resource. For evaluating a system, operational tests are conducted to find out urgent requirements needed for a desired application.

When enrolling a user's fingerprint, the enroller should be sure about the finger is being dry. In other words, moisture and humidity on finger will not let the user being enrolled in secure email system and on the other hand after he has been enrolled successfully, he may not be able to authenticate himself while sending or receiving email messages with humid fingers. The indoor and outdoor environmental factors should also been considered as an increasing weather temperature or a rainy day will be resulted in increasing weather humidity.

Regarding fingerprint systems' prices, they differ from 50$ to 800$ according to their functionality, performance and specificity on scanning uni or dual finger acquisition. The most promising vendors who are manufacturing these products are Microsoft and Bayometric Inc.

For implementing proposed secure email system, the lowest price will be more than enough as there is no need for additional properties except scanning a finger in order to acquire the fingerprint. As both endpoints of email client need a fingerprint device, number of needed fingerprint devices will be equal to number of people who are using this system.

The mentioned issues on this part may be frightening to some companies but there is no need for worrying in acquiring a correct fingerprint as this biometric feature is being used worldwide even in passports known as biometric passports and in most of recent mobiles and iPhones. It is worth to mention that "Providing security has its own prices to comply with security documents, if one does not need security there is no need to pay for it."

Privacy Issues

While using fingerprint identification and authentication in a system such as secure email system, it automatically inherits common disadvantages regarding the privacy issues. The first one is that users are not satisfied to provide their fingerprint data as they are not aware of other usages of fingerprint data. Because from their background, fingerprint is related to justice and criminality environments and it makes them worrying about providing their fingerprint to a third party. The other one is their thought of a third party which will be able to gain their fingerprint and masquerade their identity to access some of their sensitive data. By hashing the fingerprint features, these disadvantages can be resolved easily. As a fingerprint hash is going to be saved in a fingerprint database server and fingerprint is the first point of user's identification, the identification will be done by both fingerprint presentation and stored fingerprint hash. The third party does not have the fingerprint, so he will not be able to access user's sensitive data.

In PKI authentication systems, this can be done by adding a physical token (alike what is done in banks) along with presenting fingerprint data. So the combination of these can be the solution for accepting or denying accesses to sensitive resources. So when implementing a fingerprint identification system, all privacy issues should be addressed correctly. The fingerprint data is sensitive as much as minutia-based data or pattern-based data are. After enrolling users by their fingerprint, for privacy issues it is better for fingerprint image not to be shown on monitor while identifying or authenticating the user because someone may capture fingerprint picture from monitor.

Implementation and Functional Issues

SSL connection protocols, secure email application and fingerprint SDK can be easily implemented in java. Fingerprint Secure Email

Endpoints System (FpSEES) may employ Java Cryptographic Extension (JCE Java2 SDK, v1.4) for cryptographic primitives such as SHA-2. In this section, FpSEES performance based on computational costs and computational complexities will be evaluated. By assuming that the identity and password are 128 bits and the output size of the secure SHA-2 hash function is 256 bits. RC4 128 bits key is used for Gmail SSL encrypted connection and database server connections. As exclusive-or operation has low computational cost, that can be ignored.

In sending process which consists of login (which uses database server connection and Gmail server connection), authenticating (hash calculation is needed) and message sending (hash calculation on sent message), the computational costs will be 4*128+2*160+2*1024+2*256=3200 bits (128 bit for RC4 encryption, 128 bit for message digest MD5, 160 bit for SHA-1 message digest, 1024 bit for RSA key exchange per secure SSL connection) for secure connection and hash function calculations. While in receiving and verification process consisting of login (which uses database server connection and Gmail server connection), authenticating (hash calculation is needed), message reading (verification is done by hash calculation on received message), and sending a receipt (which uses database server connection and Gmail server connection), the calculation cost will be 4*128+2*160+2*1024+2*256=3200 bits.

Our result for login and authentication phase is 4*128+2*160+2*1024=2688 bits which is comparable with the results obtained by (Chen, Lee, & Hsu, 2012) a fingerprint authentication in mobile system that uses 512 bits for login and authentication phase; and other results based on ElGamal public cryptosystem scheme (Lee, Ryu, & Yoo, 2002) uses 2304 bits for login and authentication phase (Chen, et al., 2012) and its improved version (Khan & Zhang, 2007; Kim, Lee, & Yoo, 2003; Lin & Lai, 2004) uses 3456 and 2432 bits for login and authentication phase (Chen, et al., 2012). It is worth mentioning that our method is being used for computer systems which are capable of doing more complex calculations, while the other methods mentioned above are implemented for mobile environment, smart phones and other portable devices which show that our model can also be useful for all portable system environments. The security provided by this model will be achievable only if both end points use the fingerprints (sender and receiver fingerprints). So if one endpoint does not use the application along with his fingerprint, the security for secure email endpoints will not be provided. As mentioned before, the database tables are including the fingerprint hashes for sender and receiver authentication to retrieve their name and pictures. Let us assume two scenarios for this, one is when the sender does not use the fingerprint and the second one is when the receiver is not using his fingerprint. In the first scenario, the user has not used the secure email application, so it is obvious that absence of fingerprint will result in absence of message hash and considering it as a spam while the other end is using the secure email application. In the second one, the sender has sent his secure email by using his fingerprint, so the first stage of this process is done. But on the other side (receiver side) without using fingerprint (i.e. no secure email application existed), email message will be received in his inbox without knowledge about sender's details and no receipt acknowledgement will be issued for sender. Also for security reasons, it is better not to apply this framework in public places. But if one needs to use it in public places, he will need to make a VPN connection to the desired database server which has a static IP address which can be accessed from outside. In the case of being in DMZ zone, making connections will face hard ways which needs the administrator to overcome this kind of issues by setting special network settings which is not the concern of this chapter.

FURTHER RESEARCH DIRECTIONS

Despite numerous efforts done in this chapter to enhance security of email at end points, the proposed system has not been tested and practiced yet. This method can prevent mailboxes from getting spams, scams, and unwanted emails. Surely, there is a lot to do to confirm and evaluate this system as an enhanced email security system in real world communication. The designed SQL database may also have security weaknesses which will be distinguished while it is being practiced by real users. This will result in enhancing the best design for table relationships by SQL programming which can be accessed by ODBC drivers through Delphi or C # Object Oriented Programming Interface (OOPI). These weaknesses and correct evaluations can also be found out by using more users in a large-scale infrastructure; so they can be omitted in large information era communications.

Enhanced customized fingerprint image processing algorithms should be implemented which will play a role in decreasing the possible error rates in human fingerprint feature extraction. Several Artificial Neural Networks (ANNs), the best pattern recognizers, can be used to recognize and classify extracted fingerprint images according to existing database. These ANNs should be customized to be used in this category to reduce existing error rates. As a result, an expert team consisting of professional programmers, image processors, intelligent system designers are needed to achieve this for secure human communications via email systems.

In practical stages, several methods of acquiring fingerprint images should be tested to prevent possibilities of fake user registration in fingerprint database. One method can be tried and confirmed through Identity Registration Office. As it was presented, this research is done to provide a secure framework for email communication. There are a lot to do it in a proper manner. At the end, I am hoping for a world without any spams, scams, and unwanted email messages in future Internet and communications.

CONCLUSION

From years ago up to now, the cryptography algorithms whether symmetric or asymmetric, have been used for encryption and digital signature purposes. Most of email websites are using cryptography techniques for their CA certificates issued by a Trusted Third Party (TTP) along with SHA-1 and MD5 fingerprints. Though all of these attributes added in emailing procedures are trying to fulfill the security properties such as confidentiality, integrity, availability, origin authentication, and non-repudiation, they still lack non-repudiation security property. In information security era, all researchers are trying to provide new methods to omit existing vulnerabilities, which attackers are using to implement an attack. Emails such as scams, spams, and spoofing are dramatically increasing these days and nothing can stop them though there are anti spammers and anti viruses to mitigate critical threats. All of mail boxes are relying on a simple password that users are trying to keep it as simple as they can, because they need to remember so many passwords in information era century. A new parameter should be added to existing email systems, to enhance the email security. Biometric techniques and devices are developing rapidly and are mostly being used in passports, ATMs, and daily operations. For what reason biometric properties which are not being forgotten (passwords) or stolen (tokens) are not being used for email communications?

Email systems can be connected to Identity Registration Office for validating user identity. By integrating these to each other, the enrollment process will be easier without any weaknesses or vulnerabilities which may threaten most of biometric data gathering systems at enrolling process. In this study a secure email system based on fingerprint identification is presented to enhance end point security and to prove the original email message sender and receiver which prevent spam and spoofing email attacks. The novel secure email collects users' fingerprints in enrolling process along with their personal information to make an assurance in receiving and sending email messages. The secure email system will automatically transparently displays full name and personal image of the real sender and receiver depending on SQL server 2005 database tables' relationships. This study shows that checking fingerprint and message hash values significantly improves misdirected emails at a glance by showing email message status as verified successful or verified failure by cheap computations of fingerprint and email message hash value in comparison with expensive cryptography algorithms. The presented method is based on what you are, rather than a password or token that is based on what you know or what you have respectively.

The performance of secure email system is totally relying on FAR and FRR rates of fingerprint reader. These parameters will also be affected by various techniques to achieve a score threshold to make a decision on accepting or rejecting a person while authenticating a person. It is hopefully a good point on fingerprints that all humans have a unique one; it can also be repaired by nano silver techniques while one's finger is cut or altered. Another good point on fingerprint biometric property is its capability for being checked on liveness feature which will reject all of fake fingerprints. So the proposed secure email system can be regarded as an end point security enhancer. The hash functions are being used in this method, so cryptography techniques are not thrown away; it is just being integrated with another human property to overcome problems of password sharing, scam email, spam email, and spoofing emails. There is no special vulnerability threatening this system if a security policy document is there to be complied with. If there are no rules, there is no security as well. This is like that to say "if some one shares his password, no one will be responsible for his password sharing and its results". By researching on this topic, the aim was on enhancing security of existing email systems, not to rejecting them.

Implementing fingerprint identification secure email system in real email system infrastructures is a hope to achieve in the future to study on this project broader where real users with real live fingerprints are widely available. So by going through this chapter, how will future email systems provide and enhance end point security properties for their users and customers?

ACKNOWLEDGMENT

First and foremost, I (Babak Sokouti) would like to thank to my supervisor of project taken in Royal Holloway University of London (RHUL), Mr. Martin Warren, for the valuable guidance and advice. He inspired me greatly to work on my project. His willingness to motivate me contributed tremendously to my project which is part of this chapter. Last but not least we wish to avail ourselves of this opportunity, express a sense of gratitude and love to our beloved parents for their support, strength, help, and encouragement.

REFERENCES

M2-EasyScan. (2012). Fingerprint reader. Retrieved from http://www.easylobby.com/pdfs/ProductSpecSheets/M2-EasyScan.pdf

Alonso-Fernandez, F., Fierrez-Aguilar, J., & Ortega-Garcia, J. (2005). An enhanced gabor filter-based segmentation algorithm for fingerprint recognition systems. In Proceedings of the 4th International Symposium on Image and Signal Processing and Analysis, (pp. 239-244). IEEE.

Antonelli, A., Capelli, R., Maio, D., & Maltoni, D. (2006). Fake finger detection by skin distortion analysis. *IEEE Transactions on Information Forensics and Security*, *1*, 360–373. doi:10.1109/TIFS.2006.879289.

Babler, W. (1991). *Dermatoglyphics: Science in transition* (*Vol. 9*). New York, NY: Wiley-Liss.

Baldiserra, D., Franco, A., Maio, D., & Maltoni, D. (2006). Fake fingerprint detection by odor analysis. Paper presented at International Conference on Biometrics. New York, NY.

Bansal, R., Sehgal, P., & Bedi, P. (2010). Effective morphological extraction of true fingerprint minutiae based on the hit or miss transform. *International Journal of Biometrics and Bioinformatics*, *4*(2), 71–85.

Bazen, A. M., & Gerez, S. H. (2002a). Elastic minutiae matching by means of thin-plate spline models. Paper presented at ICPR 2002. New York, NY.

Bazen, A. M., & Gerez, S. H. (2002b). Fingerprint matching by thin-plate spline modelling of elastic deformations. *Pattern Recognition*, 36.

Bazen, A. M., & Gerez, S. H. (2002c). Thin-plate spline modelling of elastic deformations in fingerprints. Paper presented at SPS 2002. New York, NY.

Bazen, A. M., & Gerez, S. H. (2002d). Systematic methods for the computation of the directional fields and singular points of fingerprints. *IEEE Transactions on Pattern Analysis and Machine Intelligence*, *24*(7), 905–919. doi:10.1109/TPAMI.2002.1017618.

Cappelli, R. (2003). *Handbook of fingerprint recognition*. New York, NY: Springer.

Cappelli, R., Maio, D., & Maltoni, D. (2001). Modelling plastic distortion in fingerprint images. Paper presented at the International Conference on Advances in Pattern Recognition. New York, NY.

Chang, S. H., Cheng, F. H., Hsu, W. H., & Wu, G. Z. (1997). Fast algorithm for point pattern-matching: Invariant to translations, rotations and scale changes. *Pattern Recognition*, *30*(2), 311–320. doi:10.1016/S0031-3203(96)00076-3.

Chen, C.-L., Lee, C.-C., & Hsu, C.-Y. (2012). Mobile device integration of a fingerprint biometric remote authentication scheme. *International Journal of Communication Systems*, *25*, 585–597. doi:10.1002/dac.1277.

Chen, X., Tian, J., Yang, X., & Zhang, Y. (2006). An algorithm for distorted fingerprint matching based on local triangle feature set. *IEEE Transactions on Information Forensics and Security*, *1*(2), 169–177. doi:10.1109/TIFS.2006.873605.

Diffie, W., & Hellman, M. E. (1976). New directions in cryptography. *IEEE Transactions on Information Theory*, *22*, 644–654. doi:10.1109/TIT.1976.1055638.

Donahue, M. L., & Rokhlin, S. I. (1993). On the use of level curves in image analysis. *CVGIP: Image Understanding*, *57*(2), 185–203. doi:10.1006/ciun.1993.1012.

Drahansky, M., Funk, W., & Nötzel, R. (2006). Liveness detection based on fine movements of the fingertip surface. Paper presented at the IAW'06. New York, NY.

Drahansky, M., & Lodrova, D. (2008). Liveness detection for biometric systems based on papillary lines. *International Journal of Security and Its Applications*, *2*(4), 29–37.

Endo, Y., & Matsumoto, T. (2002). Can we make artificial fingers that fool fingerprint systems? Paper presented at IPSJ for Computer Security Symposium. New York, NY.

FBI. (1991). *The FBI fingerprint identification automation program: Issues and options*. Washington, DC: FBI.

Galbally, J., Fierrez, J., Rodriguez-Gonzalez, J. D., Alonso-Fernandez, F., Ortega-Garcia, J., & Tapiador, M. (2006). On the vulnerability of fingerprint verification systems to fake fingerprint attacks. Paper presented at International Carnahan Conference on Security Technology. New York, NY.

Galton, F. (1892). *Fingerprints*. London, UK: Macmillan.

Garfinkel, S. L. (2003). Enabling email confidentiality through the use of opportunistic encryption. In Proceeding of the 2003 Annual National Conference on Digital Government Research. IEEE.

Garfinkel, S. L., Margrave, D., Schiller, J. I., Nordlander, E., & Miller, R. C. (2005). How to make secure email easier to use. In Proceeding of the SIGCHI Conference on Human Factors in Computing Systems, (pp. 701-710). ACM.

Gutmann, P. (2004). Why isn't the internet secure yet, dammit. In Proceeding of the AusCERT Asia Pacific Information Technology Security Conference 2004; Computer Security: Are we there yet? (pp. 71-79). AusCERT.

Hill, C. J. (2001). *Risk of masquerade arising from the storage of Biometrics*. Canberra, Australia: Australian National University.

Hong, L., Wan, Y., & Jain, A. K. (1998). Fingerprint image enhancement: Algorithm and performance evaluation. *IEEE Transactions on Pattern Analysis and Machine Intelligence*, *20*(8), 777–789. doi:10.1109/34.709565.

Housley, R. (1989). Electronic message security: A comparison of three approaches. In Proceedings of the Fifth Annual Computer Security Applications Conference Proceedings. IEEE.

Ismail, A., & Schnabel, U. (2004). An efficient fingerprint matching system. Paper presented at the 3rd International Conference on Electrical & Computer Engineering ICECE 2004. New York, NY.

Jain, A. K., Bolle, R., & Pankanti, S. (2005). *Biometrics: Personal identification in networked society*. Berlin, Germany: Springer.

Jain, A. K., Maltoni, D., Maio, D., & Prabhakar, S. (2003). *Handbook of fingerprint recognition*. Berlin, Germany: Springer.

Jain, A. K., Prabhakar, S., Hong, L., & Pankanti, S. (2000). Filterbank-based fingerprint matching. *IEEE Transactions on Image Processing*, *9*(8), 846–859. doi:10.1109/83.841531 PMID:18255456.

Jain, A. K., Prabhakar, S., & Pankanti, S. (2001). Twin test: On discriminability of fingerprints. *Lecture Notes in Computer Science*, *2091*, 211–217. doi:10.1007/3-540-45344-X_30.

Jain, A. K., Ross, A., & Prabhakar, S. (2004). An introduction to biometric recognition. *IEEE Transactions on Circuits and Systems for Video Technology*, *14*, 4–20. doi:10.1109/TCSVT.2003.818349.

Jiang, X., & Yau, W. Y. (2000). Fingerprint minutiae matching based on the local and global structures. In Proceedings of 15th International Conference on Pattern Recognition, (vol. 2, pp. 1042-1045). IEEE.

Khan, M. K., & Zhang, J. (2007). Improving the security of a flexible biometric remote user authentication scheme. *Computer Standards & Interfaces*, *29*(1), 82–85. doi:10.1016/j.csi.2006.01.002.

Kim, H. S., Lee, S. W., & Yoo, K. Y. (2003). On the security of ID-based password authentication scheme using smart cards and fingerprints. *ACM Operating System*, *37*(4), 32–41. doi:10.1145/958965.958969.

Lee, H. C., & Gaensslen, R. E. (2001). *Advances in fingerprint technology* (2nd ed.). New York, NY: Elsevier Publishing. doi:10.1201/9781420041347.

Lee, J. K., Ryu, S. R., & Yoo, K. Y. (2002). Finger-print based remote user authentication scheme using smart cards. *IEEE Electronics Letters*, *38*(12), 554–555. doi:10.1049/el:20020380.

Liao, I. E., Lee, C. C., & Hwang, M. S. (2006). A password authentication scheme over insecure networks. *Journal of Computer and System Sciences*, *72*(4), 727–740. doi:10.1016/j.jcss.2005.10.001.

Lin, C. H., & Lai, Y. Y. (2004). A flexible biometric remote user authentication scheme. *Computer Standards & Interfaces*, *27*(1), 19–23. doi:10.1016/j.csi.2004.03.003.

Maio, D., Maltoni, D., Cappelli, R., Wayman, J. L., & Jain, A. K. (2002). *FVC2002: Fingerprint verification competition*. Bologna, Italy: University of Bologna.

Matsumoto, T. (2001). What will you do if you find a particular weakness of a security technology? *Journal of IEICE*, *84*(3).

Matsumoto, T., Matsumoto, H., Yamada, K., & Hoshino, S. (2002). Impact of artificial gummy fingers on fingerprint systems. In Proceedings of SPIE, Optical Security and Counterfeit Deterrence Techniques, (pp. 275-289). Springer.

Menezes, A. J., Van Oorschot, P. C., & Vanstone, S. A. (1996). *Handbook of applied cryptography*. Boca Raton, FL: CRC Press. doi:10.1201/9781439821916.

Mohsen, S. M., Zamshed, S. M., & Hashem, M. M. A. (2004). Automated fingerprint recognition: Using minutiae matching technique for the large fingerprint database. Paper presented at the International Conference on Electrical and Computer Engineering ICECE 2004. New York, NY.

Molle, R. M., Connell, J. H., Pankanti, S., Ratha, N. K., & Senior, A. W. (2003). *Guide to biometrics*. Berlin, Germany: Springer.

Mosorov, V. (2001). Using tophat transformation for image fingerprint segmentation. Paper presented at the International Conference on Signals and Electronic Systems. New York, NY.

Msiza, I. S., Leke-Betechuoh, B., Nelwamondo, F. V., & Msimang, N. (2009). A fingerprint pattern classification approach based on the coordinate geometry of singularities. Paper presented at the IEEE International Conference on Systems, Man and Cybernetics, SMC 2009. New York, NY.

NIST. (2012). Tentative timeline of the development of new hash functions. Retrieved from http://csrc.nist.gov/groups/ST/hash/timeline.html

O'Gorman, L. (2002). Seven issues with human authentication technologies. In Proceedings of Workshop on Automatic Identification Advanced Technologies (AutoID), (pp. 185-186). AudoID.

Poh, N., & Bengio, S. (2005). An investigation of f-ratio client-dependent normalisation on biometric authentication tasks. Paper presented at the IEEE International Conference on Acoustics, Speech, and Signal Processing (ICASSP). New York, NY.

Prabhakar, S., Pankanti, S., & Jain, A. K. (2003). Biometric recognition: Security and privacy concerns. Paper presented at the IEEE Security and Privacy. New York, NY.

Putte, T. V., & Keuning, J. T. (2000). Biometrical fingerprint recognition don't get your fingers burned. Paper presented at the IFIP 2000. New York, NY.

Ratha, N., Connell, J., & Bolle, R. (2001). An analysis of minutiae matching strength. Paper presented at the International Conference on Audio- and Video-Based Biometric Person Authentication III. New York, NY.

Ratha, N. K., Chen, S. Y., & Jain, A. K. (1995). Adaptive flow orientation-based feature extraction in fingerprint images. *Pattern Recognition*, *28*(11), 1657–1672. doi:10.1016/0031-3203(95)00039-3.

Ratha, N. K., Karu, K., Chen, S., & Jain, A. K. (1996). A real-time matching system for large fingerprint databases. *IEEE Transactions on Pattern Analysis and Machine Intelligence*, *18*(8), 799–813. doi:10.1109/34.531800.

Ratha, N. K., Pandit, V. D., Bolle, R. M., & Vaish, V. (2000). Robust fingerprint authentication using local structural similarity. In Proceedings of Workshop on Applications of Computer Vision, (pp. 29-34). IEEE.

Rokbani, N., & Alimi, A. (2005). Fingerprint identification using minutiae constellation matching. Paper presented at the IADIS Virtual Multi Conference on Computer Science and Information Systems. New York, NY.

Ruby, B. L., Zhijie, S., & Xiao, Y. (2001). Efficient permutation instructions for fast software cryptography. *IEEE Micro*, *21*(6), 56–69. doi:10.1109/40.977759.

Schuckers, S., & Abhyankar, A. (2004). A wavelet based approach to detecting liveness in fingerprint scanners. Paper presented at the Biometric Authentication Workshop (ECCV). New York, NY.

Schuckers, S., Hornak, L., Norman, T., Derakhshani, R., & Parthasaradhi, S. (2002). *Issues for liveness detection in biometrics*. Morgantown, WV: West Virginia University.

Shen, L. L., Kot, A., & Koo, W. M. (2001). Quality measures of fingerprint images. Paper presented at the 3rd Audio and Video-Based Person Authentication, AVBPA 2001. New York, NY.

Soutar, C. (2002). Biometric system security. Retrieved from http://www.bioscrypt.com/assets/security_soutar.pdf

Tan, B., & Schuckers, S. (2006). Comparison of ridge- and intensity-based perspiration live-ness detection methods in fingerprint scanners. Paper presented at the SPIE, Biometric Technology for Human Identification III. New York, NY.

Tan, B., & Schuckers, S. (2008). New approach for liveness detection in fingerprint scanners based on valley noise analysis. *Journal of Electronic Imaging*, *17*(1). doi:10.1117/1.2885133 PMID:23087585.

Teddy, K., & Lockheed, M. (2002). Fingerprint enhancement by spectral analysis techniques. Paper presented at the 31st Applied Imagery Pattern Recognition Workshop. New York, NY.

Tulyakov, S., Farooq, F., Mansukhani, P., & Govindaraju, V. (2007). Symmetric hash functions for secure fingerprint biometric systems. *Pattern Recognition Letters*, *28*, 2427–2436. doi:10.1016/j.patrec.2007.08.008.

Wayman, J. L., Jain, A. K., Maltoni, D., & Maio, D. (2005). *Biometric systems: Technology, design and performance evaluation*. Berlin, Germany: Springer.

Xu, H., Veldhuis, R., Bazen, A., Kevenaar, T., Akkermans, T., & Gokberk, B. (2009). Fingerprint verification using spectral minutiae representations. Paper presented at the IEEE Transactions on Information Forensics and Security. New York, NY.

ADDITIONAL READING

APWG. (2011). APWG global phishing survey releases: Domain name use and trends in 2H2011. Retrieved from http://www.antiphishing.org/

Ashley, M., Copeland, M., Grahn, J., & Wheeler, D. A. (1999). The GNU privacy handbook. Retrieved from http://www.gpg.cz/rp/GnuPG/gph.pdf

Atkins, D., Stallings, W., & Zimmermann, P. (1996). PGP message exchange formats. Retrieved from http://www.ietf.org/rfc/rfc1991.txt

Balenson, D. (1993). Privacy enhancement for internet electronic mail: Part III: Algorithms, modes, and identifiers. Retrieved from http://www.faqs.org/rfcs/rfc1423.html

Bhattacharyya, M., Hershkop, S., Eskin, E., & Stolfo, S. J. (2002). MET: An experimental system for malicious email tracking. Paper presented at the 2002 New Security Paradigms Workshop (NSPW-2002). New York, NY.

Borenstein, N., & Freed, N. (1993). MIME (multipurpose internet mail extensions) part one: Mechanisms for specifying and describing the format of internet message bodies. Retrieved from http://www.ietf.org/rfc/rfc1521.txt

Callas, J., Donnerhacke, L., Finney, H., Shaw, D., & Thayer, R. (2007). OpenPGP message format. Retrieved from http://www.faqs.org/rfcs/rfc4880.html

Callas, J., Donnerhacke, L., Finney, H., & Thayer, R. (1998). OpenPGP message format. Retrieved from http://www.ietf.org/rfc/rfc2440.txt

Crocker, C., Freed, N., Galvin, J., & Murphy, S. (1995). MIME object security services. Retrieved from http://rfc1848.openrfc.org/

Crocker, D. H. (1982). Standard for the format of ARPA internet text messages. Retrieved from http://www.rfc-editor.org/rfc/rfc822.txt

Dusse, S., Hoffman, P., Ramsdell, B., Lundblade, L., & Repka, L. (1998). S/MIME version 2 message specification. Retrieved from www.ietf.org/rfc/rfc2311.txt

Edulog. (2005). Email. Retrieved from http://thinkdifferent.typepad.com/edulog/computer_forensics_i/

Freed, N., & Borenstein, N. (1996). Multipurpose internet mail extensions (MIME) part two: Media types. Retrieved from http://tools.ietf.org/html/rfc2046.txt

Hoffman, P. E., & Ramsdell, B. C. (2005). S/MIME mail security. Retrieved from http://www.ietf.org/html.charters/smime-charter.html

Kaliski, B. (1993). Privacy enhancement for internet electronic mail: Part IV: Key certification and related services. Retrieved from http://www.faqs.org/rfcs/rfc1424.html

Kaliski, B. (1998). PKCS #7: Cryptographic message syntax version 1.5. Retrieved from http://tools.ietf.org/html/rfc2315

Kavi. (2012). Kavi mailing list manager help. Retrieved from http://support.kavi.com/khelp/kmlm/user_help/html/how_email_works.html

Kent, S. (1993). Privacy enhancement for internet electronic mail: Part II: Certificate-based key management. Retrieved from http://www.faqs.org/rfcs/rfc1422.html

Leiner, B. M., Cerf, V. G., Clark, D. D., Kahn, R. E., Leinrock, L., Lynch, D. C., et al. (2012). A brief history of the internet. Retrieved from http://www.internetsociety.org/internet/internet-51/history-internet/brief-history-internet

Levi, A., & Özcan, M. (2005). Practical and secure e-mail system (PractiSES). Paper presented at the Advances in Information Systems Third International Conference. Izmir, Turkey.

Lieberman, E., & Miller, R. C. (2007). Facemail: Showing faces of recipients to prevent misdirected email. Paper presented at the 3rd Symposium on Usable Privacy and Security. New York, NY.

Linn, J. (1993). Privacy enhancement for internet electronic mail: Part I: Message encryption and authentication procedures. Retrieved from http://www.faqs.org/rfcs/rfc1421.html

Moser, H. (2002). S/MIME. Retrieved from http://www.heinzi.at/texte/smime.pdf

Namestnikova, M. (2012). Spam report: March 2012. Retrieved from http://www.securelist.com/en/analysis/204792226/Spam_report_March_2012

Obied, A. (2006). *Secure email with fingerprint recognition*. Calgary, Canada: University of Calgary.

Pharming. (2009). Wikipedia. Retrieved from http://en.wikipedia.org/wiki/Pharming

Plante, A. (2004). Stuffing spam. Retrieved from http://infosecuritymag.techtarget.com/ss/0,295796,sid6_iss386_art765,00.html

Ramsdell, B. (1999). S/MIME version 3 message specification. Retrieved from ftp://ftp.isi.edu/in-notes/rfc2633.txt

Rojkovic, D. (2010). Link analysis tool general policies version 1.0. Retrieved from https://www.fer.hr/_download/repository/LAT_Doc_General-Policies_Final_V1.0.pdf

RSA. (2009). Public-key cryptography standards (PKCS). Retrieved from http://www.rsasecurity.com/rsalabs/node.asp?id=2124

SORBS. (2002). Introduction and a bit of history. Retrieved from http://www.sorbs.net

Sukarno, P., & Bhattacharjee, N. (2008). Authentication architecture based on crypto-biometric systems. Paper presented at the International Conference on Security and Management (SAM'08). New York, NY.

Tracy, M., Jansen, W., Scarfone, K., & Butterfield, J. (2007). *Guidelines on electronic mail security, U. S. department of commerce*. Gaithersburg, MD: National Institute of Standards and Technology.

Turner, S., & Housley, R. (2008). *Implementing email security and tokens: Current standards, tools, and practices*. New York, NY: Wiley Publishing.

KEY TERMS AND DEFINITIONS

Asymmetric Encryption: This cryptosystem, known as public key encryption, is consisting of a pair of different keys (public key and private key) for encryption and decryption process.

Authentication: It is identity verification process for an entity to be claimed to be.

Email Security: A secure email environment is an infrastructure where not only a message is sent and received in a secure manner but also the end points are real authenticated humans not just by digital signature.

Fingerprint Biometrics: Fingerprints are biometrical presented of a human that can be used for real human identification and authentication based on extracted fingerprint features.

Hash Function: It is a one way function that maps a variable length data block into a fixed length value. It is mostly used for message authentication as a message digest.

Man-in-the-Middle Attack: In this kind of attack, there is an intruder between sender and receiver that intercepts and alters communicated data in order to pretend as one or more entities.

Replay Attack: In this attack an authorized and completed service can be forged and sent as a repeated command to repeat authorized commands.

Robust Non-Repudiation: It is a security service in which both end points are assured of each other's identity and reality.

Security Services: There are five main security services which are essential for an environment to be secure. They are confidentiality, integrity, message authentication, non-repudiation and availability.

Symmetric Encryption: This cryptosystem is consisting of a shared key between sender and receiver for encryption and decryption process.

Section 5
Engineering Secure Information Systems

Chapter 16
Cryptography in Electronic Mail

Hosnieh Rafiee
Hasso Plattner Institute, Germany

Martin von Löwis
Hasso Plattner Institute, Germany

Christoph Meinel
Hasso Plattner Institute, Germany

ABSTRACT

Electronic Mail (email) is a very important method of communicating across the Internet, but the protocols used to handle emails during transmission, downloads, and organizational processes are not secure. Spammers and scammers misuse these protocols to propagate spam or scams across the Internet for advertising purposes or to gain access to critical data, such as credit card information. Cryptographic approaches are applied as a tool to help in securing email components, such as the header, data, etc. This chapter classifies the approaches used according to the protection mechanisms provided to the email components, and it also briefly describes these approaches. Because scammers are continually trying to crack current algorithms, the most recent improvements in email security using cryptography are covered in this discussion. An explanation is given as to the need for verifying both receivers and senders in this process. Finally, the authors examine how the use of these approaches will work in IPv6 as compared to IPv4.

INTRODUCTION

In computer terms, email (e-mail) is short for electronic mail. It is a current method of transmitting data, text files, digital photos, and audio and video files from one computer to another over the internet. This phenomenon did not become popular until 1990 and now it is a major business in personal communications. Compared to sending mail via the post office in the traditional way (snail mail), email is faster and cheaper. Messages can be sent at any time to anywhere and the recipient can read it at his or her convenience. The same message can be sent to multiple recipients at one time and the message can be forwarded without having to retype it.

Early email was not invented; it just evolved. Early email was just a small advance on what we know these days as a file directory—it just put a message in another user's directory in a spot where

DOI: 10.4018/978-1-4666-4030-6.ch016

they could see it when they logged on. Just like leaving a note on someone's desk.

The first documented email system was MAILBOX, used at the Massachusetts Institute of Technology. Another early program used to send messages, on the same computer, was called SNDMSG (Tomlinson, 1971).

Some of the mainframe computers of this era might have had up to one hundred users - often they used what are called "dumb terminals" to access the mainframe from their work desks. Dumb terminals just connected to the mainframe—they had no storage or memory of their own and all work was done by the remote mainframe computer.

Today, a standard protocol called Simple Mail Transfer Protocol (SMTP) (Klensin, 2008) is used to send and receive mails and transport them across multiple networks (SMTP relay) by establishing a two-way transmission channel between a SMTP client and server over the internet or networks.

Here, two problems are encountered. The first is related to spamming. Spam mail is unsolicited email. It is also known as "junk" email that is typically not wanted by the user who is receiving it. The second is related to scamming. Scam mail is an email that is also unsolicited, but is attempting to acquire money or personal information from the recipient. Spammers and criminals profit from the use programs that misuse the SMTP protocol.

The U.S. Congress passed a law (15 USC Chapter 103, 2011) in 2003 that was designed to curb spam. This law makes it illegal to send messages that use deceptive subject lines and false return addresses, providing fines for as much as 6 million dollars and possible prison terms for violators. The law states that all messages, solicited or unsolicited, must have a valid postal address and an opt-out mechanism so that recipients can prevent future email solicitations. The email system is also vulnerable to hackers who can attach malicious programs to an email in hopes of infecting other computers whose resources they can then use in further attacking scenarios. This could damage the reputation of Internet Service Providers (ISPs) and/or expose critical personal information to criminals.

Email remains the most important application on the internet and is the most widely used facility that the internet has. Now more than 600 million people internationally use email. One can thus see how important it is to make it as secure as possible.

This chapter focuses on the use of cryptographic approaches to resolve the security issues inherent in SMTP. Reference will be made to many different possible cryptographic approaches based on what part of the total message they address; envelope or content. Each approach will be classified accordingly. Thus, there are cryptographic approaches for securing the SMTP envelope, such as verifying the users' authenticity to reduce spam and forged messages, and for securing the content of the message to prevent exposing critical data, such as credit card information, etc. to criminals. The necessity of verifying receivers, as well as senders, in order to avoid forged messages, will also be discussed. We start with a short introduction about electronic mail, SMTP, and problems of misusing SMTP. We discuss the advantages and disadvantages of these approaches and then introduce the most recent improvements and modifications made to enhance these approaches. Finally, we describe how to use these approaches in future internet networks, i.e., IPv6.

ELECTRONIC MAIL (EMAIL)

Email Object

An electronic mail message (or email for short) is a digital message that can be transferred over communication networks. An email consists of two components (Klensin, 2008):

- **Envelope:** The envelope is something that an email user will never see since it is part of the internal process by which an email is routed. It's added automatically by your e-mail program when you press "Send", and it's removed automatically by the recipient's mail server just before the letter (without the envelope) is placed into their mailbox. Your email program connects to your outgoing mail server, and tells it your email address (the "Sender"), and the address(es) of the recipient(s). This is called the envelope. The data in the envelope is required by the Mail Transfer Agent (MTA) (Gellens & Klensin, 2011), that is, the SMTP clients and servers that provide a mail transport service.

- **Content:** The content is sent in the SMTP DATA protocol unit and has two parts:
  - **Header:** the body is always preceded by header lines that identify particular routing information of the message, including the sender, recipient, date, and subject. Some headers are mandatory, such as the FROM, TO and DATE headers. Some mail systems do not have the equivalent of a SMTP envelope, so when a message leaves the Internet environment, it might be necessary to insert the SMTP envelope information into the message header section.
  - **Body:** The body is the part that we always see as it is the actual content of the message contained in the email.

Email Transfer Protocols

Email transfer has been available as a computer application since the early 1960s, even before the evolution of the Internet. The first attempt to provide a protocol for electronic mail delivery on different platforms was supplied by the Address and Routing Parameter Area (ARPA), which proposed the Simple Mail Transfer Protocol (SMTP). It was developed for sending and receiving mail, and transporting it across multiple networks (SMTP relay). SMTP is an application layer protocol within the TCP/IP suite. The protocol is based on the "snail" mail (Van Staden & Venter, 2010) architecture; electronic mail is sent from one "post office" to the next, until the mail is delivered to the intended "mailbox."

In October 2008, the latest version of this protocol (Klensin, 2008) was released describing the musts of backwards compatibility for this protocol. This, in a nutshell, stated that SMTP Service Extensions defined in previous versions, which are not in regular use, might not be described in later RFC documents, but are expected to remain available. Since SMTP is limited in its ability to queue messages at the receiving end, it is usually used with one of two other protocols, POP3 or IMAP. SMTP is a simple text-based protocol. It thus benefits from other standard protocols, such as Multipurpose Internet Mail Extensions (MIME) (Freed & Borenstein, 1996), for sending non-text mail formats because SMTP supports only 7-bit ASCII characters, and thus, cannot transmit data in a binary format or other such formats.

SMTP Vulnerabilities

SMTP is not a secure protocol because the information that is transmitted in the SMTP is transmitted in plain text. It can thus be easily manipulated. The vulnerabilities inherent in SMTP allow for email abuse. Email abuse occurs when electronic mail is used to advertise unethically, harass, or annoy the email recipient. Abuse takes different forms—such as, spam, scam, email threatening (malware, viruses) and email cracking. Unsolicited electronic messages sent to people who do not choose to receive them are called spam. However, unsolicited messages sent to multiple accounts are not necessarily spam—for example, the occasional funny mass messages sent from friends to friends and back again. In these cases, the sender is known, whereas with spam, the sender is unknown. Scam is used to refer to unsolicited electronic messages that are sent to someone with the intention of getting him to give money for a service or product that does not actually exist. Scam phishers try to send messages by manipulating the SMTP header or body to make them look legitimate. They search open mail relays, an SMTP server that allows anonymous users on the internet to send mail via this server, in order to deceive inexperienced users on the internet. They do this by using scammers' bluffs, which offer users lucrative business opportunities and other such things. They can also send messages to a list of mail addresses. These mail addresses are obtained by crawling through web pages on the internet using different software. For example, a scammer might ask you to cash foreign checks for which you will receive remuneration. Another example is where you are told you won prize money from a lottery (which you did not even enter). The difference between spam and scam is spam emails are emails that are sent with the intent to get you to buy a product. The product might exist, but usually does not work as described, and is not worth the money. So, the difference is that spam -while obnoxious and undesirable, is not illegal. Scams, on the other hand, are illegal. Spamming techniques are often employed by scammers. Threatening e-mail (malware attached to email) is usually sent in mass to many users with the intent to slow productivity of, or cause damage to, the recipient's computer system. These malicious programs, malwares or worms, called bots, are attached to messages sent to people in the hopes of infecting other computers on the internet. These infected computers are called zombies and they allow attackers to gain full access of the computer's resources. The attacker now controls the computers and can do Denial of Service (DoS) and phishing attacks (Suwa, Yamai, Okayama, & Nakamura, 2011) and can further propagate their attacks against other computers by using the computers that they now control. A cracker is someone who gains access to somebody's mailbox by usurping their passwords and bypassing all other security measures. They do this to gain information about the user that they can then use for their gain.

Email spoofing is another attack in this category. It is the act of editing or falsifying the SMTP header and the envelope information to hide the true origin or root of an email. Spoofing is also used to add fake validity to the content of an email by using a well-known and trusted domain, as the originating domain in order to perpetrate a phishing attack. Phishers are able to create emails with fake "Mail From:" headers in order to impersonate any organization they choose. In some cases, they may also set the "RCPT To:" field to an email address of their choice, whereby any customer replying to the phishing email will be sent to them. The growing press coverage over phishing attacks has meant that most customers are very wary of sending confidential information (such as passwords and PIN information) by email—however, in many cases, these types of attacks are still successful. The sniffing attack (Trabelsi, Rahmani, Kaouech, & Frikha, 2004) is not readily detectable. It can be accomplished by simply downloading free sniffer software from the Internet and installing it onto a Personal Computer (PC), which then becomes one of the infected computers on the network (botnet). A sniffer captures all packets and sends the important data to the attackers' computer. This data may consist of the passwords used to authenticate during an FTP session or the message of an email contained in SMTP packets that contains critical information.

Relay hijacking (see Figure 1) occurs when a malicious node finds an unsecure "SMTP Relay Server1" and misuses it to send messages to the target through other trusted relays, which are based on the trust of the "SMTP Relay Server1."

Figure 1. Relay hijacking

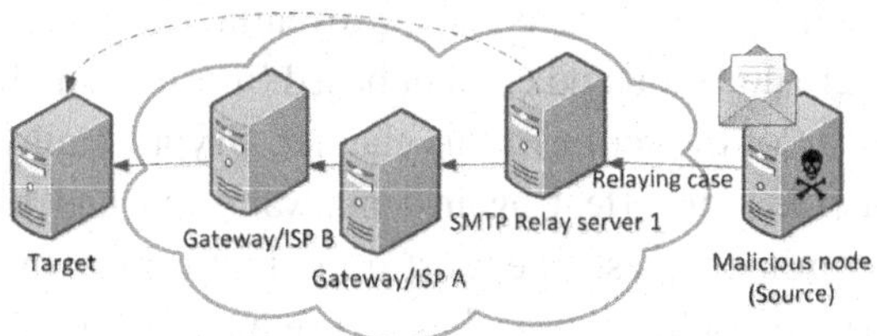

CRYPTOGRAPHIC PROTECTION MECHANISMS

People are unaware of sniffing attacks, and thus, they might include some critical personal information in their emails, which would be beneficial to thieves. For example, you might send an email to a friend asking them to watch your house while you are gone. The information contained in that email might define when you will be gone and where the location of the extra key is so that that person can gain entry to the house to check on it. A thief using a sniffing attack could garner this information and use it to steal everything from your house.

Scammers and attackers are actively looking to usurp critical information that is sent via emails. They are also interested in sending forged emails in order to pretend to be someone that they are not in order to obtain critical information from a user, such as password(s), bank account number(s) with associated PIN(s), etc. It is thus very important to insure the security of this critical information during the transfer process. Cryptography offers various methods for taking plain text data and transforming it into unreadable data for the purpose of securing the data during transmission. Using this approach, a key is used on the send side to encrypt the data, and a matching key is used on the receive side to decrypt the message.

It is important to remember that most spam messages are prevented by using approaches (Rafiee, Von Loewis, & Meinel, 2012) other than cryptographic. Cryptography thus plays a minor role in the prevention of spam. Cryptography plays no role in the prevention of scam except when the scammer uses a spamming approach—such as, forging headers or bogus domain. The two main approaches used in preventing scam are user education and content based filtering which is out of the scope of this chapter. Cryptography also has no effect against malware attached to spam messages. The most important role of the cryptographic approach is its use in email cracking which was explained in a prior section. This is because the cryptographic approach can be used to sign a domain, hash passwords, encrypt mail contents and prevent forged messages.

For the purposes of this chapter, cryptographic approaches will be classified into two main categories based on their usage in securing email components; securing the envelope and securing the content. Figure 2 shows the classification of cryptographic approaches used for each email component, i.e., the envelope and the content.

Securing the Envelope

SMTP wraps an email in an envelope for transmission. The envelope specifies what system is transmitting the mail, who the mail is from, and who it is to. This envelope might be likened to the envelope used in "snail mail." This is used by mail transport software to route and deliver the email. Because the envelope is processed before the data carrying the content, it is cheaper to reject spam based on envelope information than on content information. Likewise, the IP address of the sending system is available and can be compared with Blacklist and White list databases or other types of spam filtering. To protect this critical data, in order to reduce forged data such as forged "From", there are some cryptographic approaches available. These approaches are used to secure messages during the transfer process and during the message submission process from one MTA (Gellens & Klensin, 2011) to another.

Message Transfer

When transferring a message from your e-mail client, such as Microsoft Outlook or Thunderbird, the sending Mail Transfer Agent (MTA) (Gellens & Klensin, 2011) handles all of the mail delivery processing until the message has been either accepted or rejected by the receiving MTA. It can thus be sent either directly to the target domain, such as example.com if the "To" field is xx@example.

Figure 2. Cryptography classification for secure email

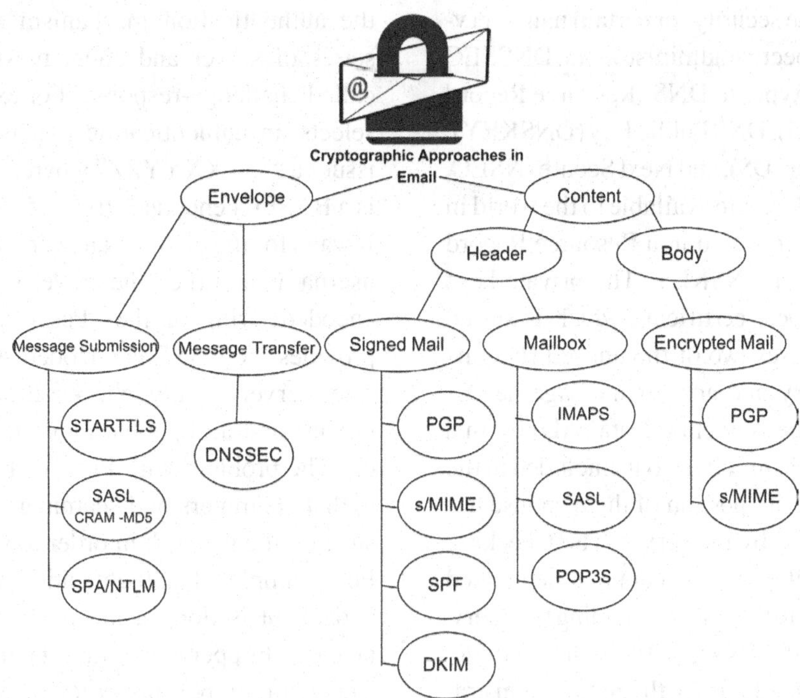

com, or to another e-mail server that is providing a relay service. Moreover, as the email clears the queue, it is routed along a host-to-host chain of servers. Each MTA in the internet network needs to ask for an IP address from the Domain Name System (DNS) in order to identify the next MTA in the delivery chain. The DNS is simply a database that defines the relationship between the name of a computer, such as http://www.example.com, to an IP address, such as 10.10.1.1. This process is called DNS resolving. DNS relies on a distributed database with a hierarchical structure. Email servers also require some specialized records in the DNS database like the MX record.

Unfortunately, the DNS is not secure enough. In particular there is currently no proof that the DNS server hasn't been corrupted. This has serious consequences for e-commerce and for the control of critical infrastructure. Ariyapperuma and Mitchell (2007) surveyed DNS attacks, such as man-in-the-middle (MITM) attacks, where the recipient of data from a DNS name server has no way of authenticating its origin or verifying its integrity. This is because the DNS does not specify a mechanism for servers to provide authentication details for the data they push down to clients. The resolver process has no way of verifying the authenticity and integrity of the data sent by name servers.

Domain Name System Security Extension (DNSSEC)

DNSSEC is an extension of the DNS (Arends, Austein, Larson, Massey, & Rose, 2005) used to validate DNS query operations. It verifies the authenticity and integrity of query results from a signed zone. In other words, if a DNSSEC is available from the requestor client to the resolver/caching nameserver to the authoritative nameservers, then the client has a level of assurance that the DNS query response is signed and trustworthy, starting from the root and chaining all the way down to the domain and subdomains. It uses asymmetrical cryptography which means that separate keys are used to encrypt and decrypt data in order to provide security for certain name servers with their respective administrators. DNSSEC adds four record types to DNS; Resource Record Signature (RRSIG), DNS Public Key (DNSKEY), Delegation Signer (DS), and Next Secure (NSEC, NSEC3). Public keys are available to the world in DNS zones and are stored in a Resource Record (RR) type called a DNSKEY. The private keys are stored in a local certificate which is stored on the server. It uses two of the unused flag bits in the DNS query and answer message header (AD and CD). The Authentic Data (AD) bit in a response indicates that all the data included in the answer and authority portion of the response has been authenticated by the server. The Checking Disabled (CD) bit indicates that unauthenticated data is acceptable to the resolver sending the query. Moreover, if it provides security for the example.com domain and subdomains, the zone administrator will then electronically sign the zone and place this signature in the RRSIG. NSEC3 records are used to provide proof that a name does not exist by providing a range of names that do not exist. When the DNS server would normally reply with an empty answer, the NSEC3 record is signed with the corresponding RRSIG record in order to confirm that the domain name does not exist.

Message Submission

SMTP (Postel, 1982) is a simple protocol that is used for sending and receiving messages across the internet networks. Originally it did not support authentication. Thus spammers, scammers and attackers were able to misuse this schema in order to send their spam or malwares. SMTP Authentication is a feature which was introduced by Myers (1999) to protect mail servers from spam. The simplest authentication mechanism is "Plain". The client simply sends the unencrypted password to the server. All clients support the "Plain" mechanism. Two other authentication mechanisms are used for Authentication purposes; "Login" and SASL (CRAM -MD5). "Login" is the authentication mechanism consisting of a series of server and client message exchanges called challenge-response. For example, a client selects an authentication mechanism, a Server issues a "334 XXYYZZ" where "334 XXYYZZ" is a BASE64 encoded string of the "Username:". It waits for the client to answer with the BASE64 username and then the server sends a BASE64 encoded string of the "Password:" The client provides the BASE64 encoded string password. The Server finally checks the authentication request and accepts the request if everything is ok. The problem with Plain text authentications is that spammers and scammers can also easily sniff on the network in order to steal passwords. For example, if authentication via mail server and client is done using a plaintext password, an eavesdropper can obtain the user's password. This not only permits him to access anything in his mailbox, but, in a worse case, he can use the same password for all of the other critical applications or servers that need to be protected. It thus gives him access to anything else that the user has protected using the same password. So Siemborski and Melnikov (2007) proposed an extension to SMTP in order to enable it to support secure authentication.

SMTP -STARTTLS (TLS Secure Password)

The Transport Layer Security (TLS) protocol was first proposed in 1991 (Dierks & Allen, 1999). Later it was updated and improved (Turner & Polk, 2011). Some of the improvements to this protocol are the replacement of the MD5/SHA-1 combination with cipher-suite-specified Pseudo Random Functions (PRFs). Additional ability was provided to the client/servers enabling them to specify their hash function and more support was offered for authenticated encryption with additional data modes. TLS is based on SSL3 to provide integrity and privacy on data. The authentication mechanism in this protocol is based on asymmetric cryptography (public/private key) such as RSA, DSA, etc. The data encryption is based on symmetric cryptography such as AES, RC4, etc. The negotiation of a shared secret is secure and it is not possible for attackers to eavesdrop on it. In the authentication process, a TLS client sends a message to a TLS server, and the server responds with the information that the server needs to do the authentication itself. The client and server perform an additional exchange of session keys, and the authentication dialog ends. When authentication is completed, SSL-secured communication can begin between the server and the client using the symmetric encryption keys that are established during the authentication process. The keys for this symmetric encryption are generated uniquely for each connection. TLS is independent of application protocol. Therefore, the other protocols such as SMTP can layer on top of the TLS protocol transparently. Hoffman (2002) offered an extension to SMTP, called STARTTLS, which enabled it to use TLS. STARTTLS will thus help in authenticating clients or servers by ensuring the identities of the parties engaged in secure communication. It protects SMTP against password disclosure. By doing this it prevents some types of attacks against SMTP. An example of this type of attack would be man-in-the-middle.

When a client wants to start a STARTTLS session, as shown in Figure 3, it sends a request to the server, the connection to the server is established and the server answers the client's request with a 220 message. The client then sends a EHLO message which the server responds to with a welcome message. The message exchange continues as shown in Figure 3 until a secure session is established between the client and the server.

Figure 3. STARTTLS session between a client and a server

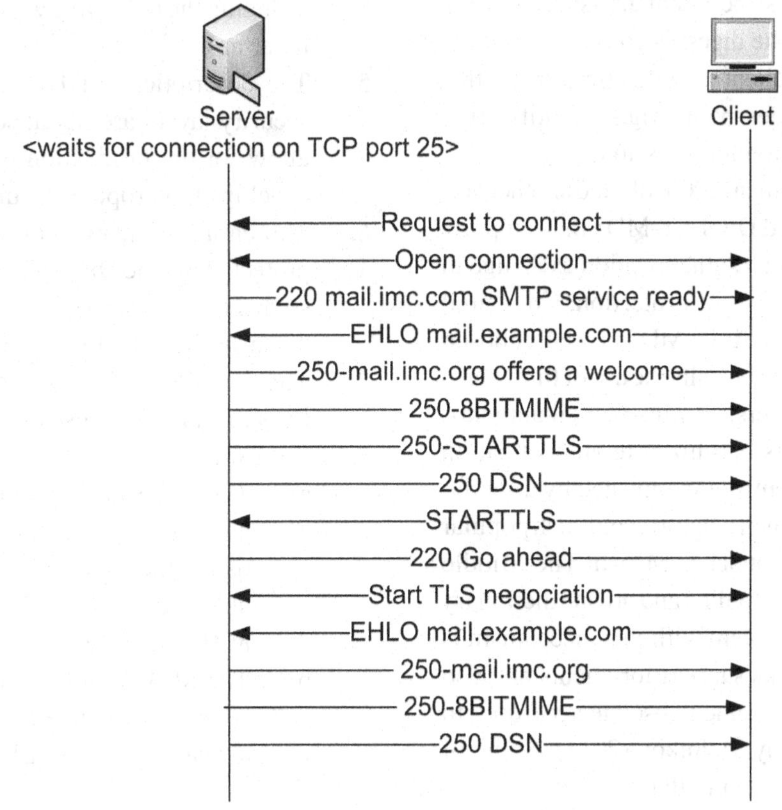

SASL (CRAM -MD5)

The old version of SASL used the Challenge-Response Authentication Mechanism (CRAM) (Klensin, Catoe & Krumviede, 1997), which is a cryptographic mechanism. This mechanism made use of the Message Digest 5 (MD5) algorithm to protect passwords against eavesdropping during transmission. Like the "Login" mechanism that is explained in the section "Message Transfer," it encoded the username in a BASE64 string. But it used the following MD5 algorithm in Hash-Based Message Authentication Codes (HMACs) (Krawczyk, Bellare & Canetti, 1997) to hash the password.

digest = MD5(('secret' XOR opad), MD5(('secret' XOR ipad), plain_data))

Where iPad is the byte 0x36 repeated B times, opad is the byte 0x5C repeated B times, and 'secret' is a string known only to the client and server. The client then sends this digest to the server. When the server receives the client message, it verifies the digest. If the digest is correct, the server assumes that the client is authenticated. So this mechanism provides both origin identification and replay protection for a session.

Leach and Newman (2000) offered another version of SASL called DIGEST-MD5 that supports data integrity after an authentication exchange in addition to other types of protection. Compared to CRAM-MD5, DIGEST-MD5 prevents chosen plaintext attacks and permits the use of third party authentication servers, permits mutual authentication, and permits optimized re-authentication if a client was recently authenticated by a server. Using this mechanism helps to avoid such popular attacks as replay attacks, Man-In-The-Middle (MITM) attacks, and online and offline dictionary attacks. But the problem with this mechanism is not only that it lacks support for clients but also this mechanism is deemed obsolete according to the list presented by Melnikov (2011). Some of the problems explained in that list are:

1. There are too many modes and too many options presented without thorough explanations or adequate implementations to back them up. Documentation is lacking in all areas. Some of the options are in conflict with each other.
2. The DIGEST-MD5 document allows an extra construct and allows for "implied folding whitespace" to be inserted in many places which is confusing and many implementations do not accept it.
3. The DIGEST-MD5 document's concept of a "realm" is used to define a collection of accounts. One or more realms can be supported by A DIGEST-MD5 server. There is no guidance provided by the DIGEST-MD5 document as to how realms should be named or how to enter them in User Interfaces (UIs).
4. Because the use of username in the inner hash is problematic it is rarely done in practice. Because it is not compatible with widely deployed UNIX password databases changing the username would invalidate the inner hash.
5. The descriptions of DES/3DES and RC4 security layers are not adequate enough to allow for the production of independently developed interoperable implementations.
6. The entire authentication exchange is not protected by The DIGEST-MD5 outer hash, so this makes the mechanism vulnerable to "man-in-the-middle" attacks.
7. The DIGEST-MD5 cryptographic primitives that are being use do not meet today's standards:
    a. The MD5 hash is not strong enough against brute force attacks initiated using the powerful hardware available today (Kim, Biryukov, Preneel, & Hong, 2006).
    b. The RC4 algorithm is prone to attack when used as the security layer without discarding the initial key stream output

   c. The DES cipher for the security layer is considered insecure due to its small key space

SPA/NTLM (Integrated Windows Authentication)

NT LAN Manager (NTLM) (Microsoft Corporation, 2012) also known as Secure Password Authorization (SPA) is the Windows Challenge-Response authentication protocol. NTLM uses three types of messages between the client and server. A message is based on the client, the format, and the use of the message. As with some other authentication mechanisms, it uses a base64 encoded data stream that is the same as POP3 or SMTP. NTLM credentials are comprised of a domain name, a username, and a one-way hash of the user's password. NTLM uses an encrypted challenge/response protocol to authenticate a user without sending the user's password over the network. Microsoft Corporation (2012) listed the following steps as outlines for this protocol:

1. (Interactive authentication only) A user accesses a client computer and provides a domain name, user name, and password. The client computes a cryptographic hash of the password and discards the actual password.
2. The client sends the user name to the server (in plaintext).
3. The server generates a 16-byte random number, called a challenge or nonce, and sends it to the client.
4. The client encrypts this challenge with the hash of the user's password and returns the result to the server. This is called the response.
5. The server sends the following three items to the domain controller:
   a. User name
   b. Challenge sent to the client
   c. Response received from the client
6. The domain controller uses the user name to retrieve the hash of the user's password from the Security Account Manager database. It uses this password hash to encrypt the challenge.
7. The domain controller compares the encrypted challenge it computed (in step 6) to the response computed by the client (in step 4). If they are identical, authentication is successful.

NTLM is widely deployed on current systems. The main disadvantage of this mechanism is that it is not very secure and that it is vulnerable to many types of attack like the credentials forwarding attack. Ochoa and Azubel (2010) have published a list of these vulnerabilities.

Securing the Content

One of the oldest shortcomings of electronic mail in the internet, and most of its predecessors, is that the content is not cryptographically secured in the standard protocols. In particular, the content can neither be reliably authenticated, nor is it protected against eavesdropping. In the first version of electronic mail used in the UNIX environment, the SNDMSG (Tomlinson, 1971), this did not pose an issue as mail was only exchanged locally between users of the same multi-tasking operating system. Here, the operating system provided both authentication (by trustfully inserting correct sender information), and integrity and confidentiality (by protecting the recipients mailbox using regular file system access control).

Once email started being transmitted over the network, both authenticity and confidentiality were lost. Many users did not consider this as a problem: the network operators were trusted to not perform eavesdropping (and intercepting email is indeed a criminal offense today in many jurisdictions). In addition, email originally was not used for any "critical" activity, such as commercial transactions. Authenticity was not a concern because, in most cases, the sender could be reliably authenticated by just verifying that the content is plausible, as recipients were familiar with the senders.

Today most users still do not consider confidentiality of email as an issue as they continue to trust network operators to not intercept their data. Some users, however, are concerned about the ability of government-supported lawful interception. In addition, a threat to confidentiality exists during message submission and postbox access. This threat is also addressed by transport-layer encryption which was discussed in the subsections on "Message Submission."

On the other hand, message authentication is a real concern for many users, as users often receive spam and scam emails from fake email accounts, and phishing emails that try to impersonate a genuine sender by talking the user into performing some action. As a consequence, a variety of approaches to deal with message and sender authenticity have been developed.

Securing the Header

Email messages delivered using SMTP usually contain headers which describe the travel path of a message between senders and recipients (Table 1). However, even though most email users are not

Table 1. Header Fields of a SMTP Message (Resnick, 2001)

Field name	Application	Required	Description
From	originator fields	Yes	The sender of the message.
Sender		No	If different than "From"
Reply-To		No	specify to whom the response shall be sent. If not set replies go to "From"
To	Destination fields	No (but usually present)	the primary recipient of the message
Cc		No	The secondary recipients of the message. A copy of message sent to them
Bcc		No	an original copy of message sent to these recipients
Date	Originator's date	Yes	Date and time stamp for the message
Message-ID	Identification fields	No (but usually present)	Unique code applied in a time of sending
In-Reply-To		No	A mechanism to Coordinate responses
References		No	If any other message ID available
Subject	International fields	No (but usually present)	Title of the message
Comments		No	Description of the message
Keywords		No	Used for searching purposes
Return-Path	Trace fields	No	Used to trace messages through email systems
Received			
Resent-Date	new fields	Depends on the status of message whether it is forwarded or not	Used to forward message
Resent-From			
Resent-Sender			
Resent-To			
Resent-Cc			
Resent-Bcc			

concerned with this, it is important to remember that the data contained in the header is critical data that needs to be protected in order to prevent the forging of messages and in order to reduce spam. There are some cryptographic approaches available for use in securing messages during the client message fetching process (mailbox security).

Mailbox

When a user wants to access or manage his emails, first he needs to use an email client which is called the Mail User Agent (MUA) (Gellens & Klensin, 2011). The most popular MUAs are Outlook, Thunderbird, Opera Mail, Eudora email software, Pegasus Mail, etc. These MUAs use some standard protocols for receiving email which are stored on the server and in managing them. One of these protocols is Post Office Protocol 3 (POP3) (Myers & Rose, 1997). POP3 is a client/server protocol. It has been built into the Netscape and Microsoft Internet Explorer browsers. POP3 is designed to delete email from the server as soon as the user has downloaded it. However, some email clients allow for users or an administrator to set an option that will allow for a longer retention period or an indefinite retention period. In POP3, users can work offline on their emails, but any changes made will not be saved on the server. Users need to periodically check the server for new emails, and if any are present, download them from the server to their PC. For these reasons, Internet Message Access Protocol (IMAP) (Crispin, 2003) was proposed to enhance the receipt of email from a server. This protocol enables users to better organize their emails on the server by creating unlimited folders. IMAP can act like a remote file server. Since it keeps original emails on the server, the user has access to all his emails from anywhere, or he can connect to the server from different computers at the same time. A user can also work live on his emails and any changes made to any email will be stored on the server. This occurs because, when a connection is established with the server, IMAP maintains that connection with the server. Messages viewed once on the server are then cached on the computer in order to save bandwidth. Users can also set up a synchronization process in order to store permanent copies of messages locally. Like other non-secure protocols that have been explained in past sections, IMAP and POP3 are vulnerable to various types of attack (Newman, 1999), such as man-in-the-middle attacks. Also passwords and usernames are sent in plaintext and thus can be sniffed easily. This is the main reason that Newman (1999) wanted to use these protocols over TLS/SSL.

IMAPS

There are two mechanisms in use to protect IMAP; IMAP over SSL which is known as IMAPS and IMAP over TLS which is known as STARTTLS (Newman, 1999). The Secure Sockets Layer (SSL) Protocol Version 3.0 (Freier, Karlton & Kocher, 2011) is the last version of SSL. It has two security features; encryption and certification. It avoids fake identity scams by asking the contacted server to present its digital certificate to prove its identity.

SSL and TLS differ in the way a secure connection is started, but both are generally considered equal in terms of security. The main difference is that, while SSL connections begin with security and proceed directly to a secured communication, TLS connections begin with an unsecured "hello" message to the server in order to determine if that server supports encryption. In other words, IMAP will use an unencrypted channel, at first, in order to determine if both the client and the server support the STARTTLS command. If they do, then the connection between them will be switched to an encrypted communication and it will then proceed to initiate the STARTTLS handshake. If the client and server both do not support the STARTTLS command, then the communication will remain unsecure. Moreover, TLS is capable of working on different ports and has more backward compatibility than SSL. Figure 4 depicts the simple IMAP handshakes over SSL and TLS. IMAP (Crispin, 2003) supports a large number of commands. In the illustration, for instance, the CAPABILITY command requests a list of the supported server capabilities. The CHANGECIPHERSPEC (Freier, Karlton & Kocher, 2011), in Figure 4, is a message used to notify the receiving party that subsequent records will be protected under the just-negotiated CipherSpec and keys. Receipt of this message causes the receiver to copy the "read pending" state into the "read current" state. The client sends a CHANGECIPHERSPEC message, initiates the handshake key exchange and the certificate verification message process. The server then sends a message, similar to that of the client, after having successfully processed the key exchange message. The NEWSESSIONTICKET is basically a ticket consisting of the session state that includes, for example, the cipher suite and master secret in use.

SASL

As explained in the section "SASL (CRAM-MD5)", the Simple Authentication and Security Layer (SASL) (Melnikov & Zeilenga, 2006) is a framework which provides authentication and data security services in connection-oriented protocols via replaceable mechanisms. IMAP and POP are among the protocols that contain SASL support. If a protocol supports SASL, then it should include a command for identifying and authenticating a user to a server, and optionally, for negotiating protection of subsequent protocol interactions. If its use is negotiated, a security layer is inserted between the protocol and the connection. For authentication purposes, any of the mechanisms can be used that were explained in the prior sections, such as CRAM-MD5 (Klensin, Catoe & Krumviede, 1997), DIGEST-MD5, PLAIN, LOGIN and NTLM (Microsoft Corporation, 2012).

Figure 4. Simple IMAP handshakes over SSL and TLS

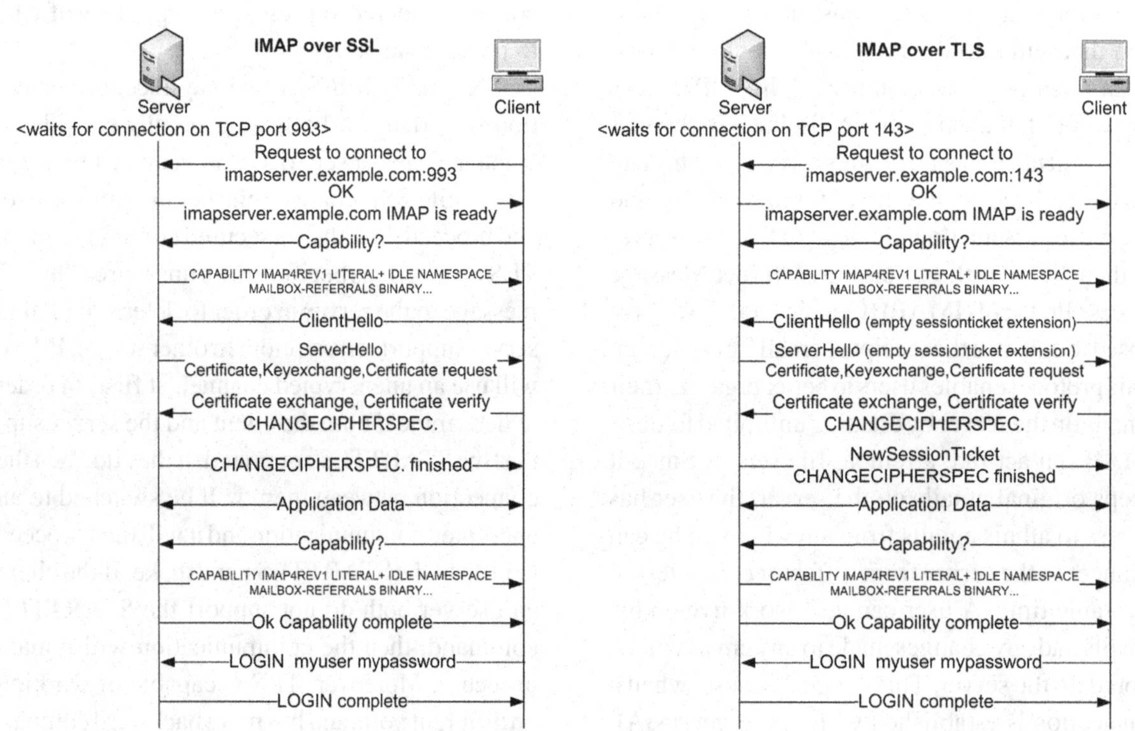

POP3S

Like IMAPS, POP3 can also be protected over SSL or TLS (Newman, 1999). The former is known as POP3S and the latter as POP3 over TLS. POP3S uses a separate SSL port, i.e. 995, where the SSL handshake procedure begins as soon as a client connects, and then, only after the session is encrypted does the regular protocol handling begin. Using two separate ports for plaintext and SSL connections was thought to be wasteful. This is why POP3 over TLS is the more popular of the two, as it uses the normal unencrypted port, i.e. 110. A client first connects to this unsecure port and immediately starts a STARTTLS command that changes the session to an encrypted one. However, the problem with POP3 over TLS occurs when a client does not support a secure connection or a client prefers using an unsecure connection instead of a secure one. This is when the POP3 over TLS tries to do a plaintext authentication, which is impossible in SSL, since the connection will be refused by the server.

Message Signing

Both Pretty Good Privacy (PGP) and S/MIME support message signatures. In email, it is essential that the message remains legible, even after signing, which causes both PGP and S/MIME to employ ASCII-armored data representations, where the original plain text becomes, literally, a part of the complete message. Additionally, S/MIME puts the MIME layer on top, allowing mail readers to recognize and display the original message; the signature then typically gets rendered as an attachment.

Again, each protocol specifies the set of supported algorithms. In addition to the asymmetric algorithms, digital signatures need to select hash algorithms. Also, some asymmetric algorithms are signature-only, so the list of algorithms for signing messages is longer than the one for encryption.

PGP requires a Digital Signature Algorithm (DSA) for the signature, and allows, but deprecates, RSA. SHA-1 is required as a hash algorithm with various alternatives also being supported (MD-5, RIPE-MD/160, SHA-256, etc.).

S/MIME requires RSA with SHA-256, and recommends various combinations of RSA and DSA with MD5, SHA-1, and SHA-256.

As with encrypting messages, verifying messages poses a challenge for the validation of the sender's public key. The challenge is slightly easier than that for encryption, though, because:

- The data format is backwards compatible, so the recipient is able to read the message even if he cannot verify the signature.
- The message typically includes an indication of how to establish trust. For S/MIME, the certificate is often included in the signed message, only requiring the recipient to receive and trust the CA certificate. Receiving the CA certificate is feasible, as the location of the CA certificate is included in the user certificate. For PGP, the key identifier is included in the message, which allows the user to retrieve the key from a key server (if the key was uploaded).

MTA Authentication

In addition to authenticating users sending email, authenticating the sender's Mail Transfer Agent (MTA) is also a useful technique for preventing faked emails. Users cannot generally assume that communication partners will be able to verify a signature due to the lack of trust; therefore, message signing is not widely used. In order to reduce spam, email administrators have been looking for alternative approaches to validate that an email message really comes from the user that claims to be the sender of the email.

Instead of having the user sign the email, the first mail transport agent receiving the original message submission will sign the email, allowing receiving mail transport agents to verify that the mail was really submitted through that host. In addition, for an internet domain, the list of authorized MTAs is published. As a consequence, spammers sending email for a different domain can be recognized; in addition, spammers sending from your own domain, that do not go through the domain's official MTAs, can also be detected. We present two protocols that have been established for this application.

Sender Policy Framework

The Sender Policy Framework (SPF) (Wong & Schlitt, 2006) defines DNS records that list authorized source MTAs for messages originating from a domain. SPF defines a new resource record type (99); for compatibility, the TXT record type (16) can also be used. The value of this resource record defines, in a micro programming language, the list of valid senders for a domain, by specification of IPv4 or IPv6 address prefixes, or redirecting through MX, A, or PTR records. A receiving MTA uses the source sender identity as indicated in the MAIL FROM SMTP command, retrieves the corresponding SPF record, and checks whether the TCP peer address of the SMTP communication is authorized to send email. Optionally, the same check can also be applied to the host name in the SMTP HELO/EHLO command, although many legitimate senders currently fail this test as they put bogus data into the HELO command. No check of the (Resnick, 2008) "From: header" is performed.

With this framework, receiving MTAs may choose to reject email if the sender domain has an SPF record, or it may quarantine or flag the message.

In itself, no cryptographic mechanism is employed in this protocol. However, a potential threat to the protocol is poisoning of the recipient's DNS cache. This would be done to introduce fake SPF records to make the receiving MTA accept a message from an unauthorized host. This threat can be avoided by using DNSSEC in addition to SPF, in order to trustfully sign all DNS records involved (i.e. the SPF record itself, and any MX and A records it refers to).

DomainKeys Identified Mail (DKIM)

DKIM (Allman, Callas, Delany, Libbey, Fenton, & Thomas, 2007) involves a cryptographic mechanism that not only authorizes senders, but to also authenticates the originating MTA. As with SPF, DNS resource records are used to publish authorized information about the domain. However, instead of publishing policy, DKIM publishes public keys in the DNS. Compared to the other technologies, the authors of the specification point out that DKIM:

- Puts signatures into email headers, leaving the body untouched;
- Does not require users to have a priori trust in certain public keys; instead, the public keys are found through DNS lookups;
- Does not mandate any specific policy for the case that verification fails.

Each domain can publish any number of keys, typically one per sending MTA. The domain keys are put into the <keyname>._domainkeys.<domain> label, using a TXT record.

A MTA emitting a message creates a signature including certain selected header fields, and the body, signs this with the key, and creates a new email header. This header includes the key name, the list of fields included in the checksum, and the actual signature value. The supported signature algorithms are RSA-SHA1 and RSA-SHA256. Allman et al. (2007) point out those keys of 4096 bits and more will not fit into the standard DNS size limit for UDP messages of 512 bytes.

As the message is forwarded from MTA to MTA, possibly being replicated at a mailing list, it may get signed multiple times. Recipients can verify each individual signature separately.

The specification leaves any policy effect of DKIM verification to the local systems. They recommend that MTAs indicate verification results in additional email headers, allowing users to filter by these headers, rather than rejecting messages. For example, a spam filter might diagnose a phishing attempt when an unsigned message is received for a domain that is known to typically sign messages. In order to determine whether a sender would normally sign messages, the Author Domain Signing Practices (ADSP) protocol (Allman, Fenton, Delany & Levine, 2009; Leiba, Thomas, & Crocker, 2011) can be used.

DKIM, as currently specified, has a shortcoming that causes verification to fail even though the message was not substantially modified: transit MTAs may restructure MIME payloads, and in particular change the character encoding of text parts. This will break the verification, as DKIM's signature algorithm is not MIME-aware.

Securing the Body

Securing the body is critical when email exchanged between users contains vital data, such as credit card information or passwords. A particular common use case for email encryption is the exchange of passwords between system administrators. In this case, users just do not want to risk having their password intercepted. As discussed later, using email encryption is a challenge in practice, and the hurdles are too high for casual non-admin users.

Message Encryption

In today's email infrastructure, message encryption relies on asymmetric cryptography. Using only symmetric cryptography would require a sender and a recipient to share a secret, which is impractical by the nature of electronic mail. With asymmetric cryptography, the practical challenge is to obtain the public key of the recipient. Two strategies have been developed to provide this information to the sender:

- A directory service allows looking up public keys by certain criteria, such as the recipient's email address or the recipient's real name. Such directories often allow any user to post information, so the challenge here is to verify that the public key really belongs to the recipient.
- In the absence of a directory, the recipient can send his public key in a first interchange, which is then followed by the actual communication. With RSA, a typical approach is to have the recipient send a signed message first: the protocols discussed below will then allow for the inclusion of the public key along with the message. This also helps to verify that the recipient really holds the corresponding private key. Verifying that the public key really belongs to the recipient (rather than belonging to a man in the middle) still remains a challenge.

Pretty Good Privacy (PGP)

In 1991, Phil Zimmermann created the first version of the Pretty Good Privacy software (Zimmermann, 1995). The current version of the protocol is OpenPGP (Shaw, 2009) which is based on version 5.0 of the PGP software. PGP offers both digital signature and encryption. Encryption is performed in the following steps (section 2.1: Shaw, 2009):

1. The sender creates a message.
2. The sending OpenPGP generates a random number to be used as a session key for this message only.
3. The session key is encrypted using each recipient's public key.
4. These "encrypted session keys" start the message.
5. The sender optionally compresses the message.
6. The sending OpenPGP encrypts the message using the session key, which forms the remainder of the message.

7. The receiving OpenPGP decrypts the session key using the recipient's private key.
8. The receiving OpenPGP decrypts the message using the session key.
9. If the message was compressed, it will be decompressed.

Messages are transmitted as a series of packets, with packets being packed by packet type. Packet types include public keys, secret keys, encrypted session keys, signatures, compressed payload, encrypted payload, etc.

The preferred public key algorithm of PGP is Elgamal; RSA is also supported, but deprecated. Various symmetric algorithms for data encryption are supported, including IDEA, 3DES, CAST5, Blowfish, and AES. 3DES is required, AES-128, CAST5, and IDEA are recommended. As compression algorithms, ZIP, ZLIB and BZip2 are supported. None of the compression algorithms must be supported, but ZIP should be implemented.

In an email message, the encrypted data is typically put in ASCII armor, with a header tag indicating the kind of data, and the actual encryption result encoded in a radix-64 encoding.

PGP keys are mutually signed in a web of trust, where users can arbitrarily sign each other's public key. Global key servers can be used to upload and download public keys and signatures to public keys. Users then need to establish trust themselves in the claimed identities, but checking whether they can establish a chain of trust between people they personally trust, following signatures that those people made, then ultimately to the identity of the message recipient. In addition, people use other means of communicating public keys, such as posting them on their home pages, or maintaining key rings within communities.

S/MIME

The Secure/Multipurpose Internet Mail Extensions (Ramsdell & Turner, 2010) use the existing MIME framework (Freed & Borenstein, 1996). The current protocol version is 3.2. In addition, it is based on the Public Key Infrastructure (PKI) (Cooper et al., 2008) and the Cryptographic Message Syntax (CMS) (Housley, 2009). While we assume that the reader is familiar with PKI, we elaborate on CMS first.

CMS is derived from PKCS#7 (Kaliski, 1998). It is an ASN.1 (Legg, 2007) based syntax for encrypted and signed data. In addition, it supports various auxiliary data records such as encrypted symmetric keys. Following the ASN.1 notion of object identifiers, arbitrary cryptographic algorithms can be used, allowing for the introduction of new algorithms without the need to change the data structures. Encrypted data is a record identified by the object identifier

{ iso(1) member-body(2) us(840)
rsadsi(113549) pkcs(1) pkcs7(7) 6 }

While CMS uses Distinguished Encoding Rules (DER) to transmit data, S/MIME now takes such messages and puts them into the MIME framework. In addition, it specifies certain cryptographic algorithms required for implementations to allow for interoperability. Finally, it also supports transmission of auxiliary data such as certificates and certificate revocation lists.

For key encryption, S/MIME specifies RSA as mandatory, and recommends RSAES-OAEP. For symmetric algorithms, AES-128 CBC is required, and AES-192 CBC and 3DES CBC are recommended. CMS messages are transmitted using the application/pkcs7-mime media type.

Trust in public keys is established through certificate authorities in the PKI. A common infrastructure for publishing certificates is LDAP, but there currently is no global directory for PKI certificates (unlike PGP). Instead, there may be organization-wide directories (such as installations of Microsoft's Active Directory), allowing for the retrieval of a certificate for a message recipient. In the absence of a directory, it is common to have the ultimate recipient (Bob) of an encrypted message send a signed message to Alice first, as this will include Bob's certificate, which then gets cached in Alice's email client, allowing Alice to then send an encrypted message. Trust in Certificate Authorities is typically achieved by relying on a list of CAs which is provided by the operating system vendor, and extended according to local policies.

FUTURE RESEARCH DIRECTIONS TO SECURE EMAIL

The fight against spam and scam will be an ever ongoing process because as the cryptographic algorithms continue to improve and as new cryptographic algorithms are proposed for use along with the current protocols which secure email components during the transfer process, the scammers continue to come up with new techniques of their own to circumvent the new security. They are making use of more powerful hardware and more intrusive software packages in order to crack cryptographic algorithms that already exist. We will thus have to focus all of our resources on trying to stay one step ahead of the spammers and scammer of email systems.

Internet Protocol version 6 (IPv6) (Deering & Hinden, 1998) is the next-generation of internet protocol and is designed to solve security issues and the lack of addresses that are present in the older version (IPv4) of this protocol. On February 3, 2011, IANA allocated the final blocks of IPv4 addresses to the regional registries thereby exhausting the central address pool. Despite the fact that the protocols related to email, such as SMTP, IMAP, POP3, etc., are application layer protocols within IPv6 networks, spammers and scammers now have another exploitable area at their disposal which resulted from the expansion of the address space and the nodes' temporary addresses used for privacy or security reasons in IPv6. If spammers and scammers gain full access to the resources of one IPv6 node in a network, then they will be able to send spam and scam through a different authorized IP address from the same node. Moreover, in a subnet, there are 2^{64} IPv6 usable addresses making it easy for spammers and scammers to change their IPv6 addresses every second or to send out each spam or scam mail with a different address. This helps them hide their identity while they flood the network with spam and scam thus complicating the life of the system administrator. Moreover, due to the fact that IPv6 addresses are 128 bits in comparison to IPv4 addresses that are 32 bits, the regular DNS Address Resource Record (RR) was created to allow a domain name to be associated with a 128-bit IPv6 address. An example of these RRs is the four "A"s, i.e. "AAAA", to indicate that the IPv6 address is four times the size of the IPv4 address. The AAAA record is structured in the same way that the A record is in both binary and master file formats, but it is just much larger. As stated in an earlier section, in order to secure DNS, as it has a vital role in many protocols, like email protocols, especially in the transfer stage, DNSSEC (Arends, Austein, Larson, Massey & Rose, 2005) was proposed. Hoffman (2010) adds the latest extension to DNSSEC which specifies how the DNSSEC cryptographic algorithm identifiers in the IANA registries are allocated. When user A sends an email to user B, it is important for user A to ensure that user B, in the other domain, really receives that message without a scammer having eavesdropped and spoofed it on its way before it reaches user B. It is the same for user B as he wants to be sure that user A really sent that email. For average users this may not be as important as it is for say governors or people who have high positions in society as there is the potential for their reputation to be sullied by bogus information contained in fraudulent emails. More to the point, as also touched briefly in section "MTA Authentication", consider this hypothetical example. The head of a large company wants to expel one of his executive managers called X, but before doing so he wants to get the opinions of his other executive managers. Since he is traveling on business he prefers to use email as the means of contacting all of the executive managers. The head of the company's email resides in a different domain than those of his executive managers. X finds out what is going on and being the devious person he is, he initiates a 'man-in-the-middle' attack. This attack enables him to capture the emails being sent to the executive managers and to then create a bogus "in his favor" response from each manager back to the head of the company. X wants to buy himself enough time so that his dismissal will not be imminent. He hopes to use this time to collect incriminating information against the head of the company so that X can blackmail him in order to keep his job. So in this example you can see how important it is to check both the sender and the receiver. If the email clients of those executive managers checked the receiver's domain, then X would not have been able to execute his attack. The same is true for the receivers. If they had checked the sender, this would not have happened and X would not have had an opportunity to send forged emails to the head of the company. This issue also applied to the content of emails. Several new studies focus on making better use of a cryptographic approach to protect data. Mantoro, Norhanipah and Bidin (2011) proposed an IPv6 framework for DNSSEC in order to provide for origin authentication of DNS data. DNSSEC is not widely implemented and this kind of framework can be the first steps for DNSSEC global implementation.

CONCLUSION

Electronic Mail (email) is a novel way of communicating using the internet. Unfortunately, protocols related to transfer, receive, or send emails do not have the protection mechanisms needed to protect the email components and to prevent spam, crack or the theft of critical data. For example, many scammers and spammers misuse SMTP, a protocol for sending and receiving emails, in order to disseminate their unwanted messages or to attach malicious programs. However, cryptographic approaches play a minor role in spam reduction. But they do have a high effect on the prevention of email cracking and forged messages.

To protect the mail data, verify authenticity, and, as a result, decrease spam and forged mail, many approaches have been proposed which were classified in this chapter as cryptographic approaches according to the level of protection afforded to email components. Their advantages and disadvantages, if any, were described. We explained the differences in the use of these approaches in the new generation of internet protocol, i.e. IPv6, in comparison to the old internet protocol, i.e. IPv4, and we covered the most recent studies in this area. We also explained the importance of verifying "sender domain" as well as "receiver domain."

REFERENCES

Allman, E., Callas, J., Delany, M., Libbey, M., Fenton, J., & Thomas, M. (2007). DomainKeys identified mail (DKIM) signatures. RFC. Retrieved from http://tools.ietf.org/html/rfc4871

Allman, E., Fenton, J., Delany, M., & Levine, J. (2009). DomainKeys identified mail (DKIM) author domain signing practices (ADSP). RFC. Retrieved from http://tools.ietf.org/html/rfc5617

Arends, R., Austein, R., Larson, M., Massey, D., & Rose, S. (2005). DNS security introduction and requirements. RFC. Retrieved March 2005, from http://www.ietf.org/rfc/rfc4033.txt

Ariyapperuma, S., & Mitchell, C. J. (2007). Security vulnerabilities in DNS and DNSSEC. In Proceedings of the Second International Conference on Availability, Reliability and Security. ACM. Retrieved from http://dl.acm.org/citation.cfm?id=1250514

15. Chapter, U. S. C. 103. (2011). Commerce and trade. Retrieved from http://uscode.house.gov/download/pls/15C103.txt

Cooper, D., Santesson, S., Farrell, S., Boeyen, S., Housley, R., & Polk, W. (2008). Internet X.509 public key infrastructure certificate and certificate revocation list (CRL) profile. RFC. Retrieved from http://www.ietf.org/rfc/rfc5280.txt

Crispin, M. (2003). Internet message access protocol - Version 4rev1. Retrieved from http://tools.ietf.org/html/rfc3501

Deering, S., & Hinden, R. (1998). Internet protocol, version 6 (IPv6) specification. RFC. Retrieved from http://www.ietf.org/rfc/rfc2460.txt

Dierks, T., & Allen, C. (1999). The TLS protocol version 1.0. RFC. Retrieved from http://www.ietf.org/rfc/rfc2246.txt

Eastlake, D. (1999). Domain name system security extensions. RFC. Retrieved from http://tools.ietf.org/html/rfc2535

Freed, N., & Borenstein, N. (1996). Multipurpose internet mail extensions (MIME) part one: Format of internet message bodies. RFC. Retrieved from http://tools.ietf.org/html/rfc2045

Freed, N., & Borenstein, N. (1996). Multipurpose internet mail extensions (MIME) part five: Conformance criteria and examples. RFC. Retrieved from http://tools.ietf.org/html/rfc2049

Freier, A., Karlton, P., & Kocher, P. (2011). The secure sockets layer (SSL) protocol version 3.0. RFC. Retrieved from http://tools.ietf.org/html/rfc6101

Gellens, R., & Klensin, J. (2011). Message submission for mail. RFC. Retrieved from http://tools.ietf.org/html/rfc6409

Hoffman, P. (2002). SMTP service extension for secure SMTP over transport layer security. RFC. Retrieved from http://www.ietf.org/rfc/rfc3207.txt

Hoffman, P. (2010). Cryptographic algorithm identifier allocation for DNSSEC. Retrieved from http://tools.ietf.org/html/rfc6014

Housley, R. (2009). Cryptographic message syntax (CMS). RFC. Retrieved from http://tools.ietf.org/html/rfc5652

Kaliski, B. (1998). PKCS #10: Certification request syntax version 1.5. RFC. Retrieved from http://tools.ietf.org/html/rfc2314

Kim, J., Biryukov, A., Preneel, B., & Hong, S. (2006). On the security of HMAC and NMAC based on HAVAL, MD4, MD5, SHA-0 and SHA-1. Retrieved from http://eprint.iacr.org/2006/187.pdf

Klensin, J. (2008). Simple mail transfer protocol. RFC. Retrieved from http://tools.ietf.org/html/rfc5321

Klensin, J., Catoe, R., & Krumviede, P. (1997). IMAP/POP authorize extension for simple challenge/response. RFC. Retrieved from http://tools.ietf.org/html/rfc2195

Krawczyk, H., Bellare, M., & Canetti, R. (1997). HMAC: Keyed-hashing for message authentication. RFC. Retrieved from http://tools.ietf.org/html/rfc2104

Leach, P., & Newman, C. (2000). Using digest authentication as a SASL mechanism. RFC. Retrieved from http://www.ietf.org/rfc/rfc2831.txt

Legg, S. (2007). Abstract syntax notation X (ASN.X) representation of encoding instructions for the generic string encoding rules (GSER). RFC. Retrieved from http://tools.ietf.org/html/rfc4913

Leiba, B., Thomas, M., & Crocker, D. (2011). Author domain signing practices (ADSP): Point and counterpoint. Internet Computing, 15(1), 76-80. Retrieved from http://doi.ieeecomputersociety.org/10.1109/MIC.2011.1

Mantoro, T., Norhanipah, S. A., & Bidin, A. F. (2011). An implementation on domain name system security extensions framework for the support of IPv6 environment. doi:10.1109/ICMCS.2011.5945627

Melnikov, A. (2011). Moving DIGEST-MD5 to historic. RFC. Retrieved from http://tools.ietf.org/html/rfc6331

Melnikov, A., & Zeilenga, K. (2006). Simple authentication and security layer (SASL). Retrieved from http://tools.ietf.org/html/rfc4422

Microsoft Corporation. (2012). Microsoft NTLM. Retrieved from http://msdn.microsoft.com/en-us/library/aa378749.aspx

Myers, J. (1999). SMTP service extension for authentication. RFC. Retrieved from http://tools.ietf.org/html/rfc2554

Myers, J., & Rose, M. (1997). Post office protocol - Version 3. RFC. Retrieved from http://www.ietf.org/rfc/rfc1939.txt

Newman, C. (1999). Using TLS with IMAP, POP3 and ACAP. RFC. Retrieved from http://tools.ietf.org/html/rfc2595

Ochoa, H., & Azubel, A. (2010). Windows SMB NTLM authentication weak nonce vulnerability. Retrieved from http://www.ampliasecurity.com/research/OCHOA-2010-0209.txt

Postel, J. B. (1982). Simple mail transfer protocol. RFC. Retrieved from http://www.ietf.org/rfc/rfc821.txt

Rafiee, H., Von Loewis, M., & Meinel, C. (2012). IPv6 deployment and spam challenges. *IEEE Internet Computing*, *16*(6). doi:10.1109/MIC.2012.97.

Ramsdell, B., & Turner, S. (2010). Secure/multipurpose internet mail extensions (S/MIME) version 3.2 certificate handling. RFC. Retrieved from http://tools.ietf.org/html/rfc5750

Ramsdell, B., & Turner, S. (2010). Secure/multipurpose internet mail extensions (S/MIME) version 3.2 message specification. RFC. Retrieved from http://tools.ietf.org/html/rfc5751

Resnick, P. (2001). Internet message format. RFC. Retrieved from http://tools.ietf.org/html/rfc2822

Resnick, P. (2008). Internet message format. RFC. Retrieved from http://tools.ietf.org/html/rfc5322

Shaw, D. (2009). The camellia cipher in OpenPGP. RFC. Retrieved from http://tools.ietf.org/html/rfc5581

Siemborski, R., & Melnikov, A. (2007). SMTP service extension for authentication. RFC. Retrieved from http://tools.ietf.org/html/rfc4954

Suwa, S., Yamai, N., Okayama, K., & Nakamura, M. (2011). DNS resource record analysis of URLs in e-mail messages for improving spam filtering. In Proceedings of the 2011 IEEE/IPSJ International Symposium on Applications and the Internet. IEEE. Retrieved from http://dl.acm.org/citation.cfm?id=2061659

Tomlinson, R. (1971). The first network email. Retrieved from http://openmap.bbn.com/~tomlinso/ray/firstemailframe.html

Trabelsi, Z., Rahmani, H., Kaouech, K., & Frikha, M. (2004). Malicious sniffing systems detection platform. *IEEE Computer Society*, *201*. doi: doi:10.1109/SAINT.2004.1266117.

Turner, S., & Polk, T. (2011). Prohibiting secure sockets layer (SSL) version 2.0. RFC. Retrieved from http://tools.ietf.org/html/rfc617

Van Staden, F., & Venter, H. (2010). Adding digital forensic readiness to the email trace header. [ISSA]. *IEEE Information Security for South Africa*, *1*. doi: doi:10.1109/ISSA.2010.5588258.

Wong, M., & Schlitt, W. (2006). Sender policy framework (SPF) for authorizing use of domains in e-mail, version 1. RFC. Retrieved from http://tools.ietf.org/html/rfc4408

Zimmermann, P. R. (1995). The official PGP user's guide. Retrieved from http://mitpress.mit.edu/catalog/item/default.asp?ttype=2&tid=5518

ADDITIONAL READING

Oppliger, R. (2009). SSL protocol, TLS protocol. In *SSL and TLS: Theory and Practice* (pp. 75–178). Norwood, MA: Artech House.

KEY TERMS AND DEFINITIONS

Cracker: Crackers transform computers into zombies by using small¬ programs that exploit weaknesses in a computer's Operating System (OS).

Cryptography (in Email Usage): The practice and study of techniques for secure communication or content of email in the presence of third parties (called adversaries). These techniques are related to various aspects in information security such as data confidentiality, data integrity, authentication, and non-repudiation.

DKIM: DomainKeys Identified Mail involves a cryptographic mechanism to not only authorize senders, but to also authenticate the originating MTA.

MIME: Multipurpose Internet Mail Extensions is an Internet standard that extends the format of email to support; text in character sets other than ASCII, non-text attachments, message bodies with multiple parts, and header information in non-ASCII character sets.

Scammer: The use of Internet services or software with Internet access to defraud victims or to otherwise take advantage of them, for example by stealing personal information.

SMTP: Simple Mail Transfer Protocol is a protocol used to send electronic mail across the Internet.

Spam: Spam is the use of electronic messaging systems to send unsolicited bulk messages, especially advertising, indiscriminately. Spam is often used for the purposes of scamming.

Spammer: A person who creates electronic spam.

SPF: The Sender Policy Framework defines DNS records that list authorized source MTAs for messages originating from a domain. With this framework, receiving MTAs may choose to reject email if the sender domain has an SPF record, or it may quarantine or flag the message.

Chapter 17
Theory and Practice of Secure E-Voting Systems

Kun Peng
Institute for Infocomm Research, Singapore

ABSTRACT

Electronic voting is a popular application of cryptographic and network techniques to e-government. Most of the existing e-voting schemes can be classified into two categories: homomorphic voting and shuffling-based voting. In a homomorphic voting, an encryption algorithm with special homomorphic property (e.g. ElGamal encryption or Paillier encryption) is employed to encrypt the votes such that the sum of the votes can be recovered without decrypting any single vote. An advantage of homomorphic voting is efficient tallying. Tallying in homomorphic voting only costs one single decryption operation for each candidate. In this chapter, the existing e-voting solutions in both categories are surveyed and analysed. The key security properties in both categories are presented and then the existing e-voting schemes in each category are checked against the corresponding security properties. Security and efficiency of the schemes are analysed and the strongest security and highest efficiency achievable in each category is estimated. Problems and concerns about the existing solutions including vulnerability to malicious voters and (or) talliers, possible failure of complete correctness, imperfect privacy, dependence on computational assumptions, and exaggerated efficiency are addressed. New approaches will be proposed in both kinds of solutions to overcome the existing drawbacks in them. In homomorphic e-voting, the authors deal with possibly malicious voters and aim at efficient vote validity check to achieve strong and formally provable soundness and privacy. It can be implemented through new zero knowledge proof techniques, which are both efficient and provably secure. In mix-network-based e-voting, the authors deal with possibly deviating operations of both voters and talliers and aim at efficient proof of validity of shuffling, which guarantees the desired security properties and prevent attacks from malicious participants. It can be based on inspiring linear algebra knowledge and the new zero knowledge proof of existence of secret permutation.

DOI: 10.4018/978-1-4666-4030-6.ch017

INTRODUCTION

Election has been playing a very important role in democracy and with the development of human society its form has kept changing. Through the past twenty centuries, different voting platforms have been adopted. The ancient Greeks dropped stones and pot shards into a vase, while the modern democracy developing from West Europe and North America adopts paper ballots, which are dropped in sealed boxes. All these traditional methods heavily depend on human intervention in tallying and so takes time and cannot avoid errors. The 2004 US president election is a typical example to demonstrate this drawback, not to mention the chaos caused by delay in tallying in countries with a large population. Moreover, in the fast-paced modern society, fewer and fewer people are willing to take the troubles to visit voting stations, especially in nations having enjoyed democracy for a long time.

With the rapid development of information technology, automatic voting becomes possible to prevent the drawbacks of traditional elections. The automation should maintain security of the traditional elections including fairness of the election and privacy of the votes. In 1869 Thomas Edison received US patent 90,646 for an "electronic voting device," but failed to sell his invention to the Massachusetts legislative bodies. Mechanical voting booths and punch cards are already employed to replace paper ballots to achieve faster tallying. Absentee ballots was adopted in 1997, when Monterey County, California experimented with the first Voting By Mail (VBM) system. Moreover, Direct Recording Electronic (DRE) systems have been employed in polling stations since the 1970s to store the talliers electromagnetically. As these methods still have drawbacks in convenience and speed, more advanced technologies are desired.

Electronic online voting on the Internet would be much more convenient as it enables voters to vote from anywhere. In the digital era, we have e-mail, e-commerce, e-passport, and many things have been automated by computers. The essential target of world wide Web is to communicate more information in a faster, cheaper and more convenient way. Internet voting enables voters to cast their votes any time anywhere and will result in higher voting rate. Moreover, votes in digital form can be counted fast and absolutely correctly. Fast, error-free and convenient voting and tallying processes could bring a great impact to the contemporary democratic societies. For example, elections can be held more often and in greater scale to make better use of democratic methods to decide more affairs by the citizens.

In 2004, Internet voting system was used in the national referendum in Geneva canton of Switzerland. In that nation, elections or referendums are held four or five times a year, while 580000 Swiss citizens living abroad among its seven million population. So it is important to provide them with a fast and convenient way to vote. Living in a wealthy country, more than half of the Swiss population had Internet access, both at home and at the workplace. Due to all these reasons, the governments, both at local and Federal levels have decided to develop Internet-voting solutions. According to a polling in 2003, about 73% of the Swiss population support online Internet voting. Besides already being applied to referendums, online Internet voting is supported by 80% of the Swiss voters to be employed in elections as well.

Internet voting was adopted in the European Parliamentary elections in the Netherlands in 2004 to help Dutch electors abroad or on trip on the Election Day. There was a registration phase before the elections so that eligible voters can choose the way they hope to use to vote: by post, by proxy holder, by Internet or by telephone. A surprisingly high rate (41%) of the eligible voters preferred the Internet voting system although most of them have access to the other methods. Actually, the rate could be much higher if more voters had receive the voting documents in time.

In the USA, there have been many attempts to employ electronic voting in elections. Among them, the most famous is Voting Over the Internet (VOI). VOI was adopted in the general elections of 2000 in four states (Florida, South Carolina, Texas and Utah). Another Internet voting project in USA is Secure Electronic Registration and Voting Experiment (SERVE), which was designed for primary and general elections in 2004. The eligible voters to use SERVE were mostly voters abroad and military personnel, which were estimated to be million in amount.

In the UK, several different electronic voting solutions have been experimented since 2002 and the most advanced of them is remote electronic voting via the Internet and digital television, which were used in the local election in 30 municipals in 2003 and attracted 27% of the voters to vote electronically (146 000 votes). The majority of all the investigated voters prefer Internet voting while only a small part of the voters is against it. Even though some eligible voters cannot guarantee to use e-voting methods themselves, they usually support to make it available to the public.

Estonia is a nation with a special interest in electronic voting. It has been developing an online Internet voting system since 2003, which was used in the municipal elections in autumn 2005. A public opinion poll in Estonia showed that 73% of voters are in favour of e-voting in general, while the target of the e-voting system is to attract 1 million users. As one of the most practical e-voting solutions, the Estonian e-voting system can be used as a specimen to show usually how e-voting works in practice.

According to (Mage, 2007), the Estonian e-voting system is implemented from the sixth day up to the fourth day before the Election Day and the following principles are followed in the Estonian e-voting system.

- Each eligible voter is able to revote. In this case the older votes are deleted.
- Classical voting in polling box cancels the voters' electronic votes.
- If considerable attacks against e-voting have been detected, Electoral Committee might stop e-voting and cancel the result of voting.

The Estonian e-voting systems consist of several main modules: voter application and network server while back-office is divided into votes storing server and votes counting server. These components are described in (Mage, 2007) as follows.

- Voter application is a web application. The encryption and authentication built into the Secure Socket Layer (SSL) protocol protect the communication between voters and network server. The Estonian e-voting system is able to run on Windows, Linux, and MacOS operation systems. In the Windows operation system, it is required to use Microsoft internet explorer. The public key PK of e-voting is integrated into voting application. Voter application uses signed ActiveX application.
- The processes of network server are authentication, the checking of franchise, sending a candidates' list to voters, receiving signed and encrypted ballots. Network server immediately transfers the received encrypted ballots to votes storing server and transposes the acknowledgements of receipt from votes storing server to voters. Network server completes the work at the moment when the period of e-voting finishes.
- Votes storing server receives encrypted ballots from Network Server and stores them until the end of voting period. One of the specific properties of the Estonian e-voting system is an option to cast a vote more than once. The last vote is taken into account. Votes storing server has a responsibility of votes' managing and canceling.

- Votes Counting Server is an offline server, which summarizes all encrypted ballots. The encrypted ballots are transferred from votes storing server to votes counting server by using data carriers. Votes counting server does not get voters' digital signatures and it does not know voters' personal data.

Those existing practical e-voting systems have several drawbacks. Firstly, strict public verification to any one is not provided. Secondly, guarantee to voters' privacy is not formal and strong enough. Thirdly, some of them are not convenient enough and still require some kind of physical appearance of voters. Fourthly, efficiency will deteriorate when stronger security is provided.

Technically, secure e-voting can be implemented through either homomorphic tallying or mix network. Both of them need to encrypt the votes and distribute the decryption power among multiple talliers in a publicly verifiable way.

Homomorphic tallying does not decrypt the encrypted votes separately but exploits homomorphism of the employed encryption algorithm to collectively tally the encrypted votes using a small number of decryptions. A homomorphic encryption algorithm can be employed to encrypt the votes. Each vote must be in a special format, so that the number of votes can be correctly counted. More precisely, in homomorphic e-voting every vote contains one or more selections (each corresponding to a candidate or a possible choice) and every selection must be one of two pre-defined integers (e.g. 0 and 1), each representing support or rejection of a candidate or choice. Then homomorphism of the encryption algorithm is exploited to recover the sum the votes for every candidate: the product of all the encrypted selections for a candidate can be decrypted into the sum of the votes for him.

Mix network is an anonymous routing network. As shown in Figure 1, it consists of multiple routing nodes, who shuffle a batch of sealed messages in turn. The shuffling operation of each routing node re-orders (using a random permutation) and randomizes (e.g. through re-encryption) the sealed messages. The output of every routing node is shuffled by the next routing node. In this way, the encrypted messages are repeatedly shuffled in succession by all the routing nodes in the mix network. If at least one routing node conceals his permutation, the repeatedly shuffled encrypted messages cannot be traced. In e-voting, a mix network can be employed to shuffle the encrypted votes before they are decrypted so that no vote can be traced back to its voter. Finally, the repeatedly shuffled votes are decrypted to count all the votes. In this way, no voter's privacy is violated although all the votes are published. Mix network is especially useful for e-voting with complex election rules like preferential election.

No matter which of the two solutions is employed in e-voting, the private key of the encryption algorithm used to seal the votes is distributed among multiple talliers. In homomorphic e-voting, they cooperate to decrypt in a distributed manner the product of the encrypted selections for every candidate. In mix-network-based e-voting, they shuffle the encrypted votes as routing nodes and then cooperate to decrypt them. Its advantage over a one-tallier solution is obvious: even if some talliers are dishonest or compromised, e-voting can still run properly and the votes are still kept secret. As our new PVSS technique is a

Figure 1. Mix network

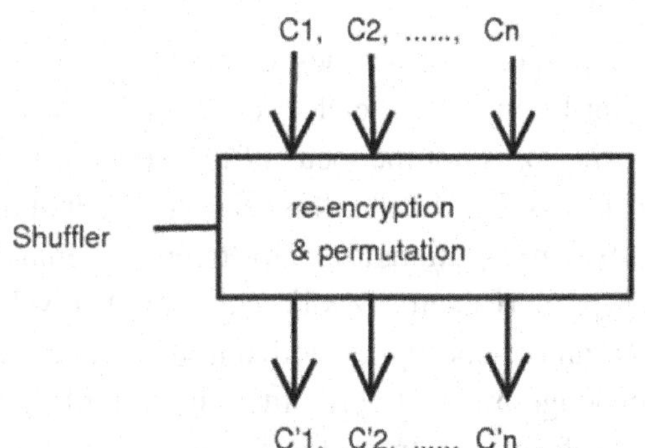

general solution more secure and efficient than the existing PVSS schemes, it can be employed to optimise e-voting schemes no matter whether they employ homomorphic tallying or mix network.

BACKGROUND

Electronic voting is a popular application of cryptographic and network techniques to e-government. An e-voting scheme should satisfy the following properties.

- **Correctness:** All the valid votes are counted without being tampered with.
- **Privacy:** No information about any voter's choice in the election is revealed.
- **Robustness:** Any dishonest behaviour or abnormal situation can be detected and solved without revealing any vote.
- **Verifiability:** Correctness of the election can be verified. It is classified into two types as follows.
- **Individual Verifiability:** Each voter can verify that his vote is counted and not tampered with.
- **Public Verifiability:** Anyone can verify that all the votes are counted and not tampered with according to public information.
- **High Efficiency:** The voting operation and tallying operation should be efficient enough for practical elections including large scale elections.

A property sometimes desired in e-voting, receipt-freeness (or called coercion-resistance elsewhere), is not the focus of this section, so is not discussed in detail in this section. Either of the two existing solutions to receipt-freeness, deniable encryption (Canetti, Dwork, Naor, & Ostrovsky, 1997) and re-encryption with untransferable zero knowledge proof of correctness by a third party (in the form of a trusted authority or a tamper-resistant hardware) linked through untappable communication channel[1] (Lee & Kim, 2000) can be employed if it is required.

Most of the existing e-voting schemes can be classified into two categories: homomorphic voting and shuffling-based voting. In a homomorphic voting scheme (Adler, Dai, Green, & Neff, 2000; Baudron, Fouque, Pointcheval, Poupard, & Stern, 2001; Damg_ard & Jurik, 2001; Hevia & Kiwi, 2002; Hirt & Sako, 2000; Katz, Myers, & Ostrovsky, 2001; Kiayias & Yung, 2002; Lee & Kim, 2000, 2002; Neff, 2000; Peng, Boyd, Dawson, & Lee, 2004; Schoenmakers, 2000), an encryption algorithm with special homomorphic property (e.g. ElGamal encryption or Paillier encryption [Paillier, 1999]) is employed to encrypt the votes such that the sum of the votes can be recovered without decrypting any single vote. An advantage of homomorphic voting is efficient tallying. Tallying in homomorphic voting only costs one single decryption operation for each candidate. However, homomorphic voting has the following drawbacks.

- **Complex Vote:** A vote must contain a ciphertext for each candidate (or possible choice) in the election. Thus, encryption cost for each voter is high. This drawback is especially serious when the number of candidates is large or in preferential election, where the preferential order of all the candidates must be contained in a vote.
- **High Cost in Vote Validity Check:** In a valid vote, each ciphertext must be in a special format. Correctness of homomorphic voting depends on validity of the votes. An invalid vote can compromise correctness of a homomorphic voting scheme, so must be detected and deleted before the tallying phase. Unfortunately, vote validity check is very costly (both for the voters to prove validity of their votes and for a tallier (and other verifiers) to verify validity of the votes) and becomes an efficiency bottleneck in homomorphic e-voting.

These two drawbacks imply that the computational and communicational cost for every voter is high, especially when the election is complex. Note that although the talliers can be several authorities with high computational power and linked with a broadband communication channel the voters are common people and some of them possibly have limited computational power and communication bandwidth, especially when mobile devices are used to cast the votes. Therefore, although homomorphic voting is suitable for a very simple election (e.g. YES/NO election) it is impractical in more complicated circumstances.

Shuffling-based voting (Abe & Hoshino, 2001; Furukawa & Sako, 2001; Furukawa, 2005; Golle, Zhong, Boneh, Jakobsson, & Juels, 2002; Groth, 2003; Neff, 2001, 2004; Park, Itoh, & Kurosawa, 1993; Peng, Boyd, Dawson, & Viswanathan, 2004; Peng, Boyd, & Dawson, 2005) is more suitable for complex elections (e.g. with multiple candidates or votes containing complex information like preference of the candidates) as it has the following merits. No matter how complex a vote is it is sealed in one ciphertext. Moreover, no vote validity check is needed. So the cost for a voter is low and low-capability devices and low-performance communication channels can be used to cast the votes. A shuffling-based voting scheme employs multiple instances of shuffling to repeatedly shuffle the encrypted votes before they are decrypted (opened) so that the opened votes cannot be traced back to the voters if at least the permutation in one shuffling instance is concealed. Secure shuffling-based e-voting applications should follow three rules to achieve critically high security requirements and otherwise may cause serious chaos and turbulence.

- The security requirements of e-voting like correctness, privacy, robustness and public verifiability must be completely and strictly satisfied.
- Validity of shuffling must be publicly and completely verified.
- Multiple shuffling operations are performed in sequence such that no opened vote can be traced back to its voter if at least one shuffling node conceals his permutation.

E-voting schemes like (Jakobsson, Juels, & Rivest, 2002; Golle & Juels, 2004; Peng, Boyd, Dawson, & Viswanathan, 2004) do not strictly follow these three rules, have looser security standards and cannot completely satisfy the security requirements of e-voting, so are not satisfactory solutions[2].

The main concerns in shuffling-based e-voting are inefficiency in public verification and weak robustness. There are two methods to implement public verification in shuffling-based e-voting. The first method is instant verification: each shuffling operation is publicly verified before the votes are sent to the next shuffling node such that any deviating operation in the shuffling is detected immediately and no vote is decrypted unless all the shuffling nodes strictly follow the shuffling protocol. A drawback of this method (Abe, 1999; Abe & Hoshino, 2001; Furukawa & Sako, 2001; Furukawa, 2004, 2005; Groth, 2003; Neff, 2001, 2004; Nguyen, Safavi-Naini, & Kurosawa, 2006; Peng et al., 2005) is low efficiency. The second method is to omit separate public verifications in all the shuffling operations and to make a final public check after the votes are shuffled and decrypted (Golle et al., 2002; Park et al., 1993). If any shuffling operation deviates from the shuffling protocol, the final check fails and a identifying function can be used to identify the dishonest shuffling node. This method is more efficient in public verification, but has its own drawback: weak robustness.

The most serious drawback of the second verification method is that it is more vulnerable to attacks against privacy. The first verification method guarantees that any dishonest behaviour of any shuffling node is instantly detected, rewound, and redone. So with the first verification method, the only concern is dishonest behaviour of the voters. With the second verification method, the e-voting procedure continues until the final decryption of the votes even if some malicious shuffling node has deviated from the protocol, and thus gives more chances to the attacks. For example, the votes are still decrypted even if they are tampered with in the shuffling in (Park et al., 1993), which is vulnerable to many ``relation attacks" (see Pfitzmann, 1994, for definition, detailed explanation and more references). The e-voting scheme in (Golle et al., 2002) takes two additional operations on the voters' side, double encryption and zero knowledge proof of knowledge of certain secrets committed in the ciphertexts, to counteract those attacks. However, it is pointed out in (Abe & Imai, 2003) that (Golle et al., 2002) is still vulnerable to attacks from dishonest talliers, not to mention the two additional operations counteract the efficiency improvement gained through omitting instant verification and compromise the advantage of shuffling-based e-voting in efficiency on the voters' side.

ISSUES, CONTROVERSIES, PROBLEMS

The existing mix network schemes cannot provide ideal support to e-voting. Among the well known mix network schemes (Abe, 1999; Abe & Hoshino, 2001; Furukawa & Sako, 2001; Groth, 2003; Groth & Lu, 2007; Groth & Ishai, 2008; Neff, 2001; Peng, Boyd, Dawson, & Viswanathan, 2004; Peng et al., 2005; Kun Peng & Bao, 2010a; Wikstrom, 2005), the most recent of them (Groth, 2003; Groth & Lu, 2007; Groth & Ishai, 2008; Peng, Boyd, Dawson, & Viswanathan, 2004; Peng et al., 2005; Kun, Peng, & Bao, 2010a; Wikstrom, 2005) (initially proposed in the past decade) are more efficient where the scheme in (Furukawa, 2005) is an extended journal version of (Furukawa & Sako, 2001) and the scheme in (Neff, 2004) is a formal publication of (Neff, 2001). In the recent mix network schemes, the shuffling protocol in (Peng, Boyd, Dawson, & Viswanathan, 2004) is very efficient. However, unlike all the other shuffling protocols it only allows the routing node to choose his permutation from a small fraction of all the possible permutations. So it is not a complete shuffling and is weak in privacy. The other recent mix network schemes employ the same idea: given random integers t_i for $i=1,2,\ldots,n$, if

$$RE(\prod_{i=1}^{n} c_i^{t_i}) = \prod_{i=1}^{n} c_i'^{t_i'} \qquad (1)$$

and $t_1', t_2', \ldots, t_n'$. is a permutation of $t_1,t_2,\ldots,t_n$, then $D(c_1'), D(c_2'), \ldots, D(c_n')$ is a permutation of $D(c_1),D(c_2),\ldots,D(c_n)$ with an overwhelmingly large probability. This idea is simple and effective and actually will be employed in the new mix network as well. However, its usage by the recent mix network schemes has two drawbacks. Firstly, they do not give a formal proof for soundness of shuffling guaranteed by this approach. Secondly, their methods to prove that $t_1', t_2', \ldots, t_n'$ is a permutation of $t_1,t_2,\ldots,t_n$ in (1) is not efficient enough as explained before.

In this section, a new proof protocol is proposed to prove that $t_1', t_2', \ldots, t_n'$ is a permutation of $t_1,t_2,\ldots,t_n$ in (1). The new proof method is simpler and more efficient than the existing ones. Moreover, for the first time a formal soundness analysis is given in a proposed mix network to illustrate why its satisfaction of (1) guarantees soundness of shuffling when $t_1', t_2', \ldots, t_n'$ is a permutation of $t_1,t_2,\ldots,t_n$. Therefore, both drawbacks in the recent mix network schemes (Groth, 2003; Groth & Lu, 2007; Groth & Ishai, 2008; Peng, Boyd, Dawson, & Viswanathan, 2004; Peng et al., 2005; Kun, Peng, & Bao, 2010a;Wikstrom, 2005) are overcome. To show its advantages, a comparison is made between the new mix network with the recent mix network schemes. The comparison avoids the imprecision, exaggeration and unfairness in the existing comparisons and is more fair and objective. To show its practical value, extending the new mix network to flexible environments and applying it to e-voting are discussed.

As stated before, the current methods to prove that $t_1', t_2', \ldots, t_n'$ is a permutation of $t_1, t_2, \ldots, t_n$ in (1) is complex and inefficient. In the mix network based on (Groth, 2003), a routing node firstly commits to his permutation $\pi()$. He then permutes $t_1, t_2, \ldots, t_n$ using $\pi()$ and commits them in $T_1, T_2, \ldots, T_n$ using a commitment function *Com*(). Neff's proof technique (Neff, 2001) is then employed to prove that $t_1, t_2, \ldots, t_n$ are permuted and committed in $T_1, T_2, \ldots, T_n$ using the permutation committed in the first step. Finally, the routing node publishes $c = \prod_{i=1}^{n} c_i^{t_i}$, $c' = \prod_{i=1}^{n} c_i'^{t_{\pi(i)}}$ and proves

$$ZP\left(t_1', t_2', \ldots, t_n' \mid c' = \prod_{i=1}^{n} c_i'^{t_i'}, T_i = Com(t_i') \text{ for } i = 1, 2, \ldots, n \right)$$

and that c' is a re-encryption of c where

$$ZP\left(x_1, x_2, \ldots, x_k \mid y_1, y_2, \ldots, y_l \right)$$

denotes ZK (zero knowledge) proof of knowledge of integers $x_1, x_2, \ldots, x_k$ to satisfy conditions $y_1, y_2, \ldots, y_l$.

In the mix network based on (Groth, 2003), given random integers t_i and t_i' for $i=1,2,\ldots,n$, a routing node has to prove that he knows secret integers s_i and s_i' for $i=1,2,\ldots,n$, such that

$$\sum_{i=1}^{n} t_i D(c_i) = \sum_{i=1}^{n} s_i D(c_i') \bmod q$$

$$\sum_{i=1}^{n} t_i' D(c_i) = \sum_{i=1}^{n} s_i' D(c_i') \bmod q$$

$$\sum_{i=1}^{n} t_i t_i' D(c_i) = \sum_{i=1}^{n} s_i s_i' D(c_i') \bmod q$$

where $s_1, s_2, \ldots, s_n$ and $s_1', s_2', \ldots, s_n'$ are permutations of $t_1, t_2, \ldots, t_n$ and $t_1', t_2', \ldots, t_n'$ respectively. In the mix network based on (Peng et al., 2005), $t_1, t_2, \ldots, t_n$ (denoted as $p_1, p_2, \ldots, p_n$) are randomly chosen from a special range and $t_1', t_2', \ldots, t_n'$ (denoted as $\rho_1, \rho_2, \ldots, \rho_n$) is guaranteed to be a permutation of $t_1, t_2, \ldots, t_n$ by proving satisfaction of

$$\prod_{i=1}^{n} t_i = \prod_{i=1}^{n} t_i' \tag{2}$$

$$\sum_{i=1}^{n} t_i = \sum_{i=1}^{n} t_i' \tag{3}$$

and that $t_1', t_2', \ldots, t_n'$ are in the same range. Besides the complexity in proving satisfaction of (2) and (3), the proof that $t_1', t_2', \ldots, t_n'$ are in the same range is left unimplemented and its cost is not included in efficiency estimation in (Peng et al., 2005). Although it is vaguely mentioned in (Peng et al., 2005) that "We then note that a standard proof of knowledge over a group of unknown order also gives an upper bound on the bit-size of the exponents, i.e., it implicitly proves that $\rho_i \in [-2^K + 1, 2^K - 1]$," there is no more efficient way to prove that a secret integer chosen from a range is in the same range than the proof protocol in (Boudot, 2000)[3], whose cost in n instances of proof is much higher than the claimed total cost of shuffling in (Peng et al., 2005).

The mix network in (Groth, 2003) is optimised into two schemes in (Groth & Lu, 2007) and (Groth & Ishai, 2008), concentrating on computational efficiency and communicational efficiency respectively; while the mix network in (Groth, 2003) is optimised into a scheme in (Kun, Peng, & Bao, 2010a). The mix network schemes in (Groth & Lu, 2007; Groth & Ishai, 2008) and (Kun, Peng, & Bao, 2010a) prove that $t_1', t_2', \ldots, t_n'$ is a permutation of $t_1, t_2, \ldots, t_n$ in (1) as well and their proof techniques follow the same principles in (Groth, 2003) and (Peng et al., 2005) respectively. In summary, the proof techniques in the recent mix network schemes are complex and costly. However, all of them claim high efficiency and the shuffling protocol in (Groth & Lu, 2007) even claim to prove validity of shuffling of *n* ciphertexts at a cost lower than *n* exponentiations. The reason for their claimed extraordinarily high efficiency is that the recent mix network schemes employ unfair estimations and comparisons to exaggerate their advantage in efficiency over the previous work. Most of them (Groth & Lu, 2007; Groth & Ishai, 2008; Peng, Boyd, Dawson, & Viswanathan, 2004; Peng et al., 2005; Kun Peng & Bao, 2010a;Wikstrom, 2005) employ much shorter exponents than usual in many computations, while assuming the previous mix network schemes still employ exponents with normal length. In this way, they can count multiple exponentiations with short exponents as one exponentiation with a normal-length exponent. For example, the shuffling protocol in (Groth & Lu, 2007) counts multiple times of *n* exponentiations it needs to prove validity of shuffling as a number smaller than *n*. In Section 5 of (Groth, 2003), an efficiency improvement mechanism is applied solely to itself and not employed in the previous shuffling schemes although it is appliable to them as well. When those efficiency improvement mechanisms are employed in the previous mix network schemes their efficiency can be dramatically improved as well. So the efficiency comparisons in the recent mix network schemes are not very fair and do not precisely measure efficiency of different mix network schemes.

SOLUTIONS AND RECOMMENDATIONS

The main idea in the new mix network technique is that a simpler and more efficient proof is given to prove that $t'_1, t'_2, \ldots, t'_n$ is a permutation of $t_1, t_2, \ldots, t_n$ in (1). We find that satisfaction of $\sum_{i=1}^{n} t_i = \sum_{i=1}^{n} t'_i$ as proved in (Peng et al., 2005) is not helpful to guarantee validity of shuffling. Moreover, to limit $t'_1, t'_2, \ldots, t'_n$ in a certain range is essential in efficient proof of validity of shuffling. For example[4], when $t_1, t_2, \ldots, t_n$ are primes, $\sum_{i=1}^{n} t_i = \sum_{i=1}^{n} t'_i$ and $\prod_{i=1}^{n} t_i = \prod_{i=1}^{n} t'_i$ but they are not limited in any range, $t'_1, t'_2, \ldots, t'_n$ may not be a permutation of $t_1, t_2, \ldots, t_n$. To guarantee that $t'_1, t'_2, \ldots, t'_n$ is a permutation of $t_1, t_2, \ldots, t_n$, we randomly choose primes $t_1, t_2, \ldots, t_n$ from a range $R = \{2^T, 2^T + 1, 2^{T+1} - 1\}$ and then prove that

$$\prod_{i=1}^{n} t_i = \prod_{i=1}^{n} t'_i \qquad (4)$$

and $t'_1, t'_2, \ldots, t'_n$ are in R where T is a security parameter. Since the product of any integers in R is out of R and $t_1, t_2, \ldots, t_n, t'_1, t'_2, \ldots, t'_n$ are in R, satisfaction of $\prod_{i=1}^{n} t_i = \prod_{i=1}^{n} t'_i$ guarantees that $t'_1, t'_2, \ldots, t'_n$ is a permutation of $t_1, t_2, \ldots, t_n$. Depending on the concrete employed encryption algorithm, the concrete proof of satisfaction of (1) and (4) is different. In the new design, the proof is described based on a popular encryption algorithms in mix network, Paillier encryption. Moreover, a very efficient proof mechanism is employed to prove that $t'_1, t'_2, \ldots, t'_n$ are in R. It is different from the range proofs in (Peng et al., 2005) and so can be much more efficient than the normal range proof techniques like (Boudot, 2000).

The message space of Paillier encryption is Z_N where N is a composite with large secret factors. The multiplicative modulus is N^2 and the public key is g, a large number with secret order modulo N^2. Encryption of a message m is $g^m r^N \bmod N^2$ where r is randomly chosen from Z_N^*. More details of it can be found in (Paillier, 1999). When Paillier encryption is employed, shuffling and proof of its validity in the new mix network is as follows where 2^{T+1} is smaller than the factors of N.

1. The routing node calculates and publishes $c_i' = c_{\pi(i)} r_i^N \bmod N^2$ where π() is the permutation he chooses and r_i is randomly chosen from Z_N^*.
2. Random primes $t_1, t_2, \ldots, t_n$ in R are chosen by some verifier(s) or generated by a (pseudo) random function.
3. The routing node calculates and publishes $C = r^N \prod_{i=1}^{n} c_i'^{t_i'} \bmod N^2$ where $t_i' = t_{\pi(i)}$ and r is randomly chosen from Z_N^*.
4. The routing node proves knowledge of a secret integer $R' = r \prod_{i=1}^{n} r_i^{t_i'} \bmod N$ such that $R'^N \prod_{i=1}^{n} c_i^{t_i} = C \bmod N^2$ using ZK proof of knowledge of root (Guillou & Quisquater, 1989).
5. The routing node calculates and publishes $e_i = e_{i-1}^{t_i'} h^{r_i'} \bmod N^2$ where $e_0 = g$, h is an integer in the same cyclic group of g, $\log_g h$ and $\log_h g$ are secret and r_i' is randomly chosen from a large subset in Z_N for i=1,2,…,n.
6. The routing node, presented in Box 1, proves as detailed in the following.
   a. The routing node randomly chooses integers $s_1, s_2, \ldots, s_n, u_1, u_2, \ldots, u_n$ from Z_N and U from Z_N^*. He calculates and publishes $C' = U^N \prod_{i=1}^{n} c_i'^{s_i} \bmod N^2$, $e_i' = e_{i-1}^{s_i} h^{u_i} \bmod N^2$ for i=1,2,…,n.
   b. Some verifier(s) or a (pseudo)random function generates a random challenge $c \in Z_L$ where L is a security parameter.
   c. The routing node publishes $w_i = s_i - ct_i'$ in Z for i=1,2,…,n, $W = U / r^c \bmod N;\ v_i = u_i - cr_i'$ in Z for i=1,2,…,n.
   d. Public verification:

$$C' = C^c W^N \prod_{i=1}^{n} c_i'^{w_i} \bmod N^2 \tag{5}$$

$$e_i' = e_{i-1}^{w_i} h^{v_i} e_i^c \bmod N^2 \text{ for } i = 1,2,\ldots,n. \tag{6}$$

Note that although w_i and v_i are calculated in Z,, the proof protocol is statistically private once s_i is statistically much larger than ct_i' and u_i is statistically much larger than cr_i'.

7. The routing node proves knowledge of a secret integer $R'' = \sum_{i=1}^{n} (r_i' \sum_{j=i+1}^{n} t_j')$ such that $e_n = g^{\prod_{i=1}^{n} t_i} h^{R''} \bmod N^2$ using ZK proof of knowledge of discrete logarithm (Schnorr, 1991).

Security of the proof protocol to guarantee satisfaction of Equations (1) and (4) is illustrated in Theorem 1 and Theorem 2.

Theorem 1: The routing node's proof in Steps 4, 6, and 7 of the proof protocol can successfully pass their verifications if he is honest and strictly follows the shuffling protocol.

Proof: If the routing node is honest and strictly follows the shuffling protocol, Equations (1) and (4) are satisfied and $t_1', t_2', \ldots, t_n'$ is a permutation of $t_1, t_2, \ldots, t_n$. Then

Box 1.

$$ZP\,(\,t_1', t_2', \ldots, t_n', r, r_1', r_2', \ldots, r_n' \mid C = r^N \prod_{i=1}^{n} c_i'^{t_i'} \bmod N^2,\ e_i = e_{i-1}^{t_i'} h^{r_i'} \bmod N^2 \ \ for\ i = 1,2,\ldots,n\,)$$

$$R'^N \prod_{i=1}^{n} c_i^{t_i} = (r\prod_{i=1}^{n} r_i^{t'_i})^N \prod_{i=1}^{n} c_i^{t_i} = r^N (\prod_{i=1}^{n} r_i^{t'_i})^N \prod_{i=1}^{n} c_i^{t_i}$$
$$= r^N (\prod_{i=1}^{n} r_i^{t'_i})^N \prod_{i=1}^{n} c_{\pi(i)}^{t_{\pi(i)}} = r^N (\prod_{i=1}^{n} r_i^{t'_i})^N \prod_{i=1}^{n} c_{\pi(i)}^{t'_i}$$
$$= r^N \prod_{i=1}^{n} (c_{\pi(i)} r_i^N)^{t'_i} = r^N \prod_{i=1}^{n} c_i'^{t'_i} = C \bmod N^2;$$

and

$$e_n = e_{n-1}^{t'_n} h^{r'_n} = (e_{n-2}^{t'_{n-1}} h^{r'_{n-1}})^{t'_n} h^{r'_n} = \ldots\ldots =$$
$$g^{\prod_{i=1}^{n} t'_i} h^{\sum_{i=1}^{n}(r'_i \sum_{j=i+1}^{n} t'_j)} = g^{\prod_{i=1}^{n} t'_i} h^{R''} = g^{\prod_{i=1}^{n} t_i} h^{R''} \bmod N^2;$$

and

$$C^c W^N \prod_{i=1}^{n} c_i'^{w_i} = (r^N \prod_{i=1}^{n} c_i'^{t'_i})^c (U / r^c)^N \prod_{i=1}^{n} c_i'^{s_i - ct'_i}$$
$$= U^N \prod_{i=1}^{n} c_i'^{s_i} = C' \bmod N^2;$$

$$e_{i-1}^{w_i} h^{v_i} e_i^c = e_{i-1}^{s_i - ct'_i} h^{u_i - cr'_i} (e_{i-1}^{t'_i} h^{r'_i})^c = e_{i-1}^{s_i} h^{u_i}$$
$$= e'_i \bmod N^2 \text{ for } i = 1,2,\ldots,n.$$

Therefore, the routing node's proof in Steps 4, 6, and 7 of the shuffling protocol successfully passes their verifications.

Theorem 2: If the routing node's proof in Steps 4, 6, and 7 successfully passes their verifications, Equations (1) and (4) are satisfied.

Proof: If the routing node's proof in Steps 4, 6, and 7 successfully passes their verifications, the routing node can calculate in polynomial time integers $t'_1, t'_2, \ldots, t'_n$, $r, R', R'', r'_1, r'_2, \ldots, r'_n$ such that the following equations hold as the ZK proof primitives in the three steps (including ZK proof of knowledge of root [Guillou & Quisquater, 1989], ZK proof of knowledge of discrete logarithm [Schnorr, 1991] and ZK proof of equality of discrete logarithms [Chaum & Pedersen, 1992]) are sound and passing their verifications guarantees their claimed knowledge and relation.

$$R'^N \prod_{i=1}^{n} c_i^{t_i} = C \bmod N^2 \qquad (7)$$

$$C = r^N \prod_{i=1}^{n} c_i'^{t'_i} \bmod N^2 \qquad (8)$$

$$e_i = e_{i-1}^{t'_i} h^{r'_i} \bmod N^2 \text{ for } i = 1,2,\ldots,n \qquad (9)$$

$$e_n = g^{\prod_{i=1}^{n} t_i} h^{R''} \bmod N^2 \qquad (10)$$

(7) and (8) imply

$$R'^N \prod_{i=1}^{n} c_i^{t_i} = r^N \prod_{i=1}^{n} c_i'^{t'_i} \bmod N^2$$

and so

$$\prod_{i=1}^{n} c_i'^{t'_i} = (R' / r)^N \prod_{i=1}^{n} c_i^{t_i} \bmod N^2 = RE(\prod_{i=1}^{n} c_i^{t_i}).$$

(9) implies

$$e_n = e_{n-1}^{t'_n} h^{r'_n} = (e_{n-2}^{t'_{n-1}} h^{r'_{n-1}})^{t'_n} h^{r'_n}$$
$$= \ldots\ldots = g^{\prod_{i=1}^{n} t'_i} h^{\sum_{i=1}^{n}(r'_i \sum_{j=i+1}^{n} t'_j)} \bmod N^2. \qquad (11)$$

So

$$g^{\prod_{i=1}^{n} t_i} h^{R''} = g^{\prod_{i=1}^{n} t'_i} h^{\sum_{i=1}^{n}(r'_i \sum_{j=i+1}^{n} t'_j)} \bmod N^2$$

and thus

$$g^{\prod_{i=1}^{n} t_i - \prod_{i=1}^{n} t'_i} = h^{\sum_{i=1}^{n}(r'_i \sum_{j=i+1}^{n} t'_j) - R''} \bmod N^2.$$

As the routing node can calculate in polynomial time $\prod_{i=1}^{n} t'_i$ and $\log_g h$ and $\log_h g$ are secret and no information about the order of g is known, (10) and (11) imply $\prod_{i=1}^{n} t_i = \prod_{i=1}^{n} t'_i$ due to the following reasons.

- If $\prod_{i=1}^{n} t_i \neq \prod_{i=1}^{n} t'_i$ and $\prod_{i=1}^{n} t_i - \prod_{i=1}^{n} t'_i$ is a multiple of the order of g, then the routing node can calculate in polynomial time a multiple of the order of g, which is a contradiction.
- If $\prod_{i=1}^{n} t_i \neq \prod_{i=1}^{n} t'_i$ and $\prod_{i=1}^{n} t_i - \prod_{i=1}^{n} t'_i$ is not a multiple of the order of g, then

$$\log_h g = (\sum_{i=1}^{n}(r'_i \sum_{j=i+1}^{n} t'_j) - R'') / (\prod_{i=1}^{n} t_i - \prod_{i=1}^{n} t'_i)$$

and given the order of g the routing node can calculate $\log_h g$ in polynomial time, which is contradictory to the widely accepted hardness of the discrete logarithm problem.

Earlier in this chapter, proof of satisfaction of (1) and (4) has been specified. However, to guarantee that $t'_1, t'_2, \ldots, t'_n$ is a permutation of $t_1, t_2, \ldots, t_n$ and thus $D(c'_1), D(c'_2), \ldots, D(c'_n)$ is a permutation of $D(c_1), D(c_2), \ldots, D(c_n)$, we still need to prove that $t'_1, t'_2, \ldots, t'_n$ are in the range R Namely, n instances of range proof is needed. The normal range proof techniques (Boudot, 2000; Camenisch, Chaabouni, & Shelat, 2008; Chaabouni, Lipmaa, & Shelat, 2010; Groth, 2005; Lipmaa, 2003; Peng & Bao, 2010b) are not efficient for mix network. Even the most efficient two of them (Boudot, 2000; Peng & Bao, 2010b.) still cost scores of exponentiations for one instance of range proof. So we have to prove that $t'_1, t'_2, \ldots, t'_n$ are in R in a different and more efficient way.

Although there is no efficient method to prove that $t'_1, t'_2, \ldots, t'_n$ are in R when $t'_1, t'_2, \ldots, t'_n$ are chosen from the primes in R, $t'_1, t'_2, \ldots, t'_n$ can be proved to be in R if they are primes chosen from a much smaller range. This idea is not strange to the research community but to the best of our knowledge the condition for it to work and the guideline to set its parameters have never been formally discussed in detail. To use this idea, there are some additional requirements on parameter setting in the proof of satisfaction of (1) and (4) in section 2.2.1 besides statistical privacy. Its parameter setting needs to be modified as follows. Firstly, $t_1, t_2, \ldots, t_n$ are chosen from the primes in a subset R_1 in the middle of R and thus $t'_1, t'_2, \ldots, t'_n$ are in R_1 as well. Then s_i is randomly chosen from a large set S_1 and c is randomly chosen from a large set S_2 If $w_i + c(2^T + 2^{T-1})$ is in a range R_2, t'_i can be guaranteed to be in R. Namely, if t'_i is chosen in a small fraction of R near its middle point $2^T + 2^{T-1}$ and $s_i - c(t'_i - (2^T + 2^{T-1}))$ is in R_2, the absolute value of $t_i(2^T + 2^{T-1})$ is guaranteed to be smaller than $2^T + 2^{T-1}$. In this way, range proof of secret integer t_i in R is implemented through a simple and public membership test of $w_i + c(2^T + 2^{T-1})$ in R_2. When R_1 is small enough and S_1, S_2 and R_2 are appropriately set, the range proof can achieve the soundness defined in Definition 1.

Definition 1: *(Soundness of range proof)* If t'_i is not in R, the probability that the verification in the range proof is passed is no more than a negligible parameter denoted as δ.

More precisely, the parameters should be chosen according to the following three rules

$$Max(S_1) + Max(R_1 \times S_2) \le Max(R_2)$$

$$Min(S_1) + Min(R_1 \times S_2) \ge Min(R_2)$$

$$(MaxAbs(\hat{R}) + 1)(Max(S_2) - Min(S_2))\delta \ge | R_2 | \quad (12)$$

where the following denotations are employed.

- $\hat{R} = \{x \mid x + (2^T + 2^{T-1}) \in R\}$
- *MaxAbs*()denotes the integer with the largest absolute value in a set;
- *Max*()denotes the largest integer in a set;
- *Min*()denotes the smallest integer in a set;
- $|T|$ denotes the size of a set T;
- dT denotes a set $\{t | t=dt, t \in T\}$ where T is a set of integers and d is an integer.

The meaning of the first two rules is very clear: an honest routing node must pass the verification. The third rule in (12) aims to guarantee soundness of the range proof, which means that if the routing node passes the verification t_i' is guaranteed to be in R with an overwhelmingly large probability. Its principle is illustrated in detail in Theorem 3.

Soundness of the range proof means that

$$(MaxAbs(\hat{R}) + 1)(Max(S_2) - Min(S_2))\delta \ge | R_2 |$$

should be satisfied.

To Prove Theorem 3, Lemma 1 is proved first.

Lemma 1: In the range proof, the number of elements falling in $(MaxAbs(\hat{R}) + 1)S_2$ should be no more than $|S_2|\delta$ in any range with a width $|R_2|$.

Proof: If the number of elements in $(MaxAbs(\hat{R}) + 1)S_2$ is more than $|S_2|\delta$ in a range with a width $|R_2|$, then there are at least $\lfloor | S_2 | \delta \rfloor + 1$ integers in both $(MaxAbs(\hat{R}) + 1)S_2$ and a range $\{t, t+1, \ldots, t+|R_2|-1\}$. Denote these integers as $b_1, b_2, \ldots, b_{\lfloor |S_2|\delta \rfloor + 1}$. The routing node chooses $s_i = Min(R_2) - t$ and then we have $b_j + s_i = b_j + Min(R_2) - t$ for $j = 1, 2, \ldots, \lfloor | S_2 | \delta \rfloor + 1$ where $0 \le b_j - t \le |R_2|-1$. As b_j is in $\{t, t+1, \ldots, t+|R_2|-1\}$,

$$Min(R_2) \le b_j + s_i \le Min(R_2) + | R_2 | - 1 = Max(R_2)$$

for $j = 1, 2, \ldots, \lfloor | S_2 | \delta \rfloor + 1$. Namely, $b_j + s_i$ is in R_2 for

$j = 1, 2, \ldots, \lfloor | S_2 | \delta \rfloor + 1.$

As $b_1, b_2, \ldots, b_{\lfloor |S_2|\delta \rfloor + 1}$ are in

$(MaxAbs(\hat{R}) + 1)S_2$,

So $b_j + s_i$ is in $(MaxAbs(\hat{R}) + 1)S_2 + s_i$ for

$j = 1, 2, \ldots, \lfloor | S_2 | \delta \rfloor + 1.$

So, $(MaxAbs(\hat{R}) + 1)S_2 + s_i \cap R_2$ at least contains $b_j + s_i$ for $j = 1, 2, \ldots, \lfloor | S_2 | \delta \rfloor + 1$. So

$$| ((MaxAbs(\hat{R}) + 1)S_2 + s_i) \cap R_2 | \ge \lfloor | S_2 | \delta \rfloor + 1$$

Namely, with $t_i' = MaxAbs(\hat{R}) + 1$, if the probability that the verification in the range proof is passed is denoted as P, then

$$P \ge | (t_i' S_2 + s_i) \cap R_2 | / | S_2 | \ge (\lfloor | S_2 | \delta \rfloor + 1) / | S_2 | > \delta,$$

which is contradictory to Definition 1. This contradiction shows that Lemma 2.2.2 must be correct.

Proof of Theorem 3

Note that if the probability that a random element in any part of a set falls into a certain subset is no more than a certain value, then the probability that a random element in the set falls into the certain subset is no more than the certain value. So according to Lemma 1, the average probability that an integer in the equation presented in Box 2 falls into $(MaxAbs(\hat{R})+1)S_2$ is no more than $|S_2|\delta/|R_2|$. So the number of integers in $(MaxAbs(\hat{R})+1)S_2$ is no more than as presented in Box 3.

Therefore,

$$((MaxAbs(\hat{R})+1)Max(S_2)$$
$$-(MaxAbs(\hat{R})+1)Min(S_2))\mid S_2 \mid \delta / \mid R_2 \mid$$
$$\geq \mid (MaxAbs(\hat{R})+1)S_2 \mid = \mid S_2 \mid .$$

and thus

$$(MaxAbs(\hat{R})+1)(Max(S_2)-Min(S_2))\delta \geq \mid R_2 \mid .$$

The analysis above shows that the n instances of range proof can be efficiently implemented after the parameters are adjusted. For example, R_1 can be

$$\{2^{T-1}+2^T-l, 2^{T-1}+2^T-l+1, \ldots, 2^{T-1}+2^T+l\}$$

where l is much smaller than 2^T. Of course, besides the three rules, l should be large enough such that it is difficult to guess which primes are chosen from R_1 as $t_1, t_2, \ldots, t_n$. Since T can be as large as several hundred, those requirements can be easily satisfied and there are many valid choices for R_2, S_1 and S_2. Together with satisfaction of Equation (4), the n instances of range proof guarantee that $t_1', t_2', \ldots, t_n'$ is a permutation of $t_1, t_2, \ldots, t_n$ as analysed in the beginning of before. Then with Equation (1) satisfied as well, validity of shuffling is guaranteed as illustrated before.

As mentioned before, although many mix network schemes guarantee validity of shuffling by proving satisfaction of (1) and that $t_1', t_2', \ldots, t_n'$ is a permutation of $t_1, t_2, \ldots, t_n$, none of them gives a formal analysis of the guarantee. In Theorem 4, it is formally illustrated why satisfaction of (1) guarantees validity of shuffling in the new mix network when $t_1', t_2', \ldots, t_n'$ is a permutation of $t_1, t_2, \ldots, t_n$.

Theorem 4: In the new mix network, the probability that Equation (1) is satisfied and $t_1', t_2', \ldots, t_n'$ is a permutation of $t_1, t_2, \ldots, t_n$ but $D(c_1'), D(c_2'), \ldots, D(c_n')$ is not a permutation of $D(c_1), D(c_2), \ldots, D(c_n)$ is negligible.

To prove Theorem 4, a lemma is proved first.

Box 2.

$$\{(MaxAbs(\hat{R})+1)Min(S_2), (MaxAbs(\hat{R})+1)Min(S_2)+1, \ldots, (MaxAbs(\hat{R})+1)Max(S_2)\}$$

Box 3.

$$((MaxAbs(\hat{R})+1)Max(S_2)-(MaxAbs(\hat{R})+1)Min(S_2))\mid S_2 \mid \delta / \mid R_2 \mid$$

Lemma 2: If $\prod_{i=1}^{n} y_i^{z_i}$ is an Nth residue with a probability larger than $1/K$ where every z_i is randomly chosen from a set S, which contains K integers smaller than the factors of N, then $y_1, y_2, \ldots, y_n$ are N^{th} residues.

Proof: $\prod_{i=1}^{n} y_i^{z_i}$ is an Nth residue with a probability larger than $1/K$ implies that for any given integer v in $\{1,2,\ldots,N\}$ there must exist integers $z_1, z_2, \ldots, z_n$ and z_v' in S and two different integers x and x' in Z_N such that

$$\prod_{i=1}^{n} y_i^{z_i} = x^N \bmod N^2 \tag{13}$$

$$\left(\prod_{i=1}^{v-1} y_i^{z_i}\right) y_v^{z_v'} \prod_{i=v+1}^{n} y_i^{z_i} = x'^N \bmod N^2. \tag{14}$$

Otherwise, for any $(z_1, z_2, \ldots, z_{v-1}, z_{v+1}, \ldots, z_n)$ in S^{n-1}, there is at most one z_v in S such that $\prod_{i=1}^{n} y_i^{z_i} \bmod N^2$ is an Nth residue. This implies that among the K^n possible choices for $(z_1, z_2, \ldots, z_n)$ (combination of the K^{n-1} possible choices for $(z_1, z_2, \ldots, z_{v-1}, z_{v+1}, \ldots, z_n)$ and the K possible choices for z_v) there is at most K^{n-1} choices to construct an Nth residue in the form $\prod_{i=1}^{n} y_i^{z_i} \bmod N^2$, which is a contradiction to the assumption that $\prod_{i=1}^{n} y_i^{z_i}$ is an Nth residue with a probability larger than $1/K$.

(13) and (14) imply $y_v^{z_v - z_v'}$ is an Nth residue. According to Euclidean algorithm there exist integers α and β to satisfy

$$\beta(z_v - z_v') = \alpha N + GCD(N, z_v - z_v').$$

Note that $GCD(N, z_v - z_v') = 1$ as z_v, z_v' are in S and thus smaller than the factors of N. So $y_v^{\beta(z_v - z_v')} = y_v^{\alpha N} y_v \bmod N^2$. Namely,

$$y_v = y_v^{\beta(z_v - z_v')} / y_v^{\alpha N} = (y_v^{(z_v - z_v')})^{\beta} / y_v^{\alpha N}$$
$$= (x / x')^{N\beta} / (y_v^{\alpha})^N = ((x / x')^{\beta} / y_v^{\alpha})^N \bmod N^2.$$

So y_v is an Nth residue. Therefore, $y_1, y_2, \ldots, y_n$ are N^{th} residues as v can be any integer in $\{1,2,\ldots,n\}$.

Proof of Theorem 4

Let A_1 be the event that $D(c_1'), D(c_2'), \ldots, D(c_n')$ is a permutation of $D(c_1), D(c_2), \ldots, D(c_n)$ A_2 be the event that Equation (1) is correct; A_3 be the event that the routing node successfully proves satisfaction of (1); $P(A)$ denote the probability of event A

$$\begin{aligned}
P(A_3 / \bar{A}_1) &= P\left((A_3 \wedge A_2) / \bar{A}_1\right) \\
&+P\left((A_3 \wedge \bar{A}_2) / \bar{A}_1\right) = P(A_3 \wedge A_2 \wedge \bar{A}_1) / P(\bar{A}_1) \\
&+P(A_3 \wedge \bar{A}_2 \wedge \bar{A}_1) / P(\bar{A}_1) \\
&= P(\bar{A}_1 \wedge A_2) P(A_3 / \bar{A}_1 \wedge A_2) / P(\bar{A}_1) \\
&+P(A_3 \wedge \bar{A}_2 \wedge \bar{A}_1) P(\bar{A}_2 \wedge \bar{A}_1) / \left(P(\bar{A}_1) P(\bar{A}_2 \wedge \bar{A}_1)\right) \\
&= P(A_2 / \bar{A}_1) P(A_3 / \bar{A}_1 \wedge A_2) \\
&+P(\bar{A}_2 / \bar{A}_1) P(A_3 \wedge \bar{A}_2 \wedge \bar{A}_1) / P(\bar{A}_2 \wedge \bar{A}_1) \\
&= P(A_2 / \bar{A}_1) P(A_3 / \bar{A}_1 \wedge A_2) \\
&+P(\bar{A}_2 / \bar{A}_1) P(A_3 \wedge \bar{A}_2 \wedge \bar{A}_1) / \left(P(\bar{A}_2) P(\bar{A}_1 / \bar{A}_2)\right) \\
P(\bar{A}_1 / \bar{A}_2) &= 1
\end{aligned}$$

as $P(A_2/A_1)=1$. So

$$\begin{aligned}
P(A_3 / \bar{A}_1) &= P(A_2 / \bar{A}_1) P(A_3 / \bar{A}_1 \wedge A_2) \\
&+P(\bar{A}_2 / \bar{A}_1) P(A_3 \wedge \bar{A}_2 \wedge \bar{A}_1) / P(\bar{A}_2) \\
&\le P(A_2 / \bar{A}_1) P(A_3 / \bar{A}_1 \wedge A_2) \\
&+P(\bar{A}_2 / \bar{A}_1) P(A_3 \wedge \bar{A}_2) / P(\bar{A}_2) \\
&\le P(A_2 / \bar{A}_1) P(A_3 / \bar{A}_1 \wedge A_2) \\
&+P(\bar{A}_2 / \bar{A}_1) P(A_3 / \bar{A}_2) \\
&\le P(A_2 / \bar{A}_1) P(A_3 / \bar{A}_1 \wedge A_2) + P(A_3 / \bar{A}_2)
\end{aligned}$$

Suppose there are k primes in R_1. If $P(A_2 / \bar{A}_1) > 1 / k$, then when $\bar{A}_1$ happens the probability that (1) is correct is larger than $1/k$. Namely, when $\bar{A}_1$ happens,

$$RE(\prod_{i=1}^{n} c_i^{t_i}) = \prod_{i=1}^{n} c_i'^{t_{\pi(i)}}$$

with a probability larger than $1/k$ where $\pi()$ is a permutation of $\{1,2,..,n\}$. Namely, when $\bar{A}_1$ happens,

$$RE(\prod_{i=1}^{n} c_i^{t_i}) = \prod_{i=1}^{n} c'^{t_i}_{\pi^{-1}(i)}$$

with a probability larger than $1/k$.

According to additive homomorphism of Paillier encryption algorithm, when $\bar{A}_1$ happens,

$$\prod_{i=1}^{n} (c_i / c'_{\pi^{-1}(i)})^{t_i} = E(0)$$

with a probability larger than $1/k$. Namely, when $\bar{A}_1$ happens, $\prod_{i=1}^{n} (c_i / c'_{\pi^{-1}(i)})^{t_i}$ is an Nth residue with a probability larger than $1/k$.

So, according to Lemma 2, when $\bar{A}_1$ happens $c_i / c'_{\pi^{-1}(i)}$ is an N-th residue for $i=1,2,\ldots,n$, and thus $D(c_1'), D(c_2'), \ldots, D(c_n')$ is a permutation of $D(c_1), D(c_2), \ldots, D(c_n)$, which is a contradiction. So $P(A_2 / \bar{A}_1) \leq 1/k$ must be true to avoid the contradiction.

As with Paillier encryption (1) is proved using a standard proof of knowledge of root (Guillou & Quisquater, 1989), $P(A_3 / \bar{A}_1 \wedge A_2) = 1$ and $P(A_3 / \bar{A}_2) < 2^{-L'}$ where L' is the bit length of the challenge in the proof of knowledge of root. Therefore,

$$P(A_3 / \bar{A}_1) \leq P(A_2 / \bar{A}_1) + P(A_3 / \bar{A}_2) = 1/k + 2^{-L'}$$

The new mix network is compared with the recent mix network schemes in Table 1. When computational cost of a routing node is estimated, the exponentiations are counted. For simplicity, they are counted in terms of multiples of *n,* the dominating part of the cost. As the re-encryption operation is efficient and costs almost the same in all the shuffling protocols, like in most existing mix network schemes, in this section only the cost of the proof of validity of shuffling is included in the comparison. As stated before, applying an efficiency improvement mechanism like small exponent to the recent mix network schemes and excluding it from other mix network schemes is

Table 1. Comparison of mix network schemes

mix network	privacy	formal analysis	computational cost of proof of validity of shuffling	other comment
(Groth, 2003)	strong	incomplete	12*n*	
(Peng, Boyd, Dawson, & Viswanathan, 2004)	weak[5]	complete	12*n*	
(Groth, 2003)	strong	incomplete	13*n*	
(Peng et al., 2005)	strong	incomplete	15*n*	*n* instances of range proofs unimplemented
(Groth & Lu, 2007)	strong	incomplete	10*n*	
(Groth & Ishai, 2008) [6]	strong	incomplete	22*n*	
New	strong	complete	7*n*	

unfair as the efficiency improvement mechanisms are simple and general techniques applicable to all the mix network schemes. For example, in the new mix network scheme, $t_1,t_2,\ldots,t_n$ and $s_1,s_2,\ldots,s_n$ can be set to be small exponents to greatly improve efficiency as well. So, for the sake of fairness and to show exactly how advanced every mix network scheme is, the efficiency improvement mechanisms are not included in any mix network scheme in the cost estimation in Table 1 and every exponentiation is counted equally. As explained before, most recent mix network schemes do not provide a complete formal security analysis as they do not formally explain why shuffling is valid when (1) is satisfied and $t'_1,t'_2,\ldots,t'_n$ is a permutation of $t_1,t_2,\ldots,t_n$. Except for in (Groth & Ishai, 2008), communicational cost of mix networks is approximately in direct proportion to their computational cost, so communicational cost is not separately estimated in Table 1 like in the efficiency analysis in most mix network schemes.

EXTENSION AND APPLICATION

Other popular encryption algorithms in mix network like ElGamal encryption can be employed in the new mix network as well. A typical ElGamal encryption algorithm employs two large primes p and q where q is a factor of p-1. Suppose g is a generator of the cyclic subgroup of order q in Z_p^* and the private key is an integer x in Z_q, and the public key is $y = g^x \bmod p$.

Encryption of a message m is $(g^r \bmod p, my^r \bmod p)$ where r is randomly chosen from Z_q. When ElGamal encryption is employed, shuffling and proof of its validity in the new mix network is as follows where 2^{T+1} is smaller than q.

1. The routing node calculates and publishes $c'_i = (a'_i, b'_i)$ where $c_i=(a_i,b_i)$, $a'_i = a_{\pi(i)} g^{r_i} \bmod p$, $b'_i = b_{\pi(i)} y^{r_i} \bmod p$, $\pi()$ is the permutation he chooses and r_i is randomly chosen from Z_q.
2. Random primes $t_1,t_2,\ldots,t_n$ in R_1 are chosen by some verifier(s) or generated by a (pseudo) random function where R_1 is in the middle of R and much smaller than it.
3. The routing node calculates and publishes $A = g^r \prod_{i=1}^n a'^{t'_i}_i \bmod p$ and $B = y^r \prod_{i=1}^n b'^{t'_i}_i \bmod p$ where $t'_i = t_{\pi(i)}$ and r is randomly chosen from Z_q.
4. The routing node proves knowledge of a secret integer $R' = r + \sum_{i=1}^n r_i t'_i \bmod q$ such that $g^{R'} \prod_{i=1}^n a_i^{t_i} = A \bmod p$ and $y^{R'} \prod_{i=1}^n b_i^{t_i} = B \bmod p$ using ZK proof of knowledge of discrete logarithm (Schnorr, 1991).
5. The routing node calculates and publishes $e_i = e_{i-1}^{t'_i} h^{r'_i} \bmod N$ where N is a composite with large secret factors, f and h are generators of a large cyclic subgroup with secret order in Z_N^*, $\log_f h$ and $\log_h f$ are secret and r'_i is randomly chosen from a large subset in Z_N for i=1,2,…,n.
6. The routing node proves

$$ZP$$

$$(t'_1, t'_2, \ldots, t'_n, r, r'_1, r'_2, \ldots, r'_n \mid A = g^r \prod_{i=1}^n a'^{t'_i}_i \bmod p,)$$

$$B = y^r \prod_{i=1}^n b'^{t'_i}_i \bmod p, e_i = e_{i-1}^{t'_i} h^{r'_i} \bmod N$$

for i=1,2,…,n as detailed in the following:

a. The routing node randomly chooses integers $s_1,s_2,\ldots,s_n$ from a large set S_1, $u_1,u_2,\ldots,u_n$ from Z_N and U from Z_q. He calculates and publishes

$$A' = g^U \prod_{i=1}^{n} a_i'^{s_i} \bmod p,\ \ B' = y^U \prod_{i=1}^{n} b_i'^{s_i} \bmod p,$$

$$e_i' = e_{i-1}^{s_i} h^{u_i} \bmod N \ \text{ for } i=1,2,\ldots,n.$$

b. Some verifier(s) or a (pseudo)random function generates a random challenge $c \in S_2$ where S_2 is a large set.

c. The routing node publishes
$w_i = s_i - ct_i'$ in Z for i=1,2,…,n,
$W = U - cr \bmod q$, $v_i = u_i - cr_i'$
in Z for i=1,2,…,n.

d. Public verification:

$$A' = A^c g^W \prod_{i=1}^{n} a_i'^{w_i} \bmod p,$$

$$B' = B^c y^W \prod_{i=1}^{n} b_i'^{w_i} \bmod p,$$

$$e_i' = e_{i-1}^{w_i} h^{v_i} e_i^c \bmod N \ \text{ for } i=1,2,\ldots,n.$$

7. The routing node proves knowledge of a secret integer $R'' = \sum_{i=1}^{n} (r_i \sum_{j=i+1}^{n} t_j')$ such that $e_n = g^{\prod_{i=1}^{n} t_i} h^{R''} \bmod N$ using ZK proof of knowledge of discrete logarithm (Schnorr, 1991).
8. It is publicly verified that $w_i + c(2^T + 2^{T-1})$ is in R_2 to guarantee that t_i' is in R where choice of R_1, R_2, S_1, S_2 must satisfy the three rules in (10), (11), and (12) and guarantee statistical privacy of the proof.

When the new mix network employs ElGamal-encryption-based shuffling, formal analysis of its security is similar to the analysis of its Paillier-encryption-based version. Due to space limit, the analysis is not repeated here. As mentioned before, the most important application of mix network is e-voting. A mix-network-based e-voting design is described in the following to show importance of the new mix network in practical applications.

1. Some talliers share the private key of an encryption algorithm, which is employed to encrypt the votes in the election. The sharing mechanism guarantees that decryption is only feasible when enough talliers (e.g. over a threshold) cooperate. For example, the private key of Paillier encryption can be shared using the technique in (Fouque, Poupard, & Stern, 2000).
2. The voters encrypt their votes and submit the ciphertexts to the talliers.
3. The talliers set up a mix network and each of them acts as a routing node.
4. The talliers take turns to shuffle the encrypted votes.
5. The talliers cooperate to decrypt the repeatedly shuffled ciphertexts and recover the votes. Each of them publicly proves validity of his part of decryption work as detailed in (Fouque, Poupard, & Stern, 2000).
6. Any election rule can be applied to count the decrypted votes and determine the result of the election.

If at least one tallier conceals his permutation used in his shuffling, the decrypted votes cannot be traced back to the voters and thus privacy of e-voting is guaranteed. As the new mix network is publicly verifiable, the voters and independent observers can verify validity of the talliers' shuffling such that any cheating in tallying can be detected.

Homomorphic tallying does not decrypt the encrypted votes separately but exploits homomorphism of the employed encryption algorithm to collectively open the encrypted votes using a small number of decryptions. The e-voting schemes employing homomorphic tallying (Adler et al., 2000; Baudron, Fouque, Pointcheval, Stern, & Poupard, 2001; Damga_ard & Jurik, 2001; Groth, 2005; Hirt & Sako, 2000; Katz et al., 2001; Kiayias & Yung, 2002; Lee & Kim, 2000, 2002; Neff, 2000; Peng, Boyd, Dawson, & Lee, 2004; Schoenmakers, 2000) are called homomorphic e-voting schemes. They usually employ an homomorphic encryption algorithm to encrypt the votes where an encryption algorithm with decryption function $D()$ is homomorphic if $D(c_1)+D(c_2)=D(c_1c_2)$ or $D(c_1)D(c_2)=D(c_1c_2)$ for any ciphertexts c_1 and c_2.

Then homomorphism of the encryption algorithm is exploited to recover the sum the votes for every candidate. With homomorphic tallying, each vote must be in a special format, so that the number of votes can be correctly counted. More precisely, in homomorphic e-voting every vote contains one or more selections (each corresponding to a candidate or a possible choice) and every selection must be one of two pre-defined integers (e.g. 0 and 1), each representing support or rejection of a candidate or choice. So each vote must be publicly checked to be valid (in the certain special format). Vote validity check usually depends on costly zero knowledge proof operations and corresponding verification operations.

Homomorphic e-voting schemes (Adler et al., 2000; Baudron, Fouque, Pointcheval, Stern, & Poupard, 2001; Damga_ard & Jurik, 2001; Groth, 2005; Hirt & Sako, 2000; Katz et al., 2001; Kiayias & Yung, 2002; Lee & Kim, 2000, 2002; Neff, 2000; Peng, Boyd, Dawson, & Lee, 2004; Peng & Bao, 2008; Schoenmakers, 2000) employ an additive homomorphic encryption algorithm with a distributed decryption function to seal the votes. The tallying operation in homomorphic e-voting decrypts the sum of the votes instead of the separate votes. So it only costs one single decryption operation to count the votes for each candidate and is quite efficient. However, correctness of homomorphic voting depends on validity of the votes. An invalid vote can be the sum of multiple valid votes to compromise correctness of a homomorphic voting scheme. So a vote validity check mechanism is necessary to detect and delete any invalid vote before the tallying phase.

A typical additive homomorphic encryption algorithm with a T-out-of-M distributed decryption function is distributed Paillier encryption proposed by Fouque et al. (Fouque, Poupard,& Stern, 2000), which is recalled as follows.

1. **Key Generation:** $N=pq$, $p = 2p' + 1$ and $q = 2q' + 1$ where p and q are primes and $gcd(N, \phi(N)) = 1$. Integers a, b are randomly chosen from Z_N^* and $g = (1+N)^a + b^N \bmod N^2$. The private key is $\beta p'q'$ where β is randomly chosen from Z_N^*. The public key consists of N, g and $\theta = a\beta p'q'$. $A_1A_2,\ldots,A_M$ are the private key holders. Let $F(x) = \sum_{k=0}^{T-1} f_k x^k$ where $f_0 = \beta p'q'$ and f_1, f_2, f_{T-1} are random integers in $Z_{p'q'}$. The share $d_j = F(j) \bmod p'q'N$ is distributed to A_j for $j=1,2,\ldots,M$, G is the cyclic subgroup containing all the quadratic residues in $Z_{N^2}^*$ where an integer y in Z_{N^2} is an Nth residue if there exist an integer x such that $x^N = y \bmod N^2$. Random integer v is a generator of G and $v_j = v^{\Delta d_j} \bmod N^2$ for $j=1,2,\ldots,M$ where $\Delta = M!$. Integers v and v_j for $j=1,2,\ldots,M$ are published.
2. **Encryption:** A message $s \in Z_N$ is encrypted into $c = g^s r^N \bmod N^2$ where r is randomly chosen from Z_N^*.
3. **Partial Decryptions of Ciphertext *c*:** For $j=1,2,\ldots,M$ A_j provides his part of decryption $d_j = c^{2\Delta d_j}$ and proves $\log_{c^{4\Delta}} d_j^2 = \log_{v^\Delta} v_j$.
4. **Combination of Partial Decryptions:** The final decryption result can be recovered as $s = L(\prod_{j \in \Psi} d_j^{2u_i}) \times \frac{1}{4\Delta^2\theta}$ where set Ψ contains the indices of T correct partial decryptions and $u_j = \Delta \prod_{1 \le j' \le M, j' \ne j} \frac{j'}{j'-j}$.

The complete decryption function in the distributed Paillier encryption including the partial decryptions and the combination is denoted as $D()$. With this encryption algorithm to seal the votes, most of the existing homomorphic e-voting schemes can be abstracted into the following protocol.

1. Suppose there are n voters and w candidates and each voter has to elect some of the candidates in his vote. It is required that $n<N$, which is satisfied in any practical election.
2. Each voter V_i chooses his voting vector $(s_{i,1}, s_{i,2}, \ldots, s_{i,w})$ where $s_{i,l}=0$ or $s_{i,l}=1$ for $l = 1,2,\ldots,w$. A rule is followed: $s_{i,l}=1$ if V_i elects the lth candidate.
3. The distributed Paillier encryption recalled above is employed to encrypt the votes where the private key is shared among talliers $A_1, A_2, \ldots, A_M$. Each vote $(s_{i,1}, s_{i,2}, \ldots, s_{i,w})$ is encrypted into $(c_{i,1}, c_{i,2}, \ldots, c_{i,w})$ where $c_{i,l} = g^{s_{i,l}} r_{i,l}^N \bmod N^2$ and $r_{i,l}$ is randomly chosen from Z_N^* for $l = 1,2,\ldots,w$.
4. Each V_i illustrates validity of his vote through proof of

$$KN\,[\, c_{i,l}^{1/N} \,] \vee KN\,[\, (c_{i,l} / g)^{1/N} \,] \text{ for } l = 1,2,\ldots,w \tag{15}$$

where $KN(x)$ denotes knowledge of x. If the number of selected candidates in a vote must be a fixed number, each V_i has to prove that $\prod_{l=1}^{w} c_{i,l}$ is an encryption of the number using ZK proof of knowledge of Nth root (Guillou & Quisquater, 1989). Proof of (15) is implemented by running the proof protocol in the following (which is a combination of ZK proof of knowledge of Nth root [Guillou & Quisquater, 1989] and ZK proof of partial knowledge [Cramer, Damgard, & Schoenmakers, 1994]) for $l = 1,2,\ldots,w$.

a. V_i publishes $a_{s_{i,l}} = r^N \bmod N^2$

$$a_{1-s_{i,l}} = u_{1-s_{i,l}}^N / (c_{i,l} / g^{1-s_{i,l}})^{v_{1-s_{i,l}}} \bmod N^2$$

where $r \in Z_N^*$, $v_{1-s_{i,l}} \in Z_N$, and $u_{1-s_{i,l}} \in Z_N^*$ are randomly chosen.

b. An integer v is randomly chosen from Z_N by a verifier or a (pseudo)random function.

c. V_i publishes u_0, u_1, v_0 and v_1 where

$$u_{s_{i,l}} = r s_{i,l}^{v_{s_{i,l}}} \bmod N^2$$

$$v_{s_{i,l}} = v - v_{1-s_{i,l}} \bmod Z_N$$

d. Public verification:

$$u_0^N = a_0 c_{i,l}^{v_0} \bmod N^2$$

$$u_1^N = a_1 (c_{i,l} / g)^{v_1} \bmod N^2$$

$$v = v_0 + v_1 \bmod Z_N$$

5. The talliers verify the voters' proof of validity of their votes. The votes failing to pass the verification are deleted.
6. For simplicity, assume all the votes pass the vote validity check. As $n<N$ and the votes are valid, T honest talliers among $A_1, A_2, \ldots, A_M$ cooperate to decrypt $\prod_{i=1}^{n} c_{i,l}$ into the number of votes for the lth candidate for $l = 1,2,\ldots,w$. After the decryption, each A_j publicly proves that his partial decryption is correct.
7. The candidate(s) with the most votes wins.

Completeness and soundness of ZK proof of knowledge of Nth root (Guillou & Quisquater, 1989) and ZK proof of partial knowledge (Cramer, Damgard, & Schoenmakers, 1994) guarantee that with a overwhelmingly large probability a voter's vote is valid if his proof of validity of his vote can pass public verification. Honest verifier zero knowledge property of ZK proof of knowledge of root (Guillou & Quisquater, 1989) and ZK proof of partial knowledge (Cramer, Damgard, & Schoenmakers, 1994) guarantees that no vote is revealed in vote validity check. Tallying is very efficient and only costs each tallier $3w$ exponentiations. Vote validity check is inefficient as it repeats the proof and verification protocol for w times. Vote validity check brings each voter even higher a cost than vote encryption and a verifier at least $O(wn)$ exponentiations. So vote validity check is the efficiency bottleneck of homomorphic e-voting.

A prototype of the new e-voting scheme is presented in this section to show its basic workflow in the classic homomorphic tally scenario; while a more important work, its efficient specification, will be addressed later. The new e-voting scheme employs Paillier encryption, a typical homomorphic encryption algorithm to seal the votes, while distributed decryption mechanism is employed to share the decryption key among multiple talliers. In the tallying phase, the sum of the votes instead of the separate votes for every candidate is decrypted. So it only costs one single decryption operation to count the votes for each candidate and is quite efficient in tallying. As correctness of the tallying depends on validity of the votes, a vote validity check mechanism is designed to detect any invalid vote before the tallying phase.

Suppose there are M talliers and the tallying power needs at least T of them to obtain. A typical homomorphic encryption algorithm suitable for e-voting is the distributed Paillier encryption with a T-out-of-M distributed decryption function proposed by Fouque et al. (Fouque, Poupard,& Stern, 2000), which is recalled in the appendix. The encryption of a message m is $g^m r^N \bmod N^2$ where N and g is defined in the appendix and r is randomly chosen from Z_N^*. The complete decryption function in the distributed Paillier encryption including the partial decryptions and the combination is denoted as $D()$. With this encryption algorithm to seal the votes, the new e-voting scheme is proposed in a prototype as follows.

1. Suppose there are n voters and w candidates and each voter has to elect some of the candidates in his vote. It is required that $n<N$, which is satisfied in any practical election.
2. Each voter V_i chooses his voting vector $(s_{i,1}, s_{i,2}, \ldots, s_{i,w})$ where $s_{i,l}=0$ or $s_{i,l}=1$ for $l = 1,2,\ldots,w$. A rule is followed: $s_{i.l}=1$ if the lth candidate is V_i election.
3. Each V_i encrypts $(s_{i,1}, s_{i,2}, \ldots, s_{i,w})$ into $(c_{i,1}, c_{i,2}, \ldots, c_{i,w})$ where $c_{i,l} = g^{s_{i,l}} R_i^{r_{i,l} N} \bmod N^2$, R_i is randomly chosen from Z_N^* and $r_{i.l}$ is randomly chosen from Z_N for $l = 1,2,\ldots,w$. All the encrypted voting vectors are submitted to the talliers.
4. The talliers $A_1, A_2, \ldots, A_M$ cooperate to generate a public set $S = \{s_1, s_2, \ldots, s_w\}$, where each s_l is a random integer in Z_K corporately chosen by all the talliers and K is a large security parameter no larger than N but guaranteeing that w / K is negligible. For example, they can generate S as follows.
   a. Each A_j randomly chooses $S_{l,j}$ in Z_K and publishes $H_{l,j} = H_j(S_{l,j})$ for $l = 1,2,\ldots,w$ where $H_j()$ is a one-way and collision-resistant hash function.
   b. After all the $H_{l,j}$ s are published, each A_j publishes $S_{l,j}$ for $l = 1,2,\ldots,w$ and any one can verify their validity against their commitments $H_{l,j}$ for $l = 1,2,\ldots,w$.
   c. $s_l = \sum_{j=1}^{M} S_{l,j} \bmod K$ for $l = 1,2,\ldots,w$.
5. Each V_i has to prove that $C_i = \prod_{l=1}^{w} c_{i,l}^{s_l} \bmod N^2$ encrypts a message in S. As illustrated in Theorem 5, this proof guarantees that the voting vector encrypted in $(c_{i,1}, c_{i,2}, \ldots, c_{i,w})$ is valid with an overwhelmingly large probability. The proof is implemented by V_i using the following proof

$$KN[\log_{R_i^N}(C_i / g^{s_1})] \vee KN[\log_{R_i^N}(C_i / g^{s_2})] \vee KN[\log_{R_i^N}(C_i / g^{s_w})] \quad (16)$$

where $KN(x)$ denotes knowledge of x and R_i can be published. It is a proof of knowledge of 1-out-of- w discrete logarithms, which can be implemented through ZK proof of partial knowledge (Cramer, Damgard, & Schoenmakers, 1994) and ZK proof of knowledge of discrete logarithm (Schnorr, 1991).

6. The talliers verify the voters' proof of validity of their votes. The votes failing to pass the verification are deleted.
7. For simplicity, assume that all the votes pass the vote validity check. As $n<N$ and the votes are valid, T honest talliers among $A_1A_2,\ldots,A_M$ cooperate to decrypt $\prod_{i=1}^{n} c_{i,l}$ into the number of votes for the lth candidate for $l = 1,2,\ldots,w$. After the decryption, each A_j publicly proves that his partial decryption is correct.
8. The candidate with the most votes wins.

Theorem 5: If the voting vector in $(c_{i,1}, c_{i,2}, \ldots, c_{i,w})$ is invalid, the probability that the message encrypted in C_i lies in S is negligible.

Proof: As $(c_{i,1}, c_{i,2}, \ldots, c_{i,w})$ is invalid, there are the following two possibilities where $(s_{i,1}, s_{i,2}, \ldots, s_{i,w})$ is the voting vector encrypted into $(c_{i,1}, c_{i,2}, \ldots, c_{i,w})$.

- There is only one non-zero integer in $s_{i,1}, s_{i,2}, \ldots, s_{i,w}$.
- There are more than one non-zero integers in $s_{i,1}, s_{i,2}, \ldots, s_{i,w}$.

In the first case, suppose $s_{i,l'} \neq 0$. As $(c_{i,1}, c_{i,2}, \ldots, c_{i,w})$ is invalid, $s_{i,l'} \neq 1 \bmod N$. So

$$D(C_i) = D(\prod_{l=1}^{w} c_{i,l}^{s_l}) = \sum_{l=1}^{w} s_{i,l}s_l = s_{i,l'}s_{l'} \neq s_{l'} \bmod N$$

and the probability that

$$D(C_i) = D(\prod_{l=1}^{w} c_{i,l}^{s_l}) = \sum_{l=1}^{w} s_{i,l}s_l = s_{i,l'}s_{l'} = s_{l''} \bmod N$$

and $l'' \neq l'$ and $1 \leq l'' \leq w$ is $(w-1)/K$ as $s_1, s_2, \ldots, s_w$ are randomly chosen in Z_K. Therefore, the probability that $D(C_i) = s_{l''} \bmod N$ and $1 \leq l'' \leq w$ is negligible.

In the second case, suppose only $s_{i,T_1}, s_{i,T_2}, \ldots, s_{i,T_\pi}$ are non-zero integers in $s_{i,1}, s_{i,2}, \ldots, s_{i,w}$ where $1 \leq T_1, T_2, \ldots, T_\pi \leq w$ and $\pi>1$. Then

$$D(C_i) = D(\prod_{l=1}^{w} c_{i,l}^{s_l}) = \sum_{l=1}^{w} s_{i,l}s_l = \sum_{l=1}^{\pi} s_{i,T_l}s_{T_l} \bmod N.$$

So, as $s_1, s_2, \ldots, s_w$ are randomly chosen in Z_K the probability that $D(C_i) = s_{l''} \bmod N$ and $1 \leq l'' \leq w$ is w / K and thus negligible.

Therefore, in both cases the probability that the message encrypted in C_i lies in S is negligible.

Correctness of the e-voting protocol is straightforward and any interested reader can follow it step by step to check it. Homomorphism of the employed encryption algorithm and soundness of the employed ZK proof primitives to verify validity the participants' operations (e.g. voters' voting and talliers' decryption) guarantee soundness of the e-voting protocol. Honest verifier ZK property of the employed ZK proof primitives guarantees that no vote is revealed if the verifier is honest (or replaced by a random oracle) in them. Tallying is very efficient and only costs each tallier $3w$ exponentiations. However, vote validity check is inefficient as it cost each voter $O(w)$ exponentiations. So vote validity check is the efficiency bottleneck of the prototype. Moreover, the prototype needs an assumption on honesty of the verifier or the random oracle assumption.

In this section, two efficient vote validity proof and verification protocols are proposed to achieve high efficiency on the base of the prototype. The first protocol only costs $O(\sqrt{w})$ exponentiations for every voter and achieves assumption-free soundness, but still needs the honest-verifier assumption. The second protocol only costs $O(1)$ exponentiations for every voter and removes the honest-verifier assumption but only achieves computational soundness.

In (Peng, 2011), an efficient membership proof technique is proposed, which can prove that a secret integer is in a set of w integers at the cost of $O(\sqrt{w})$ exponentiations. It employs divide-and-conquer strategy to use ZK proof of partial knowledge (Cramer, Damgard, & Schoenmakers, 1994) in a more efficient way. Although the membership proof protocol in (Peng, 2011) does not employ Paillier encryption as its sealing algorithm, it can be adapted to support Paillier encryption and improve efficiency of vote validity proof as follows.

1. For simplicity of description, suppose S can be divided into κ subsets $S_1, S_2, \ldots, S_\kappa$ and each S_l contains k integers denoted as $\tau_{l,1}, \tau_{l,2}, \ldots, \tau_{l,k}$.
2. V_i randomly chooses an integer s in Z_N and calculates for each S_l integers $b_{l,j}$ for j=1,2,…,k in Z_N to satisfy

$$\sum_{j=1}^{k} b_{l,j}\tau_{l,\rho}^{j} = s \bmod N \ \ for\ \ \rho = 1,2,\ldots,k. \tag{17}$$

More precisely, integers $b_{l,j}$ for l=1,2,…,κ and j=1,2,…,k must satisfy

$$\begin{pmatrix} \tau_{l,1} & \tau_{l,1}^2 & \cdots & \tau_{l,1}^k \\ \tau_{l,2} & \tau_{l,2}^2 & \cdots & \tau_{l,2}^k \\ \cdots & \cdots & \cdots & \cdots \\ \cdots & \cdots & \cdots & \cdots \\ \tau_{l,k} & \tau_{l,k}^2 & \cdots & \tau_{l,k}^k \end{pmatrix} \begin{pmatrix} b_{l,1} \\ b_{l,2} \\ \cdots \\ \cdots \\ b_{l,k} \end{pmatrix} = \begin{pmatrix} s \\ s \\ \cdots \\ \cdots \\ s \end{pmatrix}$$

for l=1,2,…,κ where in this paper computations in any matrix is carried out modulo N. As $\tau_{l,j} < N$ for l=1,2,…,κ and j=1,2,…,k and they are different integers,

$$M_l = \begin{pmatrix} \tau_{l,1} & \tau_{l,1}^2 & \cdots & \tau_{l,1}^k \\ \tau_{l,2} & \tau_{l,2}^2 & \cdots & \tau_{l,2}^k \\ \cdots & \cdots & \cdots & \cdots \\ \cdots & \cdots & \cdots & \cdots \\ \tau_{l,k} & \tau_{l,k}^2 & \cdots & \tau_{l,k}^k \end{pmatrix}$$

is a non-singular matrix for l=1,2,…,κ and there is a unique solution for $b_{l,1}, b_{l,2}, \ldots, b_{l,k}$:

$$\begin{pmatrix} b_{l,1} \\ b_{l,2} \\ \cdots \\ \cdots \\ b_{l,k} \end{pmatrix} = M_l^{-1} \begin{pmatrix} s \\ s \\ \cdots \\ \cdots \\ s \end{pmatrix}$$

for l=1,2,…,κ Therefore, functions

$$F_l(x) = \sum\nolimits_{j=1}^{k} b_{l,i} x^j \bmod N$$

for l=1,2,…,κ are obtained, each to satisfy

$$F_l(\tau_{l,i}) = s \ \text{for}\ j = 1,2,\ldots,k. \tag{18}$$

V_i publishes s. Note that $F_l()$ is actually the unique polynomial with degree at most k to satisfy (18) and $F_l(0)$=0. Readers with basic knowledge in linear algebra should know a few efficient methods, which do not cost any exponentiation, to calculate $F_l()$ from $\tau_{l,j}$ for j=1,2,…,k. Our presentation of $F_l()$ through matrix calculations is only one of them, which seems formal and straightforward. Also note that if necessary calculation of $F_l()$ can be performed beforehand once

S is published such that it is already available when the membership proof or exclusion proof starts.

3. V_i calculates $e_{i,j} = e_{i,j-1}^{m_i} R_i^{\gamma_{i,j}N} \bmod N^2$ for $j=1,2,\ldots,k-1$ where $m_i = \sum_{l=1}^{w} s_{i,l} s_l$, $e_{i,0} = C_i$ and $\gamma_{i,j}$ is randomly chosen from Z_{N}.
4. V_i proves validity of $e_{i,1}, e_{i,2}, \ldots, e_{i,k-1}$ using a zero knowledge proof that he knows m_i, $r_i = R_i^{\sum_{l=1}^{w} r_{i,l} s_l} \bmod N^2$ and $\gamma_{i,j}$ for $j=1,2,\ldots,k-1$ such that $C_i = g^{m_i} r_i^N \bmod N^2$ and $e_{i,j} = e_{i,j-1}^{m_i} R_i^{\gamma_{i,j}N} \bmod N^2$ for $j=1,2,\ldots,k-1$, which can be implemented through a simple combination of ZK proof of knowledge of discrete logarithm (Schnorr, 1991) and ZK proof of equality of discrete logarithms (Chaum & Pedersen, 1992).
5. V_i publishes $\omega_{i,l} = g^{s_i'} R_i'^N \bmod N^2$ for $l=1,2,\ldots,\kappa$ where $s_i' = \sum_{j=0}^{k-1} b_{l,j+1} m_i^{j+1} \bmod N$ and $R_i' = R_i^{\sum_{j=0}^{k-1} \Gamma_{i,j+1} b_{l,j+1}} \bmod N$ and $\Gamma_{i,j} = \Gamma_{i,j-1} m_i + \gamma_{i,j-1} \bmod N$ for $j=2,3,\ldots,k$ and $\Gamma_{i,1} = \sum_{l=1}^{w} r_{i,l} s_l \bmod N$.
6. Any verifier can check $\omega_{i,l} = \prod_{j=0}^{k-1} e_{i,j}^{b_{l,j+1}} \bmod N^2$ for $l=1,2,\ldots,\kappa$ as follows.
   a. He randomly chooses integers $\theta_1, \theta_2, \ldots, \theta_\kappa$ from Z_τ where τ is a large integer smaller than p and q.
   b. For $i=1,2,\ldots,n$ he checks

$$\prod_{l=1}^{\kappa} \omega_{i,l}^{\theta_l} = \prod_{j=0}^{k-1} e_{i,j}^{\sum_{l=1}^{\kappa} \theta_l b_{l,j+1}} \bmod N^2. \qquad (19)$$

   c. He accepts validity of $\omega_{i,1}, \omega_{i,2}, \ldots, \omega_{i,\kappa}$ if (19) holds.
7. The verifier (e.g. the talliers)
   a. calculates $b_{l,j}$ for $l=1,2,\ldots,\kappa$ and $j=1,2,\ldots,k$ to satisfy (17) like the voter does where s is provided by the voter;
   b. verifies V_i's proof of validity of $e_{i,1}, e_{i,2}, \ldots, e_{i,k-1}$.
8. Vote validity proof is reduced to proof of encryption in one of multiple ciphertexts: s is encrypted in one of the κ ciphertexts $\omega_{i,1}, \omega_{i,2}, \ldots, \omega_{i,\kappa}$ where $\omega_{i,l} = \prod_{j=0}^{k-1} e_{i,j}^{b_{l,j+1}} \bmod N^2$.
9. V_i runs ZK proof of partial knowledge (Cramer, Damgard, & Schoenmakers, 1994) and ZK proof of knowledge of Nth root (Guillou & Quisquater, 1989) to implement the proof by showing that he knows one of κ instances of Nth root: $(\omega_{i,1} / g^s)^{1/N}$, $(\omega_{i,2} / g^s)^{1/N}, \ldots, (\omega_{i,\kappa} / g^s)^{1/N}$.

The new vote validity proof protocol above employs zero knowledge proof primitives and so achieves honest verifier zero knowledge as shown in Theorem 1 in (Peng, 2011). It guarantees validity of the votes as illustrated in Theorem 6.

Theorem 6: The new vote validity proof protocol is sound. More precisely, if a polynomial voter can extract an opening (m_i, r_i) to C_i such that $m_i \neq s_l \bmod q$ for $l = 1, 2, \ldots, w$, then the probability that the voter can pass the verification for validity of his vote is negligible.

Proof: If the voter extracts m_i, r_i and passes the verification in the vote validity proof with a non-negligible probability while $C_i = g^{m_i} r_i^N \bmod N^2$ and $m_i \neq s_l \bmod N$ for $l = 1, 2, \ldots, w$, a contradiction can be found as follows. As he passes the verification in the vote validity proof with a non-negligible probability, he must have successfully proved validity of $e_{i,1}, e_{i,2}, \ldots, e_{i,k-1}$ with a non-negligible probability. As proof of validity of $e_{i,1}, e_{i,2}, \ldots, e_{i,k-1}$ is based on ZK proof of knowledge of Nth root (Guillou & Quisquater, 1989) and ZK proof of equality of discrete logarithms in (Chaum & Pedersen, 1992), whose soundness is formally proved when they are proposed, it is guaranteed with a non-negligible probability that the voter can calculate integers m_i, r_i and $\gamma_{i,j}$ for j=1,2,...,k-1 in polynomial time such that

$$C_i = g^{m_i} r_i^N \bmod N^2 \quad (20)$$

$$e_{i,j} = e_{i,j-1}^{m_i} \gamma_{i,j}^N \bmod N^2 \ \ for\ j = 1,2,\ldots,k-1 \quad (21)$$

where $e_{i,0} = C_i$.

As he passes the verification in the vote validity proof with a non-negligible probability, the voter must have successfully passed the zero knowledge proof of knowledge of one out of κ N^{th} roots (Cramer, Damgard, & Schoenmakers, 1994) with a non-negligible probability. As soundness of zero knowledge proof of partial knowledge (Cramer, Damgard, & Schoenmakers, 1994) is formally proved when it is proposed, it is guaranteed that for some l in {1,2,...,κ} the voter can calculate integers s and R in polynomial time such that $g^s R^N = \omega_{i,l} \bmod N^2$. Namely,

$$g^s R^N = \prod_{j=0}^{k-1} e_{i,j}^{b_{l,j+1}} \bmod N^2 \quad (22)$$

with a non-negligible probability where $e_{i,0} = C_i$.

(20), (21) and (22) imply that with a non-negligible probability

$$g^s R^N = \prod_{j=0}^{k-1} g^{b_{l,j+1} m_i^{j+1}} \Gamma_{i,j+1}^{N b_{l,j+1}}$$

$$= g^{\sum_{j=0}^{k-1} b_{l,j+1} m_i^{j+1}} \left(\prod_{j=0}^{k-1} \Gamma_{i,j+1}^{b_{l,j+1}}\right)^N \bmod N^2$$

where $\Gamma_{i,j} = \Gamma_{i,j-1}^{m_i} \gamma_{i,j-1} \bmod N^2$ for j=2,3,...,k and $\Gamma_{i,1} = r_i$. So

$$s = D(g^s R^N) = D\left(g^{\sum_{j=0}^{k-1} b_{l,j+1} m_i^{j+1}} \left(\prod_{j=0}^{k-1} \Gamma_{i,j+1}^{b_{l,j+1}}\right)^N\right)$$

$$= \sum_{j=0}^{k-1} b_{l,j+1} m_i^{j+1} = \sum_{j=1}^{k} b_{l,j} m_i^j \bmod N$$

with a non-negligible probability.

Note that $b_{l,1}, b_{l,2}, \ldots, b_{l,k}$ are generated through

$$\sum_{j=1}^{k} b_{l,j} \tau_{l,\rho}^j = s \bmod N \ \text{ for } \rho = 1,2,\ldots,k.$$

So with a non-negligible probability

$$\begin{pmatrix} \tau_{l,1} & \tau_{l,1}^2 & \cdots & \tau_{l,1}^k \\ \tau_{l,2} & \tau_{l,2}^2 & \cdots & \tau_{l,2}^k \\ \cdots & \cdots & \cdots & \cdots \\ \cdots & \cdots & \cdots & \cdots \\ \tau_{l,k} & \tau_{l,k}^2 & \cdots & \tau_{l,k}^k \\ m_i & m_i^2 & \cdots, & m_i^k \end{pmatrix} \begin{pmatrix} b_{l,1} \\ b_{l,2} \\ \cdots \\ \cdots \\ b_{l,k} \end{pmatrix} = \begin{pmatrix} s \\ s \\ \cdots \\ \cdots \\ s \\ s \end{pmatrix} \quad (23)$$

However, as $m_i \neq s_l \bmod N$ for $l = 1,2,\ldots,w$ and all the calculations in the matrix is performed modulo N,

$$\begin{pmatrix} \tau_{l,1} & \tau_{l,1}^2 & \cdots & \tau_{l,1}^k & s \\ \tau_{l,2} & \tau_{l,2}^2 & \cdots & \tau_{l,2}^k & s \\ \cdots & \cdots & \cdots & \cdots & \cdots \\ \cdots & \cdots & \cdots & \cdots & \cdots \\ \tau_{l,k} & \tau_{l,k}^2 & \cdots & \tau_{l,k}^k & s \\ m_i & m_i^2 & \cdots, & m_i^k & s \end{pmatrix}$$

is a non-singular matrix and thus (23) absolutely and always fails. Therefore, a contradiction is found and the probability that a voter can pass the vote validity proof is negligible if the integer he encrypts in C_i is not in *S*.

The main idea of the second new vote validity proof technique is based on the Diffie-Hellman handshake. The talliers set up w different Diffie-Hellman keys, each of whose discrete logarithm is the product of two key roots. The two key roots for the jth Diffie-Hellman key include a constant key root chosen by the talliers and $\log_{R_i^N} y_j$ where $y_j = C_i / g^{s_j} \bmod N^2$. The talliers then seal a random secret message *m* into w commitments, using a hash function *H*() and the w Diffie-Hellman keys. The talliers publish the w commitments and his Diffie-Hellman commitment to his key root and then ask the voter V_i to extract *m*. Obviously, V_i can extract *m* if he knows one of the *n* Diffie-Hellman keys, while Diffie-Hellman assumption (to be detailed later) implies that he knows the jth Diffie-Hellman key iff he knows $\log_{R_i^N} y_j$. The proof protocol is described as follows to guarantee that the voter knows one of $\log_{R_i^N} y_1, \log_{R_i^N} y_2, \ldots, \log_{R_i^N} y_w$ under Diffie-Hellman assumption.

1. For simplicity and without losing generality, suppose V_i knows $x_t = \log_{R_i^N} y_t$ where $1 \le t \le w$. A one-way and collision-resistant hash function *H*() from Z_{N^2} to Z_L is employed where *L*<<*N*.
2. The talliers randomly choose an integers *r* from Z_N and a random message *m* from Z_L. They calculate and conceal $z_j = y_j^r \bmod N^2$ for $j = 1,2,\ldots,w$. They calculate and publish $c_j = H(z_j) \oplus m$ for $j = 1,2,\ldots,w$, $z = (R_i^N)^r \bmod N^2$.
3. V_i publishes $u = H(z_t) \oplus c_t$ where $z_t = z^{x_t} \bmod N^2$.
4. The talliers verify *u*=*m*.

They accept the proof if this equation holds.

This new vote validity proof protocol is quite efficient. Especially the prover only needs a low constant computational cost independent of w. So it is suitable for low-capability voters using mobile devices. Moreover, as *L*<<*N*, it greatly improves communicational efficiency as well. Theorem 7 shows that it guarantees validity of the votes under Diffie-Hellman assumption as defined in Definition 2, while it is proved to be honest-verifier zero knowledge in Theorem 8.

Definition 2: *(Diffie-Hellman assumption)* Given $h^a \bmod N^2$ and $h^b \bmod N^2$, it is hard to calculate $h^{ab} \bmod N^2$ unless either *a* or *b* is known.

Theorem 7: Passing the new vote validity proof protocol guarantees the voter's knowledge of one of $\log_{R_i^N} y_1, \log_{R_i^N} y_2, \cdots, \log_{R_i^N} y_w$ under Diffie-Hellman assumption.

Proof: Passing the new vote validity proof protocol implies *u*=*m* and thus the user knows *m*. As the only published information about *m* is $c_j = H(z_j) \oplus m$ for $j = 1,2,\ldots,w$.

The user must know a z_J where $1 \le J \le w$. So according to Diffie-Hellman assumption, the user must know

$$x_J = \log_{R_i^N} y_J \text{ as } z_J = (R_i^N)^{x_J r} \bmod N^2$$

and *r* is kept secret from the prover.

Theorem 8: The new vote validity proof protocol achieves honest-verifier zero knowledge.

Proof: The proof transcript of the new vote validity proof protocol contains $c_1, c_2, \ldots, c_w, z, u$. A party without any knowledge of any secret can simulate the proof transcript as follows.

1. He randomly chooses an integers *r* from Z_N and a random message *m* from Z_L.
2. He calculates $z = (R_i^N)^r \bmod N^2$ and $z_j = y_j^r \bmod N^2$ for $j = 1,2,\ldots,w$.
3. He calculates $c_j = H(z_j) \oplus m$ for $j = 1,2,\ldots,w$.
4. He sets *u*=*m*.

In both the real transcript with an honest verifier and the simulating transcript,

- *u* is uniformly distributed in Z_L.
- z is uniformly distributed in the cyclic group generated by the generator R_i^N.
- $c_j = H(z_j) \oplus u$ for $j = 1,2,\ldots,w$ where $z_j = y_j^{\log_{R_i^N} z} \bmod N^2$.

As the two transcripts have just the same distribution, the proof transcript can be simulated without any difference by a party without any knowledge of any secret if the verifier is honest and does not deviate from the proof protocol. So the new vote validity proof protocol achieves honest-verifier zero knowledge.

Note that proof of zero knowledge in Theorem 8 assumes that the verifier is honest and does not deviate from the proof protocol. If the verifier is dishonest and encrypts different messages in $c_1, c_2, \ldots, c_w$, he can break privacy of the proof. When the verifier cannot be trusted, the vote validity proof protocol can be further optimised as follows such that before returning *m* the voter can verify that the verifier is honest and all the $c_1, c_2, \ldots, c_w$ are encryptions of the same message.

1. Suppose V_i knows $x_t = \log_{R_i^N} y_t$ where $1 \le t \le w$. Besides one-way and collision-resistant hash functions *H*() and $H'()$, a block cipher $E_k()$ (e.g. AES) with key *k* and a message space Z_L is employed.
2. The talliers randomly choose an integers *r* from Z_N and a random message *m* from Z_L. They calculate and conceal $z_j = y_j^r \bmod N^2$ for $j = 1,2,\ldots,w$. They calculate and publish $c_j = E_{H(z_j)}(m)$ for $j = 1,2,\ldots,w$; $c'_j = E_m(H(z_j))$ for $j = 1,2,\ldots,w$; $z = (R_i^N)^r \bmod N^2$.
3. V_i calculates $u = H(z_t) \oplus c_t$ where $z_t = z^{x_t} \bmod N^2$ and verifies $E_{D_u(c'_j)}(u) = c_j$ for $j = 1,2,\ldots,w$ where *D*() is the decryption function of *E*(). He publishes *u* if all the w equations hold. Otherwise he gives up his proof as the verifier is detected to be dishonest.
4. The talliers verify *u*=*m*.

They accept the proof iff this equation holds. As the employed hash functions are one-way and collision-resistent and it is difficult to find different integers pairs (k_1,m_1) and (k_2,m_2) in Z_L^2 such that

$$E_{k_1}(m_1) = E_{k_2}(m_2) \text{ and } E_{m_1}(k_1) = E_{m_2}(k_2),$$

the verifier is guaranteed to have committed to the same *m* in the w instances of commitment (encryption). So it is not necessary to be trusted. Except that the user returns opening of one of $c_1, c_2, \ldots, c_n$ in two steps (instead of in one step) and there is a verification against the verifier before the second step, this further optimisation actually employs the same proof principle. So it inherits the security properties proved in Theorem 7 and Theorem 8. Moreover, it optimises its zero knowledge property to achieve stronger privacy without any trust on the verifier. However, its soundness is only computational. The other vote validity proof techniques including Protocol 1 employ standard ZK proof primitives like ZK proof of knowledge of discrete logarithm and ZK proof of partial knowledge, so they can formally build an extractor to extract their claimed knowledge from their proof transcript. To achieve higher efficiency and stronger privacy, this second vote valididty proof protocol bases its soundness on the computational assumption on the Diffie-Hellman problem and the employed hash functions. So it only achieves computational soundness and cannot provide an extractor to show unconditional soundness.

FUTURE RESEARCH DIRECTIONS

In homomorphic e-voting, the work in the future should focus on two directions.

- More efficient proof and verification of validity of votes: more advanced ZK proof techniques should be designed to achieved higher efficiency and stronger soundness.
- Supporting more election rules: complex and unlimited election rules should be supported.

In mix-network-based e-voting, the work in the future should focus on two directions.

- More efficient proof and verification of validity of shuffling: more advanced ZK proof techniques should be designed to achieved higher efficiency and stronger soundness.
- Trade off on-line operations for off-line operations: costly operations should be carried out off-line to improve on-line efficiency.

CONCLUSION

The new e-voting scheme is compared with the existing e-voting schemes in Table 2. In comparison of privacy, the ZK models in different solutions are listed. In estimation of computational efficiency, computational cost of a voter and the talliers is estimated and exponentiations with full length exponents in Z_N are counted. An

Table 2. Comparison of e-voting schemes

E-Voting	Computation		Communication	privacy	soundness
	voter	talliers			
shuffling	2	$\geq 8Mn$	$\geq(8Mn+2n)$	honest	mostly
based			$\log_2 N$	verifier	computational
existing	$\geq 6w$	$\geq 4nw$	$\geq 8nw\log_2 N$	honest	unconditional
homomorphic		$+3Mw$		verifier	
Protocol 1	$2w+4k+3\kappa+4$	$n(w \mid K \mid / \mid N \mid + 4k + 3\kappa) + 3Mw$	$n(2w + 4k + 3\kappa)\log_2 N$	honest verifier	unconditional
Protocol 2	2w+1	$n(w \mid K \mid / \mid N \mid + 3) + 3Mw$	$n(w(2\log_2 N + \log_2 K + 2\log_2 L) + 2\log_2 N + \log_2 L)$	no trust needed	computational

exponentiation with an exponent in Z_K is regarded as $|K|/|N|$ full length exponents where $|\ |$ stands for bit length as the computational cost of a modulo exponentiation is approximately linear in the bit length of its exponent. As N is usually at least 1024 bits long, $|K|/|N|$ can be quite small while K is still large enough to guarantee that w / K is negligible. In estimation of communicational efficiency, the number of bits transfered between the participants is estimated. Note that N is usually much larger than L and K. For example, it is common to set $\log_2 N=1021$ and $\log_2 L=\log_2 K=128$.

The comparison clearly demonstrates that in comparison with the existing e-voting schemes our new e-voting design is more efficient and can achieve stronger privacy. In election applications emphasizing soundness, it can employ the first vote validity proof protocol; in election applications emphasizing privacy, it can employ the second vote validity proof protocol.

REFERENCES

Abe, M. (1999). Mix-networks on permutation net-works. In *Proceedings of Asiacrypt 1998* (*Vol. 1716*, pp. 258–273). Berlin, Germany: Springer-Verlag.

Abe, M., & Hoshino, F. (2001). Remarks on mix-network based on permutation networks. In *Proceedings of Public Key Cryptography 2001* (*Vol. 1992*, pp. 317–324). Berlin, Germany: Springer-Verlag. doi:10.1007/3-540-44586-2_23.

Abe, M., & Imai, H. (2003). Flaws in some robust optimistic mix-nets. In *Proceedings of ACISP 2003,* (Vol. 2727, pp. 39-50). Berlin, Germany: Springer.

Adler, J. M., Dai, W., Green, R. L., & Ne, C. A. (2000). Computational details of the vote here homomorphic election system. *VoteHere Inc*. Retrieved from http://www.votehere.net/technicaldocs/hom.pdf

Baudron, O., Fouque, P.-A., Pointcheval, D., Stern, J., & Poupard, G. (2001). Practical multicandidate election system. In *Proceedings of the Twentieth Annual ACM Symposium on Principles of Distributed Computing,* (p. 274-283). ACM.

Boudot, F. (2000). Efficient proofs that a committed number lies in an interval. In *Proceedings of the Eurocrypt 2000,* (Vol. 1807, pp. 431-444). Berlin, Germany: Springer-Verlag.

Canetti, R., Dwork, C., Naor, M., & Ostrovsky, R. (1997). Deniable encryption. In *Proceedings of Crypto 1997* (*Vol. 1294*, pp. 90–104). Berlin, Germany: Springer-Verlag.

Chaum, D., & Pedersen, T. (1992). Wallet databases with observers. In *Proceedings of Crypto 1992* (*Vol. 740*, pp. 89–105). Berlin, Germany: Springer-Verlag.

Cramer, R., Damgard, I., & Schoenmakers, B. (1994). Proofs of partial knowledge and theory and practice of secure e-voting systems. In *Proceedings of Crypto 1994* (*Vol. 839*, pp. 174–187). Berlin, Germany: Springer-Verlag.

Damgard, I., & Jurik, M. (2001). A generalisation, a simplification and some applications of Paillier's probabilistic public-key system. In *Proceedings of PKC 2001,* (Vol. 1992, pp. 119-136). Berlin, Germany: Springer-Verlag.

Fouque, P., Poupard, G., & Stern, J. (2000). Sharing decryption in the context of voting or lotteries. In *Proceedings of Financial Cryptography 2000* (*Vol. 1962*, pp. 90–104). Berlin, Germany: Springer-Verlag. doi:10.1007/3-540-45472-1_7.

Furukawa, J. (2004). Efficient, verifiable shuffle decryption and its requirement of unlinkability. In *Proceedings of PKC 2004,* (Vol. 2947, pp. 319-332). Berlin, Germany: Springer.

Furukawa, J., & Sako, K. (2001). An efficient scheme for proving a shuffle. In *Proceedings of Crypto 2001* (*Vol. 2139*, pp. 368–387). Berlin, Germany: Springer. doi:10.1007/3-540-44647-8_22.

Golle, P., & Juels, A. (2004). Parallel mixing. [CCS.]. *Proceedings of CCS, 2004*, 220–226. doi:10.1145/1030083.1030113.

Golle, P., Zhong, S., Boneh, D., Jakobsson, M., & Juels, A. (2002). Optimistic mixing for exit-polls. In *Proceedings of Asiacrypt 2002* (*Vol. 1592*, pp. 451–465). Berlin, Germany: Springer-Verlag. doi:10.1007/3-540-36178-2_28.

Groth, J. (2003). A verifiable secret shuffle of homomorphic encryptions. In *Proceedings of Public Key Cryptography 2003* (*Vol. 2567*, pp. 145–160). Berlin, Germany: Springer-Verlag. doi:10.1007/3-540-36288-6_11.

Guillou, L. C., & Quisquater, J. J. (1989). A paradoxical identity-based signature scheme resulting from zero-knowledge. In Goldwasser, S. (Ed.), *Crypto 1988* (*Vol. 403*, pp. 216–231). Berlin, Germany: Springer-Verlag.

Hevia, A., & Kiwi, M. (2002). Non-interactive zero-knowledge arguments for voting. In *Proceedings of LATIN 2002,* (Vol. 2286, pp. 415-429). Berlin, Germany: Springer-Verlag.

Hirt, M., & Sako, K. (2000). E_cient receipt-free voting based on homomorphic encryption. *Proceedings of EUROCRYPT, 2000*, 539–556.

Jakobsson, M., Juels, A., & Rivest, R. L. (2002). Making mix nets robust for electronic voting by randomized partial checking. In *Proceedings of the 11th Usenix Security Symposium 2002,* (pp. 339-353). USENIX.

Katz, J., Myers, S., & Ostrovsky, R. (2001). Cryptographic counters and applications to electronic voting. *Proceedings of EUROCRYPT, 2001*, 78–92.

Kiayias, A., & Yung, M. (2002). Self-tallying elections and perfect ballot secrecy. In *Proceedings of PKC 2002,* (p. 141-158). PKC.

Lee, B., & Kim, K. (2000). Receipt-free electronic voting through collaboration of voter and honest verifier. [JW-ISC.]. *Proceedings of JW-ISC, 2000*, 101–108.

Lee, B., & Kim, K. (2002). Receipt-free electronic voting scheme with a tamper-resistant randomizer. In *Proceedings of ICISC 2002,* (Vol. 2587, pp. 389-406). Springer-Verlag.

Lipmaa, H. (2003). On diophantine complexity and statistical zero-knowledge arguments. In *Proceedings of Asiacrypt '03* (*Vol. 2894*, pp. 398–415). Berlin, Germany: Springer-Verlag. doi:10.1007/978-3-540-40061-5_26.

Neff, C. A. (2000). *Conducting a universally verifiable electronic election using homomorphic encryption.* White Paper. VoteHere Inc.

Neff, C. A. (2001). A verifiable secret shuffle and its application to e-voting. In *Proceedings of the ACM Conference on Computer and Communications Security 2001,* (p. 116-125). ACM.

Neff, C. A. (2004). *Verifiable mixing (shuffling) of ElGamal pairs.* Retrieved from http://theory.lcs.mit.edu/_rivest/voting/papers/Neff-2004-04-21-ElGamalShuffles.pdf

Nguyen, L., Safavi-Naini, R., & Kurosawa, K. (2006). Verifiable shuffles: a formal model and a Paillier-based three-round construction with provable security. *International Journal of Information Security*, *4*, 241–255. doi:10.1007/s10207-006-0004-8.

Paillier, P. (1999). Public key cryptosystem based on composite degree residuosity classes. In *Proceedings of Eurocrypt 1999* (*Vol. 1592*, pp. 223–238). Berlin, Germany: Springer-Verlag. doi:10.1007/3-540-48910-X_16.

Park, C., Itoh, K., & Kurosawa, K. (1993). Efficient anonymous channel and all/nothing election scheme. In *Proceedings of Eurocrypt 1993* (*Vol. 765*, pp. 248–259). Berlin, Germany: Springer-Verlag.

Peng, K., Boyd, C., Dawson, E., & Lee, B. (2004). Multiplicative homomorphic e-voting. In *Proceedings of Indocrypt 2004* (*Vol. 3348*, pp. 61–72). Berlin, Germany: Springer-Verlag. doi:10.1007/978-3-540-30556-9_6.

Peng, K., Boyd, C., Dawson, E., & Viswanathan, K. (2004). A correct, private and efficient mix network. In *Proceedings of the 2004 International Workshop on Practice and Theory in Public Key Cryptography*, (Vol. 2947, pp. 439-454). Berlin, Germany: Springer-Verlag.

Pfitzmann, B. (1994). Breaking an efficient anonymous channel. In *Proceedings of Eurocrypt 1994* (*Vol. 950*, pp. 339–348). Berlin, Germany: Springer-Verlag.

Schnorr, C. (1991). Efficient signature generation by smart cards. *Journal of Cryptology*, *4*, 161–174. doi:10.1007/BF00196725.

Schoenmakers, B. (2000, July). Fully auditable electronic secret-ballot elections. *XOOTIC Magazine*.

ADDITIONAL READING

Buldas, A., & Magi, T. (2007). Practical security analysis of e-voting systems. In *Proceedings of the Security 2nd International Conference on Advances in Information and Computer Security*, (p. 320-335). IEEE.

Camenisch, J., Chaabouni, R., & Shelat, A. (2008). Efficient protocols for set membership and range proofs. In *Proceedings of Asiacrypt '08* (*Vol. 3089*, pp. 234–252). Berlin, Germany: Springer-Verlag. doi:10.1007/978-3-540-89255-7_15.

Chaabouni, R., Lipmaa, H., & Shelat, A. (2010). Additive combinatorics and discrete logarithm based range protocols. In *Proceedings of ACISP 2010,* (Vol. 6168, pp. 336-351). ACISP.

Furukawa, J. (2005). Efficient and verifiable shuffling and shuffle-decryption. *IEICE Transactions*, *88*(1), 172–188.

Groth, J. (2005). Non-interactive zero-knowledge arguments for voting. In *Proceedings of ACNS 2005*, (Vol. 3531, pp. 467-482). Berlin, Germany: Springer-Verlag.

Groth, J., & Ishai, Y. (2008). Sub-linear zero-knowledge argument for correctness of a shuffle. In *Proceedings of Eurocrypt 2008* (*Vol. 4965*, pp. 379–396). Berlin, Germany: Springer. doi:10.1007/978-3-540-78967-3_22.

Groth, J., & Lu, S. (2007). Verifiable shuffle of large size ciphertexts. In *Proceedings of PKC 2007*, (Vol. 4450, pp. 377-392). Berlin, Germany: Springer.

Kun Peng, E. D., & Bao, F. (2011). Modification and optimisation of a shuffling scheme: Stronger security, formal analysis and higher efficiency. *International Journal of Information Security*, *10*(1), 33–47. doi:10.1007/s10207-010-0117-y.

Peng, K. (2011). A general, flexible and efficient proof of inclusion and exclusion. In *Proceedings of CT-RSA 2011,* (Vol. 6558, pp. 33-48). CT-RSA.

Peng, K., & Bao, F. (2008). Efficient vote validity check in homomorphic electronic voting. In *Proceedings of ICISC 2008,* (Vol. 5461, pp. 202-217). ICISC.

Peng, K., & Bao, F. (2010a). An efficient range proof scheme. [IEEE.]. *Proceedings of IEEE PASSAT*, *2010*, 826–833.

Peng, K., & Bao, F. (2010b). Batch range proof for practical small ranges. In *Proceedings of Africacrypt 2010* (*Vol. 6055*, pp. 114–130). Africacrypt. doi:10.1007/978-3-642-12678-9_8.

Peng, K., Boyd, C., & Dawson, E. (2005). Simple and efficient shuffling with provable correctness and ZK privacy. In *Proceedings of Crypto '05* (*Vol. 3089*, pp. 188–204). Berlin, Germany: Springer-Verlag. doi:10.1007/11535218_12.

Wikstrom, D. (2005). A sender verifiable mix-net and a new proof of a shuffle. In *Proceedings of Asiacrypt '05* (*Vol. 3788*, pp. 273–292). Berlin, Germany: Springer. doi:10.1007/11593447_15.

KEY TERMS AND DEFINITIONS

e-Government: Electronic government, including but not limited to e-voting.

Encryption: Used to seal the votes before they are submitted.

e-Voting: Electronic voting.

Homomorphism: A special property of encryption algorithms, which can be exploited in collective tallying.

Mix Network: An anonymous communicational network, which is employed to shuffle the encrypted votes.

Privacy: No vote can be traced back to its voter.

Security: Security of e-voting includes correctness, soundness, and privacy.

ENDNOTES

1 The untappable communication channel is in the form of an internal channel like bus or USB cable when a tamper-resistant hardware is employed.

2 Jakobsson et al. (2002) cannot guarantee complete correctness, privacy, robustness, or public verifiability of election. Peng, Boyd, Dawson, and Viswanathan (2004) only supports a small fraction of all the possible permutations and thus is weak in privacy. Golle and Juels (2004) has a loose requirement on privacy and causes concerns with public verifiability.

3 As shown before, although there is no more efficient method to prove that a secret integer chosen from a range is in the same range, a secret integer chosen from a range can be proved to be in another much larger range efficiently.

4 A simple example is N=10, $t_1=t_2=\ldots=t_{10}=2$ while $t'_1 = t'_2 = t'_3 = t'_4 = 4$, $t'_5 = t'_6 = 2$, $t'_7 = t'_8 = 1$ and $t'_9 = t'_{10} = -1$. Another simple examples is N=10, $t_1=t_2=2$, $t_3=t_4=3$, $t_5=t_6=5$, $t_7=t_8=7$, $t_9=t_10=11$, while $t'_1 = t'_2 = 22$, $t'_3 = t'_4 = 15$, $t'_5 = t'_6 = -7$, $t'_7 = t'_8 = t'_9 = t'_{10} = -1$

5 As explained before, it only supports a very small fraction of all the possible permutations.

6 The mix network scheme in Groth and Ishai (2008) is very special in comparison with other mix network schemes. While the other mix network schemes focus on computation in efficiency analysis as their communicational cost is approximately linear in their computational cost; the mix network scheme in Groth and Ishai (2008) achieves high efficiency in communication by sacrificing computational efficiency. So although communicational efficiency is not the subject of this section, for the sake of fairness, we have to mention that the mix network scheme in Groth and Ishai (2008) has an advantage in communicational efficiency.

Chapter 18
Sealed-Bid Auction Protocols

Kun Peng
Institute for Infocomm Research, Singapore

ABSTRACT

In the Internet era electronic commerce is an important and popular industry. Electronic auctions provide a key function in e-commerce, enabling effective and fair distribution of electronic as well as non-electronic goods. Like other fields of e-commerce, e-auctions face serious security threats. Fraud can be committed by bidders or auctioneers. Most popular Internet auctions sites use an open-cry bidding process. This can add excitement to an auction in progress and possibly encourage new bidders to join an auction. However, there are serious difficulties in maintaining the security requirements often required in commercial auctions, particularly in terms of protecting bid confidentiality and bidder privacy. Additionally, some of the current auction techniques are interactive and require many rounds of communication before completion so that more time is required to determine the final winning price. Intensive communication over the insecure Internet is also a problem from the perspective of availability of service and network security. For these reasons most recent research in this area has concentrated on sealed-bid auctions. Sealed-bid auctions are the focus of this chapter. In this chapter, security requirements in e-auction including correctness, fairness, non-repudiation, robustness, public verifiability, bid privacy, and other desired properties like price flexibility and rule flexibility are introduced. The existing approaches to realize them are investigated. The authors show that the key requirement is bid privacy and the main challenge to the design of an e-auction is how to protect bid privacy without compromising other requirements and properties. Techniques to achieve bid privacy are presented in this chapter according to different application environments.

DOI: 10.4018/978-1-4666-4030-6.ch018

INTRODUCTION

The sealed-bid auction has been a useful tool to distribute resources for many years. It usually contains four phases. Various sealing functions may be used to seal the bids and keep them secret before they are opened. Different auction rules may be used.

Auctions have a long history since 500 B.C., when Herodotus reported the use of an auction (Cassady, 1967). Auction was frequently used to liquidate property and estate goods during the Roman Empire (Cassady, 1967). They are an effective method to distribute goods fairly. In the traditional auction systems both the open cry auction, such as English auction and Dutch auction, and the sealed bid auction have been widely used. In the open cry auctions, the bids are cried out openly and the bidder with the highest bid win. If each time a bidder cries out a new bid higher than the last one, it is called English auction. If the auctioneer cries out the bids from the highest possible price one by one until a bidder accept the current bid, it is called Dutch auction. In a sealed-bid auction, a bidder has to submit a sealed bid before a closing time. After the closing time one or more auctioneers open the bids to decide the winners according to a pre-defined rule. Sealed-bid auction is illustrated in Figure 1 to including at least two phases, the bidding phase when the bids are sealed and the bid opening phase when the bids are opened.

In the Internet era electronic commerce is an important and popular industry. Electronic auction is a key function in e-commerce and can be used to distribute electronic as well as non-electronic goods effectively and fairly. Although still at its early stage, e-auction is developing fast. Internet auctions accounted for approximately $3 billion in sales in 1999 and have grown significantly to $15 billion in sales for the year 2002 (Prevention & Division, 2003). The most famous e-auction website, e-bay, has more than two million visitors a day. In a network environment, sealed-bid auction is preferred not only because of its convenience and quickness but also because of its potential ability to protect bid confidentiality and bidders' privacy.

The players in an auction include:

- Seller, who has one or more items (also called goods) to sell;
- Bidder, who submits a bid (the highest price he is willing to pay);
- Auctioneer, who acts on behalf of the seller to determine a winning price (clearing price) and a bidder as the winner.
- Winner, the bidder chosen by the auctioneer(s) to pay the seller the clearing price and get the goods.

Figure 1. Sealed-bid auction

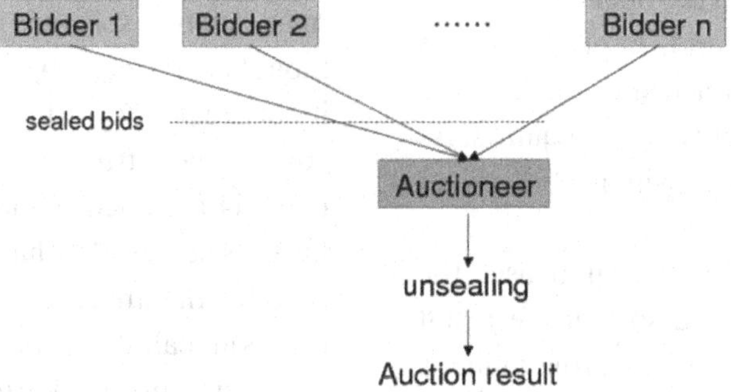

A sealed-bid auction is usually composed of four phases: preparation phase, bid submission phase, bid opening phase, and winner determination phase.

1. In the preparation phase, the auction system is set up and initialized. The auctioneers are chosen; the system parameters are generated; the item to sell is described; the auction rule is declared; the bidders winning price and the winner's identity as its output:

$$(W, ID) = F(I_1, b_1, I_2, b_2, \ldots, I_n, b_n)$$

   where n is the number of bidders, I_i is the identity of the ith bidder, b_i is I_i's bid, W is the winning price and ID is the winner's identity.
2. In the bid submission phase, every bidder submits a sealed bid through a communication network. The bids may be encrypted or signed by the bidder if needed. The employed communication network can be based on any computer network, like the Internet or a LAN. When bid sealing is applied to protect confidentiality of the bids, the communication network becomes a confidential channel. Usually, a digital signature technique is employed to upgrade the network to an authentic channel. In some cases, special techniques are used to upgrade the network to an anonymous channel.
3. In the bid opening phase, the bids are opened to determine the winning price. This is a very critical operation and the opening does not mean publish all the bids in plaintext with bidders' identities attached to them as bid privacy and anonymity may be required. As a result of bid opening, a winning bid (price) is determined.
4. In the winner determination phase, the winner(s) are identified so that the result (including the winning price and the winner's identity) of the auction can be published. If any bidder has a dispute, he can lodge it and the auctioneers must prove validity of the result publicly.

Sealing is a function used to achieve confidentiality and privacy. Usually, there are two kinds of sealing.

1. **Sealing by Hash Function:** Initially, a commitment for each bid is generated by a one-way and collision-resistant hash function. Each bidder first publishes his commitment of bid. After all the bidders have published their commitments, each bidder submits his bid (in plaintext or encrypted). This method aims to realize bid confidentiality and thus fairness—it is impossible for any bidder to know the bids of other bidders when his bid is committed even if he conspires with the auctioneer(s). Note that hash function is much more efficient than public-key encryption.
2. **Sealing by Encryption:** The bids are encrypted when submitted. As usually the bidders have not contacted the auctioneers before the auction1, it is supposed that public-key encryption algorithms are employed. This method is usually employed to implement bid privacy. In the opening phase, only necessary decryptions are performed and all the bids except the winning bid may remain encrypted at the end of auction.

The role of hash function is not recognised in many auction schemes and encryption sealing is thought to be enough. However, bid confidentiality or bid privacy achieved by encryption is often conditional—trust on some auctioneer(s) or third party is assumed while bid confidentiality and fairness achieved by hash function sealing is only based on the strength of the hash function. So hash function sealing is necessary to achieve strong bid confidentiality and fairness in some applications.

According to different auction rules, sealed-bid auctions can be further classified as follows.

1. Only one item to sell.
   a. First Bid Auction: Only one item is to be sold and the bidder with the highest bid gets the item. One drawback of this rule is that the bidders may decide their bids according to their expectation of other bids instead of according to their real evaluation of the item. So the clearing price may be different from the reasonable market price, which is a disadvantage compared to open cry auction.
   b. To overcome the problem in first bid auction, Vickrey (1961) proposed a different rule: the bidder with the highest bid wins but he only pays the second highest bid. Under this rule, the bidders tend to submit their real evaluation of the item as their bids.
2. More than one identical item to sell.
   a. In k^{th} bid auction, $k-1$ identical items are on sale, the kth bidding price is the clearing price and bidders with higher $k-1$ bids are winners. This is actually an extension of Vickrey auction and also encourages the bidder to submit their real evaluation as their bids.
3. Combination of different items to sell.
   a. In a combinatorial auctions (Suzuki & Yokoo, 2002; Yokoo & Suzuki, 2002; DeVries & Vohra, 2000; Silaghi, 2002; Holzman, Kfir-Dahav, Monderer, & Tennenholtz, 2001), more than one type of item is sold and there may be more than one item in each type. A bidder can offer a price for a chosen combination of the items. The seller chooses a distribution of the items so that the total price is the highest. Combinatorial auction is more flexible and comprehensive.

In this book, it is assumed that there is only one type of item to sell and combinatorial auction is not included.

Like other fields of e-commerce, e-auction is facing serious security concerns. For example, fraud in e-auction is a big problem. It was reported by the US Internet Fraud Watch that online auction fraud accounted for 51% of Internet fraud in the US in 2004 (Fraud, 2004). A fraud can be committed by bidders or auctioneers. Most contemporary e-auction websites use very simple auction mechanisms and require complete trust by the bidders on the auctioneers. Thus the bidders' interest is at risk due to the malicious activities of the auctioneers. The auctioneer may manipulate the price or the auction process to obtain a biased result. When a bidder uses e-coin, malicious auctioneers may misuse the e-coin. Moreover, the auctioneers can obtain personal information (identity and bid value) about the bidders as normally neither privacy nor anonymity service is provided in open cry e-auctions. Additionally, some of the current auction techniques are interactive and require many rounds of communication before completion. So more time is required to determine the final winning price. As well intensive communication over the insecure Internet is a problem from the perspective of availability of service and network security.

To defend against the increasing fraud and attacks, an auction scheme must have some desired requirements. The security requirements can be divided into two types.

Basic Requirements

Some requirements are compulsory in any auction application, so are called basic requirements.

1. **Correctness:** Correctness means the winning price and winner(s) must be determined exactly according to the auction rule. It is the most basic and important requirement

for an auction scheme. It must be achieved without any trust assumption.

2. **Confidentiality:** Confidentiality is the direct result of sealing. The sealing must be so strong that each bid remains confidential to other bidders and the auctioneer(s) before the bid opening phase starts.
3. **Fairness:** No bidder can get more information than other bidders and take advantage of them. Two necessary conditions for fairness are that no bidder has any knowledge of other bidders' bids when he submits his bid and no bid can be changed after it is submitted. Otherwise, he can choose his bid according to other bids. So the following two conditions must be satisfied.
    a. No bidder has any knowledge of any other bids before the bid submission phase ends, which is in fact confidentiality.
    b. After the bid submission phase ends, no bidder can change his bid.
4. **Non-Repudiation:** No bidder can deny his bid. A strict requirement for non-repudiation is that even though some bidders try to deny their bids, a correct auction result can still be determined. A looser standard only requires that any bidder trying to deny his bid can be identified and expelled from future auctions or is liable to other sanctions.
5. **Robustness:** Robustness is a stronger requirement than correctness. It requires that a correct auction result must be obtained not only in normal cases, but also in abnormal situations. The possible abnormal incidents include the following.
    a. A dishonest bidder submits an invalid bid.
    b. One or more malicious auctioneers perform an incorrect bid opening.
    c. One or more auctioneers fail to undertake their jobs.

As many unexpected accidents may happen in a real auction, robustness is essential for an auction system to be practical.

6. **Public Verifiability:** The validity of the auction must be publicly verifiable. In many cases, neither the bidders nor the auctioneers can be trusted. So validity of their behaviors must be publicly verifiable. In other cases, a bidder or other people may challenge the validity of the auction result and the dispute can only be solved by providing a publicly verifiable proof of correctness of the auction. The facts to be verified are as follows:
    a. Verification of validity of the bids;
    b. Verification of validity of bid opening;
    c. Verification of winner's identity.

Advanced Requirements

Other requirements are optional according to different applications, so are called advanced requirements.

1. **Price Flexibility:** The idea of sealed-bid auction is to finish the auction in one round. So the bids must be precise enough to avoid a tie situation, which means a new round of auction is needed. Therefore, the biddable prices should not be limited to a small set of prices. The range of biddable prices must be big enough for the bidders to evaluate the item on sale precisely.
2. **Rule Flexibility:** In different applications, different auction rules may be preferred. For example, first bid auction, Vickrey (second-bid) auction and k^{th} bid auction are often adopted in real auctions. So various auction rules must be supported.
3. **Bid Privacy:** Bid privacy is an extension of bid confidentiality. It requires that confidentiality of the bids must be kept not only before the bids are opened to achieve fairness, but

also after the bid opening phase to protect the bidders' privacy. Bid privacy is a complex and flexible concept. Usually bid privacy is not applied to the winning bid (namely clearing price, which is public in the end of auction in all known auction schemes) and only restricted to the other bids (losing bids and the winners' bids in Vickrey auction or k^{th} bid auction). However, stronger requirement is possible to hide even the winning bid. On the other hand, weaker requirement on bid privacy is possible in some applications. Bid privacy is a key requirement and be classified and illustrated in detail later in this thesis.

It is required that all these requirements are achieved in a computationally and communicationally efficient manner. When this target is not easy to achieve, the best trade-off between the requirements and efficiency is desired.

Anonymity is a property required in many papers about sealed-bid auction like (Franklin & Reiter, 1996; Viswanathan, Boyd, & Dawson, 2000; Peng, Boyd, Dawson, & Viswanathan, 2002b, 2003b). Obviously it is an optional property. However, this property is not included in this book. Anonymity in sealed-bid auction requires that the identities of the bidders (or the losing bidders) must be kept confidential, so that those identities are not known to other people including the auctioneers. Those papers usually claim that it is not difficult to achieve anonymity. Their methods to implement anonymity is easy: every bidder submits his bid using a pseudonym through an anonymous channel. However, it is difficult to design either an appropriate pseudonym or an appropriate anonymous channel for sealed-bid privacy.

The pseudonyms must be issued by a trusted authority after it authenticates the bidders such that no bidder can get more than one pseudonym. A possible method to implement pseudonym is blind signature2. A third party authority authenticates each bidder and blindly signs a pseudonym chosen by the bidder. Thus, each bidder gets a unique pseudonym, which cannot be linked to him by anyone else. However, this pseudonym mechanism is not recoverable, so the winner can deny his winning bid. As non-repudiation is a compulsory property in sealed-bid auctions, blind-signature-based pseudonym is not suitable for sealed-bid auction. Another method is to employ group signature, a normal method to implement recoverable anonymity. Each bidder becomes a group member and gets a signing key. Then the bidders sign their bids using the signing key in the group and submit their bids using their chosen pseudonyms. All the bids are indistinguishable without the group manager's intervention. When necessary, the group manager can recover the identity behind the winning bid. However, under this pseudonym mechanism, a bidder can submit multiple bids using different pseudonyms, which violates fairness and high efficiency of the auction. The only feasible method to implement pseudonym is authenticated temporal key, which is proposed in (Peng et al., 2002b). A trusted third party authenticates each bidder can issue a temporal signed key certificate (including a pair of public and private keys) to each bidder. The signed certificate is used as a pseudonym. The bidders use their temporal private keys to sign their bids. When necessary, the trusted third party can identify the winner from the winning bid. Although this method can work, it requires too strong a trust: the third party does not reveal the relation between the pseudonyms and the bidder's identities.

It is even more difficult to find a useable anonymous communication channel for sealed-bid auction. Existing practical anonymous communication channels like the famous onion routing3 are not publicly verifiable. The routers can delete or tamper with the transmitted messages without being detected. Public verifiability is a compulsory property in sealed-bid auction and it must be publicly verified that each bid is taken into account without being changed. So the existing anonymous channels cannot be employed in sealed-bid auction. Even if a publicly verifiable anonymous channel is available, it cannot achieve anonymity in sealed-bid auction. Since the anonymous channel is publicly verifiable, the first router's routing of each bid must be publicly verified, which reveals the bidders' identities. So anonymity is inconsistent with public verifiability, a much more important property. As a result, anonymity must be sacrificed to achieve public verifiability.

Although anonymity is an impractical requirement in sealed-bid auction, it is possible to weaken this concept and maintain as much privacy as possible for the bidders. For example, it is possible to achieve a weaker requirement: relative anonymity, which implies unlinkability between identity and data when identities are public (the data may be public or private). If the data is private, relative anonymity is automatically achieved. If the data is not private, special mechanisms must be employed to hide the link between the identities and the public data. In sealed-bid auction, when bid privacy is achieved relative anonymity is automatically achieved as the data is private. If bid privacy is not achieved in a sealed-bid auction, method to achieve relative anonymity can be explored.

Background

Bid privacy is a very important and frequently required requirement in sealed-bid auction schemes. It has a great influence on other requirements, especially public verifiability and efficiency. Bid privacy is also the most difficult to achieve among all the properties. Without bid privacy, the bidders can submit bids in any format and as precise as they like, while the auctioneer can just publicly unseal all the bids, chooses the winning bid using any auction rule and directly link it to the winner. So when bid privacy is not required, all the desired properties can be easily and efficiently achieved. A lot of sealed-bid auction schemes employ various techniques to achieve bid privacy. In this chapter, bid privacy is used as a thread when we explore sealed-bid auction schemes.

According to different strength of bid privacy, sealed-bid auction can be classified into three categories: auction without bid privacy, auction with bid privacy and a third type between them: auction with relative bid privacy. Relative bid privacy is defined in (Peng, Boyd, Dawson, & Viswanathan, 2003a) as an alternative to strict bid privacy in certain auction applications. This classification is based on the motivations of bid privacy in different auction applications. There are many motivations to support bid privacy. The following are the most common two.

1. Bidders want their bidding behaviours to be untraceable. Especially they do not want other people know that he submits a certain bid in an auction, which is a violation of their personal privacy and may violate their benefit in a later auction.
2. Sellers should be prevented from knowing the bidding values or their distribution. Otherwise they may gain some advantage when selling an identical or similar item in the future.

Standard bid privacy is necessary if both motivations exist.

Definition 1: Standard bid privacy is achieved if after the auction is finished:

- A bidder knows only his own bidding value, the results (the clearing price and identity of the winner(s)) and information that can be deduced from them;
- Seller, auctioneers or other parties only know the results and information that can be deduced from them.

However, in some applications, only the first motivation exists. In this case, only relative bid privacy need be employed.

Definition 2: Relative bid privacy means at the end of the auction, although the bids are opened and published in plaintext, the only information revealed from the auction about the link between bidders and their bids is:

- Each winner has a bid no less than the winning price;
- Each loser has a bid less than the winning price.

Relative bid privacy actually refers to unlinkability between bids and bidders when the bids are public (where the identities of the bidders may be public or private). Usually, relative bid privacy is much easier and more efficient to achieve than standard bid privacy.

The first secure sealed-bid auction scheme was proposed by Franklin and Reiter (Franklin & Reiter, 1996). To achieve bid confidentiality, threshold secret sharing is employed to seal the bids. The auction scheme is described as follows.

1. In the preparation phase, multiple auctioneers are chosen and their public keys are published. Then the auction rule and bid format are published. Any auction rule can be applied and any bidding value within the messages spaces of the auctioneers' encryption algorithms is valid.
2. In the bid submission phase, every bidder employs Shamir's threshold secret (Shamir, 1979) to share his bid among the auctioneers. Each auctioneer's share is signed by the bidder, encrypted using the auctioneer's public key and sends to the auctioneer.
3. In the bid opening phase, the auctioneers cooperate to reconstruct all the bids and determine the winning bid.
4. In the winner determination phase, the signature on the winning bid is verified and the winner is identified.

As a basic sealed-bid auction scheme, this protocol is simple and straightforward. However, the basic structure of a sealed-bid auction protocol is clearly introduced in this scheme. The roles in the auction (bidders and auctioneers) and the auction phases are introduced. Threshold trust among multiple auctioneers, a classic method to achieve confidentiality, is described and analysed. If the number of malicious auctioneers is not over the threshold, no bid can be opened before the bid opening phase and bid confidentiality is achieved. If the number of cooperating auctioneers is over the threshold, all the bids can be reconstructed to determine the winning bid. Correctness, fairness and robustness are straightforwardly based on the threshold trust. Digital signature is used to achieve non-repudiation. Bid privacy is ignored, so that public verifiability, rule flexibility and price flexibility are achieved. Although it is claimed in this scheme that anonymity is feasible, we have illustrated in Section 2.3 that anonymity is impractical in sealed-bid auctions as public verifiability and robustness are required. Relative anonymity is impossible as unlinkability between the bids and bidders are not implemented or even mentioned. This basic auction is illustrated in Figure 2.

Although this auction scheme is basic and primitive, it provides a direction for later auction schemes. Cryptographic tools used in this scheme like digital signature on the bids, secret sharing of bids, threshold trust of bid confidentiality are inherited by many following sealed-bid auction scheme. This scheme illustrates that sealed-bid auction can be easily implemented without bid privacy. Unfortunately, the incorrect understanding of anonymity in sealed-bid auction is also inherited by many following auction schemes. Another contribution of this scheme is that an e-cash mechanism is designed to implement payment after the auction. However, payment is usually considered as a question in e-cash. With the development of e-cash and e-auction, researchers gradually understand that these two techniques should be studied separately. So currently, payment is not included in a typical auction scheme.

Figure 2. Auction without bid privacy

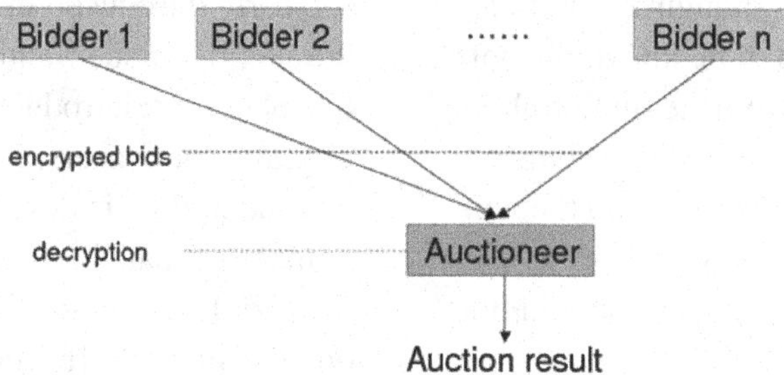

Peng et al. proposed the concept of relative bid privacy. As stated in Section 2.4, relative bid privacy conceals each individual bidder's evaluation although all the bids are revealed. As it is easier to achieve than standard bid privacy, it is more efficient in applications concealing not the bidding values but the bidder's personal privacy. With only relative bid privacy all the bids can be opened to determined the winning bid. In most of sealed-bid auction schemes with relative bid privacy (except Lipmaa, Asokan, & Niemi, 2002, as explained later in this section) simple and flexible bid rule and bid format can be used and bid opening is very simple. The key technique is how to hide the link between the bids and the bidders. As stated before, anonymity is impractical in robust and publicly verifiable auction. So identities of the bids are public. Therefore relative bid privacy and relative anonymity become identical: both the bids and the bidders' identities are public but the link between them must be kept secret. Namely, the bids must be submitted through a special untraceable but publicly verifiable communication channel.

This idea of unlinkability was first proposed in (Viswanathan et al., 2000) and (Mu & Varadharajan, 2000) in two independent papers, although relative bid privacy is not defined in these two papers. In these two schemes, the bidders submit their bids through an untraceable channel. The auctioneer publicly opens all the bids and the winning bid can be easily found. However, they did not mention how to implement the untraceable channel. As stated before, the existing anonymous communication channels cannot be employed since the auction scheme must be publicly verifiable and robust. So these two schemes are incomplete and fail to answer the most important question: how to implement the untraceable channel. Therefore, their improvement on the auction by Franklin and Reiter is not great enough and their main contribution is proposing the idea that unlinkability between the bids and bidders can be achieved if a publicly verifiable untraceable communication channel can be designed.

A practical method to implement a publicly verifiable untraceable communication channel is the special mix network used in e-voting schemes (Park, Itoh, & Kurosawa, 1993; Neff, 2001; Golle, Zhong, Boneh, Jakobsson, & Juels, 2002; Groth, 2003; Groth & Lu, 2007; Groth & Ishai, 2008; Peng, Boyd, Dawson, & Viswanathan, 2004; Peng, Boyd, & Dawson, 2005c; Peng & Bao, 2011). This kind of mix network usually consists of multiple shuffling nodes, each of whom in turn randomises (by re-encryption or decryption chain) some encrypted messages (input ciphertexts) and shuffles them to some output ciphertexts. Each node must publicly prove validity of his shuffling (the plaintexts of his output ciphertexts is a permutation of the plaintexts of his input ciphertexts). If at least one of the shuffling nodes conceals his shuffling, the unlinkability between the messages and their providers is kept secret. Lipmaa et al. (2002) proposed an auction scheme with two auctioneers (sellers). One of them shuffles the sealed bids while the other open the shuffled bids. Although relative bid privacy is achieved in Lipmaa's scheme, his scheme has three drawbacks.

1. The shuffling is not verifiable, so the auction is not verifiable.
2. Only one shuffling node is employed. So the shuffling node must be trusted. This trust is too strong.
3. Complex and inefficient bid opening operation is employed. The scheme is much less efficient than the schemes by Viswanathan and Mu and even less efficient than some sealed-bid auctions with bid privacy. At this high cost, the achievement is that if each of the auctioneers is trusted, the losing bids are only revealed to the auctioneers but not revealed to the fellow bidders. Otherwise, all the bids are revealed to anyone. The claim in their paper that their scheme only reveals some statistically negligible information about the bids is unreliable as no analysis is given to measure the amount of revealed information and show that it is statistically negligible. This property is only slightly stronger than relative bid privacy and much weaker than the standard bid privacy as an impractical trust is needed.

The most efficient and practical auction scheme in this model is (Peng et al., 2003a). It is in this paper that the concept of relative bid privacy is proposed. A special mix network composed of multiple shuffling nodes is designed in this auction schemes. The mix network is publicly verifiable and efficient. After the bids are shuffled, they are unsealed publicly and the winning bid is publicly determined. This scheme is much simpler and more efficient than Lipmaa's scheme. Relative bid privacy is completely achieved while public verifiability, reasonable trust and high efficiency are all obtained. The auction protocol in (Peng et al., 2003a) is as follows where there are n bidders B_i for $i = 1,2,\dots,n$ and m auctioneers A_j for $j = 1,2,\dots,m$, who act as the servers in the mix network.

1. **Preparation Phase:** A public key $y \in Z_q^*$ is published, while the corresponding private key $x = \log_g y$ is shared among the auctioneers by k-out-of-m verifiable secret sharing. Each A_j gets a share x_j while $y_j = g^{x_j}$ is published for $j = 1,2,\dots,m$.
2. **Bid Submission Phase:**
   a. **Submitting the Bid Commitments:** Each bidder B_i chooses a bid b_i from the biddable prices. B_i also chooses a random value $v_i \in Z_q^*$. ElGamal encryption in Group G, a cyclic subgroup of order q in Z_p^* is employed where p, q are large primes and $p = 2q + 1$. Each B_i calculates his commitment $c_i = H(b_i, v_i)$ and encrypts it as

$$e_i = (\alpha_i, \beta_i) = (g^{r_i} \bmod p, c_i y^{r_i} \bmod p)$$

   where $H()$ is a hash function and r_i is chosen randomly from Z_q^*. B_i signs e_i and submits it to the first server in the mix network. The signed e_i for $i = 1,2,\dots,n$ are published on the bulletin board and anyone can verify that they are validly signed by the bidders.

   b. **Shuffling the Commitments:** Inputs to auctioneer A_j are $e_{j-1,i}$ for $i = 1,2,\dots,n$ and his outputs are $e_{j,i}$ for $i = 1,2,\dots,n$ while inputs to the first auctioneer A_1 are $e_{0,i} = e_i$ for $i = 1,2,\dots,n$. Auctioneer A_j performs the following operations:

i. Obtains input $e_{j-1,i}$ for $i=1,2,\ldots,n$ published by A_{j-1} on the bulletin board;

ii. Performs re-encryption $e_{j,i}=(\alpha_{j,i},\beta_{j,i})=(g^{r_{j,i}}\alpha_{j-1,\pi_j(i)},\ y^{r_{j,i}}\beta_{j-1,\pi(i)})$ for $i=1,2,\ldots,n$ where π_j is a random permutation from $\{1,2,\ldots,n\}$ to $\{1,2,\ldots,n\}$ and $r_{j,i}$ for $i=1,2,\ldots,n$ are randomly chosen.

c. **Decrypting the Commitments:** A_m's outputs $e_{m,i}$ for $i=1,2,\ldots,n$ are decrypted by the auctioneers. Each auctioneer A_j publishes $d_{i,j}=\alpha_{m,i}^{x_j}$. Anyone can get the decrypted commitments $c_i'=\beta_{m,i}/\prod_{s\in S}d_{i,s}^{u_s} \bmod p$ for $i=1,2,\ldots,n$ where S is a set of over k authorities and $u_s=\prod_{A_l\in S,l\neq s}(s-l)/l$.

d. **Checking the Shuffled Commitments:** Every bidder checks that his commitment is among the published mixed commitments. If a bidder B_i fails to find his commitment, he can complain. Any dispute is solved as follows.

i. B_i publishes e_i and his signature on e_i.

ii. Each auctioneer (from the first one to the last one) has to prove his shuffling of e_i is correct by publishing his output for e_i and the random value is used in his re-encryption of e_i. If any auctioneer has performed an incorrect shuffling, he will be discovered and the next step is skipped. Otherwise, some e_j' will be revealed, which is A_m's output for e_i.

iii. Each auctioneer has to prove that he decrypted e_j' correctly using a proof of correct decryption (proof of equality of logarithms (Chaum & Pedersen, 1992) if ElGamal encryption is employed). Any incorrect decryption can be found.

iv. If any auctioneer fails to prove his innocence, he is removed (or replaced if necessary) and the mixing is performed again. If all the auctioneers prove their innocence, a commitment must have been found for e_i, so the protesting bidder is identified as a cheater and removed.

3. **Bid Opening Phase:**

a. **Providing the Committed Bidding Values:** Each bidder B_i calculates $e1_i=(\alpha1_i,\beta1_i)=(g^{r1_i},b_iy^{r1_i})$ and $e2_i=(\alpha2_i,\beta2_i)=(g^{r2_i},v_iy^{r2_i})$ where $r1_i$ and $r2_i$ are chosen randomly from Z_q. B_i signs $(e1_i,e2_i)$ and submits it to the first server in the mix network. The signed $(e1_i,e2_i)$ for $i=1,2,\ldots,n$ are published on the bulletin board and anyone can verify that they are validly signed by the bidders.

b. **Shuffling the Bids:** Auctioneer A_j with $j>1$ gets $(e1_{j-1,i},e2_{j-1,i})$ for $i=1,2,\ldots,n$ from A_{j-1} and shuffles them to $(e1_{j,i},e2_{j,i})$ for $i=1,2,\ldots,n$ while A_1 gets $(e1_{0,i},e2_{0,i})=(e1_i,e2_i)$ for $i=1,2,\ldots,n$ from the bidders. Re-encryption and permutation in the shuffling are the same as in the first round.

c. **Decrypting the Bids:** A_m's outputs $(e1_{m,i}, e2_{m,i})$ for $i = 1, 2, \ldots, n$ are decrypted by the auctioneers. Like in the first round, if more than k auctioneers are honest, b_i and r_i for $i = 1, 2, \ldots, n$ can be recovered correctly.

d. **Verifying Validity of the Bids:** Suppose (b'_i, v'_i) for $i = 1, 2, \ldots, n$ are the results of bid decryption. If $H(b'_i, v'_i)$ is not among the published commitments in the first round, $(\hat{b}_i, \hat{v}_i)$ is traced in a reverse direction through the mix network as follows to solve the problem.

   i. Each auctioneer has to prove that his partial decryption of (b'_i, v'_i) is correct using a proof of correct decryption (proof of equality of logarithms (Chaum & Pedersen, 1992) if ElGamal encryption is employed). If an incorrect decryption is found, the auctioneer performing it is identified as a cheater and the next step is skipped. Otherwise, $(e1'_j, e2'_j)$, the ciphertext corresponding to (b'_i, v'_i), is revealed.

   ii. Each auctioneer (from the last one to the first one) has to prove his shuffling leading to $(e1'_j, e2'_j)$ is correct by publishing his input for $(e1'_j, e2'_j)$ and the random value he used in his re-encryption of the input. If any auctioneer has performed an incorrect shuffling, he will be discovered.

   iii. If any auctioneer fails to prove his innocence, he is removed (or replaced if necessary) and the mixing is performed again. If all the auctioneers prove their innocence, the output in dispute has been traced back to an input of the mix network. The bidder submitting the input in dispute is identified as a cheater and removed.

4. **Winning Price and Winner Determination Phase:** The auction rule is applied to the opened bids and the winning price and the winner's price can be found easily. The winner B_I has to prove his identity by revealing $r1_I$ and illustrating the winner's price is encrypted in $e1_I$. Anyone can verify that the winner's price is encrypted in $e1_I$ and the $(e1_I, e2_I)$ on the bulletin board is signed by B_I. If the winner refuses to cooperate, the auctioneers can trace the winner's bid through the mix network (revealing their shuffling in regard to the winner's bid) to identify the winner.

MAIN FOCUS OF THE CHAPTER

Issues, Controversies, Problems

Standard bid privacy implies that all the losing bids must be kept secret. This is actually an application of secure (multiparty) computation. In a secure computation, an function is computed while the inputs are sealed (e.g. encrypted or committed). The computing entity (usually multiple parties) computes on the sealed inputs without knowledge of the inputs in plaintext. The result of the function is obtained in plaintext while no information about the inputs is revealed except what can be deduced from the result. Sealed-bid auction with bid privacy is actually a special case of secure multiparty computation, where the sealed bids are the sealed inputs and multiple auctioneers act as the computing parties.

Suppose the bids are $b_1, b_2, \ldots, b_n$. A typical method to seal the bids is to share them among the auctioneers using a threshold VSS (verifiable secret sharing) scheme or encrypt them using an encryption algorithm with a private key threshold shared among the auctioneers. Bid b_i is sealed into c_i, which is the commitment of b_i in the VSS or ciphertext of b_i in the encryption algorithm with threshold distributed decryption. To guarantee bid confidentiality and bid privacy, the commitment scheme must be at least computationally hiding and the encryption algorithm must be semantically secure. If the number of colluding auctioneers is not over the threshold, no bid can be opened and no information about the bids is revealed.

In a ρth bid auction ($\rho = 1$ in the first bid auction and $\rho = 2$ in the Vickrey auction), given $c_1, c_2, \ldots, c_n$, the auctioneers must perform a multiparty computation bid opening function f on them, which outputs a set of indexes indicating the winning bids

$$W = f(c_1, c_2, \ldots, c_n) = \{i \mid b_i \geq Th(B, \rho)\}$$

where $B = \{b_1, b_2, \ldots, b_n\}$ and $Th(S, k)$ return the kth largest integer in set S.

Secure multiparty computation is denoted as SMC later in this chapter. There are two methods to implement secure multiparty computation: evaluation circuit and homomorphic computation. The first method (Naor, Pinkas, & Sumner, 1999; Juels & Szydlo, 2002; Cramer, Damgard, & Nielsen, 2001; Jakobsson & Juels, 2000; Cachin &Camenisch, 2000; Peng, Bao, & Dawson, 2007) is based on encrypted truth tables. Namely, a truth table of each logic gate in a circuit is encrypted and the rows in every table are shuffled, so that each gate can be evaluated with its inputs and output in ciphertext. The second method (Sander, Young, & Yung, 1999; Beaver, 2000; Fischlin, 2001; Peng, Boyd, Dawson, & Lee, 2004; Peng, 2007) is based on logic homomorphism of encryption schemes and called homomorphic computation. As special encryption algorithms are designed to be homomorphic in regard of the logical relation in the gates in the circuit, the evaluation can be realized by computing the ciphertexts of the inputs to the function without the help of any truth table. An important issue in secure multiparty computation is the format of the inputs (bids). Usually, the inputs are encrypted bit by bit. Sometimes, secure computation can be improved with optimised input format.

Auction schemes in this category do not consider special characters of sealed-bid auction protocols and simply employ existing general SMC Techniques to implement the bid opening function. Several auction schemes have been proposed in this category based on different evaluation circuits (Naor et al., 1999; Juels & Szydlo, 2002; Jakobsson & Juels, 2000; Cramer et al., 2001; Cachin, 1999). All of them seal the bid by bit and employ an evaluation circuit composed of a large number of logic gates to evaluate the sealed bids. Inputs and outputs in the gates are also sealed and only the final output bits are unsealed, so that no intermediate information other than the auction result is revealed. Secure computation in each gate is implemented through a truth table mapping the sealed inputs of the gate to the sealed output of the gate. The rows in the truth table are randomly shuffled so that no information about the bids is revealed from computation in the gate. The truth tables are called randomised sealed truth table. Auction by general secure evaluation is illustrated in Figure 3.

In Naor et al. (1999), an evaluation circuit is generated by an authority AI and sent to another authority A, who uses it to process the ciphertext inputs. A hash function is employed in the truth tables to link their inputs to their outputs. Oblivious transfer4 is employed to submit the inputs to the function confidentially. Correctness

Figure 3. Auction by general secure evaluation

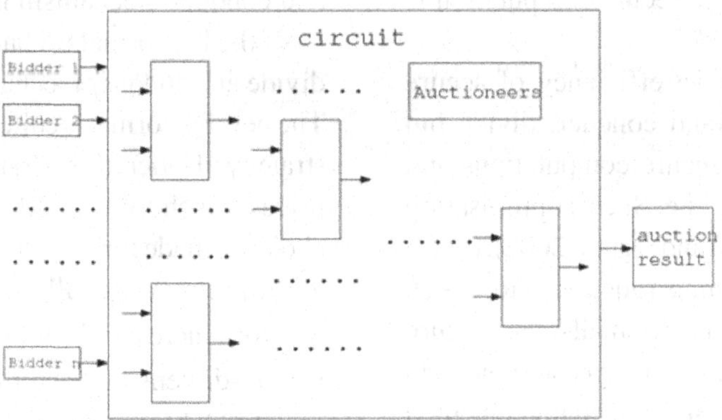

of the circuit is guaranteed by a cut-and-choose mechanism. Correctness of the computation is guaranteed by one-wayness of the hash function and an assumption that AI and A do not conspire. As the oblivious transfer primitive employed in (Naor et al., 1999) is not verifiable, AI can modify the inputs to the circuit without being detected. This problem was fixed by Juels and Szydlo (Juels & Szydlo, 2002). They design a primitive called verifiable 1-out-of-2 oblivious transfer, which is slightly less efficient than the 1-out-of-2 oblivious transfer in (Naor et al., 1999), but prevents AI from cheating alone. Other drawbacks of (Naor et al., 1999) are (1) the cut-and-choose mechanism to guarantee circuit correctness is highly inefficient in communication as a few circuits must be transported from AI to A; (2) correctness of the auction relies on trust that the two authorities do not collude and is not publicly verifiable5; (3) the oblivious transfer used for bid submission is not efficient (both in computation and communication).

In Cramer et al, (2001), Jakobsson and Juels (2000), and Cachin and Camenisch (2000), correctness of circuit and evaluation can be publicly verified with help of public-key cryptology. So the costly cut-and-choose mechanism is removed and correctness is not based on any trust. However, public-key cryptology is much less efficient in computation than the hash function computation in Naor et al. (1999) and Juels and Szydlo (2002). As the number of gates in a circuit is large and construction, evaluation and the corresponding, validity verification in each gate requires hundreds of exponentiations, an extremely high computational cost.

Bid opening through general SMC is a very simple idea. It is so straightforward that it only directly employs an existing general secure computation technique without any adaptation or any other technique. However, various problems exist in all the auction schemes in this category. The most serious problem is low efficiency, which is due to two reasons, large number of gates in the circuits and inefficient to check validity of the circuit. So this idea is not a satisfactory solution to bid privacy in sealed-bid auction.

Inefficiency of sealed-bid auction through general SMC is not surprising as secure computation through evaluation circuit is usually inefficient. For example, it is estimated in (Kurosawa & Ogata, 2002) that at least $7L$ gates are needed in an evaluation circuit to solve a simple question, comparing 2 L -bit integers. To evaluate an auction, a complex circuit containing a large number of gates are needed. For the sake of public verifiability, a large number of exponentiations are needed for each gate or costly cut-and-choose mechanism must be employed. So implement bid opening using one single secure computation is very inefficient.

A solution to improve efficiency of secure computation is divide and conquer: divide bid opening into multiple secure computations and implement them one by one. Such a optimisation is proposed in Kurosawa and Ogata (2002): dividing the whole bid opening function into $n-1$ comparisons of bid pair. A small-scale secure computation to compare two encrypted integers is designed and bid opening can be implemented by $n-1$ such comparisons. This optimisation is simple: the bid format is not changed (still bit by bit sealing of each bid) and no special auction-oriented secure computation technique is employed. Comparing two encrypted integers is an intensively studied question in secure computation, called the millionaire problem. In a millionaire problem, two millionaires compare who is richer without revealing their wealth, which is actually a comparison of two ciphertexts. Many secure computation techniques (Cachin & Camenisch, 2000; Peng, Boyd, Dawson, & Lee, 2004, 2005; Peng, Boyd, Dawson, & Okamoto, 2006; Peng et al., 2007) can be employed to solve this problem. Any of them can be directly employed to compare the sealed bids in pair and find the winning bid.

Although the auction scheme in (Kurosawa & Ogata, 2002) is more efficient than the sealed-bid auctions based on a single secure computation, its efficiency is still too low for some applications. So more efficient divide and conquer mechanism must be employed to design more efficient sealed-bid auction scheme with bid privacy. In the rest of this section, secure computation techniques with more complex divide and conquer strategy specially designed for auction and special bid formats are employed to design more efficient sealed-bid auction schemes with bid privacy. The auction scheme in (Kurosawa & Ogata, 2002) is a medium step towards the more advanced auction schemes employing more complex divide and conquer mechanism in secure computation.

If the bid format is changed, a more advanced divide and conquer mechanism can be employed. The new bid format is called one-choice-per-price strategy. Under this strategy, a definite set of prices are chosen as biddable prices. In a bid, a choice is made for each biddable price, indicating willingness or unwillingness to pay the price. Suppose there are L biddable prices, each bid b_i is a L-dimension vector containing an item for each biddable price: $(b_{i,1}, b_{i,2}, \dots, b_{i,L})$. If a bidder is willing to pay a price, he puts an value indicating ``YES" on the corresponding place in his bid vector. If a bidder is unwilling to pay a price, he puts an value indicating ``NO" on the corresponding place in his bid vector. Bid b_i is sealed into $(c_{i,1}, c_{i,2}, \dots, c_{i,L})$ and submitted. This strategy has been employed in a few auction schemes, but is only defined recently in (Peng, Boyd, & Dawson, 2005a, 2005b).

In the bid opening phase a divide and conquer mechanism called downward search is performed to search for the winning bid. Downward search divides the whole task of bid opening in a first-bid auction into multiple tasks, each for a biddable price. Every task tests whether there is a "YES" choice at the corresponding price. The search starts at the highest biddable price. A small-scale secure computation, search for "YES" choice, is performed to test whether there is any "YES" choice at the highest price. The test is very simple: open all the bid choices at the highest price and any "YES" choice can be definitely found if there is any. If there is a "YES" choice, the winning price is the highest price. If there is no "YES" choice, the search go on and the same small-scale secure computation (test of "YES" choice) is perform on the next price by opening all the bid choices at that price to test whether there is any "YES"' choice. The search goes on downwards until the winning price is met. Although every bidder's bid choices over the winning price are revealed in this bid opening through the downward search, this revealed information can be deduced from the auction result. So bid privacy is not compromised. Sealed-bid auction employing downward search is illustrated in Figure 4.

Downward search can be implemented interactively or non-interactively.

1. **Interactive Downward Search:** The bidders remain on-line during the bid opening phase to help the auctioneers open their bid choices price by price interactively. One round of communication between the bidders and the auctioneers is needed for each biddable price no lower than the winning bid. Sealed-bid auction schemes employing interactive downward search includes Sakurai and Miyazaki (1999) and Suzuki, Kobayashi, and Morita (2000).
2. **Non-Interactive Downward Search:** The bidders do not take part in bid opening online. The auctioneers cooperate the opening the bid choices price by price until the winning price is met. Sealed-bid auction schemes employing non-interactive downward search includes Watanabe and Imai (2000), Sako (2000), and Peng, Boyd, Dawson, and Viswanathan (2002a).

A typical sealed-bid auction scheme employing interactive downward search is (Suzuki et al., 2000), which is described as follows.

1. **Bid Sealing:** Bidder B_i chooses his bid vector $(b_{i,1}, b_{i,2}, \ldots, b_{i,L})$ and then employs a one-way and collision-resistant hash function $h()$ to seal his bid. He calculates a hash chain $c_{i,j} = h(c_{i,j-1} \| b_{i,L+1-j})$ for $1 < j \leq n$ and $c_{i,1} = h(r_i, b_{i,L})$ where r_i is a random integer. He them publishes $c_{i,L}$, end of the hash chain, as his bid commitment.
2. **Bid Opening:** At the highest price p_1, each bidder B_i publishes $b_{i,1}$ and $c_{i,L-1}$. Any one can verify that $c_{i,L} = h(c_{i,L-1} \| b_{i,1})$. If there is a "YES" choice at p_1, it is declared as the winning price. Otherwise B_i publishes $b_{i,2}$ and $c_{i,L-2}$ and the search goes downwards to p_2. The hash chain is opened price by price until a "YES" choice is found.

Two obvious advantages of the auction scheme in (Suzuki et al., 2000) are high efficiency in computation and strong bid privacy. As hash function is much more efficient than public key cipher, both bid sealing and bid opening are much

Figure 4. Auction with downward search

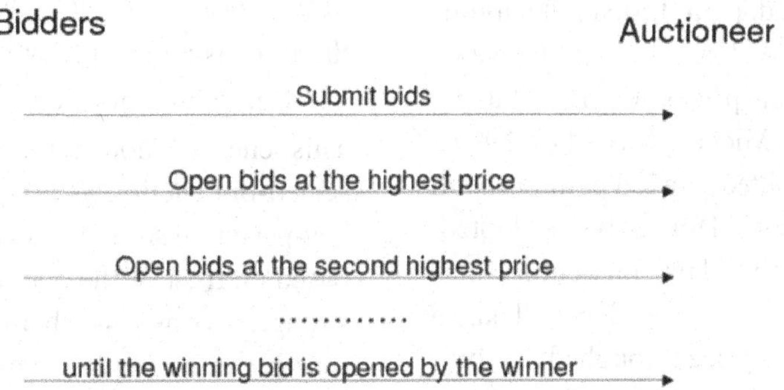

more efficient than in the auction schemes employing general SMC and the auction scheme in (Kurosawa & Ogata, 2002). Unlike auction schemes employing general SMC and the auction scheme in (Kurosawa & Ogata, 2002), bid privacy is no based on any kind of trust on the auctioneers in the auction scheme in (Suzuki et al., 2000). Instead, bid privacy is only dependent on one-wayness of the employed hash function. The drawback of the auction scheme in (Suzuki et al., 2000) is also obvious: the bidders must keep on-line during the auction opening phase and communicates with the auctioneers for $O(L)$ rounds. This is a high cost in communication. Moreover, in some applications it is impractical to keep the bidders on-line.

The auction scheme in (Suzuki et al., 2000) shows that at the cost of inefficient on-line communication bid privacy can be achieved efficiently in computation. Moreover, bid privacy can be very strong when downward search is applied. Bid privacy in (Suzuki et al., 2000) is the strongest in all the known sealed-bid auction schemes. Downward search can even obtain stronger bid privacy. For example, if an information theoretically hiding commitment function is employed to seal the bid choices and on-line communication from the bidders is used to open the commitment, unconditional bid privacy can be achieved, which is even stronger than bid privacy in (Suzuki et al., 2000).

Another sealed-bid auction scheme employing interactive downward search is (Sakurai & Miyazaki, 1999). In (Sakurai & Miyazaki, 1999), a shorter bid format is adopted. Instead of submitting a L-dimension vector, a bidder chooses a bid form the L biddable prices and signs it using undeniable signature (Michels & Stadler, 1997). The signature is submitted as a bid commitment. Although L-dimension bid format is not adopted, this auction is still classified into one-choice-per-price sealed-bid auction as the bidders still has to open their bids price by price through all the biddable prices in the downward direction until the winning price is met. The bid opening phase starts at the highest biddable price p_1, while each bidder has to interactively prove whether his bid is p_1. If there is no bid at p_1, bid opening moves to p_2 and each bidder has to interactively prove whether his bid is p_2. The interactive signature verification goes on until the highest bid is met. The auction scheme in (Sakurai & Miyazaki, 1999) can be regarded as a variant of sealed-bid auction with one-choice-per-price bid and interactive downward search. The bid format is simplified but price-by-price interactive bid opening by the on-line bidders is still employed. Although bids in (Sakurai & Miyazaki, 1999) are shorter than those in (Suzuki et al., 2000), $O(L)$ rounds of signature proof and verification are needed in (Sakurai & Miyazaki, 1999). As signature proof and verification is public key cryptographic operations with costly computation and long integers, (Sakurai & Miyazaki, 1999) is less efficient than (Suzuki et al., 2000).

The first auction scheme employing non-interactive downward search is (Sako, 2000). In this scheme, every biddable price is associated to a unique encryption-decryption key pair. A bidder uses the public encryption key corresponding to his bid to encrypt a special token corresponding to his identity. He submits the ciphertext as his sealed bid. The index of the secret decryption key that can decrypt the ciphertext into a valid token reveals the bid. In the bid opening phase, the auctioneers sharing the private keys firstly decrypt all the bids using the private key corresponding to p_1. If no valid bid is found, they decrypt all the bids using the private key corresponding to p_2. Decryption goes on until a valid bid is met. This scheme is not a typical one-choice-per-price sealed-bid auction as it actually employs a one-key-per-price strategy. As a result, bid privacy is based on trust of the auctioneers and is not very strong. Anyway, this scheme shows that downward search can be implemented off-line without interactive communication with the bidders.

A typical sealed-bid auction scheme employing non-interactive downward search is (Watanabe & Imai, 2000), which employs a technique called key chain. The principle of bid sealing and bid opening through a key chain is as follows.

1. One-key-per-price strategy is employed and each bid is a L-dimension vector.
2. At each price all the bid choices are encrypted with a public key corresponding to the price.
3. The decrypting keys at the biddable prices are shared among the bidders and an auctioneer. Only when all the bidders and the auctioneer put their shares together at a price, can the bids at that price be opened.
4. If a bidder is not willing to pay a price, at that price his bidding choice contains his share of the decryption key needed to open the bids at the next lower price. So if none of the bidders are willing to pay a price, the decryption key to open the bids at the next lower price can be constructed from their opened bids at the price.
5. If a bidder is willing to pay a price, his share of the decryption key needed to open the bids at the next lower price is not contained in the bid for the current price. In this case the key chain is broken and the decryption key to open the bids at the next lower price cannot be constructed, thus the confidentiality of the losing bids is protected.
6. In the bid submission phase, the bidders submit their bids as described above to the auctioneer together with their private key shares at the highest price p_1.
7. In the bid opening phase, the auctioneer pieces the bidders' private key shares at p_1 together to open all the bids at p_1. If there is a ``YES" choice at p_1, the winning bid is met and other private keys cannot be reconstructed. Otherwise, he can piece together the private key shares recovered from the opened bids at p_1 to decrypt all the bids at p_2. The downward search can go on without any help from the bidders until the winning bid is met.

Their auction protocol in (Watanabe & Imai, 2000) is as follows.

1. Registration Phase
   a. Bidder B_i chooses his secret share $x_{i,j}$ for price p_j. The corresponding public key share is $y_{i,j} = g^{x_{i,j}}$. Additionally $x_{i,j}$ is encrypted as $\beta_{i,j} = VE_T(x_{i,j})$ by a third party T's public key. Watanabe and Imai adopted Naccache-Stern encryption algorithm (Naccache & Stern, 1998). $\beta_{i,j}$ is recoverable by T and can be verified as a correct encryption of the secret committed in $y_{i,j}$ by zero knowledge proof of equality of logarithms (Chaum & Pedersen, 1992). B_i signs, and sends $y_{i,j}$ and $\beta_{i,j}$ for $j = 1,2,\dots,w$ to auctioneer A.
   b. A verifies B_i's signature on $y_{i,j}$ and $\beta_{i,j}$ for $j = 1,2,\dots,w$ and the correctness of encryption. If the verification is successful, A sends a certificate $cert_i = (z_{i,1}, z_{i,2}, \dots, z_{i,j})$ to B_i where $z_{i,j} = Sig_A(B_i, y_{i,j})$. Then A chooses his own secret shares $x_{A,j}$ and generates the public keys in the chain $Y_j = g^{x_{A,j}} \prod_{i=1}^{n} y_{i,j}$ for $j = 1,2,\dots,w$. Finally A publishes Y_j for $j = 1,2,\dots,w$ and the registration information of the bidders. Key generation is illustrated in Table 1 for the case of 3 bidders and 6 biddable prices, so that $n = 3$ and $w = 6$.
2. Bid Submission Phase

a. B_i publishes his bid $V_{i,j} = E_{Y_j}(I_{i,j}, y_{i,j}, z_{i,j})$ for $j = 1,2,\ldots,w$. If he is not willing to pay p_j, $I_{i,j} = (No,\ x_{i,j+1})$. If he is willing to pay p_j, $I_{i,j} = (Yes,\ proof(x_{i,j+1}))$ where $proof(x_{i,j+1})$ is a transcript for zero knowledge proof of knowledge of $x_{i,j+1}$. $I_{i,j}$ can be checked against $y_{i,j}$ and $z_{i,j}$ to show that B_i provides a valid $x_{i,j+1}$ (in a ``Yes" bid) or knows its value (in a ``No" bid). Bid format is illustrated in Table 2 (supposing there are 3 bidders and 6 biddable prices). In the table, for simplicity, only $x_{i,j}$, the basic element of bid $V_{i,j}$, is presented.

3. Bid Opening Phase
   a. B_i publishes $x_{i,1}$, $y_{i,1}$ and $z_{i,1}$.
   b. A calculates and publishes $X_1 = x_{A1} + \sum_{i=1}^{n} x_{i,1}$, the decryption key for the bids at p_1.
   c. If no "Yes" bid is found at this price, decryption key for p_2 can be constructed and opening continues. Similarly the opening can go on along the key chain until a "yes" bid is found as winning bid and the key chain is broken.

Although it is claimed in (Watanabe & Imai, 2000) that the losing bids are kept secret and stronger privacy is achieved than in (Sako, 2000), it is not true. Although the private key chain cannot extend beyond the winning price by the auctioneer, the bidders can help the auctioneer to extend the private key chain further as each bidder knows his private key shares at all the biddable prices. So the auctioneer can collude with a small number of bidders to open bid choices at prices lower than the winning price. For example, when p_j is the winning price the auctioneer can collude with the winner (who provides his private key

Table 1. Key generation in the scheme by Watanabe and Imai

	A	B_1	B_2	B_3	encryption key
p_1	$g^{x_{A1}}$	$y_{1,1} = g^{x_{1,1}}$	$y_{2,1} = g^{x_{2,1}}$	$y_{3,1} = g^{x_{3,1}}$	$Y_1 = g^{x_{A1}} \times y_{1,1} \times y_{2,1} \times y_{3,1}$
p_2	$g^{x_{A2}}$	$y_{1,2} = g^{x_{1,2}}$	$y_{2,2} = g^{x_{2,2}}$	$y_{3,2} = g^{x_{3,2}}$	$Y_2 = g^{x_{A2}} \times y_{1,2} \times y_{2,2} \times y_{3,2}$
p_3	$g^{x_{A3}}$	$y_{1,3} = g^{x_{1,3}}$	$y_{2,3} = g^{x_{2,3}}$	$y_{3,3} = g^{x_{3,3}}$	$Y_3 = g^{x_{A3}} \times y_{1,3} \times y_{2,3} \times y_{3,3}$
p_4	$g^{x_{A4}}$	$y_{1,4} = g^{x_{1,4}}$	$y_{2,4} = g^{x_{2,4}}$	$y_{3,4} = g^{x_{3,4}}$	$Y_4 = g^{x_{A4}} \times y_{1,4} \times y_{2,4} \times y_{3,4}$
p_5	$g^{x_{A5}}$	$y_{1,5} = g^{x_{1,5}}$	$y_{2,5} = g^{x_{2,5}}$	$y_{3,5} = g^{x_{3,5}}$	$Y_5 = g^{x_{A5}} \times y_{1,5} \times y_{2,5} \times y_{3,5}$
p_6	$g^{x_{A6}}$	$y_{1,6} = g^{x_{1,6}}$	$y_{2,6} = g^{x_{2,6}}$	$y_{3,6} = g^{x_{3,6}}$	$Y_6 = g^{x_{A6}} \times y_{1,6} \times y_{2,6} \times y_{3,6}$

Table 2. Bids in the scheme by Watanabe and Imai

	B_1	B_2	B_3	decryption key
p_1	$E_{y_1}(x_{1,2})$	$E_{y_1}(x_{2,2})$	$E_{y_1}(x_{3,2})$	$X_1 = x_{A1} + x_{1,1} + x_{2,1} + x_{3,1}$
p_2	$\mathbf{E}_{\mathbf{y_2}}$ **(proof($\mathbf{x_{1,3}}$))**	$E_{y_2}(x_{2,3})$	$E_{y_2}(x_{3,3})$	$X_2 = x_{A2} + x_{1,2} + x_{2,2} + x_{3,2}$
p_3	$E_{y_3}(x_{1,4})$	$\mathbf{E}_{\mathbf{y_3}}$ **(proof($\mathbf{x_{2,4}}$))**	$E_{y_3}(x_{3,4})$	$\mathbf{B_1}$ and $\mathbf{A}$ can collude to recover $\mathbf{X_3}$
p_4	$E_{y_4}(x_{1,5})$	$E_{y_4}(x_{2,5})$	$E_{y_4}(x_{3,5})$	$\mathbf{B_1}$, $\mathbf{B_2}$ and $\mathbf{A}$ can collude to recover $\mathbf{X_4}$
p_5	$E_{y_5}(x_{1,6})$	$E_{y_5}(x_{2,6})$	$\mathbf{E}_{\mathbf{y_5}}$ **(proof($\mathbf{x_{3,6}}$))**	$\mathbf{B_1}$, $\mathbf{B_2}$ and $\mathbf{A}$ can collude to recover $\mathbf{X_5}$
p_6	$E_{y_6}(x_{1,1})$	$E_{y_6}(x_{2,1})$	$E_{y_6}(x_{3,1})$	$\mathbf{B_1}$, $\mathbf{B_2}$, $\mathbf{B_3}$ and $\mathbf{A}$ can collude to recover $\mathbf{X_6}$

share at p_{j+1}) to decrypt all the bid choices at p_{j+1} and the bid choice at any price no lower than the second highest bid. With collusion from more bidders, more bid choices lower than the winning bid can be opened. This attack reveals the losing bids (some are revealed completely and some are revealed partially depending on the number of colluding bidders). So although (Watanabe & Imai, 2000) is less efficient than (Sako, 2000), it does not achieve stronger bid privacy.

The auction scheme in (Watanabe & Imai, 2000) is optimised in (Peng et al.,2002a), which guarantees that no losing bid is revealed if DL problem is hard to solve. In (Peng et al.,2002a), the key chain is modified such that no bidder knows any private key share lower than his evaluation. Therefore, it is computationally guaranteed that the key chain cannot extend beyond the winning price. The auction scheme in (Peng et al.,2002a) is described as follows.

1. **Initial Phase:** Each bidder B_i chooses a secret x_i and publishes the commitments

$$Com1_i = (B_i,\ y_i,\ Sig_{B_i}(B_i, y_i))$$

   where $y_i = g^{x_i}$ for $i = 1,2,\ldots,n$ on a bulletin board. An auctioneer chooses a secret x_A and publishes $y_A = g^{x_A}$.
2. **Pre-Bidding Phase:** Every bidder publishes a public key for every biddable price. If a

bidder B_i is not willing to pay p_j, his public key for p_{j+1} is $y_{i,j+1} = g^{x_{i,j+1}}$ where the corresponding secret key $x_{i,j+1}$ is kept secret. If bidder B_i's 's bidding price is p_j, his public key for p_{j+1} is $y_{i,j+1} = g^{r_i}\prod_{k=1,k\neq i}^{n} y_k$ where r_i is kept secret and he chooses public keys $y_{i,j+2}$, $y_{i,j+3}$, $y_{i,w}$ randomly for p_{j+2}, p_{j+3}, p_w. B_i publishes

$$Com2_i = (B_i,\ y_{i,1}, y_{i,2}, \ldots, y_{i,w},\ Sig_{B_i}(B_i,\ y_{i,1}, y_{i,2}, \ldots, y_{i,w}))$$

on the bulletin board. Key generation is illustrated in Table 3 (supposing there are 3 bidders and 6 biddable prices, so that $n = 3$, $w = 6$). The public key for price p_j is $Y_1 = y_A\prod_{k=1}^{n} y_{k,1}$ and $Y_j = \prod_{k=1}^{n} y_{k,j}$ for $j = 2, 3, \ldots, w$, which can be calculated by anybody using the public values available on the bulletin board.

3. **Bid Submission Phase:** Every bidder submits a bid for each biddable price. If a bidder B_i is not willing to pay p_j, his bid at p_j is $V_{i,j} = E_{Y_j}(x_{i,j+1})$. If B_i is willing to pay p_j, $V_{i,j} = E_{Y_j}(r_i)$. At price p_j lower than his evaluation, $V_{i,j}$ is randomly chosen. B_i publishes

$$V_i = (B_i,\ V_{i,1}, V_{i,2}, \ldots, V_{i,w},\ Sig_{B_i}(B_i,\ V_{i,1}, V_{i,2}, \ldots, V_{i,w}))$$

on the bulletin board. Bid format is illustrated in Table 4 (supposing there are 3 bidders and 6 biddable prices).

4. **Opening Phase Phase:** The bidders publish $Com3_i = (x_{i,1},\ Sig_{B_i}(x_{i,1}))$ for $i = 1, 2, \ldots, n$. After all the bidders publish their shares, the auctioneer publishes x_A. Anybody can verify the validity of the shares against $y_{i,1}$ for $i = 1, 2, \ldots, n$ and y_A. Then the decryption key for the first price $X_1 = \sum_{k=1}^{n} x_{k,1}$ can be constructed to decrypt all the bids at p_1. The meaning of B_i's decrypted bid $v_{i,1}$ can be determined by testing whether $y_{i,2} = g^{v_{i,1}}$ ($v_{i,1}$ is negative bid) or $y_{i,2} = g^{v_{i,1}}\prod_{k=1,k\neq i}^{n} y_k$ ($v_{i,1}$ is positive bid). If there is no bid showing willingness to pay at p_1, all the shares $x_{i,2} = v_{i,1}$ for $i = 1, 2, \ldots, n$ are obtained and $X_2 = \sum_{k=1}^{n} x_{k,2}$ can be recovered. Then all the bids at p_2 are opened. The opening continues until $y_{i,j+1} \neq g^{v_{i,j}}$ is met and the key chain breaks at p_{j+1}.

5. **Winner Identification Phase:** If $y_{i,j+1} = g^{v_{i,j}}\prod_{k=1}^{n} y_k$, p_j and B_i are declared as winning price and winner. Otherwise B_i is identified as a cheater.

When B_i chooses is willing to pay p_j, his choice at p_j, $y_{i,j+1} = g^{v_{i,j}}\prod_{k=1,k\neq i}^{n} y_k$, indicates that he does not know $\log_g y_{i,j+1}$ if the DL problem is hard. Namely, each bidder publicly proves that he does not know any private key shares lower than his evaluation and the key chain ends at the winning price if the DL problem is hard. Another small modification in (Peng et al., 2002a) is that the auctioneer does not participate key sharing, so that registration and key generation is simpler. Although strong bid privacy is achieved in (Peng et al., 2002a), the sealed-bid auction scheme in (Peng et al.,2002a) requires $O(L)$ exponentiations and is inefficient in computation.

Table 3. Key generation in the auction by Peng et al. (2002)

	B_1	B_2	B_3	encryption key
	p_2	p_3	p_5	
p_1	$y_{1,1} = g^{x_{1,1}}$	$y_{2,1} = g^{x_{2,1}}$	$y_{3,1} = g^{x_{3,1}}$	$Y_1 = y_{1,1} \times y_{2,1} \times y_{3,1}$
p_2	$y_{1,2} = g^{x_{1,2}}$	$y_{2,2} = g^{x_{2,2}}$	$y_{3,2} = g^{x_{3,2}}$	$Y_2 = y_{1,2} \times y_{2,2} \times y_{3,2}$
p_3	$\mathbf{y_{1,3} = g^{r_1} y_2 y_3}$	$y_{2,3} = g^{x_{2,3}}$	$y_{3,3} = g^{x_{3,3}}$	$Y_3 = y_{1,3} \times y_{2,3} \times y_{3,3}$
p_4	any $y_{1,4}$ in G	$\mathbf{y_{2,4} = g^{r_2} y_1 y_3}$	$y_{3,4} = g^{x_{3,4}}$	$Y_4 = y_{1,4} \times y_{2,4} \times y_{3,4}$
p_5	any $y_{1,5}$ in G	any $y_{2,5}$ in G	$y_{3,5} = g^{x_{3,5}}$	$Y_5 = y_{1,5} \times y_{2,5} \times y_{3,5}$
p_6	any $y_{1,6}$ in G	any $y_{2,6}$ in G	$\mathbf{y_{3,6} = g^{r_3} y_1 y_2}$	$Y_6 = y_{1,6} \times y_{2,6} \times y_{3,6}$

Although downward search can achieve strong bid privacy, sealed-bid auctions based on it have a few drawbacks. Firstly, no scheme is efficient both in computation and in communication. Secondly, the only supported auction rule is first bid auction. The divide and conquer mechanism can be further optimised to solve these two problems. In the optimisation one-choice-per-price bid format is adopted, while downward search is replaced by binary search through the biddable prices.

As binary search can find the winning price by searching for "YES" choice at $\log_2 L$ biddable prices, secure computation of bid opening is reduced to $\log_2 L$ tests of "YES" choice. Although the number of tests is dramatically reduced, each test becomes more complex. As the binary search goes through some prices lower than the winning price, revealing any bid choice in the test may violate bid privacy. So, in each test of "YES" choice, the bid choice cannot be simply opened like in the downward-search auction schemes. Instead a secure computation without revealing any bid choice must be employed to test existence of "YES" choice at each price on the binary searching route.

Normally, the secure computation to test existence of "YES" choice is implemented through homomorphic computation. As stated before, homomorphic computation is the other method of secure computation other than evaluation through circuit. The bid choices are sealed with special homomorphic encryption or commitment (usually secret sharing) functions, so that test of "YES" choice can be implemented by computation on the sealed bid choices without unsealing them. A simple description of this auction mechanism combining the merits of the existing auction schemes (Kikuchi, Harkavy, & Tygar, 1998; Kikuchi, Hotta, Abe, & Nakanishi, 2000; Chida, Kobayashi, & Morita, 2001; Kikuchi, 2001; Abe & Suzuki, 2002; Omote & Miyaji, 2002) is as follows.

- Each bid choice can only be chosen from zero and a constant non-zero integer (e.g.

Table 4. Bids in the auction by Peng et al. (2002)

	B_1	B_2	B_3	**decryption key**
	p_2	p_3	p_5	
p_1	$E_{Y_1}(x_{1,2})$	$E_{Y_1}(x_{2,2})$	$E_{Y_1}(x_{3,2})$	$X_1 = x_{1,1} + x_{2,1} + x_{3,1}$
p_2	$\mathbf{E}_{\mathbf{Y_2}}(\mathbf{r}_1)$	$E_{Y_2}(x_{2,3})$	$E_{Y_2}(x_{3,3})$	$X_2 = x_{1,2} + x_{2,2} + x_{3,2}$
p_3	random bid in	$\mathbf{E}_{\mathbf{Y_3}}(\mathbf{r}_2)$	$E_{Y_3}(x_{3,4})$	$\mathbf{B_2}$ and $\mathbf{B_3}$ must
	correct format			collude to recover $\mathbf{X_3}$
p_4	random bid in	random bid in	$E_{Y_4}(x_{3,5})$	all the bidders must
	correct format	correct format		collude to recover $\mathbf{X_4}$
p_5	random bid in	random bid in	$\mathbf{E}_{\mathbf{Y_5}}(\mathbf{r}_3)$	all the bidders must
	correct format	correct format		collude to recover $\mathbf{X_5}$
p_6	random bid in	random bid in	random bid in	all the bidders must
	correct format	correct format	correct format	collude to recover $\mathbf{X_6}$

1) and encrypted with an additive homomorphic encryption algorithm like modified ElGamal encryption (Lee & Kim, 2000, 2002) or Paillier encryption (Paillier, 1999). So the product of the encrypted choices at a price encrypts the number of "YES" choices.

- In a ρth bid auction, secure computation of test of "YES" choice at price p_j is just a range test $D(\prod_{i=1}^{n} c_{i,j}) \geq ?\rho$, where $D()$ stands for decryption or opening of commitment. When $\rho = 1$ (first bid auction), the range test is reduced to a zero test $D(\prod_{i=1}^{n} c_{i,j}) \overset{?}{=} 0$. When $\rho > 1$, the range test is reduced to a OR logic combination of zero tests

$$D(\prod_{i=1}^{n} c_{i,j}) \overset{?}{=} 0 \vee D(\prod_{i=1}^{n} c_{i,j} / E(1)) \overset{?}{=} 0 \vee \ldots \vee D(\prod_{i=1}^{n} c_{i,j} / E(\rho)) \overset{?}{=} 0.$$

- Zero test is a basic secure computation protocol, which tests whether an encrypted or committed integer is zero without revealing it. Formal definition of zero test and its implementation can be found in (Peng,

Boyd, Dawson, & Lee, 2004). Secure computation of OR logic combination of zero tests is a little more complex: randomise and shuffle the multiple zero tests and then perform zero test one by one. Details about secure computation of OR logic combination of zero tests can be found in (Peng, Boyd, Dawson, & Lee, 2004). It is pointed out in (Peng, Boyd, Dawson, & Lee, 2004) that when there is at most one true clause in the OR logic, the shuffle-and-test-one-by-one secure computation does not reveal any information other than the result of the OR logic combination.

Sealed-bid auction employing binary search and homomorphic bid opening is illustrated in Figure 5.

Sealed-bid auction schemes with binary search usually employ homomorphic secret sharing or homomorphic encryption algorithm with distributed decryption to seal the bids, where the power of secret reconstruction or decryption is shared by multiple auctioneers with a threshold sharing. As a result the sum of bid choices at any price can be recovered if the number of colluding auctioneers is over the threshold and no losing bid is revealed if the number of colluding auctioneers is not over the threshold. In the recent years, a few such sealec-bid auctions schemes (Kikuchi et al., 1998, 2000; Chida et al., 2001; Kikuchi, 2001; Abe & Suzuki, 2002; Omote & Miyaji, 2002) have been proposed.

Kikuchi (Kikuchi et al., 1998, 2000) proposed an auction scheme, employing one-choice-per-price bid format Shamir's secret sharing (Shamir, 1979) to seal the bid choices. In each bid choice, zero stands for ``NO", while an identifying token of the bidder instead of a constant integer stands for ``YES". Every bidder shares each of his bid choices among the auctioneers using Shamir's secret sharing. In the binary search, the sum of bid choices at the prices on the searching route are reconstructed from the sum of shares held a number of auctioneers over the threshold. Kikuchi's scheme is straightforward and achieves bid privacy based on a threshold trust. However, it has several drawbacks. Firstly, Shamir's secret sharing is not verifiable, which compromises public verifiability and robustness of the auction. Moreover, although the bid format in this scheme enables identify the winner efficiently without opening all the bid choices at the winning price, this format causes some problems. The first problem is that only first bid auction can be handled. The second problem is that the auction fails when there is a tie or invalid bid choice.

Another method to share the bids is proposed in (Kikuchi, 2001). Although like in Shamir's secret sharing a polynomial is employed to share a secret, unlike in Shamir's secret sharing and its variants, the highest degree of the polynomial is

Figure 5. Auction with binary search and homomorphic bid-opening

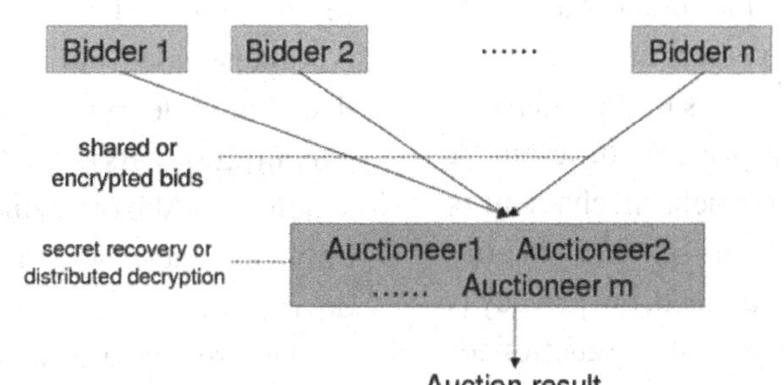

employed in (Kikuchi, 2001) to present the secret. The shares are generated from the polynomial in the same way as in Shamir's scheme. Lagrange interpolation can be employed to determine the degree of the polynomial. The sum of the polynomials is a polynomial, whose highest degree indicates the highest bid. The auctioneers perform a binary search to find the smallest number of shares needed for secret reconstruction, which is the highest degree of the sum polynomial that indicates the highest bid. This scheme is more robust than (Kikuchi et al., 1998) and (Kikuchi et al., 2000) as the highest bid can still be found when there is a tie and attack from invalid bid can be detected. However, it is not verifiable like (Kikuchi et al., 1998) and (Kikuchi et al., 2000). Another drawback of this scheme is that its winner identification function is too complex and its extension from first bid auction to the ρth bid auction is not practical. The most serious (and fatal in most circumstances) problem in this scheme is that the number of biddable prices cannot be over $m-t$ when t-out-of-m secret sharing is employed.

The auction scheme in (Chida et al., 2001) does not employ the normal threshold secret sharing, but a special 2-out-of-2 secret sharing among two auctioneers. One-choice-per-price strategy is employed. A bidder submits two same values as his choice at a price if he is not willing to pay the price, two different values as his choice at a price if he is willing to pay this price. All the bid choices at a price form two vectors, each containing one value in every bid choice. The homomorphism is achieved by the fact that if no bidders are willing to pay a price, the two vectors at this price is equal and if at least one bidder is willing to pay a price, the two vectors at this price are different. A hash-function-based commitment mechanism is employed for bid sealing in this scheme. As only the winner's commitment is opened, bid privacy is achieved with the trust that at least one auctioneer does not conspire. A flaw of this scheme is that correctness is based on trust of each auctioneer. For example, a bidder can collude with either of the auctioneers to reduce his submitted bid or deny his committed bid without being detected. As stated in Section 2.1, correctness of an auction must be achieved without any kind of trust assumption. So this auction scheme is not reliable.

The sealed-bid auction scheme in (Abe & Suzuki, 2002) employs ElGamal encryption algorithm with distributed decryption instead of secret sharing to seal the bids. The private key is threshold shared by the auctioneers to guarantee robustness and bid privacy with a threshold trust. The auctioneers cooperate to perform a binary search and at each price on the searching route check existence of "YES" choice through distributed decryption. Semantic security property of the encryption algorithm and homomorphic property of the distributed ElGamal encryption scheme are employed together with a "mix and match" technique to find out the winning price without decrypting the bids. This scheme can deal with ρ^{th} bid auction besides Vickery auction and first bid auction. One advantage of (Abe & Suzuki, 2002) over the secret-sharing-based auction schemes (except the impractical scheme in Kikuchi, 2001) is that sealing bid using encryption and opening bid using distributed decryption needs only one instance of secret sharing to share the private key while sealing bid using secret sharing and opening bid using secret reconstruction needs multiple instances of secret sharing, each for a biddable price. Another advantage of (Abe & Suzuki, 2002) is that a constant value is chosen to stand for "YES" in a bid choice, so that Vickrey auction and ρ^{th} bid auction are supported. Another sealed-bid auction scheme employing distributed decryption is proposed in (Omote & Miyaji, 2002). Its main difference from the auction scheme in (Abe & Suzuki, 2002) is that it employs only two auctioneers and 2-out-of-2 distributed decryption.

The sealed-bid auction scheme in (Abe & Suzuki, 2002) can achieve most desired properties in sealed-bid auction in normal situations.

However, it still has a few drawbacks and vulnerable to some attacks in abnormal situations, where the bidders or auctioneers deviate from the auction protocol. Peng et al. (2002b) points out that Abe and Suzuki (2002) is vulnerable to ABC (auctioneer-bidder collusion) attack against bid confidentiality and fairness, BBC (bidder-bidder collusion) attack against correctness and dispute attack against public verifiability. In (Peng et al., 2002b), a sealed-bid auction scheme is proposed to overcome the drawbacks of the previous auction scheme employing binary search including the three attacks against (Abe & Suzuki, 2002) and lack of verifiability in (Kikuchi et al., 1998, 2000; Kikuchi, 2001). The auction scheme in (Peng et al., 2002b) employs verifiable threshold secret sharing for bid sealing and bid opening as follows.

1. **Preparation Phase:** Multiple auctioneers are employed, each of which has set up a Paillier encryption system. The auctioneers' public keys and the verifiable secret sharing with unconditional hiding property (Pedersen, 1991) are published. The secret sharing scheme in (Pedersen, 1991) is verifiable, so that public verifiability can be achieved in the auction. As one-choice-per-price bid format will be adopted, the unconditional hiding property of the commitment function in (Pedersen, 1991) is necessary.
2. **Bid Submission:** The bidders use the one-choice-per-price bid format (non-zero integer standing for "YES" and 0 standing for "NO") and employ the secret sharing scheme in (Pedersen, 1991) to share their bid choices. The bidders use each auctioneer's public key to encrypt his shares and submit the encrypted shares to the auctioneers after signing them. The bidders publish the commitments of their shares as described in (Pedersen, 1991). The bidders prove that their shares encrypted in the ciphertexts sent to the auctioneers are the same shares committed in the commitments and can be used to recover their unique bids.
3. **Bid Opening:** The auctioneers verify that the bids are correctly shared. Then they cooperate to perform a binary search through the biddable prices. At each price on the searching route the auctioneers sum up their shares from the bidders and test whether the sum of the bid choices (recoverable from the summed-up shares) is zero until the winning bid is found.
4. **Winner Identification:** All the bid choices at the winning price are decrypted. The bidder submitting the winning bid is the winner. The winner 's signature on the winning bid can be publicly verified.

In summary, combination of binary search and homomorphic bid opening illustrates that downward search can be replaced by more efficient binary search if threshold trust on the auctioneers is acceptable for bid privacy. Exploitation of homomorphism unsealing and zero test (Peng, Boyd, Dawson, & Lee, 2004; Peng, 2007) can guarantee bid privacy if the number of malicious conspiring auctioneers is not over the sharing threshold. Moreover, these sealed-bid auction schemes support ρ^{th} bid auction. In addition, more biddable prices are permitted in these auction schemes to improve price flexibility as the number of searching rounds is dramatically reduced compared to in the auction schemes employing downward bid search. Although the existing auction schemes do not apply zero test and cannot achieve complete bid privacy (they usually just recover and publish the sum of bid choices at any price on the binary searching route), we believe zero test technique in (Peng, Boyd, Dawson, & Lee, 2004; Peng, 2007) will be applied to homomorphic bid opening to strengthen bid privacy.

Binary search and homomorphic bid opening seem successful with the help of zero test technique in (Peng, Boyd, Dawson, & Lee, 2004). However, there are still vulnerability and problems in this strategy. Firstly, soundless of homomorphic bid opening depends on validity of the bids. As each bidder actually can submit other bid choices than "YES" and "NO", correctness of bid opening is not guaranteed. For example, malicious bidder can submit invalid bid (e.g. submitting -1 where 1 stands for "YES") to attack the auction protocol. This attack is described and analysed in details in (Peng, Boyd, & Dawson, Chapter: Sealed-bid Auction Protocols 40, 2006a, 2005a, 2005b). From the view-point of secure computation, changing the bid from the normal format to the one-choice-per-price format is actually a pre-computation as a part of the secure computation. So correctness of this pre-computation must be publicly verified for the sake of public verifiability of secure computation and thus public verifiability of the auction scheme based on it. Therefore, the integer I standing for "YES" must be constant and proof and verification of the following equation is necessary.

$$D(c_{i,j}) = 0 \vee D(c_{i,j}) = I \ for \ i = 1,2,\ldots,n \ and \ j = 1,2,\ldots,L \quad (1)$$

Unfortunately, this important test is ignored in all the first auction schemes in Section 5.4. This test is only mentioned in ρ^{th} bid auction (Abe & Suzuki, 2002; Omote & Miyaji, 2002). It is clearly demonstrated in (Peng, Boyd, & Dawson, 2006a, 2005a, 2005b) that without this test, homomorphic bid opening in first bid auction is vulnerable to BBC attack. Moreover, it is not easy to perform this test efficiently. If standard ZK proof (by Cramer) is employed in this test, $O(L)$ full-length exponentiations are needed for each bidder and $O(nL)$ full-length exponentiations are needed for an auctioneer. This high cost counteracts the efficiency improvement through divide and conquer. Another drawback in the auction schemes in Section 5.4 is that although binary search reduces the cost of bid opening from $O(L)$ round to $\log_2 L$ rounds, each bidder still needs $O(L)$ exponentiations to seal their bids.

Therefore, advantage of binary search and homomorphic bid opening is dubious. After the cost of bid validity check is taken into account, computation cost of an auctioneer in sealed-bid auction schemes employing binary search and homomorphic bid opening is not less than that in sealed-bid auction schemes employing General SMC or sealed-bid auction schemes employing downward search. Moreover, computation cost of a bidder in sealed-bid auction schemes employing binary search and homomorphic bid opening is higher than that in sealed-bid auction schemes employing General SMC. Is binary search an unsuccessful attempt? Do we come back to the starting point after the exploration? Fortunately, several sealed-bid auction schemes are proposed recently to address these problems in sealed-bid auction schemes employing binary search and homomorphic bid opening.

Efficiency problem of bid validity check is addressed in (Peng, Boyd, & Dawson,2006a). Batch proof and verification techniques in (Aditya, Peng, Boyd, & Dawson, 2004) is adapted to batch verify validity of bid vector with the help of an original oblivious transfer mechanism. Batch proof and verification of Equation 1 is briefly described as follows where $b_{i,k}$ is the "YES" choice in bid vector $b_i = (b_{i,1}, b_{i,2}, \ldots, b_{i,L})$.

1. A verifier (e.g. auctioneer) randomly choose L integers $t_1, t_2, \ldots, t_L$, which are T bits long.
2. The bidder employs the 1-out-of-L oblivious transfer technique in (Peng, Boyd, & Dawson, 2006a) to obtain t_k from the verifier while has no knowledge of other integers.
3. The bidder make a commitment according to his bid vector and t_k.

4. The verifier publishes $t_1, t_2, \dots, t_L$ as challenges.
5. The bidder publishes a response according to his bid, t_k and the challenges, which is verified against the commitment.

The batch proof and verification technique can prove that there exist an integer k in $\{1, 2, \dots, L\}$, such that

$$\prod_{j=1}^{L} D(c_{i,j}^{t_j}) = t_k \qquad (2)$$

without revealing k. According to the batch verification theory in (Aditya, Peng, Boyd, & Dawson, 2004), Equation 2 implies that b_i is a vector containing only one non-zero items and $L-1$ zeros with a probability $1-2^{-T}$. In addition to proof that

$$\prod_{j=1}^{L} D(c_{i,j}) = 1$$

b_i is publicly proved to contain one 1 and $L-1$ zeros. As batch verification in (Aditya, Peng, Boyd, & Dawson, 2004) employs short exponents (T bits long where T can be 20 or 30) and the 1-out-of-L oblivious transfer technique in (Peng, Boyd, & Dawson,2006a) costs only $O(\log_2 L)$ full-length exponentiations, batch verification of bid validity reduces computational cost of bid validity check from $O(L)$ full-length exponentiations to $\log_2 L$ full-length exponentiations. After this efficiency improvement, a sealed-bid auction scheme employing binary search and homomorphic bid opening is more efficient than other solutions to bid privacy.

In (Peng, Boyd, & Dawson, 2005b), homomorphic bid opening is randomised to avoid bid validity check. Instead of fixing "YES" choice to a constant integer, testing $D(\prod_{i=1}^{n} c_{i,j}) \stackrel{?}{=} 0$ and depending on bid validity check, the sealed-bid auction in (Peng, Boyd, & Dawson, 2005b) uses a random non-zero integer to stand for "YES" choice, testing $D(\prod_{i=1}^{n} c_{i,j}^{t_i}) \stackrel{?}{=} 0$ without bid validity check where t_i is randomly chosen. Another contribution of (Peng, Boyd, & Dawson, 2005b) is achieving bid confidentiality and fairness without any trust, a property only achieved before in sealed-bid auction with relative bid privacy (Peng et al., 2003a). Suppose there are n bidders $B_1, B_2, \dots, B_n$ and m auctioneers $A_1, A_2, \dots, A_m$. The auction protocol in (Peng, Boyd, & Dawson, 2005b) is as follows.

Preparation Phase

A bulletin board is set up as a broadcast communication channel. Each A_j establishes his Paillier encryption (Paillier, 1999) algorithm with public key N_j (product of two secret large primes) and g_j (whose order is a multiple of N_j), message space Z_{N_j}, multiplicative modulus N_j^2, encryption function $E_j(x) = g_j^x r^{N_j} \bmod N_j^2$ and a corresponding decryption function $D_j()$. A_j publishes on the bulletin board his encryption function and public key for $j = 1, 2, \dots, m$. Large primes p and q are chosen such that q is a factor of $p-1$ and $nq^2 < N_j$ for $j = 1, 2, \dots, m$. Cyclic group G contains all the quadratic-residues in Z_p^* and has an order q. Random primes f, g and h are chosen such that $\log_g f$ and $\log_h g$ are unknown. The bid committing function is $Com(x) = f^x g^r \bmod p$ where x is a bidding choice in Z_q and r is a random integer in Z_q. A sharing threshold parameter T smaller than m is chosen. System parameters p, q, f, g, h, T and N_j for $j = 1, 2, \dots, m$ are published on the bulletin board.

Bidding Phase

Each bidder B_i selects his bidding vector $(b_{i,1}, b_{i,2}, \dots, b_{i,w})$ as his choices at $p_1, p_2, \dots, p_L$ where $b_{i,l} \in Z_q$ for $l = 1,2,\dots,w$. If he is willing to pay p_l, $b_{i,l}$ is a random non-zero integer modulo q; if he is unwilling to pay p_l, $b_{i,l} = 0$. Then he signs and publishes

$$c_{i,l} = Com(b_{i,l}) = f^{b_{i,l}} g^{r_{i,l}} \bmod p$$

for $l = 1,2,\dots,w$ on the bulletin board where $r_{i,l}$ is randomly chosen from Z_q.

Bid Opening Phase

Bid Randomization

Each auctioneer A_j publishes a commitment (e.g. one-way hash function) of random integer $R_{j,i,l}$ from Z_q for $i = 1,2,\dots,n$ and $l = 1,2,\dots,w$. After all the commitments have been published, the auctioneers publish $R_{j,i,l}$ for $j = 1,2,\dots,m$ as randomizing factors of $b_{i,l}$ on the bulletin board.

Secret Sharing

Each B_i calculates $R_{i,l} = \sum_{j=1}^{m} R_{j,i,l} \bmod q$. Then he calculates $s_{i,l} = r_{i,l} R_{i,l} \bmod q$ as his secret at p_l for $l = 1,2,\dots,w$. B_i chooses polynomials $F_{i,l}(x) = \sum_{k=0}^{T} a_{i,l,k} x^k \bmod q$ for $l = 1,2,\dots,w$ where $a_{i,l,0} = s_{i,l}$ and $a_{i,l,k}$ for $k = 1,2,\dots,T$ are randomly chosen. B_i publishes encrypted shares

$$S_{i,l,j} = E_j(F_{i,l}(j)) = g_j^{F_{i,l}(j)} t_{i,l,j}^{N_j} \bmod N_j^2$$

for $l = 1,2,\dots,w$ and $j = 1,2,\dots,m$ on the bulletin board where $t_{i,l,j}$ is randomly chosen from $Z_{N_j}^*$. B_i publishes sharing commitments $C_{i,l,k} = h^{a_{i,l,k}} \bmod p$ for $l = 1,2,\dots,w$ and $k = 0,1,\dots,T$ on the bulletin board.

Binary Search

The auctioneers cooperate to perform a binary search. At a price p_l on the searching route, the following operations are performed.

Share Verification

Each A_j calculates his summed shares $v_{j,l} = D_j(\prod_{i=1}^{n} S_{i,l,j} \bmod N_j^2)$ and the corresponding commitments $u_{l,k} = \prod_{i=1}^{n} C_{i,l,k} \bmod p$ for $k = 0,1,\dots,T$. He then verifies $h^{v_{j,l}} = \prod_{k=0}^{T} u_{l,k}^{j^k} \bmod p$. If the verification is passed, he goes on to next step. Otherwise, he verifies $h^{D_j(S_{i,l,j})} = \prod_{k=0}^{T} C_{i,l,k}^{j^k} \bmod p$ for $i = 1,2,\dots,n$ and will meet at least one failed verification. If the verification fails when $i = I$, A_j accuses bidder B_I of submitting an invalid encrypted share $S_{I,l,j}$. If B_I disputes on the accusation, the following dispute settling procedure is used. A_j publishes $z_{I,l,j} = D(S_{I,l,j})$ such that anyone can verify $h^{z_{I,l,j}} \neq \prod_{k=0}^{T} C_{I,l,k}^{j^k} \bmod p$. If $h^{z_{I,l,j}} \neq \prod_{k=0}^{T} C_{I,l,k}^{j^k} \bmod p$, B_I has to publish $t_{I,l,j}$ and proves his knowledge of $\log_{g_j}(S_{I,l,j} / t_{I,l,j}^{N_j})$ using the zero knowledge proof of knowledge of logarithm in (Schnorr, 1991)6. B_I asks the auctioneers to verify his proof and

$$S_{I,l,j} \neq g_j^{z_{I,l,j}} t_{I,l,j}^{N_j} \bmod N_j^2.$$

If

$$h^{z_{I,l,j}} = \prod_{k=0}^{T} C_{I,l,k}^{j^k} \bmod p \vee$$

$(S_{I,l,j} \neq g_j^{z_{I,l,j}} t_{I,l,j}^{N_j} \bmod N_j^2 \wedge B_I's\ proof\ is\ correct)$

The accusation against B_I is wrong and A_j is removed. Otherwise, B_I is removed from the auction and may be punished; share verification is run again.

Homomorphic Secret Recovery

Each A_j publishes $v_{j,l}$, whose validity can be verified by anyone against $C_{i,l,k}$ for $i = 1,2,\ldots,n$ and $k = 0,1,\ldots,T$. If at least $T+1$ summed shares are correct, the summed secret can be recovered. For simplicity, suppose the first $T+1$ summed shares are correct, then the summed secret is recovered:

$$d_l = \sum_{i=1}^{n} s_{i,l} = \sum_{j=1}^{T+1} v_{j,l}^{x_j} \bmod q$$

where $x_j = \prod_{1 \le k \le t+1, k \neq j} \frac{k}{k-j} \bmod q.$

Homomorphic Bid Opening

Equation $\prod_{i=1}^{n} c_{i,l}^{R_{i,l}} = g^{d_l} \bmod p$ is tested. If this equation is correct, the sum of the randomized bidding choices at p_l is zero, the binary search at p_j ends negatively and the search goes down. If this equation is incorrect, the sum of randomized bidding choices at p_l is not zero, the binary search at p_j ends positively and the search goes up.

In the end of the binary search, the winning price is found.

Winner Identification Phase

Suppose the winning price is p_w. Decrypted shares $d_{i,w,j} = D_j(S_{i,w,j})$ for $i = 1,2,\ldots,n$ are published. $h^{d_{i,w,j}} = \prod_{k=0}^{T} C_{i,w,k}^{j^k} \bmod p$ is verified for $i = 1,2,\ldots,n$ and $j = 1,2,\ldots,m$. If any bidder's secret is found to be incorrectly shared, he is removed from the auction and may be punished. If he disputes, the dispute can be solved like in Step 3(c)i. If at least $T+1$ correct shares can be found for B_i, his secret $d_{i,w}$ can be recovered:

$$d_{i,w} = \sum_{j=1}^{T+1} d_{i,w,j}^{x_j} \bmod p$$

(For simplicity, assume the first $T+1$ shares are correct). Then equation $c_{i,w}^{R_{i,w}} = g^{d_{i,w}} \bmod p$ is tested for $i = 1,2,\ldots,n$. Only when $c_{i,w}^{R_{i,w}} \neq g^{d_{i,w}} \bmod p$, is B_i a winner. Suppose $c_{I,w}^{R_{I,w}} \neq g^{d_{I,w}} \bmod p$. Then B_I must prove that he is really a winner by proving knowledge of $\log_f(c_{I,w}^{R_{I,w}} / g^{d_{I,w}})$ using the zero knowledge proof of knowledge of logarithm in (Schnorr, 1991). Any B_I failing to give this proof is a cheater and punished. The winner's signature is verified and his identity is published. If there is more than one winner, a new auction is run among the winners.

In (Peng, Boyd, & Dawson, 2005a) a modified Goldwasser-Micali encryption algorithm is designed and employed to seal the bids. Although Goldwasser-Micali encryption can only encrypt a bit, it is enough to seal bids in one-choice-per-price format as a bid choice is only a bit long. As only 2 multiplications are needed for encryption and decryption in Goldwasser-Micali encryption algorithm, both bid sealing and bid opening is very efficient. Moreover, costly bid validity check is not necessary in the new auction scheme as the plaintext space of the modified G-M encryption is the same as the message space of a bidding choice. Multiplicative homomorphism of the modified Goldwasser-Micali encryption algorithm instead of the traditional additive homomorphism in ElGamal or Paillier encryption is exploited in bid opening. Although the bid opening function must be repeated scores of times to guarantee high probability of correctness, bid opening is still much more efficient than in the previous sealed-bid auction schemes with bid privacy as decryption of G-M encryption is very efficient. Bid privacy is achieved in (Peng, Boyd, & Dawson, 2005a) as the winning bid is efficiently identified while all the losing bids are still kept secret after the auction. The auction scheme in (Peng, Boyd, & Dawson, 2005a) not only solves the problem of bid validity check, but also reduces the cost of bidders. Although one-choice-per-price strategy is used, each bidder only needs $O(L)$ multiplications instead of $O(L)$ exponentiations to seal his bid.

It seems that (Peng, Boyd, & Dawson, 2005a) is more advanced than (Peng, Boyd, & Dawson, 2005b), which is more advanced than (Peng, Boyd, & Dawson, 2006a) as (Peng, Boyd, & Dawson,2006a) partially solves the first problem, (Peng, Boyd, & Dawson, 2005b) completely solves the second problem while (Peng, Boyd, & Dawson, 2005a) completely solves both problems. However, it is not absolute. We must notice that (Peng, Boyd, & Dawson, 2006a) supports ρ^{th} bid auction while (Peng, Boyd, & Dawson, 2005a) and (Peng, Boyd, & Dawson, 2005b) only support fist bid auction. Moreover, (Peng, Boyd, & Dawson, 2005a) cannot employ threshold distributed decryption but m-out-of-m distributed decryption as it is unknown how to shared private key of G-M encryption with a flexible threshold.

SOLUTIONS AND RECOMMENDATIONS

In the past few years, several new e-auction schemes (Peng, Boyd, & Dawson, 2006b; Peng & Dawson, 2007; Peng & Bao, 2010; Peng, 2011) are proposed to achieve more advanced security propaerties, higher efficiency and wider application ranges.

The work in (Peng, Boyd, & Dawson, 2006b) focuses on micro e-auction, which is employed to distribute small-value merchandise. Compared to traditional general-purpose electronic auction, microelectronic auction has its own special requirements. Especially, micro auction must be very efficient: the cost of the auction protocol must not be over the cost of the merchandise for sale. Although the merchandise to distribute are of small value in micro auctions, bid privacy is still needed in many circumstances. So we neend to keep a balance between the high efficiency requirement of micro auction and the high cost needed to keep bid privacy.

In (Peng, Boyd, & Dawson, 2006b), after detailed analysis sealed-bid auction is chosen as an appropriate mechanism to implement micro auction. It is pointed out that all the previous sealed-bid auction schemes with bid privacy are only suitable for large-value merchandise. Although they have some achievement in high efficiency, they are still too inefficient for micro auction. They need a large number of exponentiations in computation, whose cost may be over the value of merchandise in micro auctions. So special sealed-bid auction schemes suitable for micro auction must be designed. In the paper, security and efficiency of sealed-bid micro auction are discussed and sealed-bid micro auction schemes with satisfactory security properties are designed. The simple and practical solution to efficient secure micro sealed-bid e-auction proposed in (Peng, Boyd, & Dawson, 2006b) is to modify and optimize appropriate existing secure general-purpose sealed-bid e-auction into micro auction schemes. It is pointed out that among the two common methods to design secure sealed-bid e-auction, secure evaluation and one-choice-per-price strategy, one-choice-per-price strategy is more suitable for micro auction as it can more easily achieve high efficiency in micro auction. In the paper two secure micro sealed-bid e-auction schemes are designed based on existing sealed-bid auction schemes employing one-choice-per-price strategy. Both schemes can satisfy the security requirements for micro auction and are efficient, thus are suitable for auction of small-value merchandise. The second scheme is especially efficient as it is improved in efficiency by using the idea of batch proof. Batch proof in this paper employs an idea similar to efficiency improvement measures in some micro payment systems (Micali & Rivest, 2002). It aggregately proves validity of a few random subsets of bid opening operations to publicly prove validity of bid opening with a large probability. After the improvement, only a small constant number of exponentiations are needed in the second scheme. Although the improvement sacrifices instant verifiability and cannot detect invalid operation by the auctioneers until a final verification, the sacrifice is tolerable in micro auctions.

Efficiency of bid validity check is addressed in (Peng & Dawson, 2007). It is noticed that in homomorphic auction schemes, each bidding selection is only valid when it is either "YES" or "NO". As shown in (Peng, Boyd, & Dawson,2006a) invalid bidding selections (neither "YES" nor "NO") may compromise correctness and fairness of the auction. So validity of the bids must be guaranteed in all the homomorphic auction schemes (Kikuchi et al., 1998, 2000; Abe & Suzuki, 2002; Omote & Miyaji, 2002; Peng et al., 2002b; Peng, Boyd, & Dawson, 2005b, 2005a). In most existing homomorphic auction schemes (Kikuchi et al., 1998, 2000; Peng et al., 2002b; Abe & Suzuki, 2002; Omote &Miyaji, 2002), one integer (usually 0) is chosen to stands for "NO" in a bidding selection and another integer (usually 1) is chosen to stands for "YES" in a bidding selection. In these schemes proved validity of the bids must be proved by the bidders and verified by the auctioneers and independent observers. In a publicly verifiable auction scheme, the proof must be publicly verifiable. However, proof and verification of bid validity in them is either (Kikuchi et al., 1998, 2000; Peng et al., 2002b) or inefficient (Abe & Suzuki, 2002; Omote & Miyaji, 2002). In (Peng, Boyd, & Dawson, 2005b, 2005a), all the integers in the domain of the sealing function (either secret sharing or encryption) are divided into two subsets. Any integer in one subset stands for "YES" and any integer in the other subset stands for "NO". Thus, in these two schemes there is no invalid bidding selection and no bidder has to prove validity of his bid. However, these two schemes have their own drawbacks. They only support first bid auction, so are not flexible. Moreover, they need more complicated bid opening. It is pointed out in (Peng & Dawson, 2007) that correctness, fairness, robustness, flexibility, and high efficiency are difficult to be simultaneously guaranteed. To achieve correctness and fairness, either flexibility and robustness is sacrificed (in Peng, Boyd, & Dawson, 2005b, 2005a) or costly bid validity check must be employed (in Kikuchi et al., 1998, 2000; Abe & Suzuki, 2002; Omote &Miyaji, 2002; Peng et al., 2002b). A new homomorphic auction scheme is proposed in the paper to solve the problem. More advanced batched proof and verification of bid validity than that in (Peng, Boyd, & Dawson, 2006a) is designed to batch prove and verify validity of bids in encryption-based homomorphic auction. Firstly, an ElGamal-based homomorphic sealed-bid auction scheme with normal inefficient bid validity check is proposed as a prototype. Then its bid validity check mechanism is optimised using the new batched proof and verification technique. It improves efficiency of encryption-based homomorphic auction compared to (Abe & Suzuki, 2002; Omote & Miyaji, 2002; Peng et al., 2002b), but does not have the drawbacks of (Peng, Boyd, & Dawson, 2005b, 2005a).

A design is proposed in (Peng & Bao, 2010) to apply a special membership proof technique and a range test technique to homomorphic e-auction. It answers three open questions. On one hand, the special membership proof technique has some limitations such that so far few appropriate applications have been found for it. Moreover, although only needing a constant cost and achieving very high efficiency the range test technique is so new that no appropriate application has been proposed for it. On the other hand, efficient and secure solution is in need for homomorphic e-auction, especially in bid validity check and range test of sum of bids. In the paper, the special membership proof technique and the range test technique are applied to homomorphic e-auction such that all of them benefit from the new design. Especially, after these two techniques are employed in homomorphic e-auction, most exponentiations in computation are combined into some products of multiple powers, which are more efficient than the same number of separate exponentiations according to (Bellare, Garay, & Rabin, 1998; Avanzi et al., 2005). The new e-auction scheme employs the optimisations and greatly improves efficiency of homomorphic e-auction. On one hand, the membership proof technique and the range test technique find an appropriate application and become practical technologies. On the other hand, homomorphic e-auction overcomes its bottlenecks in efficiency and achieves great improvement in performance.

A popular topic is discussed in (Peng, 2011): bidders using mobile devices in wireless network. It is illustrated in (Peng, 2011) that the existing secure e-auction schemes heavily depend on asymmetric cipher in bid sealing, bid opening and verification of validity. So attempts to improve their efficiency are limited by an unchangeable fact: asymmetric cipher operations like bid encryption and decryption and zero knowledge proof usually cost some exponentiations whose bases, exponents and multiplicative moduli are hundreds of bits long. Such exponentiations and large integers involved in them lead to much higher cost than symmetric cipher operations in both computation and communication and they are inevitable in asymmetric-cipher-based e-auction. So, the existing secure e-auction schemes are not suitable for applications with critical requirements on efficiency. On the other hand, with the development of wireless network and mobile computation-and-communication devices like mobile phone and smart cards, more and more users of e-auction hope to bid using wireless mobile devices in a wireless network. Such devices usually have much lower computation capability and communication bandwidth than the normal computers in high-speed networks. So the previous secure e-auction schemes cannot meet this new trend in e-auction application. It is pointed out that the only solution to break the efficiency limit of the existing secure e-auction schemes and design efficient e-auction for mobile users using wireless mobile devices is replacing asymmetric cipher with symmetric cipher. A symmetric-cipher-based e-auction scheme is proposed in the paper. Most operations in it are based on symmetric cipher and the only asymmetric cipher operations for a bidder are several multiplications. No costly exponentiations in asymmetric cipher is needed. With such a strict requirement on efficiency, it still achieves the common security properties desired in secure e-auction. The new e-auction scheme is proposed in two steps. An unverifiable prototype is proposed first. Then its vulnerability in robustness is pointed out in and it is optimised into a final proposal, which is verifiable and robust. The new e-auction scheme can be applied to auction applications with critical requirements on efficiency and mobile users can use it to bid in a wireless network.

FUTURE RESEARCH DIRECTIONS

In e-auction with absolute bid privacy, the work in the future should focus on two directions.

- More efficient proof and verification of validity of bids: more advanced ZK proof techiques should be designed to achieved higher efficiency and stronger soundness.
- Supporting more auction rules: complex and unlimited auction rules should be supported.

In e-auction with relative bid privacy, the work in the future should focus on two directions.

- More efficient proof and verification of validity of shuffling: more advanced ZK proof techiques should be designed to achieved higher efficiency and stronger soundness.
- Trade off on-line operations for off-line operations: costly operations should be carried out off-line to improve on-line efficiency.

CONCLUSION

Scores of sealed-bid auction schemes have been described and analysed in this chapter. It is difficult to conclude which of them is the best as various circumstances may be involved in application of sealed-bid auction. However, it is still possible to recommend the most suitable sealed-bid auction scheme in a concrete application circumstance. If bid privacy is not required, sealed-bid auction can be efficiently implemented to satisfy all the other desired properties including correctness, confidentiality, fairness, non-repudiation, robustness, public verifiability, price flexibility and rule flexibility. If only the bidder's personal privacy is concerned and the distribution of bids can be revealed, relative bid privacy is enough and the sealed-bid auction scheme in (Peng et al., 2003a) can be employed to achieve all the desired properties.

If complete bid privacy is required, factors like communication pattern, trust assumption and auction rule must be considered. If high computation efficiency is desired and on-line communication is tolerable, the downward-search sealed-bid auction scheme in (Suzuki et al., 2000) is the best choice, which very efficiently achieves bid privacy and other desired properties without any trust at the cost of intensive on-line communication between the bidders and auctioneers. If on-line communication is not tolerable but strong bid privacy without any trust is needed, another downward downward-search sealed-bid auction scheme (Peng et al.,2002a) should be employed, which non-interactively achieves all the desired properties without any trust but with a high computation cost. If high efficiency is the emphasis and bid privacy based on shared trust is acceptable, the binary-search sealed-bid auction scheme (Peng & Bao, 2010) can be employed in first bid auction. If efficient Vickrey auction or ρ^{th} bid auction is needed, the binary-search sealed-bid auction scheme in (Peng & Dawson, 2007) is suitable. If extremely high efficiency is needed for mobile bidders in wireless networks the best solution is the proposal in Peng (2011).

REFERENCES

Abe, M., & Suzuki, K. (2002). M+1-st price auction using homomorphic encryption. In Proceedings of Public Key Cryptology 2002, (Vol. 2288, pp. 115-124). Berlin, Germany: Springer-Verlag.

Aditya, R., Peng, K., Boyd, C., & Dawson, E. (2004). Batch verification for equality of discrete logarithms and threshold decryptions. In Proceedings of the Second Conference of Applied Cryptography and Network Security, ACNS 04, (Vol. 3089, pp. 494-508). Berlin, Germany: Springer-Verlag.

Beaver, D. (2000). Minimal-latency secure function evaluation. In *Proceedings of Eurocrypt '00* (*Vol. 1807*, pp. 335–350). Berlin, Germany: Springer.

Bellare, M., Garay, J. A., & Rabin, T. (1998). Fast batch verification for modular exponentiation and digital signatures. In *Proceedings of Eurocrypt '98* (*Vol. 1403*, pp. 236–250). Berlin, Germany: Springer-Verlag. doi:10.1007/BFb0054130.

Cachin, C. (1999). Efficient private bidding and auctions with an oblivious third party. In Proceedings of the 6th ACM Conference on Computer and Communications Security. ACM.

Cachin, C., & Camenisch, J. (2000). Optimistic fair secure computation (extended abstract). In *Proceedings of Crypto '00* (*Vol. 1880*, pp. 94–112). Berlin, Germany: Springer-Verlag.

Cassady, R. Jr. (1967). *Auctions and auctioneering*. Berkeley, CA: University of California Press.

Chaum, D., & Pedersen, T. P. (1992). Wallet databases with observers. In *Proceedings of Crypto '92* (*Vol. 740*, pp. 89–105). Berlin, Germany: Springer-Verlag.

Chida, K., Kobayashi, K., & Morita, H. (2001). Efficient sealed-bid auctions for massive numbers of bidders with lump comparison. In Proceedings of the Information Security, 4th International Conference, ISC 2001, (Vol. 2200, pp. 408-419). Berlin, Germany: Springer-Verlag.

Cramer, R., Damgard, I., & Nielsen, J. B. (2001). Multiparty computation from threshold homomorphic encryption. [Berlin, Germany: Springer.]. *Proceedings of Eurocrypt*, *01*, 280–299.

DeVries, S., & Vohra, R. (2000). Combinatorial auctions: A survey. Retrieved from http://www.citeseer.nj.nec.com/devries01combinatorial.html

Fischlin, M. (2001). A cost-effective pay-per-multiplication comparison method for millionaires. In *Proceedings of Topics in Cryptology, CT-RSA 2001* (*Vol. 2020*, pp. 457–472). Berlin, Germany: Springer. doi:10.1007/3-540-45353-9_33.

Franklin, M. K., & Reiter, M. K. (1996). The design and implementation of a secure auction service. *IEEE Transactions on Software Engineering*, *5*, 302–312. doi:10.1109/32.502223.

Fraud. (2004). Internet scams fraud trends 2004. Retrieved from http://www.fraud.org/2004-internet\%20scams.pdf

Golle, P., Zhong, S., Boneh, D., Jakobsson, M., & Juels, A. (2002). Optimistic mixing for exit-polls. In *Proceedings of Asiacrypt '02* (*Vol. 1592*, pp. 451–465). Berlin, Germany: Springer-Verlag.

Groth, J. (2003). A verifiable secret shuffle of homomorphic encryptions. In *Proceedings of Public Key Cryptography 2003* (*Vol. 2567*, pp. 145–160). Berlin, Germany: Springer-Verlag. doi:10.1007/3-540-36288-6_11.

Holzman, R., Kfir-Dahav, N., Monderer, D., & Tennenholtz, M. (2001). Bundling equilibrium in combinatorial auctions. Retrieved from http://iew3.technion.ac.il/~moshet/rndm11.ps

Jakobsson, M., & Juels, A. (2000). Mix and match: Secure function evaluation via ciphertexts. In *Proceedings of Asiacrypt '00* (*Vol. 1976*, pp. 143–161). Berlin, Germany: Springer-Verlag. doi:10.1007/3-540-44448-3_13.

Juels, A., & Szydlo, M. (2002). A two-server, sealed-bid auction protocol. In Proceedings of the Sixth International Conference on Financial Cryptography 2002, (Vol. 2357, pp. 72-86). Berlin, Germany: Springer-Verlag.

Kikuchi, H. (2001). (m+1)st-price auction. In Proceedings of the Fifth International Conference on Financial Cryptography 2001, (Vol. 2339, pp. 291-298). Berlin, Germany: Springer-Verlag.

Kikuchi, H., Harkavy, M., & Tygar, J. D. (1998). Multi-round anonymous auction. In Proceedings of the First IEEE Workshop on Dependable and Real-Time e-Commerce Systems, (pp. 62-69). IEEE.

Kikuchi, H., Hotta, S., Abe, K., & Nakanishi, S. (2000). Distributed auction servers resolving winner and winning bid without revealing privacy of bids. In Proceedings of International Workshop on Next Generation Internet, (NGITA2000), (pp. 307-312). IEEE.

Kurosawa, K., & Ogata, W. (2002). Bit-slice auction circuit. In Proceedings of the 7th European Symposium on Research in Computer Security, ESORICS2002, (Vol. 2502, pp. 24-38). Berlin, Germany: Springer-Verlag.

Lee, B., & Kim, K. (2000). Receipt-free electronic voting through collaboration of voter and honest verifier. [JW-ISC.]. *Proceedings of JW-ISC, 2000*, 101–108.

Lee, B., & Kim, K. (2002). Receipt-free electronic voting scheme with a tamper-resistant randomizer. In *Proceedings of Information Security and Cryptology, ICISC 2002* (*Vol. 2587*, pp. 389–406). Berlin, Germany: Springer-Verlag. doi:10.1007/3-540-36552-4_27.

Lipmaa, H., Asokan, N., & Niemi, V. (2002). Secure Vickrey auctions without thresh-old trust. In Proceedings of the 6th Annual Conference on Financial Cryptography, 2002, (Vol. 2357, pp. 87-101). Berlin, Germany: Springer-Verlag.

Micali, S., & Rivest, R. (2002). Micropayments revisited. [). Berlin, Germany: Springer.]. *Proceedings of CT-RSA*, *2271*, 149–163.

Michels, M., & Stadler, M. (1997). Verifiable homomorphic oblivious transfer and private equality test. In Proceedings of the 4th Annual Workshop on Selected Areas in Cryptology, (pp. 231-244). Springer.

Mu, Y., & Varadharajan, V. (2000). An internet anonymous auction scheme. In Proceedings of the International Conference on Information Security and Cryptology 2000, (Vol. 2015, pp. 171-182). Berlin, Germany: Springer-Verlag.

Naccache, D., & Stern, J. (1998). A new public key cryptosystem based on higher residues. In Proceedings of ACM Computer Science Conference 1998, (pp. 160-174). ACM.

Naor, M., Pinkas, B., & Sumner, R. (1999). Privacy perserving auctions and mechanism design. In Proceedings of ACM Conference on Electronic Commerce 1999, (pp. 129-139). ACM.

Neff, C. A. (2001). A verifiable secret shuffle and its application to e-voting. In Proceedings of the ACM Conference on Computer and Communications Security 2001, (pp. 116-125). ACM.

Omote, K., & Miyaji, A. (2002). A second-price sealed-bid auction with the discriminant of the p-th root. In Proceedings of the Financial Cryptography 2002, (Vol. 2357, pp. 57-71). Berlin, Germany: Springer.

Paillier, P. (1999). Public key cryptosystem based on composite degree residuosity classes. In *Proceedings of Eurocrypt '99* (*Vol. 1592*, pp. 223–238). Berlin, Germany: Springer-Verlag. doi:10.1007/3-540-48910-X_16.

Park, C., Itoh, K., & Kurosawa, K. (1993). Efficient anonymous channel and all/nothing election scheme. In *Proceedings of Eurocrypt '93* (*Vol. 765*, pp. 248–259). Berlin, Germany: Springer-Verlag.

Pedersen, T. P. (1991). Non-interactive and information-theoretic secure verifiable secret sharing. [Berlin, Germany: Springer-Verlag.]. *Proceedings of Eurocrypt*, *91*, 129–140.

Peng, K., Boyd, C., Dawson, E., & Viswanathan, K. (2002a). Non-interactive auction scheme with strong privacy. In Proceedings of ICISC 2002, (Vol. 2587, pp. 407–420). Berlin, Germany: Springer.

Peng, K., Boyd, C., Dawson, E., & Viswanathan, K. (2002b). Robust, privacy protecting and publicly verifiable sealed-bid auction. In Proceedings of ICICS 2002, (Vol. 2513, pp. 147–159). Berlin, Germany: Springer.

Peng, K., Boyd, C., Dawson, E., & Viswanathan, K. (2003a). Efficient implementation of relative bid privacy in sealed-bid auction. In Proceedings of the 4th International Workshop on Information Security Applications, WISA2003, (Vol. 2908, pp. 244-256). Berlin, Germany: Springer-Verlag.

Peng, K., Boyd, C., Dawson, E., & Viswanathan, K. (2003b). Five sealed-bid auction models. In Proceedings of the Australia Workshop of Information Security 2003. IEEE.

Peng, K., Boyd, C., Dawson, E., & Viswanathan, K. (2004). A correct, private and efficient mix network. In Proceedings of the 2004 International Workshop on Practice and Theory in Public Key Cryptography, (Vol. 2947, pp. 439-454). Berlin, Germany: Springer-Verlag.

Prevention, P. L., & Division, S. (2003). Internet auction fraud. Retrieved from http://www.psecu.com/About Us/News/Fraud/2003/20030812.html

Sako, K. (2000). An auction scheme which hides the bids of losers. In *Proceedings of Public Key Cryptology 2000* (*Vol. 1880*, pp. 422–432). Berlin, Germany: Springer-Verlag.

Sakurai, K., & Miyazaki, S. (1999). A bulletin-board based digital auction scheme with bidding down strategy -Towards anonymous electronic bidding without anonymous channels nor trusted centers. In Proceedings of International Workshop on Cryptographic Techniques and e-Commerce, (pp. 180-187). Hong Kong, Hong Kong: City University of Hong Kong Press.

Sander, T., Young, A., & Yung, M. (1999). Non-interactive cryptocomputing for NC1. In Proceedings of the 40th Annual Symposium on Foundations of Computer Science, FOCS '99, (pp. 554-567). FOCS.

Schnorr, C. (1991). Efficient signature generation by smart cards. *Journal of Cryptology*, *4*, 161–174. doi:10.1007/BF00196725.

Shamir, A. (1979). How to share a secret. *Communications of the ACM*, *22*(11), 612–613. doi:10.1145/359168.359176.

Silaghi, M.-C. (2002). An algorithm applicable to clearing combinatorial exchanges. Retrieved from http://www.citeseer.nj.nec.com/silaghi02algorithm.html

Suzuki, K., Kobayashi, K., & Morita, H. (2000). Efficient sealed-bid auction using hash chain. In Proceedings of the International Conference on Information Security and Cryptology 2000, (Vol. 2015, pp. 183-191). Berlin, Germany: Springer-Verlag.

Suzuki, K., & Yokoo, M. (2002). Secure combinatorial auctions by dynamic programming with polynomial secret sharing. In *Proceedings of Financial Cryptography 2002* (*Vol. 2357*, pp. 44–56). Berlin, Germany: Springer-Verlag. doi:10.1007/3-540-36504-4_4.

Vickrey, D. (1961, March). Counter speculation, auctions, and comatitive sealed tenders. *The Journal of Finance*, 9–37.

Viswanathan, K., Boyd, C., & Dawson, E. (2000). A three phased schema for sealed bid auction system design. In Proceedings of the Information Security and Privacy, 5th Australasian Conference, ACISP 2000, (Vol. 1841, pp. 412-426). Berlin, Germany: Springer-Verlag.

Watanabe, Y., & Imai, H. (2000). Reducing the round complexity of a sealed-bid auction protocol with an off-line ttp. [ACM.]. *Proceedings of STOC*, *2000*, 80–86.

Yokoo, M., & Suzuki, K. (2002). Secure multi-agent dynamic programming based on homomorphic encryption and its application to combinatorial auctions. In Proceedings of the First Joint International Conference on Autonomous Agents and Multiagent Systems (AAMAS-2002), (pp. 112-119). AAMAS. Retrieved from ashttp://www.kecl.ntt.co.jp/csl/ccrg/members/yokoo/PDF/aamas2002-secure-wd.pdf

ADDITIONAL READING

Avanzi, R., Cohen, H., Doche, C., Frey, G., Lange, T., & Nguyen, K. et al. (2005). *Handbook of elliptic and hyperelliptic curve cryptography*. HEHCC.

Groth, J., & Ishai, Y. (2008). Sub-linear zero-knowledge argument for correctness of a shuffle. In *Proceedings of Eurocrypt '08* (*Vol. 4965*, pp. 379–396). Berlin, Germany: Springer. doi:10.1007/978-3-540-78967-3_22.

Groth, J., & Lu, S. (2007). Verifiable shuffle of large size ciphertexts. In Proceedings of PKC '07, (Vol. 4450, p. 377-392). Berlin, Germany: Springer.

Kun Peng, E. D., & Bao, F. (2011). Modification and optimisation of a shuffling scheme: Stronger security, formal analysis and higher efficiency. *International Journal of Information Security*, *10*(1), 33–47. doi:10.1007/s10207-010-0117-y.

Peng, K. (2007). Secure multiparty computation of DNF. In Proceedings of ICICS 2007, (Vol. 4861, pp. 254-268). Berlin, Germany: Springer-Verlag.

Peng, K. (2011). Secure e-auction for mobile users with low-capability devices in wireless network. In Proceedings of WISTP 2011, (Vol. 6633, p. 351-360). WISTP.

Peng, K., & Bao, F. (2010a). A shuffling scheme with strict and strong security. [Secureware.]. *Proceedings of Secureware*, *2010*, 201–206.

Peng, K., & Bao, F. (2010b). Efficiency improvement of homomorphic e-auction. In *Proceedings of Trustbus '10* (*Vol. 6264*, pp. 238–249). Springer.

Peng, K., Bao, F., & Dawson, E. (2008). Correct, private, flexible and efficient range test. *Journal of Research and Practice in Information Technology*, *40*(4), 275–291.

Peng, K., Boyd, C., & Dawson, E. (2005a). A multiplicative homomorphic sealed-bid auction based on goldwasser-micali encryption. In Proceedings of ISC 2005, (Vol. 3650, pp. 374-388). Berlin, Germany: Springer-Verlag.

Peng, K., Boyd, C., & Dawson, E. (2005b). Optimization of electronic first-bid sealed-bid auction based on homomorphic secret sharing. In *Proceedings of Mycrypt 2005* (*Vol. 3715*, pp. 84–98). Berlin, Germany: Springer-Verlag. doi:10.1007/11554868_7.

Peng, K., Boyd, C., & Dawson, E. (2005c). Simple and efficient shuffling with provable correctness and zk privacy. In *Proceedings of Crypto '05* (*Vol. 3089*, pp. 188–204). Berlin, Germany: Springer-Verlag. doi:10.1007/11535218_12.

Peng, K., Boyd, C., & Dawson, E. (2006a). Batch verification of validity of bids in homomorphic e-auction. *Computer Communications*, *29*, 2798–2805. doi:10.1016/j.comcom.2005.10.031.

Peng, K., Boyd, C., & Dawson, E. (2006b). Sealed-bid micro auctions. In Proceedings of LFIP International Information Security Conference 2006, (pp. 246-257). LFIP.

Peng, K., Boyd, C., Dawson, E., & Lee, B. (2004). An efficient and verifiable solution to the millionaire problem. In Proceedings of ICISC 2004, (Vol. 3506, pp. 315-330). Berlin, Germany: Springer-Verlag.

Peng, K., Boyd, C., Dawson, E., & Lee, B. (2005). Ciphertext comparison, a new solution to the millionaire problem. In Proceedings of ICICS 2005, (Vol. 3783, pp. 84-96). Berlin, Germany: Springer-Verlag.

Peng, K., Boyd, C., Dawson, E., & Okamoto, E. (2006). A novel range test. In Proceedings of ACISP 2006, (Vol. 4058, pp. 247-258). Berlin, Germany: Springer-Verlag.

Peng, K., & Dawson, E. (2007). Efficient bid validity check in ElGamal-based sealed-bid e-auction. In Proceedings of ISPEC 2007, (Vol. 4464, pp. 209-224). Berlin, Germany: Springer-Verlag.

KEY TERMS AND DEFINITIONS

e-Auction: Electronic auction.

e-Commerce: Electronic commerce, including but not limited to e-auction.

Fairness: No bidder can take advantages of any other bidder.

Mix Network: An anonymous communicational network, which is employed to shuffle the encrypted bids.

Privacy: No bid can be traced back to its voter.

Routing: Transfer by a node in a noetwork.

Security: Security of e-auction includes correctness, fairness, robustness, soundness, and privacy.

ENDNOTES

1. If there is a session between the bidders and the auctioneers to distribute a symmetric key, it is possible to use more efficient secret-key encryption to encrypt the bids, but the key distribution still depends on public-key encryption.
2. A message can be signed by a signer using blind signature without being known to him.
3. Onion routing is an anonymous communciation network, through which a sender can send a message to a receiver without revealing his identity.
4. Oblivious transfer is a technique enable a receiver to extract a message among multiple messages owned by a sender where the receiver obtains no other message and the sender does not know which message has been extracted.
5. Although it is said in (Naor et al., 1999) that "A naive verification procedure is to require the auctioneer to publish the tables and garbled input values of the circuit (signed by the AI), and allow suspecting bidders to simulate its computation", this verification procedure violates the basic rule in (Naor et al., 1999) that AI alone cannot know the bids. So another verification method based on "signed 'translation' table" in (Naor et al., 1999) has to be employed. Soundness of this verification method is based on an assumption that AI does not reveal the 'translation' table to A.
6. Although the parameter setting in (Schnorr, 1991) is a little different from the parameter setting in Paillier encryption (When Schnorr, 1991, was proposed, Paillier encryption had not appeared), the proof protocol in Schnorr (1991) can be applied here without compromising its correctness, soundness, or zero knowledge property.

Chapter 19
Preserving the Privacy of Patient Records in Health Monitoring Systems

Mahmoud Elkhodr
University of Western Sydney, Australia

Seyed Shahrestani
University of Western Sydney, Australia

Hon Cheung
University of Western Sydney, Australia

ABSTRACT

The goal of this chapter is to discuss the challenges of generic security protocols and platforms for securing Electronic Health Records (EHR) in general and for their adoption in shared care environments in particular. The chapter introduces various methods and security solutions based on existing protocols, discusses their potentials, and describes some experiences with their implementations. Amongst the main challenges that e-health technology faces, security is considered as one of the major obstacles to its deployment. The chapter proposes an authentication approach, referred to as Ubiquitous Health Trust Protocol (UHTP), which aims at minimizing the security risk associated with the remote access of EHRs using portable devices. In particular, the proposed approach has been used to create ways for secure collaboration providing a set of generic services such as read/write, authentication, and trust management, as well as advanced functionality for mobile access. The experience in adopting the approach using Java on the Android platform is described.

INTRODUCTION

While the history of cryptography began thousands of years ago, academic research into computer cryptography can only be dated back to mid-1970s (D'Agapeyeff, 2008). Some of the earlier research on modern cryptography can be attributed to IBM which designed an algorithm that became the US Federal Data Encryption Standard (Smid & Branstad, 1988). Typically, cryptography has been used as a tool to generally secure communications and computer systems.

DOI: 10.4018/978-1-4666-4030-6.ch019

Recently, modern cryptography has been extended to a wide range of techniques. Credit cards with smart-card capabilities equipped with the power to execute cryptographic programs are some of the popular applications in use today. In Engineering, cryptography becomes more complicated by encompassing cryptographic theories with computer engineering hardware design and computer software algorithms. Visual cryptography is another technique used to allow visual information, such as text and images, to be encrypted in a way that decryption does not requires a computer system (Naor & Shamir, 1995). But perhaps, public-key cryptography and symmetric-key cryptography are among the popular techniques in use today. Symmetric-key cryptosystems use the same key for the encryption and decryption of a message. This was the only type of encryption publicly known until 1976 (Diffie & Hellman, 1976). A significant disadvantage of symmetric encryption is the management of keys, especially for applications on the Internet. Nevertheless, research into cryptographic techniques has been extended to include quantum physics. Quantum cryptography represents a new paradigm for securing communications systems since its security is based on the laws of quantum physics and not only on computations (Ekert, 1991). Collaborations between, mathematicians, electrical engineers, physicians, computer scientists and others have led to the state-of the-art design of various cryptography applications and the incorporation of security techniques in various applications such as in the domain of e-health. One of the major concerns with e-health systems relates to their capabilities in preserving the privacy of the patients and their medical records, which may contain highly sensitive and confidential personal information.

Electronic Health Record (EHR) provides an advanced scheme for maintaining patients' records across distributed health information systems and other health networks (B. Blobel, 2006). Compared to traditional paper-based record systems, EHRs are more efficient and reliable, providing higher degrees of availability (Hillestad, et al., 2005). But privacy and security concerns have foiled their widespread acceptance and use. To address these concerns, cryptography-based solutions have already been suggested by some researchers (Petković, Katzenbeisser, & Kursawe, 2007). But for the successful deployment of e-health systems, provision of comprehensive security measures for medical information remains a challenge that needs to be met. Cryptography is an essential element for addressing this challenge and hence the widespread acceptance of e-health systems.

Most cryptography-based solutions provide secure communication mediums for use by e-health systems (Barua, Liang, Lu, & Shen, 2011). The approaches proposed in this Chapter, use and expand such solutions. They ensure that an EHR, for instance maintained in some remote health monitoring system, is only disclosed to the authorized healthcare professionals, on their registered devices, only at the valid locations, and over a secure channel. To achieve these, building on the strengths of Transport Layer Security (TLS) protocol, a trust negotiation approach is proposed. For verification purposes, a mobile application is also constructed. The experimental works confirm that by applying the proposed approach, significant improvements in the security of the remote health monitoring systems can be achieved. The improvements in the security of the remote monitoring systems are achieved by, not only securing the communication channel, but also by providing extra protective features to the access control and authorization process before the release of any data over unsecured network. This is an enhancement to the traditional identity based only authentication's techniques.

E-Health Views and Challenges

The healthcare industry is under continuous development and growth. In the 2008–09 financial year, there were 8.1 million patients admitted to hospitals in Australia (Australian Hospital, 2010).

This number reflects an average annual increase of 3.4% for each year between 2004 and 2009 for public hospitals, and 4.4% for private hospitals. It has also been found that public hospital recurrent expenditure has increased by an average of 5.9% annually between 2004 and 2009 (Australian Hospital, 2010). Within the healthcare industry, Electronic Health Record (EHR) systems are one of the fastest growing healthcare services. Health monitoring technology, as an EHR application example, is developed as a possible solution for monitoring patients at home. The key issue is to reduce the cost on patients' care without affecting the quality of services provided (Yamazaki, Koyama, Arai, & Barolli, 2009). Remote diagnostics and patient management technologies have also been highlighted as one of the key components of healthcare for the 21st century (Weerasinghe, 2009).

In Europe, the e-health taskforce report affirms that health spending is estimated to increase by 16% in 2020 (eHealth Taskforce, 2007). The report further states that the e-health industry in Europe was worth approximately 21 billion Euros in 2009. These numbers show the increase in demand for health services, and the maintenance of the current healthcare and community care systems. The Information & Communication Technologies for Health (Health ICT) is presented as a counterbalancing solution to meet the increase in this demand. It has the potential for growth in specialized e-health services, based on EHR systems, such as Remote Monitoring Systems (RMSs) for home and community care. These e-health services have been scientifically demonstrated to improve the quality of services and result in numerous economic benefits (HealthCast 2020, 2005). The adaptation of EHRs in health operations and systems will help improving efficiency, reducing healthcare costs, and eliminating duplicative services by allowing better access to data and better sharing of patients' information amongst various organizations (Elkhodr, Shahrestani, & Cheung, 2011a).

However, there are challenges in the adaption of EHRs and they are mainly related to the deployment of this technology (Lim, Oh, Choi, & Lakshman, 2010), and to issues such as resource constraints, user mobility, cost, heterogeneity of devices, scalability, security and privacy. Privacy and security issues are regarded as serious challenges (Tyler, 2001), and the concern in privacy and security issues is more prominent in a remote health monitoring environment. In such an environment, a patient's information, which is being monitored, is collected at a home location and transmitted to a hospital for monitoring purposes. This information may contain a patient's identity, his or her medical conditions, and other information such as the location of the patient (Yao, Chu, & Li, 2010). Another important consideration is that the transmission of this information is subject to the threats of the information being intercepted, analyzed or even modified. This kind of threats lead to security and privacy concerns related, but not limited, to the confidentiality of patients' information and to the integrity of the data being exchanged. Moreover, because of the availability of information through EHR systems, access to medical data can be initiated remotely from various healthcare providers, such as private and public hospitals or clinics, pharmacies, insurance companies, research institutions and others. In such a heterogeneous shared care environment, there is a need for secure and reliable means of communications between the Internet-based healthcare information and other systems (Shahrestani, 2009). It is important not only to secure the exchange of information, but also to secure and standardize the electronic mechanisms based on strong security policies.

The goal of this Chapter is to discuss the challenges of generic security protocols and platforms for securing EHRs in general and for their adoption in remote monitoring systems in particular. The remainder of this Chapter is organized as follows. Background information on e-health and EHR systems that are relevant for the understanding of the Chapter is presented in the next section where a broad range of research topics on security and privacy issues are covered. It is followed by discussions on the approaches for securing the communication between the various components of a remote monitoring system. The section Ubiquitous Health Trust Protocol (UHTP) introduces the proposed protocol referred to as the Ubiquitous Health Trust Protocol (UHTP). UHTP secures access to the EHRs of monitored patients by healthcare professionals. It also secures the transmission of patients' EHRs between the healthcare server and the mobile device used by a healthcare professional to access these records remotely. In the section Implementation, the experiences in adopting UHTP in a mobile application based on Java on the Android platform are described. Conclusions and discussions of the potential future research are presented in the last section.

SECURING EHRS IN E-HEALTH

Brief History

The term Electronic Health Record (EHR) was first introduced almost twenty years ago (Geraci, 1996). It was defined as a concept for collecting and storing patients' health records (Gunter & Terry, 2005). While the term was considered to be new, the concept was not and could be dated back to the fifth century B.C. when Hippocrates first described what constituted a medical record. According to Hippocrates, a medical record should reflect the course and the probable cause of a disease. While these definitions are still valid, today's' EHR systems provide more functionalities. The first EHR appeared in the 1960s. By 1965, Summerfield and Empey reported that at least 73 hospital and clinic information projects, 28 projects for storage and retrieval of medical documents and other clinically-relevant information were underway (Record & Medicine, 1997). Many of today's EHRs are based on this earlier pioneering work.

Estonia is the first country that implements a nationwide Electronic Health Records System (Gunter & Terry, 2005). All of Estonia's citizens have full access to the EHR system. In Australia, the National E-Health Transition Authority (NEHTA) is undertaking a series of interdependent projects to establish the standards, specifications and infrastructure requirements for secure, interoperable electronic health information (e-health) systems (May, 2005). HealthConnect is one of the major EHR systems being developed (Goodchild, Gibson, Anderson, & Bird, 2004). MediConnect is another trial program which has implemented an EHR (Jordan, 2004), and it was designed to improve quality and safety in medication management by improving access to medication information through information technology. In the United Kingdom, projects on electronic health records are being developed with the objective of centralizing the digital records of their patients (Bergmann, Bott, Pretschner, & Haux, 2007). In Canada, the province of Alberta has already started developing and operating a large-scale electronic health record system (Binns, 2004).

Electronic Health Records

An Electronic Health Records (EHR) holds all of the necessary information of a patient, such as medical history, demographics, immunization status, results of laboratory tests, vital signs, and personal data. These can be accessible on-line via a local area network, an enterprise-wide network, and the Internet. The instant access to patients' information, provided by EHR systems, is predicted to improve healthcare services and decrease costs of the services on both patients and healthcare providers. Using the EHR digital storage feature, a larger amount of information can be stored and retrieved easily and accesses to patients' medical information become more convenient.

Security issues arise when the Internet is used to transmit sensitive data, such as EHRs. The Internet was not originally designed and optimized with security in mind. Therefore, the use of the Internet as a medium to transmit sensitive information needs to be evaluated carefully (Furnell, Gaunt, Pangalos, Sanders, & Warren, 1994). Instead of the Internet, healthcare information can be transmitted over a secure closed network, such as a grid based directory (Organisation, 2000). Unlike conventional file sharing system, it uses a messaging approach to send data to and receive data from a central database. The innovating part of this system is the ability to be mobile in a way that it can be used as a portable health record system such as in (Ruotsalainen, 2004). However, there are known limitations with the use of grid systems such as those described in (Andersson, et al., 2005).

Security Issues Within Shared Care Environments

An important functionality provided by EHR systems is the possibility of ubiquitous access to relevant health information (Elkhodr, Shahrestani, & Cheung, 2011b). This technology facilitates the exchange of medical information among different healthcare providers such as clinics, medical centers, and hospitals, and among other actors of a healthcare system such as insurance companies. In such a ubiquitous shared care environment where health information systems are interconnected, there are legal implications, social and technological considerations regarding the release, exchange and access of these medical data. Exchanging data and allowing remote access to EHRs require the information to be properly protected. The information can only be accessed by authorized personnel, especially when access control policies, privileges and security techniques could vary from a healthcare provider to another. The secure exchange of information among different healthcare providers not only depends on secure and standardized electronic mechanisms but also on standardized security policies. In fact, different healthcare providers might have different security policies, especially in terms of access privileges and release of EHRs. Standardized infrastructures, protecting the confidentiality of patients and the use of coherent security policies are essentials for the secure exchange of EHRs.

The Australian National E-health Transition Authority (NEHTA) has suggested an Interoperability Framework with a set of standards and specifications for a secure shared care environment in 2006 (Kühn & Murzek, 2006). According to this framework, the transmission of data follows point-to-point messaging through pre-installed software in the computers of an organization. In this setting, the configuration of the system has to follow pre-determined standards even if there are multiple vendors. The medium of transmission would be Web Services which set up the specifications for secure messaging from application-to-application point of view. The two main roles of this framework are maintaining EHR architecture standards that identify the logical structure, and maintaining e-Health information interchange standards of a specific format. For securing the transmission of EHRs, NEHTA proposes the use of SOAP protocol (NEHTA, 2009).

In a traditional secure file sharing structure, data are transferred as packets in an encrypted format. There are several protocols that can be used to encrypt data. Transport Layer Security (TLS) and Secure Socket Layer (TLS) are among the popular ones. Transport Layer Security (TLS) is a secure communication protocol, making use of cryptographic techniques to protect the confidentiality and integrity of information being transmitted, especially over the Internet. Secure Socket Layer (SSL) is a predecessor of TLS (TLS vs. SSL, 2010). TLS enciphers the sections of network connections at the application layer in order to guarantee end-to-end secure communication at the transport layer. TLS supports data integrity, confidentiality and client/server authentication.

Effectively, TLS provides a secure channel between a client and a server.

Apart from securing the transmission of EHRs, in a shared care environment, defining what is considered to be sensitive information as well as determining the level of permissions granted to users become vague. In fact, each participating institution of a health network would have different approaches when defining the level of sensitivity associated to the information, access rights and the level of security required in protecting privacy of patients (Bernd Blobel & Roger-France, 2001). Since the concept of security and protection of patient's privacy differ from one organization to another, a comprehensive understanding of the complexity involved in interconnecting health information systems is required for the secure exchange and release of medical data. Therefore, for an EHR system to be able to secure and protect the confidentiality of patients, it should not only incorporate security requirements but also guarantee the flow and availability of the information between different organizations.

Most of the electronic health information sharing platforms in Europe contain an interoperability and security domain. Regional and national platforms are both in use as well (Ruotsalainen, 2004). These systems use national secure infrastructures that are based on a closed network architecture (Persephone, Pekka, & Hanna, 2005). Many of these networks use Public Key Infrastructure (PKI) and some VPN (Virtual Private Network) based networks. However, there are security problems when data are shared among different organizations. As a possible solution, many European researchers proposed the use of cross-organizational approaches. The HARP model is an example of a cross-platform communications system, implementing an enhanced Trusted Third Party (TTP) server (Ruotsalainen, 2004). The server features a security policy mapping. Another proposed model suggested the use of a smart card as a method of authentication. Other studies suggested the use of grid systems as a method for securing EHRs in a shared care environment (Zhang, et al., 2011). At the initial stage, the system integrates national and regional security domains using an inter-domain zone that offers a set of common security services for domains that are interconnected. In this way, cross-organizational communication can be controlled through a central administrative system. Using existing PKI services, the system can control the authentication process through a cross-domain identification, static privilege management, certification services, and auditing services. Automatic security recognition can be used for users accessing the domains externally (Zhang, Song, & Song, 2009). To address the cross-border language issue, the platform offers semantic services as well as an EHR linking system. It also supports both distributed and centralized security management models, peer-to-peer networks, EHR cross-platform and cross-organizational language interpretation, clinical coding mapping, terminology and mapping of alternative information structures.

RELATED SECURITY WORKS

Adopting EHRs in a shared care environment will open door for various sources of security breaches, especially, when more than one party is involved in the access of data. In (Han, Skinner, Potdar, & Chang, 2006), an authentication and authorization framework for e-Health Services was proposed. Their work suggests performing authorization and authentication simultaneously. No information on the system design and implementation has been provided. In (Ouafi & Phan, 2008), an authentication protocol was developed. The protocol uses "Timestamp" to describe and verify the security properties related to the expiration of keys and the freshness of the message. The protocol heavily relies on clock synchronization of both parties, and thus trusting the users' clocks is a problematic issue by itself.

Furthermore, to make the data available for external users, maintaining a stable platform with strict authentication mechanism is also important. According to (Allaert, Le Teuff, Quantin, & Barber, 2004), generally, an EHR system uses an identifier as a common attribute for authentication along with a password. This system was designed in a way where each user is offered a separate key to decrypt a ciphertext. This unique key only works if it matches with the specific attributes included in the text. The private key is generated by a private key generator. The policy for the ciphertext is expressed in Boolean format, referring to a set of attributes which are embedded into the key. This technique is known as attributes based encryption-technique. It was proposed by (Sahai & Waters, 2005).

On the other hand, the roles of healthcare providers vary as each one of them may have different range of services. Therefore, using a role based authentication system, accesses to patients' data can be restricted for each role based on the time and location of the request (Zhang, Ahn, & Chu, 2002). This feature promote the use of role based authentication systems which has become widely adopted by a number of healthcare organizations such as the one in use in Alberta (Barrows & Clayton, 1996). The system requires healthcare professional to use an electronic tag along with a unique identification number or password; where the identification number of a tag is being changed periodically.

Authorization and authentication processes require that both recipient and sender of the data to be known to each other. The recipient must be authorized and should have the proper tool for decrypting the received data. The Public Key Infrastructure (PKI) is designed with a set of requirements, a single hierarchical dependence structure with a single line authority and single root Certification Authority. In case of regional EHR networks, a regional certification authority can be used to provide healthcare related establishments and services for that particular region.

Cryptographic-Based Solutions

Many EHR systems use cryptography to provide security and privacy. For instance, the use of Public Key Infrastructure (PKI) for securing EHR can be mentioned (Hu, Wong, Zhang, & Deng, 2006). Although these approaches use PKI for mutual authentication and the like, the overall trust and security management of the system is delegated to the health care provider, similar to that of a paper-based EHR system. Another cryptography-based solution that provides for privacy and security of EHR systems has been proposed in (Wei-Bin & Chien-Ding, 2008). This approach gives patients the control over their data and the ability to restrict access to it. When a healthcare professional needs to review the EHR, an agreement or consent from the patient needs to be obtained first. The healthcare professional will then use the keys stored on a smart card to decrypt the EHR. The authors then propose a consent exception solution for emergencies, where a trusted server possesses all the secret keys of the patients and can facilitate the retrieval of patients' information in an emergency.

Another solution based on cryptography is presented in (Yu & Chekhanovskiy, 2007). It is based on the use of a patient centric system that uses tamper resistant hardware and cryptography for authentication and provision of other security services. The main drawback of this system is the use of a dedicated hardware device for protecting the content of an EHR. Also, the authors have not provided any security analysis for the proposed solution.

A hierarchical identity-based encryption and searchable encryption to construct a privacy-preserving EHR system is proposed in (Attrapadung, Furukawa, & Imai, 2006). One of the advantages of this system is that it can implement an EHR system over any third party storage device, such as cloud storage. The proposed solution however adds some overhead on the patients and the healthcare providers. It also suffers from some other limitations, including the need to create and manage multiple keys by patients and healthcare providers and the need for the patients to verify the healthcare provider's credentials. Some of these limitations can be overcome by a more sophisticated approach (Chase, 2007). In this approach, the solution is based on a smartcard technology, which requires the users of the EHR system to have a dedicated smartcard.

The concept presented in (Sahai & Waters, 2005) on Cipher text Policy Attribute Based Encryption (CP-ABE) have been used by many researchers to develop other solutions, for instance see (Bethencourt, Sahai, & Waters, 2007) and (Hupperich, et al., 2012). CP-ABE uses Elliptic Curve Cryptography (ECC) which is a based on the algebraic calculation of elliptic curves over finite fields. With smaller curve groups, it can achieve RSA equivalent security. A 163-bit ECC key offers security levels comparable to a 1024-bit RS key (Edoh, 2004). A model for cloud based EHR that does not use PKI systems has also been developed (Akinyele, et al., 2011). It uses only one public key for encrypting the data. Only one encryption key will be used by healthcare providers, while the decryption keys vary from one provider to another.

REMOTE HEALTH MONITORING SYSTEMS

Remote health monitoring systems are among the latest e-health applications under development. They offer interesting solutions and improve the quality of care. A remote health monitoring system provides a platform for assistance to the elderly in their homes or other monitored locations. Monitoring patients can help with early detection of problems and can increase their chances of survival. It will also help healthcare providers to react before a serious medical condition, such as a heart attack or diabetic emergency occurs (Kim, et al., 2010). There are other associated benefits from the use of remote health monitoring systems specifically for people who live in remote locations or are too ill to visit hospitals or medical clinics. Although, a remote monitoring system is an opportunity for improving the healthcare sector, there are a number of limitations involved. In order for this technology to become feasible, challenges exist. These challenges relate to the deployment of this technology and to issues, such as resource constraints, user mobility, cost, heterogeneity of devices, scalability, security, and privacy.

Monitoring patients by using a remote system in patients' homes gives a clear picture of their health conditions and helps in improving their current health status. The data collected by the remote monitoring system are sent to the healthcare provider and stored on their servers in the form of patients' EHRs. It is important to secure the transmission of the patient's EHRs between the healthcare provider server and the mobile device being used by the healthcare professional, as their communication is normally via unsecure networks, such as the Internet. In the following section, we introduce an approach which guarantees that patients' EHRs are only disclosed to the authorized healthcare professionals, on the registered devices, and at the appropriate locations. The aim of the proposed protocol is to not only secure the transmission of EHRs but also the authentication and authorization mechanisms over a public network.

In a remote monitoring system designed for monitoring elderly persons, as an application example, the protocol provides healthcare professionals with a secure remote access to the patient's EHR and also secures the transmission of patients' EHR between the healthcare provider's server and the healthcare professional's portable device over the Internet. The proposed ubiquitous health trust protocol (UHTP) establishes a secure session between the user's device and the healthcare provider's server. The healthcare server is where the patient's EHRs are actually stored. This session is created using the TLS handshake mechanism. The TLS session is used to ensure the encryption of the exchanged messages and protection against attackers. After establishing the secure session, UHTP proceeds with trust negotiation. Trust negotiation in UHTP aims at performing the following authentications before granting a healthcare professional access to a particular patient's EHR:

1. Authenticating the healthcare professional.
2. Authenticating the device in use.
3. Authenticating the environment of access and the person receiving the healthcare.

These are the requirements necessary to identify the user, the device and the location involved in a single healthcare transaction. Thus, these three authentications aim to enhance the security of EHRs by providing extra protection before the release of any sensitive data.

A case scenario: In an elderly remote monitoring system, a Healthcare Professional (HP) represents the person administering healthcare and may visit the house of an elderly. The house is the location where the healthcare service occurs, e.g., to conduct a medical examination, regular check up or other required healthcare activities. There is a need for these healthcare professionals to remotely access the elderly' EHRs. The reason of accessing an EHR can vary from reading the data history to modifying or adding new data to the records. Healthcare professionals will use their portable devices such as their smart phones or tablets to remotely access the EHRs. This will lead to security and access control issues, and a number of security requirements such as authentication and authorization. Concerns about the confidentiality and the privacy of the elderly are also raised.

Trust Negotiation

Trust negotiation is the term used for exchanging the digital credentials between a healthcare professional and a server for the purpose of authenticating healthcare professionals to the server in a remote health monitoring system. It is a process of establishing trust between two negotiating entities based on their credentials or attributes. There are different approaches for trust negotiation (Seamons, 2004). Some of the approaches are as follows (Seamons, 2004):

- **Simple:** This is the case when all the credentials are disclosed with each request of service.
- **Trial/Error:** This approach has two parts. Firstly, it discloses all credentials which are not sensitive. The second part discloses sensitive credentials after establishing a required trust level.
- **Informed:** This approach starts by disclosing the relevant policy first. Based on the trust specification in the policy, it then starts disclosing the necessary credentials for a successful negotiation process. It is important to note that it only discloses the necessary credentials and not all of them.
- **Advanced:** This approach is based on cryptography technology. It requires demonstration of attributes without disclosing credentials.

Trust negotiation in e-health has been addressed in previous studies such as in (Vawdrey, Sundelin, Seamons, & Knutson, 2003). The purpose behind the use of trust negotiation is to improve the healthcare system scalability by providing authentication and access control using a wireless PDA. While, in (Asokan & Tarkkala, 2005) a trust mechanism was used to set up a secure session between strangers. In this scenario, strangers enter an ad hoc network. They provide authentication through the use of a digital certificate, which authenticates the user and the access device. However, this model is only considered suitable for a small scope authentication system. Different trust negotiation approaches have been also been proposed by the research community for the purpose of establishing an access control mechanism. In (Bharadwaj & Baras, 2003), trust negotiation is used to support access control policies in open decentralized systems. Other approaches, such as in (Bertino, Ferrari, & Squicciarini, 2004; Sears, Yu, & Guan, 2005), are based on a trust negotiation framework in a peer-to-peer environment. In (Bertino, et al., 2004), a sequence prediction module was presented. The aim of this module is to cache and manage the used credential sequence from previous trust Negotiations. In (Ajayi, Sinnott, & Stell, 2007), Dynamic Trust Negotiations are formalized where the process is to achieve a trust between strangers by using intermediate trusted entities.

In (Han, Wang, Wang, & Zuo, 2009; Seamons, et al., 2002), mutual trust between strangers is established by using iterative exchange of credentials. It is referred as an Automated Trust Negotiation which is based on what an entity has and does not rely only on the entity's identity (Jacobson, 2003). In (Kawaguchi, Russell, & Guoliang, 2003), for the purpose of authentication, the credentials are signed by a credit issuer. This issuer will have the responsibility of verifying the validity of the attributes contained in these credentials. Nevertheless, traditional trust negotiation mechanisms which are based on an iterative exchange of credentials require intensive public key cryptographic calculation and policy compliance checking. These requirements are often considered to be resource hungry and burdensome for mobile devices (Yajun & Fan, 2006).

Trust Policy

Trust and security are closely linked (Liu & Xiu, 2005). The current security technologies are associated with trust implicitly. We trust a certificate authority (CA) in verifying a digital certificate. In this closed static environment, the interaction between entities (organization, CA and users) is based on trust (Liu & Xiu, 2005). In a shared environment, the role of trust is more emphasized. This is because the system involves spontaneous interaction between parties in a decentralized network. Trust is a very complex concept and has a number of different characteristics. In regards to e-health, the following trust characteristics apply:

- **Trust Subjectivity:** Different entities can have a different trust policy on the same data. A dentist may have a different trust policy in updating some particular medical data from those given to a specialist who might also have a different trust policy on the same type of data.
- **Trust Asymmetry:** Patient A trusts doctor B but B should not necessarily trust A. The degree of trust varies, unless transitivity is used.
- **Trust Transitivity:** Doctor B trusts C, who is the entity responsible of collecting data from patients. C trusts patient A, by verifying that the collected data are genuine and by validating the credentials. Therefore doctor B trusts the collected data from patient A.
- **Relativity of Context:** The level of trust may vary between entities depending on the context. Patient A trusts nurse D on one thing and but not on everything.
- **Dynamic:** Trust varies by time and context. Trust based dynamic access control depends on an initial static trust if accessed from a dynamic trusted entity.

Trust Extending TLS

The main goal of extending the Transport Layer Protocol (TLS) protocol is to make access control decisions based on attributes rather than solely on identity. This presents a solution for a distributed environment, where identity based solutions are not enough. A person's or client's attributes can be in the form of a job title, annual salary, citizenship or others, while server attributes can include privacy policy, role, membership and others. Digital credentials encapsulate the attribute information, described above. They act as a reliable carrier for these attributes. One of the important features of digital credentials is that they are verifiable by the issuer attribute authority and auditable. Also, these credentials are treated as protected resources since the information they hold is considered to be sensitive. The disclosure of credentials is usually controlled by an access control policy. These policies contain instructions and information about the entities which have the right to disclose or access the credentials.

Therefore, before granting the right to access resources, a client must present adequate credentials for the purpose of authorization. The TLS protocol is known to provide clients with encryption and data integrity. A client negotiation request is sent in the form of a message by the initiator in order to initiate the establishment of trust, such as in (Yao, Hu, Lu, & Li, 2005). Additional messages in the extended TLS include the list of names of the trust negotiation strategy families supported by the client (Yao, et al., 2005). There are also some cases where a client might be calling for trust negotiation immediately after TLS has been completed. In such a case, the server starts the trust negotiation after the completion of the TLS handshake. In a case where a client needs just one single authenticated service, then the service name is regarded as the name of the service which is supposed to be started.

In other cases, trust negotiation is combined with TLS. This extends a pure TLS. TLS's authentication mechanism is identity based and it cannot perform attribute-based authentication (Jacobson, 2003). A client and a server are only allowed one credential presentation each, on a pass/fail basis. Incorporating trust negotiation into TLS solves these problems. In (Jacobson, 2003), it is discussed that many features would not have been accomplished if TLS hasn't been combined with trust negotiation. When TLS is extended to include trust negotiation, a client and a server are allowed to exchange a single certificate chain. The server assigns a list of names that it can regard as authenticated or certified by trusted authorities. Also, during negotiation, neither a client nor a server is allowed to request supplementary certificates. It is also very important that the server first discloses its certificate before carrying out other activities.

TLS allows both a client and a server to communicate across a network in a way that there is a total prevention of interference. In some cases, the authentication of TLS is unilateral, which means that the server is the only entity that is authenticated, while the client is provided with the server's identity. Usually, the vital information and certificates essential for TLS are addressed in the form of X.509 certificates. These certificates define the required fields and the formats of data. Although TLS and trust negotiation are combined, trust negotiation is only permitted after the completion of the TLS protocol. Thus, there is no interference between the trust negotiation mechanism and the TLS protocol. However, it is important that access-control policies be well-written.

Building on the strengths of the TLS protocol, Ubiquitous Health Trust Protocol (UHTP) implements an extended TLS to provide a strong communication security over the Internet. The TLS handshake establishes keying material to provide encryption, host-based authentication, and data integrity services to every message that follows. In a client- server model, all TLS messages are tied to the session established by the handshake. TLS guarantees that the connection between the client and the server is secured. In a remote health monitoring system the transmission of patients' Electronic Health Records (EHRs) over the Internet is secured using the TLS protocol. The TLS protocol can detect if any modification or insertion of messages occurred during the communication held between the healthcares professional (the client) and the server holding the patients EHR.

UBIQUITOUS HEALTH TRUST PROTOCOL

The proposed UHTP protocol establishes a trust relationship between the healthcare professional and the service provider where EHR is stored. The client-server model is used in the rest of this chapter to represent these two negotiating entities. It is important to note that, securing the communication is a major aspect that needs to be accomplished before disclosing any sensitive information and before the start of trust negotiation. It is vital that credentials are securely exchanged between a client and server for the purpose of establishing a trust relationship. Another aspect which needs to be considered, in UHTP, is the issue of non-expert users of technology. EHR users are considered to be non-expert users of technology. They lack the knowledge and the experience to interact and perform related security choices and decisions. Since users are from diverse backgrounds and have different understanding and experience in using technology, relying on them over the security settings of a system can lead to various problems. Consequently, individuals may misuse personal data when making security decisions, leading to incorrect individual decisions, inaccurate exchange of data, and unintentional misuse of authority.

Establishing a Secure Session

For securing the communication between the Client and the Server we use the TLS protocol version 1.0. The objective of the use of TLS is to achieve a secure and reliable connection. This will provide both entities a tool for achieving mutual authentication. Integrity is also achieved through the use of a digital certificate; while encryption ensures privacy and confidentiality.

The proposed Ubiquitous Health Transport Protocol (UHTP) first starts by establishing a secure session using a TLS handshake sequence between a client and a server as illustrated in Figure 1. In this work, the device in use by the healthcare professional is considered to be the client while the web server holding the EHRs is considered to be the server. The TLS session can also be reused once it has been established. Consequently, the server assigns to each TLS session a unique identifier. This identifier is used by the mobile device (the client) for future connections. This will reduce the handshake through the use of cashing on the Web server side. A list of the handshake sequence elements used by the client and the server is given below:

1. Negotiating the Cipher Suite to be used during the exchange of messages.
2. Sharing and establishing the session key.
3. Authenticating the server and the client to the server.

In the first step, a supported Cipher Suite by the client and the server is selected as a result of the negotiation process. For instance, the TLS protocol version 3.0 supports 21 Cipher Suites. The selection of the Cipher Suite includes the agreement on the use of the following components:

- The Key Exchange Method used during the handshake
- The Cipher used for Data Transfer
- The Message Digest used for creating the Message Authentication Code (MAC)

The Key Exchange Method

UHTP uses an RSA key exchange method which is supported by TLS. It defines the shared secret symmetric cryptography key used for the exchange of data between the device in use by the healthcare professional and the server holding the EHRs. Digital signatures are an additional option that can be used as an assurance against a man-in-the-middle-attack during the exchange of information. For encrypting the messages in a session, there are a variety of choices, including the followings:

Figure 1. Establishing a Secure Session

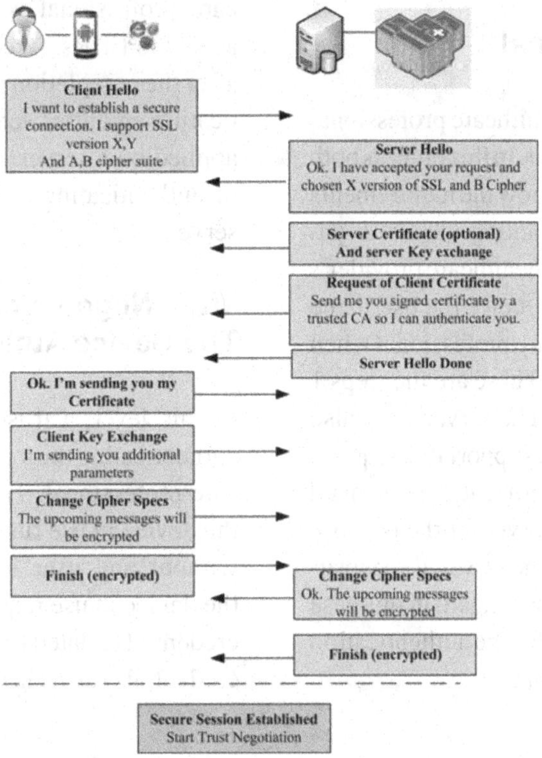

- No encryption
- Stream Ciphers
  - RC4 with 40-bit keys
  - RC4 with 128-bit keys
- CBC Block Ciphers
  - RC2 with 40 bit key
  - DES with 40 bit key
  - DES with 56 bit key
  - Triple-DES with 168 bit key
  - Idea (128 bit key)

UHTP uses Triple-DES with 168 bits key which is considered, as the International Data Encryption Algorithm (IDEA) algorithm, one of the best and strongest available cryptographic algorithms, and it uses a 128 bit key.

Digest Function

For the use of a digest function, three options are available: No digest, MD5 (128 bit), SHA-1 (160 bit) or SHA-2 (256-bit). UHTP uses the strongest digest function, the Secure Hash Algorithm (SHA-2), since it relies on a 256-bit hash. It determines how a digest is created from a record unit. This message digest is used to create a Message Authentication Code (MAC) which is encrypted with the message to provide integrity and to prevent replay attacks.

UHTP TLS Handshake Sequence

Three protocols are used during the handshake:

- The TLS Handshake Protocol for establishing the TLS session.
- The TLS Change Cipher Spec Protocol for agreeing on the Cipher Suite for the session.
- The TLS Alert Protocol for handling TLS error messages.

Trust Negotiation Level 1: Authenticating the Healthcare Professional

This level aims to verify a healthcare professional to a healthcare provider server. In this process both negotiators are assumed to know the requirements necessary for requesting/granting access to patients' EHRs. Therefore, the healthcare provider's server will be expecting to receive the username and password of the healthcare professional when requesting access to EHRs. These are the steps 1 to 4 shown in the Figure 2. The server must also be configured to receive and support this request. Digital credentials are the attributes exchanged between the client and the server for the purpose of identity authentication of the server. It encapsulates the credentials being exchanged; in this case the username and password for the authentication of the healthcare professional.

In UHTP, providing the identity of the healthcare professional is not enough to be granted access to EHRs. Access to EHRs is only granted after the completion of the three levels of authentication and after verifying access control rights applied on a server. Figure 2 details the process of authenticating a healthcare professional to a server.

Trust Negotiation Level 2: The Device Authentication

In this level, a trust negotiation proceeds into authenticating the mobile device used by a healthcare professional. The process of authenticating the device in use runs silently in the background without any user interference. Authenticating the device in use requires the exchange of digital credentials related to the device itself. The digital credentials can be in the form of attributes related

Figure 2. Authenticating the healthcare professional algorithm

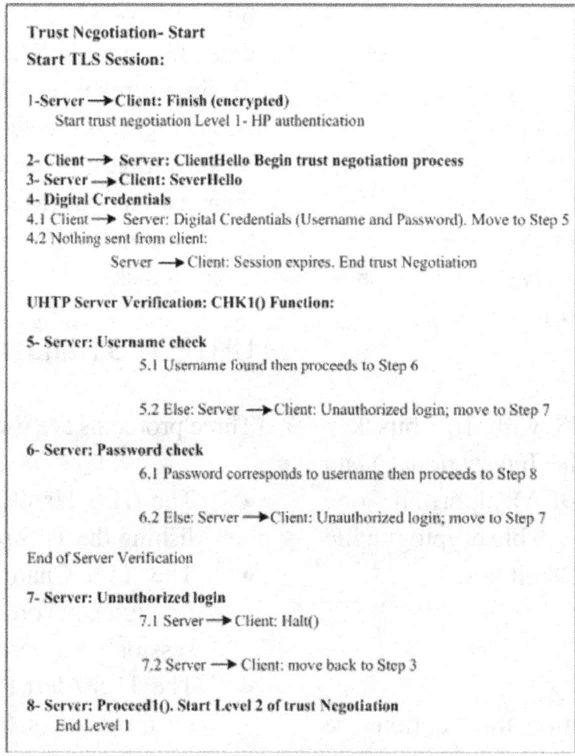

Trust Negotiation- Start
Start TLS Session:

1-Server → Client: Finish (encrypted)
Start trust negotiation Level 1- HP authentication

2- Client → Server: ClientHello Begin trust negotiation process
3- Server → Client: SeverHello
4- Digital Credentials
4.1 Client → Server: Digital Credentials (Username and Password). Move to Step 5
4.2 Nothing sent from client:
Server → Client: Session expires. End trust Negotiation

UHTP Server Verification: CHK1() Function:

5- Server: Username check
5.1 Username found then proceeds to Step 6

5.2 Else: Server → Client: Unauthorized login; move to Step 7
6- Server: Password check
6.1 Password corresponds to username then proceeds to Step 8

6.2 Else: Server → Client: Unauthorized login; move to Step 7

End of Server Verification

7- Server: Unauthorized login
7.1 Server → Client: Halt()

7.2 Server → Client: move back to Step 3

8- Server: Proceed1(). Start Level 2 of trust Negotiation
End Level 1

to a device. They allow a particular device to be identified among others. The International Mobile Equipment Identity (IMIE) number is an example of a digital credential that can be used to identify one mobile device from another. An IMIE is a unique number used for identifying mobile devices. The same requirements used for authenticating a healthcare professional also apply in authenticating a device in use. A server must be configured to request these digital credentials and must know the list of authorized mobile devices. This will allow a server to compare between the received digital credentials and the pre-registered list of digital credentials stored in the server. Analyzing and comparing these credentials enable a server to make a decision of whether or not to authenticate the device. This process of authentication is given in Figure 3. In Step 3, the client sends the device's digital credentials, which are the Mobile IMIE and the SIM serial numbers, to the server for the purpose of authenticating the device in use.

Trust Negotiation Level 3: The Environment of Access Algorithm

The environment of access is the location of a healthcare professional at the time where access to EHRs is initiated. Verifying the environment of access is the last step in the trust negotiation process which needs to be achieved. The successful completion of the trust negotiation process guarantees that patients' EHRs are trusted to the appropriate device and at the right place, and received by an authorized person. Yet, authenticating all these players is not sufficient for the release of patients' EHRs. There is still a need to meet the rights and policies enforced on a

Figure 3. Authenticating the device in use algorithm

Trust Negotiation- Start - Still within the current SSL session

Proceed1(): Server: Start

Start trust negotiation level 2- Device in use (DU) authentication

1- Server → Client: Request DU Digital Credentials

2- Digital Credentials

2.1 Client → Server: Digital credentials (IMIE and others). Move to Step 3

2.2 (Nothing sent from client)

Server → Client: Session expires. End trust Negotiation

UHTP Server Verification: CHK2() Function:

3- Server: DU Digital Credential check

3.1 Server: CHK 2() return "True"; moves to Step 5

3.2 Else: Server → Client: Unauthorized login; proceeds to Step 4

End of Server Verification

4- Server: Unauthorized login

4.1 Server→ Client: Halt()

5-Server: Proceed 2(). Start Level 3 of trust Negotiation

End Level 2

server for the purpose of controlling access to EHRs. Therefore, in verifying the environment of access, the proposed protocol checks if a particular healthcare professional is present at the monitored person's location. The assumption is that this healthcare professional is located at the monitored person's location performing a medical examination or other healthcare activities. Thus, access to the monitored patient's EHRs is required by this healthcare professional. To achieve this verification, two requirements need to be met. Firstly, we need to get the location where access to EHRs has been initiated. Secondly, the protocol needs to check if the location corresponds to the monitored person's pre-registered address on the server. Hence, the monitored person's location must be known to the server prior to the deployment of the remote monitoring system, as well. This process of verification is achieved through the use of a "Match Location (ML)" function. The algorithm for level 3 of UHTP trust negotiation is given in Figure 4. For a given location, the healthcare professional can only access the EHR of the monitored persons who are monitored at this particular location. These are the Steps 1, 2, 3, and 4 from the algorithm shown in Figure 4. The Match Location (ML) function, through Steps 4 and 5, returns true if the location of the healthcare professional, sent earlier in Step 2, matches or falls within the allowed range of the pre-registered location of the monitored person. In case the verification of the location fails, the ML function returns false (Step 4.2) and trust negotiation fails. Verifying the location of the healthcare professional is made by verifying the GPS longitude and latitude parameters of the device in use and by extracting the position from the network cell. The position parameters are the digital credentials exchanged between a client and a server. If the function ML returns true, Level 3 of trust negotiation proceeds into checking RBAC access rights. RBAC defines the access rights applied on a particular healthcare professional and the permissions assigned to access a particular EHR. RBAC works by controlling the healthcare professionals' access to EHRs based on their roles and the permissions attached. As an example: after identifying a particular healthcare professional, the server will be able to identify whether this healthcare professional is a doctor, nurse or someone else. Therefore, granting access to a particular EHR will be based on this process of identification. These are the Steps 6 and 7 shown in Figure 4.

IMPLEMENTATION

The chosen platform for simulating and developing the proposed protocol is Android. Since Android is an open development platform, it is considered a suitable platform for research and experiment. This is because access to the device hardware, ports, background services, notifications, and others are open and free to use. Android is based upon a modified version of the Linux kernel. It is a software stack for mobile devices that include an operating system, middleware, and key applications. A wide range of mobile devices and tablets, known as Android pad, run Android as an operating system. For constructing and testing the proposed protocol, we developed a simulation using the Android SDK. Android SDK includes a virtual mobile device. It is an emulator for developing and testing Android applications without using a physical mobile device.

The App consists of two parts: (1) a client side application and (2) a server side application. The first part was developed using the Android SDK (SDK, 2011), the Java Development Kit (JDK) and the Eclipse framework. The responsibility of this client side application is to generate the client's requests and to receive and process the responses sent from the server. The second part, the server side application, is responsible of generating the server's responses and requests. It holds the patients' EHR. This server side application was implemented using the Hypertext Preprocessor

Figure 4. Authenticating the environment of access algorithm

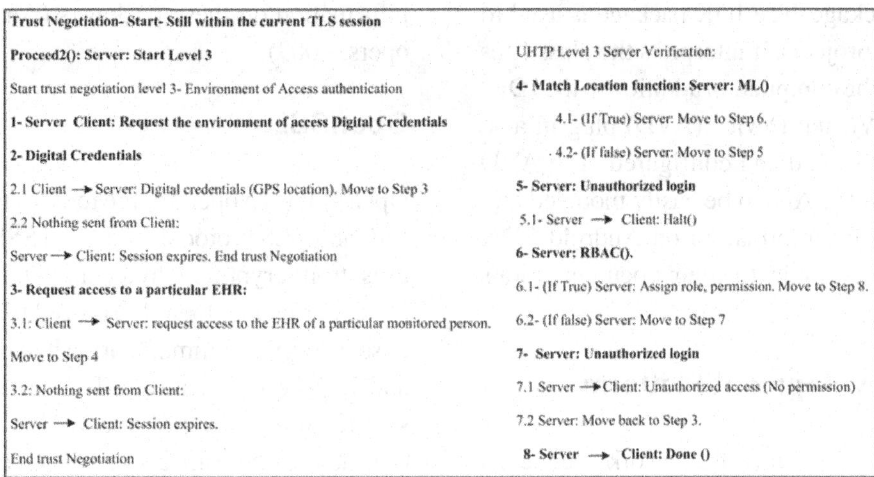

(PHP) and JavaScript Object Notation (JSON, 2010). The developed database runs on WAMP (2010). WAMP is a combination of Apache, MySQL and PHP packages. For securing the communication between the client and the server, on the Android device, TLS version 1.0 protocol was used using OpenSSL.

Configurations and Setups

The first step in the implementation phase is to set up and configure the application components and the software packages needed for implementing the App. It includes installing, configuring and setting up the environment. As shown in Figure 5, the followings are the main software packages needed for implementing the App:

Android SDK

The Android SDK is a virtual mobile device which runs locally on a computer. It includes a mobile device emulator. This emulator is used to develop the App and to test the Ubiquitous Health Trust Protocol's (UHTP) operations without the need to deploy the App on a physical mobile device. The only difference between this Emulator and a real mobile Android device is that the Emulator cannot actually receive and place calls. However, the rest of the functionalities provided by Android system can still be accessed from this Emulator in the same way they are accessed on a real mobile device. This emulator mimics all the hardware, software specifications and features of a real mobile device. The Android SDK package

Figure 5. The software packages

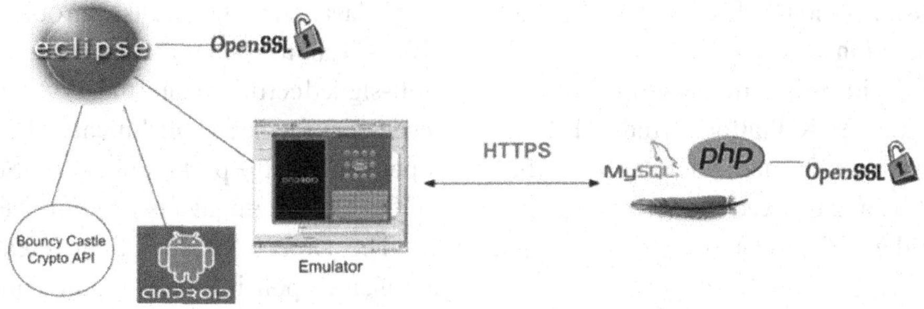

required the installation of the Java Development Kit (JDK) package. The JDK package is used to compile Java projects. It interprets the class files generated by the compiler. In addition to the JDK, the Android Virtual Device (AVD) plug-in also needs to be installed and configured. The AVD plug-in allows the App to be easily modeled and tested. For more information on Android SDK and JDK, please refer to their documentations (SDK, 2011).

Eclipse Development Platform

Eclipse is an open source framework used as an application framework for the development of the application. Eclipse is used for deploying and managing the App across the entire application lifecycle. Eclipse is popularly known as a Java IDE. Before using Eclipse, the following packages need to be added and configured:

1. Android Dalvik Debug Monitor Server (DDMS) and Android Development Tools (ADT): DDMS is used as a middleware connecting Eclipse to the applications running on the device. Also, DDMS is needed because every application on Android runs in its own process; known in java as a thread. DDMS will manage the multi-threading process. Therefore, it hosts the application on its own virtual machine. ADT is used to create the application's user interface. It uses a custom Extensible Markup Language (XML) for that purpose.
2. Android Documentation version 2.2, the Application Programming Interface version 8 (API 8), revision 1: Used for debugging the application.
3. The Android software development kit version 2.2 (SDK Platform Android 2.2), API 8, revision 2: Interaction between the application and the Android system is done through the API version 8.

Please refer to the documentation for further information on these packages (Android Developers, 2009).

OpenSSL

OpenSSL is an open source toolkit implementing SSL and TLS protocols. It has an SSL library and uses strong cryptography technologies methods. In our experiment, OpenSSL is used for the purpose of securing the communication between the client and the server by creating a TLS session. This session requires the use of a server key and a digital certificate. These are also provided by OpenSSL.

WAMP Server

WAMP stands for Windows, Apache, MySQL, and PHP. It is used to develop the server side application, mainly the database holding patients' EHRs. This server also hosts the server side application which generates the server requests and responses. The installation of WAMP is straightforward. It is also necessary to configure WAMP to include the OpenSSL module.

The Client Side Application

The first step in the application operations is to setup a secure connection between the client and the server. The application uses the protocol TLS version 1.0 for securing the communication between its browser (Web HTTP) and the web server (Apache). For the purpose of initiating a secure session, a custom Java interface called MyHttpClient was implemented within the class login.java. This interface uses an object for creating HTTPS connections. This object encapsulates the self-signed certificate and the server key; which are necessary for the establishment of TLS sessions. It operates over the port number 443. Selected code of the class login.java is given in Algorithm 1.

The Object MyHttpClient, created in class login, is responsible for communicating the client

Algorithm 1. Selected code of the class login.java

```
public MyHttpClient(Context context) {
    this.context = context; }
protected ClientConnectionManager createClientConnectionManager() {
    SchemeRegistry registry = new SchemeRegistry();
    registry.register(new Scheme("http", PlainSocketFactory.getSocketFacto-
ry(), 80));
    registry.register(new Scheme("https", newSslSocketFactory(), 443));
    return new SingleClientConnManager(getParams(), registry);
  }
  private SSLSocketFactory newSslSocketFactory() {
    try {
      // Create a new KeyStore object to store the key
      KeyStore trusted = KeyStore.getInstance("BKS");
// Fetch the key store we created which contains our server's self-signed cer-
tificate
      InputStream in = context.getResources().openRawResource(R.raw.mystore);
      try createClientConnectionManager finally {
        in.close();
      }
// validate the identity of the HTTPS server
      return new SSLSocketFactory(trusted);
    } catch (Exception e) {
      throw new AssertionError(e);     }}}
```

to the server. It generates the client messages used for establishing the handshake via the method createClientConnectionManager. The last message in Class MyHttpClient, return new TLSSocketFactory(trusted), is a method used to validate the web server. It also authenticates the certificate to the web server using a private key. The command KeyStore trusted = KeyStore. getInstance("BKS") is used to store the file containing the trusted certificate. In case a non-trusted certificate is used, the client secure socket will reject the connection during the TLS session handshake.

After establishing the secure session, the client side application collects the username and the password, from the client, using the application interface. It also collects the mobile device's IMEI and the SIM card serial numbers using the Telephony Service class and stores them into variables, as in the code shown below in Box 1.

Box 1.

```
StringsimSerial=((TelephonyManager)
getSystemService(Context.TELEPHONY_SERVICE)).getSimSerialNumber();
StringIMEI=((TelephonyManager)
getSystemService(Context.TELEPHONY_SERVICE)).getDeviceId();
```

These credentials, collected from the mobile device, are added to the array "nameValuePairs" along with the username and password, previously collected. This array is then sent to the server over HTTPS using the httpPost method, presented in Box 2. The server subsequently proceeds with the verification process as described in the UHTP method given in Section UHTP.

The Server Side Application

Upon the receipt of the client's message, the server side application starts verifying the credentials included in the array. The server side application consists mainly of the class login.php; which has the responsibility of comparing the received credentials with those stored in the database. However, for the server to be able to read, parse and respond to the clients' messages, a server API is needed as shown in Figure 6. One of the main functionality of this API is to generate the server's responses. A server's response can be of two types: 1.) a server response with a status code saying "Unauthorized Login", or 2.) an authorized login with a correct status code and a body message. The body message is the EHR requested. The server API consists of two main subclasses:

- RestUtils.php: This class is responsible for processing the incoming requests. It is also responsible for sending the appropriate responses to the client.
- RestRequest.php: The wrapper class that represents the server's request.

Therefore, using this API, the server is able to process the messages sent by the client. The client, on the other side, is specifically configured to send the array of credentials as a message to the class login.php, using the following statement presented in Box 3 (extracted from login.java class).

The class Login.php receives this message and using the server API; it reads and parses the credentials included. The process of reading and

Box 2.

```
httppost.setEntity(new UrlEncodedFormEntity(nameValuePairs));
```

Box 3.

```
HttpPost httppost = new HttpPost("https://ServerAddress/hospital/login.php");
```

Figure 6. The server API

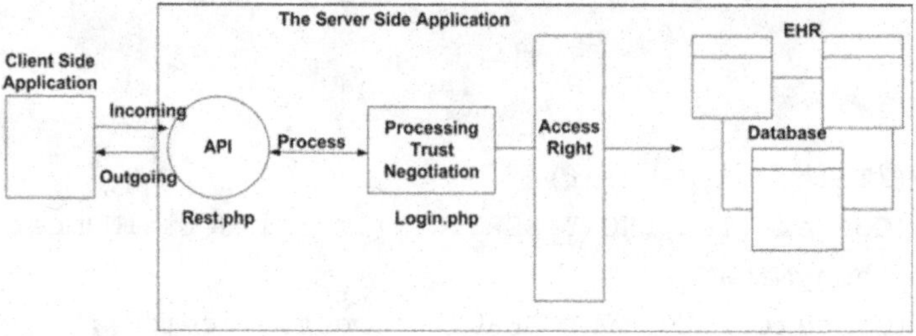

parsing the values from the array is made using the API's function Processrequest() implemented in class login.php as shown in the following codes:

```
include("rest.php");
$data = RestUtils::processRequest();
$requestVars = $data-
>getRequestVars();
```

Next, the values extracted from the array are stored in PHP variables, as shown in the code below. These are used to perform the verification process.

```
$USERNAME = $requestVars['username'];
$PASSWORD = $requestVars['password'];
$SERIAL = $requestVars['serial'];
$IMEI = $requestVars['imei'];
$LOCATION= $requestVars['loc'];
```

The server proceeds into the UHTP verification process by verifying the client's username and password, stored in the "$USERNAME" and "$PASSWORD" PHP's variables. It queries the database to verify if these values exist, as shown in the following statement, presented in Box 4.

If the server failed to verify the username and password, it generates an unauthorized message using the following statement presented in Box 5.

This instructs the server's API to send an unauthorized message to the client. The server then ends the negotiation process and waits for further actions from the client; or the session expires. If the verification succeeded, the server has successfully authenticated the client. Next, the server proceeds into verifying the device's in use credentials, the IMEI and the SIM serial numbers included in the array and the location parameters subsequently. To achieve this, the server extracts the client's identification number (ID) from the database. This ID will be used, by the server, to access his or her records on the database. Using this ID, the server is able to access the registered credentials. It compares the received IMEI and SIM serial number stored on the database, with those included in the array sent by the client. The same process is also performed to process the location information. The process is done using the "Switch" function as shown in the code in Algorithm 2.

If authentication succeeds, the server generates a status code numbered "200." However, if any of the credentials failed to authenticate, the server halts the verification process, using a break statement, and generates a different status code numbered "401." This tells the client that authentication has failed.

On the other side, the client side application is waiting for the server's response to act accord-

Box 4.

```
$checkUserQuery = "SELECT id FROM Clients WHERE username='". $USERNAME. "' AND
password='". $PASSWORD. "'";
$checkUserExecute = mysql_query($checkUserQuery);
$userRow = mysql_fetch_array($checkUserExecute);
```

Box 5.

```
RestUtils::sendResponse(401, '', 'application/json');
```

Algorithm 2. "Switch" function

```
$checkSerialQuery = "SELECT serial FROM SimSerials WHERE serial='". $SERIAL.
"' AND doctor_id='". $userId. "'";
$checkSerialExecute = mysql_query($checkSerialQuery);
$serialRow = mysql_fetch_array($checkSerialExecute);
$checkIMEIQuery = "SELECT imei FROM IMEI WHERE imei='". $IMEI. "' AND doctor_
id='". $userId. "'";
$checkIMEIExecute = mysql_query($checkIMEIQuery);
$IMEIRow = mysql_fetch_array($checkIMEIExecute);
switch($CHECK)
{case 'BOTH':
if ($serialRow && $IMEIRow)
{ RestUtils::sendResponse(200, '', 'application/json'); } else
{ RestUtils::sendResponse(401, '', 'application/json'); }
break;
case 'SERIAL':
if ($serialRow)
{ RestUtils::sendResponse(200, '', 'application/json');
else
{ RestUtils::sendResponse(401, '', 'application/json'); }
break;
case 'IMEI':
if ($IMEIRow)
{RestUtils::sendResponse(200, '', 'application/json');}
else{ RestUtils::sendResponse(401, '', 'application/json'); }
break; }}
```

ingly. Therefore, upon the receipt of the server's message, the client converts the status code into a readable message to the user. In case the status code number received was 200, the function calls the activity "ViewAccount.java". This activity displays to the requester, the client, the list of the authorized services, such as the ability to access a particular patient's EHR as shown in Figure 7.

Evaluation

The results of this experiment indicate the significant improvements in overcoming security related concerns when compared to the traditional identity-based access control techniques. The improvements in the security of EHR systems are achieved by providing extra protective features to the access control and authorization process before any data is sent over an unsecured network. The TLS handshake establishes the encryption parameters used in host-based authentication and data integrity services for every message that follows. To extend the functionality of TLS and to maximize the security of e-health systems, the notion of 'trust negotiation' is introduced and combined with TLS. In comparison with other reviewed encryptions methods, trust negotiation enhances the security levels by providing an extra authentication and access control features before the release of any data. It ensures that patients' EHRs are only disclosed over an encrypted communication channel, to the authorized healthcare

Figure 7. The application screenshot

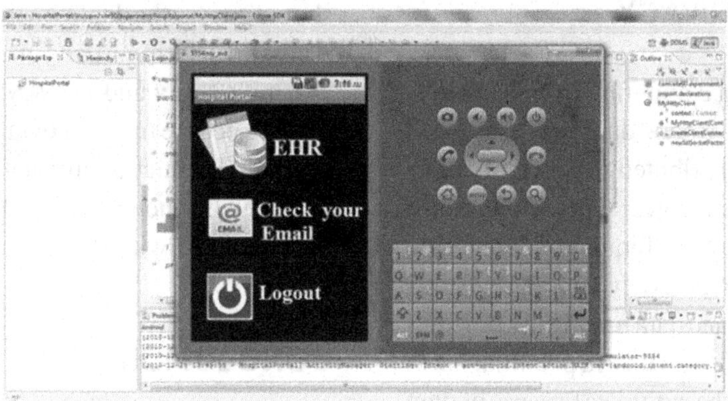

professional, using registered devices and at ratified locations. These restrictions reduce the security risks associated with the loss or theft of mobile devices.

The current versions of TLS have a vulnerability of the renegotiation procedure that can lead to successful plaintext injection attacks (Rescorla, 2009). It may allow the attacker to capture an https connection and to splice their own requests into the beginning of the handshake. This is different from a typical man-in-the-middle attack scenario. In this case, the attacker cannot decrypt the client-server communication. To fix this vulnerability, a renegotiation indication extension has been proposed for TLS (OpenSSL: SSL_CTX_Set_Options(3), 2009). However, because of the combination of the trust negotiations with the TLS protocol in our proposed approach, injection attacks are not possible without having full physical access to the mobile device and the SIM card. To mount a successful attack, the location of each patient and the credentials (username and password) of the healthcare professional also need to be known by the attacker.

Limitations

In this chapter, some major improvements to an already strong security protocol, TLS, are proposed. The proposed trust negotiations approach, improve the security of remote access to the EHR of patients stored on a healthcare provider server. One of the trust negotiation levels is based on authenticating the environment of access. This requires the verification of the location of healthcare professional through validating the GPS coordinates of their device. While the adoption of GPS coordinates enhances the security of the system, it also introduces some restrictions that need to be considered. A GPS receiver device, for instance the android mobile device, calculates the position of the healthcare professional by precisely timing the signals sent by the GPS satellites. These satellites continually transmit messages that include: the time the message was sent, the orbital information and the almanac. The use of each of these elements introduces some technical difficulty resulting in some form of limitation for the operation of the GPS device. The unavailability of GPS signals in extreme weather conditions or technical issues related to the signal time transfer, traffic signal timing, and synchronization of the cell phone base stations must also be accounted for. These issues may form a barrier to the successful completion of the third level of trust negotiation. In the future works, an alternative method to locate the device through Wi-Fi signals or cellular networks as with several other mobile applications will be used to overcome these issues.

FUTURE RESEARCH DIRECTIONS: OPEN TOPIC- PRIVACY

The paradigm shift in computing from a centralized network model where data are controlled via computers to a distributed network of smart object pose some challenges. One of the major implications is privacy as Ubiquitous Computing (UC) develops. In UC, privacy so longer means anonymity. Profiling and data mining in a e-health scenario as an example can form a potential harm to individuals due to the automate process of data collection, their storage and the way personal data can be easily shared and analyzed.

The foundations and regulations for digital privacy were established some years ago where the Internet is centralized. These regulations deal with the collection of data and their access, and ensure their correct handling. That's no longer the case today. At its simplest definition, privacy means: giving users options as to how their collected personal information might be used; specifically for secondary usage and third party access. As an example, in the online environment, privacy choices can be exercised by simply clicking a box on the browser screen that indicates a user's decision with respect to the use of the information being collected. The concept remained the same in the evolution of social networking, where users in Facebook indicate to whom and to which extent their information can be revealed. These are known as the principles of notice and choice. However, in e-health, communication of data is going to be arbitrary which lead to the following open question: Do patients own their medical data or they belong to the healthcare providers? This is a question that hasn't been answered yet. One of the major privacy concerns seen in the EHRs system is the ability to collect personal information without the individual's knowledge or consent. As medical information enter our digital world, the fine line that separates the concerns associated with the incorporation of this smart technology in your life and the possible privacy concerns becomes evident. What are the principles that should govern the deployment of such technology? And who determine that fine line between tracing, sharing of data and privacy, and to what extend sharing people medical data is accepted? How do we provide notice appropriate to circumstances to individuals when the collected data might easily be associated with that individual?

CONCLUSION

The work described in this chapter aims to improve the security of e-health systems. More specifically, it is concerned with enhancing the security of HER and its communications. Remote health monitoring systems are among the latest EHR applications under development. These systems aim to deliver high quality health care without putting too much pressure on already constrained healthcare systems. Monitoring patients by using a remote system in patients' homes, for example, gives a clear picture of their health condition and helps in improving their current health status. The data collected by the remote monitoring systems are sent over unsecured networks to the healthcare provider and stored on their servers in the form of patients' EHRs. From there, healthcare professionals can access the patients' EHR and recommend medical treatment.

To address the associated security requirements, a number of security and privacy issues were analyzed and investigated. Based on these, this work has proposed to provide healthcare professionals with a portable application that can be used to remotely access the patients' EHR from registered locations. A number of security requirements were identified as essential for securing the operations of this application. Some of the security requirements relate to the impediments of the mobile devices and their loss or theft. As with other secure systems, authorization of healthcare professionals before granting access to patients' EHRs is an obvious requirement.

TLS was chosen as the underlying protocol to provide basic security solutions needed in EHR transmission. By its design, TLS protocol provides strong communication security over the Internet, as all exchanged messages are tied to the session established by the TLS handshake. To extend the functionality of TLS and to maximize the security of e-health systems, in this work the notion of 'trust negotiation' is introduced and combined with TLS into what is referred to as the Ubiquitous Health Trust Protocol (UHTP). The experimental results have shown that UHTP is capable of achieving the security requirements needed in the EHR application system.

REFERENCES

Ajayi, O., Sinnott, R., & Stell, A. (2007). Formalising dynamic trust negotiations in decentralised collaborative e-health systems. Paper presented at the the Second International Conference on Availability, Reliability and Security, 2007. ARES 2007. New York, NY.

Akinyele, J. A., Pagano, M. W., Green, M. D., Lehmann, C. U., Peterson, Z. N. J., & Rubin, A. D. (2011). Securing electronic medical records using attribute-based encryption on mobile devices. Paper presented at the 1st ACM Workshop on Security and Privacy in Smartphones and Mobile Devices. New York, NY.

Allaert, F. A., Le Teuff, G., Quantin, C., & Barber, B. (2004). The legal acknowledgement of the electronic signature: A key for a secure direct access of patients to their computerised medical record. *International Journal of Medical Informatics*, *73*(3), 239–242. doi:10.1016/j.ijmedinf.2003.11.007 PMID:15066553.

Andersson, G., Donalek, P., Farmer, R., Hatziargyriou, N., Kamwa, I., & Kundur, P. et al. (2005). Causes of the 2003 major grid blackouts in North America and Europe, and recommended means to improve system dynamic performance. *IEEE Transactions on Power Systems*, *20*(4), 1922–1928. doi:10.1109/TPWRS.2005.857942.

Android Developers. (2009). Website. Retrieved from http://developer.android.com/index.html

Asokan, N., & Tarkkala, L. (2005). Issues in initializing security. Paper presented at the Fifth IEEE International Symposium on Signal Processing and Information Technology, 2005. New York, NY.

Attrapadung, N., Furukawa, J., & Imai, H. (2006). Forward-secure and searchable broadcast encryption with short ciphertexts and private keys. [Springer.]. *Proceedings of Advances in Cryptology–ASIACRYPT*, *2006*, 161–177.

Australian Hospital. (2010). Australian hospital statistics 2008–09. Canberra, Australia: Australian Institute of Health and Welfare.

Barrows, R., & Clayton, P. (1996). Privacy, confidentiality, and electronic medical records. *Journal of the American Medical Informatics Association*, *3*(2), 139–148. doi:10.1136/jamia.1996.96236282 PMID:8653450.

Barua, M., Liang, X., Lu, R., & Shen, X. (2011). ESPAC: Enabling security and patient-centric access control for ehealth in cloud computing. *International Journal of Security and Networks*, *6*(2), 67–76. doi:10.1504/IJSN.2011.043666.

Bergmann, J., Bott, O. J., Pretschner, D. P., & Haux, R. (2007). An e-consent-based shared EHR system architecture for integrated healthcare networks. *International Journal of Medical Informatics*, *76*(2-3), 130. doi:10.1016/j.ijmedinf.2006.07.013 PMID:16971171.

Bertino, E., Ferrari, E., & Squicciarini, A. C. (2004). Trust-&Xscr: A peer-to-peer framework for trust establishment. *IEEE Transactions on Knowledge and Data Engineering*, *16*(7), 827–842. doi:10.1109/TKDE.2004.1318565.

Bethencourt, J., Sahai, A., & Waters, B. (2007). Ciphertext-policy attribute-based encryption. Paper presented at the SP '07. New York, NY.

Bharadwaj, V. G., & Baras, J. S. (2003). Towards automated negotiation of access control policies. Paper presented at the IEEE 4th International Workshop on Policies for Distributed Systems and Networks, 2003. New York, NY.

Binns, P. (2004). The impact of the electronic health record on patient safety: An Alberta perspective. *Healthcare Papers*, *5*(3), 47–51. PMID:16278536.

Blobel, B. (2006). Advanced and secure architectural EHR approaches. *International Journal of Medical Informatics*, *75*(3-4), 185. doi:10.1016/j.ijmedinf.2005.07.017 PMID:16112891.

Blobel, B., & Roger-France, F. (2001). A systematic approach for analysis and design of secure health information systems. *International Journal of Medical Informatics*, *62*(1), 51–78. doi:10.1016/S1386-5056(01)00147-2 PMID:11340006.

Chase, M. (2007). Multi-authority attribute based encryption. Paper presented at the 4th Conference on Theory of Cryptography. New York, NY.

D'Agapeyeff, A. (2008). *Codes and ciphers - A history of cryptography*. New York, NY: Hesperides Press.

Diffie, W., & Hellman, M. (1976). New directions in cryptography. *IEEE Transactions on Information Theory*, *22*(6), 644–654. doi:10.1109/TIT.1976.1055638.

Eclipse. (2012). The eclipse foundation open source community website. Retrieved from http://www.eclipse.org/

Edoh, K. D. (2004). Elliptic curve cryptography: Java implementation. Paper presented at the 1st Annual Conference on Information Security Curriculum Development. IEEE.

Ekert, A. K. (1991). Quantum cryptography based on Bell's theorem. *Physical Review Letters*, *67*(6), 661–663. doi:10.1103/PhysRevLett.67.661 PMID:10044956.

Elkhodr, M., Shahrestani, S., & Cheung, H. (2011a). An approach to enhance the security of remote health monitoring systems. Paper presented at the 4th International Conference on Security of Information and Networks. New York, NY.

Elkhodr, M., Shahrestani, S., & Cheung, H. (2011b). Enhancing the security of mobile health monitoring systems through trust negotiations. Paper presented at the 2011 IEEE 36th Conference on Local Computer Networks (LCN). New York, NY.

European Commission. (2007). eHealth taskforce report. Luxembourg: European Commission.

Furnell, S. M., Gaunt, P. N., Pangalos, G., Sanders, P. W., & Warren, M. J. (1994). A generic methodology for health care data security. *Informatics for Health & Social Care*, *19*(3), 229–245. doi:10.3109/14639239409025329 PMID:7707744.

Geraci, A. (1996). The computer dictionary project: An update. *Computer*, *29*(7), 95. doi:10.1109/2.511973.

Goodchild, A., Gibson, K., Anderson, L., & Bird, L. (2004). The Brisbane southside healthconnect trial: Preliminary results. In Proceedings of HIC 2004. HIC.

Gunter, T., & Terry, N. (2005). The emergence of national electronic health record architectures in the United States and Australia: Models, costs, and questions. *Journal of Medical Internet Research*, *7*(1), e3. doi:10.2196/jmir.7.1.e3 PMID:15829475.

Gunter, T. D., & Terry, N. P. (2005). Gunther Eysenbach. Toronto, Canada: Centre for Global eHealth Innovation.

Han, R.-F., Wang, H.-X., Wang, Y.-H., & Zuo, K.-L. (2009). Membership-based access control for trust negotiation in open systems. Paper presented at the Information Assurance and Security, 2009. IAS '09. New York, NY.

Han, S., Skinner, G., Potdar, V., & Chang, E. (2006). A framework of authentication and authorization for e-health services. Paper presented at the 3rd ACM Workshop on Secure Web Services. New York, NY.

Hillestad, R., Bigelow, J., Bower, A., Girosi, F., Meili, R., & Scoville, R. et al. (2005). Can electronic medical record systems transform health care? Potential health benefits, savings, and costs. *Health Affairs*, *24*(5), 1103–1117. doi:10.1377/hlthaff.24.5.1103 PMID:16162551.

Hu, B., Wong, D., Zhang, Z., & Deng, X. (2006). Key replacement attack against a generic construction of certificateless signature information security and privacy. *Lecture Notes in Computer Science*, *4058*, 235–246. doi:10.1007/11780656_20.

Hupperich, T. L, H., Sadeghi, A.-R., & Winandy, M. (2012). Flexible patient-controlled security for electronic health records. Paper presented at the 2nd ACM SIGHIT International Health Informatics Symposium. New York, NY.

Jacobson, J. (2003). *Trust negotiation in session layer protocols*. Provo, UT: Brigham Young University.

Java. (2012). Java development kit (JDK). Retrieved from http://java.sun.com/products/archive/jdk/1.1.8_010/

Jordan, K. (2004). *MediConnect field test assists national HealthConnect*. Canberra, Australia: Australian Government Department of Health and Ageing.

JSON. (2010). Website. Retrieved from www.json.org

Kawaguchi, A., Russell, S., & Guoliang, Q. (2003). Security issues in the development of a wireless blood-glucose monitoring system. Paper presented at the Computer-Based Medical Systems, 2003. New York, NY.

Kim, J., Choi, H.-S., Wang, H., Agoulmine, N., Deerv, M. J., & Hong, J. W.-K. (2010). POSTECH's u-health smart home for elderly monitoring and support. Paper presented at the World of Wireless Mobile and Multimedia Networks (WoWMoM). New York, NY.

Kühn, H., & Murzek, M. (2006). Interoperability issues in metamodelling platforms. In Proceedings of the 1st International Conference on Interoperability of Enterprise Software and Applications, (pp. 215-226). IEEE.

Lim, S., Oh, T. H., Choi, Y. B., & Lakshman, T. (2010). Security issues on wireless body area network for remote healthcare monitoring. Paper presented at the Sensor Networks, Ubiquitous, and Trustworthy Computing (SUTC). New York, NY.

Liu, Z., & Xiu, D. (2005). Agent-based automated trust negotiation for pervasive computing. Paper presented at the Second International Conference on Embedded Software and Systems. New York, NY.

May, L. (2005). The national e-health transition authority (NEHTA). *The HIM Journal*, *34*(1), 19. PMID:18239225.

Naor, M., & Shamir, A. (1995). Visual cryptography. In *Proceedings of Advances in Cryptology — EUROCRYPT'94* (*Vol. 950*, pp. 1–12). Berlin, Germany: Springer. doi:10.1007/BFb0053419.

NEHTA. (2009). *Web services profile*. NEHTA.

OpenSSL. SSL_CTX_set_options(3). (2009). Website. Retrieved from http://www.openssl.org/docs/ssl/SSL_CTX_set_options.html#secure_renegotiation

OpenSSL. (2012). The open source toolkit for SSL/TLS. Retrieved from www.openssl.org/

Organisation, W. (2000). *The world health report 2000 - Health systems: Improving performance*. Washington, DC: World Health Organization.

Ouafi, K., & Phan, R. (2008). Privacy of recent RFID authentication protocols. Paper presented at the Information Security Practice and Experience (ISPEC). New York, NY.

Persephone, D., Pekka, R., & Hanna, P. (2005). *Regional health economies and ICT services: The PICNIC experience*. Boca Raton, FL: IOS Press.

PHP. (2012). Hypertext preprocessor. Retrieved from www.php.net/

PricewaterhouseCoopers. (2005). HealthCast 2020: Creating a sustainable future. New York, NY: PricewaterhouseCoopers' Health Research Institute.

Record, C. O. I. T. P., & Medicine, I. O. (1997). *The computer-based patient record: An essential technology for health care* (Revised Ed.). Washington, DC: The National Academies Press.

Rescorla, E. (2009). Understanding the TLS renegotiation attack. Educated Guesswork. Retrieved from http://www.educatedguesswork.org/2009/11/understanding_the_TLS_renegoti.html

Ruotsalainen, P. (2004). A cross-platform model for secure electronic health record communication. *International Journal of Medical Informatics*, *73*(3), 291–295. doi:10.1016/j.ijmedinf.2003.12.012 PMID:15066561.

Sahai, A., & Waters, B. (2005). Fuzzy identity-based encryption. In *Proceedings of Advances in Cryptology – EUROCRYPT 2005* (*Vol. 3494*, pp. 557–557). Berlin, Germany: Springer. doi:10.1007/11426639_27.

SDK. (2011). Website. Retrieved from http://developer.android.com/sdk/index.html

Seamons, K. (2004). TrustBuilder: Automated trust negotiation in open systems. Paper presented at the 3rd Annual PKI R&D Workshop. New York, NY.

Seamons, K. E., Winslett, M., Ting, Y., Smith, B., Child, E., Jacobson, J., et al. (2002). Requirements for policy languages for trust negotiation. Paper presented at the Third International Workshop on Policies for Distributed Systems and Networks, 2002. New York, NY.

Sears, W., Yu, Z., & Guan, Y. (2005). An adaptive reputation-based trust framework for peer-to-peer applications. Paper presented at the Network Computing and Applications, Fourth IEEE International Symposium on. New York, NY.

Shahrestani, S. A. (2009). ICT healthcare: Overcoming complex barriers for successful deployment. Paper presented at the 5th WSEAS International Conference on Dynamical Systems and Control. New York, NY.

Smid, M. E., & Branstad, D. K. (1988). Data encryption standard: past and future. *Proceedings of the IEEE*, *76*(5), 550–559. doi:10.1109/5.4441.

TLS vs. SSL. (2010). Website. Retrieved from http://msdn.microsoft.com/en-us/library/aa380515(v=vs.85).aspx

Tyler, J. L. (2001). The healthcare information technology context: A framework for viewing legal aspects of telemedicine and teleradiology. Paper presented at the 34th Annual Hawaii International Conference on System Sciences, 2001. Hawaii, HI.

Vawdrey, D. K., Sundelin, T. L., Seamons, K. E., & Knutson, C. D. (2003). Trust negotiation for authentication and authorization in healthcare information systems. Paper presented at the 25th Annual International Conference of the IEEE Engineering in Medicine and Biology Society, 2003. New York, NY.

WampServer. (2010). Install PHP 5 apache MySQL on windows: WampServer. Retrieved from http://www.wampserver.com/en/

Wei-Bin, L., & Chien-Ding, L. (2008). A cryptographic key management solution for HIPAA privacy/security regulations. *IEEE Transactions on Information Technology in Biomedicine*, *12*(1), 34–41. doi:10.1109/TITB.2007.906101 PMID:18270035.

Ya-Jun, G., & Fan, H. (2006). Trust authentication protocol on the web. *Wuhan University Journal of Natural Sciences*, *11*(1), 253–255. doi:10.1007/BF02831742.

Yamazaki, A., Koyama, A., Arai, J., & Barolli, L. (2009). Design and implementation of a ubiquitous health monitoring system. *International Journal of Web Grid Services*, *5*(4), 339–355. doi:10.1504/IJWGS.2009.030263.

Yao, H.-B., Hu, H.-P., Lu, Z.-D., & Li, R.-X. (2005). Dynamic role and context-based access control for grid applications. Paper presented at the TENCON 2005 2005 IEEE Region 10. New York, NY.

Yao, W., Chu, C.-H., & Li, Z. (2010). The use of RFID in healthcare: Benefits and barriers. Paper presented at the RFID-Technology and Applications (RFID-TA), 2010 IEEE International Conference on. New York, NY.

Yu, W. D., & Chekhanovskiy, M. A. (2007). An electronic health record content protection system using SmartCard and PMR. Paper presented at the e-Health Networking, Application and Services, 2007 9th International Conference on. New York, NY.

Zhang, J., Zhang, K., Yang, Y., Sun, J., Ling, T., & Wang, G. et al. (2011). Grid-based implementation of XDS-I as part of image-enabled EHR for regional healthcare in Shanghai. *International Journal of Computer Assisted Radiology and Surgery*, *6*(2), 273–284. doi:10.1007/s11548-010-0522-8 PMID:20694521.

Zhang, L., Ahn, G.-J., & Chu, B.-T. (2002). A role-based delegation framework for healthcare information systems. Paper presented at the Seventh ACM Symposium on Access Control Models and Technologies. New York, NY.

Zhang, X., Song, M., & Song, J. (2009). A solution of electronic authentication services based on PKI for enabling e-business. Paper presented at e-Business Engineering. New York, NY.

ADDITIONAL READING

Beckwith, R. (2003). Designing for ubiquity: The perception of privacy. *IEEE Pervasive Computing / IEEE Computer Society [and] IEEE Communications Society*, *2*(2), 40–46. doi:10.1109/MPRV.2003.1203752.

Byunggil, L., & Howon, K. (2007). Privacy management for medical service application using mobile phone collaborated with RFID reader. Paper presented at the Third International IEEE Conference on the Signal-Image Technologies and Internet-Based System, 2007. New York, NY.

Calvert, J., Hollander-Rodriguez, J., & Atlas, M. (2008). What are the repercussions of disclosing a medical error? *The Journal of Family Practice*, *57*(2), 124–125. PMID:18248735.

Dourish, P., Grinter, R., Delgado de la Flor, J., & Joseph, M. (2004). Security in the wild: user strategies for managing security as an everyday, practical problem. *Personal and Ubiquitous Computing*, *8*(6), 391–401. doi:10.1007/s00779-004-0308-5.

Eklund, J. M., Hansen, T. R., Sprinkle, J., & Sastry, S. (2005). Information technology for assisted living at home: Building a wireless infrastructure for assisted living. Paper presented at the 27th Annual International Conference of the Engineering in Medicine and Biology Society, 2005. New York, NY.

Elkhodr, M., Shahrestani, S., & Cheung, H. (2011). Ubiquitous health monitoring systems: Addressing security concerns. *Journal of Computer Science*, *7*(10), 1465–1473. doi:10.3844/jcssp.2011.1465.1473.

Guo, Y.-J., Hong, F., Zhang, Q.-G., & Li, R. (2005). An access control model for ubiquitous computing application. Paper presented at the 2nd International Conference on Mobile Technology, Applications and Systems, 2005. New York, NY.

Hess, A. (2003). *Content-triggered trust negotiation*. Provo, UT: Brigham Young University.

Hong, J. I., Ng, J. D., Lederer, S., & Landay, J. A. (2004). Privacy risk models for designing privacy-sensitive ubiquitous computing systems. Paper presented at the 5th Conference on Designing Interactive Systems: Processes, Practices, Methods, and Techniques. New York, NY.

Kargl, F., Lawrence, E., Fischer, M., & Yen Yang, L. (2008). Security, privacy and legal issues in pervasive ehealth monitoring systems. Paper presented at 7th International Conference on the Mobile Business, 2008. New York, NY.

Kawaguchi, A., Russell, S., & Guoliang, Q. (2003). Security issues in the development of a wireless blood-glucose monitoring system. Paper presented at the 16th IEEE Symposium Computer-Based Medical Systems, 2003. New York, NY.

Kim, J., Choi, H.-S., Wang, H., Agoulmine, N., Deerv, M. J., & Hong, J. W.-K. (2010). POSTECH's u-health smart home for elderly monitoring and support. Paper presented at the World of Wireless Mobile and Multimedia Networks (WoWMoM). New York, NY.

Langheinrich, M. (2001). Privacy by design - Principles of privacy-aware ubiquitous systems. Paper presented at the 3rd International Conference on Ubiquitous Computing. New York, NY.

Lederer, S., Dey, A. K., & Mankoff, J. (2002). *A conceptual model and a metaphor of everyday privacy in ubiquitous*. Berkeley, CA: University of California at Berkeley.

Malasri, K., & Wang, L. (2007). Addressing security in medical sensor networks. Paper presented at the 1st ACM SIGMOBILE International Workshop on Systems and Networking Support for Healthcare and Assisted Living Environments. New York, NY.

Marx, G. T. (2001). Identity and anonymity: Some conceptual distinctions and issues for research. Retrieved from http://web.mit.edu/gtmarx/www/identity.html

Meingast, M., Roosta, T., & Sastry, S. (2006). Security and privacy issues with health care information technology. Paper presented at the Engineering in Medicine and Biology Society, 2006. New York, NY.

Mitseva, A., Wardana, S. A., & Prasad, N. R. (2008). Context-aware privacy protection for wireless sensor networks in hybrid hierarchical architecture. Paper presented at the Wireless Communications and Mobile Computing Conference, 2008. New York, NY.

Moncrieff, S., Venkatesh, S., & West, G. (2009). A framework for the design of privacy preserving pervasive healthcare. Paper presented at the IEEE International Conference on Multimedia and Expo, 2009. New York, NY.

Ninghui, L., Mitchell, J. C., & Winsborough, W. H. (2002). Design of a role-based trust-management framework. Paper presented at the IEEE Symposium on Security and Privacy, 2002. New York, NY.

Pallapa, G., Roy, N., & Das, S. (2007). Precision: Privacy enhanced context-aware information fusion in ubiquitous healthcare. Paper presented at First International Workshop on the Software Engineering for Pervasive Computing Applications, Systems, and Environments, 2007. New York, NY.

Piramuthu, S. (2008). Lightweight cryptographic authentication in passive RFID-tagged systems. *IEEE Transactions on Systems, Man and Cybernetics. Part C, Applications and Reviews*, *38*(3), 360–376. doi:10.1109/TSMCC.2007.913918.

Price, B. A., Adam, K., & Nuseibeh, B. (2005). Keeping ubiquitous computing to yourself: A practical model for user control of privacy. *International Journal of Human-Computer Studies*, *63*(1-2), 228–253. doi:10.1016/j.ijhcs.2005.04.008.

Seamons, K. E., Winslett, M., Ting, Y., Smith, B., Child, E., Jacobson, J., et al. (2002). Requirements for policy languages for trust negotiation. Paper presented at the Third International Workshop on Policies for Distributed Systems and Networks, 2002. New York, NY.

Serjantov, A., & Danezis, G. (2003). Towards an information theoretic metric for anonymity. Paper presented at the 2nd International Conference on Privacy Enhancing Technologies. New York, NY.

KEY TERMS AND DEFINITIONS

E-Health: Also written e-health, eHealth, and E-health, is an acronym for Electronic health and a term used for managing health information in the digital world during their digital storage, electronic process and communication.

EHR: Stands for Electronic Health Record. EHR is also known as EPR (Electronic Patient Record) and EMR (electronic medical record). The term represents a patient's health record or his or her information in digital format.

IMEI: The International Mobile Equipment Identity is a unique number used to identify mobile devices. PKI: Public Key Infrastructure is a system for the handling digital certificates which are used to verify that a particular public key belongs to a certain party.

RBAC: Role-Based Access Control (RBAC) is a flexible access control technology that restricts system access to authorized users based on their functions or roles.

TLS: Transport Layer Security (TLS) is a cryptographic protocol that provides communication security over the Internet.

Trust Negotiation: It is a process of establishing trust between two negotiating entities based on their credentials or attributes rather than their identities.

Compilation of References

15. Chapter, U. S. C. 103. (2011). Commerce and trade. Retrieved from http://uscode.house.gov/download/pls/15C103.txt

3G. Americas. (2008). Security and trust in mobile applications. Technical Report. Retrieved September 16, 2012, from http://www.gemalto.com/telecom/download/security_trust_in_mobile_applications.pdf

AAP. (2005). NSW speed cameras in doubt. The Age. Retrieved March 27, 2012, from http://www.theage.com.au/articles/2005/08/10/1123353368652.html

Abe, M., & Imai, H. (2003). Flaws in some robust optimistic mix-nets. In Proceedings of ACISP 2003, (Vol. 2727, pp. 39-50). Berlin, Germany: Springer.

Abe, M., & Suzuki, K. (2002). M+1-st price auction using homomorphic encryption. In Proceedings of Public Key Cryptology 2002, (Vol. 2288, pp. 115-124). Berlin, Germany: Springer-Verlag.

Abe, M. (1999). Mix-networks on permutation net-works. In *Proceedings of Asiacrypt 1998* (*Vol. 1716*, pp. 258–273). Berlin, Germany: Springer-Verlag.

Abe, M., & Hoshino, F. (2001). Remarks on mix-network based on permutation networks. In *Proceedings of Public Key Cryptography 2001* (*Vol. 1992*, pp. 317–324). Berlin, Germany: Springer-Verlag. doi:10.1007/3-540-44586-2_23.

Aditya, R., Peng, K., Boyd, C., & Dawson, E. (2004). Batch verification for equality of discrete logarithms and threshold decryptions. In Proceedings of the Second Conference of Applied Cryptography and Network Security, ACNS 04, (Vol. 3089, pp. 494-508). Berlin, Germany: Springer-Verlag.

Adler, J. M., Dai, W., Green, R. L., & Ne, C. A. (2000). Computational details of the vote here homomorphic election system. VoteHere Inc. Retrieved from http://www.votehere.net/technicaldocs/hom.pdf

Agosta, G., Barenghi, A., & Pelosi, G. (2012). A code morphing methodology to automate power analysis countermeasures. In Proceedings of the Design Automation Conference, (pp. 77–82). IEEE Press.

Agrawal, R., & Srikant, R. (2000). Privacy-preserving data mining. In Proceedings of the 2000 ACM SIGMOD on Management of Data, (pp. 439–450). ACM Press.

Agrawal, R., Evfimievski, A., & Srikant, R. (2003). Paper. In Proceedings of the 2003 ACM SIGMOD International Conference on Management of Data, (pp. 86-97). ACM Press.

Agrawal, R., Kiernan, J., Srikant, R., & Xu, Y. (2004). Order preserving encryption for numeric data. In Proceedings of the 2004 ACM SIGMOD International Conference on Management of Data, (pp. 563–574). ACM.

Agrawal, D., Archambeault, B., Rao, R., & Rohatgi, P. (2002). The EM side- channel(s). *Lecture Notes in Computer Science*, *2523*, 29–45. doi:10.1007/3-540-36400-5_4.

Aho, Sethi, & Ullman. (1986). Compilers: Principles, techniques, and tools. Reading, MA: Addison-Wesley.

Aitken, R., Leveugle, R., Metra, C., & Nicoladis, M. (Eds.). (2006). 12th IEEE international on-line testing symposium (IOLTS 2006). Como, Italy: IEEE Computer Society.

Ajayi, O., Sinnott, R., & Stell, A. (2007). Formalising dynamic trust negotiations in decentralised collaborative e-health systems. Paper presented at the the Second International Conference on Availability, Reliability and Security, 2007. ARES 2007. New York, NY.

Akinyele, J. A., Pagano, M. W., Green, M. D., Lehmann, C. U., Peterson, Z. N. J., & Rubin, A. D. (2011). Securing electronic medical records using attribute-based encryption on mobile devices. Paper presented at the 1st ACM Workshop on Security and Privacy in Smartphones and Mobile Devices. New York, NY.

Akyildiz, I. F., Su, W., Sankarasubramaniam, Y., & Cayirci, E. (2002). A survey on sensor networks. *IEEE Communications Magazine*, *40*(8), 102–114. doi:10.1109/MCOM.2002.1024422.

Alam, M., Zhang, X., Nauman, M., Ali, T., & Seifert, J. (2008). Model-based behavioral attestation. In Proceedings of the 13th ACM Symposium on Access Control Models and Technologies, (pp. 175-184). ACM.

Alghafli, K., Jones, A., & Martin, T. (2011). Forensic analysis of the Windows 7 registry. Journal of Digital Forensics, Security and Law, 5(4).

Alioto, M., Giancane, L., Scotti, G., & Trifiletti, A. (2010a). Leakage power analysis attacks: A novel class of attacks to nanometer cryptographic circuits. *IEEE Transactions on Circuits and Systems. I, Regular Papers*, *57*(2), 355–367. doi:10.1109/TCSI.2009.2019411.

Alioto, M., Poli, M., & Rocchi, S. (2010b). A general power model of differential power analysis attacks to static logic circuits. IEEE Transactions on Very Large Scale Integration (VLSI). *Systems*, *18*(5), 711–724.

Allaert, F. A., Le Teuff, G., Quantin, C., & Barber, B. (2004). The legal acknowledgement of the electronic signature: A key for a secure direct access of patients to their computerised medical record. *International Journal of Medical Informatics*, *73*(3), 239–242. doi:10.1016/j.ijmedinf.2003.11.007 PMID:15066553.

Allman, E., Callas, J., Delany, M., Libbey, M., Fenton, J., & Thomas, M. (2007). DomainKeys identified mail (DKIM) signatures. RFC. Retrieved from http://tools.ietf.org/html/rfc4871

Allman, E., Fenton, J., Delany, M., & Levine, J. (2009). DomainKeys identified mail (DKIM) author domain signing practices (ADSP). RFC. Retrieved from http://tools.ietf.org/html/rfc5617

Alonso-Fernandez, F., Fierrez-Aguilar, J., & Ortega-Garcia, J. (2005). An enhanced gabor filter-based segmentation algorithm for fingerprint recognition systems. In Proceedings of the 4th International Symposium on Image and Signal Processing and Analysis, (pp. 239-244). IEEE.

AlSa'deh, A., Rafiee, H., & Meinel, C. (2012a). Stopping time condition for practical IPv6 cryptographically generated addresses. In Proceedings of 2012 International Conference on Information Networking, ICOIN 2012, (pp. 257-262). Bali, Indonesia: IEEE.

AlSa'deh, A., Rafiee, H., & Meinel, C. (2012b). Cryptographically generated addresses (CGAs): Possible attacks and proposed mitigation approaches. In Proceedings of 12th IEEE International Conference on Computer and Information Technology (IEEE CIT' 12). Chengdu, China: IEEE.

Alvarez, G., & Li, S. (2006). Some basic cryptographic requirements for chaos-based cryptosystems. *International Journal of Bifurcation and Chaos in Applied Sciences and Engineering*, *16*, 2129–2151. doi:10.1142/S0218127406015970.

AMD. (2005). AMD64 virtualization codenamed ''pacifica'' technology. Publication No. 33047. Secure Virtual Machine Architecture Reference Manual, Revision 3.01.

Amirbekyan, A., & Estivill-Castro, V. (2009). Practical protocol for Yao's millionaires problem enables secure multiparty computation of metrics and efficient privacy-preserving k-NN for large data sets. *Knowledge and Information Systems*, *21*, 327–363. doi:10.1007/s10115-009-0233-z.

Anderson, R., & Kuhn, M. (1996). Tamper resistance: A cautionary note. Retrieved from http://www.cl.cam.ac.uk/~rja14/tamper.html

Andersson, G., Donalek, P., Farmer, R., Hatziargyriou, N., Kamwa, I., & Kundur, P. et al. (2005). Causes of the 2003 major grid blackouts in North America and Europe, and recommended means to improve system dynamic performance. *IEEE Transactions on Power Systems*, *20*(4), 1922–1928. doi:10.1109/TPWRS.2005.857942.

Android Developers. (2009). Website. Retrieved from http://developer.android.com/index.html

Antonelli, A., Capelli, R., Maio, D., & Maltoni, D. (2006). Fake finger detection by skin distortion analysis. *IEEE Transactions on Information Forensics and Security*, *1*, 360–373. doi:10.1109/TIFS.2006.879289.

APCO. (2007). Good practice guide for computer-based electronic evidence. Retrieved April 25, 2012, from http://7safe.com/electronic_evidence/ACPO_guidelines_computer_evidence_v4_web.pdf

Arends, R., Austein, R., Larson, M., Massey, D., & Rose, S. (2005). DNS security introduction and requirements. RFC. Retrieved March 2005, from http://www.ietf.org/rfc/rfc4033.txt

Arends, R., Austein, R., Larson, M., Massey, D., & Rose, S. (2005). RFC 4033 - DNS security introduction and requirements. Retrieved from http://www.rfc-editor.org/

Ariyapperuma, S., & Mitchell, C. J. (2007). Security vulnerabilities in DNS and DNSSEC. In Proceedings of the Second International Conference on Availability, Reliability and Security. ACM. Retrieved from http://dl.acm.org/citation.cfm?id=1250514

Arkko, J., Kempf, J., Zill, B., & Nikander, P. (2005). Secure neighbor discovery (SEND). RFC 3971. Retrieved from http://tools.ietf.org/html/rfc3971

Armknecht, F., Gasmi, Y., Sadeghi, A.-R., Stewin, P., Unger, M., Ramunno, G., et al. (2008). An efficient implementation of trusted channels based on OpenSSL. In: Proceedings of the 3rd ACM Workshop on Scalable Trusted Computing, (pp. 41-50). ACM.

Asokan, N., & Tarkkala, L. (2005). Issues in initializing security. Paper presented at the Fifth IEEE International Symposium on Signal Processing and Information Technology, 2005. New York, NY.

Atallah, M. J., & Du, W. (2001). Secure multiparty computational geometry. In Proceedings of 7th International Workshop on Algorithms and Data Structures, (pp. 165-179). IEEE.

Ateniese, G., Kamara, S., & Katz, J. (2009). Proofs of storage from homomorphic identification protocols. *Lecture Notes in Computer Science*, *5912*, 319–333. doi:10.1007/978-3-642-10366-7_19.

Atiskov, A. J., & Perminov, V. I. (2007). Adaptive hybrid technology of business-process modeling. SPIIRAS Proceedings, 4(1).

Atiskov, A. J. (2008). Integration of business-process modeling with object-oriented designing using hybrid technology of transformation. Informational. *Measuring and Controlling Systems*, *6*(4), 18–20.

Atiskov, A. J. (2012). *Transformation functional diagrams into UML diagrams*. Saarbrucken, Germany: LAP LAMBERT Academic Publishing GmbH & Co..

Attrapadung, N., Furukawa, J., & Imai, H. (2006). Forward-secure and searchable broadcast encryption with short ciphertexts and private keys. [Springer.]. *Proceedings of Advances in Cryptology–ASIACRYPT*, *2006*, 161–177.

Aumuller, C., Bier, P., Fischer, W., Hofreiter, P., & Seifert, J.-P. (2002). Fault attacks on RSA with CRT: Concrete results and practical countermeasures. *Lecture Notes in Computer Science*, *2523*, 260–275. doi:10.1007/3-540-36400-5_20.

Aura, T. (2005). Cryptographically generated addresses (CGA). RFC 3972. Retrieved from http://tools.ietf.org/html/rfc3972

Aura, T. (2003). Cryptographically generated addresses (CGA). *Lecture Notes in Computer Science*, *2851*, 29–43. doi:10.1007/10958513_3.

Australian Hospital. (2010). Australian hospital statistics 2008–09. Canberra, Australia: Australian Institute of Health and Welfare.

Babenko, L. K., & Ishchukova, E. A. (2010). Differential analysis GOST encryption algorithm. In Proceedings of the 3rd International Conference of Security of Information and Networks, (pp. 149-157). New York, NY: Association for Computing Machinery, Inc.

Babenko, L. K., Ishchukova, E. A., & Maro, E. A. (2011). Algebraic analysis of GOST encryption algorithm. In Proceedings of the 4th International Conference of Security of Information and Networks, (pp. 57-62). New York, NY: Association for Computing Machinery, Inc.

Babler, W. (1991). *Dermatoglyphics: Science in transition* (*Vol. 9*). New York, NY: Wiley-Liss.

Baek, J., Safavi-Naini, R., & Susilo, W. (2006). On the integration of public key data encryption and public key encryption with keyword search. *Lecture Notes in Computer Science*, *4176*, 217–232. doi:10.1007/11836810_16.

Baek, J., Safavi-Naini, R., & Susilo, W. (2008). Public key encryption with keyword search revisited. *Lecture Notes in Computer Science*, *5072*, 1249–1259. doi:10.1007/978-3-540-69839-5_96.

Baldiserra, D., Franco, A., Maio, D., & Maltoni, D. (2006). Fake fingerprint detection by odor analysis. Paper presented at International Conference on Biometrics. New York, NY.

Bansal, R., Sehgal, P., & Bedi, P. (2010). Effective morphological extraction of true fingerprint minutiae based on the hit or miss transform. *International Journal of Biometrics and Bioinformatics*, *4*(2), 71–85.

Bao, F., Deng, R. H., Ding, X., & Yang, Y. (2008). Private query on encrypted data in multi-user settings. *Lecture Notes in Computer Science*, *4991*, 71–85. doi:10.1007/978-3-540-79104-1_6.

Bard, G. V. (2009). *Algebraic cryptanalysis*. New York, NY: Springer. doi:10.1007/978-0-387-88757-9.

Bar-El, H., Choukri, H., Naccache, D., Tunstall, M., & Whelan, C. (2006). The sorcerer's apprentice guide to fault attacks. *Proceedings of the IEEE*, *94*(2), 370–382. doi:10.1109/JPROC.2005.862424.

Barenghi, A., Bertoni, G., Parrinello, E., & Pelosi, G. (2009). Low voltage fault attacks on the RSA cryptosystem. Retrieved from http://home.dei.polimi.it/barenghi/files/FDTC2009.pdf

Barenghi, A., Bertoni, G., Santis, F. D., & Melzani, F. (2011a). On the efficiency of design time evaluation of the resistance to power attacks. In Proceedings of DSD, (pp. 777-785). IEEE Press.

Barenghi, A., Pelosi, G., & Teglia, Y. (2010b). Improving first order differential power attacks through digital signal processing. In Proceedings of the 3rd International Conference on Security of Information and Networks, (pp. 124-133). ACM Press.

Barenghi, A., Bertoni, G. M., Breveglieri, L., Pelosi, G., & Palomba, A. (2011b). Fault attack to the elliptic curve digital signature algorithm with multiple bit faults.[ACM Press.]. *Proceedings of SIN*, *2011*, 63–72.

Barenghi, A., Pelosi, G., & Teglia, Y. (2011c). Information leakage discovery techniques to enhance secure chip design. *Lecture Notes in Computer Science*, *6633*, 128–143. doi:10.1007/978-3-642-21040-2_9.

Barrows, R., & Clayton, P. (1996). Privacy, confidentiality, and electronic medical records. *Journal of the American Medical Informatics Association*, *3*(2), 139–148. doi:10.1136/jamia.1996.96236282 PMID:8653450.

Barua, M., Liang, X., Lu, R., & Shen, X. (2011). ESPAC: Enabling security and patient-centric access control for ehealth in cloud computing. *International Journal of Security and Networks*, *6*(2), 67–76. doi:10.1504/IJSN.2011.043666.

Baudron, O., Fouque, P.-A., Pointcheval, D., Stern, J., & Poupard, G. (2001). Practical multi-candidate election system. In Proceedings of the Twentieth Annual ACM Symposium on Principles of Distributed Computing, (p. 274-283). ACM.

Bayardo, R., & Agrawal, R. (2005). Data privacy through optimal k-anonymization. In Proceedings the 21st International Conference on Data Engineering, (pp. 217-228). IEEE.

Bazen, A. M., & Gerez, S. H. (2002a). Elastic minutiae matching by means of thin-plate spline models. Paper presented at ICPR 2002. New York, NY.

Bazen, A. M., & Gerez, S. H. (2002c). Thin-plate spline modelling of elastic deformations in fingerprints. Paper presented at SPS 2002. New York, NY.

Bazen, A. M., & Gerez, S. H. (2002b). Fingerprint matching by thin-plate spline modelling of elastic deformations. *Pattern Recognition*, 36.

Bazen, A. M., & Gerez, S. H. (2002d). Systematic methods for the computation of the directional fields and singular points of fingerprints. *IEEE Transactions on Pattern Analysis and Machine Intelligence*, *24*(7), 905–919. doi:10.1109/TPAMI.2002.1017618.

Beaver, D. (2000). Minimal-latency secure function evaluation. In *Proceedings of Eurocrypt '00* (*Vol. 1807*, pp. 335–350). Berlin, Germany: Springer.

Beck, F., Cholez, T., Festor, O., & Chrisment, I. (2007). Monitoring the neighbor discovery protocol. In Proceedings of the International Multi-Conference on Computing in the Global Information Technology, (pp. 57-62). IEEE.

Becker, T., & Weispfenning, V. (1993). *Gröbner bases: A computational approach to commutative algebra (corrected edition)*. New York, NY: Springer–Verlag.

Beimel, A. (1996). Secure schemes for secret sharing and key distribution. (PhD Thesis). Israel Institute of Technology. Haiifa, Israel.

Bellare, M., Boldyreva, A., & O'Neill, A. (2007). Deterministic and efficiently searchable encryption. *Lecture Notes in Computer Science*, *4622*, 535–552. doi:10.1007/978-3-540-74143-5_30.

Bellare, M., Garay, J. A., & Rabin, T. (1998). Fast batch verification for modular exponentiation and digital signatures. In *Proceedings of Eurocrypt '98* (*Vol. 1403*, pp. 236–250). Berlin, Germany: Springer-Verlag. doi:10.1007/BFb0054130.

Bello, L. (2008). DSA-1571-1 Openssl – Predictable random number generator. Debian Project. Retrieved April 22, 2012, from http://www.debian.org/security/2008/dsa-1571

Bellovin, S. M. (1995). Using the domain name system for system break-ins. In Proceedings of the Fifth Usenix Unix Security Symposium. IEEE.

Benaloh, J. (1994). Dense probabilistic encryption. In Proceedings of the Workshop on Selected Areas of Cryptography, (pp. 120-128). IEEE.

Benenson, Z. (2006). TrustedPals: Secure multiparty computation implemented with smart cards. In Proceedings of the 11th European Symposium on Research in Computer Security (ESORICS 2006), (pp. 306-314). ESORICS.

Bergmann, J., Bott, O. J., Pretschner, D. P., & Haux, R. (2007). An e-consent-based shared EHR system architecture for integrated healthcare networks. *International Journal of Medical Informatics*, *76*(2-3), 130. doi:10.1016/j.ijmedinf.2006.07.013 PMID:16971171.

Berners-Lee, T., Hendler, J., & Lassila, O. (2001). The semantic web: A new form of web content that is meaningful to computers will unleash a revolution of new possibilities. *Scientific American*, *5*, 34–43. doi:10.1038/scientificamerican0501-34.

Bernstein, D. (2005). Cache-timing attacks on AES. Technical Report. Retrieved from http://cr.yp.to/antiforgery/cachetiming-20050414.pdf

Bertino, E., Ferrari, E., & Squicciarini, A. C. (2004). Trust-&Xscr: A peer-to-peer framework for trust establishment. *IEEE Transactions on Knowledge and Data Engineering*, *16*(7), 827–842. doi:10.1109/TKDE.2004.1318565.

Bethencourt, J., Sahai, A., & Waters, B. (2007). Ciphertext-policy attribute-based encryption. In Proceedings of the IEEE Symposium on Security and Privacy, (pp. 321-334). IEEE Press.

Bharadwaj, V. G., & Baras, J. S. (2003). Towards automated negotiation of access control policies. Paper presented at the IEEE 4th International Workshop on Policies for Distributed Systems and Networks, 2003. New York, NY.

Biagioni, E., & Bridges, K. (2002). The application of remote sensor technology to assist the recovery of rare and endangered species. *International Journal of High Performance Computing Applications*, *16*(3). doi:10.1177/10943420020160031001.

Biham, E., & Shamir, A. (1991). Differential cryptanalysis of DES-like cryptosystems. *Journal of Cryptology*, *4*(1), 3–72. doi:10.1007/BF00630563.

Biham, E., & Shamir, A. (1992). Differential cryptanalysis of the full 16-round DES. *Lecture Notes in Computer Science*, *740*, 487–496. doi:10.1007/3-540-48071-4_34.

Binns, P. (2004). The impact of the electronic health record on patient safety: An Alberta perspective. *Healthcare Papers*, *5*(3), 47–51. PMID:16278536.

Biryukov, A., & Wagner, D. (1999). Slide attacks. *Lecture Notes in Computer Science*, *1636*, 245–259. doi:10.1007/3-540-48519-8_18.

Biryukov, A., & Wagner, D. (2000). Advanced slide attacks. *Lecture Notes in Computer Science*, *1807*, 589–606. doi:10.1007/3-540-45539-6_41.

Blaha, M., & Rumbaugh, J. (2005). *Object-oriented modeling and design with UML* (2nd ed.). Upper Saddle River, NJ: Pearson Prentice Hall.

Blaze, M., Feigenbaum, J., Ioannidis, J., & Keromytis, A. D. (1999). RFC 2704 – The keynote trust management system version 2. Retrieved from http://www.ietf.org/rfc/rfc2704.txt

Bleichenbacher, D., & Nguyen, P. (2000). Noisy polynomial interpolation and noisy Chinese remaindering. [EURO-CRYPT.]. *Proceedings of EURO-CRYPT, 2000*, 53–69.

Blobel, B. (2006). Advanced and secure architectural EHR approaches. *International Journal of Medical Informatics*, *75*(3-4), 185. doi:10.1016/j.ijmedinf.2005.07.017 PMID:16112891.

Blobel, B., & Roger-France, F. (2001). A systematic approach for analysis and design of secure health information systems. *International Journal of Medical Informatics*, *62*(1), 51–78. doi:10.1016/S1386-5056(01)00147-2 PMID:11340006.

Bobba, R., Fatemieh, O., Khan, F., Gunter, C. A., & Khurana, H. (2006). Using attribute-based access control to enable attribute-based messaging. In Proceedings of ACSAC, (pp. 403-413). IEEE Computer Society.

Bock, C. (1999a). Three kinds of behavior model. *Journal of Object-Oriented Programming*, *12*(4).

Bock, C. (1999b). Unified behavior models. *Journal of Object-Oriented Programming*, *12*(5).

Bogdanov, A., Khovratovich, D., & Rechberger, C. (2011). Biclique cryptanalysis of the full AES. In D. Lee & X. Wang (Eds.), 17thInternational Conference on the Theory and Application of Cryptology and Information Security – AsiaCrypt, (pp. 344-371). Berlin, Germany: Springer.

Boldyreva, A., Chenette, N., Lee, Y., & O'Neill, A. (2009). Order-preserving symmetric encryption. *Lecture Notes in Computer Science*, *5479*, 224–241. doi:10.1007/978-3-642-01001-9_13.

Boneh, D., DeMillo, R., & Lipton, R. (2001). On the importance of checking cryptographic protocols for faults. *Journal of Cryptology*, *14*(2), 101–119. doi:10.1007/s001450010016.

Boneh, D., Di Crescenzo, G., Ostrovsky, R., & Persiano, G. (2004). Public key encryption with keyword search. *Lecture Notes in Computer Science*, *3027*, 506–522. doi:10.1007/978 3 540-24676-3_30.

Boneh, D., & Franklin, M. (2003). Identity-based encryption from the weil pairing. *SIAM Journal on Computing*, *32*, 586–615. doi:10.1137/S0097539701398521.

Boneh, D., Kushilevitz, E., Ostrovsky, R., & Skeith, W. E. III. (2007). Public key encryption that allows PIR queries. *Lecture Notes in Computer Science*, *4622*, 50–67. doi:10.1007/978-3-540-74143-5_4.

Boneh, D., Sahai, A., & Waters, B. (2011). Functional encryption: Definitions and challenges. *Lecture Notes in Computer Science*, *6597*, 253–273. doi:10.1007/978-3-642-19571-6_16.

Boneh, D., & Waters, B. (2007). Conjunctive, subset, and range queries on encrypted data. *Lecture Notes in Computer Science*, *4392*, 535–554. doi:10.1007/978-3-540-70936-7_29.

Boonkrong, S., & Bradford, R. (2004). Authentication in mobile ad hoc networks. In Proceedings of the 1st Thailand Computer Science Conference (ThCSC), (pp. 202-207). ThCSC.

Bos, J. W., Özen, O., & Hubaux, J. P. (2009). Analysis and optimization of cryptographically generated addresses. In Proceedings of the 12th International Conference on Information Security, (pp. 17-32). Pisa, Italy: Springer-Verlag.

Bosch, C., Tang, Q., Hartel, P., & Jonker, W. (2012). Selective document retrieval from encrypted databse. *Lecture Notes in Computer Science*, *7483*, 224–241. doi:10.1007/978-3-642-33383-5_14.

Boudot, F. (2000). Efficient proofs that a committed number lies in an interval. In Proceedings of the Eurocrypt 2000, (Vol. 1807, pp. 431-444). Berlin, Germany: Springer-Verlag.

Boukerche, A., Camara, D., Loureiro, A., & Figueiredo, C. (2009). Algorithms for mobile ad hoc networks. In Boukerche, A. (Ed.), *Algorithms and Protocols for Wireless and Mobile Ad Hoc Networks*. New York, NY: John Wiley & Sons, Inc..

Bowers, K. D., Juels, A., & Oprea, A. (2009). Proofs of retrievability: Theory and implementation. In Proceedings of the 2009 ACM Workshop on Cloud Computing Security, (pp. 43–54). ACM Press.

Boyen, X. (2007). Mesh signatures. *Lecture Notes in Computer Science*, *4515*, 210–227. doi:10.1007/978-3-540-72540-4_12.

Brakerski, Z., Gentry, C., & Vaikuntanathan, V. (2012). Fully homomorphic encryption without bootstrapping. In Proceedings of Innovations in Theoretical Computer Science (ITCS 2012). ITCS.

Brier, E., Clavier, C., & Olivier, F. (2004). Correlation power analysis with a leakage model. Retrieved from http://www.iacr.org/archive/ches2004/31560016/31560016.pdf

Brownfield, M. I. (2006). Energy-efficient wireless sensor network MAC protocol. (Doctoral Dissertation). Virginia Polytechnic Institute and State University. Blacksburg, VA.

Bulygin, S. (2011). Algebraic cryptanalysis of the round-reduced and side channel analysis of the full PRINTCipher-48. Retrieved May 31, 2011 from http://eprint.iacr.org/2011/287.pdf

Byun, J. W., Rhee, H. S., Park, H., & Lee, D. H. (2006). Off-line keyword guessing attacks on recent keyword search schemes over encrypted data. *Lecture Notes in Computer Science*, *4165*, 75–83. doi:10.1007/11844662_6.

Cabiddu, G., Cesena, E., Sassu, R., Vernizzi, D., Ramunno, G., & Lioy, A. (2011). The trusted platform agent. *IEEE Software*, *28*(2), 35–41. doi:10.1109/MS.2010.160.

Cachin, C. (1999). Efficient private bidding and auctions with an oblivious third party. In Proceedings of the 6th ACM Conference on Computer and Communications Security. ACM.

Cachin, C., & Camenisch, J. (2000). Optimistic fair secure computation (extended abstract). In *Proceedings of Crypto '00* (*Vol. 1880*, pp. 94–112). Berlin, Germany: Springer-Verlag.

Cachin, C., Micali, S., & Stadler, M. (1999). Computationally private information retrieval with polylogarithmic communication. *Lecture Notes in Computer Science*, *1592*, 402–414. doi:10.1007/3-540-48910-X_28.

Callas, J., Donnerhacke, L., Finney, H., Shaw, D., & Thayer, R. (2007). RFC 4880 - OpenPGP message format. Retrieved from http://www.rfc-editor.org/

Canetti, R. (2000). Security and composition of multiparty cryptographic protocols. *Journal of Cryptology*, *13*(1), 143–202. doi:10.1007/s001459910006.

Canetti, R., Dwork, C., Naor, M., & Ostrovsky, R. (1997). Deniable encryption. In *Proceedings of Crypto 1997* (*Vol. 1294*, pp. 90–104). Berlin, Germany: Springer-Verlag.

Capkun, S., Hubaux, J.-P., & Buttyan, L. (2003). Mobility helps security in ad hoc networks. In Proceedings of the 4th ACM International Symposium on Mobile ad Hoc Networking & Computing (MobiHoc). ACM Press.

Capkun, S., Buttyan, L., & Hubaux, J.-P. (2003). Self-organized public-key management for mobile ad hoc networks. *IEEE Transactions on Mobile Computing*, *2*(1). doi:10.1109/TMC.2003.1195151.

Capkun, S., Hubaux, J.-P., & Buttyan, L. (2006). Mobility helps peer-to-peer security. *IEEE Transactions on Mobile Computing*, *5*(1), 43–51. doi:10.1109/TMC.2006.12.

Cappelli, R., Maio, D., & Maltoni, D. (2001). Modelling plastic distortion in fingerprint images. Paper presented at the International Conference on Advances in Pattern Recognition. New York, NY.

Cappelli, R. (2003). *Handbook of fingerprint recognition*. New York, NY: Springer.

Cassady, R. Jr. (1967). *Auctions and auctioneering*. Berkeley, CA: University of California Press.

Castelluccia, C. (2007). Securing very dynamic groups and data aggregation in wireless sensor networks. In Proceedings of the IEEE Internatonal Conference on Mobile Adhoc and Sensor Systems, (pp. 1-9). IEEE.

Castelluccia, C., Saxena, N., & Yi, J.-H. (2005). Self-configurable key pre-distribution in mobile ad hoc networks. In Proceedings of the 4th IFIP-TC6 International Conference on Networking Technologies, Services, and Protocols. IFIP.

Castelluccia, C. (2005). Efficient aggregation of encrypted data in wireless sensor networks. In *Proceedings of MobiQuitous* (pp. 109–117). IEEE Computer Society. doi:10.1109/MOBIQUITOUS.2005.25.

Chai, Q., & Gong, G. (2011). *Verifiable symmetric searchable encryption for semi-honest-but-curious cloud services. Technical Report CACR 2011-22.* Ontario, Canada: University of Waterloo.

Chang, B. J., Kuo, S. L., Liang, Y. H., & Wang, D. Y. (2008). Markov chain-based trust model for analyzing trust value in distributed multicasting mobile ad hoc networks. In Proceedings of the IEEE Asia-Pacific Services Computing Conference, (pp. 156-161). IEEE.

Chang, S. H., Cheng, F. H., Hsu, W. H., & Wu, G. Z. (1997). Fast algorithm for point pattern-matching: Invariant to translations, rotations and scale changes. *Pattern Recognition*, *30*(2), 311–320. doi:10.1016/S0031-3203(96)00076-3.

Chang, Y., & Lu, C. (2001). Oblivious polynomial evaluation and oblivious neural learning. In *Proceedings of Theoretical Computer Science* (pp. 369–384). IEEE. doi:10.1007/3-540-45682-1_22.

Chang, Y., & Mitzenmacher, M. (2005). Privacy preserving keyword searches on remote encrypted data. *Lecture Notes in Computer Science*, *3531*, 442–455. doi:10.1007/11496137_30.

Chan, H., & Perrig, A. (2003). Security and privacy in sensor networks. *IEEE Computer*, *36*(10), 103–105. doi:10.1109/MC.2003.1236475.

Charnes, C., O'Connor, L., Pieprzyk, J., Safavi-Naini, R., & Zheng, Y. (1994). *Further comments on GOST encryption algorithm.* Wollongong, Australia: The University of Wollongong.

Chase, M. (2007). Multi-authority attribute based encryption. Paper presented at the 4th Conference on Theory of Cryptography. New York, NY.

Chase, M., & Kamara, S. (2010). Structured encryption and controlled disclosure. *Lecture Notes in Computer Science*, *6477*, 577–594. doi:10.1007/978-3-642-17373-8_33.

Chaum, D., & Van Heyst, E. (1991). Group signatures. In Proceedings of the 10th Annual International Conference on Theory and Application of Cryptographic Techniques, EUROCRYPT 1991, (pp. 257–265). Berlin, Germany: Springer-Verlag.

Chaum, D., Crepeau, C., & Damgard, I. (1988). Multiparty unconditionally secure protocols. In Proceedings of the 20th ACM Symposium on the Theory of Computing, (pp. 11-19). ACM Press.

Chaum, D., & Pedersen, T. P. (1992). Wallet databases with observers. In *Proceedings of Crypto '92* (*Vol. 740*, pp. 89–105). Berlin, Germany: Springer-Verlag.

Chen, C.-L., Lee, C.-C., & Hsu, C.-Y. (2012). Mobile device integration of a fingerprint biometric remote authentication scheme. *International Journal of Communication Systems*, *25*, 585–597. doi:10.1002/dac.1277.

Cheneau, T. (2011). NDprotector an implementation of CGA & SEND that works on Linux. Retrieved from http://amnesiak.org/NDprotector/

Cheneau, T., Boudguiga, A., & Laurent, M. (2010). Significantly improved performances of the cryptographically generated addresses thanks to ECC and GPGPU. *Computers & Security*, *29*(4), 419–431. doi:10.1016/j.cose.2009.12.008.

Cheng, H., & Xiaobo, L. (2000). Partial encryption of compressed images and videos. *IEEE Transactions on Signal Processing*, *48*, 2439–2451. doi:10.1109/78.852023.

Chen, X., Tian, J., Yang, X., & Zhang, Y. (2006). An algorithm for distorted fingerprint matching based on local triangle feature set. *IEEE Transactions on Information Forensics and Security*, *1*(2), 169–177. doi:10.1109/TIFS.2006.873605.

Cheshire, S. (2008). IPv4 address conflict detection. RFC 5227. Retrieved from http://tools.ietf.org/html/rfc5227

Chida, K., Kobayashi, K., & Morita, H. (2001). Efficient sealed-bid auctions for massive numbers of bidders with lump comparison. In Proceedings of the Information Security, 4th International Conference, ISC 2001, (Vol. 2200, pp. 408-419). Berlin, Germany: Springer-Verlag.

Chiu, S., & Gamess, E. (2009). Easy-SEND: A didactic implementation of the secure neighbor discovery protocol for IPv6. In Proceedings of the World Congress on Engineering and Computer Science, WCECS 2009, (pp. 260-265). San Francisco, CA: WCECS.

Chlamtac, I., Conti, M., & Liu, J. (2003). Mobile ad hoc networking: Imperatives and challenges. *Ad Hoc Networks*, *1*, 13–64. doi:10.1016/S1570-8705(03)00013-1.

Chor, B., & Gilboa, N. (1997). Computationally private information retrieval. In Proceedings of 29th Annual ACM Symposium on Theory of Computing, (pp. 304–313). ACM Press.

Chor, B., Kushilevitz, E., Goldreich, O., & Sudan, M. (1995). Private information retrieval. In Proceedings of the 36th Annual IEEE Symposium on Foundations of Computer Science, (pp. 41–50). IEEE.

Clarke, D., Elien, J. E., Ellison, C., Fredette, M., Morcos, A., & Rivest, R. L. (2001). Certificate chain discovery in SPKI/SDSI. *Journal of Computer Security*, *9*(4), 285–322.

Clifton, C., Kantarcioglu, M., & Vaidya, J. (2004). Tools for privacy preserving distributed data mining. *ACM SIGKDD Explorations Newsletter*, *4*(2), 28–34. doi:10.1145/772862.772867.

Close, T. (2003a). Naming vs. pointing. Retrieved April 17, 2012, from http://www.waterken.com/dev/YURL/Analogy/

Close, T. (2003b). Waterken YURL: Trust management for humans. Retrieved April 17 2012, from http://www.waterken.com/dev/YURL/Name/

Close, T. (2005). Petname tool: Enabling web site recognition using the existing ssl infrastructure. Retrieved April 17, 2012, from http://www.w3.org/2005/Security/usability-ws/papers/02-hp-petname/

Close, T. (2012). Petname tool 1.7. Retrieved April 17 2012, from https://addons.mozilla.org/en-US/firefox/addon/957

Conta, A., Deering, S., & Gupta, M. (2006). Internet control message protocol (ICMPv6) for the internet protocol version 6 (IPv6) specification. RFC 4443. Retrieved from http://tools.ietf.org/html/rfc4443

Cooper, D., Santesson, S., Farrell, S., Boeyen, S., Housley, R., & Polk, W. (2008). Internet X.509 public key infrastructure certificate and certificate revocation list (CRL) profile. RFC. Retrieved from http://www.ietf.org/rfc/rfc5280.txt

Cormen, T. H., Leiserson, C. E., & Rivest, R. L. (2009). *Introduction to algorithms*. Cambridge, MA: The MIT Press.

Corporation, C. (2012). Capdesk. Retrieved April 17 2012, from http://www.skyhunter.com/marcs/CapDeskSpec.html

Courtois, N. (2011). Algebraic complexity reduction and cryptanalysis of GOST. Retrieved November 19, 2011 from http://eprint.iacr.org/2011/626.pdf

Courtois, N., & Bard, G. V. (2007). Algebraic cryptanalysis of the data encryption standard. In Proceedings of the Cryptography and Coding, 11th IMA Conference, (pp. 152-169). New York, NY: Springer.

Courtois, N., & Debraize, B. (2008). Algebraic description and simultaneous linear approximations of addition in snow 2.0. *Lecture Notes in Computer Science*, *5308*, 328–344. doi:10.1007/978-3-540-88625-9_22.

Courtois, N., & Debraize, B. (2008). Specific s-box criteria in algebraic attacks on block ciphers with several known plaintexts. *Lecture Notes in Computer Science*, *4945*, 100–113. doi:10.1007/978-3-540-88353-1_9.

Courtois, N., Goubin, L., Meier, W., & Tacier, J.-D. (2002). Solving underdefined systems of multivariate quadratic equations. *Lecture Notes in Computer Science*, *2274*, 211–227. doi:10.1007/3-540-45664-3_15.

Courtois, N., Klimov, A., Patarin, J., & Shamir, A. (2000). Efficient algorithms for solving overdefined systems of multivariate polynomial equations. *Lecture Notes in Computer Science*, *1807*, 392–407. doi:10.1007/3-540-45539-6_27.

Courtois, N., & Pieprzyk, J. (2002). Cryptanalysis of block ciphers with overdefined systems of equations. *Lecture Notes in Computer Science*, *2501*, 267–287. doi:10.1007/3-540-36178-2_17.

Cox, D. A., Little, J. B., & O'Shea, D. (1996). *Ideals, varieties, and algorithms* (2nd ed.). New York, NY: Springer-Verlag.

Cramer, R., Damgard, I., & Nielsen, J. B. (2001). Multiparty computation from threshold homomorphic encryption.[Berlin, Germany: Springer.]. *Proceedings of Eurocrypt*, *01*, 280–299.

Cramer, R., Damgard, I., & Schoenmakers, B. (1994). Proofs of partial knowledge and theory and practice of secure e-voting systems. In *Proceedings of Crypto 1994* (*Vol. 839*, pp. 174–187). Berlin, Germany: Springer-Verlag.

Cranor, L., Egelman, S., Hong, J., & Zhang, Y. (2006). Phinding phish: An evaluation of anti-phishing toolbars. Technical Report CMU-CyLab-06-018. Pittsburgh, PA: Carnegie Mellon University CyLab.

Crispin, M. (2003). Internet message access protocol - Version 4rev1. Retrieved from http://tools.ietf.org/html/rfc3501

Curtmola, R., Garay, J., Kamara, S., & Ostrovsky, R. (2006). Searchable symmetric encryption: Improved definitions and efficient constructions. In Proceedings of the 13th ACM Conference on Computer and Communications Security, (pp. 79–88). ACM.

Czarnecki, K., & Helsen, S. (2003). Classification of model transformation approaches. In Proceedings of the OOPSLA 2003 Workshop on the Generative Techniques in the Context of Model-Driven Architecture. Anaheim, CA: OOPSLA. Retrieved from http://www.swen.uwaterloo.ca/~kczarnec/ECE750T7/czarnecki_helsen.pdf

Daemen, J., & Rijmen, V. (2002). *The design of Rijndael: AES - The advanced encryption standard*. Berlin, Germany: Springer. doi:10.1007/978-3-662-04722-4.

D'Agapeyeff, A. (2008). *Codes and ciphers - A history of cryptography*. New York, NY: Hesperides Press.

Damgard, I., & Jurik, M. (2001). A generalisation, a simplification and some applications of Paillier's probabilistic public-key system. In Proceedings of PKC 2001, (Vol. 1992, pp. 119-136). Berlin, Germany: Springer-Verlag.

Deering, S., & Hinden, R. (1998). Internet protocol, version 6 (IPv6) specification. RFC. Retrieved from http://www.ietf.org/rfc/rfc2460.txt

Deng, J., Han, R., & Mishra, S. (2005). Countermeasures against traffic analysis attacks in wireless sensor networks. In Proceedings of the 1st IEEE Conference on Security and Privacy for Emerging Areas in Communication Networks, (pp.113-124). IEEE.

Denning, D., & Branstad, D. (1996). A taxonomy for key escrow encryption systems. *Communications of the ACM*, *39*(3). doi:10.1145/227234.227239.

Deutsch, H. (2008). Relative identity. In E. N. Zalta (Ed.), The Stanford Encyclopedia of Philosophy. Retrieved from http://plato.stanford.edu/archives/win2008/entries/identity-relative/

DeVries, S., & Vohra, R. (2000). Combinatorial auctions: A survey. Retrieved from http://www.citeseer.nj.nec.com/devries01combinatorial.html

Dhamija, R., & Tygar, J. D. (2006). Why phishing works. In Proceedings of the SIGCHI Conference on Human Factors in Computing Systems, (pp. 581–590). ACM Press.

Dhillon, I. S., & Modha, D. S. (1999). A data-clustering algorithm on distributed memory multiprocessors. In Proceedings of Large-scale Parallel KDD Systems Workshop (ACM SIGKDD), (pp. 245-260). ACM Press.

Di Crescenzo, G., Ge, R., & Arce, G. (2007). Threshold cryptography in mobile ad hoc networks under minimal topology and setup assumptions. *Security Issues in Sensor and Ad Hoc Networks*, *5*(1), 63–75. doi:10.1016/j.adhoc.2006.05.006.

Di-Crescenzo, G., Ishai, Y., & Ostrovsky, R. (1998). Universal service-providers for database private information retrieval. In Proceedings of the 17th Annual ACM Symposium on Principles of Distributed Computing, (pp. 91–100). ACM Press.

Dierks, T., & Allen, C. (1999). The TLS protocol version 1.0. RFC. Retrieved from http://www.ietf.org/rfc/rfc2246.txt

Dierks, T., & Rescorla, E. (2008). RFC-5246: The transport layer security (TLS) protocol version 1.2. Retrieved from http://www.ietf.org

Diffie, W., & Hellman, M. (1976). New directions in cryptography. *IEEE Transactions on Information Theory*, *22*(6), 644–654. doi:10.1109/TIT.1976.1055638.

DOCOMO Communications Laboratories USA. (2008). SEND project. Retrieved April 23, 2012, from http://www.docomolabs-usa.com/lab_opensource.html

Domingo-Ferrer, J. (1996). A new privacy homomorphism and applications. *Information Processing Letters*, *60*(5), 277–282. doi:10.1016/S0020-0190(96)00170-6.

Domingo-Ferrer, J. (2002). A provably secure additive and multiplicative privacy homomorphism. *Lecture Notes in Computer Science*, *2433*, 471–483. doi:10.1007/3-540-45811-5_37.

Donahue, M. L., & Rokhlin, S. I. (1993). On the use of level curves in image analysis. *CVGIP: Image Understanding*, *57*(2), 185–203. doi:10.1006/ciun.1993.1012.

Donnerhacke, L., Finney, H., Shaw, D., & Thayer, R. (2007). OpenPGP message format. IETF. Retrieved April 25, 2012, from https://tools.ietf.org/html/rfc4880

Douceur, J. (2002). The sybil attack. In Proceedings of the 1st International Workshop on Peer-to-Peer Systems (IPTPS). IPTPS.

Doukhnitch, E., & Ozen, E. (2011). Hardware-oriented algorithm for quaternion valued matrix decomposition. *IEEE Transactions on Circuits and Wystems. II, Express Briefs*, *58*(4), 225–229. doi:10.1109/TCSII.2011.2111590.

Dowd, J., Xu, S., & Zhang, W. (2006). Privacy-preserving decision tree mining based on random substitutions.[ETRICS.]. *Proceedings of ETRICS*, *2006*, 145–159.

Drahansky, M., Funk, W., & Nötzel, R. (2006). Liveness detection based on fine movements of the fingertip surface. Paper presented at the IAW'06. New York, NY.

Drahansky, M., & Lodrova, D. (2008). Liveness detection for biometric systems based on papillary lines. *International Journal of Security and Its Applications*, *2*(4), 29–37.

Drelie Gelasca, E., Tomasic, D., & Ebrahimi, T. (2005). Which colors best catch your eyes: A subjective study of color saliency. Retrieved April 17, 2012, from http://infoscience.epfl.ch/getfile.py?mode=best&recid=87215

Droms, R. (1997). Dynamic host configuration protocol. RFC 2131. Retrieved from http://tools.ietf.org/html/rfc2131

Droms, R., Bound, J., Volz, B., Lemon, T., Perkins, C., & Carney, M. (2003). Dynamic host configuration protocol for IPv6 (DHCPv6). Retrieved from http://tools.ietf.org/html/rfc3315

Du, W., & Atallah, M. J. (2001). Secure multiparty computation problems and their applications: Review and open problems. In Proceedings of the New Security Paradigms Workshop, (pp. 11-20). IEEE.

Du, W., & Atallah, M. J. (2002). a practical approach to solve secure multiparty computation problems. In Proceedings of the New Security Paradigms Workshop, (pp. 127-135). IEEE.

Duda, R. O., Hart, P. E., & Stork, D. G. (2001). *Pattern classification*. New York, NY: John Wiley & Sons.

Du, W., & Zhan, Z. (2002). Building decision tree classifier on private data. In *Proceedings of Electrical Engineering and Computer Science* (pp. 11–20). IEEE.

Dziembowski, S., Kazana, T., & Wichs, D. (2011). Key-evolution schemes resilient to space-bounded leakage. In P. Rogaway (Ed.), Advances in Cryptology - CRYPTO 2003, 23rd Annual International Cryptology Conference, (pp. 617-630). Berlin, Germany: Springer.

Eastlake, D. (1999). Domain name system security extensions. RFC. Retrieved from http://tools.ietf.org/html/rfc2535

Eclipse. (2012). The eclipse foundation open source community website. Retrieved from http://www.eclipse.org/

Edoh, K. D. (2004). Elliptic curve cryptography: Java implementation. Paper presented at the 1st Annual Conference on Information Security Curriculum Development. IEEE.

Eisenbarth, T., Kasper, T., Moradi, A., Paar, C., Salmasizadeh, M., & Shalmani, M. T. M. (2008). On the power of power analysis in the real world: A complete break of the Keeloq code hopping scheme. Retrieved from http://emsec.ruhr-uni-bochum.de/media/crypto/veroeffentlichungen/2010/09/11/crypto2008_keeloq_slides.pdf

Ekert, A. K. (1991). Quantum cryptography based on Bell's theorem. *Physical Review Letters*, *67*(6), 661–663. doi:10.1103/PhysRevLett.67.661 PMID:10044956.

Elkamchouchi, H., & Makar, A. M. (2005). Measuring encryption quality of bitmaps images with Rijndael and KAMKAR block ciphers. In Proceedings of 22nd National Radio Science Conference (NRSC), (pp. 1-8). NRSC.

Elkhodr, M., Shahrestani, S., & Cheung, H. (2011a). An approach to enhance the security of remote health monitoring systems. Paper presented at the 4th International Conference on Security of Information and Networks. New York, NY.

Elkhodr, M., Shahrestani, S., & Cheung, H. (2011b). Enhancing the security of mobile health monitoring systems through trust negotiations. Paper presented at the 2011 IEEE 36th Conference on Local Computer Networks (LCN). New York, NY.

Ellison, C., & Schneier, B. (2000). Ten risks of PKI: What you're not being told about public key infrastructure. Computer Security Journal, 16(1).

Ellison, C., et al. (1999). RFC 2693 - SPKI certification theory. Retrieved from http://www.ietf.org/rfc/rfc2693.txt

Ellison, C., Frantz, B., Lampson, B., Rivest, R., Thomas, B., & Ylonen, T. (1999). SPKI certificate theory. RFC 2693. Retrieved from http://www.ietf.org

Emekci, F., Sahin, O. D., Agrawal, D., & El Abbadi, A. (2007). Privacy preserving decision tree learning over multiple parties. *Data & Knowledge Engineering*, *63*, 348–361. doi:10.1016/j.datak.2007.02.004.

Emin, E. G., Bruijn, W., Reynolds, P., Shieh, A., Walsh, K., Williams, D., & Schneider, F. B. (2011). Logical attestation: An authorization architecture for trustworthy computing. In Proceedings of the 23rd ACM Symposium on Operating Systems Principles, (pp. 249-264). ACM.

Endo, Y., & Matsumoto, T. (2002). Can we make artificial fingers that fool fingerprint systems? Paper presented at IPSJ for Computer Security Symposium. New York, NY.

Enev, M., Gupta, S., Kohno, T., & Patel, S. N. (2011). Televisions, video privacy, and powerline electromagnetic interference. Retrieved from http://homes.cs.washington.edu/~sidhant/docs/TVEMI.pdf

Entity. (2012). Wikipedia. Retrieved April 17 2012, from http://en.wikipedia.org/wiki/Entity

Escala, A., Herranz, J., & Morillo, P. (2011). Revocable attribute-based signatures with adaptive security in the standard model. *Lecture Notes in Computer Science*, *6737*, 224–241. doi:10.1007/978-3-642-21969-6_14.

European Commission. (2007). eHealth taskforce report. Luxembourg: European Commission.

Even, S., Goldreich, O., & Micali, S. (1990). Online/offline digital signatures. *Crypto*, *435*, 263–277.

Evfimievski, A., Gehrke, J., & Srikant, R. (2003). Limiting privacy breaches in privacy preserving data mining. In Proceedings of the Twenty-Second ACM SIGACT-SIGMOD-SIGART Symposium on Principles of Database Systems, (pp. 211-222). ACM Press.

Evfimievski, A., Srikant, R., Agrawal, R., & Gehrke, J. (2002). Privacy preserving mining of association rules. In Proceedings of the Eighth ACM SIGKDD International Conference on Knowledge Discovery and Data Mining, (pp. 217–228). ACM Press.

Fang, W., & Yang, B. (2008). Privacy preserving decision tree learning over vertically partitioned data. In Proceedings of the 2008 International Conference on Computer Science & Software Engineering. IEEE.

Faugère, J.-C. (2002). A new efficient algorithm for computing Gröbner bases without reduction to zero (F5). In Proceedings of the 2002 International Symposium on Symbolic and Algebraic Computation (ISSAC 2002), (pp. 75–83). New York, NY: Association for Computing Machinery, Inc.

Faugère, J.-C. (1999). A new efficient algorithm for computing Gröbner bases (F4). *Journal of Pure and Applied Algebra*, *139*(1-3), 61–88. doi:10.1016/S0022-4049(99)00005-5.

FBI. (1991). *The FBI fingerprint identification automation program: Issues and options*. Washington, DC: FBI.

Fedorchenko, L. N. (2011). *Regularization of context-free grammar*. Saarbrucken, Germany: LAP LAMBERT Academic Publishing GmbH & Co..

Ferdous, M. S., Jøsang, A., Singh, K., & Borgaonkar, R. (2009). Security usability of petname systems. In Proceedings of the 14th Nordic Workshop on Secure IT systems (NordSec 2009). Oslo, Norway: NordSec.

Ferguson, N., Schroeppel, R., & Whiting, D. (2001). A simple algebraic representation of Rijndael. In *Proceedings of Selected Areas in Cryptography* (pp. 103–111). New York, NY: Springer–Verlag. doi:10.1007/3-540-45537-X_8.

Fischlin, M. (2001). A cost-effective pay-per-multiplication comparison method for millionaires. In *Proceedings of Topics in Cryptology, CT-RSA 2001 (Vol. 2020*, pp. 457–472). Berlin, Germany: Springer. doi:10.1007/3-540-45353-9_33.

Fouque, P., Poupard, G., & Stern, J. (2000). Sharing decryption in the context of voting or lotteries. In *Proceedings of Financial Cryptography 2000 (Vol. 1962*, pp. 90–104). Berlin, Germany: Springer-Verlag. doi:10.1007/3-540-45472-1_7.

Franconi, L., & Merola, G. (2003). Implementing statistical disclosure control for aggregated data released via remote access. Working Paper No. 30. Geneva, Switzerland: United Nations Statistical Commission and European Commission.

Franklin, M. K., & Reiter, M. K. (1996). The design and implementation of a secure auction service. *IEEE Transactions on Software Engineering*, *5*, 302–312. doi:10.1109/32.502223.

Fraud. (2004). Internet scams fraud trends 2004. Retrieved from http://www.fraud.org/2004-internet\%20scams.pdf

Freed, N., & Borenstein, N. (1996). Multipurpose internet mail extensions (MIME) part five: Conformance criteria and examples. RFC. Retrieved from http://tools.ietf.org/html/rfc2049

Freed, N., & Borenstein, N. (1996). Multipurpose internet mail extensions (MIME) part one: Format of internet message bodies. RFC. Retrieved from http://tools.ietf.org/html/rfc2045

Freedman, M., Nissim, K., & Pinkas, B. (2004). Efficient private matching and set intersection.[Eurocrypt.]. *Proceedings of the Advances in Cryptology Eurocrypt*, *2004*, 1–19.

Freier, A., Karlton, P., & Kocher, P. (2011). The secure sockets layer (SSL) protocol version 3.0. RFC. Retrieved from http://tools.ietf.org/html/rfc6101

Fuhr, T., & Paillier, P. (2007). Decryptable searchable encryption. *Lecture Notes in Computer Science*, *4784*, 228–236. doi:10.1007/978-3-540-75670-5_17.

Fung, B., Wang, K., & Yu, P. (2005). Top-down specialization for information and privacy preservation. In Proceedings of the 21st IEEE International Conference on Data Engineering, (pp. 205-216). IEEE Press.

Furnell, S. M., Gaunt, P. N., Pangalos, G., Sanders, P. W., & Warren, M. J. (1994). A generic methodology for health care data security. *Informatics for Health & Social Care*, *19*(3), 229–245. doi:10.3109/14639239409025329 PMID:7707744.

Furukawa, J. (2004). Efficient, verifiable shuffle decryption and its requirement of unlinkability. In Proceedings of PKC 2004, (Vol. 2947, pp. 319-332). Berlin, Germany: Springer.

Furukawa, J., & Sako, K. (2001). An efficient scheme for proving a shuffle. In *Proceedings of Crypto 2001* (*Vol. 2139*, pp. 368–387). Berlin, Germany: Springer. doi:10.1007/3-540-44647-8_22.

Galbally, J., Fierrez, J., Rodriguez-Gonzalez, J. D., Alonso-Fernandez, F., Ortega-Garcia, J., & Tapiador, M. (2006). On the vulnerability of fingerprint verification systems to fake fingerprint attacks. Paper presented at International Carnahan Conference on Security Technology. New York, NY.

Gallois, A. (2012). Identity over time. In E. N. Zalta (Ed.), The Stanford Encyclopedia of Philosophy. Retrieved from http://plato.stanford.edu/archives/sum2012/entries/identity-time/

Gallois, A. (2011). Occasional identity: Thereby hangs the tale. *Analytic Philosophy*, *52*(3), 188–202. doi:10.1111/j.2153-960X.2011.00527.x.

Galton, F. (1892). *Fingerprints*. London, UK: Macmillan.

Gandolfi, K., Mourtel, C., & Olivier, F. (2001). Electromagnetic analysis: Concrete results.[London, UK: Springer.]. *Proceedings of CHES*, *2001*, 251–261.

Garcia-Hernandez, C. F., Ibarguangoytia-Gonzalez, P. H., Garcia-Hernandez, J., & Perez-Diaz, J. A. (2007). Wireless sensor networks and applications: A survey. *International Journal of Computer Science and Network Security*, *7*(3), 264–273.

Garfinkel, S. L. (2003). Enabling email confidentiality through the use of opportunistic encryption. In Proceeding of the 2003 Annual National Conference on Digital Government Research. IEEE.

Garfinkel, S. L., Margrave, D., Schiller, J. I., Nordlander, E., & Miller, R. C. (2005). How to make secure email easier to use. In Proceeding of the SIGCHI Conference on Human Factors in Computing Systems, (pp. 701-710). ACM.

Gasmi, Y., Sadeghi, A.-R., Stewin, P., Unger, M., & Asokan, N. (2007). Beyond secure channels. In Proceedings of the 2nd ACM Workshop on Scalable Trusted Computing, (pp. 30-40). ACM.

Gavidia, D., & Van Steen, M. (2007). Enforcing data integrity in very large ad hoc networks. In Proceedings of the 2007 International Conference on Mobile Data Management, (pp. 77-85). IEEE.

Geach, P. T. (1967). Identity. *The Review of Metaphysics, 21*, 3–12.

Gebotys, C. H., & White, B. A. (2008). EM analysis of a wireless java-based PDA. ACM Transactions on Embedded Computer Systems, 7(4).

Gellens, R., & Klensin, J. (2011). Message submission for mail. RFC. Retrieved from http://tools.ietf.org/html/rfc6409

Gentry, C. (2009). Fully homomorphic encryption using ideal lattices. Paper presented at the 41st ACM Symposium on the Theory of Computation. Bethesda, MD.

Gentry, C., & Halevi, S. (2011). Implementing Gentry's fully-homomorphic encryption scheme. In Paterson, K. (Ed.), *Advances in Cryptology -- Eurocrypt 2011* (pp. 129–148). Berlin, Germany: Springer. doi:10.1007/978-3-642-20465-4_9.

Gentry, C., Halevi, S., & Smart, N. (2012). Homomorphic evaluation of the AES circuit. *Lecture Notes in Computer Science, 7417*, 850–867. doi:10.1007/978-3-642-32009-5_49.

Geraci, A. (1996). The computer dictionary project: An update. *Computer, 29*(7), 95. doi:10.1109/2.511973.

Gertner, Y., Ishai, Y., Kushilevitz, E., & Malkin, T. (1998). Protecting data privacy in information retrieval schemes. In Proceedings of the Thirtieth Annual ACM Symposium on Theory of Computing, STOC '98, (pp. 151–160). ACM Press.

Gilboa, N. (1999). Two party RSA key generation. [CRYPTO.]. *Proceedings of CRYPTO, 1999*, 116–129.

Girao, J., Schneider, M., & Westhoff, D. (2004). CDA: Concealed data aggregation in wireless sensor networks. In Proceedings of the ACM Workshop on Wireless Security. ACM Press.

Goethals, B., Laur, S., Lipmaa, H., & Mielikäinen, T. (2004). On private scalar product computation for privacy-preserving data mining. *Lecture Notes in Computer Science, 3506*, 104–120. doi:10.1007/11496618_9.

Goh, E. J. (2003). Secure indexes. Technical Report 216. IACR.

Goldman, K., Perez, R., & Sailer, R. (2006). Linking remote attestation to secure tunnel endpoints. In Proceedings of the 1st ACM Symposium on Applied Computing, (pp. 21-24). ACM.

Goldreich, O., Micali, S., & Wigderson, A. (1987). How to play any mental game - A completeness theorem for protocols with honest majority. In Proceedings of the 19th Symposium on Theory of Computer Science, (pp. 218–229). IEEE.

Goldreich, O. (2004). *Foundations of cryptography: Basic applications*. Cambridge, UK: Cambridge University Press. doi:10.1017/CBO9780511721656.

Goldreich, O., & Ostrovsky, R. (1996). Software protection and simulation on oblivious RAMs. *Journal of the ACM, 43*(3), 431–473. doi:10.1145/233551.233553.

Golle, P., & Juels, A. (2004). Parallel mixing. [CCS.]. *Proceedings of CCS, 2004*, 220–226. doi:10.1145/1030083.1030113.

Golle, P., Staddon, J., & Waters, B. (2004). Secure conjunctive keyword search over encrypted data. *Lecture Notes in Computer Science, 3089*, 31–45. doi:10.1007/978-3-540-24852-1_3.

Golle, P., Zhong, S., Boneh, D., Jakobsson, M., & Juels, A. (2002). Optimistic mixing for exit-polls. In *Proceedings of Asiacrypt '02* (*Vol. 1592*, pp. 451–465). Berlin, Germany: Springer-Verlag.

Goodchild, A., Gibson, K., Anderson, L., & Bird, L. (2004). The Brisbane southside healthconnect trial: Preliminary results. In Proceedings of HIC 2004. HIC.

Govindavajhala, S., & Appel, A. W. (2003). Using memory errors to attack virtual machine. Retrieved from http://www.cs.princeton.edu/~sudhakar/papers/memerr.pdf

Groat, S., Dunlop, M., Marchany, R., & Tront, J. (2010). The privacy implications of stateless IPv6 addressing. In Proceedings of the Sixth Annual Workshop on Cyber Security and Information Intelligence Research, CSIIRW '10, (pp. 52:1-52:4). New York, NY: ACM.

Grosek, O., Nemoga, K., & Zanechal, M. (1997). Why use bijective S-boxes in GOST-algorithm. Retrieved July 30, 1997 from http://www.mat.savba.sk/preprints/1997/97-11.PS

Groth, J. (2003). A verifiable secret shuffle of homomorphic encryptions. In *Proceedings of Public Key Cryptography 2003* (*Vol. 2567*, pp. 145–160). Berlin, Germany: Springer-Verlag. doi:10.1007/3-540-36288-6_11.

Groth, J., & Sahai, A. (2008). Efficient non-interactive proof systems for bilinear groups. *Lecture Notes in Computer Science*, *4965*, 415–432. doi:10.1007/978-3-540-78967-3_24.

Grover, J., Gaur, M., Laxmi, V., & Prajapati, N. (2011). A sybil attack detection approach using neighboring vehicles in VANET. In Proceedings of the 4th International Conference on Security of Information and Networks, (pp. 151-158). IEEE.

Guillou, L. C., & Quisquater, J. J. (1989). A paradoxical identity-based signature scheme resulting from zero-knowledge. In Goldwasser, S. (Ed.), *Crypto 1988* (*Vol. 403*, pp. 216–231). Berlin, Germany: Springer-Verlag.

Gunter, T. D., & Terry, N. P. (2005). Gunther Eysenbach. Toronto, Canada: Centre for Global eHealth Innovation.

Gunter, T., & Terry, N. (2005). The emergence of national electronic health record architectures in the United States and Australia: Models, costs, and questions. *Journal of Medical Internet Research*, 7(1), e3. doi:10.2196/jmir.7.1.e3 PMID:15829475.

Gutmann, P. (2004). Why isn't the internet secure yet, dammit. In Proceeding of the AusCERT Asia Pacific Information Technology Security Conference 2004; Computer Security: Are we there yet? (pp. 71-79). AusCERT.

Halderman, J., Schoen, S., Heninger, N., Clarkson, W., Paul, W., & Cal, J. et al. (2006). Lest we remember: Cold-boot attacks on encryption keys. *Communications of the ACM*, *52*(5).

Hamid, A., Rashid, M. O., & Hong, C. S. (2006). Defense against lap-top class attacker in wireless sensor network. In Proceedings of the 8th International Conference on Advanced Communication Technology. IEEE.

Hamilton, W. (1847). On quaternions. *Proceedings of the Royal Irish Academy*, *3*, 1–16.

Han, R.-F., Wang, H.-X., Wang, Y.-H., & Zuo, K.-L. (2009). Membership-based access control for trust negotiation in open systems. Paper presented at the Information Assurance and Security, 2009. IAS '09. New York, NY.

Han, S., Skinner, G., Potdar, V., & Chang, E. (2006). A framework of authentication and authorization for e-health services. Paper presented at the 3rd ACM Workshop on Secure Web Services. New York, NY.

Handschuh, H., & Paillier, P. (2000). Smart card crypto-coprocessors for public-key cryptography: Smart card research and application. *Lecture Notes in Computer Science*, *1820*, 372–379. doi:10.1007/10721064_35.

Harn, L., Hsin, W.-J., & Lin, C.-L. (2009). Efficient online/offline signature schemes based on multiple-collision trapdoor hash families. *The Computer Journal*. doi: doi:10.1093/comjnl/bxp044.

Harn, L., Mehta, M., & Hsin, W.-J. (2004). Integrating Diffie-Hellman key exchange into the digital signature algorithm (DSA). *IEEE Communications Letters*, *8*(3). doi:10.1109/LCOMM.2004.825705.

Harris, J., & Hill, R. (2010). Building a trusted image for embedded systems. In Proceedings of the 6th Annual Cyber Security and Information Intelligence Research Workshop, (pp. 65:1-65:4). IEEE.

Hauser, V. (2012). THC-IPv6: The hackers choice. Retrieved April 23, 2012, from http://www.thc.org/thc-ipv6

Hayes, J. M. (1998). The problem with multiple roots in web browsers - Certificate masquerading. In Proceedings of the 7th Workshop on Enabling Technologies, Infrastructure for Collaborative Enterprises (WETICE '98), (pp. 306–313). IEEE.

Herzberg, A. (2006). Trustbar firefox addon. Retrieved April 17, 2012, from http://u.cs.biu.ac.il/~herzbea/TrustBar/

Herzberg, A., & Gbara, A. (2004). Protecting (even na¨ive) web users from spoofing and phishing attacks. Technical Report 2004/155. Cryptology ePrint Archive.

Hevia, A., & Kiwi, M. (2002). Non-interactive zero-knowledge arguments for voting. In Proceedings of LATIN 2002, (Vol. 2286, pp. 415-429). Berlin, Germany: Springer-Verlag.

Hill, C. J. (2001). *Risk of masquerade arising from the storage of Biometrics*. Canberra, Australia: Australian National University.

Hillestad, R., Bigelow, J., Bower, A., Girosi, F., Meili, R., & Scoville, R. et al. (2005). Can electronic medical record systems transform health care? Potential health benefits, savings, and costs. *Health Affairs*, *24*(5), 1103–1117. doi:10.1377/hlthaff.24.5.1103 PMID:16162551.

Hirt, M., & Sako, K. (2000). E_cient receipt-free voting based on homomorphic encryption. *Proceedings of EUROCRYPT*, *2000*, 539–556.

Hoffman, P. (2002). SMTP service extension for secure SMTP over transport layer security. RFC. Retrieved from http://www.ietf.org/rfc/rfc3207.txt

Hoffman, P. (2010). Cryptographic algorithm identifier allocation for DNSSEC. Retrieved from http://tools.ietf.org/html/rfc6014

Hoffman, P., & Schlyter, J. (2012). The DNS-based authentication of named entities (DANE) protocol for transport layer security (TLS) draft-ietf-dane-protocol-18. Retrieved from http://tools.ietf.org/html/draft-ietf-dane-protocol-18

Hoffman, K., Zage, D., & Nita-Rotaru, C. (2009). A survey of attack and defense techniques for reputation systems. *ACM Computing Surveys*, *42*(1). doi:10.1145/1592451.1592452.

Hofheinz, D., & Weinreb, E. (2008). Searchable encryption with decryption in the standard model. Retrieved from http://eprint.iacr.org/2008/423

Holzman, R., Kfir-Dahav, N., Monderer, D., & Tennenholtz, M. (2001). Bundling equilibrium in combinatorial auctions. Retrieved from http://iew3.technion.ac.il/~moshet/rndm11.ps

Hong, L., Wan, Y., & Jain, A. K. (1998). Fingerprint image enhancement: Algorithm and performance evaluation. *IEEE Transactions on Pattern Analysis and Machine Intelligence*, *20*(8), 777–789. doi:10.1109/34.709565.

Hore, B., Mehrotra, S., Canim, M., & Kantarcioglu, M. (2012). Secure multidimensional range queries over outsourced data. *The VLDB Journal*, *21*(3), 333–358. doi:10.1007/s00778-011-0245-7.

Hossam, E. H., Ahmed, H. M., & Osama, S. F. (2007a). An efficient chaos-based feedback stream cipher (ECBFSC) for image encryption and decryption. *Journal of Computing and Informatics*, *31*, 121–129.

Hossam, E. H., Ahmed, H. M., & Osama, S. F. (2007b). Encryption efficiency analysis and security evaluation of RC6 block ciphers for digital images. *International Journal of Computer and Information Technology*, *3*(1), 33–39.

Housley, R. (1989). Electronic message security: A comparison of three approaches. In Proceedings of the Fifth Annual Computer Security Applications Conference Proceedings. IEEE.

Housley, R. (2009). Cryptographic message syntax (CMS). RFC. Retrieved from http://tools.ietf.org/html/rfc5652

Housley, R., Ford, W., Polk, T., & Solo, D. (1999). Internet X.509 public key infrastructure – Certificate and CRL profile. RFC 2459 (RFC 3280–2002). Retrieved from http://www.ietf.org

Hsiao, S.-F., & Delosme, J.-M. (1994). Parallel processing of complex data using quaternion and pseudo-quaternion CORDIC algorithms. In Proceedings of the ASAP 1994 Conference, (pp. 125-130). University of California.

Hsin, W.-J., & Harn, L. (2007). Practical public key solution in mobile ad hoc networks. In Proceedings of the International Conference on Security of Information and Networks. Gazimagusa, Cyprus: IEEE.

Huang, E., Hu, W., Crowcroft, J., & Wassell, I. (2005). Towards commercial mobile ad hoc network applications: A radio dispatch system. In Proceedings of the 6th ACM International Symposium on Mobile Ad Hoc Networking and Computing. Urbana-Champaign, IL: ACM Press.

Huawei Technologies Corp. & BUPT. (2009). IPv6-send-CGA an implementation of SEND protocol in LINUX kernel. Retrieved from http://code.google.com/p/ipv6-send-cga/

Hu, B., Wong, D., Zhang, Z., & Deng, X. (2006). Key replacement attack against a generic construction of certificateless signature information security and privacy. *Lecture Notes in Computer Science*, *4058*, 235–246. doi:10.1007/11780656_20.

Hubaux, J.-P., Buttyan, L., & Capkun, S. (2001). The quest for security in mobile ad hoc networks. In Proceedings of the ACM Symposium on Mobile Ad Hoc Networking and Computing (MobiHOC). ACM Press.

Hui, J., & Thubert, P. (2011). Compression format for IPv6 datagrams over IEEE 802.15.4-based networks. IETF Request for Comments (RFC): 6282. Retrieved April 20, 2012, from http://tools.ietf.org/html/rfc6282

Hupperich, T. L, H., Sadeghi, A.-R., & Winandy, M. (2012). Flexible patient-controlled security for electronic health records. Paper presented at the 2nd ACM SIGHIT International Health Informatics Symposium. New York, NY.

Hwang, Y. H., & Lee, P. J. (2007). Public key encryption with conjunctive keyword search and its extension to a multi-user system. *Lecture Notes in Computer Science*, *4575*, 2–22. doi:10.1007/978-3-540-73489-5_2.

IAIK TU Graz. (2009). jTSS project (jTSS). Retrieved May 2, 2012, from http://trustedjava.sourceforge.net

IBM. (2008). TrouSerS project – The open-source TCG software stack (TrouSerS). Retrieved May 2, 2012, from http://trousers.sourceforge.net/

Ibraimi, L., Nikova, S., Hartel, P. H., & Jonker, W. (2011). Public-key encryption with delegated search. *Lecture Notes in Computer Science*, *6715*, 532–549. doi:10.1007/978-3-642-21554-4_31.

IDEF0 Draft. (2012). Federal information processing standards publication. Retrieved from http://www.itl.nist.gov/fipspubs/idef0.doc

IDEF5. (2012). Ontology description capture method. Retrieved from http://www.idef.com/idef5.html

Identity. (2012). Wikipedia. Retrieved April 17 2012, from http://en.wikipedia.org/wiki/Identity_management.

IEEE Std 802.15.4TM-2003. (2003). IEEE standard for information technology-telecommunications and information exchange between systems-local and metropolitan area networks-specific requirements-part 15.4: Wireless medium access control (MAC) and physical layer (PHY) specifications for low-rate wireless personal area networks (WPANs). IEEE.

Iima, Y., Kanzaki, A., Hara, T., & Nishio, S. (2009). Overhearing-based data transmission reduction for periodical data gathering in wireless sensor networks. In Proceedings of the International Workshop on Data Management for Information Explosion in Wireless Networks, (pp. 1048-1053). IEEE.

Intel. (2011). Intel trusted execution technology (TXT), measured launched environment developer's guide. Document Number: 315168-008. Retrieved May 2, 2012, from http://download.intel.com/technology/security/downloads/315168.pdf

Internet Archive Wayback Machine. (2012). Snapshot on zooko's writing. Retrieved on April 17 2012, from http://web.archive.org/web/*/http://zooko.com/distnames.html

Internet Assigned Numbers Authority. (2012). IANA IPv4 address space registry. Retrieved from http://www.iana.org/assignments/ipv4-address-space/

Internet Society. World IPv6 Launch. (2012). Internet society. Retrieved April 23, 2012, from http://www.worldipv6day.org/

Ioannidis, I., & Grama, A. (2003). An efficient protocol for Yao's millionaires problem. In Proceedings of the 36th Hawaii International Conference on System Sciences, (pp. 6–9). IEEE.

Iovino, V., & Persiano, G. (2008). Hidden-vector encryption with groups of prime order. *Lecture Notes in Computer Science*, *5209*, 75–88. doi:10.1007/978-3-540-85538-5_5.

Ishai, Y., & Kushilevitz, E. (1999). Improved upper bounds on information-theoretic private information retrieval (extended abstract). In Proceedings of the Thirty-first Annual ACM Symposium on Theory of Computing, (pp. 79–88). ACM.

Islam, M., Kuzu, M., & Kantarcioglu, M. (2012). Access pattern disclosure on searchable encryption: Ramification, attack and mitigation. In Proceedings of the Network and Distributed System Security Symposium, NDSS 2012. NDSS.

Ismail, A., & Schnabel, U. (2004). An efficient fingerprint matching system. Paper presented at the 3rd International Conference on Electrical & Computer Engineering ICECE 2004. New York, NY.

Ismail, A. I., Amin, M., & Diab, H. (2006). How to repair the hill cipher. *Journal of Zhejiang University of Science A*, *7*(12), 2022–2030. doi:10.1631/jzus.2006.A2022.

ISO. (1988). *IS 7498-2: Basic reference model for open systems interconnection - Part 2: Security architecture*. Geneva, Switzerland: International Organisation for Standardization.

Isobe, T. (2011). A single-key attack on the full GOST block cipher. *Lecture Notes in Computer Science*, *6733*, 290–305. doi:10.1007/978-3-642-21702-9_17.

Jacobson, J. (2003). *Trust negotiation in session layer protocols*. Provo, UT: Brigham Young University.

Jain, A. K., Bolle, R., & Pankanti, S. (2005). *Biometrics: Personal identification in networked society*. Berlin, Germany: Springer.

Jain, A. K., Maltoni, D., Maio, D., & Prabhakar, S. (2003). *Handbook of fingerprint recognition*. Berlin, Germany: Springer.

Jain, A. K., Prabhakar, S., Hong, L., & Pankanti, S. (2000). Filterbank-based fingerprint matching. *IEEE Transactions on Image Processing*, *9*(8), 846–859. doi:10.1109/83.841531 PMID:18255456.

Jain, A. K., Prabhakar, S., & Pankanti, S. (2001). Twin test: On discriminability of fingerprints. *Lecture Notes in Computer Science*, *2091*, 211–217. doi:10.1007/3-540-45344-X_30.

Jain, A. K., Ross, A., & Prabhakar, S. (2004). An introduction to biometric recognition. *IEEE Transactions on Circuits and Systems for Video Technology*, *14*, 4–20. doi:10.1109/TCSVT.2003.818349.

Jakobsson, M., Juels, A., & Rivest, R. L. (2002). Making mix nets robust for electronic voting by randomized partial checking. In Proceedings of the 11th Usenix Security Symposium 2002, (pp. 339-353). USENIX.

Jakobsson, M., & Juels, A. (2000). Mix and match: Secure function evaluation via ciphertexts. In *Proceedings of Asiacrypt '00* (*Vol. 1976*, pp. 143–161). Berlin, Germany: Springer-Verlag. doi:10.1007/3-540-44448-3_13.

Janning, A., Heyszl, J., Stumpf, F., & Sigl, G. (2011). A cost-effective FPGA-based fault simulation environment. In Proceedings of FDTC 2011. Tokyo, Japan: FDTC.

Java. (2012). Java development kit (JDK). Retrieved from http://java.sun.com/products/archive/jdk/1.1.8_010/

Jenn, E., Arlat, J., Rimen, M., Ohlsson, J., & Karlsson, J. (1994). Fault injection into VHDL models: The MEFISTO tool. In Proceedings of FTCS, (pp. 66-75). IEEE Press.

Jha, S., Kruger, L., & McDaniel, P. (2005). Privacy preserving clustering. In Proceedings of the 10th European Symposium on Research in Computer Security (ESORICS), (pp. 397-417).

Jiang, S., & Xia, S. (2012). Configuring cryptographically generated addresses (CGA) using DHCPv6. Retrieved from http://tools.ietf.org/html/draft-ietf-dhc-cga-config-dhcpv6-02

Jiang, X., & Yau, W. Y. (2000). Fingerprint minutiae matching based on the local and global structures. In Proceedings of 15th International Conference on Pattern Recognition, (vol. 2, pp. 1042-1045). IEEE.

Jonsson, J., & Kaliski, B. (2003). RFC-3447 - PKCS#1: RSA cryptography specifications version 2.1. Retrieved from http://www.ietf.org

Jordan, K. (2004). *MediConnect field test assists national HealthConnect*. Canberra, Australia: Australian Government Department of Health and Ageing.

Jøsang, A. (1996). The right type of trust for distributed systems. In C. Meadows (Ed.), Proceedings of the 1996 New Security Paradigms Workshop. ACM.

Jøsang, A., & Lo Presti, S. (2004). Analysing the relationship between risk and trust. In T. Dimitrakos (Ed.), Proceedings of the Second International Conference on Trust Management (iTrust). Oxford, UK: iTrust.

Jøsang, A., & Pope, S. (2005). User-centric identity management. In A. Clark (Ed.), Proceedings of AusCERT 2005. Brisbane, Australia: AusCERT.

Jøsang, A., Al Fayyadh, B., Grandison, T., AlZomai, M., & McNamara, J. (2007). Security usability principles for vulnerability analysis and risk assessment. In Proceedings of the Computer Security Applications Conference, Annual, (pp. 269-278). ACSAC.

Jøsang, A., Al Zomai, M., & Suriadi, S. (2007). Usability and privacy in identity management architectures. In L. Brankovic & C. Steketee (Eds.), Fifth Australasian Information Security Workshop (Privacy Enhancing Technologies) (AISW 2007), (vol. 68, pp. 143–152). Ballarat, Australia: ACS.

Jøsang, A., AlFayyadh, B., Grandison, T., AlZomai, M., & McNamara, J. (2007). Security usability principles for vulnerability analysis and risk assessment. In Proceedings of the Annual Computer Security Applications Conference (ACSAC'07). ACSAC.

Jøsang, A., Møllerud, P. M., & Cheung, E. (2001). Web security: The emperors new armour. In Proceedings of the European Conference on Information Systems (ECIS2001). Bled, Slovenia: ECIS.

Jøsang, A., Povey, D., & Ho, A. (2002). What you see is not always what you sign. In Proceedings of the Australian UNIX and Open Systems Users Group Conference (AUUG2002). Melbourne, Australia: AUUG.

Jøsang, A., Varmedal, K. A., Rosenberger, C., & Kumar, R. (2012). Service provider authentication assurance. In Proceedings of the 10th Annual Conference on Privacy, Security and Trust (PST 2012). Paris, France: PST.

Joye, M., & Tunstall, M. (2012). *Fault analysis in cryptography*. Berlin, Germany: Springer. doi:10.1007/978-3-642-29656-7.

JSON. (2010). Website. Retrieved from www.json.org

Juels, A., & Szydlo, M. (2002). A two-server, sealed-bid auction protocol. In Proceedings of the Sixth International Conference on Financial Cryptography 2002, (Vol. 2357, pp. 72-86). Berlin, Germany: Springer-Verlag.

Jung, W., Hong, S., Ha, M., Kim, Y.-J., & Kim, D. (2009). SSL-based lightweight security of IP-based wireless sensor networks. In Proceedings of the International Conference on Advanced Information Networking and Applications Workshops, (pp. 1112-1117). IEEE.

Kaliski, B. (1998). PKCS #10: Certification request syntax version 1.5. RFC. Retrieved from http://tools.ietf.org/html/rfc2314

Kalkbrener, M. (1999). On the complexity of Gröbner bases conversion. *Journal of Symbolic Computation*, *28*(1-2), 265–273. doi:10.1006/jsco.1998.0276.

Kaminsky, D. (2008). Details. [Blog]. Retrieved from http://dankaminsky.com/2008/07/24/details/

Kantarcioglu, M., & Vaidya, J. (2003). privacy preserving naive bayes classifier for horizontally partitioned data. In Proceedings of the Workshop on Privacy Preserving Data Mining held in association with The Third IEEE International Conference on Data Mining. IEEE.

Kantarcioglu, M., & Clifton, C. (2004). Privacy preserving data mining of association rules on horizontally partitioned data. *Transactions on Knowledge and Data Engineering*, *16*(9), 639–644. doi:10.1109/TKDE.2004.45.

Kanzaki, A., Iima, Y., Hara, T., & Nishio, S. (2010). Overhearing-based data transmission reduction using data interpolation in wireless sensor networks. In Proceedings of the Fifth International Conference on Mobile Computing and Ubiquitous Networking. IEEE.

Karakehayov, Z. (2005). Using REWARD to detect team black-hole attacks in wireless sensor networks. In Proceedings of the Workshop on Real World Wireless Sensor Networks. IEEE.

Kargupta, H., Huang, W., Sivakumar, K., & Johnson, E. (2001). Distributed clustering using collective principal component analysis. *Knowledge and Information Systems*, *3*(4), 405–421. doi:10.1007/PL00011677.

Karlof, C., & Wagner, D. (2002). Secure routing in wireless sensor networks: Attacks and countermeasures. In Proceedings of the First IEEE International Workshop on Sensor Network Protocols and Applications, (pp. 113-127). IEEE.

Karlsson, J., Dooley, L., & Pulkkis, G. (2012). Routing security in mobile ad-hoc networks. Issues in Informing Science and Information Technology, 9.

Katz, J. (2007). Universally composable multiparty computation using tamper-proof hardware. *Lecture Notes in Computer Science, 4515*, 115–128. doi:10.1007/978-3-540-72540-4_7.

Katz, J., Myers, S., & Ostrovsky, R. (2001). Cryptographic counters and applications to electronic voting. *Proceedings of EUROCRYPT, 2001*, 78–92.

Katz, J., Sahai, A., & Waters, B. (2008). Predicate encryption supporting disjunctions, polynomial equations, and inner products. *Lecture Notes in Computer Science, 4965*, 146–162. doi:10.1007/978-3-540-78967-3_9.

Kauer, B. (2007). OSLO: Improving the security of trusted computing. In Proceedings of the 16th USENIX Security Symposium, (pp. 1-9). USENIX.

Kaur, R., & Rai, M. (2012). A novel review on routing protocols in MANETs. Undergraduate Academic Research Journal, 1(1).

Kawaguchi, A., Russell, S., & Guoliang, Q. (2003). Security issues in the development of a wireless blood-glucose monitoring system. Paper presented at the Computer-Based Medical Systems, 2003. New York, NY.

Kayser, R. (2007). Federal register. Government Printing Office. Retrieved March 27, 2012, from http://csrc.nist.gov/groups/ST/hash/documents/FR_Notice_Nov07.pdf

Kelsey, J., Schneier, B., & Wagner, D. (1996). Key-shedule cryptanalysis of IDEA, G-DES, GOST, SAFER, and Triple-DES. *Lecture Notes in Computer Science, 1109*, 237–251. doi:10.1007/3-540-68697-5_19.

Kent, S., & Seo, K. (2005). RFC-4301: Security architecture for the internet protocol. Retrieved from http://www.ietf.org

Kerschbaum, F., & Sorniotti, A. (2011). Searchable encryption for outsourced data analytics. *Lecture Notes in Computer Science, 6711*, 61–76. doi:10.1007/978-3-642-22633-5_5.

Kesterson, H. L., II. (2007). PKI & identity: Technical and legal aspects. Retrieved April 17, 2012, from http://www.itu.int/dms_pub/itu-t/oth/15/04/T15040000110001P-DFE.pdf

Khader, D. (2007a). Attribute based group signature with revocation. Report 2007/241. Cryptology ePrint Archive.

Khader, D. (2007b). Attribute based group signatures. Report 2007/159. Cryptology ePrint Archive.

Khan, M. K., & Zhang, J. (2007). Improving the security of a flexible biometric remote user authentication scheme. *Computer Standards & Interfaces, 29*(1), 82–85. doi:10.1016/j.csi.2006.01.002.

Kiayias, A., & Yung, M. (2002). Self-tallying elections and perfect ballot secrecy. In Proceedings of PKC 2002, (p. 141-158). PKC.

Kikuchi, H. (2001). (m+1)st-price auction. In Proceedings of the Fifth International Conference on Financial Cryptography 2001, (Vol. 2339, pp. 291-298). Berlin, Germany: Springer-Verlag.

Kikuchi, H., Harkavy, M., & Tygar, J. D. (1998). Multi-round anonymous auction. In Proceedings of the First IEEE Workshop on Dependable and Real-Time e-Commerce Systems, (pp. 62-69). IEEE.

Kikuchi, H., Hotta, S., Abe, K., & Nakanishi, S. (2000). Distributed auction servers resolving winner and winning bid without revealing privacy of bids. In Proceedings of International Workshop on Next Generation Internet, (NGITA2000), (pp. 307-312). IEEE.

Kim, J. (1986). A method for limiting disclosure in microdata based on random noise and transformation. In Proceedings of the American Statistical Association on Survey Research Methods, (pp. 370–374). IEEE.

Kim, J., Biryukov, A., Preneel, B., & Hong, S. (2006). On the security of HMAC and NMAC based on HAVAL, MD4, MD5, SHA-0 and SHA-1. Retrieved from http://eprint.iacr.org/2006/187.pdf

Kim, J., Choi, H.-S., Wang, H., Agoulmine, N., Deerv, M. J., & Hong, J. W.-K. (2010). POSTECH's u-health smart home for elderly monitoring and support. Paper presented at the World of Wireless Mobile and Multimedia Networks (WoWMoM). New York, NY.

Kim, C. H., & Quisquater, J.-J. (2007). Fault attacks for CRT based RSA: New attacks, new results, and new countermeasures. *Lecture Notes in Computer Science, 4462*, 215–228. doi:10.1007/978-3-540-72354-7_18.

Kim, H. S., Lee, S. W., & Yoo, K. Y. (2003). On the security of ID-based password authentication scheme using smart cards and fingerprints. *ACM Operating System*, *37*(4), 32–41. doi:10.1145/958965.958969.

Kipnis, A., & Shamir, A. (1999). Cryptanalysis of the HFE public key cryptosystem by relinearization. *Lecture Notes in Computer Science*, *1666*, 19–30. doi:10.1007/3-540-48405-1_2.

Klein, T. (2006). All your private keys are belong to us - Extracting RSA private keys and certificates from process memory. Trapkit. Retrieved April 22, 2012, from http://www.trapkit.de/research/sslkeyfinder/keyfinder_v1.0_20060205.pdf

Klensin, J. (2008). Simple mail transfer protocol. RFC. Retrieved from http://tools.ietf.org/html/rfc5321

Klensin, J., Catoe, R., & Krumviede, P. (1997). IMAP/POP authorize extension for simple challenge/response. RFC. Retrieved from http://tools.ietf.org/html/rfc2195

Klusch, M., Lodi, S., & Moro, G. (2003). Distributed clustering based on sampling local density estimates. In Proceedings of the Eighteenth International Joint Conference on Artificial Intelligence (IJCAI 2003), (pp. 485–490). IJCAI.

Kocher, P. C. (1996). Timing attacks on implementations of Diffie-Hellman, RSA, DSS, and other systems. Retrieved from http://www.cryptography.com/public/pdf/TimingAttacks.pdf

Kocher, P. C., Jaffe, J., & Jun, B. (1999). Differential power analysis. Retrieved from http://www.cryptography.com/public/pdf/DPA.pdf

Kohlas, R., Jonczy, J., & Haenni, R. (2008). A trust evaluation method based on logic and probability theory. In Proceedings of the Joint iTrust and PST Conferences on Privacy, Trust Management and Security (IFIPTM 2008). IFIPTM.

Ko, Y., Hong, S., Lee, W., Lee, S., & Kang, J.-S. (2004). Related key differential attacks on 27 round of XTEA and full round of GOST. *Lecture Notes in Computer Science*, *3017*, 299–316. doi:10.1007/978-3-540-25937-4_19.

Krawczyk, H., Bellare, M., & Canetti, R. (1997). HMAC: Keyed-hashing for message authentication. RFC. Retrieved from http://tools.ietf.org/html/rfc2104

Krontiris, I., Dimitriou, T., & Giannetsos, T. (2007). Intrusion detection of sinkhole attacks in wireless sensor networks. In Proceedings of the 3rd International Conference on Algorithmic Aspects of Wireless Sensor Networks, (pp. 150-161). IEEE.

Kühn, H., & Murzek, M. (2006). Interoperability issues in metamodelling platforms. In Proceedings of the 1st International Conference on Interoperability of Enterprise Software and Applications, (pp. 215-226). IEEE.

Kuipers, J. B. (1999). *Quaternions and rotation sequences*. Princeton, NJ: Princeton University Press.

Kukec, A., & Zeeb, B. A. (2010). Native SeND kernel API for* BSD.[Tokyo, Japan: Tokyo University of Science.]. *Proceedings of AsiaBSDCon*, *2010*, 1–9.

Kumar, Y., Munjal, R., & Sharma, H. (2011). Comparison of symmetric and asymmetric cryptography with existing vulnerabilities and countermeasures. *International Journal of Computer Science and Management Studies*, *11*(3).

Kurosawa, K., & Ogata, W. (2002). Bit-slice auction circuit. In Proceedings of the 7th European Symposium on Research in Computer Security, ESORICS2002, (Vol. 2502, pp. 24-38). Berlin, Germany: Springer-Verlag.

Kushilevitz, E., & Ostrovsky, R. (1997). Replication is not needed: Single database, computationally private information retrieval. In Proceedings of the 38th Annual IEEE Computer Society Conference on Foundation of Computer Science, (pp. 20–22). IEEE.

Kuzu, M., Islam, M., Mohammad, S., & Kantarcioglu, M. (2012). Efficient similarity search over encrypted data. In Proceedings of the 2012 IEEE 28th International Conference on Data Engineering, (pp. 1156–1167). IEEE Computer Society.

Law, Y. W., Hartel, P., den Hartog, J., & Havinga, P. (2005). Link-layer jamming attacks on S-MAC. In Proceedings of the Second IEEE European Workshop on Wireless Sensor Networks, (pp. 217-225). IEEE.

Law, L., Menezes, A., Qu, M., Solinas, J., & Vanstone, S. (2003). An efficient protocol for authenticated key agreement. *Designs, Codes and Cryptography*, *28*(2), 119–134. doi:10.1023/A:1022595222606.

Lazos, L., & Poovendran, R. (2004). SeRLoc: Secure range-independent localization for wireless sensor networks. In Proceedings of the 3rd ACM Workshop on Wireless Security, (pp. 21-30). ACM Press.

Le, H.-C., Guyennet, H., & Felea, V. (2007). OBMAC: An overhearing based MAC protocol for wireless sensor networks. In Proceedings of the International Conference on Sensor Technologies and Applications, (pp. 547-553). IEEE.

Leach, P., & Newman, C. (2000). Using digest authentication as a SASL mechanism. RFC. Retrieved from http://www.ietf.org/rfc/rfc2831.txt

Lee, B., & Kim, K. (2002). Receipt-free electronic voting scheme with a tamper-resistant randomizer. In Proceedings of ICISC 2002, (Vol. 2587, pp. 389-406). Springer-Verlag.

Lee, E. (2011). Security in wireless ad hoc networks. Science Academy Transactions on Computer and Communication Networks, 1(1).

Lee, B., & Kim, K. (2000). Receipt-free electronic voting through collaboration of voter and honest verifier.[JW-ISC.]. *Proceedings of JW-ISC*, *2000*, 101–108.

Lee, B., & Kim, K. (2002). Receipt-free electronic voting scheme with a tamper-resistant randomizer. In *Proceedings of Information Security and Cryptology, ICISC 2002* (*Vol. 2587*, pp. 389–406). Berlin, Germany: Springer-Verlag. doi:10.1007/3-540-36552-4_27.

Lee, H. C., & Gaensslen, R. E. (2001). *Advances in fingerprint technology* (2nd ed.). New York, NY: Elsevier Publishing. doi:10.1201/9781420041347.

Lee, J. K., Ryu, S. R., & Yoo, K. Y. (2002). Fingerprint based remote user authentication scheme using smart cards. *IEEE Electronics Letters*, *38*(12), 554–555. doi:10.1049/el:20020380.

Lefevre, K., Dewittd, J., & Ramakrishnan, R. (2005). Incognito: Efficient full-domain k-anonymity. In Proceedings of the 2005 ACM SIGMOD International Conference on Management of Data, (pp. 49-60). ACM.

Legg, S. (2007). Abstract syntax notation X (ASN.X) representation of encoding instructions for the generic string encoding rules (GSER). RFC. Retrieved from http://tools.ietf.org/html/rfc4913

Leiba, B., Thomas, M., & Crocker, D. (2011). Author domain signing practices (ADSP): Point and counterpoint. Internet Computing, 15(1), 76-80. Retrieved from http://doi.ieeecomputersociety.org/10.1109/MIC.2011.1

Lenstra, A., Hughes, J., Augier, M., Bos, J., Kleinjung, T., & Wachter, C. (2012). Ron was wrong, Whit is right. Report 2012/064. Cryptology ePrint Archive.

Leveugle, R., Ammari, A., Maingot, V., Teyssou, E., Moitrel, P., & Mourtel, C. … Tria, A. (2007). Experimental evaluation of protections against laser-induced faults and consequences on fault modeling. In Proceedings of DATE 2007, (pp. 1-6). IEEE Press.

Levy-Abegnoli, E., Van de Velde, G., Popoviciu, C., & Mohacs, J. (2011). IPv6 router advertisement guard. RFC 6105. Retrieved from http://tools.ietf.org/html/rfc6105

Lewko, A., & Waters, B. (2011). Decentralizing attribute-based encryption. *Lecture Notes in Computer Science*, *6632*, 568–588. doi:10.1007/978-3-642-20465-4_31.

Li, H. (2006). Security evaluation at design time for cryptographic hardware. Tech. Rep. UCAM-CL-TR-665, 1:1. Cambridge, UK: University of Cambridge.

Li, J., & Kim, K. (2007). Attribute-based ring signatures. Report 2008/394. Cryptology ePrint Archive.

Li, J., Au, M. H., Susilo, W., Xie, D., & Ren, K. (2010). Attribute-based signature and its applications. In Proceedings of the 5th ACM Symposium on Information, Computer and Communications Security, ASIACCS 2010, (pp. 60–69). New York, NY: ACM.

Liang, W., & Wang, W. (2005). On performance analysis of challenge/response based authentication in wireless networks. *International Journal of Computer and Telecommunications Networking*, *48*(2), 267–288.

Lian, S., Sun, J., & Wong, Z. (2005). Security analysis of chaos-based image encryption algorithm. *Physics Letters. [Part A]*, 645–661.

Liao, I. E., Lee, C. C., & Hwang, M. S. (2006). A password authentication scheme over insecure networks. *Journal of Computer and System Sciences*, *72*(4), 727–740. doi:10.1016/j.jcss.2005.10.001.

Li, B., & Sarkar, S. (2006). A tree-based data perturbation approach for privacy-preserving data mining. *IEEE Transactions on Knowledge and Data Engineering*, *18*(9), 1278–1283. doi:10.1109/TKDE.2006.136.

Li, J., & Kim, K. (2010). Hidden attribute-based signatures without anonymity revocation. *Information Sciences*, *180*(9), 1681–1689. doi:10.1016/j.ins.2010.01.008.

Lim, S., Oh, T. H., Choi, Y. B., & Lakshman, T. (2010). Security issues on wireless body area network for remote healthcare monitoring. Paper presented at the Sensor Networks, Ubiquitous, and Trustworthy Computing (SUTC). New York, NY.

Lim, S., Yu, C., & Das, C. R. (2005). Rcast: A randomized communication scheme for improving energy efficiency in MANETs. In Proceedings of the 25th International Conference on Distributed Computing Systems, (pp. 123-132). IEEE.

Lin, Y.-C., & Slay, J. (2005). Non-repudiation in pure mobile ad hoc network. In Proceedings of the Australian Information Security Management Conference, (pp. 59-66). IEEE.

Lin, Y.-C., & Slay, J. (2006). QoS issues of using probabilistic non-repudiation protocol in mobile ad hoc network environment. In Proceedings of the 4th Australian Information Security Management Conference. Perth, Australia: IEEE.

Li, N., Grosof, B., & Feigenbaum, J. (2003). Delegation logic: A logic based approach to distributed authorization. *ACM Transactions on Information and System Security*, *6*(1), 128–171. doi:10.1145/605434.605438.

Lin, C. H., & Lai, Y. Y. (2004). A flexible biometric remote user authentication scheme. *Computer Standards & Interfaces*, *27*(1), 19–23. doi:10.1016/j.csi.2004.03.003.

Lindell, Y., & Pinkas, B. (2000). Privacy preserving data mining. In Proceedings of Advances in Cryptology (Crypto 2000), (pp. 36–54). Crypto.

Linn, J., & Branchaud, M. (2004). An examination of asserted PKI issues and proposed alternatives. In Proceedings of the 3rd Annual PKI R&D Workshop. Gaithersburg, MD: NIST.

Lipmaa, H., Asokan, N., & Niemi, V. (2002). Secure Vickrey auctions without thresh-old trust. In Proceedings of the 6th Annual Conference on Financial Cryptography, 2002, (Vol. 2357, pp. 87-101). Berlin, Germany: Springer-Verlag.

Lipmaa, H. (2003). On diophantine complexity and statistical zero-knowledge arguments. In *Proceedings of Asiacrypt '03* (*Vol. 2894*, pp. 398–415). Berlin, Germany: Springer-Verlag. doi:10.1007/978-3-540-40061-5_26.

Liu, Z., & Xiu, D. (2005). Agent-based automated trust negotiation for pervasive computing. Paper presented at the Second International Conference on Embedded Software and Systems. New York, NY.

Liu, J., & Li, J. (2010). A better improvement on the integrated Diffie-Hellman-DSA key agreement protocol. *International Journal of Network Security*, *11*(2), 114–117.

Li, Y., Sakiyama, K., Gomisawa, S., Fukunaga, T., Takahashi, J., & Ohta, K. (2010). Fault sensitivity analysis. *Lecture Notes in Computer Science*, *6225*, 320–334. doi:10.1007/978-3-642-15031-9_22.

Lopez, J., Roman, R., Agudo, I., & Fernandez-Gago, C. (2010). Trust management systems for wireless sensor networks: Best practices. *Journal of Computer Communications*, *33*(9), 1086–1093. doi:10.1016/j.comcom.2010.02.006.

Lu, B., & Pooch, U. (2005). A lightweight authentication protocol for mobile ad hoc networks. *International Journal of Information and Technology*, *11*(2).

Lubimov, A. V. (2008). The functional structure of common criteria. In Proceedings of XI St. Petersburg International Conference "Regional Informatics–2008" (RI–2008), (pp. 103-104). St. Petersburg, Russia: RI.

Lu, C. Y., Browne, D., Yang, T., & Pan, J. W. (2007). Demonstration of a compiled version of Shor's quantum factoring algorithm using photonic qubits. *Physical Review Letters*, *99*(25). doi:10.1103/PhysRevLett.99.250504 PMID:18233508.

Lucas, M. W. (2006). *PGP & GPG: Email for the practical paranoid*. New York, NY: No Starch Press Inc..

Lunin, A. (2008). Government and business collaboration in the standardization of cryptographic methods. World and Security, 1.

Luo, H., Zerfos, P., Kong, J., Lu, S., & Zhang, L. (2002). Self-securing ad hoc wireless networks. In Proceedings of the 2002 IEEE Symposium on Computers and Communications. IEEE.

Lupu, T. G. (2009). Main types of attacks in wireless sensor networks. In Proceedings of the 9th WSEAS International Conference on Signal, Speech and Image Processing, (pp. 180-185). WSEAS.

Lynn, C., Kent, S., & Seo, K. (2004). X.509 extensions for IP addresses and AS identifiers. RFC 3779. Retrieved from http://tools.ietf.org/html/rfc3779

M2-EasyScan. (2012). Fingerprint reader. Retrieved from http://www.easylobby.com/pdfs/ProductSpecSheets/M2-EasyScan.pdf

Machanavajjhala, A., Gehrke, J., & Kifer, D. (2007). l-Diversity: Privacy beyond k-anonymity. In Proceedings of ACM Transactions on Knowledge Discovery from Data, (pp. 24-35). ACM Press.

Mainwaring, A., Culler, D., Polastre, J., Szewczyk, R., & Anderson, J. (2002). Wireless sensor networks for habitat monitoring. In Proceedings of the 1st ACM International Workshop on Wireless Sensor Networks and Applications. ACM Press.

Maio, D., Maltoni, D., Cappelli, R., Wayman, J. L., & Jain, A. K. (2002). *FVC2002: Fingerprint verification competition*. Bologna, Italy: University of Bologna.

Maji, H., Prabhakaran, M., & Rosulek, M. (2008). Attribute-based signatures: Achieving attribute-privacy and collusion-resistance. Report 2008/328. Cryptology ePrint Archive.

Maji, H., Prabhakaran, M., & Rosulek, M. (2011). Attribute-based signatures. *Lecture Notes in Computer Science*, *6558*, 376–392. doi:10.1007/978-3-642-19074-2_24.

Malekian, E., & Zakerolhosseini, A. (2010). OTRU: A non-associative and high speed public key cryptosystem. In Proceedings of the 15th CSI International Symposium Computer Architecture and Digital Systems (CADS), (pp. 83-90). CADS.

Malekian, E., & Zakerolhosseini, A. (2010). NTRU-like public key cryptosystems beyond dedekind domain up to alternative algebra. *Transactions on Computational Science*, *10*, 25–41.

Mangard, S. (2004). Hardware countermeasures against DPA: A statistical analysis of their effectiveness. *Lecture Notes in Computer Science*, *2964*, 222–235. doi:10.1007/978-3-540-24660-2_18.

Mangard, S., Oswald, E., & Popp, T. (2007). *Power analysis attacks - revealing the secrets of smart cards*. Berlin, Germany: Springer.

Mangard, S., Oswald, E., & Standaert, F. (2011). One for all - All for one: Unifying standard differential power analysis attacks. *Information Security*, *5*(2), 100–110. doi:10.1049/iet-ifs.2010.0096.

Manola, F., & Miller, E. (2004). RDF primer. W3C Recommendation 10 February 2004. Retrieved from http://www.w3.org/TR/rdf-primer

Mano, M. (1988). *Computer engineering hardware design*. Upper Saddle River, NJ: Prentice-Hall, Inc..

Mantoro, T., Norhanipah, S. A., & Bidin, A. F. (2011). An implementation on domain name system security extensions framework for the support of IPv6 environment. doi:10.1109/ICMCS.2011.5945627

Marins, J. L., Xiaoping, Y., et al. (2001). An extended kalman filter for quaternion-based orientation estimation using MARG sensors. In Proceedings of the 2001 IEEE/RSJ, International Conference on Intelligent Robots and Systems, (pp. 2003-2011). Maui, HI: IEEE.

Martin, T., & Jones, A. (2011). An evaluation of data erasing tools. Paper presented at the 9th Australian Digital Forensics Conference. Perth, Australia.

Marvel, L. M., Boncelet, G. G., & Retter, C. T. (1999). Spread spectrum image steganography. *IEEE Transactions on Signal Processing*, *8*, 1075–1083. PMID:18267522.

Matsui, M. (1998). Linear cryptanalysis method for DES cipher. *Lecture Notes in Computer Science*, *765*, 386–397. doi:10.1007/3-540-48285-7_33.

Matsumoto, T., Matsumoto, H., Yamada, K., & Hoshino, S. (2002). Impact of artificial gummy fingers on fingerprint systems. In Proceedings of SPIE, Optical Security and Counterfeit Deterrence Techniques, (pp. 275-289). Springer.

Matsumoto, T. (2001). What will you do if you find a particular weakness of a security technology? *Journal of IEICE*, *84*(3).

May, L. (2005). The national e-health transition authority (NEHTA). *The HIM Journal*, *34*(1), 19. PMID:18239225.

McAfee. (2012). SiteAdvisor and SiteAdvisor plus. Retrieved September 09, 2012, from http://home.mcafee.com/store/siteadvisor-live?ctst=1

McCune, J. M., Li, Y., Qu, N., Zhou, Z., Datta, A., Gligor, V., & Perrig, A. (2010). TrustVisor: Efficient TCB reduction and attestation. In Proceedings of the 2010 IEEE Symposium on Security and Privacy, (pp. 143-158). Washington, DC: IEEE Computer Society.

McGrath, N., Gladyshev, P., & Carthy, J. (2010). Cryptopometry as a methodology for investigating encrypted material. *International Journal of Digital Crime and Forensics*, *2*(1), 29–35. doi:10.4018/jdcf.2010010101.

McGuinness, D., & Deborah, L. (2009). OWL 2 web ontology language. W3C Recommendation 27 October 2009. Retrieved from http://www.w3.org/TR/owl2-overview

McKnight, D. H., & Chervany, N. L. (1996). The meanings of trust. Technical Report MISRC Working Paper Series 96-04. Minneapolis, MN: University of Minnesota, Management Information Systems Reseach Center.

Mehrolhassani, M., & Elзi, A. (2008). OLS: An ontology based information system. In Proceedings of International Workshop on Ontology Alignment and Visualization (OnAV-2008), held in conjunction with the Second International Conference on Complex, Intelligent and Software Intensive Systems (CISIS 2008), (pp. 892-896). Barcelona, Spain: IEEE.

Melnikov, A. (2011). Moving DIGEST-MD5 to historic. RFC. Retrieved from http://tools.ietf.org/html/rfc6331

Melnikov, A., & Zeilenga, K. (2006). Simple authentication and security layer (SASL). Retrieved from http://tools.ietf.org/html/rfc4422

Menezes, A. J., Van Oorschot, P. C., & Vanstone, S. A. (1996). *Handbook of applied cryptography*. Boca Raton, FL: CRC Press. doi:10.1201/9781439821916.

Menezes, A., van Oorschot, P., & Vanstone, S. (1997). *Handbook of applied cryptography*. Boca Raton, FL: CRC Press.

Merugu, S., & Ghosh, J. (2003). Privacy-preserving distributed clustering using generative models. In Proceedings of the 3rd IEEE International Conference on Data Mining (ICDM 2003), (pp. 211–218). IEEE.

Messerges, T. S., Dabbish, E. A., & Sloan, R. H. (1999a). Investigations of power analysis attacks on smartcards. Retrieved from http://static.usenix.org/events/smartcard99/full_papers/messerges/messerges.pdf

Messerges, T. S., Dabbish, E. A., & Sloan, R. H. (1999b). Power analysis attacks of modular exponentiation in smartcards. Retrieved from http://saluc.engr.uconn.edu/refs/sidechannel/messerges99power.pdf

Meyer, B. (1988). *Object-oriented software construction*. Hemel Hempstead, NJ: Prentice Hall.

Micali, S., & Rivest, R. (2002). Micropayments revisited. [). Berlin, Germany: Springer.]. *Proceedings of CT-RSA*, *2271*, 149–163.

Michels, M., & Stadler, M. (1997). Verifiable homomorphic oblivious transfer and private equality test. In Proceedings of the 4th Annual Workshop on Selected Areas in Cryptology, (pp. 231-244). Springer.

Micro, T. (2012). TrendProtect. Retrieved September 09, 2012, from http://www.trendsecure.com/portal/en-US/tools/security_tools/trendprotect

Microsoft Corporation. (2012). Microsoft NTLM. Retrieved from http://msdn.microsoft.com/en-us/library/aa378749.aspx

Microsoft. (2001). Microsoft security bulletin MS01-017 (March 22, 2001): Erroneous VeriSign-issued digital certificates pose spoofing hazard. Retrieved from http://www.microsoft.com/technet/security/bulletin/MS01-017.asp

Miller, M. (2000). Lambda for humans: The PetName markup language. Retrieved April 17, 2012, from http://www.erights.org/elib/capability/pnml.html

Mills, E. (2011). Fraudulent Google certificate points to internet attack. Retrieved form http://news.cnet.com/

Misaghi, M., da Silva, E., & Albini, L. C. P. (2012). Distributed self-organized trust management for mobile ad hoc networks. *Communications in Computer and Information Science*, *293*, 506–518. doi:10.1007/978-3-642-30507-8_43.

Mohsen, S. M., Zamshed, S. M., & Hashem, M. M. A. (2004). Automated fingerprint recognition: Using minutiae matching technique for the large fingerprint database. Paper presented at the International Conference on Electrical and Computer Engineering ICECE 2004. New York, NY.

Moldovyan, N. A., & Moldovyan, A. A. (2007). *Data-driven block ciphers for fast telecommunication systems*. New York, NY: Talor & Francis Group. doi:10.1201/9781420054125.

Molle, R. M., Connell, J. H., Pankanti, S., Ratha, N. K., & Senior, A. W. (2003). *Guide to biometrics*. Berlin, Germany: Springer.

Monnet, Y., Renaudin, M., Leveugle, R., Feyt, N., Moitrel, P., & Nzenguet, F. M. (2006). Practical evaluation of fault countermeasures on an asynchronous des crypto processor. In Proceedings of IOLTS, (pp. 125-130). IEEE Press.

Montenegro, G., Kushalnagar, N., Hui, J., & Culler, D. (2007). Transmission of IPv6 packets over IEEE 802.15.4 networks. IETF Request for Comments (RFC): 4944. Retrieved April 20, 2012, from http://tools.ietf.org/html/rfc4944

Moore, N. (2006). Optimistic duplicate address detection (DAD) for IPv6. Retrieved from http://tools.ietf.org/html/rfc4429

Moore, D. (2009). *The basic practice of statistics*. New York, NY: WH Freeman & Co..

Moradi, A., Barenghi, A., Kasper, T., & Paar, C. (2011). On the vulnerability of FPGA bitstream encryption against power analysis attacks: Extracting keys from XILINX Virtex FPGAs. Retrieved from http://eprint.iacr.org/2011/390

Mosorov, V. (2001). Using tophat transformation for image fingerprint segmentation. Paper presented at the International Conference on Signals and Electronic Systems. New York, NY.

Msiza, I. S., Leke-Betechuoh, B., Nelwamondo, F. V., & Msimang, N. (2009). A fingerprint pattern classification approach based on the coordinate geometry of singularities. Paper presented at the IEEE International Conference on Systems, Man and Cybernetics, SMC 2009. New York, NY.

Mu, Y., & Varadharajan, V. (2000). An internet anonymous auction scheme. In Proceedings of the International Conference on Information Security and Cryptology 2000, (Vol. 2015, pp. 171-182). Berlin, Germany: Springer-Verlag.

Murugan, R., & Shanmugam, A. (2012). Cluster based node misbehaviour detection, isolation and authentication using threshold cryptography in mobile ad hoc networks. *International Journal of Computer Science and Security*, *6*(3).

Musen, M. (2012). Protégé. Stanford, CA: Stanford University. Retrieved from http://protege.stanford.edu

Myers, J. (1999). SMTP service extension for authentication. RFC. Retrieved from http://tools.ietf.org/html/rfc2554

Myers, J., & Rose, M. (1997). Post office protocol - Version 3. RFC. Retrieved from http://www.ietf.org/rfc/rfc1939.txt

Naccache, D., & Stern, J. (1998). A new public key cryptosystem based on higher residues. In Proceedings of the 5th ACM Conference on Computer and Communications Security, (pp. 59–66). ACM Press.

Nagase, T., Koide, R., Araki, T., & Hasegawa, Y. (2004b). A new quadripartite public-key cryptosystem. In Proceedings of the International Symposium on Communications and Information Technologies 2004 (ISCIT 2004), (pp. 74-79). Sapporo, Japan: ISCIT.

Nagase, T., Komata, M., & Araki, T. (2004a). Secure signals transmission based on quaternion encryption scheme. In Proceedings 18th International Conference on Advanced Information Networking and Application (AINA 2004), (pp. 35-38). IEEE Computer Society.

Nagase, T., Koide, R., Araki, T., & Hasegawa, Y. (2005). Dispersion of sequences for generating a robust enciphering system. *ECTI Transactions on Computer and Information Theory*, *1*(1), 9–14.

Naor, M., & Nissim, K. (2001). Communication preserving protocols for secure function evaluation. In Proceedings of the 33rd Annual ACM Symposium on Theory of Computing. Heraklion, Greece: ACM.

Naor, M., & Pinkas, B. (1999). Oblivious transfer and polynomial evaluation. In Proceedings of the 31st Symposium on Theory of Computer Science, (pp. 245–254). IEEE.

Naor, M., Pinkas, B., & Sumner, R. (1999). Privacy perserving auctions and mechanism design. In Proceedings of ACM Conference on Electronic Commerce 1999, (pp. 129-139). ACM.

Naor, M., & Pinkas, B. (2005). Computationally secure oblivious transfer. *Journal of Cryptology*, *18*(1), 245–254. doi:10.1007/s00145-004-0102-6.

Naor, M., & Shamir, A. (1995). Visual cryptography. In *Proceedings of Advances in Cryptology — EUROCRYPT'94* (*Vol. 950*, pp. 1–12). Berlin, Germany: Springer. doi:10.1007/BFb0053419.

Narten, T., Draves, R., & Krishnan, S. (2007). Privacy extensions for stateless address autoconfiguration in IPv6. RFC 4941. Retrieved from http://tools.ietf.org/html/rfc4941

Narten, T., Nordmark, E., Simpson, W., & Soliman, H. (2007). Neighbor discovery for IP version 6 (IPv6). RFC 4861. Retrieved from http://tools.ietf.org/html/rfc4861

National Institutes of Standards and Technology. (2001). Announcing the advanced encryption standard (AES). Retrieved April 25, 2012, from http://csrc.nist.gov/publications/fips/fips197/fips-197.pdf

Nayak, A., & Stojmenovic, I. (2010). *Wireless sensor and actuator networks: Algorithms and protocols for scalable coordination and data communication.* New York, NY: Wiley-Interscience. doi:10.1002/9780470570517.

Neff, C. A. (2000). Conducting a universally verifiable electronic election using homomorphic encryption. White Paper. VoteHere Inc.

Neff, C. A. (2001). A verifiable secret shuffle and its application to e-voting. In Proceedings of the ACM Conference on Computer and Communications Security 2001, (p. 116-125). ACM.

Neff, C. A. (2004). Verifiable mixing (shuffling) of ElGamal pairs. Retrieved from http://theory.lcs.mit.edu/_rivest/voting/papers/Neff-2004-04-21-ElGamalShuffles.pdf

NEHTA. (2009). *Web services profile.* NEHTA.

Netcraft Ltd. (2010). Certification services: Netcraft report. Retrieved from https://ssl.netcraft.com/ssl-samplereport/CMatch/certs

Newman, C. (1999). Using TLS with IMAP, POP3 and ACAP. RFC. Retrieved from http://tools.ietf.org/html/rfc2595

Newsome, J., Shi, E., Song, D., & Perrig, A. (2004). The sybil attack in sensor networks: Analysis and defenses. In Proceedings of the Third International Symposium on Information Processing in Sensor Networks, (pp. 259-268). IEEE.

Nguyen, L., Safavi-Naini, R., & Kurosawa, K. (2006). Verifiable shuffles: a formal model and a Paillier-based three-round construction with provable security. *International Journal of Information Security*, *4*, 241–255. doi:10.1007/s10207-006-0004-8.

Nikander, E. P., Kempf, J., & Nordmark, E. (2004). IPv6 neighbor discovery (ND) trust models and threats. RFC 3756. Retrieved from http://tools.ietf.org/html/rfc3756

Nikander, P. (2002). Denial-of-service, address ownership, and early authentication in the IPv6 world. In Proceedings of the 9th International Workshop on Security Protocols, (pp. 12–21). London, UK: Springer-Verlag. Retrieved from http://dl.acm.org/citation.cfm?id=647219.720869

NIST. (2001). FIPS-197: Advanced encryption standard (AES).[Washington, DC: NIST.]. *Federal Information Processing Standards Publication*, *197*, 441–0311.

NIST. (2012). Tentative timeline of the development of new hash functions. Retrieved from http://csrc.nist.gov/groups/ST/hash/timeline.html

Ns2. (2012). Website. Retrieved September 5, 2012, from http://www.isi.edu/nsnam/ns/

O'Gorman, L. (2002). Seven issues with human authentication technologies. In Proceedings of Workshop on Automatic Identification Advanced Technologies (AutoID), (pp. 185-186). AudoID.

Ochoa, H., & Azubel, A. (2010). Windows SMB NTLM authentication weak nonce vulnerability. Retrieved from http://www.ampliasecurity.com/research/OCHOA-2010-0209.txt

Oechslin, P. (2003). Making a faster cryptanalytic time-memory trade-off. In D. Boneh (Ed.), Advances in Cryptology - CRYPTO 2003, 23rd Annual International Cryptology Conference, (pp. 617-630). Berlin, Germany: Springer.

Okamoto, T., & Takashima, K. (2011). Efficient attribute-based signatures for non-monotone predicates in the standard model. *Lecture Notes in Computer Science*, *6571*, 35–52. doi:10.1007/978-3-642-19379-8_3.

Oleshchuk, V., & Zadorozhny, V. (2007). Secure multiparty computations and privacy preservation: Results and open problems. Telektronikk: Telenor's Journal of Technology, 103(2).

Oliveira, S., & Zaiane, O. R. (2003). Privacy preserving clustering by data transformation. In Proceedings of XVIII Simp'osio Brasileiro de Bancos de Dados, (pp. 304–318). IEEE.

Ølnes, J. (2006). PKI interoperability by an independent, trusted validation authority. In Proceedings of the 5th Annual PKI R&D Workshop. Gaithersburg, MD: NIST.

OMNeT++. (2012). Website. Retrieved September 5, 2012, from http://omnetpp.org/

Omote, K., & Miyaji, A. (2002). A second-price sealed-bid auction with the discriminant of the p-th root. In Proceedings of the Financial Cryptography 2002, (Vol. 2357, pp. 57-71). Berlin, Germany: Springer.

OpenSSL. (2012). The open source toolkit for SSL/TLS. Retrieved from www.openssl.org/

OpenSSL. SSL_CTX_set_options(3). (2009). Website. Retrieved from http://www.openssl.org/docs/ssl/SSL_CTX_set_options.html#SECURE_RENEGOTIATION

OPNET. (2012). Website. Retrieved September 5, 2012, from http://www.opnet.com/

Oreku, G. S., Li, J., Pazynyuk, T., & Mtenzi, F. J. (2007). Modified s-box to archive accelerated GOST. *International Journal of Computer Science and Network Security*, *7*(6), 88–98.

Organisation, W. (2000). *The world health report 2000 - Health systems: Improving performance*. Washington, DC: World Health Organization.

O'shea, G., & Roe, M. (2001). Child-proof authentication for MIPv6 (CAM). *ACM SIGCOMM Computer Communication Review*, *31*(2), 4–8. doi:10.1145/505666.505668.

Ouafi, K., & Phan, R. (2008). Privacy of recent RFID authentication protocols. Paper presented at the Information Security Practice and Experience (ISPEC). New York, NY.

Özarar, M., & Özgit, A. (2007). Secure multiparty overall mean computation via oblivious polynomial evaluation. In Proceedings of First International Conference on Security of Information and Networks (SIN 2007), (pp. 84-95). IEEE.

Özarar, M., & Özgit, A. (2008). Secure homogeneous matrix algebra with oblivious polynomial evaluation. In Proceedings of Third Information Security and Cryptology Conference (ISCTURKEY), (pp. 157-163). ISCTURKEY.

Özarar, M., & Özgit, A. (2011). *Privacy preserving hierarchical agglomerative document clustering*. Technical Report. METU.

Padmavathi, G., & Shanmugapriya, D. (2009). A survey of attacks, security mechanisms and challenges in wireless sensor networks. *International Journal of Computer Science and Information Security*, *4*(1&2).

Paillier, P. (1999). Public key cryptosystem based on composite degree residuosity classes. In *Proceedings of Eurocrypt '99* (*Vol. 1592*, pp. 223–238). Berlin, Germany: Springer-Verlag. doi:10.1007/3-540-48910-X_16.

Pappas, V., Raykova, M., Vo, B., Bellovin, S. M., & Malkin, T. (2011). Private search in the real world. In Proceedings of the 27th Annual Computer Security Applications Conference, (pp. 83–92). ACM.

Park, C., Itoh, K., & Kurosawa, K. (1993). Efficient anonymous channel and all/nothing election scheme. In *Proceedings of Eurocrypt 1993* (*Vol. 765*, pp. 248–259). Berlin, Germany: Springer-Verlag.

Parno, B. J. (2005). Distributed detection of node replication attacks in sensor networks. (MSc. Thesis). Carnegie Mellon University. Pittsburgh, PA.

Pathan, A. S. K. (Ed.). (2010). *Security of self-organizing networks: MANET, WSN, WMN, VANET*. Boca Raton, FL: CRC Press. doi:10.1201/EBK1439819197.

Pawar, P. M., Nielsen, R. H., Prasad, N. R., Ohmori, S., & Prasad, R. (2012). Behavioral modeling of WSN MAC layer security attacks: A sequential UML approach. *Journal of Cyber Security and Mobility*, *1*(1), 65–82.

Pedersen, T. P. (1991). Non-interactive and information-theoretic secure verifiable secret sharing.[Berlin, Germany: Springer-Verlag.]. *Proceedings of Eurocrypt*, *91*, 129–140.

Peeters, E., Standaert, F.-X., & Quisquater, J. (2007). Power and electromagnetic analysis: Improved model, consequences and comparisons. *Integration (Tokyo, Japan)*, *40*(1), 52–60.

Peng, K., Boyd, C., Dawson, E., & Viswanathan, K. (2002a). Non-interactive auction scheme with strong privacy. In Proceedings of ICISC 2002, (Vol. 2587, pp. 407–420). Berlin, Germany: Springer.

Peng, K., Boyd, C., Dawson, E., & Viswanathan, K. (2002b). Robust, privacy protecting and publicly verifiable sealed-bid auction. In Proceedings of ICICS 2002, (Vol. 2513, pp. 147–159). Berlin, Germany: Springer.

Peng, K., Boyd, C., Dawson, E., & Viswanathan, K. (2003a). Efficient implementation of relative bid privacy in sealed-bid auction. In Proceedings of the 4th International Workshop on Information Security Applications, WISA2003, (Vol. 2908, pp. 244-256). Berlin, Germany: Springer-Verlag.

Peng, K., Boyd, C., Dawson, E., & Viswanathan, K. (2003b). Five sealed-bid auction models. In Proceedings of the Australia Workshop of Information Security 2003. IEEE.

Peng, K., Boyd, C., Dawson, E., & Viswanathan, K. (2004). A correct, private and efficient mix network. In Proceedings of the 2004 International Workshop on Practice and Theory in Public Key Cryptography, (Vol. 2947, pp. 439-454). Berlin, Germany: Springer-Verlag.

Peng, K., Boyd, C., Dawson, E., & Lee, B. (2004). Multiplicative homomorphic e-voting. In *Proceedings of Indocrypt 2004* (*Vol. 3348*, pp. 61–72). Berlin, Germany: Springer-Verlag. doi:10.1007/978-3-540-30556-9_6.

Perkins, C., Johnson, D., & Arkko, J. (2011). Mobility support in IPv6. RFC 6275. Retrieved from http://tools.ietf.org/html/rfc6275

Perrig, A., Stankovic, J., & Wagner, D. (2004). Security in wireless sensor networks. *Communications of the ACM*, *47*(6), 53–57. doi:10.1145/990680.990707.

Perrig, A., Szewczyk, R., Tygar, J. D., Wen, V., & Culler, D. E. (2002). SPINS: Security protocols for sensor networks. *Wireless Networks*, *8*(5), 521–534. doi:10.1023/A:1016598314198.

Persephone, D., Pekka, R., & Hanna, P. (2005). *Regional health economies and ICT services: The PICNIC experience*. Boca Raton, FL: IOS Press.

Pfitzmann, B. (1994). Breaking an efficient anonymous channel. In *Proceedings of Eurocrypt 1994* (*Vol. 950*, pp. 339–348). Berlin, Germany: Springer-Verlag.

PHP. (2012). Hypertext preprocessor. Retrieved from www.php.net/

Pieprzyk, J., & Tombak, L. (1994). *Soviet encryption algorithm*. Wollongong, Australia: The University of Wollongong.

Pinkas, B. (2003). In Explorations, S. I. G. K. D. D. (Ed.), *Cryptographic techniques for privacy-preserving data mining* (pp. 12–19). ACM.

Poh, N., & Bengio, S. (2005). An investigation of f-ratio client-dependent normalisation on biometric authentication tasks. Paper presented at the IEEE International Conference on Acoustics, Speech, and Signal Processing (ICASSP). New York, NY.

Popov, V., Kurepkin, I., & Leontiev, S. (2006). Additional cryptographic algorithms for use with GOST 28147-89, GOST R 34.10-94, GOST R 34.10-2001, and GOST R 34.11-94 algorithms. Retrieved January 2006 from http://www.ietf.org/rfc/rfc4357

Postel, J. B. (1982). Simple mail transfer protocol. RFC. Retrieved from http://www.ietf.org/rfc/rfc821.txt

Prabhakar, S., Pankanti, S., & Jain, A. K. (2003). Biometric recognition: Security and privacy concerns. Paper presented at the IEEE Security and Privacy. New York, NY.

Prevention, P. L., & Division, S. (2003). Internet auction fraud. Retrieved from http://www.psecu.com/About Us/News/Fraud/2003/20030812.html

PricewaterhouseCoopers. (2005). HealthCast 2020: Creating a sustainable future. New York, NY: PricewaterhouseCoopers' Health Research Institute.

Putte, T. V., & Keuning, J. T. (2000). Biometrical fingerprint recognition don't get your fingers burned. Paper presented at the IFIP 2000. New York, NY.

Quisquater, J.-J., & Samyde, D. (2002). Eddy current for magnetic analysis with active sensor. In Proceedings of E-Smart 2002. Nice, France: E-Smart.

Quisquater, J., & Samyde, D. (2001). Electromagnetic analysis (EMA): Measures and counter-measures for smart cards.[London, UK: Springer.]. *Proceedings of E-SMART, 2001*, 200–210.

Radosavac, S., Crdenas, A. A., Baras, J. S., & Moustakides, G. V. (2007). Detecting IEEE 802.11 MAC layer misbehavior in ad hoc networks: Robust strategies against individual and colluding attackers. *Journal of Computer Security*, *15*(1), 103–128.

Rafiee, H., AlSa'deh, A., & Meinel, C. (2011). WinSEND: Windows secure neighbor discovery. In Proceedings of the 4th International Conference on Security, SIN 2011, (pp. 243-246). Sydney, Australia: ACM.

Rafiee, H., AlSa'deh, A., & Meinel, C. (2012). Multicore-based auto-scaling secure neighbor discovery for windows operating systems. In Proceedings of the 2012 International Conference on Information Networking, ICOIN 2012, (pp. 269-274). Bali, Indonesia: IEEE.

Rafiee, H., Von Loewis, M., & Meinel, C. (2012). IPv6 deployment and spam challenges. *IEEE Internet Computing*, *16*(6). doi:10.1109/MIC.2012.97.

Rafsanjani, M., & Shojaiemehr, B. (2012). Improvement of self-organized public key management for MANET. *Journal of American Science*, *8*(1).

Ramsdell, B., & Turner, S. (2010). Secure/multipurpose internet mail extensions (S/MIME) version 3.2 message specification. RFC. Retrieved from http://tools.ietf.org/html/rfc5751

Ratha, N. K., Pandit, V. D., Bolle, R. M., & Vaish, V. (2000). Robust fingerprint authentication using local structural similarity. In Proceedings of Workshop on Applications of Computer Vision, (pp. 29-34). IEEE.

Ratha, N., Connell, J., & Bolle, R. (2001). An analysis of minutiae matching strength. Paper presented at the International Conference on Audio- and Video-Based Biometric Person Authentication III. New York, NY.

Ratha, N. K., Chen, S. Y., & Jain, A. K. (1995). Adaptive flow orientation-based feature extraction in fingerprint images. *Pattern Recognition*, *28*(11), 1657–1672. doi:10.1016/0031-3203(95)00039-3.

Ratha, N. K., Karu, K., Chen, S., & Jain, A. K. (1996). A real-time matching system for large fingerprint databases. *IEEE Transactions on Pattern Analysis and Machine Intelligence*, *18*(8), 799–813. doi:10.1109/34.531800.

Raya, M., & Hubaux, J.-P. (2007). Securing vehicular ad hoc networks. *Journal of Computer Security*, *15*, 39–68.

Raykova, M., Cui, A., Vo, B., Liu, B., Malkin, T., Bellovin, S. M., & Stolfo, S. J. (2012). Usable, secure, private search. *IEEE Security & Privacy*, *10*, 53–60.

Raymond, D. R., & Midkiff, S. F. (2008). Denial-of-service in wireless sensor networks: Attacks and defenses. *IEEE Pervasive Computing / IEEE Computer Society [and] IEEE Communications Society*, *7*(1), 74–81. doi:10.1109/MPRV.2008.6.

Record, C. O. I. T. P., & Medicine, I. O. (1997). *The computer-based patient record: An essential technology for health care* (Revised Ed.). Washington, DC: The National Academies Press.

Renauld, M., Standaert, F.-X., Veyrat-Charvillon, N., Kamel, D., & Flandre, D. (2011). A formal study of power variability issues and side-channel attacks for nanoscale devices. Retrieved from http://perso.uclouvain.be/fstandae/PUBLIS/94.pdf

Rescorla, E. (2009). Understanding the TLS renegotiation attack. Educated Guesswork. Retrieved from http://www.educatedguesswork.org/2009/11/understanding_the_TLS_renegoti. html

Resnick, P. (2001). Internet message format. RFC. Retrieved from http://tools.ietf.org/html/rfc2822

Resnick, P. (2008). Internet message format. RFC. Retrieved from http://tools.ietf.org/html/rfc5322

Rhee, H. S., Park, J. H., Susilo, W., & Lee, D. H. (2010). Trapdoor security in a searchable public-key encryption scheme with a designated tester. *Journal of Systems and Software*, *83*(5), 763–771. doi:10.1016/j.jss.2009.11.726.

Rivest, R. L., Adleman, L., & Dertouzos, M. L. (1978). On data banks and privacy homomorphisms. In *Foundations on Secure Computation* (pp. 169–179). New York, NY: Academia Press.

Rivest, R. L., Shamir, A., & Adleman, L. M. (1978). A method for obtaining digital signatures and public-key cryptosystems. *Communications of the ACM*, *21*(2), 120–126. doi:10.1145/359340.359342.

Rivest, R., Shamir, A., & Tauman, Y. (2001). How to leak a secret. *Lecture Notes in Computer Science*, *2248*, 552–565. doi:10.1007/3-540-45682-1_32.

Rizvi, S. J., & Harista, J. R. (2002). Maintaining data privacy in association rule mining. In Proceedings of 28th International Conference on Very Large Data Bases (VLDB), (pp. 682-693). VLDB.

Rizvi, S., Sultana, Z., Sun, B., & Islam, W. (2010). Security of mobile agent in ad hoc network using threshold cryptography. World Academy of Science, Engineering and Technology, 70.

Roessler, T., & Saldhana, A. (2010). W3C security context: User interface guidelines. Retrieved April 17 2012, from http://www.w3.org/TR/wsc-ui/

Rogaway, P., & Shrimpton, T. (2004). Cryptographic hash-function basics: Definitions, implications, and separations for preimage resistance, second-preimage resistance, and collision resistance. In Proceedings of the Fast Software Encryption, 11th International Workshop, (pp. 371-388). Springer.

Rokbani, N., & Alimi, A. (2005). Fingerprint identification using minutiae constellation matching. Paper presented at the IADIS Virtual Multi Conference on Computer Science and Information Systems. New York, NY.

Rubenking, N. J. (2009). Web of trust review and rating, August 13, 2009. Retrieved September 09, 2012, from http://www.pcmag.com/article2/0,2817,2351536,00.asp

Ruby, B. L., Zhijie, S., & Xiao, Y. (2001). Efficient permutation instructions for fast software cryptography. *IEEE Micro*, *21*(6), 56–69. doi:10.1109/40.977759.

Ruotsalainen, P. (2004). A cross-platform model for secure electronic health record communication. *International Journal of Medical Informatics*, *73*(3), 291–295. doi:10.1016/j.ijmedinf.2003.12.012 PMID:15066561.

Saarinen, M.-J. (1998). A chosen key attack against the secret s-boxes of GOST. Retrieved August 12, 1998 from http://www.researchgate.net/publication/2598060_A_chosen_key_attack_against_the_secret_S-boxes_of_GOST

Sadeghi, A.-R., & Schulz, S. (2010). Extending IPsec for efficient remote attestation. In Proceedings of the 14th International Conference on Financial Cryptograpy and Data Security, (pp. 150-165). IEEE.

Sadeghi, A.-R., & Stüble, C. (2004). Property-based attestation for computing platforms: Caring about properties, not mechanisms. In Proceedings of the 2004 Workshop on New Security Paradigm, (pp. 67-77). New York, NY: ACM.

Saha, H., Bhattacharyya, D., & Banerjee, P. (2012). A novel approach for attacks mitigation in mobile ad hoc networks using cellular automata. International Journal of Ad Hoc, Sensor & Ubiquitous Computing, 3(2).

Sahai, A., & Waters, B. (2005). Fuzzy identity-based encryption. In *Proceedings of Advances in Cryptology – EUROCRYPT 2005* (*Vol. 3494*, pp. 557–557). Berlin, Germany: Springer. doi:10.1007/11426639_27.

Sailer, R., Zhang, X., Jaeger, T., & van Doorn, L. (2004). Design and Implementation of a TCG-based integrity measurement architecture. In Proceedings of the 13th USENIX Security Symposium, (pp. 223-238). USENIX.

Sako, K. (2000). An auction scheme which hides the bids of losers. In *Proceedings of Public Key Cryptology 2000* (*Vol. 1880*, pp. 422–432). Berlin, Germany: Springer-Verlag.

Sakurai, K., & Miyazaki, S. (1999). A bulletin-board based digital auction scheme with bidding down strategy -Towards anonymous electronic bidding without anonymous channels nor trusted centers. In Proceedings of International Workshop on Cryptographic Techniques and e-Commerce, (pp. 180-187). Hong Kong, Hong Kong: City University of Hong Kong Press.

Sander, T., Young, A., & Yung, M. (1999). Non-interactive cryptocomputing for NC1. In Proceedings of the 40th Annual Symposium on Foundations of Computer Science, FOCS '99, (pp. 554-567). FOCS.

Sangwine, S. J. (1996). Fourier transforms of color images using quaternions, or hypercomplex numbers. *Electronics Letters*, *32*(21), 1979–1980. doi:10.1049/el:19961331.

Saxena, N., Tsudik, G., & Yi, J.-H. (2009). Efficient node admission and certificateless secure communication in short-lived MANETs. *IEEE Transactions on Parallel and Distributed Systems*, *20*(2), 158–170. doi:10.1109/TPDS.2008.77.

Saxena, N., & Yi, J.-H. (2009). Noninteractive self-certification for long-lived mobile ad hoc networks. *IEEE Transactions on Information Forensics and Security*, *4*(4), 946–955. doi:10.1109/TIFS.2009.2031946.

Schmidt, J.-M., & Herbst, C. (2008). A practical fault attack on square and multiply. Retrieved from http://conferenze.dei.polimi.it/FDTC08/fdtc08-schmidt.pdf

Schneier, B. (1996). *Applied cryptography, protocols, algorithms and source code in C* (2nd ed.). New York, NY: John Wiley & Sons, Inc..

Schnorr, C. (1991). Efficient signature generation by smart cards. *Journal of Cryptology*, *4*, 161–174. doi:10.1007/BF00196725.

Schoenmakers, B. (2000, July). Fully auditable electronic secret-ballot elections. XOOTIC Magazine.

Schreiber, F. (1973). *Sybil*. New York, NY: Warner Books.

Schuckers, S., & Abhyankar, A. (2004). A wavelet based approach to detecting liveness in fingerprint scanners. Paper presented at the Biometric Authentication Workshop (ECCV). New York, NY.

Schuckers, S., Hornak, L., Norman, T., Derakhshani, R., & Parthasaradhi, S. (2002). *Issues for liveness detection in biometrics*. Morgantown, WV: West Virginia University.

Schwiebert, L., Gupta, S. K. S., & Weinmann, J. (2001). Research challenges in wireless networks of biomedical sensors. In Proceedings of the 7th Annual International Conference on Mobile Computing and Networking, (pp. 151-165). New York, NY: ACM.

SDK. (2011). Website. Retrieved from http://developer.android.com/sdk/index.html

Seamons, K. (2004). TrustBuilder: Automated trust negotiation in open systems. Paper presented at the 3rd Annual PKI R&D Workshop. New York, NY.

Seamons, K. E., Winslett, M., Ting, Y., Smith, B., Child, E., Jacobson, J., et al. (2002). Requirements for policy languages for trust negotiation. Paper presented at the Third International Workshop on Policies for Distributed Systems and Networks, 2002. New York, NY.

Sears, W., Yu, Z., & Guan, Y. (2005). An adaptive reputation-based trust framework for peer-to-peer applications. Paper presented at the Network Computing and Applications, Fourth IEEE International Symposium on. New York, NY.

Sen, J. (2009). A survey on wireless sensor network security. *International Journal of Communication Networks and Information Security*, *1*(2), 55–78.

Shacham, H., & Waters, B. (2008). Compact proofs of retrievability. *Lecture Notes in Computer Science*, *5350*, 90–107. doi:10.1007/978-3-540-89255-7_7.

Shahandashti, S., & Safavi-Naini, R. (2009). Threshold attribute-based signatures and their application to anonymous credential systems. *Lecture Notes in Computer Science*, *5580*, 198–216. doi:10.1007/978-3-642-02384-2_13.

Shahrestani, S. A. (2009). ICT healthcare: Overcoming complex barriers for successful deployment. Paper presented at the 5th WSEAS International Conference on Dynamical Systems and Control. New York, NY.

Shakarian, P. (2011, April). Stuxnet: Cyberwar revolution in military affairs. Small Wars Journal.

Shamir, A., & Van Someren, N. (1999). Playing hide and seek with stored keys. In M. Franklin (Ed.), Financial Cryptography, Third International Conference Proceedings, (pp. 118-124). Springer.

Shamir, A. (1979). How to share a secret. *Communications of the ACM*, *22*(11), 612–613. doi:10.1145/359168.359176.

Shamir, A., & Tauman, Y. (2001). Improved online/offline signature scheme. *Advances in Cryptology*, *2139*, 355–367.

Shannon, C. E. (1948). Communication theory of secrecy systems. *The Bell System Technical Journal*, *28*, 656–715.

Shanqing, G., & Yingpei, Z. (2008). Attribute-based signature scheme. In Proceedings of the 2008 International Conference on Information Security and Assurance (ISA 2008), (pp. 509–511). Washington, DC: IEEE Computer Society.

Shapiro, J. S. (2000). Pet names, true names, and nicknames. Retrieved April 17 2000, from http://www.eros-os.org/~majordomo/dcms-dev/0036.html

Sharma, S., & Jena, S. K. (2011). A survey on secure hierarchical routing protocols in wireless sensor networks. In Proceedings of the International Conference on Communication, Computing & Security, (pp. 146-151). IEEE.

Shaw, D. (2009). The camellia cipher in OpenPGP. RFC. Retrieved from http://tools.ietf.org/html/rfc5581

Shen, L. L., Kot, A., & Koo, W. M. (2001). Quality measures of fingerprint images. Paper presented at the 3rd Audio and Video-Based Person Authentication, AVBPA 2001. New York, NY.

Shen, E., Shi, E., & Waters, B. (2009). Predicate privacy in encryption systems. *Lecture Notes in Computer Science*, *5444*, 457–473. doi:10.1007/978-3-642-00457-5_27.

Shirey, R. (2007). RFC-4949: Internet security glossary, version 2. Retrieved from http://www.ietf.org

Shirky, C. (2002). Domain names: Memorable, global, non-political? Retrieved April 17, 2012, from http://shirky.com/writings/domain_names.html

Shirude, A., Muley, G., Nikam, A., & Marathe, S. (2012). Detection node misconduct in MANET. *International Journal of Engineering and Social Science*, *2*(5), 2249–9482.

Shor, P. (1994). Algorithms for quantum computation: Discrete logarithms and factoring. In Proceedings of the 35th Annual Symposium on Foundations of Computer Science, (pp. 124-134). IEEE.

Sider, T. (2000). Recent work on identity over time. *Philosophical Books*, *41*(2), 81–89. doi:10.1111/1468-0149.00183.

Siemborski, R., & Melnikov, A. (2007). SMTP service extension for authentication. RFC. Retrieved from http://tools.ietf.org/html/rfc4954

Silaghi, M.-C. (2002). An algorithm applicable to clearing combinatorial exchanges. Retrieved from http://www.citeseer.nj.nec.com/silaghi02algorithm.html

Simmons, G. J., & Meadows, C. (1995). The role of trust in information integrity protocols. *Journal of Computer Security*, *3*(1), 71–84.

Singh, K., & Yadav, R., & Ranvijay. (2007). A review paper on ad hoc network security. *International Journal of Computer Science and Security*, *1*(1).

Singh, V. P., Jain, S., & Singhai, J. (2010). Hello flood attack and its countermeasures in wireless sensor networks. *International Journal of Computer Science*, *7*(3), 23–27.

Sirrix, A. G. (2010). Trusted GRUB project (tGRUB). Retrieved May 2, 2012, from http://projects.sirrix.com/trac/trustedgrub

Skorobogatov, S. P., & Anderson, R. J. (2002). Optical fault induction attacks. Retrieved from http://www.cl.cam.ac.uk/~sps32/ches02-optofault.pdf

Smid, M. E., & Branstad, D. K. (1988). Data encryption standard: past and future. *Proceedings of the IEEE*, *76*(5), 550–559. doi:10.1109/5.4441.

Soghoian, C., & Stamm, S. (2011). Certified lies: Detecting and defeating government interception attacks against ssl (short paper). Financial Cryptography, 250–259.

Sokullu, R., Dagdeviren, O., & Korkmaz, I. (2008). On the IEEE 802.15.4 MAC layer attacks: GTS attack. In Proceedings of the Second International Conference on Sensor Technologies and Applications, (pp. 673-678). IEEE.

Sokullu, R., Korkmaz, I., Dagdeviren, O., Mitseva, A., & Prasad, N. R. (2007). An investigation on IEEE 802.15.4 MAC layer attacks. In Proceedings of the International Symposium on Wireless Personal Media Communications. IEEE.

Sokullu, R., Korkmaz, I., & Dagdeviren, O. (2009). GTS attack: An IEEE 802.15.4 MAC layer attack in wireless sensor networks. *IARIA International Journal on Advances in Networks and Services*, *2*(1), 104–114.

Song, D. X., Wagner, D., & Perrig, A. (2000). Practical techniques for searches on encrypted data. In Proceedings of the IEEE Symposium on Security and Privacy, (pp. 44–55). IEEE Computer Society.

Soutar, C. (2002). Biometric system security. Retrieved from http://www.bioscrypt.com/assets/security_soutar.pdf

SPARQL Query Language for RDF. (2008). W3C recommendation 15 January 2008. Retrieved from http://www.w3.org/TR/rdf-sparql-query

Srinivasan, A., Teitelbaum, J., Liang, H., Wu, J., & Cardei, M. (2008). Reputation and trust-based systems for ad hoc and sensor networks. In Boukerche, A. (Ed.), *Algorithms and Protocols for Wireless, Mobile Ad Hoc Networks*. New York, NY: Wiley. doi:10.1002/9780470396384.ch13.

Srivastava, M. B., Muntz, R. R., & Potkonjak, M. (2001). Smart kindergarten: Sensorbased wireless networks for smart developmental problem-solving enviroments. In Proceedings of the 7th Annual International Conference on Mobile Computing and Networking, (pp. 132-138). New York, NY: ACM.

Stajano, F., & Anderson, R. (1999). The resurrecting duckling: Security issues for ad-hoc wireless networks. In Proceedings of the 7th International Workshop on Security Protocols. IEEE.

Stallings, W. (2006). *Cryptography and network security*. Upper Saddle River, NJ: Prentice Hall.

Stevens, M., Lenstra, A., & Weger, B. (2007). Chosen-prefix collisions for MD5 and colliding X.509 certificates for different identities. In Naor, M. (Ed.), *Advances in Cryptology -- Eurocrypt 2007* (pp. 19–35). Springer. doi:10.1007/978-3-540-72540-4_1.

Stiegler, M. (2005). Petname systems. Retrieved April 17 2012, from http://www.financialcryptography.com/mt/archives/000499.html

Stiegler, M., Karp, A. H., Yee, K. P., & Miller, M. (2004). Polaris: Virus safe computing for windows xp. Retrieved April 17 2012, from http://www.hpl.hp.com/techreports/2004/HPL-2004-221.pdf

Stüble, C., & Zaerin, A. (2010). µTSS - A simplified trusted software stack. In Proceedings of the 3rd International Conference on Trust and Trustworthy Computing, (pp. 124-140). IEEE.

Sugawara, T., Suzuki, D., & Katashita, T. (2012). Circuit simulation for fault sensitivity analysis and its application to cryptographic LSI. In Proceedings of FDTC, (pp. 16-23). IEEE Press.

Sun, Y., Han, Z., & Liu, K. J. R. (2008). Defense of trust management vulnerabilities in distributed networks. *IEEE Communications Magazine*, *46*(2), 112–119. doi:10.1109/MCOM.2008.4473092.

Sutter, G. (2011). Modular multiplication and exponentiation architectures for fast RSA cryptosystem based on digital serial computation. *IEEE Transactions on Industrial Electronics*, *58*(7), 3101–3109. doi:10.1109/TIE.2010.2080653.

Suwa, S., Yamai, N., Okayama, K., & Nakamura, M. (2011). DNS resource record analysis of URLs in e-mail messages for improving spam filtering. In Proceedings of the 2011 IEEE/IPSJ International Symposium on Applications and the Internet. IEEE. Retrieved from http://dl.acm.org/citation.cfm?id=2061659

Suzuki, K., Kobayashi, K., & Morita, H. (2000). Efficient sealed-bid auction using hash chain. In Proceedings of the International Conference on Information Security and Cryptology 2000, (Vol. 2015, pp. 183-191). Berlin, Germany: Springer-Verlag.

Suzuki, K., & Yokoo, M. (2002). Secure combinatorial auctions by dynamic programming with polynomial secret sharing. In *Proceedings of Financial Cryptography 2002* (*Vol. 2357*, pp. 44–56). Berlin, Germany: Springer-Verlag. doi:10.1007/3-540-36504-4_4.

Sweeney, L. (2002). k-Anonymity: A model for protecting privacy. International Journal on Uncertainty. *Fuzziness and Knowledge-Based Systems*, *10*(5), 557–570. doi:10.1142/S0218488502001648.

Tan, B., & Schuckers, S. (2006). Comparison of ridge- and intensity-based perspiration live-ness detection methods in fingerprint scanners. Paper presented at the SPIE, Biometric Technology for Human Identification III. New York, NY.

Tan, B., & Schuckers, S. (2008). New approach for liveness detection in fingerprint scanners based on valley noise analysis. *Journal of Electronic Imaging*, *17*(1). doi:10.1117/1.2885133 PMID:23087585.

Tandel, P., Valiveti, S., Agrawal, K., & Kotecha, K. (2010). Non-repudiation in ad hoc networks. Communication and Networking. *Communications in Computer and Information Science*, *120*, 405–415. doi:10.1007/978-3-642-17604-3_48.

Taneja, K., & Patel, R. (2007). Mobile ad hoc networks: Challenges and future. In Proceedings of the National Conference on Challenges & Opportunities in Information Technology (COIT-2007). RIMT-IET.

Tang, Q. (2010). Privacy preserving mapping schemes supporting comparison. In Proceedings of the 2010 ACM workshop on Cloud Computing Security Workshop, (pp. 53–58). ACM Press.

Tang, Q. (2011). Towards public key encryption scheme supporting equality test with fine-grained authorization. *Lecture Notes in Computer Science*, *6812*, 389–406. doi:10.1007/978-3-642-22497-3_25.

Tang, Q. (2012a). Public key encryption schemes supporting equality test with authorization of different granularity. *International Journal of Applied Cryptography*, *2*(4), 304–321. doi:10.1504/IJACT.2012.048079.

Tang, Q. (2012b). Public key encryption supporting plaintext equality test and user-specified authorization. In *Security and Communication Networks*. New York, NY: Wiley. doi:10.1002/sec.418.

Tang, Q., & Chen, L. (2009). Public-key encryption with registered keyword search. *Lecture Notes in Computer Science*, *6391*, 163–178. doi:10.1007/978-3-642-16441-5_11.

tBook. (2012). Trusted boot project (tboot). Retrieved May 2, 2012, from http://tboot.sourceforge.net/

Teddy, K., & Lockheed, M. (2002). Fingerprint enhancement by spectral analysis techniques. Paper presented at the 31st Applied Imagery Pattern Recognition Workshop. New York, NY.

Thanh, D. V., & Jørstad, I. J. (2007). The ambiguity of identity. *Telektronikk*, *103*(3/4), 3–10.

Thomas, S. (2000). *SSL and TLS essentials, securing the web*. New York, NY: Wiley.

Thomson, S., Narten, T., & Jinmei, T. (2007). IPv6 stateless address autoconfiguration. RFC 4862. Retrieved from http://tools.ietf.org/html/rfc4862

Tiri, K., & Verbauwhede, I. (2005). Simulation models for side-channel information leaks. Retrieved from http://www.cosic.esat.kuleuven.be/publications/article-669.pdf

Tiri, K. (2010). Side-channel resistant circuit styles and associated IC design flow. *Secure Integrated Circuits and Systems*, *1*, 145–157. doi:10.1007/978-0-387-71829-3_8.

TLS vs. SSL. (2010). Website. Retrieved from http://msdn.microsoft.com/en-us/library/aa380515(v=vs.85).aspx

Toegl, R., Winkler, T., Nauman, M., & Hong, T. (2009). Towards platform-independent trusted computing. In Proceedings of the 2009 ACM Workshop on Scalable Trusted Computing, (pp. 61-66). ACM.

Tomlinson, R. (1971). The first network email. Retrieved from http://openmap.bbn.com/~tomlinso/ray/firstemailframe.html

Trabelsi, Z., Rahmani, H., Kaouech, K., & Frikha, M. (2004). Malicious sniffing systems detection platform. *IEEE Computer Society*, *201*. doi: doi:10.1109/SAINT.2004.1266117.

Tromer, E., Osvik, D., & Shamir, A. (2010). Efficient cache attacks on AES, and countermeasures. *Journal of Cryptology*, *23*(2), 37–71. doi:10.1007/s00145-009-9049-y.

Trusted Computing Group. (2005). TCG infrastructure working group (IWG) subject key attestation evidence extension: Version 1.0 revision 7, 2005. Retrieved September 16, 2012, from https://www.trustedcomputinggroup.org/files/resource_files/876A7F79-1D09-3519-AD321B21144AE93C/IWG_SKAE_Extension_1-00.pdf

Trusted Computing Group. (2007). TCG software stack: Version 1.2 level 1 errata A, 2007. Retrieved September 16, 2012, from http://www.trustedcomputinggroup.org/files/resource_files/6479CD77-1D09-3519-AD89EAD-1BC8C97F0/TSS_1_2_Errata_A-final.pdf

Trusted Computing Group. (2010). TCG mobile trusted module, specification, v. 1.0, revision 7.02. Retrieved May 2, 2012, from http://www.trustedcomputinggroup.org/files/static_page_files/3D843B67-1A4B-B294-D0B5B407C36F4B1D/Revision_7.02-_29April2010-tcg-mobile-trusted-module-1.0.pdf

Trusted Computing Group. (2011a). TCG TPM main part 1 design principles: Version 1.2 level 2 revision 116, 2011. Retrieved September 16, 2012, from https://www.trustedcomputinggroup.org/files/static_page_files/72C26AB5-1A4B-B294-D002BC0B8C062FF6/TPM%20Main-Part%201%20Design%20Principles_v1.2_rev116_01032011.pdf

Trusted Computing Group. (2011b). TCG TPM main part 2 TPM structures: Version 1.2 level 2 revision 116, 2011. Retrieved September 16, 2012, from https://www.trustedcomputinggroup.org/files/static_page_files/72C2B624-1A4B-B294-D0E07C5F7F49140D/TPM%20Main-Part%202%20TPM%20Structures_v1.2_rev116_01032011.pdf

Trusted Computing Group. (2011c). TCG TPM main part 3 commands: Version 1.2 level 2 revision 116, 2011. Retrieved September 16, 2012, from https://www.trustedcomputinggroup.org/files/static_page_files/72C33D71-1A4B-B294-D02C7DF86630BE7C/TPM%20Main-Part%203%20Commands_v1.2_rev116_01032011.pdf

Trusted Computing Group. (2012). TCG PC client specific implementation specification for conventional BIOS, version 1.21 errata, revision 1.00. Retrieved May 2, 2012, from http://www.trustedcomputinggroup.org/files/resource_files/CB0B2BFA-1A4B-B294-D0C3B9075B5AFF17/TCG_PCClientImplementation_1-21_1_00.pdf

Tulyakov, S., Farooq, F., Mansukhani, P., & Govindaraju, V. (2007). Symmetric hash functions for secure fingerprint biometric systems. *Pattern Recognition Letters*, *28*, 2427–2436. doi:10.1016/j.patrec.2007.08.008.

Turner, S., & Polk, T. (2011). Prohibiting secure sockets layer (SSL) version 2.0. RFC. Retrieved from http://tools.ietf.org/html/rfc617

Tyler, J. L. (2001). The healthcare information technology context: A framework for viewing legal aspects of telemedicine and teleradiology. Paper presented at the 34th Annual Hawaii International Conference on System Sciences, 2001. Hawaii, HI.

UK e Envoy. (2002). Registration and authentication. Retrieved from http://e-government.cabinetoffice.gov.uk/assetRoot/04/00/09/60/04000960.pdf

UML. (2012). Website. Retrieved from http://www.uml.org

Vaidya, J., & Clifton, C. (2003). Leveraging the "multi" in secure multiparty computation. In Proceedings of the Workshop on Privacy in the Electronic Society, (pp. 53-59). IEEE.

Vaidya, J., & Clifton, C. (2003). Privacy-preserving k-means clustering over vertically partitioned data. In Proceedings of the Ninth ACM SIGKDD International Conference on Knowledge Discovery and Data Mining, (pp. 206–215). ACM.

Vaidya, J., & Clifton, C. (2004). Privacy preserving naive bayes classifier for vertically partitioned data. In Proceedings of the 2004 SIAM International Conference on Data Mining, (pp. 522-526). SIAM.

Van der Merwe, J., Dawoud, D., & McDonald, S. (2007). A survey on peer-to-peer key management for mobile ad hoc networks. *ACM Computing Surveys*, *39*(1).

Van Staden, F., & Venter, H. (2010). Adding digital forensic readiness to the email trace header.[ISSA]. *IEEE Information Security for South Africa, 1*. doi: doi:10.1109/ISSA.2010.5588258.

Vanishree, H., & George, K. (2009). A novel unconditionally secure oblivious polynomial evaluation protocol. In Proceedings of 2009 International Workshop on Information Security and Application (IWISA 2009). IWISA.

Vasudevan, A., McCune, J., Newsome, J., Perrig, A., & van Doorn, L. (2012). CARMA: A hardware tamper-resistant isolated execution environment on commodity x86 platforms. In Proceedings of the 7th ACM Symposium on Information, Computer and Communications Security. IEEE.

Vasudevan, A., Parno, B., Qu, N., Gligor, V. D., & Perrig, A. (2012). Lockdown: Towards a safe and practical architecture for security applications on commodity platforms. In Proceedings of the 5th International Conference on Trust and Trustworthy Computing, (pp. 34-54). Vienna, Austria: IEEE.

Vawdrey, D. K., Sundelin, T. L., Seamons, K. E., & Knutson, C. D. (2003). Trust negotiation for authentication and authorization in healthcare information systems. Paper presented at the 25th Annual International Conference of the IEEE Engineering in Medicine and Biology Society, 2003. New York, NY.

Verykios, V. S., Bertino, E., Parasiliti, L., Favino, I. N., Saygin, Y., & Theodoridis, Y. (2004). State-of-the-art in privacy preserving data mining. ACM SIGMOD, 33(1).

Vickrey, D. (1961, March). Counter speculation, auctions, and comatitive sealed tenders. *The Journal of Finance*, 9–37.

Viejo, A., Wu, Q., & Domingo-Ferrer, J. (2011). Asymmetric homomorphisms for secure aggregation in heterogeneous scenarios. Information Fusion. Retrieved April 20, 2012, from http://dx.doi.org/10.1016/j.inffus.2011.03.002

Viswanathan, K., Boyd, C., & Dawson, E. (2000). A three phased schema for sealed bid auction system design. In Proceedings of the Information Security and Privacy, 5th Australasian Conference, ACISP 2000, (Vol. 1841, pp. 412-426). Berlin, Germany: Springer-Verlag.

W3Schools. (2012). OS platform statistics. Retrieved from http://www.w3schools.com/browsers/browsers_os.asp

Wagner, D. (2004). Resilient aggregation in sensor networks. In Proceedings of the 2nd ACM Workshop on Security of Ad Hoc and Sensor Networks. New York, NY: ACM.

WampServer. (2010). Install PHP 5 apache MySQL on windows: WampServer. Retrieved from http://www.wampserver.com/en/

Wang, X., Feng, D., Lai, X., & Yu, H. (2004). Collisions for hash functions MD4, MD5, HAVAL-128 and RIPEMD. Cryptology ePrint Archive. Retrieved March 27, 2012, from http://eprint.iacr.org/2004/199

Wang, X., Yu, H., & Yin, Y. (2005). Efficient collision search attacks on SHA-0. In V. Shoup (Ed.), Advances in Cryptology - CRYPTO 2005, 25th Annual International Cryptology Conference, (pp. 1-16). Springer.

Wang, X., & Yu, H. (2005). How to break MD5 and other Hash functions. In Cramer, R. (Ed.), *Advances in Cryptology -- Eurocrypt 2005* (pp. 19–35). Springer. doi:10.1007/11426639_2.

Ward, J. P. (1997). *Quaternions and cayley numbers.* Dordrecht, The Netherlands: Kluwer Acadmic Publishers. doi:10.1007/978-94-011-5768-1.

Watanabe, Y., & Imai, H. (2000). Reducing the round complexity of a sealed-bid auction protocol with an off-line ttp.[ACM.]. *Proceedings of STOC, 2000*, 80–86.

Waters, B. (2011). Ciphertext-policy attribute-based encryption: An expressive, efficient, and provably secure realization. *Lecture Notes in Computer Science, 6571*, 53–70. doi:10.1007/978-3-642-19379-8_4.

Wayman, J. L., Jain, A. K., Maltoni, D., & Maio, D. (2005). *Biometric systems: Technology, design and performance evaluation.* Berlin, Germany: Springer.

Wei-Bin, L., & Chien-Ding, L. (2008). A cryptographic key management solution for HIPAA privacy/security regulations. *IEEE Transactions on Information Technology in Biomedicine, 12*(1), 34–41. doi:10.1109/TITB.2007.906101 PMID:18270035.

Weinmann, R.-P. (2009). Algebraic methods in block cipher cryptanalysis. (Doctoral Dissertation). Technische Universität. Darmstadt, Germany.

Westhoff, D., Girao, J., & Acharya, M. (2006). Concealed data aggregation for reverse multicast traffic in sensor networks: Encryption, key distribution, and routing adaptation. *IEEE Transactions on Mobile Computing*, *5*(10), 1417–1431. doi:10.1109/TMC.2006.144.

Whitten, A., & Tygar, J. D. (1999). Why johnny can't encrypt: A usability evaluation of PGP 5.0. In Proceedings of the 8th USENIX Security Symposium. USENIX.

Wilcox-O'Hearn, Z. (2001). Names: Decentralized, secure, human-meaningful: Choose two. Retrieved April 17 2012, from http://www.zooko.com/distnames.html

Wong, M., & Schlitt, W. (2006). Sender policy framework (SPF) for authorizing use of domains in e-mail, version 1. RFC. Retrieved from http://tools.ietf.org/html/rfc4408

Wood, A. D., & Stankovic, J. A. (2004). A taxonomy for denial-of-service attacks in wireless sensor networks. In *Handbook of Sensor Networks: Compact Wireless and Wired Sensing Systems*. Boca Raton, FL: CRC Press.

WOT Services Ltd. (2012). Web of trust. Retrieved September 09, 2012, from http://www.mywot.com/

WOT. (2012). Wiki. Retrieved September 09, 2012, from http://www.mywot.com/wiki/WOT

Wright, P., & Greengrass, P. (1988). *Spycatcher: The candid autobiography of a senior intelligence officer*. New York, NY: Dell.

Wyman, B. (2006). The persistence of identity. Retrieved April 17, 2012, from http://www.wyman.us/main/2006/12/the_persistence.html.

Xiao, Y., Sethi, S., Chen, H. H., & Sun, B. (2005). Security services and enhancements in the IEEE 802.15.4 wireless sensor networks. In Proceedings of IEEE Global Telecommunications Conference. IEEE.

Xu, H., Veldhuis, R., Bazen, A., Kevenaar, T., Akkermans, T., & Gokberk, B. (2009). Fingerprint verification using spectral minutiae representations. Paper presented at the IEEE Transactions on Information Forensics and Security. New York, NY.

Xu, S., & Capkun, S. (2008). Distributed and secure bootstrapping of mobile ad hoc networks: Framework and constructions. *ACM Transactions on Information and System Security*, *12*(1). doi:10.1145/1410234.1410236.

Ya-Jun, G., & Fan, H. (2006). Trust authentication protocol on the web. *Wuhan University Journal of Natural Sciences*, *11*(1), 253–255. doi:10.1007/BF02831742.

Yamazaki, A., Koyama, A., Arai, J., & Barolli, L. (2009). Design and implementation of a ubiquitous health monitoring system. *International Journal of Web Grid Services*, *5*(4), 339–355. doi:10.1504/IJWGS.2009.030263.

Yang, G., Tan, C., Huang, Q., & Wong, D. S. (2010). Probabilistic public key encryption with equality test. *Lecture Notes in Computer Science*, *5985*, 119–131. doi:10.1007/978-3-642-11925-5_9.

Yang, P., Cao, Z., & Dong, X. (2011). Fuzzy identity based signature with applications to biometric authentication. *Computers & Electrical Engineering*, *37*(4), 532–540. doi:10.1016/j.compeleceng.2011.04.013.

Yao, A. C. (1986). How to generate and exchange secrets. In Proceedings of the 27th IEEE Symposium on Foundations of Computer Science. IEEE.

Yao, H.-B., Hu, H.-P., Lu, Z.-D., & Li, R.-X. (2005). Dynamic role and context-based access control for grid applications. Paper presented at the TENCON 2005 2005 IEEE Region 10. New York, NY.

Yao, W., Chu, C.-H., & Li, Z. (2010). The use of RFID in healthcare: Benefits and barriers. Paper presented at the RFID-Technology and Applications (RFID-TA), 2010 IEEE International Conference on. New York, NY.

Yaobin, M. A., & Guanrong, C. H. (2004a). Chaos-based image encryption. In Bayro-Corrochano, E. (Ed.), *Handbook of Computational Geometry for Pattern Recognition, Computer Vision, Neural Computing and Robotics*. Berlin, Germany: Springer-Verlag.

Yaobin, M. A., Guanrong, C. H., & Shiguo, L. (2004b). A symmetric image encryption scheme based on 3D chaotic cat maps. *Chaos, Solitons, and Fractals*, *21*, 749–761. doi:10.1016/j.chaos.2003.12.022.

Yee, K. P., & Sitaker, K. (2006). Passpet: Convenient password management and phishing protection. In Proceedings of SOUPS, (pp. 32–43). SOUPS.

Yeh, Y.-S., Lin, C.-H., & Wang, C.-C. (1998). Dynamic GOST. *Journal of Information Science and Engineering*, *16*(6), 857–861.

Yokoo, M., & Suzuki, K. (2002). Secure multi-agent dynamic programming based on homomorphic encryption and its application to combinatorial auctions. In Proceedings of the First Joint International Conference on Autonomous Agents and Multiagent Systems (AAMAS-2002), (pp. 112-119). AAMAS. Retrieved from ashttp://www.kecl.ntt.co.jp/csl/ccrg/members/yokoo/PDF/aamas2002-secure-wd.pdf

Yu, W. D., & Chekhanovskiy, M. A. (2007). An electronic health record content protection system using SmartCard and PMR. Paper presented at the e-Health Networking, Application and Services, 2007 9th International Conference on. New York, NY.

Yu, Y., Li, K., Zhou, W., & Li, P. (2012). Trust mechanisms in wireless sensor networks: Attack analysis and countermeasures. *Journal of Network and Computer Applications*, *35*(3), 867–880. doi:10.1016/j.jnca.2011.03.005.

Zhang, L., Ahn, G.-J., & Chu, B.-T. (2002). A role-based delegation framework for healthcare information systems. Paper presented at the Seventh ACM Symposium on Access Control Models and Technologies. New York, NY.

Zhang, X., Song, M., & Song, J. (2009). A solution of electronic authentication services based on PKI for enabling e-business. Paper presented at e-Business Engineering. New York, NY.

Zhang, J., Zhang, K., Yang, Y., Sun, J., Ling, T., & Wang, G. et al. (2011). Grid-based implementation of XDS-I as part of image-enabled EHR for regional healthcare in Shanghai. *International Journal of Computer Assisted Radiology and Surgery*, *6*(2), 273–284. doi:10.1007/s11548-010-0522-8 PMID:20694521.

Zhang, R., & Imai, H. (2007). Generic combination of public key encryption with keyword search and public key encryption. *Lecture Notes in Computer Science*, *4521*, 159–174. doi:10.1007/978-3-540-76969-9_11.

Ziedan, I., Fouad, M., & Salem, H. D. (2006). Application of data encryption standard to bitmap and JPEG images. In Proceedings of 20th National Radio Science Conference (NRSC), (pp. 1-16). NRSC.

Zimmermann, P. R. (1995). The official PGP user's guide. Retrieved from http://mitpress.mit.edu/catalog/item/default.asp?ttype=2&tid=5518

About the Contributors

Atilla Elçi is Full Professor and Chairman of the Department of Electrical and Electronics Engineering at Aksaray University, Aksaray, Turkey, since August 2012. He was Full Professor and Chairman of Computer and Educational Technology at Süleyman Demirel University, Isparta, Turkey (May 2010 – June 2012). He served as Full Professor of Computer Engineering, the Founding Director of the Graduate School of Science and Technology, and the Dean of Engineering Faculty at Toros University, Mersin, Turkey (July 2010 – June 2011); with the Computer Engineering Program, Middle East Technical University (METU NCC, Spring 2010); Eastern Mediterranean University (2003-2009), where he established the Internet Technologies Research Center and Semantic Robotics Lab; Haliç University, Istanbul, Turkey, Founder and Chair of the Computer Engineering Department (2000-2003); the International Telecommunication Union, Geneva, Switzerland, as Chief Technical Advisor (1985-1997); METU Ankara, Turkey, where he was Chair and Assistant Chair of Computer Engineering Department (1976-1985); Purdue University, W. Lafayette, Indiana, USA, as Research Assistant (1974-1975). He has organized or served in the committees of numerous international conferences. He has been organizing IEEE Engineering Semantic Agent Systems Workshops since 2006, Security of Information and Networks Conferences since 2007, and IJRCS Symposiums 2007 and 2009. He has published over a hundred journal and conference papers; edited the book titled Semantic Agent Systems (Springer 2011), Theory and Practice of Cryptography Solutions for Secure Information Systems (IGI 2013); Proceedings of SIN 2007, 9 – 12 by ACM, ESAS 2006-12 by IEEE CS, and IJRCS 2009; special issues. He was the program chair for the 36th COMPSAC (2012). He obtained B.Sc. in Computer/Control Engineering at METU, Ankara, Turkey (1970), M.Sc. & Ph.D. in Computer Sciences at Purdue University, USA (1973, 1975). His research and experience encompass Web semantics, agent-based systems, robotics, machine learning, knowledge representation and ontology, information security, software engineering, and natural language translation.

Josef Pieprzyk is a Professor, Chair of Computing, at Macquarie University. His main research interest focus is cryptology and computer security and includes design and analysis of cryptographic algorithms (such as encryption, hashing, and digital signatures), secure multiparty computations, cryptographic protocols, copyright protection, e-commerce, Web security, and cybercrime prevention. Professor Pieprzyk is a member of the editorial boards for International Journal of Information Security, Journal of Mathematical Cryptology, International Journal of Applied Cryptography, Fundamenta Informaticae, Journal of Research and Practice in Information Technology, International Journal of Security and Networks, and International Journal of Information and Computer Security. Professor Pieprzyk was instrumental in creation of both Auscrypt and ACISP conference streams. The Auscrypt stream was renamed as Asiacrypt and later included by IACR as one of the flagship conferences along with Eurocrypt and Crypto. The ACISP conference is the main cryptographic event in Australia and New Zealand. In 2008, he was the Program Chair of Asiacrypt 2008 (Melbourne, Australia). In 2010, he was serving the Program Chair of CT-RSA 2010 (San Francisco, USA). He is serving on many program committees of international conferences. Professor Pieprzyk published 5 books, edited 10 books (conference proceedings published by Springer-Verlag), 6 book chapters, and ~200 papers in refereed journals and refereed international conferences.

Alexander G. Chefranov holds the degrees of a Ph.D. (Computer Science) and a Doctor of Engineering Sciences. He is currently an Associate Professor of the Department of Computer Engineering, Eastern Mediterranean University, Famagusta, North Cyprus. There he was one of the founders of Internet Technologies Research Center and served as its Director in 2008/09. Prior to joining Eastern Mediterranean University, he was a Professor at the Department of Software Engineering at Taganrog State University of Radio-Engineering in Russia. His research interests in information security include symmetric and asymmetric ciphers, authentication and key exchange protocols, database security. He served as a program committee chair of SIN 2009 held in North Cyprus in 2009 and a program committee co-chair of SIN Conferences held in Russia, Australia, and India in 2010-2012.

Mehmet A. Orgun is a Professor at Macquarie University, Sydney, Australia. He received his B.Sc. and M.Sc. degrees in Computer Science and Engineering from Hacettepe University, Ankara, Turkey in 1982 & 1985, respectively; and his PhD degree in Computer Science from the University of Victoria, Canada, in 1991. Prior to joining Macquarie University in September 1992, he worked as a Post-Doctoral Fellow at the University of Victoria. He was elevated to the grade of a Senior Member of IEEE (SMIEEE) in 1996. He researches in the broad area of intelligent systems, with specific research interests in knowledge discovery, trusted systems, multi-agent systems, and industry applications of these research areas. He was the Program Committee Co-Chair of the 20th Australian Joint Conference on Artificial Intelligence (AI'07) and the Conference co-chair of the 2nd International Conference on Security of Information and Networks (SIN 2009). He has been serving as Program Committee Co-Chair of the 14th Pacific-Rim International Conference on Artificial Intelligence (PRICAI'2010), and the Conference Co-Chair of the 3rd International Conference on Security of Information and Networks (SIN 2010). He serves on the editorial boards of The Journal of Universal Computer Science, and Expert Systems: The Journal of Knowledge Engineering.

Huaxiong Wang received a PhD in Mathematics from University of Haifa, Israel, in 1996 and a PhD in Computer Science from University of Wollongong, Australia, in 2001. He joined Nanyang Technological University, Singapore, in 2006, and is currently an Associate Professor in the Division of Mathematical Sciences. Prior to that, he held positions in several universities, including Macquarie University, Australia; City University of Hong Kong; University of Wollongong, Australi; National University of Singapore; Kobe University, Japan. His research interests include cryptography, information security, coding theory, combinatorics, and theoretical computer science. He has been on the editorial boards of Designs, Codes, and Cryptography, International Journal of Foundations of Computer Science, Journal of Communications (JCM), and Journal of Communications and Networks. He was the Program Co-Chair of 9th Australasian Conference on Information Security and Privacy (ACISP'04), Sydney,

Australia, 2004, and 4th International Conference on Cryptology and Network Security (CANS05), Xiamen, China, 2005. He received the inaugural Award of Best Research Contribution awarded by the Computer Science Association of Australasia in 2004.

Rajan Shankaran is a Senior Lecturer at Macquarie University, Sydney, Australia. He received the MBA (MIS) degree in Information Systems Maastricht School of Management in 1994; and MSc (Honours) and PhD degrees in Computing from the University of Western Sydney in 1999 and 2005, respectively. He joined Macquarie University as a Lecturer in 2001 and was promoted to Senior Lecturer in 2011. Prior to Macquarie University, he was employed, first as an Associate Lecturer and then as a Lecturer, at the University of Western Sydney. He mainly works in the areas of network security and trust in mobile networks. He has served as a program committee member for a number of conferences in computer networking and security. More recently, he has been serving as the Program Co-Chair as well as local arrangements chair of the 4th International Conference on Security of Information and Networks (SIN 2011) held in Sydney in November 2011.

* * *

Ahmad AlSa'deh is a PhD student at the Hasso-Plattner-Institut at the University of Potsdam, Germany. His research interests include networking security, particularly IPv6 security. Alsa'deh has an MS in scientific computing from Birzeit University in Palestine.

Alexey Jurievich Atiskov was born in Saint-Petersburg in 1983. Graduated from Saint-Petersburg State Electrotechnical University in 2006, specialty "Automated Systems of Information Processing and Control." Was employed at SPIIRAS Laboratory of Computer Systems and Information Security Problems in 2006 as Senior Researcher. Developed the semi-automatic system that transforms business-process diagrams into class diagrams of UML based on hybrid adaptive technology. Defined transformation rules that use ontological description in OWL format. Obtained PhD in 2011 by thesis "Development of Technology and Software of the Automated Transformation of Functional Design Diagrams into Diagrams UML." Wrote more than 12 papers including monograph and 4 theses of the report for international conferences.

Liudmila Babenko, Professor, Department of Security of Information Technologies, Taganrog, Southern Federal University (SFedU, former Taganrog State University of Radio Engineering), Russia; Director of the Scientific Educational Center "Modern Security Technology," SFedU; Full Member of Russian Academy of Natural History; Corresponding Member of Russian Academy of Natural Science; Program Chair of International Conference on Security of Information and Networks (SIN); Expert of Russian Foundation for Basic Research (RFBR), Dep. 07; Member of dissertation councils in Southern Federal University and Stavropol State University on the following domains: Methods and Systems of Information Security, Information Security, Software for Computers, Computing Systems and Networks, Mathematical Modeling, Numerical Methods, and Software. Main areas of research: mathematical models and methods of protection, conversion and transmission of information, modern technologies of information security. Cryptographic methods and tools for information security. Parallel algorithms applied to problems of mathematical physics, pattern recognition, and evaluation of cryptographic security.

Alessandro Barenghi received his M.Sc. degree in Computer Engineering (2007) and the Doctoral degree in Information Technology (2011) at Politecnico di Milano, where he is currently a Post-Doctoral Researcher. The main area of interest for his researches is computer, embedded and network security, and, in particular, applied aspects of cryptography. In addition, he also works in the field of formal languages and compilers, where his current interest concerns techniques for parallel parsing.

Luca Breveglieri received both the M.Sc. degree in Electronic Engineering and the B.Sc. degree in Electronic Engineering of Information Technology and Systems from the Politecnico di Milano, Italy, in 1986 and 1992, respectively. From 1991 to 1998, he was a Computer Technician and a part-time Researcher. Since 1998, he has been an Associate Professor of Computer Science at the Politecnico di Milano. He has over 100 publications in refereed journals and conferences. His current research interests include architectures of computing systems, application specific VLSI synthesis, computer arithmetic, applied cryptography, and automata and formal languages theory.

Giovanni Cabiddu is a PhD student at Politecnico di Torino. His current research interests include trusted computing, virtualization, secure programming, and vulnerability exploitation techniques. He graduated with an M.Sc. in Computer Engineering from Politecnico di Torino in 2009.

Hon Cheung graduated from The University of Western Australia in 1984 with First Class Honours in Electrical Engineering. He received his PhD degree from the same university in 1988. He is currently with the School of Computing, Engineering, and Mathematics, and the Networking, Security, and Cloud Research group at the University of Western Sydney. Dr Cheung has research experience in a number of areas, including conventional methods in artificial intelligence, fuzzy sets, artificial neural networks, digital signal processing, image processing, and network security and forensics. In the area of teaching, Dr Cheung has experience in development and delivery of a relative large number of subjects in computer science, electrical and electronic engineering, computer engineering, and networking.

Orhan Dagdeviren received the BSc. degree in Computer Eng. and MSc. degree in Computer Engineering from Izmir Institute of Technology, Turkey. He received Ph.D. degree from Ege University, International Computer Institute. He is an Assistant Professor in same institute. His interests lie in the computer networking and distributed systems areas. His recent focus is on graph theoretic middleware protocol design for wireless sensor networks, mobile ad hoc networks, and grid computing.

Mehmet Emin Dalkilic received his BSc. degree in Electrical and Electronics Engineering in 1985 from Hacettepe University, Turkey. He obtained his MSc. and PhD. degrees in Electrical and Computer Engineering Department at Syracuse University, USA, in 1989 and 1994, respectively. Currently, he is a Professor and the Director of the International Computer Institute, Ege University, Turkey. His research interests include algorithms, computer networks, network security, and parallel and distributed computing.

Fabrizio De Santis received his M.Sc. degree in Computer Engineering (2010) at Politecnico di Milano. In January 2011, he joined the Institute for Security in Information Technology, Department of Electrical Engineering at Technische Universitaet Muenchen working towards his PhD. His research investigates advanced physical attacks and countermeasures for development of secure cryptographic devices.

Evgueni Doukhnitch received PhD and DSc from Taganrog State Radio-Technical University, Russia, in 1973 and 1985, respectively. From 1999-2010, he was with the Department of Computer Engineering, Eastern Mediterranean University, Northern Cyprus, as a Professor. Now he is a Professor at Computer Engineering Department, Istanbul Aydin University, Turkey. His research interests are in the areas of hardware-oriented algorithms, hardware realization of linear algebra problems, and special-purpose processors.

Mahmoud Elkhodr, awarded the International Postgraduate Research Scholarship and the Australian Postgraduate Award, is pursuing his PhD studies in Information Technology and Communications at the University of Western Sydney (UWS). He is also with the Networking, Security, and Cloud Research (NSCR) group at UWS. Mahmoud received a B.Sc. in Information Technology and Computing (Hons) from the Arab Open University, Lebanon, and the Open University, UK (2006), a Master of Science (Hons) and Master of Information and Communication Technologies from the School of Computing, Engineering, and Mathematics at UWS, Australia (2009-2011). His main teaching and research interests include: computer networking, ubiquitous computing, e-health, Internet of things, privacy, and object oriented approach.

Ludmila Nickolayevna Fedorchenko graduated from Leningrad State University (presently SPbSU) and completed postgraduate in "Software Engineering" at Mathematics & Mechanics faculty SpbSU in 1975. Ph.D. in Computer Sciences by thesis "Regularization of Context-Free Grammars on the Base of Syntax-Graph Scheme." The fields of her science interests are syntax-directed data processing, methods and algorithms of grammar regularization, parsing, translating systems, software SynGT (Syntax Graph Transformations). Senior researcher at the laboratory of Applied Informatics of Saint-Petersburg Institute for Informatics and Automation RAS (SPIIRAS). Written more than 55 papers and two monographs.

Md. Sadek Ferdous is a second year PhD student at the School of Computing, University of Glasgow, UK, where he is investigating the ways smart phones can be used for managing user identities. Before that he worked as a Research Assistant for a year at the University of Kent, UK, participating in a JISC funded project (Logins4Life) where he was responsible for investigating and developing mechanism to integrate Social Network sites into the Federated Identity Management System to allow users to use their Social Networking accounts to access restricted resources in academia. He holds double Masters in Security and Mobile Computing from the Norwegian University of Science & Technology (NTNU), Norway, and the University of Tatu in Estonia. His research interests include identity management, pet-name systems, privacy enhancing technologies, trust management, security usability, and information security. He is the author of several publications on different aspects of networking, security, and identity.

Lein Harn received the B.S. degree in Electrical Engineering from the National Taiwan University in 1977, the M.S. degree in Electrical Engineering from the State University of New York-Stony Brook in 1980, and the Ph.D. degree in Electrical Engineering from the University of Minnesota in 1984. In 1984, he joined the Department of Electrical and Computer Engineering, University of Missouri-Columbia as an Assistant Professor, and in 1986, he moved to Computer Science and Telecommunication Program (CSTP), University of Missouri, Kansas City (UMKC). While at UMKC, he went on development leave to work in Racal Data Group, Florida, for a year. His research interests include cryptography, network security, and wireless communication security. He has published a number of papers on digital signature design and applications and wireless and network security. He has written two books on security. He is currently investigating new ways of using secret sharing in various applications.

Wen-Jung Hsin received an M.S. degree in Computer Science from the University of California, San Diego, and an interdisciplinary Ph.D. in Computer Science and Telecommunications at the University of Missouri – Kansas City. Currently, she is a Professor in the Department of Computer Science, Information Systems, and Mathematics at Park University, Parkville, Missouri, USA. She has been with Park University since 2004. Prior to her Ph.D. study, she was a Senior Associate Programmer at International Business Machines (IBM), Endicott, New York. Her teaching and research interests are in the areas of computer science education, computer networking, network security, and cryptography.

Evgenia Ishchukova is the Assistant Professor at Southern Federal University, Taganrog, Russia. In 2003, she graduated from Taganrog State University of Radioengineering, Russia, in Information Security Area (diploma with honors). In 2007 she received Candidate of Technical Sciences degree (PhD equiv.) for the work titled "Research and Development of Algorithms for Strength Assessment of Modern Block Ciphers with Differential Cryptanalysis." She has more than 50 published papers on cryptography and cryptanalysis. The scope of research interests includes cryptography, cryptanalysis, block encryption algorithms, and distributed multiprocessing calculations. Since 2002 she regularly takes part in national and international research and engineering conferences and seminars devoted to information security problems, e.g. in Security of Information and Networks (SIN) conference series, 2010-2012.

Audun Jøsang is Professor at the University of Oslo, where he teaches and conducts research on trust management and information security. In particular, Prof. Jøsang is well known for his work on user-centric identity management and on computational trust based on subjective logic. Prior to joining Oslo University, he was Associate Professor at QUT, Research Leader of the Security Unit at DSTC in Brisbane, worked in the telecommunications industry for Alcatel in Belgium and for Telenor in Norway. He was also Associate Professor at the Norwegian University of Science and Technology (NTNU). Prof. Jøsang has a Masters degree in Information Security from Royal Holloway College London, and a PhD from NTNU in Norway. Prof. Jøsang has more than 100 scientific publications that together have been cited more than 10,000 times.

Ilker Korkmaz received the BSc. degree in Electrical and Electronics Engineering and MSc. degree in Computer Science from Ege University, Turkey. He is a PhD candidate at International Computer Institute at Ege University, working under the supervision of Prof. Dr. Mehmet Emin Dalkilic. He is also an instructor at the Department of Computer Engineering at Izmir University of Economics. His research interests include computer networks, mobile systems, network security, and password security. He is also interested in studying any kind of distributed systems. His recent focus is on secure aggregation protocols in wireless sensor networks.

Antonio Lioy holds a M.Sc. degree (summa cum laude) in Electronic Engineering and a Ph.D. in Computer Engineering. Currently, he is Full Professor at the Politecnico di Torino, where he leads the TORSEC research group active in information systems security. His current research interests are in the fields of network security (especially optimization and automatic configuration), PKI applications (e-identity and electronic workflows), and policy-based system protection. Since 2007, Prof. Lioy has been cooperating with ENISA (the European Network and Information Security Agency of the EU), first as member of the PSG (Permanent Stakeholders' Group) and then as scientific expert in the workgroups "Government Cloud Computing" and "Consumerization of IT." Prof. Lioy is a registered Professional Engineer in Italy, a member of the IEEE and the IEEE Computer Society.

Martin von Löwis is a lecturer at the University of Potsdam's Hasso-Plattner-Institut in the Operating Systems and Middleware Group. His research interests include compiler construction and embedded systems, as well as IPv6 and public-key infrastructure. Löwis has a PhD in computer science from the Humboldt-University in Berlin.

Ahmed Mahmoud received a BSc. in Computer Science from Al-Zaytoonah University, Amman, Jordan, in 1997, an MSc. in Applied Mathematics and Computer Science and PhD in Computer Engineering from Eastern Mediterranean University, North Cyprus, in 2001 and 2012, respectively. From 2001 to 2006, he was a Lecturer in the Computer Science Department at Al-Azhar University, Gaza Strip, Palestine. From September 2006 to September 2011, he was with the Computer Engineering Department at Eastern Mediterranean University, Famagusta, North Cyprus. Since January 2012, he has been an Assistant Professor in the Information Technology Department at Al-Azhar University, Gaza Strip, Palestine. His research interests are in the areas of information security, discrete geometry, parallel programming, and distributed systems.

Ekaterina Maro graduated from Southern Federal University in 2009. She studied postgraduate course on "Methods and Tools of Information Security" (supervised by Ludmila Babenko). She is a Researcher at South Russian Regional Center for Education and Research on Information Security since 2010. She has 17 research publications on cryptography and information security. She was awarded in a public competition of the Russian Ministry of Education for the best student work in natural science, engineering, and humanities among universities of the Russian Federation (2009). She is the winner of the Russian competition in the area of information security "Infoforum-New Generation" in "Student of the Year" (2009) and "Young Specialist of the Year" (2012) categories. She takes part in national and international conferences since 2009. Her research interests are cryptography, evaluation of information systems complexity, digital signatures, and privacy.

Thomas Martin has ten years' experience in Information Security Research. His research interests include: cryptography, multi-party communications, digital rights management, identity management, penetration testing, risk assessment, and computer forensics. While at BT, he developed several security related patents, as well as participated in such projects as the EU FP7 MASTER Project (Managing Assurance, Security, and Trust for sERvices). He is one of the Lecturers in the M.Sc. in Information Security Program at Khalifa University, UAE. He also supervises several M.Sc. and Ph.D. students in such topics as spear phishing detection, block cipher design, android forensics, and cloud computing security.

Christoph Meinel is a Professor and Director of the Hasso-Plattner-Institut at the University of Potsdam, where he leads the Internet Technologies and Systems research group. His research interests include security and trust engineering, Web 3.0, and eLearning. Meinel has a PhD in computer science from Humboldt University in Berlin.

Filippo Melzani received the Laurea degree (M.Sc. Italian equivalent, 5 years) in Computer Engineering in 2005 at the Politecnico di Milano, Italy. Since 2006, he works within the Advanced System Technology group at STMicroelectronics. The main area of interest covers hardware implementations of cryptographic algorithms and side-channel attacks and countermeasures.

Nikolay Andreevich Moldovyan, Head of the Cryptology Laboratory, Dr. Sci.(Tech.), Prof., Honored Inventor of Russian Federation. The field of his science interests are synthesis and analysis of the commutative and deniable encryption algorithms; digital signature and public encryption algorithms; collective signature, blind signature, public key distribution, and zero knowledge protocols; public key cryptosystems based on difficulty of simultaneous solving two independent hard problems; cryptographic primitives for designing block ciphers, data-driven block ciphers, and software suitable ciphers. He is author or coauthor of 200 papers, 70 patents, and 10 books.

Fedor Alexandrovich Novikov graduated from Leningrad State University in 1974. He received his Ph. D. in Computer Science in 1983 and Dr. Sc. in Software Engineering in 2011. His fields of interest are automated program synthesis, visual construction of applications, and modeling with UML. Born in Saint-Petersburg in 1951. Graduated from Leningrad State University, Mathematics and Mechanics Department in 1974. Was employed at several institutions of Russian Academy of Sciences for more than thirty years. Obtained Ph. D. degree in Computer Science in 1983 and Dr. Sc. degree in Software Engineering in 2011. Fields of interest: automatic program synthesis, visual construction of applications, and modeling with UML. Written more than 50 scientific papers and 20 monographs.

Mert Özarar has completed his Ph.D. studies in Computer Engineering Department at Middle East Technical University (METU). His research focuses on using algorithmic techniques from cryptography and secure multiparty computation to design and model secure protocols for data communications and networking. His primary academic interests are cryptography, security, algorithms, and machine learning. Most recently, his work has focused on the security and privacy issues of data mining and applied cryptography. Other academic interests of his include complexity theory, pattern recognition, and game theory. In 2004, he opted to join a startup company, TÜRKTRUST Inc., which is the leading certification authority and IT-Security company in Turkey. Dr. Özarar has received double Master's degrees in Computer Engineering in 2003 and in Cryptography in 2004 both from METU. As an undergraduate, he studied at METU as well where he has received degrees in Computer Engineering and Mathematics in the double major program. In the past, he has worked for IBM, ZIB, TU-Darmstadt, and METU.

Attila Özgit is a graduate of Middle East Technical University (METU). He worked abroad as Software Engineer and Technical Support Manager for several years before rejoining the METU. He has served as the Assistant Director, and then as the Director of Computer Center at METU, where he initiated and managed several forerunner projects. Dr. Özgit is currently working in Dept. of Computer Engineering of METU as a faculty member, where he is doing research in information security, particularly on defense technologies. He is also the ccTLD manager of ".tr" domain.

Andrea Palomba received his M.Sc. degree in Computer Engineering (2010) at Politecnico di Milano. Since January 2011, he is a Ph.D. student at Dipartimento di Elettronica e Informazione – DEI of Politecnico di Milano, and his advisor is Prof. Luca Breveglieri. His current research investigates the development of secure design methodologies for cryptographic devices.

Gerardo Pelosi received his Laurea degree (M.Sc. Italian equivalent, 5 years) in Telecommunications Engineering in 2003 and the Ph.D. degree in Information Technology in 2007 at the Politecnico di Milano, Italy, where he is currently Assistant Professor. He was previously a Research Assistant at University of Bergamo (Italy) and a Research Consultant at STMicroelectronics. His research fields cover (1) the area of information security and privacy (including access control models, models for encrypted data management in relational databases and secure data outsourcing), and (2) the area of applied cryptography (including embedded system security, side-channel cryptanalysis, system-level attacks, and efficient hardware and software design of cryptographic algorithms). Other research interests are in designing security support into computer architectures and the logic synthesis of combinatorial circuits.

Kun Peng received his Bachelor's degree in Software Engineering and his Master degree's in Computer Security from Huazhong University of Science and Technology, China. He graduated from the Information Security Institute, Queensland University of Technology, Australia, in 2004, obtaining his PhD degree in Information Security. His main research interest is in applied public key cryptology. His main research interests include applied cryptology, network security, and secure e-commerce and e-government. He is now a scientist at the Institute for Infocomm Research, Singapore.

Hosnieh Rafiee is a PhD student at Hasso-Plattner-Institut at the University of Potsdam. Her research interests are in network security—including spam filtering approaches and DNS security, focused on composing cryptographic mechanisms in IPv6 networks—and deployment of SEcure Neighbor Discovery (SEND). Rafiee has a MSc in IT-Computer Networks Engineering from Amirkabir University of Technology in Tehran.

Gianluca Ramunno is a Researcher in the security group of Politecnico di Torino, where he received his M.Sc. (2000) in Electronic Engineering and Ph.D. (2004) in Computer Engineering. His initial research interests were in the fields of digital signature, e-documents, and time stamping, where he performed joint activity within ETSI. Since 2006, he has been investigating the field of Trusted Computing, leading the Politecnico di Torino activities in this area within the EU FP6 project OpenTC. His current activity is focused on the security of Cloud Computing, and he is leading the Politecnico di Torino activities in this area within the EU FP7 project TClouds.

Seyed Shahrestani completed his PhD degree in Electrical and Information Engineering at the University of Sydney. He joined University of Western Sydney (UWS) in 1999, where he is currently a Senior Lecturer with the School of Computing, Engineering, and Mathematics. He is also the head of the Networking, Security, and Cloud Research (NSCR) group at UWS. Seyed has established collaborations with several researchers and groups around the globe. Seyed's research in complex systems has resulted in establishment of a framework for global control of complex nonlinear, and possibly chaotic, systems. In addition to introducing new concepts and strategies, the framework utilizes established methods for analysis and control of complex nonlinear systems but with new intent. In computer networking, Seyed's research has provided some original solutions to problems in two important aspects of the Internet, namely network security and management. His research interests include but not limited to computer networking, wireless and mobile computing, network management and security, artificial intelligence, and e-health.

Babak Sokouti has over 15 years IT technical management and consulting experience, including managing and maintaining sophisticated network infrastructures. He has obtained Bachelor of Science in Electrical Engineering with a specialization in Control from Isfahan University of Technology, Isfahan, Iran; a Master of Science in Electrical Engineering with a specialization in Electronics (with background of biomedical engineering) from Tabriz Branch, Islamic Azad University, Tabriz, Iran; a Master of Science in Information Security with Distinction from Royal Holloway University of London, London, UK; and is currently a PhD student in Structural Bioinformatics at Biotechnology Research Center, Tabriz University of Medical Sciences, Tabriz, Iran. In addition, he has obtained IT industry certifications including MCP, MCSA 2003, MCDBA 2000, MCSE 2003, and MCTS 2008. His research interests include cryptographic algorithms, information security, network security and protocols, image processing, protein structure prediction, and hybrid intelligent neural network systems based on genetic algorithms.

Massoud Sokouti obtained a Bachelor of Science in Information Technology Engineering with a specialization in IT from University of Tabriz, Tabriz, Iran. Currently, he is a last year Master of Science student in Computer Engineering with a specialization in Computer Architecture of Electrical and Computer Engineering Department at Shahid Beheshti University, Tehran, Iran, and an excellent member of Computer Society of Iran. He has been awarded the first prize of scientific and technical innovation in 6th National Conference on Electronic Commerce and Economy. He has worked on database design and software development using Microsoft SQL Server 2005, Net beans, and Eclipse (Java programming environment), MATLAB, and C++ programming. His main research work is in the area of m-commerce, e-commerce, cryptographic algorithms, network security and protocols, information security, tree-based cryptographic systems, robust eye detection using image processing, wavelet, and genetic algorithms.

Qiang Tang is a Postdoc Researcher from the APSIA group, SnT, University of Luxembourg. Over the years, his research interest has been focused on designing and analyzing cryptographic protocols. Currently, he is working on pragmatic cryptographic protocols, which facilitate clients to securely outsource their data and related operations to third-party service providers in the cloud-computing paradigm. Before moving to Luxembourg, he worked as a Postdoc Researcher at Ecole Normale Superieure, Paris, France, and University of Twente, The Netherlands. He received his PhD degree from Royal Holloway, University of London, in 2007, and obtained his Master and Bachelor degrees from Peking University and Yantai University, respectively, in China.

Fatih Tekbacak was born in 1982. He received the BSc. degree in Computer Engineering and MSc. degree in Computer Software from Izmir Institute of Technology, Turkey. He is a PhD candidate in Computer Engineering at Ege University, working under the supervision of Prof. Dr. Oguz Dikenelli and Assist. Prof. Dr. Tugkan Tuglular. He is also a Research Assistant in Izmir Institute of Technology. His main research interests include linked data, Semantic Web, provenance, and access control. His recent focus is on provenance based linked data query execution.

Vladimir Ivanovich Vorobiev was born in Vyazniki, Vladimir region of Russia in 1942. Graduated with honour from Leningrad Hydro-Meteorologic Institute in 1965. After post-graduate studies obtained his Ph.D. (in Physics and Mathematics). In 1968 was employed at the Institute of Oceanology RAS as a Junior Researcher. In 1975 was employed as a Senior Researcher at the Institute of Physics and Technology named after A.F. Ioffe. In 1978, Vorobiev V.I. got an appointment of a Head of Software Laboratory in Leningrad Research Computer Centre. From 1991 until now, Vorobiev V.I. is a Head of the Laboratory of Information Computer Systems. Received degree of Dr.Sci. (Engineering) in 1994. Received the title of Professor in 1999. His scientific interests include modeling and design of information security assurance systems, software qualimetry, parallel and distributed programming, cluster, GRID and cloud computing technologies, e-documents circulation. Published more than 100 papers and monographs.

Piyi Yang is a Lecturer in the Department of Computer Science and Engineering at University of Shanghai for Science and Technology, China. He earned his PhD in 2009 and Bachelor of Science in Computer Science in 2003 from Shanghai Jiao Tong University. He is actively involved in the academic community of cryptography and information security since 2008, serving as an Editor for International Journal on Advances in Security, Co-Chair of DEPEND 2010 and 2011, Technical Program Committee Member of DEPEND 2012, and reviewer for several internationally recognized journals (such as Information Science Journal of Systems and Software, IEEE Transactions on Systems, Man, and Cybernetics). Piyi has published papers in various well-known international journals and conferences such as IEEE Communications Letters, Computers & Electrical Engineering, IPCCC, and NSS. He is also a member of Chinese Association for Cryptology Research since 2005.

Tanveer A. Zia is a Senior Lecturer in Computing, Course Coordinator for the Doctor of Information Technology, and Associate Head of School, School of Computing & Mathematics, Faculty of Business, Charles Sturt University (CSU) in NSW, Australia. He has earned his PhD from the University of Sydney in 2008, Master of Interactive Multimedia (MIMM) from University of Technology Sydney in 2004, MBA from Preston University USA in 1997, and Bachelors of Science in Computer Sciences from Southwestern University, Philippines in 1992. Tanveer's broader research interests are in Information and Communication Technology (ICT) security. Specifically, he is interested in security of low powered mobile devices. He is also interested in biometric security, cyber security, cloud computing security, information assurance, protection against identity theft, trust management, forensic computing, and law and ethics in ICT. He is serving on technical and program committees of several international conferences in his area of research. He actively publishes in international conferences, symposiums, workshops, and refereed journals. Tanveer is a Senior Member Australian Computer Society and Certified Professional (MACS Snr CP), Senior Member Institute of Electrical and Electronics Engineers (IEEE), Senior Member International Association of Computer Sciences and Information Technology (IACSIT), Member IEEE Computer Society, Member Australian Information Security Association (AISA), Member ISACA, and Academic Advocate for CSU.

Index

3-entity communications 216

A

additively homomorphic cryptosystem 260
algebraic cryptanalysis 36-37, 40-41, 50, 53, 57-58
Android 499, 502, 514-516, 521, 523, 526
anonymous routing network 431
Asymmetric Encryption 64-65, 335, 337, 380, 404
Attribute-Based Encryption (ABE) 164
Attribute-Based Messaging (ABM) 160, 171
Attribute-Based Signature (ABS) 159-161
Authentication and Key Agreement (AKA) scheme 205
Authorized Delegation Discovery (ADD) 190

B

Back-off Manipulation 228, 244
Bellcore attack 142
bid privacy 460, 462, 464-469, 471-476, 479-481, 483-485, 487, 490, 492-493, 495
Biometrics 301, 362, 373-375, 393, 399-402, 404
blacklist sites 306
Brute Force Search 37

C

CapDesk 319, 329
chosen plaintext attack 126
CIA (Confidentiality, Integrity and Availability) 366
ciphertext-only attacks 240
ciphertexts 65, 71-73, 75-76, 85, 87, 90, 92-93, 97-98, 100, 108, 229, 240, 251, 434, 436, 445-446, 451, 458, 468, 472, 474, 485, 494, 497, 523
cloud computing 2, 30, 65, 85, 105-106, 523
Cognitive Walkthrough 321, 332
Computer Forensics 62
cracker 409, 427

D

Denial-of-Service (DoS) attacks 179, 189
Differential Electromagnetic Attacks (DEMA) 134
Differential Power Attacks (DPA) 134
Diffie-Hellman assumption 453
DIGEST-MD5 414, 418, 426
Direct Recording Electronic (DRE) systems 429
Discretionary Direct Trust model 288
DNSSEC (DNS Security Extension) 292
Domain Name System (DNS) 411
Domain Name System Security Extension (DNSSEC) 411
Downward Search 474-477, 481, 485-486
Duplicate Address Detection (DAD) 179, 181-182, 185, 197

E

e-auction 314, 460-461, 463, 467, 490-492, 497-498
e-commerce 311, 411, 429, 460-461, 463, 494, 496, 498
e-Health Services 501, 504, 525
Electronic Health Record (EHR) 500-502
ElGamal encryption 307, 370, 428, 432, 444, 469-471, 482, 484
Email Mining Toolkit (EMT) 364
Extended Linearization method 51-53, 55, 57, 61

F

Fault-Based Attacks 141
Federal Security Service of Russia 34
File Carving 72, 82
fingerprint identification system 361, 363, 395
full-domain search 87-89, 100
Fully Homomorphic Encryption (FHE) 65

G

global namespace 303, 310
GnuPG 72-73, 75-76, 364, 370, 402
GOST encryption algorithm 34-35, 44, 54-58
GOST-H 37, 40
Guaranteed Time Slot (GTS) 230

H

Hamming Distance Problem (HDP) 269
Hardware Design Workflow 143, 157
Hardware-Oriented Octonion Encryption Scheme (HW-OES) 110, 112, 120-128
Hardware Synthesis Process 157
Hash Functions 2, 34, 60, 64-70, 74, 82, 100, 127, 164-165, 167, 184, 204-208, 210-211, 216, 219, 307-308, 338-339, 380-382, 386, 388-389, 393-394, 396, 398, 401-402, 404, 412, 448, 453-455, 462, 469, 472-473, 475-476, 488
Hierarchical Agglomerative Clustering (HAC) 258
Hill cipher (HC) 111
homomorphic e-voting 428, 431-432, 446-448, 455, 458
hyper-complex number systems 110-111

I

Ideal Model Paradigm 255
IDEF0 5-15, 31-32
identity management process 309
Identity Management System (IdMS) 310
index-based search 85, 88, 100-101
index privacy 95-96, 98
Information & Communication Technologies for Health (Health ICT) 501
Internet Engineering Task Force (IETF) 243
IPv4 address space 178, 196

K

k-anonymity 261, 275-276
key chain 477-480
Key Management 102, 174, 202-203, 205, 216, 218-222, 339, 349, 362, 369, 372, 403, 527
key matrix 111, 113, 115, 118, 120, 127
keyword-based search 88
Known Plaintext-Ciphertext Attack (KPCA) 110-111

L

leaf certificate owner 283
Linear cryptanalysis 37-39, 59
Link Layer Jamming 228

M

Mail Transfer Agent (MTA) 172, 408, 410, 419
Mail User Agent (MUA) 172, 364, 417
malicious adversary 255
Malicious CA 287
Malicious Last Hop Router 179
Man-In-The-Middle (MITM) Attacks 182, 411, 414
Message Authentication Code (MAC) 510-511
Message Security Protocol (MSP) 364, 371
mix-network-based e-voting 428, 431, 445, 455
mix network schemes 434-436, 441, 443-444, 459
Mobile Ad hoc NETwork (MANET)
    centralized server 200-201, 203, 216, 222
    distributed server 200, 204, 216, 222
    self-organized 205
Moore's Law 215
multiplicative homomorphism 489

N

Neighbor Discovery Protocol (NDP) 178-179, 181, 195
Neural network applications 258
Nightly Tester Tool 321, 325
Node Tampering 227, 239, 244
Noisy Polynomial Interpolation problem 262, 271
non-repudiation protocol 205, 218

O

oblivious transfer 258, 260, 262, 275-278, 472-473, 486-487, 495, 498
octonions 110-111, 119, 121, 127
ontological engineering 3, 29
ontological modeling 4, 15, 30
OpenPGP 71-72, 80, 294, 299, 319, 370, 403, 421-422, 426
Out-of-Band Channel 283, 285-287, 289-291, 301

P

Paillier encryption 428, 432, 436, 443, 445-448, 450, 482, 485, 487, 489, 498
Parameter Spoofing 179

Personal Health Record 108
Petname Model 302, 304, 310-314, 317-319, 327-329, 333
Pharming 368, 403
Phishing 294-295, 297-299, 302-303, 306-307, 309-311, 321, 329-331, 361-362, 364, 368, 389, 402, 409, 416, 421
Polaris 319, 331
Post Office Protocol 3 (POP3) 417
Privacy Enhanced Email (PEM) 363
Privacy Homomorphism (PH) 239
Private Information Retrieval (PIR) 90, 257
probabilistic polynomial-time algorithms (PPTA) 265
Public Key Cryptography Standard 362, 371
public key cryptosystem 59, 129, 141, 275, 307-308, 333, 457, 495
public key encryption 63-64, 72, 84-85, 91-93, 100, 104-107, 177, 369, 380, 404, 462, 498
Public Key Encryption Supporting Equality Test 92
Public-Key Ring 290

Q

Quantum Computing 64
quantum cryptography 500, 524
Quaternion Encryption Scheme (QES) 110-111
quaternions 111, 116, 118, 128-129

R

Radio Jamming 226, 228
Random Number Generator (RNG) 337
Real Model Paradigm 255
Redirect Attack 183
Regional Internet Registries (RIRs) 178
remote health monitoring systems 500, 506, 522, 524
Replay Attack 182, 187, 231, 244, 390, 404
REWARD 237
Rogue Router Attack 183
Role-Based Access Control (RBAC) 529

S

S-Boxes 35-44, 46-47, 53, 57, 59-61
sealed-bid auction 460-462, 464-468, 471-477, 480, 483-487, 490-491, 493-497
Searchable Encryption 87, 93, 104-105, 108, 505
Search in Encrypted Data (SED) scheme 84
Secure Multiparty Computation (SMC) 253-254, 256, 264-265, 272-273, 276, 278, 471-472, 497
Secure Multipurpose Internet Mail Extensions (S 364, 372
Semantic Web 5, 15, 30, 32-33
semi-honest adversary 255
Sender Policy Framework (SPF) 420, 426
sequence diagrams 17, 382-383
Side-Channel Attacks (SCA) 134
sign-off validation tools 144
Silo Model 306
Simple Mail Transfer Protocol (SMTP) 407-408
Simple Public Key Infrastructure (SPKI) 314
(Simulated) Power Trace 157
SIV (System Integrity Verifier) 338
Slide attacks 39, 58, 60
sniffing attack 409-410
Spam 361-362, 364-365, 368, 389, 396-398, 403, 406-410, 412, 416-417, 419, 421, 423-424, 426-427
SPARQL 5, 12-13, 15, 30-32
StateLess Address Auto-Configuration (SLAAC) 179-180
Stuxnet 287, 300
symmetric block cipher 35, 57
symmetric-key cryptosystems 215
SynGT 22, 24, 26-28

T

threshold cryptography 202, 204-205, 217-218
threshold secret sharing 204, 467, 484-485
Transport Layer Security (TLS) 299, 335, 356, 412, 500, 503, 529
trapdoor hash family 211-213, 219
trapdoor privacy 89, 95-100
TrueCrypt 75, 78, 80
TrustBar 298, 316-317, 321, 325-328, 330
Trusted Channel 346
Trusted Computing Group (TCG) 335, 360
Trusted Platform Agent (TPA) 346-347
Trusted Platform Module (TPM) 335-336, 360
Trusted Third Party (TTP) 255, 278, 397, 504
trust negotiation 500, 507-510, 512-514, 520-521, 523, 525-526, 528-529
Turing machine 19-20
Type 2B IdM 307
typo squatting 309

U

Ubiquitous Health Trust Protocol (UHTP) 499, 502, 506, 509, 523
unforgeability 160, 163-164, 173-174, 177

Unified Modeling Language (UML) 32
unlinkability 456, 466-468
User Authentication 173-174, 203, 298, 388, 400-401
User-Centric Id Management 306-307
User Privacy-Preserving 173-174

V

verifiable secret sharing (VSS) 278, 469, 472, 485, 495
VeriSign 287-288
Voting Over the Internet (VOI) 430

W

Web Ontology Language (OWL) 33
Wireless Sensor Networks (WSNs) 223

Z

zero test 482-483, 485
Zooko's triangle 310-314, 328, 333